WEST ACADEMIC PUBLISHING'S LAW SCHOOL ADVISORY BOARD

JESSE H. CHOPER
Professor of Law and Dean Emeritus
University of California, Berkeley

JOSHUA DRESSLER
Distinguished University Professor, Frank R. Strong Chair in Law
Michael E. Moritz College of Law, The Ohio State University

YALE KAMISAR
Professor of Law Emeritus, University of San Diego
Professor of Law Emeritus, University of Michigan

MARY KAY KANE
Professor of Law, Chancellor and Dean Emeritus
University of California, Hastings College of the Law

LARRY D. KRAMER
President, William and Flora Hewlett Foundation

JONATHAN R. MACEY
Professor of Law, Yale Law School

ARTHUR R. MILLER
University Professor, New York University
Formerly Bruce Bromley Professor of Law, Harvard University

GRANT S. NELSON
Professor of Law Emeritus, Pepperdine University
Professor of Law Emeritus, University of California, Los Angeles

A. BENJAMIN SPENCER
Justice Thurgood Marshall Distinguished Professor of Law
University of Virginia School of Law

JAMES J. WHITE
Robert A. Sullivan Professor of Law Emeritus
University of Michigan

CONTRACTS
Ninth Edition

Robert D. Brain
Clinical Professor of Law
Loyola Law School, Los Angeles

QUICK REVIEW SERIES

The publisher is not engaged in rendering legal or other professional advice, and this publication is not a substitute for the advice of an attorney. If you require legal or other expert advice, you should seek the services of a competent attorney or other professional.

Sum & Substance Quick Review Series is a Publication of West Academic Publishing.

© 1996, 1997 by West Professional Training Programs Inc., d/b/a Sum and Substance
© 2000 by West Publishing Corporation d/b/a West Group
© West, a Thomson business, 2006
© 2013 Thomson Reuters
© 2018 LEG, Inc. d/b/a West Academic
    444 Cedar Street, Suite 700
    St. Paul, MN 55101
    1-877-888-1330

Printed in the United States of America

ISBN: 978-1-68328-676-9

*As always, to Pam, who is my rock,
and to Donna, who has my hopes.*

ACKNOWLEDGMENTS

In revising the Book for the Ninth Edition, I had the help of four very bright students. Their input has helped me think about things differently and put ideas more understandably. So I wanted to thank Gloria Dorriz and Sona Patel, Loyola Law School Los Angeles, Class of 2020, and Fady Saleh and Samantha Santopoalo, Harvard Law School, Class of 2020. I would also like to continue to acknowledge and thank my former colleague, Mark S. Scarberry of Pepperdine University School of Law for his allowing me to use and reproduce some of the exam materials in this Book.

TABLE OF CONTENTS

ACKNOWLEDGMENTS V

PART I. INTRODUCTION TO CONTRACT LAW

Chapter 1. An Introduction to Contract Law: Sources of Contract Law, Definitions of Contract, Types of Contracts, and the Basic Components of Contracts............3
A. Sources of Contract Law. [§ 1–1] 3
   1. Common Law. [§ 1–2] 4
   2. Treatises. [§ 1–3]...4
   3. Restatement of Contracts. [§ 1–4]..4
   4. The Uniform Commercial Code. [§ 1–5] 5
   5. The British Sales of Goods Act. [§ 1–6] 7
   6. The American Uniform Sales Act. [§ 1–7] 7
   7. The United Nations Convention on Contracts for the International Sales of Goods. [§ 1–8]....................................7
B. Definition of a Contract. [§ 1–9]...8
   1. Restatement Definition. [§ 1–10] 8
   2. UCC Definition. [§ 1–11] 9
   3. Distinction Between Restatement and UCC Definitions. [§ 1–12] 9
C. Elements of a Contract. [§ 1–13]...10
D. Types of Contracts. [§ 1–14] 11
   1. Unilateral Contracts. [§ 1–15]..11
   2. Bilateral Contracts. [§ 1–16] 11
   3. Express Contracts. [§ 1–17]...11
   4. Implied-in-Fact Contracts. [§ 1–18].....................................11
      a. Example of *Wrench LLC v. Taco Bell Corp.* [§ 1–19].....12
   5. Implied-in-Law Contracts or "Quasi-Contracts." [§ 1–20] 12
      a. Example. [§ 1–21]...12

PART II. MUTUAL ASSENT, OFFER, AND ACCEPTANCE

Chapter 2. Mutual Assent.. 17
A. Mutual Assent: Defined and Discussed. [§ 2–1] 17
   1. Example of Mutuality of Obligation. [§ 2–2] 17
B. Mutual Assent Judged by Objective Theory of Contracts. [§ 2–3] 18
   1. Elimination of "Meeting of the Minds." [§ 2–4]..................19
      a. Example of *Lucy v. Zehmer*. [§ 2–5] 19
   2. Presumption Against Mutual Assent to Contract in Domestic or Social Situations. [§ 2–6] 20
      a. Example of *Balfour v. Balfour*. [§ 2–7] 21

TABLE OF CONTENTS

C. Precise Time of Making of Contract Irrelevant for Determining Mutual Assent. [§ 2–8] 21
D. Mutual Assent as to All Terms Not Required: Only as to Essential or "Material" Ones. [§ 2–9] 22

Chapter 3. Offers 23
A. Offer: Defined and Discussed. [§ 3–1] 23
B. Effect of Offer: Powers and Rights of Acceptance. [§ 3–2] 23
    1. The Right to Accept: Option Contracts. [§ 3–3] 24
        a. Example of *Beall v. Beall*. [§ 3–4] 24
    2. The Right to Accept: Merchants Firm Offer Under the UCC. [§ 3–5] 25
    3. Implied Unilateral Option Contract upon and Offeree's Beginning of Performance in Response to an Unambiguous Offer to Enter into a Unilateral Contract. [§ 3–6] 25
    4. Implied Option Contract Based on Substantial Reliance. [§ 3–7] 25
C. Test to Determine Whether an "Offer" Was Made: The Objective Theory of Contracts. [§ 3–8] 26
    1. Example of *Lonergan v. Scolnick*. [§ 3–9] 26
    2. Distinguishing Offers from Other Types of Communications. [§ 3–10] 27
        a. Offer Must Contain Terms That Are Reasonably Certain. [§ 3–11] 27
        b. Offer Distinguished from Statement of Future Intention. [§ 3–12] 27
            (1) Example. [§ 3–13] 27
        c. Offer Distinguished from Request for Price Quotation. [§ 3–14] 28
            (1) Example. [§ 3–15] 28
        d. Offer Distinguished from a Preliminary Negotiation or Invitation to Make an Offer. [§ 3–16] 28
            (1) Example. [§ 3–17] 28
        e. Offer Distinguished from Advertisements/Catalogue Descriptions. [§ 3–18] 29
            (1) Rationale for Rule. [§ 3–19] 29
            (2) Example. [§ 3–20] 30
            (3) Example of *Lefkowitz v. Great Minneapolis Surplus Store*. [§ 3–21] 30
            (4) Special Considerations for Some Kind of Catalogues. [§ 3–22] 31
        f. Offer Distinguished from Statements Made in Jest, in Anger, as an Opinion, in a Grumbling Manner, or While Intoxicated. [§ 3–23] 31
            (1) Example. [§ 3–24] 32
            (2) Example of *Hawkins v. McGee*. [§ 3–25] 32

TABLE OF CONTENTS

- D. Types of Offers. [§ 3–26] 33
  1. Offer to Enter into a Unilateral Contract. [§ 3–27] 33
  2. Offer to Enter into a Bilateral Contract. [§ 3–28] 33
  3. Ambiguous/Indifferent Offers. [§ 3–29] 33
     a. Significance of the Distinction Between Unilateral, Bilateral, and Ambiguous Contract Offers. [§ 3–30] 34
  4. Ambiguous Offers Under the UCC. [§ 3–31] 35
  5. "General" Contract or "Reward" Offers. [§ 3–32] 35
- E. The Offeror Is the "Master of the Offer." [§ 3–33] 35
- F. Special Rules Regarding Offers Made at Auctions. [§ 3–34] 36
  1. Auctions with Reserve. [§ 3–35] 36
  2. Auctions Without Reserve. [§ 3–36] 36
  3. Withdrawal of Bid. [§ 3–37] 37
- G. Offers Under the CISG. [§ 3–38] 37
- H. Exam Approach to Offer Issues. [§ 3–39] 37

Chapter 4. Acceptance 39
- A. Acceptance: Defined and Discussed. [§ 4–1] 39
- B. Effect of Acceptance. [§ 4–2] 39
- C. Test to Determine Whether Acceptance Has Taken Place: The Objective Theory of Contracts. [§ 4–3] 39
  1. Example. [§ 4–4] 40
  2. Cross-Offers. [§ 4–5] 40
- D. Who Is Entitled to Accept the Offer. [§ 4–6] 41
  1. Who Constitutes an "Offeree" Is Judged by the Objective Theory of Contracts. [§ 4–7] 41
  2. Power to Accept Is Not Generally Transferable. [§ 4–8] 41
     a. Example. [§ 4–9] 41
     b. Exception: Right to Accept Under an Option Contract Is Generally Transferable. [§ 4–10] 42
     c. Example. [§ 4–11] 42
  3. Special Problems Concerning Acceptance of "General" or "Reward" Offers. [§ 4–12] 42
     a. "General" or "Reward" Offers Can *Presumptively* Be Accepted by Only the First Person to Do the Required Acts. [§ 4–13] 43
        (1) Example. [§ 4–14] 43
        (2) Example. [§ 4–15] 43
        (3) Exception: General Offer Whose Conditions Make It Unlikely That an Unlimited Number of People Can Accept Is Effective as to All Who Meet Those Conditions. [§ 4–16] 44
            (a) Example of *Carlill v. Carbolic Smoke Ball Co.* [§ 4–17] 44
     b. Offeree Must Know of General Offer in Order to Accept It. [§ 4–18] 44
        (1) Example. [§ 4–19] 45

TABLE OF CONTENTS

    (2) Example. [§ 4–20] 45
    (3) Rationale for Rule That Offeree Must Know of Reward Offer to Accept It. [§ 4–21] 45
    (4) Police Officers and Other Governmental Workers. [§ 4–22] 46
  c. Revocation of General Offers: The "Equal Publicity Rule." [4–23] 46
    (1) Example. [§ 4–24] 47
  d. Notice of Intent to Accept General Offer Not Required. [§ 4–25]..47
    (1) Example of *Carlill v. Carbolic Smoke Ball.* [4–26]..47
E. When An Offer May Be Accepted: Duration of the Power of Acceptance. [§ 4–27] 48
 1. Acts and Events That Terminate an Offeree's Power of Acceptance Under Revocable Offers. [§ 4–28]........................48
  a. Termination of Revocable Offers Through Rejection and Counter-Offer by the Offeree. [§ 4–29]....................49
    (1) Example. [§ 4–30] 49
    (2) Rejections and Counter-Offers Immediately Cut off Power of Acceptance Even if Offer Was to Be Held Open. [§ 4–31]..50
      (a) Example. [4–32] 50
      (b) Exception: When Offer Specifically States It Will Be Kept Open Despite Rejection or Counter-Offer. [§ 4–33] 50
    (3) Counter-Offer Need Not Explicitly Reject Offer. [§ 4–34]..50
    (4) Rejections and Counter-Offers Are Judged Under the Objective Theory of Contracts. [§ 4–35] 51
    (5) Common Law Rule: Counter-Offer Found if Purported Acceptance Differed from the Offer in the Slightest Respect. [§ 4–36] 52
    (6) Rejections and Counter-Offers Distinguished from Other Types of Communications. [§ 4–37].....52
      (a) "Neutral Comments." [§ 4–38] 52
      (b) Mere "Inquiries" or Preliminary Negotiations. [§ 4–39]..53
      (c) Requests for Modification. [§ 4–40] 53
      (d) "Grumbling" Acceptances. [§ 4–41] 53
      (e) "Intention to Take the Offer Under Further Advisement." [§ 4–42] 53
    (7) When a Rejection Is Effective. [§ 4–43] 54
  b. Termination of the Power of Acceptance in Revocable Offers Through Lapse of Time. [§ 4–44] 54
    (1) Determination of "Reasonable Time." [§ 4–45].......54

- (2) Common Presumptions About What Constitutes "Reasonable Time." [§ 4–46] 55
  - (a) Offers Made in Direct Negotiations: Reasonable Time Terminates at End of Negotiation. [§ 4–47] 55
  - (b) Offers in Letters: Acceptance Timely if Made on the Day of Receipt, Otherwise Acceptance Transmitted in the Same Medium as the Offer Is Timely. [§ 4–48] 55
  - (c) Offers in Telegram, Overnight Delivery, Facsimile, Text, or E-Mail: Indications That Acceptance Must Be Expedited to Be Timely. [§ 4–49] 56
  - (d) Offers Dealing with Price-Volatile Subject Matter: Acceptances Usually Need to Be Expedited to Be Effective. [§ 4–50] 56
    - (i) Example. [§ 4–51] 56
- (3) Interpretation of Ambiguous Time Provisions in an Offer. [§ 4–52] 57
- (4) Effect of Delayed Transmission of Offer. [§ 4–53] 57
- (5) When an Acceptance Is Effective. [§ 4–54] 57
- c. Termination of Offers by Revocation. [§ 4–55] 58
  - (1) Revocation Defined. [§ 4–56] 58
  - (2) Revocations Are Judged Under the Objective Theory of Contracts. [§ 4–57] 58
  - (3) General Rule: To Be Effective, a Revocation Must Be Transmitted by the Offeror to the Offeree. [§ 4–58] 58
    - (a) Exception: The Indirect Revocation Doctrine. [§ 4–59] 59
      - (i) Example of *Dickinson v. Dodds*. [§ 4–60] 59
      - (ii) Rationale for the Indirect Revocation Doctrine. [§ 4–61] 60
    - (b) Exception: Revocation of General Offers via "The Equal Publicity Rule." [§ 4–62] 60
    - (c) Revocations Are Typically Effective Only upon Receipt. [§ 4–63] 60
- d. Traditional Rule: Termination of Offeree's Power to Accept a Revocable Offer upon Death or Incapacity of Offeror. [§ 4–64] 61
  - (1) Criticism of Traditional Rule. [§ 4–65] 61
  - (2) Example. [§ 4–66] 61
- e. Termination of Offeree's Power to Accept upon Death or Incapacity of the Offeree. [§ 4–67] 62

TABLE OF CONTENTS

    f.   Termination of Offeree's Power to Accept by Non-Occurrence of an *Implied* Condition: Death or Destruction of a Person or Thing Essential for Performance (Other than the Offeror or Offeree). [§ 4–68] 62

    g.   Termination of Offeree's Power of Acceptance by Non-Occurrence of an *Implied* Condition: Supervening Illegality. [§ 4–69] 62

        (1)   Example. [§ 4–70] 63

    h.   Termination of Offeree's Power of Acceptance of Revocable Offers by the Non-Occurrence of an *Express* Condition of Acceptance Specified in the Offer. [§ 4–71] 63

2.   Acts and Events That Terminate an Offeree's Power of Acceptance Under Irrevocable Offers. [§ 4–72] 63

    a.   The Four Situations in Which an Offer Will Be Deemed "Irrevocable." [§ 4–73] 64

        (1)   Option Contracts: Defined and Discussed. [§ 4–74] 64

            (a)   Example. [§ 4–75] 64

            (b)   Effect of Option Contract: Elevating the Offeree's <u>Power</u> to Accept to the Offeree's *Right to* Accept. [§ 4–76] 65

            (c)   Option Contracts and "Purported" Consideration. [§ 4–77] 65

        (2)   Merchant's Firm Offer. [§ 4–78] 66

            (a)   Example. [§ 4–79] 66

        (3)   Making Unambiguous Unilateral Contract Offers Temporarily Irrevocable Under Restatement 2d § 45. [§ 4–80] 67

            (a)   The "Brooklyn Bridge" Hypothetical. [§ 4–81] 68

            (b)   Problems Associated with Restatement § 45's Approach in Making a Unilateral Contract Offer Temporarily Irrevocable. [§ 4–82] 68

                (i)   Problems Associated with "Beginning Performance," "Tender Performance," or "Tender the Beginning of Performance." [§ 4–83] 69

                (ii)   Fairness of Making the Option Contract Unilateral Only. [§ 4–84] 70

        (4)   Making Certain Contract Offers Temporarily Irrevocable by Substantial Reliance Under Restatement 2d § 87(2). [§ 4–85] 71

            (a)   Example of *Drennan v. Star Paving Co.* [§ 4–86] 72

xii

TABLE OF CONTENTS

    b. Acts and Events That Terminate the Power of Acceptance Even Under Irrevocable Offers. [§ 4–87] 73
      (1) Example. [§ 4–88] 74
      (2) Example. [§ 4–89] 74
      (3) Example. [§ 4–90] 74
      (4) Example. [§ 4–91] 74
F. How an Offer May Be Accepted: Permissible Methods or Modes of Acceptance. [§ 4–92] 75
  1. General Rule Regarding Acceptance of an Offer Which Unambiguously Specifies Method of Acceptance: The Offeree Must Follow the Directions of the Offeror. [§ 4–93] 75
  2. General Rules Regarding Acceptance of an Offer Which Does Not Explicitly Specify the Method of Acceptance: Ambiguous or Indifferent Offers: It May Be Accepted in Any Reasonable Manner. [§ 4–94] 76
    a. Example of *Hamer v. Sidway*. [§ 4–95] 76
    b. Review Problem. [§ 4–96] 76
  3. Special Rules for Offer to Purchase Goods for Prompt Shipment Under UCC: The Offeror May Promise Shipment, or Actually Ship. [§ 4–97] 77
  4. Special Problems When Beginning Performance Is Intended to Act as an Acceptance. [§ 4–98] 77
    a. Beginning Performance in Response to an Unambiguous Offer for Unilateral Contract. [§ 4–99] 77
    b. Beginning Performance in Response to an Unambiguous Offer for Bilateral Contract. [§ 4–100] ... 77
    c. Beginning Performance in Response to an Ambiguous or Indifferent Offer. [§ 4–101] 78
      (1) Treatment of Beginning Performance in Response to an Ambiguous or Indifferent Offer. [§ 4–102] 78
        (a) Example. [§ 4–103] 78
      (2) Necessity of Giving Notice to Offeror When Beginning Performance Validly Acts as Acceptance. [§ 4–104] 79
        (a) Exceptions: When an Offeree Need Not Give Notice. [§ 4–105] 79
      (3) Effect of Failing to Give Notice. [§ 4–106] 80
  5. Ordering Goods for Prompt Shipment: The "Unilateral Contract Trick" Under the UCC. [§ 4–107] 81
    a. Accommodation Shipments. [§ 4–108] 82
  6. Notice Problems in Acceptance Under Unilateral Contracts. [§ 4–109] 82
    a. Example. [§ 4–110] 82
    b. Example of *Carlill v. Carbolic Smoke Ball*. [§ 4–111] ... 83

TABLE OF CONTENTS

    7. Acceptance by Silence or Inaction. [§ 4–112] 83
        a. Silent Acceptance of Services. [§ 4–113] 83
            (1) Example. [§ 4–114] 84
        b. Silent Acceptance at Direction of Offeror. [§ 4–115] 84
        c. Silence Can Act as a Valid Acceptance Because of Previous Conduct. [§ 4–116] 84
        d. Silent Acceptance of Property by Acting Inconsistently with Owner's Interest. [§ 4–117] 84
  G. Posting Problems: The Mailbox Rule. [§ 4–118] 85
    1. Offers Effective upon Receipt. [§ 4–119] 85
    2. Acceptances Effective on Dispatch. [§ 4–120] 86
        a. Communication Must Be Properly Addressed and Deliverable. [§ 4–121] 86
        b. Acceptance by the Mode of Communication Used Must Be an Authorized Mode of Acceptance. [§ 4–122] 86
        c. Offeror Loses Power to Revoke After a Properly Dispatched Acceptance. [§ 4–123] 87
        d. Special Mailbox Rules Regarding Acceptances Under Option Contracts. [§ 4–124] 87
            (1) Example. [§ 4–125] 87
    3. Rejections Effective upon Receipt. [§ 4–126] 88
    4. Revocations Effective upon Receipt Under Majority Rule. [§ 4–127] 88
    5. Effect of First Sending a Rejection, Followed by an Acceptance. [§ 4–128] 88
    6. Effect of First Sending an Acceptance, Followed by a Rejection. [§ 4–129] 88
    7. Graphic Summary of Mailbox Rule. [§ 4–130] 88
  H. Exam Approach to Acceptance Issues. [§ 4–131] 89

Chapter 5. When the "Acceptance" Varies from the Offer: The "Mirror Image" and "Last Shot" Rules and UCC § 2–207 91
  A. Common Law View: The "Mirror Image" Rule. [§ 5–1] 92
  B. Unfairness of the Mirror Image Rule. [§ 5–2] 92
    1. Example of Unfairness Where One Party Doesn't Perform. [§ 5–3] 92
    2. Example of Unfairness Where the Parties Perform: The "Last Shot" Doctrine. [§ 5–4] 93
  C. UCC § 2–207: An Overview. [§ 5–5] 94
  D. Analysis of § 2–207 Problems. [§ 5–6] 94
    1. First Step: Do the Parties Have a Contract Based on Their Writings Under § 2–207(1)? [§ 5–7] 95
        a. First Sub-Step: Does the Offeree's Document Act as a "Definite and Seasonable Expression of Acceptance?" [§ 5–8] 95
            (1) Example. [§ 5–9] 96

		b.	Second Sub-Step: Does the Offeree's Document "Expressly Make [Acceptance] Conditional on [the Offeror's] Assent to the Additional or Different Terms"?: Herein the "Special Language." [§ 5–10] 96

        b. Second Sub-Step: Does the Offeree's Document "Expressly Make [Acceptance] Conditional on [the Offeror's] Assent to the Additional or Different Terms"?: Herein the "Special Language." [§ 5–10] 96
           (1) Example. [§ 5–11] 97
           (2) Example of the Incorrect Approach Taken by a Court Under § 2–207(1): *Roto-Lith v. F.P. Bartlett & Co.* [§ 5–12] 98
           (3) Examples of the Correct Approach Under § 2–207(1): *Dorton v. Collins & Aikman Corp* and *C. Itoh & Co. v. Jordan International.* [§ 5–13] 99
    2. Second Step: If the Parties Have a Contract Based on Their Exchanged Writings Under § 2–207(1), Then § 2–207(2) Governs What Terms Make up the Contract. [§ 5–14]..........99
        a. If Either Party Is a Non-Merchant, the Offeror's Terms Control. [§ 5–15] 100
        b. If Both Parties Are Merchants, the Offeree's Terms Control *Unless* One of the Three § 2–207(2) Exceptions Apply. [§ 5–16] 100
           (1) Example. [§ 5–17] 100
           (2) Example. [§ 5–18] 101
           (3) Example. [§ 5–19] 101
           (4) Example. [§ 5–20] 101
        c. The Curious Absence of "Different" Terms Under § 2–207(2). [§ 5–21] 102
           (1) Example. [§ 5–22] 103
    3. Third Step: If No Contract Is Formed Under § 2–207(1) Based on the Exchanged Writings, an Implied-in-Fact Contract May Be Formed by the Parties' Conduct Under § 2–207(3); if So, the "Knockout" Rule of § 2–207(3) Will Determine Which Terms Become Part of the Contract. [§ 5–23] 105
        a. The "Knockout" Rule. [§ 5–24] 105
    4. When the Additional or Different Terms Are Found in a "Confirmation" Instead of an Acceptance. [§ 5–25] 106
        a. The Effect of a "Confirmation" Containing Additional or Different Terms. [§ 5–26] 106
           (1) Review Problem. [§ 5–27] 107

E. Practical Differences Between the Common Law and UCC § 2–207. [§ 5–28] 108
F. Exam Approach to § 2–207 Issues. [§ 5–29] 108
    1. Example. [§ 5–30] 109
    2. Example. [§ 5–31] 111
G. Analysis Under Revised UCC. [§ 5–32] 112
H. The Restatement View. [§ 5–33] 112
I. "Battle of the Forms" Under the CISG. [§ 5–34] 113

TABLE OF CONTENTS

Chapter 6. The Indefiniteness Doctrine 115
A. The Indefiniteness Doctrine: Defined and Discussed. [§ 6–1] 115
    1. Rationales for the Indefiniteness Doctrine. [§ 6–2] 115
        a. Example. [§ 6–3] 116
    2. Types of Indefiniteness Cases. [§ 6–4] 116
        a. Example Where Parties Have Not Agreed to a Term. [§ 6–5] 117
        b. Example Where an Agreed upon Term Is Too Ambiguous to Be Enforced: *Varney v. Ditmars*. [§ 6–6] 117
        c. Example When There Is an "Agreement to Agree." [§ 6–7] 117
    3. Indefiniteness Distinguished from Failure to Make a Contract. [§ 6–8] 117
    4. Indefiniteness Doctrine Only Applies to Essential Terms. [§ 6–9] 118
B. Common Law Rule on Indefiniteness. [§ 6–10] 118
C. Modern Rule on Indefiniteness. [§ 6–11] 118
    1. The UCC Approach to Indefiniteness: The Gap Fillers. [§ 6–12] 119
        a. Gap Fillers Are NOT Effective Unless an Otherwise Enforceable Contract Has Been Formed. [§ 6–13] 119
        b. Gap Fillers ARE Effective When the Parties Make Agreements to Agree. [§ 6–14] 120
        c. Gap Fillers Are NOT Effective if the Parties Make a Specific Agreement to the Contrary. [§ 6–15] 120
    2. Specific Gap Fillers Under the UCC. [§ 6–16] 120
        a. Gap Filler as to Price: Reasonable Price. [§ 6–17] 120
        b. Gap Filler Regarding Mode of Delivery: Delivery in a Single Lot. [§ 6–18] 120
        c. Gap Filler Regarding Place of Delivery: The Seller's Place of Business. [§ 6–19] 121
        d. Gap Filler Regarding Time of Delivery: Reasonable Time. [§ 6–20] 121
        e. Gap Filler Regarding Time of Payment: Payment Due at Time and Place of Delivery. [§ 6–21] 121
        f. No Gap Fillers Regarding Subject Matter of the Contract or Quantity. [§ 6–22] 121
    3. The Restatement Approach to the Indefiniteness Doctrine. [§ 6–23] 122
        a. Agreements to Agree in Non-UCC Transactions. [§ 6–24] 122
D. Part Performance as a Cure for Indefiniteness. [§ 6–25] 123
E. Usage of Trade, Course of Dealing, and Course of Performance as Cures for Indefiniteness. [§ 6–26] 124
F. Indefiniteness Under the CISG. [§ 6–27] 124
G. Exam Approach to Indefiniteness Issues. [§ 6–28] 125

TABLE OF CONTENTS

PART III. CONSIDERATION AND ITS "SUBSTITUTES" (WITH A SPECIAL TREATMENT OF MODIFICATIONS)

Chapter 7. Consideration **129**
- A. The Consideration Doctrine. [§ 7–1] 129
- B. Definitions of Consideration. [§ 7–2] 130
  1. The "Will" Theory. [§ 7–3] 130
  2. The "Benefit/Detriment" Theory. [§ 7–4] 130
     - a. Example: Analysis of a Unilateral Contract Using the "Benefit/Detriment" Theory. [§ 7–5] 131
     - b. Example: Analysis of a Bilateral Contract Using the "Benefit/Detriment" Theory. [§ 7–6] 131
  3. The Restatement's "Bargain" Theory. [§ 7–7] 131
     - a. Example: Analysis of a Unilateral Contract Using the "Bargain" Theory. [§ 7–8] 132
     - b. Example: Analysis of a Bilateral Contract Using the "Bargain" Theory. [§ 7–9] 132
  4. Modern Contract Law's Acceptance of the Benefit/Detriment and Bargain Theories of Consideration. [§ 7–10] 132
  5. Criticism of Consideration Definitions. [§ 7–11] 133
- C. Types of Consideration in Unilateral Contracts Under the Restatement's Bargain Theory. [§ 7–12] 133
  1. Example of an "Act" Serving as Consideration. [§ 7–13] 134
  2. Example of "Forbearance" to Serve as Consideration: *Hamer v. Sidway*. [§ 7–14] 134
  3. Example of "Destruction of a Legal Relationship" as Consideration. [§ 7–15] 134
  4. Example of "Modification of a Legal Relationship" as Consideration. [§ 7–16] 134
  5. Example of No Consideration Making Agreement Unenforceable. [§ 7–17] 135
- D. Types of Consideration in Bilateral Contracts Under the Restatement's Bargain Theory. [§ 7–18] 135
  1. Example. [§ 7–19] 135
- E. The Return Promises or Performances by the Promisee Can Be Valid Consideration Even if Given to a Third Party. [§ 7–20] 136
  1. Example. [§ 7–21] 136
- F. Transactions Without Consideration Due to the Lack of a Bargained for Exchange. [§ 7–22] 136
  1. Gratuitous or Gift Promises. [§ 7–23] 137
     - a. Traditional Rule: Gift Promises Are Unenforceable Because They Are Not Supported by Consideration. [§ 7–24] 137
       - (1) Example. [§ 7–25] 137

(2) Completed Gift Not Affected by Lack of Consideration. [§ 7–26] 137
(3) Acts "Incidental" to a True Gift Promise Are Insufficient Consideration to Enforce the Promise. [§ 7–27] 137
    (a) Example. [§ 7–28] 138
    (b) Example of *Kirksey v. Kirksey*. [§ 7–29] 138

2. "Past" Consideration (or "Moral Obligation"). [§ 7–30] 139
  a. Traditional Rule: "Past" Consideration and Moral Obligation Have the Same Effect as "Gift Promises"—They Are Insufficient to Make the Promise Enforceable. [§ 7–31] 139
    (1) Example of *Mills v. Wyman*. [§ 7–32] 140
  b. Modern Rule: "Past" Consideration and Moral Obligation Can Make *Some* Promises Enforceable. [§ 7–33] 140
    (1) Gift Promises Made Enforceable by Past Consideration Under Restatement 2d § 86. [§ 7–34] 140
      (a) Example of *Webb v. McGowin*. [§ 7–35] 141
      (b) Example of *Mills v. Wyman*. [§ 7–36] 141
      (c) Review Problem. [§ 7–37] 142
    (2) Promises to Pay Debts Made Unenforceable Under the Statute of Limitations or by Bankruptcy Under Restatement §§ 82 and 83. [§ 7–38] 142
      (a) Example. [§ 7–39] 143

3. Unsolicited Actions Are Insufficient to Act as Consideration. [§ 7–40] 143
  a. Example. [§ 7–41] 143

G. Specific Types of Transactions Raising Consideration Issues. [§ 7–42] 144
  1. Transaction in Which the Consideration of One Party Is Worth Substantially Less than the Other: The "Peppercorn" Theory of Consideration. [§ 7–43] 144
    a. Inadequate Consideration May Be Evidence of Fraud, Duress, or Undue Influence. [§ 7–44] 144
    b. Inadequate Consideration May Be Evidence of "Sham" Consideration. [§ 7–45] 145
      (1) Example. [§ 7–46] 145
  2. Illusory Promises. [§ 7–47] 145
    a. Traditional Rule: Contracts with Personal Satisfaction Clauses Were Not Enforceable. [§ 7–48] 146
    b. Modern Rule: The Implied Duty of Good Faith and Fair Dealing Renders Contracts with Personal Satisfaction Clauses Enforceable. [§ 7–49] 146

TABLE OF CONTENTS

    (1) Example. [§ 7–50] 146
    (2) Exception: "Sale on Approval" and "Sale or Return" Contracts. [§ 7–51] 147
  c. "Exclusive Dealing" Contracts. [§ 7–52] 147
    (1) Example. [§ 7–53] 148
    (2) Example of Exclusive Dealing Contract: *Wood v. Lucy, Lady Duff Gordon*. [§ 7–54] 148
    (3) Example Based on *Kubik v. J & R Foods of Oregon*. [§ 7–55] 149
  d. "Requirements" and "Output" Contracts. [§ 7–56] 149
    (1) Example. [§ 7–57] 150
    (2) Requirements and Output Contracts Probably Have No Implied Floor, but Do Have an Implied Ceiling. [§ 7–58] 151
    (3) If a Target Quantity Is Specified in an Output or Requirements Contract. [§ 7–59] 152
  e. Contracts with Expressly Conditional Promises: Such Contracts Are Enforceable Unless the Condition Is Within the Unfettered Discretion of the Promisor. [§ 7–60] 152
    (1) Example. [§ 7–61] 153
    (2) Example. [§ 7–62] 153
    (3) Example: Aleatory Promises. [§ 7–63] 153
    (4) Even if the Occurrence of a Condition Is to *Some* Extent Within the Discretion of the Promisor, the Promise Is Nonetheless Enforceable if Any Restriction on the Promisor's Discretion Can Be Implied. [§ 7–64] 153
      (a) Example. [§ 7–65] 154
  f. Special Illusory Promise Problems Regarding Termination-at-Will Clauses. [§ 7–66] 154
    (1) Traditional Rule: Contracts with Termination-at-Will Clauses Were Deemed Illusory and Hence Unenforceable. [§ 7–67] 154
      (a) Example: *Miami Coca-Cola Bottling Co. v. Orange Crush Co.* [§ 7–68] 154
    (2) Modern Rule: Contracts with Termination-at-Will Clauses Are Probably Enforceable. [§ 7–69] 155
    (3) The UCC Approach to Terminable-at-Will Contracts: The Reasonable Notification Requirement Avoids Most Illusory Promise Issues. [§ 7–70] 156
3. Modification of Existing Agreements: The Pre-Existing Duty Rule. [§ 7–71] 156

  a. The General Common Law Rule: "New" Consideration Is Required for an Enforceable Modification. [§ 7–72] 156
   (1) Example of the Extortionist. [§ 7–73] 157
   (2) Example of the Profiteer. [§ 7–74] 158
   (3) Example of the "Dishonest Compromiser." [§ 7–75] 158
  b. Restatement 2d § 73: The Pre-Existing Duty Rule. [§ 7–76] 158
   (1) "Getting Around" the Pre-Existing Duty Rule. [§ 7–77] 159
   (2) Example. [§ 7–78] 159
   (3) Example. [§ 7–79] 160
   (4) Example of *Foakes v. Beer*. [§ 7–80] 160
  c. Exceptions to the Pre-Existing Duty Rule. [§ 7–81] 161
   (1) Modifications Enforceable Without Consideration Under the UCC. [§ 7–82] 162
   (2) Modifications Enforceable Without Consideration in Light of Unanticipated Circumstances. [§ 7–83] 162
   (3) Modifications Enforceable Without Consideration if Statutorily Permitted. [§ 7–84] 163
   (4) Modifications Enforceable Without Consideration in Light of Material Reliance. [§ 7–85] 163
  d. The Pre-Existing Duty Rule and Public Officials and Other Governmental Workers. [§ 7–86] 163
   (1) Example. [§ 7–87] 164
 4. Settlement of Claims Based on Incorrect Information. [§ 7–88] 164
  a. Example Based on *Fiege v. Boehm*. [§ 7–89] 165
 5. Purported, but Unperformed, Consideration Is Not Effective Consideration. [§ 7–90] 165
  a. Exception: Purported Consideration Sufficient for Option Contracts. [§ 7–91] 166
 6. Voidable Promises Can Serve as Valid Consideration. [§ 7–92] 166
  a. Example. [§ 7–93] 166
H. Exam Approach to Consideration Issues. [§ 7–94] 166

Chapter 8. Promissory Estoppel and the Seal 169
A. The Promissory Estoppel Doctrine. [§ 8–1] 169
B. Promissory Estoppel Is Not a "Substitute" for Consideration. [§ 8–2] 169
C. Elements of Promissory Estoppel Under the Second Restatement. [§ 8–3] 170

TABLE OF CONTENTS

	1. Example of *Ricketts v. Scothorn.* [§ 8–4]	170
	2. Difference Between Promissory Estoppel Under the First and Second Restatement of Contracts. [§ 8–5]	171
D.	Types of Promises Made Enforceable Under Promissory Estoppel. [§ 8–6]	171
	1. Gift Promises. [§ 8–7]	171
	2. Oral Promises to Convey Land. [§ 8–8]	172
	3. Charitable Subscriptions. [§ 8–9]	172
	a. Example. [§ 8–10]	172
	4. Offers That Induce Foreseeable Reliance of a Substantial Nature Become Irrevocable. [§ 8–11]	172
	a. Example. [§ 8–12]	173
	b. Offers by Sub-Contractors. [§ 8–13]	173
	5. Actions Taken in Reliance on Promises Made in Preliminary Negotiations. [§ 8–14]	174
	a. Example of *Hoffman v. Red Owl Stores.* [§ 8–15]	174
E.	Remedies When a Promise Is Enforced Under Promissory Estoppel. [§ 8–16]	175
	1. Example. [§ 8–17]	175
	2. Example of *Hoffman v. Red Owl Stores.* [§ 8–18]	175
F.	Exam Approach to Promissory Estoppel Issues. [§ 8–19]	176
G.	The Common Law Seal. [§ 8–20]	176

Chapter 9. Modifications (with an Emphasis on UCC § 2–209) 177

A.	Modification, Generally. [§ 9–1]	177
	1. The Concern Regarding Modifications. [§ 9–2]	177
B.	Modification Under the UCC. [§ 9–3]	178
	1. Modifications Under the UCC Are Enforceable Even Without Consideration. [§ 9–4]	179
	a. Example. [§ 9–5]	179
	2. An Oral Modification Is Unenforceable Under the UCC if the Parties Have Agreed to a "No Modification Except by Signed Writing" Clause. [§ 9–6]	179
	3. The Contract, as Modified, Must Satisfy the Statute of Frauds to Be Enforceable Under the UCC. [§ 9–7]	180
	a. Example. [§ 9–8]	180
	b. Example. [§ 9–9]	181
	4. A Modification That Is Unenforceable Because It Is Not in Writing Can Still Operate as an Enforceable Waiver Under the UCC. [§ 9–10]	181
	a. The First Interpretation of How § 2–209(4) Operates: The Only Way a No Modification Except in Writing Clause, or the Statute of Frauds, May Be "Waived" Is by Written Agreement of the Parties Specifically Waiving the Clause or Applicability of the Statute. [§ 9–11]	182

TABLE OF CONTENTS

- b. The Second Interpretation of How § 2–209(4) Operates: An Attempted Oral Modification Acts as an Implied Waiver of Both a No Modification Except in Writing Clause and the Statute of Frauds. [§ 9–12] 182
- c. The Third Interpretation of How § 2–209(4) Operates: The Terms of a Bilateral Oral Modification Are Inadmissible, but Evidence of One Party's Unilateral Waiver Is Admissible upon a Showing of Good Faith. [§ 9–13] 183
- d. The Fourth Interpretation of How § 2–209(4) Operates: Evidence of the Modification Is Freely Admissible if the Party Seeking to Establish the Modification Can Show Reliance on the Modified Agreement. [§ 9–14] 184
- e. Example of *Wisconsin Knife Works v. National Metal Crafters.* [§ 9–15] 185
5. Retraction of Waivers in Modifications Controlled by the UCC. [§ 9–16] 186
   - a. Example. [§ 9–17] 187
6. Party Proposing the Modification Must Act in Good Faith in Order for a Modification Under a UCC Agreement to Be Enforceable. [§ 9–18] 187
   - a. Example. [§ 9–19] 187
C. Modifications at Common Law and Under the Restatement. [§ 9–20] 188
   1. "No Modification Except in Writing" Clauses and Statute of Frauds Concerns Are Not Applicable to Oral Modifications Governed by Common Law Rules. [§ 9–21] 188
   2. Restatement Rules. [§ 9–22] 188
      - a. Instances Where Restatement Allows *Some* Modifications to Be Enforceable Without Consideration. [§ 9–23] 188
      - b. Restatement Rule Requires Statue of Frauds to Be Satisfied for the Contract, as Modified. [§ 9–24] 189
      - c. Difference Between Modification and Rescission of Prior Agreement Followed by Entry into New Contract. [§ 9–25] 189
D. Graphic Summary of UCC and Common Law Rules Regarding Modification. [§ 9–26] 190
E. Modification Under the CISG. [§ 9–27] 190
F. Distinguishing Modification from the Parol Evidence Rule. [§ 9–28] 190
   1. Example. [§ 9–29] 191
G. Exam Approach to Modification Issues. [§ 9–30] 191

TABLE OF CONTENTS

PART IV. "VOIDABILITY" AND DEFENSES TO CONTRACT FORMATION

Chapter 10. The Statute of Frauds 195
- A. The Statute of Frauds Doctrine. [§ 10–1] 195
  1. Purposes of the Statute. [§ 10–2] 195
  2. Effect of the Statute Applying. [§ 10–3] 196
- B. Major Types of Cases Covered by the Statute. [§ 10–4] 196
  1. Nomenclature Under the Statute of Frauds Doctrine. [§ 10–5] 197
- C. Type One: Contracts for the Transfer of an Interest in Land. [§ 10–6] 197
  1. The Transfer of Virtually All Interests in Land, Except Licenses, Are Covered by the Statute. [§ 10–7] 198
     a. "Transfer of Interest in Land" Includes Option Contracts. [§ 10–8] 198
     b. Promises to Pay in Return for a Present Conveyance Are Outside the Statute. [§ 10–9] 198
  2. Satisfying the Statute. [§ 10–10] 198
     a. The "Merger" Doctrine. [§ 10–11] 199
  3. Reasonable Reliance by the Purchaser Also Makes a Promise to Transfer an Interest in Land Enforceable: The Part Performance Exception. [§ 10–12] 199
     a. Example. [§ 10–13] 199
- D. Type Two: Contracts Which, by Their Terms, Cannot Be Performed Within a Year of Their Making. [§ 10–14] 200
  1. It Is Only When, by Its Own Terms, Completed Performance of a Promise Is *Impossible* Within a Year of Its Making That the Statute Applies. [§ 10–15] 200
     a. Example. [§ 10–16] 200
     b. Example. [§ 10–17] 200
     c. Example. [§ 10–18] 201
  2. Split of Opinion as to Whether Contracts Terminable Within a Year Are Within the Statute. [§ 10–19] 201
  3. The Full Performance Exception: Complete Performance by One Party Takes the Contract Outside the Statute. [§ 10–20] 201
     a. Part Performance Does Not Take the Contract Outside the Statute. [§ 10–21] 202
  4. Satisfying the Statute in a Contract Which, by Its Terms, Cannot Be Performed Within a Year. [§ 10–22] 202
     a. Merger Doctrine Applies. [§ 10–23] 203
- E. Type Three: Contracts Made in Consideration of Marriage. [§ 10–24] 203
  1. Pre-Nuptial Agreements. [§ 10–25] 203

xxiii

TABLE OF CONTENTS

- F. Type Four: Contracts Where One Party Acts as Surety for Another. [§ 10–26] 203
  1. Definition of Surety. [§ 10–27] 204
     a. Example. [§ 10–28] 204
  2. Where the Supposed Surety Is Primarily, Not Secondarily, Liable, No Suretyship Exists and the Contract Is Outside the Statute. [§ 10–29] 204
     a. Example. [§ 10–30] 204
  3. The "Main Purpose" or "Leading Object" Exception. [§ 10–31] 205
     a. Example. [§ 10–32] 205
     b. Example. [§ 10–33] 205
  4. Satisfying the Statute in Suretyship Contracts. [§ 10–34] 205
- G. Type Five: Contracts for the Sale of Goods for $500 or More Under UCC § 2–201. [§ 10–35] 206
  1. Structure of UCC § 2–201. [§ 10–36] 206
  2. Satisfying the Statute Under § 2–201(1). [§ 10–37] 207
     a. Example. [§ 10–38] 207
     b. Typical Problems Under § 2–201(1). [§ 10–39] 208
        (1) Divisible Contracts. [§ 10–40] 208
        (2) Decision to Limit Enforcement of Agreement to Less than $500. [§ 10–41] 208
        (3) A Contract Cannot Be Enforced Beyond the Quantity Shown in the Writing. [§ 10–42] 208
        (4) A Contract Containing No Formal "Signature" Can Nonetheless Fulfill the "Signed by" Requirement. [§ 10–43] 209
  3. Satisfying the Statute Under § 2–201(2): The Merchant's Confirmatory Memorandum. [§ 10–44] 209
     a. Example. [§ 10–45] 209
     b. Effect on the Recipient of a Valid Merchant's Confirmatory Memorandum. [§ 10–46] 210
        (1) Example. [§ 10–47] 210
     c. Effect of Objecting Within Ten Days. [§ 10–48] 211
     d. Effect of Either Party Not Being a Merchant. [§ 10–49] 211
     e. Effect of the Confirming Memorandum Not Satisfying § 2–201(1) Against the Sender. [§ 10–50] 211
  4. Satisfying the Statute Under § 2–201(3). [§ 10–51] 212
     a. Specially Manufactured Goods. [§ 10–52] 212
     b. Admission. [§ 10–53] 212
     c. Performance. [§ 10–54] 213
        (1) Part Performance. [§ 10–55] 213
           (a) Example Based on *Allied Grape Growers v. Bronco Wine Co.* [§ 10–56] 213

		d.	Review Problem. [§ 10–57] 214
H.	Enforcement of Oral Promises in Contracts Within the Statute, Other than Transfer of Land Interests, by Reliance and Estoppel. [§ 10–58] 214		
	1.	Example Based on *Allied Grape Growers v. Bronco Wine Co.* [§ 10–59] 215	
I.	The Statute as Applied to Modifications of Existing Contracts. [§ 10–60] 215		
J.	Consequence of Not Satisfying the Statute of Frauds. [§ 10–61] 216		
	1.	Example. [§ 10–62]..216	
	2.	Example. [§ 10–63]..216	
	3.	Restitution Required upon Disaffirmance. [§ 10–64] 217	
K.	Mnemonic Summary. [§ 10–65] 217		
L.	Exam Approaches to Statute of Frauds Issues. [§ 10–66]...........217		

Chapter 11. Capacity 219

A.	Capacity, Generally. [§ 11–1] 219			
B.	Incapacity Due to Infancy/Minority. [§ 11–2] 219			
	1.	Example. [§ 11–3]..219		
	2.	Ratification of a Contract Entered into by a Minor. [§ 11–4] 220		
		a.	Express Ratification. [§ 11–5] 220	
		b.	Implied-in-Fact Ratification. [§ 11–6]...........................220	
		c.	Ratification by Silence: Implied-in-Law Ratification. [§ 11–7]...220	
	3.	Restitution upon Disaffirmance of Contracts Entered into by Minors. [§ 11–8]..221		
		a.	Majority Rule Regarding Treatment of the Economic Benefit Received by the Minor While in Possession of the Goods: No Restitutionary Recovery Permitted in Credit Sales. [§ 11–9]...221	
			(1)	Minority View: The "New Hampshire" Rule Allows for Restitutionary Recovery in Some Situations Even in Credit Sales. [§ 11–10]...........222
		b.	Treatment of the Economic Benefit Received by the Minor While in Possession of the Goods or Services: Restitutionary Recovery Permitted in Cash Sales. [§ 11–11]..222	
		c.	Treatment of the Economic Benefit Received by the Minor While in Possession of the Goods or Services: Restitutionary Recovery Permitted in Contracts for "Necessities," Even in Credit Sales. [§ 11–12] 223	
		d.	Treatment of the Economic Benefit Received Procured by the Minor via Misrepresentation of Age by Minor. [§ 11–13] 223	
			(1)	Example. [§ 11–14]...223

TABLE OF CONTENTS

- C. Incapacity Due to Mental Infirmity. [§ 11–15] 224
  1. Rules When a Guardian Has Been Appointed Due to "Mental Illness or Defect." [§ 11–16] 224
  2. Rules When a Party Lacks the Mental Capacity to Contract Under Either the "Cognition" or "Acts" Tests. [§ 11–17] 225
     a. Avoidability Under the "Cognition" Test. [§ 11–18].....225
     b. Avoidability Under the "Volition" or "Acts" Test. [§ 11–19]...225
        (1) Example of *Ortelere v. Teacher's Retirement Board*. [§ 11–20] 225
     c. Ratification of Contracts Entered into by Individuals with Mental Incapacity Under the "Cognition" or "Acts" Tests. [§ 11–21] 226
     d. Limitation on Avoidability of Contracts Entered into by Individuals with Mental Incapacity Under the "Cognition" or "Acts" Tests. [§ 11–22]....................226
        (1) Example. [§ 11–23] 227
  3. Rules When an Individual Temporarily Lacks Mental Capacity Due to Intoxication from Alcohol or Other Drug Use. [§ 11–24] 227
     a. Restatement Rule. [§ 11–25] 227
        (1) Example. [§ 11–26] 227
     b. Majority Rule. [§ 11–27] 228
- D. Exam Approach to Incapacity Issues. [§ 11–28] 228

Chapter 12. Mistake and Misunderstanding 229
- A. The Mistake Doctrine. [§ 12–1]..229
- B. Definition of "Mistake." [§ 12–2]..229
  1. Erroneous Belief as to the Future Is Not a "Mistake." [§ 12–3] 229
  2. Mistake of Law Can Be a Mistake of Fact. [§ 12–4] 229
  3. "Mistake" Distinguished from "Misunderstanding." [§ 12–5] 230
- C. Unilateral and Mutual Mistake. [§ 12–6] 230
- D. Mutual Mistake Defined. [§ 12–7] 230
  1. Elements Necessary to Establish Mutual Mistake. [§ 12–8] 230
     a. The Mistake Must Be as to a "Basic Assumption" on Which the Contract Was Made. [§ 12–9] 231
     b. The Mistake Must Have a "Material Effect" on the Agreed Transaction. [§ 12–10]...................................231
     c. The Party Seeking to Avoid the Contract Must Not Bear the Risk of Making the Mistake. [§ 12–11] 231
  2. Examples Applying Mutual Mistake Principles. [§ 12–12] 232
     a. Example of *Sherwood v. Walker*. [§ 12–13] 232

		b.	Example of *Wood v. Boynton*. [§ 12–14] 233
			(1) Conscious Ignorance. [§ 12–15] 233
		c.	Example of Land Sales. [§ 12–16] 234
	3.	Limitation on When a Party May Void a Contract Based on Mutual Mistake: Reasonable Time After Discovery. [§ 12–17] 234
	4.	Effect of Mutual Mistake. [§ 12–18] 234
		a.	Restitution Required if Contract Avoided on the Basis of Mutual Mistake. [§ 12–19] 234
	5.	Review Problem. [§ 12–20] 234
E.	Unilateral Mistake Defined. [§ 12–21] 235
	1.	Elements Necessary to Establish Unilateral Mistake. [§ 12–22] 235
		a.	Example of Mistaken Bid Cases. [§ 12–23] 236
		b.	Example of Mistaken Payment Cases. [§ 12–24] 237
	2.	Limitation on When a Party May Void a Contract Based on Unilateral Mistake: A Reasonable Time After Discovery. [§ 12–25] 237
	3.	Effect of Unilateral Mistake. [§ 12–26] 237
		a.	Restitution Required upon Avoidance of Contract Entered into Under Unilateral Mistake. [§ 12–27] 237
F.	The "Misunderstanding" Doctrine. [§ 12–28] 238
	1.	Distinguishing "Misunderstanding" from "Mistake." [§ 12–29] 238
	2.	Effect of Misunderstanding. [§ 12–30] 238
		a.	Example of *Raffles v. Wichelhaus*. [§ 12–31] 238
		b.	Example. [§ 12–32] 239
		c.	Example. [§ 12–33] 239
G.	Exam Approach to Mistake and Misunderstanding Issues. [§ 12–34] 239

Chapter 13. Duress **241**

A.	The Problem of Duress. [§ 13–1] 241
B.	Duress by Physical Compulsion. [§ 13–2] 241
C.	Duress by "Improper" Threat. [§ 13–3] 242
	1. What Constitutes an "Improper" Threat? [§ 13–4] 242
	2. Improper Threat When Terms of the Exchange Appear Fair. [§ 13–5] 242
	a. Example. [§ 13–6] 243
	b. Example. [§ 13–7] 243
	c. Example. [§ 13–8] 243
	d. Example. [§ 13–9] 244
	3. Improper Threat Where Terms of the Exchange Appear Unfair. [§ 13–10] 244
	a. Example. [§ 13–11] 244
	b. Example. [§ 13–12] 244
	c. Example. [§ 13–13] 245

TABLE OF CONTENTS

       d.   Review Problem: Economic Duress. [§ 13–14] 245
D. Restitution Recoverable upon Avoidance of Contract for Duress. [§ 13–15] 245
E. Exam Approach to Duress Issues. [§ 13–16]................................246

Chapter 14. Undue Influence 247
A. The Undue Influence Doctrine. [§ 14–1] 247
B. Elements Necessary to Establish Undue Influence. [§ 14–2] 247
    1. The First Element: A "Special Relationship." [§ 14–3] 247
    2. The Second Element: Improper Persuasion. [§ 14–4]...........248
C. Restitution Recoverable upon Avoidance of the Contract for Undue Influence. [§ 14–5] 248
D. Exam Approach to Undue Influence Issues. [§ 14–6]................249

Chapter 15. Misrepresentation.. 251
A. The Misrepresentation Doctrine. [§ 15–1] 251
B. Types of Misrepresentation. [§ 15–2] 251
C. Effect of Misrepresentation. [§ 15–3] 252
D. "Void" Contracts Resulting from Fraud in the *Factum*. [§ 15–4] 252
    1. Example. [§ 15–5]..252
E. Elements Necessary to Establish Fraud in the Inducement. [§ 15–6] 253
    1. Misrepresentation of "Fact." [§ 15–7] 253
        a. Distinguishing "Fact" from "Opinion." [§ 15–8] 253
            (1) Exceptions When Even a Statement of "Opinion" Can Serve as the Basis for a Misrepresentation Claim. [§ 15–9]...254
                (a) Example. [§ 15–10] 254
        b. Distinguishing "Existing Fact" from "Prediction of Future Events." [§ 15–11]...255
        c. Distinguishing "Fact" from "Statement of Intention": The Difference Between Ordinary Breach and Misrepresentation. [§ 15–12]...255
            (1) Example. [§ 15–13] 255
        d. Distinguishing "Fact" from "Puffing" or "Trade Talk." [§ 15–14] 256
        e. When a Party's Silence Can Act as a Factual Misrepresentation: The Duty to Disclose. [§ 15–15] 257
            (1) Example. [§ 15–16] 258
            (2) Example. [§ 15–17] 258
            (3) Example. [§ 15–18] 258
            (4) Example. [§ 15–19] 259
            (5) Example. [§ 15–20] 259

TABLE OF CONTENTS

      f.   Silence Does Not Act as an Actionable Misrepresentation When the Parties Are Dealing at "Arm's Length" and None of the Exceptions Apply. [§ 15–21] 260
    2.   The Misrepresentation Must Be Either *Fraudulent* or *Material*. [§ 15–22] 260
      a.   Definition of "Fraudulent." [§ 15–23] 260
        (1)   Example. [§ 15–24] 261
        (2)   Example. [§ 15–25] 261
        (3)   Example. [§ 15–26] 261
      b.   Definition of "Material." [§ 15–27] 262
        (1)   Example. [§ 15–28] 262
    3.   The Misrepresentation Must Induce Actual Reliance. [§ 15–29] 262
    4.   The Reliance Must Be Reasonable. [§ 15–30] 262
      a.   Example. [§ 15–31] 263
      b.   Example. [§ 15–32] 263
F.   Limitation on Voidability of Contract Based on Misrepresentation: The Claim Must Be Asserted Within a Reasonable Time After Discovery. [§ 15–33] 263
G.   Restitution Required upon Avoidance of Contract Based on Misrepresentation. [§ 15–34] 263
H.   Exam Approach to Misrepresentation Issues. [§ 15–35] 264

Chapter 16. Unconscionability **265**
A.   The Unconscionability Doctrine. [§ 16–1] 265
B.   Unconscionability Applies to UCC and Non-UCC Transactions. [§ 16–2] 265
C.   Effect of Unconscionability Under Modern Contract Law. [§ 16–3] 266
    1.   Effect of Unconscionability Under Common Law. [§ 16–4] 266
D.   Elements Necessary to Establish Unconscionability Under Modern Contract Law. [§ 16–5] 267
    1.   Definition of "Procedural" Unconscionability. [§ 16–6] 267
    2.   Definition of "Substantive" Unconscionability. [§ 16–7] 267
    3.   Some Combination of Both Procedural and Substantive Unconscionability Is Necessary for Application of the Doctrine: The "Sliding Scale" Test. [§ 16–8] 267
      a.   *Williams v. Walker-Thomas Furniture Co.* [§ 16–9] 268
        (1)   Criticism of, and Additional Facts Relevant to, *Williams v. Walker-Thomas Furniture Co.* [§ 16–10] 269
    4.   Unconscionability Applies to Conditions Present at the Time of Making the Contract. [§ 16–11] 271
    5.   Note on Adhesion Contracts. [§ 16–12] 271

TABLE OF CONTENTS

E. Unconscionability Not Limited to Consumer Transactions. [§ 16–13] 271
F. Unconscionability Applied to Clauses Which Limit Remedies or Disclaim Warranties. [§ 16–14] 271
G. Exam Approach to Unconscionability Issues. [§ 16–15] 272

Chapter 17. "Illegality" or Contracts "Against Public Policy" **273**
A. Illegality Discussed. [§ 17–1] 273
B. Definition of "Illegal" Contracts. [§ 17–2] 273
C. Common Types of "Illegal" Contracts. [§ 17–3] 273
    1. Agreements for the Performance of Criminal Acts. [§ 17–4] 274
    2. Gambling Contracts. [§ 17–5] 274
    3. Contracts Obtained by Bribery. [§ 17–6] 274
        a. Example. [§ 17–7] 274
    4. Contracts in Which a Party Releases Another from Tort Liability. [§ 17–8] 274
        a. Example. [§ 17–9] 274
    5. Agreements for Services Provided by Parties Who Should Be, but Are Not, Licensed. [§ 17–10] 275
        a. Example. [§ 17–11] 275
        b. Example. [§ 17–12] 275
    6. Agreements in Which the Seller Knows of Buyer's Illegal Purpose. [§ 17–13] 275
        a. Example. [§ 17–14] 275
        b. Example. [§ 17–15] 276
        c. Example. [§ 17–16] 276
D. General Rule: If an "Illegal" Agreement Is Wholly Executory, Neither Party Can Enforce It. [§ 17–17] 276
    1. Exception: Ignorance of Facts at Time Contract Made. [§ 17–18] 276
        a. Example. [§ 17–19] 276
    2. Exception: Statutes Designed to Protect a Particular Class. [§ 17–20] 277
        a. Example. [§ 17–21] 277
E. When "Illegal" Agreements Are Performed: Parties Are Generally Left as the Court Finds Them. [§ 17–22] 277
    1. Exception: The *In Pari Delicto* Doctrine. [§ 17–23] 277
        a. Example of *"in pari deicto"* in action: *Bateman Eichler v. Berner*. [§ 17–24] 277
    2. Exception: The *Locus Poenitentiae* Doctrine. [§ 17–25] 278
F. Divisibility and Severability. [§ 17–26] 278
G. Exam Approach to Illegality Issues. [§ 17–27] 279

TABLE OF CONTENTS

PART V. THE PAROL EVIDENCE RULE AND INTERPRETATION

Chapter 18. The Parol Evidence Rule 283
- A. The Parol Evidence Rule Generally. [§ 18–1] 283
  1. The Real Problem Giving Rise to the Parol Evidence Rule. [§ 18–2] 283
  2. Definition of "Parol Evidence." [§ 18–3] 284
- B. Statement of, and Steps to Analyze, the Parol Evidence Rule. [§ 18–4] 284
- C. Integration of a Document Under the Parol Evidence Rule. [§ 18–5] 285
  1. "Partial" and "Total" Integration: Defined. [§ 18–6] 285
  2. Effect of Classification as a "Partially" or "Totally" Integrated Contract. [§ 18–7] 286
  3. How to Determine Whether an Agreement Is Partially or Totally Integrated. [§ 18–8] 286
     - a. Williston's "Four Corner" Test to Determine Integration. [§ 18–9] 286
       - (1) The Williston View Today. [§ 18–10] 287
     - b. Corbin/Restatement View: Extrinsic Evidence Should Be Examined to Determine Integration. [§ 18–11] 287
     - c. Example Illustrating the Difference Between Williston and Corbin/Restatement Views. [§ 18–12] 288
- D. Determination of Whether a Term Is "Contradictory" or "Consistent": The Restatement's "Might Naturally" Test. [§ 18–13] 288
  1. Example of *Mitchell v. Lath*. [§ 18–14] 289
  2. Example. [§ 18–15] 289
  3. Effect of "Merger" or "Integration" Clauses. [§ 18–16] 290
  4. Effect of the Determination to Admit Parol Terms. [§ 18–17] 290
- E. Operation of Parol Evidence Rule Under Restatement. [§ 18–18] 291
- F. Situations When the Parol Evidence Rule Does Not Apply. [§ 18–19] 291
  1. Agreements Made After the Contract Has Been Formed. [§ 18–20] 291
  2. Where a Party Introduces Evidence to Show There Was No Valid Agreement. [§ 18–21] 291
  3. Evidence of a Condition Precedent. [§ 18–22] 292
  4. Evidence of a Failure to Pay Consideration. [§ 18–23] 292
     - a. Exception: Option Contracts. [§ 18–24] 292
  5. Evidence of Facts Establishing That the Contract Is Voidable. [§ 18–25] 292

TABLE OF CONTENTS

   6. Evidence That Contradicts "Precatory" Language or "Recitals of Fact." [§ 18–26]...292
   7. Evidence as to a Meaning of a Term Found in the Written Contract. [§ 18–27]...293
    a. Example. [§ 18–28]..293
 G. Relationship of the Parol Evidence Rule to the Statute of Frauds. [§ 18–29] 293
   1. Example. [§ 18–30]..294
 H. Review Problem. [§ 18–31]..294
 I. The Parol Evidence Rule Under the CISG. [§ 18–32] 295
 J. Exam Approach to Parol Evidence Rule Issues. [§ 18–33]..........295
 K. Graphic Summary of Parol Evidence Rule. [§ 18–34] 296

Chapter 19. Interpretation 297
 A. Interpretation Generally. [§ 19–1] 297
 B. Rules of Construction. [§ 19–2] 297
   1. An Interpretation That Gives Meaning to All Terms Is Preferable to an Interpretation Making a Part of the Agreement Surplusage. [§ 19–3]..297
   2. If Two Clauses Conflict, the More Specific Acts as an Exception to the General. [§ 19–4]..298
   3. Separately Negotiated Terms Are Given Greater Weight than Standardized Terms. [§ 19–5] 298
   4. Handwritten Terms Generally Control over Typed or Printed Ones; Typewritten Terms Generally Control over Printed Ones. [§ 19–6] 298
   5. If a Term Is Ambiguous, It Should Be Resolved Against the Drafting Party. [§ 19–7] 298
   6. The Expression of One Thing Is the Exclusion of Others. [§ 19–8] 298
 C. Rules of Interpretation. [§ 19–9]...299
   1. General Rules. [§ 19–10] 299
    a. Language Is Given Its Generally Prevailing Meaning in Society. [§ 19–11]...299
    b. Technical Terms to Be Given Their Technical Meaning in a Transaction Within That Field. [§ 19–12]..300
    c. Terms to Be Interpreted in Light of Their Meaning Within the Usage of Trade, Course of Dealing, or Course of Performance. [§ 19–13] 300
     (1) Hierarchy of Terms: Express, Course of Performance, Course of Dealing, Usage of Trade. [§ 19–14]...300
     (2) The "Reasonable Reconciliation" Doctrine. [§ 19–15]...301
      (a) Example of *Nanakuli Paving & Rock Co. v. Shell Oil Co., Inc.* [§ 19–16] 301

2. Admissibility of Extrinsic Evidence to Prove the Parties Had Their Own Special Meaning for a Term. [§ 19–17] 303
    a. Traditional Williston/Holmes View: The Plain Meaning Rule. [§ 19–18] 303
    b. More Contemporary Corbin/Restatement View: The "Reasonably Susceptible" Test. [§ 19–19] 304
       (1) Example of *Trident Center v. Connecticut General Life Ins. Co.* [§ 19–20] 305
3. Review Problem. [§ 19–21] 306
D. Exam Approach to Interpretation Issues. [§ 19–22] 307

Chapter 20. UCC § 2–202 309
A. UCC § 2–202: Combining the Parol Evidence Rule with Interpretation Rules. [§ 20–1] 309
B. How to Approach a § 2–202 Parol Evidence Rule Problem. [§ 20–2] 309
  1. Integration: Partially or Totally Integrated Contracts. [§ 20–3] 310
  2. When the Agreement Is Totally Integrated: No Parol Evidence Is Admissible. [§ 20–4] 310
  3. When the Writing Is Partially Integrated: "Contradictory" Parol Terms Are Inadmissible; "Consistent" Parol Terms Are Admissible. [§ 20–5] 310
    a. Determining Whether a Term Is "Contradictory": The "Would Certainly" Test. [§ 20–6] 310
       (1) Example. [§ 20–7] 311
       (2) Potential Limitation on the "Would Certainly" Test. [§ 20–8] 311
  4. Evidence of Course of Performance, Course of Dealing, and Usage of Trade Can Be Introduced to *Explain* a Term Found in the Contract, Regardless Whether the Agreement Is Partially or Totally Integrated. [§ 20–9] 312
    a. Course of Performance. [§ 20–10] 313
       (1) Example. [§ 20–11] 313
       (2) "Waiver" and Course of Performance. [§ 20–12] 313
    b. Course of Dealing. [§ 20–13] 314
       (1) Example. [§ 20–14] 314
    c. Usage of Trade. [§ 20–15] 314
       (1) Example. [§ 20–16] 314
       (2) Example of *Frigaliment Importing Co. v. B.N.S. International Sales Corp.* [§ 20–17] 315
    d. Hierarchy of Interpretation: Express Terms; Course of Performance, Course of Dealing, and Usage of Trade. [§ 20–18] 315
C. Situations Where UCC § 2–202 Does Not Apply. [§ 20–19] 316
D. Exam Approach to § 2–202 Issues. [§ 20–20] 316

E. Graphic Summary of § 2–202. [§ 20–21] 317

PART VI. CONDITIONS, PERFORMANCE, AND BREACH

Chapter 21. Conditions, Performance and Breach (with an Emphasis on Common Law Rules)..................................... **321**
A. Introduction and Overview. [§ 21–1] 321
B. Types of Conditions. [§ 21–2] 322
    1. Express, Implied-in-Fact, and Constructive Conditions. [§ 21–3] 322
        a. Express Conditions: Defined and Discussed. [§ 21–4] 322
            (1) Example of Express Condition. [§ 21–5] 322
        b. Implied-in-Fact Conditions: Defined and Discussed. [§ 21–6] 322
            (1) Example of Implied-in-Fact Condition. [§ 21–7] 323
        c. Constructive or Implied Conditions: Defined and Discussed. [§ 21–8] 323
            (1) Example of Constructive Condition. [§ 21–9] 324
    2. Conditions Precedent and Conditions Subsequent. [§ 21–10] 324
        a. Conditions Precedent: Defined and Discussed. [§ 21–11] 324
            (1) Example of Express Condition Precedent. [§ 21–12] 324
            (2) Effect of Classification as Express Condition Precedent. [§ 21–13] 325
                (a) Example of Effects of Contract with Express Condition Precedent. [§ 21–14] 325
        b. Conditions Subsequent: Defined and Discussed. [§ 21–15] 325
            (1) Example of Express Condition Subsequent. [§ 21–16] 326
            (2) Effect of Classification as Express Condition Subsequent. [§ 21–17] 326
                (a) Example of Effects of a Contract with Express Condition Subsequent. [§ 21–18] 326
        c. How to Tell Whether a Condition Is "Precedent" or "Subsequent." [§ 21–19] 327
        d. Restatement 2d Rejects Terms "Condition Precedent" and "Condition Subsequent." [§ 21–20] 328
    3. Concurrent Conditions. [§ 21–21] 328
C. Issues Involving Express Conditions. [§ 21–22] 328
    1. Express Conditions Are "Strictly Construed." [§ 21–23] 328
        a. Example of "Strict Construction" in an Express Condition Precedent. [§ 21–24] 329

- b. Example of "Strict Construction" in Express Condition Subsequent. [§ 21–25] 329
2. Why a Party Would Make a Duty Expressly Conditional on the Happening of an Event. [§ 21–26] 329
3. Issues Involved in Determining Whether a Contractual Obligation Is an Expressly Conditional Promise, an Unconditional Duty, or Both. [§ 21–27] 330
    - a. Example. [§ 21–28] 330
    - b. How a Court Determines Whether an Obligation Is a Conditional Promise, an Unconditional Duty, or Both. [§ 21–29] 331
        - (1) Interpretation That a Promise Is an Unconditional Duty, Rather than a Conditional Obligation, Is Favored When the Event Necessary to Fulfill the Condition Is Within the Obligee's Control. [§ 21–30] 332
            - (a) Example. [§ 21–31] 332
        - (2) Interpretation That Reduces Promisor's Risk of Forfeiture Is Preferred. [§ 21–32] 332
            - (a) Example. [§ 21–33] 332
        - (3) When in Doubt, a Promise Should Be Interpreted as an Unconditional Duty Rather than a Conditional Promise. [§ 21–34] 333
        - (4) Interpretation of a Term as Both a Duty and a Condition Is Very Unusual. [§ 21–35] 333
        - (5) Interpreting an "Ordinary" Promise as an Express Condition. [§ 21–36] 334
4. Issues Involved with Specific Types of Express Conditions. [§ 21–37] 334
    - a. Express Conditions of Satisfaction. [§ 21–38] 334
        - (1) Where Satisfaction Is Dependent upon the Subjective "Taste, Fancy, or Personal Judgment" of a Party to the Contract. [§ 21–39] 334
        - (2) Where Satisfaction Is Dependent upon Objective "Market" Factors. [§ 21–40] 335
        - (3) Where Satisfaction Is Dependent upon Satisfaction of a Third Party. [§ 21–41] 335
    - b. "Pay-if-Paid" Clauses Interpreted as "Time of Payment" Clauses. [§ 21–42] 336
D. Issues Associated with Constructive Conditions: Performance and Breach. [§ 21–43] 337
1. Role of Constructive Conditions. [§ 21–44] 337
    - a. Constructive Conditions Necessary for Reasonable Operation Under a Contract. [§ 21–45] 337
        - (1) Example. [§ 21–46] 337

- b. Concurrent Conditions of Exchange and Tender of Performance as a Constructive Condition. [§ 21–47] 338
  - (1) Tender: Defined and Discussed. [§ 21–48] 339
  - (2) Resolution of Scenarios. [§ 21–49] 339
- c. Constructive Conditions Regulating the Order of Performance. [§ 21–50] 340
  - (1) Order of Performance Where Simultaneous Exchange of Performance Is Possible. [§ 21–51] 340
  - (2) Order of Performance Where One Party's Performance Will Take Time and the Other Does Not. [§ 21–52] 341
    - (a) Example. [§ 21–53] 341
    - (b) Issues in the Order of Performance Rules Where a Simultaneous Exchange of Performance Is Not Possible. [§ 21–54] 342
- d. Performance and Constructive Conditions' Role in Immaterial, Material and Total Breach. [§ 21–55] 342
  - (1) Definitions of Immaterial, Material, and Total Breach. [§ 21–56] 343
    - (a) Immaterial Breach. [§ 21–57] 343
    - (b) Material Breach. [§ 21–58] 344
    - (c) Total Breach. [§ 21–59] 344
  - (2) Consequences of Deciding That a Breach Is Immaterial, Material, or Total. [§ 21–60] 345
  - (3) Role of Constructive Conditions in Determining the Consequences of Material and Immaterial Breach. [§ 21–61] 347
  - (4) The Only Situation in Which the Materiality of the Breach Matters: Bilateral Contracts in Which There Are Executory Duties Remaining on Both Sides at the Time of the Breach. [§ 21–62] 348
    - (a) The Doctrine of Material/Immaterial Breach Does Not Apply to Unilateral Contracts. [§ 21–63] 348
    - (b) The Doctrine of Material/Immaterial Breach Does Not Apply to Bilateral Contracts When All the Duties of One Party Have Been Completely Performed. [§ 21–64] 349
  - (5) How to Determine Whether a Breach Is Material or Immaterial. [§ 21–65] 350
  - (6) The "First" Material Breach Doctrine. [§ 21–66] 351
    - (a) Example. [§ 21–67] 352

- (7) The Substantial Performance Doctrine: Classic Application of the Immaterial Breach Doctrine. [§ 21–68] 352
  - (a) How to Determine Whether a Promise Has Been Substantially Performed. [§ 21–69] 353
  - (b) *Jacob & Youngs v. Kent.* [§ 21–70] 353
  - (c) Example. [§ 21–71] 356
- (8) Doctrines That "Transform" Material Breaches into Immaterial Breaches. [§ 21–72] 357
  - (a) The Divisibility (or Part Performance) Doctrine. [§ 21–73] 357
    - (i) Requirements for Applying the Divisibility Doctrine. [§ 21–74] 358
  - (b) Example. [§ 21–75] 358
  - (c) Example. [§ 21–76] 358
  - (d) Cure. [§ 21–77] 359
    - (i) Breaching Party Has a *Right* to Cure Until the Breach Becomes Total. [§ 21–78] 359
  - (e) Waiver. [§ 21–79] 359
    - (i) Example. [§ 21–80] 360
- (9) Total Breach. [§ 21–81] 360
  - (a) How a Material Breach Becomes a Total Breach. [§ 21–82] 360
    - (i) How to Determine What Is "a Reasonable Time" for Purposes of Transforming a Material Breach into a Total Breach. [§ 21–83] 361
  - (b) Example. [§ 21–84] 362
  - (c) Example. [§ 21–85] 362
  - (d) Effect of "Time Is of the Essence" Clauses. [§ 21–86] 363
  - (e) Total Breach Found upon Immaterial Breach Accompanied or Followed by a Repudiation. [§ 21–87] 363
    - (i) Example. [§ 21–88] 364
    - (ii) Exception: Failure to Make Installment Payments, Even When Accompanied by a Repudiation, Does Not Become a Total Breach. [§ 21–89] 364
  - (f) Example. [§ 21–90] 365
- (10) Restitution Available to Both Parties upon a Material Breach. [§ 21–91] 365
- E. Excuse of Conditions. [§ 21–92] 365
  - 1. Excuse of a Condition by Waiver, Estoppel and Election. [§ 21–93] 366
    - a. When a Waiver Can Take Place. [§ 21–94] 367

TABLE OF CONTENTS

		(1) Waivers Before, or Contemporaneous with, Contract Formation. [§ 21–95]	367
		(2) Waivers Made After Contract Formation, but Before Performance Is Due. [§ 21–96]	368
		(3) Waivers Made After Performance Was Due. [§ 21–97]	368
	b.	Implied Waivers: Waiver by Conduct. [§ 21–98]	369
		(1) Example. [§ 21–99]	370
	c.	Retraction of Waivers. [§ 21–100]	370
		(1) Example. [§ 21–101]	370
2.	Excuse of a Condition by Wrongful Prevention, Hindrance, and Noncooperation by the Party Benefitted by the Condition. [§ 21–102]		371
	a.	Example of Express Condition Precedent Being Excused by Affirmative Wrongful Prevention Based on *Barron v. Cain*. [§ 21–103]	372
	b.	Example of Express Condition Precedent Being Excused by Inaction Leading to Wrongful Prevention or Hindrance. [§ 21–104]	373
	c.	Example of Breach of Duty of Cooperation Stemming from the Duty of Good Faith and Fair Dealing Becoming a Material Breach Based on *Swartz v. War Memorial Comm'n*. [§ 21–105]	373
	d.	Review Problem. [§ 21–106]	374
3.	Excuse of Condition to Avoid Disproportionate Forfeiture. [§ 21–107]		374
	a.	Example. [§ 21–108]	375
	b.	Example Based on *Jacob & Youngs v. Kent*. [§ 21–109]	375

F. Exam Approach to Condition, Performance and Breach Issues. [§ 21–110] 376
   1. Approach to Express Conditions. [§ 21–111] 376
   2. Approach to Breach Issues. [§ 21–112] 377

Chapter 22. Conditions, Performance and Breach (with an Emphasis on Contracts Governed by the UCC) 379

A. Performance and Breach in Contracts Governed by the UCC, Generally. [§ 22–1] 379
B. Tender and Implied Conditions of Exchange Under the Code. [§ 22–2] 380
   1. The Acts Necessary to Fulfill a Seller's Obligation to Tender Delivery. [§ 22–3] 380
      a. Example. [§ 22–4] 381
   2. The Acts Necessary to Fulfill a Buyer's Obligation to Tender Payment. [§ 22–5] 381
   3. Order of Performance. [§ 22–6] 381

TABLE OF CONTENTS

- C. The Perfect Tender Rule Under the UCC. [§ 22–7] 382
  - 1. Example. [§ 22–8] 383
  - 2. Example. [§ 22–9] 383
  - 3. Example. [§ 22–10] 384
  - 4. Limitations on the Perfect Tender Rule. [§ 22–11] 384
    - a. The Seller's Right to Cure Under § 2–508. [§ 22–12] 385
      - (1) The Seller Has a Right to Cure When the "Time for Performance" Under the Contract Has Not Passed. [§ 22–13] 386
        - (a) Example. [§ 22–14] 386
      - (2) A Seller's Ability to Cure After the "Time for Performance" Under the Contract Has Expired. [§ 22–15] 387
        - (a) Example. [§ 22–16] 388
        - (b) Example. [§ 22–17] 388
      - (3) The Manner in Which a Seller May Cure: Cure by Replacement, Cure by Repair, or Cure by Cash Discount. [§ 22–18] 389
        - (a) Exception to the Rule That Cure by Repair Is Acceptable: The "Shaken Faith" Doctrine. [§ 22–19] 390
          - (i) Example Based on *Zabriske Chevrolet v. Smith*. [§ 22–20] 390
        - (b) Quality of Cure by Replacement: Majority View Does Not Require Repaired Good Sufficient to Satisfy Perfect Tender Rule. [§ 22–21] 391
      - (4) Buyer's Rights and Duties When Seller Attempts to Cure. [§ 22–22] 391
    - b. Installment Contracts. [§ 22–23] 392
      - (1) A Buyer May Reject a *Particular Shipment* Due to a Non-Conforming Tender of That Shipment *Only* if the Non-Conformity Both "Substantially Impairs" the Value of the Shipment and Is Not Cured. [§ 22–24] 392
        - (a) Example. [§ 22–25] 393
        - (b) Example. [§ 22–26] 393
      - (2) A Buyer May Terminate *the Entire Installment Contract* Due to a Non-Conforming Tender in a Particular Shipment or Shipments *Only* When the Non-Conformity in the Particular Shipment(s) Substantially Impairs the Value of the *Whole Contract*. [§ 22–27] 394
        - (a) Example. [§ 22–28] 394

TABLE OF CONTENTS

			(3) Rationale for Different Treatment of Buyer's Right to Reject Goods in Installment and Single Lot Contracts. [§ 22–29]..........395	
		c.	*De Minimis Non Curat Lex.* [§ 22–30] 396	
		d.	The "Complex Machine" Exception. [§ 22–31]..........396	
			(1) Example. [§ 22–32]..........396	
		e.	Usage of Trade; Course of Dealing; and Course of Performance. [§ 22–33] 396	
			(1) Example. [§ 22–34]..........397	
		f.	Revocation of Acceptance. [§ 22–35] 397	
D.	Performance in Contracts Governed by the UCC: Acceptance, Rejection, and Revocation of Acceptance. [§ 22–36] 397			
	1.	"Acceptance" of Goods Under the UCC. [§ 22–37] 397		
		a.	Effect of Acceptance. [§ 22–38]..........398	
	2.	Rejection of Goods Under the UCC. [§ 22–39] 399		
		a.	Actions a Buyer *Must* Take in Order to Reject Effectively. [§ 22–40]..........399	
		b.	Action a Buyer *Cannot* Take in Order to Reject Effectively. [§ 22–41]..........400	
			(1) Example. [§ 22–42]..........400	
		c.	Actions Which a Rejecting Buyer Is *Permitted to* Take Which Do Not Render Acceptance Ineffective. [§ 22–43]..........401	
		d.	Grounds for Rejection. [§ 22–44] 401	
	3.	Revocation of Acceptance. [§ 22–45] 402		
		a.	Elements of an Effective Revocation of Acceptance. [§ 22–46]..........402	
			(1) Example. [§ 22–47]..........403	
			(2) Example. [§ 22–48]..........403	
			(3) Example. [§ 22–49]..........403	
		b.	Rationale for Having Different Standards for Rejection than for Revocation of Acceptance. [§ 22–50]..........404	
		c.	The Relationship Between Cure and Revocation of Acceptance. [§ 22–51]..........404	
		d.	Typically No Restitution Is Recoverable upon Revocation. [§ 22–52] 405	
		e.	A Buyer of an Imperfect Good Who Neither Rejects nor Revokes: Breach of Warranty. [§ 22–53]..........405	
E.	Exam Approaches to Performance and Breach Issues Under the UCC. [§ 22–54]..........405			

Chapter 23. Prospective Nonperformance or Anticipatory Repudiation 407

A. The Anticipatory Repudiation (Also, Incorrectly, Called the "Anticipatory Breach") Doctrine. [§ 23–1]..........407

TABLE OF CONTENTS

- B. *Hochster v. De La Tour:* The Beginning of the Modern Anticipatory Repudiation Doctrine. [§ 23–2] 407
  1. Effect of Anticipatory Repudiation Under Modern Contract Law. [§ 23–3] 409
- C. Elements of Anticipatory Repudiation in Non-UCC Transactions. [§ 23–4] 410
  1. There Must Be a Repudiation of a Bilateral Contract with Executory Duties by Both Parties. [§ 23–5] 410
     a. Example. [§ 23–6] 411
     b. Example. [§ 23–7] 411
     c. Exception: Where Performance by the Innocent Party Is a Condition of the Repudiated Duty. [§ 23–8] 411
        (1) Example. [§ 23–9] 412
  2. The Repudiated Duty Must Be Important Enough That Its Non-Performance Would Be Deemed a Total Breach. [§ 23–10] 412
     a. Example. [§ 23–11] 412
  3. The Repudiation Must Be *Definite* and *Unequivocal*. [§ 23–12] 413
     a. Repudiation by Words. [§ 23–13] 413
        (1) Distinguishing Repudiation from a Request for Modification. [§ 23–14] 413
        (2) Distinguishing Repudiation from a Good Faith Difference of Opinion as to the Meaning of the Contract. [§ 23–15] 414
     b. Repudiation by Conduct. [§ 23–16] 414
        (1) Example. [§ 23–17] 415
        (2) Example. [§ 23–18] 415
  4. An Effective Repudiation May Only Repudiate Some Duties. [§ 23–19] 415
- D. Effect of Anticipatory Repudiation in Contracts Governed by the UCC. [§ 23–20] 415
  1. Anticipatory Repudiation Under UCC § 2–610. [§ 23–21] 416
  2. Anticipatory Repudiation by Failing to Provide Reasonable Assurances Under UCC § 2–609. [§ 23–22] 416
     a. What Constitutes "Reasonable Grounds for Insecurity" Under § 2–609(1) and (2)? [§ 23–23] 418
        (1) The Grounds for Demanding Assurances Need Not Be True; They Need Only Reasonably Appear to Be True to the Insecure Party. [§ 23–24] 419
        (2) Grounds for Insecurity Must Become Known to the Insecure Party *After* the Contract Is Formed, Not Before. [§ 23–25] 419

TABLE OF CONTENTS

		(3)	A Demand for Assurances Cannot Effectively Demand Only a Particular Kind of Assurance. [§ 23–26]	420
	b.		What Constitutes "Adequate Assurances" of Performance? [§ 23–27]	420
	c.		What an Insecure Party May Do While Waiting for a Response to a Justified Demand for Assurances. [§ 23–28]	421
	d.		Consequence of Failing to Respond Adequately to a Justified Demand for Assurances. [§ 23–29]	421
	e.		Right to Demand Adequate Assurances in Contracts Not Governed by the UCC. [§ 23–30]	422

E. Mechanics of Anticipatory Repudiation. [§ 23–31] 422
F. The Repudiating Party's Right to Retract the Repudiation. [§ 23–32] 423
    1. Example. [§ 23–33] 424
G. Exam Approaches to Anticipatory Repudiation Issues. [§ 23–34] 424

Chapter 24. Discharge of Duties by Subsequent Agreement—Substituted Performances, Substituted Contracts (Including Novations), Accords, Mutual Rescission, and Releases 427

A. Discharge of Duty by Subsequent Agreements, Generally. [§ 24–1] 427
B. Substituted Performance. [§ 24–2] 428
    1. Example. [§ 24–3] 428
    2. Example. [§ 24–4] 429
C. Substituted Contracts, Including Novations. [§ 24–5] 429
    1. Effect of Substituted Contract or Novation. [§ 24–6] 429
        a. Example. [§ 24–7] 430
        b. Example. [§ 24–8] 430
D. Accords. [§ 24–9] 430
    1. Example. [§ 24–10] 431
    2. Example. [§ 24–11] 431
    3. Recurring Problems Under the Most Frequent Use of Accords: Offers to Compromise a Disputed Debt. [§ 24–12] 431
        a. Consideration Issues When a Debtor Offers to Pay the Creditor Less than the Full Amount the Creditor Is Seeking. [§ 24–13] 432
        b. The Effect of Attempted Settlement by Tender of a Check in "Full Satisfaction" of a Debt. [§ 24–14] 433
            (1) A Creditor Who Cashes a Check Tendered "in Full Satisfaction" of a Debt Is Typically Held to Have Accepted the Offer of an Accord. [§ 24–15] 433

		(2)	The Effect of a Creditor Who Crosses out the "in Full Satisfaction" Language and Replaces It with "Without Prejudice" Language Instead: The Effect of UCC § 3–311. [§ 24–16] 433

- 4. How to Determine if a Subsequent Contract Is a Substituted Contract or an Accord. [§ 24–17] 434
- E. Mutual Rescission and Unilateral Renunciation. [§ 24–18] 434
  - 1. Unilateral Renunciation. [§ 24–19] 435
  - 2. Example. [§ 24–20] 435
  - 3. Example. [§ 24–21] 435
  - 4. General Rule: Mutual Rescissions Can Be Oral. [§ 24–22] 435
    - a. Exception: Mutual Rescission of a Duty to Transfer an Interest in Land Must Be in Writing. [§ 24–23] 436
  - 5. Distinguishing Mutual Rescission from Substituted Performance, Substituted Contracts, and Accords. [§ 24–24] 436
- F. Releases. [§ 24–25] 436
  - 1. Distinguishing Releases from Substituted Performance, Substituted Contracts, and Accords. [§ 24–26] 436
- G. Exam Approach to Substituted Performance, Substituted Contract, Novation, Accord, Mutual Rescission, and Release Issues. [§ 24–27] 437

Chapter 25. Discharge of Duties by Impossibility, Impracticability, or Frustration of Purpose 439

- A. Impossibility, Impracticability and Frustration, Generally. [§ 25–1] 439
  - 1. Effect of Establishing a Defense Based on Impossibility, Impracticability, and Frustration: Discharge of Remaining Duties. [§ 25–2] 440
- B. Impossibility: Defined and Discussed. [§ 25–3] 441
  - 1. Elements Necessary to Establish Impossibility. [§ 25–4] 441
    - a. An Event Must Occur That Makes Performance Objectively Impossible. [§ 25–5] 442
      - (1) Example. [§ 25–6] 442
      - (2) Example. [§ 25–7] 443
    - b. The Non-Occurrence of the Event Making Performance Impossible Must Have Been a "Basic Assumption" of Both Parties When They Entered into Their Agreement. [§ 25–8] 443
      - (1) *Taylor v. Caldwell*. [§ 25–9] 443
      - (2) Example. [§ 25–10] 443
      - (3) Example. [§ 25–11] 444

    c. The Event Making Performance Impossible Must Have Occurred Without the Fault of the Party Asserting the Defense. [§ 25–12]..................................444
      (1) Example. [§ 25–13]..445
    d. The Party Asserting the Impossibility Defense Must Not Have Assumed the Risk of the Occurrence of the Event Making Performance Impossible. [§ 25–14]......445
      (1) Example. [§ 25–15]..445
  2. Common Fact Situations Presenting Impossibility Issues. [§ 25–16]...446
    a. Death or Incapacity of a Particular Person Necessary for Performance ("Personal Service" Contracts). [§ 25–17]...446
      (1) Example. [§ 25–18]..447
      (2) Example. [§ 25–19]..447
    b. Death, Destruction, Deterioration, or the Failure to Come into Existence, of a Thing Necessary for Performance. [§ 25–20]..447
      (1) Example. [§ 25–21]..447
      (2) Example. [§ 25–22]..448
    c. Impossibility Due to Government Regulation or Order Making Performance Illegal. [§ 25–23]...............448
      (1) Example. [§ 25–24]..449
    d. Contracts to Repair Existing Building. [§ 25–25]........449
    e. Contracts to Erect New Buildings. [§ 25–26]..............449
    f. Labor Strikes. [§ 25–27]..449
    g. Land Sale Contracts. [§ 25–28].....................................450
  3. Partial Impossibility. [§ 25–29]..450
    a. Example. [§ 25–30]..450
C. Commercial Impracticability: Defined and Discussed. [§ 25–31]...451
  1. Elements Necessary to Establish an Impracticability Defense. [§ 25–32]...452
    a. An Event Must Occur That Makes Performance Commercially Impracticable. [§ 25–33].......................452
      (1) Example. [§ 25–34]..453
      (2) Example. [§ 25–35]..453
    b. The Non-Occurrence of the Event Making Performance Impractical Must Have Been a Basic Assumption of Both Parties When They Entered into Their Agreement. [§ 25–36]...453
      (1) Example. [§ 25–37]..454
    c. The Event Making Performance Impractical Must Occur Without the Fault of the Party Asserting the Defense. [§ 25–38]..454
      (1) Example. [§ 25–39]..454

TABLE OF CONTENTS

		d.	The Party Asserting the Defense Must Not Have Assumed the Risk of the Occurrence of the Event Making Performance Impractical. [§ 25–40]	454
			(1) Example. [§ 25–41]	455
			(2) Example of Construction of a New Structure. [§ 25–42]	456
			(3) Exception: Example of *Alcoa Co. v. Essex*. [§ 25–43]	457
	2.	Contrasting Impossibility and Impracticability. [§ 25–44]		458
D.	Frustration of Purpose: Defined and Discussed. [§ 25–45]			458
	1.	Elements Necessary to Establish the Frustration of Purpose Defense. [§ 25–46]		459
		a.	An Event Must Occur That Frustrates the Principal Purpose for Entering into a Contract. [§ 25–47]	459
			(1) Example. [§ 25–48]	460
		b.	The Non-Occurrence of the Event Frustrating Performance Must Have Been a Basic Assumption of Both Parties on Which the Contract Was Made. [§ 25–49]	461
			(1) Example of Leased Premises Destroyed During Term of Lease. [§ 25–50]	461
		c.	The Event Causing Frustration of Purpose Must Have Occurred Without the Fault of the Party Asserting the Defense. [§ 25–51]	461
			(1) Example. [§ 25–52]	461
		d.	The Party Asserting the Frustration Defense Must Not Have Assumed the Risk of the Occurrence of the Event Frustrating Performance of the Duty. [§ 25–53]	462
			(1) Example. [§ 25–54]	462
	2.	Examples of Frustration Cases. [§ 25–55]		462
		a.	Example of *Krell v. Henry (The Coronation Cases)*. [§ 25–56]	462
		b.	Example of *Lloyd v. Murphy*. [§ 25–57]	463
		c.	Example of *LaCumbre Golf & Country Club v. Santa Barbara Hotel*. [§ 25–58]	464
E.	Timing of Events Giving Rise to Impossibility, Impracticability, and Frustration: Relation to the "Mistake" Doctrine. [§ 25–59]			465
F.	Temporary Impossibility, Impracticability, or Frustration. [§ 25–60]			465
	1.	Example. [§ 25–61]		466
	2.	Example. [§ 25–62]		466
	3.	Example of *Autry v. Republic Prod'ns*. [§ 25–63]		466
G.	The Effect of a "Force Majeure" Clause on Impossibility, Impracticability, and Frustration. [§ 25–64]			467

TABLE OF CONTENTS

H. Restitution Available in Contracts Discharged Due to Impossibility, Impractibility, and Frustration. [§ 25–65] 467
I. Exam Approach to Impossibility, Impracticability, and Frustration of Purpose Issues. [§ 25–66] 467

PART VII. CONTRACTS INVOLVING THIRD PARTIES

Chapter 26. Third Party Beneficiary Contracts 471
A. Third Party Beneficiary Contracts Generally. [§ 26–1] 471
B. Terminology of Third Party Beneficiary Contracts. [§ 26–2] 471
    1. Example. [§ 26–3] 472
C. Issues Arising Under Third Party Beneficiary Contracts. [§ 26–4] 472
D. The Rights of the Beneficiary to Sue the Promisor. [§ 26–5] 473
    1. Early American Law: "Creditor" and "Donee" Beneficiaries Could Enforce the Promisor's Promise; "Incidental" Beneficiaries Could Not. [§ 26–6] 473
        a. "Donee" Beneficiaries: Defined and Discussed. [§ 26–7] 474
            (1) *Seaver v. Ransom.* [§ 26–8] 474
        b. "Creditor" Beneficiaries: Defined and Discussed. [§ 26–9] 475
            (1) *Lawrence v. Fox.* [§ 26–10] 476
        c. "Incidental" Beneficiary: Defined and Discussed. [§ 26–11] 477
            (1) Example. [§ 26–12] 477
    2. Modern Contract Law: "Intended" Beneficiaries Can Enforce the Promisor's Promise; "Incidental" Beneficiaries Cannot. [§ 26–13] 478
        a. "Intended" Beneficiaries: Defined and Discussed. [§ 26–14] 478
            (1) Example of *Seaver v. Ransom.* [§ 26–15] 479
            (2) Example of *Lawrence v. Fox.* [§ 26–16] 479
        b. "Incidental" Beneficiary: Defined and Discussed. [§ 26–17] 480
            (1) Example. [§ 26–18] 480
        c. Situations in Which Analysis Under the First and Second Restatements Would Yield Different Results. [§ 26–19] 481
            (1) Example. [§ 26–20] 482
            (2) Example. [§ 26–21] 482
        d. Important Principles in Analyzing Third Party Beneficiary Contracts Under Modern Contract Law. [§ 26–22] 483

(1) Performance of the Promisor's Promise Need Not Be Made Directly to the Third Party in Order for the Third Party to Be an Intended Beneficiary. [§ 26–23].................483
(2) The Identity of the Intended Beneficiary Need Not Be Known at the Time the Promisor/Promisee Contract Is Made. [§ 26–24].................484
(3) An Intended Beneficiary Need Not Manifest Any Agreement to the Promisor/Promisee Contract in Order to Gain Enforceable Rights Against the Promisee. [§ 26–25].................484
(4) A Beneficiary May Disclaim His or Her Rights to Enforce the Promisor's Promise. [§ 26–26].......485
(a) Example. [§ 26–27].................485
3. Recurring Fact Situations Concerning Whether a Beneficiary Is Intended or Incidental. [§ 26–28].................486
a. A Citizen's Right to Enforce a Government's Contract with a Private Party to Perform a Municipal Service. [§ 26–29].................486
b. Construction Contracts. [§ 26–30].................487
E. Rights of the Promisor in a Suit Brought by the Beneficiary. [§ 26–31].................488
1. An Intended Beneficiary Is Subject to Any Defense the Promisor Has Against the Promisee. [§ 26–32].................488
a. Example. [§ 26–33].................488
b. *Rouse v. United States.* [§ 26–34].................489
2. An Intended Beneficiary's Right to Sue the Promisor Is Subject to Any Limiting or Conditional Terms of the Promisor/Promisee Contract. [§ 26–35].................491
a. Example. [§ 26–36].................491
3. An Intended Third Party Beneficiary's Recovery Against the Promisor Is Subject to Offset by the Amount of Any Damages the Promisor Suffers as a Result of an Immaterial Breach by the Promisee. [§ 26–37].................491
a. Example. [§ 26–38].................492
F. Rights of an Intended Beneficiary to Sue the Promisee. [§ 26–39].................492
1. Example. [§ 26–40].................493
2. Example. [§ 26–41].................493
G. Rights of the Promisee Against the Promisor. [§ 26–42].................494
1. Example. [§ 26–43].................494
H. Rights of the Promisee and Promisor to Modify Their Contract to the Disadvantage of an Intended Beneficiary. [§ 26–44].................494
1. View of the Second Restatement: An Intended Beneficiary's Rights Vest upon His or Her Reliance on the Promisor's Promise. [§ 26–45].................495
a. Example. [§ 26–46].................495

TABLE OF CONTENTS

    2. Minority View: An Intended Beneficiary's Rights Vest Immediately upon Execution of the Promisor/Promisee Contract. [§ 26–47] 496
    3. Second Minority View: The Beneficiary's Rights Vest upon Knowledge of the Promisor's Promise. [§ 26–48] 496
I. Distinction Between Creditor-Like Intended Third Party Beneficiary Contracts and Accords or Novations. [§ 26–49] 497
    1. Example. [§ 26–50] 497
    2. Example. [§ 26–51] 497
J. Distinction Between a Third Party Beneficiary Contract Situation and an Assignment Situation. [§ 26–52] 498
K. Exam Approach to Third Party Beneficiary Issues. [§ 26–53] 498

Chapter 27. Assignments 499
A. Assignments Generally. [§ 27–1] 499
B. Definition, Terminology, and Major Effects of Assignments. [§ 27–2] 499
    1. Example. [§ 27–3] 500
C. Types of Assignments. [§ 27–4] 501
    1. "Gratuitous Assignments": Defined and Discussed. [§ 27–5] 501
        a. Example. [§ 27–6] 501
        b. Example. [§ 27–7] 501
    2. "Assignments for Value": Defined and Discussed. [§ 27–8] 502
        a. Example. [§ 27–9] 502
D. Elements Necessary to Make an Effective Assignment. [§ 27–10] 503
    1. The Assignor Must Manifest a Present Intention to Transfer an *Existing* Contractual Right. [§ 27–11] 503
        a. Example. [§ 27–12] 503
        b. Example. [§ 27–13] 504
        c. Special Rule Under Article 9 of the UCC: After-Acquired Property Clauses. [§ 27–14] 504
    2. There Must Be No Prohibition Against Assignment of the Particular Right. [§ 27–15] 505
        a. A Purported Assignment That Violates Public Policy Is Ineffective. [§ 27–16] 505
        b. A Purported Assignment That Materially and Adversely Affects the Obligor's Rights, Duties, and Justified Expectations as to Return Performance Is Ineffective. [§ 27–17] 506
            (1) Example. [§ 27–18] 507
            (2) Example. [§ 27–19] 507
            (3) Example. [§ 27–20] 508

TABLE OF CONTENTS

    c. A Purported Assignment That Violates a Valid "No Assignment" Provision in the Assignor/Obligor Contract Is Ineffective. [§ 27–21] 508
  3. General Rule: The Assignee Must Agree to the Assignment to Make It Effective. [§ 27–22] 510
   a. The Two Exceptions to the General Rule That the Assignee Must Agree Before the Assignment Is Effective. [§ 27–23] 510
    (1) Example. [§ 27–24] 510
    (2) Example. [§ 27–25] 511
    (3) Review Problem. [§ 27–26] 511
E. Recurring Issues That Arise in Determining the Effectiveness of Assignments. [§ 27–27] 512
 1. Notification to the Obligor of the Assignment Is Not Necessary for an Assignment to Be Effective. [§ 27–28] 512
 2. An Effective Assignment Can Be Partial. [§ 27–29] 512
  a. Example. [§ 27–30] 512
 3. An Effective Assignment Can Be Conditional or Otherwise Limited. [§ 27–31] 513
  a. Example. [§ 27–32] 513
 4. Distinction Between an Assignment and a Third Party Beneficiary Contract. [§ 27–33] 513
  a. Example. [§ 27–34] 514
  b. Example. [§ 27–35] 514
 5. Interpretation of the Phrase "Assignments of the Contract" or ". . . of All My Rights Under the Contract." [§ 27–36] 515
  a. Example. [§ 27–37] 515
 6. Oral Assignments Are Effective Unless the Subject Matter of the Assignment Is Within the Statute of Frauds. [§ 27–38] 515
  a. Example. [§ 27–39] 515
F. Rights of the Assignee, and Duties of the Obligor, After Valid Assignment. [§ 27–40] 516
 1. Example. [§ 27–41] 516
G. Claims and Defenses the Obligor Can Assert Against Assignee. [§ 27–42] 517
 1. Example. [§ 27–43] 517
 2. "Holder in Due Course" Exception. [§ 27–44] 518
  a. Definition of "Holder in Due Course." [§ 27–45] 519
  b. Effect of "Holder in Due Course" Status. [§ 27–46] 519
   (1) Example. [§ 27–47] 520
  c. Limitation on Holder in Due Course Doctrine. [§ 27–48] 520
H. Rights of the Assignee to Sue the Assignor: The Implied Warranties Inherent in Assignments for Value. [§ 27–49] 521
 1. Example. [§ 27–50] 521

TABLE OF CONTENTS

	2.	Example. [§ 27–51]...522
I.	Assignee's Rights upon Attempted Modification of Assignment by the Assignor and the Obligor. [§ 27–52]..................................522
	1.	Modification Rules Regarding Assignments for Value. [§ 27–53] 522
	2.	Modification Rules Regarding Gratuitous Assignments. [§ 27–54] 523
J.	Rights of the Assignee Among Competing Claims of Ownership. [§ 27–55]...523
	1.	The "New York" Rule: The First Assignee Always Has Priority. [§ 27–56] 523
		a.	Example. [§ 27–57]..524
	2.	The "English Rule": The First Assignee to Notify the Obligor Has Priority. [§ 27–58] 524
		a.	Example. [§ 27–59]..524
	3.	The Massachusetts/Restatement 2d Rule: The First Assignee Generally Prevails, Subject to Four Exceptions. [§ 27–60] 524
		a.	Example. [§ 27–61]..525
	4.	Article 9 of the UCC Rule: First to File or Perfect Gets Priority. [§ 27–62] 525
K.	Exam Approaches to Assignment Issues. [§ 27–63] 526

Chapter 28. Delegation **527**

A. Delegation Generally. [§ 28–1]...527
B. Terminology of Delegation. [§ 28–2] 527
    1. Example. [§ 28–3]...528
C. Elements of an Effective Delegation. [§ 28–4] 528
    1. The Delegating Party Must Manifest an Intention to Delegate a Duty. [§ 28–5] 529
        a. Construction of a Clause "Assigning the Contract." [§ 28–6]..529
            (1) Example. [§ 28–7]..529
    2. There Must Be No Prohibition Against Delegation of This Particular Duty. [§ 28–8]..529
        a. A Purported Delegation That Violates Public Policy Is Ineffective. [§ 28–9]...530
        b. A Purported Delegation of a Duty in Which the Obligee Has a "Substantial Interest" in Having the Delegating Party Perform the Duty Is Ineffective. [§ 28–10]..530
            (1) Example. [§ 28–11]...531
            (2) Example. [§ 28–12]...531
            (3) Example. [§ 28–13]...531
            (4) Example of *Sally Beauty Co. v. Nexxus Products Co., Inc.* [§ 28–14] 531

(5) Example of *Macke Co. v. Pizza of Gaithersburg, Inc.* [§ 28–15] 532
      c. A Purported Delegation That Violates a Specific "No Delegation" Clause in a Contract Is Ineffective. [§ 28–16]..533
  3. The Obligee Need Not Assent to, or Even Be Aware of, the Delegation for It to Be Effective. [§ 28–17] 533
      a. Example. [§ 28–18]...533
D. Principal Consequences of an Effective Delegation. [§ 28–19] 533
  1. Upon a Valid Delegation, the Delegate Acquires *a Right* to Perform the Delegated Duty. [§ 28–20]....................534
      a. Example. [§ 28–21]...534
  2. Delegation Does Not Discharge the Duty of the Delegating Party to Render Performance to the Obligee. [§ 28–22] 535
  3. Full Performance by the Delegate Discharges the Duty Owed by the Delegating Party. [§ 28–23]....................535
      a. Example. [§ 28–24]...535
  4. A Delegate Has an Enforceable Obligation, as Opposed to a Right, to Perform the Transferred Duty Only When He or She Specifically Assumes Such a Duty. [§ 28–25]..........536
      a. Example. [§ 28–26]...536
      b. Example. [§ 28–27]...537
  5. Relationship Between Delegations and Third Party Beneficiary Contracts. [§ 28–28]..537
      a. Example. [§ 28–29]...538
      b. Example. [§ 28–30]...539
E. Distinction Between Novation and Delegation. [§ 28–31] 539
  1. Example. [§ 28–32]...539
F. Exam Approach to Delegation Issues. [§ 28–33] 540

PART VIII. REMEDIES

Chapter 29. Equitable Remedies 543
A. Equitable Relief Generally. [§ 29–1]...543
B. Types of Equitable Remedies. [§ 29–2]..543
  1. Specific Performance. [§ 29–3] 544
  2. Prohibitory Injunctions. [§ 29–4] 544
      a. Example of *Lumley v. Wagner*. [§ 29–5] 544
  3. Reformation. [§ 29–6] 545
C. Requirements for Obtaining Equitable Relief for Breach of Contract. [§ 29–7]...545
  1. Equitable Relief Will Not Be Awarded Unless an Award of Damages Would Be "Inadequate" to Put the Non-Breaching Party in the Position He or She Would Have Been in Had the Contract Been Performed. [§ 29–8] 546

TABLE OF CONTENTS

- a. The Difficulty of Proving Damages with Reasonable Certainty. [§ 29–9] 547
  - (1) Example of *Laclede Gas Co. v. Amoco Oil Co.* [§ 29–10] 547
  - (2) Example. [§ 29–11] 548
  - (3) Example. [§ 29–12] 548
- b. The Difficulty of Procuring Suitable Substitute Performance. [§ 29–13] 549
  - (1) Example. [§ 29–14] 550
  - (2) Example. [§ 29–15] 550
  - (3) Example. [§ 29–16] 550
  - (4) Review Problem. [§ 29–17] 550
- c. The Likelihood That an Award of Damages Could Not Be Collected. [§ 29–18] 551
  - (1) Example. [29–19] 551

2. Equitable Relief Will Not Be Awarded if There Are Undue Practical Limitations on a Court's Ability to Grant Such Relief. [§ 29–20] 551
   - a. Whether the Terms of the Contract Are Too Uncertain to Provide a Basis for a Specific Performance Order. [§ 29–21] 552
     - (1) Example. [§ 29–22] 553
   - b. Whether the Supervisory Burden on the Court Outweighs the Advantage to Be Gained by an Order for an Equitable Remedy. [§ 29–23] 553
     - (1) Example. [§ 29–24] 554
     - (2) Example. [§ 29–25] 554
     - (3) Example of *Walgreen Co. v. Sara Creek Property Co.* [29–26] 554
   - c. Contracts Calling for the Performance of "Personal Services" Will Not Be Specifically Enforced. [§ 29–27] 555
     - (1) Example. [§ 29–28] 556
     - (2) Example. [§ 29–29] 557
     - (3) Example. [§ 29–30] 557
     - (4) "Personal Services" Contract with Covenant Not to Compete. [§ 29–31] 558

3. Equitable Relief Will Not Be Granted if Certain "Equitable Principles" Are Violated. [§ 29–32] 559
   - a. Whether Such an Order Would Violate Public Policy. [§ 29–33] 560
     - (1) Example. [§ 29–34] 560
   - b. Whether Such an Order Would Be Unjust Because the Breaching Party's Assent to the Contract Was Induced by Unfair Practices. [§ 29–35] 560
     - (1) Example. [§ 29–36] 561

TABLE OF CONTENTS

        c. Whether Such an Order Would Be Sufficiently "Unjust" as to Cause Unreasonable Hardship or Loss to the *Breaching* Party. [§ 29–37] 561
            (1) Example Based on *Peevyhouse v. Garland Coal & Mining Co.* [§ 29–38] 562
        d. Whether There Is Sufficient Security to Believe the Non-Breaching Party Will Perform. [§ 29–39] 563
            (1) Example. [§ 29–40] 563
D. Exam Approach to Equitable Relief Issues. [§ 29–41] 564

Chapter 30. Money Damages **565**
A. The "Interest" Analysis of Contract Law and the Concept of Economic Breach. [§ 30–1] 565
    1. The "Efficient Breach" Doctrine Defined and Explained. [§ 30–2] 565
B. Defining, Identifying, and Valuing the Economic Interests Resulting from Contract Formation. [§ 30–3] 567
    1. The Expectation (or "Benefit of the Bargain") Interest. [§ 30–4] 568
        a. Example. [§ 30–5] 568
    2. The Reliance (or "Out-of-Pocket") Interest. [§ 30–6] 569
        a. Example. [§ 30–7] 569
    3. The Restitutionary Interest. [§ 30–8] 570
    4. Types of Damages Recoverable by the Non-Breaching Party. [§ 30–9] 570
C. A Glossary of Damages Terminology. [§ 30–10] 570
    1. Benefit of the Bargain Damages. [§ 30–11] 570
    2. Consequential Damages. [§ 30–12] 571
        a. Example. [§ 30–13] 571
    3. Direct Damages. [§ 30–14] 572
        a. Example. [§ 30–15] 572
    4. Exemplary Damages. [§ 30–16] 573
    5. Expectation Damages. [§ 30–17] 573
    6. General Damages. [§ 30–18] 573
    7. Incidental Damages. [§ 30–19] 573
        a. Example. [§ 30–20] 574
    8. Liquidated Damages. [§ 30–21] 574
    9. Nominal Damages. [§ 30–22] 574
    10. Out-of-Pocket Damages. [§ 30–23] 575
    11. Punitive Damages. [§ 30–24] 575
    12. Reliance Damages. [§ 30–25] 575
    13. Special Damages. [§ 30–26] 575
    14. Stipulated Damages. [§ 30–27] 575
D. Expectation Damages: The General Measure of Contract Damages. [§ 30–28] 576
    1. Calculating Expectation Damages. [§ 30–29] 576
        a. Lost Value 576

b. Incidental Loss. 577
c. Consequential Loss. 577
d. Cost Avoided. 577
e. Loss Avoided. 578
2. Employment Contracts: Breach by Employer. [§ 30–30] 579
3. Employment Contracts: Breach by Employee. [§ 30–31] 581
4. Construction Contracts: Breach by Builder. [§ 30–32] 582
a. Example. [§ 30–33] 584
b. Example. [§ 30–34] 584
c. Example of *Jacob & Youngs, Inc. v. Kent.* [§ 30–35] 584
5. Construction Contracts: Breach by Landowner. [§ 30–36] 585
6. Real Estate Contracts: Breach by Buyer. [§ 30–37] 586
7. Real Estate Contracts: Breach by Seller. [§ 30–38] 587
a. Example. [§ 30–39] 587
8. Expectation Damage Recovery Under Contracts Governed by the UCC. [§ 30–40] 588
a. Buyer's Damages. [§ 30–41] 588
(1) Example. [§ 30–42] 589
(2) Different Formulation for Buyer's Warranty Damages. [§ 30–43] 590
b. Seller's Damages. [§ 30–44] 590
(1) Example. [§ 30–45] 591
(2) Different Formulation for Lost Volume Sellers. [§ 30–46] 592
9. Expectation Damages in "Losing" Contracts. [§ 30–47] 592
E. Three Limitations on the Recoverability of Expectation Damages: Certainty, Foreseeability, and Avoidability. [§ 30–48] 593
1. The "Certainty" Limitation: Damages Cannot Be Recovered Unless Proven with "Reasonable Certainty." [§ 30–49] 593
a. Modern Rules as to How "Certain" a Damage Must Be Proven to Be Recoverable. [§ 30–50] 594
(1) The Reasonable Certainty Test Typically Limits Recovery of Damages Only Where a Non-Breaching Buyer Is Suing for Consequential Lost Profits Resulting from a "Collateral" Transaction. [§ 30–51] 595
(2) Example. [§ 30–52] 597
(3) Example. [§ 30–53] 598
2. The "Foreseeability" Limitation: Damages Unrecoverable Unless the Breaching Party Either Foresaw, or Should Have Foreseen the Type of Damage at the Time of Contracting. [§ 30–54] 598
a. *Hadley v. Baxendale.* [§ 30–55] 599

		b.	Analysis of *Hadley v. Baxendale* and the "Foreseeability" Limitation of Contract Damages. [§ 30–56]...601

        b. Analysis of *Hadley v. Baxendale* and the "Foreseeability" Limitation of Contract Damages. [§ 30–56]..601

        c. The Modern Test for Whether a Loss Is a "Direct" or an "Indirect" Consequential Damage. [§ 30–57]..........602

        d. Example. [§ 30–58]...604

     3. The Avoidability Limitation. [§ 30–59]................................605

        a. Example of *Rockingham County v. Luten Bridge Co.* [§ 30–60]..606

        b. Limits on the Avoidability Principle: An Injured Party Need Not Take Steps to Avoid Damages if Doing So Would Cause the Injured Party Undue Risk, Burden or Humiliation. [§ 30–61] 606

           (1) Example. [§ 30–62]...606

           (2) Example. [§ 30–63]...607

           (3) Example of *Parker v. Twentieth Century-Fox Film Corp.* [§ 30–64]..608

F. Reliance Damages. [§ 30–65] 609

     1. The Availability of Reliance Damages. [§ 30–66] 609

        a. Example. [§ 30–67]...610

     2. Limitations on Reliance Damage Recovery. [§ 30–68] 610

        a. Reliance Damages Must Be Proven with Reasonable Certainty. [§ 30–69] 611

        b. Limitation on the Recovery of Reliance Damages in "Losing Contract" Situations. [§ 30–70] 611

           (1) Example. [§ 30–71]...611

        c. The Value of Any Salvageable Materials Must Be Subtracted from a Recovery of Reliance Damages as a Cost Avoided. [§ 30–72] 612

        d. Damages Must Not Be Avoidable Without Undue Risk, Burden, or Humiliation. [§ 30–73] 612

     3. Recovery Based on the Reliance Interest in Other Situations. [§ 30–74] 612

G. Emotional Distress Damages Are Generally Not Available in Breach of Contract Suits. [§ 30–75] 613

     1. Exception: Emotional Distress Damages Are Available When the Breach of Contract Also Results in Tangible Personal Injury. [§ 30–76] 614

        a. Example. [§ 30–77]...614

        b. Example of *Sullivan v. O'Connor*. [§ 30–78] 614

     2. Exception: Recovery for Emotional Distress Is Permitted When Such Harm Is "Particularly Likely" to Result from a Breach. [§ 30–79] 615

H. Liquidated Damages. [§ 30–80] 615

     1. Requirements for an Enforceable Liquidated Damage Provision. [§ 30–81] 617

lv

TABLE OF CONTENTS

        a.   The Amount of the Liquidated Damage Must Be Reasonable in Light of the Anticipated or Actual Loss. [§ 30–82] 617
           (1)   Example. [§ 30–83] 617
        b.   Actual Damages Must Be Somewhat Difficult to Prove in Order for a Liquidated Damage Provision to Be Enforceable. [§ 30–84] 618
           (1)   Example. [§ 30–85] 618
      2.   Alternative Performance Clauses Distinguished from Liquidated Damage Clauses. [§ 30–86] 619
I.   Punitive Damages Are Generally Not Recoverable in Breach of Contract Actions. [§ 30–87] 620
      1.   Exception to General Rule: Punitive Damages Can Be Recovered for "Bad Faith" Breaches of Insurance Contracts. [§ 30–88] 621
J.   The Injured Party's Right to Recover Pre-Judgment and Post-Judgment Interest on Any Award. [§ 30–89] 622
K.   Reduction of "Future" Awards to Present Value. [§ 30–90] 623
L.   Exam Approach to Damage Issues. [§ 30–91] 623

Chapter 31. Restitution 625
A.   Restitution Overview. [§ 31–1] 625
      1.   Some General Principles of Restitution. [§ 31–2] 625
      2.   When Restitution Is Available. [§ 31–3] 627
B.   Rules Common to All Restitution Actions. [§ 31–4] 628
      1.   Two Common Methods of Valuing the Restitution Interest: The "Cost Avoided" and the "Net Benefit" Methods. [§ 31–5] 628
        a.   The "Cost Avoided" Method: Defined. [§ 31–6] 628
        b.   The "Net Benefit" Method: Defined. [§ 31–7] 629
        c.   Example Applying "Cost Avoided" and "Net Benefit" Methods. [§ 31–8] 629
        d.   Additional Example Applying "Cost Avoided" and "Net Benefit" Methods. [§ 31–9] 629
        e.   Determining Which Method of Valuing the Restitutionary Interest Should Be Used. [§ 31–10] 630
      2.   The "Mutual Restitution" Requirement. [§ 31–11] 630
        a.   Example. [§ 31–12] 631
        b.   Example. [§ 31–13] 631
C.   Limitations of Restitutionary Recovery for Breach of Contract. [§ 31–14] 631
      1.   Restitution Is Available Only if the Breach Would Give Rise to Damages for Total, and Not Just Immaterial, Breach. [§ 31–15] 632
        a.   Example. [§ 31–16] 632

TABLE OF CONTENTS

- 2. Restitution Is Not Available if the Non-Breaching Party Has Performed All of His or Her Duties Under the Contract, and No Performance by the Breaching Party Remains Due Other than the Payment of a Definite Sum of Money. [§ 31–17] 632
  - a. Example. [§ 31–18] 633
  - b. Example. [§ 31–19] 633
- 3. Majority Rule: Restitution Unavailable to a *Willful* Breacher. [§ 31–20] 634
- D. Common Fact Situations Involving the Non-Breaching Party Seeking Restitution. [§ 31–21] 634
  - 1. Restitution Is Almost Always Used in "Losing Contract" Situations. [§ 31–22] 634
    - a. Example. [§ 31–23] 634
  - 2. Restitution Is Almost Always Used When the Value of the Benefits Provided Exceeds the Reasonable Value of Those Services. [§ 31–24] 635
    - a. Example. [§ 31–25] 635
  - 3. Restitution Is Never Used When the Value of the Benefits Is Less than the Contract Price. [§ 31–26] 636
    - a. Example. [§ 31–27] 636
- E. Issues When Restitutionary Recovery Is Sought by the Party in Breach. [§ 31–28] 636
  - 1. Calculating the Value of the Restitutionary Award in Cases Brought by the Breaching Party. [§ 31–29] 637
    - a. Example. [§ 31–30] 637
- F. Recovery in Restitution for Quasi-Contract. [§ 31–31] 638
  - 1. Example. [§ 31–32] 639
- G. Restitutionary Recovery in Voidable Contracts. [§ 31–33] 639
  - 1. Example. [§ 31–34] 640
- H. Exam Approach to Restitution Issues. [§ 31–35] 640

Chapter 32. Remedies for Breach Under the UCC 641
- A. UCC Remedies Generally. [§ 32–1] 641
- B. Equitable Remedies Available to Buyers Under the UCC. [§ 32–2] 641
  - 1. Specific Performance. [§ 32–3] 641
    - a. Example. [§ 32–4] 642
    - b. *Sedmak v. Charlie's Chevrolet, Inc.* [§ 32–5] 642
    - c. Review Problem. [§ 32–6] 643
  - 2. Replevin. [§ 32–7] 643
- C. Comparison of UCC and Common Law Money Damage Provisions. [§ 32–8] 644
  - 1. Consequential Damages Under the UCC: § 2–715(2). [§ 32–9] 644
  - 2. Incidental Damages Under the UCC. [§ 32–10] 646

TABLE OF CONTENTS

- D. Buyer's Right to Sue for Damages in Cases Where He or She Does Not Have the Goods at the Time of Suit. [§ 32–11] 646
  1. UCC § 2–712: Cover Damages. [§ 32–12] 647
     a. The Formula for Recovery of Cover Damages. [§ 32–13] 648
        (1) Example. [§ 32–14] 648
  2. UCC § 2–713: Market Differential Damages. [§ 32–15] 650
     a. The Formula for Market Differential Damages. [§ 32–16] 650
        (1) Issues in Determining the "Market Price." [§ 32–17] 650
            (a) Determining the "Temporal" Market. [§ 32–18] 650
                (i) Exception Based on *Oloffson v. Coomer.* [§ 32–19] 651
            (b) Determining the Geographic Market. [§ 32–20] 651
        (2) Example. [§ 32–21] 652
  3. Buyer's Right to Market Differential Damages Even if Buyer Has Covered. [§ 32–22] 653
- E. Buyer's Right to Damages for Breach of Warranty and Other Non-Conforming Tender When the Buyer Has Possession of the Goods at the Time of Filing of the Breach of Contract Suit. [§ 32–23] 653
  1. The Formula for Breach of Warranty Recovery Under UCC § 2–714. [§ 32–24] 654
     a. The Difference Between the Value of the Goods as Promised and the Value of Goods Received. [§ 32–25] 654
  2. The Formula for Other Non-Conforming Tenders. [§ 32–26] 655
  3. Buyer's Right to Offset Damages Under § 2–717. [§ 32–27] 655
  4. Buyer's Right to Recover Deposits, Down Payments and the Like. [§ 32–28] 656
- F. Seller's Right to Sue for the Full Contract Price upon Buyer's Breach: Sellers "Specific Performance." [§ 32–29] 656
  1. When Buyer Has Accepted the Goods. [§ 32–30] 657
  2. When the Goods Are Lost or Destroyed After the Risk of Loss Passed to the Buyer. [§ 32–31] 657
  3. When Seller Attempts to Re-Sell Goods Wrongfully Rejected by Buyer, but Cannot Obtain a Reasonable Price upon Re-Sale. [§ 32–32] 658
  4. When Seller Establishes That Resale of the Wrongfully Rejected Goods Would Be Unavailing. [§ 32–33] 658

TABLE OF CONTENTS

- G. Seller's Right to Sue for Damages Other than the Full Contract Price upon Buyer's Breach. [§ 32–34] 659
  1. Recovery Under § 2–706: Seller's "Cover" Damages. [§ 32–35] 659
     - a. The Formula for Calculating a Seller's "Cover" Damages. [§ 32–36] 659
       - (1) Example. [§ 32–37] 660
  2. Recovery Under § 2–708(1): Seller's Market Differential Damages. [§ 32–38] 660
     - a. The Formula for Calculating a Seller's Market Differential Damages. [§ 32–39] 661
       - (1) Problems in Determining the "Market Price." [§ 32–40] 661
         - (a) Determining the Temporal Market. [§ 32–41] 661
         - (b) Determining the Geographic Market. [§ 32–42] 661
       - (2) Example. [§ 32–43] 662
  3. Seller's Right to Market Differential Damages Even if Buyer Has Covered. [§ 32–44] 662
  4. Recovery Under § 2–708(2): Seller's Lost Profit Recovery. [§ 32–45] 662
     - a. "Lost Volume" Sellers. [§ 32–46] 663
       - (1) The Formula for Lost Volume Seller's Recovery of Lost Profits Under UCC § 2–708(2). [§ 32–47] 664
     - b. Recovery upon Buyer's Breach When the Manufacturer/Seller Has Only Partially Completed the Good. [§ 32–48] 664
- H. Liquidated Damages Under Article 2. [§ 32–49] 665
- I. Emotional Distress Damages, Punitive Damages, and Recovery of Pre-Judgment Interest Under the UCC. [§ 32–50] 666
- J. Limitation on, or Modification of, Contract Remedies. [§ 32–51] 666
  1. When a Limited Remedy "Fails of Its Essential Purpose" Under UCC § 2–719(2). [§ 32–52] 666
     - a. When a "No Consequential Damages" Clause Is Linked with a "Repair or Replacement" or "Warranty Disclaimer" Clause. [§ 32–53] 667
  2. Distinction Between Limitation of Remedy Under UCC § 2–719 and Disclaimer of Warranty Under § 2–316. [§ 32–54] 669
- K. Exam Approach to UCC Remedies Issues. [§ 32–55] 669

TABLE OF CONTENTS

PART IX. MISCELLANEOUS UCC AND CISG DOCTRINES

Chapter 33. Applicability of Article Two of the UCC and the CISG 673
A. Applicability of Article Two of the UCC Generally. [§ 33–1] 673
B. Article Two Is Not Limited to Merchants. [§ 33–2] 673
C. UCC § 2–102: Article Two Applies to "Transactions in Goods." [§ 33–3] 674
    1. The Meaning of "Transaction." [§ 33–4] 674
        a. Sales. [§ 33–5] 674
        b. Leases. [§ 33–6] 674
    2. The Meaning of "Goods." [§ 33–7] 676
        a. Example. [§ 33–8] 676
        b. Example. [§ 33–9] 677
D. Article Two Applicability to Sales/Services "Hybrid" Transactions. [§ 33–10] 677
    1. The "Predominant Purpose" Test. [§ 33–11] 677
    2. The "Gravamen" Test. [§ 33–12] 678
E. Article Two Applicability When There Is a Sale of Something Attached to Realty. [§ 33–13] 678
F. Applicability of the CISG. [§ 33–14] 679
G. Exam Approach to Article Two/CISG Applicability Issues. [§ 33–15] 680

Chapter 34. Risk of Loss and Mercantile Terms 681
A. Risk of Loss, Generally. [§ 34–1] 681
    1. Consequences of Risk of Loss Allocation. [§ 34–2] 681
    2. Risk of Loss Rules in the Absence of Breach. [§ 34–3] 682
        a. Shipment Contract. [§ 34–4] 682
        b. Destination Contract. [§ 34–5] 682
    3. Effect of Breach on Risk of Loss. [§ 34–6] 683
        a. When a Seller Breaches in Such a Way to Give the Buyer a Right of Rejection. [§ 34–7] 683
        b. UCC § 2–510(2): When a Seller Breaches and Buyer Revokes Acceptance. [§ 34–8] 684
        c. UCC § 2–510(3): When a Buyer Repudiates or Otherwise Breaches Before the Risk Has Shifted to Him or Her. [§ 34–9] 684
B. Risk of Loss Under the CISG. [§ 34–10] 684
C. Mercantile Terms. [§ 34–11] 685
    1. F.O.B. [§ 34–12] 685
    2. F.A.S. [§ 34–13] 686
        a. "F.O.B." When Used with a Vessel. [§ 34–14] 686
    3. C.I.F. [§ 34–15] 686
    4. C. & F. [§ 34–16] 687

Chapter 35. Warranties 689
A. Warranties Under the UCC Generally. [§ 35–1] 689
B. Express Warranties. [§ 35–2] 689
    1. An Express Warranty Is Created by an Affirmation, Promise, Description, or Sample. [§ 35–3] 689
    2. The Affirmations Made by the Seller Must Become Part of "the Basis of the Bargain." [§ 35–4] 691
        a. Theory One: "Basis of the Bargain" Means "Reliance." [§ 35–5] 691
        b. Theory Two: "Basis of the Bargain" Means the Affirmation Was Made Before the Sale Took Place. [§ 35–6] 692
    3. Disclaiming an Express Warranty. [§ 35–7] 693
C. Implied Warranty of Merchantability. [§ 35–8] 696
    1. The Buyer Must Establish That the Seller Was a "Merchant." [§ 35–9] 696
    2. The Buyer Must Establish That the Goods Were Not "Merchantable." [§ 35–10] 696
    3. Disclaimer of Implied Warranty of Merchantability. [§ 35–11] 697
D. The Implied Warranty of Fitness for a Particular Purpose. [§ 35–12] 698
    1. Example. [§ 35–13] 698
    2. Example. [§ 35–14] 699
    3. Disclaiming the Implied Warranty of Fitness for a Particular Purpose. [§ 35–15] 699
E. Doctrines Applicable to All Warranty Claims: Notice and Privity. [§ 35–16] 700
    1. The Notice Requirement Under UCC § 2–607(3). [§ 35–17] 700
    2. Who Is a Proper Defendant: Vertical Privity. [§ 35–18] 700
    3. Who Is Entitled to Sue: Horizontal Privity. [§ 35–19] 702
F. Warranty Defenses. [§ 35–20] 703
    1. Assumption of the Risk. [§ 35–21] 703
        a. Comparative Negligence. [§ 35–22] 703
    2. Unforeseeable Misuse of the Product. [§ 35–23] 704
G. Damages for Breach of Warranty. [§ 35–24] 704
H. Warranties Under CISG. [§ 35–25] 704
I. Exam Approach to Warranty Issues. [§ 35–26] 704

Sample Multiple Choice Questions 707

Answers to Sample Multiple Choice Questions 729

Sample Essay Questions 747

Suggested Analysis of Sample Essay Questions 761

TABLE OF CONTENTS

Case Squibs.. 815
TABLE OF CASES 863
TABLE OF RESTATEMENT OF CONTRACTS 867
TABLE OF UCC SECTIONS..873
TABLE OF CISG SECTIONS 877
INDEX 879

CONTRACTS
Ninth Edition

PART I

INTRODUCTION TO CONTRACT LAW

CHAPTER 1

AN INTRODUCTION TO CONTRACT LAW: SOURCES OF CONTRACT LAW, DEFINITIONS OF CONTRACT, TYPES OF CONTRACTS, AND THE BASIC COMPONENTS OF CONTRACTS

A. SOURCES OF CONTRACT LAW. [§ 1–1*]

Contract law is derived from several different sources but is reasonably uniform throughout the United States. This is, in part, because lawyers, judges, and legislatures generally agree on the basic principles of contract law, and also because contracts are so frequently made and so heavily relied upon nationwide that a common set of rules governing the formation, operation, and interpretation of contracts is a contemporary economic imperative. The main sources for the study of contract law are: (1) common law judicial decision-making; (2) treatises; (3) the Restatement of Contracts; and (4) the Uniform Commercial Code. Each is described further below, along with a description of some of the older influences on contract law and a note on a newer treaty governing international agreements, the "CISG."

---

* For more information, listen to CD # 1, Track 2 of *Sum and Substance Audio on Contracts*.

CHAPTER 1

1. **Common Law. [§ 1–2]**

    Most American contract law is common law based. As you will discover in law school, the term "common law" has different meanings based on different contexts. Here, it means that contract law has mostly been shaped through judicial decisions, rather than through statutes. Each state has its own court system, and so the law varies a bit from state to state. However, as indicated above, for the most part, contract law is reasonably uniform throughout the country.

2. **Treatises. [§ 1–3]**

    Every contracts student comes across references to Professor Williston's and Professor Corbin's treatises. Professor Williston taught at the Harvard Law School and his treatise was published between 1920–1922 in five volumes. Professor Corbin, who taught at Yale, published his treatise between 1950–1960 in eight volumes. Each was extremely influential and largely shaped common law decisions after its publication. Each author read virtually all of the cases and writings on contracts existing at the time they were published. Both of these professors then extracted the rules governing contractual agreements from those cases and articles, and structured those rules into an organized set of legal principles with citations to support them. Modern day authors of contracts law treatises include Professors Farnsworth, Murray, Calamari and Perillo, and White and Summers.

3. **Restatement of Contracts. [§ 1–4]**

    The American Law Institute, a prestigious group of law professors, judges, and practitioners, published the Restatement (First) of Contracts in 1932. The Restatement set forth a series of black letter rules governing contract formation, operation, breach, etc., by restating the **majority rules** governing those principles adopted by courts throughout the country in an orderly fashion. Some thirty years later, the First Restatement was revised to take into account newer thinking about contract law, and the Restatement (Second) of Contracts was published in 1962. Both Restatements also include Comments and Illustrations further explaining the rules.

    The Restatement is not "the law" anywhere, in that it has not been adopted by any legislature but, for the most part, it does set forth the mutually shared and agreed principles and vocabulary of modern contract law. Due to the prestige of its drafters, the "Restatement (Second)" is frequently cited in modern case law as articulating the correct rule of law, and thus shapes common law contract making. In a few places, the drafters of the Restatement (Second) came up with rules and vocabulary that reflected where they saw the law going (or perhaps where they wanted it to go) somewhat more so than the drafters of Restatement (First), who attempted merely to restate the rules that existed at the time of its making. Most of the time the drafters of the Restatement (Second) proved prescient and their "forward-looking" rules were eventually adopted by a majority of the courts. However, there are a few instances, pointed out in the text, where the courts have refused to go along with the drafters of the second version. Nevertheless, the overwhelming majority of the Restatement (Second) provisions can reliably be viewed as setting forth current contract law.

One thing all law students are asked to do in the first year is "extract the rule" from the cases. This is the "R" in the famous IRAC structure. The Restatement contains nearly all the "rules" of the cases. As such, one of the differences between Contracts and many other first year courses is that students are required to determine *which* of the Restatement's rules govern the cases, and then how to apply that rule in other situations.

Unless indicated otherwise, all citations to the Restatement in this book are to the Restatement 2d.

4. **The Uniform Commercial Code. [§ 1–5]**

The Uniform Commercial Code ("UCC" or the "Code") is a set of statutes that governs commercial transactions throughout the United States. It is divided into nine substantive sections, called "Articles," only two of which are usually cited in a first year Contracts course: Article 1, dealing with general rules and general definitions used under all Articles of the Code, and Article 2, entitled "Uniform Commercial Code—Sales." (A few professors might cite a few sections of Article 9, entitled "Uniform Commercial Code—Secured Transactions" and of Article 3, entitled "Uniform Commercial Code—Negotiable Instruments").

Article 2 has the most influence on contract law, and its rules are discussed in some detail in this book. The first edition of the UCC was published in 1952 and it has been revised several times since then. The UCC was drafted as a joint project by the American Law Institute ("ALI") and the National Conference of Commissioners on Uniform State Laws ("NCCUSL"), which is a group similar to, but has a different membership from, the ALI (which drafted the Restatement).

Unlike the Restatement, the UCC is "the law" throughout the United States. That is, 50 state legislatures (and the governing bodies for various affiliates and territories, including Washington DC, Puerto Rico, etc.) have adopted the UCC as the Commercial Code for their state or territory, although each state amended the UCC slightly when enacting it into each state's commercial code.

CHAPTER 1

While the provisions of the UCC thus apply with the force of law to contractual relations within its scope, it is important to understand that **the UCC does not apply to all contracts**. By its terms, Article 2 applies only to "transactions in goods," and thus does not apply to contracts for the sale of land, to contracts for services, or to leases of goods [UCC § 2–102]. Thus, the first step in analyzing any problem is to determine whether the UCC and its rules apply, or whether more general common law contract rules apply. The rules for Article 2 applicability are covered in Chapter Thirty-Three.

The drafters of the UCC are continually revising portions of it. This book cites primarily to the 2002 version of Article 2 and the 2010 version of Article 1, the versions adopted by most states and the ones found in most casebook supplements designed for Contracts courses.

Occasionally, however, reference will be made in this Book to the *2003* version of Article 2. The story of its passage and subsequent non-adoption is an interesting one. The basics of Article 2 had remained the same since 1972. However, commerce had changed quite a bit between 1972 and 2003. E-mail and texts had replaced faxes and phones, computers had become a staple in homes and businesses, e-commerce was established, computer software was being directly downloaded, and generally American commerce was being swept into a digital era. The drafters tried to get ahead of the technology curve and adopted a heavily revised Article that dealt with some of these changes, and wanted to clean up a few drafting ambiguities that they had inadvertently allowed when drafting Article 2.

Despite the lobbying by the NCCUSL, not one state adopted even a single provision of the 2003 version of Article 2. The thought was that these new changes, and the inevitable unintended consequences that so radical a revision would necessarily engender, might well change the dependable interpretation of countless existing agreements drafted under the "old" Article 2 rules. Accordingly, state legislatures have left it to their courts to adapt the older rules and existing documents to the new digital age. Faced with the inevitable, the NCCUSL has now "withdrawn" the 2003 version and there is no hope for its passage into law anywhere. Nevertheless, because its "fixes" to various problems posed by the 2002 version of the UCC are taught by several professors and instructive as to more modern thinking on commercial issues, some mention is made of the a few 2003 provisions throughout this book.

So that there is no confusion, when just the "normal" citation to a UCC provision is given, e.g., UCC § 2–207, that refers to the 2002 version of the Code. The citation form UCC § 2R–207 refers to the revised, 2003 version.

5. The British Sales of Goods Act. [§ 1–6]

The British Sales Act (or English Uniform Sales Act) was the first attempt to codify contract rules in Anglo-American law, and was published in 1893. To the modern eye, its scope was very limited. Indeed, it did not cover much more than offer and acceptance and warranty rules, and had no provisions regarding remedies for contract breach. It is mentioned here because there are references to the English Uniform Sales Act in some very old contracts cases.

6. The American Uniform Sales Act. [§ 1–7]

Many early American contracts cases refer to the **Uniform Sales Act ("USA")**, which is the American version of the similar-sounding British Act, and was published by its drafters in 1903. Like the British Act, its scope was severely limited and dissatisfaction with the limited scope was, in some ways, the catalyst for the UCC.

7. The United Nations Convention on Contracts for the International Sales of Goods. [§ 1–8]

In 1980, the United States, along with 11 other countries, signed an multi-national treaty known as **The United Nations Convention on Contracts for the International Sales of Goods ("CISG")**, which became effective in 1988. Currently over 85 countries have adopted the CISG.

While this puts it far too simply, the CISG is a kind of international Article 2 of the UCC, i.e., it sets forth contracts rules for those who enter into trans-national contracts. As a treaty, it is "the law" in the United States and thus governs those international transactions to which it applies. CISG applicability is discussed in Chapter Thirty-Three.

The drafters of the CISG—commercial scholars from all over the world—essentially started with UCC Article 2 and then either adopted, modified, or rejected the principles of the UCC. While an in-depth analysis of the CISG is beyond the scope of this book, occasional reference is made to important CISG provisions, both to show that reasonable people can view commercial law policy differently, and because many contracts professors cover the CISG as part of the growing trend of introducing international law principles into the first year curriculum. The CISG is codified in 52 Fed. Reg. 6262, *et seq.*

CHAPTER 1

B. DEFINITION OF A CONTRACT. [§ 1–9*]

Perhaps surprisingly, there is not one agreed upon definition of a contract. What follows are the two most frequently cited definitions.

1. Restatement Definition. [§ 1–10]

Section 1 of the Restatement 2d states that, "A contract is a promise or a set of promises for the breach of which the law gives a remedy, or the performance of which the law in some way recognizes as a duty." In essence, under the Restatement, a contract is a promise or set of promises that are enforceable in a court if one party fails to perform what he or she promised.

Note that the definition does not treat oral and written contracts differently. We will see in Chapter Ten that there are a few types of contracts that are voidable unless they are in writing due to something called "the Statute of Frauds," but these are the exceptions. Despite that old saying, "An oral contract is not worth the paper it is written on," in general oral contracts are just as valid and enforceable as written contracts and courts will enforce the promises made in such agreements.

Note also that in some ways, the concepts expressed before the comma in § 1, and the concepts expressed after the comma, are repetitive. That is, if the law provides a remedy for a breach of a promise, it is because the law recognizes a duty that the "other" party perform that promise.

You might be wondering what sorts of promises the law won't enforce. There are a couple of main categories. One is "gift promises," e.g., where Joe promises to give his niece $1,000 when she turns 21. If Joe doesn't come through, it is unlikely the niece can sue him for breach of contract because Joe has just promised to make a gift, and they have not entered into a contract. Another category are "social compacts" where, e.g., Fred promises to wash his sister's clothes if she washes his car. If the sister washes the car, but Fred doesn't wash the clothes, again it is unlikely Fred will be answerable for breach of contract. These issues are discussed in greater detail in the Offer and Acceptance and in the Consideration sections of this book, as are the other kinds of "promises" that the law won't enforce and thus are not part of a "contract." But the above will give you a sense of the kinds of agreements which are not "contracts" and not subject to contract rules.

---

* For more information, listen to CD # 1, Track 3 of *Sum and Substance Audio on Contracts*.

AN INTRODUCTION TO CONTRACT LAW

2. **UCC Definition. [§ 1–11]**

   Section 1–201(b)(12) of the UCC defines a contract as "the <u>total legal obligation</u> that results from the parties' *agreement* . . ." and § 1–210(b)(3) of the UCC defines "agreement" as "the bargain of the parties . . . as found in their language <u>or inferred from other circumstances</u>." Hence, under the UCC a contract is a legal obligation (meaning that a court will enforce it if breached) consisting of all terms agreed to by the parties, plus terms that are implied by courts or by the Code itself.

3. **Distinction Between Restatement and UCC Definitions. [§ 1–12]**

   In most cases, a contract under the Restatement will also be one under the UCC. The one place where there will be a contract under the UCC, but not one under the Restatement, is when *both* parties complete all performance called for under the contract contemporaneous with their agreement and where their agreement contains implied obligations under the UCC. For example, assume June buys a watch from Watches R' Us for $100. There is likely no "contract" under the Restatement 2d because there are no "promises" of either party left to be enforced. There would be a UCC contract, however, for their agreement gives rise to continuing legal obligations, e.g., if the watch is defective, June likely has the continuing protection of something called the "implied warranty of merchantability" which the UCC implies in sales by a merchant seller, even if the parties do not specifically refer to such a warranty as part of their bargain [UCC § 2–314; *see* Chapter Thirty-Five]. So the implied warranty obligation is part of the total obligations of the parties, which extends beyond the simple exchange of the watch for the money, making it a UCC "contract."

   Note that if they agreed to a deal where June put $10 down today for the watch, and agreed to return next Thursday and pay the balance, there *would* be a contract under the Restatement because each party would have promised something now that he or she had to do in the future—June to show up next Thursday with $90, and Watches R' Us to provide the watch. So if one of the parties fails to perform on Thursday, the other can sue in court for breach. Similarly, if June paid the entire amount on the day they made the contract, but agreed to return for the watch next Thursday, there would still be a Restatement contract for there would be at least one unperformed (or, in contract terms, "unexecuted" or "executory") promise remaining after the agreement had been made.

   Most contracts cases deal with contracts having at least some executory performance, i.e., with at least some promised acts remaining unperformed at the time the contract is formed, and so when this book refers to a "contract," it will usually be a contract under both the Restatement and UCC.

Note that the UCC defines the term "agreement" in § 1–201(b)(3) as "the bargain of the parties in fact as found in their language or inferred from other circumstances . . ." You will find that often cases and classroom discussion use "agreement" and "contract" synonymously. The Code defines them differently and you should keep that distinction in mind as you proceed in the course.

C. ELEMENTS OF A CONTRACT. [§ 1–13*]

A contract is formed after there has been:

1) a valid **offer** by one party;
2) a valid **acceptance** by the other; and
3) **consideration**.

A brief description of each of these terms follows. For a more detailed discussion, see the chapter indicated in this book. Note that some professors add a "fourth" element: an **absence of defenses to contract formation**. These defenses are discussed in Chapters Ten through Seventeen.

An **offer** is a manifestation by one party reasonably indicating a willingness to be legally bound to a particular transaction on certain terms [Restatement 2d § 24; Chapter Three].

An **acceptance** is a manifestation by the "other" party of a similar willingness to be legally bound to that same transaction [Restatement 2d § 50; Chapters Four and Five].

Consideration is the main doctrine governing which promises made by the parties will be enforceable through our legal system. Courts will not enforce all promises exchanged between two parties. As mentioned earlier, for example, courts will not enforce "gift promises"—"I'll give you a ride to the game next week"—and will only enforce those with "consideration." For valid consideration, the promises of one party must induce (or at least appear to induce) the promises or actions of the other, i.e., the parties' promises must be the result of a "bargained for exchange," and something of value must be promised or exchanged between the parties, e.g., I'll give you a ride to the game if you promise to buy the beers when we get there. [Restatement 2d § 71; Chapter Seven.] If consideration is not present, a party's promises may still be enforced to some extent if **promissory estoppel** (loosely defined as "a moral obligation") is present. For the doctrine of promissory estoppel to apply, the party seeking to enforce the promise of another must both reasonably and actually rely on

---

* For more information, listen to CD # 1, Track 4 of *Sum and Substance Audio on Contracts*.

AN INTRODUCTION TO CONTRACT LAW

that promise, and it must be demonstrated that it would be unjust if the promise were not enforced. (Restatement 2d § 90; *see* Chapter Eight.)

D. TYPES OF CONTRACTS. [§ 1–14*]

1. **Unilateral Contracts. [§ 1–15]**

   Unilateral contracts are those in which only **one party makes a promise, in the form of an offer, which calls for the other to render some sort of** *performance as acceptance.* For example, Jill and Ed agree that Jill will pay Ed $1,000 if Ed paints Jill's house. If Ed finishes the painting, they have entered into a unilateral contract because only one party, Jill, has made *a promise*, i.e., to pay; and that promise is made in exchange for *an act* by Ed, i.e., the painting, in order to accept. In other words, Ed's performance in painting the house (as opposed to his *promise* to paint) acted as the acceptance of Jill's offer [§ 3–27].

2. **Bilateral Contracts. [§ 1–16]**

   Bilateral contracts are those in which **both parties make mutual promises to each other**. For example, suppose Jill promises to pay Ed $1,000 if he will *agree* to paint her house next Thursday. At this point, Jill has made an offer to enter into a bilateral contract for she seeks a promise of performance in return from Ed. If, in response to Jill's offer, Ed promises to do the painting next Thursday, then Ed has accepted Jill's offer and a bilateral contract has been formed [§ 3–28].

3. **Express Contracts. [§ 1–17]**

   An express contract is one in which **the parties' contract results from words**, whether oral or written.

4. **Implied-in-Fact Contracts. [§ 1–18]**

   An implied-in-fact contract is one that **is reasonably implied by the parties' conduct**, rather than by express words. For example, a sign in Sally's Barber Shop states, "We only give haircuts and we only charge $25.00." Bruce walks in, sits in the barber chair and allows Sally to cut his hair, all without saying a word. An implied-in-fact contract has been formed, for it is reasonable factually to imply that he is agreeing to the $25 contract price when he sits in the chair. **The legal effect of an implied-in-fact contract is exactly the same as that of an express contract.**

---

* For more information, listen to CD # 1, Track 5 of *Sum and Substance Audio on Contracts*.

CHAPTER 1

a. Example of *Wrench LLC v. Taco Bell Corp.* [§ 1–19]

Wrench created a caricature dog named "Psycho Chihuahua," portrayed as a feisty, edgy and confident dog. Wrench sent these drawings to Taco Bell Corp. Both parties concede that they had a basic understanding that Taco Bell would compensate Wrench if it used "Psycho Chihuahua" in advertising, even if no express agreement with those terms were agreed to. Taco Bell. did in fact use such portrayal in its commercials, having a live dog named Gidget emulate "Psycho Chihuahua," but did not pay Wrench.

Held: Judgment for Wrench under an implied-in-fact contract theory. Wrench disclosed an idea to Taco Bell, at its request, and it was reasonably understood that Wrench expected compensation for the use of its ideas. By using Wrench's caricature, an implied-in-fact contract was established whereby Taco Bell had to pay reasonable compensation to Wrench. [*Wrench, LLC v. Taco Bell Corp.*, 256 F.3d 446 (6th Cir. 2001)].

5. Implied-in-Law Contracts or "Quasi-Contracts." [§ 1–20]

Implied-in-law contracts or "quasi-contracts" (the terms are synonymous) **are not really contracts at all**, for there is no "offer" and "acceptance" agreed to by the parties, and no "consideration" exchanged at the time of its making. Rather, quasi-contracts refer to a limited group of *situations* where, to avoid inequity and one party being unjustly enriched by the actions of the other, a court will hold that the benefitted party to pay the party who performed the services. This is true even though the benefitted party neither explicitly nor implicitly agreed to pay for such services. In these situations courts **imply, as a matter of *law***, that the benefitted party would have agreed to pay for the benefits received if given a chance to do so. If a quasi-contract is found, the benefitted party is required to pay a "reasonable amount," or the "fair market value" for those services. Note that because there is no "contract" in these cases, some modern commentators do not use the terms implied-in-law contract, or "quasi-contract" at all. Instead they describe such situations as giving rise to "quasi-contractual *claims*" or "quasi-contractual *recovery*" [*see* § 31–31 for a further discussion of quasi-contractual recovery].

a. Example. [§ 1–21]

Georgia, a doctor, sees Fred lying unconscious in the street and renders emergency medical treatment that saves Fred's life. Fred is liable for the fair market value of Georgia's services under an implied-in-law contract, or quasi-contract theory. Even though Fred never promised to pay for those services, and Georgia never formally offered to provide medical help, the court will nevertheless impose that obligation on Fred as a matter of law. The idea is that, under the circumstances, Fred probably would have agreed to pay for such aid if given the chance to do so, and it would thus be inequitable and unjust under the circumstances for Fred to benefit from Georgia's treatment without paying the fair market value, or "going rate," for it.

PART II

MUTUAL ASSENT, OFFER, AND ACCEPTANCE

CHAPTER 2

MUTUAL ASSENT

A. MUTUAL ASSENT: DEFINED AND DISCUSSED. [§ 2–1]

For a contract to be valid, the parties must manifest a **mutual assent to be bound** [Restatement 2d §§ 17, 18]. In other words, subject to the objective theory of contracts, *see* § 2–3, it is necessary to show that one party promised something, or began a performance, in return for a promise by the other, and that the other party agreed to that same exchange.

The rationale for this requirement, also known as **mutuality of obligation**, is that contract making is a form of risk allocation and it is important that the financial risks associated with a contract be shared symmetrically. This concept is illustrated immediately below.

1. **Example of Mutuality of Obligation. [§ 2–2]**

    Joe contracts to sell his car to Sally for $5,000. By offering his car at that price, Joe is taking a risk that he is making a "bad" (for him) deal in that other buyers might offer him $6,000 for the car. However, Joe is also taking the chance he has made a "good" (for him) deal in that no other buyer would offer him more than $4,000 for the car. By accepting the offer, Sally is taking reciprocal risks. That is, she is taking a risk that she has entered into a "bad" (for her) deal, whereby she has agreed to purchase a $4,000 car for $5,000. But she also may have made a "good" (for her) deal in that she bought a $6,000 car for $5,000. Because Joe and Sally share equal, but opposite, risks in the same bargain, their transaction is said to evidence **mutuality of obligation** and thus would be enforceable.

    If there were a point at which only one party, say Joe, was bound to sell the car for $5,000, but Sally was not bound to purchase it at that price, Sally could engage in speculation at Joe's expense. That is, she could explore the market, find out if there were better deals available to her and, if so, simply walk away from the deal and leave Joe hanging. Obviously Sally is free to make such inquiries **before** she enters the contract, but if they have an enforceable agreement, both must be bound for a "contract" to be found.

CHAPTER 2

There is one exception to the above rule, i.e., a legally viable situation where one party is bound but the other is not. This is known as an "option contract" situation [*See* Restatement 2d § 25]. Typically this would occur where, e.g., Sally would pay Joe some money to give her the option to purchase the car for $5,000 over the next few months. Because she has paid for the right, and because Joe agreed to take the money to give her the right, Joe is bound to sell the car for the next three months to Sally, but Sally is not obligated to buy it. [*See* § 4–74 *et seq.* for a further discussion of option contracts.]

However, absent an option contract, contract law views a situation where one party is bound and the other is free to speculate as unfair. Indeed, this idea of symmetrical risk allocation is at the heart of modern contract doctrine. It is often said that contract making is a form of mutual risk allocation. Therefore, if parties do not share mutual, but opposite, risks, then they do not have mutuality of obligation, and there is no enforceable contract.

B. MUTUAL ASSENT JUDGED BY OBJECTIVE THEORY OF CONTRACTS. [§ 2–3]

The **objective theory of contracts** judges whether mutual assent exists, i.e., whether a *reasonable* person would conclude that a contract had been formed [Restatement 2d § 19, Cmt. b]. Under this test, it is irrelevant what a party subjectively meant by what he or she said or did during contract negotiation. That is, it may be possible that one party to an enforceable contract does not believe that he or she has entered into a contract, but nevertheless finds him or herself bound. If a reasonable person in the position of the **other** party would believe a contract had been formed, both parties will be bound [Restatement 2d § 19(2)]. Similarly, a person may believe himself or herself bound, but if a reasonable person would not, there is no enforceable contract.

Under Restatement 2d § 19(1), a party's manifestation of assent to enter into a transaction can be made by written or spoken words, or by acts. The key is whether the party to be bound either intended to demonstrate an intent to enter into an enforceable agreement or had "reason to know" that the other party would believe he or she had such intent [Restatement 2d § 19(2)]. A party has "reason to know" that the other party would believe he or she would have such intent if a hypothetical "person of ordinary intelligence" would believe the intent exists [Restatement 2d § 19, Cmt. b]. Whenever contract law speaks of the objective theory of contracts, it is referencing this hypothetical reasonable person of ordinary intelligence.

It is sometimes said that there is no longer a mutual assent requirement in light of the objective theory of contract. That is not true. Modern mutual assent does not turn on whether both parties *subjectively* believe they have a deal, but rather whether a reasonable person would believe that both parties have objectively agreed to be bound to the same bargain.

MUTUAL ASSENT

Restatement 2d § 17 states that a contract must have "manifestation of mutual assent" to be enforceable. Restatement 2d § 18 provides that such manifestation of mutual intent occur by promise or act. Where the "objective" theory, i.e., reasonable belief by the other party, comes in is in Restatement 2d § 19(2), which provides that manifestation of mutual assent occurs when one party has "reason to know" that the other party can infer the first party's assent. The "reason to know" standard is an objective one, and means that a reasonable person in the other party's position would believe an intent to be bound has been demonstrated. Note that while it is thus incorrect to state that the mutual assent requirement has been eliminated, it *is* accurate to say the *subjective* "meeting of the minds" requirement of early common law has been eliminated as discussed in § 2–4.

1. **Elimination of "Meeting of the Minds." [§ 2–4]**

   While the phrase "there was no contract because there was no **meeting of the minds**" is still bantered about, it is now virtually meaningless. Many years ago, contract law used a subjective test to determine mutuality and so it was important that the parties' minds in fact "met," and that they both subjectively agreed to the same deal. Today, however, it is only important that a reasonable person in the position of one party would conclude that the other party intended to be bound **even if at the time that party did not intend to be contractually bound.**

   a. **Example of *Lucy v. Zehmer*. [§ 2–5]**

      After a night of some drinking and "needling" conversation, Zehmer offered in writing to sell the Lucy brothers his farm for $50,000, a fair price. The Lucys accepted. Zehmer later contended that no contract had been formed in part because he was "higher than a Georgia Pine" when he made the offer, and mostly because he subjectively believed the offer to be a joke—a kind of dare to see if the Lucy brothers really would commit to pay the $50,000.

      Held: Zehmer made a valid offer to sell the farm because, to a reasonable person in the position of the offeree (the Lucy brothers), it appeared that Zehmer made a sincere offer. Some of the acts Zehmer undertook which made it appear to a reasonable person that there was an offer included: (1) a 40 minute discussion of the deal with the Lucys, including a detailed discussion of the kind of title that was to be conveyed; and (2) a rewrite of the offer that night to include Zehmer's wife as a co-seller. It was thus irrelevant what Zehmer subjectively believed or that Zehmer and the Lucys did not have a "meeting of the minds." The key was that the Lucys were reasonable in believing Zehmer was serious under the objective theory of contracts [*See* Case Squibs, *Lucy v. Zehmer*, 84 S.E.2d 516 (Va. 1954)].

Note that if one party specifically states at the time of the agreement that he or she does not intend to enter into a transaction with binding force, those words will keep the transaction from becoming an enforceable contract if a reasonable person on the other side of the deal would believe the speaker did not intend to be bound to an enforceable contract [Restatement 2d § 21; Cmt. b, Ill. 3].

2. **Presumption Against Mutual Assent to Contract in Domestic or Social Situations. [§ 2–6]**

Many contract cases are about a court trying to find the intent of the parties—did the parties' intend to be bound; did they intend 5 days to be 5 calendar days or 5 business days, etc. The problem is, if a court could stop time just after the deal was concluded, the parties often would say they didn't know what they intended at the time because the issue never came up, and never entered their minds. To help solve that problem, contract law uses **presumptions**, which allows a court to say, "Well, if you guys didn't think about it, and there is no evidence one way or the other, I will *presume* you intended "X." Of course if there is evidence that the parties' meant or intended something else, the presumption can be overcome (in legal terms it can be "rebutted") and the parties' true intentions fulfilled. But without such evidence, presumptions are a useful tool for a court.

Under modern contract law, there is a **presumption** against finding a mutual assent to contract if the parties are social friends making promises to each other (e.g., if you'll give me a ride to the football game, I'll buy you a hot dog at the game), or if the parties are living in an amicable domestic situation (e.g., where a brother promises to iron his sister's clothes in return for her promise to wash his car, or a husband promises to take out the trash if his wife will take the kids to school next week) [Restatement 2d § 21, Cmt. c]. As noted above, the presumption against contractual intent can be overcome by admissible evidence that a binding legal commitment was intended, e.g., if a husband and wife sign an ante-nuptial agreement, but the general rule is that these promises are unenforceable. The rationale for this rule is that it is unlikely that a reasonable person on either side of the transaction would believe that friends or family intended to be legally bound when making such casual promises.

Sometimes a court will engage in fact-finding to decide whether a promise was intended to be enforces or not. For example, suppose a Cousin A promises Cousin B she can live with Cousin A's family for the rest of her life, rent free, in exchange for her companionship. Whether that was a serious, enforceable promise by Cousin A would depend on the facts, e.g., was it said at a family party where other such promises were made?; was it said after Cousin B's spouse had just passed away?; were Cousin A and Cousin B close?, etc. A court would have to take evidence to determine whether the promise would be enforceable as viewed by a reasonable person.

   a. **Example of *Balfour v. Balfour*. [§ 2–7]**

   In *Balfour*, a husband promised to make certain monthly payments to his wife in England, with whom he was living amicably at the time of the promise, while he was posted in Sri Lanka. He failed to pay. After the parties separated, the wife sued for payments due under the agreement.

   Held: the alleged contract was not enforceable because family members do not normally contemplate legal consequences when they make promises to each other. Since a reasonable person would not expect that Mr. Balfour intended to be bound by such a promise, it was unenforceable. [*Balfour v. Balfour*, 2 K.B. 571 (1919)].

Note, many find the result in *Balfour* disgusting, and the result of a different age. Not surprising, it was decided by three male, privileged, English judges. It is unlikely it would come out the same way today in the United States, but it is a good example of the principle that social compacts are suspect as legally binding contracts.

C. PRECISE TIME OF MAKING OF CONTRACT IRRELEVANT FOR DETERMINING MUTUAL ASSENT. [§ 2–8]

Occasionally, it is difficult to tell exactly when the parties entered into a contract. For example, sometimes two companies will negotiate a contract by phone, and instead of signing a single document as a contract, they will sign identical duplicates of the same agreement so that each duplicate will be an "original" contract. However, it is unlikely they will sign those separate documents at the same time. Rather than say they had no contract (the argument being that one party was bound for a time while the other was not), and they therefore lacked mutuality (*see* § 2–1), both the Restatement and the UCC take the position that so long as mutual intent to be bound can be found at *any* point in time, a valid contract is formed. Thus, under modern contract law, **mutuality of obligation can still be satisfied even if the precise moment of contract formation cannot be precisely determined** [Restatement 2d § 22(2); UCC § 2–204(2)].

D. MUTUAL ASSENT AS TO ALL TERMS NOT REQUIRED: ONLY AS TO ESSENTIAL OR "MATERIAL" ONES. [§ 2–9]

To have a binding contract, it is not necessary that the parties manifest mutual agreement to all terms. Rather, it is only necessary that there be an agreement as to the **essential or "material" terms** [Restatement 2d § 33]. For example, if Sue has a contract with Fred to wash Fred's dog Fido for $25, they probably have an enforceable agreement even if Fred thinks Sue will use Petco-brand shampoo and Sue intends to use PetSmart-brand shampoo. That's because the brand of shampoo is likely not an essential or material term. However, if for some reason the brand of shampoo is important to them both, then the failure to agree on the shampoo renders the agreement unenforceable since there has been no mutual assent to the essential terms. [*See* Chapter Six: Indefiniteness for further discussion of this point.]

CHAPTER 3

OFFERS

A. OFFER: DEFINED AND DISCUSSED. [§ 3–1]

An "offer" is the manifestation by one party (the offeror) of a willingness to enter into a bargain with another (the intended offeree or offerees) on certain terms. To be valid, the manifestation must raise a reasonable expectation in the offeree(s) that nothing more than acceptance is needed by the offeree(s) to create a contract [Restatement 2d § 24]. Offers can be written, oral, or expressed by conduct. In a simple negotiation, offers are typically the next-to-last communication before contract formation (acceptances being the last), but in complicated, long-distance negotiations, it may be difficult to pinpoint exactly which document or draft was an offer [§ 2–8].

B. EFFECT OF OFFER: POWERS AND RIGHTS OF ACCEPTANCE. [§ 3–2*]

A valid offer invests the offeree with the **"power" of acceptance**. An offeree with the power of acceptance has the power to conclude a contract merely by accepting a valid, outstanding offer [§§ 4–6 *et seq.*], assuming consideration is present [*see* Chapter Seven for a discussion of consideration].

In certain situations, in addition to a "power" of acceptance, the offeree also obtains a **"right" of acceptance**. The principal difference between a power and a right to accept is that a *power to accept* can be taken away by the offeror—called a "revocation" of the offer [Restatement 2d § 42]—and can also be lost by some action of the offeree himself or herself—such as "rejection" of the offer, or making a "counter-offer" [Restatement 2d §§ 38, 39]. There are eight situations in total in which a *power to accept* can be lost. These are discussed in greater detail in §§ 4–29 to 4–43.

However, once an offeror gives the offeree a **right** to accept, in addition to a *power* to do so, the instances in which the offeree loses the ability to validly accept are far fewer. [*See* § 4–87 for an explanation of when an offeree with the **right** of acceptance can lose it.]

---

* For more information, listen to CD # 2, Track 1 of *Sum and Substance Audio on Contracts*.

CHAPTER 3

The question is thus when an offeror gives the offeree only a power to accept and when the offeree also gets the right to do so. The vast majority of offers only provide the offeree with a power to accept. In fact, there are only four situations in which a right to accept is also given: (1) Option contracts; (2) Merchant's Firm Offers under the UCC; (3) Where an offeree begins performance in response to a unilateral contract offer; and (4) Where the offeree "substantially relies" on the offer. Because students tend to be initially curious about the right to accept, the situations in which an offer provides a right to accept is <u>briefly</u> discussed below. However, they are more extensively and properly discussed beginning with § 4–73.

1. **The Right to Accept: Option Contracts. [§ 3–3*]**

    An option contract is a special contract where the subject matter is the offeree's right to accept **another** offer for a stated period of time or, if no time is stated, for a reasonable period of time [Restatement 2d § 25]. If Jane and Bill make a deal where, for a payment of $100 today, Jane acquires the exclusive right to accept Bill's offer to buy his car for $15,000 anytime in the next two months, they have entered into an option contract. In this case, Jane has acquired the **right** to accept the car offer in addition to the *power* to do so. [*See* §§ 4–27 *et seq.* for further explanation of the differences between the "power" and "right" of acceptance].

    a. **Example of *Beall v. Beall*. [§ 3–4]**

        The parties entered into a valid option contract for the sale of a farm, allowing the offeree to purchase the farm at a set price for five years. At the expiration of the five-year period, the parties entered into a second option contract for an additional five years. The third time the parties extended, they did not enter into a valid option contract, but rather the seller merely promised to hold the offer open and allow the offeree to purchase the farm. When push came to shove, the putative seller in the third promise situation withdrew the offer, i.e., in contracts terms, "revoked" it, before the buyer accepted it.

        Held: For the period during which the two option contracts were valid, the buyer (offeree) had **both the right and the power** to accept the offer. Because the third period was <u>not</u> the subject of a separately negotiated and paid for option contract, but merely a promise by the seller to hold the offer open, the offeree-buyer had **only a power** to accept the offer within the time limit stated, which meant it could be withdrawn by the offeror. [*Beall v. Beall*, 413 A.2d 1365 (Md. App. 1980)].

---

* For more information, listen to CD # 2, Track 2 of *Sum and Substance Audio on Contracts*.

OFFERS

2. **The Right to Accept: Merchants Firm Offer Under the UCC.** **[§ 3–5]**

   If a merchant seller makes an offer to sell a good, and promises to hold that offer open in a signed writing, the buyer obtains **both a power and a right to accept** for the time stated, not to exceed three months, or if no time is stated, for a reasonable time [UCC § 2–205] (*See* § 4–78 for a further explanation). This doctrine is known as the Merchant's Firm Offer. Hence, if merchant Art Dealer makes a signed, written offer extending to Customer the exclusive ability to purchase a particular painting for the next thirty days, Customer has acquired a **right**, in addition to a **power**, to accept, even though the parties did not enter into a valid option contract because Customer did not pay anything for it. [*See* §§ 4–78 *et seq.* for further explanation of the differences between the "power" and "right" of acceptance].

3. **Implied Unilateral Option Contract upon and Offeree's Beginning of Performance in Response to an Unambiguous Offer to Enter into a Unilateral Contract. [§ 3–6*]**

   A **right of acceptance** in the offeree is also created when an offeree "begins performance" or "tenders performance" in response to an unambiguous offer to enter into a unilateral contract [Restatement 2d § 45]. That is, once the offeree begins or tenders performance in response to an offer that requires a completed act for its acceptance (a unilateral contract, *see* § 1–15), the law implies a unilateral option contract, and the offeree has the unilateral **power and right to accept** by completing the performance within a reasonable time after performance has begun [§ 4–80 for a further explanation].

4. **Implied Option Contract Based on Substantial Reliance.** **[§ 3–7]**

   An offeree who foreseeably and substantially relies on an offer can, in some circumstances, obtain a **power and a right** to accept that offer for a reasonable period [Restatement 2d § 87(2)]. For example, where Seller-landlord promises to give Buyer-tenant the ability (as opposed to an "option") to purchase a building in which the business takes place for $25,000 at the end of the lease, and Buyer-tenant, with Seller's-landlord's knowledge and acquiescence, spends $20,000 to make improvements in the building, Buyer likely has both the power and right to accept the offer because Buyer foreseeably and substantially relied on the offer [*See* Restatement 2d § 87(2) Cmt. e, Ill. 4; § 4–85

---

* For more information, listen to CD # 2, Track 2 of *Sum and Substance Audio on Contracts*.

CHAPTER 3

C. TEST TO DETERMINE WHETHER AN "OFFER" WAS MADE: THE OBJECTIVE THEORY OF CONTRACTS. [§ 3–8*]

Whether an "offer" has been made is judged by **whether a hypothetical reasonable person, in the position of the *offeree*,** would believe that only his or her expression of assent is necessary to form an enforceable contract [Restatement 2d § 24]. In other words, offers are judged under the **objective theory of contracts**. That is, a court may determine that someone has made an offer even when the person himself or herself had no intention of making a legal commitment or believes that he or she offered to do so. So long as a reasonable person in the **offeree's** position would believe an offer was made, that offer is enforceable. Note that this is an objective test, so if a particular offeree legitimately believed that an offer had been made, but a reasonable person in the offeree's position would not have had such a belief, then no offer has been extended. [*See also* the discussion of *Lucy v. Zehmer*, § 2–5, for another illustration of this issue].

In making the determination as to whether an offer was made under the objective theory, the words and conduct of the offeror, as well as the context in which such words or actions were made, are all relevant. For example, a reasonable person would take the statement, "I'm going to offer to sell you this new $1,000 iPad for $500," very differently depending on whether it was made sarcastically to a friend while sharing beer and pizza than if it was made earnestly by a sales representative in an electronics store to a prospective customer in a going out of business sale.

1. Example of *Lonergan v. Scolnick*. [§ 3–9]

The seller placed an ad in the paper regarding a tract of land for sale. The plaintiff wrote a letter to the seller, asking about the parcel and indicating his interest in buying it. The seller sent a "form letter" as a response and indicated the plaintiff would need to act fast if interested as he expected to have a buyer "in the next week or so." The putative buyer sent what was arguably an acceptance and wanted to purchase the property.

Held: The ad and the form letter did not constitute an offer since they did not indicate to a reasonable person in the position of the offeree that the seller intended to be bound by the plaintiff's acceptance. [*Lonergan v. Scolnick*, 129 Cal. App. 2d 179 (1954)].

---

* For more information, listen to CD # 1, Track 8 of *Sum and Substance Audio on Contracts*.

OFFERS

2. **Distinguishing Offers from Other Types of Communications. [§ 3-10]**

   Over time, problems with common fact patterns have surfaced in analyzing whether an offer has been extended. Each of these is discussed below, but it is important to remember that the key question is **whether, to a reasonable person in the offeree's position, the offeror's statement creates an immediate power of acceptance in the offeree**. If it does, an enforceable offer has been made. This turns on whether, objectively, the offeror has indicated a willingness and commitment to enter into a deal on sufficiently described terms.

   a. **Offer Must Contain Terms That Are Reasonably Certain. [§ 3-11]**

   An offer that contains sufficient terms to determine whether there has been a breach and how to fashion a remedy for it is a valid offer and will not fail for indefiniteness, even if some terms are missing or are to be agreed upon at a later date [Restatement 2d § 33(1)]. The fact that some terms are missing may indicate however, that the parties did not intend the communication to be an "offer" and instead meant it to be a preliminary negotiation [Restatement 2d § 26]. The courts will look at the words, actions and context to determine whether an offer was intended.

   b. **Offer Distinguished from Statement of Future Intention. [§ 3-12]**

   A statement that a party is thinking about making an offer, or may be willing to be bound in the future, is not an offer. Instead, such statements are deemed only **"statements of future intention" or "invitations to make an offer"** [Restatement 2d § 26, Cmt. d]. Typically, phrases such as "I'm thinking about selling this item . . .," or "I may be interested in buying . . ." are only statements of future intention/preliminary negotiations, and thus not offers. On the other hand, phrases like "You can have it for . . ." or "I'll sell you . . ." or "I will buy . . ." will be deemed offers, all other things being equal.

   (1) **Example. [§ 3-13]**

   Ted tells Barbara, "I decided last night to sell my sailboat for $5,000!" Barbara immediately says, "I accept." No contract is formed. This is because a reasonable person in Barbara's position would conclude that Ted was merely stating his *future intention* to make an offer to sell the boat, and is not presently offering Barbara a chance to bind him to those terms. In other words, Ted's statement is not a commitment to sell the boat to Barbara. However, Barbara would be found to have made an offer, for a reasonable person in *Ted's* position would conclude that she is manifesting a commitment to be bound to the deal if Ted accepts.

c. **Offer Distinguished from Request for Price Quotation. [§ 3–14]**

When someone asks for, or gives, a **price quotation**, no offer is usually found, for there is no manifestation of intention to be bound, and such a statement does not create a power of acceptance in the other party. Again this is only a presumption and can be overcome.

(1) **Example. [§ 3–15]**

Sam calls up the hardware store and says, "Could you please give me a price quote for three boxes of 2 1/2-inch finishing nails?" Sam is not making an offer to purchase the nails for he is not manifesting an intention to be bound no matter what the price turns out to be [Restatement 2d § 26 Cmt. c].

Similarly, if a seller provides that the price for widgets at his or her store is $200/dozen, that also is not considered an offer, but rather a solicitation for an offer from a prospective buyer [Restatement 2d § 26 Cmt. c].

d. **Offer Distinguished from a Preliminary Negotiation or Invitation to Make an Offer. [§ 3–16]**

A statement that solicits the other party to make an offer is not an offer itself, but rather a **"preliminary negotiation"** or **"invitation to make an offer"** [Restatement 2d § 26]. Phrases such as: "Are you interested in . . ." or "Would you give . . ." are typically deemed invitations to make an offer, for a reasonable person would not find a power of acceptance created in the presumptive offeree by such statements. Once again, there is simply no commitment to be bound in a transaction expressed by these kinds of statements.

(1) **Example. [§ 3–17]**

Bruce tells Gloria, "Would you consider selling your car for $10,000?" and Gloria, responds, "It's yours." There is no contract for it is Gloria, not Bruce, who has made the offer. This is because to a reasonable person in Gloria's position, Bruce has merely entered into a preliminary negotiation with Gloria and is really trying just to solicit an offer from her, rather than make an offer himself. That is, he has not agreed to pay Gloria $10,000 for her car, but instead has merely invited Gloria to begin to negotiate with him. Gloria is the party making the offer for she has expressed a willingness to be bound to a contract to sell her car for $10,000.

e. **Offer Distinguished from Advertisements/Catalogue Descriptions. [§ 3–18]**

A staple of first year contracts classes is analyzing the effect of an advertisement or a description of an item in a mail-order catalogue. **The general rule is that an advertisement or a description in a catalogue is not an offer, but rather a solicitation to make an offer.** Thus, it is the reader of the advertisement who is deemed to make the offer when he or she tries to purchase the item.

However, if the advertisement or catalogue description, both:

(1) Specifies a particular quantity of goods to be offered at the invited price; and

(2) Indicates to the offeree what specific steps need to be followed in order to accept that offer without further communication from the seller (such as the goods are being sold on a first come, first-served basis) such an advertisement or catalogue description will be considered a binding offer [Restatement 2d § 26 Cmt. b].

(1) **Rationale for Rule. [§ 3–19]**

The rationale for the general rule is, in part, based on the consequence of deciding whether or not a contract is formed. If the advertisement or catalogue were an offer, and the customer accepted that offer by attempting to purchase the item, the seller would be in breach of contract every time the seller ran out of the advertised item in inventory and couldn't produce it when an "acceptance" was tendered.

However, if the seller specifically offers buyers a particular quantity of goods, and explains to buyers how they may accept the offer, then the store has taken sufficient steps to protect itself from the breach problem described above and has manifested an intention to be bound on the described terms. That is, to a reasonable person in the position of a buyer, there is no expectation that the store is offering an unlimited supply of goods; rather, the reasonable expectation is that once the specified quantity of goods has been sold to others, the offer expires by its own terms. There thus cannot be an over-acceptance of the offered goods.

CHAPTER 3

(2) Example. [§ 3–20]

A clothing store advertised a famous line of suits in these terms, "Nationally advertised suits. Normally $220, today only $150." Alvin came to the store in response to the advertisement, selected a suit, and tendered $150. Is there a contract? No; the advertisement stated no quantity. Such advertisements are mere statements of an intention to sell, or solicitations for the buyer to make an offer. It is Alvin who has made an offer to purchase the suit for $150.

Note that some courts have modified this doctrine and fashioned the "display theory." That is, they hold that if the customer goes into the store and there is a rack of suits offered for sale, in that case the store is held to have made an offer to sell suits up to the number of suits "displayed" in the rack. The same would also be true, e.g., if a shopper went into a grocery store and saw a display of apples or went into Costco and saw a stack of a particular model of Panasonic 75-inch televisions. That is, under traditional theory, the shopper would be the offeror, but under a minority yet more modern, view, the grocery store and Costco would be considered the offeror for the amount of apples or televisions contained in the display or out on the floor. [*Giant Food v. Washington Coca-Cola*, 332 A.2d 1 (Md. 1975)].

(3) Example of *Lefkowitz v. Great Minneapolis Surplus Store*. [§ 3–21]

The following advertisement appeared in a store window: "3 Black Lapin Stoles, Beautiful, Worth Up to $139, $1 First-Come First-Served . . ." Plaintiff was the first customer to enter the store and tendered the $1, but was told he was not eligible to buy the coat since the offer was only for women (although that was never mentioned in the ad but was asserted to be a "house rule). In court, the seller argued that if the "house rule" argument did not fly (which it did not), it was still not obligated to sell the coat to Mr. Lefkowitz because of the presumption that advertisements were not offers.

Held: Because a quantity was given and because the advertisement stated what steps needed to be taken to accept without further communication from the store, the advertisement constituted an offer. Thus, since the coats were still in stock, an enforceable contract for the stole was formed upon Mr. Lefkowitz's tender of the $1. [*Lefkowitz v. Great Minneapolis Surplus Stores*, 86 N.W.2d 689 (Minn.

1957)]. If the store had sold out before the plaintiff had tendered the $1, there would be no breach because the offer limited itself to a particular quantity and informed the offeree that it was subject to prior sale.

(4) Special Considerations for Some Kind of Catalogues. [§ 3–22]

Some catalogues are for products and look just like advertisements, and so are analyzed under the rules above. However, some catalogues are much more detailed, e.g., the catalogue for prospective students put out by your law school. The rule is that such a catalogue is still a solicitation for offers from prospective students, and not an offer itself. The idea that is sometimes hard for law students to accept is that when the student applies to law school, the terms of the offer are those set forth by the school in the catalogue. That is, it's not like a prospective student can send it an application and check and validly offer, "I'm cool with everything except having to take Contracts the first year." So even though all the terms of the offer are dictated by the school, and even though those terms are non-negotiable, the way it is analyzed is that the applicant is the one making the offer on the terms set forth in the catalogue, which itself was merely a request for solicitation for offers. What is commonly referred to as an "offer" from the school is really a contingent acceptance, binding the student to the tuition, disciplinary rules, etc., set forth in the catalogue, *contingent on* whether the student attends. That is, the terms of the catalogue make it clear that the student is not bound to come if the school has a place for him or her, and that option is incorporated into their contract.

f. **Offer Distinguished from Statements Made in Jest, in Anger, as an Opinion, in a Grumbling Manner, or While Intoxicated. [§ 3–23]**

Under the objective theory of contracts, it is irrelevant whether a party intended his or her statements or conduct to create an offer. Thus, **so long as an offeree reasonably believes that the offeror was manifesting an intention to be bound upon acceptance by the offeree, the fact that the offeror truthfully protests that he or she was only kidding, was grumbling, etc., does not prevent a valid offer from being made** [*see* §§ 2–3 *et seq.*].

So when an offeror is intoxicated, the resulting contract is voidable (because the offer was not valid) *only if* the offeree had reason to know of the intoxication, and even then only if (a) the offeror is so intoxicated so as to be unable to understand the nature of the transaction or (b) the offeror is so intoxicated that he or she is unable to act in a reasonable manner with regard to the transaction [Restatement 2d § 16]. Hence, if the offeror does understand the transaction somewhat, it will be enforceable unless the intoxication was induced by the offeree, the consideration was inadequate, or the transaction was a departure from "the normal pattern of similar transactions," so that a reasonable offeree would realize the offer was not intended to be acted upon [Restatement 2d § 16 Cmt. B; *see also* the discussion of *Lucy v. Zehmer*, § 2–5, for another illustration of this issue].

(1) **Example. [§ 3–24]**

Joe has just purchased a $30,000 car, which he loves. He tells Larry, "I'll sell my new car to you for $1,000." With only this much of the story, it is impossible to tell whether Joe has made an enforceable offer or not. To determine whether a valid offer was made, it is important to know the circumstances surrounding the communication, e.g., were Joe and Larry joking, were they old friends, did they make "offers" like this often between themselves, did Joe really need $1,000 at that point in his life and seemed serious, had they been drinking, did Larry have reason to know knew of the intoxication, etc. Obviously the disparity between the offer and the value of the car makes one question whether it will be deemed an enforceable offer, but that alone is not enough to conclude that the offer was not a serious one. The question is whether a reasonable person in Larry's position would conclude that Joe had manifested a commitment to be bound to a deal on the proffered terms.

(2) **Example of *Hawkins v. McGee*. [§ 3–25]**

A surgeon told the parents of a boy ready for hand surgery that he would "**guarantee** to make the hand '100% perfect'" if the parents agreed to contract for his services. At trial, the doctor claimed he did not intend for his statements to act as a contractual commitment, especially in light of all his warnings that it was experimental surgery. Dr. McGee claimed he was merely giving an **opinion** as to an anticipated outcome, and not making a commitment to be bound.

Held: The question of whether the doctor had entered into a contract with the parents is one for the jury to determine under an objective test. As the jury concluded that a reasonable person in the position of the parents would believe that the doctor made an offer to be legally bound to produce a 100% perfect hand, and that the parents accepted that offer, a contract was formed, regardless of whether the doctor subjectively believed he had made a "contractual" promise to cure the hand. Of significance to the court was Dr. McGee's use of the word "**guarantee**." It had the effect of creating a contract whereas a mere prediction about the outcome, e.g., "I believe he has a good chance of regaining movement in his hand," would not have. [*See* Case Squibs, *Hawkins v. McGee,* 146 A. 641 (N.H. 1929)].

D. TYPES OF OFFERS. [§ 3–26*]

A discussion of the various types of offers studied in a first year Contracts course are discussed immediately below. As discussed further in § 3–33 below, these rules stem from the concept that the offeror is the "Master of the Offer."

1. **Offer to Enter into a Unilateral Contract. [§ 3–27]**

    A unilateral contract offer is one in which the offeror seeks actual *performance* of an act by the offeree as the acceptance. For example, "I promise to pay you $1,000 if you actually paint my house." The offeror is **not** seeking the painter's *promise* to paint the house, but instead is saying that he or she is offering to pay only on completion of the specified act. [*See* §§ 1–15 for a discussion of unilateral contracts and §§ 4–59 *et seq.* for a discussion of the special problems involved in accepting unilateral contract offers.)

2. **Offer to Enter into a Bilateral Contract. [§ 3–28]**

    An offer to enter into a bilateral contract is one in which the offeror seeks a *promise* of performance by the offeree as the acceptance. For example, "I promise to pay you $1,000 if you agree to paint my house by the end of the month." Obviously the offeror expects that the offeree will eventually follow through and paint the house if the offeree accepts, but at the time the offer is made, the offeror is only <u>bargaining for the promise</u> of performance, not for the performance itself. [*See* § 1–16 for a discussion of bilateral contracts].

3. **Ambiguous/Indifferent Offers. [§ 3–29]**

    Most offers are not unambiguously unilateral or bilateral. That is, the offer is sufficiently ambiguous such that a person in the offeree's position could reasonably believe that the offer could be accepted either by promising to do what the offer asked, or by actually doing it. For example, it is not clear whether an offeror who says, "I'll pay you $1,000 to paint my house" is seeking a promise by the offeree to

---

* For more information, listen to CD # 1, Track 9 of *Sum and Substance Audio on Contracts.*

CHAPTER 3

paint the house or is seeking completion of the painting job by the offeree as acceptance. An offer is deemed an **"indifferent"** or **"ambiguous" offer** if it is unclear whether the offeree may accept by promising to perform or by beginning performance [Restatement 2d § 32]. In this situation, acceptance by either mode is deemed both invited and valid, and whether it is an indifferent offer or not is judged under the objective theory of contracts. [*See* § 4–3 for a further explanation of the objective theory of contracts].

a. **Significance of the Distinction Between Unilateral, Bilateral, and Ambiguous Contract Offers. [§ 3–30]**

Many first year students wonder why anyone would ever make an ambiguous or, especially, a bilateral contract offer, and are surprised to learn that most offers are either ambiguous or bilateral in nature. That is, the question is why would someone only want a promised performance when you could bargain for performance itself? The answer lies in the concept of breach and settled expectations. If an offeror says, "I will only pay you if you complete painting my house," he or she cannot reasonably rely on the house being painted, even if the offeree promises to paint the house. The offer was only that the painter would be paid *if* he or she actually painted the house and if the offeree decided he or she did not want the money or the hassle of painting the house, he or she could not paint it without contractual liability. [*See* § 4–80 *et seq.* for a more thorough discussion of this issue].

On the other hand, if the offeree *promises* to paint the house by a certain date for $1,000, the offeror/homeowner has a right to expect that the work will be done at the promised price. If it is not, she will have a right to sue for breach of contract, get the work done by someone else, and charge the breaching painter the difference between what she had to pay the "new" painter and $1,000, assuming there is no justifiable excuse for the painter's non-performance. In other words, once the painter *promises* to paint the house, he or she can't just change his or her mind and escape contractual liability.

Note there is a difference in how these types of offers may be accepted. A unilateral contract offer can only be accepted by actually performing and completing the task specified in the offer whereas a bilateral contract offer can only be accepted by promising to perform. If the offer calls for performance (unilateral contract) and the offeree promises to perform, the acceptance is invalid. The same is true where the offer calls for a promise to perform (bilateral) and the offeree begins performance without promising the offeror that he will perform. However, an ambiguous offer, it can be accepted either by promising to perform, or performing, the act.

OFFERS

The distinction also affects the offeror's ability to revoke the offer. A bilateral contract offer can be revoked at any time before acceptance by the offeree. A unilateral contract offer can also be revoked at any time before acceptance, unless the offeree has begun or tendered the beginning of performance. In that case, the offeree can stop performing at any point. Of course, if the painter doesn't finish painting the house, he or she hasn't "accepted" and would not be entitled to the contract price. But if he or she *does* stop, there has been no breach, since the offeror has specified that the way to accept the offer is by <u>completing</u> performance. On the other hand, as we will discuss in further detail in Chapter Four, once the offeree has begun or tendered performance, the offeror cannot revoke the offer for a reasonable time and must allow the offeree a reasonable opportunity to complete performance. [Restatement 2d § 45].

4. Ambiguous Offers Under the UCC. [§ 3–31]

The UCC explicitly recognizes the principle of ambiguous offers by allowing for acceptance in any manner and by any medium "reasonable in the circumstances." An offer to purchase goods by "prompt or current shipment" is viewed as allowing the offeree to accept by either shipping or promising to ship the goods that are the subject of the offer [UCC § 2–206].

5. "General" Contract or "Reward" Offers. [§ 3–32*]

A "general" offer is an offer phrased in such a way that a large, and in some cases, potentially unlimited, number of people are given the power to accept it [Restatement 2d § 29 Cmt. b]. For example, Bank offers a reward for information leading to the arrest and conviction of someone who robbed one of its branches. Almost always, general contract offers are unilateral in nature, i.e., the offeror is only offering to pay upon the completion of some act. However, general offers carry with them peculiar problems regarding acceptance and revocation, which is why they are typically discussed separately from normal unilateral contract rules. (*See* § 4–12 for a discussion of the acceptance and revocation problems associated with general offers.)

E. THE OFFEROR IS THE "MASTER OF THE OFFER." [§ 3–33**]

It is often said that the offeror is the "master of the offer." This means that the offeror is free to dictate all the terms of the offer. However, when cases

---

* For more information, listen to CD # 1, Track 9 of *Sum and Substance Audio on Contracts*.

** For more information, listen to CD # 1, Track 8 of *Sum and Substance Audio on Contracts*.

CHAPTER 3

speak of the offeror as being the "master of the offer," they generally are referring to two specific things:

> (1) **The offeror's power to specify *how, when, and where* the offer is to be accepted,** [Restatement 2d §§ 30, 60] e.g., the offeror may validly say that the offer can only be accepted by singing Lady Gaga's *"Born That Way"* in Swedish in front of the Washington Monument before 10:00 a.m. tomorrow; and

> (2) **The offeror's power to dictate *who* may validly accept the offer,** [Restatement 2d § 29] e.g., the offeror may validly say that offer may only be accepted by members of the local Yacht club.

Once an offeror has validly limited either how the offer can be accepted or who may accept it, an offeree is required to abide by such limitations in accepting the offer, assuming the restrictions do not violate any anti-discrimination laws [§§ 4–6, 4–92].

F. SPECIAL RULES REGARDING OFFERS MADE AT AUCTIONS. [§ 3–34]

There are special rules for dealing with offers made at auctions, including on-line auctions. The key to analyzing an auction transaction is to determine, as between the auctioneer and the bidder, which party is the offeror and which is the offeree. The answer depends on whether the auction was **"with reserve"** or **"without reserve"** [Restatement 2d § 28; UCC § 2–328].

1. Auctions with Reserve. [§ 3–35]

   Auctions are assumed to be "with reserve" unless otherwise indicated [Restatement 2d § 28(1)(a); UCC § 2–328(3)]. "Reserve" means that the auctioneer reserves the right to remove the goods from the auction at any time before the "hammer falls," or, in an on-line auction, before the timer counts down to 00:00 time remaining, usually because a minimum price has not been bid. **Thus, in an auction with reserve, the auctioneer is deemed merely to solicit offers from bidders and it is the bidders themselves who are the offerors.** The auctioneer, as offeree, has the power to accept or decline the bids, and signifies acceptance of the last offer (if it exceeds the minimum price) by letting the hammer fall or the time expire. Thus, even if there are bids outstanding, the auctioneer can reject them if they are below the minimum price for the lot simply by never letting the hammer fall or withdrawing the goods with time remaining and thus never "accepting" any offer.

2. Auctions Without Reserve. [§ 3–36]

   If the auction is specifically stated to be without reserve, the auctioneer is the offeror and each successive bidder is an offeree [Restatement 2d § 28(1)(b); UCC § 2–328(3)]. By placing the goods on sale without reserve, the auctioneer is deemed to have made an irrevocable offer to sell, which cannot be withdrawn after the first bid is made. Each bid acts as a conditional acceptance, subject to the conditions that: (a) it is not withdrawn before the hammer falls or time expires and (b) no higher bid is made. Once the hammer falls without a retraction of the final bid, and without a higher bid being made, the conditional acceptance becomes an enforceable acceptance, and a contract is formed with the last bidder. As discussed further in § 3–37, note that the rule concerning the conditional acceptance above deals with retraction of the *bid*, not withdrawal of the good itself from the auction. In an auction without reserve, once the auctioneer starts taking bids, the owner of the good cannot withdraw it for any reason, including the fact that a hoped for minimum price is not met.

3. **Withdrawal of Bid. [§ 3–37]**

Whether or not an auction is with reserve, absent an agreement to the contrary, the <u>bidder</u> is free to withdraw his or her bid at any time prior to the auctioneer's announced completion of the sale. In such an event, earlier bids are **not** automatically restored [Restatement 2d § 28(1)(c); UCC § 2–328(3)].

G. OFFERS UNDER THE CISG. [§ 3–38*]

In general, the CISG focuses more on whether an agreement has been reached, rather than analyzing which communication might be an offer and which might be the acceptance. However, to the extent the CISG focuses on one communication as an offer, the rules are virtually identical to those of the Restatement. Under Article 14(1), "A proposal for concluding a contract addressed to one or more specific persons constitutes an offer if it is **sufficiently definite** and **indicates the intention of the offeror to be bound** in case of acceptance." If the communication is "other than one addressed to one or more specific persons" it is considered "merely as an invitation to make [an] offer[ ]" [Article 14(2)].

H. EXAM APPROACH TO OFFER ISSUES. [§ 3–39**]

The typical way "offers" are tested on a Contracts exam is to give the student several communications between the parties (multiple conversations, phone calls, letters, e-mails, etc.), and then require the student to identify which of these communications constituted the offer. The key is whether a **reasonable person** in the position of the other party would believe the communication by the offeror signified an

---

* For more information, listen to CD # 3, Track 3 of *Sum and Substance Audio on Contracts*.

** For more information, listen to CD # 3, Track 4 of *Sum and Substance Audio on Contracts*.

CHAPTER 3

intention and commitment to be bound [§ 3–8]. In making that call, remember the rules distinguishing offers from other communications as a matter of law [§ 3–10 *et seq.*], and that the subjective intent of the offeror is irrelevant [§ 3–8]. Typically, an exam question will not just focus on the "offer." The student will also have to deal with acceptance issues as well. Hence, grasping the information in both this and the next Chapter is necessary to fully analyze such a question.

CHAPTER 4

ACCEPTANCE

A. ACCEPTANCE: DEFINED AND DISCUSSED. [§ 4–1]

An "acceptance" is a manifestation by the offeree that he or she is willing to be bound to the agreement proposed by the terms of the offer [Restatement 2d § 50(1)]. An acceptance can be written, oral, or expressed by conduct. In most situations, the acceptance is the last communication required for contract formation, although in some complex negotiations, it may be difficult to pinpoint what is the "offer" and what is the "acceptance." see § 3–1. To be valid under § 50 of the Restatement 2d, an acceptance must be made:

(1) **By someone entitled to accept the offer** [§ 4–6]

(2) **At a time when the power of acceptance has not been terminated** [§ 4–27]

(3) **In a manner required or permitted by the offer** [§ 4–92].

B. EFFECT OF ACCEPTANCE. [§ 4–2]

Assuming the existence of valid consideration, or its "substitutes," [Chapter Seven] timely acceptance of a valid offer in a permissible way by an authorized offeree creates an enforceable contract. A valid acceptance cuts off the offeror's right to revoke the offer, and also cuts off the offeree's right to reject the offer.

C. TEST TO DETERMINE WHETHER ACCEPTANCE HAS TAKEN PLACE: THE OBJECTIVE THEORY OF CONTRACTS. [§ 4–3*]

Whether or not an offeree has accepted an offer is judged under the **objective theory of contracts. The test is whether, to a reasonable person in the position of the *offeror*, the offeree has manifested a willingness to be bound by the terms of the offer**. If so, a valid acceptance has been made. The test is not whether the *actual* offeree believed he or she had accepted the offer, but rather whether **a**

---

* For more information, listen to CD # 1, Track 8 of *Sum and Substance Audio on Contracts*.

hypothetical person, standing in the shoes of the offeror, would believe that the offeree has manifested a willingness to be bound.

A somewhat strange, and relatively uncommon (except in law school hypotheticals), effect of the objective theory of contracts is that sometimes an offeree may accept an offer without even knowing its contents or having the slightest idea that he or she has entered into a contract. That is, so long as the offeree at least knew that some sort of offer had been tendered (even if its exact terms are unknown), and as long as a reasonable person in the offeror's position would have believed an acceptance had been tendered or expressed, the acceptance will be valid.

1. **Example. [§ 4–4]**

    Frank, a law student, sends a letter to his college roommate, Jim, offering Jim one-half of his upcoming summer's earnings if Jim will pay one-half of Frank's spring semester tuition. Frank truthfully and seriously explains that he is experiencing cash flow problems and figures Jim, who now has a high paying corporate job, may want to make such an investment and help Frank out. Jim receives the letter, but loses it before he gets a chance to read it. Frank calls and asks, "Do we have a deal as outlined in the letter?" and Jim replies (because he's embarrassed about losing the letter), "You bet we do, good buddy." A contract is formed because a reasonable person in Frank's shoes would believe Jim had manifested an intention to be bound. Jim's ignorance of the exact terms of the offer is irrelevant, for he knew from Frank's question that an offer had been made.

    Note the result would be the same even if the offeree thought he or she was accepting another offer. For example, Tim and his friend Jack plan a party for the following week. While at work, Tim receives a hand-written letter from Jack, thinking it is an invitation to the party. However, the letter was really an offer for Jack to purchase Tim's car. Later in the week, but before the party, the two run into each other, and Jack asks Tim what he thinks of the proposal in the letter. Tim, embarrassed about not reading the letter, quickly replies, "Great! Let's do it," thinking Jack is referring to the party. However, Jack now thinks that Tim has accepted his offer to purchase his car, while Tim thinks he has accepted a party invitation. Since a hypothetical reasonable person in the offeror's (Jack's) shoes would believe his or her offer was accepted, Tim's acceptance is valid in light of the fact that he was unaware of what he was accepting and believed he was accepting another offer.

2. **Cross-Offers. [§ 4–5]**

    Occasionally parties will exchange identical offers to each other in the mail. That is, the buyer will send an offer to the seller stating that he or she is willing to buy particular goods on certain terms, and the seller will also send an offer to the buyer indicating a willingness to sell those same goods on those same terms. **The exchange of cross-offers does not form a contract**, for while both parties have manifested a willingness to be bound on his or her own suggested terms, **neither has manifested a willingness to accept the offer of the other party** [Restatement 2d § 23, Cmt. d]. Recall that the definition of acceptance requires a "manifestation of *assent*" by the offeree, and there is no such manifestation in a cross-offer.

In the era of e-commerce, cross-offers are becoming increasingly rare, but they do occur every once in a while.

D. WHO IS ENTITLED TO ACCEPT THE OFFER. [§ 4–6]

When an offer is made to someone, the offeree is said to have a **power of acceptance**. The general rule is that **an offer may only be accepted by the person or persons in whom it is reasonably apparent that the offeror intended to create the *power of acceptance* when the offer was made** [Restatement 2d §§ 29, 52, 58, 60]. When an offeror specifically limits who may accept the offer, such a limitation is effective, because the offeror is the "master of the offer." However, when no specific person is mentioned, an offer may be accepted by anyone to whom it reasonably appears the offeror was intending to give the power of acceptance. In cases of doubt, the court decides who is in the class of authorized, but unspecified, offerees. A court makes such a determination through an examination of the circumstances under which the offer was made, e.g., was it made in a face-to-face meeting, on a phone call, in a text message, on line, in front of a large group, in a newspaper, etc.

1. **Who Constitutes an "Offeree" Is Judged by the Objective Theory of Contracts. [§ 4–7]**

    The **objective theory of contracts** determines whether an individual is an authorized offeree, and thereby eligible to accept an offer. Thus, if a hypothetical reasonable person in the purported offeree's shoes would believe the offer was being made to him or her, that person has the power to accept it. Hence, once again, the subjective intention of the offeror as to whom the offer was intended is not controlling.

2. **Power to Accept Is Not Generally Transferable. [§ 4–8]**

    On occasion, an eligible offeree will try to transfer his or her power of acceptance to another. In the absence of an option contract [§ 4–74], such a transfer has **no legal effect** [Restatement 2d § 52]. That is, the power to accept an offer is not legally transferable.

    a. **Example. [§ 4–9]**

        In a face-to-face conversation, Barbara offers to sell her stereo to Elaine for $500 and states that the offer will remain open for a week. After a few days Elaine decides she does not want the stereo, but mentions the offer to Mary and tells Mary she can go ahead and buy Barbara's stereo if she wants, for Elaine will give Mary her power of acceptance. Mary thereafter walks up to Barbara and says, "I'll take the stereo you offered Elaine for $500." No contract is formed, for Elaine cannot assign her power to accept. Barbara is still the master of the offer and could decide to not sell her stereo to Mary if she does not wish to do so. However, Mary will be judged as having made an offer to purchase the stereo, and thus, Barbara can decide to accept or decline *Mary's* offer.

b. **Exception: Right to Accept Under an Option Contract Is Generally Transferable. [§ 4–10]**

Absent an express agreement to the contrary, if the offeree has entered into a valid option contract, the offeree gains a **right** to accept the offer rather than merely a **power** to do so [Restatement 2d § 25]. As such, the right of acceptance is transferable under the general rules governing the assignability of all other contract rights (*see* § 4–76 and Chapter Twenty-Seven).

c. **Example. [§ 4–11]**

Joe has an option contract to buy Steve's house for $150,000 cash, the option being exercisable within the next 30 days. This means that Joe has the right to exercise the option and purchase the house at any time during that 30-day period. Steve also cannot revoke the offer during that 30-day window. If Joe decides he does not want to buy the house, but he knows that Andrea does, he can transfer or "assign" his right to buy the house to Andrea. Since Joe had the right to accept the offer to buy the house, and the option contract is transferrable, upon assignment, Andrea has the right to accept the offer to buy the house for $150,000 cash during the remainder of the 30-day window.

3. **Special Problems Concerning Acceptance of "General" or "Reward" Offers. [§ 4–12*]**

A "general" offer is an offer that creates powers of acceptance in a large, and in some cases, an unlimited number of people. For example, an offer by a bank of $5,000 for information leading to the arrest and conviction of the party who robbed the local branch is a "general" or, as it is sometimes known, a "reward" offer. [§ 3–32.]

---

* For more information, listen to CD # 2, Track 4 of *Sum and Substance Audio on Contracts.*

ACCEPTANCE

A general offer presents four problems regarding acceptance:

(1) Whether acceptance by one person extinguishes the power of all others to accept the general offer [§ 4–13];

(2) Whether the offeree must know of the general offer in order to accept it [§ 4–18];

(3) How a general offer can be revoked by the offeror so as to terminate the power of acceptance [§ 4–23]; and

(4) Whether an offeree must give notice to the offeror of his or her intention to accept before beginning performance [§ 4–25].

These issues are discussed below largely in the context of rewards, which are the most common form of general offers.

a. "General" or "Reward" Offers Can *Presumptively* Be Accepted by Only the First Person to Do the Required Acts. [§ 4–13]

Presumptively, a general reward offer, e.g., the bank will offer $5,000 "for information leading to the arrest and conviction of the person who robbed the Main Street branch," can only be accepted by the **first** person supplying such information. The terms of, and circumstances surrounding, the offer may rebut the presumption, but if nothing is said one way or the other as to who may accept, only the first supplier of information can validly accept the offer [Restatement 2d § 29, Cmt. b, Ill. 1].

(1) Example. [§ 4–14]

City posts a reward for information leading to the conviction of the individual who assaulted the Mayor on Tuesday night. On Monday, Julie calls the police and gives some information about the assault which leads to the conviction of the guilty party. On Tuesday, Bruce provides different, but truthful and helpful information. Even if Bruce's information was essential to the conviction, and even if Bruce did not know about Julie's previous call, Bruce is not entitled to the reward because he was not the first person to comply with the terms of the offer.

(2) Example. [§ 4–15]

The owner of a large company promises a $500 bonus to "any employee" who doesn't take a sick day for two years. The words and circumstances of the offer itself make it clear that the *presumption* of valid acceptance only by the first authorized offeree to do the requested act **is overcome or rebutted**, and any and all employees who meet the requisite conditions are free to accept this offer.

CHAPTER 4

(3) Exception: General Offer Whose Conditions Make It Unlikely That an Unlimited Number of People Can Accept Is Effective as to All Who Meet Those Conditions. [§ 4–16]

Contract law holds that a general offer that imposes conditions which make it likely that only a small number of people can accept, because only a small number of people are likely to meet all the conditions, is effective as to any and all persons who do, in fact, meet the conditions, and not just to the first to do so.

(a) Example of *Carlill v. Carbolic Smoke Ball Co.* [§ 4–17*]

Manufacturer of a "carbolic smoke ball" (a kind of incense, shaped into a ball, with medicinal qualities claimed by the manufacturer) placed advertisements in several publications offering a £100 reward to anyone who caught the flu after purchasing the product and using it as directed. The ad also stated that £1,000 was deposited with the manufacturer's bank for purposes of paying the reward to those who qualified.

Held: A valid general offer existed to any and all who met the conditions. The Court held that it was likely that only a limited number of people would meet the conditions in the ad, and thus, under the rule set forth in § 4–16, the offer was valid as to *all* who actually met the conditions and otherwise performed the acts necessary to accept the offer. [*Carlill v. Carbolic Smoke Ball Co.*, 1 Q.B. 256 (1893); *see also* §§ 4–26; 4–111 for other holdings from the case.]

b. Offeree Must Know of General Offer in Order to Accept It. [§ 4–18]

An offeree must know of the existence of the offer before he or she can validly accept it. Note that the offeree need not know of the offer before **starting** the actions necessary to collect it, but must know of the offer before *finishing* those acts and claiming the reward [Restatement 2d §§ 51, 23 (*see* esp. Cmt. c, Ill. 2)]. Note also that the offeree need not know exactly what the terms of the reward offer are in order to accept it (*see* §§ 4–3; 2–9). The requirement is only that he or she must at least know that some sort of a reward is being offered for the kinds of actions being

---

* For more information, listen to CD #2, Track 4 of *Sum and Substance Audio on Contracts*.

undertaken by the offeree. Lastly, this rule is also supported by the "unsolicited action" rule outlined in consideration [§ 7–40].

(1) Example. [§ 4–19]

On Friday, Bank posts a reward offer. The following Monday, a spirited public citizen reports that she saw a certain individual climbing out of the bank window at 2:00 a.m. The next Wednesday, Citizen hears for the first time about the bank's reward for information leading to the conviction of the robber. Regardless whether the individual she named is convicted of the crime, the public-spirited citizen is not entitled to the reward because she did not know of the reward offer before she gave the information. [*Broadnax v. Ledbetter*, 100 Tex. 375 (1907)].

(2) Example. [§ 4–20]

On Friday, Bank posts a general reward offer promising to pay for information that will lead to the conviction of anyone who has, or will in the future, rob one of its branches. The following Monday, a spirited public citizen sees something suspicious at 2:00 a.m. in the bank. She begins her own investigation, not knowing of the offer. On Wednesday, she learns for the first time that the bank is offering a reward of some sort for information leading to the conviction of the robber. On Thursday, she tells what she knows to the police, and ultimately the information she provided is instrumental in securing the conviction of the robber. She is entitled to the reward, even if she didn't know about it when she started investigating, or even if she did not know of the **amount** of the reward when she turned over the information to the police because she knew that a reward was offered at the time she finished the acts called for by the offer.

(3) Rationale for Rule That Offeree Must Know of Reward Offer to Accept It. [§ 4–21]

The rationale for the rule that an offeree must at least know of the existence of a reward offer before it can be validly accepted is twofold. First, the offer of a reward is designed to motivate people into taking actions that they would not otherwise take. Thus, if a person was going to come forward with incriminating information about a criminal anyway, by definition the reward offer played no part in his or her decision. Second, a party who doesn't know of the reward has no legitimate expectation of payment. Accordingly, it is thought that there is no reason for the legal system to reward actions that carry with them no promissory expectations.

(4) Police Officers and Other Governmental Workers. [§ 4–22]

The majority rule is that a police officer who arrests a criminal may collect a reward offered for the apprehension of that criminal only if the officer performs acts which are outside of his or her official duties. If the required acts are within the officer's official duties, as is likely the case, the promise to pay the reward is unenforceable due to lack of consideration under the pre-existing duty rule [§ 7–76]. Perhaps more realistically, the reward is unenforceable because it would be against public policy to allow wealthy citizens to offer extra compensation to police officers to do the jobs they are already paid to do at the expense of less affluent victims who cannot offer such reward. The same is true for other governmental workers as well, although many law school hypotheticals seem to deal with the police. So a county building inspector cannot enforce a promised "promptness bonus" for moving Mr. Moneybag's building project to the top of the list.

c. Revocation of General Offers: The "Equal Publicity Rule." [4–23]

As we will explain in detail later in this Chapter, the general rule is that until an offer is accepted, it can be revoked at will by the offeror [§ 4–55]. Typically though, the offeree must be specifically told about the revocation before the revocation is effective. [§§ 4–58 *et seq.*]. The problem with a general offer is that the offeror, such as a bank making a reward offer, will usually not know who has seen the original published offer and may be working to try and collect the reward. Accordingly, if the bank wishes to revoke the offer before it is accepted, it will not know who to contact in order to revoke it.

Contract law has solved this problem by means of the **"equal publicity rule,"** which provides that if the offeror of a general offer gives *equal publicity to its retraction as it did in making the offer*, i.e., publishes it in the same places, with the same prominence and frequency, *the offer will be retracted as to all offerees, <u>regardless whether they ever had actual notice of the retraction</u>* [Restatement 2d § 46; § 4–62]. In some instances though, since a reward offer is an offer for a unilateral contract, the offeror may be prevented from revoking the offer where the offeree has already begun performance [§ 4–24].

ACCEPTANCE

(1) Example. [§ 4–24]

Cereal company advertises a tablet computer to anyone who collects and turns in 250 cereal box tops. The promotion turns out to be very popular, and after a month, there are many more people turning in box tops than the company contemplated. The company runs a similar ad with equal publicity thanking all who participated in the promotion, but announces that it is putting an end to the program. The ad effectively revokes the offer against someone who heard about the promotion after the retraction was published and who never heard or knew about the retraction. However, those who were already collecting box tops because of the ad at the time of the retraction have a reasonable time to complete their collection, turn them in, and collect the tablet [*see* Restatement 2d § 45, Cmt. d, Ill. 8].

d. Notice of Intent to Accept General Offer Not Required. [§ 4–25]

Unless specifically and unambiguously required by the offer itself, an offeree need not give notice to the general offeror of his or her intent to accept the offer.

(1) Example of *Carlill v. Carbolic Smoke Ball.* [4–26*]

Manufacturer placed an advertisement in several publications promising to pay £100 to anyone who caught the flu after purchasing and using its product as directed. Carlill purchased and correctly used the product, but nevertheless caught the flu. Manufacturer asserted that it should not have to pay because Carlill did not give the manufacturer notice that she was intending to accept the general offer before she began performance.

Held: Carlill (the offeree) was under no duty to inform the manufacturer (the offeror) of her intention to accept a general offer before beginning performance. The court held that the notification requirement was for the benefit of the offeror and thus could be waived by it. According to the court, the manufacturer (offeror) here had implicitly waived the notice by the wording of its ad and the structure of its promise. [*Carlill v. Carbolic Smoke Ball,* 1 Q.B. 256 (1893); *see also* §§ 4–17 and 4–111 for additional holdings from the case].

---

* For more information, listen to CD #2, Track 4 of *Sum and Substance Audio on Contracts.*

CHAPTER 4

E. WHEN AN OFFER MAY BE ACCEPTED: DURATION OF THE POWER OF ACCEPTANCE. [§ 4–27*]

A purported acceptance of an offer after the power of acceptance has been terminated is invalid. There are different rules regarding what acts and events terminate the power of acceptance depending on whether the offer is "revocable" or "irrevocable," and these rules are discussed extensively below in §§ 4–28 *et seq.* and 4–72 *et seq.* respectively. However, it is important to understand that regardless of whether the offer was revocable or irrevocable when made, once it has been effectively terminated, the offeree has thereafter neither the power nor right to accept the offer, *and any <u>purported</u> acceptance by the offeree is often itself an offer.*

Note that you will often see in cases and other sources a reference to "termination of an offer." While this phraseology is descriptive, it is not technically accurate. **What terminates is not the offer, but rather the offeree's *power* (or legal ability) to validly accept the offer**. Nonetheless, on occasion this book uses the terms "termination" (or "expiration") of an offer to be consistent with the cases and other sources that use these words to mean termination of the power of acceptance.

1. Acts and Events That Terminate an Offeree's Power of Acceptance Under Revocable Offers. [§ 4–28]

Under Restatement 2d § 35(1), a *revocable* offer may be accepted so long as the power of acceptance under it has not been terminated. Hence, it is important to learn what a "revocable" offer is, and what acts and events can terminate the offeree's power of acceptance under it.

The definition of "revocable offer" is a catchall, i.e., a revocable offer is any offer that is not an "irrevocable" one. Since there are only 4 situations in which an offer will be deemed "irrevocable," [*see* §§ 4–73 *et seq.* for a discussion of those situations] most offers are *"revocable."*

The power of acceptance can be terminated upon the happening of 8 separate acts or events under a "revocable" offer:

(1) **Rejection or counter-offer by the offeree** [§ 4–29; Restatement 2d §§ 36(1)(a), 38, 39];

(2) **Lapse of time** [§ 4–44; Restatement 2d §§ 36(1)(b), 41];

(3) **Express or implied revocation by the offeror** [§ 4–55; Restatement 2d §§ 36(1)(c), 42, 43, 46];

---

* For more information, listen to CD # 2, Track 1 of *Sum and Substance Audio on Contracts*.

ACCEPTANCE

(4) **Death or incapacity of the offeror** [§ 4–64; Restatement 2d §§ 36(1)(d), 48];

(5) **Death or incapacity of the offeree** [§ 4–67; Restatement 2d §§ 36(1)(d), 48];

(6) **Non-occurrence of an implied condition: death or destruction of a person or thing (other than the offeror or offeree) essential for the contract's performance** [§ 4–68; Restatement 2d § 36(2) Cmt. c];

(7) **Non-occurrence of an implied condition, including supervening illegality** [§ 4–69; Restatement 2d § 36(2) Cmt. c]; and

(8) **Non-occurrence of an express condition of acceptance** under the terms of the offer [§ 4–71; Restatement 2d § 36(2) Cmt. b].

a. **Termination of Revocable Offers Through Rejection and Counter-Offer by the Offeree. [§ 4–29]**

A **rejection** occurs upon any manifestation by the offeree that he or she does not accept the offer and is unwilling to be bound under its terms [Restatement 2d §§ 36(1)(a), 38].

A **counter-offer** is an offer made by the offeree to the original offeror relating to the same subject matter as the original proposal, but on different terms than those proposed in the original offer. It has the effect of *implicitly rejecting* **the original offer** (thereby terminating the power of the offeree to accept the original offer) and **proposing a new offer in its place** [Restatement 2d §§ 36(1)(a), 39].

Both rejections and counter-offers may be communicated by words or by actions, and to reiterate, *their effect is to terminate immediately the offeree's power to validly accept the original offer.*

(1) **Example. [§ 4–30]**

Alice offers to sell her old lawn mower to Joe, her neighbor, for $25. After inspection, Joe immediately rejects her offer, noting that it was too old. Immediately thereafter, Joe changes his mind, and told Alice he'd take it, figuring he could fix it up and make it work. Joe's initial denial of Alice's offer is deemed a rejection, and thus terminates his power of acceptance. When Joe changes his mind and says he *will* purchase the mower, Joe has now made an offer to do so, which can be accepted or not by Alice.

The result would be the same if Joe had said, "I'll take it for $20," in response to Alice's original offer and then agreed to take it for $25 before Alice said anything. Joe's $20 proposal was a counter-offer, i.e., an offer relating to the same subject matter as the original offer but on different terms, and *implicitly* **acts as a *rejection* of the original offer**, thus terminating his power to accept it. At this stage, once again Joe has made an offer to purchase the mower for $25, which Alice can accept or reject.

(2) **Rejections and Counter-Offers Immediately Cut off Power of Acceptance Even if Offer Was to Be Held Open. [§ 4–31]**

Except in the rarest of cases [§ 4–33], a rejection or counter-offer of a **revocable offer** immediately cuts off the offeree's power to accept, *even if the offeror has indicated the offer will be held open* [Restatement 2d § 38].

(a) **Example. [4–32]**

Antique Store owner offers to sell Jack a grandfather clock for $7,500, and tells him to "take a week to think it over." Jack immediately responds, "I'll give you $6,000 for it." Even though the owner has indicated the offer will be open for a week, Jack's counter-offer **immediately** cuts off his power of acceptance. If later in the week Jack comes back to the store and says that he'll "take the clock for $7,500," it will be Jack making a new offer to purchase the clock, which the owner can accept or reject [Restatement 2d § 38, Cmt. a, Ill. 1].

(b) **Exception: When Offer Specifically States It Will Be Kept Open Despite Rejection or Counter-Offer. [§ 4–33]**

Very occasionally, an offeror may say something like, "I'll sell my car to you for $5,000, and I'll let you have 30 days to think about it. However, I'll be willing to consider a counter-offer in the meantime." In such a case, because of the clear intent of the offeror as the "master of the offer," a counter-offer by the offeree will not terminate his or her power to accept the $5,000 offer within a month of its making [Restatement 2d § 39(2), Cmt. c].

(3) **Counter-Offer Need Not Explicitly Reject Offer. [§ 4–34]**

All counter-offers are effective as rejections of the original offer, regardless whether they specifically mention the original offer. In effect, **when the offeree makes a** counter-offer, he or she is implicitly rejecting the original offer and telling the offeror, "I do not want to make a deal on the terms you proposed, and instead, am willing to be bound only on the different terms I am now proposing" [Restatement 2d § 39, Cmt. a]. For example, Sam offers to sell his car to Bob for $5,000. Bob replies, "I'll give you $4,000 for it." At this point, even without mentioning Sam's offer specifically, Bob has implicitly rejected it. Thus, Bob has terminated his power to accept Sam's $5,000 offer and Bob can no longer validly accept it. If a minute later Bob reconsiders and says, "OK, I'll pay $5,000," it is now Bob who will be deemed to have made a new offer to purchase the car at that price, which Sam may accept or reject.

(4) Rejections and Counter-Offers Are Judged Under the Objective Theory of Contracts. [§ 4–35]

The test for whether an offeree has rejected an offer, whether by counter-offer or outright rejection, is determined under the **objective theory of contracts**. That is, whether a hypothetical reasonable person, in the position of the offeror, would believe that the offeree was rejecting the offer or making a counter-offer. Once again, even if the offeree did not subjectively intend to reject an offer, or to make a counter-offer, such intention is irrelevant. In making the determination, the context of the situation, as well as the words and actions of the offeree, are taken into account.

An issue that sometimes arises with regard to counter-offers is the effect of changing many of the terms of the offer. The issue is whether that is a counter-offer, terminating the power to accept under the original offer, or whether it is a completely separate offer. Let's take an absurd example, Gary offers to sell his car to Mary for $10,000. Mary says in response, "I'll give you $25,000 for your baseball card collection." Mary has made a separate offer, which can be accepted or not by Gary, but since it is so different from the offer, the power of acceptance to buy the car for $10,000 is not terminated.

The problem comes when, e.g., in response to the offer to sell the car for $10,000, Mary says, "I'll take it if you also throw in your baseball card collection." Assuming the collection itself is worth $25,000, there is a factual question whether Mary was making a counter-offer or a separate, new offer where the car is not a significant part of the transaction any longer. The answer is that a court would take evidence and decide whether Mary's statement meets the test of a counter-offer, i.e., "an offer made by the offeree to the original offeror relating to the same subject matter as the original proposal, but on different terms."

(5) Common Law Rule: Counter-Offer Found if Purported Acceptance Differed from the Offer in the Slightest Respect. [§ 4–36]

At common law, if the terms of a purported acceptance deviated from the terms of an offer in the *slightest respect* it was deemed to be a counter-offer and not an acceptance. This was known as the "mirror image" rule. The UCC has changed this rule substantially [Chapter Five].

(6) Rejections and Counter-Offers Distinguished from Other Types of Communications. [§ 4–37]

As with any legal classification, in close cases it is difficult to say whether an offeree's statement falls on the rejection/counter-offer side of the line or should be interpreted as something else. Of course the answer to such an inquiry is often of crucial importance, for it will often decide whether or not a contract was formed and, if so, what its terms are. Over time, contract law has been able to classify various situations and develop rules for determining when statements are rejections, counter-offers, or something else. Each of these situations is described below. However, once again the guiding principles in determining whether a statement is a rejection, counter-offer, or something else are:

> (1) **To be an effective rejection, the offeree must manifest an intention not to accept the offer as judged by a reasonable person in the position of the offeror**; and
>
> (2) **To be an effective counter-offer, the offeree must manifest an intention to be bound only on different terms from those made in the offer as judged by a reasonable person in the position of the offeror.**
>
> **(a) "Neutral Comments." [§ 4–38]**
>
> Dave offers to sell a ring to Sally for $10,000. Sally says, "Gee that's expensive. I don't know if I can afford it." Sally has made only a **neutral comment**, and has not rejected the offer, for a reasonable person would not believe her to have manifested an intention not to

ACCEPTANCE

be bound. Thus, Sally still retains the power to accept Dave's offer.

(b) Mere "Inquiries" or Preliminary Negotiations. [§ 4–39]

Bernice offers to sell her watch to Jane for $500. Jane replies, "Would you consider $450?" Jane has not rejected the offer under the objective theory, and has made a **"mere inquiry,"** or entered into only a **"preliminary negotiation"** as to whether Bernice might be willing to negotiate the price [Restatement 2d § 26]. Jane's statement does not rise to the level of a counter-offer because Jane has neither expressed a commitment to be bound to a $450 price, nor manifested an intention to proceed only on different terms from those made in the offer [§ 3–16]. Therefore, Jane still retains the power to accept Bernice's $500 offer [Restatement 2d § 39, Cmt. b, Ill. 2].

(c) Requests for Modification. [§ 4–40]

In response to an offer to sell him a $2,000 stereo on no-interest 90-day credit, Moe says, "O.K. I'll take it, but will you give me a 5% discount for cash?" Moe has accepted the stereo at $2,000 and has made a **request for modification** of the contract regarding the cash discount, which may be accepted or rejected by the store [*see* Chapter Nine for a further discussion of modification]. Note that if Moe had said, "I'll accept only if you give me a 5% discount for cash," then it would be a counter-offer, as a reasonable person would believe Moe was rejecting the offered terms and was willing to be bound only upon agreement as to the discount.

(d) "Grumbling" Acceptances. [§ 4–41]

In response to an offer to sell him a used refrigerator for $500, Bernie says, "O.K. I'll take it, but the price is way too high. I should only have to pay you $400 for it." Bernie has accepted, even if he is not happy about it. Such a situation is known as a "grumbling acceptance."

(e) "Intention to Take the Offer Under Further Advisement." [§ 4–42]

Laura offers to sell her watch to Jean for $600 and tells Jean to "take a week to think about it. I won't sell to anyone else before then." The next day Jean says, "I'm leaning towards not paying $600, but I tell you what, how about $525 to close the deal right now. Of course, if you say no, I'll keep your $600 offer under advisement for the rest of the week like you promised." Jean's power to accept the $600 deal has **not** been terminated, for she has manifested an intention to keep the offer open. To a reasonable person in the position of the offeror, Jean would not be seen as manifesting an unwillingness to be bound by the original offer, but rather making a **preliminary inquiry** as to whether the price was negotiable. As such, Laura is not entitled to rely on Jean's statements as terminating the offer, and, if nothing more is said, Jean may validly accept the $600 offer later in the week [Restatement 2d § 38(2), Cmt. b; § 39(2), Cmt. c, Ill. 3].

(7) **When a Rejection Is Effective. [§ 4–43]**

The general rule is that a **rejection is effective upon receipt by the offeror**. In the vast majority of cases, the determination of exactly when a rejection is received is undisputed or unimportant, e.g., the rejection comes during a face-to-face conversation, by e-mail, during a phone conversation, or for other reasons the parties do not contest the time of rejection. However, occasionally a party will mail an acceptance and then change his or her mind and want to signify rejection (e.g., by a phone call, e-mail, or presumably text message) before the offeror has received the mailed acceptance. Similarly, an offeree may originally mail a rejection and then want to accept by phone before the offeror receives the mailed rejection. These situations, and others, are covered by the **mailbox rule** [§§ 4–118 *et. seq.*].

b. **Termination of the Power of Acceptance in Revocable Offers Through Lapse of Time. [§ 4–44]**

Sometimes an offer specifies when it will terminate, e.g., "This offer is valid until 5:00 p.m. on October 1." The offeror, as "master of the offer," is entitled to make such a specification and if the offeree has not accepted it within the specified time, the offeree's power of acceptance terminates. *If there is no mention of an expiration time in the offer, the power to accept terminates after a "reasonable time"* [Restatement 2d §§ 36; 41(1)].

(1) **Determination of "Reasonable Time." [§ 4–45]**

A reasonable time regarding the termination of an offer with no specified time limit will vary depending on the circumstances existing when the offer was extended and when the acceptance was made [Restatement 2d § 41(2)]. The circumstances used to determine when a reasonable time has elapsed include the subject matter of the contract, the manner in which the offer was made, any previous dealings between parties, etc. **The test of what constitutes a reasonable time for acceptance is how long would a reasonable person in the position of the offeree believe he or she had to accept** [Restatement 2d § 41, Cmt. b]. If the acceptance is dispatched before that "reasonable time" elapses, it is effective.

(2) Common Presumptions About What Constitutes "Reasonable Time." [§ 4–46]

There are some general rules regarding what is a "reasonable time" in certain types of recurring transactions that have developed over the years. As with all presumptions, these rules can be overcome or rebutted depending on exactly what is communicated between the parties and other relevant circumstances, but the general presumptions are as follows:

(a) Offers Made in Direct Negotiations: Reasonable Time Terminates at End of Negotiation. [§ 4–47]

When parties deal directly over the phone, face-to-face, and probably via text messaging, **the offeree's power to accept the offer presumptively terminates when the negotiation session has concluded** [Restatement 2d § 64]. For example, if Ann offers Bill her record collection for $300 in a telephone conversation and Bill fails to accept during the conversation, Bill could not accept it during a face-to-face meeting a few hours later for the offer terminated when the phone conversation ended. However, if Ann said in the phone conversation, "I'll sell you my record collection for $300. You don't have to decide now—let me know by Friday," Ann's words overcome the presumption and the power of acceptance extends after the conversation terminates.

(b) Offers in Letters: Acceptance Timely if Made on the Day of Receipt, Otherwise Acceptance Transmitted in the Same Medium as the Offer Is Timely. [§ 4–48]

Generally, an acceptance of an offer by letter is timely if the acceptance is mailed on the date the offer is received, or early the next day if it was received towards the close of business. However, more (or less) time may be allowed before the power of acceptance terminates depending on the circumstances surrounding the particular offer. Note that the general presumption provides that when the parties are at some distance from each other, the time for acceptance extends at least to the normal time for transmission of the offer [Restatement 2d § 41(3), Cmt. e]. Also, sending of the offeree's reply by the same medium as that used to transmit the offer is presumptively timely and valid [Restatement 2d § 65].

(c) Offers in Telegram, Overnight Delivery, Facsimile, Text, or E-Mail: Indications That Acceptance Must Be Expedited to Be Timely. [§ 4–49]

Anytime an *offer* is made via an expedited mode of communication, such as by fax, text, e-mail, or overnight mail, it is evidence that acceptance also must be expedited to be effective. In any situation, all the circumstances will have to be weighed, but the fact that an offeror chose a quick means of communication is an important factor in assessing how long the offeree's "reasonable time" period will extend before the offer lapses.

(d) Offers Dealing with Price-Volatile Subject Matter: Acceptances Usually Need to Be Expedited to Be Effective. [§ 4–50]

As a general rule, the more the subject matter of a contract is subject to rapid price fluctuations, e.g., commodities, the shorter the period of time the offeree has to accept.

(i) Example. [§ 4–51]

Because of a catastrophic event, the price of gold on international exchanges was fluctuating wildly minute-by-minute. An e-mail offer to purchase gold at $1,750/ounce made to a dealer on the exchange would most likely have to be accepted within a minute or two to be viable under such circumstances.

ACCEPTANCE

(3) Interpretation of Ambiguous Time Provisions in an Offer. [§ 4–52]

Even if an offer specifically limits the time period for an effective acceptance, such limitation may nevertheless be ambiguous. For example, if a letter ends with, "This offer is effective for 10 days," it is not clear on its face whether the offer can be accepted 10 days from the date of the letter, from the date of the postmark, from the date of receipt, whether it means 10 calendar days or 10 business days, what happens if the 10th day is a weekend day, etc. In such cases, it is up to the court to interpret what the offer meant in light of all relevant circumstances, such as any previous dealings between the parties, the business practices of the industry, etc. [§§ 6–20; 6–23]. The general principle is that a court will try to ascertain what was reasonable for a person in the position of the offeree to believe as to how long the offer was open. If, after applying such rules of interpretation, a court still cannot come up with a definitive answer, generally any ambiguity is resolved *against* the offeror since, after all, the offeror could have made the provisions clearer.

(4) Effect of Delayed Transmission of Offer. [§ 4–53]

While it doesn't happen often, occasionally offers sent, for example, by U.S. mail, are delayed through no fault of either the offeror or offeree. This could also happen to e-mailed offers which somehow got hung up in a server and never delivered, or (perhaps delivered to the "junk" mail folder. The rule in this situation is that **if the offeree knows or has reason to know of the delay in communication at the time he or she receives the offer, the delay does not extend the time during which the offeree can accept** [Restatement 2d § 49]. Thus, if on November 15, an offeree first receives a letter dated and post-marked October 1, notifying her that the offer described in the letter may be accepted during the next 10 days, the offeree cannot accept it because she has reason to know of the delay in transmittal. That is, the offeree's power to accept terminated sometime in mid-October [Restatement 2d § 49, Ill. 1].

(5) When an Acceptance Is Effective. [§ 4–54]

The general rule is that **acceptances are effective upon dispatch** by the offeree. However, occasionally (in real life, but frequently on law school examinations), an offeree will change his or her mind and mail a rejection followed by a (telephoned, texted, or e-mailed) acceptance or visa-versa. These situations, and others, are covered by the **mailbox rule** [§§ 4–118 *et. seq.*].

c. **Termination of Offers by Revocation. [§ 4–55]**

Revocable offers can be freely rescinded or "revoked" by the offeror up until the moment of acceptance. So long as it has not been accepted, the offeror can "take back" an offer, even if he or she promised to keep it open. Thus, if an offeror says, "I'll sell you my watch for $500. You don't have to decide now—I'll give you a week to think about it," and five minutes later says, "I've changed by mind, I don't want to sell my watch to you," the offer is validly revoked and with it the offeree's power to accept. Even if an offeree is on his or her way to accept an offer, but the offeror sees the offeree first and says, "I revoke, the deal is off!" the revocation is immediately effective, the power to accept is terminated, and the offer cannot be accepted [Restatement 2d § 36; 42].

(1) **Revocation Defined. [§ 4–56]**

Revocation occurs when the offeree receives from the offeror a manifestation of an intention not to enter into the previously proposed contract [Restatement 2d § 42].

(2) **Revocations Are Judged Under the Objective Theory of Contracts. [§ 4–57]**

The **objective theory of contracts** judges whether a revocation has occurred. Thus, **the test is whether by words or actions, and in light of all other relevant circumstances, it would appear to a hypothetical reasonable person in the position of the offeree that the offeror has manifested an unwillingness to continue to be bound by the terms of the offer.** Once again, whether the offeror subjectively believes he or she has revoked an offer is not controlling.

(3) **General Rule: To Be Effective, a Revocation Must Be Transmitted by the Offeror to the Offeree. [§ 4–58]**

The general rule is that a revocation must be actually transmitted or communicated by the offeror to the offeree in order to be effective. However, there are two important exceptions to that rule, discussed below.

ACCEPTANCE

(a) Exception: The Indirect Revocation Doctrine. [§ 4–59]

An indirect revocation occurs when the offeree hears from a third party, rather than from the offeror directly, that the offeror has revoked the offer.

There are two requirements for an effective indirect revocation:

(1) The offeror must have taken a <u>definite act inconsistent with an intention to enter into the proposed contract</u>; and

(2) The offeree must have learned of the offeror's conduct from a <u>reliable and trustworthy source</u> [Restatement 2d § 43].

According to the Restatement 2d, the "definite act" requirement is to be construed narrowly, and essentially means that the offeror must have taken some act that makes performance by him or her under the proposed contract *impossible or virtually impossible,* e.g., selling the subject matter of the contract to another person. Similarly, the source from which the offeree hears of the alternate disposition of the subject matter of the contract must appear to be reliable to a person acting in good faith [Restatement 2d § 43, Cmt. d].

(i) Example of *Dickinson v. Dodds.* [§ 4–60]

Dodds offered to sell a piece of land to Dickinson for a given price and promised Dickinson two days to think it over. The next day, before Dickinson had either accepted or rejected the offer, Dodds sold the property to Allan. Dickinson heard from a reliable source that Dodds was selling (or perhaps had sold, the case isn't absolutely clear on that point) the property to Allan, but nevertheless thereafter sent Dodds what would otherwise have been an effective acceptance.

Held: There was not a valid acceptance by Dickinson because the offer was indirectly revoked and with it Dickinson's power of acceptance was terminated [*Dickinson v. Dodds*, 2 Ch. D. 463 (Eng. 1876)].

CHAPTER 4

(ii) **Rationale for the Indirect Revocation Doctrine. [§ 4–61]**

The rationale behind the indirect revocation doctrine is straightforward. If the original offeree really knew that the offeror had already sold the goods, property, etc. in question, then there is only one reason the offeree would still try to "accept" the offer—namely to make the offeror a breaching party liable to the offeree for damages. That is, by "accepting" the offeror's promise to deliver what the offeree knows the offeror can't produce, the offeree is unjustifiably setting the offeror up for a breach of contract action. Contract law will not allow the offeree to set up the offeror in this manner.

(b) **Exception: Revocation of General Offers via "The Equal Publicity Rule." [§ 4–62]**

Recall that a general offer is one that can potentially be accepted by an unlimited number of people [§ 4–12]. A problem thus arises when the maker of a general offer wants to revoke that offer, since there is no way to ensure that everyone who saw the offer will also see the revocation. This problem is solved by the **equal publicity rule,** which states that **so long as the revocation of a general offer is given equal publicity as the offer itself, the offer will be deemed revoked as to all, including those who have no personal knowledge of the revocation** [Restatement 2d § 46; § 4–23]. Note how this is an exception to the general rule, that a revocation must be actually transmitted or communicated by the offeror to the offeree in order to be effective: if the offeror gives equal publicity of its revocation as it did its offer, it is deemed revoked to all, even those who never learn of it.

(c) **Revocations Are Typically Effective Only upon Receipt. [§ 4–63]**

The general rule is that **a revocation is deemed effective only upon its receipt by the offeree** or the offeree's place of business, and **not** upon its dispatch by the offeror [Restatement 2d § 42; UCC § 1–202]. Thus, a revocation lost in the mail is ineffective, and an offeree who accepts an offer, e.g., by fax, while the revocation is making its way to him or her via snail mail, has validly accepted the offer. The rule that revocations are effective upon receipt has implications under the **mailbox rule** [§ 4–118].

d. **Traditional Rule: Termination of Offeree's Power to Accept a Revocable Offer upon Death or Incapacity of Offeror. [§ 4–64]**

The traditional rule, embraced by the Restatement 2d, is that upon the death of the offeror, the offeree's power to accept an outstanding revocable offer is immediately terminated, even if the offeree has no notice of the death and accepts the offer in good faith after the offeror died. Similarly, mental incapacity of the offeror occurring after an offer is made, but before it is accepted, also immediately terminates the offeree's power to accept, even if the offeree has no notice of such incapacity and accepts the offer in good faith [Restatement 2d §§ 36(1)(d), 48].

(1) **Criticism of Traditional Rule. [§ 4–65]**

The rule that death or incapacity of the offeror immediately terminates the offeree's power of acceptance, even without notice to the offeree of the death or incapacity, has been criticized as being incompatible with the objective theory of contracts. That is, if a reasonable person in the position of the offeree would believe that an offer could still be accepted, the objective theory of contracts would seem to indicate that an acceptance by that person should be validated [Restatement 2d § 48, Cmt. a]. Case law has retreated from the traditional rule in the Restatement and today favors the modern, objective theory of contracts approach.

(2) **Example. [§ 4–66]**

Kevin offered to sell Bill his motorcycle by email on Monday afternoon. Bill checked his email on Tuesday morning, saw the offer, and accepted the offer by email that day. Unbeknownst to Bill, Kevin died Monday evening. Under the Restatement approach, Bill's power to accept the offer terminated when Kevin died on Monday, so Bill's acceptance was not valid. Under the more modern approach though, Bill's power to accept the offer did not end when Kevin died. This is because, without knowledge of Kevin's death, it would be reasonable for Bill to believe that Kevin's offer could still be accepted, and thus Bill's email acceptance could be enforced against Kevin's estate.

CHAPTER 4

e. **Termination of Offeree's Power to Accept upon Death or Incapacity of the Offeree. [§ 4–67]**

In general, only a designated "offeree" has the power to accept an offer [§ 4–6]. Thus, if the offeree dies or becomes incapacitated before acceptance, the offeree cannot accept the offer. Of course, if an offer is made to more than one offeree, the death or incapacity of one offeree will not affect the rights of the others to accept.

f. **Termination of Offeree's Power to Accept by Non-Occurrence of an *Implied* Condition: Death or Destruction of a Person or Thing Essential for Performance (Other than the Offeror or Offeree). [§ 4–68]**

If a thing or person necessary for the contract's performance either is destroyed or dies after the offer is made, but before its acceptance, the offeree's power to accept thereby terminates, even without notice to the offeree of such death or destruction [Restatement 2d § 36(2), Cmt. c]. If Charles offers to sell Bluebelle, a prize-winning racehorse, to Tony for $100,000, and if before Tony accepts the offer Bluebelle dies, Tony cannot thereafter validly accept because the "thing essential for performance" is "destroyed" prior to acceptance, regardless whether Tony knew about the horse's death when he accepted. The continued existence of the subject matter of the offer is an implied condition of the offer, i.e., contract law will *imply* Charles' offer to be, "I will offer you Bluebelle for $100,000 **on the condition that Bluebelle is still alive when you accept**" even though Charles never uttered the words in bold.

Note that if the horse died **after** acceptance, it would be an impossibility/impracticability issue, not an acceptance issue [*see* UCC § 2–613; Chapter Twenty-Five for a further discussion of these issues].

g. **Termination of Offeree's Power of Acceptance by Non-Occurrence of an *Implied* Condition: Supervening Illegality. [§ 4–69]**

Sometimes a transaction proposed in an offer is legal at the time the offer is made, but is rendered illegal by legislative act or judicial decision before the offer is accepted. The moment the act called for by the offer is made illegal, the offeree's power of acceptance terminates and the offer may no longer be validly accepted [Restatement 2d § 36(2)]. At the time the offer is made, it is implied that the subject matter of the offer will remain legal in order for the power of acceptance in the offeree to continue.

ACCEPTANCE

The non-occurrence of this condition will terminate the offeree's power of acceptance.

Note that when the act called for by the offer is illegal at the time of its making, or the act becomes illegal after the contract has been entered into, the issue is one of illegality [Chapter Seventeen], rather than formation.

(1) Example. [§ 4–70]

Buyer offered to purchase a particular pesticide from Manufacturer. Before the manufacturer accepted, the EPA outlawed the sale or use of the pesticide. Upon the EPA's ruling, Manufacturer's (the offeree's) power of acceptance was terminated due to supervening illegality. Note that it is the non-occurrence of the implied condition—that the particular pesticide would remain legal before acceptance took place—that terminated the manufacturer's (offeree's) power of acceptance.

h. Termination of Offeree's Power of Acceptance of Revocable Offers by the Non-Occurrence of an *Express* Condition of Acceptance Specified in the Offer. [§ 4–71]

Just as the offeror may specify a time limit for an offeree's acceptance, the offeror may also make the offeree's right to accept conditional upon the occurrence (or non-occurrence) of an event. Thus, if the specified event does not occur (or does occur), the power to accept is terminated. For example, assume Mike says to Al, "I'll sell you my car for $10,000 and hold the offer open for a week, but if the prime interest rate falls below 3% before you accept, the deal's off." Mike has made a valid offer but has also made Al's acceptance conditional on an event. If the prime rate falls below 3% before Al accepts, the occurrence of that express condition terminates Al's power to accept.

2. Acts and Events That Terminate an Offeree's Power of Acceptance Under Irrevocable Offers. [§ 4–72*]

There are far fewer events and acts terminating an offeree's power of acceptance under an irrevocable offer than under a revocable one. Learning the law in this area is thus a two-step process. First, it will be necessary to determine under what circumstances an offer will be deemed "irrevocable" (§ 4–73 *et seq.*), and second, to establish which acts and events will terminate the offeree's power of acceptance even under an "irrevocable" offer (§ 4–87 *et seq.*).

---

* For more information, listen to CD # 2, Track 2 of *Sum and Substance Audio on Contracts*.

CHAPTER 4

a. **The Four Situations in Which an Offer Will Be Deemed "Irrevocable." [§ 4–73]**

There are only four situations in which an offer is deemed irrevocable:

(1) When the parties have entered into an **option contract** [Restatement 2d § 25; *see* §§ 4–74 *et seq.*];

(2) When a merchant fulfills the requirements of a **merchant's firm offer** pursuant to UCC § 2–205 [§ 4–78];

(3) The temporary irrevocability that results under a **unilateral option contract** when the requirements of **Restatement 2d § 45** are met [§ 4–80]; and

(4) The temporary irrevocability that results from an **equitable option** when the offeree **substantially and foreseeably relies** on the offer, and when the requirements of **Restatement 2d § 87(2)** are otherwise met [§ 4–85].

(1) Option Contracts: Defined and Discussed. [§ 4–74]

An option contract is a special contract that defines the length of time an offeree has to accept an offer made in an "underlying" agreement [Restatement 2d § 25].

Note, however, that an option contract is itself a separate *contract,* and thus must have its own separate offer, acceptance, consideration, and freedom from defenses to be enforceable.

(a) Example. [§ 4–75]

Joe offers Clara the chance to purchase some vacant land for $50,000. Clara asks for some time to think about it. They subsequently enter into an agreement whereby Clara pays Joe $500 for the exclusive right to purchase the property for $50,000 during the next 6 months.

The $500 agreement is an option contract, because it defines the length of time Clara (the offeree) has to accept an offer (purchase of the land for $50,000) made in the "underlying" agreement. As a result of the option contract, Joe's original offer is now "irrevocable," so Joe may not revoke the offer during the option period and must allow Clara to accept the offer and buy the land for $50,000 if she chooses. Clara is under no obligation to buy the land and can choose not to proceed for any reason or for no reason. She has the complete and unfettered discretion to buy the land or not. On the

ACCEPTANCE

other hand, regardless whether Clara eventually purchases the property, Joe gets to keep the $500 for it serves as consideration for the option contract and his promise to keep his offer open during the six-month period.

(b) Effect of Option Contract: Elevating the Offeree's <u>Power</u> to Accept to the Offeree's *Right to* Accept. [§ 4–76]

As discussed earlier, when a revocable offer is made to an offeree, the offeree has, in contract terms, a **power** to accept the offer [Restatement 2d § 35]. Under an option contract, however, the offeree has a contractual **right** to accept the underlying offer. The importance of the distinction between a power and a right to accept is two-fold:

> (i) An offeree with a contractual **right** to accept is entitled to assign the right to accept the offer, whereas an offeree with only a **power** to accept may not assign the power of acceptance to another [§ 4–8]; and

> (ii) the circumstances under which the offeree's right to accept the offer can terminate are much fewer than the circumstances under which an offeree's power to accept the offer can terminate [§ 4–87].

(c) Option Contracts and "Purported" Consideration. [§ 4–77]

Ordinarily a contract is not enforceable unless the parties' promises are supported by consideration [Chapter Seven]. In the context of an option contract, the consideration requirement would mean that the offeror's promise to hold open the underlying offer without revoking it would not be enforceable unless the offeree paid money (or incurred some other legal detriment) to secure the option. However, the Restatement 2d takes the view that so long as:

> (i) The underlying (original) deal is **fair**;

> (ii) The option contract is in **writing**; and

> (iii) The option contract is **signed by the offeror**,

the option contract is enforceable even if there is only "purported" or "recited" consideration [Restatement 2d § 87(1)].

That is, if the above conditions are met, then the underlying offer will be deemed irrevocable, i.e., the option contract will be enforceable, if the parties *merely state in their written option contract that consideration was paid,* even if no money actually changed hands [Restatement 2d § 87(1), Cmt. C; § 7–94]. Hence, in the example given in § 4–75, if Clara never actually paid Joe the $500, their option contract would still be valid if the requirements of § 87(1) were otherwise met.

(2) Merchant's Firm Offer. [§ 4–78]

Under UCC § 2–205, a merchant's offer may become irrevocable even in the absence of real or purported consideration which would be necessary to establish an option contract. For this to occur, the following must be established:

(a) the **offeror** (but not necessarily *the offeree*) must be a **merchant,** within the definition of UCC § 2–104(1);

(b) the offer must be **in a writing signed by the merchant offeror** [§ 1–201(b)(43),(37)]; and

(c) the record/writing must **expressly state** that the **offer** is intended to be **irrevocable or will be held open.**

If those three criteria are met, then the offer will be deemed irrevocable for the amount of time stated in the letter, or if no time is stated, for a reasonable period of time, *but in no event will the offer be deemed irrevocable for more than 3 months* [UCC § 2–205].

If the parties wish to extend the period for greater than 3 months, they may do so either by having the merchant send another letter at or near the end of the original three month period, or by entering into a separate option contract supported by consideration.

(a) Example. [§ 4–79]

Tom owns an antique store. His customer Pat loves a particular chest of drawers. On January 15, Tom writes Pat a signed letter telling her that she may have until June 15 to buy the piece at the current price.

ACCEPTANCE

Tom has made a merchant's firm offer to Pat, meaning that the offer to sell the chest of drawers to her at the current price is irrevocable by Tom for the next 3 months. Note that the fact that Tom promised to hold the offer open for greater than 3 months does not invalidate the offer—it just means that the offer will only be deemed irrevocable for a three-month period, and revocable thereafter. If Tom sells the chest to anyone else before April 15, he runs the risk of being in breach should Pat tender the purchase price to him before that date.

Tom may revoke the offer after April 15 though, or he may extend it another 3 months by a separate letter since this would be a new firm offer for the next 3-month period. Note that if Pat originally paid Tom $10 to keep the offer open for 6 months, the offer would be irrevocable for the full 6 months since Pat gave consideration and they would have entered into an option contract.

(3) Making Unambiguous Unilateral Contract Offers Temporarily Irrevocable Under Restatement 2d § 45. [§ 4–80*]

A unilateral contract offer seeks actual performance, not the promise of performance [§§ 1–15; 3–27]. Hence, by definition, a unilateral contract offer cannot be accepted until the requested performance is actually completed. If the performance takes some time to complete, the offeree is presented with a potential problem. That is, the offeree may have spent a good deal of time, money, and effort getting to a point where performance is almost completed, and thus the acceptance almost completely tendered, only to have the offeror revoke the offer at the last minute on the theory that offers are freely revocable until accepted.

After various fits and starts, contract law has now solved this problem by stating that once an offeree faced with an ***unambiguous*** unilateral contract offer either **"begins performance"** or **"tenders performance"** or **"tenders the beginning of performance,"** a **unilateral *option* contract is implied** whereby the *offer becomes temporarily irrevocable for a reasonable period of time* in order to allow the offeree to complete performance [Restatement 2d § 45]. Note that the offeror's duty under

---

* For more information, listen to CD # 2, Track 3 of *Sum and Substance Audio on Contracts*.

the contract does not arise until the offeree has <u>completed</u> the performance required by the offer [Restatement 2d § 45, Cmt. e].

To illustrate this principle, and its ramifications, probably the most famous hypothetical in contract law is discussed below.

(a) The "Brooklyn Bridge" Hypothetical. [§ 4–81]

Bill offers John $100 to be paid upon John's completion of a walk across the Brooklyn Bridge. John eagerly starts out and just before he takes his last step, Bill yells, "I revoke," and asserts that no contract had ever been formed because his was an offer for a unilateral contract which can only be accepted by completion of performance. (Your Professor may update this hypothetical to illustrate the point, e.g., Bill offers John $800 upon the completion of the painting of his house, or upon winning "The Biggest Loser" competition and yells, "I revoke" before the final brush stroke, the final episode of the show, etc.)

Under Restatement 2d § 45, as soon as John **began performance**, i.e., *started* walking across the bridge, **Bill's offer became irrevocable for a reasonable period of time** in order to allow John to finish. As soon as John began walking, a unilateral option contract between John and Bill was deemed to be in effect. Hence, when Bill yells, "I revoke" as John gets to the end of the bridge, his words have no legal effect for, at that point, Bill's offer is irrevocable for a reasonable period to give John the ability to finish.

(b) Problems Associated with Restatement § 45's Approach in Making a Unilateral Contract Offer Temporarily Irrevocable. [§ 4–82]

While the approach of § 45 works well in a majority of cases, there are usually two problems Professors want to discuss when you get to this part of the course:

(1) when does an offeree "begin performance," "tender performance," or "tender the beginning of performance?" [§ 4–83]; and

(2) is it fair that the option contract is unilateral in effect, i.e., that it forces the offeror to leave open the offer, but does not require the offeree to complete performance? [§ 4–84].

ACCEPTANCE

(i) Problems Associated with "Beginning Performance," "Tender Performance," or "Tender the Beginning of Performance." [§ 4–83]

Under § 45's approach, obviously the big event is the offeree's "beginning performance," or "tendering performance" or "tendering the beginning of performance" for it is at one of those points the unilateral offer becomes irrevocable for a reasonable time. Exactly when performance "begins" or is "tendered" though, is not always easy to discern.

For example, suppose Bill offered to pay John, a house painter, $800 upon completion of painting the exterior of Bill's house. The next day, John shows up ready to begin painting and before he gets out of his truck, Bill runs up to John saying he's changed his mind and is revoking his offer because he no longer wants the work to be done.

Bill will say that John has not "begun performance"—he hasn't put one dab of paint yet on the house. On the other hand, John will say he "began performance," e.g., when he went to the paint store and purchased the paint for the job, or perhaps when he started his drive to Bill's house, etc.

There is no universally accepted test to determine when performance has officially begun. The general idea is that the more specific acts the offeree can point to that were done to enable him or her to perform under the particular contract, the more likely it is that performance has begun. Some factors to consider include: the extent to which the conduct of the offeree is connected to the offer, the character of the conduct, the extent to which the conduct is of benefit to the offeror, and the terms agreed to by the parties including course of dealing and usage of trade [Restatement 2d § 45, Cmt. f].

Tender is defined as the manifestation of the <u>willingness and ability</u> to perform. So if Owner makes a unilateral offer to Landscaper to mow the lawn and trim the trees for $200, when Landscaper shows up with the lawnmower, and says, "I'm ready to mow and trim," she has tendered performance as she has shown a willingness and ability to perform. At that point she has an option to complete performance. But if she shows up and says, "I am ready to mow and trim as soon as my assistant brings the equipment in the second truck," some courts would hold there is no "tender" because there was an expression of <u>willingness</u> to perform, but without the <u>ability</u> to do so.

(ii) Fairness of Making the Option Contract Unilateral Only. [§ 4–84]

This time assume that Bill offers John, a furniture maker, $800 upon the completion of a custom desk, so long as John can deliver it within 4 months. John starts work right away, and Bill is delighted. However, after a few weeks John decides the desk is too big a job for too little money, and simply stops working on it, without informing Bill. At the end of four months Bill expects the desk, and is disappointed to learn no work has been done on it for over 3 months.

Under the approach of Restatement 2d § 45, Bill has no remedy in the above situation, because the implied option contract that springs into existence upon the beginning of performance is unilateral only. That means while Bill is bound to leave open the offer for a reasonable period of time once John starts work, John is not obligated to finish the desk, attempt to finish the desk, or even notify Bill if he decides not to work on the desk. The option is one way, i.e., unilateral, only. (It is true that the above hypothetical is actually governed by the UCC since it is for the sale of goods. However, it is easier to illustrate the effect of § 45 with this example, so you should assume it is decided by common law principles as you work your way through the hypothetical).

Contract law justifies this result by saying it was, after all, Bill's choice to make John a unilateral contract offer and since he chose that type of offer, he's stuck with its effects. If Bill wanted a commitment by John to finish the project, he should have sought John's *promise* that he would deliver the desk on time via a bilateral contract

ACCEPTANCE

offer. If John didn't timely tender the desk under a bilateral contract, Bill would at least have a breach of contract claim against him.

One way to think about this is to suppose a reward offer where a bank makes a unilateral reward offer for information leading to conviction of someone who robbed a branch. Assume Bill starts looking for the robber. Contract law does not want to say Bill has breached if he doesn't find any information. It accomplishes this goal by giving Bill the option, but not the obligation, to find the information and allows Bill to quit whenever he wants and not "exercise" his option.

(4) Making Certain Contract Offers Temporarily Irrevocable by Substantial Reliance Under Restatement 2d § 87(2). [§ 4–85*]

Sometimes an offeree will substantially rely on an offer even before he or she accepts it. Such reliance may be shown by use of the offer in another presentation, by incurring substantial expense in anticipation of accepting the offer, etc. Under Restatement 2d § 87(2), **an offer will be deemed irrevocable for a reasonable period of time if reliance on it is substantial and foreseeable enough**. The provision states:

An **offeror's power to revoke is terminated**, and an option contract is completed, whereby an **offer is deemed irrevocable** to the extent necessary to avoid injustice, when:

(a) an offeree takes action (or forebears to take action) of a *substantial* nature in response to an offer; and

(b) such action is *reasonably foreseeable* given the nature of the offer.

In other words, when an offeree detrimentally *relies on the offer* to a **"substantial"** degree in making pre-acceptance preparations, and when that reliance is reasonably foreseeable, the offer becomes irrevocable for a reasonable period. Sometimes this doctrine is known as providing an **equitable option** for the offeree.

---

* For more information, listen to CD # 2, Track 3 of *Sum and Substance Audio on Contracts*.

CHAPTER 4

(a) Example of *Drennan v. Star Paving Co.* [§ 4-86*]

Star Paving, a subcontractor, submitted a bid to Drennan, a general contractor, for paving work to be done on a large project. Drennan used Star Paving's bid in preparing its own price quote to the developer of the project for the entire project. Drennan also had to put up a "performance bond," which cost it $37,000, when it submitted its bid to the developer to assure its ability to complete the project if it was awarded the contract. Drennan was eventually awarded the contract to build the overall project by the developer. However, before Drennan could tell Star Paving its bid to do the paving work was accepted, Star Paving tried to revoke its bid. Notwithstanding the attempted revocation, Drennan went ahead and "accepted" anyway.

Star Paving's argument was that normal contract rules provide that, absent an option contract [§ 4–74], a merchant's firm offer [§ 4–78], or a situation under Restatement 2d § 45 [§ 4–80], offers are freely revocable until accepted, and its offer had not been accepted by Drennan before the revocation. Drennan, on the other hand, said it could hardly be expected to accept Star Paving's offer before it knew whether it was awarded the contract to build the entire project by the developer, for unless it had such a contract, it would have no use for Star Paving's services.

Held: Drennan prevailed under the rules of Restatement 2d § 87(2). That is: (a) Drennan took action of a substantial nature in reliance on Star Paving's offer (using Star's bid as part of its overall bid and buying the performance bond); (b) such reliance was foreseeable (given the nature of a general contractor's business); and (c) it would be unjust not to allow Drennan to accept Star Paving's bid after it had used Star Paving's quote in preparing its own bid to the developer (and make Drennan go find another subcontractor willing to do the job, probably at a higher price). As such, Star Paving's offer to do the paving work at a set price was deemed irrevocable for a reasonable period of time, which in this case was defined as a day or two after Drennan learned that it had been awarded the entire job by the developer. As

---

* For more information, listen to CD # 2, Track 3 of *Sum and Substance Audio on Contracts*.

ACCEPTANCE

Drennan had accepted within this period, its acceptance was valid and Star Paving's attempted revocation was a nullity. [*See* § 8–13 for a more detailed discussion of the general contractor/subcontractor relationship] [*See* Case Squibs *Drennan v. Star Paving Co.*, 51 Cal.2d 409 (1958)].

b. **Acts and Events That Terminate the Power of Acceptance Even Under Irrevocable Offers. [§ 4–87*]**

The following acts and events will terminate even "irrevocable" offers:

(1) Upon the **expiration of a reasonable time**, or the *time specified for acceptance:*

(a) in an *option contract* [Restatement 2d §§ 25, 87(2)]; or

(b) in a *merchant's firm offer* (so long as that time does not exceed three months) [UCC 2–205];

or upon the expiration of a reasonable time for implied option contracts established under Restatement 2d §§ 45 or 87(2);

(2) The **supervening destruction or death of a thing essential for performance** (non-occurrence of an implied condition) (*see* § 4–68) [Restatement 2d § 37];

(3) **Supervening illegality** (non-occurrence of an implied condition) (*see* § 4–69) [Restatement 2d § 37];

(4) **The non-occurrence of an express condition, the occurrence of which is necessary to accept the offer** (usually specified in the option contract or merchant's firm offer) [Restatement 2d § 37; § 4–71]; and

(5) Under the *majority rule,* **rejection or counter-offer by the offeree,** *followed by reasonable, foreseeable, and detrimental reliance by the offeror* [Restatement 2d § 37 Cmt. b, Ill. 2].

Accordingly, the following acts or events, which **will** terminate the power of acceptance under revocable offers, **do *not* terminate the power of acceptance under irrevocable offers:**

(1) Rejection and counter-offer by the offeree, so long as the **rejection is <u>not</u> followed by reliance** by the offeror [§ 4–29];

---

* For more information, listen to CD # 2, Tracks 2 and 3 of *Sum and Substance Audio on Contracts.*

73

CHAPTER 4

(2) Attempted revocation by the offeror [§ 4–55];

(3) Death or capacity by the offeror [§ 4–64]; and

(4) Death or incapacity of the offeree [§ 4–67].

(1) Example. [§ 4–88]

Under a valid option contract, Laura has 30 days from January 15 to purchase Bob's car for $5,000. On January 17, Laura drives to Bob's house and says, "There is no way I am going to buy your crummy car for $5,000. I'll offer you $3,500 and that's it."

If Bob does nothing, Laura still has until February 14 to purchase the car for $5,000 because rejections and counter-offers, in and of themselves, do not terminate the offeree's right to accept under an *irrevocable* offer. Note the distinction with **revocable** offers: where rejections and counter-offers, in and of themselves, do terminate the offeree's power of acceptance [§ 4–29].

(2) Example. [§ 4–89]

Same as above, except this time, in light of Laura's talk with Bob, Bob sells the car to Steve on January 20. At this point, under the majority rule, Laura's power *and* right to accept, even though it was "irrevocable" via their option contract, have nonetheless terminated, due to: (a) Laura's rejection and counter-offer; and (b) Bob's subsequent reasonable, foreseeable, and detrimental reliance on the rejection in selling the car to another [Restatement 2d § 37].

(3) Example. [§ 4–90]

Same as above, except before Laura accepts, the car is destroyed in an accident that is not Bob's fault. Laura's right to accept, even under an irrevocable option contract, is terminated upon the destruction of the "thing necessary for performance." Contract law is not going to say Bob is in breach for failure to produce what is now a non-existent item.

(4) Example. [§ 4–91]

Same as above, except before Laura's acceptance the government declares ownership of the type of car that is the subject matter of the agreement illegal because of safety concerns. Upon the government's mandate, Laura loses the right to exercise the option and purchase the car.

ACCEPTANCE

F. HOW AN OFFER MAY BE ACCEPTED: PERMISSIBLE METHODS OR MODES OF ACCEPTANCE. [§ 4-92*]

As "master of the offer," the offeror can set forth four possible ways in which an offer may be accepted:

(1) By requiring the offeree to **promise to perform** the action requested in the offer;

(2) By requiring the offeree to **actually perform** the action requested in the offer;

(3) By requiring the offeree to **begin to perform** the action requested in the offer; or

(4) In certain cases, by **silence and/or inaction** of the offeree.

When an offer is clear as to how an offer can be accepted, determining the permissible mode of acceptance for the offeree is, of course, no problem. However, when an offer is unclear as to how it should be accepted, there can be a problem in determining which of these methods is "permissible" in response to a particular offer. The rules governing this problem are discussed below.

1. General Rule Regarding Acceptance of an Offer Which Unambiguously Specifies Method of Acceptance: The Offeree Must Follow the Directions of the Offeror. [§ 4-93]

When the offer specifically states how it is to be accepted, the offeree must comply with the terms of the offer in order to have a valid acceptance [Restatement 2d §§ 30, 58, 60]. This means that an unambiguous offer to enter into a unilateral contract can only be accepted by performing the acts (or by beginning to perform, or by tendering performance, of these acts if completion will take time [§§ 4-83 *et seq.*]) called for in the offer. In addition, it also means that an offeror is entitled to limit acceptance to particular words or conduct. Thus, if an offer says that no other acceptance will be honored but the delivery of a telegram containing the words, "I accept wholeheartedly," then transmitting an e-mail with that message, or sending a telegram with just the words, "I accept" does not act as a valid acceptance. Rather, those communications would themselves be counter-offers.

---

* For more information, listen to CD # 2, Tracks 1 and 2 of *Sum and Substance Audio on Contracts*.

CHAPTER 4

2. General Rules Regarding Acceptance of an Offer Which Does Not Explicitly Specify the Method of Acceptance: Ambiguous or Indifferent Offers: It May Be Accepted in Any Reasonable Manner. [§ 4–94*]

If an offer does not unambiguously specify how it is to be accepted, it may be accepted in any manner and by any medium reasonable under the circumstances [Restatement 2d § 30(2); UCC § 2–206(1)(a)]. Thus, if the offer, and the circumstances under which it was made, do not explicitly specify a method of acceptance, the offeree may accept either by performing, by promising to perform, or by beginning performance, so long as such action is reasonable. [Restatement 2d § 32]. Such offers are known as "indifferent" or "ambiguous" offers since the offeror appears to be indifferent as to the acceptable mode of acceptance or, at least, the offeror was ambiguous as to what he or she intended.

In making the determination whether a particular form of acceptance is reasonable, it is important to examine the surrounding circumstances. It may well be that even though the offer is silent as to whether a promissory acceptance or acceptance by performance is permitted, the circumstances clearly point to one of these options being the only "reasonable" method of acceptance.

a. Example of *Hamer v. Sidway*. [§ 4–95]

Uncle writes to his nephew, who is then 16, offering to pay nephew $5,000 if nephew will refrain from drinking or using tobacco until age 21. Under the circumstances, an immediate promise by the nephew to refrain from drinking and using tobacco would be ineffective to bind Uncle, for Uncle clearly, if not expressly, is bargaining for performance, not a promise of performance. As such, it will be deemed an offer for a unilateral contract. Note virtually all reward offers are deemed unilateral contract offers for the same reason. [*Case Squibs, Hamer v. Sidway,* 27 N.E. 256 (N.Y. 1891), (4–84; § 7–14)]

b. Review Problem. [§ 4–96]

Jeff says to Grace "I'll pay you $1,000 to paint my house next week."

Question:

How can Grace validly accept?

---

* For more information, listen to CD # 2, Tracks 3 and 4 of *Sum and Substance Audio on Contracts.*

ACCEPTANCE

Answer:

It is unclear whether Jeff is asking exclusively for a promise to paint his house or for actual performance. Jeff's offer thus is an ambiguous or indifferent one. As such, Grace may validly accept by promising to paint the house or by beginning to paint the house within a reasonable time.

3. **Special Rules for Offer to Purchase Goods for Prompt Shipment Under UCC: The Offeror May Promise Shipment, or Actually Ship. [§ 4–97*]**

Unless there is an unambiguous indication to the contrary by the offeror, **an order to buy goods for prompt shipment invites acceptance either by prompt shipment of, or by a prompt promise to ship, the goods.** Thus, if Jack places an order to a lighting store for "3 halogen lamps, Model No. XB–15, A.S.A.P.," the store may accept either by promising to ship the lamps or by actually shipping the lamps. If the store accepts by actually shipping, however, it must notify Jack of its acceptance within a reasonable time or else the contract becomes unenforceable [UCC § 2–206; see § 4–104, for a further discussion of the subsequent notice requirement].

4. **Special Problems When Beginning Performance Is Intended to Act as an Acceptance. [§ 4–98]**

When an offeree begins performance in response to an offer, the question as to whether such activity serves as a valid acceptance can be a complicated one, depending on the type of offer it is, and on the circumstances surrounding its making.

   a. **Beginning Performance in Response to an Unambiguous Offer for Unilateral Contract. [§ 4–99]**

   As noted earlier, Restatement 2d § 45 provides that a unilateral option contract is formed upon the beginning of performance in response to a clear and unambiguous offer to enter into a unilateral contract. Once performance has begun, the offer becomes irrevocable for a reasonable period of time, which ensures that the offeree will have reasonable time to complete performance and thus accept the offer [§§ 4–80, et seq.].

   b. **Beginning Performance in Response to an Unambiguous Offer for Bilateral Contract. [§ 4–100]**

   If there is a clear offer to enter into a bilateral contract, i.e., one which unambiguously calls for a promissory acceptance and only

---

* For more information, listen to CD # 3, Track 2 of *Sum and Substance Audio on Contracts*.

a promissory acceptance, then beginning performance will not be an effective acceptance for it was not what the offeror requested.

c. **Beginning Performance in Response to an Ambiguous or Indifferent Offer. [§ 4–101*]**

As noted in § 4–94, an offer that is unclear as to the mode of acceptance called for can be accepted by beginning performance, so long as such action is "reasonable in the circumstances." [Restatement 2d § 30(2); UCC § 2–206(1)(a)]. However, there are some special considerations when the offeree attempts to accept in this manner, which is discussed below.

(1) **Treatment of Beginning Performance in Response to an Ambiguous or Indifferent Offer. [§ 4–102]**

If the commencement of performance is a reasonable means of acceptance in response to an ambiguous offer, the **beginning of performance will simultaneously also imply a promise by the offeree to complete performance** and thus result in an enforceable bilateral contract between the parties. That is, if the offeror does not make it clear whether he or she is seeking actual performance, or promised performance, as acceptance, then either mode of acceptance is permitted [Restatement 2d § 62(1)].

But once the offeree begins or tenders performance, he or she is bound and is deemed to have made an implied promise to complete the performance [Restatement 2d § 62(2)]. In other words, once an offeree begins or tenders performance in response to an offer whose mode of acceptance is ambiguous, a bilateral contract is formed. If the offeree unjustifiably does not thereafter complete performance, a breach has occurred.

(a) **Example. [§ 4–103]**

John offers Nina $1,000 to paint his house next Wednesday. The mode of acceptance called for under that offer is ambiguous, so Nina may accept either by painting the house next Wednesday or by promising to do so. However, suppose Nina starts painting and John later orders her off his property. At that point, she has neither performed nor made an express promise to perform, and thus John would argue that since his offer has not been accepted, he may revoke it. However,

---

* For more information, listen to CD # 2, Track 3 of *Sum and Substance Audio on Contracts*.

as soon as Nina began working, she is deemed to have accepted John's offer by promising to finish, thereby completing the formation of a bilateral contract. As there has been a valid acceptance to an outstanding offer, John would be in breach if he does not allow Nina to finish. Similarly, if Nina walked off the job after starting to paint (without a justifiable reason), she would be in breach, for by beginning performance, she has made an implied promise to finish.

This is different than the situation under Restatement 2d § 45, where John's offer is <u>unambiguously</u> a unilateral one. In that situation, Nina's beginning of performance would only trigger a temporary and unilateral option contract, where John was bound and had to give Nina a reasonable time to finish and pay her if she finishes, but Nina would not be bound to finish and could walk off the job without contractual penalty.

(2) Necessity of Giving Notice to Offeror When Beginning Performance Validly Acts as Acceptance. [§ 4–104]

A problem may arise in those cases where beginning of performance acts as an effective acceptance, because the offeror may not know that the offeree has accepted. This will almost always be true when the offeror and offeree are in different cities, and will also be true, e.g., where the offeree is a company who begins performance by boxing up goods in its plant. Under Restatement 2d § 54(2), if the offeree has reason to know that the offeror has **no adequate means of learning about the beginning of performance**, the offeree must notify the offeror of his or her actions within a reasonable time. The UCC, in § 2–206(2), makes the requirement even plainer—an offeree who accepts by beginning performance must *always* give the offeror notice of the acceptance within a reasonable time. [§§ 4–109, 4–110 and 4–111.]

(a) Exceptions: When an Offeree Need Not Give Notice. [§ 4–105]

An offeree who reasonably accepts an offer by beginning performance need not give notice that he or she has accepted by starting to perform in three cases:

(1) If the nature of the performance is such that the offeror would know of the acceptance, e.g., an offer to paint a house that the offeror lives in so

that when the offeree starts, such performance would come to the offeror's attention;

(2) When the offeror states in the offer that such notice is unnecessary; and

(3) If past dealings between the parties indicate that such notice is not required [Restatement 2d § 54(2)].

While these exceptions are only explicitly set forth in the Restatement, it is difficult to imagine they would not also apply to contracts governed by the UCC.

(3) Effect of Failing to Give Notice. [§ 4–106*]

Under the Restatement, if an offeree who has validly accepted by beginning performance fails to give the required notice after a reasonable time, the contractual duties of the offeror are "discharged" [Restatement 2d § 54]. Thus, sending the notice in such situations is treated as a condition subsequent to the offeror's duties under the contract. That is, a valid contract is formed upon the beginning of performance, but on the condition that notice is sent. If the condition is not fulfilled (i.e., if the notice is never sent), the duties of the offeror become unenforceable (*see* § 21–15 for a more thorough discussion of conditions subsequent).

Under the UCC, if the offeree fails to give notice of his performance to the offeror, the offer is treated as having "lapsed" before it was accepted and the situation is treated as if no contract was ever formed [UCC § 2–206(2)]. Although the ultimate result is the same under both the Restatement and the UCC, they have different paths to get there. Under the UCC, there was never a contract, whereas under the Restatement, there was a contract, but without the notice it is unenforceable.

However, note that under § 54 of the Restatement 2d, once an offeree begins performance, he or she is promising to finish regardless whether the offeree gives notice. That is, while the offeror is not bound to accept the offeree's completed performance in such a case (since his duties under the contract are not enforceable), the offeror can **sue** the offeree under breach of contract for any damages suffered if the offeree does not complete timely performance. So when the offeree begins performance

---

* For more information, listen to CD # 3, Tracks 2, 4 and 6 of *Sum and Substance Audio on Contracts*.

without giving notice when notice is required, the offeror is in a very strong position—he or she need not accept performance, but is entitled to sue for breach if the failure to complete the performance causes the offeror damage.

5. **Ordering Goods for Prompt Shipment: The "Unilateral Contract Trick" Under the UCC. [§ 4–107]**

Under common law rules, a breach did not always occur when an offeror sent non-conforming goods; sometimes this was deemed a counter-offer. For example, assume a retailer (offeror) orders one hundred 46-inch flat screen television sets from a manufacturer (offeree) and does so on a unilateral contract basis, i.e., the retailer makes clear that payment will be forthcoming only when the 46-inch sets arrive. If the manufacturer shipped 42-inch sets instead, at common law there was no breach because there was never an acceptance. That is, the only way the offer could be accepted was to ship 46-inch sets. As such, shipment of the 42-inch sets acted as a counter-offer. This was known as the "unilateral contract trick" where the offeror was "tricked" after making a unilateral contract offer. This rule was unfair to the offerors, for such party was relying on receiving conforming goods in response to the offer. Therefore, while the offerors could reject the non-conforming 42-inch sets when the sets arrived, at that point the offeror had to start over, at some inconvenience (if not at some financial sacrifice), and place another order for 46-inch sets with someone else. Further, the offeror could not bring a breach of contract suit against the seller, for there was never an enforceable contract on which to sue. Often the retailer would just accept the non-conforming goods to avoid the hassle.

UCC § 2–206(1)(b) has changed the common law rule. Now, when sending goods is a reasonable means of acceptance, the offeree (in the case above, the manufacturer) who sends the 42-inch sets is deemed to have both simultaneously accepted the offer to send 46-inch sets and to have breached that contract by sending non-conforming goods. Thus, by avoiding the "unilateral contract trick" and replacing it with simultaneous formation and breach, when non-conforming goods are sent, the buyer is entitled either to accept the non-conforming goods (and pay the lesser price for the 42-inch sets), or to reject them and **sue for breach of the promise to deliver conforming goods**.

Note that the UCC § 2–206 applies whenever it is "reasonable" to accept by shipment. Thus, despite its name, the "unilateral contract trick" does not apply *only* to situations where the offeror has made a unilateral contract offer; **rather, it applies whenever there is an ambiguous or indifferent offer**. That is, when an offer is ambiguous as to calling for shipment or a promise of shipment, the sending of non-conforming goods by the offeree acts as a simultaneous promissory acceptance of the offer and a breach of the resulting contract.

a. Accommodation Shipments. [§ 4–108]

If the offeree wishes to send non-conforming goods, but also to keep such action as a counter-offer and not have it be treated as a simultaneous acceptance and breach under § 2–206(1), the offeree may send an "accommodation shipment." Under an accommodation shipment the seller notifies the buyer (typically in a cover letter or e-mail) that the goods the seller has shipped are not what was requested in the offer, but also expresses a good-faith belief or hope that the buyer can use them anyway [UCC § 2–206(1)(b)]. With such notice there is no unilateral contract trick, and the seller's actions can only be deemed a counter-offer, to be accepted or not as the buyer wishes.

6. Notice Problems in Acceptance Under Unilateral Contracts. [§ 4–109*]

When an offeror makes an offer for a unilateral contract, an issue sometimes arises as to whether the offeree need give the offeror notice of his or her **intention** to accept. The answer is no. That is, if an offer can be accepted by performance, then the acceptance is effective regardless of whether the offeree has previously given notice of his or her intention to accept. However, **upon actual acceptance,** the offeree may have to give reasonably prompt notice that he or she has performed the acts specified in the offer. Under Restatement 2d § 54, the offeree must give notice of acceptance if the offeror has no adequate means of learning the performance with reasonable promptness or certainty. If such notice is not given, then the offeror's duties are discharged and he or she will not be in breach for failing to perform.

a. Example. [§ 4–110]

Laura has a vacation cabin 200 miles from her principal residence. She has made a unilateral offer over the phone to a painter that she will pay him $500 to paint her cabin by June 1. The painter need not give Laura notice that he intends to accept her offer, and may validly accept it by painting the cabin in accordance with the terms of the offer. However, as Laura will not have an adequate means of learning of the acceptance within a reasonable time after the painter's performance, he is under an obligation to give her reasonably prompt notice once he actually accepts. If he does not, her duties under the contract will be discharged.

---

* For more information, listen to CD # 2, Tracks 2–6 of *Sum and Substance Audio on Contracts.*

ACCEPTANCE

b. **Example of *Carlill v. Carbolic Smoke Ball*. [§ 4–111*]**

Manufacturer placed an advertisement in several publications promising to pay £100 to anyone who caught the flu after purchasing and using the manufacturer's product as directed. Carlill purchased and correctly used the smoke ball, but nevertheless caught the flu.

Held: Carlill was under no duty to inform the manufacturer of her intention to accept the unilateral offer (i.e., purchasing the ball, using it correctly, and catching the flu). Thus, by doing the acts called for in the offer, her acceptance was effective, despite the lack of prior notice. However, she was obligated to let the company know of her acceptance within a reasonable time after catching the flu and <u>completing</u> performance, as it would have no other adequate means of learning of Carlill's performance with reasonable promptness and certainty and thus would not be liable to her until she let the company know of her acceptance [Case Squibs, *Carlill v. Carbolic Smoke Ball Co.*, 1 Q.B. 256 (1893); *see also* §§ 4–17; 4–26].

Carlill can be distinguished from the Example in § 4–110 because the court held that the manufacturer impliedly waived notice of the beginning of performance in how it structured its offer and the means it used to communicate it.

7. **Acceptance by Silence or Inaction. [§ 4–112**]**

The general rule is that an offeree's silence cannot act as a valid acceptance. However, there are a few particular situations where the offeree's silence may act to bind him or her to the terms of an offer [Restatement 2d § 69, Cmt. a].

a. **Silent Acceptance of Services. [§ 4–113]**

Where an offeree silently takes the benefit of offered services, having reason to know the offeror expected to be paid for them, and having an opportunity to reject them, the offeree's silence operates as an acceptance. This rule is a specialized application of the general rule regarding implied-in-fact contracts, i.e., a situation where an acceptance is deemed effective because, to a reasonable person in the position of the offeror, the conduct (rather than the words) of the offeree indicates the offeree's intention to be bound by the terms of the offer [Restatement 2d § 69(1)(a);§ 1–18].

---

* For more information, listen to CD # 2 Track 5 of *Sum and Substance Audio on Contracts*.

** For more information, listen to CD # 2 Track 5 of *Sum and Substance Audio on Contracts*.

CHAPTER 4

(1) Example. [§ 4–114]

A medical clinic has a sign outside that says, "Today only. Physicals $5." Ann enters the clinic, waits in line for the physical, and receives the physical, all without saying anything. Ann is liable for the $5.

b. Silent Acceptance at Direction of Offeror. [§ 4–115]

Sometimes an offeror will try to structure an offer so that the offeree's silence or inaction will be deemed an effective acceptance, e.g., an unsolicited offer may state, "I am so sure you will want our product, just keep it and we will bill you in 30 days." Perhaps surprisingly, such an offer **may** be effective and silence **can** serve to bind the recipient. The key factor is *whether the offeree intends to accept the offer or not*. That is, if the offeree remains silent but intends to accept the offer, the silent acceptance is valid. However, if the offeree remains silent and intends to reject the offer, then the silence is not a valid acceptance [Restatement 2d § 69(1)(b)]. While this puts the offeror in a position of uncertainty as to whether or not the offer is accepted and makes the offer dependent upon the offeree's unilateral and unexpressed intent (contrary to the objective theory of contracts), it is the offeror's fault for phrasing the offer as he or she did in the first place.

c. Silence Can Act as a Valid Acceptance Because of Previous Conduct. [§ 4–116]

So long as the parties' previous dealings make it reasonable, silence and inaction by the offeree may act as effective acceptance [Restatement 2d § 69(1)(c)]. A typical contemporary example of when the parties' prior conduct is sufficient to create acceptance by silence is, e.g., subscription to a paid Internet radio service like Spotify. When the customer signs up for a paid membership, he or she is given the right to cancel at any time, but also promises that silence and inaction on the subscriber's part acts as acceptance of the subscription for the next month, and an authorization for an automatic credit card debit is valid.

d. Silent Acceptance of Property by Acting Inconsistently with Owner's Interest. [§ 4–117]

If an offeree acquires property (personal or real) as part of an offer, and acts inconsistently with the offeror's ownership interest in that property, there has been an acceptance by conduct, even if no express acceptance was ever made [Restatement 2d § 69(2); UCC § 2–606(1)(c)]. For example, through the mail Bud is sent a DVD along with a letter saying, "If you wish to purchase this exciting movie, do nothing and it's yours. We will bill you $20 later. However, if you don't want it just put it in the prepaid envelope and return it to us." If Bill gift wraps it and gives it to his daughter for her birthday, he has accepted the offer to purchase the DVD by silence, for he has acted inconsistently with the offeror's ownership interest [Restatement 2d § 69, Cmt. e, Ill. 7]. This is true even if in his mind Bill has not subjectively intended to accept the offer (*see* § 4–115) because, e.g., he believes it was a gift from the seller [Restatement 2d § 69, Cmt. e]. If he just keeps the DVD without opening it and with no intent to accept the offer, there is no contract. Once again, this rule is a particularized example of an implied-in-fact contract [§ 4–113]. Note that if he sets the DVD aside on a shelf, waiting for UPS to pick it up, however, this not a valid acceptance [Restatement 2d § 69, Cmt. e, Ill. 8].

G. POSTING PROBLEMS: THE MAILBOX RULE. [§ 4–118*]

On a cost-benefit analysis, most students put learning the mailbox rule far on the debit side. However, it is not as confusing as it first appears, and when you understand the problems the mailbox rule seeks to resolve, rather than just trying to learn some disjointed rules, the doctrine makes a good deal of sense and solves some recurring problems.

There are two types of posting problems inherent in transmitted offers and acceptances. The first concerns **when a particular communication is effective**, e.g., when an offer or a rejection is effective, when it is sent or when it is received.

The second issue revolves around when a party **changes his or her mind**, e.g., if an offeree accepts by mail, but two hours later, before the offeror gets the letter, the offeree telephones the offeror and rejects, which is the effective communication—the previously sent written acceptance or the later made oral rejection? Although it will be necessary to learn the rules for each situation, the general rule set down in the 1818 English case *Adams v. Lindsell* (*see* Case Squibs) and Restatement 2d § 63, is:

(1) **offers, revocations, and rejections are effective on *receipt*;** but

(2) **acceptances are effective on *dispatch.***

1. Offers Effective upon Receipt. [§ 4–119]

   Under the mailbox rule, and in the absence of any contrary intention of the parties, an **offer** is *not* effective until **the offeree receives it** [Restatement 2d § 63(a); *see also* § 4–53 for a discussion of the effect if the transmission of an offer is lost in the mail.]

---

* For more information, listen to CD # 2, Track 6, and CD # 3, Track 1 of *Sum and Substance Audio on Contracts.*

CHAPTER 4

2. Acceptances Effective on Dispatch. [§ 4–120]

Acceptances have the opposite rule from offers: an **acceptance** is **effective on dispatch**. This means that a properly dispatched acceptance will be effective, *even if it never gets to the offeror*. However, it is important to note the "time of dispatch" means more than just, e.g., giving a letter to an assistant to mail—it means putting the letter out of the offeror's ability to recall it. Usually, this is the time of actually delivering the letter to a mailbox [Restatement 2d § 63], hitting the "send" button for a fax, text, or e-mail, etc. so that it is dispatched to the offeror and is not recallable by the offeror. Note that for the acceptance on dispatch rule, two criteria must be met:

(1) **The communication must be properly addressed and (in the case of a letter) stamped**; and

(2) **Acceptance by the type of communication used must be a permissible mode of acceptance**.

Each of these requirements is discussed below.

a. Communication Must Be Properly Addressed and Deliverable. [§ 4–121]

The acceptance must be properly addressed for it to be effective upon dispatch [Restatement 2d § 66]. If the communication is not properly addressed, it is usually effective only upon *receipt*. Note however, under § 67 of the Restatement 2d, even if an acceptance is misaddressed it will nonetheless be treated as effective on dispatch **if** it arrived within the time a properly addressed letter would normally have arrived. Thus, if the sender transposed two numbers of the zip code, but the post office was able to timely deliver the letter anyway, the acceptance will be effective upon dispatch. Note that for a letter, it must also be properly stamped.

b. Acceptance by the Mode of Communication Used Must Be an Authorized Mode of Acceptance. [§ 4–122]

An offer may specify that acceptance can only be effective upon receipt by the offeror. If it does, then the general acceptance upon dispatch rule is not followed. Similarly, the offer may validly indicate that acceptance by another medium, such as a telegram, or by performance, is the only way to accept the offer. If the offer specifically limits the mode of acceptance so that acceptance by dispatch of a letter is not an authorized mode of acceptance, then the dispatch rule will also not control. Lastly, even if the offer is silent as to how and when it is to be accepted, any purported method of acceptance must be "reasonable under the circumstances" [Restatement 2d § 65; § 4–94 *et seq.*].

ACCEPTANCE

Thus, if the circumstances, such as where the offeree knows that the offeror has competing bids, indicate a quicker form of acceptance should be used, then a mailed acceptance will only be effective upon receipt. Note, however, that under § 67 of the Restatement 2d, even if the offeree uses an unauthorized means of communication to transmit an acceptance or fails to exercise reasonable diligence to insure safe transmission, it will nonetheless be treated as effective on dispatch **if** that communication arrives within the time in which a properly dispatched acceptance would normally have arrived.

c. **Offeror Loses Power to Revoke After a Properly Dispatched Acceptance. [§ 4–123]**

One consequence of acceptance is that the offeror thereafter loses the power to revoke the offer. Hence, even if the offeror has not yet received the properly dispatched acceptance, and thus reasonably believes he or she still has the power to revoke, he or she may not be allowed to do so because acceptances are effective on dispatch. [Case Squib, *Adams v. Lindsell*.]

d. **Special Mailbox Rules Regarding Acceptances Under Option Contracts. [§ 4–124]**

Unless explicitly provided to the contrary, **acceptance of the underlying offer that is the subject of an option contract is not effective until it is *received* by the offeror** [Restatement 2d § 63(b)]. This is clearly an exception to the normal rule and is a codification by the Restatement of normative conduct. Note: this rule does **not** address acceptance of an offer to enter into an option contract. Rather, it is acceptance of the *underlying offer* that is **the subject of** an option contract that is effective. In other words, this rule assumes an option contract has previously been entered into and the offeree is now exercising his option granted under the option contract.

(1) **Example. [§ 4–125]**

Jane has entered into a valid option contract whereby she has the right to purchase Bob's car for $5,000 during the next seven days. On the seventh day, she sends Bob a letter indicating her acceptance of the underlying deal, along with a check for $5,000. If the letter is received by Bob on the eighth day, it is invalid, for acceptances of the underlying transactions in option contracts are only effective upon receipt, not dispatch.

CHAPTER 4

3. **Rejections Effective upon Receipt. [§ 4–126]**

   A **rejection** of an offer is *not effective* until it is **received**. A communication need not be read to be "received." Rather, it is received when it is in the control of the addressee. Thus, a rejection typically becomes effective when it arrives at the offeror's address (including e-mail address: UCC § R2–213) or if the offeror knows of it [UCC § 1–202].

4. **Revocations Effective upon Receipt Under Majority Rule. [§ 4–127]**

   The majority rule states that **revocations** of revocable offers *are effective* on **receipt** [Restatement 2d § 63, Cmt. c]. However, a minority of jurisdictions has adopted the rule that an offeror's revocation should be effective on dispatch. The minority rule has been criticized because under it, an offeree can lose his or her power to accept before he or she even knows it, i.e., as soon as the offeror puts the revocation in the mailbox.

5. **Effect of First Sending a Rejection, Followed by an Acceptance. [§ 4–128]**

   If an offeree first mails a rejection, and then changes his or her mind and communicates an acceptance, the rule is: **the acceptance is effective if it arrives first; and the rejection is effective if it arrives first**.

6. **Effect of First Sending an Acceptance, Followed by a Rejection. [§ 4–129]**

   If an offeree first mails an acceptance, and then changes his or her mind and communicates a rejection, the rule is: **the acceptance is effective on dispatch unless: (1) the rejection arrives first; *and* (2) the offeror changes his or her position in reliance on the rejection**. For example, if the rejection overtook the acceptance, and upon receiving it the offeror entered into a contract for the same goods with someone else, the offeror changed position in reliance on the rejection and it is thus effective. Otherwise the initial acceptance of the offer will be binding on the offeree.

7. **Graphic Summary of Mailbox Rule. [§ 4–130]**

   The chart below summarizes the mailbox rule:

   In the absence of a contrary indication from the parties themselves, specifically including contrary instructions in the offer itself, the following rules apply:

ACCEPTANCE

COMMUNICATION	EFFECT
1. Offer ---->	Effective on receipt
2. Acceptance ---->	Effective on dispatch
3. Rejection ---->	Effective on receipt
4. Revocation ---->	Effective on receipt (maj.) Effective on dispatch (min.)
5. Rejection followed by acceptance ---->	Rejection effective if it gets there first; acceptance effective if it gets there first
6. Acceptance followed by rejection ---->	Acceptance effective unless: (a) rejection gets there first; **and** (b) offeror detrimentally relies on the rejection

H. EXAM APPROACH TO ACCEPTANCE ISSUES. [§ 4–131*]

Use the following approach when addressing "acceptance" issues on an examination:

1. Make sure the offer is still open when it is purportedly accepted, i.e., determine whether the offer is revocable or irrevocable, and whether any act or event has occurred that will terminate the offeree's power or right to accept [§§ 4–27, *et seq.*];

2. Make sure the party who accepts the offer has a valid power of acceptance, meaning the offeror gave the party the power to accept when making the offer [§§ 4–6 *et seq.*], or that the accepting party has been assigned the right to accept under a valid option contract by a proper offeree [§§ 4–10; 4–74];

3. Make sure the offer is accepted by a proper method or mode of acceptance, i.e., one that is either specified in the offer, or is reasonable under the circumstances if the offer is ambiguous [§§ 4–92 *et seq.*];

4. Make sure the acceptance is timely, either in light of the time specified for acceptance in the offer, or a reasonable time if no time is mentioned [§§ 4–44 *et seq.*], always keeping in mind the mailbox and delayed communication rules regarding the effectiveness various communications [§§ 4–118 *et seq.*]; and

---

* For more information, listen to CD # 3, Track 4 of *Sum and Substance Audio on Contracts*.

CHAPTER 4

5. Lastly, keep in mind that acceptances are judged under the objective theory of contracts [§ 4–3], so that the intent of the accepting party is not controlling. Watch out for the special problems associated with specific issues such as cross-offers [§ 4–5)] and general or reward offers [§ 4–12].

CHAPTER 5

WHEN THE "ACCEPTANCE" VARIES FROM THE OFFER: THE "MIRROR IMAGE" AND "LAST SHOT" RULES AND UCC § 2–207

AUTHOR'S NOTE:

In coming up with § 2–207 the drafters of the UCC had the laudable goal of developing rules to deal with a "real-world" problem—namely what to do when buyers and sellers made contracts by exchanging their own forms which didn't have exactly the same terms. As you know from the previous chapters, under strict common law rules, unless the parties agreed on the same terms, there was never a contract—one of the parties always was deemed to have made a counter-offer. The statutory scheme the drafters developed to deal with these issues, § 2–207, is, in almost everyone's view, too complicated, cumbersome, and with astonishing gaps and inconsistencies—the proverbial cow developed by a committee that ended up being a camel.

Different individuals drafted each of the three sections of § 2–207, and yet another person drafted the comments. Indeed, the first draft had only two sections; another draft had six sections; and the drafters couldn't get agreement on just how the provision would work. (The 2003 revised UCC simplifies the rules to a great degree, but, as with the rest of the 2003 revision, that provision has not been adopted in any state. Just so you are aware of it, this book explains § 2R–207 in § 5–32.) But until there is a groundswell for change, contract law is "stuck" with the § 2–207 contents, structure and comments that have bedeviled students for over 30 years.

CHAPTER 5

The good news is that § 2–207 is only 4 sentences, and so once you understand how the sentences operate, it is not too bad. But be prepared to spend some time getting to that level of understanding.

A. COMMON LAW VIEW: THE "MIRROR IMAGE" RULE. [§ 5–1*]

Under common law, an effective acceptance must have accepted the offer unconditionally and entirely. That is, the acceptance had to be the "mirror image" of the offer. If the purported acceptance added an additional term, had one fewer term, or even slightly changed a term, it was considered a counter-offer, not an acceptance.

B. UNFAIRNESS OF THE MIRROR IMAGE RULE. [§ 5–2]

The mirror image rule makes sense in face-to-face transactions, for it seems only fair to say in those situations that unless the parties agree as to all the same terms, they have not manifested the mutual assent necessary for a valid contract. However, in modern commercial transactions, where the parties often do not deal face-to-face and where offer and acceptance are often made via pre-printed forms emailed or faxed between locations, the mirror image rule often leads to unfairness. This unfairness comes about in two ways, each of which is described by example below.

1. Example of Unfairness Where One Party Doesn't Perform. [§ 5–3]

On September 1, a farmer in Kansas sends a "Purchase Order" to a grain supplier in Illinois. The Purchase Order contains blanks, which the farmer fills in by hand to indicate she wants 1,000 pounds of corn to be delivered on or before next February 15, at a price she fills in. Clause 36 of her Purchase Order is pre-printed and states that delivery of the corn shall be made by U.P.S.

Upon receiving the Purchase Order, the grain supplier sends out a pre-printed "Acceptance of Purchase Order." The owner fills in the blanks to indicate the grain company is promising to supply 1,000 pounds of corn to be delivered on or before February 15, and promises to sell the corn at the same price quoted in the Purchase Order. However, clause 31 of the Acceptance is also pre-printed and says that delivery is to be made by "any common carrier."

When the Acceptance form arrives, Farmer checks only to ensure that the handwritten quantity, price, and delivery dates are correct, and puts the document in her files. If the grain company never

---

* For more information, listen to CD # 3, Track 5 of *Sum and Substance Audio on Contracts*.

delivers the corn, under the mirror image rule there is no breach of contract since no contract was ever formed. Because of the discrepancies in the delivery term ("U.P.S." versus "any common carrier") the acceptance was not a mirror image of the offer, and thus was a counter-offer, which was never itself accepted by Farmer. Obviously, this is unfair to Farmer who thought her grain needs had been covered and now has to start over, and situations like this were an impetus to develop § 2–207.

2. **Example of Unfairness Where the Parties Perform: The "Last Shot" Doctrine. [§ 5–4]**

Builder places an order for 100 doors from lumber company. On the Purchase Order Builder uses to order the doors is the following clause: "Supplier warrants that all doors supplied under this contract shall be of stainable quality." Lumber company sends back an acknowledgment form that is identical to the Purchase Order in every respect, except that the third page of its pre-printed form provides: "Supplier represents that its products are only of paintable, not stainable, quality." Neither party looks at the other's form except for the price, delivery and quantity terms, and the doors are timely delivered and paid for. Later, when the doors turn out to be unstainable, Builder sues Lumber company.

The difference between the farmer hypothetical and this one is that here, the parties actually performed. As before, under the common law's mirror image rule, the parties never had a contract based on the exchange of forms. However, because Lumber company's form was the last pending offer at the time the parties performed, common law held that when the builder paid for the doors, he or she implicitly accepted the lumber company's counter-offer, and thus became bound to a contract whose terms included the paintable-only quality warranty. This rule is sometimes called the "last shot" doctrine and resulted in a contract by performance being made on the terms of the last party to submit a form or other communication. While perhaps not quite as unfair as the situation described in § 5–3, because Builder could have checked Lumber company's form on as to the stainable/paintable term, which presumably was an important one to Builder, the last shot doctrine also deprived offerors of some of the benefits they thought they were getting under these types of contracts. Recall, the scenario is that neither party reads the fine print and boilerplate (pre-printed language contained in the other party's form) and thus neither party really knows what the terms of the deal truly are or what the other party is offering to do. The drafters of the UCC attempted to deal with these issues and cure these types of unfairness in § 2–207, which is discussed below.

CHAPTER 5

C. UCC § 2–207: AN OVERVIEW. [§ 5–5*]

Section 2–207 of the UCC was intended to lessen, if not eliminate, the unfairness of the common law mirror image and last shot rules. It does so by eliminating the strict requirement that the terms must be identical for a contract to be formed, i.e., that there is no contract when the second form contains terms "**different from**," or "**additional to**," the original offer. However, it is important to note that not only does § 2–207 govern *whether* the parties *have* a contract (i.e., whether there was a valid offer and acceptance to satisfy mutual intent), but it also determines what **the terms** of that resulting contract are. It does the first job reasonably well; but it is in the latter area—determining the terms—that many of § 2–207's problems arise.

D. ANALYSIS OF § 2–207 PROBLEMS. [§ 5–6]

After ascertaining that the rules of Article 2 of the UCC govern the transaction [Chapter Thirty-Three], nearly all § 2–207 problems can be analyzed in only three steps:

> **(1) Do the parties have a contract based on the exchange of their writings under § 2–207(1)?** That is, does the purported acceptance from the offeree act as an effective acceptance of the offeror's offer, or is it a counter-offer as would be true under common law mirror image rule? [§ 5–7];
>
> **(2) If the offeree's form is an effective acceptance, then the terms of the contract are dictated by the rules § 2–207(2)** [§ 5–14] **and;**
>
> **(3) If the offeree's form is *not* an effective acceptance, then the parties do not have a contract based on their writings.** In that case it is necessary to examine whether they have a contract by <u>conduct, and</u> if they do, § 2–207(3) determines the terms of that contract [§ 5–23].
>
> To summarize, the *existence* of a contract will be found either under § 2–207(1) by the exchange of the writings, or because there is a contract by conduct under § 2–207(3). Those are the only two ways contracts can be formed under § 2–207.
>
> However, the *terms* of any contract formed under § 2–207 are determined either by § 2–207(2) (if there is a contract based upon the exchange of writings under § 2–207(1)) or by § 2–207(3) (if there is a contract only by conduct.)
>
> Example. Throughout the next several sections we will use the following example:

---

* For more information, listen to CD # 3, Track 6 of *Sum and Substance Audio on Contracts.*

UCC § 2–207

The offeror is a buyer who orders a product on a "Purchase Order" form, and the offeree is a seller who purports to accept that order by an "Acknowledgement" form that differs from the Purchase Order in some respect.

1. **First Step: Do the Parties Have a Contract Based on Their Writings Under § 2–207(1)? [§ 5–7*]**

   The first issue is whether the parties have a contract based on their exchanged writings. This is determined by judging their writings under the provisions of § 2–207(1). **The only function of § 2–207(1) is to determine if the Purchase Order and Acknowledgement together constitute a binding offer and acceptance.** That is, whether the exchange of the two writings forms an enforceable agreement even though they are dissimilar. This is done in two sub-steps:

   > (1) Determining whether the seller/offeree's Acknowledgement is a "definite and seasonable expression of acceptance;" and

   > (2) Ascertaining whether the seller's purported acceptance is "expressly made conditional" on the buyer/offeror's "assent to [any] different or additional terms" or is otherwise a counter-offer because it made its acceptance conditional on the offeror's acceptance of the additional or different terms [*see* Restatement 2d § 59].

   The analysis for each of these sub-steps is described below.

   a. **First Sub-Step: Does the Offeree's Document Act as a "Definite and Seasonable Expression of Acceptance?" [§ 5–8]**

      The first questions are: (1) whether the purported acceptance will be deemed to have accepted the offer at all (in the words of § 2–207, is it a "definite ... expression of acceptance") and (2) whether the offer has lapsed (in the words of the statute, is it a "seasonable expression of acceptance"). Usually this is not a problem, as most sellers' forms evidence a desire to sell the same goods the buyer wishes to purchase, at the same price the buyer wants to pay, and the acceptance is sent seasonably.

      However, if the purported acceptance is too different from the offer, if the offer has lapsed due to time, or if it contains special language (discussed below in § 5–10) that would make it a counter-offer at common law, the offeree's document is **not** an acceptance, but will be deemed a counter-offer, and the

---

* For more information, listen to CD # 3, Track 7 of *Sum and Substance Audio on Contracts*.

determination of whether the parties have a contract is judged under § 2–207(3) not § 2–207(1).

(1) Example. [§ 5–9]

Buyer submits a Purchase Order for 1,000 apples at a price of $2 per apple. After receiving the Purchase Order, Seller sends an Acknowledgement "confirming" the order for 1,000 oranges at a price of $15 per orange. Since the seller's confirmation contains product and price terms that are too different from the buyer's offer, the Acknowledgement is not a "definite . . . expression of acceptance" of an offer for apples, but is instead a counter-offer for oranges. If, however, the Acknowledgement had confirmed 1,000 apples at $2 each, the Acknowledgement would be an effective acceptance, even if there were some additional or different terms, e.g., the Acknowledgement had a different mode of delivery for the apples. Similarly, if the Acknowledgement said the seller was "considering" supplying the apples, there would be no valid acceptance because there would be no "definite . . . *expression* of acceptance."

Same result if the Purchase Order stated it could only be accepted before June 1, and seller sent the Acknowledgement on June 10. There the purported acceptance in the Acknowledgement is not a "*seasonable* expression of acceptance," and thus is treated as a counter-offer.

Same result if the Acknowledgement would be judged a counter-offer at common law because it had the "special language" (discussed below in § 5–10) which made the acceptance conditional on the offeror's acceptance to the additional or different terms.

b. Second Sub-Step: Does the Offeree's Document "Expressly Make [Acceptance] Conditional on [the Offeror's] Assent to the Additional or Different Terms"?: Herein the "Special Language." [§ 5–10]

While § 2–207(1) holds that most purported acceptances with different or additional terms are, in fact, acceptances and not counter-offers, a question remains as to how an offeree can make a valid counter-offer if he or she does not want to accept one or more of the offeror's terms. To solve this problem, § 2–207(1) provides that if the seller's form makes acceptance "*expressly . . . conditional on assent to the additional or different terms*" found in seller's form, then the Acknowledgement will be treated as a counter-offer and not an acceptance. Once again this makes sense under the objective theory of contract, for if the seller indicates: (a) that the seller is proposing a deal on different terms; and (b) that the seller is only willing to go forward if the buyer agrees to the seller's terms, then a reasonable person in the position of the buyer would know that its offer is not being "accepted" by the Acknowledgement and the seller is treated as having made a counter-offer and not an acceptance.

This is also the result under Restatement 2d § 59. In the previous paragraphs, this was referred to as "special language." In truth, § 2–207 does not *require* that the seller's form contain the exact "expressly made conditional language" of § 2–207(1). But most lawyers who draft contracts figure why not use the language of the UCC, and so most of the cases where there is an effective counter-offer use that language. But, if it can be fairly ascertained from other language that the offeree is not willing to go forward unless the offeror assents to the additional or different terms in the Acknowledgement, the latter document is a counter-offer, not an acceptance.

(1) Example. [§ 5–11]

Buyer submits a Purchase Order for 1,000 stereos at a price of $100 per stereo. Seller then submits an Acknowledgement confirming 1,000 stereos at $100 each. However, the seller's Acknowledgement also adds a damages disclaimer and contains the following clause: "Seller's Acceptance is hereby expressly made conditional on Buyer's assent to the additional and different terms of this Acknowledgement." Although Seller's Acknowledgement appears to be an acceptance, the presence of the "expressly made conditional" clause actually makes it a counter-offer which the buyer is free to accept or decline.

In order for the Acknowledgement to be treated as a counter-offer, the seller must require an affirmative act by the buyer to indicate Buyer's agreement to the counter-offer (in the words of § 2–207, the additional terms must be "expressly made conditional on Buyer's *assent* to the additional and different terms").

If instead the Acceptance says something like "Buyer's failure to object to the additional or different terms of this acceptance will be deemed an acceptance of such terms," the Acknowledgement **will be an acceptance** of the offer and NOT a counter-offer. Section 2–207(1) does not permit the silence or inaction of Buyer to act as a wholesale acceptance of the seller's different terms. To determine which party's terms control when the Acknowledgement is an acceptance, see § 5–8.

(2) Example of the Incorrect Approach Taken by a Court Under § 2–207(1): *Roto-Lith v. F.P. Bartlett & Co.* [§ 5–12*]

Perhaps the most criticized § 2–207 case ever is the one many first-year students are initially assigned, *Roto-Lith, Ltd. v. F.P. Bartlett & Co.* The reason the case is so widely criticized is that it fails to recognize the point made above, i.e., that the seller cannot make its form a counter-offer simply by the silence or inaction of the buyer.

In *Roto-Lith,* the seller-offeree's acknowledgement form both disclaimed all warranties and contained the following clause, "[I]f these terms [including the one that disclaimed warranties] are not acceptable, buyer must notify seller at once." Buyer did not notify the seller of any objection and eventually purchased the goods. When the goods turned out to be sub-standard, the buyer sued for breach of warranty, and the seller defended by asserting that the buyer's silence constituted an acceptance of the warranty disclaimer. The court agreed with the seller and held that the quoted language made the offeree's acknowledgement a counter-offer, which was implicitly accepted by the buyer when it accepted the goods [*Roto-Lith, Ltd. v. F.P. Bartlett & Co.*, 297 F.2d 497 (1st Cir. 1962)].

However, this analysis is incorrect, **for a clause that does not call for an *express* manifestation of the buyer's assent to the different terms found in the offeree's document is insufficient to render that document a counter-offer under § 2–207(1)**. Rather, the seller's document should have been classified as an *acceptance* under § 2–207(1), (and because the warranty disclaimer **materially altered the offer)** [*see* § 5–18 for a discussion of the material alteration issue], under § 2–207(2) the disclaimer should not have been deemed to be part of the contract.

While frustrating sometimes to study a case that is wrongly decided, *Roto-Lith* should give you some solace—§ 2–207 is so confusingly drafted that it can gave even experienced judges and lawyers fits.

---

* For more information about this case, listen to CD # 3, Track 8 of *Sum and Substance Audio on Contracts.*

(3) **Examples of the Correct Approach Under § 2–207(1): *Dorton v. Collins & Aikman Corp* and *C. Itoh & Co. v. Jordan International*. [§ 5–13*]**

The two cases cited in the heading, taken together, establish the correct analysis under § 2–207(1). In both cases the seller was the offeree, and its form contained an additional term calling for arbitration of certain disputes under the contract, rather than litigation of those claims.

In *Dorton,* the seller's form also stated, ". . . [our] acceptance of your order is subject to all the terms and conditions [in this document], including arbitration." The court correctly held that the "is subject to" language was insufficient to transform the purported acceptance into a counter-offer because the language did not expressly require the buyer's **affirmative assent** to those terms before they became part of the contract. Hence, the seller's form became a valid acceptance, not a counter-offer, and the question of whether the arbitration term became part of the contract was decided by reference to § 2–207(2) (*see* § 5–14).

In *Itoh,* the seller's form stated that its acceptance was "expressly conditional on Buyer's assent to the additional . . . terms and conditions set forth below [one of which was arbitration]." The court correctly held that the "expressly made conditional on Buyer's assent" language was sufficient to turn the purported acceptance into a counter-offer, and thus the parties had no contract based on the exchange of their writings. Whether they had a contract at all was thus determined by reference to § 2–207(3) and whether they had a contract by conduct. [*See* Case Squibs, *Dorton v. Collins & Aikman Corp.*, 453 F.2d 1161 (6th Cir. 1972) and *C. Itoh & Co. v .Jordan Int'l*, 552 F.2d 1228 (7th Cir. 1977)].

2. **Second Step: If the Parties Have a Contract Based on Their Exchanged Writings Under § 2–207(1), Then § 2–207(2) Governs What Terms Make up the Contract. [§ 5–14**]**

Once it is determined that a contract is formed by the exchanged writings under § 2–207(1), i.e., it is determined that the offeree sent a definite and seasonable expression of acceptance and that it was not a counter-offer, the provisions of § 2–207(2) provide the rules to determine what the terms of that contract are. The proper analysis

---

* For more information about these cases, listen to CD # 3, Track 8 of *Sum and Substance Audio on Contracts.*

** For more information, listen to CD # 3, Track 8 of *Sum and Substance Audio on Contracts.*

under § 2–207(2) begins with a determination of whether both parties are merchants, or whether at least one of them is a consumer.

a. **If Either Party Is a Non-Merchant, the Offeror's Terms Control. [§ 5–15]**

   If *either* party to the contract is a non-merchant, then any additional terms contained in the acceptance are deemed merely "proposals" for addition to the contract, which may or may not be accepted by the offeror. That is, such terms do not automatically become part of the contract, and are treated as nothing more than suggestions for possible additions to the deal presented to the offeror, which can be accepted or not by that party. If the offeror wants to accept them, the offeror must signify that intent in some objectively verifiable way.

   Note the definition of a "merchant" is given in § 2–104(1) [*see also* § 35–9 for a further discussion of who is and is not a merchant.]

b. **If Both Parties Are Merchants, the Offeree's Terms Control *Unless* One of the Three § 2–207(2) Exceptions Apply. [§ 5–16]**

   § 2–207(2) is rather awkwardly phrased on this issue, but it says that when two merchants are involved, the additional terms in the offeree's acceptance *become* part of the contract *unless*:

   (1) The **offer expressly limits acceptance to the terms of the offer** [§ 2–207(2)(a); § 5–17];

   (2) The additional terms in the acceptance **materially alter** the offer [§ 2–207(2)(b); § 5–18]; or

   (3) **Notification of objection** to the additional terms by the offeror is given within a reasonable time after notice of them has been received [§ 2–207(2)(c); § 5–19].

   Thus, only if **none** of these three conditions apply will the additional terms in the Acknowledgement become part of the contract. It is very rare that such will be the case; so, as you will see, the probable result under § 2–207(2), even with merchants, is that the offeror's terms will still likely control the deal.

   In the four examples given below, assume both parties are merchants.

   (1) Example. [§ 5–17]

   Offeror/Buyer's Purchase Order provides: "Acceptance of this offer is limited to the terms of this offer." Offeree/Seller's Acknowledgement is the same as the offer, except it does not contain the quoted language above, and contains a "no modification except in writing" clause. The "no modification except in writing" provision does **not** become part of the contract, because the **offer expressly limited acceptance** to only those terms found in the offer [UCC § 2–207(2)(a)].

(2) **Example. [§ 5–18]**

Offeree/Seller's Acknowledgement is the same as the offeror/buyer's Purchase Order, except that it provides: "No goods sold under this contract shall be sold with any warranty, express or implied, including the warranty of merchantability." If seller's Acknowledgement form is judged an acceptance under § 2–207(1), the warranty disclaimer does **not** become part of the contract because it **materially alters** the contract [UCC § 2–207(2)(b)]. (For examples of those terms that do, and do, not materially alter a contract, *see* UCC § 2–207, Cmts. 4 and 5, respectively.)

The general test for whether a term "materially alters" the deal is whether it "would . . . result in surprise or hardship if incorporated without express awareness by the other party" [§ 2–207, Cmt. 4]. Since most "other parties" will correctly claim that just about any "slipped in" term would be an unjust surprise, most additional or different terms of the purported acceptance will be deemed to have "materially altered" the deal.

(3) **Example. [§ 5–19]**

Seller's Acknowledgement is the same as the offeror's Purchase Order, except it provides: "Any objection to the quality of goods must be brought to seller's attention within 90 days after delivery." If the buyer does not object to this term, and if the offer does not limit acceptance to only the terms found in the offer, the clause requiring 90-day notification *will* become part of the deal because, under Cmt. 5 to § 2–207, such clauses do **not** materially alter the transaction, i.e., they are common enough that insertion of such a term would not "unfairly surprise" the buyer.

(4) **Example. [§ 5–20]**

Seller's Acknowledgement is the same as the offeror's Purchase Order, except it provides: "Any dispute arising under this agreement shall be resolved by arbitration, not litigation." A day after receiving the seller's form, the buyer notices the arbitration provision and notifies the seller that he or she objects to that provision. Because the **offeror's**

CHAPTER 5

objection to the additional term is made within a reasonable time after Buyer has notice of it, the arbitration provision does not become part of the contract [UCC § 2–207(2)(c)].

c. **The Curious Absence of "Different" Terms Under § 2–207(2). [§ 5–21*]**

Section 2–207(1) states that an expression of acceptance can act as an effective acceptance, "even though it states terms additional to or **different from** those offered or agreed upon." However, in § 2–207(2), there is no mention of "different" terms. The provision states only, "[T]he **additional** terms are to be construed as proposals for addition to the contract." Thus, often the parties will end up in a situation where an acceptance is found under § 2–207(1) despite the presence of a different term in the acceptance; however, there is no guidance under § 2–207(2) as to whether that "different" term is or is not part of the resulting contract.

Three main theories have arisen to explain how "different" terms should be handled under § 2–207(2). (1) The <u>first</u> is that different terms should be treated the same as additional terms, for it was just a drafting oversight that the word "different" was left out of § 2–207(2). Proponents of this approach believe that the omission of "different" terms was essentially a typo, and "different" terms should be treated exactly as "additional" terms. There is support for this theory in Comment 3 to § 2–207, which states: "Whether or not additional **or different** terms will become part of the agreement depends upon the provisions of subsection (2)." Of course the comments do not have the force of the text, but Comment 3 at least provides some support for this approach to dealing with "additional terms."

(2) The second theory is often called the "literalist" approach. Under this view, different terms simply drop out altogether and can never become part of the agreement without the offeror separately and specifically agreeing to them. Unlike proponents of the first approach, proponents of this view assume that the omission of "different" terms in 2–207(2) was deliberate, and so while "different" terms in the acknowledgement form will not prevent a contract from being formed via an exchange of the writings under 2–207(1), the fact that the term does not appear in 2–207(2) means that such "different" terms will never become part of the contract. The support for this theory comes from the plain "literal" language of the statute, i.e., the phrase "different

---

* For more information, listen to CD # 3, Track 10 of *Sum and Substance Audio on Contracts*.

terms" is included in § 2–207(1) and not in § 2–207(2). The policy behind it is that the second party (typically the seller) has accepted the terms of the offer in its Acknowledgement and thus cannot reasonably expect the "different" terms in its purported acceptance to be controlling. That is, if the first form says there is to be a 12-month warranty, it is not reasonable for the seller to believe it has "accepted" that offer with a 6-month warranty clause which is in its form. So the 6-month clause just disappears and never becomes part of the contract and the warranty term would be 12 months.

The last theory is known as the "Comment 6" approach. Comment 6 to § 2–207 provides that, "[w]here clauses on confirming forms sent by both parties conflict each party must be assumed to object to a clause of the other conflicting with one on the confirmation sent by himself." Hence, under this view, the different terms found on each of the forms will be "knocked out" of the deal, and either there will be no term on that issue, or a "gap filler" or other implied term of the UCC will control. One of the objections to this approach is that the above quote refers to "confirmations" and "confirming forms," and not to the initial exchange of the buyer's and seller's forms, and that the "knock out" rule generally is limited to situations in which § 2–207(3) controls, not 2–207(2) (*see* § 5–23). This differs from the "literalist" approach because under the "literalist" view, the terms of the offer become operative, whereas under Comment 6 approach, *neither* party's terms become operative. It is either that there is no term at all on that issue or a supplementary term under the UCC will be implied. Those that favor this view believe it is fairer, because it doesn't favor one party of the other depending on which exchanged their form first.

By happenstance it could turn out that the supplementary term under the Code matches a term suggested by one of the parties, e.g., seller says no warranty of merchantability and the buyer says there is a warranty of merchantability. Under this approach both would be knocked out, but because the Code implies a merchantability warranty, the warranty would be part of the deal [§ 2–314]. So the buyer's term would control in such an instance, but not because it was in the buyer's form, but because it just happened to be the same term as the Code implied after both party's express term got knocked out.

(1) Example. [§ 5–22]

The following example will illustrate how an acceptance containing a different term would be handled under each of the three theories.

A merchant buyer uses a Purchase Order to place an order for 500 picture frames at a price of $10 per frame from a merchant seller. The Purchase Order specifies that the frames be delivered to Buyer's place of residence by November 1. Upon receipt of the Purchase Order, Seller submits an Acknowledgement form confirming the purchase of 500 frames at $10 each. However, Seller's form states that the frames will be delivered by November 5. Since the buyer's Purchase Order initially specified a delivery date of November 1, the November 5 date is a different term, rather than an additional one.

Under the first approach to "different" terms, the different term is treated as if it was an additional term. Since Seller's Acknowledgement confirms the same quantity and price of frames as the buyer's Purchase Order, the Acknowledgement is a definite and seasonable expression of acceptance. Therefore, § 2–207(2) will dictate whether the November 5 delivery date would become part of the contract. Accordingly, since both buyer and seller are merchants, the November 5 delivery date would become part of the contract unless any of the exceptions of § 2–207(a)–(c) apply.

Here, the offer did not expressly limit acceptance to the terms of the offer, so § 2–207(a) is not triggered nor did buyer object to the term once it received seller's form, so § 2–207(2)(c) is not applicable either. As such, under the first view, the "different" term—the November 5 delivery date—would become part of the contract unless the different delivery date materially alters the offer. We would have to know more facts to determine whether the four day delay "materially alters" this particular deal.

Under the literalist approach, different terms cannot become part of the contract unless specifically agreed to by the offeror. However the different term will not prevent the contract from being formed based on the writings. So, as explained above, the parties have a contract based on their writings since Seller's Acknowledgement is an effective acceptance. Although the parties have a valid contract, according to the literalist approach the November 5 delivery date would not become part of the contract unless Buyer specifically assented to it. If Buyer does not agree to the November 5 delivery date, the original November 1 date will control as the Seller will be deemed to have accepted the terms of the offer.

Lastly, the third, "Comment 6" theory purports that the different delivery terms should knock each other out. As a result, the time for delivery would be a "reasonable time" under the UCC gap filler regarding time of delivery, § 2–309.

3. **Third Step: If No Contract Is Formed Under § 2–207(1) Based on the Exchanged Writings, an Implied-in-Fact Contract May Be Formed by the Parties' Conduct Under § 2–207(3); if So, the "Knockout" Rule of § 2–207(3) Will Determine Which Terms Become Part of the Contract. [§ 5–23*]**

If the offeree's form is found not to constitute an effective acceptance, either because it was not a "definite or seasonable expression of acceptance," or because it was expressly made conditional on the offeror's assent to additional or different terms, then analysis of a § 2–207 problem must proceed directly to § 2–207(3). That is, § 2–207(2) plays absolutely no role in such a case, and is bypassed completely in analyzing such a problem. This is because § 2–207(2)'s only function is to provide the rules for determining what terms become a part of the contract if a contract is made by the exchange of the writings under § 2–207(1).

Contrast that with § 2–207(3): "conduct by both parties which recognizes the existence of a contract is sufficient to establish a contract although the writings of the parties do not establish a contract." Thus, even if the offeree is deemed to have sent a counter-offer that is never formally accepted, the parties can establish an implied-in-fact contract by their conduct. Therefore, if the seller sends the goods called for in the offer, and the buyer accepts them, they have made a contract by conduct under § 2–207(3).

Note that if the seller does not send the goods at all in a § 2–207(3) situation, there simply is no contract since the exchanged writings did not constitute an enforceable agreement.

(Note also that if the parties do have a contract based on the exchange of their writings, its terms **must** be governed by § 2–207(2) even if the seller ships the goods and the buyer accepts them. In other words, resort to § 2–207(3) can only be made when **no** contract is formed based on the parties' exchanged writings as judged by application of the rules in § 2–207(1).)

a. **The "Knockout" Rule. [§ 5–24]**

Under the common law's "last shot" doctrine, the terms of an implied-in-fact contract made under § 2–207(3) would be the

---

* For more information, listen to CD # 3, Track 9 of *Sum and Substance Audio on Contracts*.

terms stated in the last form exchanged between the parties, i.e., the other party would be deemed to have impliedly accepted whatever offer (or counter-offer) was last exchanged between them [§ 5–4]. Section 2–207(3) changes the rule. Once a contract by conduct has been found under the first sentence of § 2–207(3), i.e., "[c]onduct by both parties which recognize[s] the existence of a contract," the second sentence of that provision provides that the **terms** of such a contract "consist of those **terms** on which the writings of the **parties agree, together with any supplementary terms** incorporated under any other provision of this Act." Thus, all the terms found in both parties' writings become part of the contract, but any term that is not found in **both** documents is "knocked out," and does not become part of the contract.

In other words, the contract consists of all the terms both parties agreed on, but no term on which only one party put forward. If at the end of the "knockout" process the contract is left with no term regarding price, time of delivery, place of delivery, time of payment, or place of payment, warranty, etc., such terms can be supplied by the UCC's "gap fillers," or other "default" provisions of the Code which are the "supplementary terms" referred to in § 2–207(3) [*see* § 6–12 for a discussion of gap fillers].

4. **When the Additional or Different Terms Are Found in a "Confirmation" Instead of an Acceptance. [§ 5–25*]**

   Until now, the analysis under § 2–207 has assumed that the parties have exchanged a written offer and a written "acceptance" that differs from the offer. However, a close reading of § 2–207(1) reveals that it also applies where one party sends the other "a written confirmation ... within a reasonable time which states terms additional to and different from those ... agreed upon." In other words, if the parties have made, e.g., an oral contract over the telephone, and one party thereafter sends the other a written confirmation of the oral contract, but the confirmation contains different or additional terms than those agreed to on the phone, § 2–207 is implicated [*See* § 2–207, Cmt. 1].

   a. **The Effect of a "Confirmation" Containing Additional or Different Terms. [§ 5–26]**

      The § 2–207 analysis of a problem where the confirmation, rather than the acceptance, is the operative document varies only slightly from the "normal" § 2–207 analysis. The principal difference is that there is no need to inquire whether the parties have entered into a contract based on their exchanged writings

---

   * For more information, listen to CD # 3, Track 11 of *Sum and Substance Audio on Contracts*.

under § 2–207(1). By definition, a "confirmation" confirms that a contract exists, and merely serves to restate the terms of that contract. Thus, if the confirmation recites that it is intended to confirm a contract previously made by the parties, analysis proceeds directly to § 2–207(2) to determine the terms of the contract.

Under § 2–207(2), the terms of the confirmation are compared against the terms of the previously made oral contract. To analogize a "confirmation" situation to a more typical § 2–207 analysis, think of the oral *contract* **as the "offer"** and the ***written confirmation* as the "acceptance"** under § 2–207(2). As a result, it is unlikely that the party sending the confirmation will be able to slip in an operative term not present in the original oral contract. Only when: (a) both parties are merchants; (b) the party to whom the confirmation is sent does not notify the other of his or her objection to the additional terms of the confirmation (§ 2–207(2)(c)); and (c) those additional terms do not materially alter the contract (§ 2–207(2)(b)), do the additional terms of the confirmation become part of the contract. Otherwise, the additional terms are only proposals that may be accepted or not by the recipient of the confirmation. (If the terms of the confirmation are "different" rather than "additional," the analysis would proceed as described in § 5–21.) This rule makes sense, for it would be manifestly unfair for a party sending a written confirmation to be able to slip in a material term not agreed to by the other party.

(1) Review Problem. [§ 5–27]

Charles, the owner of a retail fitness store, telephones Terri, the owner of a company that manufactures exercise equipment. Charles places an order for fifteen $1,000 home exercise machines. Both are merchants. They agree that the machines will be delivered to Charles's store on Monday, April 10, and that Charles will pay for them within 30 days after their receipt. Nothing is said as to whether Charles is liable for interest if he is late in paying. Later that day, Terri sends Charles a "confirmation," stating accurately the terms of the deal, except she has added a term stating "Buyer will owe interest to seller at a rate of 8% per year if seller does not pay within 30 days of delivery." Charles receives the confirmation, checks only the quantity, price, and delivery terms, and thus does not object to the interest term found in the prolix of the pre-printed confirmation form.

Question: Does their contract now contain the 8% per year interest clause?

Answer: YES. The analysis is as follows:

First, since the writing at issue is a confirmation, § 2–207(1) is bypassed and the situation is analyzed under § 2–207(2).

Next, for a § 2–207(2) analysis, the oral contract, without the interest term, is to be compared with the confirmation containing the interest term. Under § 2–207(2), because both parties are merchants, the interest provision becomes part of the contract unless § 2–207(2)(a), (b), or (c) applies. Section 2–207(2)(a) does not apply, for the contract says nothing explicitly about being limited only to its terms. Section § 2–207(2)(b) does not keep out the provision, because according to Cmt. 5 to § 2–207, an interest-on-overdue-balance clause does not materially alter the transaction. Section 2–207(2)(c) does not apply because Charles did not object. Thus, the additional term of the confirmation "become[s] part of the contract" under § 2–207(2).

E. PRACTICAL DIFFERENCES BETWEEN THE COMMON LAW AND UCC § 2–207. [§ 5–28]

At common law, there was an incentive to be the last party to submit its form because, under the "last shot" doctrine, the terms in the form of the last party to submit would control if the contract was formed by performance. [§ 5–4]. However, § 2–207 changes this preference. Now, the incentive would be for each party to be the offeror. If either party to the transaction is a non-merchant, then the additional terms in the "last" document are merely proposals, and the offeror's terms control [§ 5–15]. Similarly, if both parties are merchants, it is still likely that the offeror's or counter-offeror's terms will control since additional terms in the acceptance document will become part of the contract only if none of the conditions of § 2–207(2) apply [§ 5–16], which is unlikely and limited to non-materially altering provisions.

F. EXAM APPROACH TO § 2–207 ISSUES. [§ 5–29*]

Recall, there are only three steps to applying § 2–207 in a typical case:

1. Determine whether the purported acceptance is truly an acceptance under § 2–207(1) despite the presence of additional or different terms, or is a counter-offer (because it contains a clause, e.g., "this Acceptance is expressly conditioned on Buyer's assent to any additional or different terms" or because it is not a "definite" or a "seasonable expression of acceptance.") [§§ 5–7 *et seq.*];

---

* For more information, listen to CD # 3, Track 13 of *Sum and Substance Audio on Contracts.*

UCC § 2–207

2. If the purported acceptance is deemed a valid acceptance, then the terms of the contract are determined under § 2–207(2) (and § 2–207(3) is never used) [§ 5–14]; and

3. If the purported acceptance is found not to be a valid acceptance, the parties have no contract based on their exchanged writings (and § 2–207(2) is never used). However, if the parties perform, they have a contract by conduct, and the rules of § 2–207(3) determine that contract's terms [§ 5–23].

Remember the three alternatives to analyzing a 2-207 problem if the term in the purported acceptance is a "different" term [§ 5–21].

For those who prefer a diagram, a flow chart of the steps involved in analyzing a § 2–207 problem is as follows:

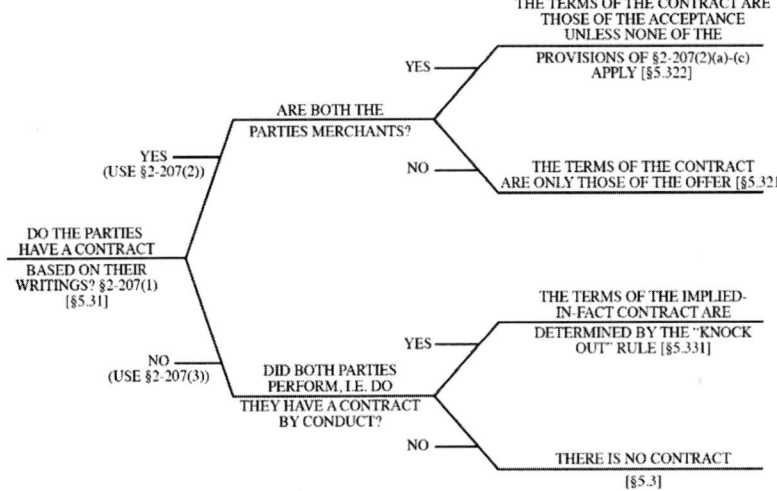

1. **Example. [§ 5–30]**

   Construct Co. sends a Purchase Order form to Door Co., seeking to purchase 100 oak doors, and stating that it is relying on Door Co. to produce doors of stainable quality. Door Co. timely sends an Acknowledgement of Order form back to Construct Co., acknowledging the order. The pertinent portions of these forms are as follows:

Purchase Order	**Acknowledgement of Order**
100 oak entry doors, 6 ft. x 3 ft.	100 oak entry doors, 6 ft. x 3 ft.
$300/door, payment due on delivery	$300/door, payment due on delivery
Delivery on 4/1/12	Delivery on 4/1/12

CHAPTER 5

Doors of Stainable Quality	No Warranty, Either Express or Implied, Including the Implied Warranty of Merchantability Regarding the Stainable Quality of the Doors

Question: Is there a contract and, if so, what are its terms?

Analysis: (1) Is there a contract based on these writings under § 2–207(1)? YES.

First, the Acknowledgement is clearly a definite and seasonable expression of acceptance under the UCC, as the presence of the different warranty terms is insufficient, in and of itself, to make the Acknowledgement a counter-offer and the Acknowledgement was sent in a "timely" manner.

Second, there is no "expressly made conditional on [buyer's] assent to different or additional terms" clause, thus the Acknowledgement is a valid acceptance under § 2–207(1), despite the fact it contains different warranty provisions. Thus the analysis must proceed under § 2–207(2) to determine the terms of the contract.

(2) Does the different term found in the Acknowledgement become part of the contract under § 2–207(2)? NO.

First, are the parties merchants? *YES*. So, there is a small chance that the "no stainable quality" term might become part of the contract. (If either party were not a merchant, there is no chance the term would become part of the contract absent express agreement by Construct Co.)

Second, are any of the provisions of § 2–207(2)(a)–(c) implicated? *YES*. There is no objection by the buyer to any different terms, either in the Purchase Order itself, or afterwards. Hence neither § 2–207(2)(a) or (c) are satisfied. However, the "no stainable quality" warranty term certainly materially alters the deal, and thus, it could not become a term of the contract under § 2–207(2)(b). (Recall there are three theories as to how to deal with "different" as opposed to "additional" terms under § 2–207(2), each of which yields the same result in this situation. [§ 5–21.] One would treat additional and different terms identically, as the above analysis dictates. The "literalist" approach provides the "different" term in the Acknowledgement cannot become part of the deal, so the "no warranty" clause would be out. Under the third, "Comment 6" approach, both warranty provisions would knock each other out, but the stainable quality requested by the offeror would trigger the implied warranty of fitness for a particular purpose requiring stainable quality doors [UCC § 2–315; *see also* § 35–12 for an explanation of that warranty]. That "different" term drops out altogether, and thus under this approach, the no stainable warranty provision would never have legal significance. Either way, the "no warranty" term is out.)

2. **Example. [§ 5–31]**

   Same parties as above, except this time the relevant forms are as follows:

Purchase Order	Acknowledgement of Order
100 oak entry doors, 6 ft. x 3 ft.	100 oak entry doors, 6 ft. x 3 ft.
$300/door, payment due on delivery	$300/door, payment due on delivery
Delivery by 4/1/12	Delivery by 4/1/12
Doors of Stainable Quality	No Warranty, Either Express or Implied Including the Implied Warranty of Merchantability. SELLER IS NOT ACCEPTING BUYER'S OFFER UNLESS BUYER EXPRESSLY ASSENTS TO THE ADDITIONAL OR DIFFERENT TERMS FOUND IN THIS ACKNOWLEDGEMENT, INCLUDING THOSE REGARDING THE STAINABLE QUALITIES OF THE DOORS.

   Neither party looks at the form of the other, except to ensure that the quantity, price, and delivery terms are correct. Non-stainable quality doors are shipped and accepted, and three months later Construct Co. sues for breach of warranty, claiming the doors are not of stainable quality as called for in the contract.

   Question: Is there a contract and, if so, what are its terms?

   Analysis: (1) Is there a contract based on the writings under § 2–207(1)? NO.

   While the Acknowledgement is a definite and seasonable expression of acceptance, its final clause turns the document into a counter-offer. It clearly states Door Co. is unwilling to go forward on anything other than its own terms and states that no contract based on the writings can be formed without the *express* assent of Construct Co. Therefore, analysis must proceed to § 2–207(3).

(2) Is there a contract by conduct under § 2–207(3)? YES.

Door Co. shipped doors to Construct Co., who accepted and paid for them. Thus, a contract by conduct was formed.

(3) Does the different warranty term in the Acknowledgement become part of the contract under § 2–207(3)? NO.

Under § 2–207(3), the terms of an implied-in-fact contract by conduct consist of only the terms *both* parties agreed upon, plus the supplemental terms of the UCC. Here, the contract was for 100 doors, at $300/door, with payment and delivery due on April 1. However, under the knockout rule [*see* § 5–24] the quality terms of each party are knocked out (for they only appear in their own forms) and do not become part of the contract. However, as discussed above, the Code's implied warranty of fitness for a particular purpose will apply and require stainable quality doors. (UCC § 2–315.) (*See* § 35–8 for a discussion of the warranty of merchantability.)

G. ANALYSIS UNDER REVISED UCC. [§ 5–32]

The drafters of the revised UCC greatly simplified the analysis of these issues. They made it essentially a **two-step process**, whereby the "knockout rule" applies to all transactions. First, so long as there has been a "definite and seasonable expression of acceptance" in the second form, then a contract has been formed [§ 2R–206(3)]. Then, the terms of the contract are just those on which the parties agree and any supplemental terms implied by Article 2R. That is, any additional or different terms are "knocked out."

H. THE RESTATEMENT VIEW. [§ 5–33]

Sections 59 and 61 of the Restatement 2d embody some of the provisions of 2–207, most specifically regarding formation. Section 61 allows an acceptance to be valid if it has additional or different terms, "unless the acceptance is made to depend on an assent to the changed or added terms." Section 59 provides the converse, namely that "a reply to an offer which purports to accept it" but which is "conditioned on the offeror's assent to" the additional or different terms is a counter-offer.

What the Restatement does not directly confront is whether, if the purported acceptance is judged a counter-offer under § 59, does the last shot doctrine still apply or does a "knockout" rule similar to 2–207(3) apply. The cases are mixed, with some adopting 2–207(3) "by analogy" and others using common law's mirror image rule.

I. "BATTLE OF THE FORMS" UNDER THE CISG. [§ 5–34*]

Article 19 of the CISG is the "battle of the forms" provision of the CISG. Article 19(1) is the general rule, and Article 19(1) provides that **any purported acceptance with any dissimilarity from the offer is presumptively a counter-offer**: "A reply to an offer which purports to be an acceptance but contains additions, limitations, or other modifications is a rejection of the offer and constitutes a counter-offer." Hence, the general rule adopts the "last shot" doctrine of our common law.

However, the effect of Article 19(1) is limited by Article 19(2), which provides that despite the language of Article 19(1), a purported acceptance containing any "additional or different terms *which do not materially alter the terms of an offer*" **constitute an acceptance**, and the resulting contract contains those non-materially altering terms, unless the offeror objects. Hence, if the purported acceptance contains only non-essential additional or different terms it operates as an acceptance. However, when the offeree's term is "material," it is a counter-offer. The question becomes what terms are material under the CISG? This is answered below.

Article 19(3) sets forth examples of terms in the purported acceptance which materially alter the deal, which include terms relating to price, time of payment, quality of goods, quantity of goods, place and time of delivery, and procedures to settle disputes under the agreement such as arbitration.

---

* For more information, listen to CD # 3, Track 12 of *Sum and Substance Audio on Contracts*.

CHAPTER 6

THE INDEFINITENESS DOCTRINE

A. THE INDEFINITENESS DOCTRINE: DEFINED AND DISCUSSED. [§ 6–1*]

The indefiniteness doctrine provides that a contract is not enforceable when a court cannot determine the agreement's essential or material terms, or cannot, with sufficient precision, fashion an appropriate remedy for its breach. Indefiniteness is an issue both with respect to the offer itself [Restatement 2d § 33(1)], and with respect to the *entire* agreement [Restatement 2d § 33(2)]. In the former situation, even if the communication is understood to be an offer, "it cannot be accepted so as to form a contract" unless "the terms of the contract are reasonably certain" [Restatement 2d § 33(1)]. In the latter situation, the resulting agreement of the parties is not enforceable unless "they provide a basis for determining the existence of a breach and for giving an appropriate remedy" [Restatement 2d § 33(2)].

Most indefiniteness cases deal only with the resulting contract, and not just the offer. Accordingly, the remainder of this chapter will deal with the situation in which there has been an offer and acceptance and the issue is whether the agreement is definite enough to be enforced.

1. Rationales for the Indefiniteness Doctrine. [§ 6–2]

Three reasons are generally given as to why a court will not enforce a contract when it cannot ascertain essential terms with sufficient certainty:

(1) if a court does not know what a term to a contract is, the court cannot tell whether that term was breached;

(2) if a court does not know what a term to a contract is, it cannot fashion an appropriate remedy for the breach of that term; and

---

* For more information, listen to CD # 9, Track 3 of *Sum and Substance Audio on Contracts*, Part 8, Tracks 1 and 2.

(3) courts have traditionally expressed a reluctance to rewrite a contract for the parties, which they would have to do in order to enforce an indefinite agreement. In other words, the traditional view is that, "courts interpret contracts, but do not write them."

a. **Example. [§ 6–3]**

Max enters into a contract with Kathleen whereby Kathleen is to build a custom made grandfather clock for Max. They agreed as to the price and the design of the clock, but they did not agree as to when delivery was due. Eight months later, the clock had not been delivered and Max sued for breach of contract. Under a strict application of the common law indefiniteness doctrine (*see* § 6–10), Kathleen would prevail because the agreement would be unenforceable. This is so because:

(1) the court cannot tell when delivery is due, so it cannot tell whether the contract has been breached;

(2) even if the court could tell that the contract has been breached, because the clock had to be delivered *sometime,* it cannot fashion an appropriate remedy, for it is impossible to tell on what date damages began to run; and

(3) to make the contract definite, the court would have to rewrite it and insert a delivery term, something courts at common law at least were generally unwilling to do.

2. **Types of Indefiniteness Cases. [§ 6–4*]**

There are three types of fact situations where the indefiniteness doctrine comes into play:

(1) **Where the parties to a contract have not agreed to a term, i.e., a term like delivery or price or delivery date is left out of their agreement for some reason** [§ 6–5];

(2) **Where the parties have agreed to a term, but the term itself is so ambiguous that it is impossible to ascertain its meaning, e.g., the parties agree to the purchase and sale of a "schemer" of televisions** [§ 6–6]; **and**

(3) **Where the parties have "agreed to agree" to negotiate a term sometime after contract formation, but then never reach an agreement on that point** [§ 6–7].

---

* For more information, listen to CD # 9, Track 3 of *Sum and Substance Audio on Contracts.*

THE INDEFINITENESS DOCTRINE

a. **Example Where Parties Have Not Agreed to a Term. [§ 6–5]**

The hypothetical between Kathleen and Max described in § 6–3, is an example of a case where the parties **have not agreed to a term**.

b. **Example Where an Agreed upon Term Is Too Ambiguous to Be Enforced:** *Varney v. Ditmars.* **[§ 6–6*]**

Employer promises employee a salary "plus a fair share of the profits" if employee does good work. This is an example of a situation where the parties have reached an agreement as to a term, but the **term is so ambiguous** that a court has no basis on which to determine whether it has been breached, or no basis to fashion a remedy even if it could be determined that a breach occurred for it does not know what a "fair" amount of the profits would be, especially when the parties likely have different interpretations of the term. [*See* Case Squibs, *Varney v. Ditmars*, 111 N.E. 822 (N.Y Ct. App. 1911)].

c. **Example When There Is an "Agreement to Agree." [§ 6–7]**

Elliot tells June, "We've got a deal. I'll touch base with you later and we'll work out the payment terms." June agrees with this statement. However, if the parties never reach an agreement as to the payment terms, either because they never discuss it or because they do discuss it but cannot reach a subsequent agreement, it is an example of the **"agreement to agree"** type of indefiniteness problem. The contract fails for indefiniteness because a court can't figure out when the buyer would be in breach for failing to pay the purchase price—maybe the terms are "You'll pay me in 10 years." The court doesn't know and does not want to rewrite the contract without authority to do so.

3. **Indefiniteness Distinguished from Failure to Make a Contract. [§ 6–8]**

The more essential terms the parties leave out of a deal, the greater the likelihood that they never had a contract in the first place. However, whether they exhibited sufficient mutual assent to establish a contract is an issue of formation, not indefiniteness. The indefiniteness doctrine presupposes the parties had a contract, but states that one or more terms may be so indefinite that a court cannot enforce the contract.

---

* For more information, listen to CD # 9, Track 4 of *Sum and Substance Audio on Contracts*.

CHAPTER 6

4. **Indefiniteness Doctrine Only Applies to Essential Terms. [§ 6–9]**

There does not have to be agreement or clarity as to <u>all</u> terms in order for an offer or an agreement to satisfy indefiniteness. Only "material" or "essential" terms must be set forth with clarity. Typical "essential" terms are set forth in the next section.

B. COMMON LAW RULE ON INDEFINITENESS. [§ 6–10*]

While scholars disagree as to exactly what terms were so essential to a contract before a common law court would find an agreement sufficiently definite and thus enforceable, the general thinking was that the parties had to manifest understandable agreement about:

(1) The **subject matter** of the contract;

(2) The **quantity** to be purchased;

(3) The **price**;

(4) The **time of performance**;

(5) The **place of performance**; and

(6) **Payment terms**.

The early common law courts were relatively strict in applying the rule and so failure to include any one of these terms in a particular deal probably was enough to run afoul of the indefiniteness doctrine and render a contract unenforceable.

C. MODERN RULE ON INDEFINITENESS. [§ 6–11]

Modern contract law has relaxed, but not eliminated, the indefiniteness rule. It has **not** done so by changing the wording of the rule itself, for under both the Restatement and the UCC a contract will fail for indefiniteness if the court cannot find a reasonably certain basis to determine the existence of a breach or to fashion an appropriate remedy [Restatement 2d § 33(2); UCC § 2–204(3)]. Rather, modern contract law has relaxed the indefiniteness rule by applying it differently and by granting a court the authority to insert terms into the agreement to "save" it from becoming enforceable due to indefiniteness. It has done so in two ways.

First, regarding cases in which the parties have agreed to a term, but the term seems ambiguous on its face, courts are now more willing to examine the circumstances surrounding a transaction so as to **interpret** the

---

* For more information, listen to CD # 9, Track 4 of *Sum and Substance Audio on Contracts*.

THE INDEFINITENESS DOCTRINE

language in a way to give definite effect to an ambiguous term (*see* Chapter Nineteen for an explanation of interpretation rules).

Second, as to those cases in which the parties have not reached an agreement as to a particular term, modern courts are far more willing to examine the circumstances surrounding a transaction so as to **imply** a reasonable term that may fill in the "gaps" left by the parties. In other words, if a court finds evidence that a bargain has been made, it will try to enforce that bargain if there is a means of doing so. Hence, the adage given above that courts "will interpret contracts but not rewrite them" has subsided a bit because the law gives the courts the authority to rewrite the agreement and insert a term in many circumstances.

There are, however, limitations to each of these doctrines. The real question in modern law is: under what circumstances will a court act, and under what circumstances will it refuse to act, to cure any indefiniteness problem? Article 2 of the UCC is cited as the forefront of the thinking on how to ease the indefiniteness rules, and its approach is discussed in the next few sections.

1. **The UCC Approach to Indefiniteness: The Gap Fillers. [§ 6–12*]**

   The drafters of the UCC approached indefiniteness by including provisions that become operative if the parties have not reached a final agreement on certain terms under their contract. That is, when the parties have left "gaps" in their contract regarding these terms, the UCC provides "gap fillers" that a court can insert into the agreement so that it has a basis to decide whether a party is in breach, and how to fashion a remedy to deal with it if a breach is found. The UCC-gap fillers govern:

   (1) The **price of the goods** the buyer must pay and the price the seller must accept [UCC § 2–305; § 6–17];

   (2) The **mode of delivery** [UCC § 2–307; § 6–18];

   (3) The **place of delivery** [UCC § 2–308; § 6–19];

   (4) The **time of delivery** [UCC § 2–309; § 6–20]; and

   (5) The **time and place for payment** [UCC § 2–310; § 6–21].

   Before discussing each gap filler individually, three points need be made.

   a. **Gap Fillers Are NOT Effective Unless an Otherwise Enforceable Contract Has Been Formed. [§ 6–13]**

      While gap fillers play an important role in the operation of a contract, they play **no** role in its formation. Thus, if the parties

---

* For more information, listen to CD # 9, Track 5 *Sum and Substance Audio on Contracts*.

agree on all terms except time of delivery, and leave a negotiation saying, "We've almost got a deal; if we can just work out the time of delivery, we will have a contract," the fact that there is a gap filler for time of delivery is irrelevant because the parties do not have an otherwise enforceable contract. [UCC § 2–305(4).]

b. **Gap Fillers ARE Effective When the Parties Make Agreements to Agree. [§ 6–14]**

Under the UCC, a gap filler is effective when the parties evidence a mutual intent to be bound, but "agree to agree" later on about a term covered by a gap filler. If, after contract formation, they do not reach an agreement as to that term, either because they forget to talk about it or because they cannot later agree, an applicable gap filler will be operative [UCC § 2–305, Cmt. 1].

c. **Gap Fillers Are NOT Effective if the Parties Make a Specific Agreement to the Contrary. [§ 6–15]**

Gap fillers only spring into existence if the parties to an enforceable contract have not agreed about a term covered by a gap filler. If the parties otherwise reach an agreement on that term, it is their agreement, not the gap filler, which controls.

2. **Specific Gap Fillers Under the UCC. [§ 6–16]**

The gap fillers are located in Part 3 of Article 2 of the UCC. Each is discussed below.

a. **Gap Filler as to Price: Reasonable Price. [§ 6–17]**

One of the more remarkable aspects of the UCC is that it allows parties to enforce a contract even though they did not agree on the price to be paid for a particular good. **If nothing is said as to price, or if the price is left to be agreed upon by the parties and they later fail to agree, the price for the goods will be "a reasonable price at time of delivery"** [UCC § 2–305]. Thus, when a builder calls a hardware store and orders 100 feet of PVC pipe to be delivered to a job site, the contractor has implicitly made an enforceable promise to pay a reasonable price pending at the time of delivery for the pipe. Generally, the reasonable price under the UCC is the market price for the goods.

b. **Gap Filler Regarding Mode of Delivery: Delivery in a Single Lot. [§ 6–18]**

As a general rule, a **buyer is entitled to demand delivery of all goods called for in a single contract in one lot, i.e., at** one time; similarly, **the seller is entitled to deliver them in one lot** [UCC § 2–307]. However, where circumstances make it **reasonable** either to make or accept delivery in several lots and, in **good faith**, the other party would **not be harmed** by such action, delivery or acceptance in multiple lots is required [UCC § 2–307, Cmt. 3]. For example, if the buyer does not have the storage space to accept the entire order at once, and if delivering the shipment in lots would not unduly inconvenience the seller, the buyer can demand delivery in lots.

c. **Gap Filler Regarding Place of Delivery: The Seller's Place of Business. [§ 6–19]**

As a general rule, **if the place of delivery is not agreed upon by the parties, delivery is to occur at the <u>seller's</u> place of business or residence. However, for specific goods located somewhere else (e.g., a racehorse in a particular paddock), delivery is to take place at the location of the specified goods if the parties know of the place at the time of contracting** [UCC § 2–308]. In other words, in the absence of a contrary agreement, the cost of delivering the goods to the buyer is always a post-contractual cost to be paid for by the buyer and not assumed to be included in the sales price.

d. **Gap Filler Regarding Time of Delivery: Reasonable Time. [§ 6–20]**

If no time for shipment or delivery is agreed upon, **the seller must tender the goods within "a reasonable time."** What is reasonable depends on all the circumstances, e.g., how complicated the good is to make, past dealings of the parties, the practice within the industry, the needs of the buyer, etc. [UCC § 2–309].

e. **Gap Filler Regarding Time of Payment: Payment Due at Time and Place of Delivery. [§ 6–21]**

In the absence of an agreement as to payment terms, **payment is due at the time and place at which the buyer is to receive the goods** [UCC § 2–310(a)].

f. **No Gap Fillers Regarding Subject Matter of the Contract or Quantity. [§ 6–22]**

In deciding what the gap fillers would be, the drafters of the UCC tried to decide what the parties probably would have chosen had they reached an agreement on the matter. However, there are two things about which it is impossible to say what the parties "probably" would have done had they reached an agreement: (1) **what** the parties bargained for, i.e., the subject matter of the contract; and (2) the **quantity** of goods the parties would want to exchange. There is no gap filler for these terms, thus the failure to agree on them results in an unenforceable contract due to indefiniteness even under the UCC [UCC § 2–204].

3. **The Restatement Approach to the Indefiniteness Doctrine. [§ 6–23]**

Like the UCC, the Restatement directs that the common law indefiniteness rule should be loosened. However, unlike the UCC, the Restatement does not provide specific gap fillers for specific terms like price, etc. Nonetheless, Restatement 2d § 204 gives a court broad powers in trying to "save" a contract from indefiniteness: "When the parties to a bargain sufficiently defined to be a contract have not agreed with respect to a term which is essential to a determination of their rights and duties, **a term which is reasonable under the circumstances is supplied by the court.**" In some ways this is a broader mandate even than under the UCC for it is not limited to particular areas such as price and delivery, but potentially allows a court to insert any reasonable term to determine the rights of the parties. Section 204, coupled with the comments to Restatement 2d § 33 suggest that some of the "reasonable" terms to be supplied would include UCC gap fillers.

For example, in a contract for the sale of a residence where no date for transfer of the deed is mentioned, if the buyer can show that the seller has hired a moving van to move out of the house on July 1, a court is entitled to imply July 1 as the closing date for the transaction. Even if there is no such objective evidence, a court can examine the trade practice and assign a reasonable date for closing for it is a term necessary to determine the rights of the parties [Restatement 2d § 33, Cmt. a; Restatement 2d § 204].

   a. **Agreements to Agree in Non-UCC Transactions. [§ 6–24]**

   Traditionally, courts have been reluctant to enforce non-UCC contracts where the parties have "agreed to agree," but subsequently failed to do so. The Restatement, however, suggests that, at least for some terms, courts should take the UCC approach and imply a reasonable term to fill in when the parties fail to reach a post-contractual agreement after agreeing to do so. [Restatement 2d § 33, Cmts. d and e]. Thus, there is reason to think the modern trend will lean towards a greater enforcement of contracts where particular promises left for future negotiation and agreement are never reached, but there are still plenty of cases which hold to the old rule and do not insert a term where there is an express agreement to agree, followed by a failure to reach agreement on that term.

THE INDEFINITENESS DOCTRINE

For example, assume that under a lease the parties provide a fixed rent for the first ten years, but then give the tenant the right to lease the premises for the subsequent ten years at a rent "to be agreed on after the initial ten year term." The tenant wants to continue to occupy the premises for years 11–20, but the parties are unable to reach agreement on a rental amount. If this were a UCC agreement, the court is empowered to supply a reasonable rental amount. However, because a lease is not governed by the UCC, the traditional (and still majority) rule is that a court will not enforce the lease for years 11–20 because there was an agreement to agree on a material term, and no agreement as to that term was reached. The majority rule rests on the notion that the parties themselves have agreed that they will have no future enforceable contract unless they actually and subjectively agree, and a court is reluctant to impose a "reasonableness" requirement in light of the express intent of the parties. For example, maybe the landlord only wants to rent out the space for the next ten years if she can get a premium on the space; otherwise, she will use it for her own purposes. And suppose the tenant believes that rents will go down in the area over the next ten years and so thinks a "reasonable" rate is one below the current market. It is because these subjective rationales are practically unknowable to a court that allows for the common law and Restatement rule that when there is an "agree to agree" clause, and no agreement is reached, the court will not force the parties into a "reasonable" contract.

However, as noted above, there is some growing support to allow a court to insert a "fair" rent amount and enforce the contract even in non-UCC contracts. Of course, if the parties specifically agreed to renew the lease at "market rates" a court could take testimony as to the appropriate rent and insert a price term because the parties have agreed to use a commercial standard, even if they do not agree at the time as to what that standard is.

D. PART PERFORMANCE AS A CURE FOR INDEFINITENESS. [§ 6–25*]

Under both the UCC and the Restatement, past performance of a contract may act to cure an indefinite contract and make it enforceable. For example, a grocery store makes a contract with a fruit wholesaler for the delivery of, "10 bushels of apples per week for the next year." The contract, as written, may fail for indefiniteness as it is not possible to tell on its face what kinds of apples are contemplated. However, if the wholesaler delivers Granny Smith apples each week for three months, and the store

---

* For more information, listen to CD # 9, Track 6 of *Sum and Substance Audio on Contracts*.

CHAPTER 6

accepts them, this past performance has likely cured any future indefiniteness problem as to the subject matter of the contract. [*See* the discussion of course of dealing in § 6–26].

E. USAGE OF TRADE, COURSE OF DEALING, AND COURSE OF PERFORMANCE AS CURES FOR INDEFINITENESS. [§ 6–26*]

When appropriate, a properly proven usage of trade, course of dealing, or course of performance can be used to cure an indefinite contract. For example, a contract calls for Contractor to deliver "a load" of gravel to a building. If within the trade "a load" has a more specific meaning, e.g., 100 pounds, then understood **usage of trade** will make the contract enforceable. [UCC § 1–303(c); Restatement 2d § 222]

Course of dealing refers to the performance of the parties in similar transactions in the past under the same or similar contractual language. For example, suppose last year the parties had a contract with a term requiring delivery "10 days after ordering," and under that contract, they had operated such that it was 10 business days and not 10 calendar days. Today they enter into a separate contract with the same "10 day" term. It is likely the "10 day" term in the current contract would be interpreted as 10 calendar days as well, based on their prior course of dealing. [UCC § 1–303(b); Restatement 2d § 223]

Course of performance looks at how the parties have operated under the current contract to interpret a potentially ambiguous term. The example with the Granny Smith apples above in § 6–25 is an example of a court being able to interpret the term "apples" to mean Granny Smith apples and cure any indefiniteness concerns using the parties "course of performance." [UCC § 1–303(a), (c); Restatement 2d §§ 219–222]

[*See* §§ 20–9 *et seq.* for a definition and discussion of these terms.]

F. INDEFINITENESS UNDER THE CISG. [§ 6–27**]

In Article 14(1), the CISG provides that an offer (or in CISG terms, a "proposal") is ineffective if it is not "sufficiently definite." That provision continues and states that an offer is "sufficiently definite if it indicates the goods [i.e., the subject matter] and expressly or implicitly fixes or makes provision for determining the quantity and the price."

---

* For more information, listen to CD # 9, Track 6 of *Sum and Substance Audio on Contracts.*

** For more information, listen to CD # 9, Track 6 of *Sum and Substance Audio on Contracts.*

THE INDEFINITENESS DOCTRINE

G. EXAM APPROACH TO INDEFINITENESS ISSUES. [§ 6–28*]

As you analyze your fact situation on an examination, first check to see if just the offer itself is definite. If it is not, it cannot be validly accepted. If you are presented with a completed contract to analyze, check to see whether the contracting parties:

1. have failed to agree to a term [§ 6–5];

2. have agreed to a term that is ambiguous (*see* [§ 6–6]; or

3. have "agreed to agree" to a term sometime after contract formation [§ 6–7].

If you have any of those situations, next determine whether the term is "essential," for only the absence of a clear enough essential or material term will make a contract unenforceable due to indefiniteness.

Next, determine whether one of the modern doctrines designed to encourage the enforceability of indefinite contracts can save the contract at issue, i.e., determine whether the contract can be made enforceable due to:

A. The "agree to agree" rules of modern contract law under the UCC [§§ 6–14; 6–24];

B. Gap Fillers or the general authority given in Restatement 2d § 204 [§§ 6–12; 6–23];

C. Interpretation [§ 6–11];

D. Past Performance, Usage of Trade, or Course of Dealing [§§ 6–25; 6–26]; or

E. Reference by the parties to a commercial or fair market standard in their contract, e.g., "The contract can be renewed by the tenant for an additional ten years at then-pending 'market rates.'"

---

* For more information, listen to CD # 9, Track 7 of *Sum and Substance Audio on Contracts*.

PART III

CONSIDERATION AND ITS "SUBSTITUTES" (WITH A SPECIAL TREATMENT OF MODIFICATIONS)

Chapter 7

Consideration

A. THE CONSIDERATION DOCTRINE. [§ 7–1*]

Not all promises, even those made in offers and acceptances, are enforceable. The doctrine of consideration is the theory that separates those promises that will be enforced from those that will not. If a promise, or subsequent agreement, is not supported by valid consideration, that promise or agreement is generally not enforceable.

A few points on the history of consideration. First, consideration is totally made up. There is nothing inherent in the law of contracts requires it. We could decide, as a legal community, to enforce all "serious" promises, and then consideration would not be necessary. But we do not. There will be many examples given in the chapter of the types of promises we do not enforce, but one of them is the so-called "gift" promises. So if Uncle promises to give Niece $10,000 when she turns 21 to give her a start in life, it may be a "serious" promise, but as we will see, it lacks consideration and so will not be enforceable in contract.

Second, there was no consideration doctrine until the seventeenth century at the earliest, and even then it took decades for it to be flushed out by the common law courts.

Thirdly, all western legal systems have independently generated consideration as a principle of its contract law. There are some variations among them, but the gist of each is similar. So while consideration may not be an "inherent" part of contract law, all legal systems recognize that all promises cannot be enforced by the courts, and so some sort of consideration has been developed.

Finally, many contracts classes and texts begin with a study of consideration. If your class proceeds that way, note that much time is spent in the first few weeks learning that consideration must be present for a valid contract. Indeed, the title of the section covering Restatement 2d §§ 71–81 (the sections usually covered at first) is, "The *Requirement* of Consideration."

---

* For more information, listen to CD # 4, Track 1 of *Sum and Substance Audio on Contracts*.

However, most classes thereafter move to Restatement 2d §§ 82–96, which are part of the Restatement section entitled "Contracts [Enforceable] *Without* Consideration." So know from the beginning that while most contracts require consideration to be enforceable, *not all do.* There will be situations in which valid contracts are formed without consideration. Also, there are situations in which the definition of consideration is met, but the agreement is nevertheless unenforceable. Finally, know that even if a contract is rendered unenforceable due to a lack of consideration, some of the promises made in the agreement may be enforceable to some extent by promissory estoppel, which is covered in this book in Chapter Eight.

B. DEFINITIONS OF CONSIDERATION. [§ 7–2]

Over time, the generally accepted definition of consideration has changed. However, as noted in § 7–11, while it is important to study these definitions, none of them completely explain <u>all</u> the situations in which consideration will or will not be found by modern courts. Thus, while the concepts contained in the various definitions are important and need to be learned, you should keep in mind that **no one definition completely describes all the contours of the consideration doctrine**.

1. The "Will" Theory. [§ 7–3]

   This theory was most prevalent in *early* common law. Under it, a promise was supported by consideration (and thus enforceable) as long as the promisor had the "will" to be legally bound at the time the promise was made. This is close to the "serious promise" theory mentioned above. While courts tried to look at objective factors to determine the "will" of the parties, in truth it was a highly subjective test, and given both the trend and need for a more objective test of consideration, the "will" theory is no longer used. However, a few casebooks still include cases decided under the will theory.

2. The "Benefit/Detriment" Theory. [§ 7–4]

   Under this theory, a promise is deemed supported by consideration (and thus enforceable), whenever:

   (1) The promisee either acts, or promises to act, **in exchange for the promisor's promise;** *and*

   (2) The promisee's act, or promised act, is *either* a **legal detriment to the promisee** or a **legal benefit to the promisor.**

   Note that each party to a bilateral contract is both a promisor (the maker of a promise) and a promisee (the recipient of a promise). The offeror makes the initial promise, but then is the promisee of the offeree's return promise in the acceptance. The offeree is a promisee of the offer, but a promisor with regard to his, her, or its acceptance.

CONSIDERATION

While the definition sounds a bit complicated and technical, in practice it is fairly straightforward as illustrated immediately below.

    a. **Example: Analysis of a Unilateral Contract Using the "Benefit/Detriment" Theory. [§ 7–5]**

Eric makes an offer to enter into a unilateral contract with Holly, promising to pay her $1,000 for her watch. If Holly gives Eric her watch in exchange for his promise to pay the $1,000 (thereby accepting the offer), Eric's promise to pay the $1,000 is enforceable under the benefit/detriment theory. That is, Holly, the promisee, suffered a **legal detriment** (i.e., she gave up possession of her watch), and Eric, the promisor, received a **legal benefit** (i.e., he obtained possession of a watch that he previously did not have a right to). Further, the detriment and benefit were given **in exchange for Eric's promise** to pay the $1,000. Thus, the parties have entered into a valid, enforceable unilateral contract with a promissory offer, an acceptance by conduct, and consideration under the "benefit/detriment" theory to enforce Eric's promise to pay.

    b. **Example: Analysis of a Bilateral Contract Using the "Benefit/Detriment" Theory. [§ 7–6]**

Assume that instead of immediately handing the watch to Eric in response to his offer to pay $1,000 for her watch, this time Holly promises to give Eric her watch at a later point. Eric's promise to pay is enforceable, for Holly suffered a **legal detriment** (she promised to give up possession of the watch), and Eric received a **legal benefit** (he was promised possession of the watch) **in exchange for his promise** of the $1,000 payment. Note also that **Holly's** promise to give up the watch (i.e., her promissory acceptance) is also enforceable. Eric suffered a legal detriment (he promised to pay $1,000), and Holly obtained a legal benefit (receipt of Eric's promise to pay), **in exchange** for Holly's promise to tender the watch. As such, the parties have entered into a valid, enforceable bilateral contract, with a promissory offer, a promissory acceptance, and consideration under the "benefit/detriment" theory to support the executory promises.

3. **The Restatement's "Bargain" Theory. [§ 7–7]**

The Restatement (both First and Second) rejected the benefit/detriment theory in favor of the "bargain" theory. Under this approach, "[t]o constitute consideration, a performance or return promise must be bargained for" [Restatement 2d § 71(1)]. Thus, under the Restatement, it is irrelevant that a party either suffers a detriment or reaps a benefit [Restatement 2d § 79(a)], as long as the return promise or requested performance sought by the promisor is **bargained for**.

Of course, this definition raises the question of when is a promise "bargained for." Under § 71(2) of the Restatement 2d, a performance is *bargained for* if:

(1) It is **sought by** the promisor *in exchange* for his or her promise; and

(2) It is **given by** the promisee *in exchange* for that promise.

Once again, while the definition may seem formidable, application of the bargain theory is also relatively straightforward as seen below.

a. **Example: Analysis of a Unilateral Contract Using the "Bargain" Theory. [§ 7–8]**

(Assume the same facts in the Holly/Eric transaction as set forth in § 7–5.) Eric's promise to pay the $1,000 is enforceable under the bargain theory. That is, Holly's act in giving up the watch was "bargained for" because it was both **sought by** Eric (the promisor), and **given by** Holly (the promisee), **in exchange** for Eric's promise to pay. Thus, the parties entered into a valid enforceable unilateral contract, with a promissory offer, an acceptance by conduct, and consideration under the "bargain" theory sufficient to enforce Eric's executory promise.

b. **Example: Analysis of a Bilateral Contract Using the "Bargain" Theory. [§ 7–9]**

(Assume the same facts in the Holly/Eric transaction as analyzed in § 7–5.) Eric's promise to pay the $1,000 is enforceable, for Holly's promised performance (her promise to tender the watch at a later time), was legally "bargained for"; i.e., it was **sought by** Eric, and **given in exchange** for Holly's promise to pay. Similarly, Holly's promise to tender the watch is enforceable, for Eric's performance (his promise to pay $1,000), was **sought by Holly**, and **given in exchange** for her promise to deliver the watch. Thus, the parties entered into a valid, enforceable bilateral contract, with a promissory offer, a promissory acceptance, and consideration under the "bargain" theory sufficient to enforce the executory promises.

4. **Modern Contract Law's Acceptance of the Benefit/Detriment and Bargain Theories of Consideration. [§ 7–10]**

The Restatement 2d's bargain theory of consideration is the preeminent view of consideration used in modern contract law. However, the idea that the promisee must suffer a legal detriment or the promisor must obtain a legal benefit is still recited to a great extent by modern courts when discussing consideration principles. Indeed, on occasion some courts have even combined the two tests, stating that consideration is present when there has been a *benefit and/or detriment* that was **bargained for** (rather than merely given "in exchange" as required by the benefit/detriment test.) The reason benefits and detriments are still recited so frequently by courts is probably that, as a practical matter, there are few occasions in which a promise will be enforceable under one theory and not the other, and also probably because the benefit/detriment theory is studied so much in law school.

5. Criticism of Consideration Definitions. [§ 7–11]

Many prominent contracts scholars have criticized both the benefit/detriment and bargain theories of consideration as insufficient to explain all cases. As indicated above, there are times when a promisee suffers a legal detriment or a promisor reaps a legal benefit in exchange for a promise, and for policy reasons, we have determined there will be no consideration present and the resulting agreement unenforceable. Similarly, there are cases in which a party's promises or performances are clearly bargained for, yet they still will not be enforced [*see* e.g., § 7–71]. As a result, it is probably more accurate to think of *consideration as the general doctrine that governs which promises will be enforced*, and to recognize there are going to be discrete factual situations in which the definition does not explain the result. So you should concentrate on learning the rules governing the "exceptions," rather than trying to "fit" the definitions of consideration into each of these types of transactions.

To be consistent, most of the examples in this Chapter will be analyzed using the language of the "bargain" theory, but the results would be the same using "benefit/detriment" terminology as well.

C. TYPES OF CONSIDERATION IN UNILATERAL CONTRACTS UNDER THE RESTATEMENT'S BARGAIN THEORY. [§ 7–12]

In a unilateral contract, the consideration supporting the offeror's promise consists of one of the following bargained for elements under the Restatement:

(1) An **act;**

(2) A **forbearance;** or

(3) The **creation, modification, or destruction of a legal relationship** [Restatement 2d § 71(2), (3)].

To support the enforceability of the promises made in a unilateral contract, and thus be deemed as valid consideration, **one** of these three elements must be sought by the promisor and undertaken by the promisee in exchange for the promise made in the offer.

1. **Example of an "Act" Serving as Consideration. [§ 7–13]**

   Frank offers to pay Larry $800 for Larry's couch if Larry will deliver it to Frank's house by 5:00. Larry's delivery of the couch is sufficient consideration to make Frank's promise to pay enforceable, for it is an **act** taken by the promisee (Larry), which was both **sought by the promisor** (Frank), and **given *in exchange* for the promise to pay.**

2. **Example of "Forbearance" to Serve as Consideration:** *Hamer v. Sidway.* **[§ 7–14*]**

   Uncle offers to pay 16-year-old nephew $1,000 if nephew refrains from smoking or drinking until age 21. If nephew does not drink or smoke until age 21, the uncle's promise to pay is supported by consideration (and thus enforceable), for nephew undertook a **forbearance *in exchange*** for uncle's promise, and that forbearance was **sought by** Uncle when he made his offer. [*See* Case Squibs section, *Hamer v. Sidway*.]

3. **Example of "Destruction of a Legal Relationship" as Consideration. [§ 7–15]**

   Greg has a 30-year $100,000 mortgage at 4% interest. He offers to pay $90,000 in cash today if the bank will cancel the 30-year loan. If the Bank agrees and cancels the loan, that act is sufficient consideration to enforce Greg's promise to pay, for it is a **destruction of a legal relationship**, undertaken *in exchange* for Greg's promise, and was an action Greg **sought** in making his offer.

4. **Example of "Modification of a Legal Relationship" as Consideration. [§ 7–16]**

   Same as above with Greg and his mortgage, except this time Greg offers the bank $1,500 today if the bank will lower the interest rate for the remainder of the loan to 3.75%. If the Bank agrees, sufficient consideration exists to enforce Greg's promise to pay the $1,500, for it is a **modification of a legal relationship**, undertaken **in exchange** for Greg's promise, and was an action Greg **sought** in making his offer.

   Note that the concept of contract modifications is broader than just a consideration issue. Hence, this book covers the concept of modifications generally in Chapter Nine, and so reference should be made to the consideration issues addressed in that chapter for a full

---

* For more information about this case, listen to CD # 4, Track 1 of *Sum and Substance Audio on Contracts.*

understanding of the issues. Further, the effect of consideration on contract modifications under the "pre-existing duty rule" is covered in §§ 7–71 *et seq.*, which also should be studied for a full understanding.

5. **Example of No Consideration Making Agreement Unenforceable. [§ 7–17]**

   Helen gratuitously offers to give her friend Ilene a ride to the airport next month, an offer that Ilene gratefully accepts. Ilene is so pleased, that she rushes out the next day and sends Helen flowers with a note saying, "Thanks for agreeing to give me a ride." Ilene's acts are insufficient consideration to enforce Helen's promise to provide a ride under the bargain theory, for Ilene's act in buying the flowers was not made as part of a bargained for exchange. That is, Ilene may have purchased the flowers **because of** Helen's promise, but Helen did not seek the flowers when she made her promise to drive Ilene to the airport. In other words, Ilene's purchase of the roses was a gift, and hence not part of the **bargain** necessary under the Restatement for the promise of a ride to the airport to be enforceable.

D. TYPES OF CONSIDERATION IN BILATERAL CONTRACTS UNDER THE RESTATEMENT'S BARGAIN THEORY. [§ 7–18]

Under the Restatement, in a bilateral contract, **each party's promise serves as consideration for the return promise of the other** if, but only if:

   (1) Each promise was **sought by**, and was **given in exchange for** the other; and

   (2) The performance promised by each party would be **valid consideration if it were carried out** [Restatement 2d § 75].

In other words, any promise made in a valid offer to enter into a bilateral contract serves as consideration for any promise made in the acceptance, and **vice versa**, so long as the offer and acceptance were bargained in exchange for each other, and so long as the promised performance, if completed, would be valid consideration, i.e., the promises are either of an **act**; a **forbearance**; or the **creation, modification, or destruction, of a legal relationship**.

1. **Example. [§ 7–19]**

   Ken offers to pay a furniture store $1,200 in three equal monthly payments for a living room set. Furniture store accepts that offer, promising to deliver the furniture next week. The contract is supported by consideration because:

(1) the promise to pay and the promise to deliver the furniture were **sought by** each other, and were given **in exchange for** each other; and

(2) if completed, the acts called for by each party's promise would be valid consideration, i.e., delivery of the furniture is an **"act"** sufficient to support the promise, and payment is similarly an **"act"** sufficient to support Ken's promise.

E. THE RETURN PROMISES OR PERFORMANCES BY THE PROMISEE CAN BE VALID CONSIDERATION EVEN IF GIVEN TO A THIRD PARTY. [§ 7–20*]

Consideration can still be valid even if it is a third party that either gives a return promise or undertakes an action in a transaction. So long as the promisee's performance or promised performance was bargained for and given in exchange for the promisor's promise, the consideration is valid even if it goes to or comes from a third party [Restatement 2d § 71(4)].

1. Example. [§ 7–21]

   Claire owes Barbara $10. Additionally, Claire owns a DVD that Ann wants. If Ann agrees to pay Barbara $10 to settle Claire's debt in return for Claire's promise to give Ann the DVD, the promise to pay the $10 and the promise to deliver the DVD are enforceable, even though a third party is involved. That is because each promise was sought, **bargained for**, and given *in exchange* for the other, and would be valid consideration if carried out.

F. TRANSACTIONS WITHOUT CONSIDERATION DUE TO THE LACK OF A BARGAINED FOR EXCHANGE. [§ 7–22**]

As mentioned above, to be enforceable under the bargain theory, the performance or promised performance of the promisee must be "bargained for," i.e., sought by and given in exchange for the other party's promise [Restatement 2d § 71]. There are three types of promises or actions which historically have been deemed insufficient to provide consideration for a contract, for they lack this "bargained for exchange" element: (i) gifts or gift promises; (ii) "past" consideration or moral obligation; and (iii) "unsolicited actions." These types of return promises or actions may, on occasion, be given **because of a promise**, but they do not serve as consideration to support a contract for they are not **sought by and given**

---

* For more information, listen to CD # 4, Track 2 of *Sum and Substance Audio on Contracts*.

** For more information, listen to CD # 4, Track 3 of *Sum and Substance Audio on Contracts*.

CONSIDERATION

in exchange for the promise (*see* § 7–17 above). Each of these three situations is discussed in further detail below.

1. **Gratuitous or Gift Promises. [§ 7–23]**

    a. **Traditional Rule: Gift Promises Are Unenforceable Because They Are Not Supported by Consideration. [§ 7–24]**

    The traditional common law rule was that a promise cannot act as consideration if it is made as a gift, rather than as part of a bargained for exchange. Examples are given below, but note also that the traditional rule has been modified by the Restatement so that, in a few enumerated situations, "gift promises" *can* act as consideration. Those circumstances are covered in the "Past Consideration/Moral Obligation" discussion below in §§ 7–30 *et seq.*

    (1) **Example. [§ 7–25]**

    Aunt says to Nephew, "Because today is your birthday, I promise to give you $1,000." Nephew says, "I accept your gracious gift." If the aunt does not pay, her promise cannot be enforced as part of a contract for she only made a gift promise. That is, she did not seek any return promise or action by Nephew when she made her promise. In other words, there was no "bargain" struck between them. As such, the aunt's promise is deemed only a gift or gratuitous promise, and is therefore **unenforceable**.

    (2) **Completed Gift Not Affected by Lack of Consideration. [§ 7–26]**

    The consideration doctrine only makes a **gift promise** unenforceable. If the promisor has already made the gift to the promisee, the rights of the promisor potentially to reclaim it are governed by the law of property, not of contract. Hence, with regard to the Aunt/Nephew situation described in § 7–25, if the Aunt had given Nephew the $1,000, property law, not contract law, would determine whether Nephew would have to return the money if Aunt wanted it back and retracted her promise.

    (3) **Acts "Incidental" to a True Gift Promise Are Insufficient Consideration to Enforce the Promise. [§ 7–27]**

    Occasionally, a promisor will require the promisee to take some sort of action in order to obtain the benefits of a gift promise. **If such action is deemed only <u>incidental</u> to the true gratuitous nature of the promise, the taking**

CHAPTER 7

of such action is insufficient to act as consideration. In order to determine whether the act is incidental or not, the key inquiry is whether the promisor made the promise in order to "get something" from the exchange, i.e., did the promisor <u>seek</u>, or <u>bargain for</u>, some sort of benefit resulting from the promise, or does the act called for merely make the giving of a gift more convenient or necessary for its receipt.

(a) Example. [§ 7–28]

Jay tells his friend Ted, "Drop by tonight on your way home from school because I have a present for you—the mystery novel you've been talking about." Even if Ted drives to Jay's house, such action is likely not sufficient consideration to make enforceable Jay's gift promise to give Ted the book. Jay was not benefitted from making the promise and his request for action was "incidental" to the true nature of the agreement, i.e., the making of a gift. It only made the giving of the gift more convenient. As such, because Jay did not <u>seek</u> or **bargain for** Ted's presence as a result of his promise to transfer possession of the book, the promise to give it to Ted is unenforceable. Hence, if Jay fails to deliver the book after Ted arrives, Ted cannot successfully sue him for breach of contract since the "duty" to deliver the book is not supported by consideration.

Note that if Ted can establish, e.g., that Jay was lonely, and thus actually was bargaining for Ted's company, then consideration may be present because Jay then would have "gotten something" from the transaction. That is, by promising to deliver the book, he would have sought or bargained for a return action by Ted (Ted's company), and Ted's company would have been given in exchange for the promised delivery of the book.

(b) Example of *Kirksey v. Kirksey*. [§ 7–29*]

A relative wrote to recently widowed sister-in-law, "If you come down and see me, I will let you have a place to raise your family." Sister-in-law moved to Alabama with her family, but brother-in-law would not provide her a place to live when she arrived.

---

* For more information about this case, listen to CD # 4, Track 3 of *Sum and Substance Audio on Contracts*.

Held: The offer of a place to live was only a gift promise and thus the actions requested of sister-in-law were merely incidental to the true nature of the offer. In other words, the brother-in-law's offer was a gift, and while it is true that to accept the gift she had to come to Alabama, that trip does not change the fundamental nature of brother-in-law's gift promise. Alabama was where the "gift" had to be accepted, but a gift is all it was. As such, her travel to the brother-in-law's farm was deemed only incidental to the gift and thus insufficient to make the promise of a place to live enforceable. Note that the sister-in-law could recover at least the expenses for her trip to Alabama, and perhaps more, under a theory of promissory estoppel [*see* Chapter Eight].

2. **"Past" Consideration (or "Moral Obligation"). [§ 7–30*]**

   a. **Traditional Rule: "Past" Consideration and Moral Obligation Have the Same Effect as "Gift Promises"— They Are Insufficient to Make the Promise Enforceable. [§ 7–31]**

   Traditionally, where a promise was made in response to some act or forbearance **previously undertaken,** or to some promise **previously made,** the promise was held *insufficient* to act as consideration. This is because, by definition, the promise could not have been made as part of a bargained for exchange. The promise could only have been made after the event occurred and while it may have been made *because of* the event, the person precipitating the previous event could not have sought it when the act was accomplished [§ 7–17] above for another example). As noted above, the "past consideration/moral obligation" rules were part of the "gift promise" doctrine in that a promise made in light of a previously conferred benefit was considered simply an unenforceable gift promise.

   Note this doctrine is sometimes known as "past" consideration. This is a term that many contracts scholars dislike for it is not consideration at all—it describes a situation in which a promise is unenforceable because it is not supported by consideration, rather than, as may be suggested by a literal reading of the words, a type or category of consideration with an adjective preceding it. Nevertheless, this Book will follow the case law which uses the term "past consideration" as a shorthand for an unenforceable promise made because of a past event.

---

* For more information, listen to CD # 4, Track 5 of *Sum and Substance Audio on Contracts.*

CHAPTER 7

(1) Example of *Mills v. Wyman*. [§ 7–32]

Mills cared for Wyman's adult son who fell ill during a sea voyage for a few weeks. Wyman's son did not have funds to pay Mills for his care. Wyman (the father) wrote to Mills expressing his thanks and promised to reimburse Mills for all the expenses incurred in the care of his son. Despite his promise, the elder Wyman never paid Mills, and so Mills sued the father.

Held: Wyman's promise was not supported by sufficient consideration and thus was unenforceable. While the elder Wyman may have felt a moral obligation for Mills's care of his son, the only consideration to support the promise was "past" or moral consideration—a promise made <u>after</u> the acts by Mills were undertaken. In other words Mills was not *seeking a promise of payment* from the elder Wyman when he cared for Wyman's son. As such, there was no bargained for exchange necessary to make Wyman's promise enforceable [*Mills v. Wyman*, 20 Mass. 207 (1825)].

b. Modern Rule: "Past" Consideration and Moral Obligation Can Make *Some* Promises Enforceable. [§ 7–33]

The Restatement, reflecting a general dissatisfaction with the common law rules on these issues, sets forth two situations in which moral obligations stemming from gift promises made in recognition of past acts can now make the promise enforceable:

(1) Where a promise is made **in recognition of a benefit previously conferred on the promisor**, assuming the requirements of Restatement § 86 are met [§ 7–34]; and

(2) Where a promise is made **to pay a debt rendered unenforceable due to running of the statute of limitations or due to bankruptcy** under Restatement §§ 82 and 83 [§ 7–38].

Each of these situations is described below.

(1) Gift Promises Made Enforceable by Past Consideration Under Restatement 2d § 86. [§ 7–34]

Restatement 2d § 86 provides as follows:

A promise made in recognition of a benefit previously received by the promisor is enforceable to the extent necessary to prevent injustice, *unless:*

(1) The promisee intended the benefit received by the promisor as a gift; or

CONSIDERATION

(2) The value of the promisor's promise is disproportionate to the benefit he or she received.

Note that this is not a full abandonment of the past consideration rule, and so each provision of § 86 must be read and applied carefully.

(a) Example of *Webb v. McGowin*. [§ 7–35]

Webb saved McGowin's life and was rendered partially paralyzed in the rescue. To show his gratitude, McGowin promised to make biweekly payments to Webb of $15 until Webb's death.

Under the Restatement 2d approach, McGowin's promise would be enforceable because:

(1) Webb's saving of McGowin's life was <u>not</u> intended as a gift (even though it was not induced by a promise of payment); and

(2) Its value ($15 per month) was not disproportionate to the benefit received by McGowin.

In articulating why McGowin's acts were not gifts, the drafters of the Restatement provided in Cmt. i to § 86 which provides that where a promise is made by a person in need of emergency services, "a positive showing that payment was expected is not then required." In other words, there is a presumption that the services rendered were not intended as a gift, but rather as a socially responsible action undertaken in an emergency. However, if the promisor, who has the burden of proof, can show that a gift was intended, then the promise is unenforceable for lack of consideration [*Webb v. McGowin*, 168 So. 196 (Ala. App. 1935)].

(b) Example of *Mills v. Wyman*. [§ 7–36]

[The facts of *Mills v. Wyman* are given in § 7–32]. Even under the Restatement 2d, Mills still could not enforce Wyman's promise, for the benefit conferred by Mills was received not by the <u>promisor</u> (the "father" Wyman), as required by § 86, but rather by the promisor's son [Restatement 2d § 86, Cmt. a, Ill. 1].

CHAPTER 7

(c) Review Problem. [§ 7–37]

Sue saw Elena, a friend of hers, at another table in a fancy restaurant and asked the waiter to send a bottle of champagne to Elena "with her compliments." Elena was thrilled by the gesture but came over to Sue and said, "That was lovely of you, but I insist on paying you for the champagne."

Question:

Is Elena's promise to pay for the champagne enforceable?

Answer:

Even under the Restatement 2d approach, Elena's promise is not enforceable. While the promise was made in recognition of a benefit previously received by the promisor (sending of the champagne to Elena), and while the value of the promise is proportionate to the benefit received (Elena promised to pay the price of the champagne), the promise still cannot be enforced because Sue originally intended the benefit received by Elena (the champagne) as a gift.

(2) Promises to Pay Debts Made Unenforceable Under the Statute of Limitations or by Bankruptcy Under Restatement §§ 82 and 83. [§ 7–38]

A valid obligation owing under a contract can become unenforceable either because the statute of limitations governing the claim has run, or because the debtor has discharged the obligation in bankruptcy. Despite the unenforceability of the debt, debtors will sometimes promise to "make good" the debt out of a moral obligation. At common law, such promises would be deemed gift promises rendered unenforceable under the "past" consideration rules.

However, the Restatement 2d has drafted special rules governing these situations:

If the debtor acknowledges that he or she still owes a debt, which is only made unenforceable due to the running of the statute of limitations, or if the debtor promises not to assert the statute of limitations as a defense in a subsequent collection suit, such promises are enforceable against the debtor [Restatement 2d § 82].

CONSIDERATION

In addition, if a debtor expressly promises to pay all or part of a contractual debt that is either discharged in bankruptcy, or is dischargeable in bankruptcy proceedings begun before the promise was made, that promise is binding against the debtor [Restatement 2d § 83].

Most states have adopted the rule of § 82, but require that such promises be **in writing** to be effective. Note that under this provision, it is only the *new* promise to pay that is enforceable, not the original debt.

(a) Example. [§ 7–39]

Jack borrows $10,000 from Joy, and is supposed to pay her $11,000 (the $10,000 principal and $1,000 in interest) when the loan is due. Jack fails to pay the debt when due. The statute of limitations expires, and Jack tells Joy he's sorry, and promises that he will repay her the $10,000 by next January 31. If Jack doesn't pay anything by the following January 31, Joy may only sue him for $10,000—the value of the newer promise—and not $11,000—the value of the original debt.

3. Unsolicited Actions Are Insufficient to Act as Consideration. [§ 7–40]

For a promisee's *actions* to be sufficient consideration so as to make the other party's promise enforceable, those *actions* must be sought by, and taken because of, an existing promise. Actions taken without regard to the promise are not sufficient to serve as consideration. This issue most often arises when a party fortuitously accomplishes the acts called for by an offer, but is unaware of the offer while he or she is doing them.

a. Example. [§ 7–41]

In the local newspaper, Harry places an advertisement promising a $100 reward for the return of his lost wallet. Tara, who is unaware of the ad, finds the wallet and independently returns it to Harry. Even though Tara did the acts called for in Harry's offer, her actions were not made as part of a bargain with Harry. That is, she did not return the wallet in exchange for Harry's promise to pay the reward. Thus, her acts cannot serve as consideration under the bargain theory [§ 4–18].

CHAPTER 7

G. SPECIFIC TYPES OF TRANSACTIONS RAISING CONSIDERATION ISSUES. [§ 7–42*]

There are certain types of transactions that inherently raise consideration issues. Each is discussed separately below but once again, the overriding principle is that as long as the promises or performances of one party are both <u>sought by</u> the other in making a promise, and are given *in exchange* for that promise, valid bargained for consideration is probably present.

1. Transaction in Which the Consideration of One Party Is Worth Substantially Less than the Other: The "Peppercorn" Theory of Consideration. [§ 7–43]

Typically, courts will not inquire into the adequacy of one party's consideration, even if its economic value seems disproportionate to the economic value of what the other party got in return [Restatement 2d § 79(b)]. The reason is that the courts will let parties make their own judgments as to how much a return promise or return performance is worth and will not try to impose any objective economic proportionality standards regarding the validity of consideration. Thus (at common law), a peppercorn, or (today) a dollar, etc., can generally serve as valid consideration for any promise, no matter how extravagant, so long as the promise was freely bargained for and freely given in exchange for the peppercorn, dollar, etc.

a. Inadequate Consideration May Be Evidence of Fraud, Duress, or Undue Influence. [§ 7–44]

Although no inquiry will normally be made into the adequacy of a party's consideration, the presence of an unusually great economic disproportionality in the parties' benefits and detriments under the contract may occasion a court to look closely for evidence of fraud, duress, mistake, or undue influence in the transaction. For example, if Bill "contracts" to sell his $25,000 painting to Mary for $100, the disparity in the value of the consideration coming to Bill entitles a court to examine the transaction for duress, fraud, mistake, undue influence, etc. on Mary's part. [*See* Chapters 11–17 for a discussion of these doctrines]. Thus, while a court will not declare a contract unenforceable based solely on the relative economic inadequacy of consideration, a disproportionate economic benefit by one party may serve as circumstantial evidence of the existence of a defense doctrine that would allow one party to avoid the contract, and entitles the court to examine the transaction

---

* For more information, listen to CD # 4, Track 2 of *Sum and Substance Audio on Contracts*.

CONSIDERATION

carefully to ensure that the promises of the parties were freely and voluntarily bargained for [Restatement 2d § 79 Cmt. e].

b. Inadequate Consideration May Be Evidence of "Sham" Consideration. [§ 7–45]

Sometimes a party to a "contract" is aware of the general rule that gift promises are unenforceable [§ 7–23]. To that extent, he or she may propose **sham consideration** in order to circumvent this general rule, usually to make gift promises enforceable. If evidence demonstrates such sham consideration, the "contract" is deemed unenforceable.

Note that like the term "past" consideration discussed above, many contracts scholars dislike the phrase "sham consideration" since there is no species of actionable "consideration" which can fairly be labeled "sham." In these situations there is <u>no</u> consideration because the exchange is pretext. However, most books and cases eschew such a mouthful and speak in terms of "sham consideration" and that is the convention used in this Book and in the Restatement 2d, *see* § 79, Cmt. d.

(1) Example. [§ 7–46]

Uncle wants to give his 16-year old niece his $5,000 antique desk on her 18th birthday. He knows gift promises are unenforceable, so he agrees to "sell" the desk to niece now for $1, with delivery to be in two years. The "bargain" is only a pretense to disguise a gift promise, and niece's payment of $1 is not consideration for uncle's promise to deliver the desk; it is a sham transaction. Hence, if uncle never delivers the desk, the contract cannot be enforced by niece. Hence, inadequate consideration may also serve as evidence of a sham transaction, which is unenforceable under contract law [§ 7–45].

2. Illusory Promises. [§ 7–47*]

An illusory promise is one in which the promisor gives the illusion of making a valid promise to act or forebear, but in reality does not bind himself or herself to do anything. In other words, it is a promise whereby the promisor has not put any limitation on his or her free will and leaves his or her future actions subject to his or her free will and whim, just as would be true if the promisor had not promised at all. For example, if in response to an offer to purchase a couch for $500, Bill responds, "I promise to pay you $500 for the couch if I decide I want to, otherwise I will not take the couch and will pay you nothing." Bill has made no real commitment, and thus no enforceable

---

* For more information, listen to CD # 4, Track 4 of *Sum and Substance Audio on Contracts*.

contract is formed. The rule governing illusory promises is that **a true illusory promise cannot serve as consideration**. While the general rule is of long standing and continues today, the question of what is and what is not a true illusory promise has changed over time.

a. **Traditional Rule: Contracts with Personal Satisfaction Clauses Were Not Enforceable. [§ 7–48]**

   The common law rule was clear: **a contract with a personal satisfaction clause was illusory because the promisor failed to make a definite commitment to be bound**, and thus insufficient to act as consideration. For example, if Joe promised to accept and pay $500 for a portrait, "if I like it when completed," no enforceable agreement was ever formed between Joe and the artist because Joe's promise was illusory. The personal satisfaction clause means Joe had made no definite commitment to purchase the painting.

b. **Modern Rule: The Implied Duty of Good Faith and Fair Dealing Renders Contracts with Personal Satisfaction Clauses Enforceable. [§ 7–49]**

   Modern contract law has changed the rules in two ways regarding when a promise is illusory. First, contract law now holds that *any* **restriction on a promisor's freedom of action, whether express or implied, will prevent a promise from being classified as illusory**. Second, it provides that one of the implied restrictions on a promisor's freedom of action is **an implied duty of good faith performance**. That is, in **every contract**, the parties will be deemed to have agreed to perform under the contract in good faith [Restatement 2d § 205; UCC § 1–304]. Imposition of a good faith obligation permits the courts to hold that the promisor has implicitly restricted his or her actions, i.e., the promisor is obligated to perform in good faith, and such restriction on the promisor's freedom has been deemed sufficient to keep the promise from being truly illusory.

   (1) **Example. [§ 7–50]**

   Joe hires an artist to paint his portrait, promising to pay $500 if he likes it when it is completed. Under modern contract law, this is an enforceable contract despite the personal satisfaction clause, as the court will imply that Joe must exercise his judgment as to whether he likes the painting in good faith. With this construction, Joe has promised an **"act,"** i.e., he has suffered a detriment, by obligating himself to do something he legally did not have

CONSIDERATION

to do before contracting—pay $500 if he honestly likes the picture. As such, the contract is supported by consideration. Contrast this with a promise by Joe to pay the artist $500 "if I *feel like it* when I see the painting." This is still an illusory promise even under modern contract law.

(2) Exception: "Sale on Approval" and "Sale or Return" Contracts. [§ 7–51]

The UCC allows parties to structure an enforceable agreement in which the buyer can return the good for any, or even no, reason, without imposition of the good faith requirement. In other words, even with the epitome of an unfettered personal satisfaction clause, the UCC states that the agreement is viable.

Where the buyer is a consumer and the goods are for use, this kind of contract is known as a "sale on approval" contract [UCC § 2–326(1)(a)]. Where the buyer is a retailer and the goods are for resale, the agreement is known as a "sale or return" contract [UCC § 2–326(1)(b)]. These agreements are far from the norm, overwhelmingly favorable for a buyer, and require stringent documentation to be effective [*see, e.g.*, UCC § 2–326(3)]. However, if a buyer and seller want to enter into a "sale on approval" contract, the Code allows them to do so under freedom of contract principles.

c. "Exclusive Dealing" Contracts. [§ 7–52]

An exclusive dealing contract is one in which one party promises to give the other the exclusive rights to sell his, her, or its goods or services [UCC § 2–306(2)]. The exclusive rights can be, and usually are, limited for a period of time and/or to a particular geographic region. Arguably such agreements are illusory because while the supplying party is bound to supply goods or services, the other party is often not contractually obligated to sell (or even try to sell) the goods or services. As such, the agreement could be characterized as illusory. [§ 7–47].

Contract law makes these kinds of agreements enforceable by implying a duty of good faith on the selling party. That is, the selling party is obligated to act in good faith in attempting to sell the supplied product.

There is some controversy over the extent of the obligation the selling party has by virtue of the good faith obligation. Most courts require only a duty of "reasonable efforts," that is, the party must make a reasonable effort to market the goods or services supplied. However, UCC § 2–306(2) states that the seller must use its "best efforts" to promote the sale of the product or services. Despite this language, most courts still only imply a reasonable effort for the reasons explained in the following example.

(1) Example. [§ 7–53]

Dell Computers enters into an exclusive dealing agreement with Costco whereby Costco is granted the exclusive right to sell its computers nationwide in return for 70% of the sales price. Costco, on the other hand, is free to sell computers manufactured by others and is not obligated to sell any set number of Dell computers.

Arguably the contract lacks consideration because Dell is bound to supply computers and, at least by its terms, Costco is not obligated to sell any set number of computers, or even obligated to attempt to market them. However, modern contract law will use the implied duty of good faith on Costco to save the contract, meaning that Costco must, in good faith, try to sell Dell computers. Since Costco must do something it did not otherwise have to do—make a good faith attempt to sell the computers—there is sufficient consideration to make the contract enforceable.

The controversy mentioned above appears here in the question of the extent of Costco's obligation imposed by the implied good faith duty. If it were interpreted to require Costco's "best efforts," Costco might be subject to liability if it did not give the most shelf space or signage to Dell, promoted other computers with more fervor, or even if a sales representative suggested another brand to a customer. As a consequence, most courts would interpret the good faith requirement to require Costco to use only "reasonable efforts" to sell the computers, despite the language of 2–306.

(2) Example of Exclusive Dealing Contract: *Wood v. Lucy, Lady Duff Gordon.* **[§ 7–54*]**

Lady Duff Gordon granted Wood an exclusive right to sell her clothing line for a year in return for his promise to pay her half of any profits he might make from selling them. Under their agreement she provided him with the exclusive rights to sell her clothing line, but he was not specifically obligated to sell (or even to try to sell) any. He only promised to split any profits he made with her, but had no specific

---

* For more information about this case, listen to CD # 4, Track 4 of *Sum and Substance Audio on Contracts.*

CONSIDERATION

obligation to generate or attempt to generate any profits at all. When Lady Duff Gordon sold the rights to sell her clothing to someone else during the year, Wood brought suit to enforce the exclusive dealing provision. Her defense was that the contract with Wood was unenforceable because Wood's promise was illusory in that he promised to do nothing under the contract.

Held: Wood's promises under the agreement were enforceable as they were supported by sufficient consideration, Lady Duff Gordon's promise of an exclusive right to sell, for the court *implied a duty of good faith,* i.e., a duty of "reasonable efforts," on Wood's part. Thus, the court found that Wood impliedly bound himself in good faith to try and market the clothes (meaning that Lady Duff Gordon could sue him for breach of his duty of good faith performance if he did nothing), and therefore his promise was a sufficient legal detriment to Wood to constitute consideration. *See* § 2–306(2) of the UCC regarding exclusive dealing contracts. [Case Squibs, *Wood v. Lucy, Lady Duff Gordon,* 222 N.Y. 88, 118 N.E. 214 (1917); *see also* § 7–52].

(3) Example Based on *Kubik v. J & R Foods of Oregon*. [§ 7–55]

Restaurant negotiated an exclusive dealing agreement whereby it would be the only restaurant in the State of Oregon that could purchase barbeque sauce manufactured by Manufacturer for the next year. After a period of time under the agreement, in which it ordered several gallons of sauce a month, Restaurant thought it could reverse engineer the sauce and started producing internally a similar tasting sauce for less money. Hence, it stopped ordering the sauce from Manufacturer, and Manufacturer sued.

Held: Verdict for Manufacturer. Restaurant had a good faith obligation to order the sauce (more particularly, a good faith obligation to try and sell the sauce as part of its dishes), and hence Restaurant was liable for the profits realized by Manufacturer for a reasonable amount of sauce each month (based on what the restaurant had previously ordered) for the remainder of the contract. [*Kubik v. J & R Foods of Oregon,* 577 P.2d 518 (Or. 1978)].

d. "Requirements" and "Output" Contracts. [§ 7–56]

A requirements contract is one in which a buyer agrees to purchase all of a particular good or service it requires from one seller. An output contract is one in which a seller agrees to sell all its output of a particular good or service to one buyer. [UCC § 2–306(1).] Such contracts are arguably illusory because, in a requirements contract for example, the buyer may say it requires none of the goods or services that are the subject of the contract, and thus not be obligated to buy anything. Similarly, in an output contract, the seller may say it will not provide any of the services, or produce any of the goods, that are the subject of the contract, again arguably not obligating itself at all under the contract. Nonetheless, such contracts are common. Accordingly, contract law has determined such agreements to be enforceable by again imposing a good faith requirement on the parties to them. That is, UCC § 2–306(1) states that under output and requirements contracts, the parties have bargained for "such actual output or requirements **as may occur in good faith**." The rule for non-UCC requirements and output contracts, such as those concerning services, is similar.

(1) Example. [§ 7–57]

> Gas Co. signs a contract agreeing to provide any and all pure oxygen needed by Metal Co. in manufacturing steel over the next two years. A year and a half into the contract, Metal Co. decides it is paying too much for the oxygen, and tells Gas Co. if it does not reduce its price, Metal Co. will simply stop producing steel for the next six months, and Gas Co. will have no sales. (At the end of the six months, Metal Co. plans to work its plant overtime to make up for the steel it did not make during this six months period.) Gas Co. refuses to lower its price, Metal Co. stops manufacturing steel, and Gas Co. sues for breach of contract.
>
> Metal Co. may try to defend such a suit by asserting that the parties never had a contract because Metal Co.'s promise was illusory as it never bound itself to do anything. It would argue that it agreed to buy oxygen from Gas Co. only if it needed any, and that it could decide it did not need the gas at any time. However, this defense would fail, for the contract is enforceable because of the implied obligation of good faith. That is, under modern contract law, Metal Co. will be deemed to have bound itself to purchase (in good faith) all the oxygen it needed. In a case like this, where Metal Co.'s asserted lack of need for oxygen was made for a bad faith reason, the contract will be enforced and sufficient consideration found. Thus, in the subsequent lawsuit, Metal Co. will be deemed to have breached its implied duty of good faith, and Gas Co. can recover damages resulting

from Metal Co.'s failure to purchase a good faith amount of oxygen during the last six months of the contract.

(2) Requirements and Output Contracts Probably Have No Implied Floor, but Do Have an Implied Ceiling. [§ 7–58]

Occasionally, a buyer will enter into a requirements contract and then, due to some event or another, end up **honestly** not needing to purchase any of the goods or services that are the subject matter of the contract. For example, assume a tire company who supplied tires to Ford enters into a requirements contract with a rubber producer. A few months into the contract, the tire company loses its contract with Ford and can find no one else to purchase its tires. At that point, it may legitimately have no rubber requirements. The majority of courts and commentators have interpreted UCC § 2–306(1) as providing that so long as the buyer acts in good faith in such a circumstance, and really does not need any of the product that was the subject matter of the agreement, he or she is not obligated to purchase any. In other words, where no estimated or target amount is set forth in the agreement, there is no implied floor of a minimal order present in requirements contracts. The idea is that the rubber supplier implicitly took that risk when it entered into the requirements contract.

However, note that 2–306(1) provides that "in the absence of a stated estimate [in the agreement] any normal or otherwise comparable prior . . . requirements may be . . . demanded." Those courts and commentators who disagree with the majority view set forth above point to this language and state that, unless the manufacturer has ordered no product in the past, it may not, without breach, order no product under a requirements contract. That is, even if the tire company does not need any rubber after losing the Ford contract, it still must pay for some reasonable amount of rubber. The amount would be the low amount it needed in a comparable prior time period. Besides the language of 2–306, the justification for this view is that the supplying company (the rubber supplier) has likely made an investment in to be in a position to supply the tire manufacturer's needs, and so should not be in a position where its investment is for naught. To these courts and commentators, it is up to the recipient of the goods or services (the tire manufacturer) to include an express provision in the contract itself allowing for the possibility that its requirements could go down to "zero" under certain circumstances, and then in only those circumstances will it not be in breach for failing to order any rubber if it legitimately had no rubber needs.

On the other hand, there is unanimity among courts and commentators that § 2–306(1) contains an implied ceiling on the amount that can be ordered under a requirements contract. For example, suppose that in the middle of the agreement the tire company mentioned above got contracts to supply tires not just for Ford, but also for Toyota, General Motors, and Chrysler. As a result, instead of the amount of rubber it might have needed under the contract when signed, it now needs 25 times more. Under § 2–306(1), the tire company cannot require the rubber supplier to supply a "disproportionately" large amount of rubber under the contract, even if in good faith it needs more rubber. The rationale for that rule is that it would be unfair to hold the supplier in breach for failure to deliver an unreasonably large amount of product in those circumstances.

The rules are similar and reciprocal for output contracts. That is, if a supplier in good faith produces none of the goods that are the subject matter of the agreement, the majority view is that it may do so without fear of breach, for there is no implied floor as to the amount of goods it must produce. However, it is not entitled to suddenly start producing a "disproportionately" large amount of product and require that the buyer accept it.

(3) If a Target Quantity Is Specified in an Output or Requirements Contract. [§ 7–59]

Under UCC § 2–306(1), if the parties put a stated estimate of the amount to be provided or used in an output or requirements contract, the parties will be held to either producing or requiring an amount not disproportionate to the stated estimate. Again, however, as explained in § 7–58 above, if in good faith its requirements or output goes to zero, most courts would allow it to do so without penalty.

e. **Contracts with Expressly Conditional Promises: Such Contracts Are Enforceable Unless the Condition Is Within the Unfettered Discretion of the Promisor. [§ 7–60]**

When a party's promise under a contract is expressly conditioned upon the occurrence or non-occurrence of a particular event, there is an issue as to whether such a promise may be sufficient consideration under the illusory promise rule. To determine whether a conditional promise is illusory, it is necessary to examine who controls the occurrence of the

CONSIDERATION

condition. **If the occurrence of the condition is in the unfettered discretion of the promisor, then the promise is illusory**. However, if the occurrence of the condition is **at all** outside the **unfettered** control of the promisor, the promise is enforceable.

(1) **Example. [§ 7-61]**

Rich makes an offer to purchase Ed's air conditioner next Friday for $500 "on the condition that the temperature doesn't fall below 70 degrees by then." Ed accepts that offer. They have made an enforceable contract, for Rich's promise is not illusory, since the occurrence of the condition (the temperature falling), is outside of Rich's control.

(2) **Example. [§ 7-62]**

Bill says to Mary, "I'll pay you $1,000 for your couch on the condition I enter my living room Tuesday night." Even if Mary accepts the offer they will not have an enforceable contract. Bill's promise is unenforceable under the illusory promise doctrine, as the occurrence of the condition is within his unfettered discretion.

(3) **Example: Aleatory Promises. [§ 7-63]**

An aleatory promise is one conditional upon the happening of a reasonably chance event. An aleatory promise is not illusory because, by definition, the occurrence of the event is not within the complete unfettered discretion of the promisor. For example, if Sid promises Sally that he will share half of any future legal lottery winnings with her if she will pay him $1,000 today, such promise will be enforceable, assuming Sally agrees to it, and so long as the promise was bargained for and not made under duress, undue influence, or the like [Restatement 2d § 76, Cmt. c].

(4) **Even if the Occurrence of a Condition Is to *Some* Extent Within the Discretion of the Promisor, the Promise Is Nonetheless Enforceable if Any Restriction on the Promisor's Discretion Can Be Implied. [§ 7-64]**

If a bargained for contractual promise is expressly made conditional on the occurrence (or non-occurrence) of an event which is dependent only to *some* extent upon the discretion of the promisor, such promise is sufficient consideration to make the contract enforceable if any limitation on the promisor's exercise of discretion can be found. As with the case of promises, which are not expressly conditional, modern contract law has found such limitations on the exercise of a promisor's discretion by implying a duty of good faith on the promisor's performance.

(a) Example. [§ 7–65]

Rob agrees to purchase Holly's house for $150,000, "on the condition a loan for purchase of the house can be obtained from Central Bank." It is arguable that Rob has explicitly promised nothing, for while he has agreed to buy the house *if* he gets the loan, he has not promised *to apply* for the loan. Nevertheless, because the duty of good faith is implied in such a circumstance, a court will find that he implicitly promised to try in good faith to obtain a loan. Such restriction on Rob's actions is a sufficient legal detriment so as to prevent his promise from being deemed illusory, and the contract is thus valid. Note that implying the duty of good faith to Rob means that if he does not apply for the loan, he could be liable in a contract action for a breach of his implied duty, and his hindrance of the occurrence of the condition might transform his conditional promise into an unconditional one. [§ 21–102].

f. Special Illusory Promise Problems Regarding Termination-at-Will Clauses. [§ 7–66]

A contract that is terminable at will presents illusory promise issues. For example, assume that Rex's Pizza House places an order with Sandy's Cheese Company for 100 pounds of cheese per week for the next year, but Rex reserves the right "to terminate at any time." It is arguable that Rex has made an illusory promise, i.e., he has merely said, "I promise to order from you unless I change my mind and immediately terminate the contract." The treatment of such situations has changed over time.

(1) Traditional Rule: Contracts with Termination-at-Will Clauses Were Deemed Illusory and Hence Unenforceable. [§ 7–67]

At common law, a termination-at-will clause rendered a contract unenforceable under the illusory promise doctrine.

(a) Example: *Miami Coca-Cola Bottling Co. v. Orange Crush Co.* [§ 7–68]

In a 1924 case, Orange Crush granted a perpetual license to Coca-Cola Bottling to bottle and distribute the Orange Crush brand soft drink. While the license was perpetual, the contract had a clause allowing Coca-Cola to terminate the license at will. Even though the contract only gave Coca-Cola the right to terminate, Orange Crush gave notice that *it* was terminating the agreement, and Coca-Cola sued for damages.

Held: Verdict for Orange Crush. The court held that mutuality of obligation requires that contracts be interpreted such that if one party has the right to terminate at will, both parties must have that right. And when both parties have that right, the contract is unenforceable due to a lack of consideration, since the promises of both parties were thus illusory. That is, both parties were promising, in essence, "I will perform until I decide I do not want to." They could have decided they didn't want to proceed one second after signing the agreement, and thus they had not bound themselves to do anything. Hence, while the payment and delivery obligations under the contract had to be performed up until the termination notice since the parties had an implied-in-fact contract up until that point, the termination was effective as the written contract was unenforceable from the beginning. [Case Squibs, *Miami Coca-Cola Bottling Co. v. Orange Crush Co.*, 296 F. 693 (5th Cir. 1924)].

(2) Modern Rule: Contracts with Termination-at-Will Clauses Are Probably Enforceable. [§ 7–69]

Today most courts hold that even under a termination-at-will clause, the party terminating the contract must give "reasonable notice" to the other before ending the agreement. Under this theory, the fact that the terminating party must give notice is itself a sufficient detriment, i.e., a sufficient restriction on the promisor's actions, so as to render the promise enforceable. In other words, the requirement that the promisee give "reasonable" notice is a sufficient bargained for restriction on the promisee's actions to constitute consideration because the agreement is enforceable at least until the time of expiration of the implied reasonable notice period.

Note that if there is a specified notice period in the contract, e.g., "I will hire you for a one year period, but either of us can terminate this contract upon 30 days' notice," there is no consideration problem because each party has himself, herself or itself to perform for at least 30 days.

Note also that if the *Miami Coca-Cola Bottling* case discussed in § 7–68 above were decided today, a reasonable notice period would likely be implied and thus Orange Crush's termination would not be immediately effective, and it would be forced to pay damages, or continue to perform under the contract, for a reasonable period of time to be determined by the court.

(3) The UCC Approach to Terminable-at-Will Contracts: The Reasonable Notification Requirement Avoids Most Illusory Promise Issues. [§ 7–70]

Under UCC § 2–309(3), in order to validly terminate a UCC contract, termination must take place either upon the happening of an agreed event or after "reasonable notification" is received. Thus, because reasonable notice must be given before termination is effective is an *explicit* requirement under the UCC, termination-at-will clauses in contracts governed by the Code do not present illusory promise issues, as each party is bound to perform for at least the reasonable notice period.

If the parties specifically agree that no notification is necessary, the Code states that such a provision is invalid if its operation proves unconscionable [UCC § 2–309(3)]. Hence it is the rare case where a termination at will clause without notification will be enforceable under the UCC.

3. Modification of Existing Agreements: The Pre-Existing Duty Rule. [§ 7–71*]

Modifications to existing contracts pose a number of problems for contract law. Many of these problems are dealt with by consideration issues, which are explained below. Others deal with a mix of contractual and evidentiary issues and are explained in Chapter Nine.

a. The General Common Law Rule: "New" Consideration Is Required for an Enforceable Modification. [§ 7–72]

A paraphrase of the **general rule**, subject to a number of exceptions discussed below, is that **if the parties wish to validly modify an existing contract, new consideration must be exchanged.** [Restatement 2d § 73]. This is known as the "**pre-existing duty rule**," meaning that when one party already has a pre-existing contractual duty to do something, a subsequent promise to do that same thing will not be enforced unless new consideration is exchanged between both parties so

---

* For more information, listen to CD # 4, Track 6 of *Sum and Substance Audio on Contracts*.

CONSIDERATION

that both "get something" from the new deal. Otherwise, it is looked to as a gift promise.

The rationale for the general rule and some problems affecting its application can be illustrated by example. Imagine yourself as the judge in the following situation:

Sugar Co. in January signed a contract to supply 100 tons of sugar to Soft Drink Co. at $1/pound, with the sugar to be delivered on March 1. Soft Drink needed the sugar on that date to be able to manufacture enough soda to meet Soft Drink's contracts with various stores around the country who want the drink in time to stock up for summer.

However, Sugar Co. walks into your court in September waiving a written contract modification in which it certainly appears Soft Drink Co. agreed to pay it $1.50/pound for the sugar instead of the original $1. Otherwise, everything in the modified agreement is identical to the terms in the original contract. Sugar is now suing because Soft Drink only paid it $1/pound, the price under the original agreement.

You might think if Soft Drink agreed to pay more, then, heck, it should live up to the agreement. But then you start to think—why would Soft Drink agree to pay 50 cents more per pound when Sugar already had the duty to deliver for $1? It *might* have agreed to do so; but it seems kind of fishy. You want to know more.

The basic rule contract law follows is that such situations typically are fishy, which is why it looks for some additional consideration from Sugar Co. which would justify the payment of the additional 50-cents/pound.

Specifically, the pre-existing duty rule presumes that the benefitted party (Sugar Co.) is either: (a) an extortionist; (b) a profiteer, or (c) a "dishonest compromiser," unless it can come up with additional consideration or a pretty good reason for getting the 50-cent bonus.

(1) Example of the Extortionist. [§ 7–73]

One reason Soft Drink might have agreed to pay the extra 50 cents a pound is because Sugar came to it on February 28 and said, "We're not going to deliver unless you pay us an extra 50 cents." At that point, Soft Drink could never find another supplier for 100 tons of sugar in time to meet its own delivery obligations and so it agreed to pay the extra fifty cents because it felt it had no other choice. Because Soft Drink got nothing out of the modified bargain, the modification is not enforceable because it lacked consideration. [Restatement 2d § 176(1)(d); §§ 13–9 and 13–12].

(2) Example of the Profiteer. [§ 7–74]

Another reason Soft Drink might have agreed to the extra 50 cents/pound stems from changed market conditions. That is, assume $1/pound was the market rate when the contract was signed in January. But soon thereafter, for some reason, the market for sugar went up to $2/pound. Sugar may have come to Soft Drink in February and said, "We're not going to deliver for $1/pound. You can go out and buy sugar from somebody else for delivery by March, but it will cost you $2/pound and I don't know if you can afford it. Sure you could sue us for the difference, but that will take a long time and it will be an expensive lawsuit. So let's just split the rise in the market." Again, Soft Drink would agree because it felt it had no choice, and the pre-existing duty rule would not permit the enforceability of the 50-cent extra promise.

(3) Example of the "Dishonest Compromiser." [§ 7–75]

A third potential reason for the agreement could be that Sugar may have said, "Look, we want more money for the sugar. If you don't agree, we are going to claim that you breached the contract, and we were justified in not delivering the sugar to you. We'll find something under the contract you did wrong; our lawyers are very aggressive. Maybe we'll lose, but you'll be in litigation for a couple years, have to pay your lawyers, appear in depositions, the whole nine yards. Plus you're going to have to find another sugar supplier. So what do you say—let's agree to settle our "dispute" by your paying an extra 50 cents/pound?" Again, Soft Drink may have felt agreeing was the best and cheapest resolution of a bad situation.

b. Restatement 2d § 73: The Pre-Existing Duty Rule. [§ 7–76]

To protect against the extortionist, profiteer, and dishonest compromiser, the Restatement requires that in most cases the modified agreement must be supported by "new" consideration, different from that supporting the original agreement, as if it were a separate contract standing on its own. The language used to convey this concept is not immediately obvious, however. Restatement 2d § 73 provides:

> Performance of a **legal duty owed a promisor** which is *neither* **d**oubtful *nor* **the subject of honest dispute** is not consideration.

CONSIDERATION

As applied to the three Sugar/Soft Drink situations described above, we would say that the **legal duty** to deliver sugar at $1/pound was *neither* **doubtful** *nor* **the subject of an honest dispute**. Therefore, the promise to pay the extra 50 cents/pound was not supported by consideration, and as with most promises not supported by consideration, is unenforceable.

(1) "Getting Around" the Pre-Existing Duty Rule. [§ 7–77]

Restatement 2d § 73 does not prohibit all modifications, quite the contrary. It allows for modifications so long as there is new consideration given. The test for new consideration under that provision is: "[A] similar performance is consideration if it differs from what was required by the duty in a way which reflects more than the pretense of a bargain." This is simply a reaffirmation of the "peppercorn" and sham theories of consideration [§ 7–43], i.e., the law will not invalidate an agreement on consideration grounds just because of an economic inequality of the two promises. So long as the duties of the benefitted party are changed in a way that is not a sham— i.e., is "more than a pretense of a bargain"—the modification will be enforceable.

In the Sugar/Soft Drink hypothetical, if, e.g., Sugar promised to deliver 25 tons of sugar on February 25, with the remainder on March 1, in return for the increased price to $1.50/pound, the modification will be enforced if, as is likely, the court determines that the new delivery schedule is "more than a pretense" to justify the increased price. In this scenario, Soft Drink gets some benefit that it did not have before—some of the sugar early, so it can start production sooner.

To continue with the Sugar/Soft Drink hypothetical, what if Sugar was an extortionist, but comes up with some relatively minor extra duty that it agrees to do in order to get around the pre-existing duty rule? If Soft Drink can establish that Sugar violated the covenant of good faith and fair dealing [Restatement 2d § 205; UCC § 1–304], which it can do if it can prove the extortion, then the modification still will not be enforceable. [§ 21–102].

(2) Example. [§ 7–78]

Worker accepts a position with Company for six months employment at $100/week. Shortly after beginning work, Worker gets an offer from a competitor for $125/week and explains the situation to Company. Company's President offers Worker $120/week for the remainder of the contract to stay. Worker agrees to stay. Company is under no enforceable obligation to pay the additional $20/week under the pre-existing duty rule. Worker's obligation to work for $100/week was neither doubtful nor the subject of any dispute; hence Company's promise to pay more for the same, pre-existing duty lacked consideration and is unenforceable. If Worker and Company had agreed that Worker would have undertaken additional, more-than-pretextual, duties for the increased pay, then Worker would be entitled to the increased rate of pay.

(3) **Example. [§ 7–79]**

Farmer and Winery entered into a contract where Farmer was to supply 25 tons of "wine-quality" grapes at $75/ton for three years, a fair price. Wine quality grapes are more expensive than "consumable" quality grapes. A genuine dispute arose after the first delivery, with Winery claiming the grapes were consumable quality and Farmer asserting they were wine quality. Rather than go to court, they agreed that Winery would pay the $75/ton this year, but that Farmer would deliver 25 tons of grapes at $55/ton for the next two years.

In that case, the modification would be enforceable, and Farmer would not be entitled to sue for the $75/ton price for the last two years. This is because, under Restatement 2d § 73, the obligation of Winery to pay $75/ton for the first delivery was "the subject of honest dispute." As such, its promise to pay less for future deliveries to settle that honest dispute was enforceable as a modification.

(4) **Example of *Foakes v. Beer*. [§ 7–80*]**

Dr. Foakes had borrowed £2,090 from Ms. Beer, which was due and payable in a lump sum on a fixed date. If he did not pay on that date, he would owe her interest, plus principal, until the loan was completely repaid. Shortly before the due date, Dr. Foakes pled relative poverty and asserted he could neither pay the full £2,090 nor could he afford to pay any interest. He proposed a repayment plan where he would pay £500 instead on the due date, with the remainder of the principal to be paid on an agreed schedule, but without interest. Ms. Beer agreed to the modification. Dr. Foakes paid according to the revised payment schedule, and after

---

* For more information about this case, listen to CD # 4, Track 6 of *Sum and Substance Audio on Contracts*.

CONSIDERATION

the last payment was made, Ms. Beer nevertheless sued him for the interest per the original contract.

Held: Dr. Foakes was liable for the interest under the pre-existing duty rule. That is, Dr. Foakes was already under a pre-existing duty to repay the principal under the original contract, so his reaffirmance of that debt did not provide any consideration for Ms. Beer's promise to waive the interest. [*Foakes v. Beer,* L.R. 9 App. Cas. 605 (H.L. 1884)].

Foakes has come under criticism by some scholars over the years who argue that Ms. Beer did receive an additional benefit under the revised payment plan since she may well have gotten nothing from Dr. Beer on the due date, and may not have been able to collect a judgment against him. However, these "benefits" to Ms. Beer are insufficient under contract law to constitute consideration, for contract law looks at the issue more simply, i.e., before the due date Dr. Foakes promised to pay £2,090 plus interest; after the new agreement Dr. Foakes, promised only to pay £2,090, albeit on a different schedule, without interest. As nothing new was added in the settlement that benefitted Ms. Beer, no consideration was present.

Note also that if Dr. Foakes had promised, e.g., to provide free medical service to Ms. Beer until the principal was repaid under the revised payment schedule, the modification likely would have been enforceable because Ms. Beer would have obtained a bargained for a non-pretextual benefit (medical care), and Dr. Foakes incurred a bargained for detriment (having to provide medical care), that did not exist under the original contract.

c. **Exceptions to the Pre-Existing Duty Rule. [§ 7–81]**

The pre-existing duty rule is not free from criticism. To ameliorate some of its harsh effects, various exceptions have been crafted to it:

1. Modifications are enforceable without consideration under the UCC [UCC § 2–209(1); § 7–82];

2. Modifications are enforceable without consideration if they are both fair in amount and the result of changed circumstances that the parties did not anticipate when the contract was entered into [Restatement 2d § 89(a); § 7–83];

3. Modifications are enforceable without consideration if a statute allows it [Restatement 2d § 89(b); § 7–84];

4. Modifications are enforceable without consideration if justice requires the modification be enforced in light of one

CHAPTER 7

party's material change of position in reliance on the modified terms. [Restatement 2d § 89(c); § 7–85].

Each is discussed below.

(1) Modifications Enforceable Without Consideration Under the UCC. [§ 7–82]

The drafters of the UCC have rejected the pre-existing duty rule and have taken the position that contract modifications should be enforceable without consideration. [UCC § 2–209(1)]. That is, the UCC provides that if a seller calls a buyer and gets permission to deliver the goods on the 5th instead on the 3rd as called for under the contract, there is no need to make up some additional duties to satisfy the consideration doctrine just to make the later delivery term enforceable. Note that the UCC's position raises other difficulties, however, which are discussed in Chapter Nine.

(2) Modifications Enforceable Without Consideration in Light of Unanticipated Circumstances. [§ 7–83]

Under the Restatement, a modification is enforceable without consideration if: (a) the terms of the modification are fair; (b) in light of circumstances that were not anticipated when the contract was entered into. [Restatement 2d § 89(a)].

For example, Catering Co. signs a 5-year contract with law school to provide dinner for all attendees at the law school annual alumni dinner. The price is $10,000 for the first year, with an additional $1,000 each subsequent year. The price was arrived at by looking at past attendance figures for the alumni dinner.

Two years into the contract, the current Chief Justice of the Supreme Court steps down and agrees to be the new Dean of the law school. Attendance at the upcoming dinner is through the roof. Law School and Catering Co. agree to modify the agreement so that Catering Co.'s fee will be $50,000. Assuming the amount is reasonable, the modification is enforceable without consideration because it is due to an "unforeseen circumstance" at the time the contract was entered into. Hence Catering Co. does not have to promise to perform some additional service to make the promised $50,000 payment enforceable.

Note that this rule only deals with agreed modifications. If the law school did not agree to the extra payment, Catering Co. could not demand it based on § 89(a).

CONSIDERATION

(3) Modifications Enforceable Without Consideration if Statutorily Permitted. [§ 7–84]

There are certain consumer protection statutes that allow for modifications to be enforceable without consideration. Under Restatement 2d § 89(b), if a legislature has made a determination via statute that the pre-existing duty rule should not apply to certain types of transactions, that determination controls over common law.

(4) Modifications Enforceable Without Consideration in Light of Material Reliance. [§ 7–85]

If one party justifiably and materially relies on a contractual modification promised by the other, the modification is enforceable to the extent justice requires.

For example, Tenant and Landlord have a one-year lease at $1,000/month. Tenant loses his job and asks Landlord to reduce the rent for a few months while she looks for work. Landlord agrees to a rent of $600/month for 2 months. The modification is enforceable if tenant relies on the reduction and stays for the two months. In other words, the Landlord cannot sue for the "missing" $400/month at the end of the two-month period in the absence of some extra duty undertaken by Tenant to satisfy the consideration requirement of the pre-existing duty rule. [Restatement 2d § 89, Cmt. d, Ill. 7.]

d. The Pre-Existing Duty Rule and Public Officials and Other Governmental Workers. [§ 7–86]

Government workers and public officials owe legal duties to the public. But sometimes, certain members of the public want more than their fair share. For example, Moneybags may want to jump the line in getting his remodel plans approved by Building and Safety right away, rather than waiting his turn to have his plans reviewed three months after submission. To be clear, Moneybags is not seeking to bribe the Inspector to approve something the Inspector wouldn't otherwise approve. That would be illegal and contracts procured by bribes are unenforceable [§ 17–6]. Instead, he promises the Inspector $5,000 to stay and work overtime to review his remodel plans and approve them, but only if the Inspector would otherwise do so. Moneybags just wants to jump the queue.

Even if Inspector is motivated by the promise to do something he otherwise did not have the obligation to do (and would not have done) i.e., stay late to review the plans, under Restatement 2d § 73, such actions are not consideration sufficient to make the promise enforceable under the pre-existing duty rule. That is, the Inspector is already under a pre-existing duty to review the plans.

Note also that many scholars say this is not so much a result compelled by the pre-existing duty rule but rather one compelled by the public policy of not allowing the wealthy to pay for preferential treatment by government workers [Restatement 2d § 73 Cmt. b.]

(1) Example. [§ 7–87]

Police officer investigates a residential burglary at Homeowner's abode. Homeowner promises to pay officer $1,000 if officer gets the homeowner's stereo back to him in a week. Even if officer performs such action, there is no consideration for the promise to pay, because the officer was under a pre-existing duty as a public official to recover stolen property and return it to its true owner. This is true even if the parties can establish that the promise of the $1,000 payment was bargained for, and even if the officer can establish she took action because of the promise and worked especially hard to try to find homeowner's stereo.

4. Settlement of Claims Based on Incorrect Information. [§ 7–88]

Parties get in disputes. Most of the time those disputes are settled. When parties settle, typically there is consideration for the settlement agreement since the parties are creating a new legal obligation in their settlement agreement [Restatement 2d §§ 71(c); 74, Cmt. c] or, possibly, modifying an existing agreement that is the subject of honest dispute [Restatement 2d § 73].

However, sometimes, a party may agree to surrender, or settle, a claim or a defense as a result of erroneous information. That is, one party may believe the other arguably has a valid claim and so settling is worthwhile to get rid of the claim or to pay something so as not to face the defense in court. But what if the party finds out later that the claim or defense he or she settled in fact turns out to be invalid? In that case, arguably the promise made in the settlement is illusory. That is, in promising to pay Frank $1,000 to settle a claim that turns out to be invalid, Julie really doesn't "get" anything out of the transaction. She promised to pay $1,000 for nothing, and so Julie might argue her promise is unsupported by consideration.

On the other hand, the legal system does not want to keep opening up settlements in light of later acquired information. Accordingly, the Restatement takes the view that the promises made in such settlements are generally enforceable, even if it later turns out to be

CONSIDERATION

based on incorrect information. However, it structures the rule oddly—stating that such promises are <u>not</u> supported by consideration unless one of two things are true.

Restatement 2d § 74 provides:

> Forbearance to assert or the surrender of a claim of defense which proves to be invalid is not consideration unless:
>
> **(a) The claim or defense is in fact doubtful because of uncertainty as to the facts or the law** [Restatement 2d § 74(a)], or
>
> **(b) The forbearing or surrendering party believes [at the time the promises are made in the settlement] that the claim or defense may be fairly determined to be valid** [Restatement 2d § 74(b)].

a. **Example Based on *Fiege v. Boehm*. [§ 7–89]**

> Woman claimed her child was fathered by Man. They entered into a contract requiring Man to pay child support on condition that Woman does not report him to District Attorney for criminal proceedings for "bastardy," which was then a crime, and would probably require him to make child care payments. Later, blood tests established Man was not the father. Man sought to have the settlement agreement voided on the grounds that his promise to pay child support was not supported by consideration, since he paid and got nothing in return. That is, he argued that he would have been found not guilty of bastardy and would not have owed Woman any child care payments, so his settlement was essentially a gift.
>
> **Held:** There was consideration to support the settlement agreement. The court found Woman honestly believed that Man was the father and so she believed the criminal prosecution she could have instituted was valid. Hence Man did "get" something out of the settlement—the surrender of a claim Woman fairly and in good faith believed to be valid. Under Restatement 2d § 74(b), consideration was present. [*Fiege v. Boehm*, 210 Md. 352 (1956)].

5. **Purported, but Unperformed, Consideration Is Not Effective Consideration. [§ 7–90*]**

   Purported consideration is consideration that is intended to have taken place in exchange for a promise, but which in fact never occurred. For example, a signed document may say, "For $500 received from buyer, I hereby sell to him my antique desk." If the

---

* For more information, listen to CD # 4, Track 3 of *Sum and Substance Audio on Contracts*.

CHAPTER 7

$500 is never actually paid, the buyer cannot seek to enforce the seller to deliver the desk because purported, but not actual, consideration is insufficient to make a promise enforceable.

a. Exception: Purported Consideration Sufficient for Option Contracts. [§ 7–91]

Under § 87 of the Restatement 2d, purported consideration is sufficient to make effective the promises made in an option contract, as long as the offer for the option contract is in writing, is signed by the offeror, and proposes a fair exchange [Restatement 2d § 87, Cmt. c].

Hence, if a written option contract recites that for $20 received, seller gives buyer an option to purchase her car for $5,000 within 30 days, the seller is obligated to sell the car to the buyer if he tenders the $5,000 within 30 days, even if the buyer never paid the original $20.

6. Voidable Promises Can Serve as Valid Consideration. [§ 7–92]

If a party makes a promise that is voidable, e.g., because the promisor is a minor and lacks capacity, or because the promise violates the statue of frauds, etc., the promise may still act as valid *consideration* for the contract [Restatement 2d § 78; *See* Chapters 11–17 for a listing and discussion of those defenses to formation that make a contract voidable].

a. Example. [§ 7–93]

Kevin, a 15-year-old, promises to pay $300 for Rebecca's stereo. The contract may be voidable by Kevin because of his age, but if he wishes to enforce it, his voidable promise nevertheless serves as valid *consideration* for Rebecca's promise to tender the stereo. Hence, Kevin can enforce the contract if he wishes to.

H. EXAM APPROACH TO CONSIDERATION ISSUES. [§ 7–94*]

1. Where consideration is an issue, make sure you analyze:

   A. Whether the promise involved was **bargained for**, i.e., was sought by the promisor in exchange for his or her promise and given by the promisee in exchange for that promise §§ 7–7 *et seq.*]; and

   B. Whether, as a result of the bargain, the relevant party or parties suffered a **legal detriment**, i.e., he or she became

---

* For more information, listen to CD # 5, Track 3 of *Sum and Substance Audio on Contracts*.

obligated to do something that he or she was not obligated to do before the agreement [§ 7–4].

2. If you determine that the promise involved cannot meet the above test, then determine whether one of the modern "exceptions" to the consideration requirements is present:

   A. The implication of "good faith" performance to save output, requirements, and exclusive dealing contracts, and contracts with "personal satisfaction" clauses [§ 7–47];

   B. A gift promise for past benefits or "moral" consideration enforceable via Restatement § 2d 86 [§ 7–34];

   C. A promise to pay a debt otherwise unenforceable because of the statute of limitations or bankruptcy [§ 7–38];

   D. The implication of a "notice" requirement to save termination-at-will clauses [§ 7–66];

   E. A valid modification of the original contract [§ 7–84]; or

   F. A valid settlement [§ 7–88].

3. If the promise is not supported by either the bargain/legal detriment theory, or by one of the modern exceptions to the rule, then classify it properly as a promise that is unenforceable because it is:

   A. A gift promise [§ 7–23];

   B. An example of past or moral consideration [§ 7–30];

   C. An unsolicited action § 7–40];

   D. An illusory promise [§ 7–47];

   E. Subject to a pre-existing duty [§ 7–71];

   F. Sham consideration [§ 7–45]; or

   G. Purported consideration [§ 7–93].

However, if the promise is unenforceable because of one of these rules, determine whether it is arguably enforceable under a promissory estoppel theory, which is discussed in the next Chapter.

CHAPTER 8

PROMISSORY ESTOPPEL AND THE SEAL

A. THE PROMISSORY ESTOPPEL DOCTRINE. [§ 8–1*]

The doctrine of promissory estoppel is based on the moral premise that where the promises of one party have led the other to justifiably and reasonably rely on those promises being performed, the promises should be enforced **even if they were only gratuitous, or not otherwise supported by consideration**. In essence, the doctrine "estops" (prevents) a party from denying an obligation foreseeably resulting from reliance on his or her promise, and also estops a party from being able to deny liability on the technical ground that no "bargained for exchange" resulted upon the acceptance of an offer. At its heart, promissory estoppel is a moral and equitable doctrine that makes promises enforceable where our collective sense of justice (as decided by a judge) suggests they should be enforced.

B. PROMISSORY ESTOPPEL IS NOT A "SUBSTITUTE" FOR CONSIDERATION. [§ 8–2]

It is often said that promissory estoppel is a "substitute" for consideration, i.e., that it will "step in" when a deserving contract is held unenforceable due to a lack of consideration and render that contract enforceable. This is not technically true for a number of reasons:

First, recovery under a promissory estoppel theory is not a recovery based on "contract." Rather, it is a recovery based on a mixture of equitable and tort law principles.

Second, even when promissory estoppel applies to a promise, it does not automatically make that promise fully enforceable. Rather, promises governed by promissory estoppel are only enforceable to the extent that "justice requires," which may fall short of full enforceability (*see* § 8–3).

---

* For more information, listen to CD # 5, Track 2 of *Sum and Substance Audio on Contracts*.

Third, promissory estoppel does more than make enforceable gratuitous promises exchanged as "offers" and "acceptances." For example, it also serves to make some offers irrevocable [§§ 8–11 and 8–14], and to enforce some promises which do not rise to the level of offers, such as those made during preliminary negotiations [§ 8–13].

Lastly, promissory estoppel only applies to certain discrete *promises*. It does not "step in" and automatically make all the provisions of an entire *contract* enforceable. If it applies, only the promises in the agreement that were actually and foreseeably relied upon become enforceable.

Note, however, that despite the above, some cases have held promissory estoppel to be a "species" of consideration, but this idea has not been generally adopted [Case Squibs, *Feinberg v. Pfeiffer*, 322 S.W.2d 163 (Mo. App. 1959)].

C. ELEMENTS OF PROMISSORY ESTOPPEL UNDER THE SECOND RESTATEMENT. [§ 8–3]

Section 90 of the Restatement 2d states that a **promise is binding if:**

(a) **in making the promise the promisor should reasonably expect to induce action or forbearance on the part of the promisee;**

(b) **the promise does in fact induce foreseeable action or forbearance by the promisee; and**

(c) **injustice can be avoided only by enforcement of the promise.**

If each of these criteria are met, the promise may be enforced, but only to the extent "justice requires."

1. Example of *Ricketts v. Scothorn*. [§ 8–4]

In another age, a grandfather was upset to find his granddaughter working and gives her a $2,000 promissory note, redeemable on demand, telling her the note will ensure that she will never have to work to survive. The granddaughter quit work immediately, but did not attempt to redeem the promissory note until several years later, after her grandfather had died. His executors refused to pay on the grounds it was a gratuitous, gift promise.

Held: The promise to pay the $2,000 is enforceable under a promissory estoppel theory. The promise could not be upheld under a consideration theory, for the grandfather pretty clearly just wanted to make a gift [§ 7–23]. However, because it was a promise that: (a) **reasonably could be expected to induce action** on the part of the granddaughter in reliance on it (quitting her job); (b) **actually did induce such action** (she did quit); and (c) **would be unjust not to enforce** under the circumstances, the promise was enforceable under promissory estoppel to the extent justice requires. In this case, justice required full enforcement of the promise. [*Ricketts v. Scothorn*, 57 Neb. 51 (1898)].

2. Difference Between Promissory Estoppel Under the First and Second Restatement of Contracts. [§ 8–5]

Many contracts professors and a few casebooks ask students to compare the differences between § 90 the Restatement (First), and § 90 of the Restatement (Second). There are three main differences:

(1) The Restatement (First) required that the reliance by the promisee be actual, reasonable, and "of a definite and substantial character." The Restatement (Second) only requires the reliance to be actual and reasonable for promissory estoppel to apply;

(2) The Restatement (First) states that if promissory estoppel applies to a promise, it will be enforced *in its entirety,* **regardless whether the promisee relied completely on the promise**. For example, if a grandfather tells his adult granddaughter that he will give her $1,000 to purchase a stereo, and the granddaughter buys only a $750 stereo, a strict reading of the Restatement (First) would enforce the promise entirely, and the grandfather would have to pay $1,000 (the full value of the promise) to his granddaughter even though she only spent $750. While some commentators have questioned whether that is what § 90 of the Restatement (First) truly meant, it is what Professor Williston, the reporter for the Restatement (First), has said he intended it to mean, and it is what the section, on its face, says. Section 90 of the Restatement (Second) only enforces such promises to the extent justice requires, and so in the Grandfather/Granddaughter example, the grandfather's promise would only be enforceable to $750 (*see* § 8–16 for a further discussion of this issue); and

(3) The Restatement (First) did not make any special provision for promises to make donations to charities (or to marriage settlements), whereas the Restatement (Second) contains § 90(2), which states that such promises are binding even without any reliance by the promisee.

D. TYPES OF PROMISES MADE ENFORCEABLE UNDER PROMISSORY ESTOPPEL. [§ 8–6]

1. Gift Promises. [§ 8–7]

By far, the most common types of promises supported by promissory estoppel are gratuitous or gift promises (*see* § 7–23). Hence, if a gift promise meets the requirements of § 90, it will be enforceable to the extent justice allows.

2. **Oral Promises to Convey Land. [§ 8–8]**

If Paul makes an unbargained for, oral promise to convey Blackacre to Dan, and Dan relies on the promise by moving onto the land, making improvements, etc., and Dan is reasonable in believing he is entitled to take these actions because of the promise, most courts will hold that the promise to convey is binding against Paul under a promissory estoppel theory [Restatement 2d §§ 90, 139]. (Note this is also known as the "part performance" exception to the Statute of Frauds regarding transfers of interest in land [§ 10–12].) Whether Dan will get specific performance of the promise, i.e., actually get title to the land as promised, or simply be recompensed for his work and improvements on the land, will depend on what "justice requires" given all the circumstances (*see* § 8–16). Note that in this type of case the promissory estoppel doctrine not only overcomes a "no consideration" defense, but also overcomes a Statute of Frauds defense (*see* Chapter Ten), thereby making enforceable an <u>oral</u> promise to convey an interest in land.

3. **Charitable Subscriptions. [§ 8–9]**

The rule regarding the enforceability of promises to donate to a charity is different from the rules governing most promissory estoppel situations. Under § 90(2) of the Restatement 2d, **a pledge to a charity is enforceable even without proof that the promise induced any reliance whatsoever by the organization.**

　　a. **Example. [§ 8–10]**

Ellen calls a March of Dimes telethon and pledges $100. The promise is enforceable by the March of Dimes under § 90(2) of the Restatement 2d, even though it was gratuitous (and thus without consideration) and <u>even if the March of Dimes did not take any action in reliance on Ellen's promise</u>.

4. **Offers That Induce Foreseeable Reliance of a Substantial Nature Become Irrevocable. [§ 8–11]**

Under § 87(2) of the Restatement 2d, promissory estoppel will also serve to make any other type of offer irrevocable (at least to the extent necessary to avoid injustice) if:

　　(a) **The offeror should reasonably and foreseeably expect the offeree to undertake substantial action in reliance on the offer;** and

　　(b) **The offer actually does induce that reliance.**

PROMISSORY ESTOPPEL AND THE SEAL

a. **Example. [§ 8–12]**

Food Co. makes an offer to Farmer promising her that it is willing to buy all the carrots Farmer grows this season at a fixed price. Food Co. tells Farmer she may think about the offer for a month and need not accept before then. Farmer immediately purchases carrot seed and informs Food Co. of her actions. Within two weeks Farmer has dedicated a substantial portion of her farm to growing carrots. At this point, Food Co.'s offer is likely irrevocable until the end of the month, since Food Co. should reasonably have expected Farmer to rely on the offer to a substantial degree, and because Farmer has, in fact, relied on Food Company's promise.

b. **Offers by Sub-Contractors. [§ 8–13]**

The most common application of the rule in § 87(2) of the Restatement 2d is in dealings between general contractors and subcontractors. To fully appreciate the applicability of § 87(2) to this kind of situation, some understanding of the general contractor/subcontractor relationship is necessary.

In the construction industry, general contractors are awarded contracts by developers for constructing large projects. General contractors almost never do all the work on a large project by themselves. Thus, in preparing their proposals to submit to the developer, general contractors ("generals") solicit offers to complete various parts of the project from subcontractors, e.g., a subcontractor ("sub") will make a bid (i.e., make an offer) to do the paving work, the electrical work, etc. The general will then compile all the various proposals from all the subcontractors, and add them to the price for its own work to determine the fee it will charge the developer for the entire project.

Occasionally a sub will change its mind about its bid after the general has already relied on it by using it as part of the general's proposal to the developer, but before the general has formally "accepted" the sub's proposal. (That is, although a general will use the sub's bid in making its proposal to the developer, it will not accept the sub's offer until the developer has accepted the general's proposal to develop the entire project. The reason is that a general will not want to commit to paying the sub unless the general is awarded the development contract.) Under normal formation rules, an offer such as the one made by the sub is freely revocable until the time of acceptance [§§ 4–28 *et seq.*].

However, under § 87(2), **promissory estoppel makes the promisor's (i.e., the subcontractor's) offer irrevocable until the general contractor has a reasonable chance to**

accept. Typically, that "reasonable time" extends to a day or two after the developer has awarded the project to the general. That is, within the construction industry, a general contractor using a sub's bid to develop its own proposal is considered reasonable, foreseeable, and an act of substantial reliance. As such, it is deemed unjust to allow the sub to revoke the offer once it has been communicated to the general [*See* § 4–86 for a discussion of *Drennan v. Star Paving*].

5. **Actions Taken in Reliance on Promises Made in Preliminary Negotiations. [§ 8–14]**

   A few courts have held that a rather vague promise made in preliminary negotiations, as opposed to an offer, may be enforceable to some extent if reliance on that promise was both foreseeable and reasonable.

   a. **Example of *Hoffman v. Red Owl Stores*. [§ 8–15]**

      Red Owl franchised stores. Its representative promised Hoffman that he would be awarded a franchise if he gained the necessary experience and invested $18,000. Hoffman started a two-year quest to gain the necessary experience by quitting his job, moving to another city to go to work in another store, borrowing $18,000 from a relative, and taking a few other like-actions. At the end of the two years, Red Owl stated for the first time that the $18,000 franchise fee could not be paid with borrowed money and refused to award Hoffman a franchise.

      Held: No contract existed under the indefiniteness doctrine (*see* Chapter Six) because there were simply too many details left open as to the terms of the proposed franchise to call it an offer, e.g., where the store was to be located, how soon he could operate it, what percentage of profits he would owe Red Owl under a franchise agreement, etc. At most, Red Owl's promises were part of a preliminary negotiation. Nevertheless, because Red Owl should have foreseen Hoffman would have relied on the promise to his detriment, and because Hoffman did in fact rely on the promise, it would now be unjust not to enforce the promise to some degree. Thus, under a promissory estoppel theory, Hoffman could recover the out of pocket costs he spent in reliance on the pre-contractual promise. [*Hoffman v. Red Owl Stores*, 133 N.W.2d 267 (Wis. 1965)].

      Note that this case also sets forth the rather controversial doctrine that the parties owe a duty of good faith to each other not only in the performance and enforcement of a completed contract, but also during its **negotiation**. To that extent, the case extends dramatically and (virtually) uniquely the obligation of good faith set forth in the Restatement 2d § 205 and

UCC § 1–304, which limit good faith just to only the performance and enforcement of contractual promises after the contract is signed.

E. REMEDIES WHEN A PROMISE IS ENFORCED UNDER PROMISSORY ESTOPPEL. [§ 8–16]

When a promise is made enforceable under promissory estoppel, it is not necessarily enforceable to its full extent. Rather, under the Restatement 2d, when a party breaches a promise that is made enforceable under promissory estoppel, "the remedy granted for breach may be limited as justice allows" [Restatement 2d § 90(1)]. Sometimes the promisee is entitled to recover his or her full expectation interest, i.e., the full amount to which he or she would have been entitled had the contract gone forward. However, where the expectation interest is greatly disproportionate to the promisee's actual reliance, or where the circumstances make it unjust (or impossible) to award the complete expectation interest, a promisee is only entitled to his or her reliance damages, i.e., the amount actually expended in reliance on the promise (*see* §§ 30–28 and 30–65 for a discussion of reliance damages).

1. **Example. [§ 8–17]**

    A famous hypothetical illustrating this principle assumes that a well-dressed, obviously wealthy woman becomes concerned about a man who is not warmly dressed standing outside during a snow flurry. The woman tells the man she will give him $300 to buy a warm coat at a nearby store. The man goes into the store and buys a coat for $200. The question is, should he be entitled to $200 from the woman (the value of his out-of-pocket reliance), or $300 (the value of the full promise made by the woman)? Although Professor Williston disagreed, most commentators hold that in these circumstances, justice requires that enforcement of the promise should be limited to the man's actual reliance.

2. **Example of *Hoffman v. Red Owl Stores*. [§ 8–18]**

    (The facts of *Hoffman* are given in § 8–15.) It was impossible to award Hoffman any expectation damages because it was impossible to ascertain what profits, if any, he would have made running the grocery store. Given the uncertainty of the expectation interest, it was proper to award him his reliance, or out of pocket, damages.

F. EXAM APPROACH TO PROMISSORY ESTOPPEL ISSUES. [§ 8–19*]

Contracts professors are usually wary of students relying too heavily on promissory estoppel to enforce promises, and thereby relying too little on the intricacies of consideration when writing exam answers. In theory, many (if not most) of the promises supported by consideration could just as easily be supported by promissory estoppel. That is, most of the time, in a contract supported by consideration, it is also reasonable to foresee that a bargained for promise will be relied upon by the other party, the promise is usually relied upon, and it would be just to enforce it. However, as Justice Holmes once said, "[a] pervasive use of promissory estoppel would cut up the doctrine of consideration by the roots." Accordingly, in your analysis of formation issues for your essay tests, you should **first** determine whether a promise can be supported by consideration. If it can, your analysis should proceed from there [§ 7–97]. It is only after you analyze thoroughly whether the promise can meet the requirements of consideration that you should examine whether the promise can be enforced by promissory estoppel.

G. THE COMMON LAW SEAL. [§ 8–20]

At common law, any promise contained in a document delivered with the promisor's seal (i.e., a wax impression, usually formed by pressing a signet ring, corporate seal, or the like into molten wax dripped onto the document) was binding even in the absence of consideration. However, the UCC in § 2–203, has formally declared seals to be inoperative, and most states have followed suit in non-UCC transactions as well. However, § 95 of the Restatement 2d still permits a sealed document to be enforced without consideration so long as the document is "delivered," and so long as the promisor and promisee are either named or identifiably described in the document. Despite this provision, the seal as a substitute for consideration is, for the most part, a dead issue.

---

* For more information, listen to CD # 5, Track 3 of *Sum and Substance Audio on Contracts*.

CHAPTER 9

MODIFICATIONS (WITH AN EMPHASIS ON UCC § 2–209)

A. MODIFICATION, GENERALLY. [§ 9–1*]

Parties to a contract sometimes wish to vary the terms of their agreement. If they want to make the changes to their initial contract enforceable by a court, they must enter into a valid **"modification"** of their original agreement.

A valid modification is itself a separate, enforceable contract. It is sometimes called "a contract on a contract," that is, a subsequent contract whose terms are largely the same as those in the original contract, but with one or more of the deal points changed.

Many modification issues are related to consideration. The common law and Restatement modification rules relating to consideration are discussed in Chapter Seven and briefly summarized below in §§ 9–20 *et seq.* However, consideration, especially under the UCC, presents unique issues, and the focus of this chapter is on the special consideration issues presented by UCC § 2–209 beginning with § 9–3.

Often enforcing a modification does not pose any particular problems, for the parties live up to their modified agreement. However, where one party asserts that a modification took place and the other disagrees, or where they both agree that a modification took place but don't agree as to its terms, modifications can present some of the most sophisticated problems of contract law. An example of how the issues can arise is illustrated below.

1. **The Concern Regarding Modifications. [§ 9–2]**

    One problem in learning the issues giving rise to the modification doctrine is that usually you are told up front in a hypothetical whether a modification actually took place. With that knowledge, it

---

* For more information, listen to CD # 5, Track 1 of *Sum and Substance Audio on Contracts*.

is tempting to try and make sure the case comes out the "right" way and reward the innocent party.

To realize the complexity of the issues surrounding modification, assume you are a judge. Two contracting parties, Ed, the President of Boutique (a clothing store), and Sally, the owner of Sweaters-R-Us (a clothing manufacturer) have a written contract calling for the delivery of 100 sweaters—50 green and 50 yellow. They both agree there was timely delivery of the sweaters, and both agree that there were no green sweaters in the delivery; instead there were 100 yellow ones. Sally claims this was not a breach, however, as she says she telephoned Ed a few days before delivery was due, and he told her it was alright to substitute the extra yellow sweaters for the green ones called for in the contract. Sally says that in the phone call, she told Ed that she was temporarily out of green sweaters, and was willing to work her factory overtime to produce the green sweaters if Ed really wanted them, but if Ed could live with the extra yellow ones, she'd appreciate it. She says Ed agreed. Ed denies that such a conversation ever took place.

As judge, if you go by the contract only, and say that Sally's company is in breach for not delivering the green sweaters, you may be fostering fraud, because what Sally said may well have happened. However, if you allow Sally to testify about this alleged oral modification, you may also be perpetuating fraud, for Sally may just be trying to cover up a breach on her part by making up the conversation with Ed. Contract law has to have rules that govern whether Sally gets to testify about the alleged modification, and those rules are discussed throughout the remainder of this chapter.

B. MODIFICATION UNDER THE UCC. [§ 9–3]

In § 2–209, the UCC sets forth a number of rules regarding the enforceability of modifications. Section 2–209 has five sections, which provide the following:

1. A modification under the UCC is enforceable **even without consideration** [UCC § 2–209(1); § 9–4];

2. A **"no modification except in writing" clause** *is enforceable*, i.e., if such a clause is in the original contract, any modification of that agreement must be in a writing or record to be enforceable [UCC § 2–209(2); § 9–6];

3. The agreement, as modified, **must satisfy the Statute of Frauds** to be enforceable [UCC § 2–209(3); § 9–7];

4. An **oral modification, unenforceable because of a "no modification except in writing" clause or because it does not satisfy the Statute of Frauds**, "*can* operate as a *waiver*" [UCC § 2–209(4); § 9–10]; and

MODIFICATIONS (WITH AN EMPHASIS ON UCC § 2–209)

5. If an oral modification is being enforced as a waiver, **the waiver may be retracted *with reasonable* notice,** so long as the other party has **not relied on the waiver** [UCC § 2–209(5); § 9–16].

1. **Modifications Under the UCC Are Enforceable Even Without Consideration. [§ 9–4]**

   UCC § 2–209(1) provides that **modifications are enforceable even without separate consideration** to support them. This is a change from the common law, which required that new consideration had to be present to make modified agreements enforceable under the pre-existing duty rule [§§ 7–71 *et seq*.]. Hence the drafters of the UCC chose to reject the pre-existing duty rule and allow for enforceable modifications without the need to generate some new consideration.

   a. **Example. [§ 9–5]**

      Richard makes volleyballs. He is under a contract to deliver 100 volleyballs to Karen on March 1. On February 20, he calls and asks Karen if it would be acceptable if he delivered the balls on March 15, and Karen says it will be no problem.

      At common law, Karen and Richard would have had to exchange new consideration to make the new delivery date effective, e.g., Karen would need to have ordered more volleyballs, or Richard would have had to promise to deliver the volleyballs at a different shipping charge, etc. However, under § 2–209(1), the modification can be enforced even without new consideration.

      Note that while the Richard/Karen modification is enforceable under § 2–209(1), it may not be enforceable under § 2–209(3) (*see* § 9–7).

   As will be explained further below (*see* § 9–20) one of the benefits of the common law's consideration requirement is that it provided evidence that a modification took place. That is, unless the parties really had made a modification, there was little reason for Richard to promise to throw in a few more volleyballs. To replace this evidentiary benefit, the UCC requires generally that the modification be in writing to be enforceable as a modification. These rules are explained in the next few sections.

2. **An Oral Modification Is Unenforceable Under the UCC if the Parties Have Agreed to a "No Modification Except by Signed Writing" Clause. [§ 9–6]**

   On occasion, buyers and sellers will enter into an agreement in which both parties agree that no modification may be effectively made to their contract unless the terms of the modification are reduced to a record signed by both parties. There is an obvious evidentiary

CHAPTER 9

advantage to requiring that no provision of a contract can be altered unless it is in writing. Also, if the requirement is that it must be in writing and signed by someone in the "home office," it stops the remote sales representative from making extravagant promises in the field just to close the deal or make an important customer happy.

UCC § 2–209(2) provides that "no modification except by signed writing" clauses (or, as they are sometimes known, "private statute of frauds" clauses) are enforceable. Thus, while a modification need not have consideration to be binding under § 2–209(1), if the parties have agreed to a no modification except in writing clause, the modification itself must be in a signed writing or it is generally unenforceable. These clauses were generally unenforceable at common law [§ 9–21].

3. **The Contract, as Modified, Must Satisfy the Statute of Frauds to Be Enforceable Under the UCC. [§ 9–7]**

Section 2–209(3) provides that the Statute of Frauds set forth in UCC § 2–201 must be satisfied if the contract, **as modified**, is within the Statute. Thus, if the parties' amended contract is for the sale of goods for $500 or more, the modified agreement must satisfy UCC § 2–201 or it is unenforceable. If the modified contract is unenforceable, then the original contract's terms are binding. Again, while the modification need not be supported by consideration under UCC § 2–209(1) to be enforceable, the modified agreement **must satisfy the Statute of Frauds under § 2–209(3)** to be effective.

Usually the Statute of Frauds under § 2–201 is satisfied by the existence of a signed memorandum, there are other ways to satisfy it, e.g., under the merchant's confirmatory memorandum doctrine of § 2–201(2), by the sending of specially made goods, by an admission made under penalty of perjury, or by performance under § 2–201(3). Hence, if the contract as modified can satisfy any portion of § 2–201, it will be enforceable.

   a. **Example. [§ 9–8]**

   Bob and Janet have signed a contract whereby Bob has agreed to sell his Poussin painting to Janet for $100,000. Under the contract, Bob is to deliver the painting on September 1. Bob claims that he and Janet modified their agreement in a telephone conversation after the contract was signed so as to allow Bob to deliver the painting a month later, on October 1.

   Janet denies she ever agreed to a later delivery. Even if the telephone conversation occurred the way Bob said it did, under the majority view the modified delivery date would be unenforceable, and inadmissible in a breach of contract action, under § 2–209(3) because the contract as modified, i.e., the contract with the October 1 delivery date, did not satisfy the Statute of Frauds under § 2–201. That is, there is no signed writing evidencing a contract with an October 1 delivery date. As such, the enforceable terms of Bob and Janet's agreement are those found in the original contract, which calls for the September 1 delivery. Hence, if Bob delivers the painting after September 1, he has breached.

Although such an agreement cannot be enforced as a *modification* under § 2–209(3), note that there is the possibility Bob may prevail by means of *waiver* as discussed in § 9–10.

b. **Example. [§ 9–9]**

Larry and Gina have a written contract calling for Larry to sell his stereo to Gina for $550. Gina claims they orally modified the price term to $490. Evidence of the alleged modification is freely admissible and the modification is enforceable because the contract, as purportedly modified, is not within the UCC's Statute of Frauds since it is for the sale of goods for less than $500.

4. **A Modification That Is Unenforceable Because It Is Not in Writing Can Still Operate as an Enforceable Waiver Under the UCC. [§ 9–10]**

Section 2–209(4) is probably the most complicated provision in Article 2, although it does not seem so at first glance. The provision says that if an attempted oral modification is unenforceable, either because the contract as modified does not satisfy the Statute of Frauds under § 2–209(3), or because there is a valid and unsatisfied "no modification except by writing" clause under § 2–209(2), the attempted modification nonetheless "can operate as a waiver." The interpretive problems concerning this provision have centered around three questions:

(1) What is it that can be "waived" under § 2–209(4);

(2) How can an otherwise unenforceable oral modification "operate" at all; and

(3) Since the provision does not say that an unenforceable modification "must" operate as a waiver, but only that it "can" operate as a waiver, under what circumstances "can" it so operate?

The courts have developed four different approaches to these questions:

CHAPTER 9

a. **The First Interpretation of How § 2–209(4) Operates: The Only Way a No Modification Except in Writing Clause, or the Statute of Frauds, May Be "Waived" Is by Written Agreement of the Parties Specifically Waiving the Clause or Applicability of the Statute. [§ 9–11]**

This view holds that § 2–209(4)'s "waiver" provision means that the parties are permitted, if they so choose, to waive the effects of either a no modification except by writing clause, or the Statute of Frauds, but can only do so via a signed writing that expressly waives those provisions. That is, § 2–209(4) gives permission to the parties to vary the operation of an otherwise binding writing requirement. However, the only effective way to make such a waiver, according to this interpretation, is via a signed, writing, which, by its own terms, specifically authorizes the parties to make subsequent binding oral modifications.

This interpretation has only limited traction among courts and commentators, and does not make a lot of sense. If the parties are going to exchange a signed writing, why would they have it say "we waive the writing requirement" and not just recite the attempted modification? And even if they recited the modified term, it is not reasonable to expect, e.g., two small business people not up on the intricacies § 2–209 to also say in their writing, "Oh, and by the way we agree also to waive the effects of the statute of frauds and/or any otherwise enforceable no modification except by signed writing clause."

b. **The Second Interpretation of How § 2–209(4) Operates: An Attempted Oral Modification Acts as an Implied Waiver of Both a No Modification Except in Writing Clause and the Statute of Frauds. [§ 9–12]**

This interpretation of § 2–209(4) provides that every time one party asserts that an oral modification took place, the court should initially examine the testimony and other evidence of that party concerning the alleged modification out of the presence of the jury. If the court finds such evidence sufficiently credible, i.e., evidence from which the jury could believe the modification occurred, the court is instructed to let the party present that same evidence before the jury.

The rationale for allowing the introduction of evidence of an oral modification even when the contract as modified does not satisfy the Statute, or when there is a "no modification except in writing" clause, is that **by agreeing to an oral modification, both parties simultaneously, albeit implicitly, agreed to a waiver of any writing requirement that formerly bound them**. That is, if the parties truly agreed to an oral modification,

MODIFICATIONS (WITH AN EMPHASIS ON UCC § 2–209)

obviously the presence of a writing requirement such as the Statute of Frauds was of no concern to them. Hence, upon their making such an agreement, there must have been a mutual, but implied, waiver of the Statute. That being so, this view holds that since courts are directed to enforce the contract in such a way as to effectuate the parties' intentions whenever possible, the modification, if truly agreed to, should be enforced and all credible evidence surrounding its making should be admitted. This was largely how common law treated oral modifications in light of a no modification except in writing clause, but again, recall that common law also had the consideration requirement which, if satisfied, lent credence to the fact that the modification was made. [*See* the further discussion of this issue in § 9–21].

c. **The Third Interpretation of How § 2–209(4) Operates: The Terms of a Bilateral Oral Modification Are Inadmissible, but Evidence of One Party's Unilateral Waiver Is Admissible upon a Showing of Good Faith. [§ 9–13]**

There are several "background" concepts that must be discussed before this theory can be completely understood.

The first such concept is the difference between a waiver and a modification in traditional contract terms. A waiver is sometimes defined as the intentional relinquishment of a known right and this definition will be used throughout this chapter. (Note that technically, a waiver is more properly defined as the excuse in the non-occurrence of, or delay in the occurrence of, a constructive condition [§ 21–79], but this is a more technical application of the waiver doctrine than is generally learned when modification issues are discussed in a first year Contracts course).

The important things about a waiver for § 2–209(4) purposes are: (a) that a *waiver* is the result of *unilateral* action, whereas a **modification** requires the agreement of **both** parties to a substitution of terms; and (b) a waiver focuses solely on the choice not to enforce a particular duty, whereas a modification concerns both the old term that the parties have canceled **and** the new term they have substituted in its place.

The second concept that needs to be understood is that inherent in any bilateral modification is one party's waiver. For example, assume a written contract calls for delivery of certain goods on August 10, and that the parties orally agree to modify that date to September 1. While a modification has occurred, so has a waiver. That is, there has been a modification since both the parties agreed to substitute the September 1 date for the August 10 date. Inherent in that transaction, however, is also the buyer's waiver, i.e., the intentional relinquishment of his or her right, to declare a breach if the goods are not delivered on August 10, so long as they are delivered by September 1.

Putting those ideas together, this interpretation of § 2–209(4) holds that while evidence of what **both** parties orally agreed to in their modification is inadmissible, evidence of one party's waiver of a particular term is admissible. That is, evidence that the parties got together and orally changed the August 10 delivery date to September 1 would be inadmissible. However, evidence that the buyer unilaterally relinquished his or her right to declare a breach if the goods were delivered between August 10 and September 1 **would be** admissible, so long as the parties appear to the court to have acted in good faith, i.e., there does not seem to be any extortion or unfair profiteering.

If you think that this emphasizes form over substance to some respect, you are correct. That is because the same conversation—the same words—constitutes both a modification and a waiver.

The justification for this theory is that it gives credence to the words of § 2–209(4). It says that when a modification can't be enforced because it does not satisfy §§ 2–209(2) and (3), it "can" operate as a waiver. So the mutual agreement of the parties can't be enforced, but one party's waiver of the right to sue can be admitted and enforced.

Critics of this approach argue that it makes all asserted modifications theoretically enforceable, meaning that any party who breaches a contract could simply come into court and say that the parties had a phone call and modified the original agreement in such a way as to make the resulting performance not a breach. The proponents of this view acknowledge that it does make modifications somewhat easier to establish, but point out that is what the drafters of the UCC appeared to want. Further, they note that modifications still have to be done in good faith [§ 9–18], and that the good faith requirement means the main worries of the modification doctrine—rewarding the extortionist, profiteer, and dishonest compromiser [§§ 7–72 *et seq.*]—are largely eliminated.

d. **The Fourth Interpretation of How § 2–209(4) Operates: Evidence of the Modification Is Freely Admissible if the Party Seeking to Establish the Modification Can Show Reliance on the Modified Agreement. [§ 9–14]**

Under this interpretation of § 2–209(4), a party seeking to establish a modification will not be allowed to do so unless he or she can establish reliance on the alleged modification. If such reliance can be shown, then evidence of the entire oral modification is freely admissible and the modification will be enforceable.

As touched on above, the proponents of this view note that one of the reasons behind the common law requirement that consideration be present to enforce a modification was that consideration provided evidence that the modification had, in fact, occurred. In other words, if Joe paid Rebecca $50, and now says the reason he did so was to move the delivery date of the contract back 10 days, the check itself provides some evidence that a modification did, in fact, occur. (Of course the $50 could have been for the re-payment of an independent loan, but at least it provides some basis to believe Joe other than just his unsupported testimony.)

Since reliance is often used to enforce a contractual promise in the absence of consideration [Chapter Eight], this view posits that when the drafters of the Code removed the common law consideration requirement as a requisite for enforcing modifications in § 2–209(1), it is reasonable to assume they intended to include reliance in its place in § 2–209(4) to serve as an evidentiary substitute, or even if that wasn't the intent of the drafters, such an approach makes sense and explains when a waiver "can" operate and when it cannot. That is, if a party can show he or she took some action in reliance on the modified promise, it is some objective evidence that the modification in fact took place.

While this interpretation makes some sense from a policy point of view, its critics point out that it has no linguistic support in the statute. That is, there is nothing in § 2–209(4) that speaks in terms of "reliance." Since the drafters did use the term "reliance" in § 2–209(5) [§ 9–16], and chose not to use it in § 2–209(4), its absence in the latter must mean that a reliance requirement cannot be read into subsection 4, or so say those who disagree with this view.

e. **Example of *Wisconsin Knife Works v. National Metal Crafters*. [§ 9–15]**

Wisconsin Knife Works ("Wisconsin") entered into a series of contracts with National Metal Crafters ("National") calling for National to deliver spade bit blanks. Some of the contracts had a "no modification except in writing" clause, and the court found no modification except in writing was the intent in all the contracts. National appeared to miss several delivery deadlines under these contracts, and eventually Wisconsin terminated the contracts, declaring that the cumulative effect of the late deliveries amounted to a material breach.

Wisconsin thereafter sued National seeking damages for that material breach. In its defense, National claimed that it had not missed the **operative** delivery deadlines of the contract because the original delivery dates called for in the written contract had been orally modified. As a consequence, National counter-claimed against Wisconsin, asserting that Wisconsin had breached by anticipatorily repudiating the agreement in its termination letter. The trial court admitted the evidence proffered by National that changes had been made to the delivery dates, and the jury apparently believed National, for it awarded National $30,000 on its counter-claim, and awarded Wisconsin nothing.

Judge Posner wrote the majority opinion for the Seventh Circuit, reversing the trial court and adopting the "fourth interpretation" given above of § 2–209(4)'s operation. He stated that unless National could establish reliance on the alleged waivers, it could not introduce evidence of them and they would not be enforceable. Therefore, he remanded the case to allow National the opportunity to prove some sort of reliance, like ordering more raw materials after the original date of delivery passed in order to supply Wisconsin.

Judge Easterbrook dissented, holding that National's evidence of the changed delivery dates was properly received. He stated that the "third interpretation" was the proper one, and hence National was freely entitled to introduce evidence of Wisconsin's unilateral waiver of the original delivery dates so long as it appeared the parties acted in good faith, and if the jury believed National's evidence as to the existence and good faith of the modifications, the modifications were enforceable [*Wisconsin Knife Works v. National Metal Crafters,* 781 F.2d 1280 (7th Cir. 1986)].

5. **Retraction of Waivers in Modifications Controlled by the UCC. [§ 9–16]**

An enforceable **modification** made under § 2–209 cannot be unilaterally retracted, for it is the result of the agreement of both parties. Of course, it can be mutually rescinded, released, further modified, etc., but it cannot simply be rendered a nullity just because one party later changes his or her mind and wants to "retract" it.

However, a **waiver** of an executory duty ***can*** be unilaterally retracted, for a waiver concerns the rights of only one party to enforce an obligation. The rules governing when such waiver can be retracted in the modification context are set forth in § 2–209(5), and are

MODIFICATIONS (WITH AN EMPHASIS ON UCC § 2–209)

identical to the rules in non-UCC contracts [§ 21–100]. That is, upon reasonable notice, a waiver of executory duties due under a contract is freely retractable *unless* such retraction would be unjust under the circumstances due to a material change of position by the other party in reliance on the waiver.

  a. **Example. [§ 9–17]**

   Alex purchased a boat and was obligated to make payments to the Boat Yard of $1,000/month for 48 months. Six months into the contract Alex asked Julie, the owner of Boat Yard, if she would be willing to take $700/month for the next 60 months rather than insist on the remaining forty-two $1,000 payments. Julie orally agreed, and for a year accepted the $700 payments. However, she thereafter changed her mind and demanded that Alex go back to making $1,000/month payments. As Julie's initial waiver of the right to insist on $1,000 payments was only as to executory portions of the contract, i.e., as to future unmade payments, she is entitled unilaterally to rescind the waiver and demand $1,000 payments from now on, **unless** Alex can show some sort of changed position in reliance on Julie's waiver, e.g., he took a lesser paying job, incurred another $300/month obligation, etc.

6. **Party Proposing the Modification Must Act in Good Faith in Order for a Modification Under a UCC Agreement to Be Enforceable. [§ 9–18]**

  Although it is not specifically set forth in § 2–209, it is clear that under the UCC, just as under the common law (§ 9–20), the party proposing the modification must do so in **good faith** in order to have the subsequent modification enforceable [UCC § 1–304].

  a. **Example. [§ 9–19]**

   Joe has a contract to supply Tilly's Restaurant with 5 dozen of a special kind of cookie that is especially popular with Tilly's customers each week, along with whatever cakes Tilly's may order for that week. One day, because he was mad at Tilly for failing to order some carrot cake, on which he made a large profit, Joe lied and told Tilly he was having some production problems and asked if would be OK to deliver only 1 dozen of the cookies. Tilly agreed.

   There has been a modification of their contract, reducing the quantity from five dozen to one dozen cookies. However, because Joe offered the modification in bad faith, it isn't enforceable. Hence, if she wishes, Tilly could sue Joe for failing to deliver four dozen cookies, even though she agreed to take the lesser amount.

Note that if Joe had really had some sort of difficulty, e.g., his ovens had broken or he had labor problems, etc., and so proposed the modification in good faith, it would be enforceable and Tilly could not sue for the failure to deliver the "missing" four dozen cookies.

C. MODIFICATIONS AT COMMON LAW AND UNDER THE RESTATEMENT. [§ 9–20]

Common Law:

A valid modification at common law required only two things:

1. Good faith by the party seeking the modification [§ 9–21]; and
2. New consideration to support the modification [§ 9–24].

Without these criteria fulfilled, the modification was unenforceable under the pre-existing duty rule [§ 7–71].

1. "No Modification Except in Writing" Clauses and Statute of Frauds Concerns Are Not Applicable to Oral Modifications Governed by Common Law Rules. [§ 9–21]

An oral modification with consideration was generally enforced at common law, even if the original contract had a no modification except in writing clause or even if the modified agreement, if viewed by itself, did not satisfy the statute of frauds. This is because it viewed that in making an oral modification, the parties inherently waived any writing requirement.

2. Restatement Rules. [§ 9–22]

The <u>general</u> Restatement rule is the same as that of common law: to surmount the pre-existing duty rule [Restatement 2d § 73] separate consideration must be present, as well as good faith [Restatement 2d § 205] to make the modification enforceable. However, the Restatement departs from pure common law and allows some modifications to be enforced even without new consideration.

a. Instances Where Restatement Allows *Some* Modifications to Be Enforceable Without Consideration. [§ 9–23]

The Restatement 2d allows modifications to be enforceable without consideration to be enforceable in three situations given in Restatement 2d § 89:

(a) Where the modification was made in good faith; and is **fair** in view of **circumstances not reasonably foreseen** when the contract was made [Restatement 2d § 89(a)];

MODIFICATIONS (WITH AN EMPHASIS ON UCC § 2–209)

    (b) Where a **statute provides that no consideration need be provided for the modification to be enforceable** [Restatement 2d § 89(b)]; or

    (c) Where **justice otherwise requires** that it be enforced due to a **material change of position, or reliance**, on the modified promise [Restatement 2d § 89(c)].

A further discussion of each of these exceptions is given in § 7–81.

b. Restatement Rule Requires Statue of Frauds to Be Satisfied for the Contract, as Modified. [§ 9–24]

Restatement 2d § 149 requires that the contract, as modified, must satisfy the statute of frauds. In this respect it is thus like the UCC's rule in § 2–209(3) [§ 9–7], and unlike the common law rule as discussed § 9–20.

c. Difference Between Modification and Rescission of Prior Agreement Followed by Entry into New Contract. [§ 9–25]

An issue sometimes arises as to whether a purported modification can be classified as the rescission of the old contract and entry into a new agreement with the modified terms. That is, assume the original contract called for delivery on June 1, and that the modified agreement calls for delivery on June 15. We normally would view this as a modification, defined as the continuation of the existing contract, but with one or more of its terms altered. But some have argued that it can equally be looked at as the rescission of the contract with the June 1 delivery date and entry into a new contract with a June 15 delivery date.

Distinguishing between the two views is significant for consideration purposes. This is because the destruction of a legal relationship is an act that qualifies as consideration [Restatement 2d § 71(3)(c)], as does the creation of a new contract [*Id.*]. This is because both parties give up something when they rescind the old contract and both gain something when they enter into a new contract. However, if every modification could be viewed as a rescission and creation of a new contract, then the requirement of "new" consideration for a modification under the pre-existing duty rule [Restatement 2d § 73] would largely be a nullity.

Common law contract law solves this potential dilemma by requiring additional overt acts before a mutual rescission is found. Typically this is something like physically ripping up the old agreement, tearing off the signatures on the old agreement, "X'ing" through the old agreement, or entering into a new agreement that recites that the parties had a previous agreement that they have mutually cancelled or rescinded.

The UCC deals with this issue by including the term "rescission" in both § 2–209(2) and § 2–209(4) so that the analysis is the same regardless whether the party seeks to enforce a modified agreement or a new one after rescinding the old one.

D. GRAPHIC SUMMARY OF UCC AND COMMON LAW RULES REGARDING MODIFICATION. [§ 9–26]

A summary of the common law and UCC rules regarding modifications is presented graphically below:

	UCC	Restatement	Common Law
Good Faith required?	Yes	Yes	Yes
Consideration required?	No	Yes*	Yes
No mod. except in writing enforceable?	Yes	No	No
Stat of Frauds gen. have to be satisfied?	Yes	Yes	No

* Subject to exceptions in Restatement 2d § 89

E. MODIFICATION UNDER THE CISG. [§ 9–27]

Article 29(2) sets forth the rules for the enforceability of oral modifications under the CISG. As there is no Statute of Frauds under the CISG, the only issue is the enforceability of no modification except in writing clauses. Article 29(2) provides: "A contract in writing which contains a provision requiring any modification . . . to be in writing may not otherwise be modified." Hence, it affirms the enforceability of such clauses.

The provision continues, however, with one exception to the general rule: "However, a party may be precluded by his conduct from asserting such a provision to the extent the other party has relied on that conduct." Hence, like the "fourth" interpretation of UCC § 2–209 discussed above [§ 9–14], one party's demonstrated reliance on the oral modification (the "conduct of the other") makes the oral modification enforceable, even with a no modification except in writing clause.

F. DISTINGUISHING MODIFICATION FROM THE PAROL EVIDENCE RULE. [§ 9–28]

A frequently made mistake by first year students is to confuse analysis under modification rules with analysis under the parol evidence rule. [The

MODIFICATIONS (WITH AN EMPHASIS ON UCC § 2–209)

parol evidence rule is discussed in Chapter Eighteen]. The standard is this:

If the alleged oral agreement of the parties was made **before**, or **contemporaneous with**, execution of the written contract, it is a parol evidence rule issue.

If the alleged oral agreement of the parties was made **after the contract was signed, it is a modification issue.**

That is, the key to determining which set of rules applies is to determine **when** the alleged oral agreement was made.

1. **Example. [§ 9–29]**

   Fred negotiated with Computer Co. over the sale of a XT–100 computer. Fred thought he and the salesman had reached an agreement during the bargaining process that Computer Co. would include an extra 1 Megabyte of RAM in his computer at no extra charge, but that term did not appear in their final written and signed contract. In addition, the final contract called for delivery of the computer on September 30, but after the contract was executed Computer Co. says it asked, and claims Fred agreed, to extend the delivery date to October 15.

   The issue of whether Fred can enforce the promise to install an extra 1 Mb of RAM is a parol evidence question, for it concerns agreement as to a term allegedly made prior to execution of the contract. Resolution of the proper delivery date is a modification issue, for it concerns an alleged agreement made after the contract was signed.

G. EXAM APPROACH TO MODIFICATION ISSUES. [§ 9–30]

When a contract is modified, use the following approach to assess whether the modification will be enforceable, or whether the terms of the original contract will control:

1. Determine whether it is a contract governed by the UCC (Chapter Thirty-Three), the common law, or the common law modified by the Restatement.

2. If it is a UCC contract, remember that the modification need not be supported by consideration to be enforceable [§ 9–4], but it must be offered in good faith [§ 9–18].

   A. If the modification is oral, recall the contract as modified must satisfy the Statute of Frauds to be enforceable **as a modification** [§ 9–7], and any "no modification except by signed writing" clause in the original contract is given effect [§ 9–6].

   B. If the oral modification cannot be enforced for the reasons given above, recall that the doctrine of waiver may allow some enforcement of the new agreement [§ 9–10]. However, also remember that waivers can be retracted so long as no reliance by the other party can be shown [§ 9–16].

3. If common law rules control, there must be new consideration and good faith present to enforce the modification under the pre-existing duty rule. However, with consideration, typically oral no modifications were enforceable even if the modified agreement satisfied the statute of frauds and even if there was a no modification except in writing clause.

4. If Restatement 2d contract rules control, the *general* rule is that, as with the common law, new consideration is needed under the pre-existing duty rule [Restatement 2d § 73], as well as good faith, to enforce the modification. However, the problem should be examined to determine whether one of the three exceptions to the new consideration requirement set forth in § 89 applies [7–81; 9–23], and realize that the Statute of Frauds must be satisfied for the contract as modified [§ 9–24].

PART IV

"VOIDABILITY" AND DEFENSES TO CONTRACT FORMATION

INTRODUCTORY NOTE ON THE CONCEPTS OF VOIDABILITY AND CONTRACT DEFENSES:

An agreement may be formed by a valid offer with a matching acceptance, and be supported by valid consideration, yet nonetheless still be unenforceable. This can happen if the agreement is "voidable" by a party, or is "void" from the beginning (void *ab initio*). The defenses discussed in this Section of the book are defenses *to formation*. That is, if any of the defenses apply, either the resulting contract can be treated as never having come into existence by the choice of a party with the defense (if voidable), or the law treats the contract as never validly came into existence at all (if void).

If a contract is voidable by a party, that party holds the option either to enforce it, or to disaffirm (avoid) it, i.e., terminate the contract without contractual liability. Another way to look at it is *that the party who has the option to disaffirm the contract based on a defense to formation has a defense to his or her non-performance*. That is, the party with the defense can refuse to perform what he or she promised in the contract, and assert the reason excusing such behavior is the facts that give rise to the defense in a subsequent breach action brought by the other party. Alternatively, the party with the defense making the resulting contract voidable can insist the other party go through with the deal and enforce the contract.

If a contract is "void," a party cannot enforce it even if he or she wishes to do so, for a "void" contract has no legal effect.

A contract is VOIDABLE if:

(a) It is a type of contract that is "within" the **Statute of Frauds** and does not satisfy the Statute of Frauds [Chapter Ten];

(b) One of the parties to the agreement is **without the capacity to contract** [Chapter Eleven];

(c) It is entered into under **mistake** [Chapter Twelve];

(d) One of the parties entered the contract under **duress by improper threat** [Chapter Thirteen];

(e) One party **unduly influenced the other** into entering into the contract [Chapter Fourteen];

(f) It was entered into by means of **fraud as to the inducement** [Chapter Fifteen]; or

(g) One or more of its terms is **unconscionable** [Chapter Sixteen].

A contract is "VOID" if:

(a) It is entered into **under duress by physical force** [§ 13.1];

(b) One party enters into it under a **fraudulent misrepresentation as to the very nature of the document itself (fraud in the *factum*)** [§ 15.3]; or

(c) It calls for a performance that is **illegal, or otherwise violates public policy** in certain cases [Chapter Seventeen].

CHAPTER 10

THE STATUTE OF FRAUDS

A. THE STATUTE OF FRAUDS DOCTRINE. [§ 10–1*]

The Statute of Frauds evidences **contract law's preference to enforce written, rather than oral, agreements** in *certain* situations. In other words, the law provides that some types of contracts will be enforced only if they are in writing. (For a list of those types of contracts, *see* § 10–4 below). Sometimes this serves a good purpose, as the Statute of Frauds can *prevent* fraudulent practices. For example, suppose Phil and Georgia never entered into a contract. Nevertheless, assume Phil tries to sue her for "breach" of oral contract anyway, hoping to win a nuisance settlement. If it is the type of contract to which the Statute of Frauds applies, Georgia has a complete defense to the suit.

However, sometimes the operation of the Statute serves an unjust purpose as it can serve to *protect* fraudulent practices. For example, suppose Phil and Georgia actually did enter into an oral contract, that Georgia does not perform, and that Phil sues her for breach. The Statute of Frauds, if applicable, would still provide Georgia with a complete defense to the action.

It is partly out of concern for the type of unfairness in the Phil/Georgia situation immediately above that the English Parliament (which passed the original Statute of Frauds in 1677) repealed most parts of the Statute in 1954, so that it does not apply to most kinds of contracts in England any longer. It is also why the CISG decided to allow oral agreements to be equally enforceable as written ones in all cases, i.e., there is not Statute of Frauds in the CISG. (*See* CISG Art. 11, providing, "[a] Contract of sale need not be concluded in or evidenced by writing. . . .")

1. Purposes of the Statute. [§ 10–2]

By requiring a signed written agreement in order to make a contract enforceable, the Statute of Frauds is said to serve several purposes:

---

* For more information, listen to CD # 7, Track 6 of *Sum and Substance Audio on Contracts*.

CHAPTER 10

(1) **evidentiary:** to provide *evidence that the parties truly entered into a contract* and to provide a written record of what they agreed to rather than trust the parties' memories;

(2) **precautionary:** to avoid a fraudulent assertion that a contract was entered into when it actually was not; and

(3) **cautionary:** to make unsophisticated parties aware that they are entering into an *agreement with legal ramifications,* i.e., when a party has to "sign" something, it appears more formal, and thus more significant, than just making an oral promise.

2. Effect of the Statute Applying. [§ 10–3]

Students spend a lot of time learning what contracts are covered by the Statute [§ 10–4] and what it takes to satisfy a contract that is covered by the Statute [§ 10–10]. Sometimes, however, the exact effect of the Statute gets overlooked.

The best way to think of the Statute is that, **when it applies and is not satisfied, it gives a party a complete defense to a breach of contract lawsuit**. For example, assume that Janet orally contracts with Bob to sell him her wine collection for $6,000. Their contract is never reduced to writing. This kind of contract is subject to the Statute [§§ 10–4 *et seq.*], and thus must be in writing to be enforceable. Now assume that Janet never delivers the wine and Bob sues her for breach. The Statute, because it applies and is not satisfied, provides Janet with a complete defense to the breach action. She did not perform what she promised, but her non-performance is excused, because she has a legally recognized *defense*—the defense of the Statute of Frauds. The way it works practically is that Bob cannot introduce any evidence of the oral contract because, under the Statute, it cannot be enforced. And if he cannot introduce evidence of the contract at trial, he cannot prove that the agreement was "breached." So Janet has a complete defense to her non-performance.

Note that the Statute has *nothing whatsoever* to do with contract formation. Just because the Statute was satisfied does not mean that a contract was formed—someone could make up or forge a signed writing for example, but that doesn't mean they had an enforceable contract. [§§ 10–46; 10–57.]

B. MAJOR TYPES OF CASES COVERED BY THE STATUTE. [§ 10–4]

While contract law refers to a "Statute of Frauds," in fact there is not a single Statute, clause, or provision that governs all the issues dealt with in this chapter. (Nevertheless, for convenience's sake, this book will go

THE STATUTE OF FRAUDS

along with the majority and discuss the doctrine as "the Statute.") However, it is more accurate to think of the Statute as a general doctrine that affects five major types of contracts studied in first year contracts classes:

(1) **Contracts for the transfer of an interest in land** [§ 10–6];

(2) **Contracts which, by their terms, cannot be performed within a year** [§ 10–14];

(3) **Contracts made in consideration of marriage** [§ 10–24];

(4) **Contracts where one party agrees to act as a surety for another** [§ 10–26]; and

(5) **Contracts for the sale of goods for $500 or more** [§ 10–35].

There is a sixth category, contracts of an executor to answer for the debts or duties of a decedent, but it is not typically studied in first year classes and will not be further discussed in this Book.

(*See* § 10–65 at the end of the chapter for a mnemonic to summarize the types pf cases subject to the Statute.)

1. Nomenclature Under the Statute of Frauds Doctrine. [§ 10–5]

Often the hardest part of mastering the Statute of Frauds is learning the terminology. The following paragraphs explain most of the seemingly tricky word choices.

If a contract **must be in writing to be enforceable**, the contract is said to be "**within the Statute**." If it *can be enforced even though oral*, it is said to be "without the Statute" or, more often, "*outside the Statute.*"

If a contract is **within the Statute**, it will **only be enforced if the Statute is "satisfied**," usually by some sort of signed writing containing the essential terms. When the contract is *within the Statute* and the necessary party *fails to satisfy the Statute* (e.g., because that party has not "signed" a "writing"), then any *oral promises made by that party are unenforceable* by the other.

C. TYPE ONE: CONTRACTS FOR THE TRANSFER OF AN INTEREST IN LAND. [§ 10–6*]

In general, **any contract for the transfer of an interest in land, other than a license, must be in writing to be enforceable** [Restatement 2d § 125].

---

* For more information, listen to CD # 7, Track 8 of *Sum and Substance Audio on Contracts*.

CHAPTER 10

1. **The Transfer of Virtually All Interests in Land, Except Licenses, Are Covered by the Statute. [§ 10–7]**

   The scope of the term "interests in land," the transfer of which must be in writing to be enforceable, is quite broad. Essentially, it includes any interest in real property other than licenses, which are only permissive uses of property. Thus, agreements to transfer homes, leases, easements, future interests, rights under restrictive covenants, or any other legal or equitable interest in land, except licenses, are within the Statute [Restatement 2d § 127].

   a. **"Transfer of Interest in Land" Includes Option Contracts. [§ 10–8]**

   An option contract regarding the sale of land must be in writing in order to be enforceable. Note that offers alone, whether offers for option contracts or offers for some other transfer of land, need not be in writing to be effective **offers**. It is only the resulting **contract** that must be in writing to be enforceable.

   b. **Promises to Pay in Return for a Present Conveyance Are Outside the Statute. [§ 10–9]**

   If a purchaser makes a promise to pay in the future in exchange for the present transfer of an interest in land, **the executory promise to pay may be enforced even if it is oral**. This is because all that is unperformed under the contract is the buyer's obligation to pay money, and not the seller's obligation to transfer a land interest. As such, the agreement at this point is outside the Statute and is looked at as only a promise to pay. However, **the opposite is not true**. A contract whereby the purchaser pays presently in return for the seller's promise to transfer land in the future *is* within the Statute, for there remains an obligation to transfer land, and not just an obligation to pay money. [Restatement 2d § 125, Cmt. e].

2. **Satisfying the Statute. [§ 10–10*]**

   If a contract for the transfer of an interest in land is within the Statute, the party seeking to enforce the contract must show:

   (a) the existence of a writing reasonably identifying all material terms of the transaction, including the interest in land that is being transferred and the price being paid for it. [Note that for all parts of the Statute, the "writing" requirement is also fulfilled by an electronic record capable of being reduced to written form, i.e., a "writing" that is on email, text, or otherwise transmitted electronically that can be printed. Note also that

---

* For more information, listen to CD # 7, Track 7 of *Sum and Substance Audio on Contracts*.

this writing is known as a "memorandum" under the Restatement 2d § 131].

(b) that the writing is signed by the other party, i.e., signed by the party against whom the contract is being enforced [Restatement 2d § 134]; and

(c) that the writing sufficiently evidences the parties' intent to transfer that interest [Restatement 2d § 131].

a. The "Merger" Doctrine. [§ 10–11]

Sometimes, all the essential terms, the signature of the party to be charged, and the intent to enter into the transaction cannot be found on only one writing, but can be found if two or more writings are taken together. All modern courts allow a party to "merge" the terms of two or more writings to create a sufficient memorandum to satisfy the Statute of Frauds. So piecing together a sale and signature from a couple of e-mails exchanged between buyer and seller is a perfectly acceptable way to establish that the Statute was fulfilled. Some courts require that these serial communications specifically refer to each other in order to "count" for statute of frauds purposes, but most courts will not require such cross-referencing if it is clear from the documents themselves that they relate to the same transaction [Restatement 2d § 132].

3. Reasonable Reliance by the Purchaser Also Makes a Promise to Transfer an Interest in Land Enforceable: The Part Performance Exception. [§ 10–12]

Even an oral contract to transfer an interest in land can be enforced if the purchaser can establish that:

(a) He or she has relied on the oral promise of the seller to sell the property, and on the continuing assent of the seller to sell the property;

(b) Such reliance was foreseeable and reasonable; and

(c) Injustice can only be avoided by enforcing the promised transfer [Restatement 2d §§ 90, 129].

Whether the buyer will be able to obtain specific performance, or is limited to reliance damages, depends on the circumstances surrounding the transaction and what justice requires. This is known as satisfying the Statute via "reliance," or via the "part performance" exception.

a. Example. [§ 10–13]

Manny orally sells Whiteacre to Jack. With Manny's knowledge, Jack moves onto the property and begins to make substantial improvements to it. Manny now tries to evict Jack, stating that their agreement for the sale of the property is unenforceable because it was oral.

Jack may equitably enforce Manny's promise to sell him the land, even though oral, because the elements listed in the previous section have been met. Whether Jack will only be permitted to recover his out-of-pocket expenses in improving the land (i.e., his reliance interest), or will be permitted to take title to the property (i.e., to get specific performance), depends on what "justice requires" after evaluating all the circumstances.

D. TYPE TWO: CONTRACTS WHICH, BY THEIR TERMS, CANNOT BE PERFORMED WITHIN A YEAR OF THEIR MAKING. [§ 10–14*]

The general common law rule is that if even a single promise made in a contract cannot be fully performed in a year from when the contract is made, all the promises in the contract are within the Statute of Frauds and thus must be in a signed writing to be enforceable. This rule is not quite as broad as it sounds, for the requirement that a promise "cannot" be performed within a year is construed quite strictly.

1. It Is Only When, by Its Own Terms, Completed Performance of a Promise Is *Impossible* Within a Year of Its Making That the Statute Applies. [§ 10–15]

If completed performance of a promise is theoretically possible, even if factually unlikely, within one year from the date it was made, the contract is outside the Statute and can be enforced even if oral.

a. Example. [§ 10–16]

Phil's Construction Company is awarded a contract for $2 billion to build an office tower twice as high and twice as large as the Willis Tower in Chicago. While it is factually unlikely that such a project could be completed in less than a year, there is nothing inherent in the contract itself that makes the completion of performance impossible within a year, and therefore the Statute does not apply. Thus, the contract can be enforced, even if oral.

b. Example. [§ 10–17]

Brian agrees to serve as Rose's butler for a two-year period. Since by the terms of the contract itself Brian's full performance cannot be completed within a year, the contract is within the Statute and must be in writing to be enforceable.

---

* For more information, listen to CD # 7, Track 9 of *Sum and Substance Audio on Contracts*.

THE STATUTE OF FRAUDS

c. Example. [§ 10–18]

On January 1, 2019, Sam agrees to work as a research assistant to Professor Smith for a three-month period beginning November 15, 2020. The contract is within the Statute, for **by its terms** it <u>cannot</u> be <u>completed</u> within one year **of its making**. Thus, it must be in writing to be enforceable.

2. Split of Opinion as to Whether Contracts Terminable Within a Year Are Within the Statute. [§ 10–19]

There is a difference of opinion as to whether contracts that are for fixed terms greater than a year, but which also give one or both parties the power to terminate them within a year, are within the Statute. An example of such a contract is where Steel Company contracts with Gas Company to purchase a supply of pure hydrogen for three years, but the contract allows either party to terminate the contract on 30 days' notice. The **majority** view holds that the **Statute applies**, as, under this view, "termination" is not "completed performance," and thus by its terms the promise to deliver gas cannot be completely performed within a year. The holders of this view would therefore require the contract to be in writing to be enforceable.

However, a **minority** view holds that exercising the right to terminate is simply an alternative means of performance under the contract. That is, Steel Company <u>can</u> completely perform either by accepting the hydrogen every month for three years and paying for it, or by terminating the contract with 30 days' notice. Either action is a completed performance under the contract under this view. Since exercising the termination provision can be done within a year, full performance is not impossible within a year of its making, and thus the minority view holds such a contract to be outside the Statute, and enforceable even if oral.

3. The Full Performance Exception: Complete Performance by One Party Takes the Contract Outside the Statute. [§ 10–20]

The majority of courts hold that where one party has **completely** performed his or her obligations under an oral contract where the other party's performance cannot be completed within a year, the contract is taken outside the Statute and can be enforced by the party who has performed. For example, Lou and Gina orally contract whereby Lou promises to deliver a load of firewood to Gina next week, in return for Gina's promise to make 18 monthly payments of $30 to Lou. At the time of its making, the contract would not be enforceable because Gina's promise cannot be completed within a year from the making of the contract. However, once Lou delivers the wood, Lou's performance is completed and at that point most courts would find the contract is taken outside the Statute, and Gina's oral promise to make monthly payments is enforceable by Lou. This rule makes sense for there is obviously evidence that the parties made a contract, i.e., it is unlikely Lou would deliver the wood otherwise, and to leave him no contractual recovery until 18 months have passed would be unfair. Those states that do not allow Lou to recover under the contract would nevertheless allow him to recover in restitution for unjust enrichment. (*See* Chapter Thirty-One for an explanation of restitution). The difference would be that under unjust enrichment, Lou would be entitled to the "fair market value" of the goods. Under a breach of contract remedy, Lou would get whatever the contract called for, regardless whether it was more or less the fair market value for the wood.

a. **Part Performance Does Not Take the Contract Outside the Statute. [§ 10–21]**

Where one party has only partially performed his or her obligations under a contract and the other party's performance cannot be completed within a year, most courts hold that the contract is still within the Statute, even if theoretically divisible. For example, in the Lou and Gina hypothetical stated above, if Lou promised to make two deliveries of firewood, one next week and one three months later, **no part** of the contract would be enforceable by Lou after delivery of only the first load. Of course, after the second load is delivered, Lou's performance is then complete and the majority of courts would find the contract outside the statute.

4. **Satisfying the Statute in a Contract Which, by Its Terms, Cannot Be Performed Within a Year. [§ 10–22*]**

A party seeking to enforce a contract which, by its very terms, cannot be performed within a year of its making, must establish:

(a) the existence of a writing or "memorandum" reasonably identifying the subject matter and essential terms of the contract [Restatement 2d § 131];

(b) that the writing is signed by the other party, i.e., the party against whom the contract is being enforced or the "adverse" party [Restatement 2d § 134]; and

(c) that the writing sufficiently evidences that the parties have intended to make a binding agreement [Restatement 2d § 131].

---

* For more information, listen to CD # 7, Track 9 of *Sum and Substance Audio on Contracts*.

THE STATUTE OF FRAUDS

a. Merger Doctrine Applies. [§ 10–23]

Note that the merger doctrine, described in § 10–11 above, applies to satisfy the Statute in these types of contracts as well [Restatement 2d § 132].

E. TYPE THREE: CONTRACTS MADE IN CONSIDERATION OF MARRIAGE. [§ 10–24*]

A contract for which all or part of the consideration is marriage, or the promise to marry, is within the Statute, and thus must be in writing to be enforceable [Restatement 2d § 124]. For example, assume Julia proposes to Richard, and to induce Richard to agree, she also promises to give him a new car if he accepts her proposal. If Richard accepts her offer, both the promise to marry and the promise to give Richard a car are within the Statute, and thus must be in writing to be enforceable. This is because the promise to give Richard the car was, in part, bargained for and given in exchange for Richard's promise to marry. Primarily this provision applied in olden days when the father of the bride promised a "dowry" to the putative husband. It does not come up very often anymore.

1. Pre-Nuptial Agreements. [§ 10–25]

The key in determining whether a pre-nuptial agreement is within or without the Statute is to determine whether it was made in **consideration of marriage**, i.e., as part of a bargain in which one party wanted to induce the other to marry (or to promise to marry), **or whether it was made only in *contemplation* of marriage**. In the former case, it is within the Statute. In the latter, it is outside the Statute and thus, enforceable even if oral.

For example, if Lisa and Rod agree to be married and a few weeks later begin discussions and eventually agree on a pre-nuptial agreement, the agreement is outside the Statute, for it was only made in *contemplation* of marriage, and not as a bargained for promise made in return for one party's <u>promise</u> to marry. That is, it was not entered into with one party's agreement of marriage being part of the bargained for exchange.

F. TYPE FOUR: CONTRACTS WHERE ONE PARTY ACTS AS SURETY FOR ANOTHER. [§ 10–26**]

In general, **a promise to pay the debt of another is within the Statute, and thus must be in writing to be enforceable**

---

* For more information, listen to CD # 7, Track 10 of *Sum and Substance Audio on Contracts*.

** For more information, listen to CD # 7, Track 11 of *Sum and Substance Audio on Contracts*.

CHAPTER 10

[Restatement 2d § 112]. This part of the Statute is known as the "suretyship" provision. It has many contours, which are described below.

1. **Definition of Surety. [§ 10–27]**

    A **surety** is a person who is ***secondarily* liable for the duty (usually debts) of another**, called the *principal* (or the debtor). As a result of **a suretyship agreement, both the surety and the principal are liable to a third party**, called the *obligee* (or creditor).

    However, it is important to note that **the surety is only liable if the principal does not perform his or her duty**. In other words, in a suretyship the creditor must seek performance by the principal first, for the principal is primarily liable, before he or she can look to the surety, who is only secondarily liable.

    a. **Example. [§ 10–28]**

       The most common example of a surety is where the surety agrees to pay a debt if the principal defaults on some credit obligation. Assume Paul wants to buy a car but his credit rating is not the best and the bank won't lend him any money unless he gets a co-signer. If Sally co-signs the loan, typically she will promise to pay any of Paul's remaining obligations under the car loan should Paul default. Sally is a surety; Paul is a principal (or debtor); and the bank is the obligee (or creditor). Should Paul default, the bank must first look to Paul to pay the remaining balance, and only if he does not or cannot pay may the bank seek to enforce Sally's promise.

       Because she is a surety, her promise is within the Statute and, absent one of the exceptions applying, it must be in writing to be enforceable.

2. **Where the Supposed Surety Is Primarily, Not Secondarily, Liable, No Suretyship Exists and the Contract Is Outside the Statute. [§ 10–29]**

    If the obligee extends credit or other services based on the credit or representations of the putative **surety**, rather than of the principal, no suretyship exists because the liability of the purported surety is primary rather than secondary. Accordingly, any oral promises made in such a contract are enforceable, as the transaction is not within the Statute [Restatement 2d § 112, Cmt. c].

    a. **Example. [§ 10–30]**

       Shirley telephones Flower Shop and instructs the shop to deliver a dozen roses to Peter, telling the florist that, "if Peter doesn't pay for them, I will." In this case, Shirley is primarily, not

THE STATUTE OF FRAUDS

secondarily, liable because the flower shop extended credit based on her representations, not Peter's. Accordingly, she is not a "surety." Thus the contract is outside the Statute, and her promise to pay the flower shop is enforceable by the shop even though it is oral.

3. **The "Main Purpose" or "Leading Object" Exception. [§ 10–31]**

If the main purpose for which the surety makes the promise to answer for the duty of the principal is to secure an economic advantage for the **surety**, rather than to provide a direct financial benefit for the **principal**, the transaction is outside the Statute under the **"main purpose"** (or **"leading object"**) exception [Restatement 2d § 116]. This rule is illustrated below.

   a. **Example. [§ 10–32]**

   Jim owes Claude $1,000. To collect, Claude is about to levy an attachment on Jim's house. Ron, who is also a creditor of Jim's, is afraid that if Claude levies on Jim's house, Jim will declare bankruptcy and the chance of Jim paying Ron the full amount of the debt would be reduced. Thus, Ron orally promises Claude that if Claude will hold off any attachment proceedings for six weeks, Ron will pay Claude the $1,000 if Jim doesn't pay it during this period. Even though Ron's promise was an oral surety, it is nonetheless enforceable under the **main purpose**, or **leading object exception**. That is because the main purpose of Ron's promise was to benefit himself (the surety) financially, not Jim (the principal) [Restatement 2d § 116, Cmt. b, Ill. 2].

   b. **Example. [§ 10–33]**

   Jim owes Claude $1,000. To collect, Claude is about to levy an attachment on Jim's house. Ron, a friend of Jim's, wants to avoid his friend's embarrassment, and so orally promises Claude he will pay the $1,000 if Jim does not, so long as Claude promises to hold off any attachment for six weeks. The **main purpose** of Ron's promise was to **benefit Jim, the principal**, financially and not Ron, the surety. As such, the main purpose rule does not apply and Ron's oral promise is within the Statute and unenforceable [Restatement 2d § 116, Cmt. b, Ill. 1].

4. **Satisfying the Statute in Suretyship Contracts. [§ 10–34*]**

A party seeking to enforce a contract for suretyship against the surety must establish:

---

* For more information, listen to CD # 7, Tracks 7 and 11 of *Sum and Substance Audio on Contracts*.

(a) The existence of a writing or "memorandum" reasonably identifying the debtor, surety, obligor, and the essential terms of the suretyship agreement;

(b) That the writing is signed by the surety [Restatement 2d § 134]; and

(c) That the writing sufficiently evidences an intent by the parties to enter into a suretyship agreement [Restatement 2d § 131].

Note that the merger doctrine (§ 10–11) applies to satisfy the statute in suretyship contracts. [Restatement 2d § 132]

G. TYPE FIVE: CONTRACTS FOR THE SALE OF GOODS FOR $500 OR MORE UNDER UCC § 2–201. [§ 10–35*]

The general rule provided by UCC § 2–201 is that to enforce a **contract for the sale of goods for $500 or more against a party, that party must have an enforceable "writing"—usually a signed and written contract.** (The threshold under the revised § R2–201 is $5,000). However, that general rule is subject to several exceptions and alternate means of satisfaction other than by a signed writing, and thus, each of the sections of § 2–201 needs to be studied carefully and independently.

1. **Structure of UCC § 2–201. [§ 10–36]**

    Section 2–201 is divided into three sections, which provide the substantive rules of the Statute:

    § 2–201(1) sets forth the general rule given in § 10–35 and describes what sort of writing is usually necessary to meet the requirements of that rule [§ 10–37].

    § 2–201(2) sets forth an alternative way to satisfy the Statute when the contract is made between merchants [§ 10–44].

    § 2–201(3) sets forth exceptions to the general rule of § 2–201(1), describing three situations in which contracts for the sale of goods in excess of $500 can be enforced even though there is no writing signed by the party against whom the contract is sought to be enforced [§ 10–51]. Unlike the exception of § 2–201(2), the three exceptions in § 2–201(3) apply regardless whether the parties are merchants.

    A party need not satisfy or meet the requirements of § 2–201(1), (2), *and* **(3) to have satisfied the Statute.**

---

* For more information, listen to CD # 7, Track 12 of *Sum and Substance Audio on Contracts*.

THE STATUTE OF FRAUDS

If a contract satisfies only **one** section of § 2–201(1)–(3), it is enforceable, i.e., the other party has lost its Statute of Frauds defense.

Note that the "merger" doctrine [§ 10–11] can be used to help satisfy the Statute for contracts for the sales of goods for $500 or more.

2. **Satisfying the Statute Under § 2–201(1). [§ 10–37]**

Under § 2–201(1), a contract for the sale of goods for $500 or more is not enforceable unless a party can establish:

(1) There is a "writing" [Note "writing" is defined in UCC § 1–201(b)(43) and includes electronic communications, like emails and texts];

(2) It is **signed** by (or on behalf of) the party (usually the defendant) against whom enforcement of the contract is sought [Note "signed" is defined in UCC § 1–201(b)(37) and includes a business's letterhead if the letter is sent on behalf of the business, i.e., if sent on letterhead which was used with the present intention to adopt the writing as being from the business, then it is "signed" solely by means of the letterhead];

(3) The writing **evidences that a contract for sale** (as opposed to merely an offer, preliminary negotiation, etc.) has been made between the parties; and

(4) The writing contains a **subject matter** and a **quantity term**.

a. **Example. [§ 10–38]**

Fred orally agrees to sell his car to Bill for $6,000. Fred sends Bill a letter saying, "I'm glad you agreed to buy my car. I think $6,000 is a fair price. As we discussed, I'll deliver it to you next Friday. /s/ Fred." Bill later changes his mind and refuses to accept delivery of the car or to pay for it. If Fred sues Bill, **Bill will prevail**, for the contract is not enforceable against him.

While the contract is for the sale of goods for $500 or more, and while there is a writing which specifies a quantity and evidences that a sale was made, **the writing was not signed by the party against whom it is being enforced, i.e., Bill**. Instead, it was only signed by the party seeking to enforce it, *Fred*. Thus, as to **Bill**, it is unenforceable.

Note that if Fred decided to breach by failing to tender the car, the contract **would** be enforceable against him, and Bill could sue him successfully. This is because in that case there is a writing signed by the party against whom the contract is being

CHAPTER 10

enforced, i.e., Fred, evidencing a contract for the sale of a specified quantity of specified goods.

b. Typical Problems Under § 2–201(1). [§ 10–39]

The following sections discuss and explain how to resolve the typical issues arising under § 2–201(1).

(1) Divisible Contracts. [§ 10–40]

Suppose the parties agree on the sale of three identical vases for a total of $600. There is an issue as to whether such agreement is one contract, and thus within the Statute, or whether it is really three contracts for $200 each, each of which is outside the Statute. The general rule is that if the parties intended to make one contract, it is within the Statute. If they intended to make three contracts, all are outside the Statute. Ascertaining the parties' intent is an issue of interpretation for the court [Chapter Nineteen].

(2) Decision to Limit Enforcement of Agreement to Less than $500. [§ 10–41]

Suppose Wanda and Susan had an oral contract for the sale of a good costing $550. If Wanda decided not to go through with the deal, could Susan sue for breach and only seek to enforce the contract for $499? The answer is no. Either the contract, as a whole, is within the Statute or it is not. If it is within the Statute, as this one is, it cannot be enforced *at all* if it is oral.

(3) A Contract Cannot Be Enforced Beyond the Quantity Shown in the Writing. [§ 10–42]

The Statute is fulfilled if there is a quantity term in the signed writing, even if the quantity term is in fact "wrong" because it misstates the true agreement of the parties. However, in that case, the contract cannot be enforced beyond the quantity set forth in the writing [UCC § 2–201(1)].

However, if the writing contained an incorrect term other than quantity, e.g., it said the price was $3,000 when the agreement was for $4,000, there is no prohibition on the seller being able to argue in court that the higher price was what was agreed to, so long as the Statute is satisfied. As § 2–201 provides, "a writing is not insufficient because it omits or incorrectly states a term agreed upon," with the exception of quantity as discussed above. [§ 10–61 *et seq.*].

THE STATUTE OF FRAUDS

(4) A Contract Containing No Formal "Signature" Can Nonetheless Fulfill the "Signed by" Requirement. [§ 10–43]

Occasionally a case will arise where, e.g., a company issues an unsigned written purchase offer on its letterhead, which the other party accepts by signing at the bottom. At that point, there is no formal signature by the company-offeror and thus, there is an issue as to whether the contract can be enforced against the company. As mentioned above, the answer is that such a document is deemed "signed" by the offeror, even if it does not contain a formal signature. This is because under UCC § 1–201(b)(37) a writing or record is considered "signed" if it includes "any symbol . . . adopted [by a party] with present intention to adopt or accept a writing." As a party's letterhead is a symbol that is conventionally adopted so as to authenticate that the written offer was presented by that company, it is a "signed" writing for purposes of § 2–201(1).

3. Satisfying the Statute Under § 2–201(2): The Merchant's Confirmatory Memorandum. [§ 10–44]

Under § 2–201(2), the sending of a "confirmatory writing," i.e., a writing that confirms the making of an oral contract, can satisfy the Statute **against the one who receives it** if:

(1) The transaction is **between merchants** [Note "merchants" is defined in UCC § 2–104(1)];

(2) The **writing is sent within a reasonable time** after the contract was made **and is sufficient against the sender** [meaning sufficient to bind the sender under UCC § 2–201(3)];

(3) It is actually **received by the other party** and that party **has reason to know of its contents**;

(4) The confirmatory **writing satisfies the requirements of 2–201(1) against the recipient**; and

(5) It is **not objected to in writing within ten days** after its receipt.

The effect of such a confirmatory writing is that, if all these elements are met, a party who has not signed anything will still lose its defense under the Statute.

a. Example. [§ 10–45]

Acme Company telephones an order for a new $10,000 transducer to Nadir Company, which is accepted on the phone by Nadir. (At this point, the contract is not enforceable against either party as the contract is not in writing).

The next day, Nadir sends a "Confirmation of Order" to Acme in which it confirms Acme's promise to pay for, and Nadir's promise to ship, a new transducer for $10,000. The confirmation is signed by a Nadir Vice-President. At this point, Nadir has lost its Statute of Frauds defense and the contract can be enforced against it. That is, Nadir has signed a writing evidencing a sale of one transducer, and thus the contract can be enforced against it under § 2–201(1). However, Acme is **not** bound at this point for it has not signed anything and has only made an oral promise to pay.

Thereafter, Acme receives the confirmation, and does not respond to it within ten days. At this point, **both** parties have lost their Statute of Frauds defense and either can enforce the contract against the other. Nadir lost its defense under § 2–201(1) when it sent the signed writing; Acme lost its defense under § 2–201(2) because it failed to object to the merchant's confirmatory writing within ten days, and the other elements of § 2–201(2) as set forth above were met. Hence, even though Acme failed to sign anything, it has no Statute of Frauds defense if it fails to timely tender payment to Nadir.

b. **Effect on the Recipient of a Valid Merchant's Confirmatory Memorandum. [§ 10–46]**

The only effect of a party's failure to object within ten days to an otherwise valid Merchant's Confirmatory Memorandum is that the party loses its Statute of Frauds defense. The failure to object has **nothing to do with contract formation**. This is a **common** mistake that is frequently tested on and, thus, is important to learn.

(1) Example. [§ 10–47]

Ralph's Tire Company ("Ralph's") has never had anything to do with Joe's Rubber Supply Co. ("Joe's"). Nevertheless, one day Ralph's gets a trumped up confirmatory memorandum from Joe's "confirming" an order of 600 pallets of rubber st $100/pallet to be delivered next month. Thinking it is a joke, Ralph's throws the confirmation away and does not object. Joe's tenders delivery of the rubber a month later and when Ralph's does not accept and pay for it, Joe's sues.

The fact that Ralph's didn't object to an otherwise valid memorandum means **only** that Ralph's has lost its Statute of Frauds defense in the suit by Joe's. It does **not** mean that

THE STATUTE OF FRAUDS

Ralph's has somehow implicitly consented to the existence of the contract, or implicitly waived its right to try and prove the alleged contract never existed. Ralph's still will have the chance to prove at trial it never ordered from, or had any dealings with, Joe's. Assuming truth will prevail at trial, Ralph's will win and is not obligated to pay for the rubber [§ 2–201, Cmt. 3].

c. **Effect of Objecting Within Ten Days. [§ 10–48]**

If the party receiving an otherwise valid merchant's confirmatory memorandum objects within ten days, whether it keeps its Statute of Frauds defense or not depends on what it says in its objection. If it disclaims knowledge of the contract, i.e., if it says something like, "Our company has never dealt with you, we do not know what you are talking about, and we certainly have no contract with you," the objecting party has preserved its Statute of Frauds defense. But if the receiving party says something like, "You have misstated our deal. Our contract was for one transducer at $9,500, not $10,000," **it loses its Statute of Frauds defense**. It does not lose the defense under § 2–201(2), for the seller's confirmatory memorandum was timely objected to. However, it loses the defense under *§ 2–201(1)*, for in its objection it has sent a **signed writing/record**, evidencing a **sales transaction**, with a given **quantity** term. Thus, it has satisfied the Statute against itself under § 2–201(1).

d. **Effect of Either Party Not Being a Merchant. [§ 10–49]**

Section 2–201(2) applies only where **both parties are merchants**. Thus, if Willie (an individual) receives a "Confirmation of Order" from a Bicycle Shop, confirming an oral order for a new 10-speed bicycle for $250, the stated agreement cannot be enforced against Willie based only on the confirmation regardless whether Willie objects to the writing within 10 days. That is, because Willie is not a merchant, and because there is nothing he has signed, the contract cannot be enforced against him under either § 2–201(1) or § 2–202(2).

e. **Effect of the Confirming Memorandum Not Satisfying § 2–201(1) Against the Sender. [§ 10–50]**

Assume manufacturer sends a written confirmation to retailer stating, "This will confirm our telephone conversation today whereby you ordered the transducers for shipment on April 10. As we agreed, we will expect payment 30 days after you receive the transducers. /s/ V.P. Manufacturer." This letter does not satisfy the requirements of § 2–201(2), and thus, the contract is still unenforceable against the retailer, and will continue to be so even if there is no objection by the retailer. The reason is that while both parties are merchants; while the confirmatory writing is signed by the manufacturer; and while it was received by the retailer, **the letter was not sufficient to bind the sender under § 2–201(1)** because there is no mention of a particular quantity. Thus, because the letter does not satisfy the requirements of § 2–201(1) so that it could be used to enforce the agreement against the sender, it is not an effective confirmatory memorandum. As a result, the agreement is voidable at the option of the retailer under the Statute, despite the merchant-retailer's failure to object.

4. **Satisfying the Statute Under § 2–201(3). [§ 10–51]**

Section 2–201(3) provides three exceptions to the writing requirement set forth in § 2–201(1). These exceptions are not limited to merchants.

   a. **Specially Manufactured Goods. [§ 10–52]**

   Under § 2–201(3)(a), an oral contract for the sale of goods for $500 or more is enforceable if the contract is for specially manufactured goods and the seller has at least begun manufacture or made commitments in reliance on the buyer's order. Perhaps surprisingly, there is no definition of "specially manufactured goods" in the UCC. However, under the most widely agreed definition, a specially manufactured good is one the manufacturer could not readily sell in the ordinary course of its business to anyone other than the original buyer. That is, it is in some sense a "custom made" product.

   b. **Admission. [§ 10–53]**

   Under § 2–201(3)(b), if the party against whom enforcement of the contract is sought admits in a deposition, at trial, or otherwise while under oath, that an oral contract was made for the sale of goods for $500 or more, the oral contract becomes enforceable. According to most modern commentators, this provision means that no motion to dismiss on Statute of Frauds grounds is possible until the plaintiff at least has had the opportunity to ask the defendant under oath whether a contract was formed or whether an offer, acceptance, and consideration took place [*See* § 2–201, Cmt. 7].

   Note that the party being deposed does not have to admit a contract was formed in order to lose its Statute of Frauds under this provision. For example, assume letter X would be considered an offer under the objective theory of contract. And assume letter Y would be considered an acceptance under the objective theory of contract. Finally, assume the letters evidence

THE STATUTE OF FRAUDS

the promises in them were bargained for. The party being deposed may testify that she never formed a contract with the plaintiff, for that is what she really believes. But if she admits that she sent letter X and received letter Y, a court would find that she "admitted" the existence of a contract by admitting its components: an offer, an acceptance, and bargained for consideration.

c. Performance. [§ 10–54]

Under § 2–201(3)(c), if the buyer has completely paid for the goods ordered under an oral contract for the sale of goods for $500 or more, or if the seller has completely delivered all goods called for under such a contract, the remaining promises under the contract are enforceable.

(1) Part Performance. [§ 10–55]

The issue is the effect on the Statute when a party only partly performs under a contract. That is, does part performance take the <u>entire</u> contract outside the Statute, or can only that part that has been performed be enforced? Section 2–201(3)(c) provides for only the latter, i.e., in such case the contract is enforceable only "with respect to goods for which payment has been made and accepted or which have been received and accepted."

(a) Example Based on *Allied Grape Growers v. Bronco Wine Co.* [§ 10–56*]

Farmer (Allied) claimed it had an oral contract with Winery (Bronco) for the delivery of 850 tons grapes. Farmer delivered about 15 tons of grapes to Winery, which were accepted and paid for by Winery. However, Farmer refused to deliver any additional grapes, claiming the amount in the first delivery was the extent of the oral contract.

Held: Verdict for Farmer on this issue under § 2–203(3)(c). Because this was an oral contract for the sale of goods in excess of $500, it was within the Statute. There was no writing that satisfied the Statute. Under § 2–201(3), the contract could be enforced, but only "with respect to goods . . . which have been received and accepted." Only the first shipment had been received and accepted, and thus the obligation to accept and pay for the remaining alleged tonnage, even if that was the oral agreement, could not be enforced

---

* For more information about this case, listen to CD # 7, Track 12 of *Sum and Substance Audio on Contracts*.

under § 2–201(3). [*Allied Grape Growers v. Bronco Wine Co.*, 203 Cal. App. 3d 432 (1988)].

However, Winery ultimately prevailed, *see* the additional discussion of this case in § 10–59.

d. Review Problem. [§ 10–57]

Printing House has a slow month and decides, on its own, to print 100,000 calendars with the "Acme Department Stores" logo on the bottom. It sends the calendars, with a bill for $50,000, to Acme, which Acme refuses. Printing House sues Acme for breach of contract.

Question:

Analyze the contractual liability of the parties and the effect of the Statute of Frauds.

Answer:

The Statute of Frauds applies because it is a sale of goods for $500 or more [§ 10–35], and the Statute is satisfied under the "specially manufactured goods" exception of § 2–201(3)(a) [§ 10–52]. Hence, Acme cannot use the Statute of Frauds as a defense to the lawsuit. However, because it never entered into a contract in the first place, it has no contractual liability to Printing House, i.e., losing the defense of the Statute of Frauds does not mean a contract is enforceable where no contract otherwise exists [§§ 10–3; 10–46 and Cmt. 3 to § 2–201.]

H. ENFORCEMENT OF ORAL PROMISES IN CONTRACTS WITHIN THE STATUTE, OTHER THAN TRANSFER OF LAND INTERESTS, BY RELIANCE AND ESTOPPEL. [§ 10–58*]

Reliance by a party as to an oral agreement to transfer an interest in land is a universally recognized way to satisfy the Statute [*see* the discussion of this issue § 10–12]. However, there is a difference of opinion as to whether reasonable reliance on an oral promise by one party will make other agreements subject to the Statute enforceable.

The *Restatement*, and a *majority of states*, provide that a **reliance exception to the Statute exists** for all contracts. Thus, upon reasonable and foreseeable reliance on an oral promise, the promise is enforceable by the relying party to the extent justice requires [Restatement 2d § 139]. These courts hold that when reasonable reliance occurs, the promising party is estopped to deny its promise and it can be enforced.

---

* For more information about this case, listen to CD # 8, Track 2 of *Sum and Substance Audio on Contracts.*

THE STATUTE OF FRAUDS

In many ways, this is a specialized application of the promissory estoppel doctrine (*see* Chapter Eight). Further, while "reasonable reliance" is not a specified statutory exception under UCC § 2–201, many jurisdictions have nevertheless recognized the doctrine even in sales of goods transactions, arguing that it applies to all code transactions via UCC § 1–103(b), which provides, "Unless displaced by the particular provisions of the Uniform Commercial Code, the principles of law and equity, including the law . . . [of] estoppel . . . supplement its provisions." The courts espousing this view thus will enforce oral sales of goods contracts for $500 or more where one party reasonably relied on the promises made in the agreement. A minority view argues that the UCC drafters carefully set out three exceptions to the Statute in § 2–201(3) and chose not to include estoppel there, and so it should not be considered an exception.

1. **Example Based on *Allied Grape Growers v. Bronco Wine Co.* [§ 10–59*]**

    [The facts of the case were set forth in § 10–56] While the court reasoned that the contract for the sale of grapes was limited to the amount of the first delivery which was accepted and paid for by Winery under a strict reading of *§ 2–201(3)*, the court nevertheless found the oral agreement for the remaining tonnage was enforceable on estoppel grounds for Winery could show it had prepared for delivery of the greater tonnage of grapes by buying bottles, labels, etc., for the full amount.

I. THE STATUTE AS APPLIED TO MODIFICATIONS OF EXISTING CONTRACTS. [§ 10–60**]

If the parties to a written contract within the Statute wish to modify it orally, there is a question as to whether such oral modification is enforceable. The Restatement provides that if the contract, as modified, is within the Statute, then all its terms must be in writing for the newly modified contract to be enforceable. If they are not in writing, only the originally agreed upon terms are effective [Restatement 2d § 149]. The UCC takes a similar position [§ 9–3]. Of course, as discussed in § 9–10, even if the agreement cannot be enforced under the Statute, it might operate as a waiver [UCC § 2–209(4)].

---

* For more information on this case, listen to CD # 8, Track 2 of *Sum and Substance Audio on Contracts*.

** For more information, listen to CD # 8, Track 1 of *Sum and Substance Audio on Contracts*.

CHAPTER 10

J. CONSEQUENCE OF NOT SATISFYING THE STATUTE OF FRAUDS. [§ 10–61*]

While there are varying tests to determine whether a particular type of transaction is within the Statute, **the *effect* of any type of contract falling within the Statute is the same:**

If the Statute applies and is not satisfied, the contract is *voidable* by the party who has the Statute of Frauds defense. Thus:

(a) the party with the defense can enforce the contract against the other, so long as the other party has satisfied the Statute; and

(b) if the party with the defense does not wish to go through with the contract, he or she does not have to. Thus, that party can simply refuse to perform what he or she promised without contractual liability. If the other party brings a breach of contract action because of such nonperformance, the action will fail for the Statute provides a complete defense. [§§ 10–3; 10–47; 10–57, § 2–201, Cmt. 4].

Some have characterized the Statute as an "evidentiary gate" which controls whether the jury will hear **any** evidence about the contract. If the Statute applies and its requirements are met (or if the Statute does not apply), the evidentiary gate is lifted and all evidence that either party wants to introduce about the contract is admissible. Of course the rules of evidence and the parol evidence rule may limit such evidence, but the point is that once the Statute has been satisfied, the *Statute of Frauds doctrine* will not limit evidence surrounding the making of the contract or its terms. On the other hand, if the Statute applies and is not satisfied, the evidentiary gate remains closed and the party seeking to allege a breach of contract against the party who never signed a contract will **never** get to put on any evidence of the contract or its terms.

1. **Example. [§ 10–62]**

    Paul agrees to sell his car to Mary for $6,000 and both parties sign a written contract to that effect. The Statute has been satisfied and thus, there is nothing in the Statute to prevent Paul from suing Mary claiming that the deal really was for $6,250. Note of course that there are other doctrines that might limit such evidence, but once the Statute is satisfied, there will be no prohibition under the *Statute of Frauds* limiting any evidence either party wishes to introduce about the contract or its terms.

2. **Example. [§ 10–63]**

    Mark orally agrees to sell his leasehold interest in a mobile home park to Terry. A few weeks later, Mark decides not to go through with

---

* For more information, listen to CD # 7, Track 6 of *Sum and Substance Audio on Contracts*.

216

THE STATUTE OF FRAUDS

the deal and Terry sues him. Since the Statute applies and is not fulfilled, Mark has a complete defense to the breach action, and Terry will not be permitted to introduce evidence that he and Mark ever entered into a contract. Without evidence of the contract, Terry's breach of contract action will thus have to be dismissed.

3. **Restitution Required upon Disaffirmance. [§ 10–64]**

The party who avoids a contract under the Statute is entitled to restitutionary recovery from the other. However, that party must also make restitution, if appropriate. That is, each party to such a contract will have to pay the other the fair value for any benefits received under the agreement before it was avoided (*see* Chapter Thirty-One for a discussion of restitution).

K. MNEMONIC SUMMARY. [§ 10–65]

For those who use mnemonics to help summarize legal principles, a well-used one in the Statute of Frauds area is "**MY LEGS**," which is explained below:

Marriage Contracts—**Only** contracts where consideration is Marriage or the promise of marriage.

Year Contracts—Contracts that **by their very terms** cannot be performed in a Year.

Land Contracts—Contracts for the transfer of an interest in Land of anything other than a license.

Estoppel (reliance) exception—A party that reasonably relies on an oral promise otherwise subject to the SOF may enforce the promise to the extent justice allows. Tis exception always applies to land contracts; and the majority rule is that applies to other contracts as well. (Some say the "E" stands for Contracts by an Executor)

Guaranty (Surety) Contracts—Contracts where one party Guarantees the debt of another.

Sale of Goods Contracts—A UCC contract for the Sale of goods for $500 or more.

You should approach a Statute of Frauds issue in the following manner:

L. EXAM APPROACHES TO STATUTE OF FRAUDS ISSUES. [§ 10–66*]

1. Ascertain whether the contract is within to the Statute, i.e., is one of the 5 types of contracts covered in this Chapter [§ 10–4];

---

* For more information, listen to CD # 8, Track 3 of *Sum and Substance Audio on Contracts*.

2. If it is a contract within the Statute, next check to see if the Statute is satisfied by a writing or "memorandum", i.e., determine whether: (a) at common law, there is a writing containing the material terms of the transaction, signed by the "party to be charged," i.e., the party who fails to perform and (b) under the UCC, there is a signed writing that evidences a contract, with subject matter and quantity terms; and

3. If it is a contract covered by the Statute, and if there is no sufficient writing signed by the appropriate party that satisfies the Statute, then check to see if one of the "exceptions" applies that make contracts enforceable even against a party who has not signed anything.

These exceptions are:

    A. For "transfer of an interest in land" contracts:

        — the part performance or reliance (estoppel) exception [§ 10–12];

    B. For "agreements that by their very terms cannot be performed in a year" contracts:

        — the full performance exception [§ 10–20];

    C. For "suretyship" contracts:

        — the "leading object" or "main purpose" exception [§ 10–31];

    D. For "sales of good" contracts:

        — the merchant's confirmatory memorandum exception [§ 10–44];

        — the specially manufactured goods exception [§ 10–52];

        — the admission exception [§ 10–53]; and

        — the full/part performance exception [§ 10–54]; or

        — the estoppel exception [§ 10–58]; and

4. If the Statute applies and is not satisfied, then it is voidable by the party with the contract defense, and his, her, or its non-performance is excused.

CHAPTER 11

CAPACITY

A. CAPACITY, GENERALLY. [§ 11–1*]

In order to enter into a contract the courts will enforce, a party must have sufficient judgment to decide whether to bind himself or herself to an enforceable promise [Restatement 2d § 12(1)]. There are two classes of persons that the law presumes not to have such judgment—minors and those who lack mental capacity.

B. INCAPACITY DUE TO INFANCY/MINORITY. [§ 11–2**]

The general rule is that until a person reaches the age of majority (in all **states 18 years of age**), any contract entered into by that person is **voidable** at the option of the minor [Restatement 2d §§ 12(2)(b); 14, although note that in § 14 the *Restatement 2d* provides that the last day on which a contract is freely voidable is, *"the beginning of the day before the person's eighteenth birthday"*].

The test is **not** whether the **particular** minor who entered into a contract is sufficiently mature to understand the nature of entering into a legal bargain. Rather, the test turns solely on the age of the individual, so very mature 17 1/2 year olds lack capacity while very immature 18 1/2 year olds have legal capacity. Note also that the minor is entitled to void the contract at any time while remaining a minor, even if he or she has enjoyed the benefits under the contract for some period of time.

1. **Example. [§ 11–3]**

   Fred just turned 17 and signs a contract to purchase a used car on credit for $6,000. If Fred wants to go through with the deal, he is entitled to do so, for he is not required to terminate (or avoid) the transaction. However, if he does not wish to go through with the deal, he does not have to. As the contract is **voidable at his option**, he may terminate it anytime up to the age of majority, and retains the ability to avoid the contract for a reasonable time attaining majority

---

* For more information, listen to CD # 5, Track 5 of *Sum and Substance Audio on Contracts*.

** For more information, listen to CD # 5, Track 6 of *Sum and Substance Audio on Contracts*.

[§ 11–7]. If he takes possession of the car for six months and makes six months' worth of payments, and then (while still 17) decides he does not want to go through with the deal, he is entitled to avoid the contract at that point. He simply has to return the car, and he will be entitled to the return of all the payments he has made. In some states he will have to account for his use of the car for six months; in other states and under the Restatement he will not have to make such an accounting [§ 11–8].

2. **Ratification of a Contract Entered into by a Minor. [§ 11–4]**

Upon reaching majority, a (former) minor can **ratify** a contract, thereby turning it from a voidable one into a binding one. Note that **ratification cannot validly take place until the minor reaches majority,** for it is only then that contract law assumes the individual has attained the capacity necessary to enter into a binding contract [Restatement 2d § 14, Cmt. c.] **Ratification needs no new consideration to be valid** [Restatement 2d § 85], and can occur in three ways:

 (a) Express ratification [§ 11–5];

 (b) Implied-in-fact ratification [§ 11–6]; or

 (c) Ratification by silence [§ 11–7].

 a. **Express Ratification. [§ 11–5]**

If a former minor expressly indicates by words, whether written or oral, that he or she wishes to be bound by the promises made in a contract entered into during minority, such ratification is valid and will serve to deprive the former minor of the further power to avoid the contract.

 b. **Implied-in-Fact Ratification. [§ 11–6]**

If the former minor manifests by action that he or she is willing to be bound to the promises made in a contract entered into during minority, such ratification is valid and will take away the former minor's further power to avoid the contract.

For example, in the hypothetical with Fred in § 11–3, if Fred continues making car payments after he turns 18, he will be deemed to have made an implied in-fact ratification of the contract. Thus, he may no longer avoid it and, if he stops making payments and tries to return the car, he will be deemed in breach.

 c. **Ratification by Silence: Implied-in-Law Ratification. [§ 11–7]**

Ratification by silence, or implied-in-law ratification, is the most common form of ratification. This occurs where a former minor says and does nothing one way or the other about a contract entered into during minority. The rule is that **a minor is given a reasonable time to disaffirm the contract after reaching majority. If it is not disaffirmed within such reasonable time, ratification will be implied.**

While the facts surrounding each contract need to be examined to determine what is a reasonable time, in general, the more benefits the minor has received under the contract, the less the amount of time he or she will have to disaffirm upon attaining majority. Conversely, the more benefits under the contract that are still executory (i.e., unperformed) as to the former minor, the greater the amount of time the former minor will have to disaffirm.

3. **Restitution upon Disaffirmance of Contracts Entered into by Minors. [§ 11–8]**

When an individual validly disaffirms a contract based on minority, an issue arises as to whether the minor must account for the benefits attained while in possession of the goods. In the Fred/car hypothetical in § 11–3, suppose Fred decided to disaffirm the car he bought on credit six months into the deal. He will be entitled to the return of all his payments upon disaffirmance. The restitution question, however, is whether he will have to account to the seller for the six months use of the car. As demonstrated below, there are many answers to the restitution question depending on the jurisdiction and the circumstances of the transaction.

a. **Majority Rule Regarding Treatment of the Economic Benefit Received by the Minor While in Possession of the Goods: No Restitutionary Recovery Permitted in Credit Sales. [§ 11–9]**

Suppose Ace Car Company sells a new car to Larry, a mature looking 17-year-old, for 24 monthly payments of $600. Larry keeps the car for ten months (until just before he turns 18) and then tells Ace he is disaffirming the contract. Because the contract is voidable, Larry is entitled to disaffirm it and is entitled to all his money back. However, the car Ace gets back is not the car it sold, i.e., the car has been used during the ten months and is worth less than when Larry drove it off the lot.

Under the majority rule, including that of the Restatement [Restatement 2d § 14, Cmt. c], **the non-minor (Ace) has no right to recover in restitution for this lost value**. That is, Ace would not be entitled to recover any fair rental value, depreciation, mileage, any damage, etc. of or to the car. This inability to seek an offset would be true even if Larry smashed the car and totally wrecked it. All Larry would have to do is disaffirm the contract (assuming it had not yet been ratified) and he would then be entitled to all his payments back, while Ace would only be entitled to the return of the wrecked automobile. If the car is stolen, the same result would follow except that Ace would not be entitled to anything back except the transfer of Larry's right to get the car back if it is ever found and/or the right to Larry's insurance payment, but only after the seller returns all of Larry's payments.

Note, however, this majority rule is subject to several exceptions discussed below.

(1) Minority View: The "New Hampshire" Rule Allows for Restitutionary Recovery in Some Situations Even in Credit Sales. [§ 11–10]

A few states have agreed with the New Hampshire Supreme Court that where a minor has contracted with someone who is not a minor, the **non-minor is entitled to restitutionary (fair market value) recovery upon the disaffirmance of a credit sale by a minor**, so long as the minor would be unjustly enriched from the use of the goods without having to pay for such use. So applying the "New Hampshire" rule in the Ace/Larry example above, if Larry avoided the contract, Ace would be required to give Larry the value of his payments, but could offset against that sum the depreciation, wear and tear, damage etc. of and to the car while in Larry's possession. If that depreciation was in excess of the payments, Ace would be entitled to recover that excess amount in a suit in restitution against Larry. [*See* the discussion of the majority and minority views in Restatement 2d § 14, Cmt. c].

b. Treatment of the Economic Benefit Received by the Minor While in Possession of the Goods or Services: Restitutionary Recovery Permitted in Cash Sales. [§ 11–11]

A different situation occurs when the minor pays cash for goods or services and later seeks disaffirmance. For example, assume Joyce gives guitar lessons for $30 per hour. If Paula, a 17-year old, pays the $30 and gets the lesson, it would be unfair to allow Paula to turn around at the end of the lesson and say she was disaffirming the contract and demand her money back. However, the minor is still deemed to be without the judgment necessary to contract.

Contract law solves this dilemma as follows: **where the minor receives goods or services in return for a *cash* payment, the minor is still entitled to avoid the contract**. However, upon disaffirmance by the minor, the non-minor is entitled to full restitutionary recovery. Thus, in the Paula/Joyce example, Paula is entitled to avoid the contract and demand her $30 back (because she is a minor) at the end of the lesson. However, when that occurs, Joyce is entitled to offset the refund by the reasonable (restitutionary) value of her services from Paula, which is most likely $30.

c. **Treatment of the Economic Benefit Received by the Minor While in Possession of the Goods or Services: Restitutionary Recovery Permitted in Contracts for "Necessities," Even in Credit Sales. [§ 11–12]**

If a minor contracts for "necessities," generally including food, clothing, and shelter (and perhaps other things if, e.g., the minor is emancipated and/or married), he or she will be liable in restitution for such necessities upon disaffirmance of the contract in many jurisdictions.

For example, assume Lloyd and Nan are both 17 years old and married to each other. They enter into a month-to-month lease for an apartment for $600 per month. At the end of the month they are entitled to disaffirm the lease contract based on their minority, but if they do so they will be liable in restitution for the fair rental value of the apartment for the month, which is likely $600 because shelter is a "necessity."

d. **Treatment of the Economic Benefit Received Procured by the Minor via Misrepresentation of Age by Minor. [§ 11–13]**

If a minor affirmatively misrepresents his or her age to the other contracting party as being 18 or older, the non-minor generally can get full restitutionary recovery for any benefits conferred on the minor should the minor later disaffirm, even in a credit sale. *Some* states go even further and hold that upon an affirmative misrepresentation of majority, a minor is **bound under the contract** and may no longer disaffirm it.

(1) **Example. [§ 11–14]**

Jane is 17 and purchases a round trip plane ticket on Airline for $500. The gate agent who sold her the ticket questions her age, but Jane shows a fake ID indicating she is 18 years old.

After the trip is completed, Jane may disaffirm the contract and is entitled to her $500 back since she is a minor. However, that amount is subject to offset because she misrepresented her age.

Under the "restitutionary" view discussed above, the airline would be entitled to offset the reasonable value of the flight from what is due Jane. If, for example, Airline was expensive, and Jane can show the "reasonable value" of the flight was only $400, she would be entitled to $100 back. On the other hand, under the "bound by the contract" view, Jane would be entitled to nothing because Airline is entitled to offset the entire amount of the contract, regardless whether it was a reasonable amount or not.

C. INCAPACITY DUE TO MENTAL INFIRMITY. [§ 11–15]

The Restatement rules regarding the avoidability of contracts by virtue of mental incapacity depend on the status of the mentally infirm individual. The first thing that has to be done is to correctly characterize the infirm individual's status as one of the following:

— Someone for whom a guardian has been appointed [Restatement 2d §§ 12(2)(a), 13; § 11–16];

— Someone who is incapacitated under the "cognition" test [Restatement 2d §§ 12(2)(c), 15(1)(a); § 11–18];

— Someone who is incapacitated under the "acts" test [Restatement 2d §§ 12(2)(c), 15(1)(b); § 11–19]; or

— Someone who is temporarily incapacitated by virtue of intoxication due to alcohol or other drug consumption [Restatement 2d §§ 12(2)(d), 16; § 11–24].

The rules and tests under each of these situations are discussed below.

1. Rules When a Guardian Has Been Appointed Due to "Mental Illness or Defect." [§ 11–16]

If a guardian has been appointed for an individual due to a "mental illness or defect," the rule is clear: the individual has no capacity to contract and any contract entered into by such a party is voidable by the guardian [Restatement 2d § 13].

Guardianship results from a court proceeding whereby someone, often a relative but sometimes the state or local government or a close friend, makes a showing to a judge that an individual is no longer capable of handling his or her legal affairs. Once a guardian is appointed, the guardian (and not the individual) has the right to avoid any contract entered into by the individual subject to the guardianship, or can affirm such a contract within a reasonable time after learning of it. [See § 11–4 above for the different ways a contract can be affirmed].

CAPACITY

The general rule is that restitution is required by the guardian for the use of the good or service by the individual subject to guardianship if: (a) the contract was for "necessities" or (b) the non-incapacitated person neither knew or should have known of the individual's incapacity at the time of contracting.

2. **Rules When a Party Lacks the Mental Capacity to Contract Under Either the "Cognition" or "Acts" Tests. [§ 11–17]**

   If no guardian has been appointed, and the mental incapacity is not temporary due to intoxication or other drug use, there are two tests for when mental incapacity will allow an individual to avoid a contract: (a) the cognition test and (b) the "acts" test. Note that the avoidability as to each is subject to an important limitation described in Restatement 2d § 15(2) and discussed below in § 11–22.

   a. **Avoidability Under the "Cognition" Test. [§ 11–18]**

      An individual incurs voidable contractual duties if he or she entered into a contract "unable to understand in a reasonable manner the nature and consequences of the transaction" [Restatement 2d § 15(1)(a)]. This is known as the "cognition" test, and under it, a court asks whether the affected individuals understood they were binding themselves to a transaction with legal consequences. If not, the contract is voidable.

   b. **Avoidability Under the "Volition" or "Acts" Test. [§ 11–19]**

      An individual also incurs voidable contractual duties if he or she entered into a contract at a time when "he [or she] is unable to act in a reasonable manner in relation to the transaction and the other party has reason to know of his [or her] condition" [Restatement 2d § 15(1)(b)]. This is known as the "volition" or "acts" test, and under it, a court asks whether the affected individuals have the mental ability to control their actions in a reasonable manner. Note that **under the "volition" or "acts" test**, but not under the "cognition" test, **voidability only occurs when the other party has reason to know of the condition**.

      (1) **Example of *Ortelere v. Teacher's Retirement Board*. [§ 11–20]**

         Ortelere was a public school teacher who participated in a public retirement system for over 40 years before she went on leave for mental illness. After going on leave, Ortelere was required to make an election regarding her retirement benefits. One option called for a greater payment per month, but was only payable while she was alive. A second option called for a smaller monthly payment, but continued the retirement payments to her husband if she predeceased him. There was some evidence that she and her husband were very close and that before her mental infirmity, she had chosen the option that would have financially protected the husband after her death. However, after her infirmity, and while in poor health, she changed her selection and chose the first option described above. Ortelere died two months after making the change and her Husband sued to avoid the changed election of benefits made by his wife on the ground that she lacked the mental capacity to do so.

Held: The election was voidable because she lacked capacity under the "acts" test. She also likely did not have the capacity to make the choice under the cognition test (although this was vigorously challenged by the dissent), but the majority held that even if she was competent under the "cognition" test, she was unable to control her actions and, because the Ortelere Teacher's Retirement Board was put on notice of Ortelere's mental incapacity when she went on leave for such infirmity, her choice was voidable for failing the "acts" or "volition" test [*Ortelere v. Teacher's Ret. Bd.*, 25 N.Y.2d 196 (1969)].

c. **Ratification of Contracts Entered into by Individuals with Mental Incapacity Under the "Cognition" or "Acts" Tests. [§ 11–21]**

Within a reasonable time after termination of the mental incapacity, as measured by either the "cognition" or "acts" tests, the individual must either avoid the contract or ratify it.

d. **Limitation on Avoidability of Contracts Entered into by Individuals with Mental Incapacity Under the "Cognition" or "Acts" Tests. [§ 11–22]**

Restatement 2d § 15(2) limits substantially the avoidability of contracts entered into by individuals judged mentally incapable under either the "cognition" or "acts" tests. It provides that, "[w]here the contract is made on fair terms and the other party is without knowledge of the mental illness or defect, the power of avoidance under Subsection (1) terminates to the extent the contract has been so performed in whole or in part or the circumstances have so changed that avoidance would be unjust" (emphasis added). Hence, if the other party does not reasonably know of the incapacity and the terms are fair, the party with mental incapacity cannot avoid the contract.

CAPACITY

(1) Example. [§ 11-23]

Individual walks into a toy store and buys a squirt gun believing it to have special powers to kill the numerous invisible Klingons he believes stalk the earth. Individual has no concept of what a contract is and pulled out some money to pay for the squirt gun just because he saw others in line do something similar. Despite lacking mental incapacity under the "cognition" test, Individual will not be able to avoid the transaction if the cashier had no reason to believe Individual suffered from any mental condition and if the price paid for the squirt gun was fair.

3. Rules When an Individual Temporarily Lacks Mental Capacity Due to Intoxication from Alcohol or Other Drug Use. [§ 11-24]

a. Restatement Rule. [§ 11-25]

Under Restatement 2d § 16, an individual incurs only voidable duties if he or she enters into a contract when:

The other party has <u>reason to know</u> that **by reason of intoxication**:

— the individual is unable to understand in a reasonable manner the nature and consequences of the transaction (the cognition test); <u>or</u>

— the individual is unable to act in a reasonable manner in relation to the transaction (the "volition" or "acts" test).

Once the intoxication no longer affects the individual, the individual has a reasonable time to either disaffirm or ratify the contract.

(1) Example. [§ 11-26]

Eric owns a Les Paul guitar coveted by Layla. Layla has made several offers to Eric seeking to buy the guitar, but he continually refused them. One night, Layla gets Eric drunk and, while intoxicated, he agrees to sell her the guitar for a fair price. Despite the fact that the price was fair, Eric has the ability to disaffirm the contract for a reasonable time after he sobers up for Layla had reason to know that by reason of the intoxication and given their history, Eric was unable to act in a reasonable manner with respect to the guitar. Of course, if Eric has changed his mind and is willing to sell her the guitar, he could always ratify the contract once he is no longer intoxicated.

b. Majority Rule. [§ 11–27]

Most states provide that **a party who is rendered incompetent under the cognitive test due to intoxication by alcohol or other drug use at the time of making a contract is entitled to disaffirm the contract to the same extent as all other classes of mental incompetents**. This is true **regardless of whether the intoxication is voluntary or involuntary and regardless whether the other party knows of the intoxication**. That is, it would apply equally to someone who voluntarily became drunk at a bar, or to someone who had taken prescription medication and was unaware of its mind-altering side effects. So long as the individual was incapacitated under the cognition test due to a temporary intoxication event, the contract remains voidable for a reasonable time after the intoxication wears off.

D. EXAM APPROACH TO INCAPACITY ISSUES. [§ 11–28*]

As a precaution, whenever you are given two parties entering into a contract on an examination, scan the question to determine whether any facts exist to argue that either party lacks the capacity to contract. That is, whether either party:

1. Is a minor [§ 11–2]; or

2. Has a mental incapacity [§ 11–15].

If so, then search for a theory under which the non-incapacitated party is nonetheless entitled to recovery from the incapacitated party. That is, look for:

1. Whether it is a cash purchase by a minor [§ 11–11];

2. Whether it is a credit purchase for necessities by a minor [§ 11–12];

3. Whether the New Hampshire Rule might apply (if you are not told one way or the other) [§ 11–10];

4. Whether the individual has a guardian [§ 11–16];

5. Whether the individual fails the "cognition" or "acts" tests and, if so, whether the other party had reason to know of the mental infirmity [§§ 11–17, 11–22];

6. Whether the incapacity was temporary due to intoxication [§ 11–24];

7. Whether the contract was ratified [§§ 11–4; 11–25].

---

* For more information, listen to CD # 5, Track 8 of *Sum and Substance Audio on Contracts*.

Chapter 12

Mistake and Misunderstanding

A. THE MISTAKE DOCTRINE. [§ 12–1*]

The mistake doctrine is easily stated: a contract entered into by mistake is voidable. While easy to state, the doctrine is difficult to apply for several reasons. The first is that the term "mistake" has a legal meaning that is different from its colloquial one. Second, when applying it, courts do not always use the same term to mean the same thing. Third, the doctrine is intended to be flexible, so that different courts can apply it differently in similar fact situations, leading to inconsistent decisions. The most important thing to keep in mind in studying the mistake doctrine is to learn a structure for analyzing mistake problems. Such a structure is provided below.

B. DEFINITION OF "MISTAKE." [§ 12–2]

For purposes of contract law, **a mistake is a belief that is not in accord with the facts at the time the contract was entered into** [Restatement 2d § 151]. Note that a mistake does not mean an improvident or regrettable act, e.g., the making of a contract in which a party lost money. Thus, a person who enters into a "bad" deal cannot, without more, use the mistake doctrine to avoid the contract.

1. **Erroneous Belief as to the Future Is Not a "Mistake." [§ 12–3]**

   Mistake is measured by the facts as they exist at the time the contract is made. Thus, a poor prediction or erroneous belief as to what will occur in the future is not a "mistake" entitling the poor predictor to relief under the mistake doctrine.

2. **Mistake of Law Can Be a Mistake of Fact. [§ 12–4]**

   A contracting party may have an erroneous belief as to the legal consequence of its promise in a contract. The existing law at the time the contract is made is generally considered a "fact," and thus, relief

---

* For more information, listen to CD # 5, Track 9 of *Sum and Substance Audio on Contracts*.

can be granted for a mistaken belief as to the operation of the law, assuming all the other elements for applying the mistake doctrine are present [Restatement 2d § 151, Cmt. b].

3. **"Mistake" Distinguished from "Misunderstanding." [§ 12–5]**

A misunderstanding occurs when two parties attach different meanings to the same term in their agreement. As such, it is not an erroneous belief as to a fact, and it is analytically distinct from (although often confused with) the mistake doctrine. The doctrine of misunderstanding is explained beginning at § 12–28.

C. UNILATERAL AND MUTUAL MISTAKE. [§ 12–6]

The Restatement 2d and the courts treat differently the situations where only *one* party to a contract is under a mistaken belief as to the true facts, versus those in which *both* parties are under such a mistake. In general, **it is easier for the party adversely affected by the mistake to get relief when the mistake is mutual rather than when it is unilateral**. The rules regarding mutual mistakes are treated immediately below, and those regarding unilateral mistakes are explained beginning at § 12–21.

D. MUTUAL MISTAKE DEFINED. [§ 12–7*]

Mutual mistake occurs when both parties to a contract are under substantially the same erroneous belief as to the true facts present at the time of the exchange [Restatement 2d § 152]. If a party is adversely affected by a contract entered into under mutual mistake, the contract is **voidable** at the option of that party. For example, Dan sold Linda an antique painting for $60 that both he and Linda reasonably believed was junk. Linda later found out it was worth $6 million. Dan, the party adversely affected by their agreement, may be able to void the contract if he can establish the necessary elements of mutual mistake, which are discussed below.

1. **Elements Necessary to Establish Mutual Mistake. [§ 12–8]**

Under Restatement 2d § 152(1), the elements of mutual mistake are:

(1) The mistake of both parties must be as to a **basic assumption** on which the contract was made [§ 12–9];

(2) The mistake must have **a material effect** on the agreed exchange of performances [§ 12–10]; and

(3) The party seeking to avoid the contract **must not bear the risk** of that mistake [§ 12–11].

---

* For more information, listen to CD # 5, Track 10 of *Sum and Substance Audio on Contracts*.

MISTAKE AND MISUNDERSTANDING

Each of these elements is discussed below.

a. The Mistake Must Be as to a "Basic Assumption" on Which the Contract Was Made. [§ 12–9]

There is no agreed upon definition for "basic assumption," but the idea is that the shared mistake must change the **essential nature** of the contract. That is, whatever the parties thought they were agreeing to must be vastly different, i.e., different not just in kind, but in essential nature, from what they actually agreed to.

b. The Mistake Must Have a "Material Effect" on the Agreed Transaction. [§ 12–10]

To meet this requirement, it must be demonstrated that it would simply be **too unfair to enforce the bargain as called for in the contract**, for one party would get far more than both parties thought he or she was bargaining for. Alternatively, one party would get far less than both parties thought he or she was bargaining for. In other words, if it appears one party is getting too large an **unbargained for windfall**, or the other is suffering too large a reasonably and **unknowingly-risked detriment**, the mistake has a material effect on the transaction. The availability of other remedies is taken into account in determining whether a party will reap a sufficiently large windfall or suffer a sufficiently large detriment [Restatement 2d § 152(2)].

c. The Party Seeking to Avoid the Contract Must Not Bear the Risk of Making the Mistake. [§ 12–11]

Under the Restatement 2d § 152, if the party seeking relief under the mistake doctrine "bears the risk of the mistake," that party cannot avoid the contract under the mistake doctrine. Under Restatement 2d § 154, there are three alternative grounds for finding whether a particular party bore the risk of the mistake:

(1) **The risk was allocated to that party by express agreement of the parties;**

(2) **The party is aware, at the time the contract is made, that he or she has only a limited knowledge of the true facts, but decides to treat that limited knowledge as sufficient;** or

(3) **As a matter of law the court finds it reasonable to place the risk of the mistake on that party.**

The first of these alternatives is almost never an issue, for if the risk was expressly allocated in the contract, usually the parties do not dispute it. The second and third alternatives are frequently litigated in mistake cases. The key to both is whether the party seeking to avoid the agreement was reasonable in believing there was no appreciable risk that his or her benefit was untrue.

2. **Examples Applying Mutual Mistake Principles. [§ 12–12]**

   a. **Example of *Sherwood v. Walker*. [§ 12–13]**

   Buyer and seller contract for the sale of a cow, the now infamous (to contracts students) Rose II of Aberlone. According to the seller, both parties were experienced farmers and reasonably believed the cow to be unable to breed, and thus worth the $80 contract price. If Rose could breed, she would have been worth around $800. After delivery to the buyer, it was discovered that Rose was pregnant and seller sought to avoid the contract based on mutual mistake.

   Held: Mutual mistake is available:

   > (1) **First**, the difference between a breeding cow and a non-breeding one is a change in the **essential nature** of the contract—i.e., what the buyer thought he was buying and what the seller thought he was selling turned out to be a completely different thing than what was actually exchanged between them. Students often argue this element was not met for they bargained for a cow and the buyer got a cow. But the testimony in the case was that breeding and barren cows are substantially different things, thus satisfying the first element.

   > (2) **Second**, the buyer would receive such a **great unbargained for windfall** in the transaction that it would be unfair to enforce the contract. Note that this was not a case where the buyer thought there was a chance the cow was breedable and thus entered the contract hoping it would end up a good deal for him, i.e., a case where he bargained for at least the *risk* of a favorable result. This was a case where any benefit he received from the breeding capabilities of the cow was a fortuity, and thus an **unbargained for windfall**.

   > (3) **Third**, the **risk of this mistake was not on the seller**, for none of the provisions of Restatement 2d § 154 apply, i.e., the seller did not expressly assume the risk, it was not a case where he entered into the contract aware that he did not know very much about the breeding properties of cattle (he was an experienced farmer), and there is nothing in the contract that would make it

MISTAKE AND MISUNDERSTANDING

reasonable for the seller, as opposed to the buyer, to bear the risk of the mistake. *Sherwood v. Walker*, 66 Mich. 568, 33 N.W. 919 (1887).

b. **Example of *Wood v. Boynton*. [§ 12–14]**

The owner of a small, unpolished stone did not know what kind of stone it was, or its value. Owner took it to a jeweler who, in good faith, also professed an uncertainty as to what it was. The jeweler suggested that it "might" be a topaz. The owner left the store but returned a few days later and sold it to the jeweler for $1, a fair price for a topaz. In fact, it turned out to be a diamond worth $700. Thereafter, the seller sought to avoid the transaction based on mutual mistake.

Held: The seller was not entitled to relief based on mutual mistake.

It is arguable that (1) the mistake changed the essential nature of the deal, i.e., a contract for the sale of a supposed topaz is essentially different from a contract for the sale of a diamond. Similarly, it is arguable that (2) the jeweler would reap a huge **unbargained for windfall**, as the thing he thought was probably a $1 topaz turned out to be worth 700 times what he paid. However, under Restatement 2d § 154, the owner bore the risk of the mistake, for **she knew she did not know exactly what the stone was, but instead of investigating further, she went ahead with the deal**. [Case Squibs, *Wood v. Boynton*, 64 Wis. 265, 25 N.W. 42 (1885)].

(1) **Conscious Ignorance. [§ 12–15]**

As some have put it, *Wood* was not a case of "mistake," but rather of **conscious ignorance** on the part of the seller. In other words, because contract making is risk allocation, seller consciously took the risk that the stone might turn out to be more valuable than seller thought and cannot avoid the contract under Restatement § 2d 152(1). Put more simply, even though seller did not explicitly agree to bear the risk, she was aware when she made the contract that her knowledge of the value of the stone was limited. Since she went ahead anyway, she is deemed to bear the risk that the stone turned out to be more valuable and cannot use the mistake doctrine to void the transaction. That is, she was not reasonable in assuming there was no appreciable risk she was under a mistaken belief [Restatement 2d § 154, Cmt. b].

CHAPTER 12

c. **Example of Land Sales. [§ 12–16]**

Occasionally, a party will sell land at a price which would be fair if the land is used for farming or for residential purposes, but later turns out to be much more valuable because, unbeknownst to both parties at the time of contracting, there are, e.g., mineral deposits hidden underneath the land. The seller, of course, wants to avoid the contract. In this type of case, the courts will generally not permit the seller to disaffirm based on mutual mistake, holding that, as a matter of law, the nature of land sales transactions makes it reasonable to impose the risk of making such a mistake on the seller, who could, after all, exclude minerals in the soil from the sale land contract or have the land tested for such minerals before it was put up for sale.

3. **Limitation on When a Party May Void a Contract Based on Mutual Mistake: Reasonable Time After Discovery. [§ 12–17]**

The adversely affected party in a contract entered into under mutual mistake must seek to disaffirm or avoid it within a reasonable time after discovery of the mistake. What constitutes a reasonable time will vary depending on the circumstances, but if disaffirmance is not sought within such time, the contract will be deemed "ratified" by the adversely affected party.

4. **Effect of Mutual Mistake. [§ 12–18]**

A party who can prove mutual mistake is entitled to either avoid the contract, or to waive the mistake and go through with the deal at that party's option. In addition, certain types of mutual mistake may justify reformation of the contract where a court will essentially rewrite the contract to make it fairer and more in line with what the parties' intended [Restatement 2d § 152].

a. **Restitution Required if Contract Avoided on the Basis of Mutual Mistake. [§ 12–19]**

If the party whose expectations under the contract were adversely affected because of a mutual mistake chooses to avoid the contract, full restitution is required for any benefits conferred under the contract up until the time it was avoided. Of course, that party must also make restitution (i.e., pay the reasonable value for any benefits received before the contract was avoided) [*See* Chapter Thirty-One for a discussion of Restitution].

5. **Review Problem. [§ 12–20]**

For a review, we will analyze the Dan/Linda problem set forth above in § 12–7, where the valuable painting was sold for $60.

MISTAKE AND MISUNDERSTANDING

(1)   The first question is whether the painting turning out to be valuable is a change in the **essential nature** of the contract—i.e., did the buyer and seller believe the transaction was for completely different thing. The answer would depend on the circumstances— was the painting marked as "poster art" for the home? Sold in a garage sale? Sold by a dealer in the "bargain" section of her gallery? Likely, however, Dan could establish that a painting he sold for $60 and a masterpiece that was worth $6 million are essentially different in kind, similar to the cow in *Sherwood*.

(2)   The second question is whether the buyer would receive such a **great unbargained for windfall** in the transaction that it would be unfair to enforce the contract. Buying a $6 million painting for $60 would seem to fulfill this element, but recall that it has to be an unbargained for windfall. If some speculation as to the value of the painting was inherent in the bargain, then the buyer's risk taking paid off and there is no actionable mistake.

(3)   The third question is whether the **risk of the mistake was allocated to the seller**, i.e., did the seller expressly assume the risk, did the seller enter into the contract aware that he did not know very much about the painting or the painter, and would the circumstances of the transaction make it reasonable for the seller, as opposed to the buyer, to bear the risk of the mistake? For example, were both Dan and Linda art experts and agreed there was "no reasonable chance" that the painting was anything more than a $60 wall hanging? Did Dan have doubts whether the painting was a masterpiece or not and went ahead with the transaction anyway, i.e., a conscious ignorance situation?

As you can see, the mistake analysis is very fact intensive.

E.   UNILATERAL MISTAKE DEFINED. [§ 12–21*]

A unilateral mistake occurs when only one party to a contract has an erroneous belief as to the true facts present in an exchange [Restatement 2d § 153].

1.   Elements Necessary to Establish Unilateral Mistake. [§ 12–22]

If only one party entered a contract under a mistake, it is relatively difficult for that party to avoid the contract due to his or her unilateral mistake. Under Restatement 2d § 153, the party seeking to void a contract mistake must show that he or she did not bear the risk of the mistake for any of the reasons set forth in Restatement 2d

---

* For more information, listen to CD # 5, Track 11 of *Sum and Substance Audio on Contracts*.

§ 154, i.e., did not expressly or reasonably assume the risk of the mistaken belief, *plus* **either** of the following:

(1) The effect of the mistake is such that enforcement against the mistaken party would be "unconscionable"; **or**

(2) The non-mistaken party either had reason to know of the mistake or caused the mistake.

There are two kinds of cases in which unilateral mistake has frequently been applied: mistaken bid cases and mistaken payment cases. Each are discussed below:

a. **Example of Mistaken Bid Cases. [§ 12–23]**

One of the most common examples of unilateral mistake cases are those in which a general contractor submits a very low bid on a project and that bid is then accepted by a developer, or a subcontractor makes a similar mistake in calculating and transmitting its bid to a general contractor. After the contract has been awarded, the general (or sub) finds that he or she has made an arithmetic or like error in the bidding process, and will end up losing money on the project (or, perhaps, making much less than expected). To get relief in these situations, the affected party must show that he or she does not bear the risk of the mistake under the test of Restatement 2d § 154. In addition, because the mistake is only unilateral, the affected party must *also* prove: (a) that enforcement against it would be "unconscionable"; or that (b) the developer had reason to know of the mistake.

Unconscionability is dealt with in Chapter Sixteen, but the idea is that the affected party must convince a court that, in good conscience, it could not force him or her to go through with the deal. If the affected party cannot establish unconscionability, then he or she must show that the other party knew of the mistake or caused it in order to get relief. For example, if all the other bids for a project were $10–13 million, and the bid of the general who was awarded the contract was $6 million, a case could be made that the developer had reason to know of the mistake.

Note that several scholars have recently insisted that mistaken bid cases really present mutual mistake, not unilateral mistake, fact situations. That is, to assume in these cases that the contractor was mistaken, but that the developer was not, is to accuse the developer of acting in bad faith by accepting a bid he or she knew was mistakenly too low. It makes more sense, and is probably more accurate, to say that both parties were mistaken. However, these scholars note that requiring

MISTAKE AND MISUNDERSTANDING

contractors to meet the more stringent unilateral mistake rules in mistaken bid cases may be justified as a matter of policy, given the nature of the contracting business and the contractor/developer relationship.

b. Example of Mistaken Payment Cases. [§ 12–24]

Another example of the use of unilateral mistake is in the so-called "mistaken payment" cases. These occur when a debtor, often a commercial tenant, makes a payment mistake, e.g., the rent is really $350/month but for some reason the accounting department messes up and issues checks for $700. Assuming the debtor can establish it did not bear the risk of this mistake under the test of Restatement 2d § 154, generally it can also establish that failure to refund the excess payments is both unconscionable and a situation in which the other party had reason to know of the mistake. [*McDonald's Corp. v. Moore*, 237 F. Supp. 874 (W.D.S.C. 1965)].

2. Limitation on When a Party May Void a Contract Based on Unilateral Mistake: A Reasonable Time After Discovery. [§ 12–25]

As with mutual mistake, the party seeking to rescind a contract based on unilateral mistake grounds must do so within a reasonable time after discovering the mistake, or the contract will be deemed implicitly ratified by that party [§ 12–17].

3. Effect of Unilateral Mistake. [§ 12–26]

If a party can establish the requisites for relief under a unilateral mistake theory, the contract is voidable by that party. That is, the mistaken party can enforce it, or may disaffirm it, at that party's option.

a. Restitution Required upon Avoidance of Contract Entered into Under Unilateral Mistake. [§ 12–27]

If the party who makes the unilateral mistake avoids a contract on that theory, he or she must make full restitution for (i.e., pay the fair value of) any benefits received under the contract up until the time of avoidance. Of course, that party may also be entitled to restitution for any benefits he or she provided as well [*See* Chapter Thirty-One for a discussion of Restitution].

CHAPTER 12

F. THE "MISUNDERSTANDING" DOCTRINE. [§ 12–28*]

A topic usually studied along with mistake, but distinguishable from it, is "misunderstanding." **Misunderstanding occurs when the parties agree to a term in their contract, but each ascribes a different meaning to the term** [Restatement 2d § 20]. For example, if the parties agree to the purchase and sale of chickens, but one party believes "chickens" to mean frying chickens and the other believes the term to refer to stewing chickens, the issue is one of misunderstanding, not of mistake [Case Squibs, *Frigaliment Importing Co. v. B.N.S. Int'l Sales Corp.*, 190 F. Supp. 116 (S.D.N.Y. 1960). Note the case raises other issues as well, which are discussed in more detail in § 20–17].

1. **Distinguishing "Misunderstanding" from "Mistake." [§ 12–29]**

   Misunderstanding is a **formation issue**, i.e., the misunderstanding doctrine governs whether the parties in fact have an enforceable contract and, if so, what its terms are. The mistake doctrine, on the other hand, assumes the existence of a valid contract, and the issue is whether a party may avoid it due to a mistaken belief that is not in accord with the true facts.

2. **Effect of Misunderstanding. [§ 12–30]**

   The effect of the misunderstanding doctrine on a transaction depends on the understandings of the parties. **If neither party knows, or has reason to know, of the meaning of a material term attached by the other, then no contract is formed** [Restatement 2d § 20(1)(a)]. **Similarly, if both parties know the other ascribes a different meaning to the term, no contract is formed** [Restatement 2d § 20(1)(b)]. However, if the parties have different meanings of a material term, but one party knows of the misunderstanding and the other party does not, a contract is formed and the meaning of the disputed term is the one believed by the party who did not know of the misunderstanding [Restatement 2d § 20(2)]. Note that the misunderstanding must be as to a **material term** for the misunderstanding doctrine to apply and, if established, entitles the party to rescission.

   a. **Example of *Raffles v. Wichelhaus*. [§ 12–31]**

      Buyer and seller agreed upon the sale of cotton to be sent on the ship *The Peerless* from Bombay, India. It turns out there were two ships named *The Peerless* docked in Bombay, and they left Bombay a few months apart. The "1st *Peerless*" left in October; the "2nd *Peerless*" in December. The buyer believed the contract

---

* For more information, listen to CD # 6, Track 1 of *Sum and Substance Audio on Contracts*.

MISTAKE AND MISUNDERSTANDING

called for shipment on the 1st *Peerless*; the seller believed it called for shipment on the 2nd *Peerless*.

Held: As neither party knew (or had reason to know) of the meaning attached to the term "*The Peerless*" by the other, no contract was ever formed since there was no mutual manifestation of agreement to go forward on the same material terms, as is necessary for contract formation (*see* Chapter Two). Thus, while the seller was not in breach for sending the goods on the 2nd *Peerless*, the buyer was also not in breach for refusing to accept them when they arrived later than the buyer expected for no contract was ever formed between them [*Raffles v. Wichelhaus*, 159 Eng. Rep. 375 (1864); Restatement 2d § 20(1)(a)].

   b. **Example. [§ 12–32]**

   The facts are the same as in *Raffles*, except assume both buyer and seller knew there were two ships named *The Peerless*, and the buyer knew the seller meant the 2nd *Peerless*, but the seller knew the buyer meant the 1st *Peerless*. In that case, once again no contract would be formed, regardless of which ship the goods were eventually shipped on, for each party was aware of the other's misunderstanding, and chose to go ahead anyway without correcting it [Restatement 2d § 20(1)(b)].

   c. **Example. [§ 12–33]**

   The facts are the same as in *Raffles*, except assume only the seller (who is in Bombay) knows there are two ships called *The Peerless*. Seller intends to ship on the later departing ship, but is confident that buyer expects the goods to be shipped on the 1st *Peerless*. In that case a contract **is** formed, and it is for shipment on the 1st *Peerless* [Restatement 2d § 20(2)].

G. EXAM APPROACH TO MISTAKE AND MISUNDERSTANDING ISSUES. [§ 12–34*]

An analysis under both mistake and misunderstanding requires extensive use of the facts you are given in your examination problem. To be attuned to the issues:

   1. Make sure you ascertain whether either party was laboring under a mistake as to an existing **fact** *at the time of the making* of the contract [§ 12–4 for purposes of mistake or laboring under a different meaning of a contractual term; § 12–28 for purposes of misunderstanding]. Remember, it is not a "mistake" (in the contracts

---

* For more information, listen to CD # 5, Track 12, and CD # 6, Track 1 of *Sum and Substance Audio on Contracts.*

sense) that a deal turns out to be a bad one, e.g., because the market for the product the buyer purchased unexpectedly collapses.

2. Once you determine the proper doctrine, set forth the elements that control its application [§ 12–8 for mutual mistake; § 12–21 for unilateral mistake; and §§ 12–28 *et seq.* for misunderstanding]; find the facts in the problem that correspond to each element of the doctrine; and then argue those facts, making sure to reach a definite conclusion.

Be especially attentive in mistake cases to whether there was "conscious ignorance," thus shifting the risk of the mistake to one party or the other. This is one of the most heavily tested issues in this area.

CHAPTER 13

DURESS

A. THE PROBLEM OF DURESS. [§ 13–1*]

When a person enters into a contract under duress, the principles of free choice and voluntary decision-making necessary for freedom of contract are imperiled. The consequence of the duress doctrine on a particular contract depends on whether the contract is entered into under **physical compulsion** or whether the contract is entered into under an **improper threat**. Each of these situations is discussed below.

B. DURESS BY PHYSICAL COMPULSION. [§ 13–2**]

If a party enters into a contract solely because he or she has been compelled to do so by use of physical force, the contract is "**void**" (not voidable) [Restatement 2d § 174]. This means there is no "contract" and neither party can enforce its terms. Thus, if Ed says to Bill, "You had better sign this contract or I will stab you with this knife," the contract Bill signs cannot be enforced by Ed, or by Bill, even if Bill later wishes to do so. They have no legally enforceable agreement.

An issue arises as to how imminent the threat has to be. That is, suppose the threat is, "Sign this contract or I will kill you someday," and there is otherwise no imminent threat. The answer is that there must be some imminence of the threat to make the contract void. [*U.S. for Use of Trane Co. v. Bond,* 586 A.2d 734, 740 (1991): "[I]t is presently the law . . . that a contract may be held void where, in addition to actual physical compulsion, a threat of *imminent physical violence* is exerted upon the victim of such magnitude as to cause a reasonable person, in the circumstances, to fear loss of life, or serious physical injury, or actual imprisonment for refusal to sign the document. In other words, duress sufficient to render a contract void consists of the actual application of physical force that is sufficient to, and does, cause the person unwillingly to execute the document; as well as the threat of application of *immediate physical force* sufficient to place a person in the position of the signer in

---

* For more information, listen to CD # 6, Track 2 of *Sum and Substance Audio on Contracts.*

** For more information, listen to CD # 6, Track 3 of *Sum and Substance Audio on Contracts.*

actual, reasonable, and imminent fear of death, serious personal injury, or actual imprisonment." (Emphasis added)].

If the threat is not imminent, the situation must be analyzed as duress by improper threat, which is discussed below in § 13–3.

C. DURESS BY "IMPROPER" THREAT. [§ 13–3*]

If a party enters into a contract because of an improper *threat* that leaves the victim no reasonable alternative but to assent to the proposed deal, the contract is **voidable** by the victim [Restatement 2d § 175]. Thus, the issue is to determine which threats are "proper" and which are "improper." This issue is discussed and explained below.

1. **What Constitutes an "Improper" Threat? [§ 13–4]**

    Not all threats made in the bargaining process are improper, e.g., the statement, "If you cannot promise to have the goods to me by November 10, I do not want to enter into a contract with you," is a threat of sorts, but it obviously is not improper when made during contract negotiations. The Restatement 2d provides two different sets of tests to determine when a threat is "improper," depending on whether the resulting exchange appears to be on fair terms or not.

    That is, perhaps surprisingly, sometimes duress results in an exchange that appears to be fair. The problem is that the contract is a "forced" sale, e.g., where Joe uses improper threats to get Mary to sell her house to him, when Mary does not want to, but where he agrees to pay her a fair price for it. On the other hand, sometimes duress results in an exchange on unfair terms, e.g., when Les uses duress to get June to sell her car to him at an unbelievably cheap price. Each situation is discussed below.

2. **Improper Threat When Terms of the Exchange Appear Fair. [§ 13–5]**

    Under Restatement 2d § 176(1), a threat made to induce a party to enter a contract where the resulting exchange is *fair* is "improper" if:

    (1) What is threatened (or the threat itself) is a **crime or tort** [Restatement 2d § 176(1)(a); § 13–6];

    (2) What is threatened is **criminal prosecution** [Restatement 2d § 176(1)(b); § 13–7];

    (3) What is threatened is the **bad faith use of the civil process** [Restatement 2d § 176(1)(c); § 13–8]; or

---

* For more information, listen to CD # 6 Track 4 of *Sum and Substance Audio on Contracts*.

DURESS

(4) The threat is a **breach of the duty of good faith and fair dealing with regard to the modification of an existing contract** [Restatement 2d § 176(1)(d); § 13–9].

Each of these provisions is discussed below.

Once again, recall that if a contract is made under the duress of an improper threat, it is voidable by the party against whom the threat was made.

a. **Example. [§ 13–6]**

Larry badly wants to buy Bernice's car, but Bernice won't sell. Larry thereafter credibly threatens to poison Bernice's husband unless she agrees to sell the car to him at a fair price. Bernice agrees to sell. Bernice can disaffirm the contract based on duress, for Larry has threatened her with both a criminal and a tortious act.

b. **Example. [§ 13–7]**

Brenda, the Bank Manager, believes Cathy, a teller, has embezzled $10,000. Brenda threatens to report Cathy to the police as an embezzler unless Cathy signs an agreement to "repay" the $10,000. If Cathy signs the agreement, she can avoid it under the duress doctrine, for the threat of criminal prosecution is an improper threat under contract law.

Note that this is true regardless of whether Cathy actually embezzled the money. The issue is whether she freely and voluntarily entered into the contract where she promised to repay the money. Since contract law presumes she did not voluntarily enter into the agreement given the threat, the contract can be avoided. On the other hand, if such agreement were reached as part of a settlement of a **civil** suit for conversion brought by the bank, it would likely be enforceable, so long as the Bank had a good faith belief that Cathy had embezzled the funds. [*See* the discussion of settlement agreements in § 24–12.]

c. **Example. [§ 13–8]**

Norma is happy with the work done by Ted, a contractor she hired to build a room addition onto her home. However, she tells Ted that she will sue him for breach of warranty unless Ted agrees to install a fountain in her backyard, a term that was not in their original agreement. Ted does not want to build the fountain, even though Norma has agreed to pay him a fair price to do so. Ultimately he agrees to do the work rather than go to the expense of fighting the suit. Ted can disaffirm the fountain agreement, as Norma threatened the use of the civil process in bad faith. Note that if Norma really believed she had a claim against Ted, her threat would not be in bad faith. Thus, if Ted offered to build the fountain in order to settle the dispute, the promise would be enforceable.

    d. **Example. [§ 13–9]**

Ellen is an interior decorator. She has signed a contract to decorate one of Rick's homes for $50,000. When she is halfway through, she unambiguously threatens not to finish unless Rick enters into another contract with her allowing her to decorate his vacation home as well. If Rick signs the vacation home contract, he may avoid it, as Ellen's threat was a breach of her duty of good faith and fair dealing with regard to the modification and therefore "improper." This is an example of the "extortionist" discussed previously in § 7–73.

3. **Improper Threat Where Terms of the Exchange Appear Unfair. [§ 13–10]**

Under Restatement 2d § 176(2), if a threat induces an exchange which is *unfair*, the threat is "improper" if:

    (1) The threatened act would **harm the recipient and not really benefit the party making the threat** [§ 13–11];

    (2) **Prior dealing** between the parties significantly **increases the effectiveness of the threat** [§ 13–12]; or

    (3) The threatened action is a **use of power for illegitimate ends** [§ 13–13].

    a. **Example. [§ 13–11]**

Ben tells Ted he will make public Ted's extra-marital affair unless Ted sells Ben his $15,000 stereo for $50. Ted agrees to sell. Since the bargain is unfair, and since the threatened act would harm Ted and not significantly benefit Ben, Ted can avoid the agreement.

    b. **Example. [§ 13–12]**

On the 10th of each month for the last two years, Ed's Food Company has delivered 20 pounds of ground coffee to Pete's Diner for $100. The coffee was a special blend made by Ed's and helped to make Pete's Diner popular. On June 11, the local gourmet club was to meet for the first time at Pete's. At 4:00 p.m. on June 10, Ed's threatens not to deliver any coffee unless Pete's agrees to pay $800 for a normal 20-pound delivery. As Pete's was out of coffee and had the gourmet club coming the next day, Pete agreed. Pete's can avoid the agreement for the resulting exchange was unfair and the prior dealings between the parties increased the effectiveness of Ed's threat (i.e., Pete's relied on the customary delivery at $100).

c. Example. [§ 13–13]

Gas Company, a monopoly, typically charges developers $200 per home to connect houses in a new real estate development. However, it seeks to charge Build Company $1,500 per home to hook up houses in Build Company Acres because it wants to pay bonuses to its executives. Build Company can disaffirm any agreement to pay the $1,500 because Gas Company has used its monopoly power to supply gas for an illegitimate end [Restatement 2d § 176, Cmt. f, Ill. 16].

d. Review Problem: Economic Duress. [§ 13–14]

Larry is in desperate need of money. Frank knows this and credibly tells Larry that unless Larry immediately accepts Frank's offer of $100 for Larry's $5,000 watch, the offer will be withdrawn. Larry agrees.

Question:

Is the contract voidable on grounds of duress?

Answer:

Even though the terms of the exchange are very unfair, if Larry accepts Frank's offer the contract will not be voidable on the grounds of duress. This is true even though Larry may legitimately feel he is under **economic duress** and that Frank is taking unfair advantage of him. The problem (for Larry) is that Larry's economic duress was not of Frank's making, and so none of the provisions of Restatement 2d § 176(2) apply. That is, **economic duress not of the advantaged party's making is not a defense to contract formation.**

D. RESTITUTION RECOVERABLE UPON AVOIDANCE OF CONTRACT FOR DURESS. [§ 13–15]

When the victim of a contract entered into under duress avoids a contract, the victim is entitled to restitution. Additionally, if appropriate, the victim may also have to make restitution to the party who made the improper threat. [*See* Chapter Thirty-One for a discussion of restitution.]

CHAPTER 13

E. EXAM APPROACH TO DURESS ISSUES. [§ 13–16*]

First determine whether a contract was entered into by threat of imminent physical harm, or by improper threat. If it is the former, the resulting agreement is void.

If one party enters into a contract or contract modification by means of improper threat, the question is whether the resulting deal is fair or not.

If the terms are fair, determine whether any of the provisions of Restatement 2d § 176(1) apply [§§ 13–5 *et seq.*]; if the resulting terms are unfair, determine whether any of the provisions of Restatement 2d § 176(2) apply [§§ 13–10 *et seq.*].

Finally, recall that economic duress not caused by the party getting a favorable deal is **not** grounds for avoiding the contract [§ 13–14].

---

* For more information, listen to CD # 6, Track 5 of *Sum and Substance Audio on Contracts*.

CHAPTER 14

UNDUE INFLUENCE

A. THE UNDUE INFLUENCE DOCTRINE. [§ 14–1*]

Undue influence occurs when a contracting party suffers from some sort of temporary or permanent mental weakness (short of incapacity) and is subject to improper persuasion (short of duress) by someone who is in a "special relationship" with that party [Restatement 2d § 177]. When it is determined that a party's assent to a contract has been induced by undue influence, the contract is **voidable** by the victim because he or she is deemed to have entered into it without sufficient voluntariness.

B. ELEMENTS NECESSARY TO ESTABLISH UNDUE INFLUENCE. [§ 14–2]

To establish a claim of undue influence, two elements must be proven:

(1) That there is a **special relationship** between the victim and the other party; and

(2) That there has been **improper persuasion** of the victim by the "stronger" party [Restatement 2d § 177].

Each of these elements is discussed below. Note, however, that it is **not** a *requirement* that the ensuing contract be "unfair" to the weaker party for undue influence to apply. That is, a contract can be objectively "fair" (the exchanged items economically proportionate) and still be voidable by the weaker party if entered into by undue influence.

Note, however, that often in undue influence situations, the resulting exchange *is* unfair, and such unfairness is a characteristic a court will use to determine whether to invoke the doctrine [§ 14–4].

1. The First Element: A "Special Relationship." [§ 14–3]

The first element a plaintiff must prove to utilize the undue influence doctrine is the existence of a "special relationship" between the contracting parties. For purposes of undue influence, a "special relationship" occurs either when the victim is under the **domination of the other**, or when the relationship between the parties is such

---

* For more information, listen to CD # 6, Track 6 of *Sum and Substance Audio on Contracts*.

that the victim is **justified in assuming the other party will not jeopardize the victim's welfare.**

The gist of this requirement is that if the circumstances surrounding the relationship of the parties make the victim particularly susceptible to influence by the other, a sufficient special relationship exists. Typical examples of such a relationship are: parent/child; lawyer/client; clergyman/parishioner; nurse/elderly patient; accountant/client; and physician/patient. However, these are not the only qualifying relationships. Also, typically the victim is weak, infirm, and/or aged, but these characteristics are neither requirements nor limitations on who can be a victim of undue influence [Restatement 2d § 177, Cmt. a].

By means of contrast, an "arms' length" transaction between two disinterested parties is the opposite of a situation giving rise to a special relationship.

2. The Second Element: Improper Persuasion. [§ 14–4]

In addition to establishing a special relationship, a party seeking to avoid a contract based on undue influence must also show that the stronger party used "improper persuasion" to gain the victim's assent to a transaction. The test for when improper persuasion has been used is whether the stronger party **seriously impaired the free exercise of judgment by the victim**. Common features of a contract entered into by unfair persuasion are:

(a) An unfair exchange (economic disproportionality);

(b) The unavailability of independent advice given to the victim before assenting to the contract;

(c) The lack of time for reflection by the victim before assenting to the agreement; and/or

(d) A high degree of susceptibility to persuasion exhibited by the victim [Restatement 2d § 177, Cmt. b].

Note the above are simply features frequently found contracts voidable on undue influence grounds. They provide circumstantial evidence that undue influence occurred. They are **not**, however, elements and thus, undue influence can be found even without them. [*See* Case Squibs, *Methodist Mission Home v. N.A.B.*, for a classic application of the undue influence doctrine].

C. RESTITUTION RECOVERABLE UPON AVOIDANCE OF THE CONTRACT FOR UNDUE INFLUENCE. [§ 14–5]

When the victim of a contract entered into by undue influence avoids the contract, the victim is entitled to restitutionary recovery and must also

UNDUE INFLUENCE

make restitution to the stronger party. (*See* Chapter Thirty-One for a discussion of restitution.)

D. EXAM APPROACH TO UNDUE INFLUENCE ISSUES. [§ 14–6]

Any time you are presented with a "special relationship" between two contracting parties, i.e., where one party is relying on the other for care or advice [§ 14–3], undue influence is potentially implicated. If such a relationship exists, look for evidence of improper persuasion [§ 14–4]. If such improper persuasion exists, the contract is voidable by the "weaker" party.

CHAPTER 15

MISREPRESENTATION

A. THE MISREPRESENTATION DOCTRINE. [§ 15–1*]

During the bargaining process, parties make representations to each other. When those representations turn out to be wrong, and when they have induced the other party to enter into a contract, the process under which parties voluntarily enter into an informed bargain can be upset. Thus, in certain situations, contract law provides relief from bargains entered into as a result of misrepresentation. These situations are described below.

B. TYPES OF MISREPRESENTATION. [§ 15–2]

Misrepresentation can be of three types:

   (1) **Innocent**, e.g., where the seller honestly and reasonably thought the property was 40 acres and not the 30 acres it turned out to be (for example, where the owner of the property hired an independent, licensed surveyor to tell her how large the property was, and the surveyor incorrectly stated it was 40 acres);

   (2) **Negligent**, e.g., where the seller honestly believed that the property was 40 acres, but "should have known" it was really 30 (for example, where she truly believed it was 40 acres because she personally, but carelessly, measured it); or

   (3) **Fraudulent**. Fraudulent representations are of three types:

   (a) Where the seller **consciously lies**, e.g., where she knew the property was 30 acres but said it was 40 anyway just to close the deal;

   (b) Where the seller **knows she does not know the true facts**, e.g., where she really had no idea of how big the property was and just made up the 40-acre figure to close the deal; or

   (c) Where the seller has a **reckless disregard for the truth or falsity of the statement**, e.g., where she may have believed the property was 40 acres when she said so to the buyer, but such belief was based exclusively on a brief glimpse at a

---

* For more information, listen to CD # 6, Track 7 of *Sum and Substance Audio on Contracts*.

complicated map, and where she really had no expertise in reading such maps and estimating acreage.

As a matter of tort law, distinguishing among these different types of misrepresentation is quite important, for each can provide the innocent party with different remedies. However, in contract law these distinctions are not as important, for the same remedies apply in contract regardless the type of misrepresentation. Those remedies are described below.

C. EFFECT OF MISREPRESENTATION. [§ 15–3]

The effect of an actionable misrepresentation made during contract negotiations depends on what was misrepresented to the innocent party. If there was a misrepresentation as to the very nature of the agreement itself, the contract is "**void**." These "fraud in the *factum*" cases are discussed in § 15–4.

If however, as is most often the case, the misrepresentation goes only to the inducement to enter into the contract, the resulting agreement is **voidable** at the option of the innocent party. These "fraud in the inducement" cases are discussed in § 15–6.

D. "VOID" CONTRACTS RESULTING FROM FRAUD IN THE *FACTUM*. [§ 15–4*]

Typically misrepresentations, even fraudulent ones, merely go to the **inducement** to enter into a contract, e.g., a party falsely tells another that a freezer will chill foods down to −20 degrees when in fact it will only chill them to 0 degrees. However, sometimes the "guilty" party will misrepresent **the very nature of the document** presented to the innocent party. In that case, there is said to be fraud in the **factum**, and the agreement is never enforceable, i.e., it was a "void" contract from its inception [Restatement 2d § 163].

1. Example. [§ 15–5]

   Insurance agent tells customer that the form customer is signing is only a release of medical records to the insurance company, which needs to be executed "just in case" the customer eventually decides to go ahead and purchase life insurance. In fact, the document is the life insurance contract itself, obligating the customer to $800 per year in premiums. The agreement is void because the very nature of the agreement was fraudulently misrepresented to the customer.

---

* For more information, listen to CD # 6, Track 8 of *Sum and Substance Audio on Contracts*.

MISREPRESENTATION

E. ELEMENTS NECESSARY TO ESTABLISH FRAUD IN THE INDUCEMENT. [§ 15–6*]

The **vast** bulk of misrepresentation cases involve fraud in the inducement. To establish that such an actionable misrepresentation occurred, and thereby **obtain the right to avoid the contract**, the innocent party must establish the following elements under Restatement 2d § 164:

(1) **A misrepresentation of existing *fact*** was made by the other party [§ 15–7];

(2) The misrepresentation was *either* **fraudulent** *or* **material** [§ 15–22];

(3) The misrepresentation was **actually relied upon by the innocent party** [§ 15–29]; and

(4) Such **reliance was reasonable** [§ 15–30].

1. Misrepresentation of "Fact." [§ 15–7]

A misrepresentation is an assertion that is not in accord with the facts [Restatement 2d § 159]. To be actionable, the assertion giving rise to a claim of misrepresentation must be about a **fact in existence at the time the assertion was made**, as opposed to an opinion, a prediction of future events, statements of intention, puffery, etc.

a. Distinguishing "Fact" from "Opinion." [§ 15–8]

The general rule is that the assertion of an opinion cannot serve as the basis of a misrepresentation claim. The problem then is determining when a statement is a fact and when it is an opinion. There is no universally agreed upon definition of opinion in contract law, but the Restatement and case law provide that the more *verifiable* or *provable* an assertion, the more likely it is to be a fact. Conversely, the more the statement expresses only an *uncertain* or *unascertainable subjective belief or judgment* about a good, the more likely it is to be an opinion [Restatement 2d § 168(1)]. In other words, if a statement can be proven true or false, it is probably a fact. If it is incapable of being proven true or false, it is likely only an opinion. So, with the exceptions and clarifications discussed below, when the misrepresentation involves a "judgment as to the quality, value, authenticity, or similar matter," it is likely an opinion and not an actionable fact [Restatement 2d § 168(1).]

---

* For more information, listen to CD # 6, Track 9 of *Sum and Substance Audio on Contracts*.

CHAPTER 15

(1) Exceptions When Even a Statement of "Opinion" Can Serve as the Basis for a Misrepresentation Claim. [§ 15–9]

Contract law provides that when a party asserts even a "pure" opinion, the party also impliedly asserts two facts: (1) what the speaker says is truly the speaker's opinion; and (2) that the speaker knows sufficient facts to justify forming the opinion. If this is not the case, i.e., if the speaker truly believes something different than what he or she opines, then such an assertion is actionable, for it will be deemed the misrepresentation of a fact—the fact of what the speaker's opinion truly was [Restatement 2d § 168(2)].

In addition, Restatement 2d § 169 sets forth several other instances in which an "opinion" may nevertheless be actionable:

> (a) When the misrepresenting party "stands in a relation of trust and confidence" to the innocent party;
>
> (b) When the innocent party reasonably believes the other party "has special skill, judgment, or objectivity with regard to the subject matter," and
>
> (c) If the innocent party is "particularly susceptible" to a misrepresentation of the type involved.

(a) Example. [§ 15–10]

> Frank is selling his home. He tells Bill that while the air conditioning system is "not perfect, in my opinion it works pretty well." In fact, Frank knows the air conditioning system is unworkable. Even though the phrase "it works pretty well" generally is taken as only expressing a subjective belief, without certainty, as to the quality of something (and therefore normally would be a non-actionable opinion), in this case Frank knew that his statement of opinion was not true, i.e., he misrepresented the "fact" of what his opinion truly was. As such, his assertion is actionable as a misrepresentation of "fact.".
>
> Same result if, e.g., a seller-appraiser gives an "opinion" that the painting she is selling is an authentic Rembrandt when she knows that it is not or knows that she does not have sufficient facts to render such an opinion. Even if the opinion was genuine, but wrong, the innocent party might be able to avoid the transaction based on the opinion since it is likely the innocent party reasonably believes appraiser "has the

MISREPRESENTATION

special skill, judgment or objectivity" to make the opinion actionable [Restatement 2d § 169(b)].

b. **Distinguishing "Existing Fact" from "Prediction of Future Events." [§ 15–11]**

A prediction of future events beyond the control of the speaker cannot serve as the basis for a misrepresentation claim. For example, assume the seller of a house says to a prospective buyer, "You should buy this house. It will only increase in value." Even if the buyer purchases the house based on the quoted statement, and even if a year later the house is worth less than what the buyer paid for it, the buyer still cannot avoid the contract based on misrepresentation. The reason is that the seller did not make a statement of existing fact about the house. Rather, the seller made only a prediction of future events beyond his or her control, which is not actionable.

c. **Distinguishing "Fact" from "Statement of Intention": The Difference Between Ordinary Breach and Misrepresentation. [§ 15–12]**

An easy mistake students sometimes make is to assert that every time a contract is breached, there must have been fraud or some other kind of actionable misrepresentation. That is, if the party promised to deliver 100 55-inch televisions on April 10, and did not do so, it is tempting to say that the seller is liable in fraud or some other form of misrepresentation. The misrepresentation doctrine is not that broad.

Whether an ordinary breach rises to the level of misrepresentation depends on the intention of the promisor *at the time the promise was made*. If the promisor knew that he or she had no intention of carrying out the promise at the time it was made, or was misrepresenting a fact at the time of contracting, then it is a misrepresentation issue, and the innocent party can avoid the contract. However, if the promisor intended to carry out the promise at the time it was made, but later failed to perform for some other reason, then the resulting suit is for a breach of contract only. Thus, in the latter case the innocent party can sue for damages as a result of the breach, but may not avoid the contract under the misrepresentation doctrine.

(1) Example. [§ 15–13]

Pam owns a lumberyard and promises Bob she will deliver firewood to his house in two weeks. She fails to deliver the wood without legal justification. Whether Bob can disaffirm the contract based on misrepresentation, or instead can only sue for breach, depends on what Pam's intentions were when she made the promise. If Pam never intended to deliver the wood, there is fraudulent inducement and her promise is actionable as a misrepresentation of "fact," i.e., the fact of what her intention truly was. If, however, at the time she made the promise she intended to carry it out, and later ran out of wood, or got mad at Bob, or for any other post-contracting reason she chose not to deliver the wood, then Bob's remedy is for breach of contract only, for there was no misrepresentation of a fact existing at the time the assertion was made.

d. **Distinguishing "Fact" from "Puffing" or "Trade Talk." [§ 15–14]**

Today it is widely recognized that assertions adjudged to be mere "puffing" or "trade talk" are insufficient statements on which to base a misrepresentation claim. Once again, the key inquiry is how to determine whether a statement is a factual one or puffing. While there is no generally agreed upon definition of puffing, the main attribute of this kind of speech is that it is so amorphous as to really be nothing more than opinion. Thus, phrases like "X brand of peanut butter is the *best*" or "This is a *superior* product," or "This deal is an *excellent value*" are not actionable. They are simply considered statements that puff up a product's or service's desirability without really promising anything concrete about the product. That is, there is no objective way to prove one brand of peanut butter is "the best," for the statement is full of ambiguity, e.g., is the speaker saying the product is the best value, the best tasting, the best for you, etc. As such, there is really no way of proving such claims true or false, and thus by definition, no way to establish that they are misrepresentations of **fact**.

Lately, the closest cases as to whether the assertion is non-actionable puffing or an actionable misrepresentation involve the word "good" or like representations. For example, assume a seller says, "This is a good car," and also assume the car completely breaks down while the buyer drives it home. Some courts hold that the words "good," "very good," etc. are too amorphous to mean anything concrete, and thus, are puffing only. However, the modern trend is to find that while it may be difficult to give those terms an exact meaning, it is not hard to find that the term means **something**, e.g., that the car was at least drivable for a little ways. Hence, if the car breaks down on the way home, an actionable misrepresentation will have occurred. Note this is even more often applied when the speaker has some expertise, e.g., if a mechanic said the car was "good"

MISREPRESENTATION

makes it more likely that an actionable misrepresentation would be found than if the same statement were made by a lay person with no mechanical training.

e. When a Party's Silence Can Act as a Factual Misrepresentation: The Duty to Disclose. [§ 15–15*]

It is almost never true that two parties to a contract have exactly the same information when negotiating a deal. Naturally, a party who lawfully and fairly obtains favorable information will be reluctant to disclose it, as it might make the bargain far less profitable for him or her. For example, a party who finds out where a road will be built because she was at the public city council meeting the night the council approved the plans will not want to share that information with the owner of property next to the road who hasn't taken the trouble to find out about the city's plans.

Most of the time the law allows a party to keep lawfully and fairly obtained information to himself or herself. However, there are five situations in which the **failure** to speak acts as a factual misrepresentation. In these cases it is said the party who is silent is under a "duty" to disclose the facts, and the failure to do so acts as an affirmative and actionable representation to the contrary. For example, if the woman who attended the council meeting was under a duty to disclose that a road was being built for some reason, then her silence would be taken as an affirmative statement that there were no plans by the city to build a road in that location, and the seller f the property could avoid it on misrepresentation grounds.

The five situations in which a party's silence can act as a misrepresentation are:

> (1) When a party has taken **affirmative action to conceal a fact**, with the intent to make it unlikely the innocent party will discover it [Restatement 2d § 160; § 15–16];
>
> (2) When, *before the contract is executed,* a party learns of **subsequent information** about which disclosure is necessary to prevent a previous assertion (which may have been true when made) from being a misrepresentation [Restatement 2d § 161(a); § 15–17];
>
> (3) Where one party knows that disclosure of a fact is **necessary to correct a mistake of the other as to a basic assumption** on which the contract is based, so long

---

* For more information, listen to CD # 6, Track 10 of *Sum and Substance Audio on Contracts.*

as non-disclosure of that fact would be a breach of good faith and reasonable standards of fair dealing [Restatement 2d § 161(b); § 15–18];

(4) Where **one party knows that disclosure of a fact is necessary to correct a mistake of the other** as to the *effect of a writing* which evidences the agreement of the parties [Restatement 2d § 161(c); § 15–19]; and

(5) Where the innocent party is entitled to know of a fact due to the **relation of trust and confidence** between the innocent and misrepresenting parties [Restatement 2d § 161(d); § 15–20].

Each of these rules is illustrated in order by an example below.

(1) Example. [§ 15–16]

Jason's car had recently been in an accident, which resulted in the engine falling out. Jason glued it back on to the engine mounts with glue and then offered it for sale to Jerry without saying anything about the engine. The "active concealment" of the engine problem will be treated as if there was an affirmative assertion by Jason that there were no problems with the engine mounts. Accordingly, Jerry can avoid the contract based on the **affirmative action to conceal a fact** which will be taken as misrepresentation of the fact that no problem with the engine existed.

(2) Example. [§ 15–17]

In applying for life insurance, Kal truthfully tells the agent he has never been diagnosed as having cancer. However, in a physical taken a few days later, **before the life insurance application is accepted by the company, and the contract is executed**, Kal learns he has cancer. He is under a duty to disclose the new diagnosis in order to prevent his previous assertion (which was true when it was made) from becoming an actionable misrepresentation. If he does not, the insurance company can disaffirm the contract.

Note that if Kal is diagnosed **after** having entered into the insurance contract, he is no longer under a misrepresentation duty to disclose that fact to the insurance company, for that is the kind of risk the company impliedly takes by entering into such a contract.

(3) Example. [§ 15–18]

Pete knows his television set does not have a picture tube, but does not disclose it to Sam, who buys the set. Pete does

MISREPRESENTATION

not say anything about the lack of a picture tube because Sam never asked about it, and Sam never asked about it because he figured when someone sells a television, it comes complete with a picture tube. Because a television having a picture tube is a **basic assumption** on which the contract is made, and because failing to disclose the problem would amount to a **breach of good faith and fair dealing**, Pete is under a duty to disclose the picture tube problem. Hence, his silence on the matter will be treated as an affirmative representation that the television has a picture tube, and that assertion can serve as the basis for a misrepresentation claim by Sam.

(4) **Example. [§ 15–19]**

Larry seeks to entice Sandra to sign a contract to purchase his home for $150,000. Although Larry does not say anything about it, Larry knows from what Sandra says that Sandra believes the mortgage provides that she can assume it. In fact, Larry's mortgage has a due-on-sale clause (meaning it is not assumable). If Sandra signs the contract, Larry's silence about the true nature of the assumability of his mortgage will be taken as a representation by him that the mortgage is assumable. Since it is not assumable, Larry's representation can serve as the basis for a misrepresentation claim by Sandra, and she is entitled to avoid the contract [Restatement 2d § 161, Cmt. e, Ill. 12].

(5) **Example. [§ 15–20]**

Accountant has handled the business affairs of client for the past 30 years. Accountant learns that oil has been discovered on client's property, a fact unknown to client. Accountant offers client a fair price for the property without oil on it, which client accepts. Nothing is said or asked during negotiations about oil being discovered on the property, either by the accountant or the client. The accountant is under a duty to speak because the **special fiduciary nature of their relationship** is one in which it **is reasonable for the client to repose trust and confidence** in accountant. The accountant's failure to disclose this information is thus actionable and will be taken as an implied representation that there was no oil on the property.

CHAPTER 15

f. **Silence Does Not Act as an Actionable Misrepresentation When the Parties Are Dealing at "Arm's Length" and None of the Exceptions Apply. [§ 15–21]**

The general rule is that when a party legally obtains information that would materially affect a transaction, and the transaction is made at "arm's length" (i.e., between parties who are not in a confidential relationship), the party with the information need not disclose it during negotiations with the other. That is, there is no duty of good faith negotiation or any other theory that makes silence while negotiating a deal in such a situation actionable. The party with the information cannot mislead the other, but as long as he or she says nothing, and none of the five situations set forth in § 15–15 apply, no action for misrepresentation can be successfully pled. [*See* Case Squibs, *Laidlaw v. Organ*, 15 U.S. (2 Wheat.) 178 (1817), for an example of a case in which the silence by a party, who had obtained information lawfully and who was in an arm's length transaction, was held not to be actionable in a misrepresentation claim.]

2. **The Misrepresentation Must Be Either *Fraudulent* or *Material*. [§ 15–22]**

To recover under a theory of deceit in *tort,* a plaintiff must show that the misrepresentations were *both* fraudulent **and** material. To be entitled to relief in contract, however, a party need only establish that a misrepresentation is **either** fraudulent or material. Each of these terms is defined and discussed below.

a. **Definition of "Fraudulent." [§ 15–23*]**

Under Restatement 2d § 162(1), a statement is "fraudulent" if:

1. The deceiving party **intended to induce** the innocent party to enter a contract, or knew with substantial certainty that his or her actions would do so; and

2. The deceiving party acted with "**scienter**." Scienter is a word referring to the mental state of the deceiving party. The deceiving party can meet the scienter requirement in three different ways. That is, scienter is present if the deceiving party made the misrepresentation either:

(a) *Knowing that what he or she represented was not true,* i.e., the deceiving party told a conscious lie;

(b) *Knowing that he or she was being reckless* in making the representation, because he or she did not

---

* For more information, listen to CD # 6, Track 9 of *Sum and Substance Audio on Contracts.*

have sufficient confidence in the truth of what was asserted; or

(c) *Knowing that he or she did not have the basis* to make the representation.

See examples of these definitions in § 15–2.

(1) Example. [§ 15–24]

Tom wants to sell his Acme Stereo receiver to Joe. During negotiations, Joe tells Tom that Acme made two types of receivers, one with copper internal wiring and one with silver internal wiring, and that he is only interested in buying Tom's if it is the silver wire model. Tom knows that the wire in his receiver is copper, but tells Joe that it is silver. Tom has made a fraudulent misrepresentation because: (a) he made the statement with the desire to induce Joe into making the contract; and (b) he made it with scienter, i.e., he consciously lied about the type of internal wiring to just to induce the sale.

(2) Example. [§ 15–25]

Same example as above: Joe wants to buy Tom's receiver only if the internal wiring is silver. Tom saw some silver looking stuff inside the receiver, but knows he really has no idea whether the wiring is silver. Nevertheless, he tells Joe that the wires are silver. If the wires are copper, Tom has made a fraudulent misrepresentation because: (a) he made the statement with the desire to induce Joe into making the contract; and (b) he made it with scienter, i.e., he recklessly told Joe the wires were silver despite the possibility that they are, in fact, copper.

(3) Example. [§ 15–26]

Same example as above, but this time, Tom, who has no idea what type of wiring is in his receiver, and has never investigated the internal wiring, assures Joe that he just inspected the receiver, and his unit is a silver wire model. If the wire turns out to be copper, Tom has made a fraudulent misrepresentation because: (a) he made the statement with the desire to induce Joe into making the contract; and (b) he made it with scienter, i.e., he knew he had no basis for making the claim.

CHAPTER 15

b. Definition of "Material." [§ 15–27]

A misrepresentation is "material" if it is likely to make a difference to a reasonable person in deciding whether to go through with the transaction [Restatement 2d § 162(2)].

(1) Example. [§ 15–28]

Charles told his wife Helen that their car got, on average, 25 miles per gallon (m.p.g.). When selling the car after Charles died, Helen repeated Charles's claim to Sally, the buyer. In fact, the car only got 17 m.p.g. Even though Helen's statement was not fraudulent, because she made it innocently and without scienter, it is actionable in contract because it was false and material. That is, the correct number of miles per gallon of a car is something a reasonable person would want to know in deciding to purchase the car, and thus Helen's statement is a material falsehood, even though innocently made.

3. The Misrepresentation Must Induce Actual Reliance. [§ 15–29]

The innocent party in a transaction induced by a misrepresentation must show actual reliance on the misrepresentation before he or she can disaffirm the contract. Such reliance is usually established by pointing to some change of position taken by the innocent party, which was motivated, **even if only in part**, by the misrepresentation. Generally, the change of position is the buyer's payment of money, or signing of a contract, in reliance on the representations of the seller.

For example, suppose Jane purchases a used smart phone. She bought it because it fit her hands nicely and she liked the screen. She was told by the seller that it was an Acme 7 model. It turns out to be an Acme 6. If Jane was going to buy the phone anyway, and it made no difference to her whether it was an Acme 6 or 7, then she has no claim to avoid the transaction under a misrepresentation theory because she did not rely on the misrepresentation in changing position, i.e., in buying the phone. That is, the misrepresentation was not a "but for" cause of the purchase.

4. The Reliance Must Be Reasonable. [§ 15–30]

In addition to showing actual reliance on an erroneous factual assertion, a party seeking to avoid a contract based on misrepresentation must also show that such reliance was reasonable. The general rule is that reliance on a misrepresentation is reasonable, even if the innocent party is "at fault" in not knowing, or

MISREPRESENTATION

failing to discover, the true facts, so long as such fault does not amount to a failure to act in good faith [Restatement 2d § 172].

a. Example. [§ 15–31]

Libby is inspecting a house she is interested in purchasing and notices a water stain on the ceiling. She asks Dennis, the seller, about it and he says there used to be a leak in the roof, but that he has repaired it. She purchases the house without having the roof inspected. If she had gotten up on the roof, she would have clearly and easily seen that there were several roof tiles missing.

Libby's reliance was nonetheless reasonable under the misrepresentation doctrine. Even if it can be argued that she was somewhat "at fault" in failing to inspect the roof, her actions did not constitute a breach of the duty of good faith. That is, even if it could be argued that the innocent party was, in *tort* terms, contributorily negligent in not discovering the true facts, such conduct is *irrelevant* to a contract-based recovery for misrepresentation unless the innocent party's actions amount to a breach of the duty of good faith.

b. Example. [§ 15–32]

Phil asks a used car salesman whether a car he is considering purchasing has air conditioning, and is erroneously told that it does. Phil then takes the car on a test drive for two hours on a very hot day and ends up buying the car. He cannot avoid the contract based on the misrepresentation about the air conditioner for, given the situation, his reliance on the assertion that the car had an air conditioner was not reasonable and amounts to a violation of his duty of good faith.

F. LIMITATION ON VOIDABILITY OF CONTRACT BASED ON MISREPRESENTATION: THE CLAIM MUST BE ASSERTED WITHIN A REASONABLE TIME AFTER DISCOVERY. [§ 15–33]

An innocent party seeking to disaffirm a contract on misrepresentation grounds must do so within a reasonable time after discovery of the misrepresentation. At the expiration of the reasonable time, the contract will be deemed ratified and the party's right to avoid it terminates.

G. RESTITUTION REQUIRED UPON AVOIDANCE OF CONTRACT BASED ON MISREPRESENTATION. [§ 15–34]

A party avoiding a contract on the grounds of misrepresentation is entitled to restitutionary recovery upon the disaffirmance. In addition, the avoiding party may also be liable for restitution to the misrepresenting party as well. (*See* Chapter Thirty-One for a discussion of restitution).

H. EXAM APPROACH TO MISREPRESENTATION ISSUES. [§ 15–35*]

Any time a party is induced to enter a contract by means of an untrue statement:

    1.   Check to see if the misleading statement is one of "fact" and not puffing, opinion, prediction, of future events, etc. [§§ 15–7 *et seq.*], or whether it was one of the situations in which silence can be taken as an actionable misrepresentation of fact [§§ 15–15 *et seq.*].

    2.   If the misrepresentation is one of "fact," determine if it was fraudulent *or* material [§§ 15–22 *et seq.*].

    3.   If the misrepresentation is of a "fact," and was either fraudulent or material, determine whether the innocent party actually, foreseeably, and reasonably relied on the statement in entering into the contract [§§ 15–29 *et seq.*, and §§ 15–30 *et seq.*].

    4.   If all these elements are met, the contract is avoidable by the innocent party.

    5.   Make sure also to check for fraud in the *factum* [§ 15–4] as well, in which case the contract is void.

---

* For more information, listen to CD # 6, Track 11 of *Sum and Substance Audio on Contracts*.

CHAPTER 16

UNCONSCIONABILITY

A. THE UNCONSCIONABILITY DOCTRINE. [§ 16–1*]

As the term is used today, unconscionability is a flexible doctrine that largely prevents one party to a contract from taking undue advantage of the other and enforcing a "too good" or "too one-sided" a deal. Some courts have suggested that unconscionability "incorporates a sense of business ethics and community morality into contract law," while others have said a contract is unconscionable if it sets forth a deal "no man in his senses . . . would make on the one hand, and no honest or fair man would accept on the other." In any event, the gist of the doctrine is that a court is directed to step in and correct a situation in which one party makes too good a deal for himself or herself, even in the absence of duress, undue influence, misrepresentation, or the other traditional contract doctrines by which deals are avoided.

Although most of our modern unconscionability jurisprudence comes from the UCC, somewhat surprisingly, the term is not defined there, nor is it defined in the Restatement 2d. The lack of a definition is intentional by the drafters of the UCC and Restatement 2d, for the idea is to give the courts as much flexibility as possible in deciding when to apply the doctrine and prohibit enforcement of unreasonably unfair transactions. Probably the most difficult part of learning about unconscionability is trying to understand a **structure** for analyzing the doctrine. Such structure is provided in § 16–5.

B. UNCONSCIONABILITY APPLIES TO UCC AND NON-UCC TRANSACTIONS. [§ 16–2]

The modern unconscionability doctrine emanates from § 2–302 of the UCC. However, it has been routinely applied to non-UCC transactions and is now generally recognized as a limitation on the enforcement of unreasonably one-sided deals throughout contract law, and is also specifically authorized by Restatement 2d § 208.

---

* For more information, listen to CD # 6, Track 12 of *Sum and Substance Audio on Contracts*.

C. EFFECT OF UNCONSCIONABILITY UNDER MODERN CONTRACT LAW. [§ 16–3]

The decision as to whether a contract, or any part of it, is unconscionable is a **decision for the court** and not the jury [UCC § 2–302; Restatement 2d § 208]. Once a court determines unconscionability is present, it is empowered to:

(1) **refuse enforcement of the entire contract;**

(2) **enforce the remainder of the contract without the unconscionable clause or clauses**; or

(3) **modify or limit application of any clause to avoid an unjust result**.

UCC § 2–302(1); Restatement § 2d 208.

Note that the unconscionability doctrine thus proves an exception to the general rule that courts interpret contracts but do not get involved in re-writing them. Under the express provisions of UCC § 2–302(1) and Restatement 2d § 208, a court is authorized to change what the parties agreed to, and to re-write a contract to avoid its unconscionable features.

1. Effect of Unconscionability Under Common Law. [§ 16–4]

Unconscionability was recognized at common law but in a much different form. Essentially (although this puts it a bit too simply), unconscionability was a specialized application of the "unclean hands" doctrine and prevented a party from being granted equitable relief. That is, a party to a contract having an unconscionably good term in its favor was not entitled to an *equitable* remedy such as specific performance.

The theory was that if a party did not proceed equitably in negotiating the contract, he or she was not entitled to an equitable remedy as a result of its breach. However, the "sharp" party was free to seek *legal* remedies, such as damages, in the event the party that was taken advantage of did not perform under the contract. Note that the unconscionable provision did not have to be the provision breached for the prohibition on equitable relief to apply. So long as there was **any** unconscionable provision in a contract, the benefited party was not entitled to an equitable remedy. [*See* Case Squibs, *Campbell Soup Co. v. Wentz* for an example of a case applying the common law approach.]

D. ELEMENTS NECESSARY TO ESTABLISH UNCONSCIONABILITY UNDER MODERN CONTRACT LAW. [§ 16–5*]

One of the frustrations resulting from the flexibility inherent in the modern unconscionability doctrine is that it is difficult to construct a structured analysis for when the doctrine should apply. However, while different courts may use different terms, **all clauses or contracts found to be unconscionable have some combination of**:

(1) *Procedural* unconscionability; and

(2) *Substantive* unconscionability.

1. **Definition of "Procedural" Unconscionability. [§ 16–6]**

   The essence of procedural unconscionability is the **absence of meaningful choice** provided to one party to the contract. This absence of meaningful choice is, in turn, made up of:

   (1) **Oppression**, i.e., unequal bargaining power between the parties; and

   (2) **Surprise**, i.e., the fact that the unconscionable clause is typically hidden in the numerous terms and legal jargon of a written agreement and is not really a bargained-for term.

2. **Definition of "Substantive" Unconscionability. [§ 16–7]**

   The essence of substantive unconscionability is that there are **terms which are unreasonably favorable to one party to the contract**.

3. **Some Combination of Both Procedural and Substantive Unconscionability Is Necessary for Application of the Doctrine: The "Sliding Scale" Test. [§ 16–8]**

   For a court to find a contract or a particular clause of a contract unconscionable, there must be some combination of both procedural and substantive unconscionability involved in the making of the contract. The greater the presence of one type of unconscionability, the less the presence of the other is necessary before the doctrine applies. This is known as the "sliding scale" test.

   To be clear, a contract may be entered into without much meaningful choice on the part of one party, but if its terms are all scrupulously fair, no unconscionability will be found. For example, if only one company makes a popular and unique good, there is no meaningful

---

* For more information, listen to CD # 7, Track 1 of *Sum and Substance Audio on Contracts*.

choice if the consumer wants the product. But if the price is fair, there is no unconscionability.

Similarly, if the parties enter into a transaction that seems very much to favor one party over another, the courts will not upset that deal if both parties entered into it knowingly, by free choice, and after serious negotiation. For example, if a consumer wants to pay $800 for a T-shirt from a fancy clothier, there is no unconscionability if the consumer enters the transaction knowingly.

It is only when the terms are unfair **and** one party's meaningful choices are limited that the doctrine applies.

SPECIAL CASE SQUIB

a. *Williams v. Walker-Thomas Furniture Co.* [§ 16–9*]

Ms. Williams purchased different items of appliances, furniture, and (finally) stereo equipment on different occasions from a retail store known as Walker-Thomas. Each of these purchases was made on credit and each was "cross-collateralized." The cross-collateralization clause provided that until the outstanding balance for **each** item was paid in full, the store retained a security interest or lien against **all** the items she had ever purchased from the store. Thus, if she ever failed to make a payment on any one piece of furniture, the store could repossess any or all other items previously.

To illustrate this idea, assume she bought a couch for $1,200 in January of 1989 and agreed to pay $100 per month for it. Assume in December 1989 (when only $100 principal remained on the couch), she bought a stereo for $600 and agreed to pay an additional $50 per month for the stereo. If she signed a cross-collateralization agreement during the stereo purchase, the store would retain its right to foreclose on the **couch** throughout 1990 should she default on making any of the payments for the **stereo**. This is true even though the couch would have been fully paid for under the original contract by January 1990.

In May 1962, Ms. Williams defaulted on her credit obligation to the store and Walker-Thomas sought to repossess everything she had purchased at the store including some items she had originally purchased as far back as 1958.

Held: The cross-collateralization clause was unconscionable as applied to Ms. Williams, because both types of unconscionability were present.

---

* For more information about this case, listen to CD # 7, Track 1 of *Sum and Substance Audio on Contracts*.

Procedural unconscionability was found because Ms. Williams had an absence of meaningful choice, i.e., due to Ms. Williams' poor financial situation, credit history, and lack of transportation which would give her easy access to other stores, she did not have any real choice but to buy her furniture on credit from Walker-Thomas (or a store like Walker-Thomas) that insisted on cross-collateralization clauses in its credit sales. That is, there was no real or meaningful equality of bargaining power between Ms. Williams and the store, for she could not have bargained for a contract without the cross-collateralization provision. Further, the court found that the cross-collateralization clause was not pointed out or explained to her, and was in small type on her contract, and thus was an example of "prolix" that was "hidden" in the contract.

Additionally, the court held the clause substantively unfair, especially in light of the fact that the store was not seeking just to repossess the last goods purchased (the stereo) but all the goods she had bought there since 1958, many of which had been fully paid for [*Williams v. Walker-Thomas Furniture Co.*, 350 F.2d 445 (D.C. Cir. 1965)].

(1) Criticism of, and Additional Facts Relevant to, *Williams v. Walker-Thomas Furniture Co.* [§ 16–10]

> This case is a staple in most first year contracts classes and usually leads to spirited discussion. It has been criticized on the following grounds:
>
> > (a) The unconscionability doctrine should not apply where the lack of meaningful choice is derived from a party's own poor financial condition. In other words, if Ms. Williams was such a bad credit risk that Sears, Wal-Mart, etc., would not extend her credit (thereby making her only choice Walker-Thomas or a like store that insisted on cross-collateralization), then she should not be able to claim she had no meaningful choice, for she did—she could have saved her money and paid cash, or she could have chosen not to purchase the goods. In the same way economic duress is not a defense to contract formation [§ 13–14], an individual's poor economic circumstance should not be a trigger for unconscionability analysis. Those who find this criticism persuasive say that unconscionability should only apply when virtually everyone in an industry gives a buyer the same choice, e.g., if every manufacturer in the car industry only offered a 1-year/15,000 mile warranty on a new car, for it is only

CHAPTER 16

then that there truly is an absence of meaningful choice as to **all** purchasers;

(b) Even if the unconscionability doctrine is to have some effect on Walker-Thomas's contract with Ms. Williams, the doctrine should just apply for "necessities" e.g., beds, refrigerators, stoves, etc., and not for things like stereos (although it turns out that many of the purchases she made before the stereo were for beds, etc. for her children, *see below*);

(c) She apparently did not read the contract and thus should not be allowed to complain about a provision she did not ask about or even try to understand; and

(d) Cross-collateralization clauses cannot be substantively unfair for purposes of unconscionability for they were expressly permitted by the UCC at the time she entered into the agreements, and so they could not, as a matter of law, be substantively unfair.

Some students find these criticisms of greater weight than others, but from *Williams* came the idea that unconscionability consists of the absence of meaningful choice (procedural) and unfair terms (substantive) and thus, it is an important case from that perspective alone. Further, it has stood as the fountainhead for all unconscionability cases following it, and thus, its general reasoning has been found persuasive by virtually all.

This case is famous and professors have delved into the facts more than is revealed in the court's opinion. It turns out that Ms. Williams was a single mother who had a government job. She, in fact, spent her money wisely and mainly on her children. As noted above, her purchases at Walker-Thomas over the years were for her home and children—appliances, beds, etc. The stereo at issue in the case was to allow her children to listen to educational tapes from their school.

She often paid her rent in cash. On the month when all this took place, she had enough money for the rent set aside in cash in her appointment, but she was robbed. So she had to choose between paying the rent or making the payment to Walker-Thomas. She chose the former, thus defaulting on her credit agreement with Walker-Thomas, which then foreclosed upon, and repossessed all her purchases under the cross-collateralization clause.

UNCONSCIONABILITY

4. Unconscionability Applies to Conditions Present at the Time of Making the Contract. [§ 16–11]

The procedural and substantive aspects of unconscionability are examined at the time the contract was made, not at the time of its performance. Hence, an exchange that appeared fair at the time it was made, but in retrospect appears one-sided, will not be affected by the unconscionability doctrine.

5. Note on Adhesion Contracts. [§ 16–12]

It is sometimes said that all adhesion contracts, i.e., contracts where one party dictates non-negotiable terms and the other party must agree to "adhere" to them or not enter into the bargain, are unconscionable. This is not true. While the existence of an adhesion contract is evidence of a lack of bargaining power on one side, it is not conclusive evidence either that the terms were unfair or that the "weaker" party did not know, appreciate, and freely agree to be bound by those terms. After all, you entered into an adhesion contract when you signed up for the LSAT, since you did not have any choice on who you contracted with or the terms of the contract you signed. The LSAT contract was offered to you on a take-it-or-leave-it basis. Nevertheless, the contract was not unconscionable as its terms, when they have been challenged, have been judged "fair."

E. UNCONSCIONABILITY NOT LIMITED TO CONSUMER TRANSACTIONS. [§ 16–13]

By far the most common application of unconscionability is to consumer transactions, like *Williams v. Walker-Thomas* (see § 16–9). However, the doctrine is not limited to consumer transactions and has recently been applied with greater frequency in merchant-to-merchant business contracts. As long as an absence of meaningful choice, along with terms unreasonably unfair to one party, can be demonstrated, the doctrine will apply. [*See* Case Squibs, *A & M Produce v. FMC Corp.*, 135 Cal. App. 3d 473 (1982), for an example of unconscionability in a merchant-to-merchant case].

F. UNCONSCIONABILITY APPLIED TO CLAUSES WHICH LIMIT REMEDIES OR DISCLAIM WARRANTIES. [§ 16–14]

In §§ 2–719 and 2–316 respectively, the UCC explicitly provides that a party's remedies upon breach can be limited, and that a buyer's warranties can be disclaimed. The argument is sometimes made that such clauses cannot be unconscionable when they appear in a contract as they are specifically permitted by the Code. This argument has not found much favor. While such clauses are specifically permitted by the Code, they are only enforceable if they are not unreasonably unfair under the circumstances, and if the other party is not the victim of oppression and/or surprise [§ 32–51]. (Recall that a similar argument was made in *Williams v. Walker-Thomas* [§ 16–9]. In that case, cross-collateralization clauses were specifically permitted by the UCC, but their inclusion in the contract at issue was nevertheless found to be unconscionable).

G. EXAM APPROACH TO UNCONSCIONABILITY ISSUES. [§ 16–15*]

When confronted with a contract that is extremely favorable for one party, first check for evidence of incapacity [Chapter Eleven]; duress [Chapter Thirteen]; undue influence [Chapter Fourteen]; or misrepresentation [Chapter Fifteen]. If there are no facts to support any of those theories, *then* check to *see* if:

1. There is an absence of meaningful choice on the part of the aggrieved party [§ 16–6]; and

2. The terms of the contract are sufficiently unfair to the aggrieved party [§§ 16–7 and 16–8].

Recall the doctrine is flexible and that the court seeks to do equity. If unconscionability is found, the court may strike the entire contract; enforce the contract without the unconscionable term or terms; or even re-write the contract so that it operates fairly.

---

* For more information, listen to CD # 7, Track 2 of *Sum and Substance Audio on Contracts*.

CHAPTER 17

"ILLEGALITY" OR CONTRACTS "AGAINST PUBLIC POLICY"

A. ILLEGALITY DISCUSSED. [§ 17–1*]

An agreement is "illegal" if either its formation or its performance is **criminal**, or otherwise **against public policy**. The general rule, subject to several exceptions, is that **such agreements are unenforceable by either party**, and thus are often said to be **"void"** contracts. (Know that many contracts scholars do not use the term "void contract," considering it as an oxymoron because if a "contract" is "void," it cannot be considered any type of contract.)

B. DEFINITION OF "ILLEGAL" CONTRACTS. [§ 17–2]

While common law calls these contracts "illegal," the Restatement does not use this term. Instead, it states that such contracts are unenforceable because the societal interest in their enforcement is clearly outweighed by public policy [Restatement 2d § 178]. While the broader idea of a contract being unenforceable because of "public policy" concerns has been adopted by the courts, the courts still tend to use the term "illegal" to refer to such agreements. Note, however, that a contract need not call for a criminal act to be illegal. Rather, "illegal" in this context is a kind of shorthand for agreements unenforceable because of public policy.

C. COMMON TYPES OF "ILLEGAL" CONTRACTS. [§ 17–3]

Given the flexibility of the term "against public policy," there is no all-inclusive list of what kinds of contracts will be deemed illegal. However, what follows is a discussion of the most frequently litigated of such agreements.

---

* For more information, listen to CD # 7, Track 3 of *Sum and Substance Audio on Contracts*.

CHAPTER 17

1. **Agreements for the Performance of Criminal Acts. [§ 17–4]**

   Any contract calling for performance of a criminal act is an illegal contract. For example, contracts for prostitution, the purchase and sale of restricted drugs, contracts calling for the killing or assault of someone, etc. are all void and cannot be enforced by either party.

2. **Gambling Contracts. [§ 17–5]**

   In most states, contracts involving wagering or gambling are illegal, and thus void.

3. **Contracts Obtained by Bribery. [§ 17–6]**

   Any agreement: (a) for the payment of a bribe, (b) procured by a bribe, or (c) performed due to bribery, is "illegal" and thus unenforceable.

   a. **Example. [§ 17–7]**

      For a $500,000 "consulting fee," Middleman promises Client that he will make sure Foreign Government will hire Client's company to construct a hospital in Foreign Country. Both Middlemen and Client know Middleman intends to bribe a foreign government official with part of the consulting fee. Sure enough Foreign Government awards Client the contract for a fair price.

      Not only is the consulting fee contract unenforceable because it is for the payment of a bribe, but the resulting hospital contract is also unenforceable because it was **procured** by a bribe.

4. **Contracts in Which a Party Releases Another from Tort Liability. [§ 17–8]**

   The general rule is that any contract in which one party seeks to release another from liability for an intentional tort is illegal and will not be enforced. However, a release of liability for negligent torts will probably be upheld, if it is entered into knowingly and in good faith.

   a. **Example. [§ 17–9]**

      Leo owns a private racetrack. In order to race a car on the track, Leo requires the driver to sign a "Release and Waiver," releasing Leo from any liability due to his own, or his employees', negligence in operating the racetrack. Such a release will usually be upheld so long as the car owner is aware that he or she is releasing a potential cause of action.

      However, if Leo tried to get the car owner to sign a release from liability for his own, or his employees', intentional torts (e.g., battery), such an agreement would not be enforced. The reason is that society views the commission of an intentional tort as a much more heinous act, and thus will not allow parties (absent

"ILLEGALITY" OR CONTRACTS "AGAINST PUBLIC POLICY"

other factors) to contractually exonerate themselves for such conduct.

In most cases, a release from injury caused by the "gross negligence" of a party is treated as a release from intentional torts, not negligence.

5. **Agreements for Services Provided by Parties Who Should Be, but Are Not, Licensed. [§ 17–10]**

If the appropriate governmental agency requires that all persons engaged in a certain occupation must be licensed so as to control the skill and moral quality of persons engaged in that trade, then a contract for services with an unlicensed individual is illegal. However, if the reason for a government-granted license is principally a revenue raising measure, a contract with an unlicensed person is not illegal in the contracts sense, and can be enforced.

   a. **Example. [§ 17–11]**

   Municipality requires all tradesmen with offices in the city to have a "Business License." Municipality does not test or screen those to whom it gives licenses, and enacted the business license statute just as a way to raise revenue. Bob is a contractor whose office is in Municipality but who does not have a business license. If Bob contracts with a church to install hardwood floors in the pulpit, the contract is not illegal, for the business license statute was not designed to control the quality of contractors.

   b. **Example. [§ 17–12]**

   Mary seeks legal advice from Mel, who is practicing as an attorney, but who in fact is not licensed as an attorney. Any contract Mary enters into for Mel's services is "illegal," for the licensing statute serves to control the skill and moral qualities of those who practice law.

6. **Agreements in Which the Seller Knows of Buyer's Illegal Purpose. [§ 17–13]**

If a seller provides legal goods to a buyer who the seller knows will use them for an illegal purpose, the prevailing rule is that the agreement is illegal only if the buyer's intended purpose involves "serious moral turpitude," or if the seller acts to assist in the illegal purpose in some way in addition to merely supplying the goods.

   a. **Example. [§ 17–14]**

   The owner of an exterminator business sells Ralph rat poison knowing Ralph intends to poison his wife with it. The contract is illegal, for murder is a crime of serious moral turpitude.

CHAPTER 17

b. Example. [§ 17–15]

It is illegal to trade with Country. Nevertheless, Frank sells 1,000 pairs of sunglasses to Jim, knowing that Jim intends to smuggle them to a supplier in Country. The contract between Frank and Jim is probably enforceable because such smuggling is probably not a crime of "serious" moral turpitude.

c. Example. [§ 17–16]

Same facts as above, except this time, in addition to supplying the sunglasses, Frank also fills out a false invoice and bill of lading, indicating the glasses are to be shipped to the Philippines. The agreement between Jim and Frank is now illegal and thus unenforceable, for Frank has now assisted and furthered the illegal enterprise by doing an act in addition to merely supplying goods.

D. GENERAL RULE: IF AN "ILLEGAL" AGREEMENT IS WHOLLY EXECUTORY, NEITHER PARTY CAN ENFORCE IT. [§ 17–17]

If an "illegal" agreement is wholly executory, then, as a general rule, neither party can enforce it, and a court will leave the parties as they find them. However, there are a few exceptions:

1. Exception: Ignorance of Facts at Time Contract Made. [§ 17–18]

If one party is justifiably ignorant of the facts making the contract illegal at the time the contract is made, that party may treat the contract as **voidable** at his or her option within a reasonable time after learning of such facts.

a. Example. [§ 17–19]

Bill hires Irv, who is an accountant, to do work only a CPA can do, but Irv has never taken the CPA exam. Because the CPA license is intended to do more than just raise revenue, and instead test the skill and moral character of the applicant, the contract is illegal and neither Bill nor Irv may enforce it [§ 17–10]. However, if it is reasonable that Bill did not know that Irv did not have a license when he hired him, Bill may avoid the contract, or enforce it, at his option when he discovers the true facts. If he avoids it, he is entitled to restitution, but he may also have to make restitution to Irv. [*See* Chapter Thirty-One for a discussion of Restitution].

"ILLEGALITY" OR CONTRACTS "AGAINST PUBLIC POLICY"

2. **Exception: Statutes Designed to Protect a Particular Class. [§ 17–20]**

   If a statute that makes an agreement illegal is designed to protect a particular class, then the party so protected has the option of disaffirming or enforcing the contract.

   a. **Example. [§ 17–21]**

   State has a usury rate of 12%. Department store, subject to the usury statute, enters into a credit agreement with customer whereby customer promises to pay 18% interest on the outstanding balance. Customer has the option to enforce or to avoid the contract. That is, because the usury law was designed to protect a particular class of persons of which she is a part (i.e., consumers) the contract is voidable, not void. However, if the store were to try to enforce it, the store could not, for as to it, the contract is illegal.

E. WHEN "ILLEGAL" AGREEMENTS ARE PERFORMED: PARTIES ARE GENERALLY LEFT AS THE COURT FINDS THEM. [§ 17–22]

The general rule regarding partially or fully executed illegal agreements is that neither party may enforce them, nor may obtain restitution, and the court will leave the parties as it finds them. For example, if Ed pays Don $10,000 to kill Noel, and Don fails to perform, Ed cannot sue Don seeking recovery of his payment. However, once again, this general rule is subject to several exceptions, discussed below.

1. **Exception: The *In Pari Delicto* Doctrine. [§ 17–23]**

   A party to an illegal contract is entitled to restitutionary recovery for the value of the products or services provided if the party can establish:

   (1) **That he or she was not guilty of "serious moral turpitude;"** and

   (2) **That the other party was more blameworthy in the transaction.**

   The rationale for this rule is that since the less blameworthy party is not "in equal fault," i.e., the party is not *in pari delicto*, he or she should be entitled to at least restitutionary recovery.

   a. **Example of *"in pari deicto"* in action: *Bateman Eichler v. Berner*. [§ 17–24]**

   Stockbroker falsely claimed to have "inside" non-public information about a stock and told some of his customers about it. The customers in turn purchased the stock, thinking they were privy to information that would soon make the stock rise in value, and paid a commission to the brokerage. When the information proved false, the customers sued the broker seeking to recover their commissions. The broker defended on the ground that the customers were *in pari delicto*, as they admitted trading only because they thought they were getting inside information.

Held: The customers' wrongdoing was not as egregious or blameworthy as the broker's, and trading on inside information did not involve "serious moral turpitude." Accordingly, the customers could seek restitutionary relief from the broker (their commissions back) even though performance under the illegal agreement had already taken place [Case Squibs, *Bateman Eichler v. Berner*, 472 U.S. 299 (1985); *see* Chapter Thirty-One for a discussion of restitution.]

2. **Exception: The *Locus Poenitentiae* Doctrine. [§ 17–25]**

If a party to an illegal agreement seeks to repudiate that agreement **before its illegal purpose has been either attempted or obtained**, he or she will be entitled to restitution, as long as the bargain is not one involving serious moral turpitude. In other words if the illegality is minor, the law allows a *"place to repent,"* i.e., a *locus poenitentiae*, and if such repentance is forthcoming, restitution can follow.

For example, assume Harry gives Tony $1,000 and asks that Tony use it to bribe a high school basketball player to throw a game. If Harry repents and tries to repudiate the deal before Tony has approached the player, Harry may be entitled to the $1,000 back from Tony in restitution. If a court determines that bribery in such a case does not involve "serious moral turpitude" and Harry would be entitled to the money back in restitution because Harry's repentance came before the illegal purpose of the arrangement had been either **attempted or obtained**.

F. DIVISIBILITY AND SEVERABILITY. [§ 17–26]

In all cases involving illegal contracts, if the contract does not involve serious moral turpitude, and if it is possible to sever, or divide out the illegal portion, a court is entitled to do so and enforce the remainder of the contract.

"ILLEGALITY" OR CONTRACTS "AGAINST PUBLIC POLICY"

G. EXAM APPROACH TO ILLEGALITY ISSUES. [§ 17–27*]

Illegality issues are usually easy to spot on examinations because the facts must tell you that the contract may contravene a statute of the appropriate jurisdiction, or that fact is obvious, e.g., it is a "contract" for murder. The only other contract subject to the rule that might not, on its face, appear to violate a statute is a contract to release intentional tort or criminal liability.

If you have an "illegal" contract, determine:

1. Whether it is "void" or voidable at the option of the aggrieved party [§§ 17–3 *et seq.*]; or

2. Whether one of the "exceptions" applies that will allow restitutionary recovery for the aggrieved party [§§ 17–23; 17–25].

---

* For more information, listen to CD # 7, Track 5 of *Sum and Substance Audio on Contracts*.

PART V

THE PAROL EVIDENCE RULE AND INTERPRETATION

INTRODUCTORY NOTE:

This Section deals with two related, but distinct, issues. The first is the determination as to what terms actually comprise the final, enforceable contract of the parties. This issue arises when a party to a written contract wants to show that one or more other terms were previously agreed upon, but somehow ended up not being included in the final writing that memorializes the contract. The **parol evidence rule** governs whether the party seeking to establish these additional terms will be permitted to do so in a breach of contract action and is discussed in Chapter Eighteen.

The second issue in this section is how to determine what a term means once it has been established that the term is part of the final enforceable contract. This topic includes both the question of how the courts are to construe language, and how much "extrinsic" evidence (evidence not evident in the contract itself) should be allowed where one party asserts that the parties had a "special meaning" for a word that is contrary to the normal usage of that term. Contract law calls the rules governing the resolution of these issues **rules of interpretation**, and they are discussed in Chapter Nineteen.

The UCC combines the parol evidence and interpretation rules into a single section, UCC § 2–202, which also contains slight twists to the common law versions of these doctrines. UCC § 2–202 is thus treated separately in Chapter Twenty.

CHAPTER 18

THE PAROL EVIDENCE RULE

A. THE PAROL EVIDENCE RULE GENERALLY.
[§ 18–1*]

The parol evidence rule determines when a party to a written contract may introduce evidence in court that the parties had reached an agreement as to a particular term during negotiations but when that term, for some reason, did not appear in the final version of the written contract. If the parties **both** agree that a term was left out, the parties are, of course, free to rewrite the contract and put the term back in. This is called **reformation**.

The parol evidence rule comes into play, however, when one party claims that a term was previously agreed to as part of the final contract, but the other disagrees and says either that it was a term agreed to in a draft of the final contract, but removed from the deal in the final negotiations, or otherwise asserts that the term was never part of the final agreement. At the heart of this rule, contract law holds a common sense preference for only enforcing the final agreement of the contracting parties. When parties cannot agree as to what terms their final agreement contained, **the parol evidence rule provides a way for a court to determine what terms the court will enforce**.

1. The Real Problem Giving Rise to the Parol Evidence Rule.
   [§ 18–2]

   One problem for students studying the parol evidence rule is that most of the time you are told what actually happened during the negotiation process. Thus, before you begin analyzing the problem, you already know which party is the "bad guy," i.e., which party is lying about a term being part of an agreement. Once that fact is known, there is a tendency to try to end up with a just resolution of the problem.

---

* For more information, listen to CD # 8, Track 4 of *Sum and Substance Audio on Contracts*.

However, to understand the dilemma the parol evidence rule seeks to solve, think of yourself for a moment as a judge with parties before you who are trying a breach of contract suit. The written and signed contract calls for the seller to deliver her stereo to the buyer, and for the buyer to pay $750 for it. The seller says the buyer is in breach because she timely delivered her stereo to the buyer and the buyer refused to pay for it. The buyer says the reason he did not pay is because the seller did not live up to her bargain. That is, he says they orally agreed that he was to pay $750 for the seller's stereo <u>and</u> her compact disc collection. As the seller never delivered the discs, he claims he does not have to pay and can return the stereo.

The seller points to the written contract, which does not mention the disc collection, but the buyer is insistent that he and the seller spent a lot of time negotiating this point and that he ultimately agreed to pay $750 (for what he claims is only a $600 stereo) solely because the seller had agreed to include the compact discs. The seller says the compact disc conversations never took place and asserts the used stereo is worth at least $750.

As the judge, how would you decide the case? If you decide this case in the seller's favor based on the written contract only, you may well be permitting fraud if the seller did in fact agree to include the discs. On the other hand, if you decide to let the buyer put on evidence to the jury of the alleged compact disc agreement, you also may be permitting fraud, for the seller may be right and the compact disc conversations may never have taken place.

The parol evidence rule sets forth the approach contract law has determined should be used to resolve this kind of dispute. [*See* § 19–21 for an analysis of this problem under both a parol evidence rule and an interpretation analysis].

2. **Definition of "Parol Evidence." [§ 18–3]**

   Parol evidence is the evidence of a term that one party claims was agreed to as part of the final contract, but does not appear in the final written agreement of the parties. Parol evidence may be written or oral.

B. STATEMENT OF, AND STEPS TO ANALYZE, THE PAROL EVIDENCE RULE. [§ 18–4]

A statement and three-step analysis of the parol evidence rule is given below. Inherent in it is a new type of vocabulary. Without knowing the vocabulary, it will be impossible to understand. The remainder of the chapter explains that vocabulary. So once you learn the vocabulary, you should come back here and the rule will be more understandable.

THE PAROL EVIDENCE RULE

The parol evidence rule regulates when a party can introduce parol evidence to supplement a written agreement. It states (with the new vocabulary terms italicized):

> When an agreement is *completely integrated*, no parol evidence is admissible. However, when an agreement is *partially integrated*, parol evidence of *consistent additional terms* will be admissible, whereas parol evidence of a *contradictory* term will not.

To let you know where we are going, any parol evidence rule problem can be analyzed in three steps:

1. Determine whether the agreement is *partially integrated* or *totally integrated*.
2. (a) If *totally integrated*, the analysis is over. No parol evidence is admissible.

   (b) If *partially integrated*, then some forms of parol evidence might be admissible. The forms admissible are set forth in Step 3.
3. (a) If the parol term is a *"contradictory" term*, the analysis is over. It will not be admissible to supplement even a partially integrated agreement.

   (b) However, if the parol term is a *"consistent additional term,"* evidence of it is admissible to supplement a partially integrated agreement.

Let's now learn the vocabulary.

C. INTEGRATION OF A DOCUMENT UNDER THE PAROL EVIDENCE RULE. [§ 18–5]

1. "Partial" and "Total" Integration: Defined. [§ 18–6]

A writing is **"integrated"** if it contains at least one term intended by the parties to be their final expression of agreement as to that term, i.e., the term is no longer meant to be part of a preliminary draft or negotiation, but rather is the term to which both parties have agreed to be bound [Restatement 2d § 209(1)].

A writing is **"partially integrated"** if the parties intended it to be the final expression of at least one of the terms it contains, but did not intend it to be a final expression of *all* terms of their agreement [Restatement 2d § 210(2)]. In other words, it appears there may be at least one term "out there" that the parties agreed to, which did not end up in their final contract.

A writing is **totally integrated** if it is intended to be the complete and exclusive expression of *all* the terms of the deal [Restatement 2d § 210(1)].

CHAPTER 18

2. **Effect of Classification as a "Partially" or "Totally" Integrated Contract. [§ 18–7]**

   If a writing is found to be **totally integrated**, **no evidence** of any parol term **can be admitted** [Restatement 2d §§ 210, 213, 215, and 216]. This makes sense, for if a writing is found to be a wholly integrated contract (a final representation of the parties' contract), by definition the parties have intended for it to be the **complete** statement of their final agreement.

   If a writing is found to be **partially integrated**, **some parol evidence** might be admissible to supplement the writing. What **is admissible** is something called a *"consistent additional term."* What is still <u>not admissible</u>, even with a partially integrated document, is something called a *"contradictory term."*

   The definitions of "consistent additional terms" and "contradictory terms" are discussed below [§ 18–13]. As you will see, their definitions have a special legal meaning in this context, and thus are not the same as the meaning of those terms in colloquial conversation. However, before getting to them we need to understand *how* an agreement is classified as totally or partially integrated.

3. **How to Determine Whether an Agreement Is Partially or Totally Integrated. [§ 18–8]**

   Obviously, the decision whether an agreement is partially or totally integrated is crucial to the party seeking to introduce parol evidence. One thing is clear. It is a decision **for the judge** made *outside the presence of a jury*. As such, it is considered a **question of law** (which a judge makes) and not a *question of fact* (which is left to the jury) [Restatement 2d § 210(3)].

   There are two views as to which test a judge should use in making the partial/total integration decision.

   a. **Williston's "Four Corner" Test to Determine Integration. [§ 18–9]**

      Professor Williston's test called for a judge to examine only the final writing itself—the "four corners" of the document—to determine if the contract **appeared complete on its face**. If it did, Williston argued it should be deemed totally integrated.

      However, if it appeared from the writing itself that some, but not all, of the terms agreed to were found in the written document, then Williston believed it should be deemed partially integrated.

      For example, if a contract called for "the sale of the home located on 123 Main St. for $150,000," a judge would consider it totally integrated under the Williston view for it appears complete on its face.

However, if the agreement called for "the sale of something to buyer for $150,000," then the agreement on its face seems incomplete, as it did not specify what was to be sold. So even Williston would say this was a partially integrated document.

(1) The Williston View Today. [§ 18–10]

A few states still claim to adhere to the Williston view, but generally it has fallen out of favor. The "Corbin" view, presented below, is now the more prevalent and it is explained below.

b. Corbin/Restatement View: Extrinsic Evidence Should Be Examined to Determine Integration. [§ 18–11]

Professor Corbin argued that the party seeking to introduce evidence of a parol agreement should be free to put on evidence tending to substantiate that claim, <u>at least to the judge</u>, out of the presence of the jury. Thus his view, which has been adopted by the Restatement 2d in §§ 210 and 214 and is the prevalent view today, is that a party can introduce all relevant evidence (at least to the judge) to show the circumstances surrounding the making of the writing in order to show the writing might not be completely or totally integrated. The thought is that letting a judge hear the evidence out of the presence of the jury will not harm the fact-finding process even if the parol term is ultimately ruled inadmissible because it is a "contradictory" term.

If after hearing this testimony a judge decides that there is enough evidence so that a jury *could* find that the written document is not the complete and final agreement of the parties, it will be deemed partially integrated and evidence of "consistent" parol terms can be admitted.

Using the example above in explaining the Williston view, take the agreement that specified "the sale of the home located on 123 Main St. for $150,000." Now, suppose the buyer wanted to introduce parol evidence <u>to the jury</u> that the price also included the seller's vintage car. Under the Corbin view, she would *first* have to introduce evidence to the judge, out of the presence of the jury, from which a jury could find the buyer's evidence credible. For example, the buyer could show the judge that the appraised value of the house was only $100,000, and so the only way the deal made sense is for something else to have been included. If the judge were persuaded that a jury, if it believed the buyer, *could* find his story credible, then a judge would find the agreement "partially integrated."

c. Example Illustrating the Difference Between Williston and Corbin/Restatement Views. [§ 18–12]

On October 1, Janet and Bob sign a written contract that states, in its entirety, "Seller, Janet, hereby agrees to sell her 1965 Mustang automobile, License No. ABC123, to buyer, Bob, for $8,000. Bob agrees to pay the purchase price at time and place of delivery, 1:00 p.m. on October 10, at Seller's house." Bob pays for and picks up the car on October 10, but later discovers that the car has not been given a polymer undercoating to protect against salt on the road during winter. Bob brings suit and wants to put on evidence that he and Janet agreed she would undercoat the car as part of the purchase price. Under the Williston view, Bob would not get to put on this evidence because the "four corners" of the contract seem complete and thus the contract would be deemed totally integrated.

Under the Corbin/Restatement view, Bob would get to argue his point and put on evidence of the circumstances surrounding the making of the agreement to the judge. If after hearing that, and any other relevant, evidence (e.g., testimony from others that Bob made offers on three other cars and always demanded the undercoating be made part of the price), the court was persuaded that a jury **could** find that the written contract did not state the entire deal between Bob and Janet, the judge would find the agreement partially integrated.

We move next to the contradictory/consistent additional term analysis.

D. DETERMINATION OF WHETHER A TERM IS "CONTRADICTORY" OR "CONSISTENT": THE RESTATEMENT'S "MIGHT NATURALLY" TEST. [§ 18–13]

This section explains how to determine whether a proffered parol term is "contradictory"—in which case it will not be admissible to supplement even a partially integrated agreement, or whether it is "consistent"—in which case it is admissible.

Under Restatement 2d § 216, a parol term does not "contradict" a term in the writing as long as it is a "consistent additional term." In other words, the term "contradictory" is not given a broad colloquial meaning, for its legal antonym under the parol evidence rule is "consistent additional term." It is binary: parol terms are either "consistent" or "contradictory."

Under the Restatement, **a term is a consistent additional term if, under the circumstances, it is one that** *"might naturally be omitted* **from the writing."** In other words, the test is the following: if the parties had really agreed to such a term, is it the kind of term which

THE PAROL EVIDENCE RULE

"might naturally" have been left out when they finally reduced their agreement to writing given the type of contract it is and the circumstances under which it was made [Restatement 2d § 216(2)(b)].

If the contested parol term **might naturally have been left out**, it is deemed a *consistent additional term* and <u>can be introduced to supplement a partially integrated writing</u>. However, if it is a term that, had the parties agreed to it, probably **would have been included** in the writings, i.e., it is a kind of term that **naturally would *not* be left out of a final writing**, then it is a *contradictory* term and <u>cannot be introduced</u>.

1. **Example of *Mitchell v. Lath*. [§ 18–14*]**

    Purchaser of land attempted to show that, as a part of the purchase price, seller had orally agreed to remove an ice house from an adjacent piece of property that seller also controlled. The ice house interfered with the view from the piece of property buyer had purchased. The written contract of sale, however, made no mention of the removal of the ice house.

    Held: If the seller had really agreed to remove the ice house, it was the type of term which probably would have been included somewhere in the documents exchanged by the parties. As such, it was *not* the kind of term that "might naturally" be omitted from the writings. Hence, it was a "contradictory" term, and evidence of its having been agreed to could not be presented to the trier of fact, even if the contract was partially integrated [*Mitchell v. Lath,* 160 N.E. 646 (N.Y. 1928)].

    The dissent in *Mitchell* saw it quite differently. To those justices, a contract for the sale of land included things in it like covenants of title, descriptions of easements on the property being sold, financing terms, and the like. An agreement to move an ice house on another piece of property is exactly the kind of thing that the parties "might naturally" have omitted from a contract for the sale of land. As such, the dissenting justices would have deemed the "ice house removal" clause as a "consistent" term, and allowed its admission into evidence by the buyers to the trier of fact.

2. **Example. [§ 18–15]**

    Jeff was interested in selling some property he owned for $7,500. Jeff was also about to undergo some plastic surgery and asked his doctor, Elizabeth, if she would be interested in purchasing it. She said she would. Elizabeth's fee for the surgery was $7,500, so they agreed to a barter exchange. However, for tax reasons, the conveyance documents recited that the price for the land was "$7,500" and said nothing about the barter agreement. Jeff, feeling clever, sues for

---

* For a further discussion of the case, listen to CD # 8, Track 5 of *Sum and Substance Audio on Contracts.*

$7,500 in cash. Elizabeth will be able to introduce evidence of the agreed barter payment term, for it is the kind of term that, under the circumstances, "might naturally" be omitted from a contract for the sale of land [Restatement 2d § 216, Cmt. d, Ill. 5].

3. **Effect of "Merger" or "Integration" Clauses. [§ 18–16*]**

A "merger" or "integration" clause (the terms are synonymous) is usually found at the end of a written agreement and typically will say something like, "The parties to this contract hereby affirm that this writing expresses the final, complete and exclusive statement of the terms of their agreement. There are no inducements to enter this contract other than those appearing in this document, and all prior agreements, written or oral, are discharged and/or merged into this contract." The intent of such clauses is to ensure that a court will find the document totally integrated and permit no parol evidence of other terms discussed during bargaining or at the time the contract was signed. **The general rule is that such clauses have a persuasive, but not determinative, effect on the question of whether the parties intended the agreement to be totally integrated**. A court can still find an agreement partially integrated even in light of a merger clause. Of course the greater the detail and specificity of such clause, the greater its persuasiveness. For example, if there were a detailed merger clause at the end of a 50-page contract between Microsoft and Dell that clearly had been negotiated over a long period of time by experienced lawyers for both sides, a court is likely to interpret the merger clause as establishing total integration. On the other hand, such a clause on the back side of a pre-printed form in an Internet sale where there is no negotiation has little persuasive effect in answering the question of whether the parties truly intended the agreement to be totally integrated.

4. **Effect of the Determination to Admit Parol Terms. [§ 18–17]**

A common misconception is that where a court permits the introduction of parol evidence, those terms automatically become part of the contract. This is **not** the case. All that happens when a judge allows the admission of parol evidence is that the party proffering the evidence has a **chance to convince** the trier of fact that the previous agreement existed. That is, he or she can put on evidence of a prior agreement as to a term. If the trier of fact does not believe the party seeking to prove the agreement, the parol term does **not** become part of the contract. If, but only if, the trier of fact believes the evidence, then those terms become part of the agreement, and any claim of breach is viewed in light of the final written contract plus the parol terms.

---

* For more information, listen to CD # 8, Track 6 of *Sum and Substance Audio on Contracts*.

THE PAROL EVIDENCE RULE

E. OPERATION OF PAROL EVIDENCE RULE UNDER RESTATEMENT. [§ 18–18]

Up to now, what has been described is a mix of common law and Restatement rules. The Restatement has added some different language in a couple of areas which should be understood if your class is Restatement heavy.

When the agreement is totally integrated, the Restatement provides that it is "binding," and then goes onto say, "A binding ... agreement discharges prior agreements" [Restatement 2d § 213(1)]. Hence it acknowledges the possibility of prior agreements of the parties during the bargaining process, but states that upon a finding of total integration, those prior agreements, to the extent they existed, are discharged.

With regard to partially integrated documents and consistent terms, it provides that consistent terms are outside "the scope" of the integrated document. It then says an integrated document "discharges prior agreements to the extent that they are within its scope" [Restatement 2d § 213(2)]. So the consistent additional terms, being outside the scope of the final writing, are not discharged and are thus admissible.

F. SITUATIONS WHEN THE PAROL EVIDENCE RULE DOES NOT APPLY. [§ 18–19*]

There are recurring fact situations to which the parol evidence rule does not apply. That is, in the situations discussed below, the parol evidence rule does not in any way limit the introduction of evidence concerning any terms agreed to by the parties regardless of whether the final contract is fully, totally, and completely integrated, and regardless of whether they contradict the writing.

1. **Agreements Made After the Contract Has Been Formed. [§ 18–20]**

    The parol evidence rule has no effect on agreements to a contract made after the contract has been entered into. Such agreements, whether oral or written, are **modifications** to an existing contract and are governed by the rules on modifications [Chapter Nine]. In other words, the cut off for when the parol evidence rule applies is the time of contract formation, and only allegations of an agreement made prior to execution of the contract will be subject to it.

2. **Where a Party Introduces Evidence to Show There Was No Valid Agreement. [§ 18–21]**

    The parol evidence rule will not act to keep out any evidence of pre-contractual bargaining if the purpose of such evidence is to show that

---

* For more information, listen to CD # 8, Track 4 of *Sum and Substance Audio on Contracts*.

no contract ever existed. This is true even if, on its face, the writing appears to be completely integrated. Thus, if the evidence is intended to show the writing was a joke, a forgery, etc., it is freely admissible.

3. **Evidence of a Condition Precedent. [§ 18–22]**

   The parol evidence rule will also not exclude evidence that the contract was subject to a parol condition precedent. The reason is that if such a condition was agreed to, and if it has not been fulfilled, no duty set forth in the written agreement would be enforceable. For example, if the parties had agreed on a written transaction, but had also orally agreed that neither party would have to perform under the written agreement "unless the Dow Jones Average exceeded 20,000," the party who did not perform because the Dow Jones Average never hit the mark would be permitted to testify to the jury about the oral condition [Restatement 2d § 217; *see* Chapter Twenty-One for a discussion of conditions]

4. **Evidence of a Failure to Pay Consideration. [§ 18–23]**

   If a party wants to introduce proof that the purported consideration evidenced in the writing was never exchanged, or that the agreement was for sham consideration, the parol evidence rule will not keep such evidence from being presented [Restatement 2d § 218(2)].

   a. **Exception: Option Contracts. [§ 18–24]**

      Because option contracts can be enforced on the basis of purported, but unperformed, consideration, this exception does not apply to them. In other words, if the final written option contract states that the prospective purchaser paid consideration for the option, no parol evidence as to the fact that no such consideration was ever actually transferred will be permitted. [Restatement 2d § 87; § 4–74].

5. **Evidence of Facts Establishing That the Contract Is Voidable. [§ 18–25]**

   A party who wants to introduce evidence that would entitle him or her to avoid the contract on the grounds of misrepresentation, duress, undue influence, illegality, mistake, unconscionability or other invalidating cause will not be prohibited from doing so by the parol evidence rule for the rule does not apply to the facts giving rise to the voidability defense.

6. **Evidence That Contradicts "Precatory" Language or "Recitals of Fact." [§ 18–26]**

   The parol evidence rule does not prevent a party from introducing evidence that contradicts: (1) "precatory" language, i.e., preliminary language in a contract without substantive effect; or (2) non-

THE PAROL EVIDENCE RULE

operative recitals of fact that are sometimes found in the beginning of relatively complex contracts.

7. Evidence as to a Meaning of a Term Found in the Written Contract. [§ 18–27]

The parol evidence rule operates to keep out pre-contractual evidence of certain terms when no mention of those terms are made in the final written contract. However, when the evidence is as to the *meaning* of a term that *is* found in the written contract, the issue is one of interpretation (*see* §§ 19–1 *et seq.*), and not of the parol evidence rule.

a. Example. [§ 18–28]

Student purchases a computer at Computer America. Her sales draft says that the computer she purchased comes with a "fully loaded software package." She wants to introduce evidence that the quoted clause means that the newest version of Windows was intended to be loaded on her computer.

The parol evidence rule does not apply to this situation because of the exception discussed in § 18–27. That is, Student is not trying to introduce evidence of a parol agreement that is not found at all in the written contract. Rather, she is introducing evidence as to the ***meaning*** *of a term* ("fully loaded software package") *that all parties agree **is already in** the contract.* Hence, admission of such testimony is dependent on interpretation rules, and not the parol evidence doctrine [Chapter Nineteen].

Contrast this example with the "Review Problem" analyzed in § 18–31, where the issue involved is the parol evidence rule, rather than interpretation.

G. RELATIONSHIP OF THE PAROL EVIDENCE RULE TO THE STATUTE OF FRAUDS. [§ 18–29]

The Statute of Frauds only regulates whether a contract may be enforced [Chapter Ten]. It has nothing to do with governing which terms are to be included in the contract, which is the function of the parol evidence rule. If the Statute of Frauds is satisfied, there is nothing in the Statute that will keep any and all evidence surrounding the contract, its making, its terms, etc. from being introduced. However, application of the parol evidence rule may keep such evidence from being admissible. That is, if the written contract is totally integrated, no such evidence can be introduced to supplement the writing, and only non-contradictory terms may be admitted if the written contract is partially integrated.

CHAPTER 18

1. **Example. [§ 18–30]**

   Buyer, the owner of a retail record store, receives a merchant's confirmatory memorandum from a record company confirming an order of specified rock videos for $12.50/video. Buyer does not object to the memorandum for ten days. The Statute of Frauds has thus been satisfied under § 2–201(2) [§ 10–44]. Accordingly, the *Statute of Frauds* will not bar evidence that she and the record company had agreed that the videos would be recorded on professional-quality, rather than standard quality, video cassettes. However, whether *the parol evidence rule* will bar such evidence depends on whether the party's agreement was totally or partially integrated, and if partially integrated, on whether such term contradicts the written contract.

H. REVIEW PROBLEM. [§ 18–31]

Student buys a computer at Computer America for $1,500. It does not come pre-loaded with any application software. The sales draft, signed by student, specifies the correct amount of RAM, the size of the hard disc, the speed, etc. of the computer and has a pre-printed integration clause on it. However, the draft says nothing about software, and Student claims the sales representative at the store promised her that the computer would come pre-loaded with the latest version of Windows. (Although this is a UCC problem, because it deals with goods, it is analyzed below under Restatement rules as an illustration)

Question:

Is the Windows agreement enforceable?

Answer:

It depends. **First**, a court will have to determine whether the sales draft is a partially or totally integrated document. Under the modern Restatement view [§ 18–7], a judge will do this by listening to Student's evidence of the circumstances involved in the making, and negotiation, of the contract and deciding whether a jury <u>could</u> believe student, taking into account the merger clause found in the draft. If the court decides a jury <u>could</u> believe her, it will declare the contract partially integrated.

If the court declared the contract to be partially integrated, the **second** step then is to determine if the Windows term is "contradictory term" or a "consistent additional" term. The test is whether it is the type of agreement that "might naturally" have been left out of the final contract [§ 18–13]. If, for example, the sales draft form had only blanks for amount of RAM, size of hard drive, etc. that were filled in by hand, Student may have a good argument, for it is unrealistic to expect a salesperson to handwrite in on the form the Windows inclusion. On the other hand, if the sales draft form had a blank for "Included Software" which was blank, Student's argument is weaker.

THE PAROL EVIDENCE RULE

If Student passes this test, i.e., if the court holds that the sales draft is only partially integrated and that the Windows term is not "contradictory" to the other terms of the agreement and is instead a "consistent," she will be permitted to testify about the Windows agreement at trial. If the jury believes her evidence, Computer America will be in breach for failing to include the software. If the jury disbelieves her evidence, the Windows agreement will be deemed not part of the contract, and the store will thus not be in breach for failing to include it.

I. THE PAROL EVIDENCE RULE UNDER THE CISG. [§ 18–32*]

The CISG has no parol evidence rule. Indeed, under Article 8(3), a court is directed to examine the negotiations of the parties "[i]n determining the intent of a party or the understanding a reasonable person would have had" as to the meaning, or terms in, the agreement.

J. EXAM APPROACH TO PAROL EVIDENCE RULE ISSUES. [§ 18–33**]

This chapter has gone into some detail on certain aspects of the parol evidence rule, and thus it is easy to "get lost in the trees" when trying to learn what to do when confronted with a parol evidence rule issue. In fact, the analysis is not that complicated:

    1. Determine whether the written contract itself is partially or completely integrated [§§ 18–8 *et seq.*], remembering that the "Corbin" test is the majority view today [§§ 18–9 *et seq.*].

    2. If it is totally integrated, no parol evidence can be introduced [§ 18–4].

    3. If it is partially integrated, then parol evidence is admissible to supplement the written contract, but not to contradict it [§ 18–4], recalling that the "might naturally" test determines whether the parol language contradicts or supplements the written contract [§ 18–13].

    4. If you are able to introduce the parol evidence, the term does not automatically become part of the contract. That is up to the trier of fact [§ 18–17].

    5. Always check to see if one of the "exceptions" to the parol evidence rule applies that will allow admission of the evidence anyway [§§ 18–19 *et seq.*].

---

    * For more information, listen to CD # 8, Track 5 of *Sum and Substance Audio on Contracts*.

    ** For more information, listen to CD # 8, Track 8 of *Sum and Substance Audio on Contracts*.

CHAPTER 18

K. GRAPHIC SUMMARY OF PAROL EVIDENCE RULE. [§ 18–34]

For those who prefer a flow chart, a graphic summary of the parol evidence rule follows:

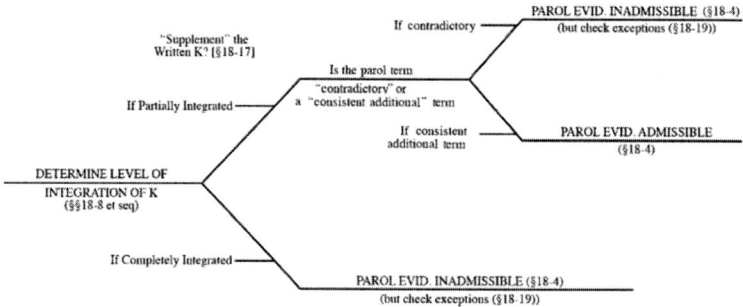

CHAPTER 19

INTERPRETATION

A. INTERPRETATION GENERALLY. [§ 19–1*]

The parol evidence rule helps courts decide whether a parol term should be added to a contract. Separate and apart from that inquiry is what **meaning** should be given to the terms that the parties agree *are* in the final written contract. **Interpretation is the process a court uses to determine the meaning of those terms** [Restatement 2d § 200]. When commentators speak of interpretation, they generally refer to two separate sets of rules:

(1) **Rules of construction**, which apply generally to any contract [§ 19–2], and

(2) **Rules of interpretation**, which regulate how a court will discern the meaning to be given terms under a particular contract [§ 19–9].

B. RULES OF CONSTRUCTION. [§ 19–2**]

Rules of construction are the generalized set of rules that apply to every contract. Often such rules are said to be "maxims" of law and provide at least a first step in determining how to interpret a contract. As generalized rules, they can be changed by the parties in any particular contract, **and only apply in the absence of admissible proof that the parties intended a different construction for their agreement**. The rules of construction are discussed below.

1. An Interpretation That Gives Meaning to All Terms Is Preferable to an Interpretation Making a Part of the Agreement Surplusage. [§ 19–3]

If two meanings of an agreement are possible, the preferable one is the one that interprets the contract in such a way that each part of it has some meaning, rather than in a way that one or more terms are left meaningless or duplicative [Restatement 2d § 203(a)].

---

* For more information, listen to CD # 8, Track 9 of *Sum and Substance Audio on Contracts*.

** For more information, listen to CD # 8, Track 10 of *Sum and Substance Audio on Contracts*.

2. If Two Clauses Conflict, the More Specific Acts as an Exception to the General. [§ 19-4]

Where two terms in a contract are in conflict, the preferred approach is to characterize the more specific of the two as an exception to the more general term [Restatement 2d § 203(c).] In other words, specific terms are given greater weight than general language terms. Thus, if one general clause in a contract says that buyers "shall be charged extra for delivery," but another very specific provision provides that the price for the particular shipment due on November 1 includes shipping charges, no extra shipping charge will likely be added for the November 1 shipment because the more specific term acts as an exception to the general.

3. Separately Negotiated Terms Are Given Greater Weight than Standardized Terms. [§ 19-5]

If a particular clause in a contract was a dickered, bargained for term, such term will generally be enforced even if it is in conflict with a more general, standardized, or pre-printed term [Restatement 2d § 203(d)].

4. Handwritten Terms Generally Control over Typed or Printed Ones; Typewritten Terms Generally Control over Printed Ones. [§ 19-6]

If a contract is printed but spaces are left to be filled in by hand, or if the parties agree to handwritten (or typewritten/computer) changes to a printed form, <u>generally</u> such handwritten or typewritten clauses are to be enforced when in conflict with the preprinted terms [Restatement 2d § 203(d)]. Handwritten terms are believed to be a more realistic view of the parties' intent, since the parties took the time to actually handwrite the terms into the contract. This is in accordance with the general rule that the parties' intent should be enforced [§ 19-10].

5. If a Term Is Ambiguous, It Should Be Resolved Against the Drafting Party. [§ 19-7]

Generally, an ambiguous term is construed against the drafter on the theory that the drafter could have made it clearer in the first place. This doctrine has had special prominence in construing insurance contracts (i.e., construing such contracts against insurance companies), and is often used in other adhesion contract situations as well.

6. The Expression of One Thing Is the Exclusion of Others. [§ 19-8]

If the parties to a contract make a list as to certain items, it may be construed that if an item is not on the list, it is intended to be excluded. For example, in selling a house, the buyer and seller list the specific light fixtures in the house that are to be included in the sale. The general rule is that if a particular fixture is not on such a list, it was intended to be excluded from the sale.

C. RULES OF INTERPRETATION. [§ 19–9*]

Rules of interpretation govern how a court derives the meaning to be given to a term in a particular contract [Restatement 2d § 200]. As shown below, most of the time this is not difficult, for the parties usually mean the same thing when they use a word, and that meaning is usually the customary one generally understood in society. However, on occasion this is not the case. Sometimes the parties to the contract do not mean the same thing when they agree on the same word, e.g., "10 days" may be 10 calendar days to one party and 10 working days to the other.

Also, sometimes one party to a contract claims that the parties **had agreed on a special meaning** for a term that is different from its generally understood meaning. On occasion, the failure to agree on the meaning of a term can mean that there is no contract at all between the parties [see § 12–28, regarding misunderstanding]. More often, however, the parties intend to be bound, and it is up to the court to determine their meaning. The rules of interpretation set forth contract law's approach in determining the meaning of contract terms.

1. **General Rules. [§ 19–10]**

    The principal goal of contract interpretation is to give effect to the intent of the parties as to the meaning of their words in the contract [Restatement 2d § 201(1)]. However, most often the parties do not explicitly define a term or otherwise express their views as to the meaning of a particular word. Thus, courts must use presumptions to ascribe a meaning to the parties' chosen words. The following sections set forth these interpretative presumptions, which control the interpretation of a contract in the absence of admissible evidence showing the parties' contrary intention.

    a. **Language Is Given Its Generally Prevailing Meaning in Society. [§ 19–11]**

        The general rule is that words are to be interpreted in light of their generally accepted societal meaning [Restatement 2d § 202(3)(a)].

---

* For more information, listen to CD # 8, Track 11 of *Sum and Substance Audio on Contracts*.

b. **Technical Terms to Be Given Their Technical Meaning in a Transaction Within That Field. [§ 19–12]**

If a term has a technical meaning to those who operate in that area, the term should be given that technical meaning if the contract deals with that field [Restatement 2d § 203(2)(b)].

c. **Terms to Be Interpreted in Light of Their Meaning Within the Usage of Trade, Course of Dealing, or Course of Performance. [§ 19–13]**

The concepts of usage of trade, course of dealing, and course of performance seem principally at issue in cases under the UCC and are defined and discussed in detail in § 6–26. However, even in non-UCC transactions, absent any admissible evidence indicating a contrary interpretation by the parties, courts will give contractual terms the meanings they have in a particular trade or vocation (usage of trade), or the meanings they have been given by the parties themselves in prior contracts (course of dealing) or in their present contract (course of performance) [Restatement 2d §§ 202(4); 219–223].

(1) **Hierarchy of Terms: Express, Course of Performance, Course of Dealing, Usage of Trade. [§ 19–14]**

A court is directed, wherever possible, to construe the meanings of express terms, i.e., the terms that appear in the construct itself, **consistently** with the meaning given such terms in the usage of trade, course of dealing, or course of performance. However, **if there truly is a conflict** among those meanings, under Restatement 2d § 203(b), the following rules govern which meaning controls:

(i) The meaning of express terms shall prevail over any conflicting meaning given such terms in the course of dealing, course of performance, and usage of trade;

(ii) The meaning given a term in the course of performance prevails over any conflicting meaning given to that term in the course of dealing or usage of trade; and

(iii) The meaning given a term in the course of dealing controls over any conflicting meaning given that term in the usage of trade.

INTERPRETATION

(2) The "Reasonable Reconciliation" Doctrine. [§ 19–15]

Under what is known as the "reasonable reconciliation" doctrine, terms which have different meanings under usage of trade, course of performance and the like can sometimes be viewed as consistent with each other. As demonstrated in the *Nanakuli* case below, sometimes courts will go to great lengths to find seemingly inconsistent meanings can, in fact, be reasonably reconciled and thus the hierarchy mentioned in § 19–4 need not apply.

(a) Example of *Nanakuli Paving & Rock Co. v. Shell Oil Co., Inc.* [§ 19–16]

> **AUTHOR'S NOTE:** (*Nanakuli* is a UCC case, but it provides a good example as to how courts deal with reconciling different meanings. As such, it is discussed in this chapter, and not Chapter Twenty, which deals more specifically with UCC rules).

Nanakuli was a general contractor. It used bids from subcontractors to assemble its bids to developers. [*See* § 8–13 for an explanation of the contractor-subcontractor relationship and how developer bids are generated.] One of its subcontractors was Shell, from whom it ordered asphalt. The nature of the business was that Nanakuli would get the a job from the developer for, e.g., paving a road. Business was good, so it would not actually start the paving until several months after it was awarded the contract. As was customary in the industry, Nanakuli would order the asphalt from Shell a day or two after it was awarded the paving contract, which was several months in advance of the needed delivery.

The Nanakuli-Shell contract had an express provision that provided that the price Shell would charge Nanakuli was the price pending *at the time of delivery*. The problem arose because Nanakuli used the price pending *at the time of the Shell-Nanakuli contract was entered into* when it prepared its bid for the developer.

In this case, Shell raised the price between the date of contracting and the time of delivery. Nanakuli claimed it should not have to pay the higher price since it relied on the time-of-contracting price in making its bid to the developer, and it was reasonable in doing so since price protection between ordering and delivery was the course of dealing between the parties and, in any event, was the usage of trade within the asphalt industry in Hawaii. Shell claimed the course of performance and usage of trade was irrelevant because the *express* pricing term—price at time of delivery—should control under the hierarchy set forthin § 1–103.

Held: The hierarchy rules (express terms prevail over course of performance, which prevails over course of dealing, which prevails over usage of trade) apply when the terms are <u>inconsistent</u> and truly in conflict [Restatement 2d § 202(5); UCC 1–303(e)]. However, the court found that the express terms and the course of dealing and usage of trade could be **"reasonably reconciled"** by noting that, in some cases, the rise in price in between the order and the delivery would not financially hurt Nanakuli because Nanakuli had bid the jobs on a "cost plus" basis, meaning that the developer agreed to pay whatever costs Nanakuli had to bear, plus a % above that, which would be Nanakuli's profit. So in those cases, charging Nanakuli the cost pending at the time of *delivery* made sense, because Nanakuli would just pass those increases through to the developer as part of its cost.

However, in other cases, Nanakuli bid the job on a "fixed price" basis, using the price pending at the time of *ordering* in preparing its price. In the "fixed price" cases, where Nanakuli had relied on the price pending at the time of ordering, it would lose money if it could not rely on the earlier price pending at the time of ordering, and Shell had provided price protection in such cases in the past. The court noted the unfairness of requiring Nanakuli to lose money on the fixed price contract, and thus held Shell was stuck with the lower, price pending at the time of ordering figure when Nanakuli used that price in fixed price contracts; but Shell could charge the higher, price pending at the time of delivery figure, when Nanakuli entered into "cost plus" agreements. Hence, under the court's reasoning, the express and course of dealing/usage of trade meanings were not in conflict at all.

Some have commented that it was a large stretch to "reconcile" the different meanings of the express and course of dealing/usage of trade terms into a "consistent" whole in this case, but the decision is indicative of how a court will approach a problem where terms appear to be in conflict, i.e., it will try to

INTERPRETATION

"reasonably reconcile" them so no conflict exists [*Nanakuli Paving & Rock Co. v. Shell Oil Co., Inc.*, 664 F.2d 772 (9th Cir. 1981)].

2. Admissibility of Extrinsic Evidence to Prove the Parties Had Their Own Special Meaning for a Term. [§ 19–17*]

Sometimes a party will assert a breach of contract, but on the face of the contract the alleged breacher seemed to do nothing wrong. However, the party bringing the action will claim the parties had a special meaning for the term that is different from the one generally given to such a term. This special meaning can be a specialized application of a common term, e.g., when the contract calls for delivery of 7,000 tons of asphalt it means 7,000 metric tons and not 7,000 English tons. In addition, the special meaning can be part of a secret code between the parties.

For example, a famous hypothetical assumes a customer who believes people are spying on her agrees with her stockbroker that when the customer tells the broker to "sell" some stock, she really means "buy" those shares and vice versa. One day the customer tells her broker to "buy" 1,000 shares of a certain stock, and her broker ends up buying, not selling, the shares. Obviously if the customer sues for breach, she would like to be able to introduce evidence (even if it is only her own testimony) of their "secret meaning." Note that this is not a parol evidence problem, because both parties agree that the term "buy" was in the contract. The dispute is over the special *meaning* of the term used by the parties—to them "buy" meant "sell" (*see* § 18–27). The test for when such extrinsic evidence, i.e., evidence by a party of a term's meaning other than the normal definition of that term, is admissible has changed over time.

a. Traditional Williston/Holmes View: The Plain Meaning Rule. [§ 19–18]

According to the approach set forth by Professor Williston and endorsed by Justice Holmes, a party cannot introduce extrinsic evidence to explain the meaning of a term unless the term is, on its face, ambiguous. If the term had a "plain meaning" as understood in society, that was the meaning it would be given. Thus, if the parties agreed to the delivery of 14 "dweeboids" of cotton at a price of 25 "units" per dweeboid, extrinsic evidence would be allowed to explain that the parties meant a dweeboid to be 1,000 lbs. and that a "unit" was intended to be $1,000. However, in the stockbroker example given above in § 19–17, no evidence of the "buy-means-sell" agreement would be admitted

---

* For more information, listen to CD # 9, Track 1 of *Sum and Substance Audio on Contracts*.

under this view, for the words used in the contract, i.e., "buy" the stock, appeared clear on their face.

b. More Contemporary Corbin/Restatement View: The "Reasonably Susceptible" Test. [§ 19–19]

The modern trend of cases sets forth a more liberal view regarding the admission of such extrinsic evidence. Under this view, if the contract term is **"reasonably susceptible"** to the proffered meaning urged by one party under all the circumstances, that party may introduce extrinsic evidence establishing that the proffered meaning was the one actually shared by the parties [Restatement 2d § 202(1)]. The idea behind this more liberal view is that, if the primary goal of contract interpretation is to give the meaning the parties ascribed to that term when they entered the contract, then courts should not reject a proffered special meaning given for the term, or at least should not do so automatically when the term itself is unambiguous as is required under the Williston/Holmes test.

The "reasonably susceptible" test involves a two-step process. First, a court is directed to decide whether the meaning offered by a party is a "reasonably susceptible" one before that party testified to the jury about such individualized meaning. The idea is that words must mean something, so the party offering a specialized meaning must make a reasonably convincing case to the court that in this particular transaction the normal meaning of the word should not control. It is up to the party asserting the special meaning to show the circumstances that would make his or position reasonable. Thus, in the stockbroker case, if the customer were prominent and could show with reasonable conviction that she was being spied upon, a court might well determine under those circumstances that a secret meaning where buy means sell was held by the parties. If so, she would be permitted to testify as to that meaning to the trier of fact. Note that this does not mean that the trier of fact will necessarily believe the party asserting the secret meaning and may or may not find the secret meaning as controlling. However, it does mean that the party will at least get a chance to introduce evidence of that meaning to the trier of fact.

The "reasonably susceptible" test hit its zenith in the California Supreme Court's decision in *Pacific Gas & Electric v. G.W. Thomas Drayage* ("*PG & E*"). There the court held that, no matter how contradictory a special meaning might be to the express term, either party is entitled introduce evidence as to that special meaning to the Court. [*Pacific Gas & Electric Co. v. G.W. Thomas Drayage & Rigging Co.*, 69 Cal. 2d 33 (1968)].

INTERPRETATION

Some commentators have criticized the approach, stating that it renders the words used in a contract meaningless and could, if pushed to its limit, render the parol evidence rule a nullity (*see* the Review Problem in § 19–21 for a further explanation of the effect of this interpretation rule on the parol evidence rule). An example of how this most liberal "PG&E" interpretation rule is applied is discussed below.

(1) Example of *Trident Center v. Connecticut General Life Ins. Co.* [§ 19–20]

Trident was a company which built an office building, using financing from Connecticut General, an insurance company. Their loan agreement called for a set interest rate for the loan, and a clause provided that Trident did not have the right to refinance or pre-pay the loan for the first 12 years after the loan was made. Their contract also had a provision whereby if Trident defaulted on the loan, Connecticut could make the entire amount of the loan, plus a 10% surcharge, immediately due and payable.

About five years into the deal, market interest rates dropped significantly, and Trident found itself paying interest well in excess of the amount it would have to pay if it could refinance the loan. Trident argued, among other things, that despite the language of the clause that said it could not refinance or pre-pay the loan for the first 12 years, the parties did, in fact, have a special meaning for that clause, which was that Trident *could* refinance the loan within the first 12 years if it wanted to pay a 10% penalty. It pointed to the default clause as making its proffered meaning "reasonably susceptible."

Held: Trident should be able to at least present testimony as to its proffered "secret" meaning to a judge. Judge Kozinski, who wrote the opinion, noted that he could not see how a heavily negotiated term in a commercial lease that said Trident could not refinance the loan could possibly mean that Trident could refinance the loan if it was willing to pay a 10% penalty. Nevertheless, he said that under *PG & E*, finding the parties' subjective meaning of the term, and not automatically using the objective meaning of the words they used, was the key. As such, Trident must be given the opportunity to present its understanding of what the words meant. [*Trident Center v. Connecticut General Life Ins. Co.*, 847 F.2d 564 (9th Cir. 1988)].

CHAPTER 19

3. **Review Problem. [§ 19–21]**

Recall the example given in § 18–2, where the written contract calls for the seller to deliver her stereo to the buyer, and for the buyer to pay $750 for it. The seller says the buyer is in breach because she timely delivered her stereo to the buyer and the buyer refused to pay for it. The buyer says the reason he did not pay is because the seller did not live up to her bargain. That is, he says they orally agreed that he was to pay $750 for the seller's stereo <u>and</u> her compact disc collection.

Under a *parol evidence analysis*, **first**, a court will have to determine whether the contract is a partially or totally integrated document, either using Williston's or Corbin's view. If it is determined to be totally integrated, the analysis is over and no parol evidence is admissible. However, if the document is partially integrated, then consistent parol terms are admissible, while contradictory parol terms are not. That is, if the court determines that the CD term is the kind of term that, had the parties agreed to it, it might naturally be omitted from their final contract because, e.g., this was an informal agreement between friends where every "i" didn't need to be dotted, then the buyer would be able to introduce evidence of the CD agreement to the trier of fact. (When you get to Chapter 20, you will find the test for "contradictory terms" is different in the UCC than the Restatement. If it were analyzed under Article 2 you would ask whether the parol terms were the kinds of terms that "would naturally have been included" in any final agreement, and, if so, no evidence of their making will be allowed.)

But note that the problem could also be analyzed using interpretation rules. The buyer could claim that the two friends had a special meaning for the term "stereo"—to them, they used the term "stereo" as a shorthand for both the machine and the CD collection. Under this *interpretation analysis*, the **first** step is to discover when extrinsic evidence of this special meaning will be allowed. Under the Williston/Holmes view, the "Plain Language" test, the word "stereo" has a plain meaning, and so evidence that stereo means stereo plus CDs would be allowed.

Under the "Reasonably Susceptible" test authored by Corbin, if the buyer could convince a court that the term "stereo" was **reasonably susceptible** of the meaning "stereo plus CDs" in this situation, the buyer would be allowed to testify as to that meaning to the jury.

Notice that an *interpretation analysis* under a court following *PG & E* affords a party a much better chance of getting a term like the CD collection into a contract than does the parol evidence rule. That is, it is much easier to pick a term that is already in the contract, and argue a special meaning applies to it, than to argue levels of

INTERPRETATION

integration and consistency of terms as is required under the parol evidence rule. Thus, some have argued that the interpretation analysis under *PG & E* diminishes the effect of the parol evidence rule.

D. EXAM APPROACH TO INTERPRETATION ISSUES. [§ 19–22*]

To analyze an interpretation issue, first make sure that both parties agree there is a term in the contract. If they don't, then it becomes a parol evidence problem or a modification problem, depending on when it was alleged to be agreed to.

As you analyze an interpretation issue, make sure the contract complies with:

1. The rules of constructions, or "maxims":

    A. An interpretation that gives meaning to all terms is preferable to an interpretation making a part of the agreement surplusage [§ 19–3];

    B. If two clauses are in conflict, the more specific acts as an exception to the general [§ 19–4];

    C. Separately negotiated terms are given greater weight than standardized terms [§ 19–5];

    D. Handwritten terms generally control over typed or printed ones; typewritten terms generally control over printed ones [§ 19–6];

    E. If a term is ambiguous, it should be resolved against the drafter [§ 19–7]; and

    F. The expression of one thing is the exclusion of others [*see* § 19–8].

2. The rules of interpretation:

    A. The main goal is to give effect to the intent of the parties [§ 19–10];

    B. Language is given its generally prevailing meaning in society [§ 19–11];

    C. Technical terms are to be given their technical meaning within that field [§ 19–12]; and

    D. Terms are to be interpreted in light of their meaning within the usage of trade, course of dealing or course of performance, only when the terms are inconsistent [§ 19–13].

---

* For more information, listen to CD # 9, Track 2 of *Sum and Substance Audio on Contracts*.

CHAPTER 19

To determine when evidence of a special meaning is permissible, use the following tests:

1. Williston's Plain Language Test: does the word have a plain meaning? If yes, that is what it means and no evidence of a special meaning is allowed [§ 19–18]; or

2. Corbin's Reasonably Susceptible Test: whether the offered extrinsic evidence is relevant to prove a meaning to which the language of the instrument is reasonably susceptible [§ 19–19].

If the party asserting the special meaning through extrinsic evidence convinces the judge under the applicable test above, that party will then be permitted to provide testimony as to that meaning to the trier of fact, which can accept or reject it.

CHAPTER 20

UCC § 2–202

A. UCC § 2–202: COMBINING THE PAROL EVIDENCE RULE WITH INTERPRETATION RULES. [§ 20–1*]

In § 2–202, the UCC has combined the parol evidence rule (Chapter Eighteen) with the rules of interpretation (Chapter Nineteen). That is, the provision attempts to regulate both: (a) what terms are included in the contract (the parol evidence rule), **and** (b) when extrinsic evidence is admissible to show the parties' particular meaning of a term (interpretation). In the words of the statute, it governs both how terms in a written document may be "supplemented" and "explained."

B. HOW TO APPROACH A § 2–202 PAROL EVIDENCE RULE PROBLEM. [§ 20–2]

The approach to a parol evidence rule problem in a contract governed by the UCC is quite similar to the approach used under common law/Restatement rules [§§ 18–4 *et seq.*]. You should:

First, ensure that the transaction is one to which Article 2 of the UCC applies [§§ 33–3 *et seq.*].

Second, ascertain whether the writing is partially integrated or totally integrated. If it is **totally integrated**, your analysis is over, as **no parol evidence will be allowed**, although usage of trade, course of dealing and course of performance may be used to supplement the contract [UCC § 2–202(a)]. If it is a **partially integrated agreement, some parol evidence can be admitted**.

If the parol term is "contradictory," it will not be admitted, even if the agreement is partially integrated. However **if the parol term is a "consistent" term, it <u>will</u> be admitted to supplement a partially integrated agreement**. Once again, usage of trade, course of dealing and course of performance may be used to supplement a partially integrated contract [UCC § 2–202(a)].

---

* For more information, listen to CD # 8, Track 5 of *Sum and Substance Audio on Contracts*.

309

CHAPTER 20

As we will see, while the steps are similar, some of the substantive tests under the UCC parol analysis are different from their common law counterparts.

1. **Integration: Partially or Totally Integrated Contracts. [§ 20–3]**

   The test for whether the agreement is partially or totally integrated is the same under the UCC as it is under common law rules [*see* §§ 18–8 *et seq.* for a discussion for the standards and methodology used in that analysis].

2. **When the Agreement Is Totally Integrated: No Parol Evidence Is Admissible. [§ 20–4]**

   As with the common law parol evidence rule, if the agreement is judged totally integrated, <u>no parol evidence will be admitted</u>. [UCC § 2–202].

3. **When the Writing Is Partially Integrated: "Contradictory" Parol Terms Are Inadmissible; "Consistent" Parol Terms <u>Are</u> Admissible. [§ 20–5]**

   Just as with the common law parol evidence rule, any parol term judged **"contradictory" will <u>not</u> be admitted to supplement even a partially integrated document**. However, if the parol term is deemed **"consistent"** it **will be admitted to supplement a partially integrated document**. [UCC § 2–202].

   By definition, the proffered parol term must be either contradictory or consistent. They are antonyms.

   The substantive difference between the common law and UCC parol evidence analysis is that the standard for determining whether the term is "contradictory" is different.

   a. **Determining Whether a Term Is "Contradictory": The "Would Certainly" Test. [§ 20–6]**

      Under the common law parol evidence rule, the test for determining whether a term is "contradictory" or not is the Restatement's "might naturally be omitted" test, i.e., whether the proffered parol term is of a type that might naturally be omitted from the agreement [*See* § 18–13)].

      Under the UCC, the test is similar, but different. It is known as the **"would certainly"** test [UCC § 2–202, Cmt 3]. Under the "would certainly" test, the question is **whether the proffered parol term is the type that *would certainly* have been included in the final agreement of the parties had it, in fact, been agreed to.**

310

(1) Example. [§ 20–7]

Although *Mitchell v. Lath* is a non-UCC case (since it deals with the sale of real estate), it can be used to illustrate how the UCC's "would certainly" test applies, and thus this example analyzes it as if it were a UCC case (the case is analyzed using the Restatement's "might naturally" test in § 18–14).

In *Mitchell,* a seller of property owned two adjacent lots. He sold one to the buyer, and the buyer later claimed that buyer and seller had made an oral agreement, not reflected in the final written contract, that the seller would remove an ice house from the second property which blocked the view from the buyer's newly purchased lot. The seller claimed that agreement was never made.

Under the UCC the first step (assuming Article 2 applicability) would be to determine if the written agreement was partially integrated. Assuming it was, the next step would be to determine if the "move the ice house" term was an admissible consistent additional term or an inadmissible contradictory term.

To determine whether it is a consistent or contradictory term the question is: had the parties agreed to it, *is it of the type that **would certainly** have been included in their written agreement*? If a court held it was the kind of term that would certainly have been included, then it is a "contradictory" term, and therefore inadmissible. If a court holds that it is not the kind of term that would certainly have been included in a land contract, because land contracts deal with title issues and not terms about ice houses moving on adjacent property, then it is a "consistent additional term," which would be admitted.

(2) Potential Limitation on the "Would Certainly" Test. [§ 20–8]

Some scholars believe there is an inherent limitation on the application of the "would certainly" test, namely that it does not apply to a contract where it is facially obvious that a material term has not been inadvertently omitted from the final writing. For example, assume two companies have heavily negotiated a thirty-page contract, and after it is signed, it is discovered that there is no price term in the contract. The seller would like to introduce evidence that the agreed-upon price was $1,800,000, a generous, but not unconscionably high, price for the goods involved. The buyer wants to introduce evidence that the agreed-upon price was $1,600,000, a low, but not unreasonable, price for the goods.

A court examining the agreement would doubtless find it only partially integrated given that it has no price term and is otherwise so heavily negotiated. But, under the "would certainly" test, evidence of either party as to the supposedly agreed-upon term would not be admissible. This is because a price term is the sort of term that **had** the parties agreed to one, it "would certainly" have been in the agreement. Since it is very unlikely in such a heavily negotiated agreement that the parties would not have made some arrangement as to price, the argument is that the "would certainly" test simply should not be applicable to such a case. That is, where it is reasonably apparent from the face of the written contract that a material term was inadvertently omitted from the final writing, these commentators hold that the parol evidence rule should not apply and all evidence of what the parties had agreed-upon concerning that term should be freely admissible.

Those that oppose this view state that if the term was important enough to a party, he or she should have ensured that it was included in the final draft of the contract before signing it. If such an effort was not made, then he or she should be subject to the parol evidence rule like everyone else, which in the hypothetical above likely means that the price term for the contract would be a "reasonable price" under the gap filler of UCC § 2–305 [§ 6–17].

4. **Evidence of Course of Performance, Course of Dealing, and Usage of Trade Can Be Introduced to *Explain* a Term Found in the Contract, Regardless Whether the Agreement Is Partially or Totally Integrated. [§ 20–9*]**

Under UCC § 2–202, course of performance, course of dealing, and usage of trade can *always* be introduced to explain what the parties mean by a particular term, regardless whether the agreement is totally or only partially integrated. In other words, these terms can be used in the **interpretation** of what the parties intended by the terms in their agreement. These terms are defined and discussed below.

---

* For more information, listen to CD # 8, Track 5 of *Sum and Substance Audio on Contracts*.

a. **Course of Performance. [§ 20–10]**

"Course of performance" consists of a sequence of consistent actions taken by two parties involving a term **under the particular contract at issue** [UCC § 1–303(a)].

   (1) **Example. [§ 20–11]**

   The contract obligates the buyer to place 5 orders for widgets in a year, and obligates the seller to deliver them within "10 days" of the order. On the first 3 orders, seller delivered widgets, without objection, within 10 *working* days of the order, but not within 10 calendar days. If the buyer attempts to refuse delivery of the fourth order because it was not made within ten calendar days (although it was delivered within 10 business days), the seller will be able to introduce evidence of the **course of performance** under the current contract to explain what the parties meant by the delivery term, and that evidence will likely be very persuasive.

   (2) **"Waiver" and Course of Performance. [§ 20–12]**

   Let's say a seller delivers goods on the twenty-fifth of the month, without objection by the buyer, under a contract calling for delivery the fifteenth of the month. If that happened for the first seven deliveries under a year-long agreement, a course of performance has been established. However, suppose it only happened on the first delivery under that agreement. Has a course of performance been established, or has there only been a "waiver" as to the one delivery by the buyer? The difference is significant, because a course of performance becomes very persuasive evidence as to how the parties interpret the delivery term. But a one-time waiver can be retracted, and so the buyer is not "stuck" with delivery on the twenty-fifth for the remainder of the contract.

   The seller would argue that it may only have happened once, but there was only one occasion for it to have occurred. The fact that it happened in 100% of the possible instances establishes a course of performance for delivery on the twenty-fifth. The buyer would argue that she did the seller a favor on the first delivery, and shouldn't be stuck with an interpretation that the fifteenth means the twenty-fifth for the rest of the contract.

   Neither the UCC nor case law provides a test for when it is a retractable waiver and when it should be interpreted as a course of performance. What is clear is that the more times it occurs, the more likely it will be a course of performance. But when it only happens once or twice—but those were the only occasions on which it *could* have happened—the question of whether it is a waiver or a course of performance will always be raised, and a court will have to determine what it believes the parties' intent was based on an evaluation of all the circumstances.

b. **Course of Dealing. [§ 20–13]**

Course of dealing consists of a sequence of consistent actions taken by the two parties in response to repeated situations involving a similar contractual term under **previous** contracts between them [UCC § 1–303(b)]. Again, the idea is that if the parties have had previous dealings where construction of the same term is at issue, how the parties acted is persuasive evidence of what they intended that term to mean in the present contract.

(1) **Example. [§ 20–14]**

In three different contracts over the past two years with a "10 day" delivery term, the buyer has accepted delivery without objection so long as the goods were delivered within ten working days after the order was placed. Such conduct would amount to a **course of dealing**, which is persuasive evidence of what the parties intended in the present contract by the "10 day" delivery term.

c. **Usage of Trade. [§ 20–15]**

Usage of trade is any practice or method of dealing having such a regular occurrence in a particular place, vocation or trade that a party to the agreement should know of its existence [UCC § 1–303(c)]. The meaning given a particular term in the trade can be introduced as evidence of what the parties to a contract must have meant when they used that same term.

(1) **Example. [§ 20–16]**

A neophyte buyer orders a "ton" of rock from a merchant seller, and if in the industry, a "ton" is a metric, and not an English, ton that trade usage will be admissible to establish how the court should interpret the term in this contract. Note this is true regardless of the fact that the neophyte buyer may have subjectively believed he was buying an English ton of rock.

(2) **Example of *Frigaliment Importing Co. v. B.N.S. International Sales Corp.* [§ 20–17]**

Buyer agreed to purchase 100,000 pounds of "US Fresh Frozen Chicken, Grade A, Government Inspected" from seller. However, buyer contends "chicken" means a young chicken, suitable for broiling and frying. Seller contends "chicken" means any bird of that genus, and includes the less desirable stewing chickens. Seller delivered 100,000 pounds of the older, stewing fowls. Buyer rejected, contending there was a usage of trade whereby "chicken" means a young, frying chicken.

Held: Judgment for Seller. Buyer was correct as to the law—usage of trade should be used to interpret the contract. However, that "chicken" meant young, frying chickens was *not* the common understanding of the word in the chicken trade at the time the contract was entered into. [*Frigaliment Importing Co. v. B.N.S. Int'l. Sales Corp.*, 190 F. Supp. 116 (S.D.N.Y 1960)].

d. **Hierarchy of Interpretation: Express Terms; Course of Performance, Course of Dealing, and Usage of Trade. [§ 20–18]**

When possible, a court is instructed to interpret express terms, course of performance, course of dealing, and usage of trade in such a way that they are consistent with each other [UCC § 1–303(e)]. However, under § 1–303(e), **when those terms are in conflict**, the hierarchy as to which terms control are the same as for non-UCC transactions [§ 19–14], i.e.:

Express terms control over conflicting meanings under course of performance, course of dealing, or usage of trade.

The meaning as determined by course of performance controls over conflicting meaning under course of dealing, or usage of trade.

The meaning as determined by course of dealing controls over a conflicting meaning under a usage of trade.

[*See* § 19–16 for a discussion of the *Nanakuli* decision, which is a UCC case applying the hierarchy of the terms given above.]

C. SITUATIONS WHERE UCC § 2–202 DOES NOT APPLY. [§ 20–19*]

A list of situations in which the common law parol evidence rule does not apply is given in §§ 18–19 *et seq*. Those same rules apply to UCC § 2–202, i.e., the UCC parol evidence rule does not apply:

(a) To modifications agreed to after the contract has been made;

(b) To evidence introduced to prove either that no contract was ever made, that a condition precedent has not been fulfilled or waived, or that consideration has not been paid;

(c) To show the facts necessary to establish that the contract is voidable;

(d) To contemporaneous **written** documents. Thus evidence of such writings, typically "side letter" agreements, is freely admissible either to explain terms in the writing or to add terms to the writing, regardless of whether the writing is totally or partially integrated;

(e) To precatory language or recitals of fact;

(f) To interpret the language found in the final written agreement; or

(g) To show the consideration was "sham."

D. EXAM APPROACH TO § 2–202 ISSUES. [§ 20–20]

Please see the exam approach set forth in § 18–33 for the common law parol evidence rule. The only major change is that the test for whether the parol term supplements or contradicts the written contract is the "would certainly" test under § 2–202 [§ 20–6], rather than the "might naturally" test of common law [§ 18–13].

---

* For more information, listen to CD # 8, Track 7 of *Sum and Substance Audio on Contracts*.

E. GRAPHIC SUMMARY OF § 2–202. [§ 20–21*]

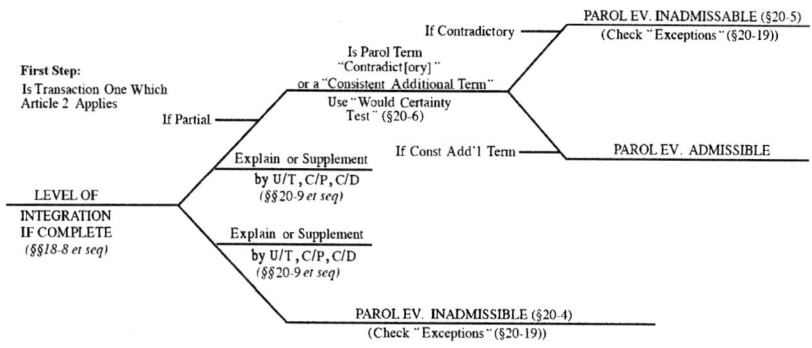

---

* For more information, listen to CD # 8, Track 8 of *Sum and Substance Audio on Contracts.*

Part VI

Conditions, Performance, and Breach

INTRODUCTORY NOTE REGARDING CONDITIONS, PERFORMANCE AND BREACH:

This section of the book discusses how duties become enforceable under a contract and what can happen to those duties once they become enforceable. Absent a highly unusual situation, the following are the only things that can happen when one party owes the other an enforceable contractual duty:

(1) The duty may be **discharged by performance**, i.e., the party can do what he or she promised under the contract;

(2) The duty may be **breached**, because it was not fully and completely performed and because there was no defense or other justification for such non-performance, or no subsequent agreement modifing or otherwise changing that duty;

(3) The unperformed duty can be discharged because of **anticipatory repudiation**;

(4) The unperformed duty may be **discharged by subsequent agreement that modifies, extinguishes or replaces the original agreement**;

(5) The unperformed duty may be **discharged due to impossibility, impracticability, or frustration of purpose**; or

(6) The unperformed duty may be **discharged by the other party's total breach**, meaning that if *one party* materially breached, all unperformed duties owed by the *other* party are cancelled and may go unperformed without incurring contractual liability.

The common law, Restatement, and basic UCC rules regarding performance, breach and the effect of conditions are discussed in **Chapter Twenty-One**.

A more detailed review of the UCC rules regarding performance and breach is discussed in **Chapter Twenty-Two**.

PART VI

Chapter Twenty-Three explains the process and effects of *anticipatory repudiation* (often, but mistakenly, called anticipatory breach) under **both common law and UCC contracts**.

The different ways *duties under one contract can be extinguished or exchanged for duties under a separate agreement,* and the effects of which device the parties choose to structure such an exchange of duties, are the subject of **Chapter Twenty-Four**.

The defenses of *impossibility, commercial impracticability, and frustration of purpose* are discussed in **Chapter Twenty-Five**.

Chapter 21

Conditions, Performance and Breach (with an Emphasis on Common Law Rules)

A. INTRODUCTION AND OVERVIEW. [§ 21–1]

At the end of the course, most students will rank the study and understanding of conditions as one of the most difficult part of contracts. The subject usually takes over a month of class time and is laced with new vocabulary and concepts. However, the study of conditions is really the heart of contract law, and so the time spent is well-justified.

To put the study of conditions in context, we assume that there is a valid contract, i.e., there has been a valid offer, acceptance, consideration, and an absence of defenses to formation. Conditions are typically about **performance** and **breach**. Specifically, a study of conditions in this Chapter allow us to answer the following questions:

1. When is a **duty** under a contract **enforceable**?

2. If a duty is enforceable, **has that duty been discharged due to performance** or has it been **breached**?

3. If **breached**, is the **breach material, immaterial, or total**?

4. What are the **consequences** of determining whether a breach is *material, immaterial or total*?

This Chapter discusses all the common law/Restatement rules dealing with conditions, along with a mention of the basic UCC provisions as well. For those classes where the Professor emphasizes the UCC, Chapter Twenty-Two discusses principles of condition under the UCC in some detail.

CHAPTER 21

Part B below discusses the **definitions of conditions** and explains the **different types of conditions**.

Part C deals with the issues associated with **express conditions**.

Part D discusses the issues associated with **constructive conditions**, including **tender, order of performance, and immaterial, material and total breach**.

Finally, Part E deals with the various ways **both express and constructive conditions** can be **excused**.

B. TYPES OF CONDITIONS. [§ 21–2*]

Conditions can be classified in two different ways:

1)—Express conditions (including implied-in-fact conditions) vs. constructive or implied conditions;

2)—Conditions precedent vs. conditions subsequent vs. concurrent conditions.

The nomenclature and definitions of each should be studied before the effects and consequences of those classifications can be understood. The nomenclature of each category is discussed below.

1. **Express, Implied-in-Fact, and Constructive Conditions. [§ 21–3]**

   a. **Express Conditions: Defined and Discussed. [§ 21–4]**

   An express condition is a condition expressly agreed upon by both the parties as evidenced by their words. Typically, phrases like, "on the condition that," "if, but only if," "unless," "in the event that," and "provided" are used to signify express conditions.

   (1) **Example of Express Condition. [§ 21–5]**

   If the parties contractually agree that John will buy Mary's house for $250,000 "on the condition that John is able to secure a loan for $200,000," John and Mary have entered into a contract with an express condition.

   b. **Implied-in-Fact Conditions: Defined and Discussed. [§ 21–6]**

   An implied-in-fact condition is a condition agreed upon by the parties as evidenced by the *conduct* of one or both parties, rather than their words. Whether the actions of the parties constitute an implied-in-fact condition is judged under an objective test, i.e., whether a reasonable person would believe

---

* For more information, listen to CD # 9, Track 8 of *Sum and Substance Audio on Contracts*.

CONDITIONS, PERFORMANCE AND BREACH (WITH AN EMPHASIS ON COMMON LAW RULES)

a condition had been agreed to by the parties. **Implied-in-fact conditions have the same legal effect as express conditions**. As a consequence, whenever a rule is given as to express conditions throughout the book, the rule applies equally to implied-in-fact conditions as well.

(1) Example of Implied-in-Fact Condition. [§ 21–7]

Buyer says, "I'll buy your autographed Mickey Mantle baseball card for $500, on the condition that the signature is authenticated by an independent handwriting expert." Seller says nothing, but hands over the card. The parties have entered into a valid contract with an implied-in-fact condition. The condition of signature authentication is not "express" since there was no express agreement to it via the words of both parties. Rather, Seller's **conduct** in handing over the card evidences and communicates his or her agreement with the authentication condition proposed by Buyer.

c. **Constructive or Implied Conditions: Defined and Discussed. [§ 21–8]**

A constructive or implied condition is a condition the parties have not expressly agreed upon, but which contract law either "implies" or "constructs" in every contract to help analyze the duties of the parties, or a condition which a court might decide is necessary in a particular contract to determine and carry out the parties' performance obligations [Restatement 2d § 226, Cmt. c]. Constructive conditions are equitable in nature, and thus are intended to be flexible in their application.

In deciding whether to imply a condition, a court is directed to impose a constructive condition if it believes either that:

(a) Such a condition would have been agreed to by the parties had they considered it; or

(b) Justice requires such a condition be imposed so the rights and duties of the parties under the agreement can be fairly ascertained.

Constructive conditions are, at best, distant cousins of express and implied-in-fact conditions. They operate differently and have wholly different purposes than do express conditions. As such, except for a couple of mentions in this Part B, constructive conditions are addressed separately in this chapter in Part C beginning with § 21–43.

CHAPTER 21

(1) Example of Constructive Condition. [§ 21–9]

In a one-year lease starting January 1, Landlord promises to keep Tenant's appliances in working order. Nothing is said about Tenant having to notify Landlord when an appliance breaks down. In March, Tenant's oven stops working. She does not tell Landlord. In April, Tenant tries to argue that she is entitled to move out as Landlord has breached the lease contract by failing to keep a major appliance in working order.

In this situation, a court would either "construct" or "imply" a condition that the Tenant must give Landlord notice before she can argue that Landlord has breached the contract. In other words, even though the parties did not expressly agree to this, a court will **construct a condition** so that the agreement is interpreted as if it provided, "Landlord has a duty to keep the appliances in working order *on the condition that Tenant inform Landlord when one is not in such working order.*"

2. Conditions Precedent and Conditions Subsequent. [§ 21–10]

a. Conditions Precedent: Defined and Discussed. [§ 21–11]

A condition precedent is:

(a) **An event, not certain to occur**, which

(b) **Must occur before performance under a contract is enforceable**, unless

(c) **The non-occurrence of the event is excused** [Restatement 2d § 224].

Most express conditions are conditions precedent. Note that some constructive conditions may also be classified as conditions precedent. In the Landlord/Tenant example of § 21–9 the notice requirement imposed on the tenant is a constructive condition precedent.

(1) Example of Express Condition Precedent. [§ 21–12]

In the John and Mary example given above in § 21–5, the language that John is to purchase Mary's home, "on the condition that John is able to secure a loan for $200,000," is an example of a contract with an express condition precedent. This is because loan approval is: (a) an event, which is not certain to occur, but which (b) must occur in order for the duties under the contract to become enforceable, unless (c) the non-occurrence of the condition is excused, e.g., if John agrees to buy the house even if his

CONDITIONS, PERFORMANCE AND BREACH (WITH AN EMPHASIS ON COMMON LAW RULES)

loan is not approved. Note, however, that if a contract called for a payment of $10,000, "on the condition that 30 days pass," the promise would **not** be conditional in the contract law sense, for the passing of 30 days is an event that is certain to occur.

(2) Effect of Classification as Express Condition Precedent. [§ 21-13]

There are two consequences or effects of classifying a condition as an express condition precedent. It is crucial to understand them both.

The first is <u>substantive</u>: **parties to a contract with an as yet unfulfilled express condition precedent are in a valid, binding agreement. However, the** *duties* **subject to the conditions are <u>unenforceable</u> until the conditional event occurs** [Restatement 2d § 225].

The second is <u>procedural</u>: **under an express condition precedent, the party who claims a duty is owed after the condition occurred bears the burden of proof to establish that the condition was satisfied.**

(a) Example of Effects of Contract with Express Condition Precedent. [§ 21-14]

In the John/Mary house selling agreement in § 21–5, at the time John and Mary sign the contract they are in a contract with an unfulfilled express condition precedent. That is, they are in what contract law considers a valid contract, but the **duties** under that contract—John's duty to pay $250,000 and Mary's duty to tender title—are **unenforceable** until the *condition*—obtaining the loan—is fulfilled (or excused).

If the loan comes through and John still refuses to go through with the deal it is <u>Mary</u>, **as the party claiming a duty is owed to her after the condition is fulfilled** who bears the **burden of proof to show the condition actually occurred** in any subsequent litigation.

b. Conditions Subsequent: Defined and Discussed. [§ 21-15]

A condition subsequent is:

(a) **An event, the occurrence of which is not the result of a breach of the obligor's duty of good faith**, which

CHAPTER 21

(b) **If it occurs, terminates a party's duty to perform**, unless

(c) **Its occurrence is excused** [Restatement 2d § 230].

Both express and constructive conditions can be classified as conditions subsequent.

(1) Example of Express Condition Subsequent. [§ 21–16]

On May 1, Bill and Sandra enter into a contract where Bill is obligated to purchase Sandra's home for $500,000 on June 2, "unless the Dow Jones Industrial Average has fallen to 7,500 points any time before June 1." This is an example of an express condition subsequent.

This is because the falling of the Dow Jones average is: (a) **an event**, the occurrence of which would not be a breach of Bill's duty of good faith, which, (b) **if it occurs, will terminate Bill's duty to perform**, unless (c) it is excused, e.g., by Bill deciding to go ahead and purchase the house even though the Dow Jones Average has fallen below 7,500 points.

(2) Effect of Classification as Express Condition Subsequent. [§ 21–17]

There are two consequences or effects of classifying a condition as an express condition subsequent. It is essential to understand them both.

The first is <u>substantive</u>: **parties to a contract with an as yet unfulfilled condition subsequent are in a valid, binding agreement whose terms** *are enforceable* **but are subject to the condition being fulfilled. If the condition is fulfilled, the parties are still in a valid binding contract, but the <u>duties</u> under the agreement <u>can no longer be enforced</u>** [Restatement 2d § 230(1)].

The second is <u>procedural</u>: **under a condition subsequent, the party who at one time owed a duty but now claims the duty is unenforceable because of the occurrence of the condition bears the burden of proof to establish that the condition has occurred.**

(a) **Example of Effects of a Contract with Express Condition Subsequent. [§ 21–18]**

In the Bill/Sandra example of § 21–16, when they sign their contract Bill and Sandra are in a valid and enforceable agreement with an unfulfilled condition subsequent. Bill is obligated to pay $500,000 on June

CONDITIONS, PERFORMANCE AND BREACH (WITH AN EMPHASIS ON COMMON LAW RULES)

2; Sandra is obligated to provide good title. However, if the Dow Jones Average falls below 7,500 points by June 1, their **duties become unenforceable**.

Assume the Dow Jones average fell below the target by June 1, but Sandra nevertheless sues Bill for breach if Bill refuses to tender payment. It is Bill, as **the party who at one time owed a duty, but now claims the duty is unenforceable because of the occurrence of the condition**, who **bears the burden of proof** to establish that the condition has occurred and thus he is not liable for failing to purchase the home.

c. **How to Tell Whether a Condition Is "Precedent" or "Subsequent." [§ 21–19]**

There are important consequences to determining whether a condition is "precedent" or "subsequent." There are no hard and fast rules, but the key to examine the **effect** of the condition occurring, and not how a condition may be phrased.

For example, suppose an insurance contract has a provision that any liability of the insurance company "is discharged if proof of loss by the insured is not submitted within 30 days after the incident giving rise to the claim." The way it is written has the form of a condition subsequent—liability is discharged if something happens. But, in fact, it is a condition precedent, because the **effect** is that the insurance company has no liability until the proof of loss is submitted, i.e., the condition is fulfilled. At that point, its obligation to pay the insured is enforceable. That makes the term a condition precedent.

With that said, typically words and phrases in a contract like "if," "but only if," "subject to," "on the condition that" and "provided that," typically denote conditions precedent; whereas words and phrases like "so long as," "unless" and "but not if," typically denote conditions subsequent.

As noted above, most express conditions turn out to be precedent. At least in "real world" contracts, there are few true conditions subsequent.

One important thing to note is that most duties in contracts are not subject to express conditions, e.g., Arnie promises to deliver a watch; Susan promises to pay for it. These are sometimes referenced as "unconditional duties." It is the unusual case where an express condition arises. The effect of structuring a promise as subject to a condition or an unconditional duty is discussed below [§§ 21–27 *et seq.*].

CHAPTER 21

d. Restatement 2d Rejects Terms "Condition Precedent" and "Condition Subsequent." [§ 21–20]

The Restatement 2d rejects the terms "condition precedent" and "condition subsequent." Instead, what at common law would be known as a condition precedent is simply called a "condition" under the Restatement [Restatement 2d § 224]; and what at common law would be known as a condition subsequent, is called an "event that terminates a duty" in the Restatement [Restatement 2d § 230]. However, the Restatement terminology has not proven persuasive as courts and commentators still tend to use the words "precedent" and "subsequent" as adjectives modifying conditions. Accordingly, this book will use the term condition precedent to refer to the Restatement's "condition," and condition subsequent to refer to the Restatement's "event that terminates a duty."

3. Concurrent Conditions. [§ 21–21]

Concurrent conditions are conditions that are capable of being fulfilled at the same time. For example, Arnie contractually promises to sell his watch "on the condition Susan pays me $100 on Wednesday at 1:00." Susan similarly contractually promises to "pay Arnie $100 on the condition he brings me his watch on Wednesday at 1:00." Since the exchange of the watch and the money can occur at the same time, they are known as "concurrent conditions."

There are very few express concurrent conditions. Instead, concurrent conditions are much more important in analyzing constructive conditions and most of the explanation of concurrent conditions is found beginning in § 21–51.

C. ISSUES INVOLVING EXPRESS CONDITIONS. [§ 21–22]

There are several issues that are unique to express conditions. There are addressed in this section. The issues unique to constructive conditions begin in § 21–43.

1. Express Conditions Are "Strictly Construed." [§ 21–23]

Courts "strictly construe" express conditions. This means, for express conditions precedent, that unless the condition **occurs completely and totally**, the duties subject to that condition will usually *never be enforceable*, no matter how insignificant the failure to fulfill it in its entirety seems. With regard to express conditions subsequent, the rule is similar: unless the condition is **completely and totally fulfilled**, the duties under the contract will *remain enforceable*. As will be discussed below, there are a few doctrines which excuse even express conditions, so that there are some exceptions to the strict

CONDITIONS, PERFORMANCE AND BREACH (WITH AN EMPHASIS ON COMMON LAW RULES)

construction rules [§§ 21–92 *et seq.*]. However, for the most part, the strict construction rule means that parties should enter into contracts with express conditions carefully, because their effects are significant and they will likely be enforced if the event occurs.

a. **Example of "Strict Construction" in an Express Condition Precedent. [§ 21–24]**

The parties agree that buyer will only have to accept delivery of goods and pay for them "on the condition they are delivered by 4:00 p.m. on October 1." The goods arrive at 4:05 p.m. on October 1. They are conforming goods, and the buyer has not been inconvenienced in the slightest by the five-minute delay. Nevertheless, because express conditions are "strictly enforced," buyer does not have to accept the goods or pay for them.

The rationale for the "strict construction" rule is that if the parties have gone to the trouble of inserting an express condition into their agreement, they must really mean it *literally*, and so a court will attempt to effectuate their intention.

Two points must be made. **First**, if the situation is too unfair, a court *might* be willing to excuse the failure to fulfill the condition under the "disproportionate forfeiture" rule [Restatement 2d § 229; § 21–107].

Second, contrast the "strict construction" rule of express conditions with the more relaxed rule regarding constructive conditions. For example, suppose the agreement just called for an unconditional duty that the goods were due at 4:00 p.m. on Oct. 1. Where an immaterial failure to perform, such as a five minute delay in the time called for in the agreement, it will ordinarily be classified only as an immaterial breach, and not excuse the performance of the other party, meaning the buyer would have to pay for the good [§§ 21–55 *et seq.*].

b. **Example of "Strict Construction" in Express Condition Subsequent. [§ 21–25]**

Let's return to the Bill/Sandra hypothetical in § 21–16 where Bill was to purchase Sandra's house "unless the Dow Jones Industrial Average has fallen to 7,500 points by June 1." If the DJA falls to 7,501, Bill remains obligated to purchase the home under the "strict construction" rule.

2. **Why a Party Would Make a Duty Expressly Conditional on the Happening of an Event. [§ 21–26]**

As detailed below in § 21–27, contractual duties can be structured to be expressly conditional or unconditional. The reason parties use conditions is that making a duty expressly conditional on the happening of an event shifts the risk of the non-occurrence of that event to the other party. This concept is more easily illustrated by example.

Let's use the Mary/John example in § 21–5 where John wants to purchase Mary's home. There are two ways John's contractual purchase obligation can be structured. If it was made unconditional, John would unconditionally bind himself to purchase Mary's home for $250,000. In that case, the risk of John not qualifying for a loan would be on him, for he will be obligated for the purchase price even if the loan doesn't come through.

However, if the deal is structured so that John will purchase Mary's house "on the condition that John is able to secure a loan for $200,000," the risk of John not qualifying for the loan is on Mary. That is, if John fails to get the loan, Mary will get nothing out of the transaction, as John's purchase obligation will never become enforceable.

3. **Issues Involved in Determining Whether a Contractual Obligation Is an Expressly Conditional Promise, an Unconditional Duty, or Both. [§ 21–27]**

Under Restatement 2d § 227, a contractual obligation can be structured:

(1) **As a conditional promise**;

(2) **As an unconditional duty**; or

(3) **As both a conditional promise and an unconditional duty**.

Important ramifications exist as to which of these structures applies. These are illustrated below.

a. **Example. [§ 21–28]**

A television station in California needs a special lens for one of its cameras. The lens is sold by a New York manufacturer and the seller is under a contractual obligation to deliver the lens by overnight messenger.

The three ways for the buyer and seller to structure the "messenger" provision are:

(1) **Scenario One:** They could agree that the manufacturer's delivery of the lens by overnight messenger was an express condition of the station's duties to accept and pay for the lens;

(2) **Scenario Two:** They could make the duty to use overnight messenger an unconditional duty of the seller; or

(3) **Scenario Three:** They could agree **both** that the manufacturer has a duty to deliver the lens by overnight messenger, **and** that the station's duty to accept and pay for the lens is expressly conditional on timely overnight delivery.

Assume the lens is shipped by regular mail, not overnight messenger, and arrives two days "late."

(1) In **Scenario One** described above, the station can walk away from the deal and simply reject the late delivery and not have to pay for the lens. This is because the condition necessary to make enforceable its obligation to accept and pay for the lens was never fulfilled. However, the station will not be able to sue for damages resulting from late delivery if it rejects the shipment. That is, because of the express condition, the contract means the parties agreed only that *if* the lens was timely delivered via overnight messenger, the station would be obligated to accept and pay for it.

(2) In **Scenario Two**, the station can sue for damages resulting from the delay in receiving the lens, for the manufacturer breached its unconditional duty to deliver via overnight messenger. That is, by structuring the manufacturer's obligation as a duty rather than a condition, the parties have set up a situation whereby the failure to carry out the promised duty can serve as the basis for damages arising from a breach of contract action. However, even though the lens is delivered late, the station may still have to live up to its promised duty to accept the lens and pay for it depending on whether manufacturer's breach is classified as material or not [*See* § 21–58 for a discussion of material breach].

(3) In **Scenario Three**, the station could reject the lens (for the condition to its duties to accept and pay for the lens was never fulfilled) **and** sue the manufacturer for breach of contract for any damages suffered as a result of the lens being tendered late, because the manufacturer breached its promised duty to deliver the lens via overnight messenger.

b. **How a Court Determines Whether an Obligation Is a Conditional Promise, an Unconditional Duty, or Both. [§ 21–29]**

The principal determinant in interpreting a contractual term is the intention of the parties. A court will examine the words used in the contract, the negotiating history of the parties, etc. in making that determination. However, when the intent of the

CHAPTER 21

parties is unclear as to whether an obligation is intended to be a conditional promise, an unconditional duty, or both, contract law has adopted the following presumptions to govern a court's interpretation of such terms.

(1) Interpretation That a Promise Is an Unconditional Duty, Rather than a Conditional Obligation, Is Favored When the Event Necessary to Fulfill the Condition Is Within the Obligee's Control. [§ 21–30]

If it is unclear whether a promise is intended as an unconditional duty or as a conditional obligation, it should be interpreted as a duty if the action necessary to fulfill the condition is within the obligee's control [Restatement 2d § 227(2)].

(a) Example. [§ 21–31]

In April, Jed enters into a contract with Alice's Pet Shop calling for the purchase of a pedigree beagle from a specified litter currently in Alice's shop. The contract does not specify which puppy is Jed's. Rather, in the sales agreement Jed promised that he would "select which puppy he wished to purchase from the litter before June 1." Jed does not select a puppy by June 1 and refuses to pay for a dog. Alice's sues, claiming breach of contract. Jed's defense is that selection of a puppy by June 1 was a condition precedent to his obligation to pay for the dog and, since the condition was never fulfilled, his duty never became enforceable.

Jed's promise to select the puppy will be interpreted as an unconditional duty on his part to do so, rather than as a condition to his duty to pay, for the selection of a puppy was an event within his (the obligee's) control. As Jed failed to perform an enforceable unconditional duty owed to Alice's, the pet store will prevail in the breach action [Restatement 2d § 227, Cmt. d, Ill. 9].

(2) Interpretation That Reduces Promisor's Risk of Forfeiture Is Preferred. [§ 21–32]

If it is unclear whether or not a duty is conditional, an interpretation that reduces the promisor's forfeiture risk is preferred [Restatement 2d § 227(1)].

(a) Example. [§ 21–33]

Subcontractor contracts with general contractor to do electrical work on a building. Under the contract, the general promises to pay the sub $70,000, "which shall be due five days after payment of general contractor by developer." If the developer does not pay the general contractor, the general will still have to pay the subcontractor $70,000 within a reasonable time if the subcontractor completes performance. The reason is that the payment term in the contract will be interpreted as setting forth an unconditional duty of the general contractor to pay the subcontractor $70,000 for acceptable work.

The "five days after payment of the general contractor by the developer" clause will be interpreted only as setting forth a suggested time for payment, rather than as a conditional promise making the developer's payment to the general contractor a condition precedent of the general's duty to pay the sub. This is because interpreting the term as a condition would shift the risk of the developer's non-payment, i.e., the risk of **forfeiting** all the electrical work for no payment to the subcontractor, and such an interpretation is disfavored [*See also* § 21–107 for a more detailed discussion of forfeiture].

(3) **When in Doubt, a Promise Should Be Interpreted as an Unconditional Duty Rather than a Conditional Promise. [§ 21–34]**

When in doubt, even in the absence of forfeiture or an event within the obligee's control, courts generally opt to interpret a provision as an unconditional duty rather than a conditional promise. There is no Restatement provision directing that result, but, since conditions are the unusual event, courts assume that, where ambiguous, an interpretation that the obligation is an unconditional duty is more likely to effectuate the parties' intent.

Hence, only when special language is used, e.g., "but only if," "subject to," "on the condition that," "provided that," "so long as," "unless," or "but not if," will a court deem a promise conditional. But in the absence of such special phraseology, most likely a contractual promise will simply be interpreted as setting forth an unconditional duty to perform.

(4) **Interpretation of a Term as Both a Duty and a Condition Is Very Unusual. [§ 21–35]**

To have a term to be construed both as conditioned on an event <u>and</u> establishing an enforceable duty is very, very unusual, and very special language must be used to bring that about. Something like, "Joe agrees to provide the service no later than Tuesday at 2:00 and acknowledges that if it is not provided on time, Melinda may reject the tendered service and sue for damages."

(5) Interpreting an "Ordinary" Promise as an Express Condition. [§ 21–36]

Finally, there are very few occasions in which the parties negotiating history reveals that a term that reads like a simple promise should be interpreted as an express condition. For example, suppose a buyer makes abundantly clear during negotiation that getting e-mail notice within 10 minutes after the goods have been shipped is so important to it that, without such notice, it doesn't want the goods. Even if the contract provides, "Seller to promptly inform buyer upon shipment," which reads like an unconditional duty, in light of the extreme importance of the notice requirement to the buyer as described above occurring during the contract negotiations, a court might *interpret* the notice obligation as a condition, and so the buyer would not have to accept the goods even, if promptly delivered, it did not get the required notice. This is because the "condition" making enforceable its duty to accept the goods was never fulfilled. But again, this is a highly unusual case.

4. Issues Involved with Specific Types of Express Conditions. [§ 21–37*]

Over time rules have developed with regard to specific types of express conditions. These are discussed below.

a. Express Conditions of Satisfaction. [§ 21–38]

A common clause in certain types of contracts makes payment conditional on the satisfaction of someone. The rules depend on who that "someone" is.

(1) Where Satisfaction Is Dependent upon the Subjective "Taste, Fancy, or Personal Judgment" of a Party to the Contract. [§ 21–39]

Some contracts have payment made expressly made conditional on the personal satisfaction of a party. For example, a tailor might make a contract in which final payment for a hand-made suit is made conditional on the personal satisfaction of the customer. Where the subject matter of the contract is something that reasonably is

---

* For more information, listen to CD # 9, Track 9 of *Sum and Substance Audio on Contracts*.

dependent upon the **subjective taste, fancy or personal judgment of the party**, the condition remains unfulfilled if the individual honestly and in good faith remains unsatisfied, even if a "reasonable" person would be satisfied with it [Restatement 2d § 228, Cmt. a; and Cmt. b, Ill. 4].

If the customer were to lie and say that he was dissatisfied when he, in fact, was highly pleased with the suit, it would be a breach of the covenant of good faith [Restatement 2d § 205; UCC § 1–304]. As such, a court would enforce the contract against the customer by excusing the condition on "wrongful prevention" grounds [*See* § 21–102 for a discussion of wrongful prevention].

(2) Where Satisfaction Is Dependent upon Objective "Market" Factors. [§ 21–40]

A typical provision in a commercial lease prevents subleasing without the approval of the landlord. In other words, the landlord must be "personally satisfied" with the sublessee before the sublease can effectively operate. In a commercial setting, the condition is satisfied if a **reasonable person** in the position of the landlord **would be satisfied**. Hence if the proffered sublessee has acceptable credit, a business history, etc., such that a similarly situated, hypothetical reasonable landlord would be satisfied with the sub-tenant, the condition is satisfied even if the particular landlord is honestly not personally satisfied, and withholds approval [Restatement 2d § 228, Cmt. b].

A similar rule applies to other situations in which the condition involves "objective," commercial standards as opposed to those involving personal taste.

(3) Where Satisfaction Is Dependent upon Satisfaction of a Third Party. [§ 21–41]

A common clause in certain types of construction contracts makes the contractor's payment expressly conditioned upon the approval of an engineer or architect. The majority rule is that the strict construction rule applies to these situations and if the named engineer or architect honestly and in good faith is not satisfied, then the condition is not fulfilled, even if a "reasonable" engineer or architect would be. The rationale is that if the contractor is willing to make its payment dependent upon an engineer's or architect's certificate of approval, the fact that the engineer or architect might not approve is a risk that the developer took at the time of contracting [Restatement 2d § 228, Cmt. b].

CHAPTER 21

There is a minority view which would apply reasonable commercial standards in these situations, so if a reasonable engineer or architect would be satisfied, then the condition will be deemed fulfilled even if the individual or firm named in the contract is not satisfied [*Nolan v. Whitney*, 88 N.Y. 648 (1882)].

Again, even under the majority view, the architect or engineer must act in good faith. So if the homeowner slips the architect a $100 bribe to not issue the "Architect's Certificate," meaning that the homeowner does not have to pay the contractor for certain work, such bad faith would allow the condition to be excused and the payment promised enforced on wrongful prevention grounds [See § 21–102 for a further discussion of wrongful prevention].

b. **"Pay-if-Paid" Clauses Interpreted as "Time of Payment" Clauses. [§ 21–42]**

A formerly common clause in contracts between general contractors and subcontractors provided that the general contractor's obligation to pay the subcontractor was expressly conditioned on the general contractor being paid by the homeowner or developer. The clause would read something like, "payment to subcontractor shall be due five days after payment of general contractor by developer [or homeowner]." Courts will not interpret these "pay-if-paid" clauses as imposing payment by the homeowner or developer as a condition to the general contractor's duty to pay the subcontractor. Some courts justify such a decision on the grounds that the condition should be excused by forfeiture [§ 21–107], while others simply refuse to enforce the payment clause as a condition as a matter of policy explaining that it was the general contractor, not the subcontractor, who signed the contract and thus the former bore the risk that the homeowner or developer would not pay. Many states have now enacted that rule by statute.

Instead of a condition, the clauses are now interpreted as indicating an estimated time of payment, i.e., in the clause above, the contractor would have to pay the subcontractor five days after the developer would be contractually obligated to pay the general contractor.

CONDITIONS, PERFORMANCE AND BREACH (WITH
AN EMPHASIS ON COMMON LAW RULES)

D. ISSUES ASSOCIATED WITH CONSTRUCTIVE CONDITIONS: PERFORMANCE AND BREACH. [§ 21–43*]

1. Role of Constructive Conditions. [§ 21–44]

As noted earlier, constructive conditions are equitable in nature and are conditions that are *implied* by contract law generally, or inserted by a court in a particular case, to regulate the performance duties under a contract [Restatement 2d § 226; § 21–8]. The **only** time constructive conditions have an effect is in a **bilateral contract** with **executory (unperformed) duties on both sides**. Hence, they have no effect in unilateral contracts, or when one party to a bilateral contract has already completed performance.

Constructive conditions have four basic uses:

(a) To allow a court to insert a term into a contract that a court believes is **necessary to carry out the intent of the parties** and to **make operation under a contract feasible** [§ 21–45];

(b) To regulate **tender of performance** and make duties enforceable when the parties' performance obligations under the contract can be accomplished simultaneously [§ 21–47];

(c) To regulate **order of performance** [§ 21–50]; and

(d) To regulate the **occurrence and consequence of immaterial, material, and total breach** [§ 21–55].

a. Constructive Conditions Necessary for Reasonable Operation Under a Contract. [§ 21–45]

One role of constructive conditions is to allow a court to insert a reasonable and equitable term into a contract when necessary to carry out the obvious intent of the parties or to make operation under a contract reasonably feasible.

(1) Example. [§ 21–46]

In a lease, a landlord is required to maintain the plumbing so as to make the apartment habitable and allows the tenant to withhold the rent if the plumbing falls below that standard. However, in the lease agreement, there is no express provision that allows the landlord to enter the leased premises during the lease term to repair any broken fixtures. A court will imply a condition that allows such access, and so the ability of the tenant to withhold the rent will be constructively conditioned on allowing landlord

---

* For more information, listen to CD # 9, Track 10 of *Sum and Substance Audio on Contracts*.

access to the apartment to make necessary repairs [*See also* §§ 21–8 and 21–9 for examples of constructive conditions].

b. **Concurrent Conditions of Exchange and Tender of Performance as a Constructive Condition. [§ 21–47]**

Sometimes performance duties under a bilateral contract with executory duties remaining can be performed simultaneously. For example, Harry contractually agrees to buy Draco's magic wand for $500, with the exchange to take place next Wednesday at 1:00 in Hufflepuff Room 300. At the time of contracting, they are in a bilateral contract, with executory duties that can be performed simultaneously next Wednesday at 1:00, i.e., Harry can hand over the money at the same time Draco gives up the wand.

Imagine the following scenarios:

Scenario One: Neither Harry nor Draco show up at Hufflepuff next Wednesday at 1:00.

Scenario Two: Both show up at the appointed time and place, but Harry says he won't show Draco the money until Draco shows him the wand; and Draco says he won't show Harry the wand until Harry shows Draco the money.

Scenario Three: Both show up at the appointed time and place, and Harry shows Draco he has the $500 and says, "I'm willing to proceed," but says he won't give the money to Draco until Draco shows him the wand. Draco says he has the wand, but refuses to show it to Harry until Harry gives him the money. When Harry does not hand over the money, Draco leaves without ever showing or delivering the wand to Harry.

Scenario Four: Both show up at the appointed time and place; Harry says he's ready to go forward and shows Draco the $500; Draco says he's ready to go forward and shows Harry the wand. However, when push comes to shove, neither party wants to be the first to actually hand over the cash or the wand, and both leave without exchanging the money for the wand.

Contract law uses the <u>constructive condition of tender</u> to resolve the legal status of the parties in these scenarios [Restatement 2d § 238].

Tender is defined and discussed below, and then applied to the resolution of the four scenarios listed above.

CONDITIONS, PERFORMANCE AND BREACH (WITH AN EMPHASIS ON COMMON LAW RULES)

(1) Tender: Defined and Discussed. [§ 21–48]

"Tender" is a constructive condition that is fulfilled by a party's **offer of performance** coupled with a **manifest present ability** to perform [Restatement 2d § 238]. Note that "tender" of performance is not actual performance of the promised duty under a contract. Rather, it is an *offer* of performance coupled with a *manifestation* of a present ability to do so.

Where some or all of the parties' performances under a contract are due simultaneously, **a constructive condition precedent to one party's duties under a contract is the tender of performance by the other** [Restatement 2d § 238].

It is important to understand what this means. In a bilateral contract with executory duties remaining and where the performance obligations are due simultaneously, at the time of the making of the contract *neither party's duties are enforceable*. This is because they are subject to the constructive condition of tender. Hence, in the hypothetical above, Harry's duty to pay Draco is subject to the constructive condition that Draco tender performance. Only after such tender of performance, which fulfills the constructive condition, does Harry's duty to pay become enforceable by Draco.

Similarly, at the time of the making of a contract, Harry has no enforceable right to the wand. Draco's duty to deliver becomes enforceable only if the constructive condition of tender is satisfied, and Harry tenders payment.

(2) Resolution of Scenarios. [§ 21–49]

Applying these rules to the four scenarios set forth above, the following results:

Scenario One: When neither party showed up, neither Harry nor Draco breached the contract and neither has a viable breach of contract claim against the other. This is because both of their duties were subject to the constructive condition of tender, and the constructive condition precedent was never fulfilled. In other words, neither owed the other an enforceable duty (even though they were in a valid contract) until the constructive condition was fulfilled, and in this scenario, neither party tendered performance, and so each party's condition remained unfulfilled.

Scenario Two: Where both show up but neither demonstrates a willingness to proceed to the other, the result is the same as Scenario One. That is, tender is more than showing up at the appointed time and place for exchange. There must be a **manifested willingness** and **ability** to perform. Since neither party did anything more than just stare at the other, there was no tender. As such, the constructive condition precedent that would make their performance obligations enforceable never occurred, and so the condition remained unfulfilled.

Scenario Three: Where both show up and Harry shows Draco the money and says he's willing to proceed, but Draco essentially does nothing, Harry's actions constitute tender of performance. That is he **manifested** a **willingness** ("I'm willing to proceed") and **ability** (showing Draco the cash) to perform. As such, Harry's tender fulfills the constructive condition, making Draco's delivery obligation enforceable. When Draco leaves without handing over the wand, he has breached the contract by failing to perform an enforceable duty, and Harry has a viable breach of contract action against Draco.

Scenario Four: Where both show up and tender performance, both parties performance obligations became enforceable under Restatement 2d § 234(1). So when they each walked away without performing, each breached the contract and can be validly sued by the other.

c. **Constructive Conditions Regulating the Order of Performance. [§ 21–50]**

Once duties are enforceable, the question becomes who has to perform first. This is known as the "order of performance." Contract law provides a different view depending on whether:

(a) performance of both parties can occur simultaneously [Restatement 2d § 234(1); § 21–51]; or

(b) performance of one duty takes time and the other does not [Restatement 2d § 234(2); § 21–52].

The rules for each circumstance are given below.

(1) **Order of Performance Where Simultaneous Exchange of Performance Is Possible. [§ 21–51]**

Once the duties under an executory contract become enforceable, i.e., once the other party has tendered performance: "[w]here all or part of the performances to be exchanged under an exchange of promises can be rendered simultaneously, they are to that extent due simultaneously" [Restatement 2d § 234(1)].

CONDITIONS, PERFORMANCE AND BREACH (WITH AN EMPHASIS ON COMMON LAW RULES)

Hence, once the constructive condition of tender has been fulfilled, then the parties are under an obligation to perform concurrently if that can be done. That is, there is a **concurrent condition of exchange**. In Scenario Four above with Harry and Draco, because each party tendered performance, thereby making their respective duties enforceable, and because the exchange of money for the wand can be done simultaneously, the rule of Restatement 2d § 234(1) provides that each must perform simultaneously.

Note that the rule of Restatement 2d § 234(1) is presumptive only, and if the language or circumstances indicate the parties intended a different order of performance, it is their intention that controls.

(2) Order of Performance Where One Party's Performance Will Take Time and the Other Does Not. [§ 21–52]

If performance of one party will take time and performance of the other will not, complete performance by the party whose performance will take time is a constructive condition of the performance of the party whose performance will not take time [Restatement 2d § 234(2)].

Once again, note that this rule is presumptive only and if the language of the agreement, or the circumstances of the parties, indicate they intended a different order of performance, then such intent will control.

(a) Example. [§ 21–53]

Holly has agreed to mow John's lawn for $25. Holly shows up on time, but refuses to start until she has been paid. Holly is in breach. This is because, since Holly's performance will take time to complete (mowing) while John's performance (paying) will not, John's obligation to pay is constructively conditioned on completion of Holly's performance under Restatement 2d § 234(2).

The rule has been criticized by some commentators who claim it is no more "fair" to make Holly complete performance before she gets paid (risking that John will not pay her) than it is to require John to pay first (risking that Holly will take the money and run).

CHAPTER 21

(b) Issues in the Order of Performance Rules Where a Simultaneous Exchange of Performance Is Not Possible. [§ 21–54]

There are two recurring issues in this type of situation, and contract law does not provide a clear resolution of either.

The first is whether, in regard to the Holly/John hypothetical in § 21–53, Holly's duty to mow the lawn constructively conditioned on John's <u>tender</u> of payment? That is, even if Holly has no right to be paid up front, can she at least demand that John show her the money and promise that he will give it to her upon completion, i.e., require John to tender, i.e., **manifest a willingness** and **ability** to pay before her mowing obligation becomes enforceable? Such a requirement seems equitable, but the tender rule of Restatement 2d § 238 only applies by its terms to situations where concurrent performance is possible. Likely, however, <u>tender</u> by John would be required to make Holly's duty enforceable, and then she would have to perform first in order to make John's duty to pay enforceable.

The second issue is what happens if <u>both</u> performances take time to complete, e.g., the contract is I'll wash your car if you mow my lawn? There is no real answer provided by the Restatement. One resolution would be to have performance by the party whose performance would take longer a condition of the other, but that has no more basis than to require both to begin at the same time.

d. Performance and Constructive Conditions' Role in Immaterial, Material and Total Breach. [§ 21–55*]

When a party fully and completely performs a contractual duty, the duty is said to be **discharged by performance** [Restatement 2d § 235(1)].

However, <u>any</u> lack of **full** and **complete** performance is considered a breach [Restatement 2d § 235(2)]. In this regard then, breach is a strict liability concept. That is, for purposes of determining whether there was a breach, it does not matter if the failure to perform was willful, negligent, innocent, or even as a result of a party sincerely and colorably believing that it was behaving correctly under the contract. If there is any failure

---

* For more information, listen to CD # 10, Track 1 of *Sum and Substance Audio on Contracts*.

CONDITIONS, PERFORMANCE AND BREACH (WITH AN EMPHASIS ON COMMON LAW RULES)

to perform fully and completely a duty that a court later considers enforceable, a breach has occurred.

For example, suppose Larry contracts to paint Maria's kitchen lemon yellow. Larry goes to the paint store, buys a can of lemon yellow paint, and completes the job. However, unknown to Larry, the paint manufacturer made a mistake and the color in the can was really canary yellow, not lemon. Even though Larry acted in good faith, and even though he was reasonable in believing he was fully performing, he has still breached the contract with Maria because he has not fully and completely performed an enforceable contractual promise.

There are **three** and only three types of breaches:

(a) immaterial (sometimes called "partial" or "minor") breaches;

(b) material (sometimes called "serious" breaches); and

(c) total breaches.

The definitions, consequences, and frameworks for determining which type of breach has occurred follow.

(1) Definitions of Immaterial, Material, and Total Breach. [§ 21–56]

The definitions of the different types of breaches are very technical. To make matters worse, while scholars tend to agree on the situations which constitute the different types of breaches, they differ on how to articulate their definitions.

(a) Immaterial Breach. [§ 21–57]

The Restatement does not define immaterial breach. Essentially its position is that immaterial breach is a "catch-all" whereby all breaches that are neither material nor total are immaterial ones.

Some scholars would define an immaterial breach as, **"the failure of a party to perform a duty due under a contract that results in the *excused* non-occurrence of a constructive condition of exchange."**

The gist of immaterial (or partial or minor) breach is that it is a breach that is not as serious as a material breach, and one in which the other party gets a substantial amount, but not all, of the performance he or she is due under a contract.

For example, assume Pat has agreed to install a swimming pool with a working pool light at Mary's home. Pat builds the pool perfectly, except he didn't install a light bulb in the pool light. There has been an immaterial breach because Mary has received a substantial amount, but not all, of the performance she is due under the contract.

(b) Material Breach. [§ 21–58]

Under the Restatement's definition, a material breach is "**an uncured material failure ... to render ... [a] performance due at an earlier time**" [Restatement 2d § 237].

Other scholars would define it as "**the failure to perform a duty due under a contract which results in the *unexcused* non-occurrence of a constructive condition of exchange.**"

As we will see, the gist of a material breach is that it is a serious breach, in which one party is deprived of all, or a substantial amount, of the performance he or she is due under a contract.

In the Pat/Mary pool example, suppose Pat shows up on the first day of construction, turns over a shovel full of dirt, and then quits for no reason. This would be a material breach because Mary has been deprived of a substantial amount of the performance she is due under the contract.

(c) Total Breach. [§ 21–59]

Under the Restatement, a total breach occurs when "a party's **uncured material failure** to render or to offer performance **discharges the other party's remaining duties**" [Restatement 2d § 242].

Although this puts it too simply, the idea is that, due to the passage of time, or some other factor, a material breach can "ripen" into a total breach. Once it becomes a total breach, then the contract is over and the remaining duties of the innocent party under it are terminated or discharged [*See* §§ 21–81 *et seq.* for a fuller explanation of total breach].

In the Pat/Mary pool example, as discussed above, if Pat only digs a shovel full of dirt and then walks out, a material breach has occurred. As will be explained below [§ 21–60], at that point Mary is entitled to

CONDITIONS, PERFORMANCE AND BREACH (WITH AN EMPHASIS ON COMMON LAW RULES)

suspend, but not terminate, her duties under the contract. Pat's departure is not yet a total breach because, e.g., Pat could decide after an hour that he was wrong and come back to finish the job. All things being equal, if Pat offered to come back, he would probably be entitled to do so, but he would have to pay for any damage caused by the one-hour delay and the one-hour delay would be deemed an immaterial breach. However, if after a few days Pat does not come back (passage of time), or the parties take some other specified action [§§ 21–82 *et seq.*] the material breach becomes a total breach. At this point, the contract is over and Mary's duty to pay Pat is discharged or terminated [*See* § 21–65 for a further discussion of material breach].

Note that when a party is in "material breach," it is somewhat of a temporary situation. Either the material breach will become a total breach, and the duties of the innocent party will be discharged, or the material breach will become fixed or "cured," and the material breach will become an immaterial one.

Obviously, by themselves, these definitions do not explain all the ramifications of the breach doctrine. In the following sections, the definitions are applied so that their significance can be appreciated.

(2) Consequences of Deciding That a Breach Is Immaterial, Material, or Total. [§ 21–60]

If you understand the consequences of declaring a breach to be immaterial, material, or total, you will have a big leg up in understanding breach. The most important effects of deciding what kind of a breach it is are:

1. **Upon an *immaterial* breach, the non-breaching or innocent party *must* continue to perform or itself be in breach.** That is, the non-breaching party cannot suspend, or otherwise cease, performance without incurring liability when the breaching party has only *immaterially or partially* breached the agreement. Of course, the non-breaching party can sue for damages as a result of the immaterial breach, but must continue his or her performance as well.

In the Pat/Mary pool example where Pat didn't put in the light bulb, Mary cannot suspend her obligation to pay Pat $25,000 for the pool as called for in the contract. She must pay Pat what he is owed, although because Pat breached,

Mary is entitled to offset what she owes him by the damage caused from the failure to install the bulb. But the point is, even though she is the innocent or non-breaching party, she cannot suspend or terminate her payment obligations under the contract upon only an immaterial breach by Pat.

2. **Upon a material breach, the non-breaching party is entitled immediately to *suspend* his, her, or its duties under the contract without liability.**

In the Pat/Mary pool example where Pat walks off after digging only one shovel full of dirt, Mary's performance obligations (her duty to pay Pat) are immediately suspended. Thus, even if she had to make a progress payment of $100 after the first day, she could suspend that obligation in light of Pat's material breach. This is her right in addition to being able to sue Pat for damages.

3. **Once the material breach becomes a total breach, the contractual obligations of the non-breaching party are terminated.**

Hence in the Pat/Mary pool example, once Pat stays away long enough or one of the other actions occurs that transforms the material breach into a total breach, any remaining payment obligations of Mary under the contract are terminated, and she can sue for any damages suffered as a result of the breach. (Note, however, that sometimes a breaching party can obtain restitution from the innocent party [*see* Chapter Thirty-One for a discussion of Restitution]. Even if that might be true in this situation, the point here is that Mary's payment obligations under the contract are terminated, regardless whether there might be restitutionary recovery).

It is worth emphasizing that no matter what kind of breach, the non-breaching party has the right to sue the breaching party for damages. That's true whether the breach is immaterial, material, or total. For purposes of the breach doctrine, the crucial thing is that the non-breaching party in an *immaterial* breach situation **must go forward with his or her duties under the contract** or find himself or herself in breach. When the breach is *material,* in ***addition*** **to the right to collect damages from the breacher**, the non-breaching party is **also entitled to suspend performance**; and when the breach is *total*, in ***addition*** **to the right to collect damages from the breacher, the non-breaching party's duties are discharged.**

CONDITIONS, PERFORMANCE AND BREACH (WITH AN EMPHASIS ON COMMON LAW RULES)

(3) Role of Constructive Conditions in Determining the Consequences of Material and Immaterial Breach. [§ 21–61]

At this point you may be wondering what role constructive conditions play in the breach doctrine. Contract law uses constructive conditions to achieve the results and consequences set forth in the previous section. It does this by implying a condition whereby one party's duties under a contract are constructively conditioned on there not being a material breach by the other. In § 237, the Restatement 2d phrases this concept as follows:

> [I]t is a condition of each party's remaining duties to render performances to be exchanged under an exchange of promises that there be no uncured material failure by the other party to render any such performance due at an earlier time.

This is a **constructive condition subsequent**. That is, a party in a viable contract is under an enforceable duty to perform <u>unless</u> an event—material breach by the other—occurs, at which point the remaining duties are unenforceable if the non-breaching party chooses to suspend them.

Using the Pat/Mary pool example, we would say that Mary's duty to pay is constructively conditioned upon there being no material breach by Pat. So if there is only immaterial breach, Mary's payment obligations are enforceable. However, once Pat has committed a material breach, the condition is fulfilled and Mary's payment duties under the contract become unenforceable for a period of time and, if the breach becomes total, the duties become entirely discharged.

Alternatively, we could say Mary's duty to pay is conditioned on there not being an unexcused failure of Pat to fulfill a constructive condition, i.e., the condition that he not be in breach [§§ 21–58, 21–65]. When there is only an immaterial breach, we "excuse" the condition, and Mary's duties remain enforceable. When the breach is material, we regard it as an "unexcused" failure to fulfill the condition, and Mary's duties are thus suspended.

CHAPTER 21

(4) The Only Situation in Which the Materiality of the Breach Matters: Bilateral Contracts in Which There Are Executory Duties Remaining on Both Sides at the Time of the Breach. [§ 21–62]

As noted earlier [§ 21–44], the only time constructive conditions are relevant is when there are remaining duties for both parties under a bilateral contract. This is worth emphasizing with regard to material and immaterial breaches.

There are many instances in which it is irrelevant whether a breach is "material" or "immaterial." In these cases, a breach is just a breach. The only time it matters whether it is material or not is when the parties have entered into a bilateral contract, and there are unperformed duties remaining on the side of the innocent, non-breaching party at the time of the breach.

This idea is illustrated in the following sections.

(a) The Doctrine of Material/Immaterial Breach Does Not Apply to Unilateral Contracts. [§ 21–63]

The concept of a breach being material or immaterial, as opposed to just being a breach, has no relevance whatsoever in unilateral contract situations. This is because the only purpose of labeling a breach material is to allow the non-breaching party a way to suspend and ultimately terminate his or her duties under a contract without such action constituting a breach itself. In a unilateral contract, the contract is not formed until the offeree has completed performance for that is the only way an offer for a unilateral contract can be accepted [§ 4–80].

For example, in the Pat/Mary pool example, suppose Mary makes an offer for a unilateral contract to Pat, promising to pay him $25,000 "upon completion of the pool." Assume that Pat completely finishes building the pool, thereby accepting Mary's offer to enter into a unilateral contract and completing the contract. Assume also that Mary refuses to pay him. At this point her refusal to pay is simply a breach for which he can collect damages.

Because Pat has already performed, any question as to whether or not he can suspend performance is irrelevant at that point. This is because the non-breaching party only cares about a "material" breach finding when he or she has duties yet to be performed. That is, with a material breach, the non-breacher need not perform such executory duties, but with an immaterial breach, he or she must perform them or be in breach himself or herself. Here, Pat does not need the protection of a material breach finding, entitling him to cease further performance, because, by definition, he has already finished performing. He just sues for breach.

Also, if Pat just walks off the job, Mary doesn't need the protections of the "material" breach doctrine because, by walking off, Pat has indicated an unwillingness to accept Mary's offer, so they have no contract. So Mary's payment obligations do not need to be "suspended." She has no payment obligations because her unilateral contract offer was never accepted.

(b) The Doctrine of Material/Immaterial Breach Does Not Apply to Bilateral Contracts When All the Duties of One Party Have Been Completely Performed. [§ 21–64]

If one party fully completes all duties required under a bilateral contract, and the other party then breaches, once again it is irrelevant whether that breach is material or immaterial.

Returning to the Pat/Mary swimming pool problem where the parties have this time entered into a bilateral contract, assume Pat has completely and seasonably built the pool, but Mary refuses to pay him. It is irrelevant whether Mary's actions are classified as an immaterial or a material breach because there are no remaining duties left owing by Pat that need to be made subject to an implied condition that Mary pay in order to protect Pat's rights. Rather, Mary's failure to pay is simply classified as a "breach," for which Pat could recover damages.

Note that if there were supposed to be **progress payments**, e.g., where Pat was to get one-half the money when the hole was dug, and the remainder upon completing the pool, and Mary refused to pay half the money when Pat finished digging the hole, then it would matter that her failure to pay is a "material" breach. It would matter because if it were material, Pat would not have to continue working on the pool and could suspend his performance obligations. In other words, to protect his rights in such a case it is important that the implied condition that accompanies a material breach be imposed [§§ 30–32 *et seq.*].

(5) **How to Determine Whether a Breach Is Material or Immaterial. [§ 21–65]**

Obviously, there is an enormous difference to the parties between classifying a breach of a bilateral contract with executory duties on both sides as material or immaterial. As a common-sense rule of thumb, if the breach is serious enough so that it would be unjust to require the innocent, non-breaching party to perform, it is material. Conversely if the breach is minor enough so that it would be unjust to the breaching party to have him or her walk away with nothing under the contract, the breach is immaterial. However, of course, contract law makes it more complicated.

In deciding whether a particular breach results in an unexcused failure of a constructive condition, i.e., whether a material breach has occurred, Restatement 2d § 241 states that the following factors need to be weighed:

(a) The extent to which the non-breaching party will be **deprived of the reasonably expected benefit of his or her bargain**;

(b) The extent to which the non-breaching party can be **fully compensated** for the breach if made to stay in the contract and complete performance;

(c) The extent to which the breaching party will **suffer a forfeiture** if the breach is declared material and the non-breaching party need not perform under the contract;

(d) The likelihood the breaching party will **cure his or her failure**; and

(e) The extent to which the breaching party **performed within the standards of good faith and fair dealing**.

Applied to the Pat/Mary pool example, these factors would have the following effects:

(a) Where Pat simply walked off after turning one shovel full of dirt, Mary was severely deprived of the expected benefit under the contract, which argues for a material breach;

CONDITIONS, PERFORMANCE AND BREACH (WITH AN EMPHASIS ON COMMON LAW RULES)

(b) Let's say that Mary needed the pool built by a particular date for an important party she was hosting for her clients, and that date was coming soon. Assume Pat walked off the job with much of the work done, but there were still some issues with the decking to be dealt with. It would be difficult for Mary to find another pool builder who would be willing to work only on the decking problems. If it were declared an immaterial breach, Mary could sue Pat for damages, but the value to her business of her clients being disappointed by an unfinished pool would be hard to calculate with any certainty. However, if the breach was considered material, she would have a better chance of obtaining specific performance, forcing Pat to finish the pool in time for the party, since specific performance is generally granted only if the breach were material.

(c) In the situation in which the only breach was Pat's failure to install the light bulb, if the breach were material, Pat would forfeit payment for all the other work on the pool under the contract. Hence, this situation would argue for the breach to be considered immaterial.

(d) The more likely Pat is to come back and finish the pool after walking off ("curing" his breach) the more likely his breach will be considered immaterial [*See* § 21–77 for a further discussion of cure];

(e) if Pat willfully breached in order to get back at Mary in retribution for some perceived, unrelated slight, Pat would have breached the obligations of good faith [Restatement 2d § 205], and in that circumstance he would be likely be found to have committed a material breach.

(6) The "First" Material Breach Doctrine. [§ 21–66]

Occasionally, contracting parties will find themselves in a situation where each party accuses the other of material breach, each suspends performance, and eventually claims the other is liable for total breach. Contract law solves this dilemma such that **upon the first material breach**, the first non-breaching party's duties under the contract are suspended. However, if the first party's breach is only immaterial, then the other party must perform or be in material breach.

Note that this obviously puts a lot of pressure on the non-breaching party (or more likely the non-breaching party's lawyer). That is, if the non-breaching party believes the other's breach to be material, probably that party will suspend performance thereafter. However, if the assumption was wrong, and the breach will ultimately be deemed immaterial, then the original non-breaching party's subsequent failure to perform will itself be a material breach, and the original (immaterially) breaching party may now cease further performance.

(a) Example. [§ 21–67]

> Desmond hires Kathleen to paint his house for $2,000, with $1,000 due to be paid when the front of the house is completed. Kathleen paints most of the front, but does not do some of the trim. Desmond refuses to pay her the $1,000, claiming he is entitled to suspend performance due to her material breach.
>
> If Desmond turns out to be right, he is indeed entitled to suspend performance and withhold payment of the $1,000 without breaching the contract. However, if Desmond is wrong and Kathleen's breach is deemed to be only immaterial, then it is Desmond who will be in material breach by not paying the $1,000, and Kathleen need not finish painting the remainder of the house and can sue her for breach.
>
> Hence, under the first material breach doctrine, Desmond must weigh carefully the adverse consequences of his being wrong in characterizing her breach as material, for if it is not, it will be Desmond, not Kathleen, who will be judged in material breach.

(7) The Substantial Performance Doctrine: Classic Application of the Immaterial Breach Doctrine. [§ 21–68]

The substantial performance doctrine provides that so long as a party has "substantially performed" a duty under a contract, any discrepancy between the actual performance and the promised performance will be deemed an immaterial breach. Thus, the substantial performance doctrine can be thought of as a specialized application of the general immaterial breach doctrine.

It says that when there has been "substantial performance" (as opposed to full and complete performance) of the duties owed by the breaching party, the breach involved is only an

CONDITIONS, PERFORMANCE AND BREACH (WITH AN EMPHASIS ON COMMON LAW RULES)

immaterial one. In theory, analysis under the substantial performance doctrine could be applied to every breach of bilateral contract with unperformed duties remaining on both sides. In practice, however, it is often applied to breaches of contracts involving services, especially those dealing with construction contracts and where there is "economic waste," i.e., where the defect is small and where the costs of repair are relatively great [Restatement 2d § 237, Cmt. d].

(a) How to Determine Whether a Promise Has Been Substantially Performed. [§ 21–69]

The most important factors to be weighed in determining whether a party has substantially performed are:

(1) How much of the reasonably expected benefit under the contract has the non-breaching party received under the contract at the time of the breach;

(2) How great of a forfeiture will the breaching party suffer if the breach is deemed material;

(3) How completely will damages alone compensate the non-breaching party;

(4) The good or bad faith of the breaching party; and

(5) How likely is it that rectifying the breach will result in "economic waste," rather than actually providing a benefit for the non-breaching party [*See* § 21–68 for a further discussion of economic waste].

SPECIAL CASE SQUIB

(b) *Jacob & Youngs v. Kent.* [§ 21–70*]

Kent entered into a contract with Jacob & Youngs, a general contractor, to construct a vacation house on Kent's property. The contract specified that all plumbing in the home was to be with "Reading" galvanized pipe, i.e., pipe made by the Reading Company. Through oversight, the pipe actually used in approximately sixty percent of the home was that of another manufacturer, Cohoes.

The substituted Cohoes pipe was of equal quality and price as Reading pipe. Further, by the time the inadvertent breach was discovered, most of the pipe

---

* For more information about this case, listen to CD # 10, Track 1 of *Sum and Substance Audio on Contracts*.

had been installed and was concealed within the walls of the house.

Nevertheless, Kent's argument was that the contractor had to rip out the walls and relay the Reading pipe, or Kent would not have to make the remaining progress payment due under the contract. In other words, Kent's argument was that if Jacob & Youngs did not fully perform the Reading pipe promise, the contractor would be in material breach, thereby suspending and ultimately discharging Kent's duty to make the remaining payment due under the contract.

Held: The inadvertent use of the wrong pipe by Jacob & Youngs only amounted to an immaterial breach under the substantial performance doctrine. That is, because the contractor "substantially performed" its duties, the breach it committed was only an immaterial one.

Note the court did not say there was no breach. There was. Kent did not receive full and complete performance of the Reading pipe promise by Jacob & Youngs. As such, Kent could sue for any damage he might have suffered as a result of the wrong pipe being installed (which admittedly in this instance would likely be nothing). However, because performance was substantial and the breach was thus immaterial, Kent was not excused from performing his remaining duties of payment under the contract.

As Justice Cardozo put it, "The courts never say that one who makes a contract fills the measure of his duty by less than full performance" (hence, Jacob & Youngs was liable for breach). "They do say, however, that an omission, both trivial and innocent, will sometimes be atoned for by allowance of the resulting damage, and will not always be the breach of a condition to be followed by forfeiture" (hence, the breach is an immaterial one). [*Jacob & Youngs v. Kent,* 230 N.Y. 239, 129 N.E. 889 (1921)].

An analysis of the factors set forth in § 21–69 yields the same result. That is, the substantial performance doctrine applies here to make the breach an immaterial one because:

(1) Kent had received substantially all the benefit he could reasonably expect under the contract; i.e., he got

CONDITIONS, PERFORMANCE AND BREACH (WITH AN EMPHASIS ON COMMON LAW RULES)

a completed house for the price stated, with an equivalent quality of pipe throughout;

(2) To have the breach declared material would result in an unfair forfeiture to Jacob & Youngs, i.e., to deny the company the last payment under the contract for an inadvertent mistake that resulted in no objective detriment to Kent would be unjust;

(3) Damages could compensate Kent for any harm he might have suffered due to the breach;

(4) The breach was inadvertent, and thus was a "good faith" breach; and

(5) Having the breach declared material would result in economic waste, i.e., it would cost Jacob & Youngs a huge amount of money to rip out the walls and relay the pipe, with no corresponding benefit to Kent for doing so. Thus, any money spent remedying the breach (as opposed to paying for damages resulting from the breach) would be an economic waste. (Indeed, many have speculated that when Kent sued, he really was not all that concerned about having the Reading pipe installed. Rather, he just wanted leverage to get Jacob & Youngs to reduce its price on the house by foregoing the last progress payment. That is, if it would have cost Jacob & Youngs $5,000 to rip out the dry wall and relay Reading pipe, Kent would simply have offered to keep the pipe that was already in place if Jacobs & Young would agree to waive the last $3,000 progress payment.) [See § 30–32 for further discussion of economic waste].

Note that Justice Cardozo held open the possibility that breach of the Reading pipe promise could, in a particular fact setting, be a material breach. For example, if Kent were the owner of Reading Pipe Co. it might be sufficiently important to him to have his company's pipe installed so that a breach of the promise would be material. However, Justice Cardozo also cautioned that if the Reading brand pipe really was so important, Kent could have made the final payment expressly conditioned on use of that kind of pipe. Under the "strict construction" rule [see § 21–23], the court would have an easier time enforcing an expressly conditional promise and allowing Kent to forego the last payment [*But see* the discussion on forfeitures, § 20–109]. However, in the absence of an express condition, or other facts which might plausibly indicate the importance of the particular brand (as opposed to the particular quality) of the pipe, Jacob & Youngs substantially performed, and thus were liable for only an immaterial breach.

Finally, Justice Cardozo emphasized that the breach here was inadvertent, and that if the contractor had purposely installed Cohoes pipe because he thought it was just as good and had it lying around, he might not be as willing to find substantial performance.

(c) Example. [§ 21–71]

Bert contracted with Amy to paint Bert's living room "Robin's Egg Blue" so as to complement, in a precise way, Bert's couch and chairs. Amy knew of the importance of the color. Through inadvertence, Amy paints the room in "Sky Blue." The colors are similar and the actual paint job is well done, but Bert is unhappy with the "Sky Blue" because he feels it genuinely contrasts with, rather than complements, his furniture. In this case Amy's breach is a material one as the substantial performance doctrine does not apply. This can be seen again by using the factors given in § 21–69:

(1) Bert has *not* received substantially all the benefits he reasonably expected under the contract, for the walls clash with the furniture;

(2) While it is true that Amy will have done a lot of work without benefit under the contract if the breach is declared material, it is also true that such action is **not** an *unfair forfeiture,* given that she has failed to provide many of the benefits Bert bargained for under the contract;

(3) Simply paying Bert for the discrepancy in colors, i.e., giving him the difference, if any, between the cost of painting the room with Robin's Egg Blue paint versus painting it with Sky Blue paint, will not adequately compensate Bert for the loss of bargain Amy's breach occasioned;

(4) While Amy's breach may have been in good faith, this factor alone is not determinative; and

(5) Repainting the room, i.e., rectifying the breach, will not result in economic waste. This is because while it will cost Amy some time and effort to repaint the

CONDITIONS, PERFORMANCE AND BREACH (WITH AN EMPHASIS ON COMMON LAW RULES)

room, Bert will reap a corresponding benefit from such efforts.

(8) Doctrines That "Transform" Material Breaches into Immaterial Breaches. [§ 21–72*]

As noted above, a material breach does not last forever. Either action is taken that transforms it into an immaterial one (or at least some duties under the contract will still be made enforceable), or it "ripens" into a total breach and all executory duties are terminated. The actions that can transform a material breach into an immaterial breach (or at least to allow some duties still to be enforced even after a serious breach) are discussed in this section. How a material breach ripens into a total breach is discussed beginning in § 21–82.

There are three doctrines that, when applicable, transform a material breach into an immaterial one, or at least allow some part of the contract to be enforced even after a serious breach:

(1) **Divisibility**, or **part performance** [§ 21–73];

(2) **Cure** [§ 21–77]; and

(3) **Waiver** [§ 21–79].

Each is discussed below.

(a) The Divisibility (or Part Performance) Doctrine. [§ 21–73]

Courts are empowered to "save" contracts in some circumstances and prevent the termination of all duties under a contract even in the face of a serious breach.

One way a court can accomplish this is through "divisibility" whereby a court finds that some duties under a contract are still enforceable even though there has been a material breach as to the remainder. Hence it will require the innocent party to partially perform under the contract.

---

* For more information, listen to CD # 10, Track 2 of *Sum and Substance Audio on Contracts*.

CHAPTER 21

(i) Requirements for Applying the Divisibility Doctrine. [§ 21-74]

According to the Restatement 2d, a court will declare a contract divisible upon a material breach whenever it is possible:

(1) to **apportion the agreement into corresponding pairs of part performances**; and

(2) to regard the parts of each pair as **agreed equivalents** [Restatement 2d § 240].

(b) Example. [§ 21-75]

Norma purchases three separate framed posters from Leroy's Art Shop. The posters are $150 each and are to be delivered next Thursday. On Thursday, Leroy's delivers only one of the posters and refuses to deliver the other two.

Arguably there has been a material breach of the entire contract, as Norma has not received two-thirds of the value she legitimately expected to receive. However, if the contract is divisible—and likely it is—then a court can "save" part of it whereby Norma is obligated to accept and pay for the one poster that was delivered.

The contract is likely divisible because it is **possible to apportion the agreement into three separate pairs of part performances**, i.e., the performance of 3 separate $150 payments in exchange for each poster. And payment of $150 for the poster she received is an **agreed equivalent** once the part performances are segregated into three separate acts.

Of course, Norma does not have to pay for the two posters that were not delivered, and may in addition sue for any damages she suffers as a result of the store's failure to deliver the two posters. However, if divisibility applies, she must pay for the one poster she got and cannot suspend her performance for that one claiming a material breach of the whole.

(c) Example. [§ 21-76]

Same facts as above, except the three posters together make a triptych. Norma is not obligated to accept and pay for the one that was delivered, for the contract is not divisible. That is, it is impossible to separate the

CONDITIONS, PERFORMANCE AND BREACH (WITH AN EMPHASIS ON COMMON LAW RULES)

agreement into pairs of part performances, even if each panel was separately priced. In effect, Norma bought one triptych, not three posters, and so delivery of only one part is a material breach of the whole.

(d) Cure. [§ 21–77]

Cure is the name given to the acts of a breaching party to correct or ameliorate a breach, thereby transforming what would be a material breach into an immaterial one. For example, a homeowner is scheduled to make a $10,000 progress payment to a contractor by 5:00 p.m. on Tuesday and fails to do so. The failure to make a progress payment is generally considered a material breach and at that point, contractor can suspend performance. Now, assume homeowner tenders a $10,000 check by 9:00 a.m. the next day. So long as the material breach has not turned into a total breach by that time, the homeowner has the ability to fix or "cure" the material breach, thus transforming it into an immaterial one. Hence while the contractor may sue for any damages resulting from the sixteen-hour delay in getting the check (because there still was a breach, even if it was immaterial), the contractor must also continue performance after the check's tender or be in breach itself.

(i) Breaching Party Has a *Right* to Cure Until the Breach Becomes Total. [§ 21–78]

A breaching party has a **right** to cure until the breach becomes total. That is, if the breaching party tenders a cure before a material breach becomes total, then the non-breaching party **must** accept the cure and must, thereafter, timely perform any remaining duties under the contract or the initial non-breaching party himself or herself will be in breach.

Cure is an important remedy in UCC contracts, and is discussed in that context extensively beginning in § 22–12.

(e) Waiver. [§ 21–79]

A non-breaching party may waive (excuse) a material breach, thereby transforming the breach into a partial one.

CHAPTER 21

(i) Example. [§ 21–80]

Landscaper is to mow Owner's lawn weekly for a year under a written contract. Landscaper does not show up for the first three weeks, and Owner hired someone else to mow the lawn for those weeks. If Landscaper's failure to show the first three weeks is a material breach, which it likely is, Owner's duties under the contract are suspended, meaning she does not have to allow, or pay for, Landscaper to mow the lawn during the remainder of the contract.

However, if Landscaper shows up the fourth week, and Owner wished to continue with Landscaper for the remainder of the contract, she can do so by "waiving" the material breach, and electing to treat it as an immaterial one. In that circumstance, Landscaper is still liable for whatever damages Owner has suffered by virtue of hiring someone else to mow the lawn those first three weeks, but Owner has chosen to waive her rights to declare the contract over and hence must proceed as if Landscaper has only immaterially breached the contract.

(9) Total Breach. [§ 21–81*]

This section deals with the different ways a total breach can be declared. There are two:

(a) A material breach can "ripen" into total breach [Restatement 2d §§ 242, 243]; or

(b) An immaterial breach, accompanied or followed by a repudiation of future performance, also becomes a total breach in most instances [Restatement 2d § 243(2)].

(a) How a Material Breach Becomes a Total Breach. [§ 21–82]

Before the process by which a material breach becomes a total one is discussed, it is important to recall the difference between the two. Under a material breach, the non-breaching party is justified in immediately suspending performance, but his or her performance duties are not terminated or discharged. It is only

---

* For more information, listen to CD # 10, Track 1 of *Sum and Substance Audio on Contracts*.

CONDITIONS, PERFORMANCE AND BREACH (WITH AN EMPHASIS ON COMMON LAW RULES)

when the material breach becomes a total breach are the remaining duties under a contract discharged. [Restatement 2d §§ 242, 243].

Usually a material breach becomes a total one through the passage of time. That is, one party fails to perform and the other suspends performance. If there is no cure by the breaching party or waiver by the innocent one, after the expiration of a reasonable period of time, the material breach becomes a total breach.

(i) How to Determine What Is "a Reasonable Time" for Purposes of Transforming a Material Breach into a Total Breach. [§ 21–83]

There are no hard and fast rules regarding how much time needs to elapse before an uncured and unexcused material breach becomes a total one. The idea is that the more serious the breach, the more likely it was done intentionally, the more unlikely it is that substitute performance can be quickly found for the non-breaching party, etc., the shorter the time period between material and total breach.

Sometimes material and total breaches occur simultaneously. This is usually when prompt performance is key, and so any delay in performance by the breaching party means the innocent party would get no benefit from delayed performance [Restatement 2d § 243(4)].

While the breach is material, the breaching party can "cure" it or take some other action to make it into an immaterial one [§ 21–77]. Once the breach is total, however, the breach cannot be "cured" and the remaining duties become discharged.

According to Restatement 2d § 242, the following factors should be examined in determining the length of time before a material breach turns into a total one:

(1) The extent to which the non-breaching party will be deprived of the benefit of the bargain reasonably expected under the contract;

(2) The extent to which the non-breaching party can be adequately compensated for any losses suffered before the breach is declared total;

(3) The extent to which the breaching party will suffer forfeiture if the breach is declared total;

(4) The good or bad faith of the breaching party;

(5) The likelihood of cure by the breaching party;

(6) The extent to which any further delay will prevent or hinder the non-breaching party from making substitute arrangements; and

(7) The extent to which prompt performance is part of the bargain of the parties.

(b) Example. [§ 21–84]

Ent Co. purchased a dilapidated Amusement Park and had plans to renovate it. Ent Co. entered into a contract with Fix-It Corp. to do much of the renovation. Under the contract, Fix-It was to start work on March 1 and have the park in working order by the following February 1. No one from Fix-It showed up for work on March 1. At this point Fix-It has probably committed a material breach, and Ent Co.'s duty of payment is suspended.

The next day, the president of Fix-It calls Ent Co. and says that he wasn't going to send people to the construction site, but when he slept on it, he had a change of heart. He says that Fix-It is now willing to perform under the contract, and that Fix-It will have its employees work overtime at Fix-It's expense to make up for the one-day delay. Given the nature of the contract, its length, and the ability of Ent Co. to receive its bargained for benefits under the contract given Fix-It's proposed "cure" for its material breach, probably a "reasonable time" has not yet passed, and Fix-It's material breach has not been transformed into a total one. Thus, at that point, Ent Co.'s duties have not been discharged, and it must allow Fix-It to do the work and pay Fix-It the contract price for the job or Ent. Co will be the party in breach.

(c) Example. [§ 21–85]

Sports Arena enters into a contract with Clean-Up, a janitorial service, whereby Clean-Up promises to clean the arena after a Saturday night basketball game to get the arena ready for a Sunday afternoon rock concert. On Saturday evening, just after the basketball game, the general manager of Clean-Up calls up the director of Sports Arena and says that Clean-Up will not send any employees to clean up the arena. At this point there is probably a simultaneous material and total breach given the nature of the contract, the fact that Sports Arena would be hindered in its ability to secure a replacement if the breach is not deemed total, etc. In other words, under these circumstances, the "reasonable time" given before the material breach ripens into a total breach is no time at all, and Sports Arena is entitled to treat the contract as terminated as soon the phone call was made.

(d) **Effect of "Time Is of the Essence" Clauses. [§ 21–86]**

The seventh factor listed in Restatement 2d § 242 and discussed in § 21–83 deals, in part, with "time is of the essence" clauses. When these clauses are negotiated as part of the dickered (i.e., bargained) terms agreed to in a contract, they carry a substantial evidentiary weight. As a consequence a viable "time is of the essence" clause makes what would otherwise be an immaterial breach (capable of being cured) simultaneously into a total breach, which ends the contract.

On the other hand, if the clause is part of the pre-printed standard boilerplate language in a contract, it is likely not to carry much evidentiary weight, and there would still be a reasonable period of time before a material breach became total.

(e) **Total Breach Found upon Immaterial Breach Accompanied or Followed by a Repudiation. [§ 21–87]**

Under Restatement 2d § 243(2), **a total breach occurs upon either a material of an immaterial breach accompanied or followed by a repudiation of any further willingness or ability to further perform under the contract by the breaching party.**

There is often much confusion between this doctrine and the doctrine of anticipatory repudiation [Chapter Twenty-Three]. Such confusion is understandable, but the two concepts are quite distinct. For a repudiation to turn a breach into a total one, the repudiation must either **accompany or follow** the breach, i.e., the breaching party must have failed to perform a duty that was due under the contract, and later send a repudiation either simultaneously with, or after, the breach indicating the party will no longer perform under the contract.

In an *anticipatory repudiation* situation, the injured party gets a right to sue because of a repudiation made **before** performance is due. Further, for an *anticipatory* repudiation to be effective, the repudiated duty must be material, i.e., its non-performance must give rise to a material breach if it ultimately were not performed. In the rule given in this section, a simultaneous or subsequent repudiation turns a **partial** breach into a total one.

(i) Example. [§ 21-88]

Jill agrees to pay Lon $5,000 to paint her house, including the trim. Lon painted most of the house professionally but did not paint the rain gutters. Nevertheless, he submitted a bill for the full $5,000. Typically, the failure to paint the rain gutters would likely be considered only an immaterial breach. However, if such action is accompanied by a repudiation, i.e., a declaration by Lon that he refuses to paint the gutters as promised, Jill becomes entitled to sue for total breach [Restatement 2d § 243, Cmt. b, Ill. 3]. That does not mean Lon will get nothing for what he has done. But his recovery will be in restitution, not contract. [*See* Chapter Thirty-One for a discussion of Restitution].

(ii) Exception: Failure to Make Installment Payments, Even When Accompanied by a Repudiation, Does Not Become a Total Breach. [§ 21-89]

Under Restatement 2d § 243(3) if: (a) one party's performance is complete; and (b) the wrongful party's breach is a failure to make one or more installment payments followed or accompanied by a repudiation of the payment obligations in the future, such actions *do not* become a material breach. Hence, without more, the non-breaching party has only the right to sue for those payments actually missed, and not a right to sue for the entire debt.

(f) Example. [§ 21–90]

Fred borrows $12,000 from Central Bank and promises to repay the loan at $1,000 per month plus interest starting August 1. Fred unjustifiably fails to make the August, September and October payments, and on October 10, Fred writes to the bank stating that he will not be making any payments in the future. At that point, despite the material breach plus repudiation, the bank has the right to sue only for the three missed payments, and may not treat the breach as total and sue for the remainder of the payments. It can only sue for the remaining missed payments after they become due and remain unpaid [Restatement 2d § 243, Cmt. d, Ill. 4].

Note that this rule only applies in the absence of a contractual promise by the debtor to the contrary. Often to avoid such a result, lenders will include "acceleration" clauses in their contracts, stating that after one or more payments are missed, the remaining payments can be accelerated at the lender's option so that the entire loan balance becomes due, and can be sued for immediately [Restatement 2d § 243, Cmt. d; UCC § 1–309].

(10) Restitution Available to Both Parties upon a Material Breach. [§ 21–91]

In the event of a material breach, typically the non-breaching party will sue for breach of contract and seek to recover damages. However, the non-breaching party is also permitted to sue for restitution, which in some cases will produce a larger monetary recovery. In addition, the **breaching** party in a material breach situation is entitled to sue for restitution for benefits provided before the breach, even though he or she cannot sue the non-breaching party under the contract [*See* Chapter Thirty-One for a discussion of Restitution].

E. EXCUSE OF CONDITIONS. [§ 21–92*]

Conditions can operate harshly, especially express conditions because of the strict enforcement rule. A party may not get any benefit from a

---

* For more information, listen to CD # 10, Track 3 of *Sum and Substance Audio on Contracts*.

transaction because of some trivial failure to satisfy a condition. Most of the time, courts will say that a harsh result was a risk the parties agreed to when they made some of their performance obligations conditional.

However, sometimes a court will "**excuse**" the condition, or, more properly, excuse the non-occurrence of the condition precedent or excuse the occurrence of the condition subsequent. For both conditions precedent and conditions subsequent, excuse means the court will excuse the fact that the condition did not occur, i.e., it will interpret the contract as if the condition did occur.

For conditions precedent, this means that the promise of the party who heretofore had only a conditional duty will see that duty become an unconditional promise. For conditions subsequent, this means that the remaining duties under the contract are unenforceable because the contract will be interpreted as if the condition occurred.

The most common reasons for conditions to be excused are:

(1) **Waiver, estoppel, and election by the party benefitted by the condition** [§ 21–93];

(2) **Wrongful noncooperation, prevention, and hindrance by the party benefitted by the condition** [§ 21–102]; and

(3) **Disproportionate forfeiture caused by treatment of the promise as conditional** [§ 21–107].

These "excuses" can apply to both express and constructive conditions.

1. **Excuse of a Condition by Waiver, Estoppel and Election. [§ 21–93]**

   A party who is benefitted by a condition can choose to forego its benefits. For example let's revisit the hypothetical where John is contractually obligated to purchase Mary's home for $250,000 "on the condition that John is able to secure a loan for $200,000." The condition benefits John, for if he doesn't secure the loan, he doesn't have to buy the house. But suppose John gets a large inheritance after signing the contract. John can forego the benefits of the condition and simply tender cash for the home. In such case, Mary must accept it.

   By foregoing the benefits of a condition, a party has made a "waiver." Sometimes a waiver is referred to as "the intentional relinquishment of a known right." While such a term is highly descriptive of what actually occurs, it is not technically accurate. As can be seen in the John/Mary example, more properly, **a waiver is characterized as one party's excuse of the non-occurrence of, or of a delay in the occurrence of, a condition precedent, or the excuse of the occurrence of a condition subsequent.**

   Waivers can be made by words or by actions.

CONDITIONS, PERFORMANCE AND BREACH (WITH AN EMPHASIS ON COMMON LAW RULES)

"**Estoppel**" has many meanings under the law. With regard to conditions, "estoppel" is essentially synonymous with "waiver" but is perhaps a bit more descriptive of the process. An estoppel occurs when a party benefitted by a condition promises to not to enforce it, and a court determines it is equitable to require the party to live up to that promise. For example, assume delivery is due under a contract on June 1. The seller calls up and asks if she can deliver on June 15, and Buyer agrees. Buyer's promise to accept delivery on June 15 means that he is "estopped" from denying that promise, and cannot declare a breach (possibly allowing Buyer to suspend performance if the breach is material) if the goods are delivered after June 1, so long as they are delivered by June 15.

Note that estoppel in the context of conditions is a fairly outmoded term. Most modern courts just use the term "waiver" regardless whether the waiver is by conduct or by words. Accordingly, the remainder of this Chapter will refer to estoppel situations simply as "waivers."

An "election" is a waiver made after performance was due and cannot be retracted. [*See* §§ 21–97 and 21–101 for a fuller explanation of these concepts].

a. When a Waiver Can Take Place. [§ 21–94]

A waiver can take place:

(a) before, or contemporaneous with, contract formation; [*see* § 21–95];

(b) after the contract is signed, but before performance is due [*see* § 21–96]; or

(c) after performance was due when such performance was not rendered fully and completely [*see* § 21–97].

The rules governing each situation are a little different, and are explained below.

(1) Waivers Before, or Contemporaneous with, Contract Formation. [§ 21–95]

A waiver of a contract term before a contract is entered into is a rare occurrence, but it is possible. For example, assume a pre-printed contract where, e.g., Clause 18 says that payment is conditioned on delivery by the seller via the U.S. Mail. If the buyer tells the seller at the time they sign the contract that she won't enforce that condition and will pay regardless how the goods are delivered so long as they get there on time, the buyer's "waiver" is valid and the buyer could not rely on the lack of fulfillment of the condition as a reason not to pay if delivery were made, e.g., by Federal Express.

You might wonder whether a pre-contract waiver can be proven under the parol evidence rule. [Chapter Eighteen]. Recall, however, one widely adopted "exception" to the parol evidence rule allows evidence to show that oral conditions have either been agreed to or waived. [*See* § 18–22].

(2) Waivers Made After Contract Formation, but Before Performance Is Due. [§ 21–96]

Returning to the situation where John was obligated to buy Mary's home "on the condition John is able to secure a loan for $200,000," as noted earlier, if John wishes to waive the condition, he can, and if he tenders cash to Mary she must take it. But rarely does contract law get involved in such a case because if John wants to buy the house for cash, Mary almost undoubtedly be willing to sell it to him.

Where it gets interesting for contract law is when John, in all seriousness, promises Mary that he will buy her home even if he does not get the loan, but then claims this promise never took place and/or refuses to live up to the promise.

At common law, such waivers were treated as modifications to the contract, and had to be supported by consideration to be enforceable under the pre-existing duty rule. [§ 7–72]. So, without consideration, the waiver would have been a nullity and John could not be held to it.

However, there are now recognized exceptions to the "new" consideration rules:

(1) in UCC contracts, no consideration is necessary for a modification [UCC §§ 2–209(1), 1–306];

(2) under the Restatement 2d, there are three situations in which post-contractual modifications and waivers are enforceable without new consideration, including where the other party has made a material change of position in reliance on the waiver [Restatement 2d § 89; § 7–85]; and

(3) in a few cases, courts have allowed enforcement of post-contractual modifications without new consideration in the absence of statutory authority when the waived condition isn't material to the transaction.

(3) Waivers Made After Performance Was Due. [§ 21–97]

A non-breaching party is entitled to "waive" a breach. We have seen one example of this above when the non-

CONDITIONS, PERFORMANCE AND BREACH (WITH AN EMPHASIS ON COMMON LAW RULES)

breaching party elected to treat what would be a material breach as an immaterial breach [§ 21–79].

For another example, suppose Owner was to pay Contractor a $2,000 progress payment upon excavation of the ground for a swimming pool, and another $3,000 once the cement was poured. Suppose Owner approaches Contractor after the excavation and pleads cash flow problems, promising to make it up and pay $5,000 after the cement pouring. If Contractor agrees, it has made a post-due performance waiver.

Three points must be made about this last hypothetical. First, up until now, the examples have been of waivers of express conditions. This is an example of a waiver of a constructive condition—the constructive condition that Contractor's continued performance obligations are constructively conditioned on there being no uncured material breach by Owner. (The failure to make a progress payment is a material breach) [§ 21–64].

The second point is that while it is less of a mouthful to say that Contractor "waived" the breach or "waived" his rights to sue, in truth the Contractor, who is benefitted by the constructive condition (he could have stopped working because of the material breach) decided **to excuse the occurrence of the constructive condition subsequent** and not exercise its right to cease further performance [*see* § 21–93].

The third point is that because this **waiver took place after performance was due**, it is known as an "**election**." As explained in the next section, an election is a special kind of waiver that **cannot be retracted by the party making the waiver** [*See* § 21–100 for a further discussion of retraction].

Elections are enforceable in the absence of consideration [UCC § 1–306].

b. **Implied Waivers: Waiver by Conduct. [§ 21–98]**

Waivers can be by words or by conduct. Typically an implied waiver is found when the **party benefitted by the condition accepts benefits under the contract, knowing or having reason to know of the non-occurrence of the condition precedent or the occurrence of the condition subsequent** [Restatement 2d § 246].

(1) Example. [§ 21-99]

Computer technician is contractually obligated to teach a class on a new operating system to Business's employees on June 1. Payment is conditioned upon timely performance. Inadvertently, technician double booked her time and isn't available until June 10. Assume that late training in such circumstances would be a material breach. If Business nevertheless allows technician to teach the class on June 10, it has impliedly waived its right to suspend or terminate the duty to pay technician. This is because Business, **which was benefitted by the condition**, accepted the benefits of the contract knowing of the non-occurrence of the condition. Because it did so after the time for performance had passed, it is an election.

c. Retraction of Waivers. [§ 21-100]

Under certain conditions, the party making a waiver may retract it. A waiver is retractable if:

(1) It involves an **executory duty under a bilateral contract**;

(2) The party retracting the waiver gives **reasonable notice** of the retraction; and

(3) The *other party* has **not materially relied on the waiver**.

The first element—that retractions can only be to executory (remaining) duties under a contract—is why waivers made after performance is due cannot be retracted.

(1) Example. [§ 21-101]

Dan has entered into a contract with Diane's Bakery whereby he agrees to deliver 150 pounds of flour each month for a year. Under their agreement, Dan is to deliver the flour on the first of the month. For the first four months, Dan has delivered the flour on the 15th of the month. After the fourth delivery, he realizes that he has been delivering the flour late and apologizes to Diane. She says, "It's no problem; I'm fine with it." At this point, Diane has made an **election** to excuse the four late deliveries, which is irrevocable.

Dan now asks Diane whether it's OK in the future to keep to the 15th, or whether she will insist on delivery on the 1st. Diane says the 15th is fine.

CONDITIONS, PERFORMANCE AND BREACH (WITH AN EMPHASIS ON COMMON LAW RULES)

Two months later, Diane says she is going to insist that the last six deliveries be made on the 1st. What she has done is **retract** her waiver.

The first element for an effective retraction is met, as waiver concerned **unperformed duties** (the remaining six deliveries) **under a bilateral contract**.

It is unclear whether the second element is met. It would depend on what is reasonable under the circumstances. Certainly Diane could not call Dan on the last day of the sixth month, retract her waiver, and demand delivery the next day. But <u>if</u> she gave Dan enough **notice**, this element would be met.

Whether the third element is met will depend on whether Dan can show that he has relied on the 15th as the new delivery date, e.g., by making his own orders for the raw ingredients due on the 12th, which can't be changed, etc.

2. **Excuse of a Condition by Wrongful Prevention, Hindrance, and Noncooperation by the Party Benefitted by the Condition. [§ 21–102]**

A court will excuse the non-occurrence of a condition precedent, or the occurrence of a condition subsequent, if the reason the condition precedent is not fulfilled (or the condition subsequent occurs) is because the party who benefits from the condition has breached his or her **duty of good faith and fair dealing** with regard to the condition [Restatement 2d § 205; UCC § 1–304]. That is, a court will not allow a party to benefit from his or her own wrongful conduct. In addition, breach of the duty of good faith can also itself act as a material breach, allowing the other party to suspend performance [§ 21–105].

For a quick example, let's return to the situation in which John is contractually obligated to purchase Mary's home on the condition that he secures a loan. It is one thing if the loan condition is not fulfilled because John went to a few banks and got turned down because he was a poor credit risk. That was the risk Mary took in entering into a contract where the payment promise was conditional.

But it's another thing if the loan condition is not fulfilled because John got cold feet about buying the house and slipped the loan officer $100 to turn down his loan application, or if he never went to the bank at all to apply for the loan.

The way contract law deals with this situation to say that, <u>for conditions precedent</u>, a benefitted party whose actions or inactions **wrongfully prevented, hindered, or failed to cooperate in bringing about a condition**, loses the benefit of the condition. That is, the non-occurrence of the condition is excused and the formerly conditional duty becomes an unconditional promise. For <u>conditions subsequent</u>, contract law says that a benefitted party, whose actions or inactions **wrongfully prevented, hindered, or failed to cooperate in allowing the condition to occur**, loses the benefit of the condition, and the duties under the contract are unenforceable because the condition will be deemed to have occurred.

That is, encompassed within the duty of good faith is a duty not to wrongfully prevent, hinder, or fail to cooperate in seeing to it that the condition occurs; and, for conditions subsequent, to see to it that the condition does not occur. A breach of that duty of good faith excuses the condition. In the words of Restatement 2d § 245, "Where a party's breach by non-performance [of the duty of good faith and fair dealing] contributes materially to the non-occurrence of a condition of one of his duties, the non-occurrence is excused."

So in the John/Mary example, the contract started out with John's promise to pay being conditioned on his getting a loan. If he bribes the loan officer to turn down his loan application, or never applies for it, he has breached the duty of good faith, and has **wrongfully prevented, hindered, and failed to cooperate** in the occurrence of the condition, i.e., getting the loan. Accordingly the court will excuse the non-occurrence of the condition precedent, and his formerly conditional promise becomes unconditional, and he has to purchase the home or be in breach for failing to do so. In other words, the contract will be interpreted to read: "John promises to purchase Mary's home for $250,000," and the language "on the condition John gets a loan for $200,000" will be stricken and have no effect.

Students sometimes get a bit hung up in trying to decide whether it's a "hindrance" or a "prevention" case, etc. Those terms are not terms of legal significance. The words come from Comment (a) to Restatement 2d § 245 and are descriptive only. So don't worry about identifying which classification applies. The key is deciding whether the actions of the party who was benefitted by the condition acted against accepted mores or in bad faith in bringing about the failure of the condition, or, for conditions subsequent, bringing about the occurrence of the condition.

a. **Example of Express Condition Precedent Being Excused by Affirmative Wrongful Prevention Based on *Barron v. Cain*. [§ 21–103]**

In a bilateral contract, Nephew promised to care for Uncle until Uncle died in exchange for a legacy from Uncle's estate. Things didn't go well. After awhile, Uncle grabbed his shotgun and ordered Nephew permanently off the property, warning he'd be killed if he ever came back.

CONDITIONS, PERFORMANCE AND BREACH (WITH AN EMPHASIS ON COMMON LAW RULES)

Held: Nephew was entitled to the legacy right away. Originally Uncle's payment obligation was conditional—on Nephew taking care of Uncle until he died. However, Uncle's <u>actions</u> **wrongfully prevented the condition from occurring**. As such, <u>the condition was excused</u> and the formerly conditional promise to pay became unconditional and immediately payable. [*Baron v. Cain*, 4 S.E.2d 618 (N.C. 1939)].

b. **Example of Express Condition Precedent Being Excused by Inaction Leading to Wrongful Prevention or Hindrance. [§ 21–104]**

Return to the John/Mary example where John was obligated to buy Mary's home on the condition he obtained a loan for $200,000. If John never applies for a loan, a violation of his duty of good faith has occurred. Because he was the party benefitting from the condition, and because his <u>inaction</u> **wrongfully hindered and prevented the condition from occurring**, the <u>condition is excused</u> and his obligation to purchase Mary's home for $250,000 becomes enforceable even though he never got the loan.

c. **Example of Breach of Duty of Cooperation Stemming from the Duty of Good Faith and Fair Dealing Becoming a Material Breach Based on *Swartz v. War Memorial Comm'n*. [§ 21–105]**

A concessionaire had the right to sell all food and beverage at a municipally owned arena. The parties split the profits. As such maximizing revenues was important to both parties.

At the time the contract was entered into, it was against the law to sell alcoholic beverages at the arena. However, the contract provided that if concessionaire ever sold alcoholic beverages at the arena, the split of the profits on alcohol sales would be the same as the split on everything else. A couple of years into the deal, the law changed and it became legal to serve alcohol. However, for some reason, despite the urging by the owner of the arena, the concessionaire refused to apply for a liquor license.

Held: Inherent in the duty of good faith and fair dealing is a **duty to cooperate** in maximizing revenues to both parties. The concessionaire's failure to even apply for the liquor license was a breach of its cooperation duty. The breach of that duty can be, and was here, a material breach. Upon the material breach of one party (the concessionaire) the innocent party (the arena owner) had the right to suspend performance, i.e., it had the right to suspend the concessionaire's exclusive right to sell food and beverage in the building. When the concessionaire failed to cure the material breach, after a reasonable time (which was spelled out in the contract) the breach became total and the arena's duties to the concessionaire terminated. [*Swartz v. War Memorial Comm'n*, 267 N.Y.S.2d 253 (App. Div. 1966)].

d. Review Problem. [§ 21–106]

Team promises Star a $100,000 bonus if he leads league in free throw attempts. Going into the final game, Star is 5 free throws attempts behind the leader, and the leader has finished playing for the season. Star is averaging 10 free throw attempts per game. Star is benched for the final game and Team does not pay the bonus.

Analysis: Team has entered into a bilateral contract with a contingent payment obligation. Team is benefitted by the condition for it will not have to pay unless the condition is fulfilled. Whether Star can recover the bonus even though the condition did not occur will depend on the reason Star was benched. If Team did so to deny him the bonus, it has breached the duty of good faith. Its actions thus **wrongfully hindered and prevented the condition from occurring**. The condition would thus be excused and Team's payment obligation would become unconditional.

Note you might argue that even if Star played there was no guarantee that he would have had enough free throw attempts to qualify for the bonus. True, but Restatement 2d § 245 does not require that the condition would have occurred but for the wrongful prevention. It only requires that the wrongful conduct contributed "materially" to the non-occurrence [Restatement 2d § 245, Cmt. b].

3. Excuse of Condition to Avoid Disproportionate Forfeiture. [§ 21–107]

Courts will also excuse conditions if:

(1) **Enforcement of the condition will lead to disproportionate forfeiture**; *and*

(2) **The condition is not as to a material part of the bargained for exchange** [Restatement 2d § 229].

This rule applies to both express and constructive conditions.

In determining whether a forfeiture is "disproportionate," a court is directed to balance how important the condition is to the obligor against the extent of loss to be suffered by the obligee should the condition be enforced.

As with other "excuses," if the court excuses the condition because of forfeiture, for a condition precedent, the result is that the conditional

CONDITIONS, PERFORMANCE AND BREACH (WITH AN EMPHASIS ON COMMON LAW RULES)

obligation becomes an absolute duty; for a condition subsequent, the result is the duties remain enforceable.

a. Example. [§ 21–108]

Sally agrees to build an addition to Bill's home for $50,000. However, the contract states that Bill's obligation to pay Sally is "on the express condition all work on the addition is completed by March 1." Sally finishes on March 3. Bill is not inconvenienced by the delay, but refuses to pay her. A court is empowered to excuse the payment-only-if-completed-by March express condition if it determines: (a) a "disproportionate" forfeiture will occur if Bill is allowed to enforce the condition; and (b) completion of the work by the March 1 deadline was not a material part of their bargain. If a court finds that both those elements are met, Bill will be deemed to have unconditionally obligated himself to pay $50,000 for the work, and Sally will be deemed to have made an unconditional promise to finish by March 1, which she breached. As a result, while Sally is liable for any damages suffered by Bill as a result of the two-day delay, Bill is also liable to pay her $50,000 and cannot strictly enforce the condition [Restatement 2d § 229, Cmt. c, Ill. 3].

Note that if completion by March 1 was truly a material (important) part of their deal, e.g., because Bill was hosting an important party at his home on March 2, the condition would be enforced despite the forfeiture and Bill would not be obligated under the contract to pay the $50,000.

b. Example Based on *Jacob & Youngs v. Kent.* [§ 21–109]

[The facts of this case are set forth in § 21–70]. Assume for this problem that use of the Reading pipe was an express condition of the final progress payment, but otherwise the facts are the same. A court might still excuse the condition if it determines: (a) a "disproportionate" forfeiture will occur if Kent is allowed to enforce the condition; and (b) use of the Reading pipe was not a material part of their bargain. Whether it would be a material part of their bargain depends on the reason the term was inserted [Restatement 2d § 229, Cmt. a, Ill. 1].

CHAPTER 21

F. EXAM APPROACH TO CONDITION, PERFORMANCE AND BREACH ISSUES. [§ 21–110]

1. Approach to Express Conditions. [§ 21–111*]

The existence and effect of conditions help establish whether a party who has not performed what he or she promised in a contract is in breach for failing to perform, or has an excuse for not performing, i.e., the non-occurrence of a condition.

Hence the steps that should be used in analyzing a conditions issue in an exam where a party's non-performance of a contractual promise is an issue, are as follows:

1. Ascertain whether the contractual promise that was not performed is: (a) subject to a condition; (b) an unconditional duty; or (c) both subject to a condition and a duty [§§ 21–2 *et seq.*; 21–22 *et seq.*].

2. If the promise is subject to a condition, determine whether the condition is a condition precedent or subsequent [§§ 21–11; 21–15], and then determine whether it is an:

   a. express condition [§ 21–4]; or

   b. implied in fact condition [§ 21–6],

   and know the substantive and procedural effects of each.

3. Ascertain whether the condition has been satisfied, remembering that satisfying a condition precedent has different effects than satisfying a condition subsequent [§ 21–19 *et seq.*], and that express conditions are subject to the strict construction rule [§ 21–23].

4. If the condition exists and has not been satisfied, ascertain whether it has been excused by either:

   a. waiver [§ 21–93];

   b. wrongful noncooperation, prevention, and hindrance [§ 21–102]; or

   c. disproportionate forfeiture [§ 21–107].

If a condition exists and is neither satisfied nor excused, the party who failed to perform will be in breach. The analytical approach to breach issues is described below.

---

* For more information, listen to CD # 11, Track 3 of *Sum and Substance Audio on Contracts*.

CONDITIONS, PERFORMANCE AND BREACH (WITH AN EMPHASIS ON COMMON LAW RULES)

2. Approach to Breach Issues. [§ 21–112*]

The following approach should get you through an analysis of breach on an examination:

1. Make sure that a breach has occurred, i.e., that a party's failure to perform completely what has been promised under a contract is not subject to a defense or some other doctrine whereby the failure to perform is justified or excused, including checking to make sure performance by the other party was tendered [§§ 21–60; 21–47].

2. If a breach has occurred, then check to see whether the contract was a bilateral one with unexecuted duties at the time of the breach.

   (a) If it was, determine whether the breach was material or immaterial [§§ 21–55 *et seq.*], realizing that in a material breach, the aggrieved party may suspend performance, and keeping in mind the "first" material breach doctrine [§ 21–66].

   (1) If the breach was material, check to see if it has ripened into a total breach [§ 21–81], or if it has been cured, waived, or divided so that some or all of the duties are still enforceable.

   (b) If the contract was not a bilateral contract with unexecuted duties by both sides at the time of the breach, then go directly to step 3.

3. Make sure you write on your exam that the non-breaching party is entitled to damages regardless whether the breach is material or immaterial, and, if you have covered the subject, analyze the damages recoverable by the aggrieved party.

4. Check to see if the condition was excused [§ 21–92] by either:

   a. waiver [§ 21–93];

   b. wrongful noncooperation, prevention, and hindrance [§ 21–102]; or

   c. disproportionate forfeiture [§ 21–107].

5. Check to see if the failure to cooperate resulted in a material breach [§ 21–105].

---

* For more information, listen to CD # 11, Track 3 of *Sum and Substance Audio on Contracts*.

CHAPTER 22

CONDITIONS, PERFORMANCE AND BREACH (WITH AN EMPHASIS ON CONTRACTS GOVERNED BY THE UCC)

A. PERFORMANCE AND BREACH IN CONTRACTS GOVERNED BY THE UCC, GENERALLY. [§ 22–1]

Article 2 of the UCC is divided into seven "Parts." Part 5 (made up of the § 2–500's) is entitled "Performance." Part 6 (made up of the § 2–600's) is entitled "Breach, Repudiation and Excuse." In these provisions the UCC regulates the concepts discussed in the previous chapter.

As you will note as you go through this chapter, the general common law/Restatement concepts regarding tender, material breach, etc., discussed in Chapter Twenty-One are followed in contracts governed by the UCC. Hence, the material in this chapter is presented on the assumption that you have already digested the material in Chapter Twenty-One (and, if not, there is a fair amount of cross-referencing).

At the end, you will find that there are really only three main differences between breach at common law and breach under the UCC:

(1) In certain cases the UCC uses different nomenclature to describe and define these concepts;

(2) The Code has, in some cases, made it somewhat easier to establish what common law would call material breach [§§ 22–7 *et seq*]; and

(3) The UCC is more detailed and specific in describing the rights and duties of the contracting parties after a breach.

Most contracts professors do not require their students to master the differences between common law and UCC performance in the detail presented in this chapter. Most of what is separately covered is just the "perfect tender rule" under UCC § 2–601 and covered in §§ 22–7 *et seq.*

If you know the concepts presented in Chapter Twenty-One and learn the slightly different terminology of the UCC in this area, you should be fine and this Chapter need not be studied extensively. *But for those courses where Article 2 is stressed, or for students using this book in a Sales class, the UCC doctrines are explained in this chapter in some detail.*

B. TENDER AND IMPLIED CONDITIONS OF EXCHANGE UNDER THE CODE. [§ 22–2]

As with non-UCC transactions, tender of performance by one party is necessary to make the other party's duties enforceable under the UCC [*see* §§ 21–48 *et seq.*]. One difference between the Code and common law is that the Code prescribes an order for tender to take place. UCC § 2–511(1) provides "Unless otherwise agreed, tender of payment is a condition to the seller's duty <u>to tender</u> *and* complete any delivery." **Accordingly, the buyer must demonstrate a willingness and ability to pay before the seller must <u>tender</u> delivery and, eventually, deliver them. Once the buyer had tendered payment**, "Tender of delivery is a condition to the buyer's duty to accept the goods and, unless otherwise agreed, to his duty to pay for them" UCC § 2–507(1). Hence a seller must establish a willingness and ability to deliver the goods before he has a right to payment: "Tender entitles the seller to acceptance of the goods and to payment according to the contract." *Id.*

Putting it all together then, the buyer must show it is willing, and has the ability, to pay. Then the seller must tender delivery. At that point, the duties of both parties are enforceable. As with common law, these are only "default" rules, and the parties can vary them. So when Amazon wants payment before delivery, it is perfectly entitled to do so.

Setting forth the rules of § 2–507(1) and § 2–511(1) leaves two questions:

(1) What acts are necessary under the UCC to complete tender for each party [§ 21–48]; and

(2) Once tender has been made, what is the order of performance, i.e., which party must perform first or be in breach for not doing so [*See* § 21–50 for a discussion of common law rules on this subject]?

1. The Acts Necessary to Fulfill a Seller's Obligation to Tender Delivery. [§ 22–3]

As noted above, § 2–507 states that a seller's "tender of delivery" is necessary to make the buyer's duty to pay enforceable. Section 2–503 states that to fulfill a seller's obligation to tender delivery, he or she must:

CONDITIONS, PERFORMANCE AND BREACH (WITH AN EMPHASIS ON CONTRACTS GOVERNED BY THE UCC)

(1) Put and hold **conforming** goods at the buyer's disposition;

(2) Give the buyer **reasonable notice** so that the buyer may take delivery; and

(3) Either:

(a) **Make the goods available at a reasonable time and place** if they are to be picked up by the buyer; <u>or</u>,

(b) **Offer delivery of the goods at a reasonable time** if they are to be delivered by the seller.

a. Example. [§ 22–4]

Electronics store orders 100 smart phones from wholesaler, with delivery to be made at the wholesaler's place of business. Once the wholesaler notifies the buyer that it has the smart phones at its warehouse, and that the buyer can pick them up during regular business hours, tender has been accomplished. Note, however, that if the phones are **non-conforming** goods, e.g., they are the wrong brand, they don't work, etc., then the seller's tender is ineffective, and the buyer's duty to pay for them remains unenforceable.

2. The Acts Necessary to Fulfill a Buyer's Obligation to Tender Payment. [§ 22–5]

Under UCC § 2–511(1), tender of payment is a condition to the seller's obligation to complete delivery. Section 2–511(2) provides that so long as the buyer demonstrates a willingness and ability to pay "by any means or in any manner current in the ordinary course of business," the buyer's tender obligation is fulfilled.

Note, however, that if the seller does not want a check or other documentary forms of payment, and instead wants cash, the seller has the right to demand a cash payment under § 2–511(2). However, if the seller makes such a demand, the seller must give the buyer a reasonable extension of time in which to obtain the cash for payment.

3. Order of Performance. [§ 22–6]

In the absence of an express rule, it is likely that the general contracts rule on order of performance will apply even in UCC transactions, i.e., if one party's performance will take time to complete and the other's will not, completion of performance by the party whose performance takes time is a constructive condition to the obligation of the party whose performance does not take time [Restatement 2d § 234(2)]. Conversely, if the parties can perform at the same time, performance is due simultaneously [Restatement 2d § 234(1)]. So if the delivery obligations of the seller will take time, the seller must perform first. However, if the parties' performances can be done simultaneously, e.g., turn over the goods to the buyer and payment, the performances are due simultaneously absent a contrary agreement between the parties. [*See* §§ 21–50 *et seq.* for a discussion of the non-UCC rules governing order of performance].

C. THE PERFECT TENDER RULE UNDER THE UCC. [§ 22–7*]

In its initial reading, the so-called "perfect tender rule" of the UCC seems relatively straightforward and pretty unremarkable. In some respects, all it does is require the seller to live up to his or her bargain, which is the reason the buyer entered into the contract in the first place. However, as discussed below, the rule changes substantially the analysis of breach in contracts to which it applies. The perfect tender rule is set forth in UCC § 2–601 and provides:

> **In a "single lot" contract, i.e., a contract in which delivery of all the goods called for by the agreement is to be made in only one shipment, if either the goods or the tender of delivery fail in *any* respect to conform to the contract, the buyer may:**
>
> **(a) Reject the entire shipment,**
>
> **(b) Accept the entire shipment, or**
>
> **(c) Accept any commercial unit or units in the shipment, and reject the rest.**

Upon a careful read, it can be seen why the perfect tender rule alters so dramatically the analysis of breach in contracts governed by § 2–601 versus those governed by common law/Restatement rules [§§ 21–55 *et seq.*]. Under the UCC rule, **every breach by the seller in a single lot contract is a material breach**, for the failure of the seller to render promised performance "in *any* respect" gives the buyer the right to reject the shipment and relieves the buyer from having to pay for the goods.

In traditional contract terms, under the perfect tender rule, at least as it is written [§ 21–11] **any** non-performance by the seller, no matter how minor, discharges all remaining duties of the buyer under the contract at the buyer's option. Thus, **for contracts subject to the Code's perfect tender rule, the immaterial breach and substantial performance doctrines are eliminated**. The rule provides there is no breach minor enough to keep the buyer in the contract and make him or her pay for the goods sent by seller and limit the buyer's remedy only to a breach action for immaterial breach [§§ 21–57 *et seq.*, and § 21–68, for discussions of the immaterial breach and substantial performance doctrines, respectively].

Note, this is true regardless of whether the result will cause the seller to suffer a substantial forfeiture, or regardless of whether the seller's breach

---

* For more information, listen to CD # 13, Track 2 of *Sum and Substance Audio on Contracts*.

CONDITIONS, PERFORMANCE AND BREACH (WITH AN EMPHASIS ON CONTRACTS GOVERNED BY THE UCC)

was delivering 999,999 units when 1,000,000 were ordered. Under the rule, whenever the seller has failed to perform "in *any* respect" from what he or she promised, the buyer's duties to accept and pay for the goods are discharged if the buyer so chooses, i.e., the buyer can "reject the entire shipment."

Similarly, **the doctrine of divisibility is also eliminated for contracts subject to the perfect tender rule**, for upon any deviation from the seller's promised performance, the rule provides that the buyer is entitled to reject the **entire** shipment, and cannot be compelled to accept any conforming divisible unit of that shipment [*see* § 21–73 for a discussion of the divisibility doctrine]. Indeed, it is even worse (for the seller) under the perfect tender rule, for upon an imperfect tender, the buyer can decide it only wants *some* of the goods tendered. In other words, it's not all or nothing, but allows the buyer to change its mind and just take some of what was sent.

It should be noted that White & Summers have done an extensive study of how courts actually apply the perfect tender rule and have not found even a single case like those above, e.g., where a buyer like Costco was sent 4,999 widgets when it ordered 5,000, and then subsequently declared a material breach and decided to take only 2,500 of the widgets.

History shows that the perfect tender rule was passed more as a protection for consumers than businesses, i.e., a consumer shouldn't be forced to take a couch that was forest green when he or she ordered the couch in lime green, no matter how close forest and lime green might be. But with that said, the language of § 2–601 does not make any distinction between consumers and businesses, and so by its terms, Costco would be entitled to act as described above.

1. **Example. [§ 22–8]**

    Betsy owns a hardware store and orders 300 faucets of a certain type from Sheila, a plumbing wholesaler. The goods arrive timely, but when Betsy counts them, she discovers that only 298 faucets were delivered. At that point, under the perfect tender rule, there has been what common law would call a material breach and (subject to the limitations discussed §§ 22–11 *et seq.*) Betsy is entitled to reject all 298 faucets, to accept all 298 faucets, or to keep, e.g., 100 (or any other number), and return the rest to Sheila.

2. **Example. [§ 22–9]**

    Same facts as above, except this time 300 faucets are timely delivered by Sheila, but one of them is broken. Same results, for there is no divisibility doctrine under the perfect tender rule. Subject to some limitations [§§ 22–11 *et seq.*] § 2–601 provides that when there has been **any** failure of promised performance by the seller, there has been a material breach of the contract. Betsy is thus entitled to accept the 299 conforming faucets, to reject them all, or to accept some and reject the rest.

3. **Example. [§ 22–10]**

Benny ordered a custom-made couch from a furniture manufacturer. When he ordered it, the manufacturer showed Benny a sample color swatch for the couch, which Benny approved. When the couch was delivered, Benny discovered that the manufacturer used 1% more blue dye in the couch fabric than in the swatch. There has been lack of perfect tender under § 2–601, and Benny is thus entitled to reject the couch and need not pay for it.

4. **Limitations on the Perfect Tender Rule. [§ 22–11]**

The perfect tender rule is massively beneficial for the buyer. While it is true the seller need not worry about the perfect tender rule if he or she completely performs what is promised under the contract, as a practical matter there will be times when a seller is going to make good faith mistakes during his or her performance. Workers on the loading dock will mistakenly send the wrong goods; something will break during transit; someone will transpose a number and the wrong quantity will be sent, or the right quantity will be sent but on the wrong date; a plane will crash and the delivery will be late, etc. Further, in some of these cases it may well be that the buyer is not very inconvenienced, or perhaps not inconvenienced at all, by the imperfect tender, and yet the perfect tender rule nonetheless permits the buyer to get out of his or her obligations under a contract.

Thus, to combat instances of potential unfairness under § 2–601, the courts and the Code limit application of the perfect tender rule in the following major respects:

(1) While a buyer is initially entitled to reject a shipment for less than absolutely perfect tender, **a seller is granted fairly extensive rights to *cure* the imperfect tender** under the Code [*see* § 22–12 for a discussion of cure under the Code];

(2) The perfect tender rule applies only to "single lot" contracts. **In *installment contracts*, i.e., contracts where the goods are to be delivered in more than one shipment, the standards governing when a buyer can reject the goods and terminate the agreement in light of an imperfect tender are much more difficult for the buyer to meet** [*see* § 22–23 for a discussion of the rules under installment contracts];

(3) By judicial decision, **some courts have held that the perfect tender rule does not apply when the *breach is very minor***, i.e., they have engrafted a *"de minimis non curat*

CONDITIONS, PERFORMANCE AND BREACH (WITH AN EMPHASIS ON CONTRACTS GOVERNED BY THE UCC)

lex" exception to the perfect tender rule [*see* § 22–30 for a further discussion of the *de minimis non curat lex* exception];

(4) Some courts have also established a perfect tender rule exception for complex machinery [*see* § 22–31 for a further discussion of this exception];

(5) Under the Code, **the perfect tender rule must be read in conjunction with usage of trade, course of dealing, and course of performance**. Thus, even if a seller's actions seem to constitute a "breach" based on one meaning of the words used in the contract, it may be that when those words are properly interpreted in light of trade usage or prior dealings of the parties, in fact no breach has occurred [*see* § 22–33 for a further discussion of the operation of usage of trade, course of dealing, and course of performance in conjunction with the perfect tender rule]; and

(6) **The perfect tender rule does not apply to situations where the buyer has already "accepted" the goods**, but later decides that he or she wishes to return them due to a defective tender. That is, the Code's standards under which a buyer can revoke his or her acceptance are more difficult for a buyer to meet than those standards governing when he or she can *reject* those same goods when they are initially tendered [*see* § 22–35 for a further discussion of revocation of acceptance].

a. **The Seller's Right to Cure Under § 2–508. [§ 22–12]**

Probably the most significant limitation on the perfect tender rule is the right of the seller to cure certain imperfect tenders. Cure is the process by which the seller rectifies or "cures" a breach by, e.g., sending a replacement faucet if one is defective, or by shipping two more faucets if the promised quantity was deficient in that amount in the original shipment. In colloquial terms, the effect of cure is to take an originally imperfect tender and repair or "cure" it so that it is subsequently "perfect." In common law contract terms, the effect of cure is to take a material breach, and restore enough of the benefits under the contract to the injured party so that it is thereafter fair to treat the former material breach as an immaterial one [*See* § 21–77 for a discussion of cure under common law].

Thus, after an effective cure, the buyer is kept in the contract and must both accept and pay for the goods, but has the right to sue the seller for any damages caused by what common law would label as an immaterial breach after the cure [*see* § 21–60 *et seq.*].

CHAPTER 22

To understand how cure works, the following questions need to be resolved:

(1) Under what circumstances is a seller entitled to cure? [This issue is discussed further in §§ 22–13 and 22–15)]

(2) After it is determined that a seller has the right to cure, what kinds of actions constitute an effective cure? [This issue is discussed further in § 22–18]; and

(3) What are a **buyer's** rights upon accepting a cure? [This issue is discussed further in § 22–22].

(1) The Seller Has a Right to Cure When the "Time for Performance" Under the Contract Has <u>Not</u> Passed. [§ 22–13]

Under § 2–508(1) a seller has the **<u>right</u> to cure if the time for performance under the contract has not yet expired**, so long as the seller provided adequate notice of his or her intention to do so. The idea behind giving the seller an absolute right to cure in this situation is that the buyer is not likely to suffer serious harm due to an imperfect tender so long as the seller ultimately delivers conforming goods to the buyer within the time the seller originally promised to perform under the contract. That is, because the buyer has no right to rely on having the goods before the seller's "time for performance" expires, if the buyer ultimately receives conforming goods within that time anyway, it is only fair that the buyer be forced to accept and pay for them.

(a) Example. [§ 22–14]

A contract entered into on February 1 called for the delivery of 100 55-inch television sets in a single shipment to an electronics store on or before April 1. On March 16, seller delivered 100 televisions, but it turned out that one was defective. Under the perfect tender rule, the store is entitled to treat the breach as material and either send all the televisions back, or accept some and send the rest back. However, the seller has an absolute right for the next two weeks to cure the defective tender, because the seller's "time for performance" under the contract (April 1) has not yet expired.

Hence, so long as the seller first gives timely notice of its intention to cure, and so long as the seller has acted in good faith, the retailer must accept and pay for all 100 sets if the seller cures its imperfect tender by

386

sending the retailer a replacement television by April 1. This is because once the replacement television set arrives, the imperfect tender will be made perfect, and the retailer thus has no basis on which to reject.

(2) A Seller's Ability to Cure After the "Time for Performance" Under the Contract Has Expired. [§ 22–15]

After the seller's "time for performance" has run under a contract, the seller's ability to cure is more circumscribed. Section 2–508(2) provides that in such a situation, the seller has a right to cure only if:

(a) The seller had reasonable grounds to believe what was originally tendered would be acceptable to the buyer;

(b) The buyer would not be unduly inconvenienced by the delay in receiving the cured tender; and

(c) Cure is made within a reasonable time under the circumstances.

The reasons the seller's right to cure is more circumscribed in this situation is that (1) unlike the case where cure is made before the time for performance has expired, it may well be that the buyer needed a perfect and timely tender to recognize the benefits under the contract and (2) the law does not want to reward a seller who has intentionally breached. That is, there are situations where if the promised delivery date is missed by the seller, the buyer simply cannot wait until the seller is able to procure replacement goods and send them to the buyer, or some missing goods causes the buyer real inconvenience. In those cases, it is only fair to permit the buyer to reject a subsequently cured tender, and to declare a total breach of the contract. Similarly, if the seller knows what is being tendered is non-conforming, there is no reason to allow the seller to "cure" the intentional wrongdoing.

Thus, it is only when there is not an undue inconvenience to the buyer upon waiting for the cure, **and** where the seller made an inadvertent mistake in breaching the contract (or was otherwise reasonable in believing what he or she tendered was acceptable to the buyer), that the Code grants the seller the right to cure after the time for performance has expired.

CHAPTER 22

(a) **Example. [§ 22–16]**

On March 15, a retailer of televisions has twenty 42-inch flat screen televisions in stock. Because the store manager does not want to run low on inventory, she orders another 100 42-inch televisions from the manufacturer, to be delivered on or before April 1. The televisions are delivered late in the day on April 1st, when the retailer still has a dozen 42-inch sets remaining in stock. The next day the manager begins unpacking the newly delivered sets, and discovers the manufacturer has sent 100 32-inch sets. At this point, the seller has materially breached under the perfect tender rule and so the buyer can reject all 100 sets. Because the time for the seller's performance under the contract has expired, the seller does not have the absolute right to cure under § 2–508(1). Thus, if the seller is going to salvage the contract, it must establish that it has a right to cure under § 2–508(2).

To do so the seller must prove: (1) that **it acted in good faith** (e.g., that its shipping department made an honest mistake and the company thought it actually was sending working 42-inch sets); (2) that **the buyer would not suffer too much of a commercial loss** in waiting for a new shipment of 42-inch sets, i.e., that cure is "appropriate and timely under the circumstances" (which the seller would likely be able to establish here, given that the buyer still has twelve 42-inch televisions in stock); and (3) that **it will affect the cure in a reasonably timely basis** and has given timely notice of its intention to do so. In addition, the seller must compensate the buyer for any reasonable expenses caused by the breach and cure.

(b) **Example. [§ 22–17]**

Ned is leaving on a European vacation on Friday the 10th and orders from an electronics store an electric shaver that will work in all the countries he will be visiting. Under the terms of the contract, the shaver is to be delivered to Ned no later than Thursday the 9th. The store does not have such a shaver in stock, but promptly orders one from a reputable manufacturer and it is delivered to the store on the 9th. Near the close of business on that day, Ned comes into the store to pick up the shaver and discovers it does not work. Even though the store had reasonable grounds to think that the shaver would be acceptable (because the manufacturer from which it ordered the shaver was reputable), the store will **not** have the right to cure its defective tender because, under the circumstances (Ned leaving for Europe the next day), the buyer would suffer too much inconvenience waiting for the cured tender. In other words, a cure would still leave Ned without most of the value he had a right to expect from the contract.

(3) **The Manner in Which a Seller May Cure: Cure by Replacement, Cure by Repair, or Cure by Cash Discount. [§ 22–18]**

Often a seller's imperfect tender is the delivery of a non-working good, e.g., a television whose picture is consistently green, or a new car whose transmission fails. In such cases, even assuming the seller has a right to cure under § 2–508, there is often a disagreement between buyer and seller as to how the cure should be effected.

That is, usually the buyer will want a brand new television or a brand new car as a replacement, while the seller will want to try to repair the defect (or, perhaps, even refund a portion of the purchase price) before it offers a brand new good to the buyer. The buyer, of course, often does not want a repaired good or a few dollars refunded and would rather have all his or her money back than be forced to accept a repaired item.

The Code says nothing definitively about what manner of cure is effective. However, the courts have established the following general rules:

> (a) **A seller who has a right to cure under § 2–508 is *usually* entitled first to attempt to cure by repair, so long as such repair, if successfully carried out, will result in the buyer ending up with substantially all of the benefit of his or her bargain**. [*See* §§ 22–19 for a limitation on, and further explanation of, this rule].
>
> (b) **If cure by repair does not result in the buyer having the substantial benefit of his or her bargain, it is an ineffective cure and the buyer must be given a new replacement good. If the seller does not tender a new replacement good in this kind of a situation, the buyer is entitled to reject the repaired one and sue for total breach.**

(c) A seller, even one with a right to cure under § 2–508, cannot *require* the buyer to accept a cure by refund of all or any portion of the purchase price. If the seller is unwilling either to repair or replace the defective good, the buyer is entitled to terminate the contract and sue for total breach.

Thus, if the seller of the television wants to fix the problem of a consistently green picture by installing a brand new chip that controls picture quality, *generally* the courts will allow it (assuming of course the problem is fixed), and the buyer cannot insist on a brand new television. That is, in cases involving a successful cure by repair with brand new parts, the Code deems that the purchaser has received the benefit of his or her bargain, which the courts would define as a working television or car with all new parts.

One thing that is clear is that all expenses of cure must be borne by the seller [UCC §§ 2–508(1) and (2)].

(a) Exception to the Rule That Cure by Repair Is Acceptable: The "Shaken Faith" Doctrine. [§ 22–19]

Case law has engrafted one exception to the rule given above that cure by repair is generally an acceptable cure. This is known as the "shaken faith" doctrine and provides that where the breach is serious enough that a reasonable buyer would have a shaken faith in the *safety and dependability of the good*, a seller can only cure by providing a brand new replacement good.

(i) Example Based on *Zabriske Chevrolet v. Smith*. [§ 22–20]

Smith bought a new Chevrolet. While driving the car home after leaving the showroom the vehicle broke down due to a defective transmission. The dealership replaced the transmission with one from another brand new car of a different Chevrolet model that was on the lot. The Chevrolet dealership insisted the engines and transmissions of the two models were identical. Smith said he wanted a brand new car, not one with a replaced transmission.

Held: The dealership could only cure by giving Smith a completely brand new car. As the court held, "For a majority of people the purchase of a

CONDITIONS, PERFORMANCE AND BREACH (WITH AN EMPHASIS ON CONTRACTS GOVERNED BY THE UCC)

new car is major investment, rationalized by the peace of mind that flows from its dependability and safety. Once that faith is shaken, the vehicle ... becomes an instrument ... whose operation is fraught with apprehension" [*Zabriskie Chevrolet, Inc. v. Smith*, 240 A.2d 195 (N.J. Super. 1968)].

The "shaken faith" rule has been applied only sparingly and only in cases in which a reasonable buyer would fear for his or her own *safety* with a repaired versus a replacement good.

(b) Quality of Cure by Replacement: Majority View Does Not Require Repaired Good Sufficient to Satisfy Perfect Tender Rule. [§ 22–21]

An issue sometimes arises when the cure results in a good that substantially gives the buyer the benefit of his or her bargain, but is not "perfect." The issue here is, can the buyer reject a cure if what results is a good that could have been rejected under the perfect tender rule, but is still almost perfect? Most courts provide that a good that substantially provides the buyer with his or her benefits under the contract is sufficient. Some courts, however, require the cured good to meet the standards of a perfectly tendered good.

(4) Buyer's Rights and Duties When Seller Attempts to Cure. [§ 22–22]

There are certain rules regarding a buyer's rights and duties in a cure situation that need to be understood in order to understand sufficiently how the doctrine of cure operates:

(1) Section 2–508 sets forth a seller's **right** to cure, which conversely means it is the **duty** of a buyer to allow a cure if the seller can meet the requisites provided in § 2–508. Thus, if the seller is entitled to cure under § 2–508, and timely tenders the cure in an effective manner, the buyer **must** accept the cured tender or be in breach himself or herself. However, if the seller is adjudged not entitled to cure under § 2–508, or if the method of cure is not an effective one, then it is the seller who is in breach, and the buyer can reject the re-tendered goods without contractual liability.

(2) The effect of cure is to turn what would at common law be a material breach under the perfect tender rule

into an immaterial one [§§ 21–77 *et seq.*]. Hence, even if the seller is entitled to cure and does so in an effective manner, the buyer is still entitled to sue the seller for immaterial breach and recover any damages suffered while waiting for the cure.

b. **Installment Contracts. [§ 22–23]**

Section 2–601 provides that the perfect tender rule does not apply to installment contracts. An installment contract either **requires or authorizes the delivery of goods in more than one lot** [UCC § 2–612(1)]. When the seller's tender of a particular shipment under an installment contract is non-conforming, the buyer is faced with two issues: (1) on what grounds is he or she entitled to reject **that particular shipment** due to the non-conforming tender associated with that shipment; and (2) on what grounds is he or she entitled to reject **all future shipments** and to **terminate the entire contract** due to the non-conforming tender of a particular shipment or shipments? UCC § 2–612 sets forth the applicable standards governing the buyer's right of rejection in these situations, which are discussed below.

(1) **A Buyer May Reject a *Particular Shipment* Due to a Non-Conforming Tender of That Shipment *Only* if the Non-Conformity Both "Substantially Impairs" the Value of the Shipment and Is Not Cured. [§ 22–24]**

Under § 2–612(2), a buyer may reject *a particular shipment* of an installment contract due to a non-conforming tender of that shipment if:

(a) The nonconformity **substantially impairs** the value of **that shipment;** and

(b) Either:

(1) The non-conformity **cannot be cured,** or

(2) The seller **refuses to give adequate assurance** of cure.

Thus, for installment contracts under the UCC, the Code has adopted a kind of substantial performance doctrine to regulate a buyer's rights [§ 21–68 for a discussion of the substantial performance doctrine under common law]. A minor breach by the seller in the tender of a particular shipment in an installment contract, i.e., a breach that does not "substantially impair" the value of the shipment, is treated as an immaterial breach. Hence, while the buyer is entitled to sue for any damages caused by the breach, the

CONDITIONS, PERFORMANCE AND BREACH (WITH AN EMPHASIS ON CONTRACTS GOVERNED BY THE UCC)

buyer cannot reject the shipment and refuse to pay for them without incurring contractual liability. In other words, the buyer is "stuck" with having to accept imperfect (or otherwise imperfectly tendered) goods, and cannot tell the seller to take them back when the seller makes an immaterial breach of a particular installment under § 2–612. In such a case, the buyer's only recourse is to sue for the damages resulting from the breach or hope for a cure by the seller.

If the breach were serious enough that it did "substantially impair" the value of the shipment, then the buyer is entitled to reject the shipment and need not pay for the goods. However, even then the seller is entitled to cure such a breach if he or she can establish the right to do so under § 2–508 [*See* § 22–12 for a discussion of the seller's right of cure]. If the seller effectively cures the breach, once again the buyer cannot reject the shipment and must accept and pay for the goods, for his or her only recourse is to sue for damages caused by the imperfect tender.

(a) **Example. [§ 22–25]**

Betsy orders 300 faucets from Sheila, to be delivered in two lots of 150 faucets each. The first shipment was timely delivered, but when Betsy examined the faucets, she discovered that one was broken.

If this were a single lot contract for 150 faucets, Betsy would be entitled to reject all 150 faucets (or any portion thereof), and refuse to pay for them, subject to the seller's right to cure and the other applicable limitations discussed in § 21–11. However, because this is an *installment* contract, Betsy most likely would not be entitled to reject the shipment because the failure of one faucet to work out of 150 likely does not "substantially impair" the value of that shipment. As a result, Betsy must accept the shipment (although, of course, she doesn't have to pay for the broken one [UCC § 2–717]).

(b) **Example. [§ 22–26]**

Same as above, except this time 120 of the 150 faucets in the first shipment are broken. At this point, the magnitude of the breach "substantially impairs" the value of the shipment, and Betsy may reject the entire amount, or keep the 30 working models and reject the rest, subject to Sheila's right to cure.

(2) A Buyer May Terminate *the Entire Installment Contract* Due to a Non-Conforming Tender in a Particular Shipment or Shipments *Only* When the Non-Conformity in the Particular Shipment(s) Substantially Impairs the Value of the *Whole Contract*. [§ 22–27]

Under § 2–612(3), a buyer may not effectively terminate the remainder of an installment contract based on the seller's non-conforming tender in one or more of the previously received installments unless the breach of the particular installment (or the sum of the breaches in the previous installments) **substantially impairs the value of the *whole contract*.** In other words, once again the Code directs that the breach of an installment contract be treated as a partial breach until the substantial impairment test is met.

Thus, if a breach of one delivery is so bad that the value of the **whole** contract is substantially impaired, the buyer is entitled to treat the entire contract as materially breached, and may suspend his or her own performance without liability. However, if the non-conformity as to one or more shipments does not seriously impair the value of the **whole** contract, *even if the breach justifies rejection of that particular installment*, then the buyer must perform the remainder of the agreement or be in breach.

Note, however, that a seller's failure of perfect tender in one or more installments under an installment contract may give the buyer the right to demand reasonable assurances of future performance as provided in § 2–609 [*See* §§ 23–22 *et seq.* for a discussion of the requirements and effects of such a demand for reasonable assurances].

(a) Example. [§ 22–28]

A grocery store contracts for the delivery of 100 pounds of apples per month over the next two years from Wholesaler. In the first shipment, 85 pounds of apples are spoiled and Wholesaler refuses to cure by sending replacements.

The store can reject that shipment (for there was a substantial impairment in the value of the shipment). Most likely the store management will have lost confidence in the wholesaler and will wonder whether the seller is going to deliver conforming goods in the future. Probably the store would like to cancel the contract at that point and find a new supplier.

However, it is not entitled to do so, although it is entitled to send a request for reasonable assurances of its future conduct under UCC § 2–609 [*See* §§ 23–23 *et seq.* for a discussion of reasonable assurance demands].

According to Comment 6 to § 2–612, an insecurity as to the completeness of future performance based on a seller's past shipments is insufficient, in and of itself, to justify cancellation of the contract. It is only when the failure of tender in a particular shipment **substantially impairs the value of the whole** contract that the store will be entitled to declare a material breach of the whole, and cancel the remainder of the contract under § 2–612(3). Obviously, if the wholesaler continues to send a large amount of spoiled fruit with each installment (and does not cure the defective shipments), at some point the aggregate effect of those acts will be to substantially impair the value of the whole contract to the store.

It is rare that the imperfect tender in the first shipment of an installment contract can meet the "substantial impairment of the whole" standard of § 2–612(3).

(3) Rationale for Different Treatment of Buyer's Right to Reject Goods in Installment and Single Lot Contracts. [§ 22–29]

As you no doubt have ascertained, in this area form controls substance under the UCC. That is, the same breach by the seller will enable a buyer to reject a shipment under the perfect tender rule if the contract calls for a single lot delivery, but will not allow the buyer to reject the shipment under the substantial impairment test if the contract calls for more than one shipment. There is some disagreement as to the rationale for this disparate treatment. While it does not explain the issue completely, the most frequently given reason is that it is more likely that merchants enter into installment contracts, whereas ordinary consumers enter into single lot ones. This theory holds that merchants are better prepared to deal with less than perfect tender than consumers. However, if this were truly the reason for the different treatment, it would seem likely the Code would simply provide separate rejection standards for merchant and consumer buyers.

CHAPTER 22

c. ***De Minimis Non Curat Lex.*** **[§ 22–30]**

Another limitation on the perfect tender rule is described by one of the few remaining Latin phrases that is mentioned occasionally in the commercial case law, *de minimis non curat lex.* Loosely translated, the phrase means "the law does not deal in trifles." The idea is that if the breach is truly *de minimis,* i.e., truly trifling, some courts have found that the perfect tender rule should not apply even to a single lot contract despite the wording of § 2–601. Thus, to these courts, a *de minimis* breach should be treated as an immaterial one and not subject to the perfect tender rule, meaning that the buyer cannot reject the good based on the non-conformity, must pay the purchase price, and is limited to suing the seller for damages resulting from the imperfect tender.

d. **The "Complex Machine" Exception. [§ 22–31]**

An offshoot of the *"de minimis"* rule explained in the previous section is another exception to the perfect tender rule engrafted by case law. This exception is known as the "complex machine" exception and provides that it is not realistic that a car or some complex machine used in manufacturing, etc., be absolutely perfect. A consumer should expect some amount of imperfection. To be sure, the consumer should have the right to have the defect cured, and/or can sue for damages resulting therefrom, but should not be entitled to reject the good for such imperfections.

(1) **Example. [§ 22–32]**

Buyer purchases a new car. The day after bringing it home she discovers the cigarette lighter doesn't work. Under both the *de minimis* and "complex machine" exceptions, Buyer may not rely on the perfect tender rule to reject the car. Even if the dealer does not fix the problem, under these exceptions, if applicable, she is entitled to sue for damages as a result of the defect, but she is not entitled to send the car back.

e. **Usage of Trade; Course of Dealing; and Course of Performance. [§ 22–33]**

Section 2–601 does not, on its face, use the words "perfect tender." Instead, it states that buyer has the right to reject any commercial unit of a single lot shipment if seller fails "to conform to the contract." Sometimes a usage of trade, course of dealing, or course of performance may modify the duties of the seller so that even though the seller's tendered performance fails to fulfill the express words of the contract, the performance nonetheless "conforms to the contract."

CONDITIONS, PERFORMANCE AND BREACH (WITH AN EMPHASIS ON CONTRACTS GOVERNED BY THE UCC)

(1) **Example.** [§ 22–34]

Roger owns a golf shop and orders 10,000 tees from a golf supplier. Assume that in the golf industry it is a well-known and accepted practice that a supplier need not count each tee separately to fulfill an order. Rather, tees are measured by weight and the custom is that 1,000 tees weigh 12 ounces. Accordingly, the supplier sends Roger ten 12-oz. packages. Roger is obsessive and counts the tees and it turns out that only 9,987 were sent. Roger will not be able to reject the shipment under § 2–601 because given the custom, the tender of the tees by the supplier "conformed to the contract."

f. **Revocation of Acceptance.** [§ 22–35]

As explained in detail in § 22–45, a party who "accepts" a good and later tries to revoke that acceptance cannot do so under the standards of the perfect tender rule. Once acceptance has taken place, a buyer cannot reject a good unless the non-conformity **substantially impairs the value of the good to the buyer, and** *either* *was:* (a) difficult to discover when it was accepted, or (b) accepted knowingly by the buyer with the reasonable assumption the seller would fix it [UCC § 2–608]. Thus, revocation of acceptance situations are also governed by a type of substantial impairment test, which limits the harshness to sellers of the perfect tender rule [*See* the further discussion of revocation of acceptance beginning in § 22–45].

D. PERFORMANCE IN CONTRACTS GOVERNED BY THE UCC: ACCEPTANCE, REJECTION, AND REVOCATION OF ACCEPTANCE. [§ 22–36]

When a buyer receives the seller's tender of goods under a transaction governed by Article 2 of the UCC, there are three things the buyer may do:

(1) **Accept** the goods [§ 22–37],

(2) **Reject** the goods [§ 22–39], or

(3) Accept the goods at first, but later **revoke his or her acceptance** of them [§ 22–45].

1. **"Acceptance" of Goods Under the UCC.** [§ 22–37]

Once goods have been duly tendered to a buyer, most often the buyer accepts them. What constitutes acceptance is governed by § 2–606, which says there are three ways a buyer may effectively accept a seller's tender:

(1) By **informing the seller he or she will accept the goods** after having a reasonable opportunity to inspect them [UCC § 2–606(1)(a)];

(2) By keeping them and saying nothing one way or another about acceptance, i.e., by **failing to reject them effectively after a reasonable period of time** [UCC § 2–606(1)(b)]; and

(3) By taking **any act inconsistent with the seller's ownership** of the tendered goods [UCC § 2–606(1)(c)].

It is important to note that mere possession of the goods by the buyer, or even payment for the goods by the buyer, does not necessarily constitute acceptance of the goods [UCC § 2–606, Cmt. 3]. The buyer is entitled (absent an agreement to the contrary) to possess and inspect the goods for a reasonable period of time before "accepting" them [UCC § 2–513]. **"Inspection" in this context means more than just a quick glance at the goods; it means a reasonable chance to investigate them to determine if they are conforming goods.**

The most common form of acceptance is under § 2–606(1)(b), i.e., where the buyer receives the goods, inspects them, and simply keeps them without further communication with the seller. After a reasonable inspection period, acceptance by silence of the goods has taken place.

Note: Sometimes confusion arises between the concepts of "acceptance" of an offer and "acceptance" of a good. However, you must keep them analytically separate, for they are completely different concepts. For example, while an offeree generally cannot accept an offer to enter into a contract by silence [§ 4–112], acceptance of *a good* by silence (failing to reject for a reasonable period of time) under § 2–606(1)(b) is quite routine. It simply signifies the buyer is willing to keep and pay for the good tendered by the seller after the inspection period has expired.

a. Effect of Acceptance. [§ 22–38]

Acceptance is a significant event in the buyer-seller relationship. Upon a buyer's acceptance of goods, the rights and duties of the buyer and seller toward each other change. Upon acceptance of the goods:

(1) **The buyer must pay for the goods at the contract price [UCC § 2–607(1)]**. Note that even if the goods later turn out to be defective, the buyer must still pay for them upon acceptance. Obviously the buyer can later sue for damages resulting from receiving the defective product, but the purchase price must nevertheless be paid after acceptance or the buyer will also be liable for breach.

(2) **The buyer can no longer reject the goods [UCC § 2–607(2)]**, and so the buyer's right to rely on the perfect tender rule to reject a shipment is lost.

(3) The **burden of proof to establish that the seller's tender was non-conforming shifts from the seller to the buyer [UCC § 2–607(4)]** If a buyer rejects a good as non-conforming *before acceptance, the seller has the burden of proof to establish that his or her tender **was** conforming* in the subsequent breach of contract suit. **After acceptance, it is up to the buyer to prove that the seller's tender was not conforming**; and

(4) The **buyer is obligated to notify the seller of any breach** regarding the tender of the goods within a reasonable time, or the buyer is barred from recovery [UCC § 2–607(3)]. Typically, this requirement is important in breach of warranty actions when reasonable notification to the seller is a condition precedent to allowing a breach of warranty claim to continue [*See* Chapter Thirty-Five for a further discussion on breach of warranties].

2. **Rejection of Goods Under the UCC. [§ 22–39]**

If a buyer does not accept goods tendered to him or her in a transaction governed by the UCC, by definition he or she "rejects" them. In other words, any non-acceptance of goods under the Code is a rejection. For the rejection to be **effective**, certain things **must** be done by the buyer and one thing **cannot** be done by the buyer. If the buyer fails to do one of the things he or she is obligated to do, or does the one thing he or she is not supposed to do, the attempted rejection is deemed ineffective, and the goods will be judged accepted under § 2–606(1)(b). These issues are discussed immediately below.

a. **Actions a Buyer *Must* Take in Order to Reject Effectively. [§ 22–40]**

Under the UCC, a buyer who wishes to effectively reject a good is under an obligation to do the following upon rejection:

(1) Reject the good **within a reasonable time** after delivery [UCC § 2–602(1)];

(2) **Seasonably** (i.e., within a commercially reasonable time under the circumstances) **notify the seller** of the rejection [UCC § 2–602(1)];

(3) **Hold and store the goods with reasonable care**, if he or she has taken possession of them before rejection [UCC § 2–602(2)(b)]. As noted earlier in § 22–37, mere possession of a good does not signify acceptance of it. The

buyer has a reasonable period within which to inspect the good before acceptance takes place. Thus, the buyer may well have possession of the good when the decision to reject it is made, and if so, the buyer must hold the good with reasonable care;

(4) If the buyer is a merchant, **the buyer must try to sell any rejected perishable good as soon as possible**, assuming the seller or the seller's agent has no place of business "in the market of rejection" [UCC § 2–603(1)]. That is, if the seller is in the same city or "market" as the buyer, the seller has to come and retake possession of rejected *perishable* goods and try to sell them if he or she can. If the seller is not in that market, however, a merchant buyer has an obligation to attempt to sell them. However, the buyer is entitled to recover his or her costs in selling the goods, including a reasonable commission [UCC § 2–603(2)]; and

(5) **If the buyer is a merchant**, the rejected goods are not perishable, and the seller is not located in the "market of rejection," **the buyer must follow any reasonable instructions from the seller concerning the disposition of goods** [UCC § 2–603(1)]. Thus, if the seller asks the merchant buyer to ship back the rejected goods, the merchant buyer must do so. However, the buyer may demand indemnity from the seller for any expenses incurred in shipping the goods back [UCC § 2–603(1)].

b. **Action a Buyer *Cannot* Take in Order to Reject Effectively. [§ 22–41]**

Under § 2–602(2)(a), if a buyer exercises any indicia of ownership over goods he or she either is considering rejecting or has previously rejected, no rejection is possible as the buyer will be deemed to have accepted the goods.

(1) **Example. [§ 22–42]**

Megan purchased an electric lawn mower from Ralph's Hardware on Tuesday. Later that day Megan discovered it didn't work, and promptly notified Ralph that she was rejecting it. Ralph promised to pick it up from Megan's house on Friday. On Thursday, a worker repairing roof tiles at Megan's home drops a tile on the mower and destroys it. The worker immediately offers Megan a check to pay for the mower, which Megan accepts. By accepting the check made out in her name, Megan's rejection of the mower has become ineffective, for she exercised an indicia of ownership of the mower, i.e., accepting payment for its destruction. Thus, while she may keep the check, she must also pay Ralph the contract price for the mower as she has now "accepted" it under both UCC § 2–602(1)(a) and § 2–606(1)(c).

c. **Actions Which a Rejecting Buyer Is *Permitted to* Take Which Do Not Render Acceptance Ineffective. [§ 22–43]**

Upon rejection, the Code sets forth a series of options that a rejecting buyer is permitted, but is not required, to take. The most prominent of these are:

(1) If the rejecting buyer is a non-merchant, the buyer is permitted either:

to send rejected goods back to the seller,

to sell them for the seller's account, or

store them reasonably until the seller picks them up (and can charge the seller for such storage).

If the buyer in fact sells the goods for the seller, the buyer is entitled to withhold a reasonable commission from the amounts generated by the sale so long as such a sale is in good faith. Of course, the buyer must turn over any remaining proceeds from such sale to the seller [UCC § 2–604].

In addition, if the rejecting buyer is a non-merchant, the buyer may, but is not required to, follow the instructions of the seller as to the disposition of the goods. This is true even if the seller offers to pay the buyer for any inconvenience and expense [UCC § 2–604]. (Note that while this approach follows from the explicit wording of § 2–604, some courts and commentators disagree that it is what § 2–604 means. They contend that a non-merchant buyer's deliberate refusal to follow a seller's reasonable and easily carried out instructions may constitute a breach of the duty of good faith).

(2) If the rejecting buyer is a merchant, and if the goods are not perishable, and if the seller has not sent instructions regarding the disposition of the goods within a reasonable time, the buyer is also entitled to sell the goods for the seller's account and keep a commission for his or her services, or may store them until the seller picks them up, and charge the seller a fee for such storage [UCC § 2–604].

d. **Grounds for Rejection. [§ 22–44]**

As a review, recall that in a single lot contract, the buyer is entitled to reject the goods upon any deviation from promised performance under the perfect tender rule [UCC § 2–601; § 22–

7]. Under an installment contract, the grounds for rejection are more stringent [UCC § 2–612; § 22–23].

3. **Revocation of Acceptance. [§ 22–45]**

If a buyer initially accepts a good after sufficient inspection, but then later decides there are grounds to return it, the buyer's actions are no longer deemed a rejection, but rather constitute a **revocation of acceptance** [UCC § 2–608].

a. **Elements of an Effective Revocation of Acceptance. [§ 22–46]**

In order to establish that a buyer has sufficient grounds to revoke his or her previous acceptance effectively, the buyer must prove:

(1) The goods were accepted **with knowledge of their non-conformity, but with a reasonable expectation that the non-conformity would be cured by the seller** [§ 2–608(1)(a)]; or

(2) The goods were accepted **without knowledge of their non-conformity, and the non-conformity was not known because it was difficult or impossible initially to discover it** [§ 2–608(1)(b)].

In addition to **either** of the above grounds, the buyer must also establish **all** of the following:

(a) That the non-conformity on which the revocation is based **substantially impairs** the value of the goods **to the buyer** [§ 2–608(1)];

Note two things about this requirement. **First,** as noted previously (*see* § 22–35), it acts as a limitation on the perfect tender rule, i.e., a buyer may not revoke his or her acceptance for **any** non-conformity, even when it was delivered under a single lot contract. Instead, to revoke effectively, the non-conformity must **substantially impair** the value of the good.

Second, the test under § 2–608(1) is subjective, i.e., the non-conformity need only substantially impair the value of the good **to the particular buyer,** and not to a hypothetical, ordinary reasonable buyer.

(b) **Revocation must occur within a reasonable time after the buyer discovered or should have discovered the grounds for it** [§ 2–608(2)]; and

CONDITIONS, PERFORMANCE AND BREACH (WITH AN EMPHASIS ON CONTRACTS GOVERNED BY THE UCC)

(c) **Revocation must occur before any substantial change** in the condition of the goods not caused by the non-conformity [§ 2–608(2)].

(1) Example. [§ 22–47]

Ann buys a stereo system from a department store and when she gets it home, she discovers that the volume knob is not attached securely. She calls up the seller, who assures her the store will send someone out to her home in the next couple of weeks to fix it. On that representation Ann accepts and uses the stereo. If the seller never makes the repair, Ann is probably entitled to revoke her acceptance based on § 2–608(1)(a) after a couple of weeks. To establish her right to revoke, she will need to prove: (a) she accepted the stereo with knowledge of its non-conformity (i.e., she knew the knob was loose), but did so only on the reasonable assumption the defect would be cured; (b) the loose knob substantially impairs the value of the stereo to *her*, (c) her revocation occurred within a reasonable time after she realized the store was not sending someone out to fix it; and (d) there has been no substantial change in the condition of the stereo caused by anything other than the defect when she revokes her acceptance of it.

(2) Example. [§ 22–48]

Sam buys a television from Video, Inc., a retailer. The manufacturer of the set did not securely attach an internal wire. At first the television worked perfectly and Sam accepted it. After two weeks, however, the wire came loose and the television stopped working. Sam is likely entitled to revoke his acceptance against Video Inc. under § 2–608(1)(b). That is, his acceptance of a defective good was reasonably made without discovery of the non-conformity given the difficulty of discovering the problem and a non-working television substantially impairs the value of the contract to Sam. Assuming notice of Sam's revocation is timely made and that the revocation is done before there is any substantial change in the set not caused by the wire problem, Sam is entitled to revoke acceptance.

(3) Example. [§ 22–49]

Leonard, the conductor of the local symphony, buys a stereo. Over time it develops, at least to his ears, a shrill sound quality that greatly disturbs him. No one else can hear this shrill quality, and indeed everyone who hears the stereo is quite impressed with the system. Nevertheless, assuming he does so in a timely fashion, Leonard may revoke his acceptance because the non-conformity (i.e., the difference between what the stereo sounded like in the store and what it sounds like now) substantially impairs the value of the stereo to *him*.

b. **Rationale for Having Different Standards for Rejection than for Revocation of Acceptance. [§ 22–50]**

If a buyer wishes to send back a defective good delivered under a single lot contract, it is obviously easier to reject it (using the perfect tender rule of § 2–601) than to revoke his or her acceptance of it (under the subjective substantial impairment test of § 2–608). The principal reason for making it more difficult to revoke than to reject is that, by definition, a revocation must occur after the buyer has decided to accept the good. Thus, the buyer will almost surely have the good in his or her possession for a longer time in a revocation situation than in a rejection one. Hence, because it is more difficult to prove that the problem with the good which gives rise to the revocation was not caused by the buyer (given the buyer's longer time of possession), the Code has made it somewhat more difficult for the buyer to establish the right to get out of the contract under revocation than under rejection.

c. **The Relationship Between Cure and Revocation of Acceptance. [§ 22–51]**

There is a split of authority as to whether a seller has a right to cure a non-conformity giving rise to revocation of acceptance. Those who think a seller should have that cure right point to the general policy of the UCC to keep the parties in a contract, and to § 2–608(3), which states that a buyer who revokes has the same "duties" as one who rejects. They argue that because one of the duties of a rejecting party is to allow the seller to cure, clearly the Code provides for a seller's right to cure in revocation situations.

Those who believe a seller does not have a right to cure upon revocation of acceptance point to the language of the cure provision itself. Under § 2–508 there is no mention of a seller's right to cure in a revocation situation, only of a right to cure upon *rejection*. These commentators argue that if the drafters had meant for sellers to have a right to cure upon revocation, the drafters surely would have said so in § 2–508. Hence, those who hold this view believe that by not mentioning it, the Code's drafters intended that a seller have the right to cure a defective tender only when a good was rejected.

CONDITIONS, PERFORMANCE AND BREACH (WITH AN EMPHASIS ON CONTRACTS GOVERNED BY THE UCC)

d. Typically No Restitution Is Recoverable upon Revocation. [§ 22–52]

Assume Karen purchases a new car and after a few days begins to experience trouble with the ignition. She tries to reject the car, but the dealer assures her its service department will fix the problem. On those representations, she accepts it. Over the next six months the car is in for service numerous times, but the problem remains. Finally, Karen wants to revoke the acceptance of the car, which she is entitled do because while it was accepted with knowledge of the defect, she did so with a reasonable expectation that the problem would be fixed. Assume, however, that the dealership refuses to accept her revocation and Karen sues.

Most courts hold that Karen is entitled to the full amount of her purchase price back in addition to any other damages she can prove. Under the majority view she is **not** liable in restitution for the use of the car during the six months. Thus, the car dealership will receive nothing from Karen for the difference between the new car it gave her and the used car it gets back. Normal principles of restitution would seem to compel such recovery however [*see* Chapter Thirty-One for a discussion of restitution], but the Code does not specifically provide for it in revocation situations, and most courts do not grant it, although some do.

e. A Buyer of an Imperfect Good Who Neither Rejects nor Revokes: Breach of Warranty. [§ 22–53]

A buyer who ends up with a good with a defect may choose to keep it, either because he or she wants it even with the defect, or because the time for rejection or revocation has passed. In that case the buyer still can sue for breach of warranty, and is entitled to recover the difference between the value of the good the buyer was promised and the value of the good the buyer received. [UCC § 2–714; *see also* Chapter Thirty-Five for a further discussion of warranty.]

E. EXAM APPROACHES TO PERFORMANCE AND BREACH ISSUES UNDER THE UCC. [§ 22–54]

On an examination, when you are presented with a potential breach issue in a contract governed by the UCC, analyze the problem as follows:

1. Look at each party separately to determine who has breached.

    A. To determine whether the *seller* has breached, make sure the *buyer* has tendered performance, because the buyer's tender of performance is a constructive condition that must be satisfied to make the seller's duties enforceable [§ 22–2].

(1) If the seller has made an improper tender, analyze whether the contract is governed by the perfect tender rule allowing the buyer to reject the good or whether one of its exceptions apply, i.e.:

— Cure [§ 22–12 *et seq.*];

— Installment contract [§ 22–23];

— *De minimis non curat lex* [§ 22–30];

— Complex machinery [*see* § 22–31]; or

— The buyer is trying to revoke his acceptance of the goods [*see* § 22–45] and remember

— The general rule as set forth by White & Summers that courts do not recognize minor breaches as material ones under the perfect tender rule in commercial contracts [*See* § 22–11].

(2) If the buyer is entitled to reject the good, make sure the buyer has followed the procedures for an effective rejection. If the buyer has not followed all these procedures, the buyer has "accepted" the good and:

— Must pay for the goods [§ 22–37];

— Can no longer reject the goods [§ 22–39];

— Has the burden of proof to establish the non-conformity [§ 22–38]; and

— Is obligated to inform the seller of the breach or be barred from further recovery [§ 22–38].

A buyer who cannot reject may still:

— Try to revoke his or her acceptance [§ 22–45]; or

— Accept the good and sue for breach of warranty [§ 22–53].

B. To determine whether the *buyer* has breached, make sure the *seller has* tendered performance, i.e., sent conforming goods in a timely manner, because the seller's tender of performance is a constructive condition that must be satisfied to make the buyer's duty to pay enforceable [§ 22–2];

2. Realize (assuming you have covered the material in class) that the non-breaching party has a right to damages, restitution, or (possibly) equitable relief because of the breach [*See* Chapters Twenty-Nine through Thirty-Two for a discussion on remedies].

CHAPTER 23

PROSPECTIVE NONPERFORMANCE OR ANTICIPATORY REPUDIATION

A. THE ANTICIPATORY REPUDIATION (ALSO, INCORRECTLY, CALLED THE "ANTICIPATORY BREACH") DOCTRINE. [§ 23–1*]

At first blush, it seems no one could credibly argue with the concept of anticipatory repudiation. After all, if Larry's Appliance Store has made a contractual promise to deliver a new television to Donna on May 15, and on May 1 Larry calls up Donna and says "The contract's over! We're not delivering the T.V.," it seems Donna should be able to take Larry at his word and immediately sue him for breach.

However the doctrine, at least as we know it today, was not fully articulated until the 1850's (in a case called *Hochster v. De la Tour*, see § 23–2), and after *Hochster*, it still took decades before the doctrine was fully accepted and integrated into contract law. The facts and rationale of *Hochster* are presented below, along with a summary of the controversy surrounding the acceptance of the anticipatory repudiation doctrine.

SPECIAL CASE SQUIB

B. *HOCHSTER V. DE LA TOUR:* THE BEGINNING OF THE MODERN ANTICIPATORY REPUDIATION DOCTRINE. [§ 23–2]

In April 1852, Hochster entered into a contract whereby he promised to accompany De la Tour as a personal assistant throughout De la Tour's European boat trip. The trip was scheduled to start on June 1, 1852 and last for about three months. In early May, De la Tour wrote to Hochster

---

* For more information, listen to CD # 10, Track 4 of *Sum and Substance Audio on Contracts*.

and said that because he had canceled his European trip, he was compelled to "decline" Hochster's services. Hochster hustled and procured similar employment with another, but that second employment was to start about a month later, and end at the same time as De la Tour's trip. As a consequence, Hochster ended up with a month's less pay than he anticipated under his contract with De la Tour. When De la Tour refused to compensate Hochster for that month, Hochster brought suit for breach. What has made the case so memorable is that Hochster filed suit in late May, ten days before the date on which the trip for De la Tour was supposed to start.

One of De la Tour's defenses was that the suit was premature. That is, he claimed he could not have "breached" the contract on the day the suit was filed since, on that date, he had not failed to perform an enforceable duty owed to Hochster. He may have indicated that he was not going to perform such a duty, but on the day the suit was filed, his breach was only a possibility and had not yet occurred.

Held: The holding of *Hochster* is twofold:

(1) Upon the unequivocal repudiation of future performance from De la Tour, Hochster was entitled to treat his own duties under the contract as discharged, and was entitled immediately and lawfully to seek and to take other employment; and

(2) Hochster was entitled to file suit immediately upon receipt of the unequivocal repudiation, and need not wait until the date performance was due (in this case June 1), before instituting a breach action. [*Hochster v. De La Tour*, 2 El. & Bl. 678, 118 Eng. Rep. 922 (Q.B. 1853)].

The first part of the holding caused no controversy whatsoever. To make Hochster wait until June 1 before he was able to accept, or perhaps even to seek, other employment was manifestly unfair. Indeed, under the doctrine of mitigation of damages (*see* § 30–59), it is arguable that Hochster would be penalized in the amount of his recovery if he did not seek and accept reasonably similar work soon after the repudiation.

However, the second part of the holding was met with much criticism. Those who argued against its adoption in the common law made the following points:

(1) As a matter of language, this part of the holding was illogical. A contract is not "breached" until there is a non-excused or unjustified failure to perform an enforceable duty. In this case no such duty existed until after June 1. There clearly was a repudiation before then, but the relevant cause of action is for **breach** of contract, not *repudiation* of contract, and thus Hochster should not be entitled to sue for breach until after the date performance was due; and

(2) Allowing a suit for breach before the date of performance could cause problems in damage calculations. In *Hochster*, the potential

problem was not likely to cause much confusion because there was only a 10-day difference between the date of suit and the date of performance. But as we will see, for sales of goods, one damages measure uses the market price of the goods on the day they were supposed to be accepted under the contract [UCC § 2–714(2); § 32–24]. It would be impossible to know the market value of goods subject to price volatility on the day of acceptance if the case comes to trial before acceptance is due.

Despite those arguments which, of course, have merit, the courts and commentators have nevertheless adopted the rule that **the innocent party is entitled to sue for total breach immediately upon the receipt of an effective anticipatory repudiation** [Restatement 2d § 253(1); UCC § 2–610]. They have formulated the following answers to the criticisms set forth above:

> (1) It is not linguistically impossible to have a "breach" before performance is due. This is because implicit in a party's promise to do nothing that would substantially impair the good faith and fair dealing principles imputed in every contract is his or her promised performance before it is due. Thus, upon a repudiation there has, in fact, been a breach—a breach of the implied promise to do nothing to seriously impair a party's good faith performance obligation [Restatement 2d § 205; UCC § 1–304]. Nevertheless, scholars refer to a suit for this pre-performance "breach" as a suit for **anticipatory repudiation**, not "breach"; and

> (2) As a practical matter, it is unlikely there will be so much time between anticipatory repudiation and promised performance that a case will actually get to trial before performance is due. If it does, , contract law can (and has) come up with special rules to calculate a plaintiff's damage based on the market value of the goods at the time of the repudiation [UCC § 2–723]. So the damages recoverable may not be the exact damages that would be recovered had the plaintiff waited until performance was due, but at least he or she gets something, and, of course, if exact damages are desired, the plaintiff could always wait to sue until the date when performance is due.

Further, because it is unlikely that many cases will come to trial before the date of performance, it would be unfair to the vast majority of innocent parties not to let them sue immediately. That is, a rule requiring innocent parties to wait until the date performance was due before filing suit would only delay their ability to obtain judicial relief from the other party's breach.

1. **Effect of Anticipatory Repudiation Under Modern Contract Law. [§ 23–3]**

To summarize, under Restatement 2d § 253(1) and UCC § 2–610, the modern effect of one party's anticipatory repudiation is:

(A) To allow the aggrieved party to bring suit for breach immediately upon receipt of the repudiation; and

(B) To discharge immediately the aggrieved party's remaining duties under the contract, i.e., to treat the anticipatory repudiation as a total breach [§§ 21–81 *et seq.*].

Knowing the effects of anticipatory repudiation makes two other issues important: (1) what must the aggrieved party prove so as to establish that an unequivocal anticipatory repudiation has taken place [§§ 23–4 *et seq.*]; and (2) once a party has anticipatorily repudiated, can that action be "taken back" or retracted [§ 23–32]?

C. ELEMENTS OF ANTICIPATORY REPUDIATION IN NON-UCC TRANSACTIONS. [§ 23–4]

If a non-repudiating party wishes to take advantage of the anticipatory repudiation doctrine, i.e., if he or she wants to be able to bring suit immediately and to have all of his or her duties under the agreement discharged in the face of a repudiation received before performance is due, the innocent party must establish the following elements:

(1) The repudiation was received under a **bilateral contract in which there were executory duties remaining** at the time of the repudiation [§ 23–5];

(2) The non-performance of the repudiated duty would result in a **total breach** [§ 23–10]; and

(3) The repudiation was **definite and unequivocal** [§ 23–12; Restatement 2d §§ 243, 250].

Note that the elements of an effective repudiation in a contract governed by Article 2 of the UCC are similar, but the nomenclature and some of the analysis in such a situation are different enough to justify a separate discussion in §§ 23–20 *et seq.*

1. There Must Be a Repudiation of a Bilateral Contract with Executory Duties by Both Parties. [§ 23–5]

Just as was true under the material breach doctrine [§ 21–58], the courts have held that the anticipatory repudiation doctrine will not apply unless the repudiation is of a duty owing under a bilateral contract in which both the repudiating and the innocent party still have unperformed duties at the time of repudiation. However, unlike material breach, there really is no satisfactory explanation for this rule. Nonetheless, it appears well established that in a unilateral contract, or in a bilateral contract where one party's performance is completed, a repudiation before performance is due will usually not result in the innocent party being able to sue the repudiator immediately (although there is one small exception to this rule, explained in § 23–8).

PROSPECTIVE NONPERFORMANCE OR ANTICIPATORY REPUDIATION

a. **Example. [§ 23–6]**

Shannon enters into a unilateral contract with Kelsey whereby she will pay Kelsey $3,000 in three weeks so long as Kelsey immediately delivers her Rolex watch to Shannon. Kelsey gives the watch to Shannon, and immediately Shannon says she will refuse to pay Kelsey in three weeks. Given the rules currently governing anticipatory repudiation, Kelsey may not bring suit to recover the $3,000 for three weeks, i.e., until Shannon's performance becomes due, because the anticipatory repudiation doctrine does not operate in unilateral contracts, only bilateral ones with executory duties pending.

b. **Example. [§ 23–7]**

Sam borrows $25,000 from Bank and promises to repay the loan at a rate of $1,000 per month plus interest, starting January 15. Sam misses the January, February, and March payments, and on March 20 he sends a letter to the Bank stating that he is repudiating and will not be making any payments under the loan. In the absence of any clause to the contrary, Bank has a cause of action for the first three payments only, and may not use the anticipatory repudiation doctrine to sue immediately for the remaining payments due under the loan. This is because the repudiation was of a duty under a bilateral contract where one side (the Bank) had fully performed its duties at the time of the other's repudiation [Restatement 2d § 243(3), *see also id.,* Cmt. d, Ill. 4].

Note, however, it is because of this rule that most commercial lenders include "acceleration clauses" in their loan agreements. An acceleration clause provides that upon a specified breach of the borrower's promised payment schedule (e.g., 3 consecutive missed payments), the borrower's obligation to repay the loan is "accelerated" so that the full amount of the debt is due and payable immediately upon notice from the bank. Such clauses are specifically made enforceable under UCC § 1–309. The parties' agreement is thus enforceable over the "default" anticipatory repudiation rules.

c. **Exception: Where Performance by the Innocent Party Is a Condition of the Repudiated Duty. [§ 23–8]**

The only exception to the rule that anticipatory breach has effect only under a bilateral contract with each party having executory duties extant at the time of repudiation comes about **where performance by the innocent party is a condition precedent to the enforceability of the repudiated duty**. In those cases, which most often occur under option contracts, the innocent party may immediately bring suit for breach upon the repudiation, even if the innocent party is in a bilateral contract where one party's performance is already complete.

(1) Example. [§ 23–9]

Frank has entered into an option contract with Mary whereby Frank has the option to purchase Mary's home for $100,000 any time within the next three months. Frank has already completely paid Mary for the option. Mary calls Frank within the three-month period and tells him that she has just sold her home to someone else and so Frank is out of luck. Even though performance by Frank under the option contract has been completely rendered, Frank may immediately bring suit for breach against Mary because Frank's performance in the underlying contract, i.e., payment of the $100,000 for the house, is a condition of the repudiated duty, i.e., Mary's duty to tender the deed upon tender of payment.

2. The Repudiated Duty Must Be Important Enough That Its Non-Performance Would Be Deemed a Total Breach. [§ 23–10]

Not every repudiated duty allows the non-repudiating party to sue immediately for anticipatory repudiation and have his or her duties thereafter discharged. To take advantage of the doctrine, the innocent party must establish that the repudiated duty is important enough to the transaction that its non-performance, when due, would constitute a total breach [*See* §§ 21–81 *et seq.* for a discussion of how to tell if a breach is total]. If the duty is minor enough so that its non-performance would be only an immaterial breach, the innocent party's duties under the agreement are not discharged, and he or she must continue to perform under the contract and cannot bring suit for breach of that duty until it goes unperformed when due.

a. Example. [§ 23–11]

A term of a construction contract requires the contractor to use Acme electrical outlets throughout the building. A month before construction is scheduled to begin, contractor writes developer stating that he will not be using Acme outlets as required, but will be using Watt-Man outlets instead, which are equivalent in size, style, quality, and price. Developer cannot immediately sue claiming anticipatory repudiation because if the contractor in fact installed Watt-Man outlets, such conduct would only result in an immaterial breach. Hence, developer will have to wait until performance is due upon the contract before he can sue for

PROSPECTIVE NONPERFORMANCE OR ANTICIPATORY REPUDIATION

breach (assuming he can prove damages), and his obligations to pay contractor are not discharged upon the repudiation.

3. The Repudiation Must Be *Definite* and *Unequivocal*. [§ 23–12]

The repudiation giving rise to an anticipatory repudiation claim may be communicated either by words or through actions. However, to be actionable, **the repudiation must be *definite* and *unequivocal*, meaning that a reasonable person in the position of the innocent party must find it unmistakable that the repudiator is unwilling or unable to perform under the contract.** Because the consequences of an anticipatory repudiation are so great (i.e., cancellation of the contract, immediate suit for total breach, and a discharge of the non-repudiator's duties), contract law requires that a repudiation by words clearly and unambiguously indicate an unwillingness or inability to perform a promised duty [Restatement 2d § 250(a)]. The problems presented in analyzing whether an unequivocal repudiation has taken place differ depending on whether the repudiation is by words or by action, and each is discussed below.

a. Repudiation by Words. [§ 23–13]

Obviously, when a party says, e.g., "I refuse to go forward with our deal and will not fulfill my promised duties," there is little doubt that a repudiation has occurred. However, much of the time the words more ambiguous, making it a much closer call.

There are two recurring fact situations, discussed below, in which it is important to analyze carefully what is communicated, for if the innocent party declares an anticipatory breach and is subsequently found to be unjustified in doing so, it is the "innocent" party who is the breaching party if he or she does not perform. Once again, the guiding principle in each of these cases is to determine whether the allegedly repudiating party is definitely and unequivocally stating either an unwillingness or an inability to perform, as viewed by a reasonable person in the position of the innocent party. If so, an actionable repudiation has taken place.

(1) Distinguishing Repudiation from a Request for Modification. [§ 23–14]

Metal Co. has a contract with Electric Co. whereby it has agreed to provide Electric Co. with certain metal rods for use in generating electricity. The price is fixed at $12,000 per rod and delivery is to take place in two months. Near the time of delivery, the owner of Metal Co. calls up the president of Electric Co. and says, "The price of metal is going up. I don't think I can go forward with our deal at only

$12,000. I really need $15,000." This is not a repudiation; it is only a **request for modification**, for the owner's statement is not a definite and unequivocal manifestation of an unwillingness or inability to perform under the contract at the $12,000 price. He is only asking if Electric Co. would be willing to re-negotiate the price term.

If, however, the president of Metal Co. had said, e.g., "I refuse to deliver for the paltry price of $12,000. Unless you agree right now to pay me $15,000, the deal is off!" then an actionable repudiation has occurred. In such a case, Electric Co.'s duties would be discharged, and it would be entitled to seek the rods elsewhere without contractual liability and to sue immediately for breach.

(2) Distinguishing Repudiation from a Good Faith Difference of Opinion as to the Meaning of the Contract. [§ 23–15]

Service Co. has a contract to repair "all office equipment" at XYZ Corp. beginning October 1. In September, the president of XYZ mentions to the president of Service Co. how comforting it is to know someone will be there to service the coffee maker at the office, which always breaks down. The president of Service Co. believes the contract only covers computers, calculators, staplers, etc., but not coffee makers. Accordingly, she writes XYZ Corp. a letter noting that Service Co. does not believe it is required to fix the machine under the contract, and hence it refuses to service the machine unless it is found to be legally obligated to do so. Such a statement is not a repudiation; it is only the expression of **a good faith difference of opinion as to the rights and duties owed under the contract** [Restatement 2d § 250, Cmt. b, Ill. 3].

If the president of Service Co. had said something like, "Under no circumstances will my employees fix a stupid coffee maker," then XYZ *might* be able to establish an anticipatory repudiation. To do so, however, it will have to establish that Service Co. is in fact obligated to fix the coffee maker and that such a duty is important enough that the failure to perform it when due would be a total breach.

b. Repudiation by Conduct. [§ 23–16]

A party may also repudiate a contract by action. However, such a repudiation must also meet the "definite and unequivocal" standard, and thus, the act of the repudiator must render him or her unable, or apparently unable, to perform under the

PROSPECTIVE NONPERFORMANCE OR ANTICIPATORY REPUDIATION

contract as viewed by a reasonable person in the position of the innocent party [Restatement 2d § 250(b)].

(1) Example. [§ 23–17]

Fred has a contract with Gina whereby Gina is obligated to deliver her car to Fred on July 1. On June 15, Fred discovers Gina has sold her car to Lorraine. Gina's act of selling the car to Lorraine is a sufficiently definite act to constitute an anticipatory repudiation of the Fred/Gina agreement. Note that Gina may argue that she has not necessarily repudiated the contract because she could, after all, potentially repurchase the car from Lorraine and still deliver it timely to Fred on July 1. However, contract law provides that when a party has sold the good that he or she is contractually obligated to deliver to someone else, an actionable anticipatory repudiation by conduct has occurred [*See* UCC § 2–610, Cmt. 1].

(2) Example. [§ 23–18]

Same as above, except this time Fred discovers on June 15 that Gina has leased her car to Lorraine for six months, starting June 1. Once again this is a sufficiently definite and unequivocal act so as to constitute an actionable repudiation of the Fred/Gina contract [*See* UCC § 2–610, Cmt. 1].

4. An Effective Repudiation May Only Repudiate Some Duties. [§ 23–19]

On occasion, a party will repudiate only some of the duties called for in the contract. Contract law holds that such a partial repudiation can still serve as the basis for the innocent party to take advantage of the anticipatory repudiation doctrine (meaning an end to the entire contract and an immediate suit for breach), so long as the duties repudiated would give rise to a total breach if they were not performed, and so long as the repudiation is definite and unequivocal.

D. EFFECT OF ANTICIPATORY REPUDIATION IN CONTRACTS GOVERNED BY THE UCC. [§ 23–20]

The effect of anticipatory repudiation in contracts governed by the UCC is the same as that in non-UCC transactions, i.e., if the non-breaching party can establish the elements necessary for application of the doctrine, he or she:

(a) Can immediately bring suit for breach;

(b) Is discharged from all further duties remaining under the contract; and

(c) Is entitled to declare the contract terminated.

There are two separate Code sections, § 2–609 and § 2–610, which provide different ways for a party to establish that an anticipatory repudiation has taken place under an agreement governed by Article 2. How to establish a valid anticipatory repudiation claim under each of these provisions is explained separately below.

1. **Anticipatory Repudiation Under UCC § 2–610. [§ 23–21]**

    The elements necessary to establish anticipatory repudiation under UCC § 2–610 are quite similar to those necessary to establish anticipatory repudiation in non-UCC contracts [§§ 23–4 *et seq*.], but the nomenclature is changed in some respects. Under § 2–610, the non-repudiating party is entitled to use the anticipatory repudiation doctrine if he or she can establish that:

    (a) The contract is a **bilateral** one with **unperformed duties remaining** on both sides at the time of the repudiation;

    (b) Failure of the repudiating party to perform the repudiated duty would **"substantially impair"** the value of the contract to the innocent party (This is the UCC equivalent of the common law requirement that non-performance of the repudiated duty would result in a total breach.) [§ 23–10]; and

    (c) The repudiation, whether by words or by conduct, must **definitely and unequivocally indicate the repudiating party's unwillingness or inability to perform** his or her promised duties.

2. **Anticipatory Repudiation by Failing to Provide Reasonable Assurances Under UCC § 2–609. [§ 23–22]**

    In some ways, the common law anticipatory repudiation doctrine was not broad or strong enough. True, where the other party actually repudiated, the law gave the innocent party some powerful remedies. Still, the price for being entitled to use such extreme remedies was that there had to be a **definite and unequivocal** repudiation [*See* § 23–12]. As a practical matter, however, there are often times when a party may make statements which make the other party unsure about whether the party making the statements will perform, but where such statements do not rise to the level of an unequivocal repudiation of performance. While the innocent party may understandably be insecure as to the other party's ability or willingness to perform under these circumstances, there is little he or she can do to relieve such insecurity under the common law anticipatory repudiation doctrine. He or she cannot declare a breach given only an equivocal statement, but of course the innocent party does not want to perform or even prepare to perform, if the other will breach.

PROSPECTIVE NONPERFORMANCE OR ANTICIPATORY REPUDIATION

To illustrate this dilemma, suppose Machine, Inc., a manufacturer of custom machinery, had a contract to deliver an $800,000 carpet-weaving machine to Carpet Co. on October 1. The machine will take four months to construct, and Machine, Inc. started the manufacture of it in late June. In mid-July, the owner of Machine, Inc. has a conversation with her counterpart at Carpet Co., in which the Carpet Co. officer says, only half-jokingly, "Sure hope we'll be able to find the money to pay you for the machine." A week later, the president of Machine, Inc. reads in the *Wall Street Journal* that Carpet Co. is in deep financial trouble, is not paying its bills on time, and is likely to file for bankruptcy in the next three to four months. At this point Machine, Inc. is in an extremely vulnerable position. Carpet Co. has not repudiated its duties, and thus Machine, Inc. is not discharged from its performance and still is obligated to deliver the machine. Thus, if it chooses immediately to cease manufacture of the machine and, as a result, does not tender it as promised on October 1, Machine Inc. could well be in breach if Carpet Co. has not unequivocally repudiated before then and tenders payment. On the other hand, if Carpet Co. was really in poor financial condition, and will not pay Machine, Inc. for the machine when it is delivered, Machine Inc. might want to stop production of the carpet weaver now so as to cut its losses or try to sell the machine to someone else.

UCC § 2–609 was designed to deal with this kind of situation and provide a remedy for a party who has reason to be insecure about the other's performance. Under § 2–609, whenever one party has **"reasonable grounds for insecurity"** with respect to the other's ability or willingness to perform, he or she "may in writing demand adequate assurance of due performance." The party receiving such a demand must then provide assurances that its promised performance will be forthcoming **or else be deemed to have anticipatorily repudiated the contract**. Thus, in the Machine, Inc./Carpet Co. contract above, after the troubling conversation and upon reading the *Journal* article, Machine, Inc. is entitled to demand reasonable assurances of Carpet Co.'s ability and willingness to pay for the machine on October 1. Once the letter is received, Carpet Co. must provide some sort of assurance of payment or be deemed to have anticipatorily repudiated the contract.

Stating the rule poses four questions:

(1) When does a party have "reasonable grounds for insecurity" [§ 23–23];

(2) What kinds of things constitute "adequate assurances of due performance" by the responding party [§ 23–27];

(3) What are the rights of the insecure party while waiting for assurances, i.e., can the insecure party suspend performance until such assurances arrive [§ 23–28]; and

(4) What are the consequences of failing to provide adequate assurances [§ 23–29]?

Each of these questions is addressed below.

a. What Constitutes "Reasonable Grounds for Insecurity" Under § 2–609(1) and (2)? [§ 23–23]

The Code provides no hard and fast test for ascertaining what gives one party reasonable grounds for insecurity about the other's ability and willingness to perform under the contract. However, the courts have generally agreed on such a test which is: **if the innocent party would, in good faith, have a reasonable doubt as to the other party's willingness or ability to provide a substantial part of the bargain, reasonable grounds for insecurity exist.** [UCC § 2–609, Cmt 1.]

While not an exhaustive list, some things that give rise to legitimate grounds for insecurity include:

(1) Hearing a rumor from a reliable and knowledgeable source that the other party may be unwilling or unable to perform [UCC § 2–609, Cmt. 3];

(2) A seller's receipt of a credit report from a commercial agency indicating the buyer is falling behind in paying his, her, or its bills;

(3) An article in a trustworthy publication indicating business difficulties for the other party;

(4) Knowledge by the buyer that the seller has been making late deliveries to other purchasers [UCC § 2–609, Cmt. 3];

(5) Knowledge by the buyer that the seller has been delivering poorly performing products to others [UCC § 2–609, Cmt. 3]; and

(6) Previous imperfectly tendered deliveries by the seller to the particular buyer, including such deliveries in previous shipments under an installment contract.

Note that § 2–609 itself requires that if a party has sufficient grounds, he or she must make the demand for reasonable assurances in writing. Despite that language, a few courts have held that an oral demand is effective.

PROSPECTIVE NONPERFORMANCE OR ANTICIPATORY REPUDIATION

(1) The Grounds for Demanding Assurances Need Not Be True; They Need Only Reasonably Appear to Be True to the Insecure Party. [§ 23–24]

Suppose a reputable weekly financial magazine runs a lengthy article indicating that a buyer is in a perilous financial condition. A seller who is in a contract with that buyer sees the article and sends a demand for assurances. The article is mistaken and, in fact, the buyer is in excellent financial condition, is paying its bills on time, has a lot of cash in the bank, etc. Can the buyer ignore the demand for assurances since the source on which it is based is in error without consequence?

Answer: NO.

Under § 2–609 the grounds on which the insecurity is based need not ultimately be true. Rather, all that is required is that the grounds **reasonably appear to be true** at the time the insecure party makes the request. If the demand is reasonably based, the party receiving it *must* respond to it and objectively establish its willingness and ability to perform under the contract or face the consequences if it does not. The rationale behind this rule is that if in fact the information on which the demand is made is in error, it should not be difficult for the party receiving the demand to establish its ability and willingness to perform. On the other hand, it would be burdensome for the demanding party to verify independently what appears to be a reliable report making questionable a party's ability or willingness to perform.

(2) Grounds for Insecurity Must Become Known to the Insecure Party *After* the Contract Is Formed, Not Before. [§ 23–25]

The idea behind § 2–609 is that when a party in a contract with executory duties becomes concerned about the other's willingness or ability to perform, there should be a mechanism for alleviating that doubt short of taking a chance and declaring an anticipatory repudiation. However, if the seller knew **before** entering into the contract of grounds for such insecurity, the rationale behind § 2–609 does not apply, and the party cannot legitimately demand assurances based on that information.

If, for example, a seller knows prior to entering into a contract that the seller is in poor financial shape, contract law requires that the seller should protect himself or herself in other ways, e.g., by demanding security for the payment, negotiating for payment by letter of credit, raising the price to cover the risk of non-payment, choosing not to enter into the agreement at all, demanding payment up front, etc. Accordingly, it is only when the grounds for insecurity become known to the party **after** entering into the contract, when that party can no longer protect itself by demanding a change in the terms of the deal, that § 2–609 permits a demand for adequate assurances.

(3) A Demand for Assurances Cannot Effectively Demand Only a Particular Kind of Assurance. [§ 23–26]

Assume a seller has reasonable grounds to believe that a buyer may not pay when required under a contract and sends a demand for assurances. May the seller effectively demand a particular kind of assurance, e.g., "to satisfy me that you will perform, I demand to see an audited financial statement of your company?"

Answer: NO. If a party is entitled to demand assurance, it is up to the **receiving** party to provide such assurance and to determine what form the assurance will take. Of course if what the receiving party sends does not constitute an "adequate assurance" [§ 23–27], it must face the consequences [§ 2–609, Cmt. 4; § 23–29].

b. What Constitutes "Adequate Assurances" of Performance? [§ 23–27]

Once a party makes an effective demand for assurances, the question becomes what kinds of actions by the other party constitute "adequate" assurances. Once again, no precise test is given in the Code. However, the generally accepted formulation is that **so long as the responding party provides assurances that would indicate an ability and willingness to perform under the contract to a reasonable person in the position of the insecure party, the assurances will be adequate**. Sometimes (although rarely) even an unsubstantiated oral promise might be enough. For example, assume an electronics store has an installment contract with a reputable tube manufacturer calling for three deliveries of 500 tubes each. When the first shipment arrived, the store manager noticed that there were only 499 tubes included, and sent a written demand for assurances that the manufacturer take steps to ensure that the next delivery is complete. If in response to such a demand the manufacturer telephoned the store and told them that the defective shipment problem was being attended to and would not occur again, probably under such

PROSPECTIVE NONPERFORMANCE OR ANTICIPATORY REPUDIATION

circumstances the manufacturer's oral representation would be an adequate assurance of performance [UCC § 2–609, Cmt. 4].

However, in most cases more than just an unsupported oral intention to perform is necessary. For example, if a seller sends a request for assurances to a buyer expressing concern about the buyer's ability to pay based on a credible credit report showing that the buyer is paying its bills four months late, an oral (or even written) declaration by the buyer that "The company has plenty of money and we will pay you per the contract" will probably not be an adequate assurance of performance. In such a case, the buyer would have to provide some objective proof of its ability to pay in accordance with the contract, e.g., a financial statement, a bank statement, an explanation of its recent late payments, a reason why it expects to have funds in the future, etc.

c. **What an Insecure Party May Do While Waiting for a Response to a Justified Demand for Assurances. [§ 23-28]**

Section 2–609(1) provides that an insecure party who has sent a justified demand for assurances may, if it is commercially reasonable to do so, **suspend performance** while waiting for the assurances. Thus, as soon as the request is sent the insecure party may, if it is commercially reasonable to do so, simply cease its own performance or preparations for performance, and wait for the other party to respond. If adequate assurances arrive, and if, because of the temporary suspension, the insecure party is late in performing, such lateness is excused.

d. **Consequence of Failing to Respond Adequately to a Justified Demand for Assurances. [§ 23-29]**

A party in receipt of a justified demand for assurances under § 2–609 must adequately respond to it within a **reasonable time not exceeding thirty days**. If that party either does not respond, or does not provide an adequate response within that time, **the failure to provide adequate assurances is treated as an anticipatory repudiation, and proceed under, UCC § 2–610** [§ 23–21].

There is an issue whether the failure to respond adequately to a legitimate demand for assurances about the performance of a minor duty under a contract, i.e., a duty whose non-performance would only give rise to an immaterial breach, gives the insecure party a right to declare an anticipatory repudiation. Most courts and commentators believe that it does not. That is, to use a failure to respond to an effective demand for assurances under UCC § 2–609 as a means to declare anticipatory repudiation under UCC § 2–610, the duty subject to the demand for assurances must be one whose non-performance when due would be a total breach.

In other words, most courts believe that failure to respond adequately to a legitimate demand for assurances does not give a right to anticipatory repudiation unless the requesting party is threatened with the loss of a substantial part of what was bargained for [UCC § 2–609, Cmt. 1].

    e. **Right to Demand Adequate Assurances in Contracts Not Governed by the UCC. [§ 23–30]**

The Restatement 2d provides a similar "reasonable assurances" rule. That is, it provides that an obligee has the right to demand assurances of future performance upon reasonable grounds to believe the obligor will totally breach the agreement. Further, it also provides that the failure to respond adequately to such a justified demand should be treated as an anticipatory repudiation [Restatement 2d § 251(1), (2)].

E. MECHANICS OF ANTICIPATORY REPUDIATION. [§ 23–31]

To completely understand the anticipatory repudiation doctrine, it is important to note that receipt of a repudiation does not necessarily terminate the contract. Rather, receipt of a repudiation only gives the innocent party a **conditional right to terminate** the agreement. To fulfill the condition, the innocent party **must do something to indicate he or she is treating the repudiation as final**. This can either be done by:

    (1) *informing* the repudiator of his or her intention to treat the repudiation as final;

    (2) *bringing suit* for anticipatory repudiation; or

    (3) *materially changing his or her position* in reliance on the repudiation [Restatement 2d § 256(1); UCC § 2–611(1)].

Once such action is taken, the condition has been fulfilled; and the innocent party's duties under the contract are discharged [Restatement 2d § 253; UCC § 2–610].

This means that a party who receives a repudiation is **entitled to ignore it** and, if he or she wishes, to urge the repudiator to retract the repudiation without giving up the right to later treat the repudiation as final [Restatement 2d § 257; UCC § 2–610(1)(a) and UCC § 2–610, Cmt. 4; *see* § 23–32 for a discussion of retraction]. If the innocent party chooses to **wait before treating the repudiation as final**, he or she is entitled to suspend performance or preparation for performance during that period. Thus, if the repudiating party later retracts the repudiation, and if the

PROSPECTIVE NONPERFORMANCE OR ANTICIPATORY REPUDIATION

innocent party is late in performing under the revived contract due to the suspension in performance, such tardiness is excused [UCC § 2–610(1)(c)].

If the innocent party wants to **save the contract**, there are some obvious advantages to urging the repudiator to retract the repudiation and waiting before treating the repudiation as final. The repudiator may indeed have second thoughts and agree to continue under the contract. However, there are also risks with such a procedure. If the recipient of a repudiation made far in advance of the date performance is due under the contract does not treat the repudiation as final, the repudiator might retract his or her repudiation very close to the date on which performance was due. While in such a case the innocent party would not be required to perform on the promised date and would have a reasonable amount of time to complete performance, he or she could be hindered in such a situation by having to perform a duty that he or she genuinely thought was discharged.

Furthermore, the innocent party also may be taking somewhat of a risk if he or she decides to **continue preparation for performance** after receipt of an anticipatory repudiation. (The innocent party may choose to continue preparation either because he or she thinks the repudiating party will retract the repudiation, because he or she does not believe the repudiation to be sufficiently unequivocal in its indication of an inability or unwillingness to perform, or for other reasons.)

The UCC provides somewhat of a solution in such cases for a seller-manufacturer where the repudiation comes when a good is partially completed, however. Under UCC § 2–704(2), a seller may recover full damages if it: (a) stops production at the time it receives the repudiation; or (b) finishes making the good and tries to resell it, **so long as it uses "reasonable commercial judgment" in making the decision**. If such judgment is not shown, a manufacturer cannot recover for any costs incurred after the repudiation is received under traditional mitigation principles [See § 30–59 for a discussion of mitigation].

F. THE REPUDIATING PARTY'S RIGHT TO RETRACT THE REPUDIATION. [§ 23–32]

Both the Restatement 2d and the UCC provide that repudiations can be retracted [Restatement 2d § 256; UCC § 2–611]. That is, under certain conditions a party's anticipatory repudiation can be "taken back" or nullified. When a retraction is effectively made, both parties' duties under the contract again become enforceable (except that the aggrieved party must be entitled to more time to fulfill his or her duties than originally called for in the contract if the delay in fulfilling those duties is caused by a legitimate suspension of duties between the time of the repudiation and its retraction) [UCC § 2–611]. There are two situations, however, in which a repudiation becomes **irrevocable**:

(1) When the non-repudiating party has given notice to the repudiator that he or she considers the repudiation final (including bringing suit for breach of contract) and the contract terminated; or

(2) When the non-repudiating party has materially changed position in reliance on the repudiation [Restatement 2d § 256; UCC § 2–611(1)].

In some ways, the revocation doctrine treats an anticipatory repudiation as a revocable "offer" by the repudiator to terminate the contract. As with all other revocable offers, the party making the offer is free to revoke it (i.e., by retracting the repudiation) unless it has been accepted. In this case, the "offer" to terminate the contract can be "accepted" either: (a) by notifying the repudiator that he or she considers the repudiation final (including filing suit for total breach); or (b) by materially relying on the repudiation in such a way that justice dictates it should be irrevocable.

1. **Example. [§ 23–33]**

    Ted is a retired carpenter and has agreed to make a custom couch for Laura, to be delivered and paid for on October 1. On August 10, Laura definitely and unequivocally repudiates. Ted writes Laura and asks her to reconsider, but Laura does not respond. Ted neither takes on any more work in the interim, nor relies on Laura's repudiation in any other way. However, he also never informs Laura of his intention to treat the repudiation as final. On September 29, Laura calls up and retracts her repudiation. The retraction is effective, because Ted has neither notified Laura that he is terminating the contract nor has he relied on her repudiation in any quantifiable manner. Thus, while he does not have to tender the couch on October 1 (he has a reasonable time to complete it), he is under an obligation to supply her with the couch because the retraction came before the date on which Laura's performance was due under the original contract, and because Ted had not "accepted" her "offer" to terminate the contract by not acting on the repudiation or responding to it.

G. EXAM APPROACHES TO ANTICIPATORY REPUDIATION ISSUES. [§ 23–34*]

The following approach should be used in analyzing an anticipatory repudiation issue:

1. Make sure the elements for repudiation have been established. That is, make sure:

    A. The contract is bilateral, with executory duties by both parties extant at the time of the repudiation [§§ 23–5, 23–20];

---

* For more information, listen to CD # 11, Track 3 of *Sum and Substance Audio on Contracts*.

PROSPECTIVE NONPERFORMANCE OR ANTICIPATORY REPUDIATION

B. The repudiated duty is important enough so that its nonperformance would result in a total breach under the contract [§§ 23–10; 23–20]; and

C. The repudiation, whether by words or conduct, definitely and unequivocally establishes a refusal or inability to perform under the contract [§§ 23–12; 23–20].

> If the repudiation does not meet the definite and unequivocal test, check to see whether the innocent party is entitled to send, or has sent, a request for assurances [§ 23–22]. If the other party does not respond, or does not sufficiently respond [§ 23–27] within a reasonable time not to exceed 30 days, then the innocent party can treat the contract as having been anticipatorily repudiated.

2. If an anticipatory repudiation has occurred, determine whether the repudiator can still retract the repudiation, i.e., whether the innocent party has taken the necessary steps to discharge its duty [§§ 23–21; 23–32]. That is has the innocent party either:

A. Notified the repudiator that he or she considers the contract to be final (including bringing suit against the repudiator); or

B. Materially changed position in reliance on the repudiation.

CHAPTER 24

DISCHARGE OF DUTIES BY SUBSEQUENT AGREEMENT—SUBSTITUTED PERFORMANCES, SUBSTITUTED CONTRACTS (INCLUDING NOVATIONS), ACCORDS, MUTUAL RESCISSION, AND RELEASES

A. DISCHARGE OF DUTY BY SUBSEQUENT AGREEMENTS, GENERALLY. [§ 24–1*]

One way a party owing a duty under a contract can discharge it is by entering into a **new agreement** in its place. This Chapter discusses five types of such agreements:

(1) **Substituted performances** [Restatement 2d § 278; § 24–2];

(2) **Substituted contracts** (including **novations**) [Restatement 2d § 279; § 24–5];

(3) **Accords** [Restatement 2d § 281; § 24-9];

---

* For more information, listen to CD # 11, Track 1 of *Sum and Substance Audio on Contracts*.

(4) **Mutual rescission and Unilateral Renunciation** [Restatement 2d §§ 278, 277; § 24–19]; and

(5) **Releases** [Restatement 2d § 284; § 24–25].

Of course a **modification** is also a subsequent agreement that discharges the original duty and substitutes another in its place, keeping most of the other deal points of the original contract. Modification rules are discussed in §§ 7–71 *et seq.* and in Chapter Nine.

B. SUBSTITUTED PERFORMANCE. [§ 24–2]

"Substituted performance" describes a transaction in which a party owing a duty under a contract arranges to discharge the duty by making a different performance (as opposed to *promising* a different performance) than that called for in the original contract [Restatement 2d § 278].

A substituted performance is itself a separate contract and thus, must be formed by means of an offer, an acceptance, and consideration to be enforceable. A substituted performance is really a particular kind of unilateral contract, where the offer is a promise to discharge the duty in return for an act, the acceptance is the offeree's performance of the act called for in the offer, and the consideration constitutes the bargained for exchange of the offeror's promise to discharge a duty in return for the offeree's act.

Note that it is irrelevant whether the substituted performance is performed by the original obligor or by a third party. So long as the obligee agrees to accept a different performance as a substitute for the original duty, the original duty is discharged when the substituted performance occurs.

1. **Example. [§ 24–3]**

   Larry is a veterinarian in a rural community who has performed professional services for Byron. Larry reasonably bills Byron $300 in accordance with their agreement, but Byron complains that he is short on cash at the moment. If Larry says, "If you deliver a cord of firewood to my home by 5:00 p.m. Tuesday, I will accept it in lieu of the bill," in essence he has made an offer to enter into a unilateral contract with Byron, whereby Byron's performance will act as the acceptance of the offer. Consideration is present as Byron's act in delivering the firewood, and Larry's promise to forego enforcing the debt, evidenced by the bill, are bargained for and sought in exchange, one for the other. Thus, if Byron timely delivers the firewood, a **"substituted performance" has taken place** and Byron's debt to Larry is discharged. If Byron does not deliver the wood, Larry may sue only to enforce the $300 debt evidenced by the bill, and may **not** sue to enforce the delivery of the wood, for Byron has not promised to

DISCHARGE OF DUTIES BY SUBSEQUENT AGREEMENT

make such a delivery. Their agreement is only that <u>if</u> Byron delivers the wood, the debt will be discharged.

Note that to be a **valid substituted performance**, the obligor (Larry) must agree to <u>discharge the existing duty</u> upon actual **performance only**. If the duty is discharged on the basis of a *promised* performance, e.g., if Larry had said to Byron "If you **promise** to deliver a load of firewood to my house by 5:00 p.m. Tuesday, I will accept it in lieu of the bill," it would be a *substituted contract or accord situation* [addressed in §§ 24–5 and 24–9, respectively], not a substituted **performance**.

2. Example. [§ 24–4]

Same situation as above, except this time Larry agrees to discharge the bill if Byron's sister, Gina, delivers a cord of firewood to Larry's house by 5:00 p.m. Tuesday. If the wood is timely delivered by Gina, Byron's duty to pay the debt is discharged for it is irrelevant that a third party performed the agreed upon performance. If it is not, Larry's only recourse is to sue Byron for payment of the original debt.

C. SUBSTITUTED CONTRACTS, INCLUDING NOVATIONS. [§ 24–5]

A "substituted contract" is a transaction in which a party owing a duty under a contract discharges it by *promising* **a different performance than that originally called for under the contract** [Restatement 2d § 279]. As its name suggests, a substituted contract is itself a separate contract and thus, must be formed by means of a separate offer, acceptance, and consideration to be enforceable. A substituted contract is really a special type of bilateral contract, where the offer is a promise to discharge the debt upon the promised performance of an act, the acceptance is the offeree's promise to do the act called for in the offer, and where each party's bargained for promise serves as consideration for the other.

There are two categories of substituted contracts depending on whether the original promisee, or a third party, promises to perform the new obligation. If <u>the original obligor promises to perform</u> the new duty, contract law calls it simply a **"substituted contract,"** i.e., the substitution of the promised duties under one contract for promised duties under another. However, if the new contract is entered into between the original obligee and <u>a third party</u>, it is known as a subspecies of substituted contracts called a **"novation"** [Restatement 2d § 280].

1. Effect of Substituted Contract or Novation. [§ 24–6]

Upon the valid formation of a substituted contract or novation, **the original debt is immediately discharged**. Thus, if the duty promised under the *new* contract is breached, the obligor is entitled to sue for damages resulting from *its* non-performance, **but cannot validly sue to enforce the original duty** [Restatement 2d § 279(2)].

a. Example. [§ 24–7]

Jason owns a limousine service. One of his first clients was Rocker, a famous rock star. Jason drove Rocker for a week as Rocker made appearances on local talk shows, etc., before a big concert. At the end of the week, Rocker examines Jason's $5,000 bill and says, "If I promise to leave two front row tickets to the concert for you at the will-call booth with some back stage passes, will you agree to accept my promise in exchange for payment of the bill?" Jason was a big fan of Rocker and so accepted Rocker's offer. Upon such acceptance, a **substituted contract** was formed, and Rocker's obligation to pay Jason $5,000 was immediately discharged. If Rocker does not leave the tickets and passes, Jason may sue him for breaching **that** promise, but cannot validly sue him seeking to enforce payment of the $5,000 bill.

b. Example. [§ 24–8]

Sally lent Nancy $2,000, the repayment of which is due tomorrow. Nancy and her brother Pat, a carpenter, propose that Sally agree to discharge the debt in exchange for Pat's promise to deliver to Sally a custom made desk within 90 days. If Sally accepts the offer, she has entered into a **novation**. As such, Nancy's obligation to pay Sally is immediately discharged. Thus, if Pat does not deliver the desk, Sally's only recourse is to sue him for his failure to deliver as promised, because she can no longer enforce Nancy's promise to repay the $2,000.

D. ACCORDS. [§ 24–9]

In some respects an accord is a hybrid made up of the attributes of a substituted performance and a substituted contract. **An "accord" is a transaction in which a party owed a duty under a contract agrees to enter into what would otherwise be a substituted contract, except that the duty due under the original contract is discharged *only when the duties promised under the accord are actually performed*** [Restatement 2d § 281(1)]. Until complete performance of the newly promised duties, the original obligation is only "suspended." If the newly promised duty in the accord is fully and completely performed, the obligations under **both** agreements have been discharged or, in the words of the doctrine, the obligations under both agreements have been **"satisfied."** Thus, upon performance of the accord, it is said the original duty has been discharged by **accord and satisfaction** [Restatement 2d § 281(2)].

DISCHARGE OF DUTIES BY SUBSEQUENT AGREEMENT

If the newly made promise in the accord is breached, the duty under the original contract is no longer suspended, and can thereafter be enforced. Thus, **upon the breach of the accord**, the obligee has the **option of either suing to enforce the original duty, or suing for the breach of the promises made in the accord** [Restatement 2d § 281(3)].

As with substituted contracts, the obligor under an accord can be either the obligor under the original contract, or a third party. However unlike substituted contracts, no special name like "novation" is given to an accord made between the original obligee and a third party.

1. **Example. [§ 24–10]**

    Same facts as in the Jason/Rocker hypothetical set forth in § 24–7, except this time Rocker looks at the bill and says, "If I promise to, and actually do, leave two front row tickets for you at the will call booth along with back stage passes, will you promise to forego collecting the bill?" Jason says "O.K., I'll forget about the bill, but only if you actually follow through on your promise," and Rocker agrees. Jason has thus entered into an **accord** with Rocker for the front row tickets rather than a substituted contract. Thus, if Rocker leaves the tickets, the duties under the **accord** will be **satisfied** and the $5,000 debt will be discharged. If, however, Rocker breaches the accord by failing to leave the tickets, Jason will have the option of suing him either for breach of the promise to leave the tickets, **or** to enforce payment of the $5,000 debt.

2. **Example. [§ 24–11]**

    Same facts as the Nancy/Pat/Sally hypothetical set forth in § 24–8, except this time Sally enters into an **accord** with Pat, rather than a novation. If Pat breaches his promise to deliver the desk, Sally has the option of either suing Pat for breach of his promise, or suing Nancy to enforce her obligation to repay the $2,000.

    Note, however, that Sally could **not** legitimately sue Nancy for the $2,000 until Pat breached the promise made in the accord. By entering into the accord with Pat, Sally agreed to suspend the enforceability of the $2,000 debt until the accord was either satisfied or breached.

3. **Recurring Problems Under the Most Frequent Use of Accords: Offers to Compromise a Disputed Debt. [§ 24–12]**

    The most frequent use of accords in modern commerce is to settle disputed monetary obligations. These types of transactions raise a number of recurring issues, two of which are typically covered in a first year contracts course:

    > (1) Whether a lack of consideration makes a settlement agreement unenforceable; and

(2)(a) The effect of a debtor attempting to discharge a disputed debt by tendering a check "in full satisfaction" of the debt; and

(b) Similarly the effect of the creditor crossing out the "in full satisfaction" language and cashing the check "without prejudice."

Each issue is discussed below.

a. **Consideration Issues When a Debtor Offers to Pay the Creditor Less than the Full Amount the Creditor Is Seeking. [§ 24–13]**

Because an accord is itself a contract, traditional contract law holds that it must be supported by consideration to be enforceable to its full extent. This can present an issue when the accord consists of the debtor's promise to pay less than the full amount the creditor claims is owed. That is, under the pre-existing duty rule [Restatement 2d § 73] and the rule announced in *Foakes v. Beer* [§ 7–80], an offer to pay $6,000 to discharge a $10,000 debt raises consideration concerns.

However, if such agreements were unenforceable, debtors would have little reason to compromise and settle before trial, for there would be no enforceable benefit in doing so. In other words, the debtors of the world would not offer to pay the $6,000 as an accord to discharge the claimed $10,000 debt if the creditor could cash the check and still successfully sue the debtor for the remaining $4,000.

Even common law contract law was sensitive to the plight of the debtor in such a situation, and almost always found consideration when a debtor offered to compromise such a debt by paying less than the creditor claimed he or she was owed. Under traditional rules, for consideration **not** to be present, the creditor would have to establish that: (a) the debt was for a liquidated (not a disputed) sum; (b) there was no **bona fide** dispute as to whether the debtor owed the full amount of the debt; **and** (c) the creditor did not receive some additional benefit from the accord than he or she had under the original contract [Restatement 2d § 73].

The UCC has changed the rule and eliminated the requirement of consideration altogether. Under UCC § 1–306, a written settlement of a claim arising out of a breach of contract is enforceable even without consideration.

DISCHARGE OF DUTIES BY SUBSEQUENT AGREEMENT

b. The Effect of Attempted Settlement by Tender of a Check in "Full Satisfaction" of a Debt. [§ 24–14]

Another recurring issue in dealing with accords is determining what effect to give a debtor's attempted settlement of a debt where he or she tenders a check with the words, e.g., "This check is in full satisfaction of our dispute" written on the memo line. This issue really presents two problems:

(1) If the creditor cashes the check without doing anything to the language on the back, has the creditor implicitly accepted by silence the debtor's offer of an accord?; and

(2) If the creditor crosses out the language and writes, e.g., "Cashing of the check is without prejudice to my rights to enforce the full amount of the debt," can the creditor cash it and still sue for the remainder of the debt?

The resolution of these issues is discussed below.

(1) A Creditor Who Cashes a Check Tendered "in Full Satisfaction" of a Debt Is Typically Held to Have Accepted the Offer of an Accord. [§ 24–15]

Traditional legal analysis holds that if a creditor cashes a check that was tendered **"in full satisfaction"** of a debt, the creditor has thereby accepted an accord to discharge the debt, and any duty of the debtor to repay the greater amount the creditor claims is owed is suspended. If the check is honored and the money paid to the creditor, there has been a satisfaction of the accord, and the duty to repay the original debt is discharged.

(2) The Effect of a Creditor Who Crosses out the "in Full Satisfaction" Language and Replaces It with "Without Prejudice" Language Instead: The Effect of UCC § 3–311. [§ 24–16]

Of course, any offeree can reject an offer, and a creditor who simply returns a debtor's check with **"in full satisfaction"** language on it will be deemed to have rejected the offer to enter into an accord. However, most creditors would like to reject the accord offer **and** cash the check **and** retain the right to sue the debtor for the remainder of the debt. Typically, they attempt to accomplish these goals by crossing out the **"in full satisfaction"** language and writing something like "without prejudice" language in its stead.

UCC § 3–311 provides that if a debtor tenders a check for the full satisfaction of an unliquidated claim, or a claim subject to a *bona fide* dispute, and if somewhere on the check the debtor has **conspicuously** stated that its tender is for the full satisfaction of that claim, then if the creditor cashes the check knowing that it was intended by the debtor to resolve the dispute, an accord has taken place *even if* the creditor crosses out the "in full satisfaction" language and writes "without prejudice" or similar language [UCC § 3–311(a), (b), (d)]. However, if the check does not conspicuously state that it is being tendered in full satisfaction of the claim, or if the creditor did not know that it was being tendered to compromise the disputed debt, then if the creditor returns the amount of the check to the debtor within 90 days after cashing the check, no accord and satisfaction has occurred, and the original debt is still enforceable by the creditor [UCC § 3–311(c)]. However, the creditor cannot cash the check, retain the proceeds, and retain the right to sue the creditor.

4. **How to Determine if a Subsequent Contract Is a Substituted Contract or an Accord. [§ 24–17]**

Obviously the obligee or creditor receives greater protection when entering into an accord rather than a substituted contract. That is, if an accord is breached, the obligee can sue under either the accord or the original contract [§ 24–9], whereas the obligee under a substituted contract or novation can only enforce the breach of the new agreement [§ 24–5]. Sometimes it is easy to tell whether the parties intended their subsequent contract to be an accord or a substituted contract because the agreement is explicit. However, unfortunately often it is not so easy to tell which type of agreement was intended from the language of the new agreement alone. In close cases, whether a subsequent agreement made to discharge a duty is an accord or a substituted contract is a question of **interpretation** for a court to be made from all the surrounding circumstances [*See* Chapter Nineteen for a discussion of interpretation]. A court will enforce whatever type of agreement it finds the parties intended.

E. MUTUAL RESCISSION AND UNILATERAL RENUNCIATION. [§ 24–18]

"Mutual rescission" is an agreement whereby each party in a bilateral contract agrees to discharge all the remaining unexecuted duties of the other [Restatement 2d § 283]. A mutual rescission is itself a contract and thus must be formed by a separate offer, acceptance, and consideration to be enforceable. A mutual rescission agreement is really a particular kind of bilateral contract, where the *offer* is a promise to discharge all remaining duties under the agreement upon a reciprocal promise *from the offeree*; the acceptance is the reciprocal

DISCHARGE OF DUTIES BY SUBSEQUENT AGREEMENT

promise **by the offeree agreeing to do the act**; and consideration is the bargained for exchange of such promises and the destruction of a legal relationship [Restatement 2d § 283, Cmt. a]. In other words, when two parties to a contract want to "call off" the deal, they do so by means of mutual rescission. Note, however, that to be effective as a mutual rescission, the parties must be in a bilateral contract with executory duties remaining on both sides at the time the rescission agreement is reached, otherwise there is no consideration for their promises.

1. **Unilateral Renunciation. [§ 24–19]**

   Rescissions are mutual. However, sometimes one party who is supposed to get a performance under a contract is willing to give up that benefit. Obviously that party could simply say, "That's O.K., Bro. You don't have to pay me back." If the speaker never presses the issue, of course, there is no litigation. But the question arises, what if the party changes his or he mind?

   The problem is that at common law, unilateral renunciations were unenforceable because there was no consideration to support it. Restatement 2d § 277(1) changes the common law rule by stating that **so long as the renunciation is <u>in writing</u>, it is enforceable even without consideration**.

2. **Example. [§ 24–20]**

   Bill has promised to pay Judy $1,000 on Friday in exchange for Judy's promise to deliver to him on that day her Nolan Ryan rookie baseball card. On Thursday, both Bill and Judy agree to call off the deal. Whether they realize it or not, the means by which they have discharged each other's duty is by a mutual rescission with each party's promised non-performance (discharge) serving as consideration for the bilateral contract.

3. **Example. [§ 24–21]**

   Same as above, except this time Judy has already given over the card, and Bill, her friend, pleads a lack of funds. If Judy wants to be nice, she can renounce her rights to receive the $1,000 payment and, if she does so in writing, it is enforceable under the Restatement 2d without consideration.

4. **General Rule: Mutual Rescissions Can Be Oral. [§ 24–22]**

   As a general rule, an oral mutual rescission is enforceable [Restatement 2d § 283, Cmt. b], even though unilateral renunciations must be in writing [Restatement 2d § 277(1)].

a. Exception: Mutual Rescission of a Duty to Transfer an Interest in Land Must Be in Writing. [§ 24–23]

Rescission of a contract in which one party's duty is to transfer an interest in land must be in writing to be enforceable. [Restatement 2d §§ 148, 283, Cmt. b]. This is an application of the Statute of Frauds concerning land sale contracts. [*See* 10–6].

5. Distinguishing Mutual Rescission from Substituted Performance, Substituted Contracts, and Accords. [§ 24–24]

Mutual rescission differs from substituted performance, substituted contracts, and accords in that one party's agreement to discharge the duties of another is not given in exchange for some other performance or promised performance, but rather is given in exchange for the other party's promise to discharge the remaining duties under the original contract.

F. RELEASES. [§ 24–25]

A "release" is an enforceable unilateral promise by a party that he or she is discharging a duty owed him or her immediately or upon the occurrence of a condition [Restatement 2d § 284]. At common law, to be effective a release needed to be supported by consideration [Restatement 2d § 284, Cmt. b]. If it is a release of an obligation where there is a bona fide dispute over what the contract called for, there is no problem finding consideration. However, most states today provide <u>by statute</u> that a release is binding even in the absence of consideration such as where there is no bona fide dispute. So if Mary owes Joe $2,000, and the parties enter into a "release" of the obligation, it is enforceable by statute in most states.

1. Distinguishing Releases from Substituted Performance, Substituted Contracts, and Accords. [§ 24–26]

A release differs from substituted performance, substituted contracts, and accords because the nature of the obligee's promise is different: in a release, the discharge of the obligor's duty takes effect immediately, or immediately upon the occurrence of a condition, such as a payment of money. In the other situations mentioned above, the obligee has only made a **promise** to discharge the duty in the future in return for completion of a specified new performance or the promise of such different performance. That promise itself creates a new duty on the part of the obligee, which can later be discharged by the parties [Restatement 2d § 284, Cmt. a].

DISCHARGE OF DUTIES BY SUBSEQUENT AGREEMENT

G. EXAM APPROACH TO SUBSTITUTED PERFORMANCE, SUBSTITUTED CONTRACT, NOVATION, ACCORD, MUTUAL RESCISSION, AND RELEASE ISSUES. [§ 24–27*]

You will likely never have an essay question totally devoted to a substituted agreement issue. At most, these issues will be one of many in an essay question, or may be the subject of a multiple-choice question or two. To handle the issues when they are brought up, the following is likely all you will need to do:

1. Identify which of the substituted agreements the parties have agreed to, i.e., substituted performance, substituted contract or novation, accord, etc.

2. Make sure that all the requirements for the particular agreement are present, e.g., there was a valid offer and acceptance for the substitute agreement, there is consideration to support the substitute agreement where necessary. For renunciations, recall it must be in writing to be enforceable.

3. Lastly, know the effect of what happens when a party breaches the substituted agreement, i.e., can the innocent party sue on the original obligation, is the innocent party stuck with suing for breach of the substitute agreement, or can both be sued upon?

---

* For more information, listen to CD # 11, Track 1 of *Sum and Substance Audio on Contracts*.

CHAPTER 25

DISCHARGE OF DUTIES BY IMPOSSIBILITY, IMPRACTICABILITY, OR FRUSTRATION OF PURPOSE

A. IMPOSSIBILITY, IMPRACTICABILITY AND FRUSTRATION, GENERALLY. [§ 25–1*]

Every time parties enter into a contract, they do so with basic unstated assumptions. For example, when Sheila contracts to purchase Joe's racehorse, both assume the horse is alive when they sign the contract and will continue to be alive until its delivery, even if that fact is not actually spelled out in the contract. When a construction company contracts to build a swimming pool in a homeowner's backyard, both parties probably assume the soil in the homeowner's backyard is similar to the soil in the surrounding area, even if that assumption is unstated in their agreement. When Bernard agrees to pay a premium price for a hotel room offering a view overlooking the Rose Parade in Pasadena on January 1, both assume that the parade will take place, even if that is not specified when the reservation is made. However, things happen. The racehorse may die in its stable just after the contract is signed. The homeowner's property may unexpectedly contain a number of huge granite boulders hidden in the ground, making excavation of the property much more burdensome than anticipated. The government may prohibit the parade one year due to security concerns.

There are two ways contract law could deal with these kinds of situations. It could take an absolutist position and say that if the seller of the horse cannot timely deliver as promised, if the construction company does not bear the extraordinary expense of digging the pool, and if the guest

---

* For more information, listen to CD # 11, Track 2 of *Sum and Substance Audio on Contracts*.

refuses to pay for the room, each has breached his or her contractual promise, and is liable for damages. On the other hand, contract law could be more flexible and provide that in certain cases, i.e., when a basic assumption that both parties made when entering into a contract unexpectedly turns out not to be true, a party's failure to perform that duty is excused (technically his or her duties under the contract are discharged) and no action for breach will lie. As you might guess from the title of this chapter, contract law has chosen the latter approach and has broken these kinds of cases into three categories:

> (1) **Impossibility**, which applies when an unexpected event occurs which makes performance by a party objectively impossible, as in the case above where the horse died;

> (2) **Commercial impracticability**, which applies when an unexpected event occurs which makes performance by a party much more burdensome, as in the case above where the granite boulders were discovered in the homeowner's soil; and

> (3) **Frustration of purpose**, which applies when an unexpected event occurs which renders virtually worthless the **value** of a party's bargain, i.e., it is still possible for the breaching party to perform, but the reason he or she entered the contract has disappeared, as in the case above where the guest can occupy the Pasadena hotel room, but the **value** to him of doing so is largely eliminated if the parade is cancelled.

1. **Effect of Establishing a Defense Based on Impossibility, Impracticability, and Frustration: Discharge of Remaining Duties. [§ 25–2]**

One thing that often gets overlooked in the study of these doctrines is the realization that, at bottom, they are nothing other than contract **defenses raised when one party fails to perform**. In contract theory, the application of these doctrines is to discharge enforceable duties. But on a *practical* level, these are defenses.

Let's say Contractor can establish the elements for impracticability [§ 25–32] under a contract in which he is to build a swimming pool. As a result, he or she will not perform the duties called for under the contract. The other party to the contract may sue Contractor for failing to perform. In the breach action, Contractor will present the elements of impracticability as a defense, i.e., he or she will admit that the promised acts went unperformed, but will claim that such non-performance was justified or excused by the commercial impracticability. If the elements of the doctrine can be proven, he or she will have a defense to the breach claim.

DISCHARGE OF DUTIES BY IMPOSSIBILITY, IMPRACTICABILITY, OR FRUSTRATION OF PURPOSE

B. IMPOSSIBILITY: DEFINED AND DISCUSSED.
[§ 25–3]

Impossibility of performance provides a defense to a breach of contract suit whereby the defendant's duties under the contract have been validly discharged (legally terminated) due to the occurrence of an unexpected event or series of events rendering performance impossible. A party is entitled to assert the defense when an unexpected event occurs which both upsets a basic assumption of both parties about the contract and which makes subsequent performance by that party impossible [*See* § 25–4 for a complete list of the elements of the defense]. When the defense applies, it discharges a party's duty to perform and thus serves as an excuse justifying that party's non-performance. Of the three doctrines discussed in this Chapter, impossibility was the most readily accepted at common law, which makes sense, for it is inherently unjust to hold someone liable for a breach when subsequent events made performance of the promised duty impossible.

Like "impracticability" [§ 25–31], impossibility is a defense mostly used by *sellers* as opposed to buyers. This is because the defense usually arises when some event occurs which renders a seller's promise to supply a good, land, service, etc., impossible to perform. On the other hand, a buyer's duty is usually only to pay money, and such payment is rarely "impossible" as defined by the doctrine.

Note that both the Restatement 2d and the UCC make no distinction between impossibility and impracticability [Restatement 2d § 261; UCC § 2–615]. These sources consider impracticability to flow from the impossibility doctrine and, in effect, find them to be part of a continuum whereby a party's duties should be discharged whenever performance becomes unexpectedly too difficult. Under this view, such performance can become too difficult either because it is too expensive to complete (impracticability), or because it is objectively impossible to execute (impossibility).

As explained in greater detail below [§ 25–44] courts are more inclined to grant relief when the triggering event makes performance objectively impossible versus impracticable. Hence, this Book keeps analysis of the two doctrines analytically separate, as do most of the cases.

1. **Elements Necessary to Establish Impossibility.** [§ 25–4]

    A party seeking to use impossibility as a defense must prove the following:

    (1) The occurrence of an event which makes performance of a duty ***objectively impossible***;

(2) The non-occurrence of the event causing the impossibility was a **mutually shared basic assumption on which the contract was made**;

(3) The event causing the impossibility occurred **without fault of the party asserting the defense**; and

(4) The party asserting the defense did not implicitly or explicitly **assume the risk of occurrence of the event** causing the impossibility of performance [Restatement 2d § 261; UCC §§ 2–613, 2–615].

a. **An Event Must Occur That Makes Performance Objectively Impossible. [§ 25–5]**

The first element of the impossibility defense is that an event must have occurred that makes performance impossible. While on its face this element seems straightforward, the term "impossible" can cause confusion and is subject to interpretation. For example, there is a big difference between saying performance of a duty is impossible because **no one** can do it (e.g., when the horse dies), and saying it is "impossible" because only the person who made the promise cannot do it, while others can (e.g., when the reason Ted's Taxi Service does not get June to the airport on time is because Ted had a flat tire and no spare).

Some commentators characterize this distinction as saying it is the difference between "objective" impossibility (when no one can perform) and "subjective" impossibility (when the person who made the promise cannot perform but someone else could), and note that only objective impossibility can serve to discharge a party's duties under the impossibility doctrine. The Restatement specifically declined to use "objective" as an adjective modifying the type of impossibility needed to invoke the doctrine [Restatement 2d § 261, Cmt. e], but it is only this "objective" type of impossibility to which the doctrine applies. [*See* Case Squibs section, *U.S. v. Wegematic*, 360 F.2d 674 (2d Cir. 1966)].

(1) **Example. [§ 25–6]**

Buyer is obligated to purchase $1 million worth of products. When the time for payment arrives, it has no money to pay for the goods and has used up every available credit source. While it might be "impossible" for the particular buyer to pay, its duty to pay is not excused, for there is insufficient impossibility as required by the doctrine.

DISCHARGE OF DUTIES BY IMPOSSIBILITY, IMPRACTICABILITY, OR FRUSTRATION OF PURPOSE

    (2) Example. [§ 25–7]

    Tony is under a contractual duty to deliver his Rembrandt to Carol on Thursday. On Wednesday, Tony's house burns down through no fault of his own, destroying the painting. Tony's duty to deliver the painting is discharged, and his performance excused, for delivery of the painting is sufficiently impossible.

b. The Non-Occurrence of the Event Making Performance Impossible Must Have Been a "Basic Assumption" of Both Parties When They Entered into Their Agreement. [§ 25–8]

To fulfill this element, a party must establish that the non-happening of the event making performance impossible was an important, or basic, assumption when the contract was made. The assumption need not be (and usually is not) stated in the contract, **but it must be mutual**. That is, the purely unilateral assumptions of one party about performance under the contract are insufficient to give rise to an impossibility defense when those assumptions do not come to pass.

SPECIAL CASE SQUIB

(1) *Taylor v. Caldwell*. [§ 25–9]

    Caldwell, owner of the Surrey Gardens and Music Hall, entered into a contract with Taylor, a producer of a musical show. In their contract Caldwell promised to lease the premises in fit condition for four nights. However, before the first concert was given, through no fault of either party, a fire destroyed the hall, and the concerts could not be performed as scheduled. Taylor brought suit against Caldwell seeking the advertising costs and some other types of loss sustained from not being able to put on the concerts as scheduled.

    Held: Both parties are excused from performance because the continued existence of the Hall was a **mutually shared basic assumption** of the contract [*Taylor v. Caldwell*, 122 Eng. Rep. 309 (1863)].

(2) Example. [§ 25–10]

    A car dealer ordered $2 million worth of automobiles from the manufacturer. Their contract stated that payment for the cars was to be made by a letter of credit issued by Central Bank. A few days before payment was due, Central Bank went out of business. Neither party's duties will be discharged due to impossibility. While it is probably true that the non-occurrence of the event, i.e., the continued existence of the Bank, was an unstated assumption of both parties when they entered the contract, the continued existence of the <u>particular</u> bank was almost surely not a **basic** assumption of the transaction. Any bank could issue the letter of credit.

(3) Example. [§ 25–11]

Beverage Co. enters into a contract with Farmer for the delivery of 1 ton of apples to be made into apple juice. Beverage Co. does not care where the apples come from so long as they are of sufficient quality, but Farmer expects that they will come from her farm. An unexpected fungus destroys Farmer's crop. Farmer's duty to deliver is not discharged under the impossibility doctrine. This is because: (a) her performance has not been rendered sufficiently "impossible," for Farmer could buy someone else's apples and still perform under the contract; and (b) the non-occurrence of the event, i.e., the ability of Farmer to deliver the apples from her own crop, was not a **mutually shared basic** assumption under the contract [*Anderson v. May*, 52 N.W. 530 (Minn. 1892)].

Note that if the contract had specifically called for delivery of, say, grapes grown on a particular vineyard for a particular winery, and if the grapes were destroyed through no fault of Farmer, Farmer's duties would be discharged. In that case, performance of the delivery promise would be sufficiently impossible, and the assumption as to the continued existence of Farmer's grape crop (the only grapes which could fulfill the contract) would be a **mutual and basic assumption** under the contract. The UCC describes this concept as applying impossibility and impracticability only when "the contract requires for its performance [particular] goods identified when the contract is made" [UCC § 2–613].

c. **The Event Making Performance Impossible Must Have Occurred Without the Fault of the Party Asserting the Defense. [§ 25–12]**

In order for a party to successfully assert an impossibility defense, the event making performance impossible must have occurred without his or her fault. "Fault" here is given its tort meaning, and thus a party who is either the intentional or negligent proximate cause of the event giving rise to the impossibility cannot successfully use the defense to discharge his or her duty.

DISCHARGE OF DUTIES BY IMPOSSIBILITY, IMPRACTICABILITY, OR FRUSTRATION OF PURPOSE

(1) Example. [§ 25–13]

A winery enters into a contract with Farmer calling for the delivery of three tons of grapes from a specific vineyard on Farmer's land. If the grapes are destroyed by fungus so that there is no crop to be delivered, whether Farmer's duties are discharged by impossibility depends on the reason the infection occurred. If it turns out that the reason the grapes became diseased is because, e.g., the farmer failed to water adequately, thus substantially increasing the likelihood of fungal infection, the impossibility doctrine does not provide a defense to Farmer, and Farmer's duty to deliver is not discharged.

However, if Farmer acted as a reasonable farmer in like circumstances in growing her crop, but the fungus nevertheless infested the grapes, Farmer's failure to deliver her grapes to the winery will be excused as the delivery obligation will be discharged.

d. The Party Asserting the Impossibility Defense Must Not Have Assumed the Risk of the Occurrence of the Event Making Performance Impossible. [§ 25–14]

The final element of the impossibility defense is a requirement that the party asserting the defense must not have assumed the risk that the event making performance impossible would occur. This element is explicitly stated in UCC § 2–613, and while it is not specifically found in the Restatement 2d, it has universally been adopted by courts in impossibility, impracticability, and frustration cases.

A party may assume the risk of the occurrence of an event either explicitly or implicitly under the contract. However, as a practical manner, it is rare for the parties to contest a case when a seller has explicitly assumed the risk. For example, if under a written agreement whereby Bill is obligated to sell his watch to Mary, Bill also promises to "assume the risk of destruction of the watch from any source, and will be strictly liable if he does not deliver for any reason," it is unlikely that Bill will contest liability if he does not deliver the watch. Hence, the typical litigation involving this element focuses on whether, under the circumstances, it is fair to say that the seller has *impliedly* promised to assume the risk that this type of contingency would occur.

(1) Example. [§ 25–15]

Larry promises to deliver a perpetual motion machine to Leo's Novelty Co., despite being cognizant of the fact that physicists believe such a machine is impossible to build. Larry is not entitled to use the impossibility defense in a breach action stemming from his failure to deliver because, under the circumstances, he impliedly assumed the risk that he would not be able to perform.

Note that the implied assumption of the risk doctrine really has more application in impracticability situations than in impossibility situations. This is because it is relatively unusual to hold that someone implicitly accepts the risk that the subject matter of the contract will be destroyed, or that performance of the promise truly will be impossible [*See* §§ 25–39 *et seq.*, for examples of the implicit assumption of the risk doctrine as applied to commercial impracticability cases].

2. **Common Fact Situations Presenting Impossibility Issues. [§ 25–16]**

Over time, contract law has been able to categorize certain types of fact situations that recurrently present impossibility of performance issues, and these are discussed below. While the contours of the doctrine vary from fact situation to fact situation, the basic analytical framework for each case is the same, i.e., if the party seeking to assert an impossibility defense can establish the occurrence of an event making performance impossible; that the non-happening of that event was a basic assumption of both parties when the contract was made; that the event occurred without fault of the party asserting the defense; and that he or she has not assumed the risk of the event's occurrence, then the duty rendered impossible to perform by the event will be discharged.

a. **Death or Incapacity of a Particular Person Necessary for Performance ("Personal Service" Contracts). [§ 25–17]**

Some contracts call not just for the performance of specified duties, but also require that specified persons perform them. These are known as "personal service" contracts. If a contract calls for a performance by a particular person, and that person dies or becomes incapacitated after the contract was entered into, but before performance is due, then the duty to perform is discharged by impossibility [Restatement 2d § 262]. However, if performance of the contract does not call for a **particular** person to perform specified duties, then death or incapacity of the party will not discharge the promisor's duty.

Recall that the death of a person necessary for performance of a contract made while an offer is pending, but **before it has been accepted**, acts to terminate the offeree's power of acceptance under a revocable offer [*See* § 4–68].

(1) **Example. [§ 25–18]**

Carol is an art dealer. She enters into a contract with her customer, John, promising to deliver to John by December 1 a new painting by Lorenzo, a living artist. Shortly after the Carol/John contract is entered into, and before December 1, Lorenzo dies. Carol's duty to deliver the painting to John is discharged by impossibility.

(2) **Example. [§ 25–19]**

Studio contracts with Actor to star in film. Actor dies before filming begins. Actor's duties are discharged due to impossibility.

b. **Death, Destruction, Deterioration, or the Failure to Come into Existence, of a Thing Necessary for Performance. [§ 25–20]**

Some contracts call not just for the performance of specified duties, but also require that goods come from a specified place, or that a particular good be delivered. If the existence of a particular thing is necessary for performance of a duty under a contract, its death, destruction, deterioration, or failure to come into existence will discharge the duties remaining under a contract. Once again, however, for the defense to apply, the existence of a **particular** thing must be mutually assumed or agreed to under the contract [Restatement 2d § 263; UCC § 2–613].

(1) **Example. [§ 25–21]**

A grocery store contracts to purchase 200 gallons of whole milk daily from the Fresh Dairy Co. ("Dairy Co."). Dairy Co. expects that it will furnish such milk from its own cows, but there is no such requirement in the contract. The dairy accidentally burns down, through no fault of the dairy, and kills all the cows. Dairy Co. now asserts its duty to supply the milk to the grocery store is discharged due to impossibility. It cannot successfully use the impossibility defense.

While it may be "subjectively" impossible for the dairy to supply the milk from its own cows, it is freely able to go into the market, purchase 200 gallons of whole milk a day from someone else, and perform its delivery duties. Hence, because performance of the duties under the contract did not call for the existence of a particular thing, i.e., milk from cows owned by Dairy Co., their destruction does not give rise to sufficient "objective" impossibility for the doctrine to apply.

However, if the contract called for the milk to come only from the cows at their particular dairy, e.g., because they were supposed to produce sweeter milk, etc., then the fire would discharge the duties. This is because now the duty to supply what is called for by the contract is impossible, and the continued existence of the dairy's cows under the contract was obviously a basic assumption of both parties. As the UCC puts it, relief can be given where "the contract requires for its performance [particular] goods identified when the contract is made" [UCC § 2–613]. [*See also* the example in § 25–11.]

Note that some commentators, although only a few cases, have criticized the above rule. To them, if impossibility is going to have much practical value, it should operate in a case where both parties probably expected the goods involved would come from the supplier's farm or workshop or whatever, even if the supplier could theoretically go out on the market and find replacement goods.

(2) Example. [§ 25–22]

Tony agrees to sell to Laura a pedigree puppy from an upcoming litter of dogs born to Frieda. If Frieda dies before giving birth, the failure of the puppy to come into existence will discharge Tony's duty to deliver, assuming again Frieda's death occurred without Tony's fault.

c. Impossibility Due to Government Regulation or Order Making Performance Illegal. [§ 25–23]

Usually, a basic assumption on which a contract is made is that there will be no law or regulation that will make performance illegal when due. In a strict sense, illegality does not result in "objective" impossibility, for the party under a duty could always perform and take the legal consequences for such action. However, as a matter of public policy, i.e., so as not to encourage people to violate valid laws and regulations, contract law holds that subsequent illegality of the duty called for in a contract discharges that duty under an impossibility theory [Restatement 2d § 264; UCC § 2–614(2)]. The law or regulation making the duty impossible can be either domestic or foreign. (Recall that when a law or regulation making illegal a requested performance in an offer becomes applicable while the offer is pending but **before the offer is accepted**, the power of the offeree to accept the offer is terminated. *See* § 4–69).

DISCHARGE OF DUTIES BY IMPOSSIBILITY, IMPRACTICABILITY, OR FRUSTRATION OF PURPOSE

(1) **Example. [§ 25–24]**

Bob was a pioneer pilot for a major airline. Before FAA regulation, the airline contractually obligated itself to employ Bob as a pilot and let him fly the L.A. to N.Y. route "to age 70, so long as Bob continues to pass his annual physical examination." The FAA subsequently imposed a binding requirement on all airlines that no pilot can operate a commercial aircraft after reaching age 60. Bob was 65 when the regulation was enacted. The airline's duty to let him fly the L.A. to N.Y. route is discharged due to supervening illegality.

d. **Contracts to Repair Existing Building. [§ 25–25]**

Another recurring situation involving the impossibility doctrine occurs when a contractor is hired to do repairs on an existing building, and then, after the contract is signed, but before the repairs are completed, the building is destroyed without either party's fault. The duty of the contractor to perform the repairs in such a situation is discharged due to impossibility [Restatement 2d, § 261, Cmt. d, Ill. 6; § 263, Cmt. a, Ill. 3].

Whether impossibility provides a defense can, of course, be important in an individual case. But, to contract law, the more important issue is to have a definite rule on this issue so both the contractor and the owner of the building know which party needs to purchase insurance to cover the contingency.

e. **Contracts to Erect New Buildings. [§ 25–26]**

The rule in the last section applies only where the contract is to repair existing buildings. When there is construction of a new building, and the partially built new structure is destroyed by fire earthquake, etc., the rule is different. As that is usually analyzed under impracticability, the situation is discussed in § 25–42.

f. **Labor Strikes. [§ 25–27]**

Another recurring fact situation presents itself when a supplier's work force goes out on strike, thereby making it "impossible" for the supplier to perform in a timely fashion. The courts are split on how to treat such a case. Some hold that the impossibility defense does not apply, on the grounds that: (a) a labor strike is only a case of "subjective" impossibility for the employer can always hire new workers or (b) that the employer is somewhat "at fault" in a strike, for the employer **could** have avoided the problem by acquiescing to the demands of its workers. However, other courts hold that if a labor strike

CHAPTER 25

prevents a party from timely performing under a contract, those duties are discharged due to impossibility.

g. Land Sale Contracts. [§ 25–28]

At common law, upon execution of the land sale agreement the purchaser immediately became the equitable owner of the property and all its improvements, even if he or she did not have legal title at the time. Thus, the old rule held that any risk of destruction of the property was allocated to the buyer upon execution of the sales contract. Hence, if a building on the property burned before the purchaser had legal title, e.g., while the sale was in escrow, there was no discharge of the buyer's duty to pay for the property. A number of states have changed this rule today by statute so that destruction of the property or of an improvement on the property after a land sale contract is executed, but before legal title passes, discharges the buyer's duty to accept title and pay for the property due to impossibility.

3. Partial Impossibility. [§ 25–29]

Sometimes impossibility can be partial, e.g., where only part of a crop is destroyed; or where a large shipment was divided in two lots and sent on two airplanes, and only one crashed. Under UCC §§ 2–615 and 2–616, contract law's responses to such a situation can be summed up as follows:

(1) If all the elements of impossibility can be established as to that portion of the goods destroyed, the seller will not be in breach for failing to supply the destroyed portion;

(2) The remaining portion must be offered to the customers of the seller on a *pro rata* basis; and

(3) If the buyer does not wish only a *pro rata* amount of his or her order, he or she may reject it without incurring contractual liability.

This concept is perhaps more easily visualized by example.

a. Example. [§ 25–30]

Vintner owns some prized vineyards which produce, at a minimum, 30 tons of grapes per year. Vintner enters into a contract promising 20 tons of grapes from her vineyards to Buyer A, and 10 tons of grapes from her vineyards to Buyer B. Buyer B plans to make his 10 tons of grapes into 50,000 cases of a "single vineyard" wine, all of which he has pre-sold.

A blight, not at all Vintner's fault, destroyed half the crop so Vintner was left with only 15 tons of grapes. Under § 2–615, Vintner is excused from having to provide the portion that was destroyed, i.e., neither Buyer A nor Buyer B can sue him for breach for failing to fulfill their orders completely.

Under § 2–616, Vintner must offer the remaining grapes on a *pro rata* basis to Buyers A and B, i.e., he must offer Buyer A 10 tons and Buyer B 5 tons. At that point, either Buyer A or Buyer B can choose to accept the offer of a *pro rata* amount, or choose not to accept it without incurring contractual liability. For example, Buyer B might well decide to decline the offer of only 5 tons and instead buy a full complement of 10 tons from a single vineyard produced by another supplier to meet its orders. Hence, Buyer B may turn down Vintner's offer of a *pro rata* delivery without breaching the contract.

C. COMMERCIAL IMPRACTICABILITY: DEFINED AND DISCUSSED. [§ 25–31]

Like impossibility, impracticability also provides a defense to a breach of contract suit for failure to perform [*see* § 25–2] whereby the party asserting the defense has his or her remaining duties under a contract discharged due to the occurrence of an unexpected event or series of events that makes performance more expensive. A party is entitled to assert the defense when an unexpected event occurs which both upsets a basic assumption of both parties about the contract and which makes subsequent performance by that party impractical [*see* § 25–32 for a complete list of the elements of the defense]. When the defense applies, it discharges a party's duty to perform and thus serves as an excuse justifying non-performance. The doctrine is recognized as a defense under both the Restatement 2d and the UCC [Restatement 2d § 261; UCC § 2–615].

Under impracticability, a party's duties are discharged due to the fact that performance turns out to be more burdensome than either party expected. Thus, while it cannot be said that the event triggering impracticability makes performance under the contract "impossible," if it nonetheless makes performance sufficiently "impractical," i.e., sufficiently more expensive, contract law provides that the party need not perform.

In truth, impracticability promises much but delivers little. There are but a handful of reported cases in which the defense has been successfully asserted. The reason is that courts view an asserted impracticability claim on very different grounds than an impossibility claim. That is, while it is viewed as unjust to require a party to be liable in breach for not performing a duty which is impossible or illegal, it is viewed as quite a different matter to excuse a party from performing just because it will cost more than he or she expected it would.

This flows from the axiom of modern contract law that contract making is risk allocation. That is, modern contract law generally states that once Lance contractually promises to build a garage for Susan at a fixed price, he bears the risk that the costs of construction may be more expensive than he thought it would be. Hence, while a court may excuse a party from performing if such performance will be **significantly** more expensive than either party thought, and for a reason the party **truly** should not have foreseen, in the vast majority of cases courts will deny a party's ability to assert the defense by holding that the party implicitly accepted the risk that a contract might not be as profitable as he or she unilaterally expected when the contract was signed.

Like impossibility, impracticability is almost always asserted by suppliers of goods or services, rather than by purchasers. The reason is that while there are a number of things that can make a seller's duties more burdensome, it is unlikely there is much that can make a buyer's duty to pay a contracted-for sum more expensive.

1. **Elements Necessary to Establish an Impracticability Defense. [§ 25–32]**

    As noted earlier [see § 25–3], the drafters of the Restatement 2d and of the UCC believed that impossibility and impracticability are in essence two sides of the same coin, i.e., they both describe a doctrine which provides relief from non-performance when such performance is unexpectedly difficult. As a result, the elements necessary to establish the impracticability defense are quite similar to those for impossibility. To establish the defense, a party must prove:

    (1) The occurrence of an event which makes performance **commercially impracticable**;

    (2) The non-occurrence of the event making performance impractical was a **mutually shared basic assumption on which the contract was made**;

    (3) The event making performance impractical occurred **without fault of the party asserting the defense**; **and**

    (4) The party asserting the defense did not implicitly or explicitly **assume the risk** of the occurrence of the event making performance impractical [Restatement 2d § 261; UCC § 2–615].

    a. **An Event Must Occur That Makes Performance Commercially Impracticable. [§ 25–33]**

        The party asserting a commercial impracticability defense must establish the occurrence of an event that makes performance of a promised duty more expensive or "impractical." There are no hard and fast rules as to how much more expensive performance must be before the requisite threshold is reached, but there is some indication from the case law and elsewhere that the **minimum** amount of extra expense necessary to establish

DISCHARGE OF DUTIES BY IMPOSSIBILITY, IMPRACTICABILITY, OR FRUSTRATION OF PURPOSE

impracticability is a five or six times increase in the expected cost [*See*, e.g., the Introductory Note to Chapter 11 of the Restatement 2d, which speaks in terms of a **tenfold** increase in cost for impracticability to occur].

In any event, certainly the fact that a party is not going to make quite as much of a profit as he or she thought when the contract was signed is not enough to trigger the defense. It is likely that even a showing that an unexpected event will turn a very profitable contract into one where the supplier will lose a little money will be insufficient to invoke impracticability. The courts demand that the party asserting the defense show that performance would be very unjust and unconscionable before he or she can meet this threshold test.

(1) Example. [§ 25–34]

Laura hires Al, a contractor, to install a swimming pool in her home for $30,000, with an expected profit of $5,000. As Al begins digging the pool, he discovers that the soil a foot or so beneath the surface is so wet that the entire backyard will need to be drained, and extra steps will need to be taken to protect the pool's foundation against leakage. These procedures will triple the amount of labor needed for construction, and will cause Al to lose $4,000 on the deal. Al's duties will probably not be discharged due to impracticability.

(2) Example. [§ 25–35]

Same as above, except this time Al discovers huge granite boulders hidden a couple of feet below the surface. The cheapest way to remove them is by blasting, and the costs associated with such blasting and protecting Laura's and her neighbors' homes from the resulting debris will increase the costs of construction tenfold, and will mean that Al will lose $250,000 on the job if the pool is completed. Al probably can establish sufficient impracticability to fulfill the first element of the defense.

b. The Non-Occurrence of the Event Making Performance Impractical Must Have Been a Basic Assumption of Both Parties When They Entered into Their Agreement. [§ 25–36]

As with impossibility [§ 25–8], to satisfy this element a party must establish that the non-occurrence of the event causing the impracticability was an important, or basic, assumption held by **both** parties when they entered into the contract. There is no test to determine whether the non-occurrence of an event was a "basic assumption" of the parties, but it is clear that the assumption must be an important one to both parties, and that it must be shared by them at the time they entered the contract.

(1) Example. [§ 25–37]

Assume the facts of the Laura/Al hypothetical set forth in § 25–35, where Al discovered huge granite boulders as he begins digging a swimming pool for Laura. It may well be that the absence of such boulders was a basic assumption shared by both parties when the contract was made. If so, Al has fulfilled the second element of the defense.

c. The Event Making Performance Impractical Must Occur Without the Fault of the Party Asserting the Defense. [§ 25–38]

If the party asserting the defense of impracticability was at fault in causing the event giving rise to impracticability, the defense will fail. As with impossibility [§ 25–12], fault is used here in the tort sense and thus includes either an intentional or a negligent act that proximately causes the event giving rise to the impracticability.

(1) Example. [§ 25–39]

Assume the facts of the Laura/Al hypothetical of § 25–35, where Al is to build a pool for Laura. This time, however, assume that Al did not take soil tests before beginning construction of the pool, and also assume that a reasonable pool builder would have performed such tests before making a fixed price offer to build the pool. If such tests would have disclosed the presence of the granite boulders, Al could not successfully assert the impracticability defense.

Note that Al might try to assert that the existence of the boulders was not his fault and thus try to argue that he did not cause the event making performance impractical. This is not a valid argument, for while Al was not at fault for the boulders being there, on these facts he **was** at fault for negligently failing to locate them before entering into the fixed price contract.

d. The Party Asserting the Defense Must Not Have Assumed the Risk of the Occurrence of the Event Making Performance Impractical. [§ 25–40]

The last element a party asserting the impracticability defense must prove is that he or she did not assume the risk that the event which made performance impractical would occur. This

DISCHARGE OF DUTIES BY IMPOSSIBILITY, IMPRACTICABILITY, OR FRUSTRATION OF PURPOSE

element is also one that most parties seeking to use the doctrine cannot fulfill, for, as mentioned earlier [§ 25–31], the idea behind mutuality of obligation under modern contract law is that contract making is risk allocation. When a party makes a contractual promise to perform a task, he or she is taking a risk that the deal may be less profitable than expected. On the other hand, the party is also entitled to reap the benefits if the deal turns out to be more profitable than anticipated. Hence, freedom of contract and the "risk allocation" idea mandates that courts view with skepticism a party's plea that the courts impose a floor on the possible losses he or she may suffer under a contract which turned out to be an improvident deal.

Indeed, recall that for every break given the party claiming impracticability, benefits are taken away from the other party. That is, a "bad" deal for one party is a "good" deal for the other, and often the party receiving the "good" deal claims that the chance to get such a profitable deal was the principal reason he or she entered into the contract in the first place. Thus, when a court grants a claim of impracticability, the party resisting application of the defense usually argues that the court is depriving that party of his or her bargained for expectations. As a consequence, courts are reluctant to find that the risk of a bad deal was not assumed by the party asserting the defense.

Another factor involved in assessing whether a party implicitly assumed the risk of the event making performance impractical is whether the event was foreseeable. While a party is not expected to protect himself or herself against every potential event that could make performance impracticable, it is fair to say that **the more foreseeable an event is, the more a party will be held to have <u>implicitly</u> assumed the risk of it occurring by failing to negotiate protection for himself or herself under the agreement**.

(1) Example. [§ 25–41]

Fusion Co. promises to supply uranium to Utility for operation of Utility's nuclear power plant. After the contract is signed, but before delivery is due, there is an illegal price-fixing agreement among uranium suppliers throughout the world so that the cost of uranium on the open market increases tenfold. A court may well conclude that Fusion Co.'s duty to deliver the uranium is nevertheless **not** discharged due to impracticability despite the price fixing agreement.

A series of cases similar to this hypothetical arose in the 1970's and 1980's (known in commercial circles as the

"Westinghouse cases"), and the courts consistently denied relief to the supplier of the power plants. The rationale was that while a supplier such as Fusion Co. may not have reasonably foreseen an illegal uranium cartel, it certainly was aware that the price of uranium might rise between the date of the contract and the date of delivery for any number of reasons. Thus, it could have negotiated a price term that was conditional on uranium not exceeding a certain price for whatever reason, or it could have agreed to supply the uranium on a cost plus basis (where it charges the buyer a certain percentage over its cost for the ore), etc. By failing to protect itself, the courts held that a company such as Fusion Co. implicitly assumed the risk that the price of uranium would rise, regardless of the reason. As such, it was not entitled to successfully use the impracticability defense.

(2) **Example of Construction of a New Structure.** [§ 25–42]

A recurring fact situation raising impracticability issues occurs when, e.g., a contractor is hired to construct a building and, after it is partially finished, the building is destroyed through no fault of either party. The builders in these cases often attempt to assert that their duties under the contract should be discharged due to impracticability. The courts have consistently held that the defense is not available in such situations for two reasons. The first reason is because performance is usually not impractical enough since it will only result, at most, in a doubling of the cost [§ 25–33]. The second reason is because the builder is deemed to have assumed the risk of such an event by making an unconditional promise to finish a building by a certain date when it could have protected itself by negotiating conditional language in the contract, e.g., a clause like, "I will build at this price assuming there is no destruction of the building during construction that is not my fault." Also courts hold the availability of insurance to builders to protect against this type of loss is a factor that makes it reasonable to put the risk of destruction on the builder. So while the builder will have to finish construction [Restatement 2d § 263, Cmt. a, Ill. 4], the builder is typically given a reasonable extension of time in which to perform.

Contrast this situation, i.e., construction of a *new* building, with repair of an *existing* building [§ 25–26].

DISCHARGE OF DUTIES BY IMPOSSIBILITY, IMPRACTICABILITY, OR FRUSTRATION OF PURPOSE

(3) Exception: Example of *Alcoa Co. v. Essex*. [§ 25–43]

Perhaps the most aggressive use of the impracticability defense was in *Alcoa v. Essex*. There, Alcoa agreed to convert specified amounts of alumina supplied by Essex into aluminum for Essex. The contract was heavily negotiated and was scheduled to run from 1968 through 1988. To protect against inflation or other changes which might affect the costs of production, the price charged by Alcoa was subject to adjustment based, in part, on changes to a particular Wholesale Price Index ("WPI"). Indexing the price to the WPI was suggested by Alcoa and was the result of an enormous amount of study by various Alcoa experts who concluded that the change in WPI historically had been reliable in tracking the changes in the actual cost of transforming alumina into aluminum.

After the contract was signed, the costs of transforming alumina into aluminum ran much higher than the corresponding rise in the WPI. As a result, Essex was getting below market prices for aluminum under the contract, and began selling aluminum on the open market, as well as using it for its own consumption. While there was nothing in the contract to prevent Essex from selling aluminum, by 1978 Essex was making a profit on the open market of around $.37/pound of aluminum, while Alcoa was losing about $.10/pound in processing the aluminum it delivered to Essex. Alcoa brought a declaratory relief action seeking to be discharged from its duties under the contract on the grounds, *inter alia,* of impracticability.

Essex defended by saying Alcoa assumed the risk that the costs of production would not match the price increases for aluminum processing when it agreed to the WPI indexing formula, especially since the idea of WPI indexing was Alcoa's idea in the first place. Further, Alcoa could have protected itself by having a clause prohibiting Essex from selling aluminum on the open market or negotiated some other sort of price guarantee.

Held: Alcoa was entitled to relief under the contract. In this case the court went farther than just discharging Alcoa's duties, and ended up actually rewriting the price term, ensuring that Alcoa would make a profit of at least $.01/pound of aluminum processed [*Alcoa v. Essex*, 499 F.Supp. 53 (W.D. Pa. 1980)].

When *Alcoa* was first decided, it caused much stir in the commercial world. However, the case has proven not to be the harbinger that many expected. Hence if a case like *Alcoa* were to come along today, Essex would likely prevail on its argument that Alcoa impliedly assumed the risk that the WPI-adjusted price it charged for aluminum would not keep up with its costs when it signed the agreement, and Alcoa thus would either have to perform under the contract or be in breach for failing to do so.

2. Contrasting Impossibility and Impracticability. [§ 25–44]

Clearly the elements of impossibility and impracticability are quite similar [*Compare* § 25–4 *with* § 25–32]. However, there are reasons to treat them separately, as is done in this book. Impossibility is a defense all modern courts recognize and apply routinely; assertions of impracticability have not been very well received by modern courts, even though all courts accept that the defense exists. Moreover, there is a quantitative difference in the structure of the two defenses as well. That is, it is rare that the buyer will complain if he or she does not obtain a promised performance if such performance is truly impossible, i.e., if a one-of-a-kind painting is destroyed through no fault of the seller, there really is nothing that can be done and a buyer does not usually feel he or she is being taken advantage of if the seller does not perform. On the other hand, if the seller's performance is merely impractical, i.e., more expensive, than the seller thought it would be, a buyer is much more likely to insist that the seller perform anyway. After all, the buyer did not promise the seller a profit when they made a contract. The buyer simply agreed to pay an agreed amount for a good, some land, or a service. Since performance is still possible, and the buyer is still willing to pay the agreed upon price, the buyer typically insists on performance.

D. FRUSTRATION OF PURPOSE: DEFINED AND DISCUSSED. [§ 25–45]

Frustration of purpose is a defense to a breach of contract claim [§ 25–2] whereby the party asserting the defense asserts that his or her duties under the contract have been discharged due to the occurrence of an unexpected event or series of events that make performance by the other party unnecessary. As in impossibility or impracticability situations, frustration is triggered by the occurrence of an event, the non-occurrence of which is a basic assumption on which the contract is made. However, unlike impossibility or impracticability, in frustration situations performance of the promised duty is perfectly possible and is no more expensive or otherwise burdensome for the non-performing party. What provides the justification for the non-performance in frustration situations is that, because of the event, the principal **purpose** for which the non-performing party entered into the contract is largely gone. In other words, the **value** to one party of the other's promised performance

DISCHARGE OF DUTIES BY IMPOSSIBILITY, IMPRACTICABILITY, OR FRUSTRATION OF PURPOSE

is substantially eliminated. Thus, while the party asserting the defense can perform his or her duty, and can perform it without extra burden, contract law says he or she does not have to because the **reason** he or she entered into the contract is "frustrated."

As impossibility and impracticability are largely seller's defenses, frustration of purpose is largely a buyer's defense. That is, in the typical fact pattern giving rise to the assertion of a frustration defense, something happens which renders meaningless the purpose for which the buyer had agreed to pay money.

The frustration defense is recognized by the Restatement 2d in § 265, although, somewhat surprisingly, it is not specifically mentioned in the UCC. Nevertheless, most commentators believe that frustration is inherently included in § 2–615, even if it is not specifically mentioned in the section. There is support for this contention in Comment 9 to UCC § 2–615.

As with impracticability, in close cases the frustration defense has received scant acceptance from the American courts. However, although the American courts continue to say that the frustration defense is a viable one, there are relatively few reported cases in which a defendant has successfully asserted the defense unless the need for it is almost too plain to be contested.

1. **Elements Necessary to Establish the Frustration of Purpose Defense. [§ 25–46]**

    A party wishing to justify his or her non-performance by use of the frustration defense must establish:

    (1) The occurrence of an event which **frustrates a principal purpose** of the party asserting the defense in entering into a contract;

    (2) That the non-occurrence of the event causing frustration was a **mutually shared basic assumption** on which the contract was made;

    (3) That the event causing the frustration occurred **without fault** of the party asserting the defense; and

    (4) The party asserting the defense did not implicitly or explicitly **assume the risk** of the event causing frustration

    [Restatement 2d § 265].

    a. **An Event Must Occur That Frustrates the Principal Purpose for Entering into a Contract. [§ 25–47]**

        To establish the frustration defense, a party must show that as a result of an unexpected event, his or her **principal purpose** for entering into the contract has been **substantially** frustrated. Buyers have had trouble convincing American courts that this element has been fulfilled for two reasons.

First, courts have viewed the purpose of a party under a contract quite broadly. Hence, merely showing that a party cannot take advantage of a transaction in the particular way he or she thought would be available at the time the contract was made is insufficient to establish that the **principal** purpose has been frustrated so long as the party can realize **some** benefit from the contract.

Second, even if a degree of frustration as to the principal purpose of the agreement is found, courts have insisted that the degree of frustration be quite substantial. Hence, just because the party would not receive **all** of the benefits he or she expected under the contract, or cannot do with the goods exactly what he or she wants, does not mean frustration has been established.

(1) Example. [§ 25–48]

Myra contracted to purchase a vacant piece of property that was zoned for commercial development. Myra planned to use the site to build a mini-mall, a fact known to the seller. After she signed the contract to purchase the property, but before she took title, the land was re-zoned to allow only single family residences, apartment buildings, and condominiums. Myra's duties are not discharged under the frustration of purpose doctrine for two reasons.

First, courts would likely hold that her principal purpose in entering into the contract was broad, i.e., to use the land for income-generation purposes, rather than narrow, i.e., to build a mini-mall. Hence, they would hold that her principal purpose is not frustrated at all by the re-zoning, because she can build an apartment building or a condominium complex on the site and generate income from the property.

Second, even if she could establish some degree of frustration in the realization of her principal purpose, it would almost surely not be substantial enough to trigger the doctrine. That is, the fact that she can use the property to generate some amount of income, even if it is not as much as the mini-mall would provide, shows that the zoning change did not cause a **substantial** frustration of her purpose in purchasing the property.

DISCHARGE OF DUTIES BY IMPOSSIBILITY, IMPRACTICABILITY, OR FRUSTRATION OF PURPOSE

b. **The Non-Occurrence of the Event Frustrating Performance Must Have Been a Basic Assumption of Both Parties on Which the Contract Was Made. [§ 25–49]**

The second element of a frustration defense is that the non-occurrence of the event causing the frustration must have been an important, or basic, assumption on which the contract was based. Once again, there is no set test to determine whether this element is met, but the party seeking to assert the defense must show that the non-occurrence of the event was an **important** and **mutually held assumption** when the contract was entered into.

(1) **Example of Leased Premises Destroyed During Term of Lease. [§ 25–50]**

Peter agrees to rent an apartment from Kristen, and they enter into a one-year written lease. Two months after the contract was signed and after Peter has moved in, the apartment building burns down through no fault of either Peter or Kristen. In such a case, Peter's duty to pay rent is discharged through frustration, as the continued presence of the apartment was certainly a shared basic assumption on which the contract was made, and Peter's principal purpose in entering into the lease contract would be substantially frustrated in the absence of the building.

c. **The Event Causing Frustration of Purpose Must Have Occurred Without the Fault of the Party Asserting the Defense. [§ 25–51]**

As with impossibility and impracticability, a party may not validly use the frustration of purpose defense if he or she was at fault in causing the event giving rise to the frustration. Once again, the term fault under this doctrine is given its tort meaning, and thus includes both intentional and negligent acts of the defendant.

(1) **Example. [§ 25–52]**

Take the Peter/Kristen example set forth in § 25–50 where Peter is a tenant of Kristen's. If the fire that burnt down the apartment building was caused by Peter's negligence, then his duty to pay rent would not be discharged due to frustration.

d. The Party Asserting the Frustration Defense Must Not Have Assumed the Risk of the Occurrence of the Event Frustrating Performance of the Duty. [§ 25–53]

As noted above, the American courts have largely been unsympathetic to frustration of purpose claims. This has occurred in part because of the limitation of the requirement that a party must establish that the principal purpose of the contract has been substantially frustrated. However, it is also because of the fourth element of the defense, i.e., that the party asserting the defense has not implicitly or explicitly assumed the risk of the frustrating event's occurrence. As with impracticability, the courts have in effect held that if the kind of event that frustrates performance is relatively foreseeable, the failure of a party to explicitly guard against its occurrence in the contract means that he or she has implicitly accepted the risk that the event will occur.

(1) Example. [§ 25–54]

Assume the facts of the hypothetical set forth in § 25–48 where Myra purchased a piece of property that was zoned for commercial purposes at the time the contract was signed. Assume this time that before she took title, the City Council zoned her parcel so that she had to keep it as vacant land. Obviously this would be a severe frustration of her principal purpose to purchase income-generating property, which is why she entered into the contract in the first place. However, if, e.g., it was known that the City Council was debating zoning changes at the time she purchased the property, she probably would **not** be entitled to the frustration defense because she would be deemed to have assumed the risk of the zoning change (a foreseeable event) by not providing for such an occurrence in her contract (e.g., by making her obligations conditional on there being no zoning change).

2. Examples of Frustration Cases. [§ 25–55]

The following are examples of relatively famous cases arising under the frustration doctrines.

a. Example of *Krell v. Henry (The Coronation Cases)*. [§ 25–56]

Krell v. Henry, the most famous of *"The Coronation Cases"* was the first significant case to allow the frustration of purpose defense. (All of the *Coronation Cases* arose on similar facts). In *Krell v. Henry,* Krell owned a flat which provided a good view of the planned coronation of King Edward VII of Great Britain.

DISCHARGE OF DUTIES BY IMPOSSIBILITY, IMPRACTICABILITY, OR FRUSTRATION OF PURPOSE

Krell advertised that he would rent the flat to anyone who wished to view the ceremony for £75, a large amount of money at the time. Henry agreed to sublease the flat, paid £25 immediately upon executing the contract, and promised to pay the remaining £50 on the day of the coronation. King Edward suffered appendicitis on the day of the coronation, and the ceremony was indefinitely postponed. Henry refused to pay the remaining £50, and Krell sued. The gist of Krell's argument was that because there was nothing preventing Henry from paying the £50, his failure to do so was an unexcused breach.

Held: Henry did not have to pay the £50 as his duty to do so was discharged due to frustration of purpose. That is:

(1) The principal purpose for which Henry let the rooms (i.e., to watch the coronation) was substantially frustrated. While it was true Henry could still take occupancy, his purpose in doing so was not to see the normal street traffic; it was to see the coronation. Accordingly, the value to him of his tenancy became non-existent when the King postponed the event;

(2) Cancellation of the coronation was an event, the non-occurrence of which was a mutually shared basic assumption on which the contract was based;

(3) Cancellation of the coronation was certainly not due to any fault of Henry; and

(4) The risk of the coronation being canceled was not fairly assumed by Henry. [*Krell v. Henry*, 2 K.B. 740 (C.A.) (1903)]

For an example of an earlier case reaching the opposite decision from *Krell v. Henry*, see Case Squibs, *Paradine v. Jane*.

b. **Example of *Lloyd v. Murphy*. [§ 25–57]**

Murphy leased commercial space from Lloyd in August 1941. Under their agreement, Murphy's use of the property was initially restricted "for the sole purpose of conducting thereon the business of displaying and selling new automobiles" in Beverly Hills. The United States entered World War II shortly after the lease was signed, and the government thereafter issued restrictions on the sale of new cars. These regulations essentially meant Murphy would not be able to get any (or very, very few) new cars to sell. As a consequence, Murphy vacated the premises and refused to pay rent. Lloyd eventually agreed to remove the "car dealership only" restriction of the lease, and even lowered the rent, but Murphy nonetheless would not occupy or pay for the space. In the subsequent breach action for failure to pay rent, Murphy asserted frustration as a defense.

Held: Frustration was not available for two reasons. **First**, to the extent there was any frustration at all, there was an insufficient showing of **substantial** frustration, given Lloyd's offer to allow the premises to be used for any legal purpose, and given the prime location of the premises. That is, since the property could be used to sell any lawfully traded goods, the broad purpose of the lease (i.e., retail commercial space) was not frustrated, even if Murphy's personal expectations was to the use of the property to sell cars were frustrated.

Second, Murphy, as lessee, was deemed to have assumed the risk of the wartime regulations. At the time the lease was signed, automobile sales were brisk because the consuming public anticipated that production might be restricted in the future because the United States' potential involvement in World War II was a highly debated topic. Given those facts, Justice Traynor concluded that Murphy was on notice that such restrictions were foreseeable, and that by failing to include a provision in the lease making the absence of such restrictions a condition of his duty to pay rent, Murphy had assumed the risk that the regulations might be imposed [*Lloyd v. Murphy,* 25 Cal.2d 48, 153 P.2d 47 (1944)].

c. **Example of *LaCumbre Golf & Country Club v. Santa Barbara Hotel.* [§ 25–58]**

A hotel was in proximity to a golf course and made a multi-year arrangement to allow hotel guests to use the golf facility. The hotel paid the golf club a monthly fee for such use. The hotel burned down without fault of its owners.

Held: The frustration defense was allowed and the hotel was excused from paying the monthly fee after the fire. There was **substantial** frustration since the hotel would have no guests and so got no benefit from the contract with the golf club. The continued existence of hotel guests was a **mutually shared basic assumption** under the contract. The hotel was **not at fault** for the fire and the court believed the risk of the hotel burning down was **not implicitly or explicitly allocated** to either party [*LaCumbre Golf & Country Club v. Santa Barbara Hotel*, 205 Cal. 422 (1928)].

Note that the case was decided decades ago. Today a court may well decide that the risk of a fire or other calamity which could result in no guests at the hotel was foreseeable to the hotel, and thus implicitly allocated to it under the agreement. In other words, the hotel should have protected itself by negotiating a fire protection clause into the agreement.

E. TIMING OF EVENTS GIVING RISE TO IMPOSSIBILITY, IMPRACTICABILITY, AND FRUSTRATION: RELATION TO THE "MISTAKE" DOCTRINE. [§ 25–59]

If you look back to the mistake doctrine [Chapter Twelve] you will see that the elements for mistake, on the one hand, and for impossibility, impracticability, and frustration, on the other, are very similar. For many cases, the point of demarcation is the time of contracting. That is, it is a voidable mistake case if the events giving rise to the doctrine are in existence at the time of contracting, e.g., both parties reasonably and justifiably believed the cow was barren when they signed the contract [§ 12–13]. On the other hand, it is a dischargeable impossibility event if the cow dies after the contract is entered into [§ 25–1], or the King catches the flu and decides not to march in the coronation after the contract has been signed [§ 25–55]. Further, having the time of contracting being the separating factor is supported by Restatement 2d §§ 261, 263, and 265, all of which, by their terms apply, "[w]here, after a contract is made . . . "

However, separating mistake and the three "discharging" doctrines discussed in this Chapter based on the events occurring before or after the time the contract was entered into does not explain all cases, e.g., the boulders in the backyard giving rise to impracticability were in the ground at the time the contract was signed [§ 25–35]. Moreover, Restatement 2d § 266 specifically contemplates situations in which the events giving rise to impossibility, impracticability, and frustration are in existence, "at the time a contract is made . . . " What is true is that in cases based on discharging events in existence at the time of contracting, the party asserting the defense must neither know, or have reason to know, of the events [*Id.*].

Moreover, while substantially related, the elements of mistake and impossibility, impracticability, and impossibility are slightly different. So the rule is that when the events giving rise to the doctrines occur after the contract is signed, you should look to impossibility, impracticability, or frustration, and not mistake, to give the party relief. When, however, the events giving rise to the doctrines were in existence at the time the contract was entered into, mistake as well as impossibility, impracticability, or frustration should be considered, with the differences among the two sets of defenses turning on the differences among the elements of the doctrines.

F. TEMPORARY IMPOSSIBILITY, IMPRACTICABILITY, OR FRUSTRATION. [§ 25–60]

There may be occasions in which the event making performance impossible, impracticable, or frustrated is only temporary. Contract law holds that in such situations, the aggrieved party's duties under the contract are initially only suspended. The duties do not become discharged until and unless performance after cessation of the impossibility or frustration would be materially more burdensome than if the event had not occurred [Restatement 2d § 269; UCC § 2–615].

1. **Example. [§ 25–61]**

    A producer has leased a theatre for a six-month run of a play. Two months into the lease, a fire breaks out in the theatre, through no fault of either the producer or the landlord. The fire damages the balcony, and the theatre must be closed for two days while repairs are made. During those two days, the duties of the landlord to provide a theatre, and the duty of the producer to pay rent, are temporarily suspended. However, since it will likely not be materially more burdensome for either party to continue once the theatre reopens, the contract is not discharged, and the lease will run for two days past the original expiration date.

2. **Example. [§ 25–62]**

    Same as above, except this time the fire is severe enough to cause the theatre to close for two months. This time the theatre is leased by another production company a week after the expiration of the first producer's six-month lease term; hence, to extend the run of the play's production at the theatre after the fire occurred would result in the theatre's having to break its lease with the next production company. The duty under the contract to provide a theatre for six months is discharged because extending it would be too burdensome to the theatre owner.

3. **Example of *Autry v. Republic Prod'ns*. [§ 25–63]**

    Probably the most famous case of "temporary" impossibility arose when the actor Gene Autry was drafted into the U.S. Army in World War II, and thus, for about three years, could not fulfill his contractual duty to appear in a movie produced by Republic Productions. When Autry returned home after being discharged, the studio wanted to make the movie for the pre-war stated salary (which would have been a bargain for the studio), claiming that Autry was only temporarily discharged from appearing in the film while on active service, and that his obligation was still in force.

    Held: Autry's duties were permanently discharged. The salary and structure of the contract made sense when it was signed in 1938. However, post-war changes to the tax code and value of the dollar were unforeseeable and changed mutually shared basic assumptions of the contract, thus allowing for a permanent discharge of Autry's duties [*Autry v. Republic Prod'ns*, 30 Cal.2d 144 (1947)].

DISCHARGE OF DUTIES BY IMPOSSIBILITY, IMPRACTICABILITY, OR FRUSTRATION OF PURPOSE

G. THE EFFECT OF A "FORCE MAJEURE" CLAUSE ON IMPOSSIBILITY, IMPRACTICABILITY, AND FRUSTRATION. [§ 25-64]

One element to establish impossibility, impracticability and frustration is that the party asserting the defense must not have explicitly or implicitly assumed the risk of the event's occurrence. To take the uncertainty of whether a court may later decide that a party may have implicitly assumed a risk and has to perform in light of what the party may consider a "dischargeable event," often the parties will insert a clause into their contract explicitly stating that in light of certain events, the parties agree that neither will have to perform. Such a clause is known as a "force majeure" clause.

An example of such clause is: "Neither party shall be liable for its failure to perform hereunder if said performance is made impossible, impracticable or is frustrated due to any occurrence beyond its reasonable control, including acts of God, fires, floods, wars, sabotage, lightning strikes, accidents, labor disputes and strikes, shortages, governmental ordinances, rules and regulations."

H. RESTITUTION AVAILABLE IN CONTRACTS DISCHARGED DUE TO IMPOSSIBILITY, IMPRACTIBILITY, AND FRUSTRATION. [§ 25-65]

While a party who successfully asserts an impossibility, impracticability, or frustration defense has his or her duties under the agreement discharged and thus, cannot be liable under the contract for such excused non-performance, he or she may still be liable in restitution for any benefits already conferred. Hence, while the other party who did not suffer the event giving rise to the defense may not recover expectation or reliance damages in a breach action, he or she is not completely without remedy for a restitutionary recovery is available [*See* Chapter Thirty-One for a discussion of restitution].

I. EXAM APPROACH TO IMPOSSIBILITY, IMPRACTICABILITY, AND FRUSTRATION OF PURPOSE ISSUES. [§ 25-66*]

In an exam situation, whenever a party does not completely perform what he or she promised to do under a contract, an issue arises as to whether that party has breached, or whether there is an excuse or defense justifying such non-performance.

Three defenses which allow a party to not perform a promised duty without incurring liability are impossibility, impracticability, and

---

* For more information, listen to CD # 11, Tracks 2 and 3 of *Sum and Substance Audio on Contracts*.

frustration of purpose. Hence, whenever you find that a party didn't follow through with what he or she promised in a contract:

1. Check to determine if any of the contract defenses discussed in Chapters Ten through Seventeen are present, especially mistake if the event was in existence before the contract was signed [25–59];

2. Check to determine whether there were any unfulfilled conditions excusing such non-performance [Chapters Twenty-One through Twenty-Two];

3. Check to determine whether the duties were substituted for other duties [Chapter Twenty-Four]; and finally

4. Check to determine if the elements of impossibility [§ 25–4]; impracticability [§ 25–31]; or frustration of purpose [§ 25–45] are present. In analyzing these defenses, recall that impossibility and impracticability are generally seller's defenses, whereas frustration is generally a buyer's defense.

If any of the defenses or doctrines set forth above apply, then the party who does not perform what he or she promised is not in breach for failing to do so because the duties under the contract are discharged. If none of the defenses or doctrines apply, the party who did not perform is in breach, and is liable to the other for breach of contract damages.

Part VII

Contracts Involving Third Parties

INTRODUCTORY NOTE REGARDING CONTRACTS INVOLVING THIRD PARTIES:

Until this point in the book, we have focused on the rights and obligations of the two parties to the contract. But contracts typically affect third parties as well. For example, if a house painter does a good job painting the outside of Joe's house, Joe's neighbor, Judy, is benefitted. Or sometimes one of the parties to a contract wants to transfer the benefits under a contract to a third party—Listen, I know under our agreement you are supposed to pay me for my car, but I just found out my sister, Cindy, needs some money, so I'd rather you send the payment directly to her. Or occasionally a party will try to transfer the burdens of a contract to another—I know we have a contract whereby my store is supposed to supply you with finishing nails for your project, but I have just entered into a deal with Gene's hardware and Gene's will supply you instead.

The study of third party contracts is largely a study of the circumstances under which third parties can obtain enforceable rights and duties under a contract between others. There are other issues that flow from that determination, e.g., once rights or duties have been given to third parties, can the original parties still modify the contract, can they sue each other, etc.?

There are three types of agreements in this section of the Book:

Chapter Twenty-Six examines "Third Party Beneficiary" contracts, i.e., contracts which benefit a third party at their inception, like Joe and the painter discussed above;

Chapter Twenty-Seven examines "Assignments," i.e., agreements under an existing contract in which a party's rights under that contract are transferred to another, like the direction to pay the money for the car to Cindy above; and

Chapter Twenty-Eight examines "Delegations," i.e., agreements under an existing contract whereby a party's duties are transferred to another, like the hypothetical with the finishing nails discussed above.

CHAPTER 26

THIRD PARTY BENEFICIARY CONTRACTS

A. THIRD PARTY BENEFICIARY CONTRACTS GENERALLY. [§ 26–1*]

Third party beneficiary contracts are contracts in which the parties make an enforceable contract under which one party becomes obligated to do something that benefits someone who is not a party to the agreement.

Almost all contracts between two parties benefit a third party in one way or another. Sometimes these benefits are direct; sometimes indirect. When they are sufficiently direct, the third party benefited by a contract can sue to enforce it, even though he or she is not a party to the contract. To fully analyze this and other issues associated with such contracts, the nomenclature used to describe the parties must be learned, and is explained below.

B. TERMINOLOGY OF THIRD PARTY BENEFICIARY CONTRACTS. [§ 26–2]

The three parties involved in third party beneficiary contract analysis are:

(1) The **Promisor**.

The promisor is the party who is contractually bound to *perform an act that will benefit a third person*. That is, the promisor makes a contract with someone, and in that contract he or she promises to perform an act that benefits a third party.

(2) The **Promisee**.

The promisee is the party who *bargained for the promisor's promise to perform the act which will benefit a third person*. In other words, the promisee is the other party who is in the contract with the

---

* For more information, listen to CD # 13, Track 3 of *Sum and Substance Audio on Contracts*.

promisor, and it is the promisee who bargains for the promisor's agreement to do something to benefit the third party.

(3) The **Beneficiary**.

The beneficiary is the person who is not a party to the promisor/promisee agreement and *who stands to benefit from performance of the promisor's promise* [Restatement 2d § 302, Cmt. a].

Some students understand these concepts best visually, by means of a graph. Using that approach, the parties involved in a third party beneficiary contract would be displayed as follows:

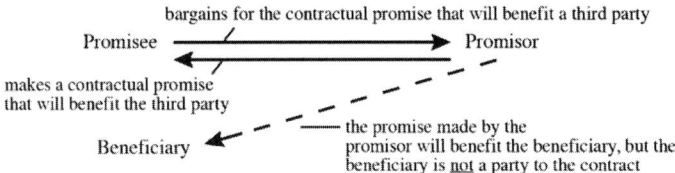

1. Example. [§ 26–3]

Mark wants to help his sister financially. Accordingly, he enters into a contract promising to sell his record collection to Janet in return for Janet's promise to pay Mark's sister $500. In this case, **Janet is the promisor**, for she is in a contract with the promisee (Mark), and she is the one making a promise, the performance of which will benefit a third person. **Mark is the promisee**, because he is the one who bargained for the promise which benefits the third party. **Mark's sister is the beneficiary**, for she is the one who benefits from the promisor's (Janet's) performance.

Graphically, this would be displayed:

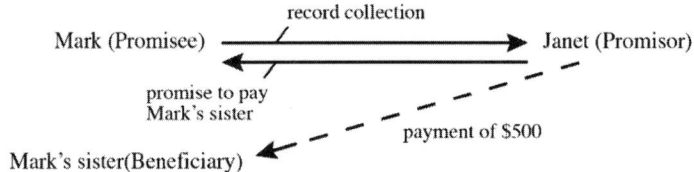

C. ISSUES ARISING UNDER THIRD PARTY BENEFICIARY CONTRACTS. [§ 26–4]

The good news is that there are five, and **only** five, issues surrounding third party beneficiary contracts. If you know the answers to these five questions, and how to analyze them, you will know all you need to know in this area. The five issues are:

(1) **When is the beneficiary entitled to sue the promisor for breach if the promisor does not perform?** [§ 26–5];

(2) Assuming the beneficiary can sue the promisor, **what defenses will the promisor be able to assert?** [§ 26–31];

(3) **Is the beneficiary entitled to sue the *promisee* if the *promisor* does not perform?** [§ 26–39];

(4) **Is the *promisee* entitled to sue the *promisor* if the promisor does not perform?** [§ 26–42]; and

(5) **May the promisor and promisee effectively modify (or even rescind) the third party beneficiary contract to the detriment of the beneficiary without first securing the beneficiary's consent** [§ 26–44]?

D. THE RIGHTS OF THE BENEFICIARY TO SUE THE PROMISOR. [§ 26–5]

The test for when a beneficiary is entitled to sue a promisor for damages arising from a promisor's failure of performance in a third party beneficiary contract has changed over time.

1. **Early American Law: "Creditor" and "Donee" Beneficiaries Could Enforce the Promisor's Promise; "Incidental" Beneficiaries Could Not. [§ 26–6]**

   From the early days of American contract law, certain kinds of beneficiaries have been entitled to enforce a promisor's promise (with the notable exceptions of those suing in Massachusetts, which did not allow recovery under a third party beneficiary theory until 1979; and of New York, which had certain restrictions on the doctrine until 1985). (For the early English common law view, see Case Squibs, *Dutton v. Poole*). However, the nomenclature and categorizations of which kinds of beneficiaries could sue the promisor has changed somewhat over time.

   The early American courts, as exemplified by the First Restatement, divided beneficiaries into three categories:

   (i) **"Donee"** beneficiaries;

   (ii) **"Creditor"** beneficiaries; and

   (iii) **"Incidental"** beneficiaries [Restatement 1st § 133].

   Of these, donee and creditor beneficiaries were entitled to enforce promises of the promisor, whereas incidental beneficiaries were not. That is, donee and creditor beneficiaries, even though they were not a party to the contract and made no promises under it, would nevertheless be able to sue the promisor for breach of contract if the promisor failed to perform without a sufficient reason.

CHAPTER 26

This categorization raises the question of what characteristics gave a beneficiary "donee," "creditor," or "incidental" status? These issues are discussed below.

a. "Donee" Beneficiaries: Defined and Discussed. [§ 26–7]

Under the First Restatement, a donee beneficiary was a beneficiary of a contractual promise made by a promisor, the **purpose** of which was either:

(i) To make **a gift** to the beneficiary; or

(ii) To confer on the beneficiary **a right against the promisor to a performance that was not already owing, nor supposed to be owing, nor asserted to be owing**, from the promisor to the beneficiary [Restatement 1st § 133(1)].

When a beneficiary could establish the elements to become a "donee" beneficiary, he or she was entitled to enforce the promisor's promise and thus to recover damages from the promisor for its breach. That is, when the promisor initially made his or her contractual promises to the promisee, he or she was also deemed to have undertaken an enforceable duty to a donee beneficiary as well [Restatement 1st, § 133(1)(a)].

SPECIAL CASE SQUIB

(1) *Seaver v. Ransom.* **[§ 26–8]**

Mrs. Beman wished to leave her home to her niece, Ms. Seaver, when she died. However, Mrs. Beman's husband had already drawn up a will for her which left the house to him. Mrs. Beman was quite ill when the will was drafted. Rather than wait for her husband, a former judge, to redraft the will, she and her husband entered into a contract whereby she agreed to sign the will as it was, leaving the house to Mr. Beman. In return, Mr. Beman promised to leave Ms. Seaver enough money in **his** will to make up for Ms. Seaver's not getting the house in Mrs. Beman's will.

When Mr. Beman died, he left no money to Ms. Seaver. Ms. Seaver sued Mr. Beman's executor, Ransom, to enforce the promise Mr. Beman made to Mrs. Beman.

Held: Ms. Seaver was a donee beneficiary of the Mr. Beman/Mrs. Beman contract, and was thus entitled to enforce Mr. Beman's promise by suing his estate for breach of Mr. Beman's promised performance.

Recall that to analyze any third party beneficiary situation, the parties must first be characterized. **Mr. Beman was the promisor**, since it was performance of his promise to

THIRD PARTY BENEFICIARY CONTRACTS

leave money in his will that would benefit a third person, Ms. Seaver. **Mrs. Beman was the promisee**, since she bargained for the promise benefiting the third party. **Ms. Seaver was the beneficiary**, since she was the party outside the promisor/promisee contract who would benefit by performance of Mr. Beman's (the promisor's) promise.

Graphically, the situation was as follows:

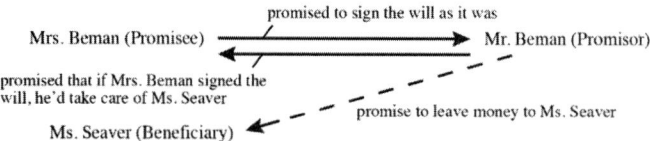

The next issue is to determine what kind of beneficiary Ms. Seaver was. Ms. Seaver met the test to be a **donee beneficiary** under Section 133(1) for two reasons. First, the purpose of Mrs. Beman in bargaining for her husband's promise to leave money in his will was to *make a gift* to Ms. Seaver. Second, Ms. Seaver also met the test for a donee beneficiary because Mr. Beman's promise conferred in Ms. Seaver the right to a performance (i.e., the payment of money), that was *neither owed to her by Mrs. Beman, nor was supposed by Mrs. Beman to be owing her, nor was asserted by Ms. Seaver to be owed to her.* Hence, Ms. Seaver was entitled to sue to enforce the promise even though she was not a party to the contract between Mr. Beman and his wife.

Note that while Mrs. Beman's intention to benefit Ms. Seaver was a gift, that does not mean that the contract failed for lack of consideration as a gift promise (*see* § 7–24). **This is because the promise made by Mr. Beman, the promisor, in the contract he entered into with his wife, was supported by consideration.** Since his promise to leave Ms. Seaver the money was clearly bargained for and given in exchange for receipt of the house, it is amply supported by consideration. The fact that his performance is promised to someone other than the one who provided the consideration is irrelevant [§ 7–20; *Seaver v. Ransom,* 120 N.E. 639 (N.Y. 1918)].

b. "Creditor" Beneficiaries: Defined and Discussed. [§ 26–9]

A "creditor" beneficiary under the First Restatement was the beneficiary of a contractual promise, the **purpose** of which was **to satisfy an actual, supposed, or asserted debt the promisee owed the beneficiary.** Once again, the effect of a beneficiary being able to establish "creditor" status was that he

CHAPTER 26

or she was entitled to sue the promisor for breach if the promisor did not perform. That is, when the promisor made an enforceable promise in his or her contract with the promisee, the effect was also to create an enforceable duty owing to the creditor beneficiary [Restatement 1st § 133(1)(b)].

SPECIAL CASE SQUIB

(1) *Lawrence v. Fox.* **[§ 26–10]**

Holly owed Lawrence $300. Holly had the money to re-pay Lawrence, but instead decided to lend the $300 to Fox in return for *Fox's* promise to re-pay the $300 to Lawrence directly to discharge Holly's obligation. Fox ended up taking the money from Holly and paying no one, so Lawrence sued Fox for re-payment of Holly's debt.

Held: Lawrence was a creditor beneficiary, and was thus entitled to sue Fox to enforce the re-payment promise Fox made to Holly. [*Lawrence v. Fox,* 20 N.Y. 268 (1859)].

Once again, the first step in analyzing the case is to identify the parties. **Fox was the promisor**, for he contractually promised to do an act (pay $300) which benefited a third party. **Holly was the promisee**, for she bargained for Fox's promise. **Lawrence was the third party beneficiary**, for performance of Fox's promise would benefit him and he was not a party to the promisor/promisee contract.

Graphically, the situation was as follows:

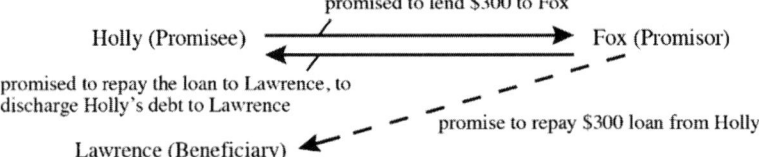

The next issue in the case is whether Lawrence could be classified as a "creditor" beneficiary so that he would be able to sue Fox for not paying him. (Note, he could not be a "donee" beneficiary for Holly was clearly not bargaining to *make a gift* of the $300 to Lawrence). Lawrence satisfies the test of a creditor beneficiary under § 133(1)(b) because Holly's purpose in seeking Fox's promise was **to satisfy a duty** that the promisee (Holly) already owed the beneficiary (Lawrence). Hence, Lawrence was entitled to sue Fox when he did not repay the $300.

THIRD PARTY BENEFICIARY CONTRACTS

c. **"Incidental" Beneficiary: Defined and Discussed. [§ 26–11]**

"Incidental" beneficiaries under the First Restatement were **all third party contract beneficiaries who were neither donee nor creditor beneficiaries.** That is, it was a "catchall" category consisting of all the third party beneficiaries in the world who might be benefited by a contract but who were neither creditor nor donee beneficiaries. The effect of being an incidental beneficiary, as opposed to a creditor or donee beneficiary, was that *an incidental beneficiary could not enforce the promisor's promise*, i.e., a merely incidental beneficiary could not sue the promisor for breach if the promisor failed to perform the contractual promise made to the promisee. A promisor simply owed no duty to an incidental beneficiary as a result of his or her contract with the promisee. This is because any benefit that would come to an incidental beneficiary as a result of the promisor's performance was deemed too indirect or "incidental" to be enforceable by the beneficiary [Restatement 1st § 133(1)(c)].

(1) **Example. [§ 26–12]**

Bob lived next door to Nancy. His yard was full of unkempt weeds, so Bob contracted with Candice to landscape his house. If Candice performed as promised, the value of Nancy's house would probably increase a bit. Candice breached, however, and did not perform the landscaping. Nancy is not entitled to sue Candice for her breach, for Nancy is only an incidental beneficiary.

Candice was the promisor (making a contractual promise whose performance would have benefited Nancy), **Bob was the promisee** (he bargained for the promise), and **Nancy was the beneficiary**.

Graphically, the situation is:

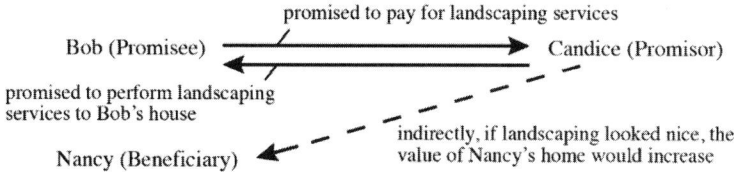

Nancy is not a donee beneficiary, for the purpose of Bob's landscaping his house was <u>**not** to make a gift to Nancy</u> of the appreciation in the value of her house. Similarly, Nancy is also not a creditor beneficiary, for the purpose of Bob's promise was <u>**not** to satisfy an asserted or real debt that Bob</u>

owed Nancy. Hence, as she is neither a donee nor creditor beneficiary, under the Restatement 1st formulation she is only an incidental beneficiary. As an incidental beneficiary, Nancy is not entitled to sue Candice to enforce her duty to landscape Bob's house, for Candice owed Nancy no duty arising out of the promisor/promisee contract.

2. **Modern Contract Law: "Intended" Beneficiaries Can Enforce the Promisor's Promise; "Incidental" Beneficiaries Cannot. [§ 26–13]**

The drafters of the Second Restatement rejected the three-tiered categorization of third party beneficiaries found in the First Restatement.

In its place, the drafters provided that there are only two types of beneficiaries:

(a) **"Intended"** beneficiaries; and

(b) **"Incidental"** beneficiaries [Restatement 2d § 302].

Intended beneficiaries are entitled to enforce the promisor's promise by directly suing the promisor for breach, whereas incidental beneficiaries cannot enforce that promise [Restatement 2d §§ 304, 315].

a. **"Intended" Beneficiaries: Defined and Discussed. [§ 26–14]**

Section 302(1) of the Restatement 2d defines intended beneficiaries as follows:

[A] beneficiary of a promise is an intended beneficiary if **recognition of a right to performance in the beneficiary is appropriate to effectuate the intention of the promisor and promisee, and either**:

(a) The performance of the promise will satisfy an *obligation of the promisee to pay money* to the beneficiary; or

(b) The circumstances indicate that the *promisee intends to give the beneficiary the benefit of the promised performance.*

Hence, there is a two-part test to achieve intended beneficiary status under § 302. The first part requires a determination of whether designation as an intended beneficiary is "appropriate to effectuate the intention of the parties." The issue is whether the **promisor and promisee intended to grant the beneficiary a right to enforce the promises** made by the promisor when they entered into their contract. This question is one that can be answered only by a fact finder's sifting through all the circumstances surrounding a particular transaction, but the idea is to determine whether the promisor and promisee were bargaining **directly to provide a benefit to the beneficiary**, or whether the promisor and promisee did not **intend to create an enforceable duty in the beneficiary** when making their contract. If the promisor and promisee did not intend to create such a duty, it would not be "appropriate to effectuate" their intentions to grant the third party intended beneficiary status.

Once it is established that the parties' intent will be furthered if intended beneficiary status is awarded to a third party, the second step is to see whether the beneficiary can meet one of the two alternative tests of Restatement 2d § 302(1)(a) or (b). That is, to determine whether performance of the promise will satisfy an antecedent *obligation* of the promisee to pay money [§ 302(1)(a)], or whether the promisee intended to *make a gift* to the beneficiary [§ 302(1)(b)].

Obviously the definitions given in §§ 302(1)(a) and (1)(b) are very close to the definitions of creditor and donee beneficiary under the First Restatement [§§ 26–7 and 26–9]. To use the language adopted by many commentators throughout the remainder of this chapter, intended beneficiaries under the Restatement 2d will be designated as either "creditor-like" intended beneficiaries under § 302(1)(a), or "donee-like" intended beneficiaries under § 302(1)(b).

(1) Example of *Seaver v. Ransom*. [§ 26–15]

The facts of *Seaver* are given in § 26–8. Under Restatement 2d § 302(1)(b), Ms. Seaver would still be able to enforce Mr. Beman's promise, for Ms. Seaver would be classified as a "donee-like" intended beneficiary of the Mr. Beman/Mrs. Beman contract. This is because: (a) recognition of her right to sue Mr. Beman (via his estate) to enforce the promise he made to his wife is appropriate to effectuate the contracting parties' intentions (i.e., Mr. and Mrs. Beman intended to confer a benefit on Ms. Seaver when they entered into their contract); and (b) the circumstances indicate a desire by Mrs. Beman to make a gift of the promised performance to Ms. Seaver.

(2) Example of *Lawrence v. Fox*. [§ 26–16]

The facts of *Lawrence* are given in § 26–10. Under the Restatement 2d § 302(1)(a), Lawrence would be classified as a "creditor-like" intended beneficiary, and thus entitled to sue Fox for Fox's failure to repay the loan. This is because: (a) recognition of Lawrence's right to enforce Fox's promise is appropriate to effectuate the contracting parties' intentions (i.e., Holly and Fox intended to benefit Lawrence when they entered into their loan agreement); and (b) performance of Fox's promise will satisfy an antecedent obligation of Holly to pay money to Lawrence.

b. "Incidental" Beneficiary: Defined and Discussed. [§ 26–17]

Incidental beneficiaries under the Restatement 2d are defined almost exactly the way incidental beneficiaries were defined under the Restatement 1st [§ 26–11]. Namely, under Restatement 2d § 302(2), "An incidental beneficiary is a beneficiary who is not an intended beneficiary." Once again, it is a catchall category. The effect of being an incidental beneficiary under the Restatement 2d is also identical to being such a beneficiary under the Restatement 1st—namely, incidental beneficiaries cannot sue the promisor for breach of the promisor's contractual duty.

(1) Example. [§ 26–18]

John was due to be paid by his employer on Friday. He had planned to use the money from his paycheck to pay off his Visa credit card bill. John's employer unjustifiably fails to pay him. Here, **Employer is the promisor** because it promised to do as act that was (indirectly) going to benefit a third party; **John is the promisee** for he bargained for that act; and **Visa is the beneficiary**.

Graphically, we have:

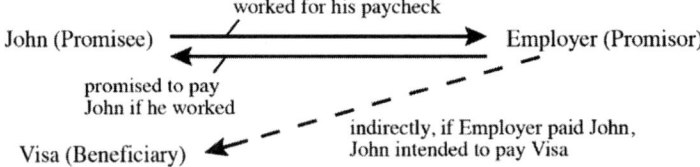

Visa may not enforce the duty of the employer to pay John under the provisions of Restatement 2d § 302(2), for Visa is only an incidental beneficiary of the employment contract. This is because:

(a) it is not appropriate in this case to give Visa a right to enforce the promise, for in entering into the employment agreement, neither John nor his employer *intended* that Visa be given a right to enforce the agreement; and

(b) performance of the employer's promise would not have satisfied John's obligation to pay money to Visa (i.e., had the employer done what it promised, i.e., paid John, John's debt to Visa would still be owing until John paid the company); thus Visa is not a "creditor-like" intended beneficiary; and

(c) John certainly did not intend a "gift" of his paycheck to Visa—thus Visa is also not a "donee-like" intended beneficiary.

Since it is not an intended beneficiary under § 302(1), Visa must be an incidental beneficiary under § 302(2), and is thus ineligible to enforce the promisor's promise.

Note that if John had somehow arranged for his employer to pay a portion of his check directly to Visa, the result would be different, for then Visa would be a "creditor-like" intended beneficiary.

c. **Situations in Which Analysis Under the First and Second Restatements Would Yield Different Results. [§ 26–19]**

As noted earlier, the Second Restatement's alternative tests for attaining intended beneficiary status seem almost identical to the First Restatement's definitions of creditor and donee beneficiary. In fact, the tests for donee beneficiaries under the two Restatements **are** very close and any donee beneficiary under the Restatement 1st would be a "donee-like" intended beneficiary under the Restatement 2d.

There are, however, a few important differences between a creditor beneficiary under the Restatement 1st and a "creditor-like" intended beneficiary under the Restatement 2d. Under § 133(1)(b) of the First Restatement, a third party is a creditor beneficiary whenever performance of the promisor's promise would "satisfy an actual, or supposed, or asserted duty of the promisee to the beneficiary." Under Restatement 2d § 302(1)(a), a third party is a creditor-like intended beneficiary only when performance of the promisor's promise "will satisfy an obligation of the promisee to pay money to the beneficiary." Hence, these provisions differ in two respects:

(1) Under the Restatement 2d, the obligation of the promisee to the "creditor-like" beneficiary **must be to pay money**. Under the Restatement 1st, the obligation could be to perform any duty; and

(2) Under the Restatement 2d, the monetary obligation owed by the promisee to the creditor-like intended beneficiary **must be an actual one**. Under the

CHAPTER 26

Restatement 1st, the obligation could be actual, or one that is merely "supposed" to be owed by the promisee, or one that is only "asserted" to be owed by the beneficiary.

(1) Example. [§ 26–20]

Dave is a gardener who is contractually obligated to mow Steve's lawn twice a month for a year. Dave enters into a contract with Jane, where in return for supplying and planting 3 large trees at Jane's house, Jane promises to perform Dave's obligation to mow Steve's lawn twice a month for the next year.

Dave and Jane have entered into a third party beneficiary contract. **Jane is the promisor**; **Dave is the promisee**; and **Steve is the beneficiary**.

Graphically, it is:

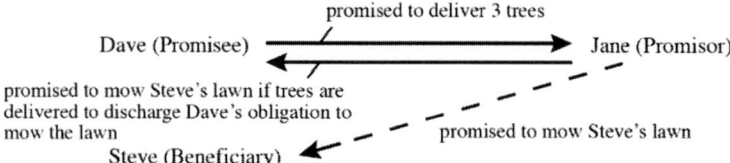

Under the First Restatement, Steve would be a creditor beneficiary under the Dave/Jane contract and hence entitled to enforce Jane's promise and sue her for breach if she failed to mow his lawn. However, because the obligation Dave (the promisee) owed to Steve (the beneficiary) is not one to pay money, Steve cannot be a "creditor-like" intended beneficiary of the promisor/promisee agreement under Restatement 2d, § 302(1). As such, he will be merely an incidental beneficiary under modern contract law, and thus unable to sue Jane if she should breach.

(2) Example. [§ 26–21]

Ryan, an 18-year old high school senior, receives in the mail an unsolicited Fruitomatic fruit slicer. Ryan keeps the product in the box and does not wish to accept it. Under traditional rules of contract formation, of course he is under no obligation to pay for it and his silence cannot be deemed an acceptance of Fruitomatic's offer to have Ryan purchase the machine [§ 4–109]. However, Ryan does not know this and 30 days later he receives an invoice from the Fruitomatic company. Thinking he has to pay the bill, Ryan thereafter enters into a contract with his parents whereby they will pay the $150 invoice if he paints the living room the next weekend.

Graphically, the relationship of the parties would be:

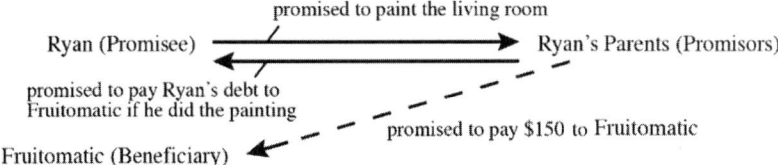

Under the First Restatement, Fruitomatic would be a creditor beneficiary of the Ryan/Ryan's parents' agreement, and thus could enforce Ryan's parents' promise to pay the invoice by suing them directly if they did not pay the $150. Fruitomatic could **not** enforce Ryan's parents' promise, however, under Restatement 2d § 302(1), because Ryan only "supposed" he owed, but did not actually owe, a monetary debt to Fruitomatic.

d. Important Principles in Analyzing Third Party Beneficiary Contracts Under Modern Contract Law. [§ 26–22]

There are certain principles which need to be understood in order to completely analyze third party beneficiary contracts. These are discussed below.

(1) Performance of the Promisor's Promise Need Not Be Made Directly to the Third Party in Order for the Third Party to Be an Intended Beneficiary. [§ 26–23]

For a third party to be an intended beneficiary under modern contract law, most often the promisor's promise will be rendered directly to the beneficiary. However, this is not a necessary requirement. For example, assume Dorothy instructs her lawyer to make sure her will includes a bequest of $10,000 to her nephew Bob.

Graphically, the parties would be:

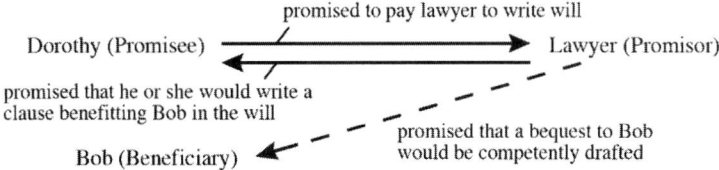

Performance of the promisor's (the lawyer's) duty is to be rendered directly to Dorothy, i.e., the making of the will

CHAPTER 26

with an appropriate clause benefiting Bob. However, Bob is nevertheless an intended beneficiary of the lawyer/Dorothy contract, and the lawyer owes a duty to Bob to ensure the bequest is made. Thus, if the lawyer does not include a provision for Bob in Dorothy's will, Bob may sue the lawyer for breach of the duty owed him even though performance was to be rendered to the promisee.

(2) The Identity of the Intended Beneficiary Need Not Be Known at the Time the Promisor/Promisee Contract Is Made. [§ 26–24]

It is not necessary that the identity of a beneficiary be known at the time the promisor/promisee contract is entered into in order to make the beneficiary an intended one [Restatement 2d § 308]. For example, assume a radio station contracts with an airline to fly the winner of a station-sponsored contest to Australia.

Graphically, the parties would be:

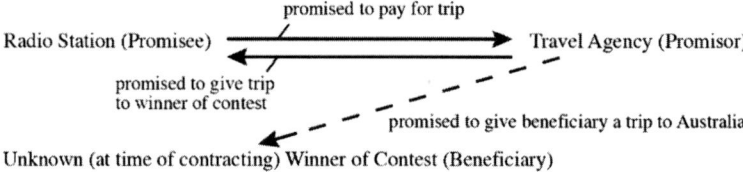

Even though the identity of the beneficiary is not known at the time of the making of the radio station/airline contract, the winner of the contest, whoever it ultimately turns out to be, is nonetheless an intended beneficiary who can sue the travel agency if it breaches its contract with the radio station by refusing to fly the contestant to Australia.

(3) An Intended Beneficiary Need Not Manifest Any Agreement to the Promisor/Promisee Contract in Order to Gain Enforceable Rights Against the Promisee. [§ 26–25]

Perhaps surprisingly, a third party can become an intended beneficiary without even knowing it. In other words, once the promisor and promisee make the contract that confers intended beneficiary status on a third party, the third party **is** a viable intended beneficiary regardless of whether he or she knows it.

Note, however, that if for some reason the beneficiary does not want to be an intended beneficiary, he or she has the

THIRD PARTY BENEFICIARY CONTRACTS

right to disclaim such status within a reasonable time after learning of the promisor/promisee agreement [§ 26–26].

(4) A Beneficiary May Disclaim His or Her Rights to Enforce the Promisor's Promise. [§ 26–26]

A third party need not acquiesce in, or even know about, the promisor/promisee agreement to become an intended third party beneficiary to that contract [*see* § 26–25]. However, sometimes when the beneficiary finds out about the agreement, the beneficiary will not find its terms acceptable. In that case, contract law provides that the beneficiary has the power to "opt out" of having to accept satisfaction of the debt by the promisor, and may continue to insist on satisfaction by the promisee only. The formal name for such a choice is "**disclaimer by the beneficiary**," and it is effectively accomplished when:

(i) the beneficiary gives **notice** of his or her decision to disclaim any obligation owing from the promisor;

(ii) such notice is given **within a reasonable time** after learning of the existence of the third party beneficiary contract; and

(iii) such **notice is not received after the beneficiary has already assented** to the contract [Restatement 2d § 306].

If the beneficiary says nothing one way or another after learning of the contract's terms, he or she is deemed to have <u>impliedly ratified the arrangement by silence</u> after the expiration of a reasonable time, and may not thereafter disclaim it [Restatement 2d § 306, Cmt. a].

(a) Example. [§ 26–27]

Ted is obligated to repay Larry $100 on August 1. On June 1, Ted enters into a contract with June whereby June promises to repay Ted's debt to Larry. At that point, whether Larry knows it or not, he is an intended creditor-like beneficiary of the Ted/June contract and is entitled to sue June if she does not pay him.

485

Graphically, we have:

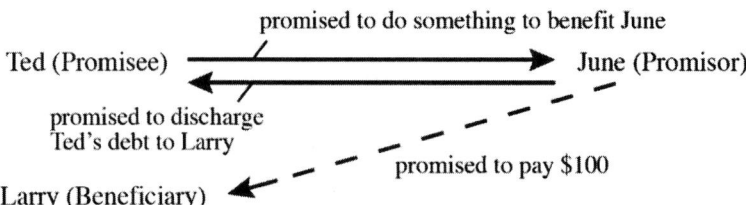

A week later, on June 7, Larry learns of the Ted/June agreement. If for some reason it is important to Larry that **Ted** repay him, Larry is entitled to notify June and Ted that he (Larry) is disclaiming his intended beneficiary status, and demanding that Ted re-pay the debt as promised on August 1. If Larry does not give such notice within a reasonable time after learning of the Ted/June contract, he will be deemed to have impliedly ratified his status as an intended beneficiary and will not thereafter be able to disclaim it.

3. **Recurring Fact Situations Concerning Whether a Beneficiary Is Intended or Incidental. [§ 26–28]**

Over time, certain recurring fact situations have arisen which present the issue of whether the beneficiary is entitled to sue to enforce the promisor's promise, i.e., whether the beneficiary is intended or incidental. The most significant of these are discussed below.

a. **A Citizen's Right to Enforce a Government's Contract with a Private Party to Perform a Municipal Service. [§ 26–29]**

One recurring third party beneficiary issue has to do with the rights of citizens as beneficiaries when the government enters into a contract with a private company to perform a municipal service. For example, assume that under the city charter a local government is under a duty to keep the streets in good repair. The city thereafter enters into a contract with Repair Co. to keep the streets in good order, but Repair Co. breaches as there are a number of unrepaired potholes.

In our diagram form, the parties would be:

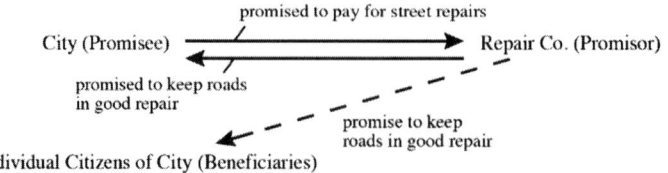

The issue is whether the citizens of the town are entitled to sue Repair Co. as intended beneficiaries of the Repair Co./City contract. The answer given by most courts is that **citizens are not entitled to sue** to enforce the promises of a private company such as Repair Co. In other words, most courts hold that citizens are only incidental, not intended, beneficiaries of such contracts with private companies performing traditionally municipal functions.

The rationale for these decisions is as follows: The citizen is an incidental beneficiary unless he or she can meet the tests of Restatement 2d § 302(1). To become an intended beneficiary under § 302, the citizen first must establish that the city and the private company **intended** to confer on the particular citizen an enforceable right to the private company's promised performance. Courts generally find that such an intention was not present.

Second, even if such intention could be found, the citizen would also have to establish that he or she was either a "donee-like" or "creditor-like" intended beneficiary. The citizen cannot be a "creditor-like" beneficiary, because the government's duty to the citizen is not one to pay money [see § 26–9]. The citizen is not a "donee-like" beneficiary, because typically there is no evidence that the municipality wanted to make a "gift" of the road repair to the citizen since it had a duty to provide such service. Hence, the citizens must be incidental beneficiaries and thus, not entitled to sue to enforce the contract [Restatement 2d § 313].

Many commentators have expressed the view that a neutral application of third party beneficiary rules to these kinds of situations would, in fact, allow the citizen to recover against the private company on a donee-like beneficiary basis. These commentators thus believe that the real reason for the rule discussed above is policy-based. That is, if contract law permitted citizens to sue private companies such as Repair Co., it would create an excessive financial burden for them, i.e., if every citizen had a right to sue when the road was not fixed properly, it would be incredibly expensive for the private company to agree to fix the road. In turn, this would lead to a decrease in the number of private companies willing to do such work, which would eventually produce an overall decline in services available to the public [Restatement 2d § 313, Cmt. a; see also Case Squibs, *Moch v. Rensselaer Water Co.*].

b. **Construction Contracts. [§ 26–30]**

The second type of recurring fact situation involving third party beneficiary issues arises out of a developer/general contractor/

subcontractor relationship. As explained previously [§ 8–13], after a developer selects a general contractor for a large construction project, the general contractor enters into contracts with one or more subcontractors to perform discrete parts of the construction project.

The parties' relationships are:

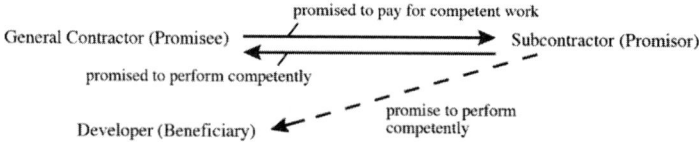

The third party beneficiary issue arises upon the subcontractor's breach. The question is whether the **developer** can bring suit against the subcontractor on the theory that the developer is an intended beneficiary of the subcontractor's promises made in the subcontractor/general contractor contract. The answer usually given is **developers are not entitled to sue subcontractors**. Once again, the courts typically find that the developer in such cases cannot establish the elements to prove he or she is an intended beneficiary. Accordingly, the developer is an incidental beneficiary, and is owed no duty by the subcontractor.

E. RIGHTS OF THE PROMISOR IN A SUIT BROUGHT BY THE BENEFICIARY. [§ 26–31]

Over time, contract law has developed rules governing the rights of the promisor in suits by the beneficiary.

1. An Intended Beneficiary Is Subject to Any Defense the Promisor Has Against the Promisee. [§ 26–32]

An intended third party beneficiary of a promisor/promisee agreement receives no more rights against the promisor than those enjoyed by the promisee. Hence any defense that could be asserted by the promisor if he or she were sued by the promisee can also be asserted against the intended beneficiary. As some courts and commentators put it, "the intended beneficiary **stands in the shoes** of the promisee," and is thus subject to any defenses that the promisor could assert against the promisee if it was the promisee who sued instead of the beneficiary.

a. Example. [§ 26–33]

Eileen is contractually obligated to pay $1,000/month to Central Bank on her mortgage. Eileen is strapped for cash and so offers to sell her car to Judy, receiving in return Judy's promise to make the next three mortgage payments.

THIRD PARTY BENEFICIARY CONTRACTS

The situation is as follows:

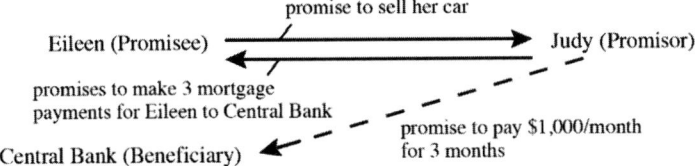

Assume that Eileen breaches by neither delivering the car nor making any mortgage payments. Because she did not receive the car, Judy of course did not make the mortgage payments either. The issue is whether Central Bank, as a creditor-like intended beneficiary of the Judy/Eileen contract, can successfully sue Judy (as the promisor) for breach? Contract law holds it cannot.

Judy has a complete defense to any such suit brought by the Bank. That is, because the beneficiary "stands in the shoes of the promisee," Central Bank's right to enforce Judy's promise is subject to any defense Judy could assert against Eileen if Eileen had sued Judy for her failure to pay. Obviously if Eileen (the promisee) sued Judy, Judy would have a material breach or failure of consideration defense (Eileen never delivered the car). Judy is entitled to raise that same defense against the Bank because a beneficiary (the Bank) "stands in the shoes" of the promisee and is subject to the same defenses as the promisor would have against the promisee if the promisee brought suit. Of course, the Bank can still sue Eileen for the payments [*See* § 26–39 for a discussion of the promisor's rights against the promise].

SPECIAL CASE SQUIB

b. *Rouse v. United States.* [§ 26–34]

Ms. Winston contracted with Associated Contractors to install a furnace in her home. She financed the purchase by signing a $1,008.37 promissory note, payable to Associated Contractors at the rate of $28.01/month. Under a program then in existence, the U.S. Government guaranteed payment in full of the promissory note if the obligor (Ms. Winston) stopped paying, i.e., if there was a "default" in the note's repayment. Thereafter, Associated Contractors sold the note to Union Trust Co., and the government's guarantee in case of default was also transferred to Union Trust.

Ms. Winston made the required monthly payments under the note until she sold her house to Rouse. In the sales contract for the house, Rouse specifically promised to assume the debt and make the $28.01 monthly payments, but never did so.

Accordingly, Union Trust sought payment of the entire outstanding balance of the note from the government under the government's guarantee. The government paid Union Trust, and thereafter brought suit against Rouse to recoup its payment. One of Rouse's defenses was that <u>Ms. Winston had misrepresented **to him**</u> the condition of the furnace when he bought the home.

Rouse had a misrepresentation defense in a suit brought by Ms. Winston. One issue in the case was whether Rouse was entitled to assert that misrepresentation defense in a suit brought by the government.

Held: Rouse was entitled to use the defense to defeat the government's claim. [*See* Case Squib, *Rouse v. United States*, 215 F.2d 972 (D.C. Cir. 1954)].

To understand the decision, the parties must first be categorized. **Rouse was the promisor**, for he promised to make payments for the benefit of Union Trust Co. (and thus for the benefit of the government as guarantor of the note). **Ms. Winston was the promisee**, for she initially owed the money and bargained for Rouse's promise to relieve her of a debt. **The Union Trust Co., and thereafter the United States, were intended "creditor-like" beneficiaries**, for performance of Mr. Rouse's promise would inure to their benefit.

The third party issues, arising only after the United States paid off the note to Union Trust as a result of its guarantee, can be diagramed as follows:

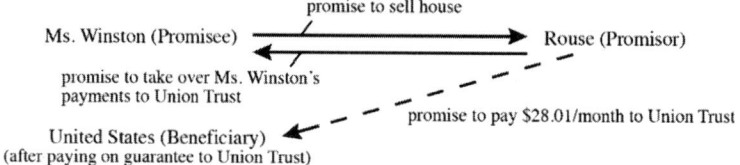

Hence, the legal question in the case was whether the promisor (Rouse) could assert a defense in a suit brought by a beneficiary (the United States) that he could have asserted had the suit had been brought by the promisee (Ms. Winston). Since Mr. Rouse clearly could have used Ms. Winston's misrepresentations about the furnace as a defense had Ms. Winston tried to sue him, he was entitled to use her misrepresentations as a defense in the suit brought by the government. That is, the United States, as an intended beneficiary, merely "stepped into Ms. Winston's shoes," and was thereby subject to the defenses that could be asserted against her had she sued Rouse [*Rouse v. United States*, 215 F.2d 872 (D.C. Cir. 1954)].

THIRD PARTY BENEFICIARY CONTRACTS

Note there are other third party issues in the case as well, but the one most focused on tends to be the issue described above.

2. An Intended Beneficiary's Right to Sue the Promisor Is Subject to Any Limiting or Conditional Terms of the Promisor/Promisee Contract. [§ 26–35]

An intended beneficiary's right to enforce the promisor's promise is subject to any limiting or conditional terms in the promisor/promisee contract. Thus, for example, if the promisor's duty is conditional upon the occurrence of an event, and that event does not occur, the beneficiary cannot bring suit for a failure of the promisor to perform. This is because the promisor's duty in such a case never became enforceable by either the promisee or the beneficiary.

a. Example. [§ 26–36]

Leo wanted to make a gift to his friend Bill. He entered into an agreement with his stockbroker Margaret whereby Margaret was contractually obligated to deliver $1,000 to Bill on December 2, "on the condition that Leo's IBM stock was worth more than $200/share at any time before Dec. 1."

Graphically, this would be depicted as:

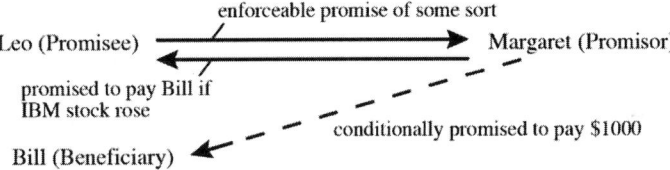

Assume the stock price never broke $200/share before Dec. 1. While Bill is clearly an intended "donee-like" beneficiary, he may not successfully sue Margaret to enforce payment of the $1,000, for his rights as beneficiary are subject to the terms of the Leo/Margaret contract.

3. An Intended Third Party Beneficiary's Recovery Against the Promisor Is Subject to Offset by the Amount of Any Damages the Promisor Suffers as a Result of an Immaterial Breach by the Promisee. [§ 26–37]

An intended beneficiary has no more rights to enforce the promisor's promise than does the promisee. This is another way of saying the beneficiary only "stands in the shoes of the promisee." Hence, if the promisor would be entitled to an offset in the damages owed due to an immaterial breach by the promisee in a suit brought by the promisee, the beneficiary's recovery is subject to that same offset.

CHAPTER 26

a. Example. [§ 26–38]

Maxine owes Keith $5,000. She enters into a contract with Tom whereby Tom promises to pay Maxine's debt to Keith in return for Maxine's promise to paint Tom's house, including the wooden windows.

In diagram fashion, the parties are:

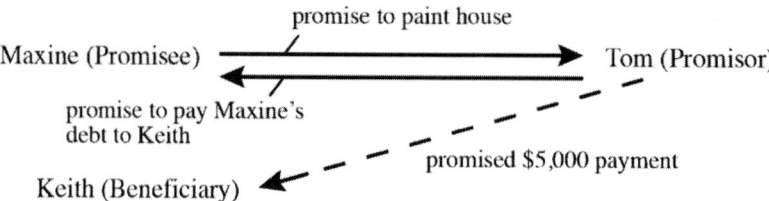

Assume that Maxine paints the house but fails to paint the wooden window frames. Tom reasonably hires another painter to paint them for $400. At that point, Tom is only obligated to pay Keith $4,600, because Keith (the beneficiary) can only enforce the contract to the extent Maxine could. Since Maxine's recovery would be subject to a $400 recoupment due to her immaterial breach, Keith's recovery is offset by that same amount.

Note, however, that while the beneficiary is said to "stand in the shoes" of the promisee, this is only true to a point. If the promisee materially breached the contract so that the promisee in fact owes the promisor damages, the promisor must sue the **promisee** to recover, not the beneficiary. For example, if Maxine had done no work on Tom's house, and Tom reasonably ended up paying another painter $5,500 to do the work, the extra $500 in damages would be due from Maxine alone. That is, Tom could not sue Keith seeking $500 in damages just because Keith "stood in Maxine's shoes" regarding his rights as an intended beneficiary.

F. RIGHTS OF AN INTENDED BENEFICIARY TO SUE THE PROMISEE. [§ 26–39]

The focus of this Chapter to this point has been on the right of the beneficiary to sue the **promisor**. However, often beneficiaries would rather sue the **promisee**. This is especially true in "creditor-like" beneficiary cases where it is the promisee that the beneficiary knew in the first place, for it was the promisee who was already indebted to the beneficiary before formation of the promisor/promisee contract. The rule regarding a beneficiary's right to sue the promisee is simple: **An intended beneficiary retains whatever rights he or she had to bring suit against the promisee before the promisor/promisee**

THIRD PARTY BENEFICIARY CONTRACTS

agreement was made, but gains no additional rights to sue the promisee as a result of the third party beneficiary contract.

In a "creditor-like" intended beneficiary situation, this rule means that an intended beneficiary can choose to enforce **either** of the two duties owed him or her: (1) the antecedent duty to pay the debt, owed by the promisee; or (2) the new duty to pay the debt, owed by the promisor. Hence, the beneficiary is entitled to bring suit and recover a judgment against either the promisee, or the promisor, or both; but, of course, the beneficiary is limited to only one satisfaction of that judgment.

In a "donee-like" intended beneficiary situation, the beneficiary likely will be able to enforce only the **new** duty of the promisor. That is, creation of the promisor/promisee contract does not create a duty where none existed. It only fails to discharge whatever duty already existed between the promisee and the beneficiary. If all the promisee intended was to make a gift to the beneficiary, then the beneficiary cannot enforce the gift promise of the promisee [*See* § 26–15 for an explanation of why the **promisor's** duty is nonetheless enforceable even when the **promisee** is only intending to make a gift].

1. **Example. [§ 26–40]**

    Betty owes Earl $10,000 and enters into a valid contract with Ralph in which Ralph promises to repay her debt to Earl.

    Graphically, the parties can be depicted:

    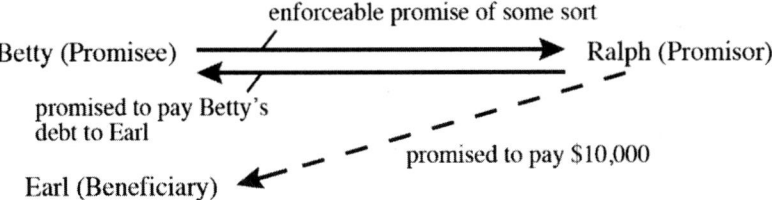

    If the debt is not repaid, Earl, the beneficiary of the Ralph/Betty contract, can either sue Betty (the promisee) on her old promise to pay, and/or Ralph (the promisor) to enforce his new promise to pay arising from the Ralph/Betty contract. However, Earl is only entitled to one complete satisfaction. That is, whether he sues only one of them, or both of them, Earl can only walk away with a total of $10,000.

2. **Example. [§ 26–41]**

    Kelly takes out a life insurance policy naming his sister Tara as his beneficiary.

    The third party beneficiary aspect of the parties' relationships can be displayed as:

CHAPTER 26

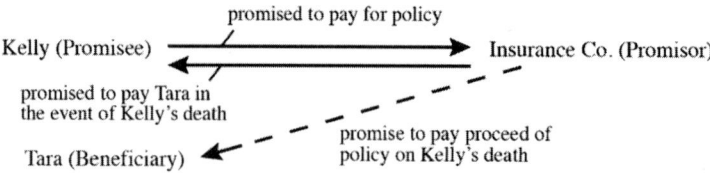

Kelly dies and the insurance company does not pay Tara. Tara as "donee-like" intended beneficiary, may not bring suit against Kelly's heirs to enforce the gift promise, for Kelly was under no obligation to name Tara as his beneficiary when he took out the insurance contract. That is, Kelly's decision to enter into a third party beneficiary contract with the insurance company does not create a duty where none existed before. Hence, Tara's only claim for breach is against the promisor, the insurance company.

G. RIGHTS OF THE PROMISEE AGAINST THE PROMISOR. [§ 26–42]

If a promisor under a third party beneficiary contract breaches the agreement, he or she is liable to **both** the promisee **and** to the beneficiary, but in different ways. The breaching promisor will likely owe the beneficiary money damages; however, the promisee can usually only get an order of specific performance ordering the promisee to perform what he or she promised.

1. Example. [§ 26–43]

Recall the Maxine/Keith/Tom hypothetical from § 26–38, whereby Maxine owes Keith $5,000, but agrees to paint Tom's house in return for Tom's promise to repay Maxine's debt to Keith. This time assume Maxine does all the painting competently, but Tom nevertheless fails to pay either Keith or Maxine. Both Keith, as an intended beneficiary, and Maxine, as promisee, are entitled to sue Tom for his non-payment. Keith is entitled to the money, whereas Maxine is only entitled to an order of specific performance requiring Tom to pay Keith. This makes sense, for performance of the promise to pay Keith was all Maxine entitled to under the contract.

H. RIGHTS OF THE PROMISEE AND PROMISOR TO MODIFY THEIR CONTRACT TO THE DISADVANTAGE OF AN INTENDED BENEFICIARY. [§ 26–44]

Once a promisor and promisee have entered into a contract making a third party an intended beneficiary, a question often arises whether promisor and promisee can later modify (or even rescind) their agreement to the disadvantage of the beneficiary. All courts agree that at some point the rights of the beneficiary vest and the promisor and promisee cannot

THIRD PARTY BENEFICIARY CONTRACTS

thereafter enforceably modify their agreement. However, there is a split of opinion as to **when** the beneficiary's rights vest. The major views are set forth below.

1. **View of the Second Restatement: An Intended Beneficiary's Rights Vest upon His or Her Reliance on the Promisor's Promise. [§ 26–45]**

   The Restatement 2d sets forth what is probably the majority view on this issue, which is that the beneficiary's rights vest upon a material change of position in justifiable reliance on the promisor's promise [Restatement 2d § 311(3)]. Hence, the promisor and promisee can freely modify or terminate the promisor's duty to the beneficiary until the beneficiary **both knows** of the promisor's promise **and relies on it**.

   Note that the promisor and promisee may not be aware of the beneficiary's reliance, and thus they may modify their contract to the beneficiary's detriment in good faith. However, under the Restatement 2d view, such a modification is not enforceable after the beneficiary's reliance, regardless of whether the modification was done in good faith or, otherwise without knowledge of the reliance by the parties to the original contract.

   a. **Example. [§ 26–46]**

      Ned and Sara have entered into an enforceable contract whereby Ned promised to pay $1,000 to Ashley in settlement of an antecedent monetary debt Sara owes Ashley. Hence, **Ned is the promisor**; **Sara is the promisee**; and **Ashley is an intended third party beneficiary**.

      Graphically, this is:

      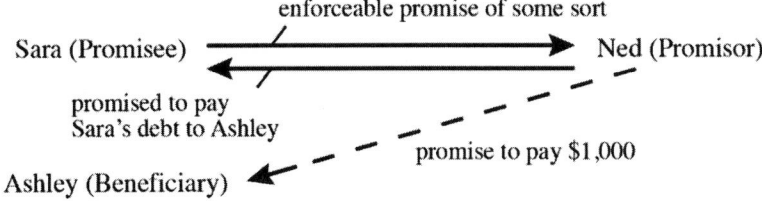

      Under the contract, Ned's performance (i.e., payment of the $1,000 to Ashley) is due August 10. On August 1, Ned and Sara meet and modify their agreement so that Ned will now pay the $1,000 directly to Sara. The issue is whether Ned and Sara (the promisor and promisee) are entitled to make an enforceable modification of their contract to Ashley's detriment.

      The answer to that question under the Restatement 2d view depends on whether Ashley both: (i) knows that she is an intended third party beneficiary; and (ii) can establish some change of position in reliance on Ned's promise. **Both** must occur before Ashley's rights are vested, i.e., before her rights as a beneficiary are irrevocable and unmodifiable by the promisor and promisee.

Thus if, for example, Sara has broken a business appointment so that she can meet Ned at a particular time and place on August 10 to receive the payment, her rights as an intended beneficiary probably have vested. If she only knows of the Ned/Sara contract but can show no reliance on it, or if she does not know of the contract, Sara and Ned's modification is enforceable. Note that even if the modification is enforceable, it really is not all that unfair to Ashley, for she still retains her right to sue Sara to repay the original debt.

Note also that Ashley may have canceled her business appointment to make time to meet Ned without letting either Ned or Sara know. That is, Ned and Sara may have modified their agreement in good faith, before becoming aware of Ashley's reliance on Ned's promise. It does not matter. Once there has been reliance, an intended beneficiary's rights are irrevocable and unmodifiable under this view.

2. **Minority View: An Intended Beneficiary's Rights Vest Immediately upon Execution of the Promisor/Promisee Contract. [§ 26–47]**

A minority view is that an intended beneficiary's rights vest immediately upon execution of the promisor/promisee contract. This is true regardless whether the beneficiary knows at the time that he or she is a beneficiary. Hence, under this view, once the promisor/promisee contract is formed, the promisor and promisee may not thereafter validly modify their agreement to the beneficiary's detriment.

3. **Second Minority View: The Beneficiary's Rights Vest upon Knowledge of the Promisor's Promise. [§ 26–48]**

Another minority view holds that the beneficiary's rights vest as soon as he or she *learns* of the promisor/promisee contract which makes him or her an intended beneficiary. Hence, under this view the beneficiary's rights can be changed so long as he or she does not know that he or she is a beneficiary. However, once the third party learns of his or her status as an intended beneficiary, no modifications to the detriment of the beneficiary may validly be made by the promisor and promisee, regardless of whether the beneficiary relies on the promise.

THIRD PARTY BENEFICIARY CONTRACTS

I. DISTINCTION BETWEEN CREDITOR-LIKE INTENDED THIRD PARTY BENEFICIARY CONTRACTS AND ACCORDS OR NOVATIONS. [§ 26–49]

It is important to be able to explain the differences between third party beneficiary contracts with a creditor-like intended beneficiary and an accord or a novation transaction. (It is important to be able to do this partly because it is a favorite question of Contracts professors on multiple choice exams). While the doctrines are related, there is one big difference between them. In novations and accords, the creditor must **agree** that performance (or promised performance) by a third party will discharge the antecedent debt [*See* §§ 24–5 and 24–9 for an explanation of accords and novations]. In a creditor-type third party beneficiary situation, the beneficiary (i.e., the creditor) need not agree to the promisee's performance of the promisee's obligation. In fact, the beneficiary need not even know about it, and once he or she **does** know of it, he or she can disclaim it [§§ 26–25, 26–26].

1. **Example. [§ 26–50]**

   Bart owes Homer $1,000. Because Bart does not have the money to repay Homer, he enters into negotiations with Homer and his friend Jennifer, hoping he can sell his watch for the necessary $1,000. After a good deal of negotiation, Homer agrees to discharge Bart's duty to pay him $1,000 and replace it with Jennifer's promise to pay Homer $1,000 upon Bart's tender of the watch to Jennifer. Depending on how they structure the deal, it can be either an accord or a novation, but in either event Homer is **not** an intended third party beneficiary of the Jennifer/Bart contract. That is, by agreeing to accept Jennifer's performance *in lieu* of Bart's debt, Homer's rights are those of an obligee in a novation or accord, which are quite different from those of an intended beneficiary.

2. **Example. [§ 26–51]**

   Same situation, except this time Bart and Jennifer have entered a contract whereby Bart agrees to sell his watch to Jennifer in return for Jennifer's promise to pay $1,000 to Homer. Homer is not involved in the negotiations. This time, Homer is a third party creditor-like intended beneficiary, even if he does not know it at the time the contract is made. When he finds out about it, he is entitled to disclaim his status as beneficiary, or he is entitled to remain silent and implicitly ratify it. However, Homer's rights are only those of an intended beneficiary. For Homer's rights to become those of an obligee in an accord or a novation situation, **Homer would have to affirmatively agree** to accept Jennifer's performance (or her promised performance) in satisfaction of Bart's antecedent obligation to Homer.

J. DISTINCTION BETWEEN A THIRD PARTY BENEFICIARY CONTRACT SITUATION AND AN ASSIGNMENT SITUATION. [§ 26–52]

The main distinction between an assignment and a third party beneficiary situation is that in the latter, **only one contract is involved**, i.e., at the time of the making of the third party beneficiary contract, an intended beneficiary gains rights.

In an **assignment**, there are **two contracts**. There is the original contract, followed by a *second one in which the rights under the first are assigned* to a third party.

The distinction between a third party beneficiary contract situation and an assignment situation is further discussed in Chapter Twenty-Seven [§ 27–33].

K. EXAM APPROACH TO THIRD PARTY BENEFICIARY ISSUES. [§ 26–53]

The first step in analyzing a third party beneficiary issue on an examination is to identify the parties and put them down graphically on your scratch paper [§ 26–2].

Next, make sure that the third party is a beneficiary as opposed to an assignee, delegate [Chapters Twenty-Seven and Twenty-Eight], or someone with some other status. If the third party is a beneficiary, determine whether he, she, or it is an intended or an incidental beneficiary [§§ 26–13 *et seq.*] for that will determine the rights of the beneficiary to enforce the agreement.

Lastly, check the list of the only 5 issues that arise in third party beneficiary situations given in § 26–2, identify which issue(s) pertains to your situation, set forth the correct rule that applies, and interweave the facts you are given with the correct legal rule.

CHAPTER 27

ASSIGNMENTS

A. ASSIGNMENTS GENERALLY. [§ 27–1*]

When a party enters into a bilateral contract, he or she obtains a right to receive the promised performance of another. While not discussed in this book until now, the right to receive promised performance under contract can be considered a property right [*see* § 30–1 for a further elaboration of this principle]. One of the attributes of property is that it is transferable. When one contracting party validly transfers the right to receive the promised performance of the other to a third person, contract law calls the transfer an "**assignment**."

B. DEFINITION, TERMINOLOGY, AND MAJOR EFFECTS OF ASSIGNMENTS. [§ 27–2]

As with third party beneficiary situations (*see* Chapter Twenty-Six), to begin understanding the rules governing assignments, you must first understand the terminology.

An assignment is a transfer of contractual *rights* to a third party [Restatement 2d § 317]. (The transfer of contractual **duties** to a third party is known as a **delegation**, and is discussed in Chapter Twenty-Eight).

There are typically three parties in an assignment:

(1) The **Assignor (or Obligee or Promisee)**. The assignor (sometimes called the "obligee" or the "promisee") is the party who transfers a right to receive contractual performance to a third party. That is, the assignor is already a party to a contract before the assignment occurs, and it is the assignor who transfers the right to *receive* the other party's performance to a third person.

(2) The **Obligor** (or Promisor). The obligor (sometimes called the "promisor") is the party who initially promised performance to the assignor but who, after the assignment, now owes that duty of promised performance to a third person.

---

* For more information, listen to CD # 13, Track 4 of *Sum and Substance Audio on Contracts*.

(3) The **Assignee.** The assignee is not a party to the initial assignor/obligor contract. The assignee is the third party who receives from the assignor the right to performance by the obligor.

As with third party beneficiary contracts, some students find that illustrating an assignment graphically is helpful to understanding assignment issues. A typical assignment scenario can be presented as follows:

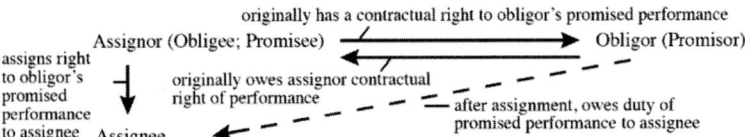

The principal consequence of an effective assignment is that the assignee acquires the right to enforce the obligor's promise. That is, the duty that the obligor had previously promised and owed to the assignor is now owed to the assignee. Further, after an assignment, it is the assignee, and **only the assignee**, who is entitled to sue the obligor for breach if the obligor unjustifiably fails to perform.

1. **Example. [§ 27–3]**

   Lorenzo is under a contractual duty to sell his watch to Lori next week for $500. Lorenzo would like to make a gift of the $500 to his sister, Darla. Accordingly, he instructs Lori to pay the $500 for the watch directly to Darla.

   An assignment has taken place. **Lorenzo is the assignor**, for it was he who had a contractual right to receive performance from Lori (payment of $500), and who transferred that right to a third party (Darla). **Lori is the obligor**, for she was under a duty to render promised performance to Lorenzo (payment of $500), but as a result of the assignment, she is now obligated to render that performance to a third person (Darla). **Darla is the assignee**, for she is the person who was not originally a party to the assignor/obligor contract, and who is now owed performance (payment of $500) by the obligor (Lori).

   Graphically, this is:

   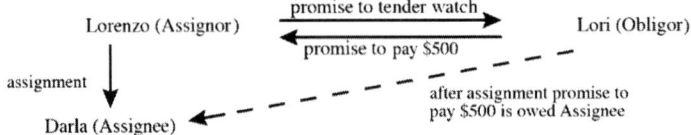

   If Lori does not pay the $500 **after the assignment**, it is **Darla, and only Darla**, who can sue to **enforce the promise**.

ASSIGNMENTS

C. TYPES OF ASSIGNMENTS. [§ 27–4]

Contract law has categorized valid assignments into two types: "gratuitous assignments" and "assignments for value."

1. "Gratuitous Assignments": Defined and Discussed. [§ 27–5]

A gratuitous assignment is one in which the assignor's **purpose** in making the transfer of the contract right is **to confer a gift** on the assignee.

a. Example. [§ 27–6]

Uncle Joe would like to give his niece Penny $5,000. Joe is owed $5,000 under a loan he made to Jill. If Joe validly transfers his right to receive the $5,000 to his niece, an assignment has taken place. **Joe is the assignor** (because he has transferred a right to performance under a contract to a third party); **Jill is the obligor** (for she was obligated to pay Joe and, as a result of the transfer, is now obligated to pay Penny); and **Penny is the assignee** (because she was not a party to the Joe/Jill contract and now has a right to enforce Jill's re-payment promise).

Illustrating this situation would show:

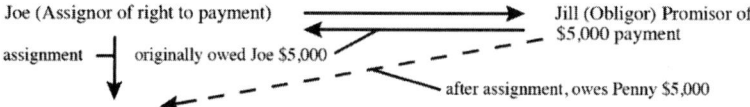

This is a **gratuitous assignment** because Uncle Joe's purpose in making the assignment to Penny was to make a gift to her. Upon the assignment it is Penny, and **only Penny**, who is owed the obligation of payment. Hence, if Jill does not re-pay the $5,000 when due, only Penny is entitled to sue her for breach.

Note that the promise to pay Penny does not fail for lack of consideration because Jill's promise to pay is supported by whatever consideration she received for it in the loan from Uncle Joe. That is, so long as her promise to pay **Uncle Joe** was supported by consideration, Uncle Joe's transfer of his right to receive payment to Penny does not make the promise unenforceable. In other words, the fact that the identity of the person Jill is supposed to pay changes does not change the fact that her promise to repay the loan is supported by consideration and thus enforceable.

b. Example. [§ 27–7]

The hypothetical among Lorenzo, Lori and Darla in § 27–3 above is also an example of a gratuitous assignment.

CHAPTER 27

2. **"Assignments for Value": Defined and Discussed. [§ 27–8]**

An assignment for value is one in which the assignee has given consideration to the assignor in order to receive the benefits of the obligor's performance. One of the most common types of assignments for value used in business transactions (and occasionally covered in a first year contracts course) is accounts receivable financing.

   a. **Example. [§ 27–9]**

   Dennis owns a wine shop and sells wine to a number of restaurants on 60 days credit. The total amount he is owed by these restaurants at any one time varies, but it averages approximately $300,000. Most businesses like the wine shop would rather have cash in hand than a promise to be paid that cash in 60 days. That is, they would prefer to sell their rights to collect the accounts to a bank, thereby getting cash immediately, and transfer the risk of the debtor's non-payment to the bank along with the wait to collect the money even if it is paid.

   Of course, a bank willing to purchase the right to collect such receivables will not pay Dennis the full amount of the debt, given both the risk of non-payment and the time value of money (i.e., getting $100 today is more valuable than getting $100 sixty days from now, because the $100 paid today can earn interest and thus will be worth more than $100 in sixty days). Hence, banks and other financial institutions will typically discount the amount of the receivables by about 20–30%. A bank thus would pay Dennis something like $225,000 today (using a 25% discount), for the right to collect $300,000 from Dennis's customers in the future.

   In the transaction giving Dennis the $225,000, an assignment has taken place. **Dennis is the assignor, the restaurants are the obligors**, and **the bank is the assignee**. This type of assignment is an "assignment for value," since the **assignee** (the bank) gave consideration **to the assignor** (Dennis) for the assignment. Specifically, it is an "accounts receivable financing" type of assignment for value because Dennis has assigned the right to receive payments (accounts receivable) from his credit account customers as a way to finance his business.

   The relationships between the parties can be shown as follows:

   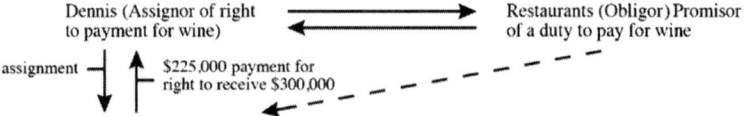

ASSIGNMENTS

D. ELEMENTS NECESSARY TO MAKE AN EFFECTIVE ASSIGNMENT. [§ 27–10]

In order to make an **effective** assignment, i.e., a legally enforceable assignment, the following elements must be satisfied:

(1) The assignor must manifest a **present intention** to transfer an *existing* contractual right to the assignee without further action by the assignor [§ 27–11];

(2) The assignment must be **permissible**, i.e., there must be *no prohibition* against the assignment of that type of contract right [§ 27–15]; and

(3) In most cases, the assignee must also manifest his or her **acceptance of the assignment** [§ 27–22].

1. The Assignor Must Manifest a Present Intention to Transfer an *Existing* Contractual Right. [§ 27–11]

The first element of an effective assignment requires the assignor to manifest an intention to transfer an *existing* contractual right to the assignee [Restatement 2d § 324]. No special words are required for an assignment, and in close cases it is for the court to determine from an examination of all the surrounding circumstances whether the words of the purported assignment actually manifest the requisite intent.

To meet this test, the assignment must be an actual present transfer of the contractual right and **not require any further action by the assignor**. If any further action is required, the parties may have entered into a separate, enforceable contract, but their agreement is **not** an "assignment," for an assignment requires the **present** transfer of an **existing** contractual right [Restatement 2d § 330].

a. Example. [§ 27–12]

Linda is under a contractual duty to pay Margaret $1,000 on May 15. Margaret owes Brian $900 on May 10. Brian expresses to Margaret his concern as to whether she will have the money to pay him. Accordingly, she promises Brian that if she does not repay Brian the $900 on May 10, on May 14 she will make an assignment to him of her right to Linda's $1,000 payment. Brian agrees to this proposition.

There has been no assignment, for Margaret has made only a promise to do something in the future. That is, while Margaret has an existing contractual right to performance from Linda, she did not transfer that right to Brian. She only promised that she **would** transfer the right in the future *upon a certain condition* which may or may not take place. Because Margaret (the assignor) would have to take further action before the assignee has an enforceable right to the obligor's (Linda's) performance, no assignment has occurred. Hence, if neither Margaret nor Linda pays Brian, Brian's rights are only against Margaret.

If Margaret and Brian had agreed that in lieu of her paying him $900 on the 10th, she would presently assign to him her right to collect the $1,000 from Linda on the 15th, then a valid assignment would have taken place. In that case, Brian would immediately acquire rights against Linda without any further action on Margaret's part, and Brian could sue Linda if she did not perform.

b. **Example. [§ 27–13]**

Sally owed David $10,000 on Monday, but did not have the cash to pay him. She asked for one day's extension, promising David that she would go to the pawn shop the next day, obtain a loan on her heirloom bracelet, and assign her rights to receive the loan proceeds to David. The next day the pawn shop offered to lend her $10,000 with her bracelet as security, and Sally told the pawn shop owner to mail the check to David.

There has been no assignment. On Monday, Sally only bound herself to make an assignment of a right under a contract not yet in existence, i.e., there was **no** existing contract right with the pawn shop. On Tuesday, she did not enter into a contract and thereafter assign rights to it to David. Rather, she entered into a third party beneficiary contract whereby David became a creditor-type intended beneficiary of the pawn shop owner's promise to pay [*See* § 27–33 for a further discussion of the difference between third party beneficiaries and assignments]. Hence, David is entitled to enforce the pawn shop owner's promise to mail him the check, but as a third party beneficiary, not as an assignee.

c. **Special Rule Under Article 9 of the UCC: After-Acquired Property Clauses. [§ 27–14]**

Recall the Dennis/restaurants/bank example of accounts receivable financing discussed in § 27–9. There, Dennis is a wine shop owner and has $300,000 in accounts receivable from various restaurants which he assigns for value to the bank for $225,000. A practical problem that arises in such financing is that every day Dennis sells more wine to the restaurants. Strict application of common law contract doctrine would require that Dennis go to the bank every night and fill out more forms for each account receivable assignment he makes, but that would be cumbersome. Hence, Article 9 of the UCC specifically permits Dennis to assign all the accounts receivable he presently has,

ASSIGNMENTS

and all "after acquired" accounts in a single transaction [UCC § 9–204].

In return, the bank will set up a line of credit that Dennis may draw upon every time he transfers a new account receivable to the bank. As such, this arrangement avoids a lot of complications and paperwork. While some claim that after-acquired property clauses are an **exception** to the rules against assignment of future rights, it really is not true. After-acquired property clauses are only promises to assign actual contract rights in the future. It is just that the promise to assign is self-executing, i.e., as soon as the account/contract with the restaurant comes in to Dennis's shop, it is automatically assigned to the bank. However, the assignment is not effective until an actual contract right from a particular restaurant is transferred. Before that, the bank merely has Dennis's promise to assign an account.

2. **There Must Be No Prohibition Against Assignment of the Particular Right. [§ 27–15]**

Even if the manifestation of the assignor's present intent to transfer an existing contractual right can be established, a purported assignment may still not be effective. This is because contract law has established several limitations as to what rights can be assigned. These rules have changed somewhat over time, and the current rules are as follows:

Generally all contract rights may be assigned [Restatement 2d § 317(2)]. A contract right may <u>not</u> be assigned only when:

(1) The assignment **violates public policy** [Restatement 2d § 317(2)(b); § 27–16];

(2) The assignment would **materially and adversely affect the obligor's rights, duties or justified expectations** under his or her contract with the assignor [Restatement 2d § 317(2)(a); § 27–17]; or

(3) An assignor's right to assign duties is **specifically and enforceably prohibited** under the assignor/obligor contract [Restatement 2d § 317(2)(c); § 27–21].

Each of these limitations is discussed and illustrated below.

a. **A Purported Assignment That Violates Public Policy Is Ineffective. [§ 27–16]**

Courts and legislatures are empowered to nullify any purported assignment if they believe it would violate public policy [Restatement 2d § 317(2)(b)]. By far the most common example of the use of such power is the prohibition against an employee's ability to assign future wages. **In almost every state an employee cannot validly assign his or her right to collect future wages to a creditor**.

The reason for voiding such an assignment on public policy grounds is, in part, based on the belief that when an employee does not receive the full value of his or her employment, there may be a lack of incentive for the employee to work as hard as he or she would otherwise.

For example, assume Doug was supposed to receive $1,000 per week from his employer. However, because of previous debts, Doug has entered into multiple assignments whereby he will only receive $300/week from his employer, and his creditors will split the remaining $700. In such a case, there is a worry that Doug may look at his employee duties differently when he only personally receives $300 as opposed to when he gets $1,000. Of course, if there is no assignment, when Doug receives the $1,000, he is free to pay $700 to his creditors if he wishes or is otherwise legally obligated to do so, and, if a court allows it, certain types of creditors may be able attach wages. It is just that Doug himself cannot assign them.

b. **A Purported Assignment That Materially and Adversely Affects the Obligor's Rights, Duties, and Justified Expectations as to Return Performance Is Ineffective. [§ 27–17]**

It is one thing for an assignor to say to an obligor, "You are under a contractual duty to pay me $1,000. I would rather you pay that money to my nephew, Adam, instead and assign to Adam the right to receive the money." It is quite another for the assignor to say, "You are under a contractual duty to paint my 2,000 square foot house for $3,000. I am assigning the right to have you paint a house for $3,000 to my rich Uncle Montesquieu, who lives in a 15,000 square foot mansion." Hence, for common sense reasons, contract law invalidates purported assignments that have a materially adverse consequence to the obligor. There are two ways such adverse consequences can occur:

(1) When the assignment results in a **material increase** in either the **burden of**, or the **risk to**, the obligor; or

(2) When the assignment results either in a **material impairment of the obligor's chance of obtaining return performance**, or in a **material reduction of the value of the return performance** due the obligor [Restatement 2d § 317(2)(a)].

ASSIGNMENTS

(1) Example. [§ 27–18]

The hypothetical case given above with the painter and Uncle Montesquieu is an example of when a purported assignment would be invalid because the obligor's **burden** in performing his or her duty is **materially increased** by the assignment.

To visualize the relationships among the parties:

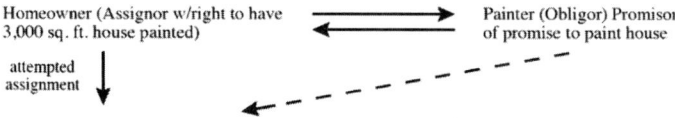

There is no hard and fast test for determining when the duty of the obligor has changed enough to make it a "materially greater" burden, but it is fair to say the courts have been more solicitous of obligors in these cases than of assignors. Hence, when an obligor will have to expend a reasonably greater amount of effort or expense to perform the assigned duty than he or she would have under the obligor/assignor contract, the assignment is likely to be invalid.

(2) Example. [§ 27–19]

Daryl takes out an automobile insurance policy with Ins. Co. Daryl is 45 years old, owns a 6 year old car, drives less than 12,000 miles per year and has neither been issued a ticket nor been in an accident for the past 10 years. His premium is $400/year. If Daryl tries to assign the right to be insured for $400/year to Tom, an 18-year old driver who has had two accidents last year, 3 speeding tickets in the last month, and who drives 30,000 miles per year in his new Corvette, the attempted assignment will be invalid.

Graphically, these parties can be represented:

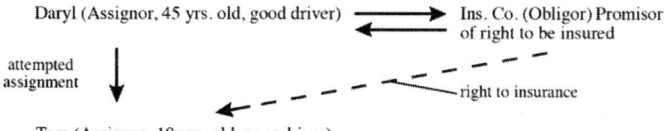

The attempted assignment will be voided because as a result of the assignment, Ins. Co.'s (i.e., the obligor's) **risks** under the insurance contract have been **materially and adversely changed**.

CHAPTER 27

(3) Example. [§ 27–20]

A concert promoter has booked Loco, a popular heavy metal band, to play at a concert for $15,000. Loco assigns its rights to receive the $15,000 to the Vienna Boys Choir. Such an assignment may be invalidated if the circumstances make it likely that what is really happening is that Loco is planning both to assign to the Vienna Boys Choir the right to receive the money, **and** to have the Vienna Boys Choir take its place at the concert.

These parties can be shown as follows:

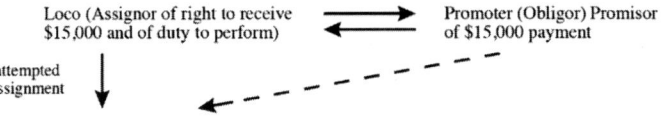

Loco (Assignor of right to receive $15,000 and of duty to perform) ⟶ ⟵ Promoter (Obligor) Promisor of $15,000 payment

attempted assignment ↓

Vienna Boys Choir (Assignee of right to receive $15,000 and of duty to perform at concert)

The attempted assignment will be voided because such an assignment will **materially impair** the promoter's right to receive its bargained for performance. That is, it seems likely concert goers who wanted to see Loco would demand their money back when the featured band turns out to be the Vienna Boys Choir. As such, the obligor (the promoter) faces a "material reduction of the value of the return performance due the obligor." If the band only assigned the rights to receive the $15,000, there is no problem.

c. A Purported Assignment That Violates a Valid "No Assignment" Provision in the Assignor/Obligor Contract Is Ineffective. [§ 27–21]

Historically, a specifically negotiated "no assignment" clause in an assignor/obligor contract was rather strictly enforced by the courts [Restatement 2d § 317(2)(c)]. However, in the last several decades, there has been a steady decline in the courts' willingness to enforce such clauses, and a simultaneous increase in contract law's desire to promote the free assignability of contractual rights. Hence, while a fully negotiated, explicit anti-assignment clause **may** still act as a bar to an assignment, courts analyze even such fully negotiated clauses carefully and with the following points in mind:

First, all courts interpret such clauses as narrowly as possible. Thus, if there is a way to find the "no assignment" clause limited in time, in subject matter, or to a particular class of persons, the courts will do so.

ASSIGNMENTS

Second, courts generally hold that such clauses operate only for the **benefit** of the **obligor**. Hence, if the obligor consents to the assignment, it is effective [Restatement 2d § 322(2)(c)].

Third, courts tend to construe a term in an agreement prohibiting "assignment of the contract" as prohibiting only **delegation** of performance, and not the assignment of rights, absent clear evidence of the parties' contrary intention [Restatement 2d § 322(1); UCC § 2–210(3)]. That is, they will interpret the phrase as denying the party the power to designate another to *perform* a promised duty under the contract, but not as prohibiting a party's ability to transfer the right *to receive* a promised benefit, such as payment of money, to another.

Fourth, many courts now interpret such clauses as creating only a contractual **duty** not to assign, and not a total bar to assignment. That is, if there is a "no assignment" clause in the assignor/obligor contract, but the assignor nevertheless assigns a right, these courts hold that the only recourse of the obligor is to sue the assignor to collect damages for breach of the duty not to assign. However, **the assignment itself is valid**, meaning the obligor must render performance to the assignee or be in breach for failing to do so despite the "no assignment" clause [Restatement 2d § 322(2)(b)]. In other words, these courts hold that "no assignment" clauses deprive the assignor of the **right** to assign, but not of the **power** to do so effectively. So the assignor is in breach after the assignment, but the obligor must still live up to the assignment.

Fifth, a number of courts have interpreted "no assignment without obligor consent" clauses in the commercial area to mean that an assignment under such a clause is effective despite the obligor's refusal to give his or her consent if the obligor's refusal is objectively **unreasonable** or made in **bad faith**. This is a common ground for interpreting no assignment clauses in commercial leases. That is, if there is a "no assignment (i.e., no sublease) without the consent of the landlord" clause in a commercial lease, many courts hold that so long as the new tenant is objectively acceptable, the landlord (i.e., the obligor) **must** accept the assignment and rent to the assignee (i.e., the sub-lessee). [*See* §§ 7–48 *et seq.* relating to personal satisfaction clauses.]

Sixth, a clause attempting to prohibit the right to assign damages for breach of the whole contract is similarly presumptively ineffective [Restatement 2d § 322(2)(a)].

CHAPTER 27

3. **General Rule: The Assignee Must Agree to the Assignment to Make It Effective. [§ 27-22]**

   The general rule is that the assignee must manifest assent to the assignment to render it effective. That is, before the assignment becomes effective and the obligor thereafter becomes bound to render performance to the assignee instead of the assignor, usually the assignee must somehow signify his or her acceptance of the transaction [Restatement 2d § 327(1)]. Once again, no special words are necessary, and whether such a manifestation of assent has been made will be judged under an objective theory, i.e., whether a reasonable person would find that a manifestation of assent to the assignment has been made as judged from all the circumstances. There are exceptions to this general rule, however, which are discussed immediately below.

   a. **The Two Exceptions to the General Rule That the Assignee Must Agree Before the Assignment Is Effective. [§ 27-23]**

      There are two situations in which an assignee does **not** have to manifest acceptance before an assignment is deemed effective:

      (1) When a third party other than the assignee has given the assignor consideration for the assignment; or

      (2) When the assignment is irrevocable **because of the delivery of a writing to a third party** [Restatement 2d § 327(1)].

      Note, however, that while an assignment without the assignee's consent is effective in these types of cases, when the assignee learns of the assignment he or she has the right to **disclaim** any rights under it within a reasonable time after learning of the assignment [Restatement 2d § 327(2)]. If no disclaimer is made after a reasonable time, the assignee may not thereafter validly disclaim it as it will be deemed implicitly ratified.

      (1) **Example. [§ 27-24]**

         Lisa owes Beverly $1,000. Dan's father contracts to paint Beverly's kitchen in return for Beverly's promise to assign her right to receive the $1,000 to Dan.

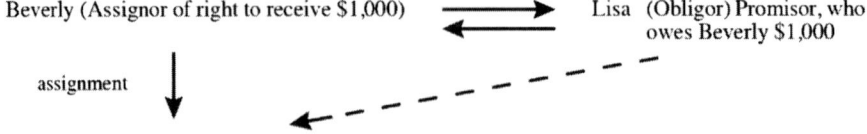

Beverly (Assignor of right to receive $1,000) → Lisa (Obligor) Promisor, who owes Beverly $1,000

assignment ↓

Dan (Assignee for value (provided by Dan's father) of the right to receive $1,000)

ASSIGNMENTS

If Beverly makes the assignment by objectively manifesting her intent to do so, the assignment is effective notwithstanding Dan's lack of knowledge or assent to the transfer. This is because **consideration for the assignment has come from someone other than the assignee**. However, when Dan finally learns of the assignment, he is entitled to disclaim his right as an assignee if he wishes, so long as he does so within a reasonable time [Restatement 2d § 327, Cmt. a, Ill. 1].

(2) Example. [§ 27–25]

Ashley has a $500 winning lottery ticket and wants to assign the rights to collect the money to her friend Rose. If she gives the ticket to Rose and says something like, "I know money is tight right now for you, so I am making you a present of the lottery winnings," a valid assignment has been made **because of the delivery of a writing to a third party**.

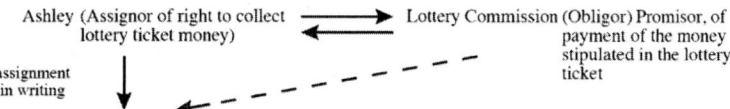

Upon the delivery of the ticket, the assignment became irrevocable.

(3) Review Problem. [§ 27–26]

Darrin is owed $1,000 from Pam. He would like to make a gift of that money to Bob, and so tells Pam he is assigning his right to receive the $1,000 to Bob.

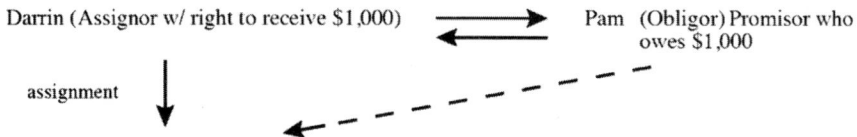

Question:

When is the assignment effective?

Answer:

The assignment is not effective until Bob manifests his acceptance of the assignment, for neither of the exceptions to the general rule set forth in § 27–23 apply.

E. RECURRING ISSUES THAT ARISE IN DETERMINING THE EFFECTIVENESS OF ASSIGNMENTS. [§ 27–27]

As noted above (§§ 27–10 *et seq.*), there are only three requirements in order to have an effective assignment. However, in the study of assignments in most first year contracts courses, there are several additional issues the Professor will bring up for discussion. Those issues are explained below.

1. **Notification to the Obligor of the Assignment Is Not Necessary for an Assignment to Be Effective. [§ 27–28]**

   While usually the **assignee** must be notified and agree to the assignment before it is effective [§ 27–22], the same is **not** true for the obligor. **That is, absent a contractual obligation to do so, the *obligor* need not be notified of the assignment before it becomes effective.** This means that once the assignment is made, the obligor is under a duty to render performance to the assignee instead of to the assignor *even if the obligor does not know that!*

   Further, once the obligor finds out about the assignment, there is no requirement that the obligor assent to the transfer. That is, contract law gives the obligor no grounds to object to, or otherwise disclaim, such an assignment, assuming that there is no prohibition against the assignment [§ 27–15]. The point is that an assignment is effective from the moment the assignor manifests his or her interest to transfer a permissible right and the assignee agrees to the assignment, even if the obligor does not yet know about it.

   Note there are situations in which an assignment is made without knowledge of the obligor, and the obligor thus renders performance to the assignor and not the assignee. The rules relating to that situation are discussed in § 27–40.

2. **An Effective Assignment Can Be Partial. [§ 27–29]**

   The assignor can make an effective assignment of only part of the duties owed by the obligor under the assignor/obligor contract [Restatement 2d § 326]. The result is that the obligor thereafter owes duties both to the assignor and the assignee.

   a. **Example. [§ 27–30]**

      Ted owes Kevin $100. Kevin owes Samantha $25. Kevin can validly assign one-quarter of his rights to receive the $100 from Ted to Samantha.

ASSIGNMENTS

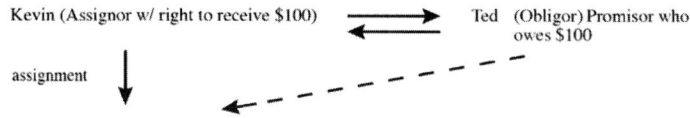

As a result of the assignment, Ted (the obligor) will owe a duty to pay Kevin (the assignor) $75, and a duty to pay Samantha (the assignee) $25. If Ted pays neither, both Kevin and Samantha can sue him to enforce their shares of the $100 repayment promise.

3. **An Effective Assignment Can Be Conditional or Otherwise Limited. [§ 27–31]**

The assignor is entitled to make an effective assignment where the assignee's rights are expressly conditional on the occurrence of a particular event, or are otherwise limited [Restatement 2d § 331].

   a. **Example. [§ 27–32]**

   Ryan is entitled to receive $1,000 from Sue. Ryan assigns his right to the $1,000 payment to David, "on the condition David gets an 'A' on his Contracts midterm."

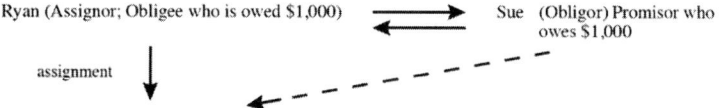

   Such an assignment is effective because it is an assignment of a present contract right. However, the assignment is not absolute, and is limited in scope by the conditional nature of the assignment itself. Thus, David's entitlement to the $1,000 is dependent on his performance on the midterm.

4. **Distinction Between an Assignment and a Third Party Beneficiary Contract. [§ 27–33]**

The principal difference between an assignment and a third party beneficiary contract is that it takes **two** agreements to make an assignment, and **only one agreement** to establish a third party beneficiary contract. That is, for an assignee to receive an enforceable duty arising from an *assignment:* **first**, there must be an existing contract between the assignor and obligor (which does not benefit the assignee) and **second**, the assignor must *later* make a transfer of rights under that contract to the assignee. On the other hand, for an intended beneficiary to receive an enforceable right arising from a third party beneficiary contract, there is only **one** transaction,

CHAPTER 27

namely the formation of one contract between the promisor and promisee which benefits a third person *at the time of its making*.

a. **Example. [§ 27–34]**

Bill enters into a contract with Mary Lee whereby he offers to sell her his watch in return for Mary Lee's promise to pay Bill's daughter Christina $500. This is a third party beneficiary situation because Christina's receipt of an enforceable duty arose out of the promises made in only one transaction—the contract between Bill (the promisee) and Mary Lee (the promisor).

Recall graphically, a third party beneficiary contract looks like:

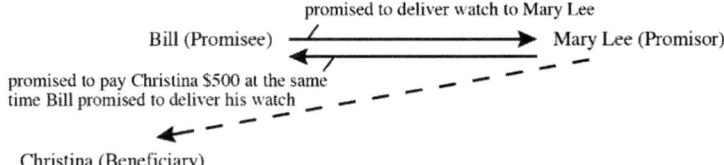

b. **Example. [§ 27–35]**

Bill is under a contractual duty to sell his watch to Mary Lee for $500. Bill is obligated to deliver the watch on May 5, and Mary Lee is obligated to pay the $500 on delivery. On May 1, Bill validly transfers his right to receive the money to his daughter Christina. This time there has been an assignment, for Christina's receipt of an enforceable duty arose from two transactions: (i) the original contract between Bill (the assignor) and Mary Lee (the obligor); and (ii) the later assignment from Bill to Christina.

Graphically this is:

(i) a straight forward two party contract

and (ii) the subsequent transfer of the right to payment to Christina.

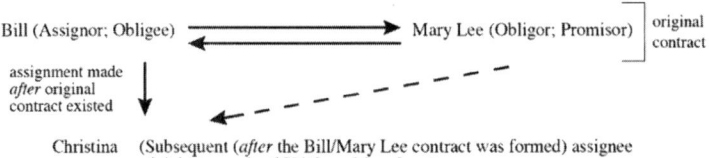

514

ASSIGNMENTS

5. **Interpretation of the Phrase "Assignments of the Contract" or ". . . of All My Rights Under the Contract." [§ 27–36]**

   Contract law has established that unless the parties evidence a different intention, when a party assigns "the contract" or "all my rights under the contract" to an assignee, such a transfer acts as *both* an assignment of rights **and** a delegation of any executory duties of that party under the agreement [Restatement 2d § 328; UCC § 2–210(3); § 28–6].

   a. **Example. [§ 27–37]**

      Louise wants to order a new book from Rich's Book Shop. She agrees to pay the $22.00 cover price upon delivery. Rich "assigns the contract" to Ed's Book Store. In the absence of a contrary intention, Ed has both been assigned the right to collect the $22 from Louise, and has been delegated the obligation to deliver the book to Louise as well.

6. **Oral Assignments Are Effective Unless the Subject Matter of the Assignment Is Within the Statute of Frauds. [§ 27–38]**

   Oral assignments are usually effective. An oral assignment is **not** effective only when the subject matter of the assignment itself is within the statute of frauds [Restatement 2d § 324, Cmt. b]. As a practical matter, a writing requirement typically becomes an issue only when the subject matter of the assignment is a right to receive an interest in land, the original transfer of which had to be in writing under the statute of frauds [§ 10–6].

   Recall that failure to satisfy the statute of frauds only makes a contract **voidable**, not void. That is, the only effect of the Statute is to deny one party to a contract the right to enforce it against the non-signing party. In the case of an assignment, it means that if the Statute applies and is not satisfied, the assignee may not enforce the assignment against the obligor. However, if the obligor wishes to go ahead with the transaction or otherwise fails to raise the Statute as a defense, the failure to satisfy the Statute does not render the transaction void.

   a. **Example. [§ 27–39]**

      Karen contracts to buy Selina's house for $100,000. Loye really wants the house and offers Karen $10,000 to assign her rights under the Selina/Karen contract to Loye and to let Loye buy the house for $100,000 from Selina.

CHAPTER 27

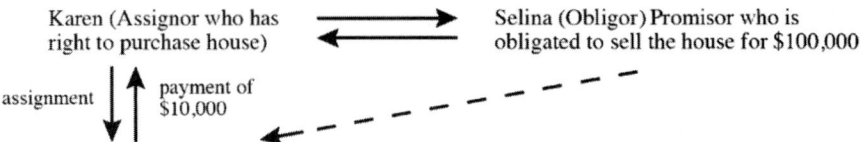

Karen accepts Loye's offer, but assume the assignment is oral. The effect of the oral assignment is to render the assignment unenforceable by Loye, the assignee. That is, Selina has a defense if Loye sues her for not transferring title to the house upon Loye's tender of $100,000 because the oral assignee of an obligation subject to the statute of frauds cannot enforce an orally transferred contract right. Only Karen (the assignor) has the enforceable right to buy the house for $100,000.

F. RIGHTS OF THE ASSIGNEE, AND DUTIES OF THE OBLIGOR, AFTER VALID ASSIGNMENT. [§ 27–40]

One of the principal effects of a valid assignment is that once the assignment occurs, the obligor no longer owes a duty to the assignor, and now owes the duty to render the promised performance to the assignee. That is, the assignee is deemed to have "stepped into the assignor's shoes" upon an assignment. After the assignment, it is the assignee, **and only the assignee**, who can enforce the obligor's duty to render the assigned performance. That also means that once the obligor receives notice of the assignment, the obligor can no longer discharge his or her duties by rendering performance to the assignor, and must render that performance to the assignee.

As mentioned earlier [§ 27–28], occasionally a situation arises whereby the obligor learns of the assignment only after he or she has rendered performance to the assignor. Because it would be unfair to the obligor to make him or her perform twice, contract law provides that if he or she does not have notice of the assignment, performance to the assignor will discharge his or her duty [Restatement 2d § 338].

1. Example. [§ 27–41]

Fred purchases a stereo on credit from Leroy's Stereo Shop ("Leroy's"). Under the terms of the credit sale, Fred must make monthly payments of $100 to Leroy's on the 1st of every month for a year, starting October 1. On September 28, Leroy's assigns the right to receive Fred's payments over the next year to Finance Co. Finance Co. immediately mails notice of the assignment to Fred.

ASSIGNMENTS

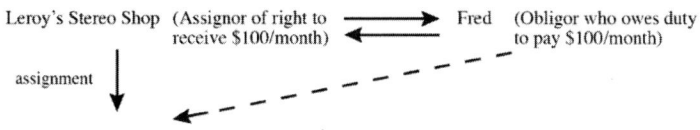

If Fred mailed the first $100 payment to Leroy's before he received notice of the assignment, his duty to make that month's payment has been discharged by performance, and Finance Co.'s only recourse is to get the $100 from Leroy's. However, if Fred had received notice of the assignment and nevertheless went ahead and paid Leroy's, thinking he was "safe" to pay the company that sold him the stereo rather than obey the dictates of some letter which told him to make his payment elsewhere, **he still is obligated to make a $100 payment to Finance Co**. If he does not make it, Finance Co. is entitled to sue Fred to recover the $100 payment. In other words, good faith does not discharge the obligor's mistaken performance to the assignee after the obligor has actual notice of the assignment. (Of course, in the case described above, Fred is entitled to sue Leroy's in restitution for return of the $100 mistakenly paid to Leroy's).

G. CLAIMS AND DEFENSES THE OBLIGOR CAN ASSERT AGAINST ASSIGNEE. [§ 27–42]

As noted earlier, upon a valid assignment, the rights of the assignor are simply transferred to the assignee. As contract law puts it, "the assignee *stands in the shoes* of the assignor." Hence, any defenses or other claims arising out of the assignor/obligor contract that could be asserted by the obligor against the assignor had there been no assignment can be asserted by the obligor in a suit brought by the assignee after an assignment has been made [Restatement 2d § 336(1)].

This sounds more complicated than it really is. What it means is that the assignment does not deprive the obligor of any defense or claim he would have had without the assignment. Hence, if an obligor could have asserted a Statute of Frauds, duress, undue influence, lack of consideration, fraud, or other defense had there been no assignment and the assignor had sued him or her, those same defenses are equally available after the assignment in a suit brought by the assignee. Further, this rule holds true regardless whether either the assignor or the assignee was aware of any such defenses at the time of the assignment [*See* § 27–44 for an important exception to this rule].

1. **Example. [§ 27–43]**

    Sara purchased a used refrigerator on credit from Ted on January 25. Ted told her the appliance was "in perfect shape" and that he had "no problems with it whatsoever." As part of the purchase transaction, Sara signed a contract calling for 10 monthly payments of $40, the first of which was due on March 1. On February 1, Ted assigned to Peter the right to collect Sara's payments under the contract. Peter promptly gave notice to Sara of the assignment, which was received by Sara before she made her first payment.

The refrigerator was delivered to Sara on January 31 and it did not operate. Sara later found out that Ted had lied to her, and that he knew the refrigerator was inoperative at the time of the sale. Not surprisingly, Sara refused to make any of the payments for the inoperative refrigerator. When her payments under the contract were not forthcoming, Peter brought suit against Sara.

There has been an assignment. **Ted is the assignor** (assigning a right to payment to a third person); **Sara is the obligor** (she initially owed a duty to pay Ted $40/month and, after the assignment, owed that same duty to Peter); and **Peter is the assignee** (for after the assignment he is owed payment of $40/month by Sara, the obligor).

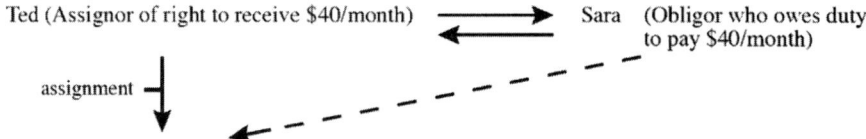

If Peter sues Sara because she refuses to pay for an inoperative refrigerator, the question is whether Sara is entitled to assert her misrepresentation defense in a suit brought by Peter, when after all it was *Ted*, not Peter, who actually made the misrepresentations. That is, can an obligor assert a defense in a suit by the assignee that she would have had if the suit had been brought by the assignor? The answer is **YES**.

The assignee (Peter) "stands in the shoes" of the assignor (Ted), and any defense that would have been assertable against Ted without the assignment is fully assertable against Peter after the assignment. Note that this is true even if Peter was absolutely unaware of the misrepresentations when the assignment was made, and in all other respects acted in good faith, including, possibly, having paid Ted for the right to receive the $40 monthly payments.

2. **"Holder in Due Course" Exception. [§ 27–44]**

In some ways it is unfair that an assignee, like Peter in the hypothetical immediately above, is subject to defenses he did not know about when he agreed to the assignment. After all, he was an innocent party as well. Thus, contract law has developed a limited exception to the general rule that assignees are subject to defenses that could be asserted against assignors called the "holder in due course" exception.

ASSIGNMENTS

a. **Definition of "Holder in Due Course." [§ 27–45]**

A "holder in due course" is a special kind of assignee for value. An assignee is a "holder in due course" when he or she has purchased the right to receive payments under a "negotiable instrument." In a Contracts course, the "negotiable instrument" involved is almost always a promissory note (a written contract whereby a buyer of a good or a service promises to make periodic payments), but another type of negotiable instrument is an ordinary check.

Hence a "holder in due course" situation arises when Buyer purchases a good (or service), like a refrigerator, from Seller and promises to pay for it by making monthly payments via a promissory note. Then Seller assigns for value the right to receive the monthly payments under the promissory note to a bank or other financial institution. The bank thus purchases the right to receive payments under a promissory note, i.e., it becomes a "holder" (of the Note).

The "due course" portion of the "holder in due course" definition requires that when the holder purchases the right to receive payment under the promissory note, the purchase be:

(i) Of a promissory note that does not bear objective evidence of forgery, alteration, irregularity, or incompleteness so as to call its authenticity into question;

(ii) Made in good faith by the holder;

(iii) Made for value; and

(iv) Made without actual knowledge by the holder of defenses to enforcement of the promissory note such as alteration, forgery, competing claims, etc. [UCC § 3–302(a)].

In essence, this means that an assignee for value of a negotiable instrument becomes a holder in due course of the promissory note so long as he, she, or it acts in good faith when buying the note, and was unaware of any defenses the obligor might have to defeat a suit brought by the assignor. [*See gen.* UCC § 3–302.]

b. **Effect of "Holder in Due Course" Status. [§ 27–46]**

A "holder in due course" assignee receives substantial benefits over ordinary assignees. Specifically, under UCC §§ 3–302 and 3–305, holders in due course are **not** subject to any defenses that could be asserted by the obligor against the assignee (with the exception of the defenses, such as lack of capacity, set forth in that provision).

CHAPTER 27

(1) **Example. [§ 27–47]**

Joe's Appliance Shop ("Joe's") orders 100 refrigerators from Manufacturer. To finance the purchase, Joe's executes a negotiable promissory note, promising to pay Manufacturer $4,500/month for a year. Manufacturer "negotiates," i.e., assigns for value, its right to receive Joe's payments under the negotiable promissory note to Credit Bank. Credit Bank purchases the note: (i) for value; (ii) in good faith; (iii) without knowledge of any defenses against Manufacturer; and in all other ways becomes a holder in due course.

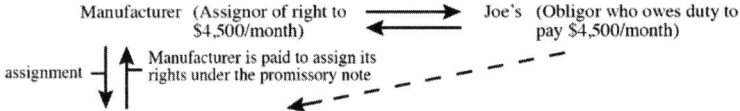

When the refrigerators arrive, they prove defective, and so Joe's refuses to make payments on the note. If Credit Bank brings suit against Joe's for its failure to pay, Credit Bank will win. As a holder in due course, Credit Bank is not subject to any defenses an obligor such as Joe's could assert against Manufacturer. Hence, Joe's (the obligor) must continue to pay Credit Bank (the "holder in due course" assignee) $4,500/month for a year or be in breach for failing to do so. To recoup its losses, Joe's must seek its recovery from Manufacturer (the assignor) for breach of warranty, misrepresentation, etc., but is "on the hook" to the Bank.

Compare this result with the Ted/Sara/Peter refrigerator transaction described in § 27–43. Where an assignee is just an ordinary assignee, as was Peter in the § 27–43 hypothetical, his rights against the obligor are subject to all the defenses that the obligor could assert against the assignee. However, when the assignee is a "holder in due course," the assignee takes free and clear from almost all of the defenses that can be caused by the assignor's conduct.

c. **Limitation on Holder in Due Course Doctrine. [§ 27–48]**

Due to various abuses practiced by assignors and holders in due course in consumer transactions, the FTC passed a regulation in the early 1970's stating that a purchaser of a negotiable instrument could not attain holder in due course status when the obligor was a consumer. Hence, today the holder in due course doctrine is alive and well in **merchant-to-merchant** situations. However, when a consumer is involved, the assignee for value is still subject to any defenses the consumer could assert against the assignor.

H. RIGHTS OF THE ASSIGNEE TO SUE THE ASSIGNOR: THE IMPLIED WARRANTIES INHERENT IN ASSIGNMENTS FOR VALUE. [§ 27–49]

Until this point, most of the focus in this chapter has been on the rights of the assignee to sue the obligor. However, there are occasions in which the assignee would like to bring suit against the **assignor** for interfering with his or her right to receive performance from the obligor. For example, suppose the assignee tries to sue the obligor for non-performance, and then finds out that the obligor has a defense to the action based on the assignor's misrepresentation, undue influence, etc. [§ 27–43]. In such cases, the assignee typically feels entitled to sue the assignor for the actions which resulted in the obligor's defense.

Contract law provides that the assignee can, in fact, sue the assignor in such cases. The theory on which the suit is based is breach of warranty. That is, contract law provides that whenever an assignment for value is made, the assignor impliedly makes certain warranties to the assignee. The Restatement 2d provides that the assignor warrants:

(1) that he or she will do nothing to impair the value of the assignment; and

(2) that the assigned right in fact exists, and is subject to no limitations or defenses other than those either told to the assignee, or those that are reasonably apparent to the assignee, at the time of assignment [Restatement 2d § 333(1)].

Note that Restatement 2d § 333(2) specifically provides that in making an assignment for value an assignor does **not** impliedly warrant that the obligor is solvent, or that the assignee is either willing or able to perform his or her obligations after the assignment is made. Those risks are assumed by the assignee in purchasing the rights of the assignment, and presumably are reflected in the price the assignee is willing to pay for the assignment.

1. **Example. [§ 27–50]**

    Assume again the facts of the hypothetical involving the sale of a refrigerator to Sara by Ted described in § 27–43. When Ted sells his rights to collect payment under the promissory note to Peter, he is impliedly warranting to Peter that he will do nothing in the future to impair the value of the assignment, and that there are no defenses to the assigned payment obligation that can be asserted by Sara. Hence when Sara successfully asserts Ted's misrepresentation as a defense to Peter's suit, there has been a breach of Ted's warranty to Peter

CHAPTER 27

that no such defense exists. As a result, Peter (the assignee) can recover from Ted (the assignor) whatever damages he suffers from the breach of that warranty, i.e., the value of the payments Sara was supposed to have made.

2. **Example. [§ 27–51]**

Hobby Shop sells a 50-inch television to Ken on credit. Ken signs a promissory note to finance the purchase, promising to pay Hobby Shop $100/month for 2 years. Hobby Shop assigns for value its right to Ken's payments to First Bank.

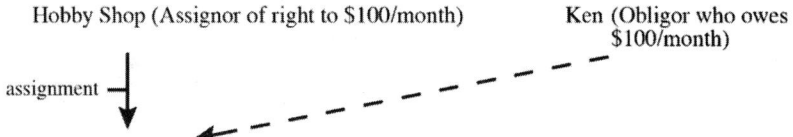

The television works well, but Ken nevertheless refuses to make any payments to First Bank. The Bank's only recourse is to sue Ken. This is because when Hobby Shop assigned the accounts receivable to First Bank, it made no implied warranty as to the solvency, ability, or willingness of Ken (the obligor) to make the payments. The risk of Ken not performing is part of what went into the price the bank was willing to pay Hobby Shop for the assignment, and thus it may only look to Ken for payment.

I. ASSIGNEE'S RIGHTS UPON ATTEMPTED MODIFICATION OF ASSIGNMENT BY THE ASSIGNOR AND THE OBLIGOR. [§ 27–52]

Sometimes after an assignment is made, the obligor and assignor attempt to modify (or even retract) the assignment, to the detriment of the assignee. The rules regarding the rights of the obligor and assignor to make an effective post-assignment modification depend on whether the assignment is gratuitous or is for value, as explained below.

1. **Modification Rules Regarding Assignments for Value. [§ 27–53]**

   Assignors and obligors have **no right to modify the assignment after an assignment for value** has been effectively made. That is, an assignment for value is *irrevocable* once validly made, and the assignee's rights vest immediately. This makes sense, for an assignment for value arises out of a separate agreement between the assignor and assignee. That agreement should not be alterable by the subsequent conduct of the assignor and obligor.

ASSIGNMENTS

2. Modification Rules Regarding Gratuitous Assignments. [§ 27–54]

The rules as to the rights of the assignor and obligor to modify a gratuitous assignment are different from, and more complex than, the rule regarding such modification rights under an assignment for value. **The general rule is that gratuitous assignments are fully revocable and modifiable.** Under § 332(1) of the Restatement 2d, a gratuitous assignment is **not** modifiable, i.e., it becomes irrevocable, **only** when:

(1) the assignment is **in writing and is signed by the assignor**;

(2) the assignment **is accompanied by delivery of a customary symbol** or so-called "token chose." For example, when a party wishes to assign the rights to recover for a winning lottery ticket, delivery of the ticket to the assignee will make the gratuitous assignment irrevocable because the ticket is a customary "symbol" or "token chose" of the right to collect, and thus evidence the assignment was made;

(3) **the assignee has relied on the assignment**; or

(4) **the assignee has received performance by the obligor of the assigned duty**. That is, once the obligor has rendered performance to the assignee, the assignor and obligor cannot go back and rescind or otherwise modify the assignee's rights in the hopes of making the assignee pay back the value of what he or she has already received.

J. RIGHTS OF THE ASSIGNEE AMONG COMPETING CLAIMS OF OWNERSHIP. [§ 27–55]

While the number and complexity of issues potentially falling under this section heading are enormous, generally Contracts courses typically focus on only one aspect of the potential problems. That is, what happens when a single assignor attempts to assign the **same** right to **two or more** different assignees? The question is which of the assignees has priority over the others. Contract law has developed four different approaches to this issue, each of which is discussed below.

1. The "New York" Rule: The First Assignee Always Has Priority. [§ 27–56]

Under the so-called "New York" rule, the first assignee automatically has priority over all later assignees. Sometimes this rule is also known as "the rule of latent equities," for in equity "first in time is first in right."

CHAPTER 27

a. **Example. [§ 27–57]**

Jerome owes Leslie $1,000 under a contract. The money is due to be paid on October 15. On September 1, Leslie makes an assignment for value of the right to collect the $1,000 to John. John does not notify Jerome of the assignment. On September 30, Leslie again makes an assignment for value of the same right to collect Jerome's payment of $1,000, this time to Karen. Karen immediately notifies Jerome of the assignment and Jerome pays Karen the $1,000 on October 15.

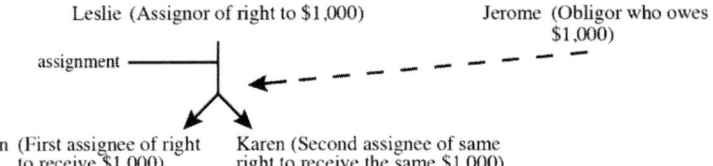

Under the New York rule, John's claim to the payment has priority over Karen's, for he was the first assignee of the right. Hence, if Jerome pays Karen, Karen will be deemed to have received the money "in trust" for John, even though she neither heard of John nor knew of the first assignment to him. As a result, John is entitled to sue Karen for the $1,000 since she is holding the money "in [constructive] trust" for him, and Karen's relief, if any, will have to come from Leslie.

2. **The "English Rule": The First Assignee to Notify the Obligor Has Priority. [§ 27–58]**

Under the so-called "English Rule," the determinative factor as to which of two competing assignees has priority is which assignee first gave notice of the assignment to the obligor. This rule has the advantage of encouraging prompt obligor notification.

a. **Example. [§ 27–59]**

Using the Jerome/Leslie hypothetical set forth in § 27–57, under the "English Rule" Karen would prevail, for she was the first to *notify* Jerome of the assignment. Hence, it would be John, not Karen, who would have to sue Leslie in a jurisdiction adopting this view.

3. **The Massachusetts/Restatement 2d Rule: The First Assignee Generally Prevails, Subject to Four Exceptions. [§ 27–60]**

Under the so-called "Massachusetts Rule," which has been adopted by the Restatement 2d in § 342, the first assignee prevails, unless a later assignee can establish one of four exceptions:

ASSIGNMENTS

(1) that the later assignee has already received satisfaction of the obligation from the obligor;

(2) that the later assignee has already obtained a judgment against the obligor resulting from the obligor's failure to perform;

(3) that the later assignee has already entered into a novation with the obligor [*see* §§ 24–5 *et seq.* for a discussion of novation]; or

(4) that the later assignee obtained possession of a symbolic writing from the obligor.

a. Example. [§ 27–61]

In the Jerome/Leslie hypothetical set forth in § 27–57 Karen would also prevail under the Massachusetts/Restatement 2d view. This time Karen would prevail because she actually received satisfaction of the obligation from Jerome before John brought suit. Thus, she would have a greater entitlement to the payment than would John, and John would again have to sue Leslie for breach of the implied warranty in making the assignment.

4. Article 9 of the UCC Rule: First to File or Perfect Gets Priority. [§ 27–62]

Article 9 of the UCC sets forth very specialized and elaborate rules regarding the function and priorities of "security interests." A security interest is an interest, akin to a lien, in personal property or fixtures, which acts as collateral to secure a payment or some other performance obligation [UCC § 1–201(35)].

While this puts it too simply, a security interest is an intangible ownership interest that the lender has in the collateral which secures a loan. For example, Jerry buys a new car with the proceeds of a car loan from a bank. Jerry gets to keep the car and drive it, and he has an ownership interest in it. However, so does the bank. The bank has a kind of lien or "security interest" in the car which serves as collateral for the loan.

One effect of the security interest is that if Jerry defaults on the loan, the bank may foreclose on its security interest and repossess the car. That is, rather than just suing Jerry for breach of contract and waiting for its money until the case comes to trial, the bank can repossess the car after default, sell it, and get its money back relatively quickly. That's why a secured loan, i.e., a loan with collateral, is usually favored by lenders, and banks secure their interest in the collateral by means of a written "security interest" governed by Article 9 of the UCC.

Under Article 9, a secured creditor can "perfect" his, her, or its security interest in personal property by, among other things, filing a "financing statement" with the appropriate governmental body, usually the Secretary of State's office for a particular state. Once filed, the financing statement gives any other interested party notice that the bank has a prior security interest in the car. Accordingly, anyone else who may wish to lend money to Jerry and use the car as collateral can determine whether an assignment of a security interest has already been made by checking with the Secretary of State [UCC §§ 9–302 *et seq.*]. Under the Code, the first assignee to file the financing statement or otherwise perfect the security interest usually has priority over any other assignees of that property [UCC § 9–322].

K. EXAM APPROACHES TO ASSIGNMENT ISSUES. [§ 27–63]

As with third party beneficiary contracts, the first, and possibly most important, step in analyzing an assignment problem is to identify the parties and know who the assignor, obligor, and the assignee are.

Next, make sure a valid assignment has taken place. That is, make sure there has been a present intention to transfer an *existing* contractual right [§ 27–11], that there is no prohibition against the assignment [§§ 27–15 *et seq.*], and that the assignee has accepted the assignment if that is necessary [§ 27–22]. Keep in mind also the other issues that arise when judging the legal effectiveness of an assignment [§§ 27–27 *et seq.*].

If an effective assignment has taken place, only four frequently tested issues remain:

1. Whether the assignor and obligor can modify the contract to the disadvantage of the assignee [§§ 27–52 *et seq.*];

2. Whether the assignee is justified in suing the non-performing obligor for breach, including an analysis of what defenses the obligor can assert in such litigation [§§ 27–40; 27–42];

3. Whether the assignee is justified in suing the assignor, and what defenses the assignor can assert in such litigation [§ 27–49]; and

4. Who is entitled to the contract right after multiple assignments of the same right by the same assignor [§§ 27–53 *et seq.*]?

Make sure you find out which issue or issues are involved in your problem and then use the facts you are given to support a reasonable conclusion based on the applicable legal standard.

CHAPTER 28

DELEGATION

A. DELEGATION GENERALLY. [§ 28–1*]

Just as a party may transfer the right to receive benefits under a contract via an assignment, a party may also transfer the obligation to perform a **duty** called for in a contract. When a party effectively **transfers a contractual obligation of performance** to a third party, it is known as a **delegation**. The terminology, mechanics, and effect of delegation are discussed in the remainder of this chapter.

B. TERMINOLOGY OF DELEGATION. [§ 28–2]

A delegation is the transfer of a contractual duty of performance to a third party [Restatement 2d § 318].

There are typically three parties involved in a delegation:

(1) The **Delegating Party**. The delegating party (sometimes known as the "obligor" or even the "delegator") is the party who transfers the duty of performance under a contract to a third party. That is, the delegating party is already a party to a contract before the delegation occurs and is under an obligation to undertake executory duties in that contract. By means of the delegation, the delegating party transfers to someone else the obligation to perform some or all of those duties.

(2) The **Obligee**. The obligee is the party who is in a contract with the delegating party before the delegation occurs, and who is owed performance of the duty the delegating party is trying to transfer. Hence, it is the obligee who, before the delegation, was expecting performance by the delegating party, and who, after the delegation, must allow a third party to perform that duty.

(3) The **Delegate**. The delegate is not a party to the original delegating party/obligee agreement. The delegate is the party to whom the delegating party transfers the obligation to perform a duty owed the obligee.

---

* For more information, listen to CD # 14, Track 1 of *Sum and Substance Audio on Contracts*.

Graphically, the parties can be depicted as follows:

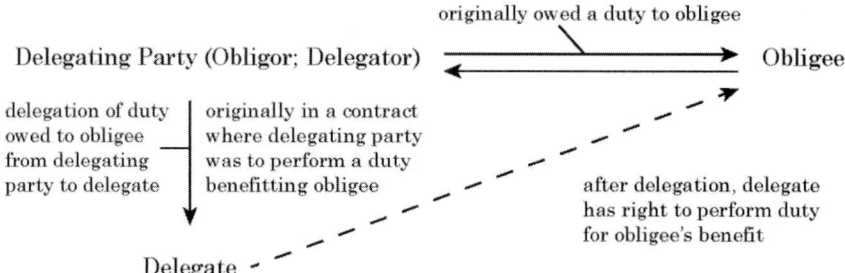

1. Example. [§ 28–3]

Sam entered into a contract with Bill's Ticket Agency for a front row ticket to a rock concert. Bill's then enters into an agreement with Lorraine's Hot Tix, transferring to Lorraine's the obligation to procure Sam's ticket. A delegation has occurred. **Bill's is the delegating party**, for it owed a contractual obligation to Sam and is now trying to transfer that obligation to another. **Sam is the obligee**, for the delegating party (Bill's) originally owed him a duty and, as a result of the delegation, Sam must now allow a third party to perform that duty. **Lorraine's is the delegate**, for it is to Lorraine's that the delegating party (Bill's) is transferring a contractual obligation.

Graphically, this would be:

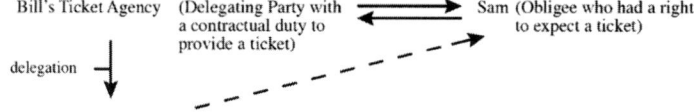

C. ELEMENTS OF AN EFFECTIVE DELEGATION. [§ 28–4]

There are only two requirements to establish an effective delegation:

(1) The delegating party must manifest an intention to delegate [§ 28–5]; and

(2) The delegation must be "permissible," i.e., there must be no prohibition against the delegation of that particular duty [§ 28–8].

Note that there is no requirement that the delegate "accept" the delegation. While initially this is surprising, it is nevertheless true that the delegate need not even know of the delegation for it to be effective. However, this is not unfair to the delegate because, as discussed later, if

DELEGATION

the delegate does not objectively and specifically "assume" the delegated duty, he or she is not liable to anyone for its non-performance [§ 28–25].

1. **The Delegating Party Must Manifest an Intention to Delegate a Duty. [§ 28–5]**

   In order to make an effective delegation, the delegating party must manifest an intention to transfer the obligation to perform a duty under an existing contract to a third party. No particular language is necessary to establish such an intention, and in close cases courts are directed to examine a party's intent from all surrounding circumstances.

   a. **Construction of a Clause "Assigning the Contract." [§ 28–6]**

   Contract law has established that, absent evidence of a contrary intention by the parties, when a party "**assigns the contract**," or "**assigns all my rights under the contract**", such a transfer acts as both an assignment of rights **and** a delegation of any executory duties owed under the contract [Restatement 2d § 328; UCC § 2–210(4); § 27–36].

   (1) **Example. [§ 28–7]**

   Jim has a contract with Vergie, a travel agent, to secure him tickets for a cruise at a price of $1,500. Vergie, thereafter, "assigns the contract" to another travel agency. Absent evidence of a contrary intention, Vergie's act both delegates the duty to provide Jim with a ticket on the cruise for $1,500, and assigns the right to receive Jim's $1,500 payment, to the other travel agency.

2. **There Must Be No Prohibition Against Delegation of This Particular Duty. [§ 28–8]**

   The second requirement for an effective delegation is that there be no prohibition against the delegation of that particular duty. The rules governing when a particular duty is delegable are as follows:

   Generally, duties in a contract are freely delegable. They are NOT delegable <u>only</u> when:

   (1) Delegation of that particular duty **violates public policy** [Restatement 2d § 318(1); § 28–9];

   (2) The obligee has a **substantial interest in having the original obligor perform the duty** [Restatement 2d § 318(2); § 28–10]; or

   (3) There is an **enforceable "no delegation" clause** in the original delegating party/obligee contract [Restatement 2d § 318(3); § 28–16].

529

Each of these limitations is discussed and illustrated below.

a. A Purported Delegation That Violates Public Policy Is Ineffective. [§ 28–9]

Courts and legislatures are empowered to nullify purported delegations that violate public policy [Restatement 2d § 318(1)]. While courts and legislatures do, in fact, use their power to nullify purported **assignments** on public policy grounds on a regular basis [§ 28–16], there are relatively few cases where a **delegation** has been voided on such grounds.

In those few cases where a court has exercised this power, it has typically nullified a municipality's attempt to delegate performance of a municipal service to a private company, e.g., where a city delegates the running a jail to a private company. There are only a handful of such cases, and both the courts and the commentators direct that the public policy nullification doctrine is valid and can serve to void a particular delegation.

b. A Purported Delegation of a Duty in Which the Obligee Has a "Substantial Interest" in Having the Delegating Party Perform the Duty Is Ineffective. [§ 28–10]

Common sense dictates that not all duties can be delegated. If, for example, a movie producer agrees to pay 'The Rock' several million dollars to star in a movie, 'The Rock' cannot delegate the duty to appear in the film to Meryl Streep. The reason is because performance of such a duty is too personal to be delegated effectively. The test for when a duty is "too personal" is nearly identical in both the UCC and the Restatement 2d:

A duty may not be delegated if the obligee has a "substantial interest" in having a particular person perform the promised acts [Restatement 2d § 318(2); UCC § 2–210(1)].

This test is intentionally flexible so as to give the courts discretion in applying it, but the courts have established the following as general criteria:

> (1) The *more* the performance depends on the **particular skills, character, training, taste, discretion, etc., of the delegating party**, the *less likely* the duty may be validly transferred. On the other hand, the more the performance is ministerial, calling for little discretion by the delegating party, the more likely it is such a delegation will be upheld; and

DELEGATION

(2) In certain contracts, the more the **delegating party retains control over the delegate**, the more likely it is that the delegation will be upheld.

Of course, if the obligee agrees to the delegation of the duty, even a "personal one," the obligor is entitled to do so. Hence, this rule does not prohibit an obligee from accepting a delegate's performance. Rather it only protects the obligee from being **forced** to accept a substitute performance of a personal duty when the obligee does not wish to do so.

(1) Example. [§ 28–11]

Law School hires Bob to teach Contracts during the next academic year. Bob cannot delegate his duties, no matter how competent the delegate may be, for the school has a "substantial interest" in seeing to it that Bob will perform [Restatement 2d § 318, Cmt. c, Ill. 5].

(2) Example. [§ 28–12]

Steve owes Jamie $100. He delegates his duty to repay the money to Ron, who tenders the $100 to Jamie. As there is no discretion or skill involved in the duty to repay money, the delegation is valid. Thus, if Jamie does not accept Ron's payment to discharge Steve's debt, she will thereafter be precluded from suing either Ron or Steve for non-payment [Restatement 2d § 318, Cmt. a, Ill. 1].

(3) Example. [§ 28–13]

Peri hires Ann, a sole practitioner, to be her attorney and Ann promises to do all legal-related work for Peri personally. Ann subsequently hires John, a paralegal. Some of the work Ann is doing for Peri is of a type that can be handled by a paralegal under professional standards. So long as Ann (the delegating party) retains **sufficient control** over John's (the delegate's) performance of such duties, she may validly delegate them to John.

(4) Example of *Sally Beauty Co. v. Nexxus Products Co., Inc.* [§ 28–14]

Best Barber & Beauty Supply Co. ("Best") entered into a contract with Nexxus to be the exclusive distributer of Nexxus hair care products to barbers throughout Texas. Best was later acquired by Sally Beauty Co., a wholly owned subsidiary of a major competitor of Nexxus. After the merger, Nexxus cancelled the contract, stating that they could not allow their products to be sold by, essentially, a direct competitor. Sally Beauty claimed Nexxus breached the contract by cancelling.

Held: The contract could not be assigned under UCC § 2-210 because the rule bars the delegation of duties if there is some reason why the non-assigning party would find performance by a delegate a substantially different thing than what he had bargained for.

Here, Nexxus had contracted for Best's best efforts in promoting the sale of Nexxus products. Nexxus would not expect a direct competitor to exercise those best efforts. The lower expected effort of Sally versus Best was not what Nexxus bargained for and it was therefore justified in cancelling the contract [*Sally Beauty Co. v. Nexxus Prods. Co., Inc.*, 801 F.2d 1001 (7th Cir. 1986)].

(5) **Example of *Macke Co. v. Pizza of Gaithersburg, Inc.* [§ 28–15]**

A pizza parlor chain ("Pizza") entered into a long term contract with a beverage company ("Virginia") to install and maintain soft drink machines in six of its locations. Approximately one year later, Virginia was purchased by Macke Co. ("Macke") The six contracts between Virginia and Pizza were assigned to Macke, and the duties to maintain the machines were similarly delegated to Macke. Pizza had dealt with Macke in the past, but wasn't happy with service it got from the company. Indeed, it entered into the Virginia contracts, in part, because it felt it got more "personalized service" from Virginia. Pizza therefore attempted to cancel the contracts shortly after the assignments, arguing the contracts were "personal service" contracts. Macke filed suit for breach

Held: The contracts were assignable, and the duties under then delegable, to Macke because the duties under the contract were not dependent on **particular skills, character, training, taste, discretion, etc., of Virginia.** Although Macke may have preferred Virginia, the duty under the contracts was only to maintain soft drink machines, and the duties under that maintenance contract was not of such a personal nature that could not be validly delegated [*Macke Co. v. Pizza of Gaithersburg, Inc.*, 259 Md. 479 (1970)].

Note that an obligee who is worried about being "stuck" with a company it does not want to deal with can always bargain for an anti-delegation clause if it does not wish to continue with a contract if the duties of the obligor are delegated to someone else (*see* § 28–16).

c. A Purported Delegation That Violates a Specific "No Delegation" Clause in a Contract Is Ineffective. [§ 28–16]

As noted earlier, anti-*assignment* clauses are not favored by the courts and, in the last 30 years, anti-*assignment* clauses have been strictly and narrowly construed (*see* § 27–21). However, **anti-*delegation* clauses face no such judicial hostility**. Thus, a "no delegation" clause in the delegating party/obligee contract that is freely bargained for and sufficiently detailed will generally be enforced.

3. The Obligee Need Not Assent to, or Even Be Aware of, the Delegation for It to Be Effective. [§ 28–17]

The obligee originally enters into a contract with the delegating party. He or she looks to the delegating party for performance. Hence, it may be somewhat surprising that, so long as the duty is properly delegable [§ 28–8], a delegation is effective even if the obligee does not know of it, or even if the obligee protests it.

a. Example. [§ 28–18]

Denise has entered into a one-year contract with Grocery Store, whereby she is under a duty to deliver 20 lbs. of Washington Delicious apples per week to the store. The contract calls for the apples to be certified Grade A–1 by the local produce board. Denise wishes to delegate her duties under the contract to Rob, another wholesale produce vendor who buys apples from the same supplier as does Denise, and who thus can supply Grade A–1 Washington Delicious apples to Grocery Store on the same terms as Denise. Accordingly, Denise delegates her delivery duties under the contract to Rob in a procedurally effective manner. Even if the owner of Grocery Store does not like Rob, and tells him she does not wish Rob to make the delivery, Rob has a right to make the deliveries, for a valid delegation can be made without the knowledge of, or even over the objections of, the obligee.

D. PRINCIPAL CONSEQUENCES OF AN EFFECTIVE DELEGATION. [§ 28–19]

Contract law identifies five principal effects of a valid delegation:

(1) The delegate acquires a **right** to perform the delegated duty [§ 28–20];

(2) The duty of the delegating party to render performance to the obligee is **not** discharged upon delegation [§ 28–22];

CHAPTER 28

(3) Performance by the delegate of the transferred duty **discharges** the duty the delegating party owed the obligee [§ 28–23];

(4) The delegate generally acquires no **duty** to perform the delegated tasks. He or she obtains an enforceable obligation to perform those delegated duties **only if** the delegate manifests **an express assumption** to undertake them [§ 28–25]; and

(5) If the delegation occurs as a result of a contract between the delegating party and the delegate (as is typically the case), the right of the delegating party to sue the delegate upon non-performance is the same as the right of the promisee to sue the promisor for non-performance under a third party beneficiary contract [§ 28–28].

1. **Upon a Valid Delegation, the Delegate Acquires *a Right* to Perform the Delegated Duty. [§ 28–20]**

   Once a delegation becomes effective, the obligee **must** allow the delegate to perform the duty or else either be in breach for not allowing such performance or be declared as having forfeited the right to sue anyone for non-performance of the duty. In some ways this rule may seem unfair since the obligee originally entered into a contract with the delegating party, not the delegate, and probably looks to the delegating party for performance. Nevertheless, if the duty is one that can be delegated, and if the delegation is done effectively, the delegate thereafter has a right to perform it.

   a. **Example. [§ 28–21]**

      Neil owes Mary $1,500 under a contract. Neil is strapped for cash, so he enters into an agreement with Letticia whereby Letticia is delegated the duty to pay Mary $1,500 in return for Neil's collection of political memorabilia. A delegation has occurred. **Neil is the delegating party**, for he is transferring the obligation to perform a contractual duty to another. **Mary is the obligee**, for she was owed performance of a duty by Neil, and as a result of the delegation, Mary must now allow another to perform the payment obligation. **Letticia is the delegate**, because Neil's contractual obligation has been transferred to her.

      Graphically, the parties would be represented:

      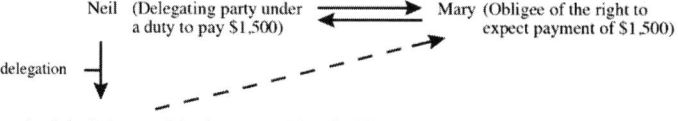

      As a consequence of the delegation, if Letticia timely tenders $1,500 to Mary, Mary must accept it or she forfeits her rights to

DELEGATION

sue either Neil or Letticia for non-performance. That is, since the obligation to pay money is a type of duty that can be delegated [§ 28–10], and since the delegation is otherwise effective, Mary may not insist on Neil making the payment, and must allow Letticia to do so if she timely performs [§ 28–26].

2. **Delegation Does Not Discharge the Duty of the Delegating Party to Render Performance to the Obligee. [§ 28–22]**

If the delegate does not perform the transferred duty after an effective delegation has taken place, the obligee still retains the right to sue the delegating party for breach [Restatement 2d § 318(3); UCC § 2–210(1)]. That is, a delegation carries with it no implied release of the delegating party's obligations. Hence, after a delegation, the delegating party is still "on the hook," and liable to the obligee in the event of the delegate's non-performance.

Note that this rule is somewhat different from the rule governing assignments. Recall that upon an effective assignment, the assignor immediately loses his or her right to receive performance under the contract [§§ 27–2 et seq.]. In other words, once the assignment is made the assignor is "out of the picture." However, upon a delegation the delegating party is still "in the picture," i.e., is still liable for his or her promised performance. [See § 28–26 for an example illustrating this rule].

3. **Full Performance by the Delegate Discharges the Duty Owed by the Delegating Party. [§ 28–23]**

As mentioned above, upon an effective delegation the delegate acquires the **right** to perform the transferred duty [§ 28–20]. If the delegate exercises that right, and tenders complete performance to the obligee, the corresponding duties owed by the delegating party to the obligee are discharged. In other words, even though one person (the delegate) renders performance, it discharges another person's (the delegating party's) duty.

a. **Example. [§ 28–24]**

As the author of this book, I hereby delegate to any and all readers the duty to make next month's payment on my Visa card.

Believe it or not, that is an effective delegation, and I have successfully delegated to you, as a reader, the obligation to make the payment. However, all that means is that if you tender the money to Visa on my behalf (admittedly a dubious proposition), Visa must accept it from you or it forfeits the right to go after me for the amount you offered. It does not mean that Visa can sue you for failing to make the payment or not look to me to pay the bill. Those consequences would only happen if you **specifically** "accepted" the delegation, as discussed in the next section. Alas, I am still on the hook for the payment if you (the reader) do not pay. You acquired the **right,** but <u>not</u> the <u>duty</u>, to pay my bill by my delegation.

4. **A Delegate Has an Enforceable Obligation, as Opposed to a Right, to Perform the Transferred Duty Only When He or She Specifically Assumes Such a Duty. [§ 28–25]**

Whether or not a delegate has an **obligation**, as well as a **right**, to perform the delegated duty depends on whether he or she objectively manifests an assumption of the obligation. That is, in a delegation transaction where the delegating party simply delegates a duty and the delegate makes no acknowledgement of any obligations arising from the delegation, the delegate obtains only a right to perform the duty, and not an obligation to do so (*see* § 28–26). This means that if the delegate does not perform the delegated duty **in such a case, the obligee is entitled only to sue the delegating party for breach**.

Note that even when there has been an "assumption" of the duties by the delegate, such action does **not** discharge the duty of the delegating party [§ 28–31; however, for a discussion of when a delegation becomes a novation, in which case the delegating party is released from his or her performance duties].

In a delegation followed by a delegate's specific assumption of the transferred duties, the **obligee is thereafter owed two enforceable duties**: (i) the original one, owed by the delegating party; and (ii) the new one, owed by the delegate. If neither the delegate nor the delegating party perform, the obligee is entitled to sue **either** the delegating party, **or** the delegate, **or both** for breach; but, of course, the obligee is entitled to only one complete satisfaction.

a. Example. [§ 28–26]

Dan writes a letter to Bank notifying it that he is delegating the duty to pay his outstanding Visa bill to the President of the United States. This is an effective delegation. Recall, however (before all the readers of this book try to do the same), that this only delegation means that the Bank must *allow* the President to pay Dan's Visa bill **if the President submits payment**. That is, upon the delegation the President has acquired the **right** to make the payment on Dan's behalf, but NOT the **duty** to do so. Only if the President **specifically assumes the duty to pay Dan's bill,** will the President have the *obligation* to make the payment as well as the right to do so, meaning that the Bank could either sue Dan or the President, or both, if payment was never made.

DELEGATION

b. Example. [§ 28–27]

Gail is contractually owed $1,000 by Ira. Ira enters into a written contract with Dennis wherein Dennis agrees to assume Ira's obligation to pay Gail $1,000 in return for Ira's watch. Ira transfers his watch to Dennis, but Dennis does not pay Gail. Gail is not aware of the delegation until after the payment was due. Gail is nonetheless entitled to sue either Ira, or Dennis, or both. That is, the manifestation by the delegate to assume the transferred duty need **not** be made **to the obligee**. As long as there is an objective manifestation of the delegate's assumption of the obligation made to the delegating party, the delegate thereafter owes an enforceable duty of performance to the obligee. As the terms of the contract between Ira and Dennis make manifest Dennis's assumption of the payment obligation, Gail can sue Dennis for non-payment even though she did not know it at the time the delegation was made.

5. Relationship Between Delegations and Third Party Beneficiary Contracts. [§ 28–28]

This is a bit tricky, but as with assignments [§ 27–33] there must be two separate agreements for a delegation, the original two-party agreement and then a separate delegation of obligation agreement; whereas, there is only one transaction for a third party beneficiary contract.

However, and here is the tricky part, the second agreement in a delegation *can itself be a third party beneficiary contract.* That is, realize that not all delegations occur as a result of a valid contract between the delegating party and the delegate, but delegations for value do so. The delegating party typically gives some sort of consideration to the delegate in order to secure the delegate's promise to perform the transferred duty. Such a contract is a third party beneficiary contract since the delegating party and the delegate have made an agreement, the performance of which will benefit the obligee, i.e., a third person who is not a party to the delegating party/delegate contract. In third party beneficiary terms, the delegating party is the promisee, the delegate is the promisor, and the obligee is the beneficiary.

An issue sometimes arises as to whether the delegating party (as well as the obligee) can sue the delegate if the delegate does not perform. Where the delegating party and the delegate have entered into a third party beneficiary contract as part of the delegation, the delegate may be sued by the delegating party for non-performance in the same manner as the promisor can be sued by the promisee for breach under a third party beneficiary contract [§§ 26–42, 28–30]. However, where the promise of the delegate to assume the delegating party's duties is only a gift promise, the delegating party has no right to sue the delegate upon the delegate's non-performance.

a. **Example. [§ 28–29]**

Lorna is contractually owed $5,000 from Michael. Michael thereafter makes a contract with Chris, promising to sell Chris his car in return for Chris's promise to assume Michael's duty to pay Lorna.

There has been a delegation. **Michael is the delegating party**, for he transferred an obligation under a contract to Chris, a third party. **Lorna is the obligee**, for she was owed a duty by Michael and, after the delegation, a third party acquired the obligation to perform the duty. **Chris is the delegate**, for Michael's duty of payment is being transferred to him.

As a delegation, it would be graphically displayed as:

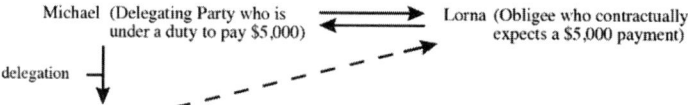

Chris (Delegate of the duty to pay Lorna $5,000, in exchange for Michael's car)

The agreement between Michael and Chris is **also** a third party beneficiary contract. In third party beneficiary language, **Chris is the promisor**, for he has undertaken a contractual promise to perform an act that will benefit a third person. **Michael is the promisee**, for he bargained for Chris's promise. **Lorna is the beneficiary**, for she is not a party to the Chris/Michael contract and will be benefitted by its performance.

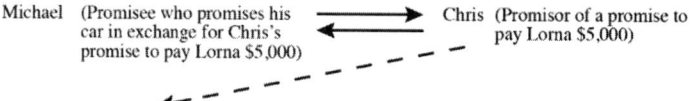

Lorna (Beneficiary of Chris's promise to pay $5,000)

Suppose Chris does not pay Lorna as he promised. The issue here is whether *Michael*, as well as Lorna, can sue Chris for his non-performance.

The answer is **YES**. Michael, as the promisee under a third party beneficiary contract, has the right to sue a breaching promisor for the promisor's breach [§ 26–42]. Of course Chris does not have to pay twice; he is liable for only one complete satisfaction. Nonetheless, both Lorna and Michael have a valid claim against him.

DELEGATION

b. Example. [§ 28–30]

Sam owes Leo $1,000 under a valid contract, the payment of which is due on Wednesday. On Tuesday, Sam calls his rich Aunt Freida and asks whether she will pay Leo for him as a favor. Freida agrees to do so, and Sam immediately calls Leo and tells Leo that Sam's payment obligation has been "delegated" to Aunt Freida. Aunt Freida does not pay the $1,000 on Wednesday.

Leo is certainly entitled to sue Sam, the delegating party, for breach when Aunt Freida does not pay. Leo is also entitled to sue Aunt Freida, the delegate, assuming that what she said in her conversation with Sam was a sufficient objective manifestation of her intention to assume Sam's payment obligation.

However, **Sam** cannot successfully sue Aunt Freida for her failure to pay, because Aunt Freida's promise to Sam was only an unenforceable gift promise. Accordingly, Sam acquired no right to enforce her promise. Thus, since Sam is not a "promisor" with third party beneficiary contractual rights against a "promisee," but merely a delegating party attempting to sue a delegate for non-performance of an unenforceable gift promise, he has no valid claim for breach resulting from Aunt Freida's failure to make the payment.

As a review problem, diagram the Leo/Sam/Aunt Freida hypothetical to see where it differs, and where it's the same, as the Michael/Chris/Lorna hypothetical of § 28–29.

E. DISTINCTION BETWEEN NOVATION AND DELEGATION. [§ 28–31]

A novation occurs when a party who is owed a duty agrees to accept the promised performance of another **in satisfaction of that duty** [§ 24–5]. Hence, a delegation differs from a novation in that an effective delegation does not carry with it a discharge of the delegating party's duties. That is, if all that occurs is a delegation, the delegating party still remains liable to the obligee for non-performance. However, if: (i) the delegate offers to perform the delegating party's duty **in return for the obligee's promise to release the delegating party from having to perform that duty**; and (ii) **the obligee agrees to such a transaction**, then a novation has occurred and the delegating party's duty is discharged.

1. Example. [§ 28–32]

In the Vergie/Jim hypothetical discussed in § 28–7, assume that the new travel agency writes Jim just after the delegation, but this time the letter says, "Vergie has retired and has asked us to look after her accounts. If you are willing to accept our agency as your exclusive travel consultant and to let us provide you with the cruise ticket for $1,500 instead of Vergie, please sign below." If Jim signs, there has now been a novation, not a delegation, and the result of which is that Jim has discharged the obligation Vergie owed him and now is entitled to enforce the promise to provide him with a ticket only against the new travel agency.

F. EXAM APPROACH TO DELEGATION ISSUES. [§ 28–33]

When faced with a delegation issue on an examination:

1. First diagram the problem so that you can tell who is the delegating party, who is the obligee, and who is the delegate [§ 28–2].

2. Next, make sure that there was an effective delegation, i.e., there was an intent to delegate [§ 28–5]; and no prohibition against a delegation [§ 28–8].

3. The third step is to check to see whether the delegate has accepted the delegation, recalling that if he has not, the obligee has no right to sue him or her for the failure of the relevant duty to be carried out [§§ 28–20; 28–25].

4. If there has been an effective delegation, then almost surely the issue turns on the fact that neither the delegating party nor the delegate (if the delegate assumed the delegation) rendered performance to the obligee. Before deciding there was a breach by either the delegate or delegating party, make sure there are no defenses justifying non-performance.

PART VIII

REMEDIES*

INTRODUCTORY NOTE REGARDING REMEDIES FOR BREACH OF CONTRACT:

Contracts professors generally hold one of two views as to where in the course remedies should be studied. Some teach it in the first month or so, on the theory that students need to know what the litigants in breach actions are really fighting about before concepts of formation, defenses, and performance, etc. make sense. Others teach it near the end of the course, on the theory that students cannot fully comprehend the intricacies of remedies until they already have a good understanding of formation, breach, and defenses. In either case, students learn that contracts remedies are categorized into three types: (i) equitable remedies; (ii) money damages; and (iii) restitution. As a consequence, this part of the book is organized as follows:

Chapter Twenty-Nine contains a discussion of the most common forms of **equitable relief**: *specific performance, prohibitory injunctions, and reformation.* It also discusses generally, the rules of equity as to when any form of equitable relief may be granted.

Chapter Thirty discusses the "legal" remedy of **money** damages, which is the most common form of remedy awarded in breach actions under American law. This Chapter focuses on damages for breaches of common law (i.e., non-UCC) contracts, but the basics of monetary recovery under contracts governed by Article 2 are also discussed.

Chapter Thirty-One discusses **restitution**, which provides a remedy when one contracting party unjustly enriches another.

Chapter Thirty-Two discusses the remedies set forth in the **UCC**, for those courses in which the Code is emphasized or for those who otherwise are curious as to UCC remedies.

---

* For more information, listen to CD # 11, Track 3 of *Sum and Substance Audio on Contracts*.

CHAPTER 29

EQUITABLE REMEDIES

A. EQUITABLE RELIEF GENERALLY. [§ 29–1*]

Early common law jurisprudence was administered by two separate court systems—courts of law and courts of equity (the latter emanating from ecclesiastical courts). While the civil procedures governing legal and equitable claims are now "merged" into one set of rules, one vestige of the dual system continues to be different substantive rules for determining when a non-breaching party is entitled to "equitable" relief (injunctions, specific performance and the like), as opposed to "legal" relief (money damages) upon the other party's breach. This Chapter deals with the most significant and frequently-awarded kinds of equitable relief: specific performance, injunctions, and reformation. (Note that equitable remedies in Article 2 contracts are governed by these same general principles. The slight differences in the UCC equity rules, as opposed to common law equity rules, are discussed in Chapter Thirty-Two).

B. TYPES OF EQUITABLE REMEDIES. [§ 29–2]

The three most common types of equitable relief granted for breach of contract claims by American courts are:

(1) **Specific Performance**: where a court orders a party to actually perform the very duty that he or she promised to perform in the contract [§ 29–3];

(2) **Prohibitory Injunctions**: where a court orders a party to refrain from doing something that would interfere with his or her ability to carry out the performance promised under the contract [§ 29–4]; and

(3) **Reformation**: where a court orders a contract to be re-written to reflect the parties' true intentions [see § 29–6].

Each of these are illustrated below and their requirements are discussed further in this Chapter [§§ 29–7 *et seq.*].

---

* For more information, listen to CD # 11, Track 5 of *Sum and Substance Audio on Contracts*.

CHAPTER 29

1. Specific Performance. [§ 29–3]

Specific performance describes an order by the court requiring a party to perform exactly what he or she promised under a contract. For example, in a valid contract, Janet promised to sell her Rembrandt painting to the County Art Museum for $1,500,000. However, on the day she is supposed to deliver it, she calls the Museum and says she has changed her mind and will no longer go through with the deal. The Museum is entitled to seek an order of *specific performance*, requiring Janet to *perform specifically* what she promised to do in the contract, namely to deliver possession of, and title to, the painting to the Museum upon the Museum's tender of $1,500,000 [Restatement 2d § 360, Cmt. b, Ill. 1]. If she disregards the court's specific performance order, the court may enforce it by holding Janet in contempt until she turns over possession of the painting.

Some have characterized **an order of specific performance** as a **"mandatory" injunction**, i.e., a court order requiring or mandating a party to take particular acts. While it is perfectly permissible to speak of the court's order in that way, the term "mandatory injunction" is more likely to be used in a Civil Procedure course, with "specific performance" the term more often referenced in contracts.

Note that in the revised 2003 version of UCC § 2R–716(1) the drafters have added a provision allowing the parties to contract so that the remedy for any breach is specific performance, with the limitation that such a provision cannot apply in consumer contracts or for the payment of money.

2. Prohibitory Injunctions. [§ 29–4]

A prohibitory injunction is a remedy whereby a party is prohibited, under penalty of court contempt, **from doing an act that would prevent performance under a contract.**

a. Example of *Lumley v. Wagner*. [§ 29–5]

Ms. Wagner, an opera singer, signed a contract agreeing to sing exclusively in Mr. Lumley's show for a three-month period. Lumley was the producer of an opera company in London. However, Mr. Gye, the producer of a competing London company, induced Ms. Wagner to sign a contract promising to sing at his theatre instead during this three-month "exclusivity" period.

Held: Mr. Lumley was entitled to obtain an *injunction prohibiting* Ms. Wagner from appearing at any other concert during the three months she had agreed to sing with Mr. Lumley's company [*Lumley v. Wagner*, 1 Deg. M. & G. 604, 42 Eng. Rep. 687 (Ch. 1852)].

An order for specific performance requiring Ms. Wagner to sing in Mr. Lumley's show would not be issued, as such orders are not given to enforce a personal service contracts [§ 29–27] on the theory that a court does not want to force parties to work together if one or both of them no longer want to. However, a court will grant the equitable remedy of a prohibitory injunction **preventing** her from singing at Mr. Gye's theatre or from undertaking any other employment that would **interfere with her ability to perform** under the original personal service contract with Mr. Lumley.

The effect of such a prohibitory injunction is to give her an "economic nudge" to perform under her original deal, since she cannot sing anywhere else during the relevant time period. But, if things have gotten sideways between Ms. Wagner and Mr. Lumley, a court will not force her to return to Mr. Lumley's employ.

As with specific performance, courts are entitled to enforce such injunctions through their contempt powers.

3. **Reformation. [§ 29–6]**

Reformation occurs when a court orders a contract to be re-written to reflect the true bargain of the parties. A party seeking reformation must establish that:

  (a) The parties had a deal that is not accurately transcribed in a contract or other operative writing; and

  (b) The mistranscription was the result of:

  (i) A clerical error, or

  (ii) Fraud on the part of the other party.

C. REQUIREMENTS FOR OBTAINING EQUITABLE RELIEF FOR BREACH OF CONTRACT. [§ 29–7]

As contract law developed, common law judges were faced with the decision of whether to award equitable relief as the normal remedy for contractual breach (making the recovery of money damages the exception), or whether to award money damages as the norm (making specific performance and injunctive relief the unusual remedy).

Scholars tend to agree that the most moral approach would have been to decide on equitable relief as the typical remedy, for it would ordinarily force a party to live up to his or her promises and actually perform what he or she said she would do. However, that approach also has significant costs for the legal system. If a court orders that some task be performed, a court must engage in some supervision of the task, not only to ensure it is done, but also that it is done acceptably well, or else its orders will

CHAPTER 29

become meaningless. If the work is not done acceptable, the court will have to hold contempt hearings, which is a further drain on its time. Due to this administrative burden, and other reasons discussed in this Chapter, contract law opted for money damages to be the typical remedy for a breach [Chapter Thirty]. Hence, it is the **extraordinary** case in which equitable relief is granted.

As a consequence, the elements a non-breaching party must meet in order to obtain an order for equitable relief are fairly stringent. To obtain an order for equitable relief, the non-breaching party must establish:

(1) An award of **money damages** is **"inadequate"** to give the innocent party the benefit of his or her bargain [Restatement 2d § 359; § 29–8];

(2) There are **no undue "practical limitations"** on a court's ability to grant equitable relief [Restatement 2d §§ 362, 366, and 367; § 29–20]; and

(3) An award of equitable relief will **not itself be unfair** by violating one of the "equitable principles" governing the grant of equitable relief [Restatement 2d §§ 364, 365; § 29–32].

1. **Equitable Relief Will Not Be Awarded Unless an Award of Damages Would Be "Inadequate" to Put the Non-Breaching Party in the Position He or She Would Have Been in Had the Contract Been Performed. [§ 29–8]**

As noted above [§ 29–7], American contract law provides that an award of money damages is the presumptive remedy granted in breach of contract cases. Hence, the <u>first</u> requirement a non-breaching party **seeking equitable relief must establish is: an award of damages would somehow be "inadequate" to compensate him, her or it fully**. In contract law, a non-breaching party is considered fully compensated when a remedy awarded by a court puts the party in the position he or she would have been in had the contract been performed [UCC § 1–305; Restatement 2d § 347, Cmt. A; § 30–4]. If an award of money damages can possibly fulfill that goal, contract law dictates that money damages should be awarded. However, when money damages are "inadequate" to meet this goal, equitable relief may be appropriate.

The Restatement 2d sets forth three factors a court must weigh in determining whether money damages are adequate to give the non-breaching party the benefit of the contract, i.e., to put the non-breaching party in the position he or she would have been in had the contract been performed:

(1) **The difficulty in proving damages with reasonable certainty**;

EQUITABLE REMEDIES

(2) **The difficulty of procuring a suitable substitute performance upon an award of monetary damages**; and

(3) **The likelihood that an award of damages could not be collected** [Restatement 2d § 360].

a. **The Difficulty of Proving Damages with Reasonable Certainty. [§ 29–9]**

Sometimes it is reasonably easy to establish a breach, but very difficult to establish with any kind of certainty what damages will flow from that breach, e.g., the breach has prevented a new business from starting and no one can predict with certainty how much money the new business owner would have realized; or where the breach is a repudiation of a future performance, where the value of the performance in the future is likely subject to a number of variables; or where the breach is a requirement or output contract where precise quantity levels are unknown before performance has actually taken place. In these kinds of situations, there is simply no accurate way to come up with an amount of money damages that would put the non-breaching party in the same position as he or she would have been in had the contract been performed. *Any* amount would be too speculative. Accordingly, contract law deems money damages "inadequate" to appropriately compensate the non-breaching party in these types of cases, thereby fulfilling the first requirement for awarding equitable relief [Restatement 2d § 360(1)].

(1) **Example of *Laclede Gas Co. v. Amoco Oil Co.* [§ 29–10]**

Laclede's predecessor entered into a long-term requirements contract with Amoco, whereby Amoco was to provide the former company, and now Laclede, with Laclede's need for propane. After operating under the agreement for some time, Amoco stated that it would be making no further deliveries. Laclede brought suit, seeking an order for specific performance compelling Amoco to continue supplying its requirements of propane. Amoco defended by noting propane gas was plentiful from other suppliers in the area, and so even if Amoco were found to be in breach, Laclede could purchase gas from another supplier and sue Amoco for the difference in price, if any. By suing for any difference in price, Amoco argued that Laclede would get gas for exactly the price it had a right to expect—the price for propane called out in the Amoco contract. Hence, it claimed damages were adequate to put Laclede in exactly the position it would have been in had the contract been performed.

Held: Laclede was entitled to an order of specific performance. The court held that specific performance was proper for three reasons. **First**, because there is difficulty in proving with reasonable certainty the damages that would flow from the breach. That is, while an award of money damages would probably be an adequate remedy if the contract called for a one-time, fixed amount delivery of propane, such was not the case under the Amoco/Laclede contract. This was a long-term requirements contract, and so it would not be possible to know exactly how much gas Laclede would order in the future, thus making a precise award of damages at trial hard to calculate.

Second, while gas from alternative sources was plentiful now, no one could predict whether that would continue, or would continue at any particular price, again making damages difficult to approximate.

Finally, a one-time award of damages at trial would not really give Laclede what it bargained for, since part of the reason Laclede entered into a long-term requirements contract was to secure the peace of mind that came from assurances of a long-term adequate supply of propane.

Accordingly, Laclede was entitled to equitable relief [Restatement 2d § 360, Cmt. b, Ill. 4 and 5; *Laclede Gas Co. v. Amoco Oil Co.*, 522 F.2d 33 (8th Cir. 1975)].

(2) **Example.** [§ 29–11]

Aimee was awarded a fried chicken franchise by a national company in a brand new location. Her contract provided that she was to receive 30% of the net profits from the franchise. Without justification, the company breached its agreement with Aimee and awarded the franchise to Gary instead. Aimee satisfies the first element necessary for an award of specific performance: it would be difficult to prove with reasonable certainty an amount of damages that would compensate her for the breach.

(3) **Example.** [§ 29–12]

Bank is contractually obligated to lend $30 million to Producer for the production of a new movie. Bank unjustifiably refuses to fund the loan. No other financial institution would lend Producer the money either, because they heard Bank refused to fund the loan. In such a case, an award of specific performance would be appropriate, since it would be difficult to estimate what profits, if any, the producer would make from the movie.

EQUITABLE REMEDIES

Note that if the producer was able to secure a loan from another bank, but at a higher interest rate, Bank would only be liable in money damages measured by the difference in interest charges the producer has to pay for the new loan versus the Bank loan.

b. **The Difficulty of Procuring Suitable Substitute Performance. [§ 29–13]**

The second factor a court will weigh in determining whether an award of money damages is "inadequate" is the difficulty the non-breaching party will have in obtaining suitable substitute performance from a third party if an award of damages is made. That is, if the goods, services, etc., which are the subject matter of the contract are fungible, or otherwise can easily be purchased elsewhere, an award of damages is appropriate. In such a case, the non-breaching party can go into the market, purchase the goods, services, etc., from a third party, and require the breaching party to pay the difference, if any, between what he or she paid in the market for the product or service and the contract price [*see* § 32–12]. That way the non-breaching party is put in exactly the same position he or she would have been in had the contract been performed.

However, **if the goods or services are not readily available elsewhere, i.e., they are in some sense "unique," an award of damages would not result in the non-breaching party ending up in the position he or she would have been in had the contract been performed**. This is because, by definition, it would be sufficiently difficult for the injured party to buy substitute goods or services promised under the contract from anyone, no matter how large an award of damages. Accordingly, **the more unique a good or a service promised to be provided under a contract is, the more likely equitable relief will be awarded for breach of that agreement** [Restatement 2d § 360(2)].

Many years ago, courts demanded that to fulfill this requirement the good truly be a one-of-a-kind item. However, today the party seeking equitable relief need only show the item to be *fairly unique*, or as some courts put it, that there "would be undue difficulty in procuring a suitable replacement."

One intractable rule governing "uniqueness" in this context is that **land is always considered unique**, and so a buyer under a contract for the purchase of land will always be able to meet this part of the test for equitable relief. [*See* Case Squibs Section, *Hilmor Sales Co v. Neushaefer Div. of Surponics Corp.* for the argument that a low price alone can make an item "unique."]

CHAPTER 29

(1) Example. [§ 29–14]

The Janet/County Art Museum hypothetical concerning the Rembrandt painting discussed in § 29–3 is an example of a "unique" good situation. That is, an award of damages to the Museum as a result of Janet's refusal to turn over the particular painting would not allow the Museum to replace what it bargained for. As such, equitable relief is appropriate.

(2) Example. [§ 29–15]

Mary contracts to sell her house to Bill. Later, she changes her mind, decides to stay in her house, and cancels the contract. She offers to pay Bill the difference, if any, between the price Bill was going to pay for her house and the price of the house next door, which has the identical floor plan to Mary's house and is presently for sale. Bill is entitled to specific performance of his contract with Mary. As noted above, each piece of land is considered unique, and even if the house next door has the identical floor plan, etc., contract law holds there will be enough differences between the two properties to make Mary's property unique. Hence, an award of damages will not be "adequate" to grant Bill the benefits to which he was contractually entitled. Thus, he is empowered to have Mary's promise to sell him her house specifically performed.

(3) Example. [§ 29–16]

Gail owns a Duisenberg automobile in pristine condition. There are only seven other known models of this type of Duisenberg in pristine condition, none of which are currently for sale. Gail contracts to sell it to Bob for $1 million but later also contracts to sell it to Dick for $1.5 million. Bob is probably entitled to specific performance. While the car is not "unique" in that it is not a "one-of-a-kind" car, it is unique enough that Bob would have sufficient difficulty procuring a suitable substitute, even with an award of damages [UCC § 2–716].

(4) Review Problem. [§ 29–17]

Leslie contracts with a Chevrolet dealership for a new Volt with specified equipment. The car dealership calls her later and refuses to deliver at the contract price.

Question:

What kind of relief can Leslie obtain?

EQUITABLE REMEDIES

Answer:

Leslie is not entitled to specific performance, for she can procure a substitute car with the same equipment at another dealership. If the car at the other dealership costs more than she was obligated to pay the first dealer, an award of damages covering the difference will give her the benefit of her bargain with the breaching dealer, i.e., the car she wants at the price she agreed to pay. Note that if the specified equipment was so specified that few cars nationwide have it, etc. then a better argument for specific performance would exist [UCC § 2–716].

c. The Likelihood That an Award of Damages Could Not Be Collected. [§ 29–18]

Courts do not want to issue orders that cannot be fulfilled by the parties. If a breaching party has no money, a court's award of money damages to the non-breaching party is likely not going to do that party much good. Thus, the inability of the breaching party to pay a damage award is one factor a court will weigh in deciding whether to order equitable relief [Restatement 2d § 360(3)].

Note that Restatement 2d § 360(3) does not set forth a rule that any time a breaching party is in poor financial health an award of equitable relief will automatically be forthcoming; nor does it say that a non-breaching party is always entitled to specific performance if the breaching party is in or near insolvency. Rather, this provision only states that a court will look at the likelihood of the non-breaching party's ability to collect an award of damages as **one factor** in deciding whether to exercise its discretion to award equitable relief.

(1) Example. [29–19]

Dorothy contracts to sell her bicycle shop to Maury for $80,000. Shortly before the transfer of ownership is to take place, Dorothy becomes insolvent and repudiates the contract. Dorothy's insolvency is just a factor indicating specific performance should be granted, as there is a genuine likelihood that an award of damages could not be collected [Restatement 2d § 360(3), Cmt. d, Ill. 9].

2. Equitable Relief Will Not Be Awarded if There Are Undue Practical Limitations on a Court's Ability to Grant Such Relief. [§ 29–20]

Whenever a court grants equitable relief, there are administrative burdens involved in supervising a party's compliance with the court's order. When those burdens get too great, a court will not order specific performance or an injunction, even if a damage award would not reliably put the innocent party in the position he or she would have been in had the contract been performed. The decision to grant equitable relief is thus always discretionary with the court.

One of the factors a court may weigh in deciding to use its discretion is how burdensome supervising the equitable decree will be. A non-exhaustive but typical list of the practical problems of enforcement that courts consider in deciding whether to order equitable relief includes:

(1) Whether the terms of the contract are sufficiently certain so as to provide a basis for an appropriate court order [Restatement 2d § 362; § 29–21];

(2) Whether the nature and magnitude of the performance promised in the contract would impose a supervisory burden on the court that is disproportionate to the advantages to be gained from specific enforcement and to the harm to be suffered from its denial [Restatement 2d § 366; § 29–23]; and

(3) Whether the contract calls for personal services [Restatement 2d § 367(1); § 29–27].

a. **Whether the Terms of the Contract Are Too Uncertain to Provide a Basis for a Specific Performance Order. [§ 29–21]**

A court is entitled to refuse equitable relief if the standards set forth in the contract are insufficiently detailed to allow the court to formulate a clear order, or to allow the court to monitor in any meaningful way whether the breaching party is complying with an order for equitable relief [Restatement 2d § 362]. The idea is that if a court orders specific performance, it wants to make its order clear enough so that the party subject to the order knows what he or she has to do to avoid being in contempt for violating the order. Further, the order must be detailed enough so that the court can easily monitor whether its order is being followed. Hence, when the terms of the contract at issue are insufficiently detailed to allow the court to issue a reasonably specific order, a court is disinclined to grant equitable relief.

Note that there is a fine line between a contract that is so indefinite that it cannot be enforced [Chapter Six], and one that is definite enough to be enforced, but too indefinite to support an award of equitable relief. While the line may be fine, there are some contracts that fall between those boundaries, and so when parties contract in very general terms, courts will often decline to specifically enforce their agreements.

(1) Example. [§ 29–22]

Darryl owns a piece of prime downtown property. He enters into a contract with Construct Co. to develop the property. Under their contract, Construct Co. will furnish the plans and eventually construct a 30-story high rise on the premises, which Construct Co. promises will be a "first class building, equivalent to other prime office space in the downtown area." Construct Co. breaches, failing either to submit the plans or build the building.

Darryl would probably not be entitled to an order of specific performance because his contract with Construct Co. is too uncertain to allow the court to fashion a sufficiently detailed specific performance order. That is, the most a court could do, would be to order Construct Co. "to build a first class building equivalent to other prime office space . . ." Issuing such an order would probably not provide Construct Co. with enough direction as to what it had to do to avoid being in contempt, e.g., would it be in violation of the order if it used tile instead of marble in the lobby? In addition, it would be difficult for the court to monitor the order and to decide whether its order had been violated. It is entirely possible the parties would come back to the court many, many times to referee the construction decisions. Hence, such a contract is too uncertain to support a specific performance order [Restatement 2d § 362, Cmt. b, Ill. 1].

b. Whether the Supervisory Burden on the Court Outweighs the Advantage to Be Gained by an Order for an Equitable Remedy. [§ 29–23]

On occasion a court will decline to issue an order for equitable relief simply because enforcement and supervision of the order will be far more burdensome than the advantages the non-breaching party will receive from the issuance of such an order [Restatement 2d § 366]. This occurs when difficult questions are raised as to the quality of performance under the decree, when the court's supervision will have to continue for a long period of time, or when the court will have to supervise a very complex operation. This is not to say that any time a complex contract comes before the court there cannot be a specific performance decree. However, a court is entitled to weigh the supervisory burdens involved in issuing an equitable remedy against the advantages gained by the non-breaching party from such an order. If the former are disproportionate to the latter, a court is entitled to use its discretion and decline to issue equitable relief, even if a damage award to the innocent party would otherwise be considered "inadequate."

(1) Example. [§ 29–24]

An airplane manufacturer promises United Air Lines that it will design, test, and have certified a new jet airplane to fulfill United's needs for such a plane in ten years. Six years into the deal, the manufacturer still has not produced a prototype. The manufacturer estimates that to meet its promised deadline, it will now have to employ 800 more individuals and take additional costly steps to speed up the work. As such, it repudiates the contract.

United will be unable to get a decree of specific performance, for the burden to the court involved in enforcing such an order outweighs the advantages to be gained from specifically enforcing the manufacturer's promise [Restatement 2d § 366, Cmt. a, Ill. 1]. The court would not know how many engineers are needed, or support personnel, or what machines have to be ordered, etc., to make sure the plane was delivered on time, and courts are disinclined to hold hearings and make rulings on such matters every time the parties disagree on what acts are necessary.

(2) Example. [§ 29–25]

Build'em is a real estate developer who sells a house to Baxter, promising Baxter that before escrow closes, there will be a sewer system in place. Build'em never constructs the sewer system. While an order of specific performance would require some supervision by the court, the administrative burden is not disproportionate to the health and safety benefits Baxter would receive from the installation of a working sewage system and thus equitable relief would be available [Restatement 2d § 366, Cmt. a, Ill. 3].

(3) Example of *Walgreen Co. v. Sara Creek Property Co.* [29–26]

Walgreen operated a pharmacy in Southgate Mall. Walgreen leased this space from Sara Creek Property (Sara). Walgreen's lease stipulated that Sara would not lease another space in the mall to anyone else who operated a competing pharmacy (a "non-competition" clause).

Sara, however, wanted to lease to Phar-Mor. Phar-Mor would occupy a huge amount of space in the mall, and would sell a large number of items, but part of the Phar-Mor store was dedicated to a pharmacy. Walgreen brought suit, seeking an injunction against Sara leasing to Phar-Mor on the basis of the non-competition clause.

Sara essentially conceded that it was breaching the contract but noted that Walgreen could be made whole by collecting damages, and thus an injunction was inappropriate. Further, it argued that there was a large administrative burden for the court, which also argued against an injunction being issued.

Held: Walgreen was entitled to a permanent injunction. The court held that Walgreen had demonstrated why damages were not adequate—its lease had 10 years to run and projecting the harm that Phar-Mor's competing pharmacy would cause it that far in the future would be no more than a guess and could well under compensate it. Furthermore, the court agreed with Walgreen that the cost to impose the injunction would be low for the court. It noted it might be high for *the parties*, because the likely result of entering an injunction would be for Sara to negotiate with Walgreen for a price to waive its no competition clause, and acknowledged that such negotiations might be long and contentious. But for the court, the only burden was to ensure that Phar-Mor didn't open a store in the mall for ten years without Walgreen's consent [*Walgreen Co. v. Sara Creek Prop. Co.*, 966 F.2d 273 (7th Cir. 1992)].

Note that the court surmised this might be a "real life" example of the efficient breach doctrine whereby Sara would be better off breaching and paying Walgreen's damages because the revenue it got from Phar-Mor would outweigh the damages owing to Walgreen. See § 30–1 for a discussion of the efficient breach doctrine.]

c. **Contracts Calling for the Performance of "Personal Services" Will Not Be Specifically Enforced. [§ 29–27]**

A court will not issue an order requiring that a contract for personal service be specifically enforced [Restatement 2d § 367(1)]. This rule leads to three questions: (1) what are "personal service" contracts; (2) why won't courts order that they be specifically performed; and (3) what rights does the innocent party have upon the breach of such a contract if he or she cannot obtain a specific performance decree? Each of these questions is answered below.

In a general sense, a "personal service" contract is any contract that calls not only for performance of a specific duty, but also for a particular person to do it. However, for purposes of the doctrine denying specific performance in "personal service" contracts, that definition is too broad. That is, there are some contracts that will meet the general definition given above, but are still be capable of being specifically enforced [§ 29–28].

While there is no universally agreed upon definition for the subset of personal service contracts that will be subject to the specific performance prohibition, the idea is that the more the contract calls for the performance by a particular person based on that particular individual's skills, character, training, talents, etc., the more likely it is to be subject to this rule. In other words, the more the performance in the contract would be non-delegable [§ 29–23], the more likely it is that the party promising to perform the service will not be ordered specifically to perform it.

To say that such contracts will not be **specifically** enforced does not mean they will not be enforced at all. The non-breaching party is, of course, free to seek a damage award. Further, the non-breaching party may also seek a prohibitory injunction preventing the breaching party from engaging in any competitive work during the period he or she was supposed to be working for the non-breaching party. However, there are limitations on when the non-breaching party is entitled to such an injunction, and these limitations are discussed below.

Under Restatement 2d § 367(2), a non-breaching party is **not** entitled to the specific performance remedy of a prohibitory injunction for breach of a personal service contract when either:

(a) The probable result of such an order will be to compel an undesirable personal relationship; or

(b) The breaching party will be left without a reasonable means of making a living if such an order were issued.

(1) Example. [§ 29–28]

Ted occasionally supplies air taxi service to remote regions in Alaska. On January 10, a scientific research team visited Ted and explained that they were just about to leave for an extended study of weather patterns in a remote area of the Alaskan tundra. They explained that while their project was to last for four months, they can only carry two months' worth of supplies with them. No other air taxi service could be found to ferry the material to the expedition. Accordingly, they signed a contract with Ted whereby he unconditionally and personally promised to fly food and other provisions to the team on March 15 to replenish their supplies.

EQUITABLE REMEDIES

In early March, Ted decides the trip is not worth the hassle, and anticipatorily repudiates the agreement. There is no other way to get the supplies to the research team. Even though this is a personal services contract in the general sense of the term, i.e., it calls for a particular person to do a particular task, it probably can be specifically enforced. That is, the contract was not awarded to Ted based on any particular skill, training, etc., that separates him from any other commercial Alaskan pilot. Any reliable air carrier would have been acceptable to deliver the supplies for the research team. Further, an order requiring Ted to perform would not end up with an "undesirable personal relationship" as dropping off the supplies is a one-time task. Accordingly, there is no reason not to grant a specific performance order compelling him to fulfill his promised performance.

(2) Example. [§ 29–29]

A prominent actor is hired to star in a movie and contractually promises the producer his exclusive services for the next four months. A few days after signing that contract, the actor signs another contract to appear in a second movie, the filming of which would entail some overlap with his four-month exclusive commitment in the first movie. The producer of the first movie is **not** entitled to an order of specific performance, for acting is a "personal service" which could not be delegated. That is, the contract was awarded based on the skills and training which separate this particular actor from all other actors, and forcing the producer and actor to work together when the actor has breached runs the risk of forcing an undesirable personal relationship. While not entitled to a specific performance order, the producer is entitled to an injunction prohibiting the actor from taking on potentially competitive work during the four-month period [Restatement 2d § 367, Cmt. b, Ill. 1].

(3) Example. [§ 29–30]

Same as above, except this time it is the producer who unjustifiably fires the actor shortly after beginning production of the movie. As is true for producer, the actor would similarly not be entitled to a specific performance order compelling the producer to hire him back, for the producer has breached the type of "personal service" contract which is not subject to a specific performance decree. Such an order would end up with a forced "undesirable" personal relationship between the actor and the producer.

(4) "Personal Services" Contract with Covenant Not to Compete. [§ 29–31]

An industrial tool manufacturer enters into employment contracts with its sales force. The contract provides, in part, that if a member of the sales force voluntarily leaves the company, "he or she will not take a position in which the employee will compete with the company for a period of two years." This type of clause is known as a "covenant not to compete" and the validity of such clauses have been the subject of much litigation and commentary.

Employers want to enforce covenants not to compete so as to prevent employees from taking the trade secrets, customer lists, and other knowledge the employee has learned while working for the employer and "selling" that knowledge to the employer's competitor upon an offer of a higher salary. Further, the employer has typically invested time and effort into the training of the employee and wants to ensure a competitor will not be freely able to purchase the fruits of that training. And a "jilted" employer does not like the idea of its ex-employee competing with it.

On the other hand, if such covenants are enforced, the employee ends up being economically tied to his or her employer, and cannot earn a living in his or her chosen profession from anyone else, at least for the period of time he or she has promised not to compete. Hence, because there are reasonable arguments on both sides, contract and labor law have struggled to find the proper approach to such covenants.

The general rule regarding such clauses today is that **if a covenant not to compete is freely negotiated and voluntarily assumed by the employee, and if a court finds that the employee did in fact have access to the original employer's <u>trade secrets</u>, such clauses will be enforced by prohibitory injunction within limits set forth below.** That is, if an employee agrees to such a clause but nevertheless accepts a position with a business rival of the employer, a court will enforce the covenant and issue a prohibitory injunction enjoining the employee from competing with his or her original employer.

However, **courts will only issue such orders if the covenant not to compete is reasonably limited in time, in geography, and in scope.** In other words, a court will not issue an injunction prohibiting an employee: (i) from working for a competing firm if the covenant is supposed to run for an unreasonably long time; or (ii) from doing the same job for a company located in a different geographical market from that in which his or her former employer competed; or (iii) from taking **any** job (not just one which would require divulging trade secrets) with another employer.

Note also that **if trade secrets are not involved, such restrictive covenants are not favored by the courts**. That is, if an employer just wants to try to make sure the former employee does not compete with the employer, courts favor voiding the restrictive covenants and allowing the employee to earn a living. Further, where the area of business is one in which the personal relationship between the employee and the customer is important, such as lawyer/client, the right of the customer to choose who he or she wishes to employ is another reason for striking covenants not to compete where no trade secrets are involved. In some states, like California, such clauses are presumptively invalid, and only enforced in narrow circumstances.

3. **Equitable Relief Will Not Be Granted if Certain "Equitable Principles" Are Violated. [§ 29–32]**

Yet another series of limitations on a court's discretion to make an equitable decree is the presence of certain equitable principles limiting the availability of equitable relief. When equity was its own branch of jurisprudence, the courts required that the non-breaching party could be guilty of no unfairness in order to qualify for equitable relief. Sometimes this was phrased "to seek equity a party must do equity," or that "a party must not come into equity with 'unclean hands.'" The broader idea was that the hallmark of equity was fairness, and hence before a court would invoke its discretion to grant equitable relief, it had to be convinced that the party seeking such relief had acted fairly in the negotiation and operation of the contract, so as to ensure that the court was not being used to further an injustice. Today, courts consider the following equitable principles in deciding whether to issue an order for specific performance or an injunction:

(1) Whether the act or forbearance compelled by the grant of equitable relief would be **contrary to public policy** [Restatement 2d § 365; § 29–33];

(2) Whether specific enforcement of the contract would be unjust because the breaching party's assent to the contract was

CHAPTER 29

induced by an unfair business practice [Restatement 2d § 364(1)(a); § 29–35];

(3) Whether specific enforcement of the contract would **cause unreasonable hardship** to the breaching party [Restatement 2d § 364(1)(b); § 29–37]; and

(4) Whether the court is satisfied that specific enforcement of the contract **would not result in the non-performance** of a substantial part of the agreed exchange [Restatement 2d § 363; § 29–39].

a. Whether Such an Order Would Violate Public Policy. [§ 29–33]

Sometimes public policy will prevent an order of specific performance, even though an award of money damages would not be adequate to place the innocent party in the same position as if the contract had been performed, and even though there is not an undue number of practical considerations weighing against the granting of equitable relief. The idea is that a court in equity should not issue an order that would be inequitable by violating some other aspect of public policy [Restatement 2d § 365].

(1) Example. [§ 29–34]

Judy is a trustee, holding a piece of property in trust for Larry, a minor. Judy enters into a contract promising to sell the property, but does so in her own name, not as trustee for Larry. In fact, she plans to abscond with the money and live on a Caribbean island. At the last minute her conscience gets the better of her and she decides she cannot go through with the deal. The purchaser is not entitled to an order of specific performance even though the subject of the contract is real property (which would ordinarily be subject to a specific performance order) and even though, as trustee, Judy has the power to sell the property. By ordering Judy to go through with the contract as written, public policy would be violated, since she is breaching a trust. Courts will not issue an equitable order forcing her to sell the property if such an order will lead to an inequitable result.

b. Whether Such an Order Would Be Unjust Because the Breaching Party's Assent to the Contract Was Induced by Unfair Practices. [§ 29–35]

A court will not issue an order of specific performance if the breaching party was induced to enter the contract by means of an unfair business practice [Restatement 2d § 364(1)(a)]. Once

EQUITABLE REMEDIES

again, the idea is that a court in equity wants "to do equity," and thus, will not issue an order compelling someone to live up to their contractual promises when these promises were not made as a result of fully informed, voluntary decision-making. Hence, if it turns out that the non-breaching party seeking equitable relief has secured the breaching party's consent to the contract by means of "unclean hands," or "sharp" practices, equitable relief will not be granted.

Note that if the actions of the non-breaching party give rise to one of the contract defenses, e.g., duress, undue influence, etc., no relief of any sort will be granted because the non-performing party is, by definition, not liable for breach. Thus, the rule of Restatement 2d § 364(1)(a) covers those situations where the practices of the **non-breaching** party during the negotiation of, or operation under, the contract are deemed "sharp" or sufficiently "unfair." In such cases, if a court determines that it would be unjust to specifically enforce the contract against the breaching party, **equity** will provide no relief, although the breaching party may well be liable in money damages arising from his or her non-performance.

(1) Example. [§ 29–36]

Sally makes an offer to purchase Bob's home for $200,000. Bob knows comparable homes in his neighborhood are selling for $140,000, and correctly suspects that Sally believes that the unfenced backyard of Bob's house is an acre. In truth, the property line is close to the house and the backyard is only 200 sq. feet. Bob accepts Sally's offer and when she finds out the true facts, she refuses to go through with the transaction. Assuming Bob's acts do not give Sally a defense to the contract such as mistake, or misrepresentation, and assuming that they do not give rise to a successful unconscionability claim, specific performance of the contract can be refused on the ground of unfairness [Restatement 2d § 364, Cmt. a, Ill. 1].

c. **Whether Such an Order Would Be Sufficiently "Unjust" as to Cause Unreasonable Hardship or Loss to the *Breaching* Party. [§ 29–37]**

When requiring a breaching party to specifically perform a promise would result in an unjust hardship to the breaching party, a court is entitled to use its discretion to deny equitable relief and require the breaching party to pay an award of money damages instead [Restatement 2d § 364(1)(b)].

CHAPTER 29

(1) Example Based on *Peevyhouse v. Garland Coal & Mining Co.* [§ 29–38]

The Peevyhouses owned a large piece of property in rural Oklahoma. Much of it lay fallow. Garland acquired from the Peevyhouses a license to strip mine for coal on their land, but a fully negotiated deal point was Garland's promise to remediate the land when it was done so that the area mined would be indistinguishable from the surrounding countryside. Indeed, the Peevyhouses took less money than their neighbors for the coal extracted from their property from Garland in return for the remediation promise.

After finishing mining, Garland discovered that it would be very expensive to fill the hole and otherwise remediate the land—there were unsupported estimates at trial that it might be as much as $29,000. Evidence at trial (again, in retrospect, unsupported) showed the decreased fair market value of the land as a result of having a large hole in it was only $300 (i.e., the fair market value of the desolate land without a hole in the middle of it minus its fair market value with such a hole was $300).

When Garland walked away after performing only minimal remediation, the Peevyhouses sued, seeking an order of specific performance requiring the hole to be filled and the land to be replanted.

Held: Verdict for Garland on disproportionate economic hardship grounds. That is, making Garland spend $29,000 to provide only a $300 value to the Peevyhouses was not something a court in "equity" would order [*Peevyhouse v. Garland Coal & Mining Co.*, 382 P.2d 109 (Okla. 1962)].

Note that some commentators defend this kind of decision using a combination of economic policy grounds and a fear that the non-breaching party may be guilty of unclean hands. To them, making a party spend $29,000 to convey only a $300 monetary benefit is an example of "economic waste," and as such should not be ordered by a court. Also, these commentators suspect that the non-breaching party really did not want Garland to specifically perform. They argue that plaintiffs in these types of cases simply **want a court to issue an <u>order</u> requiring the promisor to perform**, which they will later agree not to enforce upon a payment of an amount less than the cost of performance. That is, in the above case the fear is that the Peevyhouses were seeking a court order of specific performance just so they can later offer to "relieve" Garland of its $29,000

EQUITABLE REMEDIES

obligation upon payment to them of, e.g., $25,000, when they really didn't care about the land. Accordingly, these commentators believe that a plaintiff such as the Peevyhouses may be coming into court with "unclean hands" and should be denied equitable relief for that reason as well.

This case is the source of anger for many law students and professors. There were many evidentiary and other irregularities in the trial and appeal of the case, and the hole left by the mine essentially split the Peevyhouses' land in two. Further, by all indications the Peevyhouses genuinely cared about the land's remediation and were not acting in bad faith. Accordingly, the decision itself may not be justified on its facts. Nevertheless, the concept that economic hardship can cause a court to deny an order of specific performance is well entrenched.

d. Whether There Is Sufficient Security to Believe the Non-Breaching Party Will Perform. [§ 29–39]

A court will not order the breaching party to specifically perform a promise if the court is worried that the party ordered to perform will not thereafter receive his or her benefits under the contract. For example, a court will not order Joe to deliver his Picasso to Ellyn as he contractually promised if it does not appear that Ellyn will be able to pay Joe upon delivery. Hence, contract law provides that no order of specific performance will be issued unless a substantial part of the return performance due to the breaching party **has already been rendered**, or unless the court determines to its satisfaction that such **return performance is likely** [Restatement 2d § 363]. In older cases, this rule was sometimes put that the court will not grant equitable relief unless there is "mutuality of remedy," but this phrase is inaccurate and no longer has any validity. The idea, however, is that a court will not order the breaching party to perform if the non-breaching party has not already substantially performed, or if it does not appear likely that the non-breaching party is in a position to perform.

(1) Example. [§ 29–40]

Sara contracts to sell a piece of land to David for $100,000. Sara refuses to tender the deed, and David seeks an order compelling specific performance. Such an order will not be issued unless David can satisfy the court that he has the money to pay for the land once the deed is tendered. If he cannot establish such ability to the court's satisfaction, he may still be entitled to damages, but not to equitable relief.

The court will not order Sara to perform specifically if, as a result, Sara will end up both without her land and without David's payment.

D. EXAM APPROACH TO EQUITABLE RELIEF ISSUES. [§ 29–41]

It is very unlikely that an entire one-hour exam problem will turn on equitable relief issues. Rather, whether a party is entitled to equitable, as opposed to legal relief, will much more likely be one of several issues in a problem dealing with breach and remedies, or the subject of multiple choice questions.

As a consequence, when you are in a problem that tests remedies, you should make sure:

1. Damages will fail to put the innocent party in the position he or she would have been in had the contract been performed [§§ 29–8 *et seq.*];

2. There are no undue practical limitations in granting equitable relief [§ 29–20]; and

3. No "equitable principles" will be violated by an equitable award [§ 29–32].

4. If all of those elements are satisfied, then choose the most appropriate remedy: specific performance, injunction, or reformation, while keeping in mind that a specific performance remedy is largely within the court's discretion.

Chapter 30

Money Damages

AUTHOR'S NOTE: This chapter sets forth the rules of money damage recovery under common law/Restatement rules and the basics of UCC monetary damage recovery as well. For those classes which spend more time studying the Code, more advanced damage concepts under Article 2 are discussed in some detail in Chapter Thirty-Two.

A. THE "INTEREST" ANALYSIS OF CONTRACT LAW AND THE CONCEPT OF ECONOMIC BREACH. [§ 30–1]

As a general rule, contract law does <u>not</u> require parties to actually **perform** their promises. Instead, contract law usually requires only that a party who breaches a contractual promise pay some money to the party injured by the breach. As pointed out in the last Chapter, it is the unusual fact situation that permits a court to order a breaching party specifically to perform a contractually undertaken promise [§ 29–7].

This phenomenon can be explained by understanding the "interest" analysis of contract law. When a party enters into an enforceable contract, he or she does *not* receive a protected *right to performance* by the other party. Instead, he or she is given only a **protected economic "interest"** in the other party's performance. Hence, when a contract is breached, contract law typically does not order performance. Instead, it generally awards damages based on the interference with the non-breaching party's protected economic interest. In other words, when a contract is made, each party gets a kind of property right in the other's performance. The value of the property right is equal to the economic value of performance, i.e., a dollar amount is calculated for the value of the performance promised by each party. When the contract is breached, the injured party can thus recover money damages based on the extent to which he or she failed to receive the complete monetary value of the breaching party's performance.

1. **The "Efficient Breach" Doctrine Defined and Explained. [§ 30–2]**

    One result of the "interest" analysis is that, in certain cases, traditional contract law actually **encourages** breach and dictates that a party should **not** render performance. This is known as the "efficient breach" doctrine. The efficient breach doctrine provides that so long as a breaching party is willing to pay for any damages caused by the breach, he or she **should** breach if the end result, after the breacher pays contract damages, is that the breacher will be economically better off. The doctrine is perhaps better understood by example:

Jim's Tool and Die ("Jim's") has a contract with National Hardware Co. to manufacture and deliver one million drywall nails of assorted sizes on March 31. Producing one million nails in a month is the limit of Jim's production capacity. The contract price for the nails is $15,000, which was the market price for a million nails the previous October when the contract was signed. However, as of February 15 (approximately six weeks before delivery is due, and before Jim's has started production), the $15,000 contract price appears to make this a good deal for National Hardware, for on that date other manufacturers were charging $17,000 for identical nails. In late February, International Builders ("International") received a large building contract on a rush schedule and, as a result, offers Jim's Tool and Die $25,000 for one million assorted drywall nails, also conditioned upon delivery on March 31. Assume International Builder's had a good experience with Jim's Tool in prior dealings, and was willing to pay a premium because it was confident that if Jim' promised delivery on March 31, the nails would be there by that date and would be of good quality.

The efficient breach doctrine says Jim's should breach its contract with National Hardware and sell the nails to International Builders, for the end result would be a more economically efficient allocation of resources than if it performed. That is, if it is worth $8,000 above the current fair market value to International Builders to acquire the nails, economic efficiency dictates that such money should be allocated to a supplier such as Jim's. Hence, if Jim's breaches its contract with National Hardware so that it can supply International Builders, the end result will be that International Builders will be satisfied, for it will get what it bargained for: a million nails for $25,000. Jim's will be better off, because it will have received $10,000 more for the same goods than it would have from National Hardware.

This, of course, leaves National Hardware without nails. Obviously it is not better off after the breach by Jim's. Recall, however, that one of the principles of the efficient breach doctrine is that the breaching party must be willing to pay damages to the injured party. For National Hardware to receive what it bargained for under its contract with Jim's, Jim's will have to pay National $2,000. That is, since other nail manufacturers are now charging $17,000 for fungible nails (albeit without the reputation of Jim's), to allow National

Hardware to receive its bargain, i.e., a million nails for $15,000 out of its own pocket, Jim's will have to pay National $2,000. If Jim's does that it will still be a net $8,000 better off because of the breach and National will be "whole."

Hence, in this case the efficient breach doctrine counsels that Jim's breach the contract. This is because by virtue of the breach, both National Hardware and International will obtain the benefit of their bargains, i.e., a million nails at the prices they were willing to pay. Jim's, the breaching party, will be a net $8,000 ahead as a result of the breach, even after paying the damages caused by the breach.

There are many critics of the efficient breach idea. First, to say that National Hardware is "whole" in the above example upon a payment of $2,000 discounts the hassle National faces in having to go into the market and find someone else to supply it with nails. Second, Jim's may be, in some theoretical sense, willing to pay the $2,000, but rarely does such payment accompany the breach. It typically takes a lot of haranguing to get the breacher to pay, and perhaps even a lawsuit, with its time hassles, and its own transaction costs. Third, there is a legitimate question as to who is entitled to the premium from International—Jim's or National? After all, it was National who made what appears to be a good deal by purchasing what the market valued at $17,000 (at time of delivery) for $15,000, and as between it and Jim's, some would say it is National who should be able to decide to sell the nails to International Builder's for $25,000 and to decide the extra money is enough to put up with the hassle of going into the market and finding replacement nails for its own project. Also, arguably the relevant "market" is the $25,000 National paid, and so even if Jim's is responsible to pay [market] − [contract] the correct market price is $25,000, not $17,000.

B. DEFINING, IDENTIFYING, AND VALUING THE ECONOMIC INTERESTS RESULTING FROM CONTRACT FORMATION. [§ 30–3*]

As noted above [§ 30–1], the amount of damages an injured party is awarded upon a breach depends on the extent the breach interferes with that party realizing the full value of the economic interest arising upon contract formation. Over time, contract law has arrived at three different ways of calculating the full value of this protected economic interest, which sometimes come out to the same dollar amount resulting from the breach, but more often come out with different dollar figures. Thus, the amount of the non-breaching party's recovery may well depend on which valuation method is used to ascertain the value of the protected economic interest. **The rule is that the innocent, non-breaching party is**

---

* For more information, listen to CD # 11, Track 6 of *Sum and Substance Audio on Contracts*.

entitled to pick whichever valuation method he or she wishes, so long as the value of the interest can be adequately proven [Restatement 2d § 344].

Rather than referring to these different approaches as different valuation methods, contract law has instead chosen to say that each approach really describes its own kind of "interest." Hence, it is most accurate to say that each party receives protection for three different types of economic interests upon contract formation:

(1) The **"expectation" interest**;

(2) The **"reliance" interest**; and

(3) The **"restitution" interest**.

1. **The Expectation (or "Benefit of the Bargain") Interest. [§ 30–4]**

   The economic value of a party's expectation interest is the dollar amount that would place the non-breaching party in as good a position as he or she would have been in had the contract been performed [Restatement 2d § 344(a)]. The expectation interest is also sometimes known as the "benefit of the bargain" interest. It is made up of a number of components, but the idea is that the expectation interest is valued by taking a hypothetical situation—what would have happened had the contract been performed—and placing a dollar value on what the non-breaching party would have received under those circumstances.

   Expectation damages thus are "forward looking" in the sense that contract law looks ahead to the position the non-breaching party **would have been in** had the contract gone forward, and tries to award the innocent party an amount to put the innocent party in the same economic position.

   a. **Example. [§ 30–5]**

   Barbra bought wine futures. That is, for a $5,000 fixed price today, she bought wine that is to be delivered in eighteen months. Zipping ahead eighteen months, at the time of delivery, the wine is worth $6,500. Putting aside (for now) interest and the use of money, if the wine shop didn't deliver the wine as promised, the value of Barbra's expectation interest is $1,500. That is, she made a bargain whereby she purchased a $6,500 good for $5,000. So to give her the benefit of the bargain, the breaching seller needs to pay $1,500.

   With the $1,500 cash at hand, Barbra can either go in the market and purchase the wine for $6,500 and end up exactly where she would have been had the contract been performed—a case of wine that would cost her $5,000 out of pocket (with the

MONEY DAMAGES

additional money to make up the $6,500 purchase price coming from the breaching wine store). Or, she can simply pocket the $1,500 and realize the benefit of her bargain in cash.

If Barbra was a retailer and can prove she would have been able to sell the wine for, say $8,000 to one of her customers, her recoverable damages would be correspondingly increased. These lost profits are part of what are known as "consequential damages" [§ 30–12] and also need to be awarded in the appropriate case to put "retailer" Barbra in the position she would have been in had the contract been performed.

2. **The Reliance (or "Out-of-Pocket") Interest. [§ 30–6*]**

   The economic value of a party's reliance interest is typically the dollar amount of whatever out-of-pocket costs (including labor) were incurred by the non-breaching party up to the time of the breach in reliance on the breaching party's performance [Restatement 2d § 344(b)]. In most instances, the amount of a party's reliance interest is thus fairly easily valued, since a party usually knows how much he or she has actually spent in performance (or preparing for performance) under a contract.

   It is said that the **reliance** interest is "backward looking," i.e., an award of **reliance** damages is designed to **put the non-breaching party back in the position he or she was in before the contract was entered into** by making the breaching party refund any money the injured party has spent in reliance on the breaching party's performance.

   a. **Example. [§ 30–7]**

      Betty contracts with Archie, promising to build him a custom house for $100,000. Betty promptly begins construction and within a few days has poured the foundation and has erected the house's frame. At this point, Archie breaches by unjustifiably ordering Betty to stop construction and to leave his property. At the time of the breach, Betty has incurred costs of $20,000 (including labor) in pouring the foundation and erecting the frame. The value of her reliance interest is therefore $20,000 and awarding her that amount of money will put her in the same economic position she was in <u>before</u> the contract was signed and she had to spend the $20,000.

---

* For more information, listen to CD # 12, Track 4 of *Sum and Substance Audio on Contracts*.

CHAPTER 30

3. **The Restitutionary Interest. [§ 30–8*]**

   A contracting party's restitutionary interest is valued by the dollar amount one party has unjustly enriched the other at the time of the breach. The value of a party's restitutionary interest is the **reasonable value of the benefits that party has actually received from the other** up to the time of the breach [Restatement 2d § 344(c); *see* Chapter Thirty-One for a discussion and examples of the restitutionary interest]. Restitution is also backwards looking, but rather than trying to put the *party seeking restitution in the position he or she was in before the contract was formed*, as is true for the expectation interest, the goal of the restitutionary interest is to put the **benefitted party** in the **position he or she was in before the contract was formed** by forcing that party to pay the value of whatever benefits he or she may have received under the contract up until the breach. As is explained in § 31–2, restitution is available to both the breaching and the innocent party, where both have received benefits from the other up to the time of the breach.

4. **Types of Damages Recoverable by the Non-Breaching Party. [§ 30–9]**

   One of the interesting things about modern contract law is that, **in every contract**, each party has an expectation, a reliance, *and* a restitutionary interest. In other words, these interests are really just three different *methods* used to place a dollar value on the economic value of the other party's promised performance. Hence, upon a breach, the non-breacher has a choice of which method he or she wishes to use in seeking monetary recovery for the breach. That is, in every case, the innocent party has the option to seek recovery of either expectation damages, of reliance damages, or in restitution. It is up to that party and his or her lawyer to figure out which valuation method would provide the largest recovery in that particular situation.

C. A GLOSSARY OF DAMAGES TERMINOLOGY. [§ 30–10]

One difficulty students often have in beginning their study of contract damages is that the subject carries with it its own, rather extensive, vocabulary. Hence, the major types of contract damages are listed, defined, and illustrated below.

1. **Benefit of the Bargain Damages. [§ 30–11]**

   Benefit of the bargain damages are synonymous with **expectation** damages [§ 30–4].

---

* For more information, listen to CD # 13, Track 1 of *Sum and Substance Audio on Contracts*.

MONEY DAMAGES

2. **Consequential Damages. [§ 30–12]**

   Consequential damages are economic damages suffered as a *consequence* of the breach. They are of two types: "direct consequential damage" and "indirect" or "special" consequential loss. Direct consequential losses are those damages which a reasonable person in the shoes of the breaching party would foresee as a consequence of a breach at the time of contract formation. "Indirect or "special" economic losses" are those damages which a reasonable person present at the time of contract formation, would **not** foresee occurring as a natural result or consequence of the breach, and thus are unrecoverable unless the breaching is *on notice* at the time of contract formation that the injured party would suffer that type of loss in the event of a breach. Most often the innocent party is made aware of these "special" damages by the innocent party, e.g., the other party says, "Without a crankshaft, my mill is shut down. So if you don't get this broken crankshaft to the repair facility on time, my plant will be shut down longer and I will look to you for the lost profits I suffer because of the delay." But sometimes, the breaching party is aware of the special circumstances because of circumstances, e.g., because she is a fan, the private air charter pilot knows that Star has a live TV show that shoots in New York on Sunday nights and so knows that if there is a delay in getting Star to New York on Sunday afternoon, Star will lose his fee. Thus, the rule is that, to be recoverable, consequential loss must be foreseeable to the breaching party at the time of contracting, either because it is a "direct consequential loss," and any reasonable person would foresee the loss, or because it is an "indirect economic loss" and the breaching party has notice of it at the time of contracting.

   The rationale for consequential loss and the structure for analyzing its recovery emanate from *Hadley v. Baxendale* [§ 30–55].

   a. **Example. [§ 30–13]**

      Greg, a law student, buys a stereo from a retailer for $1,000. Greg intends to re-sell the stereo to his friend Ann for $1,500. Greg is supposed to pick up the stereo from retailer's store on Monday. Greg arrives on Monday and the retailer explains there is a delay, and promises Greg that it will be there on Wednesday. Greg comes back on Wednesday and the retailer confesses it does not have the stereo and never did. As a consequence, Greg is out the expense for the second trip and loses the profit he would have made on the sale to Ann.

      Both the cost of the second trip and the "lost" $500 profit are "consequential damages." The cost of the second trip is a "direct" consequential loss, because if a retailer told its customer to come back again, a reasonable person would recognize there will be some costs associated with the second trip. The retailer might not know exactly how much the trip cost, but that's irrelevant. It is the *type of loss* that a reasonable person in the shoes of the breaching party would expect.

The $500 profit is an "indirect" or "special" consequential loss because a reasonable person in the position of the retailer at the time the contract was made would not foresee that the failure to deliver the stereo would naturally result in a lost profit in a subsequent resale transaction. That does not mean that such a loss would be inconceivable, but it does mean that a retailer would not reasonably foresee that its failure to deliver the stereo system to a consumer, as opposed to a retailer, would cause Greg a lost profit. The likelihood is that Greg would use it as his own personal stereo, or give it as a gift to someone. Hence, the lost $500 would only be recoverable if the retailer was on notice of that potential loss in the event of a breach at the time of contracting.

3. **Direct Damages. [§ 30–14]**

The term "direct damages" has two possible meanings. The first meaning refers simply to the value of the **loss in the bargain itself**—the **lost value** involved in not obtaining the full economic performance of the subject matter of the contract. In the Barbra example with the wine futures in § 30–5, the direct loss in the value of Barbra's bargain was $1,500, which would be her "direct damage." She might have other damages as well—time spent finding a replacement wine; driving to a further store to pick up the new wine; etc. All those damages are recoverable as well, but the loss of the **bargain itself** is called the "direct damage." Similarly, suppose Jean hired a nanny to watch her kids for $1,000/week. If the rate was below market, and equivalent nannies would charge $1,300/week, then if the nanny breached the "direct damage" to Jean is $300/week, the value of the loss stemming from not obtaining the value of the subject matter of the contract itself.

The second meaning of "direct" damage is type of consequential loss. As noted in § 30–12, one type of consequential loss is known as "direct consequential damage."

a. **Example. [§ 30–15]**

Big Store, a retailer, orders 5,000 knife sets from Knife Co. at $50/set. The knives are to be delivered 6 months after the order is placed. At the time of delivery, the market has risen so that comparable sets are $55/set. If Knife Co. breaches by failing to deliver, the "direct" damage will be $5/set as Big Store's *lost value* of the **bargain itself** is $5/set—it had a contract for $50 for what the market values at $55.

Any lost profits retailer suffered resulting from the breach are a consequential damage. That is, if the breach interfered with the profits retailer was able to make because, e.g., Big Store never gets replacement knives and so loses profits from the non-existent sales as a consequence of the breach, Big Store could seek recovery for them as well. As noted in § 30–12, consequential damages can be recovered if they are a type of damage that is reasonably foreseeable to the breaching party at the time of contracting. Here, because Big Store is a retailer, it is reasonably foreseeable to someone in Knife Co.'s position at the time the contract was entered into that Big Store would attempt to make a profit when it obtained the knives. As such, this *type of* lost profit is a "direct consequential loss."

4. **Exemplary Damages. [§ 30–16]**

Exemplary damages are synonymous with **punitive** damages [§ 30–24].

5. **Expectation Damages. [§ 30–17]**

Expectation damages are damages awarded as a result of the breaching party's interference with the injured party's expectation interest [*see* § 30–4 for a discussion of the expectation interest]. Expectation damages are measured by the dollar value necessary to put the injured party in the position he or she would have been in had the contract been performed. Note, however, an award of expectation damages is subject to three important limitations: certainty, foreseeability, and avoidability [§ 30–48].

6. **General Damages. [§ 30–18]**

General damages are sometimes used as synonymous with **direct** damages. The term is used by different courts to mean different things, however, and so as not to engender confusion, it will not often be used in this book.

7. **Incidental Damages. [§ 30–19]**

Incidental damages are costs incurred by the **non-breaching** party, **after** the breach, most often in an attempt to avoid or "mitigate" further damages to be paid by the breaching party. Usually these damages are out-of-pocket costs, but they also include "accounting" losses and overhead costs, such as the value of reasonable charges for storing non-conforming goods at the buyer's place of business. "Incidental damages" are recoverable under the UCC in § 2–715, and for breach of contracts governed by the common law under Restatement 2d § 347(b). Typical incidental costs include the storage, receipt, or transportation of improperly tendered goods, interest costs, the costs to send back non-conforming goods, the time looking for and arranging substitute goods to be delivered, etc. Note that so long as the decision of the non-breaching party to incur a cost in an attempt to avoid further damages to the breacher was reasonable, and so long as the amount of the expenditure was reasonable, the loss is recoverable. [*See* § 32–10 for additional explanation of incidental damages under the UCC.]

a. **Example. [§ 30–20]**

Employer unjustly fires Larry by breaching their employment contract. Larry thereafter spends $300 hiring a search firm to help him find a new job. The $300 is a recoverable incidental damage, for it is an out-of-pocket expense incurred after the breach by the injured party (Larry), in a reasonable attempt to lessen the damages owed by the employer. That is, if Larry could find a comparable job, the amount of his salary would be offset from the damages owed by the breaching employer.

Note that the $300 incidental damage is recoverable **regardless** of whether the search firm actually finds Larry a new job. Since Larry would not have borne this expense absent his employer's breach, and since the decision to hire the firm is a reasonable one in an *attempt* to mitigate the employer's loss, and because the amount of the expenditure was reasonable, Larry is entitled to the $300, regardless of the search firm's success. Moreover, the majority view is that Larry is entitled to the $300 even if the search firm finds him employment that pays him more than his old job. That is, even if he is economically "better off" because of the breach, he still can recover his incidental damages since, when he incurred the expense, he spent the money reasonably in an attempt to lessen the breaching party's damages.

8. **Liquidated Damages. [§ 30–21]**

Liquidated damages are damages fixed by the parties in advance as the amount due upon a breach of their contract. That is, as part of their contract, the parties stipulate how much one party will have to pay the other upon a breach of the contract.

There are limitations on when liquidated damages are recoverable. They are only recoverable if: (i) the amount of actual damages resulting from a breach is hard to calculate with precision; **and** (ii) where the amount of the liquidated damage is a reasonable estimate of what the actual damages would be [Restatement 2d § 356; UCC § 2–718(1); *see* § 30-80].

9. **Nominal Damages. [§ 30–22]**

In every successful breach of contract action, the non-breaching party is entitled to damages. Usually, these will be in the form of expectation damages, reliance damages, or in restitution. However, when the non-breaching party either has not been damaged or cannot sufficiently prove the amount due him or her, the non-breaching party is still entitled to collect "nominal damages" [Restatement 2d § 346(2)].

A nominal damage is a small sum that has nothing to do with the actual amount of damage suffered. Today a typical nominal damage award is something like $1.00. The reason contract law provides an award of nominal damages for breach of contract is that a breach is considered a serious enough act that it should not go unpunished, even if the non-breaching party is otherwise not injured, or cannot sufficiently prove the extent of his or her injuries. Additionally, some contracts provide that the prevailing party in a breach action is entitled to attorneys' fees. By awarding nominal damages, an innocent party who can establish that the other party breached can still be the "prevailing party" under such a clause, even if he or she cannot otherwise establish any other contract damage.

10. Out-of-Pocket Damages. [§ 30–23]

Out-of-pocket damages are synonymous with **reliance** damages [§ 30–6].

11. Punitive Damages. [§ 30–24]

Punitive damages in contract have the same meaning as they do in tort law—they are damages awarded as punishment to the breaching party for behavior that falls below certain normative societal levels. They are not monetary damages suffered by the non-breaching party due to the breach. However, they are awarded *far* less often in breach of contract suits than they are in tort actions. That is, there are only a few situations in which the court will even consider an award of punitive damages for a contractual breach [§ 30–87].

12. Reliance Damages. [§ 30–25]

Reliance damages are damages awarded to compensate for the breaching party's interference with the injured party's reliance interest [§ 30–6]. Reliance damages are measured by the dollar value of whatever out-of-pocket costs (including labor) were incurred by the innocent party up to the time of the breach in reliance on the breaching party's performance [§ 30–6].

13. Special Damages. [§ 30–26]

The term "special damages" is most often used as a synonym of **indirect consequential damage** [§ 30–12].

14. Stipulated Damages. [§ 30–27]

Stipulated damages are synonymous with **liquidated** damages [§ 30–21].

CHAPTER 30

D. EXPECTATION DAMAGES: THE GENERAL MEASURE OF CONTRACT DAMAGES. [§ 30–28*]

The most typical measure of contract damages is an award of expectation damages. To fulfill the goal of expectation loss recovery, the amount of such damage should be an amount that will put the non-breaching party in the position he or she would have been in had the contract been performed [Restatement 2d § 347, Cmt. a; UCC § 1–305]. The amount of an expectation damage award is thus the amount that will compensate the non-breaching party completely for the economic interference to his or her expectation interest caused by the breach. Note, however, that expectation recovery is limited by three important doctrines: certainty, foreseeability, and avoidability. These doctrines are discussed in § 30–48.

The general formula for calculating expectation damages is given below, followed by application of that formula to different common types of breach.

1. **Calculating Expectation Damages. [§ 30–29]**

    Section 347 of the Restatement 2d identifies five factors that need to be accounted for in calculating expectation damages:

    a. **Lost Value.**

    Lost value is the lost dollar value of the subject matter of the bargain itself. When a party performs a contractual promise, that performance renders value to the other party. When there is a breach, some or all of that value is not received, and is thus "lost." Two quick examples can illustrate this idea. Buyer purchases a brand new computer for $1,000, a fair price. Buyer was told the computer would have an i7 chip in it. Instead, it has an i5 chip. The computer with an i5 processor is only worth $800. Buyer has suffered a "direct loss" of $200, since the value of the subject matter of the bargain itself is $200 less than he was promised.

    The second example is Jane promised to paint Tom's house for $8,000, a fair price. But Jane is a terrible painter, has left gaps in the paint, etc. The job is only worth $3,000. Tom has suffered a $5,000 direct loss, for that is the difference in value of the subject matter of the contract between what he legitimately expected to receive and what he actually got.

    Hence, one component of expectation damages takes into account the economic value that was never received by the innocent party as a result of the breach. This is done by calculating a dollar amount for the economic value that full

---

* For more information, listen to CD # 11, Track 6 of *Sum and Substance Audio on Contracts*.

performance by the non-breaching party would have rendered, and subtracting from that figure the amount of value, if any, actually received by the non-breaching party up to the time of the breach.

b. **Incidental Loss.**

The second type of harm recoverable by the injured party as part of his or her expectation damage recovery is the incidental damage suffered by the party as a result of the breach. [§ 30–19, incidental damages.]

c. **Consequential Loss.**

The third type of harm recoverable by the injured party as part of his or her expectation damage suit is the recoverable consequential damage suffered by the injured party as a result of the breach [§ 30–12].

d. **Cost Avoided.**

Recall that one consequence of another party's material breach is that the non-breaching party need not continue performance [§ 20–60]. Hence, if an injured party ceases his or her own performance due to the other party's material breach, the injured party saves whatever money it would have taken him or her to finish performance. These "**costs avoided** due to the breach" need to be accounted for in determining the injured party's expectation damages. That is, if as a result of the breach certain monies are not spent by the innocent party, the breaching party must get "credit" for those costs avoided, or else he or she will be made to pay a sum greater than necessary to put the non-breaching party in the position he or she would have been in had the contract been performed.

For example, assume Charles was contractually obligated to build a custom gazebo for Dolores. The price was $5,000, and Charles reasonably expected to make $1,000 profit, i.e., his costs to make the gazebo were $4,000. Charles starts making the gazebo and Dolores breaches. At the time of the breach, Charles has spent $1,500 in wood, paint, labor, etc. If Charles stops making the gazebo, there is a $2,500 "cost avoided." That is, he was going to spend $4,000 to make the gazebo, and now he spent $2,500 less, i.e., only $1,500.

The lost value damages are $5,000, since the value of Dolores's expected performance is $5,000 in cash and now he will be getting $0 from Dolores. But if we awarded Charles $5,000 with no offset, Charles would be in a far better position after the breach than he would have been in had the contract been performed. That is, if the contract had been performed, he would get $5,000 from Dolores, but would have had to spend $4,000 to get that $5,000, meaning he would have walked away with a $1,000 profit. But if he was now awarded $5,000 in lost value with no offset, he would walk away with a net profit of $3,500, i.e., he would get $5,000 but only have spent $1,500 to get it.

Accordingly, we offset the money Charles did not have to spend because of the breach, i.e., $2,500, from his award. That way, he gets $2,500 in damages, but has already spent $1,500, leaving him with a net profit of $1,000, exactly the same position he would have been in had the contract been performed.

We call the $2,500 Charles did not have to spend a **"cost avoided"** and subtract it from his overall recovery.

e. **Loss Avoided.**

When a non-breaching party can use in another job or application whatever materials or preparations he or she made under the contract at the time of the breach, the value of those materials and preparations must also be subtracted from any recovery. This is known as a **"loss avoided."** For example, in the Charles and Dolores hypothetical above, suppose Charles can use $250 of the wood and paint he bought to build Dolores's gazebo on his next job, which could be building a cabinet for Bob. If there was no accounting for the repurposing of the wood and paint, Charles would again be put in a better position that he would have been in had the contract been performed. That is, Dolores would pay him for those materials, and so would Bob. So he would get $250 worth of wood and paint "free" (paid for by Dolores) for Bob's job.

So Charles's recovery would be ($5,000 (in "lost value")) minus ($2,500 (in "cost[s] avoided")) and minus another ($250 (in "loss avoided)). This would leave him with a recovery from Dolores of $2,250, and he would have spent $1,500 to get it. At first blush that might sound like he is not in as good a position as if the contract would have been performed, because he only walks away from the lawsuit with a "net" $750 in cash, but remember he gets $250 in "free" supplies to make Bob's cabinet, making his overall net recovery $1,000 ($750 in cash plus $250 in supplies)., which *is* what he would have made had the contract been performed.

Accordingly, if materials or resources procured for the breached contract can be salvaged for use in another contract, but **only** if they **can** be **reasonably** salvaged, the fair market value of the salvaged materials must be subtracted from other damages as a "loss avoided" to calculate accurately the injured party's expectation recovery. It is for this reason that often the "loss

MONEY DAMAGES

avoided" is known as the "salvage value" of the materials procured in the breached contract.

Expectation Damages Determined by Formula

Expressed mathematically, the proper formula for calculating expectation damages using the criteria in Restatement 2d § 347 is:

Expectation Damages = Lost Value + Incidental Loss + Consequential Loss – Cost Avoided – Loss Avoided.

Hereafter, this formula will be abbreviated:

$$E.D. = L.V. + I + C - C.A. - L.A.$$

(Note that some find the formula cumbersome. For example, in the Charles/Dolores example with the gazebo discussed above, many find it silly to go through the formula, which would be: E.D. = ($5,000) + ($0) + ($0) – ($2,500) – ($250). This is because these students can, in their mind, see that Charles should recover a net $1,000 and can do a mental shortcut, realizing he should get his $1,000 profit + what he spent ($1,500) less the salvage value of the paint and wood ($250). Damages can be instinctual, and there is nothing wrong with taking shortcuts if you have a good handle on the concepts. But for those for whom damages are a struggle, in the sections below the full formula will be used, although a shortcut or two will be suggested for those who find the formula more of a hindrance than a solution).

In the next several sections, damage calculation using the standard formula is provided for the major categories of contract breach. Not all categories of damages are applicable from the facts of the hypotheticals so as to save them from being over-complicated, but the ideas of what to look for to recover each type of damage will often be discussed.

2. **Employment Contracts: Breach by Employer. [§ 30–30]**

> Nora is the Head of Surgery at Mercy Hospital ("Mercy"). Nora and Mercy have entered into a written employment agreement which calls for Nora to receive $240,000 in salary over the next year, plus another $36,000 in benefits. Nora and Mercy operate under the contract for 5 months, but then Mercy breaches by wrongfully firing Nora. Nora hires a physician search firm to find her a position, which costs her $400. A few weeks later, the search firm finds her a position as a staff surgeon at a large hospital in another state. Her salary at this new position is $180,000/year, and the benefit package is worth $12,000/year less at the new facility than it was at Mercy. She starts at the new position exactly one month after being fired from Mercy. To take the position, Nora incurs a moving expense of $6,000.
>
> The components of Nora's damages are valued as follows:
>
> **Lost Value**—The lost value to Nora due to the breach is relatively easy to compute. The total value to Nora of her salary

at Mercy for the year-long contract was $240,000, or $20,000/month. She was paid for five months, so she has already received $100,000 of that value. Thus, the **lost value** of the salary part of her compensation due to Mercy's breach is $240,000 − $100,000 or $140,000.

Similarly, the total value of her benefits was $36,000 for the year, or $3,000/month. She has received $15,000 worth of her benefits under the contract (5 months x $3,000/month), and thus, she has a **lost value** in benefits due to the breach of ($36,000) − ($15,000) or $21,000.

Hence, the total "lost value" as a result of Mercy's breach is ($140,000) + ($21,000) or $161,000.

Incidental Loss—Nora suffered two separate kinds of incidental damages in this hypothetical: (i) the fee Nora paid to the medical search company of $400; and (ii) moving expenses of $6,000. Both are recoverable in the breach action. That is, both are out-of-pocket expenses borne by Nora **after** the breach, and reasonably spent in an attempt to mitigate the breaching party's losses, i.e., they were expenditures reasonably made while searching for, and taking, other employment. These expenditures mitigate Mercy's damages because the salary and benefits of Nora's other employment must be subtracted from Nora's damages as losses avoided. The only question as to their recoverability by Nora is whether those amounts are "reasonable." As it appears they are, Nora is entitled to recover these amounts in her breach action against Mercy.

Consequential Loss—There are no consequential damages on these facts.

Costs Avoided—There are no costs avoided on these facts.

Loss Avoided—Nora's salary and benefits for 6 months at the other hospital are losses avoided for purposes of her expectation damages, for she is making a substitute use as to the value of the services that were the subject of the employment agreement. That is, she is "salvaging" those services and selling them to someone else.

Nora earned $15,000/month in her new job, and thus there is a 6 × $15,000 or $90,000 loss avoided as to the salary component of Nora's damages. Similarly, Nora will be able to earn 6 × $2,000/month or $12,000 in benefits at her new job during the period of time she would have been paid by Mercy if Mercy had not breached. Accordingly, her total "loss avoided" is $90,000 + $12,000 or $102,000, which must be accounted for in computing Nora's expectation recovery.

Note that if Nora could have done both jobs, she need not subtract the salary from the "new" job as a cost avoided. But, the way the problem was set up, both were full time and she could not have worked at both jobs. As such, she must subtract the amount she earned in the second position or be put in a better position than she woud have been in absent the breach.

As explained in more detail below [§ 30–59], "avoidability" is an important limitation on the recovery of a wrongfully terminated employee. An employee need not take a job that is not comparable, and hence may recover the full amount of their lost salary from the employer if he or she cannot find comparable work. But if comparable work is available, *or if the employee actually takes any other work, whether comparable or not*, the salary available because of the new work must be subtracted as a lost avoided, unless the employee can demonstrate that he or she would have been able to do both jobs.

Expectation Damages Calculation

Using the E.D. = L.V. + I + C − C.A. − L.A. formula [§ 30–29], Nora's expectation damages due from Mercy as a result of its breach are: $161,000 + $6,400 + $0 − $0 − $102,000, or **$65,400**.

3. **Employment Contracts: Breach by Employee. [§ 30–31]**

   Sid has a written employment contract in which he promised to serve as a sales representative of XYZ Corp. at an annual salary of $36,000. The contract called for Sid to work for a year, but Sid breached and left XYZ for another job after just one month. Sid had collected his salary for the month before he left. XYZ ran an ad in the paper seeking a replacement for Sid, which cost XYZ $500. As a result of the ad, XYZ was able to hire Pam as a suitable replacement for Sid. Pam started a month after Sid left and XYZ reasonably agreed to pay her $39,000/year or $3,250/month.

   Lost Value—In employee breach cases, the lost value to the employer is equal to the reasonable salary the employer has to pay the person hired to replace the breaching employee. Here, XYZ is obligated to pay Pam $3,250/month for the ten months remaining on Sid's contract, and thus the lost value to the company is 10 x $3,250 or $32,500.

   Incidental Loss—XYZ has suffered an incidental loss of $500, measured by the cost to run the advertisement in the paper. That is, the $500 is a reasonable out-of-pocket expense incurred by the injured party after Sid's breach in an effort to mitigate or lessen Sid's damages, namely to find someone who could give the company whatever benefits Sid had promised. Note that XYZ would have been entitled to recover this money regardless of whether the advertisement actually resulted in XYZ finding a replacement for Sid [§ 30–19].

Consequential Loss—In theory, any profits that Sid would have made for XYZ under the contract are recoverable by the company as a consequential loss. However, recovering the lost profits would be subject to the usual limitations of being proven with reasonable certainty [§ 30–49]. Because it would be almost impossible to prove the amount of profits Sid did not earn, and because Sid had not been on the job very long and thus did not have a "track record," it is very unlikely any consequential loss of this type could actually be recovered by XYZ. (Note this conclusion is buttressed by the fact that there are only a very few reported cases in which such consequential damages have been awarded to an employer in employee-breach cases). Accordingly, as a practical matter, there will be $0 in consequential loss recoverable by XYZ.

Cost Avoided—Due to Sid's breach, XYZ did not have to pay Sid for 11 months under the contract. Sid was to make $3,000/month under his contract, and thus XYZ avoided a cost of having to pay 11 months of his salary, or $33,000.

Loss Avoided—There are no losses avoided on these facts.

Expectation Damages Calculation

Under the E.D. = L.V. + I + C − C.A. − L. A. formula [*see* § 30–29], XYZ's expectation damages due from Sid as a result of his breach are: $32,500 + $500 + 0 − $33,000 − 0 or **$0**. Hence, XYZ is entitled only to a recovery of nominal damages [§ 30–22]—although some courts would allow the employer to recover at least the $500 in incidental damages on these facts. [§ 30–19.]

4. **Construction Contracts: Breach by Builder. [§ 30–32]**

   Before discussing examples of problems illustrating an expectation damage recovery in cases where the builder breaches, it must be noted that there are **special rules governing the calculation of "lost value" in these cases**. The reason for the special rules has to do with the fact that there are two reasonable ways of calculating lost value in a construction contract when the builder breaches. That is "lost value" could reasonably be calculated either:

   (i) by the diminution in fair market value of the property caused by the breach; or

   (ii) by the amount of money necessary to finish the job (if the builder never starts construction or quits part way through), or the amount of money necessary to remedy any problems with the construction (if the builder finished the work, but did not perform it well).

MONEY DAMAGES

Accordingly, in a rather complicated series of rules set forth in §§ 347, 348, and 350, the Restatement 2d has adopted the following rules to compute "lost value" for the breach of construction contracts where the breach is caused by the builder:

Rule No. 1: If the diminution in the fair market value of the property caused by the breach is greater than the cost of completion or repair, the injured party may only use the cost of completion or repair as the "lost value."

Rule No. 2: If the cost of completion or repair is greater than the diminution in the fair market value of the property caused by the breach, the injured party is **still** *generally* entitled to the cost of completion or repair as the "lost value" [Restatement 2d § 348, Cmt. c]. In other words, even where the cost to fix a contractor's poor workmanship, or the cost to complete a project unjustly left unfinished by a contractor, may cost more than the decrease in fair market value to the property caused by the poor workmanship or unfinished work, contract law still generally allows the owner to recover the amount of money which will allow the injured party to receive what he or she bargained for, namely an adequately constructed, completed project. This is accomplished by awarding the homeowner the cost of repair.

Rule No. 3: When the cost of completion or repair is so much greater than the diminution in fair market value to the property caused by the breach so that it is "**clearly disproportionate**" to the amount of diminution in market value, the injured party may **only** use the decreased fair market value as the "lost value" and is not entitled to use the disproportionately greater amount of the repair or completion cost in computing expectation damages [Restatement 2d § 348(2)(b)]. This Rule is thus a limited exception to Rule No. 2 above. It applies where the cost to repair the poor construction or to finish the construction would be **far** more expensive than the loss in market value occasioned by the breach. When that is so, only the lesser amount may be recovered.

Note that while there is no hard and fast test for how great the disparity between the repair/completion costs and the fair market value diminution must be to have Rule No. 3 apply instead of Rule No. 2, it is clear that the disparity must be **very** large. Some authorities also limit the applicability of Rule No. 3 to those situations where the breach is non-willful. If the contractor's breach is willful, these courts allow the land owner to use the full cost of repair or of completion as the lost value component of his or her expectation recovery.

CHAPTER 30

a. **Example. [§ 30–33]**

Barry hires Andrea to build a pool at his house for $40,000. Andrea completes the work, and is paid the contract price. Soon thereafter, however, cracks start appearing in the sides and bottom of the pool. It will cost $5,000 to repair the cracks. At trial, competent evidence demonstrates that the diminution in the fair market value of Barry's house due to the breach, i.e., the fair market value of the house with a watertight pool minus the fair market value of the house with a cracked pool, is $10,000.

The "lost value" component of Barry's expectation damages is $5,000 under Rule No. 1 above. That is, since the cost of repair ($5,000) is less than the diminution in fair market value caused by the breach ($10,000), Barry must use $5,000 as his lost value. If Barry were awarded $10,000, he would be put in a better position than if the contract had not been breached in that he could repair the pool, **plus** be left with $5,000 left over in cash.

b. **Example. [§ 30–34]**

Same as above, except this time the cracks are more extensive and it will cost $15,000 to repair the pool, but the fair market value diminution resulting from the breach is still $10,000. Barry is nevertheless entitled to use $15,000 as his "lost value" under Rule No. 2 above. That is, even though the cost to repair or complete construction is somewhat greater than the diminution in the fair market value of the property, the injured party is still entitled to use the costs of repair or completion in computing his "lost value," so long as such costs are not "clearly disproportionate" to the lost fair market value. As the $5,000 difference between the cost of repair and the loss is fair market value is not "clearly disproportionate" (as the term is used in Restatement 2d § 348), and since the only way to award Barry the full benefit of his bargain is by awarding him enough money to repair the pool, he is entitled to use $15,000 as his "lost value" in computing expectation damages.

c. **Example of *Jacob & Youngs, Inc. v. Kent*. [§ 30–35*]**

Kent hired Jacob & Youngs, Inc., a general contractor, to build a vacation home. In their contract it specified that Jacob & Youngs would use copper pipe made by the Reading Company when installing the plumbing. Shortly before construction was complete, and after most of the pipe had been covered by drywall, it was discovered that some of the pipe installed in the house was made by the Cohoes Company. It was clear that the

---

* For a further discussion of the case, listen to CD # 10, Track 1 of *Sum and Substance Audio on Contracts* or read § 30–35.

use of Cohoes pipe instead of Reading was inadvertent, and it was uncontroverted that the Cohoes pipe was functionally equivalent to the Reading pipe in quality, cost, market value, and appearance. Significantly, installation of the Cohoes pipe did not reduce the fair market value of Kent's house appreciably, if at all. However, tearing out the drywall and inspecting and replacing each pipe would have been very expensive. [*Jacob & Youngs, Inc. v. Kent*, 230 N.Y. 239, 129 N.E. 889 (1921)].

Under Rule No. 3 above, Kent was only entitled to use the diminished fair market value of his home caused by the breach as the "lost value" component of his expectation damages calculation, and not the cost to repair the construction mistake caused by using the wrong pipe. This is the type of case where the cost of completion or repair is "clearly disproportionate" to the loss in fair market value due to the breach, and hence the owner is only entitled to use the diminished fair market value as the "lost value" component of his expectation damages [Restatement 2d § 348, Cmt. c, Ill. 4]. Others have called this an example of "economic waste," i.e., if Kent were to get the cost of repair, i.e., it would be a "waste" to give him such a large economic recovery when he probably would not do anything with the house anyway, and just pocket the money.

If the breach had been willful, i.e., had Jacob & Youngs deliberately used Cohoes pipe instead of Reading, some authorities would have allowed Kent to recover the full cost of repair.

5. **Construction Contracts: Breach by Landowner. [§ 30–36]**

Wayne agrees to construct a home for Mary for $100,000. The contract calls for progress payments to be made after certain parts of the project are completed, and Wayne has appropriately been paid $20,000 in such progress payments. Mary thereafter breaches and orders Wayne off her property. At that point, Wayne has incurred costs of $25,000 in labor and materials, and he can establish that it would have cost him another $65,000 to finish the job. At the time of the breach, Wayne has also purchased $2,000 worth of 2 x 10 lumber for work on Mary's house that has not yet been used in the construction, and which can be used by Wayne on other jobs.

The components of Wayne's expectation damages are:

Lost Value—Had the contract been completed, Wayne would have been paid $100,000. He has already been paid $20,000, so the objective **lost** value as a result of the breach is $80,000.

Incidental Loss—There are no incidental damages on these facts.

CHAPTER 30

Consequential Loss—There are no consequential damages on these facts.

Cost Avoided—As a result of the breach, Wayne will not have to spend the remaining $65,000 to finish construction. Therefore, Mary's breach has resulted in a $65,000 cost avoided to him.

Loss Avoided—The $2,000 in lumber that can be used on other jobs is the kind of substitute use of resources that make up loss avoided. That is, because Wayne can salvage that lumber for work on other jobs, Mary cannot be charged for paying for it [*See* the discussion of "loss avoided" in § 30–29].

Expectation Damages Calculation

Under the E.D. = L.V. + I + C − C.A. − L.A. formula [§ 30–29], the amount of Wayne's expectation damages recoverable against Mary as a result of the breach are: $80,000 + $0 + $0 − $65,000 − $2,000 or **$13,000**.

(Some like to use a shortcut for damages in this situation, stating that recovery is the amount spent to date, plus expected profit on the job, less the loss avoided).

6. **Real Estate Contracts: Breach by Buyer. [§ 30–37]**

Connie was under a contract to sell her house to Bernie for $100,000 on March 1. At the last minute Bernie breached, and it took Connie six months to find a new buyer. The demand for real estate declined somewhat during the six-month period, and she was only able to get $98,000 when she sold it to the second buyer.

The components of Connie's expectation damages are as follows:

Lost Value—Connie lost $100,000 in value from Bernie as a result of Bernie's breach.

Incidental Loss—Connie lost the value of 6 months interest on $100,000 due to Bernie's failure to pay. Hence, at a 10% rate (which some states have as a statutory rate, regardless of what banks are paying), Connie has $500 in lost interest as an incidental damage.

Consequential Loss—There are no consequential damages on these facts.

Cost Avoided—There are no costs avoided on these facts.

Loss Avoided—Connie was able to make substitute arrangements for the house that was the subject matter of the contract by re-selling it to another for $98,000. Hence, there is a $98,000 loss avoided which must be factored in when calculating Connie's expectation recovery.

MONEY DAMAGES

Expectation Damages Calculation

Under the E.D. = L.V. + I + C − C.A. − L.A. formula (*see* § 30–29), the amount of Connie's expectation damages due from Bernie as a result of his breach are: $100,000 + $500 + $0 − $0 − $98,000 or **$2,500**.

7. **Real Estate Contracts: Breach by Seller. [§ 30–38]**

   Typically, when a seller breaches a contract to transfer an interest in land, the buyer will sue for an order of specific performance, and thus force the seller actually to transfer the property to the buyer as promised in the contract as land is considered "unique" [§ 29–13]. However, if for some reason the buyer does not wish to, or cannot, sue for equitable relief, then an award of damages is available. The courts have developed two theories of how to calculate the amount of expectation damages recoverable in these cases:

   (i) The "**American Rule**": the purchaser is entitled to recover the full amount of his or her expectation damages, i.e., the buyer can recover the difference between the contract price and the fair market value of the property, plus any down payment and any incidental damages; and

   (ii) The "**English Rule**": the purchaser is only entitled to recover his or her reliance damages, i.e., the buyer can recover any down payment, plus any out-of-pocket costs spent in acquiring title, e.g., a title insurance policy, house inspection, etc. However, benefit of the bargain damages are not permitted. That is, the buyer is not entitled to damages resulting from a "good" deal, and thus, cannot recover the difference between the fair market value of the property and the contract price under this view.

   a. **Example. [§ 30–39]**

   Don signed a contract to purchase a piece of property sold due to foreclosure at a price of **$80,000**, the price of the unpaid mortgage at the time of default. This was a good deal for Don, for competent evidence can establish that the fair market value of the property was $95,000. At the time he signed the contract, Don paid $8,000 as a down payment, and later incurred expenses of $1,000 for title insurance reports, termite inspections, etc. Shortly thereafter, just before title was to be transferred to Don, the seller breached and refused to deliver the deed.

   Most likely, Don would sue for specific performance, and thus would seek an order giving him title. However, if for some reason such a recovery was unavailable or unattractive to him, he is entitled to seek damages instead. The extent of Don's damage recovery would depend on whether he was in an "American Rule" jurisdiction or an "English Rule" jurisdiction.

If he were in an "American Rule" jurisdiction, Don would be entitled to a $23,000 expectation damage recovery, i.e., the difference between the purchase price and the fair market value of the property ($95,000–$80,000), plus the return of his $8,000 down payment. Note, he would not be entitled to the $1,000 he spent on title insurance, termite inspections, etc. because he would have had to spend that money anyway had the contract not been breached. Since he would have to have spent $1,000 had the contract gone forward to obtain the property so as to realize its $15,000 benefit in value over what he paid for it, he cannot be awarded the $1,000 as contract damages because it would put him in a better position than he would have been in had the contract gone forward.

Note the $1,000 cannot be classified as an "incidental" damage because it was money spent *before* the breach, and it was not money spent to avoid further loss.

If Don were in an "English Rule" jurisdiction, he would only be entitled to a recovery for the $1,000 he spent in reliance on the transfer of the property, along with the return of his $8,000 down payment.

8. Expectation Damage Recovery Under Contracts Governed by the UCC. [§ 30–40]

The UCC has a vast panoply of different remedies available upon breach. These are discussed in detail Chapter Thirty-Two, and it is there a student should turn if his or her professor spends significant time on the UCC. However, the "basics" are set forth below for those whose classes touch on the Code.

a. Buyer's Damages. [§ 30–41*]

There are two UCC formulas for expectation recovery for a buyer when the seller breaches. They depend on whether the buyer actually goes out into the market and purchases replacement goods (called "**cover**"—as in "covering" the breach) or whether the buyer decides he or she would just like to collect the economic value of the expectation interest under the contract, and not repurchase replacement goods.

For a buyer who "covers":

Buyer's Recovery = [(Cost of substitute goods from a second seller) − (Contract price of goods from the breaching seller)] +

---

* For more information, listen to CD # 12, Track 2 of *Sum and Substance Audio on Contracts*.

MONEY DAMAGES

(Incidental damages) + (Consequential damages) – (Expenses saved in consequence of the breach.) [UCC § 2–712].

For a buyer who does not choose to "cover":

Buyer's Recovery = [(Market value of substitute goods at the time the buyer learned of the breach) – (Contract price)] + (Incidental damages) + (Consequential damages) – (Expenses saved in consequence of the breach) [UCC § 2–713].

The choice to cover or not is completely in the discretion of the buyer.

Note that the buyer is also entitled to the recovery of any deposit, down payment, or full payment already made to the seller under UCC § 2–711.

As can be seen, while using different words, in truth the UCC formula is really just a specialized application of the more general E.D. = L.V. + I + C – C.A. – L.A. formula used previously [§ 30–29], where:

L.V. = the cost of acquiring the substitute good from another (or the market value of the goods if the buyer does not cover);

I = has the same meaning as to incidental damages as in non-UCC contracts [§ 30–19];

C = has the same general meaning as to consequential damages as in non-UCC contracts although it includes some additional factors [§§ 32–9, 30–12];

C.A. = the expenses saved as a result of the breach, including the contract price (cost) that the buyer no longer has to pay to the breaching buyer (and thus avoids); and

L.A. doesn't come into play because a *buyer* typically has no salvage value or other loss avoided.

(1) Example. [§ 30–42]

> Ben wants to buy some in-line skates from Sports Store. Sports Store is out of stock in Ben's size, but promises to order a pair for him from the manufacturer and promises delivery in a month. The price of the skates is $125. That brand of skates turns out to be particularly popular, and so when "Ben's" pair comes into Sports Store, the Store ends up selling "Ben's" skates to another for $200—the then-going price. Ben files suit.
>
> If Ben covers by buying a comparable pair of skates from another store, he is entitled to the difference between the price for replacement skates from another store minus the

contract price from Sports Store, or $200 − $125 = $75 [UCC § 2–712].

If Ben chooses not to cover, he is entitled to the difference between the current market price for the skates minus the contract price from Sports Store, or $200 − $125 = $75 [UCC § 2–713].

Such recovery makes sense for $75 is the value of Ben's "expectation" under the contract. That is, he made a "good" deal by contracting to pay $125 for an item valued by the market at $200 at the time of promised delivery. That is, he had a protected expectation interest valued at $75. So he can either pocket the $75, and realize the benefit of his bargain, or buy replacement skates for a net $125 to him, i.e., pay the purchase price of $200 to another, less the $75 recovered from Sports Store. In that way, he will be in exactly the same position as he would have been had the contract been carried out—he has his bargained for skates for $125—which, after all, is the idea behind expectation damages.

(2) Different Formulation for Buyer's Warranty Damages. [§ 30–43]

If a buyer is tendered a non-conforming good and decides to keep it and sue for breach of warranty, rather than reject it or revoke his or her acceptance of it and sue for money damages, the formula for a buyer's recovery is quite different, but the idea behind the formula is still the same—to put the buyer in the position he or she would have been in had the contract been carried out. (*See* Chapter Thirty-Five for a discussion of the substantive law regarding warranties under the Code and § 32–23 for a more detailed discussion of the damages formula used in a breach of warranty suit.)

The formula for a warranty damage recovery is:

Buyer's Recovery: [(Value of goods as warranted) − (Value of goods actually received)] + (Incidental Damages) + (Consequential Damages) − (Expenses saved in consequence of Seller's breach) [UCC § 2–714(2), (3)].

b. Seller's Damages. [§ 30–44*]

The formulas for a seller's damages recovery under Article 2 also are designed to allow the seller to recover expectation damages.

---

* For more information, listen to CD # 12, Track 3 of *Sum and Substance Audio on Contracts*.

MONEY DAMAGES

Again, there are two formulas, depending on whether the seller actually sells the goods in the marketplace to another (**"seller's cover"**) or keeps the goods.

The basic formulation is essentially the reciprocal of the buyer's damages formulation given in § 30–39, namely:

If the seller re-sells the goods ("seller's cover"):

Seller's recovery = [(Contract price from the breaching buyer) − (Price realized upon reasonable sale of the goods to another)] + (Incidental Damages) − (Expenses saved as a result of the breach) [UCC § 2–706].

If the seller does not re-sell the goods:

Seller's recovery = [(Contract price from the breaching buyer) − (Market Price of the goods at the time and place of tender)] + (Incidental Damages) − (Expenses saved as a result of the breach) [UCC § 2–708(1)].

These formulas are again no more than a specialized application of the more general E.D. = L.V. + I + C − C.A. − L.A. formula used to calculate expectation damages explained previously [§ 30–29], where:

L.V. = the contract price the seller was to receive from the buyer, i.e., the "value" of the contract that has now been "lost;"

I = has the same meaning of incidental damages as in non-UCC contracts [§ 30–19];

L.A. = the price the seller received from another buyer for the improperly rejected goods, or could have received as determined by the market;

C.A. = Costs avoided as a result of the breach.

Note that there is no authority under the Code for the seller to recover consequential loss.

(1) Example. [§ 30–45]

Sam contracts to sell his car to Betty for $5,000. Betty breaches, and Sam runs an ad in the paper for $20, and eventually finds another buyer who pays him $4,800 for the car. He sues Betty.

Under the Code, he is entitled to the contract price from Betty minus the amount he received from the other buyer, plus any incidental damages (the newspaper ad), or $5,000 − $4,800 + 20 = $220.

If he chooses not to sell the car to another buyer, assuming the $4,800 is the "market price," his recovery is the same amount, equaling the market − contract prices, plus incidentals.

Such recoveries make sense, for they protect his legitimate expectations under the Code. He made an economically good deal by contracting to sell a $4,800 item (as valued by the market) for $5,000. He can either pocket the $200 (plus the reimbursement for the ad) and keep the car, or he can sell it—which puts him in the exact position he would have been in had the contract been performed, i.e., he has a net $5,000—$4,800 from the new buyer, $200 from Betty, and a reimbursement from Betty of the $20 he had to pay for the ad.

(2) Different Formulation for Lost Volume Sellers. [§ 30–46]

The formula in § 30–43 works well for a seller who has only one item to sell. But for commercial sellers with a large supply of goods, a buyer's breach typically costs them a sale. That is, if a buyer unjustifiably backs out of a purchase of a microwave from an appliance store, the store probably can sell that same microwave to another. But had the first purchaser not breached, the store would have been able to sell two microwaves and hence realize two profits, instead of one. So the breach actually cost it a sale, even though the particular microwave that was the subject of the breached contract was eventually sold at the contract price to the second buyer.

In such situations, the Code permits the seller to recoup the profit lost because of the buyer's breach, i.e., the profit it would have made by selling the second microwave, under the formula in UCC § 2–708(2). [*See* §§ 32–45 *et seq.* for a more extensive discussion of lost volume sellers and for the formula used in such cases],

Once again, however, realize that the idea behind such a doctrine is the recovery of expectation damages, i.e., to put the retailer in the position it would have been in had the contract been performed. In other words, it would have had two profits had the contract not been breached. Since it now has only one profit, it can seek the "lost profit" on the unsold second unit from the breaching buyer and be "made whole."

9. Expectation Damages in "Losing" Contracts. [§ 30–47]

A non-breaching party in a "losing" contract, i.e., an economically improvident contract where the party would lose money had the contract been carried out, will not seek expectation damages. That is, because the goal of expectation damages is to put the party in the position he or she would have been in had the contract been carried out, an expectation damages recovery would yield no recovery at all or only nominal damages. Instead, a party to a losing contract will typically seek a restitutionary recovery [*see* Chapter Thirty-One for a discussion of restitution], or, perhaps, a reliance damages recovery [§ 30–65].

In such situations, the **burden of proof is on the *breaching party* to establish that contract would be a losing one**.

E. THREE LIMITATIONS ON THE RECOVERABILITY OF EXPECTATION DAMAGES: CERTAINTY, FORESEEABILITY, AND AVOIDABILITY. [§ 30–48*]

The recoverability of expectation damages is limited by three significant doctrines:

(1) To be recoverable, **damages must be proven with "reasonable certainty,"** i.e., the amount of the damage suffered cannot be speculative and the non-breaching party must put on proof to establish to the jury the amount of his or her losses with some degree of certainty [Restatement 2d § 352; *see* § 30–49];

(2) To be recoverable, the party in breach **must have reasonably foreseen**, at the time the contract was formed, that **the type of consequential damage** sought by the injured party would follow from the breach [Restatement 2d § 351; *see* § 30–54]; and

(3) To be recoverable, the damages sought by the injured party **must not have been avoidable** by him or her without undue risk, burden, or humiliation, i.e., the non-breaching party may not recover damages from the breaching party that could easily have been **mitigated** or avoided by the non-breaching party [Restatement 2d § 350; *see* § 30–59].

1. The "Certainty" Limitation: Damages Cannot Be Recovered Unless Proven with "Reasonable Certainty." [§ 30–49]

Generally, American courts have refused to allow an injured party to recover damages for a breach of contract unless the damages can be proven with reasonable certainty. **This rule is not limited to expectation damages**, i.e., **all** contract damages must be proven with sufficient certainty to be recoverable [Restatement 2d § 352]. However, when the reasonable certainty limitation is applied to expectation damages, it is often in the context of denying an injured

---

* For more information, listen to CD # 12, Track 1 of *Sum and Substance Audio on Contracts*.

CHAPTER 30

party's attempt to recover lost profits as a consequential damage [Restatement 2d § 352, Cmt. a; § 30–51].

a. Modern Rules as to How "Certain" a Damage Must Be Proven to Be Recoverable. [§ 30–50]

There is no precise test as to how certain proof of the amount of damages must be before they can be recovered. Indeed, the reasonable certainty doctrine is intended to be flexible so that a court can apply it more or less stringently as the facts warrant. However, over time the following rules have developed as a guide in determining whether a particular loss has been proven with enough certainty to be recoverable:

Rule No. 1: In a close case, any doubts as to whether a loss is sufficiently certain are to be resolved against the breaching party [Restatement 2d § 352, Cmt. a].

Once a court has determined that the injured party has suffered a real loss and that the breaching party caused it, any doubts about whether the loss is proven with sufficient certainty in a close case are resolved against the breaching party. The rationale is that when the choice is between denying an injured party recovery, or denying a breaching party a windfall by not having to pay for the damages that he or she caused because the magnitude of the harm cannot be precisely established, the breaching party should lose.

Rule No. 2: The requirement of certainty is less strictly applied when the breach is deliberate than when it is not.

Courts tend to give more leeway in allowing the injured party to recover for damages that can only be approximated (rather than proven with certainty) when the breach is a willful one. Once again, this is not to say that upon a deliberate breach the certainty requirement no longer applies. But it is to say that the certainty standards are relaxed in such a case as a penalty for intentional *malum in se* conduct.

Rule No. 3: So long as the injured party provides a "reasonable basis" for his or her damage calculations, those calculations are likely to be accepted as sufficient under the reasonable certainty test.

Over the past several decades, courts have required somewhat less precision in the proof of damages. In other words, modern courts place more emphasis on the modifier "reasonable" than they do on the object "certainty" in

MONEY DAMAGES

applying the rule of Restatement 2d § 352. Hence, modern courts tend to be receptive to the idea that in some cases a particular kind of loss simply is incapable of being quantified with precision, and thus, reasonable assumptions need to be made and numbers need to be approximated in order to come up with any kind of proof of loss [Restatement 2d § 352, Cmt. a]. As some courts have put it, once the *fact* of damage has been proven, the *amount* need not be established with mathematical precision.

Contrary to this trend is the fact that courts have toughened up the rules for when proof of damages are introduced through expert testimony. That is, sometimes an accountant or economist will have to be called to quantify, e.g., the amount of lost business opportunity suffered by an innocent party as a consequential damage, taking into account the sluggish economy, the trends for the industry as a whole, likely competitors, etc. While this puts it a little too simply, the Supreme Court has held that before an expert can testify as to such damage, the expert must show that the methodology used in determining the damages is generally well accepted within the field and subject to peer reviewed studies with a quantified error rate [*Daubert v. Merrell Dow Pharmaceuticals, Inc.*, 509 U.S. 579 (1993)].

(1) The Reasonable Certainty Test Typically Limits Recovery of Damages Only Where a Non-Breaching Buyer Is Suing for Consequential Lost Profits Resulting from a "Collateral" Transaction. [§ 30–51]

By far the most frequent application of the reasonable certainty test as a limitation on the recovery of contract damages takes place in cases where the non-breaching purchaser of land, goods, or services is suing for lost profits as consequential damages resulting from a "collateral" transaction that never took place because of the supplier's breach. These "collateral" transactions are of three types:

(1) Cases where the buyer planned to re-sell to another the land or good that was never delivered due to the seller's breach. In these cases, it is the lost profits from the re-sale that never took place for which the injured buyer seeks recovery;

(2) Cases where the buyer planned to use the goods or services that were never delivered due to the breach as raw materials in the manufacture or assembly of another product. In these cases, it is the lost profits

from the sales of these never fabricated products for which the injured party seeks recovery; and

(3) Cases where a breach by the supplier of services causes a delay in the opening of, or in the continued operation of, the purchaser's retail establishment. In these cases, the injured party seeks recovery of lost profits from the retail sales that never took place because the store was closed or out of inventory.

The certainty problems in these types of cases stem from the fact that there is often no proof that these other transactions would ever have taken place even if the supplier had not breached; or if they would have taken place, there is no solid proof as to what the frequency of those sales would have been or what the price would have been.

For example, suppose a furniture manufacturer never delivered a dining room set to a retailer. To recover lost profits from the sale of the dining room set that never occurred, the retailer faces problems under the certainty rule. There is rarely absolute proof as to how much the retailer would have charged for the set; when it would have been sold; *if* it would have sold; whether the retailer would have lowered the price if it did not sell right away; whether the retailer would have financed the sale rather than making it for cash, thereby incurring interest costs that would have to be subtracted from any recovery to put the retailer in the position it would have been in had the contract been performed, etc.

Because courts view it as unfair to the breaching party to make him or her pay an amount which has little or no basis in fact and is simply a guess by the injured party as to the amount of any harm suffered, contract law has developed the following considerations to help resolve the question of whether lost profits from collateral transactions that never took place should be recoverable:

(a) **When a retailer seeks to recover profits lost due to a delay in the opening, or re-opening, of commercial premises, the newer the business of the injured party, the less likely it is that a court will find that lost profits can be proven with reasonable certainty.** The converse of this rule is that the longer a party seeking lost profits in such cases has been in business, the more likely a court is to accept historical sales figures as sufficient proof of lost profits caused by the supplier's breach. However, it should be noted that even with newer businesses modern courts are increasingly willing to use subsequent sales figures, showing profits made by the business when it finally did open, as sufficiently certain proof of what the profits would have been had the business opened on time.

(b) **The more the non-breaching party's lost profits depend on uncertain tastes and preferences of the public, the more unlikely it is that such lost profits can be established with reasonable certainty.**

(c) **The longer the period of time between the breach and the expected collateral sale, or the more tenuous the connection between the breach and the anticipated collateral sale, the less likely it is that such lost profits will be established with enough certainty to be recoverable.** For example, if a supplier did not provide a chemical that the buyer says was supposed to be used in experiments for the possible development of a new non-dairy creamer, that, even if developed would not have been on the market for three years, it is unlikely the supplier will be held liable for lost profits from the delay in the sale of the creamer on certainty grounds.

(2) **Example. [§ 30–52]**

Smith Construction Co. ("Smith") agrees contractually to build a supermarket for A & B, Inc. in a small rural community. The store would be the first supermarket in the community. Smith promised to complete construction by April 1 in the contract, but did not actually finish until September 15.

It is possible that A & B can recover for lost profits from the sales that did not occur during the April 1 through September 15 period. A & B would try to establish the amount of such lost profits by its subsequent sales history, by the profits made by similar supermarkets in comparable areas around the country, by expert economic testimony as to expected profits during that time, etc. A modern court **may** find that such proof can establish A & B's lost profits with reasonable certainty. However, because the supermarket is a new enterprise and the first of its kind in the community, it is also possible that any proof as to its lost profits would not, even today, be found to be established with enough certitude to be recoverable [Restatement 2d § 352, Cmt. b, Ill. 6]. Note that if the store had been in operation for ten years or so, its sales constant, one month to the next, and Smith's breach had been the failure to finish a **remodeling** project on time, A & B could surely recover its lost profits based on historical sales figures.

(3) Example. [§ 30–53]

Jack's Publishing contracts to publish a novel written by Christie. It is to be Christie's first published book. Christie is to be paid only on a royalty basis, i.e., she is entitled only to a percentage of the purchase price of each book sold. Jack's breaches, deciding it does not want to publish the book. Despite diligent efforts, Christie finds no other publisher willing to publish the book. Christie probably cannot recover any lost profits. This is because it is unlikely Christie can prove what her royalties would have been with **any** degree of certainty given that this is her first book and that her compensation for the book is dependent totally on the uncertain tastes of the public. [Restatement 2d § 352, Cmt. a, Ill. 1].

2. The "Foreseeability" Limitation: Damages Unrecoverable Unless the Breaching Party Either Foresaw, or Should Have Foreseen the Type of Damage at the Time of Contracting. [§ 30–54]

The second limitation on recovery of expectation loss is the "foreseeability" doctrine. It is this principle that both defines consequential damages and limits the recovery of such damages. The modern rule regarding foreseeability is relatively straightforward. As stated in Restatement 2d § 351(1):

> **Damages are not recoverable for the type of loss that the party in breach did not foresee, or have reason to foresee, as a probable result of the breach when the contract was made.**

The origin of the doctrine is the most famous case in contract law, the English decision *Hadley v. Baxendale*, 9 Ex. 341, 156 Eng. Rep. 145 (1854), which is the *"Palsgraf"* of contracts. Before explaining and discussing completely the modern day applications of the rules governing the foreseeability limitation, an examination of *Hadley* is appropriate.

MONEY DAMAGES

SPECIAL CASE SQUIB

a. *Hadley v. Baxendale.* [§ 30–55]

Mr. and Mrs. Hadley owned a mill that produced flour in Glouster, England. The crankshaft of their mill broke, shutting down production at the plant. There was no feasible way to repair the shaft, so the Hadleys quickly made arrangements with W. Joyce & Co. ("Joyce"), to manufacture a new crankshaft as soon as possible. Joyce was located several hundred miles away, in Greenwich, England. Joyce told the Hadleys that its engineers needed the old shaft to serve as a model before they could manufacture a new one.

Accordingly, the Hadleys sent one of their employees to Pickford & Co. ("Pickford"), which was owned by Mr. Baxendale, and was a common carrier (i.e., the U.P.S. or FedEx of its day). A Pickford employee promised the Hadleys' employee the company would use the fastest delivery methods possible, which should get the shaft to Greenwich in two-days. There is some evidence that Pickford charged extra for the "fastest possible delivery" promise. Thus, Mr. Hadley had the old shaft delivered to Pickford the next day. Unfortunately, delivery of the shaft to Joyce took a week, not two days. As a result, the Hadleys' mill was shut down five days longer than it should have been.

The reason for the delay in shipping turned out to be a simple mistake. Pickford had included instructions with the shaft that it should be transported by railway whenever possible. When it got to the last stage of its journey, Pickford's agent either ignored or did not see the instructions to ship the shaft by rail, and instead included it with some other items that also happened to be going to Joyce, but which were being shipped by canal rather than by rail. The canal trip, as opposed to shipment by rail, accounted for the five-day delay.

When Mr. Hadley discovered what had happened, he brought suit against Baxendale, as the owner of Pickford, for breach. As part of his damages he sought five days' worth of lost profits at the mill, which he asserted was £300.

Held: Hadley was **not** entitled to recover for the lost profits from the mill's being shut down an extra five days on the grounds such damages were consequential and not sufficiently foreseeable. [*Hadley v. Baxendale,* 9 Ex. 341, 156 Eng. Rep. 145 (1854)].

Hadley set forth <u>two</u> rules regarding the recoverability of expectation damages:

(1) A **non-breaching party may recover "direct" consequential damages without having to prove specially that such damages were a foreseeable consequence of the breach**. This is because, by definition of a "direct consequential damage," any reasonable person viewing the contract at the time it was negotiated, would foresee that such type of loss would naturally follow if the contract was breached; and

(2) Any consequential damage that was not a direct consequential damage was, by definition, an "indirect" or "special" consequential damage. **To recover indirect consequential damages, the non-breaching party must prove that the breaching party either foresaw, or from the circumstances, should have foreseen, them as following from the breach**. Hence, because indirect consequential damages were, by definition, not the kind of damages a reasonable person would foresee as resulting from a breach, the burden was on the injured party to prove some notice was given the breaching party that this unusual "consequential" damage would follow from the breach of the particular contract at issue. If such a showing could be made, then the loss would be sufficiently foreseeable, and its recovery posed no special problems.

The first question in deciding the case presented in *Hadley* was thus to determine whether the lost profits due to the mill's being shut down were "direct" or "indirect" consequential damage. That is, would a loss of profits from a business having to close down production "**arise naturally, according to the usual course of things**" from the failure to deliver a package promptly. If so, the lost profits would be a direct consequential damage, and thus recoverable without a special showing of foreseeability on the Hadleys' part. If not, then the loss would be an indirect consequential loss, and thus recoverable only if Baxendale's company had notice that a delayed delivery would result in lost profits for the mill. Only by proving that Baxendale's company had such notice could Hadley prove that lost profits were a sufficiently foreseeable result of the breach so as to be recoverable should the profits be judged consequential.

Hadley held that **the lost profits from Hadleys' mill due to the delayed delivery were indirect consequential damages rather than direct ones**. Hence, they were only recoverable if Hadley could prove that "**they were in the contemplation of both parties at the time they made**

MONEY DAMAGES

the contract as the probable result of the breach." Since there was no evidence in the case that Pickford had been made aware that the mill would be shut down and losing profits while the package was in transit, and thus such loss could not have been in Pickford's contemplation at the time the contract was made as being a probable result of the breach, the Hadleys' lost profits were not recoverable under the foreseeability limitation.

Note that if extra was paid for the "fastest delivery" promise, that extra would be part of the "lost value" recovery as the Hadleys' paid for expedited service and got only regular service. Sending an employee to pick up the shaft the second time would be a direct consequential loss because it would be foreseeable at the time of contracting that if Pickford didn't deliver the shaft timely a second trip to pick it up would be necessary.

b. **Analysis of *Hadley v. Baxendale* and the "Foreseeability" Limitation of Contract Damages. [§ 30–56]**

While not expressly stated in the opinion, the rationale of the *Hadley* foreseeability doctrine is that for contract formation to work correctly, it is necessary that the parties know what economic risks they are being asked to take should the contract be breached i.e., the value of the economic "interest" (*see* § 30–1) being protected, at the time of contract formation. Freedom of contract requires that a party's decision to enter into an agreement, and to do so for a particular price, be fully informed. If a party will later be required to pay for a loss about which he or she did not reasonably know when the decision was made to enter the contract, then, by definition, his or her decision to enter the transaction in the first place was neither fully informed nor completely voluntary.

To illustrate this idea, let's update *Hadley*. Assume a woman came to Fed. Ex. and contracted with the company to deliver a package to a computer manufacturer in Palo Alto. It turns out that package contained a defective computer chip which General Motors was returning to the manufacturer. The chip was crucial to running a GM production plant, and the plant has to be shut down until a working chip is sent as a replacement. Each day the plant is shut down costs GM $1,000,000. Federal Express does not know any of these facts, other than it contracted to deliver overnight a package to a computer manufacturer. If it fails to do so, it has no way of knowing whether its breach will cause a minor inconvenience, a $50,000 loss, or a $1,000,000/day plant closure. The foreseeability doctrine holds that before Federal Express can be asked to pay $1,000,000 for one day's delay in delivery, it must be apprised that such a result is a risk it is taking by promising overnight delivery. Knowing of that risk, it may decide it does not want to enter into the contract at all; or it may decide to do so, but charge a higher price for its service; or it may negotiate with its customer a damage limitation clause, saying it will not be liable for more than the cost of the package if it does not get there overnight, etc. Whatever it may do, the point is that voluntary decision making, which is at the heart of the modern contract doctrine, requires that a party cannot be forced to pay for a kind of loss upon his or her breach that it could not have reasonably foreseen would occur when the contract was made.

The two rules of *Hadley* thus set forth the two ways a loss can be sufficiently foreseeable to be recoverable under the doctrine. If the loss is "direct," then it is, in effect, foreseeable as a matter of law. That is, because such a loss is a kind which can "fairly and reasonably be considered as arising naturally from the breach," contract law assumes that any reasonable person would foresee such a loss as occurring upon a breach, and thus factored the risk of having to pay for it upon a breach in deciding to enter the contract. Accordingly, the injured party can recover that loss without having to prove specially its foreseeability.

On the other hand, if the loss is unusual enough that a reasonable person would not foresee it as a natural result of the breach, then the injured party must prove that the breacher was aware (or at least should have been aware) of the risk of having to pay for such loss if he or she breached. Only with such proof can contract law be sure that the breaching party voluntarily entered the agreement knowing of what risks loomed if he or she should fail to perform what was promised. If the injured party cannot make such a foreseeability showing, then the consequential loss he or she suffered, no matter how real the loss may be, cannot be recovered. This is because the foreseeability doctrine states that unless it is reasonable to assume that the party is breach factored in the risk of having to pay that loss upon a breach when he or she entered the contract, he or she cannot be liable for it.

c. **The Modern Test for Whether a Loss Is a "Direct" or an "Indirect" Consequential Damage. [§ 30–57]**

In *Hadley,* the test for a direct damage was whether the loss "*may fairly . . . be considered arising naturally, i.e., according to the usual course of things, from [a] breach.*" Under the Restatement 2d, this test has been changed to state that: **damages are direct if they follow "in the ordinary course of events" from the breach** [Restatement 2d § 351(2)(a)], whereas under UCC § 2–715(2)(a) they are defined as, "loss[es] resulting from general . . . needs."

Indirect consequential losses under the Restatement are defined as losses suffered, "as a result of special circumstances, beyond the ordinary course of events, which the party in breach had reason to know." [Restatement 2d § 351(2)(b)]. Under the UCC, these losses are defined as losses, "resulting from . . . particular requirements and needs of which the seller at the time of contracting had reason to know."

There are several rules that have developed in determining whether a consequential loss is direct or indirect.

> (1) *Generally*, the only time there is any question at all regarding whether a loss was sufficiently foreseeable to be "direct" arises in **the recovery of lost profits**. That is, while the principles of foreseeability and consequential loss are not theoretically limited to lost profits (i.e., they apply to any damage that is reasonably unforeseeable at the time of contract formation), probably 90% of the time, a loss that is deemed consequential will be a lost profit.
>
> Note this does **not** mean that every time a party tries to recover a lost profit, he or she will only be able to do so upon proving the special awareness on the part of the breaching party. There are a number of situations where a lost profit so clearly will follow in the ordinary course of events after a breach that such losses will be judged direct consequential damages. For example, suppose Copymart leased a coin-operated photocopier to University, which placed it in its law library. As part of the lease, Copymart promised that it would repair any problem with the copier in 12 hours or less. If it takes Copymart three days on one occasion to repair a bank of copiers, certainly it is foreseeable that the breach of its repair obligations will cause lost revenue to University. That is why the machines are card operated. Hence, while (virtually) all consequential losses arise upon an attempt to recover lost profits, not all lost profits are consequential losses. Whether they are or not depends upon the reasonable foreseeability of the loss as determined by application of the remaining factors discussed below.
>
> (2) **The foreseeability of the loss is to be judged at the time the contract was made, not at the time the contract was breached** or any other time. Hence it is irrelevant if circumstances subsequent to the execution of the contract make it likely that a lost profit will (or will not) occur. The only relevant inquiry is whether such a loss was

reasonably foreseeable at the time the contract was entered into.

(3) **The test of foreseeability is an objective one**. The test is whether a **reasonable person**, looking at the contract when it was made, would have foreseen that the injured party would lose profits in the ordinary course of events if the other party breached. If so, such lost profit is a direct damage. If not, it is an indirect consequential loss.

(4) **It is only necessary that such loss foreseeably be "a probable result," not a certain result, of the breach**. In other words, it need not appear certain, or almost certain, that a particular kind of loss would occur upon a breach before such a loss is deemed direct. Rather, it is only necessary that a reasonable person would see such a loss as a **probable** result of the breach in the ordinary course of events.

(5) **Only the *type* of damage needs to be foreseeable in the ordinary course of events in the event of a breach, not its *amount*.**

d. Example. [§ 30–58]

Ted purchases a brand new mini-van from Dealer. Unknown to Dealer, Ted planned to use the van in his automobile repossession business. A few months after Ted purchased the van, while it is still under warranty, the van stops working. Ted has it towed to Dealer's, and it takes Dealer two days to find and fix the electrical problem. During those two days, Ted does not work, and his company loses the revenue and profits it would have made on repossessing cars for those two days.

While Ted has a valid breach of warranty case against the dealer, he probably will not be able to recover for his lost profits due to the foreseeability doctrine. That is, the lost profits suffered by Ted are not "direct" consequential damages, for a reasonable person viewing the contract at the time it was negotiated, would not foresee that if the van had electrical problems, the purchaser would probably suffer a loss of business. That is not to say that such a possibility was inconceivable, but "conceivability" is not the test. **The test is would a reasonable person have foreseen that such a type of damage result was probable in the ordinary course of events after a breach**. Since it is impossible to know whether the van's not working would cause a minor inconvenience to a "soccer dad" or a lost profit to a company, the risk of paying for the purchaser's lost profits was not reasonably in the contemplation of Dealer when it entered into the contract.

Accordingly, the lost profit from Ted's business is an indirect consequential damage on these facts.

As an indirect consequential loss, the lost profits can only be recovered by Ted if he somehow put Dealer on notice so that Dealer knew, or should have known, that one result of a breach would be that Ted would suffer lost profits. If Ted did not declare his purpose in using the van to Dealer, Dealer had no reason to foresee that it would be liable for such a loss, and hence Ted would not be able to meet his burden for recovering such real, but consequential, damages under the foreseeability limitation. Note however, that if, when contracting with the Dealer, Ted mentioned his plans regarding his company and the car to Dealer, there would be a stronger argument that Dealer had a reason to foresee that it would be liable for such a loss. In that case, Dealer may have taken other precautions, such as charging a higher price to cover additional insurance, or negotiated a "no consequential damage" limitation in the deal, etc.

3. The Avoidability Limitation. [§ 30–59]

Under the rule stated in § 350 of the Restatement 2d, a party may not recover damages that the injured party could have avoided or mitigated without undue risk, burden or humiliation.

Three points are worth noting. First, if an injured party has taken **reasonable steps** in an attempt to avoid a loss, but those steps in fact prove unsuccessful (or ultimately prove not to be the most inexpensive way of avoiding the loss), he or she is still entitled to recover the full amount of the loss suffered [Restatement 2d § 350(2)].

Second, while some courts and commentators state that the avoidability doctrine really sets forth a *"duty* to mitigate," that phrase is somewhat misleading. That is, the avoidability limitation sets forth no *"duty"* to do anything. Stating that the injured party has a *"duty"* suggests that if he or she somehow violated this "duty," the breaching party would have a right to sue the injured party for breach of the duty. That is not the case. Rather, if the injured party fails to avoid a loss that he or she could have avoided without undue risk, burden or humiliation, the *only* consequence is that the damages resulting from the failure to act may not be recovered. Hence, the worst possible case for the injured party under the avoidability principle is that he or she will not be entitled to recover anything due to the other party's breach of contract. It is never the case that the injured party will be liable for the breach of his or her "duty" to mitigate.

Third, economic consequential damages are specifically subject to the avoidability limitation, including cover [UCC § 2–715(2)(a)]. As an example, assume Fred was contractually obligated to deliver prime beef to Caterer for a big party but told Caterer he wasn't going to deliver the beef a few days before the party. If Caterer could easily "cover" by buying replacement beef, but chooses not to do so and cancels the party instead, Caterer cannot recover consequential damages for lost profits from cancellation of the party.

    a. **Example of *Rockingham County v. Luten Bridge Co.* [§ 30–60]**

        The Rockingham County Commission awarded Luten a contract for the construction of a bridge. About one month into construction, a change in the County Commission occurred, and the County clerk notified Luten that the county no longer wanted the bridge and ordered Luten to stop working on the bridge immediately. However, Luten continued to work, and completed the bridge.

        Rockingham County acknowledged that it breached, but argued that Luten should not be able to recover expenditures after it was ordered to stop work because a party may not recover damages that they could have avoided or mitigated without undue risk, burden or humiliation.

        Held: Builder could have avoided all costs after being told by the County that it no longer wanted the bridge. Hence, its recovery was limited to the costs it had expended up until the time of the breach, plus its expected profit. [*Rockingham County v. Luten Bridge Co.*, 35 F.2d 301 (4th Cir. 1929)].

    b. **Limits on the Avoidability Principle: An Injured Party Need Not Take Steps to Avoid Damages if Doing So Would Cause the Injured Party Undue Risk, Burden or Humiliation. [§ 30–61]**

        While a party injured by a breach must take appropriate steps to avoid a loss, this does not mean he or she must take **all** possible steps to do so. When avoiding the loss would force the injured party to undertake an **undue risk or burden**, or to undergo **unreasonable humiliation**, the failure to take such steps will not limit the amount of recoverable damages.

        (1) **Example. [§ 30–62]**

            Harry hires Gina to supervise his workers as they harvest crops on his farm. He agrees to pay her $30,000. A few days before the harvest is scheduled to begin, Gina breaches. Harry tries to find someone with Gina's qualifications to replace her, but because it is harvest time, all the experienced supervisors are employed elsewhere. Bill, who has little experience either as a grower or manager, and was otherwise unknown to Harry, nevertheless hears of Harry's plight and offers to take Gina's place at a salary of $20,000. Harry declines to hire Bill, and harvests his crop with no supervisor. Because there was no one in charge, some of Harry's crops did not get harvested in time and were spoiled.

Harry's recovery against Gina will **not** be affected by the avoidability doctrine, even though he could have hired, but chose not to hire, Bill. Thus, Gina is liable for the full amount of Harry's provable damages resulting from the crop failure. The reason the avoidability doctrine will not decrease his recovery is that hiring an inexperienced supervisor who Harry knew nothing about right before the harvest would have required Harry to undertake an **unreasonable risk**. Note that this result would be true even if Gina can introduce evidence indicating that had Bill been hired, some of the losses Harry suffered potentially could have been avoided. The point is that contract law will not penalize an innocent party's recovery when he or she does not take **unreasonably risky** steps to avoid a loss, even if those steps may have been successful.

(2) Example. [§ 30–63]

Ron contractually agrees to build an addition onto Jennifer's house for $20,000. Just before he is scheduled to begin construction, Ron breaches. Jennifer calls five contractors in the area to bid on the job. Jennifer ends up selecting the cheapest bid of the five, a $23,000 bid from Delores, to build the addition. Thereafter, Jennifer brings suit against Ron for breach. At trial, Ron would like to offer testimony from Sam, yet another contractor from the same town who will testify that **if** Jennifer had called **him** when she was soliciting new bids, **he would have quoted her a price of $20,000** to build the addition. As such, Ron would like to assert that he owes Jennifer nothing, for she could have avoided having to pay the extra $3,000 by just calling Sam.

Jennifer is still entitled to a $3,000 recovery against Ron. An injured party need only take reasonable steps in mitigation. In other words, contract law will not require Jennifer to bear the risk that *somewhere*, there may be *someone*, who was willing to provide replacement services for a cheaper price than the one she found. To do so would be to place an **unreasonable burden** on her. Accordingly, as long as Jennifer acted reasonably (and it appeared she did by calling five contractors), the amount of her recovery is not limited by the avoidability limitation.

CHAPTER 30

(3) Example of *Parker v. Twentieth Century-Fox Film Corp.* [§ 30–64]

The actress Shirley MacLaine (then known as Shirley MacLaine Parker) had a contract with Twentieth Century-Fox ("Fox") to star in a musical entitled Bloomer Girl for $750,000. Her contract provided that in addition to her salary, she also had the right to approve both the final screenplay and the choice of director. Shortly before filming was scheduled to begin, Fox breached by deciding not to produce the picture.

In the letter informing Ms. MacLaine of that decision, Fox offered to employ her to star in a western called Big Country, Big Man ("Big Country"). Big Country was scheduled to be shot on roughly the same time schedule as Bloomer Girl, and she was again offered $750,000 to appear in the movie. However, Big Country was a straight dramatic role, whereas Bloomer Girl was a musical in which Ms. MacLaine would have the opportunity to showcase, and enhance her reputation for, singing and dancing. Moreover, she was given neither screenplay nor director approval in Big Country, although 31 of the 34 terms in the Bloomer Girl contract were identical to the terms offered her in the Big Country contract.

Ms. MacLaine refused to accept the offer to star in Big Country, and sued for her lost $750,000 salary. Fox was willing to admit the breach, but claimed her damages were subject to avoidability limitations. That is, Fox was willing to admit its actions resulted in a $750,000 loss, but also asserted she could have avoided such loss completely without undue burden, risk, or humiliation by accepting its offer to star in Big Country. As such, the studio claimed she was only entitled to a nominal damages recovery.

Held: Ms. MacLaine was entitled to recover the total amount of her lost salary. [*Parker v. Twentieth Century-Fox Film Corp.*, 3 Cal. 3d 176 (1970)].

This case is another example of the principle that the injured party need only act reasonably to escape penalty under the avoidability limitation. In employment contracts, the rule is that the salary a non-breaching employee would have earned from a substitute job that he or she did not accept triggers the avoidability limitations of contract damages **only if the substitute employment offers reasonably comparable work**. [§ 30–30] Requiring anything else would be **unreasonably burdensome**, or perhaps, **unreasonably humiliating**, for the injured party for purposes of Restatement 2d § 350(2). Hence, the question in this case was whether starring in a dramatic western without script and director approval was reasonably comparable to starring in a musical with director and script approval rights. The court's answer was no, and hence Ms. MacLaine was entitled to recover all the damages she suffered without having that recovery limited by the avoidability principle.

Note, however, that if she *had* taken the Big Country offer, she would have had to offset the salary from that position against her damages from the loss of the Bloomer Girl role, since she could not have acted in both movies since they were to be shot on the same schedule. This is because **if an employee actually takes another job**, even if it is not comparable and wouldn't act as an offset to damages if it were turned down, **the salary from that other job must be offset against any damage recovery,** *unless the employee can prove* **that he or she could have done both jobs** [§ 30–30].

F. RELIANCE DAMAGES. [§ 30-65*]

Reliance damages are damages based on the amount of interference with the injured party's reliance interest caused by the breach. The value of reliance damages is typically equal to the amount of out-of-pocket costs, including labor, incurred by the injured party at the time of the breach either in preparation for performance, or in actual performance, under the contract. The most significant difference between reliance and expectation damages is that in the former, there is no recovery for lost profits or other consequential loss—only for out-of-pocket costs.

Reliance damages are thus "backward looking," i.e., they try to put the injured party in the position he or she was in before the contract was signed. In other words, an award of reliance damages is designed to leave the injured party just as he or she was before the contract's execution—a position in which he or she has not realized any profit from the as yet-unsigned contract, but also a position in which he or she has not incurred any expenses in performing under the contract.

1. The Availability of Reliance Damages. [§ 30-66]

Reliance damages are always available to an injured party as an option to consider, instead of seeking expectation damages [Restatement 2d § 344]. Typically, however, reliance damages are sought only when the injured party is unable to prove his or her

---

* For more information, listen to CD # 12, Track 4 of *Sum and Substance Audio on Contracts*.

expectation damages with reasonable certainty [§ 30–49], or when such damages are not sufficiently foreseeable to be recovered [§ 30–54].

a. Example. [§ 30–67]

Dick contracts to build a swimming pool for Edna. The contract price is $40,000 and Dick begins construction promptly. Two weeks into the project, Edna breaches by unjustifiably ordering Dick to cease building the pool. At the time of the breach, Dick had spent $8,000 in materials and labor.

Dick would ordinarily sue for expectation damages, which would allow him to recover for any profit he would have made in building the pool plus the amount he has spent to date. However, if Dick cannot prove with reasonable certainty how much it would have cost him to finish, and thus cannot sufficiently establish how much his profit would have been (*see* § 30–49), he is still entitled to recover his reliance damages, i.e., the $8,000 he spent in reliance on Edna's promise to pay him.

Reliance damages are thus "backwards looking"—the goal being to put the injured party in the position he or she was in **before the contract was entered into**. For Doug, that meant the position he was in before he spent $8,000 on the pool.

2. Limitations on Reliance Damage Recovery. [§ 30–68]

There are four limitations on an injured party's recovery of reliance damages:

(i) any damages claimed must be proven with **reasonable certainty** [Restatement 2d § 352; § 30–69];

(ii) if the breaching party can prove that **the injured party would have lost money** on the contract if it had been performed, i.e., it was a "losing contract," under the Restatement rule, the amount of **the loss must be subtracted** from any reliance damage recovery [§ 30–70];

(iii) the **value** of any materials purchased by the non-breaching party in performance or preparation for performance which **can be salvaged must be subtracted** from any reliance damage recovery [§ 30–72]; and

(iv) any damages claimed must **not have been avoidable** by the non-breaching party without undue burden, risk, or humiliation [Restatement 2d § 350; § 30–73].

MONEY DAMAGES

a. Reliance Damages Must Be Proven with Reasonable Certainty. [§ 30–69]

As noted previously [§ 30–49], the reasonable certainty limitation on contract damages is not limited to expectation damages. It is a limitation on recovery of reliance damages as well [Restatement 2d §§ 349, 352]. However, as a practical matter, the reasonable certainty requirement rarely serves to limit an injured party's recovery of reliance damages. This is because reliance damages are typically valued in an amount equal to the out-of-pocket costs incurred by the non-breaching party in reliance on the breaching party's performance under the contract. Hence, it is the rare case where a non-breaching party cannot prove with reasonable certainty the amount of his or her out-of-pocket costs.

b. Limitation on the Recovery of Reliance Damages in "Losing Contract" Situations. [§ 30–70]

The Restatement and many states note that the principal goal of reliance damages is to put the non-breaching party in the same position he or she would have been in *before* the contract was entered into. A necessary corollary of this goal is that contract damages should not put the party in a **better** position than he or she would have been in had the contract been performed. The **party in breach has the burden of proof**, but if that party **can prove that the non-breaching party would have lost money on the contract had it been performed, the amount of such loss must be subtracted from any reliance recovery** under the rules of the Restatement [Restatement 2d § 349].

It is because of this rule that a party in a losing contract will usually opt for restitutionary recovery instead of a reliance damage recovery [*See* Chapter Thirty-One for a discussion of restitution].

Some states reject this rule, however, and allow the injured party to recover the full amount of his or her reliance after a breach.

(1) Example. [§ 30–71]

Glenda contracted to build a swimming pool for Don at a price of $35,000. About a week after Glenda began construction, Don unjustifiably fired her. At the time of the breach, Glenda can establish she had spent $7,000 in materials and labor on the project, which Don refuses to pay. Accordingly, Glenda files suit seeking to recover her reliance damages.

During discovery, Don obtains Glenda's internal profit and loss figures for the job. As a result, Don can competently establish at trial that Glenda underbid the pool project and would have lost $5,000 had the project been completed. As a result, Glenda's reliance damage recovery would only be $2,000 (i.e., the $5,000 projected loss subtracted from the $7,000 she has already spent). Note that if she were awarded the full $7,000 she has spent in reliance up to the time of the breach, she would be in a better position than she would have been in had the contract been performed. That is, she would be "even," whereas had the contract been performed she would have been $5,000 "in the hole." Hence, the amount of such provable losses must be subtracted from her reliance damages recovery in keeping with the general goal of contract damages under the Restatement rule. Again, there are states that would allow her to recover the entire amount, not subject to offset.

c. **The Value of Any Salvageable Materials Must Be Subtracted from a Recovery of Reliance Damages as a Cost Avoided. [§ 30–72]**

As with expectation damages, the value of any salvageable materials purchased by the non-breaching party in performance or preparation for performance under the contract must be subtracted from any reliance damage recovery. The reason for this requirement is that without deducting the amount of such salvageable materials from the damages recovered, the non-breaching party would end up with an unbargained for windfall, and would once again be in a better position than he or she would have been in had the contract gone forward since the party will have materials to use in another project for "free."

d. **Damages Must Not Be Avoidable Without Undue Risk, Burden, or Humiliation. [§ 30–73]**

Reliance damages are also subject to the Restatement 2d's rules regarding avoidability or mitigation in § 350. Hence, to be recoverable, damages must not have been avoidable by the non-breacher without undue risk, burden, or humiliation [§ 30–59].

3. **Recovery Based on the Reliance Interest in Other Situations. [§ 30–74]**

In addition to being available as an alternate means of recovery for breach of contract, recovery based on the reliance interest is also used to determine recovery in other situations previously covered in this book. [Restatement 2d § 349, Cmt. b.] These situations include:

MONEY DAMAGES

(i) Recovery based on promissory estoppel [Restatement 2d § 90; Chapter Eight];

(ii) Recovery based on pre-performance preparation by the offeree which does not rise to the level of acceptance [Restatement 2d § 87(2); Chapter Four];

(iii) Recovery based on actions taken in reliance on promises that are unenforceable under the Statute of Frauds [Restatement 2d § 139; Chapter Ten]; and

(iv) Recovery based on actions taken in reliance on promises made in pre-offer, preliminary negotiations.

G. EMOTIONAL DISTRESS DAMAGES ARE GENERALLY NOT AVAILABLE IN BREACH OF CONTRACT SUITS. [§ 30–75*]

Virtually every breach of contract causes some kind of emotional distress to the non-breaching party. This is true even in merchant-to-merchant contracts. For example, assume a retailer has ordered 50 television sets from a manufacturer due to be delivered on Friday. If the sets do not come, the retailer is likely to be at least exasperated about having to deal with the breaching manufacturer, finding replacement sets if necessary, etc.

Nevertheless, contract law has been particularly unyielding in its view that emotional distress damages are not recoverable in contract, [Restatement 2d § 353] and should only be available in tort. Partly this is a reflection of the separation of tort and contract law, i.e., on the whole, tort damages are much more "personal" and designed to compensate the injured party for all personal harms (such as emotional distress), whereas contract damages are more "economic" and designed to compensate only for the lost monetary value resulting from the breach.

In addition, it is also a reflection of the idea that the amount the injured party should recover from a breach should not greatly exceed the value of the expectation, reliance, or restitutionary interests [Restatement 2d § 351(3)]. That is, awarding a non-breaching party lost value, lost profits, incidental loss, **and** emotional distress damage could result in the amount of recoverable contract damages being far in excess of the value of the non-breaching party's performance that was expected by the breaching party.

There are two exceptions to the general bar on emotional distress recovery arising from a breach of contract suit:

(i) When the breach also results in tangible personal injury [*see e.g.,* UCC § 2–715(2)(b), Restatement 2d § 353]; and

---

* For more information, listen to CD # 12, Track 5 of *Sum and Substance Audio on Contracts*.

CHAPTER 30

(ii) When emotional distress is **"particularly likely"** to result from breach of a specific contract [Restatement 2d § 353].

1. **Exception: Emotional Distress Damages Are Available When the Breach of Contract Also Results in Tangible Personal Injury. [§ 30–76]**

   When a breach of contract results in personal injury, contract law permits the non-breaching party to recover his or her emotional distress damages from the breacher. The rationale for this exception is that in such cases the interest invaded by the breach i.e., injury to the person, is a kind of interest that civil law values very highly and thus is willing to reward to a greater degree than when the interference is only a loss to the injured party's economic interest. Moreover, providing recovery for losses accompanying personal injury is the kind of interest that tort law protects. If the injured party sued in tort, recovery of emotional distress would be permitted in such situations. Hence, contract law does not deny emotional distress recovery in such cases just because a party chooses to sue in contract rather than tort.

   There are two typical ways a breach of contract can result in personal injury. One is where the breach is a breach of warranty involving a machine or other product, which, even though used foreseeably, nevertheless causes an injury. The second is where the contract is one for services involving a physician (or other health provider), where the breach is of a promise either to use reasonable care in treating a patient, or to achieve a particular result. In these types of cases, often the result is personal injury to the patient.

   a. **Example. [§ 30–77]**

      Joe buys a power mower, relying on the promise on the front of the package guaranteeing that the mower is "perfectly safe when used as directed." Joe uses the mower as directed, but it turns out the blade assembly is not bolted on tightly, and the blades came off injuring his foot. If Joe sues the manufacturer for breach of express warranty, he is entitled to recover for any emotional distress he suffers as a result of his injury.

   b. **Example of *Sullivan v. O'Connor*. [§ 30–78]**

      Ms. Sullivan contracted with Dr. O'Connor to perform plastic surgery on her nose. Ms. Sullivan claimed the doctor had promised her that the surgery would enhance her beauty and improve her appearance. However, the surgery (actually three surgeries) ended up disfiguring her nose. Because the breach of the contract between Dr. O'Connor and Ms. Sullivan resulted in a physical injury, the court allowed Ms. Sullivan to recover for the pain and suffering and mental distress she suffered with respect to her third operation.

2. Exception: Recovery for Emotional Distress Is Permitted When Such Harm Is "Particularly Likely" to Result from a Breach. [§ 30–79]

Contract law also allows emotional distress damages to be recovered if the nature of the contract is such that mental anguish is "particularly likely" to result from a breach of that agreement [Restatement 2d § 353]. This exception is **very limited**. Its principal application has been to three types of cases:

(i) Where a mortuary mishandles a corpse;

(ii) Where a telegram or other delivery company mistakenly delivers a communication informing the wrong person of a death of their loved ones; or

(iii) Where an insurance company is guilty of a "bad faith" breach [§ 30–88].

Note that a few judges have suggested that some wrongful termination of employment contracts also meet this test. That is, that the argument is that the employer should know that being fired wrongfully, and in violation of the terms of the employment contract, is "particularly likely" to cause emotional distress in the employee. While this argument has some currency, to date it is very much a minority position.

H. LIQUIDATED DAMAGES. [§ 30–80]

As a general rule, parties can enforce whatever lawful promises they voluntarily agree to in their contract. Indeed, this is largely what freedom of contract means. One of the biggest exceptions to this general rule, however, is liquidated damages. As will be seen below, liquidated damages are frequently held unenforceable [Restatement 2d § 356; UCC § 2–718].

Liquidated damages are damages the parties have agreed to in advance that will be due and payable after a breach. To examine why liquidated damage clauses are so rarely enforced, study the following hypothetical:

Ruth and Sam entered into a contract whereby Sam promised to sell his vintage record collection to Ruth for $7,000. Both parties were very anxious that the transaction actually be performed, i.e., neither wanted to have the bother of enforcing his or her expectation interest by means of a lawsuit. Hence, they agreed that if either of them breached the agreement, the breaching party would owe the other $100,000 as a liquidated damage.

CHAPTER 30

Contract law would not enforce their liquidated damage provision. At first thought, it might seem that the legal system would be happy to enforce liquidated damages. After all, by stipulating in advance to the amount of a loss one party will owe the other upon a breach, the only question in a breach of contract suit would be whether there was a breach, and no damage calculation evidence would ever have to be introduced. Accordingly, enforcing such provisions would save a court time, for there would be no need for the injured party to prove the actual amount of his or her damages, whether those damages were foreseeable, avoidable, etc., for the amount of recovery has been fixed by agreement of the parties in advance.

The reason contract law will not enforce such a liquidated damage clause has to do with the twin ideas that a party should not be better off as a result of a breach than he or she would have been had the contract been performed, and that a party should not be unfairly penalized for breaching a contract. That is, if Ruth breached the agreement to pay $7,000 for Sam's records, and if as a result of that breach Sam ended up with $100,000, Sam is in a far better economic position than he would have been in had the contract been performed.

Moreover, such a result would also penalize Ruth because the liquidated damage clause makes it too expensive for her to breach under the principles of the efficient breach doctrine [§ 30–1]. For example, suppose Ruth decided she would rather spend her money some other way than by giving it to Sam in exchange for his records. The efficient breach doctrine says that so long as Ruth is willing to pay the Sam's expectation damages, she should be able to breach when it is more efficient for her to do so, i.e., whenever she will be better off after breaching and paying damages. Here, if Ruth is willing to pay the difference between the price she was willing to pay for the records and the price someone else may offer Sam for his records, the efficient breach doctrine says she should be able to do so. However, under the liquidated damage clause, Ruth will be liable for $100,000 upon breach, not the difference between $7,000 and whatever other price Sam can get for his record collection. Hence, Ruth would be unfairly **penalized** because of her breach because she will have to give Sam $100,000 to compensate him for what is, at maximum, a $7,000 loss [Restatement 2d § 356, Cmt. a].

Note the opposite is true as well if the amount of the liquidated damage is too small. If Ruth and Sam had agreed that upon a breach, each would only owe the other $1, that clause would also be stricken because it makes it too easy for someone to breach. Courts are worried that such promises are really illusory.

Contract law likes to award the exact amount of money damages that a party suffers. Accordingly, there are only a limited number of situations in which contract law does not view the enforcement of a liquidated damage clause as extracting a penalty (or not enough of a penalty) on the

MONEY DAMAGES

breaching party and thus will allow a party to collect a liquidated amount. Those situations are described in the next section.

1. **Requirements for an Enforceable Liquidated Damage Provision. [§ 30–81]**

   In order to enforce a liquidated damage provision, the injured party must prove the following:

   (i) That the amount of the liquidated damage is **reasonable in light of the anticipated harm** to the injured party that was foreseen at the time of contract formation, or that the amount is **reasonable in light of the actual harm** suffered by the injured party; and

   (ii) That there is some reason to believe that there will be **difficulties in proving the actual loss with precision**. [UCC § 2–718(1); Restatement 2d § 356].

   Note that some courts also add a requirement that the parties not intend that the liquidated damage be a penalty [*Wassenaar v. Panos*, 331 N.W.2d 357 (Wis. 1983)].

   a. **The Amount of the Liquidated Damage Must Be Reasonable in Light of the Anticipated or Actual Loss. [§ 30–82]**

   As noted above, when a liquidated damage is considered a "penalty," contract law will not enforce it. Hence, if the amount of the liquidated damage in a contract is reasonable in light of the amount of the injured party's expectation loss that was either anticipated at the time the contract was signed, or was actually suffered by that party as a result of the breach, then by definition the liquidated amount does not extract penalty from the breaching party [Restatement 2d § 356(1); UCC § 2–718(1)].

   Note that the common law test was slightly more limited. At common law, the amount of the liquidated damage had to be a reasonable estimate of the **anticipated** harm only. If it was not, the fact that it might be reasonable in light of the actual harm suffered is irrelevant and the clause would not be enforceable.

   (1) **Example. [§ 30–83]**

   Bill was an attorney who was asked to perform legal services for Laura in 1970. Bill and his wife had just become parents of a baby boy, and Bill wished to provide for his future. Accordingly, he and Laura agreed that in consideration of Bill's legal work for Laura, she promised to transfer the deed of her beachfront property to Bill's son when he turned 21. The fair market value of the property in 1960 was $10,000, but Bill and Laura nevertheless agreed that if she breached the agreement by not turning over the deed in 1991, she would owe Bill $300,000. By 1991, the property had become extremely valuable and various appraisers valued it between $280,000 and $350,000. Laura refuses to transfer the property.

Under the rule set forth in § 356(1) of the Restatement 2d, the liquidated damage clause would be enforceable, since it calls for payment of a reasonable amount in light of the actual harm caused by Laura's breach. Under the older common law rule, however it is unlikely that the provision would be upheld because by 1970 standards, having someone pay $300,000 for the breach of a promise to transfer a $10,000 piece of property in the future, even with inflation taken into account, would almost certainly have been thought a penalty.

b. **Actual Damages Must Be Somewhat Difficult to Prove in Order for a Liquidated Damage Provision to Be Enforceable. [§ 30–84]**

While contract law generally allows parties to make reasonable estimates of actual damages in creating an enforceable liquidated damage provision, it will not do so if the precise amount of damages suffered by the breaching party can be easily determined. That is, if the precise amount of damages can be easily proven, there is no need to estimate it by means of a liquidated damage clause. In such a case, the theory of contract damages requires that the non-breaching party be compensated for the exact amount of his or her loss, and not for an estimated value of that loss.

There is an obvious tension between the two parts of the test for a liquidated damage. In other words, if the amount of a party's actual damages must be somewhat difficult to prove, then it is obviously difficult to establish that the amount of the liquidated damage is a "reasonable" amount in light of the anticipated or actual loss. While there is some truth to the argument that the two parts of the test are incompatible, it is also true they can be harmonized in many cases. That is, once it is determined that the **precise** amount of damages will be somewhat difficult to prove, then contract law will uphold a liquidated damage amount if it is a reasonable estimate of that loss.

(1) **Example. [§ 30–85]**

Dale hires Ned's Construction Co. to build a small commercial office building on some property she owns. The contract calls for construction to be completed by September

MONEY DAMAGES

1, and that if it is not, Ned's will be liable to Dale for $3,000/day thereafter until it is finished.

Depending on the circumstances, such a liquidated damage clause may or may not be enforceable. It is likely that it will be difficult to prove the exact amount of Dale's damages with precision, because her profits would depend on how much of the office building would be rented, what the exact terms of the leases would be, etc. Hence, Dale would fairly easily pass the second part of the test.

The real issue is whether she could pass the first part, i.e., whether she could prove that $3,000/day is a reasonable estimate of her actual damages in light of her real or anticipated harm. If from all the circumstances it appears that $3,000 is reasonable and is not extracting a penalty from Ned's, then it will be enforced. If $3,000 is in excess of the profit Dale reasonably would have made, then the liquidated damages clause will be judged void as a penalty.

2. Alternative Performance Clauses Distinguished from Liquidated Damage Clauses. [§ 30–86]

Compare the following two contract provisions:

Contract No. 1

Steel Co. agrees to purchase at least $300,000 of pure oxygen during the next calendar year from Gas Co. In the event of a breach of this promise, Steel Co. will pay to Gas Co. $50,000 on December 31 as a liquidated damage.

Contract No. 2

Steel Co. agrees that during the next calendar year it will either: (a) purchase at least $300,000 worth of pure oxygen from Gas Co.; or (b) pay Gas Co. $50,000 on December 31.

Result

Contract No. 1 is a standard liquidated damage clause and will only be upheld if the amount is reasonable in light of the actual or anticipated harm and if the exact amount of damages are somewhat difficult to calculate. However, a court will probably have no problem in enforcing Contract No. 2.

The difference between the two contracts is that the $50,000 payment in Contract No. 1 is triggered by a **breach**, whereas such a payment in Contract No. 2 is an alternative means of **performance**. Thus, there is no fear in Contract No. 2 that the Steel Co. will be penalized by breaching the contract in that it will be forced to pay an unreasonably high amount over and above the actual loss suffered by Gas Co. as a result of the breach. In other words, Contract No. 2 is really no different from a contract that said "Upon payment of $15, Joe is entitled to receive, at his option, either: (a) my U2 compact disc, or (b) my Mariah Carey video." Obviously in that case no one would say selection of the video presents any liquidated damage concerns, and the same holds true for Contract No. 2 above. Where the parties grant two **alternative means of performance**, as opposed to one means of performance and a liquidated damage figure for **breach** of that performance, the contract is generally enforceable.

Some courts, however, have cautioned that alternative performance clauses must be carefully scrutinized to ensure they are not really liquidated damage provisions dressed up in fancy clothes. In other words, if the substance of what is being proposed is a liquidated damage provision, then it will be stricken. Exactly where the line is to be drawn between a "real" and "sham" alternative performance clause has proven elusive, and generally, unless there is reason to doubt the intent and good faith of the parties, alternative performance clauses are enforced.

I. PUNITIVE DAMAGES ARE GENERALLY NOT RECOVERABLE IN BREACH OF CONTRACT ACTIONS. [§ 30–87]

Punitive damages are damages awarded over and above any compensatory loss suffered by the injured party as punishment for conduct that falls below socially defined norms. Because a recovery of punitive damages for breach of contract would end up putting the non-breaching party in a better position than he or she would have been in had the contract been performed, the almost universal rule is that such damages are **not** recoverable in breach of contract actions [Restatement 2d § 355] and limited to tort actions.

Despite this long-standing and relatively inflexible doctrine, over the past thirty years or so a number of commentators, plaintiff's lawyers, and some judges have tried to make a case for the recovery of punitive damages in certain contract actions. They claim that when there has been a "bad faith" breach of contract, as opposed to an "ordinary" breach, punitive damages are warranted. Under this view, an "ordinary" breach is one where a party is ultimately found to have breached a substantive term of the contract, but that the party's reasons for doing so were legitimate, e.g., it had a different, but reasonable, interpretation of what the clause meant or what the duties were. A "bad faith" breach is one where a party both breaches a substantive term of the contract, **and** does so in such a way, or for such a reason, that the breacher's conduct also violates the implied duty of good faith and fair dealing included in every contract [Restatement 2d § 205; UCC § 1–304]. In those cases, so the argument goes, punitive damages are warranted as punishment for socially reprehensible conduct.

MONEY DAMAGES

Under the Restatement 2d, punitive damages are only available when the breach of contract also turns out to be a tort. That is, the fact that tort occurred in the context of a contractual breach does not somehow deprive the court from its ability to award punitive damages for the tort (e.g., where a seller fraudulently misrepresents something as part of a sales transaction) [Restatement 2d § 355]. In all other cases, the Restatement 2d provides that no punitive damages are permitted, the "bad faith" motives of the breacher notwithstanding.

This is one area, however, where the courts have not completely followed the Restatement 2d and are willing to allow for punitive damage recovery against particularly egregious "bad faith" breachers.

1. Exception to General Rule: Punitive Damages Can Be Recovered for "Bad Faith" Breaches of Insurance Contracts. [§ 30–88]

Many states allow punitive damages to be awarded for the bad faith breach of an insurance contract, especially a life insurance contract. The doctrine became established in cases like the following hypothetical:

A husband and wife take out a life insurance policy on the husband's life for $100,000 and faithfully pay premiums on the policy for 30 years. When the husband dies, however, the insurance company does not pay the widow the $100,000. Knowing they have no real basis for saying so, they assert that the husband committed suicide (or did some other act which would allow it to avoid coverage). While, of course, this happens in only a minority of cases, when it does occur, the insurance company has been found to have made the bogus claim denying coverage for the following reasons:

> (1) It knows that the maximum extent of its contractual liability will be $100,000, i.e., there are no lost profits or consequential damages flowing from the breach that increase as time goes on. Hence, if it can keep the $100,000 for a few more months in its bank rather than paying it to the widow, it can earn interest on the funds. In other words, given the choice between having to pay $100,000 in January of year 1, or in January of year 3 (after a lawsuit, appeals, etc.), it is in the economic interest of the insurance company to pay in year 3 given the time value of money. Besides, with the interest it makes off the $100,000, it can offset some or all of the attorneys' fees needed to fight the expected suit of the widow.

> (2) It may never have to pay the $100,000 at all. While it is likely the widow may see a lawyer and file suit for breach of contract, there are a few who will not and a few who may lose even if they do file, so it may be able to keep all the money.

CHAPTER 30

(3) Even when the widow does file suit, if she desperately needs the insurance money to pay her bills after her husband dies, she might be willing to settle for less than the $100,000 just to receive some amount of money immediately. In other words, a widow badly in need of money might be willing to settle for an immediate $70,000 payment to have the matter over with, rather than wait three years or so for a trial and an appeal. If so, the insurance company has "saved" $30,000.

Hence, given the unique factual situation of the innocent party found in such a case, coupled with the particularly reprehensible nature of the breacher's acts, most states allow a jury to award punitive damages for the "bad faith" breach of an insurance contract. Initially, this doctrine was limited just to life insurance contracts, and it is with those agreements that courts still award punitive damages with the greatest frequency. However, currently, most states that recognize the bad faith doctrine allow for punitive damages whenever an insurance company makes a bad faith denial of coverage, no matter what kind of policy it is. (Recall also that most states allow for the recovery of emotional distress damages as well in "bad faith" breach cases against insurance companies) [§ 30–79; and *see* Case Squibs, *Seamen's Direct Buying Service v. Standard Oil*, 686 P.2d 1158 (Cal. 1984), regarding whether there should be a further exception to the "no punitive damages" rule in contract actions for bad faith breaches in commercial contracts.]

J. THE INJURED PARTY'S RIGHT TO RECOVER PRE-JUDGMENT AND POST-JUDGMENT INTEREST ON ANY AWARD. [§ 30–89]

In every jurisdiction, interest is awarded on a **judgment for breach of contract** from the date the award is officially entered in the courts "judgment book." That is, post-judgment interest is collectable as a matter of right up until the date the judgment is "satisfied" (the award is paid) by the breaching party.

However, a separate question is whether **pre-judgment interest** should be awarded to the non-breaching party, i.e., should interest be awarded **from the date of the breach (or the repudiation) until the day the judgment is reached**? Restatement 2d § 354 sets forth the majority rule on this issue, which is that so long as the breach consists of the failure to pay a **fixed sum of money**, or to **render a performance with a fixed or ascertainable monetary value**, the non-breaching party is entitled to prejudgment interest on the debt, *beginning on the date performance was due*. In all other cases, an award of interest is discretionary with the court [Restatement 2d § 354(1)].

In other words, so long as the amount of damages involved in the dispute is a "liquidated" amount, or can readily be calculated into a "sum certain,"

MONEY DAMAGES

interest is recoverable by the injured party as a matter of right. If the amount of damages is not liquidated, however, prejudgment interest in only awarded to the injured party when the court believes is just to do so, and the general tendency is not to award such interest [Restatement 2d § 354(2)].

The rate of prejudgment interest varies from jurisdiction to jurisdiction. Presently the rate granted by most states is in the range of 3% to 10%. Typically it is a simple interest award (not compound), and the actual calculations are done by the court, not left to the jury.

K. REDUCTION OF "FUTURE" AWARDS TO PRESENT VALUE. [§ 30–90]

Take a case where Joe sells a business in return for a promised payment of $100,000/year for ten years. To make the hypothetical easy, assume the buyer immediately repudiates and Joe quickly gets a verdict in his favor. If Joe gets $1,000,000 today ($100,000/year × 10 years), he will be overcompensated, because the last $100,000 payment in year 10 due under the contract is likely to be worth less than getting that money today. Further, Joe could invest the money today and have more than $100,000 for that last payment ten years from now.

Accordingly, contract law reduces to present value an immediate payment of damages based on future payments. Each state has its own means of calculating such deduction and the rate at which such awards are reduced. Typically, the jury is not told of this reduction, and so in Joe's case, it would likely come back with a verdict of $1 million. The court itself would then reduce the value of the award to present value and issue judgment for the reduced amount.

There is no uniform rule for when damages should be subject to reduction, but generally courts will not do so unless the award is for monies that will be paid over a year into the future.

L. EXAM APPROACH TO DAMAGE ISSUES. [§ 30–91]

When one party has breached the contract, you must always discuss the amount of damages recoverable to the non-breaching party—assuming you are to a point where you have covered damages in your class discussions.

So long as you understand the basic damage formula (§ 30–29), you should not have any problems. Just make sure that you know how to apply that general damage formula to various types of contracts. If you are given numbers regarding the costs incurred by a party or value of one party's performance, you will have to discuss each of them in your answer, even if you conclude a particular set of values do not apply in your damage analysis.

CHAPTER 30

Realize in planning your analysis that in every breach situation, you must discuss the possibility of out-of-pocket damages [§ 30–6] and restitutionary recovery [Chapter Thirty-One] as well as expectation loss. That is, because a lawyer representing the plaintiff in a breach action has the option of suing for any of these three recoveries, you must demonstrate to your Professor that you know this rule and that you will represent your future clients well. Quite often in an exam, one approach will yield a significantly higher result than the other two.

Lastly, make sure you realize that any losses the breaching party can establish must be subtracted from either expectation or out of pocket damages [§ 30–47], and that certainty [§ 30–49], foreseeability [§ 30–54], and the absence of mitigation [§ 30–59] should always be examined when discussing damage recovery.

CHAPTER 31

RESTITUTION

A. RESTITUTION OVERVIEW. [§ 31–1*]

The crux of restitution can be easily stated: a person who has been *unjustly* enriched by another must account for that enrichment. In other words, under restitution, one party can't *unjustly* get some benefits under a contract and then hold onto them. They must be paid back.

There is a scholarly debate as to whether restitution is a "remedy" for breach of contract or whether it is a separate substantive branch of law which sets forth certain occasions on which parties can recover. Regardless of which side is correct, it is certainly a theory of recovery that should be discussed anytime there has been a breach of contract [Restatement 2d § 344(c)], although there are other situations in which restitution can apply as well [§ 31–3].

Note this means that the non-breaching party in a breach suit has three choices as to the theory on which to base his or her claim for damages: (1) expectation damages [§ 30–4]; (2) reliance damages [§ 30–6]; or (3) restitutionary recovery. The non-breaching party is free to choose whichever method will maximize recovery [§ 30–3]. As a student, this means you will typically have to analyze recovery under all three methods on an exam to explain all the recoveries to which the innocent party is entitled.

Note that even though restitution is a remedy used upon contract breach, a recovery based on restitutionary principles should not be thought of as "damages." Hence, any reference to "restitution damages" is incorrect. It is more accurate to say the aggrieved party has a "restitutionary recovery."

1. **Some General Principles of Restitution. [§ 31–2]**

   Before discussing its specific application to contracts cases, there are a few general concepts regarding restitution that need to be understood:

   (1) **Recovery in restitution is based on the value of the enrichment *received* by the benefited party, and not on

---

* For more information, listen to CD # 13, Track 1 of *Sum and Substance Audio on Contracts*.

the value of the aggrieved party's *promises*. Recovery of *money damages* for breach of contract is based on the value of the promises made by the breaching party. As explained earlier, the idea behind expectation damages is that each party's promised performance is given a dollar value, and an injured party's recovery is based on the extent to which the breach prevented that party from receiving the full value of the breaching party's promised performance [§ 30–4].

On the other hand, in restitution, the measure of the aggrieved party's recovery has nothing directly to do with the economic value of the other's promised performance. Rather, it is based on the value of the **benefits** that have been *actually received* by **the benefited party**. If those benefits turn out to be worth more than the value of the promised performance, the aggrieved party may recover **more** than the contract price. If the benefits received are worth *less* than the value of the promised performance, then the aggrieved party is entitled only to that *lesser* amount if restitution is sought. The point is that the promises made under the contract are largely irrelevant for restitution purposes. What **is** relevant is the amount of benefits actually received by a party under the contract, for it is the value of those benefits upon which restitutionary relief is awarded.

(2) **Recovery in restitution is based on the value of the enrichment actually received by the benefited party, and not on the value of the efforts undertaken by the aggrieved party**. It is important to realize that restitutionary recovery is only based on the extent to which one party **actually receives** benefits provided by the other. That is, sometimes one party spends much time and effort in preparing to perform. If those efforts produce no tangible benefits to the other, there has, by definition, been no enrichment of the other. Accordingly, since there has been no benefit received, there is nothing for that party to restore, and thus no action for restitution can be successfully brought.

For example, assume that Maria's Machine Shop (Maria's) contracts to manufacture a drill press for Butler's Tool Company (Butler's) for $100,000. Maria's begins building the machine and has spent $40,000 in time and labor up until the point at which Butler's breaches by telling Maria's to discontinue performance. Maria's $40,000 expenditure is likely recoverable in a suit for reliance damages, and she may be able to sue for expectation damages as well. But she has no actionable restitutionary recovery from Butler's because her $40,000 in expenditures conferred no tangible benefit on Butler's. Because there has been no benefit received by the company that it can restore to Maria's, it owes Maria's nothing in restitution, i.e., Butler's has nothing in hand by which it has been enriched, justly or unjustly, by anything Maria's has done.

As can be seen, restitutionary recovery is thus different from recovery of reliance damages. An award of reliance damages attempts to put the **innocent party** in the position he or she was in before the contract was signed [§ 30–6]. An award of restitution, on the other hand, attempts to put the **"benefited party"** in the position he or she was in before the contract was signed. Restitution does this by making a benefited party pay for the value of any enrichment provided him or her by the other party that the benefited party did not have before the agreement was made.

(3) **Restitution is potentially available as a remedy for both the breaching and the non-breaching parties**. Because restitutionary recovery focuses only on the value of any benefits received, and not on a party's promises, it does not matter whether those benefits were received by the non-breaching party or by the breaching party. Thus, so long as the non-breaching party has received unpaid-for benefits, and so long as it would be unjust for the non-breaching party to retain those benefits without paying for them, the *non-breaching* party will be **liable to the breaching party in restitution** [*See* §§ 31–28 *et seq.*]. Although, the measure of recovery for non-breaching parties seeking restitution is different than that when the breaching party seeks to take advantage of the remedy.

2. **When Restitution Is Available. [§ 31–3]**

The predominant situations in which restitution is available are:

(a) When the contract has been totally breached [§ 31–15]

(b) When a contract is avoided because one of the defenses to formation is successfully asserted [Chapters Ten through Seventeen and § 31–33];

(c) When a contract is discharged due to impossibility, impracticability or frustration [Chapter Twenty-Five];

(d) When the breaching party seeks recovery for part performance [§§ 31–28 *et seq.*]; and

(e) When a party seeks recovery for quasi-contract [§ 31–31].

CHAPTER 31

B. RULES COMMON TO ALL RESTITUTION ACTIONS. [§ 31–4]

Once it has been determined that restitutionary recovery is appropriate, there are two rules that must be followed by the party seeking restitutionary relief:

(1) The value of the benefits conferred on the benefited party **must be properly valued under the appropriate theory** [§ 31–5]; and

(2) The party seeking restitution must "make" restitution. That is, there **must be mutual restitution** or there can be no restitution [§ 31–11].

1. Two Common Methods of Valuing the Restitution Interest: The "Cost Avoided" and the "Net Benefit" Methods. [§ 31–5]

A party's restitutionary recovery is equal to the value of the tangible benefits he or she has provided that have been received by the other party. Thus, an important question is how to value the benefits received by the other party.

There are no hard and fast rules to calculate the value of the benefits given to a party under a contract. The general idea is that the court will choose an equitable method of determining the value received in a reasonable way.

As a starting point, there are two well-known methods traditionally used to calculate the restitutionary value of a party's benefits: (1) **the "Cost Avoided" Method** and (2) **the "Net Benefit" Method**.

Sometimes these two methodologies will completely analyze a restitution problem. Other times, calculations using these methods will only be a start, and arguments can be made that an equitable adjustment should be made to more accurately reflect the value of the benefits obtained by the benefitted party.

In any event, because the "cost avoided" and "net benefit" methods are so often used (whether as complete analyses or as starting points), they are explained in detail below. Note that sometimes the dollar value of the restitutionary recovery due under these two methods yields the same result; sometimes they do not.

a. The "Cost Avoided" Method: Defined. [§ 31–6]

Calculating restitutionary recovery under the **"Cost Avoided"** method requires that the benefits received by the benefited party be valued as the market value of the benefit, as measured by dollar amount it would have cost the benefited party to obtain those same benefits from another, reasonable, provider of those benefits in the same market [Restatement 2d § 371(a)]. That is, under the cost avoided method, the question is what is the fair market value of the benefits received by the benefited party, as **measured by how much it would have cost the benefited party to hire a reasonable person in the same line of work in the same market to provide those benefits**? In that sense, it is a cost avoided by the benefitted party.

b. **The "Net Benefit" Method: Defined. [§ 31–7]**

Calculating restitutionary recovery under the **"Net Benefit"** method requires that the benefits received by the benefitted party be valued as the extent to which the *benefited party's property has been increased in value*, or his or her other interests advanced, by the actions of the aggrieved party [Restatement 2d § 371(b)]. That is, under this approach the measure of the benefits received by the enriched party is **the difference in the fair market value of his or her property, or his or her net worth, before and after the actions of the aggrieved party**.

c. **Example Applying "Cost Avoided" and "Net Benefit" Methods. [§ 31–8]**

Larry contracted to purchase a piece of land from Trish for $50,000. He pays Trish the money, but she never delivers the deed. If he sues her in restitution for return of the benefits provided to her, those benefits will be valued at $50,000 regardless of whether they are calculated under the "cost avoided" or the "net benefit" method. That is, the reasonable value of the amount of the enrichment given to Trish as measured by what it would cost someone else to give her those benefits (i.e., the "cost avoided" method) is $50,000. Similarly, the increased value of her net worth due to the benefits provided by Larry (i.e., the "net benefit" method) is also $50,000.

Where one party seeks to recover a cash payment in restitution, it does not matter which method is used because the amount of the recovery will always be the same.

d. **Additional Example Applying "Cost Avoided" and "Net Benefit" Methods. [§ 31–9]**

Where the benefits provided are *services,* however, it is **very unlikely** the two valuation methods will yield the same results. For example, assume that Alyssa hired Lance to build a custom home for her. Lance timely began construction and had done quite a bit of work on the house when Alyssa breached and ordered him off her property. Lance brings suit against Alyssa seeking to recover for his restitutionary interest. Competent evidence will show that the reasonable value of the work performed by Lance was $70,000 at the time of the breach, and that the market value of Alyssa's property increased by $30,000 as a result of having a partially completed structure on it. That is, the fair market value of the property with the structure on it, minus the fair market value without the structure, is $30,000.

Using the "cost avoided" method, Lance's actions benefited Alyssa by $70,000, for this is the amount it would have cost her to hire another reasonable builder to provide those benefits, and thus it is also the *cost* she *avoided* by not having to pay someone else for those services. Using the "net benefit" method, however, Lance benefited Alyssa by only $30,000, for this figure constitutes the extent to which the fair market value of her property increased by Lance's actions.

e. **Determining Which Method of Valuing the Restitutionary Interest Should Be Used. [§ 31–10]**

In all cases, a court has the ultimate discretion to choose either the cost avoided or net benefit valuation method in calculating the aggrieved party's restitutionary award depending on which one seems the most "just" in that particular situation [Restatement 2d § 371]. However, contract law has developed presumptions as to which method should be used:

(1) When a **non-breaching party is seeking restitutionary recovery against the breaching party**, the presumption is that the non-breaching party will be entitled to recover under the method which yields **the most generous restitutionary recovery** [Restatement 2d § 371, Cmt. b];

(2) When a **breaching party is seeking restitutionary recovery against a non-breacher**, the presumption is that the breaching party will be entitled to recover using the method which yields **the least generous restitutionary recovery** [Restatement 2d § 374, Cmt. b].

2. **The "Mutual Restitution" Requirement. [§ 31–11]**

An aggrieved party who seeks restitution of a benefit he or she has conferred on another must return whatever benefits he or she has received from the other party as part of a final restitutionary judgment. In other words, unless there is a mutual restitution of benefits, a court will not allow any restitutionary recovery [Restatement 2d § 384]. As the saying goes, "to get restitution a party must do restitution."

Sometimes, of course, the aggrieved party has received no benefits, e.g., Bill gave Darla $50,000 for a piece of property and she has not tendered the deed to him. In such cases, obviously no mutual restitution is possible, for Darla gave Bill nothing to return. But where, e.g., Ted gave Ann $25,000 in progress payments for a construction job, and Ted later breaches, Ann will have to make restitution of the $25,000 before she can obtain restitution for her services from Ted.

Where the aggrieved party has received land or goods, he or she is expected to return that same land, or those very same goods if that is possible. If the benefits obtained by the aggrieved party cannot be returned intact, e.g., when they are services, the **value** of those services, as calculated by the appropriate method [§ 31–5], must be subtracted from the net amount owing that party in ascertaining the correct net amount of restitutionary recovery [Restatement 2d § 384(2)].

a. Example. [§ 31–12]

Millie hires Frank to build an addition onto her house. Under their contract, Millie was obligated to make monthly progress payments to Frank. Frank began construction and had both laid the foundation and put up two walls when Millie unjustly fired him. At that point, Millie had paid Frank $15,000 in monthly progress payments.

To be entitled to sue Millie in restitution, Frank will have to return the $15,000 in progress payments under the rule of Restatement 2d § 384(1), and will have to be prepared to pay that money, or at least account for it as an offset, to collect a restitution judgment.

b. Example. [§ 31–13]

Same as above, except this time it was Frank who breached, and Millie sued Frank in restitution for the $15,000 in progress payments. Obviously Millie could not "return" the foundation and the walls Frank built. In cases like this where return of the exact benefits provided by the non-breaching party is either impossible or unavailing, the aggrieved party must at least offset the dollar value of such benefits in any restitutionary recovery to get the proper net restitutionary judgment amount [Restatement 2d § 384(2)]. Hence, Millie's restitution to Frank would be the fair market value for the foundation and the wall built by Frank, as measured by the appropriate method.

C. LIMITATIONS OF RESTITUTIONARY RECOVERY FOR BREACH OF CONTRACT. [§ 31–14]

There are three limitations on a non-breaching party's right to seek restitution for a breach of contract:

CHAPTER 31

(1) Restitution is only available if the injured party would be able to sue the breaching party for total, as opposed to partial, breach [Restatement 2d § 373, Cmt. a; § 31–15];

(2) A party injured by the other's breach is **not** entitled to restitution if he or she has performed all of his or her duties under the contract, and the only remaining performance due under the agreement by the breaching party is payment of a definite sum of money [Restatement 2d § 373(2); § 31–17]; and

(3) Under the majority rule, a party who has willfully breached may not recover in restitution [§ 31–20].

These limitations are discussed below.

1. **Restitution Is Available Only if the Breach Would Give Rise to Damages for Total, and Not Just Immaterial, Breach. [§ 31–15]**

   Before a party can recover in restitution, the breach involved must be serious enough to give rise to damages for a **total** breach [Restatement 2d § 373, Cmt. a; §§ 21–56 *et seq.*]. If the breach is only a partial or immaterial one, no restitution is recoverable.

   a. **Example. [§ 31–16]**

      Terry contractually agrees to build a house for Geri, and promises to use electrical wire made by Power Co. throughout the house. Geri agrees to make monthly progress payments to Terry. After two months, Terry has been paid $40,000 in progress payments, but it is then discovered that he inadvertently used nearly identical wire made by Electric Co. in various places throughout the house instead of Power Co. wire. While Geri is entitled to sue Terry for whatever damages she can prove have been caused by the *immaterial* breach, she is not entitled to recover the $40,000 that she has paid Terry in restitution because use of the wrong wire is only a non-material breach rather than a total, material breach [Restatement 2d § 373, Cmt. a, Ill. 2].

2. **Restitution Is Not Available if the Non-Breaching Party Has Performed All of His or Her Duties Under the Contract, and No Performance by the Breaching Party Remains Due Other than the Payment of a Definite Sum of Money. [§ 31–17]**

   If a non-breaching party has fully performed, and the breaching party has simply not paid the non-breaching party, restitution is not available to the non-breacher [Restatement 2d § 373(2)]. The rationale for this is two-fold: (1) in such cases, a court should not be put to the burden of determining a value for the benefits of the goods, land, or services the non-breaching party has provided the breaching

RESTITUTION

party **because the parties themselves have already set such a value of how much the goods, land, or services were worth when they made their contract**, i.e., the value of the unpaid sum of money; and (2) where a supplier's expectation damages can be so easily calculated with reference to the contract price, there is no need to resort to restitution.

a. **Example. [§ 31–18]**

> Vince has agreed to paint a portrait of Darla for $7,000. Vince paints the portrait and timely delivers it to Darla, who keeps it but refuses to pay for it. Under the rule of Restatement 2d § 373(2), Vince is not entitled to a restitutionary recovery even though he has clearly conferred a benefit on Darla, and even though Darla will be unjustly enriched if she fails to pay for it. That is because Vince (the non-breaching party), has performed all of his duties under the contract, and the only performance remaining is for Darla (the breacher), to pay of a fixed sum of money. As such, Vince must sue to recover the contract price as part of his expectation damages.
>
> This is exactly the kind of case where court believe they should not be burdened with trying to decide the value of the painting, i.e., the objective value of the benefit Vince has conferred on Darla, **because the parties themselves established that value when they made the contract**, and where the extent of Vince's expectation loss is so easily calculable from the contract price. So even if the painting is a masterpiece, and is "worth" $25,000, his recovery is limited to the $7,000 contract price. Similarly, if the painting is junk, Darla can't force Frank to settle for a smaller recovery—he gets the $7,000 contract price, which is the value the parties put on Frank' services when they entered into the contract. It is only when full performance has not been rendered to the that restitution is available.

b. **Example. [§ 31–19]**

> Marge has contracted to sell Steve a painting for $100,000. Steve makes the payment, but Marge never tenders the painting. Steve is entitled to recover $100,000 in restitution. In this case, while Steve has fully performed all of his duties under the contract, Restatement 2d § 373(2) does not bar restitutionary recovery because Marge's remaining duty is to deliver a **good**, not to pay a fixed sum of money. Accordingly, Steve would be entitled to the value of the benefit he conferred on Marge, in this case $100,000.

CHAPTER 31

3. **Majority Rule: Restitution Unavailable to a *Willful* Breacher. [§ 31–20]**

The majority rule, although there is a strong minority to the contrary, holds is that a party who willfully breaches a contract cannot recover in restitution.

D. COMMON FACT SITUATIONS INVOLVING THE NON-BREACHING PARTY SEEKING RESTITUTION. [§ 31–21]

There are recurring fact situations involving the application of restitution principles by the non-breaching party. These are detailed below.

1. **Restitution Is Almost Always Used in "Losing Contract" Situations. [§ 31–22]**

   Because restitutionary recovery is divorced from the contract price, and instead focuses on the value of benefits received, restitution quite often provides a greater recovery to the non-breaching party in a losing contract situation than a damages recovery.

   a. **Example. [§ 31–23]**

   James's construction company is hired to construct an office building on Developer's property for $1 million. James starts construction in a timely fashion and spent $600,000 in labor and materials when developer breaches by unjustifiably telling him to stop. At the time of the breach James would have had to spend another $500,000 to finish construction. The reasonable value of James's services was $600,000, for that is the amount most other contractors in the area are prepared to testify that they would have charged to perform the services James did before the breach. The market value of Developer's property increased by $350,000 as a result of the partially constructed building.

   In a suit for breach, James would not want to sue for his expectation or reliance damages. This is because the facts show that James underbid the contract and would have lost $100,000 had the contract been performed, i.e., he had already spent $600,000 and would have needed another $500,000 to finish, and he was only entitled to $1 million from Developer under the contract. In a losing contract situation the amount of the loss must be subtracted from any expectation or reliance damage recovery [§§ 30–4; 30–6].

   Accordingly, James would want to recover in restitution for the breach. As the non-breaching party, he is entitled to the greater of the two methods of valuing the benefits received by Developer. Those benefits are valued at $600,000 under the cost avoided method, for this is the cost the developer has avoided by not paying James, as measured by what other contractors would have charged to provide those same benefits. The benefits provided the Developer are valued at $350,000 under the net benefit method, for that is the net increase in the value of Developer's property as the result of James's efforts. Hence, James would be entitled to recover $600,000 in restitution. While he wouldn't make any money on the deal with a restitutionary recovery, at least he does not lose $100,000 either, as would be true where recovery was for expectation or reliance damages.

2. Restitution Is Almost Always Used When the Value of the Benefits Provided Exceeds the Reasonable Value of Those Services. [§ 31–24]

Another instance when restitution always provides a greater recovery to the non-breacher than damages is when the non-breaching party has provided services at under market rates.

a. Example. [§ 31–25]

Stuart hires Mary to paint his house for $800. Mary has almost finished when Stuart fires her. As this was Mary's first commercial painting job, she priced her services well under market just to get the work. Most other painters in the area would have charged at least $1,500 for doing the work Mary did before the breach, and her efforts in almost completely painting Stuart's house have increased its market value by $1,000.

Mary would seek a restitutionary recovery against Stuart. This is because, once again, restitution only focuses on the value of the benefits actually received, not on the value of a party's promised performance. Hence, the contract price does not provide a ceiling for restitutionary recovery, and so Mary is entitled to recover for the **value** of the enrichment her services provided to Stuart. As she is the non-breaching party seeking restitution, she is presumptively entitled to the greater of the amounts calculated under the cost avoided or net benefit methods [§ 31–10]. Under the cost avoided method, the amount of benefits received by Stuart is $1,500, for that is the cost Stuart avoided by not having to pay another reasonable painter to do the work Mary did. Under the net benefit method, the value of the services retained by Stuart was $1,000, for that is the net increase in the fair market value of Stuart's property caused by Mary's services. Hence, Mary will recover $1,500 in restitution for the breach of a contract for which she only would have been paid $800 had it been performed.

Note that if Stuart had waited until Mary had finished, and then simply not paid her, Mary would **not** have been entitled to sue in restitution for the value of her services under the rule of Restatement 2d § 373(2), since the only performance remained due was Stuart's performance of payment for a definite sum of money [§ 31–17]. In that case, she would have been limited by the contract price for her recovery.

3. **Restitution Is Never Used When the Value of the Benefits Is Less than the Contract Price. [§ 31–26]**

The converse of the rule discussed immediately above is that when the non-breaching party is an "expensive" provider of services in a non-losing contract, restitutionary recovery will give that party a smaller recovery than will damages. This is because restitutionary recovery is based on the "reasonable" value of those services, not the inflated value charged by the "expensive" non-breaching party.

a. Example. [§ 31–27]

Phil has a contract to build a custom-made wall unit for Jackie's stereo system. The contract price is $3,500. Phil timely began construction and was partially completed when Jackie breached and ordered him to stop. At that point Phil had spent $2,000 in labor and materials (applying his hourly rate), and his partially constructed wall unit has increased the value of Jackie's home by $300. It turns out that Phil is an expensive carpenter for the area, as most other carpenters would charge only $1,750 to do the work Phil did prior to the breach.

Phil's restitutionary recovery would be limited to $1,750. This is, once again, because recovery in restitution focuses only on the value of the benefits received by the other party. The question is what is the **fair market value** of the benefits conferred by Phil? Under the cost avoided method, the value is $1,750, for that is the cost Jackie avoided by not having to pay a reasonable carpenter in the area to do the work. Under the net benefit method, the value of Phil's services were $300, for that is the total appreciation of Jackie's home due to Phil's efforts. As the non-breaching party, Phil is presumptively entitled to the greater of these two figures in restitution (§ 31–10). Hence, even though Phil claims to have spent $2,000 in labor and materials on the job, he will only be able to collect $1,750 in restitution.

E. **ISSUES WHEN RESTITUTIONARY RECOVERY IS SOUGHT BY THE PARTY IN BREACH. [§ 31–28]**

As noted earlier, one of the unique features of restitution is that a *breaching* party can be (but is not always) entitled to a restitutionary recovery [Restatement 2d § 374]. This can be explained once again by the

RESTITUTION

fact that restitution focuses on the value of benefits conferred on a party and when it would be unjust for the benefited party to retain the benefits without paying for them, and by the requirement of mutual restitution. Since a breaching party will often have rendered benefits to the non-breacher before the contract was breached, it only makes sense that it would be unjust for the non-breacher to retain those benefits without paying for them, restitution should be allowed in favor of the breaching party.

1. **Calculating the Value of the Restitutionary Award in Cases Brought by the Breaching Party. [§ 31–29]**

    As noted, to calculate the proper amount of the breacher's restitutionary award, the value of the benefits received by the non-breaching party from the breacher must be calculated on both a "cost avoided" and a "net benefit" basis. Once again, a court is entitled to use whichever calculation method justice dictates should be used in the particular case to calculate the award, but there is a presumption that the method yielding the **least generous** valuation measure be used for the breaching party.

    Selecting the proper valuation method does not end the award calculation. Because it is the breaching party who is seeking recovery, **any damages suffered by the non-breacher must then be subtracted from the value of the benefits received by the non-breacher to arrive at the proper amount for the breaching party's restitutionary award**. That is, calculation of the breacher's recovery in these cases is a two-step process. First, the value of the service received by the non-breaching party must be calculated, and the least generous measure is presumptively selected. Second, the amount of any losses the non-breaching party suffered due to the breach must be subtracted from that value to arrive at the proper net restitutionary award.

    a. **Example. [§ 31–30]**

        Dave is in the business of making repairs to office buildings damaged by fire. He contracts to repair a commercial building that was severely damaged for a price of $60,000, which is to be paid on completion of the work. Dave works on the building for a few weeks, reasonably incurring $20,000 in labor and materials costs. At trial, it can be established that other builders in the area would have charged a similar amount to perform the services provided by Dave up to the point of the breach. However, Dave breaches and leaves the work site to take another, more lucrative job. The owner of the building hired someone to replace Dave, who finished the repairs for $45,000. In addition, since it took a week longer to finish the clean-up due to the delay in finding Dave's replacement, the building owner lost $2,000 in rent. Cleaning up the building from the fire damage increased its fair market value by $55,000.

The building owner would likely not bring suit against Dave, for she only had to spend $45,000 (plus $2,000 in lost rent) to get the benefits of a job for which she had contracted to pay Dave $60,000. However, **Dave** will bring suit, for he has received nothing for the benefits provided the owner. Because Dave is the breaching party, he can only sue in restitution.

The next issue is to determine the value of the benefits he provided the building owner. Under the cost avoided method of valuing the benefits received, Dave provided $20,000 in benefits, for that is the reasonable value of the services for which the owner did not have to pay, as measured by the cost others would have charged to provide those same services. Under the net benefit method, the value received by the landowner from Dave's efforts was only $10,000. That is, due to the clean-up she received a $55,000 increase in the fair market value of her property, but that $55,000 increase in value was as a result of the work of both Dave and his replacement. We know that the services of Dave's replacement were worth $45,000 (for that is how much the replacement was paid), and so the "**net benefit**" to the landowner of **Dave's** work in repairing the building would be $55,000 minus $45,000 or **$10,000**.

Because Dave is the breaching party, he is presumptively limited to using the valuation method yielding the least generous amount of recovery, or $10,000. In addition, the $2,000 lost rent suffered by the landowner must also be subtracted from Dave's recovery, so the net restitutionary relief due to Dave under these facts is **$8,000**. Note that Dave will likely consider this award unfair since he is "out-of-pocket" $20,000 in labor and materials. However, as the breaching party, contract law believes he should not be heard to complain about receiving the least generous measure of recovery. In other words, he could have ensured that the deal went forward. When he chose to breach, one of the consequences he had to suffer was the least generous method of restitutionary recovery for his work thus far.

F. RECOVERY IN RESTITUTION FOR QUASI-CONTRACT. [§ 31–31]

A party seeking to recover in "quasi-contract" must use restitution to value his or her recovery [§ 1–20]. That is, a quasi-contract, or implied-in-law contract, describes a situation in which there is no contract at all, i.e., there is no offer, acceptance, or consideration. Rather, the aggrieved party in such cases is seeking to recover for the benefit of some services provided another in a situation where it would be unjust for the benefited party to have been enriched by such services without paying for them. In these cases, while it is theoretically possible to calculate the value of the service using either the cost avoided or net benefit method, contract law has universally held that the aggrieved party is limited to a cost avoided recovery [Restatement 2d § 371, Cmt. b].

1. Example. [§ 31–32]

Roberta is a surgeon who comes across Lou, a car accident victim, lying injured and unconscious on the road. She realizes that Lou immediately needs life-saving surgery, has Lou rushed to the hospital in an ambulance, and performs surgery on him, which saves his life. Lou remained unconscious until the next day.

If Lou refuses to compensate Roberta, she is entitled to sue him in restitution. Under the "cost avoided" method of value calculation, the value of the benefit Roberta provided Lou would be equal to the reasonable value for such surgery as measured by what other surgeons in the area would charge for that procedure.

Note this value may be more or less than the fee Roberta usually charges. That is, Roberta does not automatically receive her customary fee in restitution; rather she is only entitled to the reasonable value of her service as measured by what other surgeons charge for that service.

Under the net benefit method, the value of the benefit Roberta provided Lou would be equal to the net economic benefits Lou would earn over the remainder of his life. That is, without Roberta's services, Lou would have died. Hence, his interests were advanced in an amount equal to any salary or other income he would earn for the rest of his life. For obvious reasons, recovery in quasi-contract is thus limited to the value of the benefits received as calculated under the cost avoided method.

G. RESTITUTIONARY RECOVERY IN VOIDABLE CONTRACTS. [§ 31–33]

Generally, restitutionary recovery is available to a party who decided to exercise his or her right to avoid the agreement. In these situations the idea is that *if* one party provided another a benefit under a contract that later was avoided due to any of the doctrines listed below, the party getting out of the contract must account for the benefits received, if any, while he or she was in the contract. Restitution is available when the party with the voidable defense has received benefits in the following situations:

(1) The Statute of Frauds [§ 10–64];

(2) Incapacity by minority at least for cash sales and necessities, and in some other circumstances [*see* §§ 11–8 *et seq.*];

(3) Incapacity due to mental defect in many situations [§ 11–16];

(4) Mutual mistake [§ 12–19];

(5) Unilateral mistake [§ 12–27];

(6) Duress [§ 13–5];

(7) Undue influence [§ 14–5];

(8) Misrepresentation [§ 15–34];

(9) Illegality under certain circumstances [*see* §§ 17–10; 17–13]; and

(10) Impossibility, impracticability, and frustration of purpose [*see gen.*, Restatement 2d §§ 375–377; § 25–64].

1. Example. [§ 31–34]

Fred buys a new car. He drives it for two months. He then successfully files suit to avoid the transaction based on duress. He will be entitled to whatever money he paid the dealership for the car in restitution. However, he will also have to "do" restitution, and account for the economic benefit of having the car for the time he drove it before the deal is voided.

H. EXAM APPROACH TO RESTITUTION ISSUES. [§ 31–35]

Every time you are expected to discuss damages for total breach of contract, a voidability situation, or quasi-contract, you must also consider, and likely discuss, restitutionary relief as well.

Recall that restitution is always available to the non-breaching party (subject to the limitations in § 31–14), and is often available to the breaching party as well [§ 31–28], subject to offsets for the non-breaching party's damage. Remember also that a party who decides to seek restitution must return any benefits he or she had received under the contract to the other party [§ 31–11].

If you decide that recovery in restitution is available, recall that the amount of the recovery is dependent on the value of the benefits actually received by the other party [§ 31–2]. The only "fixed" rule for determining the value of restitutionary recovery is that the result be just and reasonable, but typically the courts look to the "cost avoided" and "net benefit" methods at least as starting points in calculating those benefits (§ 31–5), and award the breaching party the least generous amount derived from those calculations, and the non-breaching party the most generous award derived from those calculations.

CHAPTER 32

REMEDIES FOR BREACH UNDER THE UCC

A. UCC REMEDIES GENERALLY. [§ 32–1]

The basics of the UCC remedies have been provided in the previous Chapters. This Chapter is for those students in classes where Code-based remedies are given more of a focus, and thus the remedies under the Code are spelled out in greater detail.

B. EQUITABLE REMEDIES AVAILABLE TO BUYERS UNDER THE UCC. [§ 32–2]

There are two principal equitable remedies specifically available to the non-breaching buyer under UCC § 2–716: (1) specific performance and (2) replevin.

1. Specific Performance. [§ 32–3*]

As with the common law, specific performance is an order by a court requiring a party to actually perform a promise he or she made in a contract. As in non-UCC contexts, the court enforces a specific performance order through the use of its contempt powers [§ 29–4]. At early common law, specific performance was available to a buyer only when the goods involved in the contract were highly unique, one-of-a-kind items. However, the Code "seeks to further a more liberal attitude than some courts have shown in connection with the specific performance of contracts for sale" [UCC § 2–716, Cmt. 1]. The Code has tried to further this "more liberal" attitude by stating that a court may order specific performance "where the goods are unique **or in other proper circumstances**" [UCC § 2–716(1)].

While the Code provides no definition for "other proper circumstances," case law has established that a court should order specific performance under § 2–716(1) when finding replacement goods cannot be done "without considerable expense, delay and inconvenience."

---

* For more information, listen to CD # 11, Track 5 of *Sum and Substance Audio on Contracts*.

CHAPTER 32

a. **Example. [§ 32–4]**

Ira contracted to buy a particular one-of-a-kind Ming vase from Jane. Jane refused to deliver possession of the vase, even though Ira timely tendered the amount of the agreed payment. Even under early common law, and certainly under the UCC rules, a one-of-a-kind Ming vase is unique and thus Ira would be entitled to an order of specific performance.

SPECIAL CASE SQUIB

b. *Sedmak v. Charlie's Chevrolet, Inc.* **[§ 32–5]**

Chevrolet sold a limited number of "Pace Car" Corvettes. Essentially, every dealer in the country got one such car. There were a limited number of option packages and colors available for the Pace Car Corvettes. In an oral agreement, Dr. Sedmak made a deal with his local dealership for a Pace Car Corvette in a particular color with special options for the list price, approximately $15,000, and he gave the dealership a $500 check to seal the deal. The limited number of cars made them valuable for collectors, and when the car arrived at the dealership, its owner told Dr. Sedmak that his $500 check was not a down payment for the purchase of car, but rather qualified him to enter an auction for the car, which the owner planned to sell to the highest bidder. Indeed, the dealer had received several bids for the car, including a $28,000 bid for the car from an out-of-state bidder.

Dr. Sedmak sued for specific performance. The dealership argued that Dr. Sedmak had not proven that the car was unique, since he had not contacted any other dealers throughout the country to see if a like car could be obtained. Indeed, there were only a limited number of colors and options available for the special car, and likely there were a few identical cars somewhere.

Held: The trial court's order of specific performance was affirmed. The court held that while the car may not be "unique" in the common law sense [like the Ming vase above], but this was a "proper circumstance" for specific performance under UCC § 2–716. The court held that specific performance was authorized under the Code whenever securing a replacement good cannot be done "without considerable expense, delay and inconvenience." Here, requiring Dr. Sedmak to make calls to Chevrolet dealers around the country hoping to find a similar car was an example of the type of considerable inconvenience that the Code sought to avoid.

REMEDIES FOR BREACH UNDER THE UCC

The *Sedmak* test has proven popular with commercial scholars and is now oft-used as the test for when specific performance is appropriate [*Sedmak v. Charlie's Chevrolet, Inc.*, 621 S.W2d 694 (Mo. 1961)].

c. **Review Problem. [§ 32–6]**

Art has contractually agreed to purchase a case of 2017 Chateau Laffite Rothschild from a big wine store in town. The wine storeowner refuses to deliver the wine. Art cannot obtain the wine from any other store in town, for the other stores have completely sold their supply. However, the wine is available via the Internet.

Question:

Can Art get specific performance?

Answer:

Even under the more liberal rules of UCC § 2–716(1), Art would *not* be entitled to an order of specific performance on these facts, because he could procure an equivalent bottle of wine "without considerable expense, delay and inconvenience."

2. **Replevin. [§ 32–7]**

Replevin is typically a pre-judgment remedy whereby a non-breaching buyer can have a law enforcement officer take possession of the goods which are the subject matter of a breach of contract action and hold them during the pendency of the lawsuit. That is, after a buyer files an action for breach, he or she can file a motion requesting an order from the court directing an officer to seize the property which is the subject of the contract.

If the court grants the motion, the officer is empowered to go to wherever the goods are kept, take possession of them, and hold onto them throughout the pendency of the lawsuit. (Indeed, some states even permit the sheriff to deliver the goods to the buyer, to be kept by the buyer until the lawsuit is over.) The reason for seeking an order of replevin is that once the goods are in the hands of the officer, the buyer knows that the goods are safe and cannot be sold or harmed by the seller until the lawsuit is over.

Replevin seems like a great pre-judgment remedy for a buyer, but it carries with it some procedural baggage. First, a court must order the buyer to post a bond, usually equal in value to the cost of the goods, before the law enforcement officer will replevy the goods. Second, even after the buyer posts the bond and the officer seizes the goods, in many states a seller can "bond back" the good by posting a similarly sized bond with the court. Once the court is convinced that a judgment in favor of the buyer can be satisfied by the bond, it will release the good from the officer, who will return it to the seller.

C. COMPARISON OF UCC AND COMMON LAW MONEY DAMAGE PROVISIONS. [§ 32–8*]

The money remedies for breach of contract governed by Article 2 of the UCC do not differ in kind from the types of money damages remedies discussed in Chapter 31. However, the Code organizes these remedies somewhat differently, gives them different names on occasion, and applies them uniquely.

As with the common law, the principal goal of UCC money damages is to put the non-breaching party in the position he or she would have been in had the contract been performed [UCC § 1–305(a)]. That is, recovery for the interference with the expectation interest is how the provisions are designed. The Code uses somewhat different terminology to get that recovery, so the E.D = L.V. + C + I − C.A. − L.A. formula is packaged in different ways [see § 30–29 for an explanation of that different terminology].

Two provisions that are a little different than their common law counterparts are the provision defining Consequential Damages, and the definition of Incidental Damages. Those provisions are discussed below.

1. Consequential Damages Under the UCC: § 2–715(2). [§ 32–9]

The recovery of a buyer's consequential damages in Article 2 contracts is governed by UCC § 2–715(2). There is an important limitation in consequential damage recovery under the UCC. **Only buyers are authorized to collect consequential loss**. There is no provision whereby a consequential damage is an authorized element of the seller's damages.

(In truth, it is the rare situation in which a seller would suffer a consequential damage. However, while it may be rare, it *is* conceivable that a seller could suffer such damages which is why in § 2R–710(2) a seller's consequential recovery is authorized.)

Section 2–715 divides consequential loss into two types: (i) consequential **economic** loss, as described in UCC § 2–715(2)(a) and (ii) consequential **personal injury and personal property** loss, as described in UCC § 2–715(2)(b). The chief difference between these two types of consequential loss is in the level of foreseeability the buyer must prove before he or she is entitled to their recovery.

The foreseeability rules governing the recovery of consequential **economic** loss under the Code are identical to the foreseeability rules for the recovery of consequential damages under common law

---

* For more information, listen to CD # 12, Tracks 2 and 3 of *Sum and Substance Audio on Contracts*.

contract principles based on *Hadley v. Baxendale* [§ 30–55]. That is, before a buyer can recover for any type of consequential economic loss, the party must show that the loss was foreseeable to a reasonable person in the breaching party's shoes at the time of contract formation. As the Code puts it, the buyer must establish that "the seller at the time of contracting had reason to know" that such type of loss would follow from the breach [UCC § 2–715(2)(a)].

As with common law, there are two ways to establish this foreseeability, depending on whether recovery is for "direct" or "indirect" economic loss. If direct, the type of loss is presumed foreseeable; if indirect, the buyer must show from the circumstances existing at the time the contract was executed that the seller was put on notice of the type of damage now claimed. As the Code expresses it, consequential economic loss includes losses, "resulting from general or particular requirements and needs the seller at the time of contracting had reason to know" [UCC § 2–715(2)(a)].

To recover for consequential **personal injury or personal property loss** under the Code, however, the buyer need only show that such losses "proximately result[ed]" from any breach of warranty. This means the foreseeability test for recovery of consequential personal injury or property loss is the lenient foreseeability test of tort, i.e., was the breach a "proximate cause" of the damage. "Personal injury" losses include medical bills, lost wages, and pain and suffering.

The second issue regarding consequential loss under the Code is whether damage to the good itself should be classified as economic loss, and thus subject to the more stringent foreseeability test of § 2–715(2)(a), or should be regarded as personal property loss, and thus recoverable under the more lenient proximate cause standard of § 2–715(2)(b). That is, suppose an airline purchases new jet engines for one of the airplanes in its fleet. The first time the engine is engaged after delivery it implodes, due to faulty construction. The accident caused much harm to the engine, but not to anything else. The question is thus whether the harm to the good itself, i.e., harm solely to the non-conforming engine, is economic consequential loss, or is personal property damage. The universal answer is that **injury to the good itself is considered economic loss** for purposes of UCC § 2–715(2). Hence, such loss would be governed by the contract-based foreseeability principles of § 2–715(2)(a), and is also subject to the warranty disclaimer rules of UCC § 2–316 and the limitation of damages rules of UCC § 2–719 [§ 32–52; *East River Steamship Corp. v. Transamerica Delaval, Inc.*, 476 U.S. 858 (1986)].

CHAPTER 32

2. Incidental Damages Under the UCC. [§ 32–10]

There are two provisions which regulate incidental damage recovery under the Code: one for buyers and one for sellers.

The buyer's provision is UCC § 2–715(1). As with common law, such damages are generally defined as out-of-pocket expenses spent after the breach, usually in an attempt to mitigate the breaching seller's damages. Specifically under § 2–715 they include, "expenses reasonably incurred in inspection, receipt, transportation and care and custody of goods rightfully rejected, any commercially reasonably charges, expenses or commissions in connection with effecting cover and any other reasonable expense incident to the delay or other breach."

Seller's incidental damages are governed by UCC § 2–710 and include, "any commercially reasonable charges, expenses or commissions incurred in stopping delivery, in the transportation, care, and custody of goods after the buyer's breach, in connection with the return or resale of the goods or otherwise resulting from the breach."

D. BUYER'S RIGHT TO SUE FOR DAMAGES IN CASES WHERE HE OR SHE DOES NOT HAVE THE GOODS AT THE TIME OF SUIT. [§ 32–11*]

There are two scenarios in which a non-breaching buyer can recover money damages. The first is when the buyer does not have the goods at the time suit is filed, and the second is when the buyer does have the goods when the suit is commenced. This section covers the Code's treatment of those situations in which a non-breaching buyer sues the breaching seller for damages where the buyer does not have the goods when suit is filed.

There are three reasons why a non-breaching buyer may not have the goods when a suit for breach is filed:

(1) The seller breached by **never tendering** the goods to the buyer;

(2) The buyer rightfully and effectively **rejected non-conforming goods** provided by the seller, and the seller did not adequately cure [§§ 22–12 *et seq.*]; and

(3) The buyer rightfully and effectively **revoked his or her acceptance** of non-conforming goods provided by the seller, and the seller did not adequately cure [§§ 22–39 *et seq.*].

In these cases, the UCC provides the buyer with two related, but distinct, remedies:

---

* For more information, listen to CD # 12, Tracks 2 of *Sum and Substance Audio on Contracts*.

REMEDIES FOR BREACH UNDER THE UCC

(1) The buyer can go into the market, purchase replacement goods ("**cover**"), and sue for the difference between the cover price and the contract price, along with other related damages [UCC § 2–712]; or

(2) The buyer can choose not to purchase replacement goods, and instead simply sue for the difference between the market price (i.e., analogous to the price pending **if** the buyer had covered) and the contract price, along with other related damages [UCC § 2–713].

Each of these remedies is discussed below.

1. UCC § 2–712: Cover Damages. [§ 32–12]

A buyer who ends up without goods due to a seller's breach is entitled to go in the market and "cover" by purchasing substitute goods. If the cost of cover is more than the contract price, the buyer is entitled to sue the breaching seller for that price differential.

It is crucial to note that under § 2–712(1) a party is allowed to effect "reasonable cover" by acting "in good faith and without unreasonable delay." This means that if the replacement goods are a little different, and perhaps a little more expensive than the goods that are the subject of the breached contract, the buyer can recover for the increased price it takes to cover for the breach as long as the buyer acts in "good faith." Similarly, if the buyer waits a few days after the breach before purchasing substitute goods, and the price of replacement increases during the interim, the buyer is entitled to seek damages based on the increased price so long as there was no "unreasonable delay" in securing replacement goods. That is, the seller cannot claim the increased price should be ignored due to mitigation [§ 30–59].

For example, suppose a large department store placed an order for 5,000 2-speed blenders from a manufacturer, to be delivered on October 15, just before the start of the store's Christmas season. The manufacturer unjustifiably fails to deliver the blenders, and the store tries to find replacements. However, it proves difficult to find 5,000 2-speed blenders, which can be delivered in time for the Christmas rush. Another manufacturer can immediately deliver 5,000 5-speed blenders, but the 5-speed blenders cost $3/per blender more than the store was obligated to pay for the 2-speed models. Because cover need only be reasonable to be recoverable, so long as the store acted in good faith in purchasing the 5-speed models, i.e., it did not do so just to increase damages to the breaching seller, it is entitled to recover the differential between the cover price and the contract price if it actually goes into the market and purchases the 5-speed models.

Accordingly, the idea of cover in UCC § 2–712(1) allows the non-breaching buyer some flexibility in proceeding after a breach. Rather than having his or her damages fixed on the day of the breach as the difference between market price for identical goods pending that day and the contract price, the buyer is entitled to spend some time looking for reasonably comparable goods. So long as the buyer acts reasonably and in good faith in purchasing replacement goods, he or she is entitled to recover the full amount of his or her cover damages.

Similarly, assume a buyer covered at $155 from a local store, but at trial the seller establishes that the buyer could have covered for $150 from another retailer. So long as the buyer acted in good faith, it can recover based on the $155 price since, "it is immaterial that hindsight may later prove the method of cover used was not the cheapest or most effective" [UCC § 2–712, Cmt. 2].

a. **The Formula for Recovery of Cover Damages. [§ 32–13]**

The formula provided in UCC § 2–712 for the recovery of cover damages is:

Buyer's Cover Damages = [(Cost of Cover) − (Contract Price)] + (Incidental Damages) + (Consequential Damages) − (Expenses Saved in Consequence of the Breach).

(1) **Example. [§ 32–14]**

DVDarama placed an order with Billy's Electronics for 100 single disc DVD players at $200/player. Billy's was supposed to make the players available for pickup by CDarama on November 1, in time for DVDarama's Christmas rush. Billy's is 100 miles away from DVDarama.

As a result of the failure to deliver, DVDarama's President spends ten hours on the phone over the next couple of days trying to find replacement units. She finally locates 100 5-disc DVD players immediately available for $207/player, and has them express shipped to her store. The express shipping cost $400 more than regular freight shipment. One of the reasons she had the new players express shipped is that she was out of stock of DVD players and had already lost two sales because she could not provide immediate delivery. At trial, she can prove she could have sold the players for $350/player to the two buyers. Additionally, she can prove that a fair value of her time is $30/hour.

Under the formula set forth in UCC § 2–712, DVDarama's recovery is determined as follows:

Cover Price—100 units × $207/unit = $20,700. (Note that the $207/unit price is recoverable even though it is for a 5-play unit. This is because, on these facts, DVDarama's decision to purchase 5-play units was neither in bad faith nor made with unreasonable delay and so is an acceptable "cover".)

Contract Price—100 units × $200/unit = $20,000.

Incidental Damages—UCC § 2–715(1) provides that "expenses reasonably incurred in . . . cure" are recoverable as incidental damage. Theoretically that would include the time spent in securing a cure. Courts tends to be reluctant to give an award for time spent because it is hard to quantify and objectively prove, and because buyer's often overvalue the hourly wage expended in cure efforts. However, the time spent in effecting cure is theoretically recoverable and, if they are included, DVDarama can recover for two types of incidental loss:

(1) The time spent by the DVDarama president in finding replacement units. If $30/hour is a reasonable figure to use for the value of her time, DVDarama is entitled to collect $300 for the ten hours she spent tracking down replacement units; and

(2) The $400 extra in express shipping charges. Given the season, it was reasonable to foresee the need for someone like DVDarama to get the units quickly. Hence, because the shipping charges represent reasonable expenses incurred after the breach in an attempt to cover, they are recoverable.

Consequential Loss—DVDarama lost two sales due to Bill's breach in not getting the units to the store as promised. The profits on those units were ($350 − $200) or $150 each. This loss was "direct" consequential loss, for if a seller does not provide a **retail** store with merchandise, it is certainly reasonably foreseeable that the store can lose sales. Hence, DVDarama also has $300 in recoverable consequential damages.

Expenses Saved in Consequence of the Breach—In the original contract DVDarama was obligated to drive 100 miles to pick up the players. This is an expense that it will no longer have to bear as a consequence of the breach. Say that cost was $100.

Accordingly, DVDarama's recovery under § 2–712 would be: [($20,700) − ($20,000)] + ($700) + ($300) − ($100) or **$1,600**.

CHAPTER 32

2. **UCC § 2–713: Market Differential Damages. [§ 32–15]**

   To be entitled to cover damages under UCC § 2–712, a non-breaching buyer must go into the market and actually purchase replacement goods. Finding such goods and coming up with the money to purchase them may be such a hassle for the buyer that he or she does not wish to do it. Or the buyer may have changed his or her mind and now really doesn't want the goods. UCC § 2–713 holds that the buyer may avoid that hassle and still recover the full extent of his or her expectation loss. That is, § 2–713(1) allows the buyer to sue for the difference between the fair market price of replacement goods and the contract price, together with associated other damages.

   a. **The Formula for Market Differential Damages. [§ 32–16]**

   The formula for recovering market differential damages provided in § 2–713 is:

   Buyer's Market Differential Damages = [(Market Price of the Goods) − (Contract Price for the Goods)] + (Incidental Damages) + (Consequential Damages) − (Expenses Saved in Consequence of the Breach).

   (1) **Issues in Determining the "Market Price." [§ 32–17]**

   The formula for market differential damages under § 2–713 requires that the contract price for the goods be subtracted from the "market price" for the goods. An issue in applying the formula is that the market price for the goods may be volatile, and change day to day. Similarly, if the buyer and seller are in different cities, it may well be that on the same day the market price for the goods in those different cities is different. Hence, a decision must be made as to which of the potentially different market prices should be selected as the proper "market price" for purposes of § 2–713 damages.

   (a) **Determining the "Temporal" Market. [§ 32–18]**

   Section 2–713(1) provides that the **temporal market price** that should be used in the formula is the **market price pending "at the time the buyer learned of the breach"** (and not, as you might expect, the price on the day delivery was due).

   Note that in the unusual case where there has been an anticipatory repudiation by the seller and case goes to trial before the delivery date, the temporal price is, "the price of . . . goods prevailing at the time when the aggrieved party learned of the repudiation" [UCC § 2–723(1)].

(i) Exception Based on *Oloffson v. Coomer*. [§ 32–19]

An exception to the rule that the date of repudiation should only be used if the case gets to trial before the trial date (which is what §§ 2–713, and 2–723(1) collectively require) was established in *Oloffson*. There, a farmer anticipatorily repudiated a contract to supply grain several months before delivery was due. The trial did not take place until after the delivery was due.

Grain prices fluctuated daily, but arranging for replacement grain on a national exchange was a relatively simple matter for the merchant buyer. In the case, the buyer decided not to cover, and sued for the difference between the market place at the time of delivery (which it claimed was the date of "breach" as called for under § 2–713, since before then it was only a repudiation) and the contract price.

Held: Where: (1) there is volatility in the price of the good; and (2) cover could be easily effectuated, a **buyer is limited to the price pending at the time of repudiation** even if it does not cover and even if comes to trial after the date of delivery. Essentially, the court said the buyer in such circumstance could not speculate on the market place pending at the date of delivery at seller's expense [*Oloffson v. Coomer*, 11 Ill.App.3d 918 (1973)].

(b) Determining the Geographic Market. [§ 32–20]

Section 2–713(2) provides that the proper **geographical market price** to be used depends on the nature of the seller's breach. *If the seller breaches by never tendering goods or by repudiation,* the **"market price"** for purposes of § 2–713 is the one pending ***at the place for tender***. *If the seller breaches by sending non-conforming goods,* and the buyer rightfully either rejects or revokes his or her acceptance of them, then the **"market price"** that should be used is the ***one pending at the place where the goods arrived***.

CHAPTER 32

(2) Example. [§ 32–21]

Roberta, a retail buyer in California, ordered 100 dozen Grade AA eggs from a seller in New York. The contract price was $10/dozen. Under their contract, tender of the eggs was to take place in New York on May 15. Hence, Roberta planned to hire a carrier to pick up the eggs on that day in New York and transport them to California.

If the contract had gone forward, the eggs were scheduled to be delivered to Roberta on May 18. On May 15, however, the seller called Roberta and told her that he would not deliver. The fair market value for such eggs on May 15 was $10.50/dozen in New York, and $11/dozen in California. On May 18, the expected date of delivery in California, the market value for the eggs was back to $10/dozen in New York, and it was $10.75/dozen in California.

If Roberta chooses **not** to cover, she is entitled to recover market differential damages under § 2–713. To do so she must select the appropriate market value for use in calculating her damages. Under § 2–713(1)(a), she must use the price pending "at the time she learned of the breach" as the temporal market value. Hence, she will have to use either the $10.50/dozen New York price, or the $11/dozen California price, which were the prices pending on May 15 (the date she learned the seller would not deliver the eggs) and not the prices pending on May 18, the delivery date under the contract.

The nature of the seller's breach was that it never tendered the goods. Hence under § 2–713(2), the geographical market to be used is the place where the goods were to be tendered. Since eggs were due to be tendered in New York, Roberta must use the $10.50/dozen price pending in New York on May 15 in determining her market differential damages.

Under the formula set forth in UCC § 2–713, Roberta's recovery is determined as follows:

Market Price—$10.50/dozen × 1,000 dozen = $10,500.

Contract Price—$10/dozen × 1,000 dozen = $10,000.

Incidental Damages—There are no incidental damages on these facts.

Consequential Damages—There are no consequential damages on these facts.

REMEDIES FOR BREACH UNDER THE UCC

Expenses Saved in Consequence of the Breach— There are no expenses saves in consequence of the breach on these facts.

Accordingly, Roberta's recovery under § 2–713 would be: $10,500 − $10,000 + $0 + $0 − $0 or **$500**.

3. Buyer's Right to Market Differential Damages Even if Buyer Has Covered. [§ 32–22]

An issue sometimes arises whether a buyer who covers at below market price can nevertheless sue for market differential damages under § 2–713. There is a split of authority on the issue. Some courts and commentators hold that if a buyer covers, he or she should be limited to cover damages since that would put the buyer in the position the buyer would have been in had the contract been performed, which is the Code's goal for damage calculation [UCC § 1–305(a)].

Those courts and commentators who take the opposite tack argue that cover damages under § 2–712 and market differential damages under § 2–713 are separate, independent remedies, and both § 2–711(1) and § 2–712(3) seem to make clear that it is the buyer's choice as to which remedy he or she chooses. The buyer does not get to recover under both sections, but can choose the theory which maximizes recovery under the law.

E. BUYER'S RIGHT TO DAMAGES FOR BREACH OF WARRANTY AND OTHER NON-CONFORMING TENDER WHEN THE BUYER HAS POSSESSION OF THE GOODS AT THE TIME OF FILING OF THE BREACH OF CONTRACT SUIT. [§ 32–23]

A buyer is entitled to accept non-conforming goods or a non-conforming tender and still bring an action against the seller based on the extent to which he or she is economically injured by the non-conformity. That is, the good may not be perfect, but it is OK for the buyer's purposes, and the hassle of rejecting and returning it may not be worth the bother. Or the problem with the good may show up several weeks after delivery, and the buyer can't return it. Nevertheless, because the buyer did not get what the buyer was promised, the buyer is entitled to damages from the breach of warranty or other non-conforming tender.

In this section, it is assumed the buyer has accepted the good despite the non-conforming tender, and thus has the good in his or her possession at the time the suit is filed. Recall that once a party accepts a good, he or she is liable for its full contract price [UCC § 2–607(1)]. Hence, in breach of warranty and other cases in this section, the buyer is liable to the seller

CHAPTER 32

for the full contract price, but is also entitled to sue the seller for the damages as described below.

1. **The Formula for Breach of Warranty Recovery Under UCC § 2–714. [§ 32–24*]**

   The general formula for a buyer's recovery breach of warranty actions set forth in §§ 2–714(2) and (3):

   Buyer's Warranty Damages = [(Value of Goods as Warranted) – (Value of Goods Received)] + (Incidental Damages) + (Consequential Damages).

   As the Code notes, this formula is only presumptive, and a buyer can recover additional damages proximately caused by seller's breach if they can be proven. [UCC § 2–714(2)]

   a. **The Difference Between the Value of the Goods as Promised and the Value of Goods Received. [§ 32–25]**

      There are two points that need to be discussed about the value differential portion of the formula regulating the amount of a buyer's recovery for breach of warranty.

      First, the focus of the recovery is on the fair market **value** of the goods as promised and as received, and **not on the contract price**. As a result, it is entirely possible that a buyer's recovery in warranty can be **greater** than the contract price he or she is obligated to pay the seller upon the decision to accept the good.

      For example, suppose Kathy is told by a sales representative in a computer store that the processor of a computer she is thinking of purchasing is powerful enough to run *Battlefield V* without buffering. Accordingly, she buys the computer for $1,500. When she gets it home, she discovers the video chip in the computer requires buffering when playing the game.

      Subsequent investigation establishes that a computer with a processor capable of running *Battlefield V* smoothly would cost at least $2,750. Similarly, most computer companies would charge no more than $1,000 for a computer with the features Kathy's computer has.

      Assuming she decides to keep the computer, the value differential to which Kathy is entitled under § 2–714(2) is $2,750 – $1,000 or $1,750, i.e., the **value** of the computer she was promised minus the **value** of the computer she actually received. Accordingly, while Kathy is still obligated to pay the purchase price of $1,500 because she has accepted, rather than rejected, the computer under § 2–607(1), she is also entitled to at least a

---

* For more information, listen to CD # 12, Track 2 of *Sum and Substance Audio on Contracts.*

$1,750 warranty recovery from the store plus any incidental or consequential damages she can establish.

The second point that needs to be mentioned about the value differential portion of the § 2–714(2) formula for recovery of breach of warranty damages is that it is often measured by the cost to repair the non-conforming good. That is, a reasonable way to estimate the difference between the value of the good as warranted and the value of the good as received is to ascertain how much it would cost to repair the good received to make it into the good promised. Hence, if a new video card would solve Kathy's problem above, damages would probably be limited to the cost of that card.

2. **The Formula for Other Non-Conforming Tenders. [§ 32–26]**

If a seller tenders conforming goods, but does so after the delivery date called for in the contract, the buyer can choose to accept the goods and waive any right to reject them. However, simply by keeping the goods the buyer does not waive his or her rights to sue for the improper tender of the goods. The formula for breach of warranty in § 2–714(2) will yield a "$0" recovery in such cases, because if the goods are conforming, their value as promised and their value as received is identical.

In such cases, the buyer can recover under the formula of § 2–714(1), which provides that, "[the buyer] may recover as damages for any non-conformity of tender the loss resulting in the ordinary course of events from the seller's breach as determined in any manner which is reasonable."

3. **Buyer's Right to Offset Damages Under § 2–717. [§ 32–27]**

Consider the following case. Colleen examines two televisions in a department store, a 42-inch model for $600, and a 32-inch model for $350. She decides on the 42-inch one, arranges for 30 days deferred billing, and for delivery the following week. When the television arrives, however, the store mistakenly delivered the 32-inch model. Obviously Colleen could reject it, but she decides to keep it and figures she'll pocket the $250 price differential between the two sets. When her bill comes, she is charged $600, i.e., she was charged the price for the set she ordered, not the one she received.

Under the rules of § 2–607(1) and § 2–714, Colleen would be entitled to sue for the difference between the value of the good she was promised ($600), and the value of the good she received ($350). However, she will also have to pay the contract price because she accepted the good. A two-step process whereby she has to pay now but sue and collect later is inefficient. Accordingly, under UCC § 2–717, a buyer is entitled to deduct from the purchase price all or any part of the damages due the buyer resulting from the seller's breach, as long as the buyer gives adequate notice of his or her intentions. Accordingly, Colleen is entitled to pay the store only $350 in response to its $600 bill, so long as she explains why she is doing so.

4. **Buyer's Right to Recover Deposits, Down Payments and the Like. [§ 32–28]**

In addition to any other recovery, a **buyer is also entitled to recover any money he or she has already paid to the breaching seller as part of a down payment, deposit, etc.**, under UCC § 2–711(1).

F. SELLER'S RIGHT TO SUE FOR THE FULL CONTRACT PRICE UPON BUYER'S BREACH: SELLERS "SPECIFIC PERFORMANCE." [§ 32–29*]

When a seller is entitled to sue the buyer for the full contract price, the action is the equivalent of specific performance [§ 29–3]. That is, the seller is seeking an order requiring the buyer actually to perform in full what the buyer promised to do under the contract. Accordingly, just as it is the unusual case where the buyer is entitled to get specific performance from the seller, it is also the unusual case where the seller is entitled to receive the full contract price from the buyer in a breach action. In many cases, the seller will only get damages for breach, i.e., a lesser recovery than the full contract price.

The Code provides that a seller is entitled to bring an action for the price in only four cases:

(1) When the buyer has **accepted** the goods [UCC § 2–709(1)(a); § 32–20];

(2) When a seller sends conforming goods to the buyer **after the risk of loss has passed to the buyer**, and when the goods are thereafter lost or destroyed before acceptance [UCC § 2–709(1)(a); see § 32–21 for a discussion of the effect of risk of loss on the seller's action for the full price; see also § 34–1 for a further discussion of risk of loss].

(3) **When the seller reasonably tries to re-sell the goods** to another after the buyer's breach, **but is unable to re-sell them for a reasonable price** [UCC § 2–709(1)(b); § 32–32]; and

(4) **When the seller does not attempt to re-sell the goods** to another after the buyer's breach **because such efforts will be unavailing** [UCC § 2–709(1)(b); § 32–33].

---

* For more information, listen to CD # 12, Track 3 of *Sum and Substance Audio on Contracts*.

REMEDIES FOR BREACH UNDER THE UCC

Note that a successful action for price is really a forced sale of the goods. That is, in such cases the seller has performed and tendered conforming goods to the buyer. For whatever reason, the buyer refuses to pay for them and does not want to go through with the sale any longer.

However, if the seller is successful in the suit and can collect the full purchase price from the buyer, he or she will have attained all the benefits due the seller under the contract. Hence, upon payment of the final judgment, the buyer is entitled to possession of the goods because in paying the seller the full contract price, he or she has "purchased" them. Accordingly, upon the full satisfaction of a judgment for the price, the seller must turn the goods over to the buyer, i.e., it truly is a "forced sale."

Each of the situations in which a seller is entitled to sue for the price is discussed below.

1. When Buyer Has Accepted the Goods. [§ 32–30]

One of the consequences of acceptance under the Code is that a buyer must pay the contract price for goods whenever he or she accepts them [UCC § 2–607(1); § 22–37]. Hence, when a party accepts goods and does not pay for them, the seller is entitled to bring an action for the full contract price [UCC § 2–709(1)(a)].

Note that the seller has the right to sue for the contract price regardless of whether the buyer keeps the conforming goods he or she has accepted, or whether the buyer ships them back to the seller. So long as there has been an "acceptance," the buyer is liable for the full contract price. If the buyer does ship the goods back to the seller, however, that act has two consequences:

(1) In addition to the purchase price, the buyer will also be liable for storage and other incidental expenses incurred by the seller as long as he or she cares for the goods [UCC §§ 2–703; 2–709(1); 2–710]; and

(2) The buyer has implicitly given the seller permission to sell the goods for a reasonable price. Hence, at any time prior to the satisfaction of a final judgment in such a case, the seller is entitled to sell the goods to another for a reasonable price. Upon such a sale, any proceeds must be credited to the breaching buyer, meaning that the damages for which the buyer is liable must be reduced by the amount of the re-sale.

2. When the Goods Are Lost or Destroyed After the Risk of Loss Passed to the Buyer. [§ 32–31]

Risk of loss is covered in some detail in Chapter Thirty-Four, but the idea is that when goods are shipped, at some point they become the buyer's responsibility. That is, if they are lost or destroyed during transit, the buyer must nevertheless pay for goods he or she has not received because he or she bears their "risk of loss." UCC § 2–709(1)(a) codifies this concept and provides that if a buyer refuses to pay for goods that are lost or destroyed after the buyer has assumed the risk of loss, the seller is entitled to sue the buyer for the full contract price.

3. **When Seller Attempts to Re-Sell Goods Wrongfully Rejected by Buyer, but Cannot Obtain a Reasonable Price upon Re-Sale. [§ 32–32]**

Suppose a seller tenders absolutely conforming goods to the buyer, but the buyer nevertheless breaches by rejecting the goods and returns them to the seller. At that point the buyer is not obligated to pay the purchase price for the goods, for there has been no acceptance of them [UCC § 2–607(1)]. Further, normal principles of avoidability dictate that the seller try to re-sell the goods to another, thereby reducing the buyer's damages [30–59].

Sometimes, however, a seller will make reasonable efforts to re-sell merchandise, but will not be able to find anyone willing to pay a reasonable price for the goods. This often happens when the good involved is custom-made, e.g., an especially long couch made to fit in a particular area in a particular buyer's home, such that there is no real market for the goods other than the breaching buyer. In these cases, when a seller is unable to re-sell wrongfully rejected goods for a reasonable price after reasonable efforts to do so, the seller is entitled to sue the buyer for the full contract price [UCC § 2–709(1)(b)].

4. **When Seller Establishes That Resale of the Wrongfully Rejected Goods Would Be Unavailing. [§ 32–33]**

Every once in awhile, a good ordered specifically for a particular buyer is so unusual that a reasonable person would conclude that any attempt to re-sell it to another would simply be unavailing. If the seller can establish that the buyer wrongfully rejected such a good, and can carry the burden of proof to establish that any efforts to re-sell the goods would be unavailing, the seller is entitled to bring an action for the full purchase price without having to go in the market and try to sell it to another [UCC § 2–709(1)(b)]. For example, buyer and seller contract for seller to build a custom-made wood carving of buyer's very unusual last name for him to hang on his wall for $300. If buyer breaches by wrongfully rejecting the carving, seller would have a strong case in demonstrating that the efforts to resell a carving of someone's last name is unavailing. Thus, seller would be able to bring an action against buyer for $300.

G. SELLER'S RIGHT TO SUE FOR DAMAGES OTHER THAN THE FULL CONTRACT PRICE UPON BUYER'S BREACH. [§ 32–34]

As noted, it is the relatively rare case where a buyer who breaches an Article 2 contract before acceptance will be liable for the full contract price. Most of the time breaching buyers in such cases breach by wrongfully rejecting conforming goods which can be re-sold to others. The Code provides three potential remedies for the non-breaching seller in such cases:

(1) The seller can resell the goods to another, and collect from the buyer any difference between the resale price and the contract price, along with other related damages under § 2–706;

(2) The seller can keep the goods, but still sue the breaching buyer for the difference between the market price at the time and place for tender and the contract price, along with other related damages under § 2–708(1); or

(3) In cases where a buyer's breach causes injury to a "lost volume" seller, or to a seller/manufacturer who has partially built the good at the time of the buyer's breach, the seller is entitled to sue for lost profits and related damages under § 2–708(2).

Each of these methods of recovery is discussed below.

1. Recovery Under § 2–706: Seller's "Cover" Damages. [§ 32–35]

Most of the time when a seller tenders conforming goods to the buyer and the buyer wrongfully rejects them, the seller will want to resell the goods to another as quickly as possible so as to realize at least some cash for the goods, and not choose to wait until a lawsuit is concluded to receive any recovery. UCC § 2–706 permits a seller to resell the goods and thereafter be entitled to recover from the breaching buyer the difference, if any, between the resale price and the contract price. Since this procedure is analogous in many respects to the non-breaching **buyer's** right to **cover** under UCC § 2–712 [§ 32–24], recovery under § 2–706 is sometimes referred to as *"seller's cover."* [See § 30–44 for a discussion of how seller's cover is really the Code's formula for the recovery of expectation damages.] However, it is formally known as "Seller's Resale" damages under the Code [UCC § 2–716].

a. The Formula for Calculating a Seller's "Cover" Damages. [§ 32–36]

Under UCC § 2–706(1), when the seller has re-sold goods wrongfully rejected by the buyer and has done so in good faith and in a commercially reasonable manner [UCC § 2–706(2)–(4)], he or she is entitled to damages computed as follows:

CHAPTER 32

Seller's Cover Damages = [(Contract Price for the Goods) − (Re-Sale Price for the Goods)] + (Incidental Damages) − (Expenses Saved in Consequence of the Buyer's Breach).

Note there is a potential problem in a seller's § 2–706 recovery, where the seller resells the goods. The potential problem is one of collusion in the resale. For example, suppose Sean owns an electronics store and has a contract to sell a 50-inch flat screen to Jessica for $1,000, a fair price. If Jessica breaches, Sean might think about trying to sell that same TV to his friend Alexa for $100, figuring he can collect the $900 difference from Jessica.

To prevent such collusion, and to protect the breaching party in such cases, § 2–706(2)–(4) set forth a number of requirements to ensure that any resale be at a fair price. The requirements are fairly detailed, but their gist is that the seller cannot obtain recovery under § 2–706 if the buyer engages in a practice that would violate his or her duty of good faith and fair dealing.

(1) **Example. [§ 32–37]**

> Manufacturer has contracted to sell 1,000 DVRs to Retailer for $200/unit. The DVRs are timely delivered and are conforming, but Retailer nevertheless rejects. Manufacturer pays to have the sets shipped back to its plant, and one of its employees spends a good deal of time trying to find a substitute buyer, which she finally does. The substitute buyer is willing, in good faith and after notice to Retailer, to purchase the DVRs at $190/unit, a commercially reasonable price given the circumstances.

> Under § 2–706(1), Manufacturer is entitled to recover ($200/unit) − ($190/unit) × 1,000 units, plus whatever incidental costs it incurred in shipping the goods back to its factory, the time spent by its employee in arranging the resale, and any other costs associated with the resale. As with the time spent by the buyer in effecting cover, the time spent in arranging the resale is theoretically recoverable as an incidental damage under § 2–710, which authorizes recovery of "any commercially reasonable charges . . . in connection with . . . resale." However, courts are reluctant to award such relief because of the difficulty in verifying the time claimed to be spent and in choosing a reasonable rate for such expenditures of time.

2. **Recovery Under § 2–708(1): Seller's Market Differential Damages. [§ 32–38]**

Just as a non-breaching buyer who chooses not to cover is still entitled to recover market differential damages upon a seller's breach

REMEDIES FOR BREACH UNDER THE UCC

[UCC § 2–713; § 32–15], a non-breaching seller is also entitled to choose not to resell wrongfully rejected goods and recover instead for market differential damages. Under § 2–708(1), upon a buyer's wrongful rejection or repudiation a seller may recover the difference between the contract price and the market price for the goods, along with other associated damages. [*See* § 30–44 for a discussion of how recovery under § 2–708(1) is a specialized application of general contract law's formulation for recovering expectation damages.]

a. **The Formula for Calculating a Seller's Market Differential Damages. [§ 32–39]**

Under UCC § 2–708(1), when a seller opts to hold onto goods that could be re-sold after a wrongful rejection or repudiation by the buyer, the seller is entitled to damages computed as follows:

Seller's Damages = [(Contract Price for the Goods) − (Market Price for the Goods)] + (Incidental Damages) − (Expenses Saved in Consequence of the Buyer's Breach).

(1) **Problems in Determining the "Market Price." [§ 32–40]**

The formula for market differential damages under UCC § 2–708(1) requires that the "market price" for the goods be subtracted from the contract price for those goods. Just as with a **buyer's** market differential damages [§ 32–16], there may be occasions when the market price for the goods is volatile, and thus will change from day to day. Further, on the same day the market price for the goods may be different in the buyer's city and the seller's city. Hence, a determination must be made as to which of the potentially different market prices should be selected as the proper "market price" for purposes of § 2–708(1) damages.

(a) **Determining the Temporal Market. [§ 32–41]**

Under § 2–708(1), when the breach is caused by the buyer's unjustified **non-acceptance of goods,** the "market price" is **the market price pending at the time . . . of tender.**

Where the breach is *repudiation by the buyer* and trial occurs before the date of tender, the Code specifies that the market price be that pending "when the aggrieved party learned of the repudiation" [UCC § 2–723(1)].

(b) **Determining the Geographic Market. [§ 32–42]**

UCC § 2–708(1) states that the proper geographic market is that pending in the place for tender.

CHAPTER 32

(2) Example. [§ 32–43]

Can Co., a manufacturer of aluminum cans in California, contracts to sell 100,000 cans at $0.20/can to Food Co., at Food Co.'s Cleveland, Ohio plant. Under their contract, tender of the cans was to take place in California on May 1, and delivery was expected in Cleveland on May 5. Due to worldwide economic uncertainty, the price of aluminum is fluctuating. On May 1, the cans were ready but Food Co. breached by not sending anyone to pick them up. The fair market value of aluminum cans on May 1, the date of tender under the contract, was $0.17/can in Cleveland and $0.16/can in California. On May 5, the date of expected delivery under the contract, the value of aluminum cans was $0.14/can in Cleveland and $0.15/can in California.

In determining its § 2–708(1) damages, Can Co. must use the market price of the cans pending at the time and place for tender. Hence, it must use the $0.16/can price that was pending in California on May 1, i.e., the date and place where tender was to take place under the contract. Hence, Can Co.'s damages under § 2–708(1) would be ($0.20/can) − ($0.16/can) × 100,000 cans, plus any incidental damages it can establish.

3. Seller's Right to Market Differential Damages Even if Buyer Has Covered. [§ 32–44]

Sometimes a seller will resell the products and yet still want to sue for market differential damages under § 2–708(1). For example, assume the contract price was $5,000; the seller found some "sucker" to pay $4,700 after the breach when the relevant market price was $4,000. Rather than limit itself to a $300 resale recovery under § 2–706, the seller would like to sue for a $1,000 market differential recovery under § 2–708.

As with the similar issue with respect to buyers, the courts and commentators are split on the issue. Some hold that if a seller chooses to resell, it should be limited to § 2–706 damages since it will be made whole upon such a recovery. Others argue that there is nothing in the Code that limits a seller who resells to § 2–706. Indeed, if anything § 2–703 seems to give the innocent seller his or her choice of which type of recovery to pursue.

4. Recovery Under § 2–708(2): Seller's Lost Profit Recovery. [§ 32–45]

A seller is entitled to recover under UCC § 2–708(2), "[i]f the measure of damages provided in [§ 2–708(1)] is inadequate to put the seller in as good a position as performance would have done . . ." If the seller can establish that recovery under § 2–708(1) would not provide the benefit of his or her bargain, then under § 2–708(2) the seller's measure of damages is the "profit which the seller would have made from full performance by the buyer, together with any incidental damages . . . due allowance for costs reasonably incurred and due credit for payment or proceeds of resale."

The question is thus under what circumstances will a seller's resort to damages under § 2–708(1) be inadequate to put the seller in as good a position as full performance would have done? There are two such situations:

1. The "lost volume seller" [§ 32–46]; and

2. The manufacturer-seller who learns of the breach when the goods are only partially constructed [§ 32–48].

a. "Lost Volume" Sellers. [§ 32–46]

The idea behind the "lost volume" seller doctrine stems from the fact that sometimes a seller is not made whole even by selling a wrongfully rejected good to another for its full contract price. This occurs when the seller has an excess supply of the goods that were the subject of the breached contract, and thus, the buyer's breach has really cost the seller a profit from a lost second sale. While this may seem a little hard to grasp in the abstract, the idea is much clearer when illustrated.

For example, a department store has thirty 42-inch flat screens in stock, and can easily and quickly get more if necessary. Devin contracts to buy one of the sets for $500, and arranges for delivery next week. Devin later changes his mind, and breaches the contract by telling the store not to deliver the television. Later that same day, the store sells the very television it was going to give Devin to another buyer—Kim. Devin would like to argue that the store has been made whole. That is, his argument is that the store had a right to expect $500 for that set from him, and it ended up getting $500 for that same set from Kim. Devin is right if the store's recovery is limited to either § 2–706 or § 2–708(1), for the result of either the (contract price) – (re-sale price) formula of § 2–706, or the (contract price) – (market price) formula of § 2–708(1), would result in a $0 recovery for the store.

The store, on the other hand, would argue that it has lost the **profit** from one sale. That is, if Devin had taken delivery of his set, the store still would have made the sale to Kim, for it would have sold her another set out of its inventory. Therefore, if Devin had not breached, it would have had the profits from **two** sales—Devin's and Kim's. As a result of Devin's breach, it only has the profit from **one** sale, i.e., Kim's. Thus, to be made whole it must be able to recover from Devin the amount of the profit it lost from the second sale that never occurred.

Contract law accepts the store's argument, and UCC § 2–708(2) gives the store the right to collect the lost profit from Devin in such a situation.

Note that in order to be a "lost volume" seller, and thus entitled to recover under § 2–708(2), the seller must truly have excess supply so that the "second" sale could take place. For example, suppose Ed had a contract to sell his Van Gough painting to Barbra for $1,000,000. Barbra breaches, but that same day Ed was able to sell it to the Getty Museum, also for $1,000,000. In this case Ed is not damaged by the breach for he has obtained all the benefits to which he was entitled under his contract with Barbra. That is, because there is no second sale possible given the limited supply of the goods, Ed did not lose a profit from the second sale, and thus is not a "lost volume" seller.

(1) The Formula for Lost Volume Seller's Recovery of Lost Profits Under UCC § 2–708(2). [§ 32–47]

The formula for recovery of a lost volume seller is:

Seller's Damages = (Profit from the Contract That was Breached) + (Incidental Damages).

Note that in § 2–708(2) there was a drafting error. § 2–708(2) provided that "due credit for payments or proceeds of any resale" had to be subtracted from the lost profits. Of course, the whole idea of lost volume recovery is that the proceeds from the re-sale of the wrongfully rejected or repudiated goods should **not** be used to offset the seller's recovery. Hence, courts and commentators routinely ignored the "due credit for the payments or proceeds of the re-sale" clause when applying § 2–708(2) in lost volume seller cases, and the phrase was deleted in revised § 2R–708(2).

b. Recovery upon Buyer's Breach When the Manufacturer/Seller Has Only Partially Completed the Good. [§ 32–48]

The second instance when a seller would resort to remedy under § 2–708(2) is when the seller is also manufacturing the item, and the buyer breaches while the item is only partway through production.

For example, suppose Trevor is making a couch for Lara. The contract price is $1,000, which will yield Trevor a $200 profit. Lara breaches when Trevor has spent $400 towards production. Part of that $400, however, is $50 worth of fabric that Trevor has not yet put on the couch and that he could use in another couch he is making for Stacey under a separate contract.

Recovery under § 2–708(1) will not put Trevor in the position he would have been in had the contact been performed, since there is no "market" price for a partially built couch. So recovery will have to be under § 2–708(2), this time using the complete formula from that provision:

> **Seller's Damages = (Profit from the Contract That was Breached) + (Incidental Damages) + (Costs reasonably incurred [up to the time of breach]) – (payments or proceeds of resale).**

Using the above facts:

> **Profit**: $200
>
> **Incidental damage**: None on these facts
>
> **Costs Reasonably incurred up to the time of breach**: $400
>
> **Payments or Proceeds of Resale:** $50 (This is what the phrase "payments or proceeds of resale" means—the scrap value of any materials which can be reused or resold by the seller).
>
> Hence, Trevor's recovery will be: ($200) + ($400) – ($50) = $550.

One last issue is whether Trevor has the option to finish making the couch, or must stop upon notification of the breach from Lara. In other words, will Trevor be limited to the damages existing at the time of the breach if he decides to finish making the couch but, in good faith, cannot get a decent price for it. The answer is that Trevor can collect full damages under each scenario, so long as the choice he makes (stopping or finishing) is a "commercially reasonable" one [UCC § 2–704].

H. LIQUIDATED DAMAGES UNDER ARTICLE 2. [§ 32–49]

As with common law rules (see § 30–80), liquidated damages are damages, the amount of which the parties have agreed in advance that will be owed upon a breach of their contract. The ability of the parties to agree to an enforceable liquidated damage provision under the Code is governed by UCC § 2–718(1). The rules of § 2–718(1), however, are the same as those governing the enforceability of liquidated damage clauses in non-UCC agreements. That is, the parties' agreement on liquidated damages will only be enforced if the amount of the liquidated damages is reasonable in light of the anticipated or actual harm caused by the breach, and where the actual amount of damages is difficult to ascertain with precision.

I. EMOTIONAL DISTRESS DAMAGES, PUNITIVE DAMAGES, AND RECOVERY OF PRE-JUDGMENT INTEREST UNDER THE UCC. [§ 32–50]

The Code has no special rules governing the recovery of emotional distress damages, punitive damages, and pre-judgment interest. Hence, the rules regarding those subjects discussed in §§ 30–75, 30–87, and 30–89, respectively, are applicable to Article 2 contracts as well.

J. LIMITATION ON, OR MODIFICATION OF, CONTRACT REMEDIES. [§ 32–51]

Under the principles of freedom of contract, UCC § 2–719 provides that contracting parties of roughly equal bargaining power may validly modify the remedies for breach provided in the Code. Indeed, they may even eliminate them entirely should they choose to do so. However, this general rule is subject to two limitations:

(1) The parties' ability to limit damages is limited by the "fails of its essential purpose" rule set forth in § 32–52 [UCC §§ 2–718(1) and 2–719(1)]; and

(2) A clause which limits the recovery of consequential damages can be avoided if unconscionable, and such a clause which limits recovery for consequential injury to the person is *prima facie* unconscionable [UCC § 2–719(3)].

1. When a Limited Remedy "Fails of Its Essential Purpose" Under UCC § 2–719(2). [§ 32–52]

A recurring issue in commercial law is the effect of a seller's breach of a clause which limits the buyer's remedies under the Code. For example, assume Felicia buys a car and in her sales agreement she agrees to an exclusive "repair or replacement" clause. That is, she agrees that if there are any mechanical problems with her car, her exclusive remedy against the dealer is to take the car back to the dealer, which in turn promises Felicia it will either repair the problem, or replace the car, at its option.

Repair or replacement clauses are quite common, are expressly permitted by the Code [UCC § 2–719(1)(b)], and are examples of clauses that limit and modify the Code's otherwise-applying remedies available for breach.

With an exclusive repair or replacement clause, a buyer like Felicia receives a benefit, but also loses a benefit. Felicia gets the benefit of the dealer's promise to repair the car. Otherwise, if the car has mechanical problems, her remedies would be things like rejection, revocation, or a breach of warranty lawsuit. Because of the dealer's repair or replacement promise, however, she now has the benefit of a promise from the dealer that any problem with her car will be taken care of relatively promptly. However, because she agreed to the repair or replacement clause as an **exclusive** remedy, she has lost the benefit of being able to resort to any other Code-based remedy should the seller breach by tendering a car that needs repairs. In other words, for the benefit of getting the seller's repair promise, she traded her rights to seek all other Code-based relief.

Assume that Felicia has mechanical problems with her car. She takes it to the dealer a number of times with the same complaints, but it is never fixed. The recurring question in these types of cases is whether the dealer's breach of its repair or replacement promise now frees Felicia to resort to **any** Article 2 remedy, or whether she is limited to suing only for money damages resulting from the dealer's breach of the *limited remedy clause,* i.e., the promise to fix the car. In other words, does breach of the clause negate the limitation of remedies clause entirely, or does it not? The dealer's argument, of course, is that by agreeing to an exclusive repair or replacement clause, Felicia forever waived her rights to recover under the panoply of Article 2 remedies and is now limited to suing for breach of that clause only.

The dealer's position in this regard is rejected by the Code. UCC § 2–719(2) makes it clear that Felicia is entitled to sue under **any** Article 2 provided remedy in such a case. Section 2–719(2) provides that whenever an exclusive or limited damage provision **"fail[s] of its essential purpose,"** the buyer is thereafter entitled to recover under **any** provision of Article 2. In other words, once the car dealership has breached its repair promise so thoroughly that there has been a failure in the essential purpose of such a clause, i.e., to give the purchaser comfort in knowing that her car will be repaired, *the limitation of remedy provision is thereafter void and without effect.* Hence, at that point there is nothing limiting Felicia from suing for breach of warranty, revoking her acceptance, etc.

a. **When a "No Consequential Damages" Clause Is Linked with a "Repair or Replacement" or "Warranty Disclaimer" Clause. [§ 32–53]**

   Another recurring issue in commercial transactions under § 2–719 is what happens when there is not just one limitation of remedy clause, but two. For example, suppose Doug's machine shop had a contract to sell a computerized drill press to Andrea's manufacturing plant. In that contract, there is **both** an exclusive repair or replacement clause, **and** a limitation on Andrea's ability to collect consequential damages upon a breach. Once again, assume there has been a failure of the essential purpose of the repair and replacement clause, as Doug has not fixed a recurring problem with the press. The issue is whether the breach of one limited damage provision acts as a breach of both of them, or whether the breach of the repair and replacement clause is independent of the consequential damages limitation.

That is, if there were only a repair and replacement clause, when it failed of its essential purpose Andrea would be entitled to recover under any UCC provision, including ones allowing for consequential loss. However, in her contract Andrea also agreed to a consequential damage limitation. Hence, Doug would argue that breach of the repair and replacement clause means that Andrea is entitled to recover under any UCC provision **except** those allowing for recovery of consequential damages. He will say that Andrea separately agreed that he would **never** be liable for such damages under their contract when she agreed to the consequential damage limitation clause.

Andrea, on the other hand, would argue that the clauses were linked, i.e., that they are dependent on each other. She would allege that the only reason she agreed to the consequential damage limitation is because Doug had provided a repair or replacement guarantee. Hence, her view would be that the breach of the repair or replacement promise should also render the consequential damage limitation unenforceable.

There is no uniform treatment of this issue by the courts. Increasingly, however, courts are seeking to discover the parties' true intentions in agreeing to these clauses, i.e., whether the parties considered them dependent or independent. If a court finds that the parties intended to link them together, then breach of the repair or replacement provision will also result in the breach of the consequential damages limitation as well, and someone such as Andrea can thus recover for her provable consequential losses. On the other hand, if the parties intended for the clauses to be independent, then they will be interpreted independently. In such a case, Doug's breach of the repair or replacement promise will not effect the consequential damage limitation and will thus supersede the effect of § 2–719(2).

Note that under some circumstances trying to insert both a warranty disclaimer clause and a consequential damages limitation in the same contract has been considered unconscionable as it leaves the buyer with essentially no remedy at all [*A & M Produce v. FMC Corp*, 135 Cal. App. 3d 473 (1982)].

REMEDIES FOR BREACH UNDER THE UCC

2. Distinction Between Limitation of Remedy Under UCC § 2–719 and Disclaimer of Warranty Under § 2–316. [§ 32–54]

Students sometimes get confused as to when the rules of § 2–719 relating to limitations of remedies apply, and when the rules of § 2–316 relating to disclaimers of warranty are operative [*see* §§ 35–11; 35–12]. When the clause in question **completely eliminates the warranty** so that it is impossible to breach that kind of warranty under the contract, the clause is a **warranty disclaimer**, and **UCC § 2–316's provisions govern**. However, if a contract provision provides that a breach of warranty can still occur, but that the *range of remedies for such breach is limited*, e.g., instead of a lawsuit the buyer is limited to repair or replacement remedy, then the *rules of § 2–719 are operative*.

K. EXAM APPROACH TO UCC REMEDIES ISSUES. [§ 32–55]

In dealing with a breach situation in a UCC agreement, the steps you should follow are:

1. Determine which party is the non-breaching one, i.e., will it be buyer or seller that will bring the suit.

2. If it is buyer who is bringing the suit:

    A. Check to see whether replacement of the good will be burdensome enough to qualify for specific performance [§ 32–3];

    B. If not (as is usually the case), then determine whether buyer has or does not have goods tendered by the seller at the time of the litigation.

    (1) If the buyer does not have the goods, recovery is based on:

       (a) Cover [§ 32–12] if the buyer reasonably purchases replacement goods; or

       (b) Market differential damages [§ 32–15] if the buyer does not go into the market and purchase replacement goods.

    (2) If the buyer retains the goods at the time the suit is filed, the suit will be for breach of warranty or the damages caused by late tender, and recovery will be based on the value of what the buyer was promised less the value of what he or she received or calculated in any other reasonable respect with regard to late tender [§ 32–23].

3. If it is the seller who is bringing suit:

   A. Check to see whether the seller can bring an action for price [§ 32–9];

   B. If not (as is usually the case), then recovery is based on:

   (1) The price received upon the resale of the goods less the contract price [§ 32–35];

   (2) The market differential [§ 32–28]; **but**

   (3) If either of these methods do not put the seller in the position he or she would have been in had the contract been performed, as is likely the case with the **lost volume seller or when a manufacturer/seller is notified of the breach during production**, then lost profit recovery is allowed, along with the other remedies of § 2–708(2) as are applicable [§ 32–45].

4. Be aware of liquidated damages and limitation of liability provisions and make sure to apply the appropriate rules [§§ 32–49, 32–51, respectively] to determine the validity of such provisions.

PART IX

MISCELLANEOUS UCC AND CISG DOCTRINES

INTRODUCTORY NOTE ON MISCELLANEOUS UCC AND CISG DOCTRINES:

There are a few doctrines that are peculiar to the UCC and the CISG in contract law.

One, the applicability of Article 2 of the UCC and the CISG, is universally studied in first year Contracts courses, and is covered in **Chapter Thirty-Three**.

The other two doctrines are only occasionally covered in Contracts course, but are routinely covered in Sales and other Commercial Law courses, for those students using this Book for those classes.

Chapter Thirty-Four covers risk of loss and the so-called "mercantile" terms, such as F.O.B. and C.I.F.

Chapter Thirty-Five covers warranties, both their applicability and their disclaimers.

CHAPTER 33

APPLICABILITY OF ARTICLE TWO OF THE UCC AND THE CISG

A. APPLICABILITY OF ARTICLE TWO OF THE UCC GENERALLY. [§ 33–1*]

One of the first issues a student or a lawyer has to confront when analyzing a contract problem is whether it is governed by the UCC the CISG, or by common law contract principles. If Article 2 applies, then the language and doctrines of the Code need to be used. Same for the CISG. Hence, determination of whether a transaction is governed by Article 2 or not is a crucial one, and sometimes may be outcome determinative for a party seeking to establish his or her right to judicial relief. The rules for deciding whether Article 2 applies to a transaction are discussed in the remainder of this Chapter, followed by a brief discussion of the applicability of the CISG.

B. ARTICLE TWO IS NOT LIMITED TO MERCHANTS. [§ 33–2]

One of the biggest misconceptions that seems to plague a good number of students is that Article 2 is limited to merchants. It is NOT. The distant origins of the UCC are found in the merchant law of England, and many of the UCC cases in contracts textbooks deal with merchants. Thus, it is understandable why some students at first believe there is a merchant limitation on the applicability of the Code. This is not the case, however. While there are about twenty provisions which set forth special rules governing merchant rights and obligations under Article 2, you must realize that the remaining sections apply equally to a contract in which a friend sells you her watch as they do to an agreement where IBM sells computers to General Motors.

---

* For more information, listen to CD # 1, Track 6 of *Sum and Substance Audio on Contracts*.

CHAPTER 33

C. UCC § 2–102: ARTICLE TWO APPLIES TO "TRANSACTIONS IN GOODS." [§ 33–3]

UCC § 2–102 provides that Article 2 "applies to transactions in goods." Hence, the general rule is simple enough to state—**any time there is a "transaction in goods," the rules of the UCC govern the agreement; when there is no "transaction in goods," common law contract rules apply**. This general rule, of course, leaves two questions: (1) What types of "transactions" are intended to be included within § 2–102; and (2) what are "goods" for purposes of Article 2 applicability? These questions are discussed below.

But before getting into the complexities, let's learn one thing that everybody agrees is true: **real estate contracts and contracts for services are not "transactions in *goods*" and so are governed by common law principles, not the UCC**.

1. **The Meaning of "Transaction." [§ 33–4]**

    One of the most surprising omissions in Article 2 is the failure to define the term "transaction." Since the question of Article 2 applicability is so important, and since applicability turns on whether the contract is a "transaction in goods," the absence of any indication as to what transactions are meant to be included is puzzling.

    While lawyers have asserted that various kinds of transactions merit Article 2 applicability, as a practical matter the courts routinely have to deal with only two types of "transactions" for Article 2 applicability purposes: (1) sales; and (2) leases. The rules governing Article 2 applicability for each of these transactions follow.

    a. **Sales. [§ 33–5]**

        There is no question that a "sale of goods" is a "transaction in goods" for purposes of Article 2 applicability. Indeed, the title of Article 2 is "Uniform Commercial Code—Sales" [UCC § 2–101]. Hence, a pure sale of goods, i.e., a transaction where title and possession of a good is transferred from the seller to the buyer, is clearly covered by Article 2 [*see* §§ 33–10 and 33–13 however for a discussion of whether Article 2 applies when the same transaction has within it both a sale of goods and a sale of a service, or where the transaction involves the sale of a good attached to real estate].

    b. **Leases. [§ 33–6]**

        For many years, the question of whether a lease of goods was a "transaction in goods" for Article 2 applicability purposes yielded conflicting answers. The rationale for the various viewpoints can be seen by examining a typical lease case where a party is seeking UCC applicability.

John leases a car for the day from a car rental facility at the airport and later gets into an accident which he claims was caused by an insufficient level of brake fluid in the car he rented. John would like Article 2 to apply to his lease so that he could validly assert a breach of warranty claim against the car rental agency [Chapter Thirty-Five]. Obviously, John's claim could also be brought in tort, but perhaps John needs to take advantage of the UCC's rather generous 4-year statute of limitations [UCC § 2–725(1)], instead of being time barred by the usual one or two year statute of limitations that applies to personal injury tort claims.

Those courts and commentators who believed that Article 2 should apply to lease transactions pointed to the plain reading of UCC § 2–102. That is, they state that a lease is certainly a "transaction" under anyone's definition of the term, and when a consumer such as John leases a "good" like a car, a "transaction in goods" has taken place and thus Article 2's provisions must apply.

Those who did not believe leases were intended to be governed by Article 2 pointed out that while UCC § 2–102 speaks in terms of transactions in goods, the substantive provisions of Article 2 do not. That is, e.g., § 2–725(1) (the statute of limitations provision), says "[a]n action for breach of any **contract for sale** must be commenced within four years." Similarly, § 2–314 (the implied warranty of merchantability provision), states that, "a warranty that the goods shall be merchantable is implied in a **contract for their sale**." Moreover, the other warranty provisions also speak in terms of "seller" rather than "lessor" or a neutral term like "transactor" [UCC §§ 2–313; 2–315]. Hence, this view holds that the more specific language of the substantive provisions of the Code makes it clear that leases should be excluded from Article 2 coverage.

Thankfully, we now have a resolution. In 1987, the Permanent Editorial Board of the UCC enacted Article 2A, which is entitled "Uniform Commercial Code—Leases" and revised that Article in 1990 [UCC § 2A–101]. As of this writing, Article 2A has already been adopted in 49 states and protectorates. In those states which have adopted it, the provisions of Article 2A will govern the formation, operation, performance obligations, etc. regarding leases. It is thus likely that within a few years, Article 2A will be applicable everywhere, and there will then be a uniform answer as to whether a lease is a "transaction" for Article 2 purposes.

CHAPTER 33

2. The Meaning of "Goods." [§ 33–7]

Unlike the word "transactions," the word "goods" *is* defined in UCC § 2–105. That statute provides that "goods" for purposes of Article 2 are "all things . . . which are movable at the time of identification to the contract."

Before discussing exactly what is meant by that definition, it is perhaps useful to get a general understanding of what is, and is not, meant by "goods." In general, a good is personal property, i.e., something which is "movable." As noted above, a contract for services is clearly not governed by Article 2, for one cannot pick up and move services like a haircut or guitar lessons. Hence, when someone makes a contract with a mechanic to tune a car, there may be a transaction, but it is not a transaction in **goods** and such a contract is thus governed by common law contract principles and not the UCC.

Similarly, a contract for real estate is also clearly not governed by Article 2, for real estate is also not "movable."

UCC § 2–105 does not just say that a good is anything "movable," however. It says that to be a good, a thing must be "movable *at the time of identification to the contract.*"

The concept of "identification" is peculiar to the Code and is described in § 2–501. As set forth in § 2–501(1)(b), identification occurs when, "goods are shipped, marked, or otherwise designated by the seller as goods to which the contract refers." That is, something is "identified" to the contract when the **particular object** that is to be provided to the **particular buyer** under the contract is determined. Depending on the type of contract involved, identification can occur either at the time of contract formation [§ 33–8] or after the contract has been executed (as when the consumer pays for the good and the particular good that is to be given to the buyer is not selected until someone in the warehouse puts it in a box with the buyer's name and address on it; § 33–9).

a. Example. [§ 33–8]

Dan enters a grocery store, selects an apple from the display in the produce section, and approaches the check-out counter. By confirming Dan's selection of the particular apple he will buy, the store has "identified" the particular good to the contract [UCC § 2–501(1)(a)]. Hence, because at the time of the identification to the contract the apple is movable, and because Dan will get title to the apple by a means of a sales transaction, the contract between Dan and the store is a "transaction in goods" governed by Article 2.

b. Example. [§ 33–9]

Mary buys a 50-inch flat-screen television from a large department store, and arranges for delivery the following Wednesday. At the time she pays for it, her television set is not "identified" to the contract, for no one knows which particular set in the department store's inventory will be Mary's. Probably her particular set will not be "identified" until the following Wednesday morning when someone from the store's warehouse will select a set from the store's inventory and designate it as the one to be delivered to Mary [UCC § 2–501(1)(b)].

Even though Mary's television was not identified at the time the contract, it is still an Article 2 transaction. Recall that to be a "good" under § 2–105, the television set does not have to be identified at the time the contract is made; rather § 2–105 says that to be a good the object must be movable **when** it is identified. Since "Mary's" television is movable on Wednesday morning when the store designates the particular set as Mary's set, it is a good. Thus, her purchase satisfies the "transaction in goods" standard of § 2–102 for Article 2 applicability even though her good was not identified to the contract until after its making.

This type of situation, where the contract is entered into before the good is specifically identified, is known as a "**contract for the sale of future goods**" [UCC § 2–501(1)(b)].

D. ARTICLE TWO APPLICABILITY TO SALES/SERVICES "HYBRID" TRANSACTIONS. [§ 33–10]

Sometimes a transaction is neither purely the sale of a good nor purely the sale of a service—it is a "hybrid." For example, suppose Martin bought a water heater from a department store for $400. Included within that price, however, was delivery to, and installation of the heater at, Martin's house. Obviously the transaction involves the sale of a good, i.e., the water heater, but it also involves the sale of a service, i.e., the delivery and installation. Two tests have developed as to whether such a sales/service hybrid transaction should be governed by Article 2: (1) the "predominant purpose" test; and (2) the "gravamen" test.

1. The "Predominant Purpose" Test. [§ 33–11]

Under the predominant purpose test, whether Article 2 applies to a sales/service hybrid transaction depends on which part of the transaction predominates. That is, the court must determine whether the principal purpose of the buyer in deciding to enter the transaction was really to acquire goods or to obtain services. If it is the former, then **all** parts of the transaction are governed by Article 2; if it is the latter, **no** part of the transaction is subject to Article 2.

For example, use the Martin/Department Store hypothetical of § 33–10, where Martin purchased a water heater and its installation for $400. If Martin's predominant purpose in the transaction was the acquisition of the heater, Martin's rights arising from the contract are exclusively governed by the UCC, regardless whether the water heater blew up because the heater itself was defective or because the installer was negligent (in the tort sense) in not tightening certain valves upon installation. Hence, on occasion, application of the predominant purpose tests results in what probably should be a tort negligence claim (failure to tighten valves) being judged under the UCC.

To determine the predominant purpose, a court examines all factors involved in the transaction. What was the total price; is it a contract for personal services, e.g., when *who* is providing the service is important; the reason a reasonable person would enter into the transaction, what the parties actually or probably intended, etc.

2. The "Gravamen" Test. [§ 33–12]

A relatively new test for Article 2 applicability in hybrid situations has developed, the "gravamen" test. Under this test, the court asks what the gravamen of the cause of action is. That is, it determines whether the buyer is complaining about a problem with non-conforming goods, or whether the buyer is complaining about negligent service. If it is the former (the heater was defective), Article 2 would apply; if it is the latter (the valve was negligently tightened), the suit is decided under tort principles regardless of the "predominant purpose" of the transaction.

A recent spate of contracts scholarship has questioned whether the gravamen test is really used that much. That is, it is mentioned in cases and the way it is portrayed in many casebooks suggests that the trend of modern decisions is towards adoption of the gravamen test, but in truth, the predominant purpose test is by far the majority rule.

E. ARTICLE TWO APPLICABILITY WHEN THERE IS A SALE OF SOMETHING ATTACHED TO REALTY. [§ 33–13]

Sometimes a contract calls for the sale of something that is attached to realty, but could be severed from it. For example, suppose a cereal maker makes a contract for the wheat growing on Farmer's land. In some senses, the wheat is identified when the contract is made, and at that point it is not movable because it is in the ground. On the other hand, when the

APPLICABILITY OF ARTICLE TWO OF THE UCC AND THE CISG

wheat is delivered to the cereal maker it certainly will be movable, which argues for the application of Article 2 to such a transaction.

UCC § 2–107 governs these kinds of cases. That provision set forth two situations as to whether Article 2 governs contracts where goods are attached to, but capable of severance from, realty.

> (1) The sale of minerals (including oil and gas), and the sale of a structure attached to real estate but due to be severed from it, **are Article 2 transactions only if the contract calls for the seller to do the severance**. That is, if the contract calls for the *buyer* to mine the minerals or remove the house, then the contract is not governed by Article 2 [UCC § 2–107(1)].

> (2) A sale apart from the land of crops, timber, and anything else attached to realty which is capable of severance without material harm to the property (but which is also not governed by the rule in part (1) above) is an Article 2 transaction **regardless of who severs the goods** [UCC § 2–107(2)]. Thus, regardless of whether it is the cereal company or the farmer who harvests the wheat crop, so long as the contract is for sale of the wheat apart from the land, Article 2 applies.

Note also that under UCC § 2–105, the unborn young of animals is considered a "good," so a contract for, e.g., a foal from a racehorse, is an Article 2 contract.

F. APPLICABILITY OF THE CISG. [§ 33–14*]

CISG applicability is tricky but important. Because the CISG was established by treaty, it "outranks" Article 2, which has been adopted by the states. Hence if the CISG applies, its terms will control—a fact that has surprised more than one lawyer and law student.

The CISG applies to a sale of goods between parties who are in different countries (Article (1)—the CISG calls countries "states" but it means countries). However, if the fact that the parties are in different countries does not appear either from the contract itself or from prior dealings between them, then the CISG does not apply.

If one of the parties has offices in the country where the other is located, as well as offices in other countries, the controlling "place of business [for determining CISG applicability] is that which has the closest relationship to the contract and its performance" [Article 10(a)]. Hence, if a U.S. company contracts with a company that has both a Canadian and a U.S. office, whether it will be a CISG contract (a contract between parties from different countries) or an Article 2 agreement depends on whether the

---

* For more information, listen to CD # 1, Track 7 of *Sum and Substance Audio on Contracts*.

Canadian office or the U.S. office of the multinational company has the closest relationship to the particular deal.

Even if the transaction is between parties in different countries, the CISG does not apply to "goods bought for personal, family, or household use," to contracts for "ships, vessels, hovercraft, or aircraft," or to contracts for the transmission of "electricity" [Article 2(a), (e) and (f)]. Further, the provisions of the CISG do not apply "to the liability of the seller for death or personal injury caused by the goods to any person" [Article 5].

Note that when someone in the U.S. orders a television from a Canadian store, it is unclear on the face of it whether the contract is governed by the CISG. The question ultimately will be whether the television is for home use or for use in a business. In any event, the idea is that the CISG only applies to transactions in goods between merchants in different countries.

Finally, the parties are free to exclude the application of the CISG if they choose to do so in their contract [Article 6].

G. EXAM APPROACH TO ARTICLE TWO/CISG APPLICABILITY ISSUES. [§ 33–15]

There are only a few things you must look at to determine whether Article 2 applies:

1. Does the contract involve a "transaction" [§ 33–4] in "goods" [§ 33–7], which means does it have a "sale" component; and

2. If so, watch for whether the "goods" are part of a sales/service hybrid [§ 33–10], or whether they are in some way attached to realty [§ 33–13].

With regard to the CISG, the applicability issues are:

1. Are the contracting parties located in different countries (and, if there is more than one office where one or more office is in the U.S. and one or more is not, whether the foreign office is the most directly involved in the deal);

2. Even if so, does the contract deal with: (a) goods bought for personal, family, or household use, e.g., a television for the buyer's home; contracts for ships, vessels, hovercraft, or aircraft; or (c) electricity; and

3. Recall the CISG can be excluded by the parties, in which case the UCC will apply if it is a sale of goods.

CHAPTER 34

RISK OF LOSS AND MERCANTILE TERMS

A. RISK OF LOSS, GENERALLY. [§ 34–1]

Very early on, who "owned" goods used to be determined by who had possession of them. But, especially after the Industrial Revolution, when goods were being transported all over the globe, there were plenty of occasions where the party in possession of the goods clearly did not own them, e.g., the shipper who transported barrels of wine from a Bordeaux seller to a London buyer certainly never owned the wine, but he or she had possession of it for a time. So contract law was left with a bit of a quandary with who should pay when the wine was destroyed, e.g., by an unexpected storm in the English Channel as the goods were being transported from Calais to Dover.

For awhile, contract law tried to solve this problem by separating "title" to the goods from possession of them. This worked for many circumstances, but did not work for others. Plus title had implications for insurance (one can only insure a good if he or she owns it) and had other ramifications as well. Mercantile lawyers put their minds to the problem and came up with **"risk of loss" rules**, i.e., **rules determining who has to pay if goods are lost, damaged, or destroyed during transit**. These rules are similar to, but are different from the rules on who has title to the goods, and so the risk of loss rules are separately studied in this chapter.

The rules regarding risk of loss under the Code are set forth in §§ 2–509 and 2–510. The rules differ depending on whether the parties have performed or breached their duties prior to the loss, damage, or destruction of the goods. These rules are set forth below. When the goods are in the control of buyer's agent, the buyer has the risk from then on because the buyer has control over them. So in every contract, the risk starts with the seller and then shifts to buyer at some point.

1. **Consequences of Risk of Loss Allocation. [§ 34–2]**

    If the seller has the risk of loss, and replaceable goods are lost, damaged, or destroyed before they reach the buyer, the seller must

CHAPTER 34

still timely tender another delivery of conforming goods, or else be in breach for failing to do so.

If the buyer has the risk of loss, and the goods are lost, damaged, or destroyed in transit, the buyer must still pay for the goods, even though the buyer will never obtain the benefit of his or her bargain, or be in breach for failing to do so.

For example, suppose a manufacturer in New York sells 100 television sets to a retailer in California. As the goods are being transported across country, through no apparent fault of either party, the sets are stolen from the back of the delivery truck. If the risk of loss is on the seller, the seller is under a duty to ensure another 100 sets will timely be delivered to the buyer to collect payment. If the risk is on the buyer, the buyer, or its insurer, will have to pay for all 100 sets, even though it will never receive them.

2. **Risk of Loss Rules in the Absence of Breach. [§ 34–3]**

Unless the parties have agreed otherwise, when the seller first acquires goods, he or she has the risk of loss; if they are destroyed at that instant, the seller still is required to perform by timely tendering replacements. Assuming neither party has breached, when the risk shifts to the buyer depends on whether the contract is a "shipment" contract or a "destination" contract.

   a. **Shipment Contract. [§ 34–4]**

   A shipment contract is one in which the seller is not required to ship the goods to any particular location [UCC §§ 2–504; 2–509(1)(a)]. In other words, it is a contract where the **buyer** agrees to make all the delivery arrangements, and will send someone to pick up the finished goods from the seller, <u>usually at the seller's place of business</u>. **In shipment contracts, where the seller has tendered conforming goods in a conforming manner, the risk of loss passes to the buyer when the goods are transferred to the buyer or to the buyer's agent, e.g., a shipping company hired by the buyer** [UCC § 2–509(1)(a)]. That is, typically the risk will pass to the buyer at the loading dock of the seller's plant when the seller gives the goods to the carrier hired by the buyer to transport the goods or to the buyer himself or herself.

   b. **Destination Contract. [§ 34–5]**

   A destination contract is one in which the contract requires the seller to deliver goods to a particular place, usually to the buyer's home or place of business. In other words, it is a contract where the seller's price includes shipping charges and under which the seller makes all the shipping arrangements [UCC § 2–509(1)(b)]. **In destination contracts, where the seller has tendered** conforming goods in a conforming manner, the risk of loss passes to the buyer only after the goods are delivered to the destination called for under the contract in a manner that enables the buyer to take delivery [UCC § 2–509(1)(b)]. That is, typically the risk will pass only after the carrier hired by the seller transfers possession of the goods to the buyer at the buyer's home or place of business.

For example, when a consumer orders something from a catalogue, typically the contract formed will be a destination contract. The company putting out the catalogue will promise to deliver the goods to a particular destination, usually the buyer's home. The price paid by the buyer thus includes a shipping charge. Hence, if the good is destroyed before it reaches the particular destination, the risk of loss is on the seller, and the seller is then obligated to re-tender another conforming shipment to the destination called for in the contract, or be in breach for failing to do so.

3. **Effect of Breach on Risk of Loss. [§ 34–6]**

UCC § 2–510 sets forth three changes to the risk of loss rules that apply when one of the parties has breached before the goods have been delivered.

a. **When a Seller Breaches in Such a Way to Give the Buyer a Right of Rejection. [§ 34–7]**

Under § 2–510(1), if a seller has breached the contract either by sending non-conforming goods, or by tendering goods in a non-conforming way, so that the buyer would have a right of rejection of the goods if they were received, then the risk of loss stays with the seller until the seller cures any problem and/or the buyer accepts goods under the contract [UCC §§ 2–601; 2–612].

Suppose Ralph purchases a blue couch from Veronica's Furniture Store by means of a shipment contract. Ralph hires a carrier to pick up the couch at Veronica's and ship it to him. However, when the carrier Ralph hires arrives at Veronica's, it is given a green couch to deliver to Ralph. Along the way, the couch is severely damaged, through no apparent fault of anyone. Under normal risk of loss rules in the absence of a breach, the risk of loss in such a case would be on Ralph (the buyer), because Veronica's contract with Ralph was a shipment contract, and the risk of loss in such contracts shifts when the seller (Veronica's) tenders the good to the buyer's carrier [UCC § 2–509(1)(a); § 34–4].

However, because Veronica's breached by sending the wrong color couch, and because the breach would have given Ralph a right of rejection had it been delivered, the risk of loss is deemed to have stayed with the breaching seller from the beginning, and Veronica's is still obligated to deliver a conforming blue couch, or be in breach for failing to do so.

b. **UCC § 2–510(2): When a Seller Breaches and Buyer Revokes Acceptance. [§ 34–8]**

Under UCC § 2–510(2), if a seller breaches by sending a non-conforming good, and a buyer later validly revokes acceptance due to that breach, the buyer is entitled to treat the loss as having rested on the seller from the beginning, but only "to the extent of any deficiency in his [or her] insurance coverage." That is, if a buyer validly revokes acceptance and later, before the goods are returned to the buyer, something happens to them, the buyer must first try to recover under his or her insurance policy. If the buyer has no policy, or if the insurance policy does not pay the full amount of the loss, e.g., there is a deductible, then the buyer may recover from the seller only for any deficiency in his or her insurance proceeds.

c. **UCC § 2–510(3): When a Buyer Repudiates or Otherwise Breaches Before the Risk Has Shifted to Him or Her. [§ 34–9]**

Under UCC § 2–510(3), when a buyer has repudiated under a contract, or is otherwise in breach before the risk of loss has passed to him or her, the seller may treat the risk as having rested on the buyer for a commercially reasonable time, but again "only to the extent of any deficiency in his [or her] effective insurance coverage." Hence, in such a case, the seller must first try to recover against his or her own insurance, and only if a deficiency still remains may he or she recover the remainder of the purchase price from the buyer.

B. RISK OF LOSS UNDER THE CISG. [§ 34–10]

The general risk of loss provision of the CISG is Article 66, which provides that loss or damage to the goods that are the subject of the contract does not discharge the buyer's duty to pay once the risk of loss has passed to the buyer.

Although it does not use the terms, Article 67(1) sets forth the same rules with regard to shipment contracts and destination contracts involving a carrier as set forth above [§ 34–4].

If no carrier is involved, and there is no "fundamental" breach (the CISG's equivalent of material breach), Article 69 provides that the risk of loss occurs when the buyer takes control of the goods, or the goods are placed at the buyer's disposal.

RISK OF LOSS AND MERCANTILE TERMS

Finally, Article 70 states that in cases where the *seller* has committed a fundamental breach, the risk of loss rules set forth above do not impair the buyer's rights on account of the breach.

AUTHOR'S NOTE: In the 2003 revision to Article 2, the drafters eliminated many of the definitions of the so-called "mercantile terms" [§§ 2–319–320] discussed below. These were eliminated not because the Permanent Editorial Board believed the definitions were wrong, but only because the Board did not see the need to define such terms in the UCC, and instead relied on other treaties and statutes to define the terms. However, "mercantile terms" are used in the version of the UCC used in most law schools, and are mentioned in various cases studied in a first year contracts course. As such, they are explained below.

C. MERCANTILE TERMS. [§ 34–11]

Mercantile terms are shorthand expressions of various terms of a contract. In other words, they are abbreviations used in commercial law to denote a lengthy series of terms in an economical way. It is the unusual contracts course that spends a lot of time studying those terms, but they are mentioned in first year cases and can occasionally be important to the outcome of a suit. Accordingly, they are briefly defined and discussed below.

1. F.O.B. [§ 34–12]

F.O.B. means "Free On Board," and is shorthand for describing whether the contract is a shipment contract or a destination contract [UCC § 2–319; *see* § 34–4 and § 34–5]. Whether the F.O.B. term connotes a shipment or destination contract depends on whether the term is followed by the place of shipment or the place of destination.

For example, suppose a **seller in Cleveland** made a contract with a **buyer in Atlanta**:

(a) If the mercantile term of the contract was **F.O.B., Cleveland**, it would mean: (i) the contract was a *shipment contract*, and thus the risk of loss shifts to the buyer when the seller tenders the goods to the buyer or the carrier hired by the carrier in Cleveland; (ii) the seller's price does not include shipping charges; and (iii) it is up to the buyer to select, hire, and pay the carrier for shipping the goods to Atlanta [UCC § 2–319(1)(a)];

(b) If the mercantile term in the contract was **F.O.B., Atlanta**, it would mean: (i) the contract was a *destination contract*, and thus the risk of loss does not pass to the buyer until the goods are duly delivered in Atlanta; (ii) the seller's price includes the cost of shipping; and (iii) it is the seller who must select, hire, and pay the carrier for shipping the goods to Atlanta [UCC § 2–319(1)(b)].

2. F.A.S. [§ 34–13]

F.A.S. means "Free Along Side," [UCC § 2–319(2)]. The term is usually followed by the name of a ship, e.g., F.A.S., S.S. Normandie. When used in this way, it means: (i) the *risk of loss* passes to the buyer when the goods are *brought **along side** the ship*, e.g., to the dock or port; (ii) the selling price only includes delivery to the dock or port; and (iii) the seller only selects and pays the carrier to get the goods to the dock; it is the buyer who selects and pays for the ship on which the goods are to be transported and who pays for loading the goods onto the ship [UCC § 2–319(2)]. Hence, if the mercantile term was F.A.S., S.S. Normandie, and if the goods were damaged or destroyed while being loaded from the dock into the cargo hold of the Normandie, the risk of loss would be on the buyer, for the goods became the buyer's risk as soon as they were safely delivered to the dock.

a. "F.O.B." When Used with a Vessel. [§ 34–14]

When used with a vessel, e.g., F.O.B., S.S. Normandie, the F.O.B. term means that the seller maintains the risk of loss until the goods are actually delivered "on board" the vessel. Hence, a seller retains the risk of loss for one more step in the process than is the rule for a F.A.S contract—delivery from alongside the ship on the dock onto the ship itself. So if the goods are damaged or destroyed during the loading process from the dock to the ship, it is the seller's responsibility under an F.O.B. contract, and the buyer's responsibility under an F.A.S. contract.

3. C.I.F. [§ 34–15]

The term C.I.F. stands for **C**ost [of goods], **I**nsurance, and **F**reight [UCC § 2–320]. By common designation, it only has meaning if it is followed by the place of destination. However, that does **not** mean it is a destination contract. To the contrary it is a shipment contract [UCC § 2–320, Cmt. 1].

For example, a **seller in New York** contracts with a **buyer in Oregon**. If they agree to use C.I.F. as the mercantile term in their agreement, it must be set forth as C.I.F., Oregon, i.e., the destination of the shipment.

A **C.I.F. Oregon** term means: (i) the contract is a **shipment** contract (even though it is the destination point which follows the "C.I.F." term), and thus the risk of loss passes to the buyer upon the seller's delivery to the carrier; (ii) the seller's price includes the cost of goods, the cost of insurance for those goods during transit, and the cost of shipping the goods; (iii) the seller must select, hire, and pay for the carrier; and (iv) the seller must obtain insurance on the goods, but the beneficiary of that insurance is the **buyer** [UCC § 2–320(1)].

Thus, if goods are lost during shipment from New York to Oregon, the risk of loss is on the **buyer** (which makes sense, because C.I.F. contracts are shipment contracts). Recall, however, that as part of the contract the seller was required to procure insurance on the goods, with the proceeds of that insurance payable to the buyer as the beneficiary. Hence, while the buyer may have to pay the seller for the goods that are destroyed, the buyer will be reimbursed for such payment by the insurance provided by the seller.

4. **C. & F. [§ 34–16]**

The term C. & F. means the same as C.I.F., except that the seller's price does not include insurance, and the seller, therefore, need not procure it [UCC § 2–320(3)]. Hence, if a buyer agrees to buy his or her own insurance to cover the risk of loss, but still wants the seller's price to include both the cost of goods and of the cost of shipment as well, a C. & F. term should be used.

CHAPTER 35

WARRANTIES

A. WARRANTIES UNDER THE UCC GENERALLY. [§ 35–1]

Article 2 of the UCC contains three warranties that are studied in first-year contracts courses:

(1) Express warranty, found in UCC § 2–313;

(2) The Implied Warranty of Merchantability, found in UCC § 2–314; and

(3) The Implied Warranty of Fitness for a Particular Purpose, found in UCC § 2–315.

Note that the Code also provides for a warranty of title in UCC § 2–312, but this provision is not typically taught in contracts courses, and thus will not be discussed in this Book.

B. EXPRESS WARRANTIES. [§ 35–2*]

A buyer seeking to prove that an actionable express warranty was made to him or her must establish that: (1) the seller made a sufficiently factual promise about the qualities or attributes of the goods which were the subject matter of the contract which turned out not to be true; (2) the factual promise was part of the "basis of the bargain;" and the failure of the good to live up to the representations of the seller caused the buyer's damage.

Each of these elements is discussed below.

1. **An Express Warranty Is Created by an Affirmation, Promise, Description, or Sample. [§ 35–3]**

    A buyer seeking to prove the existence of an actionable express warranty must show that the seller made a sufficiently factual promise to him or her relating to the qualities or attributes of the goods that were sold. Under UCC § 2–313(1), an actionable,

---

* For more information, listen to CD # 14, Track 2 of *Sum and Substance Audio on Contracts*.

sufficiently factual express warranty can be made in three separate, but related, ways:

(i) by means of an "**affirmation of fact or promise** made by the seller which relates to the goods" [UCC § 2–313(1)(a)];

(ii) by means of "**a description of the goods**" made by the seller [UCC § 2–313(1)(b)]; and

(iii) by means of "**a sample or model**" shown to the buyer as representative of the goods the buyer will receive under the contract [UCC § 2–313(1)(c)].

The Code makes clear that not every statement relating to a product's attributes becomes actionable. While there is no requirement that the word "warranty" or "guarantee" be used to create an express warranty, the Code requires that any representation made to the buyer must be **factual** before it can be actionable [UCC § 2–313]. The rules used to determine whether a particular statement is sufficiently factual to create an enforceable warranty are the same as they are for determining when a statement is sufficiently factual to serve as the basis for a misrepresentation claim [§ 15–7]. That is, the more verifiable and provable a statement is, the more likely it will be held to be an actionable affirmation of fact. The more it is an unprovable, amorphous statement about the qualities of a good, the more likely it is to be found to be an unactionable opinion or a "puffing" statement. Hence, statements like "this car will get 25 miles per gallon" will be actionable as an express warranty, whereas statements like "this car is a dilly" clearly will not.

If a seller provides a sample or model of the goods to be sold, the goods that are actually delivered must be of equivalent quality as the sample, or a breach of express warranty has occurred. The furnishing of the sample or model is the factual assertion giving rise to the actionable warranty.

Note that to be actionable, under UCC § 2–313 the statements made must "**relate to the [quality or attribute of the] goods**." For example, assume while bargaining for a contract for the sale of a photocopier, the sales representative says, "we will be able to provide service for the copier at only $25/ visit." After the contract has been entered into, assume that service visits are charged at $45. There has been a breach of contract, and perhaps even fraud. But there has been no breach of *warranty* because the sales representative's statement, while factual, did not relate to the **quality or attribute of the goods**, even though it was made during the sale of the copier.

690

WARRANTIES

2. The Affirmations Made by the Seller Must Become Part of "the Basis of the Bargain." [§ 35–4]

Once a buyer has established that a sufficiently factual statement has been made by the seller, the buyer must next prove that the statement was part of "the basis of the bargain" between the buyer and seller [UCC § 2–313(1)]. There are two views as to what "basis of the bargain" means:

(1) the first view holds that "basis of the bargain" is simply a synonym for reliance, i.e., that it sets forth a requirement that the buyer must have relied on the seller's factual promise in deciding to purchase the product before a buyer can recover for breach of warranty;

(2) the second view holds that "basis of the bargain" means only that the factual affirmations of the seller were made sometime before the sale took place.

Part of the reason different courts come to different conclusions on this issue stems from the fact that they have different views as to the purposes of the express warranty protections in the Code, as explained below.

a. Theory One: "Basis of the Bargain" Means "Reliance." [§ 35–5]

Those courts and commentators who hold that basis of the bargain is only a synonym for reliance believe that the express warranty protections of the Code are principally designed to protect the reasonable expectations of the buyer in a sales transaction. That is, they hold that if a buyer hears or reads something the seller has said about the product, and relies on that representation in making the decision to purchase the good, then the seller should be liable if the good does not have those promised qualities, for the basis on which the bargain was made has been upset.

This view also holds, however, that if the buyer did **not** rely on the seller's statements in making the decision to purchase the good, e.g., because he or she did not see or hear them before deciding to purchase the good, or because he or she would have purchased the good anyway regardless of what the seller said about that attribute, then no express warranty claim will be allowed. This is because if the buyer did not rely on the seller's promises, then the fact that the goods do not conform to what the seller promised about them caused the buyer no harm, since it resulted in no disruption of the buyer's bargain. In other words, this view holds that if the seller's statements played no role in the buyer's decision to buy the goods, those statements could not have been part of the basis of the buyer's bargain and thus there is no interest of the buyer justifying protection.

One rationale for this view is that reliance has long been a requirement for fraud and misrepresentation claims [§§ 15–29 and 15–30]. While a claim for breach of express warranty is not identical to a tort claim for misrepresentation, the two are related. That is, in each type of case a buyer is suing for damages resulting from a statement made by a seller concerning goods that turns out not to be true. Hence, as a matter of consistency, it is thought that reliance should be an element of a § 2–313 claim. Moreover, many commentators believe that a buyer truly is not deserving of recovery if he or she was not aware of, or did not rely on, the seller's warranty, for the seller's promises in these cases were, by definition, irrelevant to the bargain.

Note that there is a split even among those jurisdictions which believe that basis of the bargain means reliance. Some hold that the **burden of proving reliance should be on the buyer**, whereas *others* believe it *should be on the seller to prove the absence of reliance*. That is, this latter view holds that a buyer can prove his or her **prima facie** case for breach of express warranty without showing reliance, for reliance will be presumed. However, a seller is entitled to rebut that presumption by establishing that the buyer did not see, hear, and/or rely on the seller's affirmations in deciding to purchase the good, which, presumably it would find out during discovery [*See Hauter v. Zogarts*, 14 Cal.3d 104 (1975) for an example of a court adopting this latter rule].

b. **Theory Two: "Basis of the Bargain" Means the Affirmation Was Made Before the Sale Took Place. [§ 35–6]**

This theory holds that basis of the bargain is really only a timing requirement, i.e., that it only requires proof that the seller made the factual affirmation before the sale took place. The rationale for this view is that the Code's express warranty provisions were not designed to protect the expectations of a buyer so much as they were to punish a seller for not living up to the promises he or she made about goods. That is, this view holds that contract law does not require the seller to make any representations about his or her goods; so if the seller says nothing about them, there will be no express warranty liability.

However, once the seller does voluntarily say something about the qualities of his or her goods, he or she should be prepared to face the consequences when the goods fail to perform as promised. Hence, under this view, it is irrelevant whether the

WARRANTIES

buyer saw, heard, and/or relied on the warranty; it is only relevant that the seller made it before the sale, and that the goods did not perform as promised.

There are two justifications given for this view. First, Comment 3 to § 2–313, states that "[i]n actual practice affirmations of fact made by the seller about the goods during a bargain are regarded as part of the description of those goods; **hence no particular reliance on such statements need be shown in order to weave them into the fabric of the agreement.**" *See also* a similar statement in § 2–313, Comment 5.

The second justification is that, whether the buyer was aware of the promise or not, the price he or she paid for the goods probably reflected the costs of the warranty. That is, typically when a company makes a warranty, it will increase its price somewhat to cover the costs of having to live up to it in future litigation, to take steps in the manufacturing process to ensure the good had that attribute, and/or buy insurance to cover the risk of being sued. Thus, even if the buyer did not know about the warranty, it is likely he or she paid for its protection.

At the present time, the view that basis of the bargain means reliance is still probably the majority, but there appears to be growing acceptance of the view that the term only means that the statement must be made before the sale takes place.

3. Disclaiming an Express Warranty. [§ 35–7]

An express warranty can be disclaimed under the Code. That is, a seller can make an express warranty by making some affirmation of fact to the buyer that was part of the basis of the bargain, but then, before the contract is made, the seller can "take it back" and disclaim the previously made express promise. A caveat: while "taking it back" is what the language of the Code seems to allow, the last paragraph in this section explains why courts do not like this idea very much and sets forth the theories courts use to negate the seller's express warranty disclaimers.

Typically, the issue arises when a sales representative makes an oral express warranty to the buyer, and thereafter there is an attempt to disclaim that warranty in a written purchase agreement the parties sign to close the deal. The problem is that the buyer may not read and/or understand the written contract, and certainly does not expect that the oral warranty he or she has just been given 10 minutes before is effectively disclaimed in such a writing.

The Code regulates the disclaimer of express warranties in § 2–316(1). That provision is syntactically somewhat difficult to understand, but its approach is as follows:

(1) If it is reasonable to do so, the words of the warranty and the words of the warranty disclaimer should be construed as consistent with each other. That is, the warranty and the disclaimer should try to be harmonized so that they both can be found valid and enforceable. For example, if the oral warranty made by the sales representative was that the car got 25 m.p.g., and the warranty disclaimer disclaimed all warranties as to the qualities of the car, it might be possible to construe them as reasonably harmonious, i.e., there may be no warranty as to things like the fit and finish of the car, but there is a warranty regarding its mileage.

(2) If the express warranty and the disclaimer cannot be read consistently, as is usually the case, then the buyer's rights are circumscribed, at least under the language of § 2–316. At first the language of § 2–316(1) makes it seem as though the oral express warranty should prevail over the written disclaimer, for § 2–316(1) states that when the warranty and the disclaimer cannot be harmonized, "negation or limitation [of the warranty] is inoperative." That sounds bad for the seller.

However, application of this rule is specifically subject to the parol evidence rule, UCC § 2–202 [Chapter Eighteen]. By making the "negation is inoperative" term subject to the parol evidence rule, § 2–316(1) makes it almost impossible for an oral warranty ever to be enforceable when paired with a valid written warranty disclaimer. This is because an oral, parol statement that there *is* a warranty is almost always a "contradictory term" when compared to the written warranty disclaimer, and contradictory parol terms are typically excluded by the parol evidence rule [§ 19–1].

Obviously this is a difficult area, which perhaps can be better understood by illustration.

Susan buys a computer from Mega Byte, Inc. The Mega Byte sales representative tells Susan that the computer she is interested in will run the "DataPro" program that Susan likes to use. Relying on the representation that the computer will run DataPro, Susan buys it. When she gets home, she discovers both that the computer will not run the DataPro program and that her bill of sale provides that "Mega Byte makes no representation or warranty that its computers will be compatible with any software program on the market, and any indication to the contrary by any sales representative should be disregarded. Buyer must test the compatibility of any program prior to purchasing this computer."

In evaluating whether the disclaimer is effective under UCC § 2–316(1), the analysis is as follows:

WARRANTIES

(1) Can the warranty and the disclaimer be read consistently? Here they cannot, for an oral warranty providing that Data Pro can be run on the computer cannot be harmonized with a disclaimer providing that Mega Byte makes no enforceable warranty as to whether its computers can run any program.

(2) If the disclaimer and the warranty cannot be read consistently, then the *disclaimer* is *inoperative* under § 2–316(1), **but, that result is subject to the parol evidence rule**. Recall that under the UCC's parol evidence rule, no evidence of an oral term that "contradicts" a term in a writing can be introduced, even if the contract is only partially integrated [§ 19–1]. Here, the oral term that the computer will run DataPro certainly contradicts the written term that no representations are made as to the compatibility of any program with a Mega Byte computer.

Thus, if, somehow, evidence of the warranty and of the disclaimer could both be introduced at trial, the warranty would prevail and the disclaimer would be inoperative. However, because most such oral warranties will be found as "contradicting" the written disclaimer, parol evidence of the oral warranty will almost never be validly admitted, at least as § 2–316(1) is written. As such, the only operable provision that will be in evidence in such cases will be the disclaimer, and the disclaimer will thus control.

Note that such a result, while perhaps faithful to the language of § 2–316, is both unfair to someone in Susan's position and thoroughly disliked by the courts. Accordingly, courts often decide that written express warranty disclaimers will not be enforced either because they are unconscionable [UCC § 2–302; Chapter Sixteen]; because an oral warranty, followed by a written disclaimer, constitutes a breach of the covenant of good faith and fair dealing [UCC § 1–304], on the grounds of fraud, or on the grounds that the warranty is a misrepresentation that allows the buyer to void the contract, and facts which allow a party to void the contract are "exceptions" to the parol evidence rule, meaning that evidence of the warranty is admissible and prevails over the disclaimer [§ 18–19]. Some courts even hold that as a matter of "policy" they will not allow a written disclaimer to an oral express warranty in consumer transactions, often noting that the merger clause and/or disclaimer are just boilerplate which can more easily be disregarded than a negotiated term.

CHAPTER 35

C. IMPLIED WARRANTY OF MERCHANTABILITY. [§ 35–8*]

The implied warranty of merchantability rests on the notion that in contemporary commercial society a buyer is entitled to a representative good of the type he or she buys. If the seller wants to sell a good below the average quality of such goods without liability, it can do so, but it must specifically disclaim the merchantability warranty to put itself in that position. Many scholars state that the warranty's ascension mirrored the decline of *caveat emptor,* or "buyer beware." That is, many times a consumer now purchases goods from a seller at a distance over the Internet or the like, or buys it in a store where the good is packaged in shrink wrap and thus not available for pre-purchase inspection.

So if one, e.g., buys a computer monitor, one has the right to expect that it will be of average quality—such average quality is an **implied term of the contract**—unless the seller has disclaimed the warranty of merchantability.

A buyer seeking to establish breach of the implied warranty of merchantability under § 2–314 must prove that: (1) the seller of the good was a "merchant"; (2) the goods sold by the seller were not "merchantable"; and (3) the breach caused the buyer's damage.

1. The Buyer Must Establish That the Seller Was a "Merchant." [§ 35–9]

Not surprisingly, only **merchant** sellers are subject to liability for breach of the implied warranty of *merchantability*. Under UCC § 2–104(1), a "merchant" is someone who deals in goods of the kind, or otherwise holds himself out as having skill or knowledge peculiar to the practices or goods involved in the transaction by virtue of his or her occupation. Thus, to be liable for a breach of the merchantability warranty, the seller must be more than just an occasional seller. Rather, the seller must be someone who, by virtue of his or her occupation, regularly deals in goods of the kind involved in the sale.

Only the seller must be a merchant. The warranty is available to both consumer and merchant buyers.

2. The Buyer Must Establish That the Goods Were Not "Merchantable." [§ 35–10]

After proving that the seller is a merchant, the next element a buyer must establish to prove a breach of the implied warranty of merchantability is that the goods sold were not "merchantable." In

---

* For more information, listen to CD # 14, Track 3 of *Sum and Substance Audio on Contracts.*

WARRANTIES

Section 2–314(2), the Code gives six examples of what "merchantable" means, the most common of which are:

UCC § 2–314(2)(a)—goods are merchantable if they "**pass without objection in the trade;**"

UCC § 2–314(2)(b)—fungible goods are merchantable if they "**are of fair average quality;**" and

UCC § 2–314(2)(c)—goods are merchantable if they are "**fit for the ordinary purposes for which such goods are used.**"

3. **Disclaimer of Implied Warranty of Merchantability. [§ 35–11]**

There are two ways to disclaim the implied warranty of merchantability:

(1) Under UCC § 2–316(2), the warranty of merchantability can be disclaimed in a plain statement of disclaimer in which the word "merchantability" is used. *If* this disclaimer is *in writing*, its provisions must be *conspicuous* [§ 2–316(2)].

So a statement that "Seller makes no representations regarding the quality of goods, and disclaims all warranties, including the warranty of merchantability" would effectively disclaim the warranty so long as it was conspicuous. Note that "conspicuous" is a term defined under the Code in § 1–201(b)(10), and that provision gives some examples of fonts and colors to be used to make the writing "conspicuous." Many manufacturers will put a merchantability disclaimer in all capitals and/or in red ink to comply with the definition. Further, note also that, under the terms of § 2–316(2) the warranty of merchantability can be disclaimed orally, although many states have consumer protection statutes which require any such disclaimer to be in writing.

(2) UCC § 2–316(3)(a), if the seller wishes to disclaim **all** implied warranties, *including* the implied warranty of merchantability, the Code provides that it may do so by using expressions like "Goods are sold '*as is,*' or '*with all faults,*'" or any other language that makes it plain that no implied warranty is contemplated in the transaction.

Note that while on its face § 2–316(3)(a) does not require the "as is," "with all faults," or like disclaimer language to be conspicuous, courts have read such a requirement into the provision as a matter of fairness. After all, if a written merchantability disclaimer has to be conspicuous under § 2–316(2), logic would dictate an even broader all implied warranty disclaimer under § 2–316(3)(a) should have to be conspicuous as well.

Furthermore, as a matter of conscionability, many jurisdictions forbid a merchant seller to sell new goods on an "as is" basis. Rather, they hold that such broad disclaimers of all implied warranties are only enforceable in connection with the sale of used goods.

There is one additional way the implied warranty of merchantability can be excluded, or at least limited. Under UCC § 2–316(3)(b), if the seller allows the buyer the right to inspect the good before purchase as much as the buyer wishes, then there is no merchantability warranty as to any flaw in the good that should be discovered by such inspection.

D. THE IMPLIED WARRANTY OF FITNESS FOR A PARTICULAR PURPOSE. [§ 35–12*]

The implied warranty of fitness for a particular purpose rests on the notion that sometimes a buyer wants a good with particular attributes, but doesn't have a clue which good in the seller's inventory has those qualities. Hence, when the buyer makes his or her desired attributes known to the seller, and relies on the seller to furnish a good that has those attributes, it is only fair that the seller be held accountable if the goods do not have those qualities.

To establish that the implied warranty of fitness for a particular purpose under UCC § 2–315 has been made, a buyer must prove that:

(1) the buyer had an unusual or particular purpose in mind for the goods;

(2) the seller had reason to know of this particular purpose (usually because the buyer has told the seller of this purpose);

(3) the seller has reason to know that the buyer is relying on the seller's skill or judgment to select or furnish goods that will meet the buyer's needs;

(4) the buyer in fact relied on the seller's skill or judgment in selecting suitable goods; and

(5) the goods did not perform as warranted.

1. Example. [§ 35–13]

Jason goes into a sporting goods store and explains to Margaret, the owner of the store, that he has just been invited along to climb Mt. Everest and needs to purchase suitable shoes for use in the extreme cold and which are thick enough to give some comfort when walking along jagged peaks. Jason asks Margret what she would recommend. If Margret gives him only a pair of tennis shoes, which cause him

---

* For more information, listen to CD # 14, Track 4 of *Sum and Substance Audio on Contracts*.

WARRANTIES

injury while on the mountain climbing expedition, Jason has an implied warranty of fitness claim against the store, for (5) the goods did not perform as warranted and he:

(1) had a need for goods to perform a particular purpose;

(2) informed the seller of his needs so that the seller had reason to know of it;

(3) gave the owner reason to know he was relying on her skill and judgment in selecting the shoes; and

(4) did in fact rely on the store owner's skill and judgment in selecting the goods.

2. Example. [§ 35–14]

Same as above, but this time Jason simply walks into a store and selects the sturdiest looking and most expensive pair of shoes in the "outdoor hiking" section of the store, and figures they will satisfy his needs. No implied warranty of fitness for a particular purpose has taken place, for Jason chose the shoes on his own and did not rely on the seller to meet any needs he expressed to Margaret.

3. Disclaiming the Implied Warranty of Fitness for a Particular Purpose. [§ 35–15]

There are two ways to disclaim the implied warranty of fitness for a particular purpose:

(1) Under UCC § 2–316(2), the warranty of fitness may be disclaimed by a statement such as, "There are no warranties which extend beyond the description on the face hereof." That provision does not explicitly state that such disclaimers have to be "conspicuous," but courts typically do not give such disclaimers effect unless they are either conspicuous or otherwise known by the buyer. Also, it is apparent that no special words need be used to disclaim the implied warranty of fitness, but in "real life" it is rare to see an attempted disclaimer of the fitness warranty in particular which does not use the terms "Disclaimer" and "Implied Warranty of Fitness for a Particular Purpose" in close proximity.

(2) Under UCC § 2–316(2), a seller can exclude **all** implied warranties, *including* the implied warranty of fitness for a particular purpose, using the rules discussed above for a disclaimer of all implied warranties in the merchantability context [§ 35–11].

As with merchantability, a buyer cannot bring a viable implied warranty of fitness claim regarding a flaw that should have been discovered during a pre-purchase inspection of the goods, if the seller allows the buyer free access for such inspection [UCC § 2–316(3)(b); § 35–11].

E. DOCTRINES APPLICABLE TO ALL WARRANTY CLAIMS: NOTICE AND PRIVITY. [§ 35–16*]

There are three issues that affect all types of breach of warranty claims:

(1) The extent to which a buyer must notify the seller of the breach of warranty before he or she brings suit [§ 35–17];

(2) Whether sellers in the vertical commercial distribution chain other than the retailer, e.g., the "remote" manufacturer, can be sued successfully for breach of warranty or whether the buyer is barred from suing because of a lack of "vertical privity"? [§ 35–18]; and

(3) Whether persons other than the buyer are entitled to recover for breach of warranty, e.g., a friend to whom the buyer gave the good, or whether such individuals are barred by "horizontal privity"? [§ 35–19].

Each is discussed below.

1. The Notice Requirement Under UCC § 2–607(3). [§ 35–17]

UCC § 2–607(3) provides that a buyer must notify the seller of the breach of warranty within a reasonable time after the breach was either discovered or should have been discovered. If no such notice is provided, the buyer is "barred from any remedy" for breach.

This rule is often ignored by courts, especially in ordinary consumer transactions. After all, how many non-lawyer consumers know that one is supposed to give, e.g., Microsoft detailed notice of a claim within a reasonable time after discovering the breach of warranty or be barred from suit altogether? As such, courts will either avoid this requirement by deeming it unconscionable in a particular case, or hold that the filing of the litigation itself meets the notice requirement.

The requirement is enforced more strictly in business-to-business disputes, however.

2. Who Is a Proper Defendant: Vertical Privity. [§ 35–18]

Privity in contract law means that the parties had direct contractual dealings. For example, if Sally buys a Sony television from Sears, she is in direct vertical privity with Sears, but not with Sony, for she had no direct dealings with Sony, the "remote" manufacturer. It is called "vertical" privity because one can set up a straight vertical

---

* For more information, listen to CD # 14, Track 5 of *Sum and Substance Audio on Contracts*.

WARRANTIES

commercial line of distribution of the televisions from Sony to Sears to Sally, with each at different vertical sales levels.

At early common law, privity was a requirement in breach of contract actions because it was thought improper to allow one party to sue another for breach of contract when there was, in fact, no contract between them. So Sally could not sue Sony for breach of warranty because of the absence of an agreement between them. Indeed, at the time of the sale in a Sears store, Sony has no idea who has purchased its products.

Modern warranty law, however, has largely eliminated the vertical privity requirement in warranty cases—at least for some kinds of damages, as explained below. It is thought that since everyone in the vertical distribution chain of the goods benefits from the sale of the goods to the consumer, everyone in that chain should also share liability for goods that do not perform as are warranted. Moreover, in express warranty claims, it is often the remote manufacturer who makes the representations about the qualities of the goods that serve as the basis of the bargain, e.g., in an advertising campaign, on the package of the good itself, on a tag attached to the clothing or other good placed there by the manufacturer, etc.

Further, in a merchantability claim, it is again the remote manufacturer who is almost surely responsible for the good not being "merchantable" due to a defect in its manufacture or design. That is, the manufacturer is the "active" wrongdoer who produced a substandard good, not the retailer who only took delivery of large batch of those goods from the manufacturer and just passed the goods through to the buyer.

Moreover, to deny liability for a remote manufacturer would mean the injured buyer could not recover for injuries caused by the manufacturer when the retailer is either out of business or insolvent.

Manufacturers argued that it was unfair for them to bear responsibility for, e.g., the full price of the good (if the good was a real dud) because the consumer is suing for the retail price and the manufacturer only got the wholesale price from the retailer. Further, for many claims manufacturers asserted they should not be liable for warranties of fitness claims or for consequential damages since they do not know what the consumer is proposing to do with the goods.

Despite these arguments by the manufacturers, courts have held privity is no longer required for bringing suit for breach of warranty, and today a proper plaintiff is entitled to bring suit for express warranty against anyone in the vertical distribution chain; there is still a split whether suit for the implied warranties can be brought against anyone in the vertical chain, but the trend is to allow such suits, but to limit damages as described immediately below.

Where suit is allowed, all courts will allow a "direct damage" recovery—recovery for diminished value of the good itself as measured by the good with the qualities that were promised minus the value of the good actually received—against a remote manufacturer [UCC § 2–714(2)]. Further, all courts will allow recovery for personal injury or personal property damage against a remote manufacturer in warranty if the substantive elements for the warranty claim are met [UCC § 2–715(2)(b)]. However, some courts refuse to allow recovery of consequential economic damages against remote manufacturers in express and implied warranty cases [UCC § 2–715(2)(a)].

3. Who Is Entitled to Sue: Horizontal Privity. [§ 35–19]

The previous section discussed the privity requirement in the vertical distribution chain. There is another type of privity, i.e., "horizontal" privity, which can also be an issue in breach of warranty cases. The horizontal privity issue involves what kinds of third parties can recover in breach of warranty when their injuries are due to a breach of a warranty promise given another.

For example, suppose Dave purchases an electric lawnmower and lends it to his neighbor Julie, and then Julie becomes injured because of a product defect. Or suppose Mom buys an electric shaver for Dad, and it is Son, who is watching Dad shave, who is injured when the shaver blows up. Manufacturers argue that since no warranty was given to Julie and Son, they should not be able to recover in warranty and should be restricted to tort products liability claims.

There is universal agreement that warranty protections are not limited only to the buyer. There is disagreement, however, as to how far those protections should extend to others who are in "horizontal privity" with the buyer. It is "horizontal" privity because these users or bystanders are on the same horizontal commercial level as the buyer.

There are currently three views *in the UCC itself* as to what kinds of third parties should be entitled to bring actions for breaches of a warranty not made to them. The drafters could not decide on one view and left it up to each state to select one of the alternatives set forth in UCC § 2–318:

> (1) **UCC § 2–318—Alternative A**, provides that the only third parties who should be able to recover in warranty are "**natural persons who [are] in the household of [the] buyer or who [are] guest(s) in his home ... and who [are] injured in person.**" Hence, bystanders, people outside the home, etc., and those who suffer only economic loss are not be able to recover in warranty in the states that have adopted this view.

(2) **UCC § 2–318—Alternative B**, provides that the range of third parties entitled to sue for injuries caused by a breach of warranty include "**any natural person who may reasonably be expected to use, consume, or be affected by the goods ... and who is injured in person.**" However, *neither a corporation*, nor an individual injured other than by *personal injury*, may recover in a jurisdiction which has adopted this Alternative.

(3) **UCC § 2–318—Alternative C**, allows recovery by any "**person who may be reasonably expected to use, consume, or be affected by the good.**" Hence, corporations can recover in a state which has adopted Alternative C as well as any individual who has suffered either *economic as well as personal injuries.*

Note there is a fourth view as well, not expressed in the Code. Some jurisdictions have intentionally refused to adopt any of the three alternatives listed in § 2–318 discussed above. Instead, their rules regarding when third parties are entitled to sue for breach of warranty are left to the courts of that state.

F. WARRANTY DEFENSES. [§ 35–20]

While the rule varies somewhat among jurisdictions, it is fairly well agreed that there are two complete defenses to a breach of warranty claim: (1) Assumption of the Risk; and (2) Unforeseeable Misuse of the Product.

1. Assumption of the Risk. [§ 35–21]

In those jurisdictions where assumption of the risk remains a valid defense, i.e., where it has not been eliminated by comparative negligence, it provides a complete defense to a breach of warranty claim. Hence if a seller can prove that the plaintiff knowledgeably and voluntarily undertook a known risk in using the product as he or she did, understanding the magnitude of the risk at the time it was taken, then the seller has a complete defense to the warranty suit.

a. Comparative Negligence. [§ 35–22]

In those jurisdictions that have eliminated assumption of the risk through comparative negligence, there is a split in the courts as to whether comparative fault principles will be allowed to offset a warranty recovery. Those who allow the offset hold that the comparative inquiry is one of *fault*. So, the question is how much fault should each party be ascribed for the injury? Those states that reject the offset notion hold that it is impossible to compare *negligence* with warranty, which is a strict liability doctrine, i.e., they are apples and oranges, and

CHAPTER 35

thus a warranty recovery should not be offset by the plaintiff's negligence.

2. Unforeseeable Misuse of the Product. [§ 35–23]

If a seller can establish that a buyer was using a product in an unforeseeable manner, and that it was *such use* that caused his or her injury rather than a defect in the goods or promised attribute about the goods, once again a seller has a complete defense to a breach of warranty claim.

G. DAMAGES FOR BREACH OF WARRANTY. [§ 35–24]

Damages recoverable for breach of warranty are governed by UCC § 2–714 and are discussed in §§ 32–23 *et seq.*

H. WARRANTIES UNDER CISG. [§ 35–25]

Article 35 of the CISG sets forth the substantive warranty terms under the CISG. As will be seen below, the substance of the CISG's warranty provisions closely mirror their equivalents under Article 2 although, perhaps surprisingly, the CISG does not use the term "warranty," and, as explained below, does not specifically differ between implied and express warranties.

In Article 35(1), the seller is obligated to "deliver goods which are of the quantity, quality and description required by the contract;" in Article 35(2), the seller must deliver goods which "[p]ossess the qualities of goods which the seller has held out as a sample or model." Collectively, these provisions make up the "express warranty" provisions of the CISG.

Article 35(2)(a) is the equivalent to the UCC's implied warranty of merchantability, and requires the seller to deliver goods which "[a]re fit for the purposes for which goods of the same description would ordinarily be used."

The analog to the UCC's implied warranty of fitness for a particular purpose is Article 35(2)(b), which requires the seller to deliver goods that are "fit for any particular purpose expressly or impliedly made known to the seller at the time of the conclusion of the contract."

There is one provision under the CISG that has no UCC analog: Article 35(2)(d), which requires the seller to deliver goods which "are contained or packaged in the manner usual for such goods or, where there is no such manner, in a manner adequate to preserve and protect the goods."

I. EXAM APPROACH TO WARRANTY ISSUES. [§ 35–26]

Most contracts courses do not study warranties in any depth. Hence, it will probably be enough if you:

WARRANTIES

1. Identify which warranty is involved:

   A. Express [§ 35–2];

   B. Merchantability [§ 35–8]; or

   C. Fitness for a particular purpose [§ 35–12].

2. This determination is made based on whether:

   A. The seller said anything factual, but inaccurate, to the buyer about the good which became part of the basis of the bargain [§§ 35–4 *et seq.*];

   B. The seller was a merchant and the goods were not "merchantable" meaning it was not fit for the ordinary purpose of such goods, not of fair and average quality for such a good, or the like [§§ 35–9; 35–10]; or

   C. Whether the seller knew the buyer had some particular need in mind when he or she bought the goods and did not provide a product sufficient to live up to those needs (§ 35–13).

3. If a warranty existed and was breached, make sure to check to see whether it was effectively disclaimed or whether there any applicable defenses [§§ 35–7; 35–11; 35–15].

4. Finally, examine whether it is the type of injury the plaintiff can assert [§ 35–18] and, if so, use the formula in UCC § 2–714(2) to calculate damages [§ 32–24].

SAMPLE MULTIPLE CHOICE QUESTIONS

Questions 1–3 are based on the following fact situation:

Priscilla was a plumbing contractor. Allan and Brenda each owned an apartment building. Allan explained to Priscilla the plumbing work that was needed for his building. Brenda also explained to Priscilla the plumbing work that was needed for her building.

On January 15, Priscilla mailed offers to Allan and Brenda. Priscilla offered to do the work on Allan's building for $2,000 and offered to do the work on Brenda's building for $4,000. In each case, Priscilla's offer stated that it would be open until January 30.

On the morning of January 20, Allan mailed a properly addressed letter to Priscilla stating, "We've got a deal." That afternoon, Allan spoke to Xerxes, another plumber, who said he would do the job for $1,500. Allan immediately sent a letter by express mail to Priscilla, stating, "Please disregard my other letter. I am going to have someone else do the plumbing work."

On January 21, Priscilla received the letter Allan sent by express mail. Priscilla received Allan's other letter on January 22. Priscilla demanded that Allan permit her to do the work for $2,000, but Allan refused.

On January 24, Brenda mailed a letter to Priscilla, stating, "$4,000 is too much. I will agree to pay you $3,000 if you will agree to do the job." On January 25, Brenda spoke to Xerxes, who said he would not do the job for less than $5,000. That afternoon, Brenda sent a letter by express mail to Priscilla, stating, "Disregard my letter of 1/24. I accept your offer." Priscilla received both of Brenda's letters on January 27. Brenda thereafter spoke to Yolanda, another plumber; Yolanda said she would do the plumbing work on Brenda's building for $3,500. Brenda immediately telephoned Priscilla and said (before Priscilla could say a word), "This is Brenda. The deal is off." Priscilla then demanded that Brenda permit her (Priscilla) to do the work for $4,000. Brenda refused.

1. If Priscilla sues Allan for breach of contract, Priscilla will:

(A) **Lose**, because Priscilla received the letter Allan sent by express mail before Priscilla received Allan's first letter (the one not sent by express mail).

(B) **Lose**, because the offer in Allan's first letter (the one not sent by express mail) could be retracted up until the time Priscilla received it.

SAMPLE MULTIPLE CHOICE QUESTIONS

(C) **Win**, because the letter Allan sent by express mail did not have legal effect until Priscilla received it.

(D) **Win**, because the offer in Allan's first letter (the one not sent by express mail) had legal effect when it was sent, even though it was not received first.

2. Assume Brenda's first letter (the one not sent by express mail) was received on the morning of January 26, and Brenda's letter sent by express mail was received on the afternoon of January 26. If Priscilla sues Brenda for breach of contract, Priscilla will:

(A) **Lose**, because Priscilla received Brenda's first letter before Priscilla received the letter Brenda sent by express mail.

(B) **Lose**, because Brenda's first letter had legal effect when it was sent.

(C) **Win**, because Brenda's first letter did not have legal effect until Priscilla received it.

(D) **Win**, because the letter Brenda sent by express mail had legal effect when it was sent, even though it was not received first.

3. Assume the letter Brenda sent by express mail was received on the morning of January 26, and Brenda's first letter (the one not sent by express mail) was received on the afternoon of January 26. If Priscilla sues Brenda for breach of contract, Priscilla will:

(A) **Lose**, because the letter Brenda sent by express mail did not have legal effect when it was sent.

(B) **Lose**, because Brenda's first letter had legal effect when it was sent, even though it was not received first.

(C) **Win**, because Priscilla received the letter Brenda sent by express mail before Priscilla received Brenda's first letter.

(D) **Win**, because the letter Brenda sent by express mail had legal effect when it was sent.

Questions 4–6 are based on the following fact situation:

Professor Jones was out for a walk with his family. He heard a sudden squeal of brakes and was horrified to see that his neighbor Quigley had been run over by an automobile driven by Jones's nephew Newton. Quigley was lying in the street, unconscious. Dr. Fiscus, who happened to be driving by, stopped, gave aid to Quigley, and accompanied Quigley to the hospital. Despite Dr. Fiscus's prompt and expert medical attention, Quigley never regained consciousness; Quigley died a week later. Jones was noticeably bothered by these events; to cheer him up, three of his students washed and waxed his automobile early one morning before Jones awoke. (Jones had parked the auto on the street.) The next day, out of gratitude, Jones promised the students that he would pay each of them $10. (The reasonable value of the wash and wax job was $45.) Although

SAMPLE MULTIPLE CHOICE QUESTIONS

Jones was not legally responsible for Newton's negligence in driving over Quigley, Jones told others he felt responsible since Newton was coming to see him. For that reason, Jones promised Quigley's widow that he would pay her $10,000.

4. Who, if anyone, is obligated to pay Dr. Fiscus for his services?

(A) Jones.

(B) Quigley's estate.

(C) Both Quigley's estate and Jones.

(D) Neither Quigley's estate nor Jones.

5. Under the Restatement 2d of Contracts, Jones would:

(A) Be obligated to pay $10 to each of the students.

(B) Be obligated to pay $45 to each of the students.

(C) Not be obligated to pay anything to the students because, in washing and waxing his car without asking him first, the students deprived him of the opportunity of declining the benefit.

(D) Not be obligated to pay anything to the students because the students washed and waxed his car as a gift to him.

6. Under the Restatement 2d of Contracts, Jones would:

(A) Not be obligated to pay $10,000 to Quigley's widow.

(B) Be obligated to pay $10,000 to Quigley's widow, assuming her loss due to the death of her husband is at least equal to the $10,000 Quigley promised to pay her.

(C) Be obligated to pay $10,000 to Quigley's widow under the doctrine of promissory estoppel, assuming the jurisdiction accepts that doctrine.

(D) Be obligated to pay $10,000 to Quigley's widow under the doctrine of consideration, assuming Jones obtained some peace of mind as a result of making the promise.

Questions 7–10 are based on the following fact situation:

Rita operated a retail computer store in the State of Washegon. Diane operated a wholesale distribution business (also in Washegon) which specialized in computers and computer monitors, such as the Sony XYZ monitor. Rita telephoned Diane on February 1 and said, "I need a Sony XYZ monitor. Can you get me one?" Diane replied, "Sure, but it will take a month . . ." At that point Rita interrupted Diane to say "I have to go now; an important customer just walked in. You will deliver the monitor in a month for sure?" Diane responded "Yes," and Rita ended the conversation by saying, "I'll be waiting for it. Good-bye."

The next day Diane sent Rita a brief note (with Diane's initials at the bottom) that said, "Per agreement with Rita: one Sony XYZ monitor to be

SAMPLE MULTIPLE CHOICE QUESTIONS

delivered on March 1." Rita received Diane's note on February 4. Rita later sent Diane a letter that stated, "I never agreed to buy a monitor from you. We didn't even agree on a price."

Diane sued Rita; in Diane's complaint all of the foregoing facts were alleged.

Consider the following possible facts:

I. Rita sent her letter to Diane on February 16.

II. The wholesale price for the Sony XYZ monitor was $7,500.

III. The wholesale price for the Sony XYZ monitor was $4,000.

7. Which of those possible facts would be helpful to Diane in countering Rita's statute of frauds argument?

(A) I only.

(B) II only.

(C) I and III.

(D) III.

8. Was a contract formed?

(A) No, because Rita never promised to pay for the monitor.

(B) No, because Diane and Rita did not manifest mutual assent to the sale of the monitor.

(C) No, because Diane and Rita did not agree on a specific price.

(D) Yes, because the contract is definite enough to enforce.

9. Assume Diane's complaint also alleges (1) that XYZ monitors typically sold at wholesale for $6,500 and (2) that Rita sent her letter to Diane on February 4, the same day Rita received Diane's note. In *Diane v. Rita,* should the court grant Rita's motion to dismiss (the equivalent of a demurrer)?

(A) No, because Diane should have an opportunity to take Rita's deposition.

(B) No, because the complaint does not show that the contract is within the statute of frauds.

(C) Yes, because the complaint shows the contract is within the statute of frauds.

(D) Yes, because Rita objected to the contents of Diane's note.

10. Assume that a contract was formed, that Rita did not send any letter to Diane, that Diane failed to deliver the XYZ monitor, that the monitor's reasonable wholesale value was $6,500, that Rita sued Diane, instead of Diane suing Rita, and that Diane has asserted the statute of frauds defense. Consider the following statements:

SAMPLE MULTIPLE CHOICE QUESTIONS

I. Rita is the "party to be charged" for purposes of the statute of frauds.

II. The contract is enforceable because there is an adequate memorandum signed by "the party to be charged."

III. The contract is enforceable because there is a confirming memorandum that satisfies the statute of frauds as against the recipient of the memorandum.

Which of those statements are true?

(A) I only.

(B) I and III.

(C) II only.

(D) III only.

Questions 11 and 12 are based on the following fact situation:

Sally orally contracted to sell her home (consisting of a two story house and the surrounding quarter acre of land in the State of Arivada) to Bert. Sally owned no other real property. Their written agreement provided that "The price for the home is $100,000, which Bert agrees to pay." The written agreement described the home as "Sally's home, 4029 Smithson Street," but said nothing about the $45,000 mortgage that was on the home. During oral negotiations before the written agreement was signed, Sally and Bert had agreed that Bert could pay Sally $55,000 cash (in the form of a cashier's check) and assume the $45,000 mortgage; as they signed the written agreement they remarked to each other that the $55,000 cashier's check Bert was supposed to obtain for Sally would be the largest check either of them had ever seen. (It was much easier for Bert to come up with $55,000 cash rather than $100,000 cash, so Bert preferred to pay $55,000 cash and assume the mortgage rather than paying $100,000 cash. Of course, if the deal were for payment of $100,000 cash, Sally would have to use $45,000 of the cash to pay off the mortgage, so she could deliver title to her home to Bert unencumbered by the mortgage. Sally would have preferred an all cash deal so she could pay off the mortgage. If Bert assumes the mortgage, Sally will still be liable on the mortgage debt if Bert does not make the payments, so she is safer if the mortgage debt is paid off.)

11. Is Bert's promise to make the mortgage payments unenforceable under the suretyship section of the statute of frauds? Consider the following responses to that question:

I. Yes, because there is no writing signed by Bert that evidences the promise.

II. Yes, because there is no writing signed by both parties that evidences the promise.

III. No, because the promise was made to Sally.

SAMPLE MULTIPLE CHOICE QUESTIONS

IV. No, because Bert is not a surety for Sally.

Which of those responses is correct?

(A) I only.

(B) II only.

(C) III and IV.

(D) IV only.

12. If Bert refuses to purchase Sally's home, and Sally then sues Bert, alleging that he was obligated to pay the $100,000 price for the home by giving her a $55,000 cashier's check and assuming the $45,000 mortgage, Bert's best argument in defense will be:

(A) The alleged agreement is unenforceable because the description of the home in the written agreement does not include a city or state.

(B) The alleged promise to pay part of the price by assuming the mortgage is an essential term of the alleged agreement.

(C) The alleged agreement for him to assume the mortgage cannot be proved because of the parol evidence rule.

(D) The alleged agreement is too indefinite to enforce.

Questions 13–16 are based on the following fact situation:

Morton Manufacturing contracted in writing to sell 250 "400 day, key-wound anniversary clocks" to Store for $12,500. Delivery was due June 1. The written agreement provided that "Morton Manufacturing must provide one sample clock for Store to inspect on or before May 1." (That was so Store could decide how it wanted to advertise and display the clocks.) That is, Morton did not have to "deliver" the clocks then, but it did have to allow Store to photograph and examine a model by that date.

On April 1, Morton wrote Store to say that Morton was having difficulty obtaining parts to make all 250 of the clocks and to ask if the contract could be reduced to 200 clocks for $10,000. Store replied by phone on April 5 that the change was acceptable. The next day Store telephoned Morton to ask that the price for the 200 clocks be decreased to $9,000; the Store representative truthfully pointed out that other retail stores had recently reduced their prices on similar clocks and that Store therefore could not sell the clocks for as much as they had expected. The authorized Morton representative agreed on the phone to the price reduction.

On May 1, Morton did not provide the sample clock because the Morton employee responsible for providing it thought it was supposed to be provided on May 2. When the Morton employee showed up at Store's offices on May 2, he was unceremoniously told to get out and the President of Store told the Morton employee to pass on the word to Morton's management that, "as result of this late and sloppy practice" Store would not buy any of the clocks.

SAMPLE MULTIPLE CHOICE QUESTIONS

On May 5, after cooling off a bit, Store's President wrote to Morton and reaffirmed Store's commitment to purchase "250 clocks for $12,500, as specified in our contract." When the General Manager of Morton got the letter, she first checked to see if it was still possible for Morton to purchase the parts for 250 clocks (instead of 200) and to manufacture and deliver them on time. She was told that Morton could make the 250 clocks, but that it would need to start immediately making the additional 50 units to have them finished by June 1. After debating the issue, she finally concluded that Morton was only obligated to deliver 200 clocks. Accordingly, she instructed her manufacturing facility not to make the additional clocks, and only tendered 200 on June 1. Store rejected the delivery of 200 clocks, insisting on delivery of all 250.

All of these events took place in State which allows neither admissions nor reliance to satisfy the statute of frauds.

13. The court will most likely construe the requirement of delivery of a sample clock on May 1 as:

(A) A promise.

(B) An express condition.

(C) A promise and an express condition.

(D) Neither a promise nor an express condition.

14. The delay in delivery of the sample clock will probably:

(A) Prevent Morton from enforcing the contract against Store.

(B) Entitle Store to recover any damages caused by the delay.

(C) Prevent Morton from enforcing the contract against Store and entitle Store to recover any damages caused by the delay.

(D) Neither prevent Morton from enforcing the contract against Store nor entitle Store to recover any damages resulting from the delay.

15. As of May 3, what is the best characterization of the parties?

(A) Morton was entitled to declare the contract canceled and cease its performance.

(B) Both Morton and Store were entitled to declare the contract canceled and cease their performance.

(C) Store was entitled to declare the contract canceled and cease its performance.

(D) Neither Morton nor Store were entitled to declare the contract canceled and cease their performance.

16. As of June 1, what is the best characterization of the parties?

(A) Morton has materially breached by tendering only 200 clocks.

(B) Morton has immaterially breached by tendering 200 clocks.

(C) Store has materially breached by refusing to accept and pay for 200 clocks.

(D) Store has immaterially breached by refusing to accept and pay for 200 clocks.

Question 17

On April 1, Sy, the owner of a very well-known art gallery, had the following telephone conversation with Bob, one of his most valued customers:

S: Bob, I just procured "The Blue City" by Chagall. I know it would go nicely with your collection and I will let you have it for $25,000.

B: I'm tempted, but I couldn't begin thinking about making such a purchase until my CD matures at the end of July.

S: For you, my friend, I will hold my offer open until August 10.

The best description of Bob's right to purchase the Chagall is:

(A) Bob has an irrevocable right to purchase the Chagall for $25,000 until August 10.

(B) Bob has a power to purchase the Chagall for $25,000 until June 30, but that power is revocable by Sy.

(C) Bob has an irrevocable right to purchase the Chagall for $25,000 until June 30.

(D) Bob has only a power to purchase the Chagall for $25,000 until August 10, and that power is revocable by Sy.

Questions 18 and 19 are based on the following fact situation:

Betty Buyer owned Bower Records, a retail record store in Sacramento. On behalf of Bower, Betty ordered 150 copies of the latest CD single hit from Sorrygram Records, Luciano Pavarotti's "Boys Just Want To Have Fun," at the price listed in Sorrygram's catalogue, $1/record. A few days later, Bower received a shipment from Sorrygram which also contained the following cover letter:

SORRYGRAM RECORDS, INC.

Los Angeles, California

Ms. Betty Buyer

Bower Records

Sacramento, Calif.

Dear Betty:

Due to unprecedented demand, we are presently sold out of the CD single, "Boys Just Want To Have Fun," and thus we can neither accept nor fill your latest order. However, because you are such a valued customer, we

SAMPLE MULTIPLE CHOICE QUESTIONS

have sent instead 150 CD copies of Pavarotti's new album, "Luciano Rides the New Wave," which has "Boys Just Want To Have Fun" on the front side. As you know, we usually charge retailers $2.50 for our CD albums, but because of the inconvenience we have already caused you, we will only charge you our special accommodation price of $1.25/album and consider the matter closed.

Sincerely,

/s/Sam Seller

Sorrygram Records

As indicated in the letter, Sorrygram shipped 150 CD albums to Bower instead of the requested single CDs.

Variation One

18. The best description of the legal relationship between Bower and Sorrygram is:

(A) They have a contract for 150 "Boys Just Want To Have Fun" single CDs at $1/record, which has been breached by Sorrygram.

(B) They have no contract.

(C) If Sorrygram had reasonable grounds to believe that shipment of the albums instead of the CD singles would be acceptable by Bower with the indicated money allowance, they have a contract for 150 "Pavarotti Rides the New Wave" CD albums at $1.25/album.

(D) They have a contract for 150 "Boys Just Want To Have Fun" CD singles at $1/record, but Betty has the right to accept the CD albums as a substituted performance.

Variation Two

Betty considered keeping the CD albums, but in good faith determined that her tiny store did not have sufficient shelf space at the time to display them. Accordingly, she called Seller and told him she did not want the shipment. The next day, Betty received the following Mailgram:

Mrs. Betty Buyer

Bower Records

Sacramento, Calif.

Dear Betty:

Sorry to hear you won't be able to take the albums. Please send them back to us within the next week or so, and we will credit any shipping cots you incur to your next order from us.

/s/ Sam Seller

19. The best description of Bower Records's duties with respect to the return of the albums is:

SAMPLE MULTIPLE CHOICE QUESTIONS

(A) So long as Bower stores the albums with reasonable care, Bower is under no duty to send the albums back to Sorrygram and can charge Sorrygram a fee for storing the records until Sorrygram arranges to pick up the records.

(B) So long as Bower stores the albums with reasonable care, Bower is under no duty to send the albums back to Sorrygram, but cannot charge Sorrygram a fee for storing the albums.

(C) Bower is under a duty to send the albums back to Sorrygram, but may do so freight collect.

(D) Bower is under a duty to send the albums back to Sorrygram, but cannot do so freight collect. Rather, Bower is bound by the terms of Seller's letter and must take the shipping costs as a credit against Sorrygram's next shipment.

Questions 20–22 are based on the following fact situation:

On June 1, Owner orally offered to pay Andy $1,000 if Andy would repair the roof at Owner's beach cottage. Andy requested time to think it over. Owner told Andy that he would give Andy a couple of days to think about it, but that he had to know Andy's decision no later than June 3.

On June 3, Owner, impatient at waiting for word from Andy, offered Brenda $1,000 if Brenda would promise to repair the roof at the cottage. Brenda stated that she would take her equipment to the cottage tomorrow and, if the job looked worth it, she would start right in. Brenda also stated that if it appeared not to be worth it, she would contact Owner and give an estimate of her price. Owner consented to such an arrangement.

When Brenda arrived at the cottage on June 4, she saw Andy working on the roof. Andy truthfully explained to her that he decided to accept the job, and that he had begun working on the project on the afternoon of June 3, and that he had dispatched a letter to Owner that at about 9:30 p.m. the previous night stating he would undertake the work.

20. If Owner's offer to Andy is considered an offer looking towards a unilateral contract, which of the following is true?

(A) Andy had to notify Owner of his acceptance before he started work on the roof, or else his acceptance was ineffective.

(B) Andy's dispatch of the letter on June 3, properly addressed to Owner, was a valid acceptance of Owner's offer.

(C) Andy may cease, without breach, if he has started to perform; but Owner must hold his offer open for a reasonable period of time.

(D) Andy may not withdraw without breach once he has started to perform because by starting to work on the roof, Andy has made an implied promise to finish the work.

SAMPLE MULTIPLE CHOICE QUESTIONS

21. If Owner's offer to Andy is considered an offer looking towards a bilateral contract, which of the following is true?

(A) A contract was formed when Andy commenced work on the roof.

(B) A contract was formed when Andy dispatched the letter of acceptance, properly addressed, on June 3.

(C) A contract would be formed when Andy's letter is received by the Owner.

(D) They have no contract.

22. If Owner's offer to Brenda is considered an offer looking towards a bilateral contract, which of the following is true?

(A) A contract would be formed when Brenda communicated her promise of acceptance to Owner.

(B) Brenda could no longer effectively accept the offer because the offer was effectively revoked when Brenda saw Andy repairing the cottage and heard of Andy's acceptance.

(C) Brenda can no longer validly accept the offer because, as a matter of law, there cannot be a valid contract between Brenda and Owner if there is a prior valid contract for repair of the same cottage roof between Owner and Andy.

(D) The consideration for Owner's promise to pay Brenda $1,000 would be Brenda's actual performance of the roof repair in a satisfactory manner.

Questions 23–25 are based on the following fact situation:

Writer agreed to write a book on a then-topical subject for Publisher within twelve months. Writer was to receive $1 per page, but if he completed the book in six months, he would receive a bonus of an additional $1 per page. However, if Writer drank alcoholic beverages while under the contract, Writer would get only 50 cents per page, regardless of when the book was completed, but assuming it was completed. After four months, Writer telephoned Publisher and demanded $3 per page if he should meet the six month deadline. When asked why, the writer stated that he just felt he was worth it. Publisher agreed to such change and Writer continued working as before.

23. If Writer meets the six month deadline:

(A) Publisher owes Writer $3 per page.

(B) Publisher owes Writer $2 per page.

(C) A new modified contract has been formed for $3 per page, the old contract having been partially rescinded by mutual agreement.

(D) Writer has relied upon the new promise of Publisher by meeting the deadline and Publisher is, therefore, estopped from revoking it.

SAMPLE MULTIPLE CHOICE QUESTIONS

24. Writer does not meet the twelve month deadline and does not expect to finish in less than an additional twelve months. Which of the following best describes the consequence of this fact?

(A) Publisher must accept the book when it is completed, but is entitled to damages resulting from the breach.

(B) Publisher may waive the deadline, in which event Publisher has waived his right to damages resulting from the breach.

(C) Writer is excused from meeting the deadline if the reason he is late in producing the material is unexpected difficulty in learning how to operate his new word processor.

(D) Publisher may agree to an extension, receive the book, and still hold the Writer liable in breach of contract.

25. If Writer completed the book in six months, but drinks during the contract period, which of the following best describes the situation?

(A) Writer is entitled to receive only 50 cents per page.

(B) Writer is entitled to receive $2 per page if Publisher knew of his drinking while it was going on, but said nothing at the time.

(C) Writer is entitled to recover $2 per page if he could show that he only drank after Publisher had told him that the "no drinking" provision was designed solely to insure that Writer finished the book within a year and that, otherwise, it did not matter to Publisher whether or not Writer drank.

(D) Publisher may not enforce the no drinking condition as such a clause violates public policy.

Questions 26–28 are based on the following fact situation:

Hotel advertised in the paper that it would rent rooms to delegates to the Republican Convention for $20 a night, a drastically reduced rate, for the seven day period the convention is in progress. Delegate read such ad and wrote for a room for seven days, mentioning the ad. As specified in the ad, Delegate enclosed a non-refundable $50 deposit. Hotel answered that a room was reserved for the time requested but stating no purpose for which room was reserved.

26. If the Hotel is destroyed by fire just before the day of the convention:

(A) Delegate, assuming she comes to the convention, is entitled to sue the Hotel for the price difference between their rate and the rate she is forced to pay at another hotel, regardless of who or what is responsible for the fire.

(B) Hotel will escape liability to Delegate because performance is impossible, regardless of who or what is responsible for the fire.

SAMPLE MULTIPLE CHOICE QUESTIONS

(C) Delegate is entitled to damages from Hotel if Hotel's own carelessness caused the fire.

(D) The risk of the Hotel burning is upon Hotel, not Delegate, because Hotel can safeguard itself by insurance and is in control of the premises.

27. If Delegate becomes very ill the day before and cannot attend the convention, she is entitled to:

(A) Recover the $50 deposit from Hotel, subject to an offset for any loss suffered by Hotel due to its inability to rent the room under a frustration of purpose/restitution theory.

(B) Recover the $50 deposit from Hotel with no offset for any loss suffered by Hotel in failing to rent the room under a frustration of purpose/restitution theory.

(C) Recover nothing from Hotel, because Delegate can establish the elements of neither impossibility nor frustration of purpose.

(D) Recover the $50 deposit from Hotel, subject to a deduction for any loss suffered by Hotel due to its inability to rent the room, under temporary impossibility/restitution theory.

28. If the Republican Convention is moved suddenly to another city, which is the most accurate description?

(A) Delegate is entitled to cancel and recover the $50 deposit under an impossibility/restitution theory.

(B) Delegate will still be liable for the week's room rate, because the parol evidence rule will not permit Delegate to introduce the special propose of the contract with the Hotel.

(C) Delegate cannot cancel or recover her deposit because Hotel did not expressly restrict use of the room to any particular purpose.

(D) Delegate is entitled to cancel and recover the $50 from the Hotel under a frustration of purpose/restitution theory.

Questions 29–31 are based on the following fact situation:

Dealer, a retailer of automobiles, advertised that it will provide a "free" one-year insurance policy protecting the purchaser of one of its cars from loss due to theft. Dealer thereafter contracts with Insurance Company for a "blanket coverage policy" wherein Insurance Company promised to provide coverage on any car sold by Dealer, so long as Dealer paid the monthly premium. Later, a car is sold by Dealer to Buyer, who receives a written statement from both Dealer and Insurance Company explaining one-year "free" coverage. Buyer did not procure insurance on her car.

29. In the contract between Dealer and Insurance Company, what is the best categorization of Buyer under the Restatement 2d:

(A) A donee-like intended beneficiary.

SAMPLE MULTIPLE CHOICE QUESTIONS

(B) A creditor-like intended beneficiary.

(C) An incidental beneficiary.

(D) Not a third party beneficiary at all because Buyer's identity was unknown at the time of contract formation.

30. If Buyer's car is stolen within the year, and both Dealer and Insurance Company refuse to pay Buyer for her loss, which is the most accurate statement?

(A) Buyer is only entitled to recover from Insurance Company for breach of the Dealer/Insurance Co. contract.

(B) Buyer is only entitled to recover from Dealer for breach of the Dealer/Insurance Co. contract.

(C) Buyer is entitled to recover from either Dealer or Insurance Company for breach of the Dealer/Insurance Co. contract.

(D) Only Dealer can bring suit against the Insurance Company for breach of the Dealer/Insurance Co. contract.

31. Dealer cancels the insurance policy six months after Buyer purchases the car, and stops paying the premiums, all without telling Buyer. The car is stolen one month later, and once again, neither Dealer nor Insurance Company pays Buyer for her car. Which of the following best describes Buyer's rights?

I. Buyer may sue Dealer for breach of the Dealer/Insurance Co. contract.

II. Buyer may sue Insurance Co. for breach of the Dealer/Insurance Co. contract.

III. Buyer may sue Dealer for breach of warranty that follows a third party beneficiary contract.

(A) I only.

(B) II only.

(C) I and II.

(D) I, II, and III.

Questions 32–35 are based on the following fact situation:

Alexandra has a bilateral contract with Owen to paint Owen's house this year for $500. Alexandra assigns for value the contract to Roger, a competent painter. Alexandra thereafter informs Owen that she has "assigned the contract" to Roger because she (Alexandra) is moving out of the state and, therefore, must divest herself of rights and obligations under the painting contract.

32. Which is the most accurate statement?

SAMPLE MULTIPLE CHOICE QUESTIONS

(A) Owen must accept if Roger tenders performance, but Owen can hold either Alexandra or Roger liable for any defects in Roger's performance.

(B) Owen is entitled to refuse to accept the tender of performance by Roger, because Alexandra could not have assigned her rights under this contract.

(C) Owen is entitled to refuse to accept the tender of performance by Roger because there can be no valid delegation of a personal service contract.

(D) If Owen allows Roger to perform, and Roger performs acceptably well, such performance terminates Alexandra's duty.

33. Alexandra and Owen, after the assignment but before performance, agree that the house should not be painted by Roger because they just found out Roger is an anarchist. Which of the following best describes Roger's rights?

(A) Roger's rights and duties are extinguished.

(B) Roger may sue either Alexandra or Owen, or both, if Owen does not permit him to paint the house due to the subsequent "anarchist" agreement by Alexandra and Owen.

(C) Roger may sue only Owen if Owen does not permit him to paint the house due to the subsequent "anarchist" agreement by Alexandra and Owen.

(D) Roger may sue only Alexandra if Owen does not permit him to paint the house due to the subsequent "anarchist" agreement by Alexandra and Owen.

34. Assume Roger told Owen he "was taking over the contract" from Alexandra shortly after Alexandra "assigned" him the contract. If Roger fails to paint Owen's house after the assignment, Owen may sue:

(A) Alexandra only.

(B) Roger only.

(C) Either Alexandra or Roger, or both.

(D) Either Alexandra or Roger, but not both.

35. Roger paints Owen's house. Owen:

(A) Can discharge by performance his duties under the Owen/Alexandra contract by paying either Alexandra or Roger.

(B) Is only liable for the reasonable value of Roger's performance, if that is less than the contract price.

(C) Must pay Roger the contract price to discharge by performance his duties under the Owen/Alexandra contract.

(D) Must pay Alexandra the contract price to discharge by performance his duties under the Owen/Alexandra contract.

Questions 36–39 are based on the following fact situation:

Bill and Emily entered into a contract whereby Bill promised to build an apartment building for Emily for $100,000, with progress payments of $9,000 a month. Honest differences arose after five months over whether landscaping was extra or within the contract terms. Emily suggested that the issue be resolved by her promising to pay Bill an additional $5,000 upon Bill's current promise to do, and eventual completion of, the landscaping as set forth in the plans. Bill agreed.

36. Assume that Bill does the landscaping. If Emily can prove that landscaping was within the terms of the original contract:

(A) She need not pay the extra $5,000 for her promise to do so is unenforceable.

(B) She must pay Bill the extra $5,000 because she entered into a valid accord with Bill.

(C) She must pay Bill the extra $5,000 because she entered into a valid novation with Bill.

(D) She must pay Bill the extra $5,000 because she entered into a valid substituted performance agreement with Bill.

37. Assume that Bill does not do the landscaping. If Emily can prove that landscaping was, in fact, within the terms of the original contract, which is the most accurate statement?

(A) She may recover only for breach of the original contract.

(B) She can recover only for breach of Bill's second promise.

(C) She can recover for Bill's breach of the original promise or for Bill's breach of the second promise.

(D) She can withhold payment due under both agreements until Bill honors his second promise.

38. Emily withholds the seventh progress payment because of an honest dispute as to the amount of progress Bill has made at the end of the seventh month. Which of the following best describes Bill's rights?

(A) Bill may suspend performance, but he will be liable for breach of contract if Emily is ultimately found to be correct.

(B) Bill must continue performance until the honest dispute is resolved, but is entitled to recover damages if he is ultimately found to be correct.

(C) Bill is discharged from any further obligation to build by Emily's unilateral decision to withhold payment.

SAMPLE MULTIPLE CHOICE QUESTIONS

(D) Bill may consider himself discharged from any further obligation to build, in which event his recovery, if he is ultimately found to be correct, is the amount due under the contract at the time of suspension of work.

39. Emily now asserts that Bill also orally and separately agreed that the contract price would also include a sidewalk surrounding the structure after the structure was completed. Which of the following scenarios would most likely allow Emily to enforce such an agreement.

(A) The oral agreement was made just before they signed their written construction contract.

(B) The oral agreement was made just after the written contract was signed. Emily asserts that she had just forgotten about asking Bill about it during contract negotiations, and when she remembered (about 30 minutes after the contract was signed), Bill said no problem—I'll put it in for the same price.

(C) The oral agreement was made just after the written contract was signed, as part of a conversation in which Emily agreed to extend the completion date given that pouring and hardening of the sidewalk would take time.

(D) The oral agreement was made just before the written contract was signed as part of a conversation in which she promised not to hold Bill to the completion date in the written contact, given the amount of time it would take to make the sidewalk.

Question 40

On May 26, Jones says to Smith, "I will sell you my Chevy for $1,500 or my Dodge for $1,700. Just let me know which one by next Friday, June 1." Smith replies, "I will definitely buy one of your cars. I'll let you know which one before June 1." Which is the most accurate statement?

(A) There is no contract as of May 26, because Smith cannot accept until he designates which car he will buy; otherwise there would be a lack of mutuality.

(B) There is a contract as of May 26, with Jones guaranteeing, in return for Smith's promise to buy that Smith has a choice that can be made as late as June 1.

(C) There is no contract as of May 26, because it would be unfair to require Jones to have both cars encumbered until Smith designates which car he will buy.

(D) Smith's reply is only a counter-offer; Jones now must decide whether to accept this counter-offer, in which case he must encumber both cars until Smith decides which car he wants.

SAMPLE MULTIPLE CHOICE QUESTIONS

Question 41

Martha, in Maine, wrote to Daisy, her daughter who lived in Missouri, saying, "I am in bad shape. Promise me you will come and take care of me for the rest of my life and you can have my home when I'm gone. Write me your plans at once, because if you can't come I want to get someone else."

This letter was posted on June 1 and received by Daisy on June 4. On the morning of June 5, Daisy sent a letter to Martha saying, "Don't worry. You can depend on me. I am coming right away." On June 6, Martha became suddenly and violently insane. On June 7, Daisy resigned her job and boarded a train bound for Martha's home.

When Martha received Daisy's letter on June 8, she tore it up, and telegraphed Daisy, "Stay away from me. You are trying to hex me." Daisy was then en route, and did not receive this message. When Daisy arrived at Martha's home on June 11, Martha refused to receive her, and died the next day, June 12.

No provision was made for Daisy in Martha's will, which left everything to Martha's sister in San Diego. Daisy demanded that Martha's executor convey the home to her. On his refusal, Daisy brings suit for breach of contract by Martha. Which of the following arguments best supports Daisy's position?

(A) Daisy reasonably and detrimentally relied on Martha's promise at a time when she did not know Martha had become insane.

(B) Since Martha was insane at the time she attempted to revoke the offer, the revocation is without legal effect, and the original offer stands.

(C) Daisy gave the promise requested, and thereby entered a bilateral contract that was not lacking in mutuality or legal efficacy.

(D) A revocation is effective only on receipt, and here Martha's revocation was not received by Daisy, since she was en route to Maine as her mother had requested.

Question 42

The rule that the death of the offeror terminates the offeree's power of acceptance is:

(A) Consistent with the objective theory of contracts, but inconsistent with the subjective theory.

(B) Consistent with the subjective theory of contracts, but inconsistent with the objective theory.

(C) Equally consistent with both the objective and subjective theories of contracts.

(D) Equally inconsistent with both the objective and subjective theories of contracts.

SAMPLE MULTIPLE CHOICE QUESTIONS

Questions 43–44 are based on the following fact situation:

Bernice, the owner of an advertising agency, had the following conversation with Sheila, the owner of a 1929 Model T Ford with the license No. PIK/FAIR, on October 1:

B: You are positive that this was the car in which Douglas Fairbanks proposed to Mary Pickford?

S: Yes, it is. I bought the car at an auction from Christie's Auction House last month, and I have a letter from Christie's authenticating the car. I wouldn't ask $150,000 for it otherwise.

B: That's important to me, because we have an advertising campaign for Le Pew perfume that revolves around re-living the elegant lifestyles of Fairbanks and Pickford. We plan to feature the car as authentic in our T.V. ads, and to send the car around the country to shopping malls and the like to increase the volume of our department store sales. However, Le Pew is willing to go forward with our agency only if we are able to secure the authentic car.

S: I understand. However, I would not have bought it from Christie's if I wasn't sure it was the right car.

B: Well, O.K., I'll take it. Shall we say delivery of the car on November 1?

S: That will be fine.

Variation One

The next day, Sheila telephoned Bernice and they had the following conversation:

S: When we spoke yesterday we neglected to set any payment terms. Is it acceptable if we agree that you will pay $15,000 down by October 15, and the remainder on delivery?

B: That will be no problem at all.

On October 15, Sheila received a check from Bernice's agency for $15,000, which had the following phrase typed on the check's "Memo" line: "Dn. Pymt. for PIK/FAIR Model T." Sheila immediately deposited the check in her account.

On November 1, Bernice came to Sheila's house with a cashier's check in the amount of $135,000. However, Sheila appeared at the door and said she had changed her mind and no longer wished to sell the car. She offered Bernice $15,000 in cash and said: "We never really had a deal anyway. Our agreement was never reduced to writing."

43. In a suit by Bernice against Sheila for breach, which of the following accurately describes how the court should rule on Sheila's statute of frauds defense?

SAMPLE MULTIPLE CHOICE QUESTIONS

I.   The defense should succeed because of the part performance exception to the statute of frauds.

II. The defense should fail because of the part performance exception to the statute of frauds.

III. The defense should fail because the notation on the "Memo" line of the $15,000 check is sufficient to satisfy the UCC's statute of frauds, assuming the check was signed by Bernice.

IV. The defense should succeed because no evidence of the October 1 conversation, or of the $15,000 check, will be admissible under the parol evidence rule.

(A) I only.

(B) II only.

(C) I and IV.

(D) II and III.

Variation Two

On November 1, Sheila tendered the keys and certificate of title to Bernice, and Bernice gave Sheila a check for $150,000. However, on December 1, the man who furnished the Model T to Christie's confessed that he had perpetrated a fraud, and that the Model T with the PIK/FAIR license plates that he had auctioned through Christie's was not the authentic car in which Douglas Fairbanks had proposed to Mary Pickford. The authentic car was, in fact, owned by another antique car collector, Reginald Jackson. Subsequent investigation revealed that neither Christie's nor Sheila nor Bernice had any idea that the PIK/FAIR Model T was not authentic.

44. Which of the following warranties, if any, has Sheila breached?

I. Express Warranty.

II. Warranty of Merchantability

(A) I and II.

(B) I only.

(C) II only.

(D) Sheila has breached neither of the listed warranties.

Question 45 is based on the following fact situation:

Bruce Buyer owned a large electronics store and placed an order for 75 Sony XB–100 Cassette Decks, which were timely delivered by Sony. Upon inspecting the decks the next day, Bruce determined that none of the tape counters worked and thus told Sony he was rejecting the shipment.

45. The best description of the parties' rights and duties is:

SAMPLE MULTIPLE CHOICE QUESTIONS

I. Sony has a right to cure so long as the time for performance under the contract has not passed, acted in good faith and it seasonably notifies Bruce of its intention to do so.

II. Sony has a right to cure even if it only establishes that it had reasonable grounds to believe that the cassette decks were acceptable when shipped and seasonably notifies Bruce of its intention to do so.

III. Sony has no right to cure if the time for performance under the contract has passed.

IV. Sony has a right to cure even if the time for performance under the contract has passed, but only if it can establish that it reasonably believed the decks were acceptable when shipped, seasonably notifies Bruce of its intention to do so, acted in good faith and the delay in getting new decks to Bruce does not cause him any commercial hardship.

(A) I only.

(B) I and III.

(C) I and IV.

(D) III only.

Question 46 is based on the following fact situation:

Sid Seller owns a wine shop in Beverly Hills. Buford Buyer lives in San Francisco and regularly purchases wines from Sid.

In 1982, Sid and Buford entered into a "wine futures" contract for 1 case of 1982 Chateau Margaux, a very popular wine. Under this agreement, Buford committed to purchase the wine at a fixed price and gained the right to obtain possession of the wine in the summer of 1986, shortly after its arrival in the United States. Under their contract, Buford had to leave a $200 deposit on placing the order (which he did), and was obligated to pay the remaining $400 when the wine was tendered to him.

On April 1, 1984, the *LA. Times's* Business Section featured an article entitled, "San Francisco Mogul Hits the Skids—Buford Buyer in Serious Financial Trouble," which set forth a long list of Buford's business troubles.

Sid immediately sent Buford a telegram stating, "Saw article in *LA. Times*. Please advise whether you are willing and able to pay for the Ch. Margaux when it arrives." Buford timely dispatched the following reply:

April 5, 1984

Sid Seller

Beverly Hills, Ca.

LA. Times article in error. I am doing fine. I will be able to pay the $400 in 1986.

/s/Buford

SAMPLE MULTIPLE CHOICE QUESTIONS

Buford did not communicate further with Sid.

46. If Sid sued Buford for anticipatory repudiation on May 15, 1984, Sid should:

(A) **Lose**, because Buford responded to Sid's request for assurances within a commercially reasonable time.

(B) **Lose**, if Buford can establish that the L.A. Times article was inaccurate and that he was very well off financially in April.

(C) **Lose**, because Buford has expressed no definite and unequivocal refusal to perform as is required before an anticipatory breach action can successfully be brought under the UCC.

(D) **Prevail**, because Buford did not provide sufficient reasonable assurances in his April 5, 1984, telegram.

ANSWERS TO SAMPLE MULTIPLE CHOICE QUESTIONS

Answer to Question 1.

(D) is the correct answer.

Under the "mailbox rule," an acceptance is generally valid upon dispatch so long as it is properly addressed and acceptance by mail is an authorized method of acceptance. However, one exception to this principle is that when an offeree sends an acceptance which is followed by a rejection, it is the **rejection** that is effective so long as the rejection arrives first **and the offeror changes position in reliance on the rejection** [Text § 4–129]. Here, Allan's 1/20 letter was an effective acceptance. However, his 1/20 (express mail) rejection overtook it in the mail. Hence, if Priscilla had relied on the rejection, e.g., by taking another job during the same time period she had offered to work for Allan, the rejection would have become the operative response from the offeree. However, no reliance is shown on these facts, and thus the correct choice is D. A and B are incorrect because the express mail rejection was received first and takes precedence over the 1/20 regular mail acceptance. Thus, there is no contract on which Priscilla can successfully sue. C is incorrect because it is an incorrect statement of the substantive law under the mailbox rule.

Answer to Question 2.

(A) is the correct answer.

Under the mailbox rule, when a rejection is followed by an acceptance, the first to arrive becomes the operative response [Text § 4–128]. Brenda's 1/24 letter is a counter-offer, which, of course, also serves as a rejection. Her 1/25 letter (the one sent by express mail) is an acceptance. The 1/24 letter arrived first, so it is the operative document. Thus, A is the only correct choice. B is incorrect for it misstates the substantive rule set forth above. C and D are incorrect because for Priscilla to prevail, Brenda's acceptance letter would have had to arrive before her counter-offer/rejection letter, under the mailbox rule, which it did not.

Answer to Question 3.

(C) is the correct answer.

As noted above in the Answer to Question No. 2, in cases where an offeree first sends a rejection and follows that with an acceptance, the first

ANSWERS TO SAMPLE MULTIPLE CHOICE QUESTIONS

to arrive is operative [Text § 4–128]. Here, the 1/25 acceptance arrived first, hence the contract was made at that point. Once an offer has been effectively accepted, it can no longer be rejected, and thus Priscilla's receipt of the 1/25 counter-offer/rejection has no effect. A and B are thus incorrect, because for Priscilla to lose, Brenda's counter-offer/rejection must have been the operative document. However, as noted above, since the counter-offer arrived after the acceptance, the acceptance took precedence. D is incorrect because it misstates the substantive law under the mailbox rule.

Answer to question 4.

(B) is the correct answer.

This is an implied-in-law contract, or quasi-contract. That is, it is a situation in which it would be unjust for a party to receive benefits from another without paying for such benefits. The fact that Dr. Fiscus's efforts were ultimately unsuccessful in saving Quigley's life is irrelevant to the question of whether Quigley's estate is responsible in restitution for Dr. Fiscus's services [Text §§ 1–20; 31–31]. A is not correct for two reasons. Jones cannot be liable in contract to Dr. Fiscus because he never entered into a contract with Dr. Fiscus. He cannot be liable in restitution for quasi-contract, because Dr. Fiscus never performed any services that benefitted him (Jones). C is incorrect because A is incorrect. D is incorrect because B is correct.

Answer to Question 5.

(D) is the correct answer.

The Restatement 2d has relaxed the common law rules relating to the adequacy of past consideration to be effective consideration. Under § 86, a promise based on past consideration will be enforceable to the extent necessary to avoid injustice unless: (a) **the promisee intended the benefit received by the promisor as a gift,** or (b) the value of the promise is disproportionate to the benefits received. [Text § 7–33] Here, the students intended to make a gift of the car wash and wax to their professor, thus, Professor Jones's promise to pay them for it is unenforceable. Thus, A is incorrect for it is based on Jones's unenforceable promise. B is incorrect for it is based on the fair market value or quasi-contractual value of the student's efforts. However, because Jones was not unconscious or otherwise unavailable to bargain with the students before they began work on his car, and because there was no emergency that called for immediate car washing action by the students, this is not a quasi-contract situation [Text § 1–20]. C is incorrect because it inaccurately states the Restatement's rules regarding past consideration.

ANSWERS TO SAMPLE MULTIPLE CHOICE QUESTIONS

Answer to Question 6.

(A) is the correct answer.

Jones's promise to Quigley's widow is only a gift promise and thus unenforceable. B is incorrect because, although it accurately states one part of the rule of Restatement 2d § 86 (*see* the Answer to Question 5, above), § 86 cannot be used to enforce Jones's promise since Quigley's widow provided no benefit to Jones as is required under that provision [Text § 7–33]. C is incorrect because, on these facts, there is no evidence that Quigley's widow relied on Jones's promise. D is not correct because, even if Jones obtained some peace of mind, that benefit is not "bargained for" as the term is used in the Restatement 2d's formulation of consideration [Text § 7–7; 7–23].

Answer to Question 7.

(C) is the correct answer.

The contract is for the sale of goods, and thus governed by the UCC. The UCC's statute of frauds must be satisfied if the contract is for $500 [Text § 10–35]. Of the three choices, both I and III help Diane in overcoming Rita's assertion of the statute as a defense. Under UCC § 2–201(2), if a merchant buyer does not object within 10 days after the receipt of a record form the seller that, *inter alia,* confirms the transaction, the buyer loses his or her right to assert the Statute as a defense. [Text § 10–46] Under Choice I, Rita's memorandum was untimely, for it was sent 12 days after its receipt, and thus such a fact would be helpful to Diane. Choice III is also helpful to Diane because if a contract was formed, the price for the monitor would be a "reasonable price" under UCC § 2–305, the gap filler on price [Text § 6–17]. It is likely that the price other wholesalers in the area charged for the monitor would become the "reasonable price," and thus the contract, if it existed, would be for the sale of goods for less than $500. As such, the UCC's statute of frauds would not apply to it [Text § 10–35], and that fact is also helpful to Diane. Thus II would not be helpful, because if the monitor typically sold for more than $500, the UCC statute of frauds would apply, and that would be helpful to Rita, not Diane.

Answer to Question 8.

(D) is the correct answer.

This is a fairly close call, but under the relaxed formation rules of the UCC, a contract was formed. Under § 2–204(a), a contract may be made in any manner sufficient to show agreement [Text § 6–11]. Here, Rita gave objective indications that she was willing to be bound to purchase the monitor and Diane gave objective indications that she was willing to sell Rita a monitor. Accordingly, since the parties have agreed as to subject matter (the monitor) and quantity (one) and have indicated an intent to contract, the contract is definite enough to be enforced under the UCC, by

ANSWERS TO SAMPLE MULTIPLE CHOICE QUESTIONS

use of the gap fillers. [Text § 6–16] For these reasons, A and B are incorrect. Similarly, C is also incorrect because under the UCC, when the parties evidence an intent to contract but do not reach agreement in the price, UCC § 2–305 states that the price will be a "reasonable price." [Text § 6–17].

Answer to Question 9.

(A) is the correct answer.

While some courts disagree, the majority rule is that a party seeking to enforce an agreement governed by the UCC has a right to take deposition testimony of the party asserting the defense for purposes of eliciting an "admission" of the elements of a contract by that party, and thereby satisfying the Statute under § 2–201(3)(b) [Text § 10–53]. B is not right, because the contract is within the Statute if the reasonable price for the monitor is $6,500 (see the answer to Question 8, above). C and D are correct statements of law, but the principles set forth in each of those answers is subject to the rule discussed above, namely that a party opposing assertion of the Statute has the right to elicit an admission, under oath, under § 2–201(3)(b).

Answer to Question 10.

(C) is the correct answer.

Choice I is incorrect, because under the statute of frauds, the "party to be charged" is the party who is asserting a statute of frauds defense and claims that his or her promise cannot be enforced, i.e., "charged." Choice III is an incorrect statement of the law. UCC § 2–201(2) states that to be effective, the confirming memorandum must satisfy the statute under § 2–201(1) as against **the sender,** not the recipient [Text § 10–50]. Choice II is true because Diane is the party to be charged and she sent an adequate memorandum [Text § 10–44]. Note that while she did not "sign" the memorandum, her initials are a sufficient "signature" for statute of frauds purposes under § 1–201(37) [Text § 10–43].

Answer to Question 11.

(C) is the correct answer.

A surety is someone who promises a third party to pay the debt of another [Text § 10–27]. To be a surety, the party must only be secondarily liable on the debt, and thus called on to perform his or her promise only if the principal, who is primarily liable, does not pay the obligation [Text § 10–29]. While a suretyship promise, with some exceptions, must be in writing to be enforceable, here Bert is not a surety. He is not secondarily liable on the mortgage, for the facts say that upon assumption of the debt it is he who must make the payments and it is Sally who remains liable only if **he** defaults. Hence, Choice IV is correct. Additionally, on these facts Bert is also not a surety because he did not promise the Bank that he would be secondarily liable for Sally's debt. He only made Sally the

ANSWERS TO SAMPLE MULTIPLE CHOICE QUESTIONS

promise that he would assume the mortgage. Accordingly, Choice III is correct as well. Choices I and II would be correct only if Bert **were** a surety, which he is not.

Answer to Question 12.

(C) is the correct answer.

A modern court will use its interpretive powers to fill in gaps in an agreement, even in contracts not specifically governed by the UCC's gap fillers [Text § 6–23]. Here, given that Sally owned only one piece of property, and that the property was located at 4029 Smithson Street, a court would be able to determine sufficiently the subject matter of the contract, even in the absence of the state and city. Hence A is incorrect. B and D are also incorrect for the same reason. That is, a court would be able to use the custom of the area or the usage of trade, e.g., full payment due at the close of escrow, to interpret the proper payment terms under the contract [Text § 19–13]. C is correct. Recall that a written contract will either be considered totally or partially integrated for purposes of the parol evidence rule [Text § 18–4]. If it is considered totally integrated, then no evidence of any other term can be admitted, which, in this case, means that no evidence of the mortgage assumption could be introduced [Text § 18–4]. If it is partially integrated, evidence of any consistent term can be admitted, but the test for whether a term is consistent is the "might naturally" test for this kind of contract. That is, whether, if the parties really agreed on the term, is it the kind of term they might naturally omit from their final written agreement? [Text § 18–13] A mortgage assumption clause, if it were agreed to, would be considered such an important clause that a court would not conclude that it is the kind of term the parties might naturally have left out of their sales agreement, and thus the parol evidence rule would serve as Bert's best argument.

Answer to Question 13.

(A) is the correct answer.

The language creating the duty to provide the sample clock evidences a promise, not a condition. A condition is created with phrases like "if but only if," "on the condition that", "provided that", or any other language indicating that the entire transaction will not be enforceable until or unless something happens (i.e., occurrence of the condition is either fulfilled or excused) [Text § 21–27]. Here, the sample clause is merely a promise by Morton that it would supply one clock by a certain date. There is absolutely no evidence that the parties intended that their deal was contingent on the strict enforcement of that provision. B, C, and D are thus incorrect for the clock delivery term is a promise and not a condition.

ANSWERS TO SAMPLE MULTIPLE CHOICE QUESTIONS

Answer to Question 14.

(B) is the correct answer.

By failing to do what it promised, Morton has breached and thus, at the very least, must pay for damages caused by the breach [Text § 21–43]. Hence D is incorrect. The question is whether the breach could be classified as material or immaterial. If material, Store would be entitled to cease its own performance and to sue Morton for damages. If immaterial, Store would be obligated to continue performance and the only effect of the breach would be its suit for any damages caused by the one day delay [Text § 21–60]. The Restatement has identified various factors that go into the determination of whether a breach is material or partial [Text § 21–65]. These factors all point to Morton's breach as being immaterial, i.e., the breach did not deprive Store of most of the benefits of its bargain; Store can be fully compensated for its damages if the breach is declared only immaterial; Morton would suffer a fairly severe forfeiture under the contract if the breach were ruled material; Morton cured the breach within a day; and Morton acted in good faith. Hence, because the breach is only a partial one, B is the correct answer. A and C are both incorrect because they presume a material breach, i.e., one that would prevent Morton from enforcing the contract against Store [Text § 21–60].

Answer to Question 15.

(A) is the correct answer.

There was an anticipatory repudiation by Store when its President unequivocally told the Morton's employee that Store was not going to proceed under the contract and buy any clocks [Text §§ 23–4; 23–20]. At that point, Store was entitled to declare the contract over, cease its own performance, and sue Morton for material breach. As noted above (see the Answer to Question 14), because the failure to deliver the single clock on April 1 was only an immaterial breach [Text § 21–60], Store had no right to terminate the contract and cease its own performance at that point. Hence, A is the correct answer and B, C and D are incorrect.

Answer to Question 16.

(A) is the correct answer.

The May 5 letter by Store's President had the effect of retracting the anticipatory repudiation and reinstating the contract [Text § 23–32]. Hence, the question is whether Morton had a right to deliver only 200 clocks given the April 5 and April 6 telephone conversations, or whether it was obligated to deliver all 250 clocks. Morton would not be able to introduce evidence of the oral modification to 200 units. Under UCC § 2–209(3), if the contract as modified is within the statute of frauds (which this was), then the Statute must be satisfied before evidence of the modification is allowed [Text § 9–27]. Store did not sign anything indicating the reduced quantity, and there are no other facts that suggest

ANSWERS TO SAMPLE MULTIPLE CHOICE QUESTIONS

the Statute had been satisfied. However, there was the possibility that the reduction might be enforced as a waiver [Text § 9–10]. That is, under § 2–209(4), modifications rendered unenforceable due to a lack of writing can be enforced as waivers. However, under § 2–209(5), waivers can be retracted so long as the party benefiting from the waiver has not detrimentally relied on it. [Text § 9–16]. Here, besides retracting the repudiation, Store's May 5 letter also retracted the waiver to 200 units. Because Morton still could have performed at the time it received the retraction (and thus did not detrimentally rely on it), upon receipt of the May 5 letter the contract once again became one for 250 clocks. Hence, under the perfect tender rule [Text § 22–7] Morton's tender of only 200 clocks was therefore a material breach, and A is the correct response. B is thus incorrect because it states that Morton immaterially breached the contract. C and D are incorrect because they state that it is Store, not Morton, who has breached the contract.

Answer to Question 17.

(D) is the correct answer.

The difference between a power to accept and a right to accept turns on whether the offer is a revocable or an irrevocable one [Text § 4–72]. UCC § 2–205 rejects the common law rule that an offer may be made irrevocable only when consideration passes between the parties, i.e., when there is an option contract, and allows a merchant seller to make an enforceable irrevocable offer even in the absence of consideration [Text § 4–87]. However, to accomplish this "firm offer" effectively, the merchant seller must do so in writing. Here, the promise of the seller to hold open the offer was made orally, so the offeree (Bob) has only the power of acceptance under it, not the right to accept. A and C are thus incorrect for they state that Bob has a right to purchase the painting, and not merely a power to do so. D is incorrect for it states that Bob's power to purchase the painting only lasts to June 30, when Sy promised to hold his offer open until August 10.

Answer to Question 18.

(B) is the correct answer.

Under the "unilateral contract trick" of the UCC, a seller who is entitled to accept an offer by shipment, and who ships non-conforming goods, has simultaneously accepted and breached the contract [Text § 4–107]. However, if the seller who sent the non-conforming goods notifies the buyer that the goods are non-conforming and are being sent to the buyer as only an accommodation, the sending of such goods acts only as a counter-offer and not a breach [Text § 4–108]. The last sentence of the substantive paragraph of Sam's letter makes clear that this is an accommodation shipment, and thus since Betty has not accepted the tender of the records, their present status is that they do not have a contract. Thus A and D are incorrect.

ANSWERS TO SAMPLE MULTIPLE CHOICE QUESTIONS

Answer to Question 19.

(C) is the correct answer.

Upon a rightful rejection of goods under the UCC, a merchant buyer such as Bower's must follow any reasonable instructions of the buyer to return the goods [Text § 22–40]. However, it is entitled to be indemnified for any costs it has expended in doing so, which includes return the goods freight collect. Thus, A, B, and D are incorrect.

Answer to Question 20.

(C) is the correct answer.

Under § 45 of the Restatement 2d, beginning performance in response to an offer to enter into a unilateral contract creates a unilateral option contract exercisable by the offeree [Text § 4–80]. Hence, as soon as Andy started repairing the roof, the offer became temporarily irrevocable and Owner had to allow Andy a reasonable time to finish performance. A is not correct, for while Andy has an obligation to notify Owner within a reasonable time **after** beginning performance, he has no obligation to make such notice **before** beginning performance [Text § 4–104]. B is not correct, for a promissory offer in response to an offer for a unilateral contract is not a valid acceptance [Text § 4–93]. D is not correct under Restatement 2d § 45, although it is a minority position [Text § 4–84]. That is, under § 45, the option contract is unilateral only, and beginning performance does not obligate him or her to finish.

Answer to Question 21.

(D) is the correct answer.

A is not correct, because acceptance by beginning performance is only an acceptable method of acceptance in response to an ambiguous offer, or to an offer seeking a unilateral contract. [Text §§ 4–98; 4–100] B is also not correct. Generally, under the "mailbox rule," an acceptance is effective upon dispatch [Text § 4–119]. However, for that rule to apply, acceptance by mail must be an authorized method of acceptance [Text § 4–120]. Here, Owner made it clear that Andy's power of acceptance would lapse unless Andy told Owner of his decision by June 3. In that situation, mailing an acceptance late in the day on June 3 is not an effective method of acceptance, and thus B is incorrect. C is incorrect because the Owner would not receive the acceptance until after the offer lapsed by its own terms, i.e., after June 3 [Text § 4–45].

Answer to Question 22.

(B) is the correct answer.

Under the indirect revocation doctrine, when an offeree learns from a reliable source that an offeror has taken a definite act inconsistent with an intention to enter into the contract with the offeree, the offer is effectively revoked [Text § 4–59]. A is incorrect, because Brenda lost the

ANSWERS TO SAMPLE MULTIPLE CHOICE QUESTIONS

power to accept the offer when it was revoked as explained above [Text § 4–55]. C is incorrect as a matter of law. That is, a careless offeror can indeed have made a contract to sell the same thing to two or more different offerees. All that means is that the offeror will be liable in breach to one or more parties if the offerees accept and the seller doesn't perform. D is incorrect, for the consideration that supports a bilateral contract is the mutual promises, not performances by each party [Text § 7–18].

Answer to Question 23.

(B) is the correct answer.

The pre-existing duty rule regarding the consideration needed to enforce a contract modification has been relaxed, but not eliminated in non-UCC contracts. (It **has** been eliminated for UCC contracts, *see* UCC § 2–209(1). [Text § 9–20]) Under § 89 of the Restatement 2d, parties can make an enforceable modification to any executory duties under a contract only if the modification is fair, equitable, and either: (i) is made due to circumstances unanticipated at the time of contract formation; or (ii) has induced reliance by a party benefited by the modification [Text §§ 7–83; 9–20]. Here, the modification is not made due to unanticipated circumstances, nor has it induced reliance by Writer. Accordingly, the $3/page modification is unenforceable, so A is incorrect. C is wrong because the elements of a mutual rescission have not been established [Text § 24–19]. D is factually incorrect, i.e., there is no showing of reliance on these facts.

Answer to Question 24.

(D) is the correct answer.

The first question here is whether Writer's breach is material or immaterial. If material, Publisher is entitled to cease performance under the contract and need not accept it when it is tendered 12 months late [Text § 21–60]. If immaterial, Publisher cannot cease performance, and thus must accept its late delivery (although it will, of course, have the right to sue for any damages caused by the breach). Doubling the time agreed upon to tender a book on a then-topical subject is a material breach, and thus A is incorrect, and the Publisher need not accept the book when tendered [Text § 21–60]. B is incorrect, for when a non-breaching party waives the material breach of the other, the former material breach becomes an immaterial one [Text § 21–79]. That is, such a waiver is not a waiver of the right to sue for damages; rather it is a waiver of the right to cease performance due to the material breach. C is incorrect, for it is an example of "subjective" not "objective" impossibility/impracticability [Text § 25–5].

ANSWERS TO SAMPLE MULTIPLE CHOICE QUESTIONS

Answer to Question 25.

(C) is the correct answer.

One party's breach with the knowledge of the other does not amount to a "waiver" of the non-breaching party's right to sue for damages. To constitute a waiver, there must be some affirmative statement or action by the waiving party establishing the relinquishment of a right, or the affirmative excuse in the occurrence of, or delay in the occurrence of, a condition [Text § 21–60]. Accordingly, B is incorrect. A is a plausible answer, but it is only true if you assume facts not given, i.e., you assume that Publisher told Writer that the "no drinking" clause was important to Publisher regardless of when the book was finished. D is incorrect as a matter of law. A contract wherein someone agrees to forego a legal activity is not an "illegal" contract [Text § 17–2].

Answer to Question 26.

(C) is the correct answer.

A party's duties under a contract are discharged under the impossibility doctrine only if, *inter alia,* the impossibility-causing event occurred without the fault of the party asserting the defense [Text § 25–12]. Accordingly, A and B are incorrect, for they are too broad, i.e., they allocate liability to one party or the other regardless of who was at fault in causing the fire. D is incorrect because the contract between Delegate and Hotel did not allocate the risk of fire [Text § 25–14]. Both clearly contemplated the continuing existence of the hotel as a basic assumption of their contract [Text § 25–8].

Answer to Question 27.

(C) is the correct answer.

The fact that Delegate cannot attend the convention due to illness is an insufficient reason to trigger the impossibility, impracticability, or frustration doctrines. Her performance is not impossible of being performed by anyone, and thus, at most is only a case of "subjective" impossibility, which is insufficient to establish impossibility as a defense [Text § 25–4]. For the same reasons, her performance is not rendered impractical, for it will not cost her any additional money to perform [Text § 25–33]. There is no frustration here, for the fact that the deposit was labelled non-refundable demonstrates that the financial risk of Delegate's non-attendance, for whatever reason, was on Delegate, and not Hotel, under the contract [Text § 25–53]. A, B, and D are incorrect for they state that Delegate is entitled to her money back under either a frustration or an impossibility theory.

ANSWERS TO SAMPLE MULTIPLE CHOICE QUESTIONS

Answer to Question 28.

(D) is the correct answer.

The facts of this hypothetical are drawn almost exactly from *Krell v. Henry,* the classic case on frustration of purpose [Text § 25–56]. Here, Delegate's reference to the ad when the reservation was made, together with the timing of the reservation and the request for the special price, demonstrate that both parties knew the purpose for which Delegate entered into the contract. A is wrong because this is not an impossibility of performance case, for Delegate can still perform, and can perform for the agreed upon price [Text § 25–3]. Rather, the problem is that the value of the return performance has been frustrated. B is incorrect, for the parol evidence rule does not apply to situations giving one party the power to avoid an agreement [Text § 18–25]. C is incorrect because the value of the return performance to Delegate is sufficiently frustrated to invoke the frustration defense [Text § 25–4]. Hence, D is the correct choice, with frustration giving Delegate the power to cancel the contract, and restitution providing the theory by which she can recover her deposit [Text §§ 25–64; 31–33].

Answer to Question 29.

(A) is the correct answer.

As with any potential third party beneficiary situation, first identify the parties. Insurance Co. is the promisor, for it is obligated to do an act (provide coverage) that will benefit a third party. Dealer is the promisee, for it bargained for the promisor's promise. Buyer is the beneficiary, for she will benefit from performance of Insurance Co.'s promise [Text § 26–2]. D is incorrect because a valid third party beneficiary contract can be formed even if the precise identity of the beneficiary is not known at the time the contract is made. [Text § 26–24] C is incorrect, because granting Buyer a right to enforce Insurance Co.'s promise of coverage surely will effectuate the intentions of Insurance Co. and Dealer when they entered into their third party beneficiary contract, thereby making Buyer an intended, rather than an incidental beneficiary. [Text § 26–14] B is wrong, because to be a creditor-like intended beneficiary under Restatement 2d § 302, performance of the promisor's promise must satisfy an obligation of the promisee to pay money to the beneficiary. That is, for Buyer to be an intended creditor-like beneficiary, the third party beneficiary contract would have to have been entered into to satisfy an obligation of **the Dealer** to pay money to Buyer [Text §§ 26–14; 26–19]. As this was not the case, the correct choice is A.

Answer to Question 30.

(A) is the correct answer.

The key to this question was the focus in each of the responses on who the beneficiary (Buyer) could sue **"for breach of the Dealer/**

ANSWERS TO SAMPLE MULTIPLE CHOICE QUESTIONS

Insurance Co. contract." In other words, what rights does a donee-like intended beneficiary have against the promisor and promisee solely arising out of that contract, and that contract alone. An intended beneficiary (Buyer) has the right to sue the promisor, Insurance Co., for breach of his, her, or its promise [Text § 26–5]. Indeed, that is often the central issue arising from such agreements. However, an intended donee-like beneficiary acquires no rights **against the promisee** (here, Dealer), arising from the formation of such a contract [Text § 26–31]. Hence, while Buyer may have some rights against Dealer for breach of the direct promise made to Buyer that the Dealer would provide insurance, those rights did not arise from the Dealer/Insurance Co. agreement. Accordingly, since the only entity an intended donee-like beneficiary can sue for breach of a third party beneficiary contract alone is the promisor, the correct answer is A. Thus, B and C are incorrect. D is incorrect because Buyer, as an intended beneficiary, is entitled to bring suit against the promisor, Insurance Co [Text § 26–5].

Answer to Question 31.

(B) is the correct answer.

The issue in this question turns, in part, on the rights of the promisor and promisee to modify the third party beneficiary contract to the detriment of the intended beneficiary [Text § 26–44]. While there are three tests, reflecting different views, as to when the beneficiary's rights vest under such a contract, all three are satisfied here. Accordingly, Dealer and Insurance Co. were without power to modify the contract to the detriment of Buyer. As such, Buyer retained whatever rights she had prior to the attempted modification which, as set forth in the Answer to Question 30 above, means she could only sue Insurance Co., the promisor, for its breach of the third party beneficiary contract. Note that Choice III is incorrect because there are no warranties that follow from the creation of a third party beneficiary contract (although there are warranties that follow an assignment for value) [Text § 27–42]. Thus, choice I is incorrect.

Answer to Question 32.

(A) is the correct answer.

Absent evidence to the contrary, the phrase "assigning the contract" includes both an assignment of rights under the agreement and a delegation of the assigning party's duties [Text §§ 27–36; 28–6]. Hence, upon the "assignment of the contract," Roger acquired both a right to receive the $500 payment for the job from Owen, and the right to perform the painting, so long as the duty was validly delegable. A duty is not delegable when its performance requires the special training, skills, abilities, etc., of the delegating party, in this case Alexandra, i.e., when it is a "personal services" contract within the meaning of the term used in delegation situations [Text § 28–10]. A contract to paint a house is not a "personal services" contract in that sense, for the task is one any

ANSWERS TO SAMPLE MULTIPLE CHOICE QUESTIONS

competent painter can accomplish. Accordingly, C is incorrect and the delegation was valid. Upon a valid delegation, the obligee, in this case Owen, must allow the delegate, Roger, to perform the duties called for in the obligee/delegating party contract. That is, Owen must allow Roger to do the painting or be in breach for failing to do so [Text §§ 28–20; 28–22]; accordingly B is an incorrect choice. Upon a simple delegation, the delegating party (Alexandra) is still liable to the obligee (Roger) for breach by the delegate. The only way the delegating party can be "off the hook" is if the delegating party and the obligee enter into a novation, whereby the obligee specifically agrees to accept the delegate's performance in satisfaction of the duty owed by the delegating party [Text §§ 28–31; 24–5]. Because no novation occurred here, D is wrong and A is the correct response.

Answer to Question 33.

(B) is the correct answer.

The assignor and the obligor have no power to modify or terminate an assignment for value [Text § 27–35]. Accordingly, A is incorrect. Upon the delegation, Roger acquired the right to perform the painting duties on Owen's home. If Owen will not allow him to paint the house, Owen is in breach [Text §§ 28–20; 28–22]. Upon an assignment for value, the assignor makes an implied warranty *inter alia,* that he or she will do nothing to impair the value of the assignment [Text § 27–42]. If Alexandra conspires with Roger to terminate the assigned right, and Roger is thereby prevented from doing the acts necessary to receive the benefits of the assignment, Alexandra is also liable to him. Hence, B is the correct answer, since both Owen and Alexandra may be sued, and so C and D are incorrect.

Answer to Question 34.

(C) is the correct answer.

After a valid delegating with an express assertion by the delegate that he will assume the obligation, an obligee such as Owen has the right to sue either the delegating party or the delegate, or both, for the delegate's breach [Text § 28–25]. Of course, the obligee is only entitled to one recovery, but he or she is freely entitled to bring suit against both parties. Thus, A, B, and D are incorrect.

Answer to Question 35.

(C) is the correct answer.

After a valid assignment *with notice to the obligor,* the only way the obligor may discharge his or her duties by performance is by rendering such performance **to the assignee** [Text § 27–27]. Here, the assignment was valid, and the obligor (Owen) had notice of the assignment. Accordingly, his tender of payment to anyone other than Roger, the assignee, will not discharge his duties under the Alexandra/Owen

ANSWERS TO SAMPLE MULTIPLE CHOICE QUESTIONS

contract. Thus, A and D are incorrect. B is incorrect for if Owen prevails, he prevails because of the contract and is thus entitled to the contract price for the painting, regardless of its fair market or restitutionary value.

Answer to Question 36.

(B) is the correct answer.

The issue is whether there is sufficient consideration to enforce the promise to pay $5,000, and if so, whether their resulting agreement can be called a novation or a substituted performance. An agreement to surrender a claim under a contract is supported by consideration when the existence and/or amount of the claim is the subject of a **bona fide** dispute between the parties [Text §§ 7–82; 24–13]. Accordingly, A is incorrect. B is correct, and C and D are incorrect, because the subsequent agreement between Emily and Bill is an accord, and neither a novation nor a substituted performance agreement. A novation occurs when a party who is owed a duty under a contract agrees to discharge that duty in return for a promised performance by a third party [Text § 24–5]. Here, no third parties entered into agreements with Emily so it is not a novation. A substituted performance agreement is one in which a party who is owed a duty under a contract agrees to discharge that duty upon the actual performance of another duty [Text § 24–2]. Here, Emily's promise to discharge the debt was made in return for Bill's **promise** of completing the landscaping, and she made it clear that the duty she was compromising would not be discharged until the landscaping was completed. The promise constituted an accord, and the discharge upon completion of the landscaping would be a satisfaction [Text § 24–9].

Answer to Question 37.

(C) is the correct answer.

Upon breach of an accord, the non-breaching party is entitled to sue for breach of the original contract duty or of the accord [Text § 24–9]. Thus, A and B are incorrect. D is incorrect for Emily would only be entitled to cease performance under the contract upon a material breach by Bill. Here, the failure to provide $5,000 worth of landscaping in a $100,000 apartment building construction contract would most likely be considered only an immaterial breach under the substantial performance doctrine [Text § 21–68].

Answer to Question 38.

(A) is the correct answer.

Typically, an unjustified failure to provide progress payments in a construction contract acts as a material breach, which would allow Bill to cease (or at least suspend) performance. However, under the "first" material breach doctrine, if Emily was **justified** in withholding the progress payment and Bill nevertheless walked off the job, it would be Bill who has breached the agreement, not Emily [Text § 21–66]. In other

ANSWERS TO SAMPLE MULTIPLE CHOICE QUESTIONS

words, the fact that Bill has an honest dispute with Emily will not shield him from being a breaching party if the facts ultimately prove he was in the wrong. B is wrong because Bill is not obligated to continue performance if Emily's withholding of the progress payments was unjustified. C is incorrect because Bill will only be discharged from performance if Emily's withholding of progress payments was unjustified. D is incorrect because the amount of recovery he would be entitled to if Emily were found to be the breaching party would not be fixed at the amount then due under the contract at the time of the breach. [Text § 30–31].

Answer to Question 39.

(C) is the correct answer.

An agreement on a term like putting in a sidewalk is the kind of term that the parties would not naturally leave out of their written agreement. Accordingly, A and D are incorrect because the parol evidence rule, which applies to terms allegedly agreed upon prior to the making of the contract, would provide an obstacle to Emily in trying to prove that the sidewalk agreement was part of the contract [Text § 18–13]. B and C deal with modifications, which are not subject to the parol evidence rule, i.e., to agreements made after the contract was established [Text § 18–29]. In § 89, the Restatement 2d has relaxed somewhat the pre-existing duty rule dealing with contract modifications, providing that parties can make an enforceable modification to any executory duties under a contract only if the modification is fair, equitable, and either: (i) is made due to circumstances unanticipated at the time of contract formation; or (ii) has induced reliance by a party benefited by the modification [Text § 7–83; 9–21]. Here in, B the modification is not made due to unanticipated circumstances (Emily says she just forgot about it), nor do the facts reveal that it has induced reliance by Emily. Accordingly, to be enforceable it will need to have consideration, which is why B is incorrect. In C, unlike in B, Emily provided consideration to support the sidewalk promise (i.e., she extended the completion date under the contract), and thus C most likely would allow Emily to enforce the sidewalk promise.

Answer to Question 40.

(B) is the correct answer.

There is an offer, an acceptance, and consideration found in the Smith/Jones conversation. Jones made an offer to buy, an acceptance on those terms was agreed to by Smith, and the promises to buy and sell were mutually bargained for [Text §§ 7–4; 7–18]. The contract will not fail for indefiniteness, for the parties have given themselves until June 1 to cure any indefiniteness as to the subject matter [Text § 6–4]. A is incorrect, because both parties are bound to buy and sell, respectively, a car, and C is incorrect, because this was the offer Jones made. Thus, Jones cannot be heard to complain about its "unfairness." D is incorrect, because Smith accepted the offer on its terms and did not propose any additional terms to the bargain [Text § 4–29], and thus, his reply cannot be considered a counter-offer.

Answer to Question 41.

(C) is the correct answer.

Martha made an offer seeking a promissory acceptance, the invited method of which was by return letter. The offer did not specify an exact time, but it was posted by Daisy the morning after it was received, which seems timely enough under the circumstances [Text § 4–48]. Because acceptances are effective upon dispatch [Text § 4–119] (assuming acceptance by mail is an authorized mode of acceptance and that the letter is properly addressed), a contract was formed as soon as Daisy mailed the letter. Note that Daisy's power of acceptance was still in effect, for Martha became incapacitated only after the acceptance became effective [Text § 4–67]. A is incorrect, because while foreseeable reliance on a promise might allow Daisy to collect reliance damages from Martha's estate on a promissory estoppel theory, it would probably not allow Daisy to enforce the contract so as to provide her with the house. [Text § 8–16] B is incorrect, for by the time Martha attempted to revoke the offer it had already been accepted, and once an offer has been accepted, the offeree loses his or her right to revoke it [Text § 4–2]. D is wrong, because the receipt of Martha's revocation is irrelevant since the offer had already been accepted.

Answer to Question 42.

(B) is the correct answer.

The rule states that upon the death of the offeror, the power of acceptance of the offeree is immediately terminated, regardless whether the offeree knows of the death or not [Text § 4–67]. Hence, imagine that an offeree does not know that an offeror had died and is reasonable in not knowing that fact. To a reasonable person in the shoes of the offeree (the objective theory of contracts test) [Text § 4–3], it appears that the offer may still be effectively accepted. Because it cannot, the rule seems more consistent with the subjective theory of contracts, i.e., consistent with the idea that there can be no subjective meeting of the minds between the two contracting parties, than with the objective theory.

Answer to Question 43.

(B) is the correct choice.

Because this is a contract for the sale of goods for $500 or more, the transaction will not be enforceable unless the UCC's statute of frauds is satisfied [Text § 10–35]. Here, it is Sheila who is the "party to be charged" for it is she who is asserting the defense. [Text § 10–37] Accordingly, the Statute cannot be satisfied against her under § 2–201 by the check itself, for the check was signed by Bernice, not Sheila; hence Choice III is

ANSWERS TO SAMPLE MULTIPLE CHOICE QUESTIONS

incorrect. Choice II is correct, because under § 2–201(3)(c), performance under a contract satisfies the Statute. While the Code speaks in terms of "performance" and not "part performance" (which was true here), most courts allow part performance to satisfy the statute in a case like this on the grounds that one the cashing of a $15,000 check is sufficient indicia that any oral testimony will rest on a real transaction. [Text § 10–55] Accordingly, when Sheila cashed the check, she lost the statute of frauds defense. Choice I is thus wrong because it is an incorrect statement of the law. Choice IV is incorrect, because the parol evidence rule has nothing to do with whether the statute of frauds is satisfied. [Text § 18–29].

Answer to Question 44.

(B) is the correct answer.

The only warranty breached here is an express warranty. The implied warranty of merchantability focuses on the workmanship of the good, i.e., whether it is of average quality, or fit for the ordinary use for which such goods are put [Text § 35–10]. Here, Bernice's complaint is not that the car does not run well, but that certain factual representations made about the car, on which she relied in making the purchase, turned out to be false. As such, there has been an actionable breach of express warranty [Text § 35–2].

Answer to Question 45.

(C) is the correct answer.

Under UCC § 2–508(1), a seller has an absolute right to cure so long as the time for performance under the contract has not yet passed, and so long as the seller gives reasonable notice that he or she is intending to cure and has acted in good faith [Text § 22–12]. Hence Choice I is a correct statement of the law. Under § 2–508(2), a seller must establish that it had reason to believe that the goods were acceptable when shipped, that any delay in getting conforming goods to the buyer will not result in commercial hardship to the buyer, and that the buyer is seasonably notified of the seller's intentions, before it has the right to cure [Text § 22–15]. Hence, Choice IV is also a correct statement of the law. Choices II and III are simply incorrect statements of the law.

Answer to Question 46.

(D) is the correct answer.

Under UCC § 2–609, a party to a contract who has reasonable grounds to do so is entitled to seek reasonable assurances from the other party as to the other's willingness and ability to perform under the contract [Text § 23–22]. An article in a newspaper of general circulation disclosing a buyer's fiscal troubles is generally held to be sufficient for the seller to seek such assurances [Text § 23–23]. The failure to give adequate assurances within a reasonable time (not to exceed 30 days) when properly demanded constitutes an anticipatory repudiation [Text § 23–

ANSWERS TO SAMPLE MULTIPLE CHOICE QUESTIONS

22]. The test for whether assurances are adequate is an objective one, i.e., whether a reasonable person in the position of the insecure party would be assured of the other's willingness and ability to perform. Conclusory promises without some detail to back them up are generally not considered sufficient assurances [Text § 23–27]. Here, the article gave Sid reasonable grounds to demand assurances, and the response of Buford was insufficient. Hence, D is the correct answer. Note that C is wrong because under the UCC, an anticipatory repudiation may occur either as a result of a definite or unequivocal refusal to perform under § 2–610, or as a result of the failure to respond to adequate assurances under § 2–609. [Text § 23–20]

SAMPLE ESSAY QUESTIONS

LIST OF ISSUES COVERED IN ESSAY QUESTIONS

This is a general list of the issues covered in each of the essay questions which follow, so you know which questions will test you on material you have already covered in class.

Question 1
Offer
Acceptance
Statute of Frauds
Conditions
Modification
Damages

Question 2
Offer
Indefiniteness
Acceptance
Mailbox Rule
Revocation
Consideration

Question 3
Statute of Frauds
Breach (Material vs. Immaterial)
Frustration
Implied condition
Impracticability
Remedies (Damages and Restitution)

Question 4
Offer
Acceptance
Revocation
Statute of Frauds
UCC § 2–207
Impracticability
Cover as UCC Remedy

Question 5
Offer
Acceptance
Statute of Frauds
Breach
Damages (action for the price)
Accommodation shipment
Cure

Question 6
Preliminary negotiations
Offer
UCC § 2–207
Consideration

Question 7
Offer
Acceptance
Revocation
Mailbox Rule

Question 8
Offer
UCC § 2–207
Acceptance
Revocation

Question 9
Parol Evidence Rule
Limitation of Remedy
Unconscionability
Rejection
Revocation
Damages

SAMPLE ESSAY QUESTIONS

Question No. 1

Sally owned two adjacent houses on Park Street: 2101 Park Street and 2103 Park Street. Sally lived in the house at 2101 Park Street and rented out the house at 2103 Park Street. At all relevant times the 2101 Park Street house was worth $135,000, and the 2103 Park Street house was worth $100,000.

On June 1, Sally decided to sell 2101 Park Street, so she put a "For Sale" sign in the front yard. Bub was driving through the neighborhood that day, saw the sign, stopped, and rang the doorbell. Sally showed Bub through the house, told him she was asking $150,000 for it, and told him she wanted to deliver the deed on August 1 and receive the $150,000 on the same day. She also said she would have the house painted inside and out before August 1. (The painting would cost Sally $2,000.) In response, Bub asked if she would take $140,000 for the house. Sally said she would have to think about it. Bub told Sally that he would not be able to buy her house unless he could find a buyer for his present house (on Elm Street). Bub said, "If we do make a deal, could we understand that I have to buy your house only if by July 1 I have a contract with a buyer to buy my house on Elm Street?" Sally said that would be "OK" with her.

On June 2, Sally wrote Bub the following letter:

> June 2
>
> Dear Bub:
>
> I offer to sell you my home on Park Street for $145,000. If you wish to accept this offer you must let me know before June 10.
>
> If you accept, then you will pay me the $145,000, and I will give you a deed, all on August 1. I will maintain insurance on the house until August 1 and will also take good care of the lawns and plants until that date. My furniture is not included, except for the dining room table (which was specially made to fit the odd shaped dining room), and the six matching chairs. My insurance company has appraised the dining set at $600.
>
> Very truly yours,
>
> /s/ Sally

On June 4 Bub wrote back:

> June 4
>
> Dear Sally:
>
> I am happy to accept the offer set forth in your June 2 letter.
>
> Sincerely,
>
> /s/ Bub

SAMPLE ESSAY QUESTIONS

On June 10, Bub telephoned Sally and said it did not look like he was going to be able to find a buyer for his Elm Street house, but that he would buy Sally's home anyway. Sally said, "Great," and told Bub that she would go ahead and arrange for the house to be painted. Sally immediately called a painter and contracted with her to paint the 2101 Park Street house for $2,000.

On June 12, Bub telephoned Sally and said he had changed his mind; he said he would not buy her home unless he succeeded in finding a buyer for his house. Sally said he was obligated to buy her house anyway.

Bub did not find a buyer for his house. When Sally tendered a deed to him on August 1, Bub refused to pay her the $145,000 or any other amount.

Sally has now sued Bub for damages for breach of contract. Will she prevail? Discuss. Assuming she prevails, what amount of damages will she recover? Discuss.

Question No. 2

Leslie wrote to Tom on December 1, 1988 in an undated letter, saying, "I will lease you my house for a year, while I am away in Europe. You can have the house beginning on January 1, 1989. Write me with your answer within one week." Although Leslie mailed the letter on December 1, it was misplaced for 10 days by the postal service. Thus, it was postmarked December 11 and was delivered to Tom on December 12. The envelope bore no markings on it indicating the misplacement at the post office. But for its misplacement, the letter would have been delivered on December 2. On the morning of December 14, Tom mailed a letter back to Leslie, which stated, "I accept your offer. Please be sure all the locks and built-in appliances are in good working order." The postal service lost Tom's letter, which was properly addressed and stamped. Accordingly, it was never delivered to Leslie.

Meanwhile, on December 10, Leslie leased the house to Xerxes for calendar year 1989. Tom showed up at the house mid-morning on January 1 with a moving van he had rented full of his possessions. Unfortunately for Tom, Xerxes had already moved in. Once Tom assured himself that Xerxes had a lease, he drove straight to his lawyer. The lawyer told Tom that Tom had no claim against Leslie. (Do not necessarily assume the lawyer was competent.) Tom nevertheless sent a demand letter to Leslie, demanding $5,000 in damages to settle his breach of contract claim. Leslie responded with the following letter:

SAMPLE ESSAY QUESTIONS

Dear Tom:

I will agree to pay you $600 in full settlement of any claim you may have against me.

/s/ Leslie

Tom immediately mailed a reply, stating, "I agree to your terms."

Leslie never paid Tom anything, so Tom sued Leslie.

Assume the state landlord-tenant law requires landlords to have rented premises in "safe and decent condition" before renting them.

Please discuss the following questions:

(a) Did Tom have a valid contract to lease the house?

(b) If Tom did not have a valid contract to lease the house, can he recover the $600 from Leslie?

(c) Would your answer to (a) be changed if Leslie's December 1, 1988 letter had included the following sentence: "The monthly rent will be as agreed upon between us?"

Please assume that there are no statute of frauds issues.

Question No. 3

Novice Publishing Co. ("Novice") was a new company that was formed to publish law books. Congress was about to pass a bill that would completely rewrite the law of government ethics, so Novice contracted with Priscilla Professor to write a 15-chapter single volume treatise on government ethics law. Both Priscilla and Novice knew that there were already too many treatises in existence on government ethics law for a new one to be profitable unless there was a change in the law, and unless Novice could publish the first book to deal with the new law. Consequently, Novice's president, Newton, orally proposed the following deal to Priscilla:

- Priscilla would write a 15-chapter, one-volume, treatise on government ethics law;

- The first chapter would be "due" in four months, and then one additional chapter would be "due" each month thereafter (Priscilla had truthfully informed Novice that it would be very difficult to complete such a treatise in less than 18 months.);

- Priscilla would be paid $30,000 when the book was completed, but would receive no other payments or royalties from the treatise; and

- Novice could refuse to pay Priscilla if the text was "unsatisfactory to Novice."

SAMPLE ESSAY QUESTIONS

Priscilla was concerned that Novice might not have the money to pay her the $30,000, so Newton called Big Bucks into the room. Big Bucks was a wealthy philanthropist with a strong interest in government ethics issues. Indeed, he had suggested that Novice break into the law book market with a government ethics book. Priscilla told Big Bucks of her concern; he said that he personally would ensure that she would be paid. Big Bucks took one of his business cards, wrote on the back of it "$30,000 ensured," and handed it to Priscilla. Priscilla then accepted Novice's proposal.

Priscilla began work on the treatise, but it went more slowly than she expected. It took her four months and eighteen days to complete the first chapter. While that chapter was in the mail to Novice, the U.S. President unexpectedly vetoed the government ethics bill. It was obvious that her veto could not be overridden, and she had 3 1/2 years left in her first term of office. In truth, the government ethics bill was dead as a doornail and so government ethics law would, as a result, remain substantially unchanged for the foreseeable future.

When Priscilla heard of the veto, she called Novice's President Newton to say that she would have to restructure completely her outline of the treatise. Newton said he wasn't sure he could let her have that much time. He truthfully pointed out that publishing costs were rising 1% per month and that the prices at which law books could be sold were not rising at all.

When Newton got Priscilla's first chapter in the mail, he skimmed it quickly and then sent a letter to Priscilla. The letter said that Novice was canceling the contract for "delay and unsatisfactory work."

Discuss the issues raised by these facts.

Question No. 4

Bev owned a business that did a large amount of chrome plating of bumpers and other car parts for Ford and Chrysler. Her contracts with Ford and Chrysler were fixed-price contracts ($20 per bumper, $3 per hood ornament, etc.), so Bev always worried about increases in the price of chromium. The country of Volga was the major chromium producer in the world. Accordingly, Bev had followed the widely reported unrest in Volga since 1982. It is now 1988.

In January of 1988, Bev decided to lay in a large stock of chromium, so she pulled out of her desk a brochure she had received the previous week from Sal, a dealer in metals. The brochure discussed various metals, including chromium, which Sal offered for sale, and it included a pre-printed Order Form. Bev filled in the blanks for her name ("Bev"), the type of metal she wanted ("99% pure chromium"), the amount ("five tons"), and the delivery date ("June"). A clause in the middle of the form stated that "Buyer agrees to hold this offer open for 35 days, and Seller may accept at any time within the

SAMPLE ESSAY QUESTIONS

period." Another clause in the form stated that the price for the chromium under the contract would be the closing price on the New York Commodities Exchange for the day on which the order was accepted. Bev signed on the signature line at the bottom of the form and mailed the order form to Sal on January 10.

On February 7, Sal mailed Bev a typed sheet entitled "Confirmation of Sale." The Confirmation stated that "Seller confirms the sale of five tons of 99% pure chromium to Bev." The Confirmation of Sale also stated that "Seller will not be responsible to deliver metals if availability is materially affected by labor strike, natural disaster, or war (including civil war)." This clause was not in the Order Form. The signature line at the bottom of the confirmation was blank; Sal had forgotten to sign it.

On February 8, before Bev received Sal's Confirmation of Sale, the market price of chromium dropped 10%. Sal anticipated a further drop, so he decided to wait several weeks before buying the chromium he would need to fill Bev's order. Bev also anticipated a further drop. Accordingly, as she had not yet received Sal's Confirmation, she mailed Sal a letter on February 8 saying that she no longer wished to purchase the chromium from him.

On February 9, Bev received Sal's Confirmation of Sale. She knew it was from Sal only because the envelope in which the Confirmation came had his return address on it, and because the Confirmation of Sale referred to five tons of 99% pure chromium, the same amount of the same metal she had ordered from Sal.

On February 10, Sal received Bev's February 8 letter. Sal wrote a note to himself saying "Don't buy chromium for Bev's order."

On February 11, tensions heightened in Volga. The market price of chromium accordingly went up by 15%. Bev immediately mailed a letter to Sal on February 11. In her letter: (1) she thanked Sal for his February 7 Confirmation of Sale; (2) said that he should ignore her February 8 letter; (3) stated that she was "looking forward to delivery of five tons of chromium under our contract;" and (4) signed it "Your loyal customer, Bev."

Sal received Bev's February 11 letter on February 13. He was busy; he glanced at her letter, did not notice it was signed by Bev (although it was), thought it pertained to a deal with a different customer, and threw it away.

On April 15, full scale civil war erupted in Volga. The market price of chromium went up by a factor of ten. On April 25, Bev wrote to Sal stating that she would prefer delivery of the five tons of chromium on June 3. On April 27, immediately after receiving Bev's letter, Sal wrote back, saying, "I believe you cancelled your order and that we do not have a deal. Please advise me immediately if you believe

SAMPLE ESSAY QUESTIONS

otherwise. Regardless, it does not appear I have any responsibility to deliver chromium. Moreover, I doubt I could get together more than one ton of chromium for you in any case given the civil unrest in Volga." Sal signed the letter, "Best wishes, Sal."

It is now April 30. Bev has come to you for advice. Please advise her: (1) whether there is an enforceable contract for sale of the chromium? (2) If there is, what should she do? If Bev tells you she believes the price of chromium will rise steadily between now and the end of June, what effect will that have on your advice to her?

Question No. 5

On March 8, Byron went to the audio/video store and met the owner, Silvio, and spoke with him about ordering a new plasma screen TV. However, in the end Byron mumbled something about maybe not being able to afford the TV, but wasn't too clear in telling Silvio that he didn't want the TV. A few days later, Byron received the following letter from Silvio, dated March 10:

> Byron,
>
> It was, as usual, a pleasure seeing you again at the store. I am starting work on building the TV you ordered and I guarantee that it will fit into that unused space in your home for which you gave me the measurements. The price, as we discussed, is $6,500 and it should be ready in two or three weeks. I will call you when it is finished. Thanks again for your order.
>
> /s/ Silvio

Byron never responded to the letter and on April 1, Byron got a call from Silvio, who said, "Your beautiful TV is ready! When will you be by to pick it up or should I deliver it?" Byron replied, honestly, "Silvio this is all a misunderstanding. I never meant to order it when I was in your store last month. I suppose I could see how you might have **thought** I told you to go ahead, but I can't afford it right now and I never wanted you to make it." In response Silvio said, honestly, "It sure seemed to me like you told me you wanted it. And anyway, what about my letter?"

Byron told Silvio, "I meant to call you about that letter, but I forgot. It's still here sitting on my desk. Anyway, the letter proves nothing and I am not going to pick up the TV because I never ordered it." Byron never took delivery of the plasma screen which was tailored to fit his home.

The TV cost Silvio $4,000 to make, inclusive both of the time he spent in making it and of the materials.

On his birthday, May 1, Byron treated himself to dinner at his favorite restaurant, Le Cess Poule. He ordered shrimp cocktail to

SAMPLE ESSAY QUESTIONS

start, sirloin steak with Béarnaise sauce, apple pie, and a 1961 Laffite Rothschild as his wine.

As the waiter presented the wine, Byron noticed the waiter had made a mistake and had brought him a 1970 Laffite and not a 1961. Byron had never tasted the 1970 wine, was curious about it, and so said nothing about it. He finished drinking it at the restaurant. Le Cess Poule charges $700 bottle for the 1961, but only $575 for the 1970 Laffite. The retail values of these wines are $250 for the 1961 and $150 for the 1970.

When the waiter came with the appetizer he told Byron that the restaurant had, unfortunately, sold out of the shrimp cocktail but that he had brought Byron crab cocktail in its place as he thought this would be equally acceptable. The waiter additionally explained that while the crab cocktail was more expensive ($18 instead of $12), the restaurant would charge him only $12 due to the inconvenience they were sure Byron had been caused. Byron grumbled but said that it would be OK and ate the crab cocktail.

Byron took a bite of the sirloin when it arrived and exclaimed to the waiter, "This is Hollandaise sauce, not Béarnaise!" The waiter promised to bring Béarnaise sauce shortly, but never did. Byron took another bite or two of the meat while he was waiting, but finally it got cold and he eventually told the waiter he did not want it any longer and to take it away.

When dessert came, the waiter brought Byron a piece of pecan pie. Byron screamed that he had ordered apple and not pecan. The waiter apologized for his mistake and told Byron he would immediately bring him a slice of apple pie in its place. Byron said "forget it," and walked out of the restaurant without paying.

Discuss liability and damages:

    (A) In *Silvio v. Byron*; and

    (B) Arising out of Byron's dispute with Le Cess Poule.

Question No. 6

Sap Co. ("Sap") was a manufacturer of heavy duty equipment. Bloop Co. ("Bloop") owned a private harbor and needed a large power dredge to keep the channels in the harbor free of silt. (A power dredge is like a small powerful ship but with a scoop attached to its bottom to scoop silt up out of the channels.)

In early March, Bloop discussed its needs with Sap; after extensive discussions, Sap proposed a particular design for the type of dredge Bloop would need and asserted that Sap was capable of making such a custom-made dredge. Sap told Bloop that it would take a few days to figure out the price Sap would have to charge.

SAMPLE ESSAY QUESTIONS

Sap thereafter telegraphed Bloop on March 13. The telegram said: (1) the price for the dredge, if the parties agreed to a deal, would be $2.5 million; (2) Sap would have to do one final check of its cost figures before committing to building the dredge; and (3) Bloop would need to pay part of the price several months before delivery.

Bloop then sent Sap the following letter on March 15:

> Dear Sap Co.:
>
> Two and a half million dollars is a lot of money. It is much more than we expected, and frankly we think it is too high. However, we really need a dredge and you seem very qualified to build one. Let us know when we can expect the dredge; any time before December of this year will be OK. We expect to receive full warranties, including a warranty that the dredge will do the job for us. We do not want to be limited to arbitration if there is a dispute, even though we know it is usual to have an arbitration agreement in these sorts of contracts. We are willing to deal with you only on the above terms.
>
> We don't know how we're going to scrape together $2.5 million, so we will **very** much appreciate it if you would reduce your price.
>
> Sincerely,
>
> /s/ President Bloop Co.
>
> P.S. We will pay $100,000 of the total on June 1. We reserve the right to cancel this order at any time up to June 15, by sending you a letter that says we are canceling it. Any payments we make before then will be returned to us if we cancel by June 15.

Sap mailed the following reply to Bloop on March 19:

> Dear Bloop Co.:
>
> We will deliver the dredge in October of this year. We will give you a warranty that the dredge will be free from defects in materials and workmanship (for example, that the steel used in it will be good steel and that the parts will be welded together properly), but we will not warrant that the dredge will actually work to dredge the silt in your particular harbor. **There will be NO implied warranty of merchantability or of fitness.** We agree that you will pay $100,000 out of the 2.5 million total on June 1. We will have the same right to cancel by June 15 that you have. Let us know if you agree to these terms; otherwise we will not deliver the dredge.
>
> Sincerely,
>
> /s/ President Sap Co.

SAMPLE ESSAY QUESTIONS

No further correspondence was exchanged between Bloop and Sap until June 1, when Bloop paid Sap the $100,000 by check. Sap immediately deposited the check in its account. On June 2, Sap wrote Bloop and said that the price for the dredge would be only $2.3 million. Sap's letter said Bloop need not respond to it and Bloop did not. Bloop received Sap's price reduction letter on June 4.

On June 10, Bloop's president reviewed the file and for the first time noticed all the provisions in Sap's letter of March 19. He wrote Sap on June 10, saying that Bloop objected to the warranty limitations and to the provision allowing Sap to cancel, all of which were in Sap's March 19 letter.

Sap received the letter on June 14 and immediately telegraphed Bloop, stating that Sap would not deliver the dredge.

Bloop comes to you for advice on June 15. Is there a contract? If so, what are its terms? Discuss. Assume there are no statute of frauds issues.

Question No. 7

Joe Freelance was an independent producer of television documentaries and of television news stories. During the past few years, Joe had frequently produced stories for the CBS "60 Minutes" news program. On September 25, Joe had the following conversation with Don Hughclever, who was in charge of producing "60 Minutes."

Don: We're thinking of running a story on photocopy salespersons. Do they all look like Jack Klugman? What brand of glass cleaner do they use to clean the glass plates on their photocopiers? Inquiring minds want to know!

Joe: I could do a ten-minute story like that for you, but I'd have to ask at least $25,000.

Don: We could afford to pay that much for a high quality piece . . .

[Sound of telephone ringing. Don answers it and then turns back to Joe]

Don: Excuse me, Joe. I have to talk to our nightly news anchorman now. We'll talk again later.

The next day, Don sent the following letter to Joe:

Dear Joe:

CBS is willing to pay $25,000 for a high quality ten-minute piece on photocopier salespersons. We are scheduling it for our December 1, show.

SAMPLE ESSAY QUESTIONS

Very truly yours,

(Signed) Don Hughclever

Joe did not respond to the letter, but immediately got to work on the story. Accompanied by an associate with a TV camera hidden in a briefcase, Joe went to Maxine's Wonderful World of Photocopiers and posed as a potential buyer. Maxine herself showed Joe several models of photocopiers. Joe said he liked the Z1000 photocopier and asked what he needed to do to get one. Maxine said she could quote him a price of $1,000 for a Z1000, and that he should send in a purchase order.

Joe then returned to his office and, with the television camera focused on his desk, filled out a purchase order. As he did so, Joe said (into the microphone), "We'll send this purchase order to Maxine and see how long it takes her to respond. Television viewers, this is true drama." Joe mailed Maxine the purchase order (which merely stated that he was ordering one Z1000 for $1,000).

Maxine received the purchase order the next day and immediately drove to the post office to mail back an acknowledgement which was sent in an envelope with sufficient postage and addressed correctly. The acknowledgement stated that Maxine would fill Joe's order at the stated price. It also stated that:

(1) The Z1000 is warranted to work properly for one month or 1,000 copies, whichever comes first;

(2) There is NO IMPLIED WARRANTY OF MERCHANTABILITY OR FITNESS FOR ANY PARTICULAR PURPOSE accompanying the sale of the Z1000;

(3) The $1,000 price for the Z1000 offered by Maxine is a special low price. By ordering a Z1000 at that price, Buyer agrees to buy all photocopy supplies for the Z1000 from Maxine for the next year at Maxine's standard prices; and

(4) The terms of this acknowledgement, and only the terms of this acknowledgement, are the terms of the contract between Buyer and Maxine.

Then Maxine returned from the post office, she found a message from Joe on her telephone answering machine. The message was:

I am doing a story on photocopier salesperson for "60 Minutes." I don't really want a copier. Watch the show on December 1. This is Joe. Good-bye.

Joe never finished the story for "60 Minutes." CBS sued Joe for breach of contract. So did Maxine. Will CBS prevail? Will Maxine prevail? Discuss.

SAMPLE ESSAY QUESTIONS

Question No. 8

Sound mixing companies prepare the sound tracks for motion pictures, television shows, and commercials. Johnson worked for a sound mixing company for ten years, learned everything there was to know about sound mixing and about sound mixing equipment, and then decided to start his own sound mixing company. In the fall, he purchased a small house in an area zoned for residential and commercial uses and began to remodel it into a sound mixing studio. He ordered acoustic paneling to put on the walls. On Friday, October 16, the paneling was delivered, and Johnson started to go to the hardware store to buy nails to install it. As he was about to get in his car, he spotted Neighbor in her front yard and introduced himself. When Johnson said he was going to the hardware store to buy nails, Neighbor said, "I've got a bag of nails I don't need. You can have it for $20. I'm leaving on vacation right now, but if you want the bag, it's in the garage." Neighbor got in her car and drove off. Johnson looked in Neighbor's garage, saw the bag of nails, and saw that it still had a $15 hardware store price tag on it. Johnson took the bag and left a note for Neighbor saying he would pay her only $15 for the nails, since that is what the nails cost her.

On Monday, October 19, Sound Mixing Equipment Sales Co. ("Sales Co.") mailed a letter to Johnson. (Johnson had written Sales Co. asking for its best offer on an Acme X14 Super Sound Mixer.) Sales Co.'s letter stated:

> Pursuant to your inquiry, we are happy to quote you an Acme Super Sound Mixer for the low price of $30,000. We do not usually sell X14's for this low a price, but we intend to get lots of business from your new company. You can come by our premises any time before next Thursday, October 29 to give us an answer.

Johnson received Sales Co.'s letter on Thursday, October 22. That same day, October 22, Sales Co., mailed the following letter to Johnson:

> After further consideration, we must ask $32,000 for the Acme X14.

On Monday, October 26, Johnson received Sales Co.'s letter of October 22.

On Saturday, October 24, after he had received the 10/19 letter but before he had received the 10/22 one, Johnson mailed the following letter to Sales Co.:

> It's a deal. I insist that if any lawsuit that arises out of this deal, the losing party will pay the prevailing party's attorney's fees.

Sales Co. received Johnson's letter of October 24 on Wednesday, October 28.

SAMPLE ESSAY QUESTIONS

Discuss the following questions:

(1) Does Johnson have a contract to pay $20 for the nails?

(2) Does Johnson have a contract to buy an X14?

(3) Assuming he does, regardless of your answer to Part "(2)",

    (a) Is the attorney's fee term a part of the contract?

    (b) What price must Johnson pay for the X14?

    (c) Is Johnson obligated to buy additional items from Sales Co.?

Question No. 9

Pete, the owner of Pete's Ambulance Service ("Pete's") came into your office today, July 13, and told you the following story:

On June 1, Pete's purchased a new ambulance from Sam's Specialty Chevrolet ("Sam's") for $35,000. Just before the contract was signed, Peter told Sam he needed a reliable vehicle, and related a horror story about what happened a few weeks prior when one of his ambulances got a flat tire on the way to the hospital while transporting a critically ill patient and the driver discovered there was no spare tire. In response, Sam promised personally to see to it that two spares were installed in the new ambulance. Nonetheless, Peter discovered yesterday that no spare tires were ever installed in the vehicle he purchased from Sam's.

The purchase contract was only one page long and paragraph 6 was set out in all capital letters as follows: "SELLER'S RESPONSIBILITIES UNDER THIS AGREEMENT ARE LIMITED SOLELY TO REPAIR OR REPLACEMENT, IN ITS SOLE DISCRETION, OF ANY DEFECTIVE PART OF SUBJECT VEHICLE FOR A PERIOD OF TWELVE MONTHS. IN NO EVENT WILL SELLER BE RESPONSIBLE FOR CONSEQUENTIAL DAMAGES ARISING OUT OF ANY BREACH OF THIS AGREEMENT."

Pete's took delivery on June 1 and drove without incident for two weeks. However, starting June 15 the engine began to stall, and between June 15 and July 7, the ambulance was in Sam's service department being worked on for 10 full days. Each ambulance in Pete's fleet averages two calls a day at $500 per call.

On July 7, Sam told Peter his shop had fixed the stalling problem and indeed the ambulance operated normally until yesterday. At about noon yesterday the ambulance was on its way to the hospital with a heart attack patient when the engine stalled in the middle of an intersection. When the engine stopped, the power steering froze, and the driver crashed into a light pole, injuring herself. The ambulance would not restart, and so another ambulance had to be called to deal

SAMPLE ESSAY QUESTIONS

with the heart attack victim. The delay in getting another ambulance to the scene caused the patient further injuries.

At about 5:00 p.m. yesterday Peter called Sam to tell him to take his no-good ambulance back, and found out that Sam's was out of business.

Please advise Peter as to all his present options concerning the ambulance arising under **contract law** (do not discuss any tort claims he may have), and what procedures he must follow, if any, to take advantage of each option. Also discuss any defenses he is likely to face in pursuing each such option, and the damages, if any, available to him under each option.

SUGGESTED ANALYSIS OF SAMPLE ESSAY QUESTIONS

Answer to Question No. 1

Will Sally prevail?

Sally will prevail only if there was an enforceable contract that was breached by Bub.

There was a contract.

Sally did not offer to sell the house to Bub for $150,000 on June 1; she merely said she was asking $150,000 for it [Text § 3–16]. Anyway, Bub never accepted any offer at $150,000. Similarly, Bub did not offer to buy it for $140,000; he merely asked if she would take $140,000 for it [Text § 3–16]. Further, even if Bub somehow made an offer to buy it for $140,000, Sally never accepted any such offer.

Sally's June 2 letter **is** an offer. It says it is an offer, invites Bub to accept, includes words of commitment ("If you accept, then you **will** pay . . . and **I will** give you a deed . . ."), and its terms are reasonably definite [Text § 3–1]. It was a manifestation of commitment to enter into a bargain so made as to justify Bub in reasonably concluding that his acceptance was invited and would conclude the bargain.

Bub explicitly accepted the offer on June 4, within the time period for acceptance under the offer [Text § 4–27] and obviously Bub was a proper offeree, for the offer was plainly directed to him [Text § 4–6]. Thus, there was an offer and acceptance.

This is a bilateral contract, and thus, Bub's promise to pay was consideration for Sally's promise to hand over the deed, and **vice versa** [Text § 7–12].

Thus, there was a contract based on the terms of the June 2 and June 4 letters.

The contract may or may not be enforceable under the statute of frauds.

This is a contract for sale of an interest in real property so it is within the statute of frauds [Text § 10–7]. Thus, there must be a memorandum of the contract signed by the party to be charged, which identifies the parties, identifies the subject matter of the

SUGGESTED ANALYSIS OF SAMPLE ESSAY QUESTIONS

contract, and **contains all the essential terms** of the contract [Text 10–10]. Otherwise the contract is voidable. [Text § 10–3].

Bub is the "party to be charged" under the statute, because he is the one who is resisting enforcement of the contract. The only writing he signed was the letter of June 4. Since that letter expressly refers to the letter of June 2 and expresses his assent to it, all courts will be willing to read the two letters together (integrate them) to see if there is a sufficient memorandum. The two letters together identify the parties (Bub and Sally), more or less identify the subject matter (Sally's home on Park Street), and state a lot of the terms, but not all of them. The letters say nothing about the condition precedent that Bub find a buyer for his house by July 1, nothing about Sally's obligation to paint the house, and do not state which of Sally's houses on Park Street is the subject matter of the agreement.

The issues then are whether the identification of the house is sufficient, and whether the condition precedent and the painting term are essential terms.

You cannot tell from the letters alone what real property is being sold. However, in a sense that is always true. Even if the letters said "2101 Park Street," you still would not know what real property was involved without looking at a parcel map to find Park Street and then looking at the numbers on the houses to find out which one was 2101 and how much surrounding land came with the house. You always have to look at some external facts to apply the contract to the real world. The question should be whether the facts you have to look to are objectively verifiable facts that do not involve a risk of perjury; if so then the description should be considered adequate.

Modern courts will not be bothered by the absence of a specific mention of a particular city and state. There is no indication from these facts that Sally owned a home on any Park Street in any other city. The absence of a street number would not be a problem if Sally owned only one house on Park Street; there, the question of which house on Park Street she owns could be answered by looking to objective facts without any risk of perjury. Here, however, she owns two houses on Park Street, so the question is whether the letters provide us with enough identifying information to decide which house is being sold without there being a risk of perjury. The letters provide two important bits of information: (1) the house that is being sold is Sally's "home;" and (2) the house has an odd shaped dining room. Objective facts can be used to determine which of the two houses was being used as a "home" by Sally, and if only one of the houses has an odd shaped dining room suited for a custom made table and chair set worth $600, then that too is an objective fact that identifies the property that is being sold. A court that took a modern approach to this would almost certainly decide that the property was adequately described. The court might also consider the price in the letters to indicate that 2101 Park Street was intended, since its value is much closer to $145,000 than is the value of 2103 Park Street.

The next question then is whether omission of the painting term and of the condition precedent is fatal to the enforceability of the agreement. We must first ask if these terms were part of the contract. If they were not part of the contract, then it would not matter that they were omitted. To satisfy the statute of frauds, a memorandum must contain all the essential terms of the contract [Text § 10–10]. (Below is a discussion as to whether such terms are part of the contract under the parol evidence rule; for now just assume that they were part of it.)

The painting term is relatively minor in value—$2,000 out of $145,000 total—so a court might say it was a mere detail rather than an essential term.

The condition precedent was very important, however. Assuming that there was a real chance Bub might not be able to find a buyer in a month, the condition would make it much less likely that Sally would get the benefit of the contract. Thus, a court could well say the condition was an essential term, and thus hold that the letters were insufficient to satisfy the statute of frauds. On the other hand, conditions precedent like this one can be proved despite the parol evidence rule (as we will see below), even if the writing otherwise is treated as a complete integration. It would seem strange to allow the condition to be proved under one rule which is designed to prevent perjury (the parol evidence rule) but then to throw out the whole contract under another rule that is designed to prevent perjury (the statute of frauds). Accordingly, it is reasonable to suppose that the condition should not be treated as an essential term under the statute of frauds, or that its absence can be excused given that there is no argument that the term was, in fact, part of the contract, and that the contract is thus enforceable under the Statute.

Was the condition precedent part of the contract? Yes.

The condition precedent of Bub obtaining a contract to sell his home by July 1 was a condition that would either have to be fulfilled or excused before either party would owe any enforceable duties to the other under the contract. Thus, evidence of the condition is admissible under the doctrine that the parol evidence rule does not apply to exclude evidence that a condition precedent was not fulfilled [Text § 18–22].

Since evidence of the condition is admissible, the only question is whether that evidence will convince the trier of fact that the parties agreed to the condition. Of course, there is no way to predict how a particular jury would view this proof in advance, but there are reasons to think the evidence would be accepted. First, the evidence of the June 1 conversation will establish that both parties agreed that such a condition would be part of any bargain that they ultimately concluded. A reasonable person would therefore think that the condition was part of their ultimate agreement, unless when they formed their contract by correspondence they manifested an intent not to have such a condition. No such intent was manifested. Further, the June 10 telephone conversation indicates that both parties still thought the condition was part of their deal. Why would Bub have said he would buy the house "anyway" if he did not think the condition was part of the original deal? If Sally did not think the condition was part of the original deal, she probably would have protested that there was no such condition at all. She would not have in effect said that since Bub was waiving the condition, she would go ahead and have the painting done without waiting to see if Bub could sell his house.

Thus, evidence of the condition precedent is admissible under the parol evidence rule, and that evidence should be enough to convince the trier of fact that the condition was part of their bargain.

Did Bub waive the condition? Yes.

The condition was waived if Bub led Sally reasonably to believe that he would perform even if the event described in the condition did not occur [Text § 21–92]. He told her he would buy her home even if he could not find a buyer for his home, so even though the condition was part of the initial contract, Bub was (as of June 10) obligated to buy the house regardless whether the condition was fulfilled.

Was Bub entitled to reinstate the condition? Perhaps.

At the time of the waiver the condition had not yet failed—it was still possible that Bub might find a buyer by July 1. Thus, his waiver did not become an "election." [Text § 21–94] That means the waiver can be retracted (and the condition reinstated) if Bub gave Sally notice of the retraction before she *materially* changed position in reliance on the waiver [Text § 21–100].

Bub attempted to retract the waiver on June 12, only two days after making it. However, Sally had already entered into a contract to have the house painted by that time. That is, she had relied on the promise of the waiver of the condition to her legal detriment.

The next issue, however, is whether Sally's reliance was a "material" change of position based on the waiver. A court could say that $2,000 in absolute terms is a lot of money to the average homeowner, so Sally did materially change position if she had the house painted. However, as she apparently only **contracted** to have it painted, she should be able to get out of the painting contract for a lot less than $2,000—even if the painting contractor is unwilling to negotiate a rescission, Sally could repudiate the contract and probably pay a lot less than $2,000 in damages (although the hassle of defending a lawsuit and the possible injury to Sally's reputation if she repudiates the painting contract might lead the court to consider the whole $2,000 as Sally's reliance). A court might not think that lesser amount would represent a material change in her position.

Further, the court would consider whether Sally was going to have to paint the house anyway to sell it to someone else. If so, her injury from painting it now would be little or nothing. A court might also say that if the house needed painting, and if the painting increased the value of the house, then Sally's reliance did not represent a material change of position.

If the court concludes that Bub was entitled to reinstate the condition because Sally had not "materially" relied on his waiver, then Sally will not prevail in her lawsuit. That is, because the condition (Bub's house selling by July 1) was not fulfilled, Bub had no obligation to buy the home [Text § 21–2].

In other words, they were in a valid contract, but because of the failure of the condition precedent, the duties under the contract were never enforceable. Since the duties were unenforceable, Bub could not have breached by not performing.

If, on the other hand, the court concludes that Bub was not entitled to reinstate the condition, Sally will prevail in her lawsuit. Bub's duty to buy the home would then become unconditional [Text § 21–2]. The only condition to Bub's duty to buy the home would be the constructive condition that Sally would have to tender a deed to the home before Bub would be obligated to pay the contract price of $145,000 [Text § 21–43]. Sally satisfied that condition by timely tendering the deed. In that case, Bub would be in breach when he failed to tender the purchase price.

Another argument for Sally is that Bub's June 12 telephone conversation acted as an anticipatory repudiation of the

SUGGESTED ANALYSIS OF SAMPLE ESSAY QUESTIONS

purchase contract. That is, the argument is that Bub made a definite and unequivocal expression of his intent not to go forward with the purchase in that conversation. [Text § 23–12] His conversation probably is not an anticipatory repudiation, however. Most likely, Bub was merely expressing his view that he could retract his waiver, and not impliedly stating that if he could retract his waiver, he refused to continue with the contract. If Bub's statement **was** an anticipatory repudiation, however, Sally was entitled to treat the contract as breached at that point and sue for total breach damages [Text § 23–12].

Was the condition precedent eliminated by an enforceable modification of the parties' agreement? No.

A separate issue is whether the June 10 conversation acted as an oral modification of the contract. In other words, regardless of whether a "waiver" of the condition occurred, did the 6/10 conversation eliminate the condition from the deal altogether by means of a modification? [Text § 9–1] While Sally would like to argue this is the case, thereby making the contract enforceable, she runs into several problems with that theory. First, a modification of a contract is itself a contract: it is the substitution of a new different contract for the original contract. That means there must be mutual assent (offer and acceptance) **and consideration** for a modification to occur. There probably was an offer and acceptance. Bub certainly manifested assent in the June 10 conversation to an elimination of the condition. There may be some question as to whether Sally manifested assent in return, however. Clearly, Sally did not **expressly** manifest any assent. However, she did say she would go ahead and arrange for the painting. Accordingly, a reasonable person might well interpret that statement as assent to elimination of the condition, so probably mutual assent can be established.

While there is an offer and an acceptance of the modification, there is no apparent consideration for the deal. Bub does not say, "I will agree to eliminate the condition if you will agree to reduce the price by $500" or anything similar. It does not appear that Bub is seeking anything in exchange (i.e., is bargaining) for his action in rescinding the condition [Text § 7–89]; he just flatly says that he will buy the house even if the condition is not satisfied. Neither does it appear that Sally is giving him anything **in exchange** for eliminating the condition. She does say she will go ahead and arrange for the painting, but an objective observer would likely not think she is exchanging that promise for his elimination of the condition. Rather, she is most likely reacting to his statement that he will buy the house even if the condition is not satisfied. Thus, because the bargained for

SUGGESTED ANALYSIS OF SAMPLE ESSAY QUESTIONS

exchange requirement is not met, the "modification" is unenforceable because there is no consideration for it. (This is not a UCC Article 2 contract, so consideration or promissory estoppel is needed [Text §§ 7–72; 9–20]. There are no unanticipated circumstances so Restatement 2d § 89(a) does not apply.)

In addition, the statute of frauds bars enforcement of any modification here. The contract as modified is a contract for the conveyance of an interest in land [Text § 10–7], so the modification has to be evidenced by a memorandum signed by Bub (the party to be charged, i.e., the party who would be denying that there was a modification which eliminated the condition). [Text § 10–10] There is no such memorandum.

Damages, Assuming Sally Prevails

The contract called for Sally to get $145,000 in exchange for a $135,000 house, $2,000 worth of painting, and the $600 dining room set. Thus, if the contract had been performed, she would have gotten $145,000 in cash, but would have given up a total of $137,600 in value. Thus, she would have improved her economic condition by $7,400 [Text § 30–28]. That is, she would have to receive $7,400 to put her in the same economic position as if the contract had been fully performed. (Her expectation interest is greater than any reliance or restitution interest she may have, so she will seek enforcement of her expectation interest.)

All of this assumes Sally was obligated under the contract to paint the house. If she was not obligated to paint it, and did not paint it, her damages would be increased by $2,000. That is, in such event, the bargain would have been for her to give up only the $135,000 home and the $600 table and chairs in exchange for the $145,000. Accordingly, her expectation damages would be $9,400.

To decide whether she was obligated to paint the house, we must consider the parol evidence rule. Bub's June 4 letter expressed assent to a contract as "set forth in your [Sally's] June 2 letter." That should be enough to constitute adoption by Bub of the June 2 letter as a final statement of the parties' agreement [Text § 18–4]. (Of course, Sally adopted it as a proposed final statement of the parties' agreement by signing and sending it.) The June 2 letter does not appear to be tentative and it has some detail in it. Thus, the June 2/June 4 letter agreements, taken together, would at least constitute a partial integration, meaning that neither party could introduce evidence of prior written agreements or prior or contemporaneous oral agreements that "contradict" the terms of the letters [Text § 18–4]. Using the "might naturally" test, it would appear the painting requirement

SUGGESTED ANALYSIS OF SAMPLE ESSAY QUESTIONS

is a consistent additional term. That is, if the parties had agreed to it, it is the kind of thing that might naturally have been left out of their contract. [Text § 18–13] Thus, Bub can introduce evidence of the term unless the June 2/June 4 letters constitute a complete integration.

Depending on the jurisdiction, a court will apply one of two tests to determine if the June 2/June 4 letter agreement is a complete integration.

Under the "four corners" test, the court will probably conclude that it is a complete integration. [Text § 18–9] There is nothing obviously left out, and there is quite a bit of detail in the letter. As such, a court might well conclude the parties' agreement was completely integrated and no additional evidence of its terms will be permitted. However, a court might also say that a $145,000 transaction would probably have additional details, in which case that the letter agreement would be found incompletely integrated.

Under the "reasonably susceptible" test, [Text § 18–11] the court considers separately, out of the presence of the jury, all the relevant evidence about the contract. If the court believes the painting term was really a part of the agreement (or at least that there is credible evidence that it was), then the court allows the trier of fact to consider the evidence. Here, there is good evidence that the term was agreed to and that the parties did not intend to eliminate it. Sally's phone response on June 10 is especially persuasive. Accordingly, it is likely that under the reasonably susceptible test the contract will be considered only partially integrated.

Answer to Question No. 2

Part (a) of the question involves 5 issues:

1) Whether the letter of 12/1 was an offer;

2) The effect of the delay of the offer in the mail;

3) The effect of the lease to Xerxes ("X");

4) The effect of the loss of the December 14 letter in the mail; and

5) Whether the inclusion of the statement "Please be sure all the locks and appliances are in good working order" prevented the December 14 letter from being an effective acceptance.

    1) An offer is a manifestation of willingness (or commitment) to enter into a bargain so made as to justify another in believing that his or her assent is invited and will conclude the bargain [Text § 3–1]. The 12/1 letter showed willingness to enter into the bargain and commitment to the proposed bargain. That is, it

SUGGESTED ANALYSIS OF SAMPLE ESSAY QUESTIONS

used words of commitment ("I **will** lease you my house," "You can have the house") and it invited Tom to accept ("Write me with your answer . . ."), thus showing that Leslie was committed to leasing the house to Tom if Tom assented to the proposed deal. Because the letter asked Tom to give an answer, Tom was justified in believing that his assent was invited.

The real issue here was the indefiniteness of the December 1 letter. It did not state the rental price, when rent would be due, how much rent would be paid in advance, how much of a security deposit (if any) would be required, **etc.** [Text § 6–8]. This indefiniteness has two effects: (1) it may make it unreasonable for Tom to believe that Leslie is making a sufficient commitment to lease the house to Tom so as to make the letter an offer—a reasonable person would probably want to have these terms settled before being bound to a bargain; and (2) even if Leslie manifested enough commitment, if the bargain is too indefinite it will not be enforced.

As to the first effect, Leslie has used rather clear words of commitment, and she is concerned with nailing down a tenant for her house quickly, because she is about to leave for Europe. Tom could reasonably believe that Leslie was willing to lease the house for a reasonable amount on the usual terms.

As to the second effect, if the parties intended to conclude a bargain (as they apparently did here), courts are hesitant to destroy that bargain for indefiniteness. This is a case of omitted terms [Text § 6–5] (not an agreement to agree), so a court could reasonably conclude that the parties intended the rentals to be a reasonable amount on the usual terms; at least the court could conclude that implying such reasonable and usual terms would not unjustly violate the expectations of the parties. This is a lease of property and thus the UCC's gap fillers do not specifically apply, but courts in non-UCC transactions are increasingly willing to imply reasonable and usual terms to save a contract from indefiniteness where it does not appear that such implications will defeat the parties' expectations [Text § 6–23].

Fair market rental value can probably be determined sufficiently accurately from the rental price of similar houses in the area, and there probably are fairly standard terms in the area (for example, first and last months' rent in advance plus one month's rent security deposit, with rentals payable monthly on the first of each month). Some courts would imply terms to make the contract enforceable; others would say that more certainty is needed in contracts involving real property than in other contracts and would refuse to imply terms. Assuming a court is willing to imply terms, the contract will be enforceable.

SUGGESTED ANALYSIS OF SAMPLE ESSAY QUESTIONS

2) Assuming the December 1 letter was definite enough to be an offer, the next issue is the effect of the delay of the offer in the mail. The rule is that the time to accept an offer which gives a time period for acceptance runs from the time the offer is received, unless the offer states otherwise [Text § 4–52]. However, if the offeree has reason to know that communication of the offer has been delayed, the amount of the delay is subtracted from the period for acceptance [Text § 4–53]. This all, thus, boils down to whether Tom had reason to know that the postal service delayed the offer. If the letter had been dated, perhaps he would have had reason to know. However, since it bore no date, and the envelope gave no indication of the letter's misplacement, he had no reason to know of the delay. Accordingly, the offer was still open and he accepted it in a timely manner, unless it had been effectively revoked.

3) That takes us to the question of the effect of the lease to X. Did it revoke the offer? The answer is "no." Tom was never told by Leslie that she was revoking the offer, [Text § 4–58] hence her only argument is indirect revocation. However, an indirect revocation is only effective when the offeree obtains reliable information that the offeror has taken action that is inconsistent with an intent to enter into the offered bargain. [Text § 4–61] There is no indication here that Tom obtained **any** information about the lease to X until January 1, long after Tom sent his acceptance. An offeror cannot revoke an offer after it is accepted, of course.

4) The loss of Tom's acceptance letter in the mail does not matter. Leslie sent the offer via mail, so the mail would normally be a reasonable (and therefore invited) means of sending the acceptance. [Text § 4–94] She did not tell him he had to use some other means and she came close to actually telling him to use the mail by asking Tom to write her with his answer. Thus, the mail was an invited means of acceptance. An acceptance sent by an invited means is effective when it is sent, even if it never arrives, so long as it is properly addressed and stamped, which this one was [Text § 4–119].

5) Finally, there is the question of the statement in the acceptance that Leslie should be sure that the locks and appliances were in good working order. This is not a contract for the sale of goods, so UCC § 2–207 does not apply. The old "mirror image" rule applies, so if Tom's letter is *requiring* an added term, it is not an acceptance but rather a counter-offer (which Leslie never accepted). [Text § 5–1].

It is possible that Tom is accepting Leslie's offer and merely suggesting or requesting that she make sure the locks and appliances are working. That is, his letter could be interpreted not as adding a term upon which he is **insisting** be included in the deal, but rather as only a letter suggesting or requesting the offeror's consideration of additional terms [Text § 4–35]. However, in the letter he asks her to "be sure" about the appliances and such language sounds stronger than a mere request or suggestion, even though he does say "Please." Tom's best argument is that the landlord-tenant law already requires that locks and appliances be in good working order because it requires landlords to have their premises in safe and decent condition. Thus, responsibility for making sure the appliance worked and the locks were fixed would already be understood as part of Leslie's responsibilities without Tom saying anything, and hence he did not add any term that was not already there by operation of law. This is a stronger argument as to locks, and as to those appliances, that either are unsafe if they do not work (such as a gas heater), or which create a less than decent living situation if they do not work (water heater). It is not a very good argument as to appliances such as dishwashers or toasters. This is because such appliances do not directly relate to the "safe and decent" portion of the landlord's duties, so if there are such appliances Tom may be deemed to have added a term. On the other hand, perhaps it is usual in this area for landlords to have all appliances in good working order, and hence Leslie would already have that obligation based on the usual and customary terms of leases in the trade, which is possible because the offer is silent on this point. [Text § 19–13] If so, then Tom's letter did not add any term, and his December 14 letter is an effective acceptance.

Part (b)

The question here is whether there is consideration for Leslie's promise to pay the $600. Tom's promise to release a claim that turned out to be invalid can still be consideration. All that is required is that at the time the settlement contract was made Tom had an honest belief of a colorable claim for Leslie's promise to be enforced [Text § 7–76]. If Tom believed his attorney, then Tom did **not** honestly believe he had a claim, and there is no consideration. (Tom's quick agreement to accept much less than he demanded may show he did not have much confidence in the validity of his claim, but it will not be conclusive). If Tom did not believe his attorney, then he may have honestly believed his claim might be valid, which would be enough to enforce the promise.

SUGGESTED ANALYSIS OF SAMPLE ESSAY QUESTIONS

Part (c)

It is much less likely that there will be a contract if the parties agreed to agree. The courts have a harder time implying a reasonable term when the parties have said that they—the parties—are going to determine what the term is [Text § 6–7]. Here there is reliance by Tom, which Leslie should have expected. A reasonable rental amount will probably fall close to the amount that the parties would have agreed on if they in fact had gone ahead and agreed on the amount, and it will probably be an objectively determinable and fair amount for the court to force each party to accept. On the other hand, it is a very important term, and the court may refuse to "make an agreement for the parties."

Answer to Question No. 3

Statute of frauds on agreement to write and publish between Priscilla ("P") and Novice ("N").

This contract is not within the one year provision of the statute of frauds because the contract, by its very terms, is not impossible for P to complete in one year [Text § 10–15]. Just because all the chapters will not be **due** for 18 months does not mean P must take that long to write them. N is supposed to pay her when she completes the book, so if she completes it in less than a year, N must pay her then. This is a contract for services, rather than goods, so UCC § 2–201 does not apply. Thus, this is a contract that, by its terms, can be completed within a year and thus is enforceable even if oral.

Note that N's promise would also likely be enforceable, at least to some degree, on promissory estoppel grounds given the foreseeable and actual reliance undertaken by P in putting in 4 months' work on the first chapter [Text § 10–58].

Statute of frauds on guarantee by Big Bucks ("BB").

BB's promise is subject to the suretyship provision of the statute of frauds [Text § 10–26]. That is, BB is a "surety" because: (i) N may eventually owe a debt to P; (ii) as between BB and N, N is primarily liable, BB is only secondarily liable for the debt should it become due; and (iii) the promise was made to P, the creditor [Text §§ 10–27; 10–29]. The "leading object" or the "main purpose" doctrine probably does not apply here, for the economic benefit of the promise was for N, not BB [Text § 10–31]. Note, however, that an argument could be made that BB wanted the book written for his own purposes because he was interested in ethics (thereby invoking the "main purpose" doctrine), but as he does not stand to benefit economically, the doctrine likely does not apply.

SUGGESTED ANALYSIS OF SAMPLE ESSAY QUESTIONS

As the promise is within the Statute, P may or may not be able to enforce it. As the party seeking to enforce the promise, P must establish a sufficient writing, signed by BB [Text § 10–34]. Whether BB's business card is a sufficient writing is a close call: BB's printed name on it is probably a sufficient signature since he probably used his card (rather than just any piece of paper) to identify to P the name of the person who was making the promise. In other words, he used it to authenticate his intention to stand behind the guarantee. The writing is probably sufficient to identify the parties to the surety promise, i.e., BB's name is on it and its delivery by him to P should be enough to identify her as the promisee, especially since the identity of the promisee will not likely be disputed. However, it may not have all the essential terms. Perhaps the only essential term is that he is guaranteeing the payment of the $30,000, which the card says, but a court may believe some further description of the debt is needed, e.g., under what circumstance will it be paid, who is the principal, **etc.**

If the card is judged an insufficient writing, however, promissory estoppel may suffice to let P enforce the promise [Text § 10–58].

Effect of 18 day delay in completion of first chapter.

P promised to perform a series of services—completion of 15 chapters. Completion of each chapter on time is not an express condition of N's duty to pay [Text § 21–4], but failure to timely perform under a contract is always a breach [Text § 21–1]. The question then will be whether P materially breached by submitting the first chapter late [Text § 21–58] and, if so, whether she failed to cure that breach within an appropriate time [Text § 21–77]. If she did materially breach without curing, N's duties will be discharged and it may cancel the contract. If her delay is only an immaterial breach, N will be obligated to continue performing, but will have a claim against P for partial breach due to the delay.

The relevant factors for determining whether the breach is material or not are listed in Restatement 2d §§ 241 and 242 [Text § 21–65]:

The extent to which the breach will deprive N of the benefit which it reasonably expected (18 day delay seems trivial because it will lead to less than a 1% increase of costs, and because speed is no longer important after the veto, and because P may be able to "make up" the lost time on later chapters);

The extent to which damages can adequately compensate N (if P ends up taking longer than 18 months to finish, N can probably prove the increase in publishing costs caused by the delay, and those expenses will be recoverable for the partial breach);

The extent of forfeiture on P's part if N is permitted to cancel (P's work of more than 4 months will be forfeited);

The likelihood of cure (if P can write the later chapters slightly faster than one per month she can make up the lost time—but perhaps that will be very difficult);

The extent to which P acted in good faith and fairly (she apparently worked very hard to minimize the delay);

The extent to which any delay in allowing N to terminate will prevent N from making substitute arrangements (N does not want to make substitute arrangements for the treatise); and

The extent to which the agreement provides for performance without delay (i.e., there is no agreed upon "time is of the essence clause" here).

As a result, P's breach should only be judged immaterial, and thus the delay does not justify N's cancellation of the contract [Text § 21–60].

Effect of President's veto on N's duties.

There are two major issues raised by the President's veto: (1) did the veto frustrate N's purpose in entering into the contract [Text § 25–45]; and (2) was existence of the new law an implied-in-fact condition of either party's duties under the contract [Text § 21–6]?

Did the veto frustrate N's purpose?

Whether the contract was frustrated depends on how you define N's purposes under it. N will still get a book on government ethics if the contract proceeds, but it will not be the kind of book that will let N break into law publishing in a successful way. Is P's performance essentially worthless to N? Arguably it is, since it will not be financially worthwhile to publish the book. However, it can be used in N's business as part of the range of subjects it covers, even though it will not be profitable. There is a strong presumption against a finding of frustration just because a party will not make as much money from the contract as expected, or even if a party will lose some money [Text §§ 25–47; 25–49]. Hence, all things considered, it appears that frustration will not provide a successful defense to N because, on these facts, there is insufficient "frustration."

SUGGESTED ANALYSIS OF SAMPLE ESSAY QUESTIONS

Implied-in-fact condition.

The argument here is that since both P and N knew that the market would not support a new book on the old law, the fact that the law was passed was an implied-in-fact condition of their duties. (It is not a constructive condition for it is not implied by the court as a means of determining the parties' rights and duties.) This is a very close question. The principal argument against it is that if the condition was really that important, it is likely that the parties would have discussed it openly and made it an express condition. However, if it was well understood, even if not overtly expressed, it could be that the passage of the new law is an implied condition precedent, and thus the veto by the President made each party's duties under the contract unenforceable.

Effect of veto on P's duties.

Just as frustration is principally a buyer's remedy, impossibility and impracticability are seller's or supplier's remedies. Here, the veto did not make it impossible for P to finish the book [Text § 25–3], but it probably made it impracticable for it to be completed on time [Text § 25–31]. That is, the veto was the occurrence of an event, the non-occurrence of which was a basic assumption of both parties on which the contract was made [Text § 25–36]. It occurred without P's fault [Text § 25–38], and it does not seem that P either explicitly or implicitly assumed the risk that the veto would occur, since neither seemed to have considered its possibility [Text § 25–40]. This would likely be treated as a case of temporary impracticability, which means that P's delay is excused for a "reasonable period of time," and such delay cannot be considered a breach by N [Text § 25–60]. Note that if her delay in performance is "unreasonably" long (e.g., because P stopped working on it for nine months or so), then it would still constitute a material breach, and her failure to satisfy an unexcused constructive condition would justify N's withholding its performance. If the delay continues reasonably, but for a long enough period so that it creates a hardship to N, e.g., where P is working diligently, but it is taking a long time to re-structure her entire book, N would be thereafter justified in canceling the contract, but N would not have an action for breach against P.

The condition of satisfaction.

If the judging of the quality of a manuscript is seen as depending on the tastes of the publisher, then a subjective good faith standard would be applied [Text § 7–49]. That is, for N to cancel the contract on the grounds of dissatisfaction, N must **actually** be dissatisfied with the quality of the manuscript, not just with the terms of the deal. If so, application of the good faith promise is a sufficient restriction on N's activities as to cure any illusory promise problems. Since Newton merely skimmed the chapter, it appears he did not in good faith try to see if the chapter was satisfactory but just said it was not in order to be able to cancel the contract. Moreover, it is difficult for Newton to be able to state credibly that the **entire manuscript** would be unsatisfactory by reading just one chapter. The good faith obligations under a contract would seem to require N to at least have told P what was wrong with the chapter so that she could rewrite it and do the other chapters to N's liking. Accordingly there has been a breach of the duty of good faith and fair dealing by N.

Remedies.

If N is able to terminate the contract on grounds of frustration, P should get restitution of any benefits she has conferred on N [Text § 25–64]. It is difficult to know if N got any benefit at all. Under the "cost avoided" method of valuation, P would be entitled to the going rate for writing such a chapter for a legal publisher. Under the "net benefit" method, P's recovery would be nothing, for receipt of an unusable chapter has not advanced N's economic interests in the slightest [Text § 31–5].

If N is entitled to cancel the contract as a result of P's breach (i.e., in the unlikely event P's late tender will be judged a material breach), even then P is entitled to restitution [Text § 31–28]. However, restitution requires that when a breaching party seeks restitution, the measure of valuation used is the one least favorable to the breacher [Text § 31–10]. Hence, on these facts, should P be seeking restitution as the breacher, she would receive little or nothing because her compensation would be determined by the net benefit method.

If N wrongfully canceled, then N repudiated the contract and P can receive damages of $30,000, less whatever amount she can now reasonably earn from comparable employment that she would not have been able to earn if she were still working on the book [Text § 31–29].

Answer to Question No. 4

Offer

An offer is a manifestation of willingness to enter into a bargain, so made as to justify another in believing that his assent is invited and will conclude the bargain [Text § 3–1]. It must be definite enough to permit a court to determine the existence of a breach and to provide an appropriate remedy. If the

SUGGESTED ANALYSIS OF SAMPLE ESSAY QUESTIONS

manifestation shows that sender does not intend to be bound until he or she manifests further assent, it is not an offer.

Sal did not make an offer by sending the brochure and order form to Bev. Advertising brochures typically aren't offers, for reasons present here [Text § 3–18]. The brochure and blank order form do not include any terms of a deal (except price as set by N.Y. Commodities Exchange). When important terms are not stated, that is some indication that only preliminary negotiations are occurring [Text § 3–16]. Further, if Bev just wrote in her name and "I accept," and mailed the otherwise blank form to Sal, a court would have no idea how to determine whether a breach occurred or what remedy to give especially since neither quantity nor subject matter appear on the form [Text § 6–2]. It is up to the buyer to fill these in and then for Sal to determine if he is willing and able to undertake to fulfill the order. Further, the order from refers to "Buyer" as making an offer and "Seller" as having power to accept, so the brochure must be inviting offers for Sal to consider. It does not show any commitment by Sal to fill orders that buyers send in. For all these reasons, Bev would not be justified in believing her assent would conclude any deal.

Bev made an offer, however, by filling in the order form and mailing it in. All the terms are now definite (except for the June delivery date, which probably would be interpreted as permission to delivery at any time in June, and in any case is not a serious problem given the UCC gap filler on delivery time, § 2–309) [Text § 6–20]. The order calls itself an offer, and it expressly provides for acceptance by Sal. Sal would be justified in believing his assent would conclude the deal.

Acceptance

(Note: The analysis immediately below is with reference to the original UCC's § 2–207. A section at the end provides an analysis of §§ 2R–206(3) and 2R–207.)

Bev's offer is an offer for the purchase of goods. Accordingly, it is governed by the UCC. As the formation and terms of the contract here will be determined through an exchange of writings, the analysis of the issue is governed by § 2–207 [Text § 5–5].

Sal's 2/7 Confirmation of Sale acts as a valid acceptance under § 2–207. Under the common law mirror image rule, it would be a counter-offer since Sal added a "force majeure" clause (the strike, natural disaster, etc. clause); under § 2–207(1), however, it is a valid acceptance because it is a seasonable definite expression of acceptance not made conditional on Bev's assent to the force majeure clause [Text § 5–7].

SUGGESTED ANALYSIS OF SAMPLE ESSAY QUESTIONS

It is **seasonable** because it comes before the offer lapses. By its terms, the offer does not lapse until February 14, 35 days after Bev mailed the offer. The offer is not an **irrevocable** firm offer under § 2–205 because **Bev** (the offeror) did not separately sign the 35 day provision on the form which was provided by the offeree Sal, as is required by that section [Text § 4–87]. However, that just means Bev *could have* revoked the offer. However, as she did not revoke it (or otherwise terminate Sal's power of acceptance), the offer was accepted when Sal mailed the confirmation of Sal.

The 2/7 Confirmation is a **definite** expression of acceptance because it showed Sal's intent to go ahead with Bev's proposed deal. He confirmed that he would sell her the 5 tons of chromium, and he did not change the major, typically negotiated terms like price, quantity, subject matter, and delivery date. (Changing one of those would make it appear not to be an "acceptance" of the same basic deal proposed by Bev.) [Text § 5–8].

The 2/7 Confirmation did not say "No deal unless you assent to force majeure clause," or "Acceptance is conditional on assent to force majeure clause" or anything else that would make the acceptance expressly conditional on Bev's assent to the added term [Text § 5–10].

Thus the requirements of § 2–207(1) are met, and the 2/7 Confirmation acted as a valid acceptance.

Under UCC § R2–206(3), the analysis would be similar, and the parties writings constitute a valid offer and acceptance [Text § 5–32].

Attempted Revocation of Offer and Its Effects

Bev's letter of 2/8 was **an attempt to revoke her offer** [Text § 4–27]. A revocation is a manifestation by the offeror that he, she, or it no longer wishes to enter into the offered deal. The letter arrived too late for the revocation to be effective, however, because an offer cannot be revoked after it has been accepted. Where use of mail is an invited means of acceptance (as was true here, since the offer was sent by mail), an acceptance is effective upon dispatch [Text § 4–119]. Thus, Bev's offer was accepted on 2/7 when Sal mailed the confirmation. One of the consequences of acceptance of an offer is that the offer can no longer be revoked [Text § 4–2].

While the 2/8 letter cannot be effective as a revocation of Bev's offer, it might still have effect in one of four other ways:

SUGGESTED ANALYSIS OF SAMPLE ESSAY QUESTIONS

(1) If an offeree who receives a revocation after accepting the offer **relies** on the revocation, the offeror may be **estopped from enforcing the contract** [Text § 4–127]. Here, however, while it is true that Sal wrote a note to himself not to buy chromium for Bev, he had already planned to wait several weeks to buy the chromium anyway. Accordingly, it is not clear that he relied at all on Bev's 2/8 letter. **Perhaps** he would have bought chromium for Bev on 2/11 or 2/12 if he thought she still wanted it. (Any reliance after he received her 2/11 letter on 2/13 would not be reasonably justified.) Prices were rising so his initial thought that he should wait while prices fell might have changed. There are insufficient facts in this fact scenario to tell whether reliance occurred.

(2) The 2/8 letter could have been taken as an **anticipatory repudiation** [Text § 23–1]. In some sense the 2/8 letter could be interpreted as an unequivocal statement by Bev that she is unwilling to perform [Text § 23–20]. However, when she sent it she did not know there was a contract. Thus, a reasonable person looking solely at the 2/8 letter, would not know whether she would refuse to perform once she found out there **was** a contract. In addition, Sal should have known his acceptance and her revocation crossed in the mail, so probably he would not have been justified in treating this letter as a repudiation.

If the 2/8 letter was a repudiation, however, under § 2–611 Bev could retract it until: (1) Sal relied on it, or (2) Sal indicated to her that he was cancelling the deal or that he considered her repudiation final [Text § 23–32]. Sal's note to himself was not directed to Bev so (2) does not apply. Under (1), Bev could retract her repudiation unless Sal relied on it. (Whether he relied on it is the same fact question discussed above in relation to estoppel.) Hence, Bev's 2/11 letter would be an effective retraction of the repudiation unless Sal had relied on the repudiation before receiving the retraction on 2/13.

(3) The 2/8 letter could be treated by Sal as an **offer to rescind the contract** [Text § 24–18]. However, Sal did not accept that offer and Bev, in effect, revoked the offer of rescission in her 2/11 letter. Sal's note to himself was not communicated to Bev, so it provided no objective manifestation of his acceptance of the offer to rescind.

SUGGESTED ANALYSIS OF SAMPLE ESSAY QUESTIONS

(4) The 2/8 letter might be considered a **waiver** of Bev's right to insist on delivery of any chromium [Text §§ 9–10; 21–93]. Again the issue will be whether Sal relied on the 2/8 letter. If he did not, Bev can retract her waiver under § 2–209(5) [Text § 9–16].

Sal probably did not rely on the 2/8 letter, so Bev can still enforce the contract. (Of course, a court might strain to find reliance since Bev is shifting her position back and forth in response to market shifts, which puts her in a bad light. In fact, she may have acted in bad faith, in which case a court **might** prevent her from introducing her 2/11 letter. However, she was still at risk—if the market had dropped after 2/8, Sal could have held her to the contract. Thus, she should probably be considered as acting in good faith in claiming the benefit of the contract when the market shifted upwards. Moreover, if Sal did not rely on her 2/8 letter, any bad faith on her part did not harm him, anyway.)

Statue of Frauds

Assuming, that the N.Y. Commodities Exchange price for 5 tons of chromium on 2/7 would be at least $500, the contract is within the statute of frauds of Article 2, and thus must satisfy UCC § 2–201 to be enforceable [Text § 10–35]. Sal will want out of the deal and Bev will want to enforce it, so Sal is the "party to be charged," or, in § 2–201's words, the "party against whom enforcement is sought."

There does not seem to be an adequate writing signed by Sal to bind Sal under § 2–201(1) [Text § 10–37]. The 2/7 Confirmation was unsigned and apparently Sal's signature was nowhere in the Confirmation or on the envelope. There is, of course, an argument that the return address on the envelope would suffice to satisfy the Statute [Text § 10–43], but that argument is not a strong one. Sal probably did not put the address on the envelope to indicate that he was responsible for the contents of the envelope UCC § 1–201(37), but rather he put the return address there so that recipients of his letters would know the address to respond to.

However, under § 2–201(2), Bev's letter of 2/11 is sufficient against Sal as a merchant's confirmatory record [Text § 10–44]. This is, because: (1) it is sufficient against Bev (signed by her, shows a contract for sale was made, indicates quantity); (2) it seems to have been sent within a reasonable time after formation of the contract (only 4 days); (3) it confirms the existence of contract; (4) Sal received it; (5) Sal had reason to

SUGGESTED ANALYSIS OF SAMPLE ESSAY QUESTIONS

know its contents, even though he threw it away; and (6) Sal did not object to its contents until long after the ten days permitted in § 2–201(2), the statute is deemed "satisfied" under § 2–201(2).

Thus the contract is enforceable against Sal under the statute of frauds.

The Force Majeure Clause

If the force majeure clause in Sal's 2/7 Confirmation is part of the contract, Sal is probably excused from delivering any chromium. This is because the civil war in Volga has presumably "materially affected the availability" of chromium. (Sal says he can only get together one ton.)

Whether the clause becomes a term of the contract depends on UCC § 2–207(2) [Text § 5–16]. Under § 2–207(2), the force majeure clause becomes part of the contract if Bev and Sal are merchants (which is almost certainly the case) unless:

(1) Bev's offer limited Sal to accepting the offer on its terms [§ 2–207(2)(a)], or

(2) The force majeure clause materially changes the deal [§ 2–207(2)(b)], or

(3) Bev already objected to the force majeure clause, or objects to it within a reasonable time after getting Sal's Confirmation [UCC § 2–207(2)(c)].

There are no facts supporting any reasonable argument that UCC § 2–207(2)(a) or § 2–207(2)(c) are satisfied. Whether the force majeure clause materially changes the deal depends (according to Comments 4 and 5 of § 2–207) on whether it would cause Bev unreasonable surprise or hardship if the provision was included in the deal without her being aware of it. If the doctrine of impracticability would not excuse Sal from performing in the event of a civil war in Volga, then inclusion of the clause would probably unreasonably surprise Bev and cause hardship to her since she would be counting on the contract to protect her against such occurrences. Thus, if the clause would help Sal at all in this case, it probably materially changed the deal.

If Sal cannot establish that the force majeure provision became part of the contract under § 2–207(2), Sal might be able to argue that the clause was explicitly agreed to by Bev. That is, he may be able to establish that he and Bev entered into a contract modification including the term. Bev's 2/11 letter "thanking" Sal for the Confirmation may be construed as her implied assent to addition of the force majeure term [Text § 5–10]. Under § 2–207(2), just going ahead with a deal is not an assent. However,

SUGGESTED ANALYSIS OF SAMPLE ESSAY QUESTIONS

Bev's 2/11 letter comes close to endorsing the Confirmation—perhaps a reasonable person would view it as an assent. Under UCC § 2–209(1), no consideration is needed for a modification of a contract. As long as Sal is acting in good faith in proposing this modification, an assent to it by Bev will make it part of the contract. It seems honest and within commercial standards of fair dealing for Sal not to want to take these risks, so he is in good faith. Note that if this argument is successful, there will be no statute of frauds promise associated with the modification for it was done in writing [Text § 9–3].

Under § R2–207, only those terms agreed to by both parties become part of the contract. Hence, the force majeure term would not become part of the deal unless the argument above about the 2/11 letter from Bev constituting an implied agreement to the clause, is adopted by the court [Text § 5–32].

Impracticability

Assuming the force majeure clause would not become a part of the contract, Sal may still argue that his performance duties are discharged through normal commercial impracticability principles [Text § 25–31]. (No frustration of purpose issue is presented since Sal's purpose of getting money is not frustrated, nor is the money he would get from Bev practically worthless.) To establish impracticability, Sal must show that:

(1) Performance by him would be sufficiently impracticable (ten times increase in price may be enough of a cost increase to change the "essential nature of the performance" per § 2–615, Comment 4) [Text § 25–33];

(2) The impracticability was due to occurrence of an event (the Volga civil war), the non-occurrence of which was a basic assumption of both parties when they entered into the contract. However, the foreseeability of Volga civil war given Volga's recent civil unrest makes it doubtful that the occurrence of civil war was something neither party thought could happen when they entered the deal, especially since the very fact Sal tried to list civil wars in his force majeure clause shows that he was concerned about the occurrence of the event [Text § 25–36];

(3) That the party asserting the defense (Sal) did not assume the risk of the civil war's occurrence under the contract. Here there was a fixed price contract of a volatile commodity supplied from a country that is in a state of upheaval, and Sal did not include anything in

SUGGESTED ANALYSIS OF SAMPLE ESSAY QUESTIONS

the order form to put this risk on Bev. (If he had, it would have been part of Bev's offer and thus part of the contract. This may show that Sal implicitly assumed the risk.) [Text § 25–40];

(4) That the event causing the impracticability was not Sal's fault. Obviously Sal did not cause the civil war, but he did have a chance to buy the chromium on 2/7 or 2/8. Instead, Sal chose to speculate on the price of chromium. Further, if Sal had read his mail carefully, he would have known on 2/13 that Bev was expecting him to buy chromium for her, which would have given him two months to buy it before the war started. Arguably he was also responsible for the impracticability for his performance [Text § 25–38].

Accordingly, it appears Sal's performance obligations will not be discharged due to impracticability for he probably cannot establish several of the elements.

What should Bev do?

Bev should immediately demand reasonable assurances of performance under UCC § 2–609 [Text § 23–22]. Sal's 4/27 letter certainly gives Bev grounds for insecurity, so she should write Sal, include a copy of her letter of 2/11, and insist that he promise to perform and that he give her assurances that he will be able to perform. If he then says he will not perform, or if he fails to assure her within a reasonable time that he will perform, she is entitled to conclude that he has anticipatorily repudiated the contract under UCC § 2–610. Accordingly, at that point she is entitled to cancel the contract, buy the chromium elsewhere (cover), and seek damages based the on difference between the cover and contract prices under UCC § 2–712 [Text § 32–12]. Further, if she chooses not to cover, she is entitled to seek market differential damages based on the difference between the market price for the chromium and the contract price based on the formula given in § 2–713 [Text § 32–15].

It would not be prudent for Bev to cancel the contract without seeking assurances; however, because it is not clear that Sal's 4/27 letter was a repudiation. It was not unequivocal [Text § 23–12]; he said he "believed" there was no deal, and that it did not "appear" he had to deliver chromium, and that he "doubted" he could get together more than one ton. None of those is an unequivocal statement that he is refusing to perform or that he cannot perform, especially in light of his willingness to consider Bev's point of view if she believes there is a contract ("Please advise me . . .").

SUGGESTED ANALYSIS OF SAMPLE ESSAY QUESTIONS

If Bev cancels the contract now, it is more than likely that **she** would be repudiating the contract under the first material breach doctrine [Text § 21–66]. In that case, Sal would be entitled to cancel the agreement.

If Bev believes the price will continue to rise

Bev should immediately buy all the chromium she can if she believes the price will continue to rise. If Sal decides to perform, she can use his low price chromium in her business, or resell it at a big profit. If he does not, she can sue him for the price differential.

Answer to Question No. 5

Silvio v. Byron

The first issue is whether or not a contract was formed between Silvio and Byron. As we are not given the text of the conversation that took place in the store in the facts, it is impossible to answer definitively whether a contract was formed, or even who was the offeror and who was the offeree. However, typically the buyer will make the offer and the seller will accept it and there are enough facts to analyze the formation issue on that basis.

In the April 1 telephone conversation, Byron admitted that he understood how Silvio "might have thought" Byron told him to go ahead and make the TV. Under the objective theory of contracts, an effective offer is one in which a reasonable person would believe the person making the purported offer was willing to be bound on the terms he presented given those circumstances. [Text §§ 3–1; 3–8] Accordingly, Byron's admission suggests that he did make an effective offer in the store.

The next question is whether Silvio properly accepted. He may have accepted orally, promising to make the plasma screen set, thereby forming a valid bilateral contract. Once again, by not having the text of their conversation in the facts, it is impossible to say with certainty whether or not formation took place in that manner. However, the facts state that Silvio began performance shortly after Byron left. Under § 2–206 acceptance can be made by beginning performance, if such course of action is reasonable [Text § 4–98]. Here we have an audio/video dealer trying to get a specially made good into the hands of his customer in the shortest possible time, which would certainly pass any commercial reasonableness test. Additionally, Silvio gave prompt notice by the March 10th letter, as required in § 2–206(2) [Text § 4–104], making it sound even more like an effective acceptance.

SUGGESTED ANALYSIS OF SAMPLE ESSAY QUESTIONS

Thus, if no offer was made by Byron, obviously Byron will win since there can be no breach without a valid contract. However, if Byron is judged to have made an offer, as appears to be the case, it was properly accepted by Silvio and a valid contract was formed.

The next issue is whether the contract is enforceable under the statute of frauds. The agreement is subject to the statute of frauds under § 2–201(1) as it involved a contract for the sale of goods for of $500 or more [Text § 10–35]. The facts reveal no writing signed by Byron evidencing a contract, and thus under § 2–201(1) Byron has a valid statute of frauds defense [Text § 10–37]. Accordingly, unless one of the exceptions to the statute of frauds listed in § 2–201(2) or § 2–201(3) comes into play, Byron will prevail as the oral contract will be unenforceable.

Section 2–201(2) states that the recipient of a confirmatory record like Byron will lose his statute of frauds defense if he does not object properly to the memo within ten days after its receipt. However, the provision explicitly states that it is effective only "between merchants." Obviously Silvio is a merchant as he is in the business of selling TVs. The question is: can Byron be called a merchant? As it appears he is merely a consumer, he probably cannot [Text § 10–49].

There is no question, however, that the contract is enforceable under 2–201(3)(a). A custom made plasma screen TV is obviously a specially manufactured good [Text § 10–52], and here the TV was made to fit in Byron's home. Accordingly, the oral contract between Byron and Silvio is enforceable under § 2–201. Since Byron refuses to pay for the TV, he is in breach.

The next issue is what damages are collectible by Silvio. Obviously, Silvio would like to sue for the price under § 2–709 [Text § 32–29]. As Byron has not accepted the TV, Silvio's only chance for the price is under § 2–709(1)(b). Under that provision, Silvio may recover for the price of the TV only if he can establish that he cannot obtain a reasonable price for the TV from another despite diligent efforts, or establish that any attempt at resale would be reasonably unavailing [Text §§ 32–32; 32–33]. As the TV is specially made to fit into Byron's home, a good argument could be made that attempting a resale of the set by looking for someone with the unused measurements would be unavailing, thereby entitling Silvio to the full $6,500. If Silvo cannot find anyone to buy it for a reasonable price, upon satisfaction of a final judgment, Byron would be entitled to possession and title to the TV [Text § 32–29].

However, if a court should hold that portions of the TV could be dissembled and reused for parts, with relatively little damage, then Silvio would have to sue under § 2–708(2) [Text § 32–45]. Under that provision he could recover his profit ($6,500 − $4,000, or $2,500), plus the amount of time and materials expended in making the TV ($4,000), less the value of the components as scrap or less any proceeds upon resale of the TV to someone else [Text § 32–47].

Byron v. Le Cess Poule

The first issue is whether the transaction in the restaurant is governed by Article 2. Obviously steaks, shrimp, **etc.,** can be identified to the contract and at the time of identification they are movable. Thus, the requirements of Article 2 applicability set forth in § 2–105 are met [Text § 33–3]. Further, additional support for the premise that the food is covered by Article 2 comes from the language of § 2–314(1). Hence, these are clearly Article 2 transactions.

Wine

When Byron noticed the waiter had brought the 1970, as opposed to the 1961, bottle of wine and said nothing about it, he accepted goods under the contract with notice of the defect. Accordingly, under both § 2–607(3) and § 2–709(1), Byron is liable for the full contract price of the 1961 bottle [Text §§ 22–37; 32–24]. In other words, it would be incorrect to say that he is only liable for the price of the 1970 bottle under the **contract**, even though he received the 1970 wine. That is not how § 2–709(1) or § 2–607 read. If he accepted goods knowing of their non-conformity, he is liable for the full amount of the **contract** price.

However, because he accepted non-conforming goods, he has a breach of express warranty claim against the restaurant. Under § 2–714(2), the proper measure of damages for a breach of express warranty is the difference between the value of the goods as promised and the value of the goods received. In this case that is the difference between the 1961 price and the 1970 price i.e., $700 − $575. Thus, he ends up paying only the restaurant's price for the 1970 wine, but that figure is properly arrived at only after holding him liable for the full contract price and offsetting that against damages from his breach of warranty claim. See § 2–717 [Text § 32–27]. Since he has not paid that price to the restaurant, he is in breach.

Shrimp Cocktail

Le Cess Poule's tender of the crab cocktail instead of the shrimp cocktail is probably best characterized as an accommodation shipment [Text § 4–108]. The waiter informed Byron that the restaurant did not have what he asked for, tendered what he

SUGGESTED ANALYSIS OF SAMPLE ESSAY QUESTIONS

thought would be an equally acceptable good, and gave Byron the chance to refuse that selection. In other words, the crab cocktail was a counter-offer, which Byron accepted, and thus he is liable to the restaurant for the special price the waiter quoted him for the crab cocktail, $12. Once again, since he has not paid anything for the crab cocktail, he is in breach.

Steak

The first issue here is whether Byron accepted the steak. As it is difficult to tell by sight whether the sauce was a Hollandaise or Béarnaise, taking a bite or two initially would probably be inspection, not acceptance [Text § 22–37]. Thus when Byron told the waiter to bring the Béarnaise sauce, there was a proper rejection with an assurance of cure by Le Cess Poule [Text § 22–11]. However, when Byron took other bites of the steak while waiting for the Béarnaise sauce to be brought, there probably was acceptance under §§ 2–606(1)(c) and R2–608(4). That is, such acts appeared to be inconsistent with Le Cess Poule's ownership of the meat [Text § 22–37]. However, Byron still was within his rights at the end of the meal to revoke his acceptance since he only accepted with the assurance that the defect would be cured under § 2–608(1)(a) [Text § 22–45]. As the defective tender was never cured, Byron's revocation was effective and thus he is not liable for the purchase price of the steak. Although courts have been reluctant to adopt it, Le Cess Poule might have a claim in restitution for any benefits Byron received from eating the steak [Text § 22–52].

Pie

When the waiter brought Byron the wrong kind of pie, clearly Byron was within his rights to reject as the pie was a non-conforming good [Text § 22–39]. However, the restaurant attempted to cure by replacement under § 2–508(2), and possibly § 2–508(1) depending on whether the time for performance had passed [Text § 22–12]. As there is no evidence that waiting for the apple pie to be brought caused Byron any damage, it is he who is in breach for not allowing cure to be made. Thus, he is liable to the restaurant for the cost of the pie. Perhaps if the waiter intentionally brought him the wrong kind of pie Le Cess Poule would lose its cure rights as it would not have reason to believe that the goods tendered would be acceptable under § 2–508(2) [Text § 22–15]. However, there is no evidence of this from the facts and it is highly unlikely that is the case.

SUGGESTED ANALYSIS OF SAMPLE ESSAY QUESTIONS

Answer to Question No. 6

The 3/13 telegram and the 3/15 letter.

The 3/13 telegram was only a preliminary negotiation, because Sap ("S") expressly stated that S would have to give further assent to the proposed bargain before being committed to building the dredge. That is, there was no commitment to be found [Text § 3–16].

The 3/15 letter from Bloop ("B") was an offer [Text § 3–1]. B grumbled a lot about the price, but ended up expressing willingness to enter into a bargain at $2.5 million. There is language of commitment ("let us know when we can expect the dredge," "we are willing to deal with you . . ." "we will pay . . .," this "order").

Contract formation under § 2–207.

(Note: The analysis immediately below is with reference to the original UCC's § 2–207. A section at the end provides an analysis of §§ R2–206(3) and R2–207.)

UCC Article 2 applies because this is a contract for the sale of a good, i.e., something that will be movable at the time of the identification to the contract—the dredge [Text § 33–2]. S's "acceptance" contains additional and different terms from the offer, and so to resolve whether a contract exists and, if so, what its terms are, § 2–207 must be applied [Text § 5–5].

Under § 2–207(1), to be effective as an acceptance, a purported acceptance containing additional or different terms must be: (i) a **seasonable** expression of acceptance; (ii) a **definite** expression of acceptance; and (iii) not include a term making its effect conditional on the offeror's assent to the additional or different terms found in the document [Text § 5–7].

S's 3/19 letter is probably a definite and seasonable expression of acceptance. It is **seasonable** because it was sent only 4 days after the offer was sent and thus probably only a day or two after receipt of the offer. There is no indication that speed is important here, so the reasonable time to accept should extend beyond the minimum that the Restatement 2d gives (midnight of day of receipt) [Text § 4–48].

It may be a **definite** expression of acceptance because it assents to the typically negotiated terms in the offer (price, quantity, subject matter, and delivery terms), and it shows commitment to going ahead with the bargain ("We will deliver . . ."). However, S's attempt to add a cancellation right for S may change the bargain in such a fundamental way that there is no definite expression of acceptance; in effect S is saying that even if there

SUGGESTED ANALYSIS OF SAMPLE ESSAY QUESTIONS

is a contract S can choose not to perform—that is much more fundamental than warranty or arbitration issues, and may be as fundamental as price and quantity [Text § 5–8]. If the letter is not a definite expression of acceptance, it will have to be viewed as a counter-offer, and no contract would be formed by the exchange of writings under 2–207(1).

If the 3/19 letter **is** a definite expression of acceptance, we still have to ask whether the acceptance is expressly conditional on B's assent to the added or different terms.

S says that unless B agrees to S's terms, S will not deliver the dredge. Thus, S is saying that the deal will not go forward unless B expressly assents to S's terms, and that is the same as saying "no deal unless you agree to my terms." Thus, the acceptance is expressly conditional on B's assent to S's terms, which once again means S's letter is a counter-offer [Text § 5–10].

Accordingly, at least due to one, and possibly two, reasons, no contract was formed under § 2–207(1).

As a result, if a contract is to be formed at all from this fact situation, it must be formed by § 2–207(3) [Text § 5–23]. If both parties engage in conduct which would indicate to a reasonable person that a contract exists between them, then there is a contract under § 2–207(3). B paid $100,000; S accepted the check and deposited it. Those actions recognize that a contract exists.

Thus, a valid offer and acceptance were exchanged to form a contract by conduct between B and S under § 2–207(3).

Under UCC § R2–206(3), the analysis of whether a contract was formed based on the parties' writings is the same as above. Whether there is a contract based on conduct is determined under § R2–207, and is analyzed the same way as under the original UCC [Text § 5–32].

What are the terms? The § 2–207(3) analysis.

If there is no contract formed under § 2–207(1), but a contract is formed by conduct under § 2–207(3), then the terms are those on which the parties actually expressly agreed, plus any supplementary terms added by the UCC [Text § 5–23]. All others are "knocked-out." The parties' letters agreed on price ($2.5 million), quantity (one), subject matter (the dredge), and delivery date (B gave S authority to set the delivery date at any date before December, and S chose October), so these would be enforceable terms. (See below for possible modification of price term.)

Perhaps the parties agreed that there would be no limitation to arbitration; B proposed that term, and S did not object even though S did object to other specific proposals in B's offer. This analysis is borrowed from 2–207(2), under which at least some courts have held that objection to some added terms but not to others is the same as an express assent to the others. It is not clear a court would use this approach under § 2–207(3), but it would seem reasonable under these circumstances.

The analysis under § R2–207 is the same as above—the only terms that become part of the agreement are those to which the parties agree, plus those implied by the Code [Text § 5–32].

The parties did not agree to exclude any implied warranties, so B will get an implied warranty of merchantability (because such a warranty is implied whenever a sale of goods by a merchant occurs and is not disclaimed, see § 2–314) [Text § 35–8]; and, perhaps an implied warranty of fitness for B's particular purposes as well [Text § 35–12]. That is, B had a specific use for the goods; let S know of their particular use; and let S know it was relying on, and did in fact rely on, S's skill and judgment in selecting, designing, and building the dredge.

The parties did not agree on when the remaining $2.4 million would be paid or where delivery was to take place. However, the UCC gap filler in § 2–310(a) states that, in the absence of agreement to the contrary, a buyer must pay for goods at the time and place of delivery [Text § 6–21]. Similarly, § 2–308(a) provides that, in the absence of agreement in the contract, delivery is to be made at S's place of business [Text § 6–19].

The next issue is whether B is bound by the price modification, i.e., whether it becomes part of their contract. S's June 2 letter was a proposal to reduce the price from $2.5 million to $2.3 million. There is no consideration for the reduction but that doesn't matter—no consideration is needed for modification of a contract for the sale of goods under § 2–209(1) [Text § 9–20]. The modification has to be obtained in good faith, but B is in good faith here; B made no threats and S voluntarily proposed the reduction for S's own reasons. The question then is whether B assented to the proposal—i.e., whether the offer to reduce the price was "accepted" by B so as to say there was an enforceable modification of the contract. S said B did not have to answer the letter, so S is probably assuming B will assent and telling B that silence is an appropriate means of acceptance. B stayed silent apparently with the intention of accepting, so there was an effective acceptance. Acceptance by silence is usually ineffective as a method of acceptance, but when the offeror gives the offeree that power, and where the offeree intends to accept in such a manner, it is effective [Text § 4–115].

SUGGESTED ANALYSIS OF SAMPLE ESSAY QUESTIONS

The consideration problem (the cancellation provision).

Because it was not agreed to by both parties, the cancellation provision does not become part of the contract [Text § 5–23]. Probably that is all that needs to be said about the issue, but as a review recall that if one or both parties end up with the right to cancel the contract merely by sending a letter, there is a consideration or a mutuality of obligation issue. Suppose B has the right to cancel. B can then perform by either buying the dredge or by sending the notice of cancellation. Where a party has alternative ways that he can freely choose to perform his promise, his promise is consideration only if both alternatives are sufficient "somethings" and at least one of them was bargained for. The older cases would say there is no consideration here. They would say that sending a letter is not a sufficient detriment to B and hence B's promise to buy the dredge or send the notice would not be consideration. The newer cases would say that there is consideration. B had no pre-existing duty to send a letter, and sending such notice is an act, so it is a sufficient "something" to enforce the promise [Text § 7–49].

Note, however, that once B makes the $100,000 payment and S cashed the check, the contract should be enforceable by B, even if a court would otherwise have thought the right to cancel meant that there was no consideration for S's promise. That is, even if there as an illusory contract to that point, B's payment and S's receipt of the money constituted mutual agreement that there was a deal, and B's payment would be consideration for S's promise to deliver the dredge.

Answer to Question No. 7

CBS v. Joe

Joe did not finish the piece, so, if he had a contractual obligation to finish it, he breached that obligation, and CBS will prevail in the breach action. Thus, the question is whether Joe had a contractual obligation to finish the piece that he started.

Contracts cannot be formed without assent of both the contracting parties [Text § 2–1]. Mutual assent is usually shown by the making of an offer by one party and the acceptance of that offer by the other party [Text § 1–13]. Thus, the first question is whether either party here made an offer.

An offer is the manifestation of intent to enter into a bargain so made as to justify another in believing that his or her assent is invited and will conclude the bargain [Text § 3–1]. If the putative offeror manifests the intention not to be bound to a bargain until he or she manifests some further assent, then no offer has been made, but rather the party has just engaged in preliminary negotiations [Text § 3–16]. Further, a manifestation of assent cannot be an offer unless the proposed bargain is reasonably certain. The traditional view is that all material terms must be reasonably certain; the Restatement 2d view is that a contract is definite enough to be enforced if the parties intended to contract, and if the court can determine who breached and can determine an appropriate remedy [Text § 6–11].

Offer

1. *The face-to-face conversation on Sept. 25*

    No offers were made in the Sept. 25 conversation between Don and Joe. Even if an offer was made, it was not accepted.

    Don's initial statement does not show any commitment to any bargain with Joe and thus is not an offer. Don stated that CBS needed to run a story, but he did not state that he wanted Joe to do the piece, nor did he say that CBS would pay Joe for the piece. In the absence of any manifestation of commitment by Don, Joe would not be justified in believing that Don was inviting his assent or that his assent would conclude a bargain. Further, almost no terms are specified. The subject of the piece is specified, but neither its length, nor the price CBS would pay for it, nor the time when CBS would need it, are stated. This indefiniteness is evidence that CBS is not committed to any bargain; a reasonable person would want the terms specified much more completely before being bound to a bargain.

    Further, even if CBS did intend to commit itself to a bargain, the terms of the "bargain" are so indefinite that there would be no valid offer here [Text § 6–1]. Under the traditional approach, there are several material terms that are completely uncertain (price, length, time of delivery) [Text § 6–10]. Perhaps these could be supplied by usage of trade or course of dealing, but that is unlikely. There is probably not a sufficient usage of trade [Text § 6–26]; that is, it is unlikely that independent producers and networks almost always agree to a certain price, length, and time for delivery of such pieces. (If you could show that such news show pieces are almost always eight minutes, that the independent producers almost always get paid $20,000, and that the pieces are almost always considered due within 6 weeks, then you *might* be able to argue that there was a sufficient usage of trade to fill in the omitted terms. That seems very unlikely and is not suggested at all on these facts.) There is also probably not a sufficient course of dealing; that is, it is unlikely that Joe and CBS have repeatedly agreed on the same terms for price, length, and time for delivery in their past dealings. (Even if

SUGGESTED ANALYSIS OF SAMPLE ESSAY QUESTIONS

there were such a usage of trade or course of dealing, there still would be no offer, because CBS has not manifested commitment to the bargain, but at least the indefiniteness problem could be overcome.)

Under the Restatement 2d approach, the indefiniteness in these terms would prevent Don's initial statement from being an offer, because the court could not provide an appropriate remedy [Text § 6–2]. Perhaps the court could determine who breached. The court might say that since no time was stated, Joe had a reasonable time to produce the piece [Text §§ 6–20; 6–23], and if he failed to produce any piece within that time the court might be able to say that Joe breached the contract no matter what length the piece was supposed to be and no matter what the price was supposed to be. However, without knowing how much CBS was supposed to pay, the court would be unable to determine what CBS's expectation interest is. The court could not determine CBS's reliance interest without knowing how long the piece was supposed to be; if at the last minute CBS had to pay a lot extra to get a substitute piece done by another producer as a rush job, it might seem that the court could determine CBS's reliance interest as the extra costs a rush job caused as compared with what CBS normally would have paid for a piece—but those extra costs almost certainly depend on how long the piece was that was done on a rush basis, and we have no way of knowing how long a piece CBS could have relied on Joe providing, since no length was set. (Even if the court could determine what an appropriate remedy would be, so that the court could say that the indefiniteness problem is not insurmountable under the Restatement 2d approach, the court would still hold that there was no offer, because CBS did not manifest commitment to the bargain. That is, CBS simply did not intend to contract.)

Could Joe's first statement be an offer?

Joe's statement is more definite than CBS's first statement (we now have a length and a minimum price), but there are two reasons why it is not an offer.

First, it does not show commitment by Joe [Text § 3–1]. Joe does not say, "I will do a piece," but "I **could** do a piece." He is not committing himself to doing a piece, but rather is saying that it is possible that he could do it. Further, Joe has not said that $25,000 is acceptable to him, but rather that he would need to "ask at least $25,000." The statement of an "asking" price is usually not considered to be a statement that the party is willing to enter into a bargain at that price, but rather is simply preliminary negotiation [Text § 3–16]. Joe did not even say that

SUGGESTED ANALYSIS OF SAMPLE ESSAY QUESTIONS

he would have to ask $25,000, but that he would have to ask **at least** $25,000. Thus he is not saying that $25,000 is acceptable to him, but simply that he would not be willing to do it for any less than $25,000. A reasonable person would think that Joe would want to have the price set before being bound to a bargain, so this is additional evidence that Joe has not manifested commitment to a proposed bargain.

Second, Joe's statement may be too indefinite to be an offer even if he intended to contract [Text § 6–1]. No time for delivery of the piece is stated, and no firm price is stated.

(Even if somehow this were an offer, the presumption is that CBS's power of acceptance would have lapsed at the end of the face-to-face conversation [Text § 4–47]. Joe did not say how long his offer would be open, so contract law presumes that the reasonable time to accept, offers made in face-to-face conversations generally terminates when the conversation ends, unless one of the parties manifests a contrary intent. It is not likely that Don's general "We'll have to talk again later" would be interpreted to mean, "I accept your offer").

Could Don's final statements be an offer?

"We could afford . . ." is not the same as "we will pay;" it does not manifest commitment to any bargain, but just indicates that there is some chance CBS will want to enter into a bargain in the future. Don also manifests an intention not to be bound until he manifests a further assent, when he says, "Excuse me . . . We'll talk again later." Such a manifestation means that Don has merely engaged in preliminary negotiations and has not made an offer [Text § 3–16].

2. *Don's Letter*

Don's letter is probably an offer [Text § 3–1]. It manifests commitment to a bargain. In terms of commitment, "willing to pay" is not as strong as "we will pay," but in light of the firm scheduling of the piece for the Dec. 1 show, it does manifest commitment to a bargain. The letter is also definite enough to show commitment [Text § 6–1]. It contains price ($25,000), subject matter (ten minute piece on photocopier salespersons), and an implied delivery date (early enough before the Dec. 1 show so that CBS can work it into the show—presumably there is an industry usage on how much time is needed for that) [Text § 6–26]. There are no significant terms left open that would make a reasonable person think that CBS would want to have the deal clarified before being willing to be bound to a deal. "High quality" is somewhat indefinite, but it is very likely that Joe and Don know what they mean by a high quality piece because they

SUGGESTED ANALYSIS OF SAMPLE ESSAY QUESTIONS

have worked together numerous times in the past, i.e., there is a course of dealing between them [Text § 6–26]. The letter seems to be personally directed to Joe and not to others; thus there is no problem of over-acceptance that could lead a reasonable person to think that CBS would not want to create a power of acceptance that could lead to over-acceptance.

Acceptance

Acceptance is the manifestation of assent to the terms of the offer by a means invited or required by the offer [Text § 4–1]. Mike's letter did not specify any particular means of acceptance. Thus, any reasonable means of acceptance under the circumstances is invited [Text § 4–94].

This raises three issues. First, whether acceptance by beginning performance was a reasonable means of acceptance under the circumstances. Second, if so, whether Joe's failure to give notice to Don renders the acceptance void. Third, assuming that it does render the acceptance void, what are the rights of CBS in such a situation?

Was acceptance by beginning performance a reasonable means of acceptance?

There may be an argument that Don asked for a promissory acceptance in his letter. At the time of the offer, it was only 2 months until the piece was scheduled to be shown on the air. It is likely that in such a situation Don needed to know and know quickly whether Joe was going to accept; hence the argument that Don was seeking a promissory acceptance. If so, then there was no effective acceptance by Joe when he started performance without promising to complete performance [Text §§ 4–93; 4–100].

However, whatever benefits Don could receive by a promissory acceptance could just as easily be obtained through Joe's acceptance by beginning performance followed by prompt notice of acceptance. Since the offer is silent as to the method of acceptance, and since the seasonable notice requirement, if fulfilled, would seem to cover Don's concerns, it is likely that acceptance by beginning performance was an acceptable method of performance of the offer [Text § 4–101].

Assuming that beginning of performance was an acceptable mode of acceptance, *the next question is, what is the effect of Joe's failure to give notice to Don that he had begun performance?*

The general rule under the Restatement 2d is that acceptance by performance must be followed within a reasonable time by

SUGGESTED ANALYSIS OF SAMPLE ESSAY QUESTIONS

notice of acceptance to the offeror [Text § 4–104]. There are only three exceptions to the rule [Text § 4–105]:

(1) If the nature of the acceptance is such that the offeror would reasonably know the offer has been accepted. (In the present case, there are no facts that indicate Don would know that Joe accepted so this exception does not apply.)

(2) If the offeror gave the offeree a reason to believe that acceptance by beginning performance without notification was an acceptable mode of acceptance. (Here, again, however, there is nothing in Don's offer to indicate acceptance by silence would be acceptable so this exception does not apply either.)

(3) If due to past dealings between the parties it was reasonable for Joe to believe either that acceptance by beginning performance without notification was a proper means of acceptance. Once again, nothing in the facts indicate that to be the case here.)

Accordingly, on these facts, Joe's beginning performance without giving notice to Don was not an effective acceptance [Text § 4–106].

Note, however, that under the approach of § 54 of the Restatement 2d, Joe's beginning of performance acts as an enforceable promise by Joe to CBS that he will finish the piece, even if he does not follow-up those acts with notice. That is, the failure to give notice means that CBS is not bound to pay him upon tender of the finished piece. However, he is obligated to finish the piece for CBS because by beginning of performance he implicitly promised the offeror he would finish. Hence, even though the acceptance was not "effective" from Joe's point of view (in that he cannot enforce it against CBS), it was effective from CBS's view (in that CBS can enforce it against Joe), and thus CBS is entitled to recover from Joe any damages it suffers based on Joe's breach of his implied promise to finish [Text § 4–106].

Maxine v. Joe

Joe refused to buy the Z1000 photocopy machine. If he had an enforceable contract to buy one, he obviously breached it, and Maxine will prevail. Thus, *the issue of whether there was a contract must be examined.*

SUGGESTED ANALYSIS OF SAMPLE ESSAY QUESTIONS

Offer

The issue in this transaction turns on whether a contract for the sale of goods, i.e., a photocopier, was formed. As such, it is governed by the UCC [Text § 33–2].

Maxine's initial price quotation was probably not an offer. Price quotes are not usually treated as offers but rather as invitations for offers [Text § 3–16]. Courts **will** treat a quote as an offer if the circumstances or the language used shows a commitment to sell at the quoted price and if the terms are definite. Here the quantity seems definite based on Joe's inquiry about "one" photocopier, and the quote can provide the price. If the parties had intended to contract based on this quote, the UCC will fill in the remaining terms with its "gap filler" requirements [Text § 6–12] (time of delivery would be a reasonable time, payment is due at time and place of delivery which will be at Maxine's, and the quality required is that the machine be merchantable). However, Maxine did not say she would sell Joe a machine for the $1,000; she merely said she "could" quote him a price of $1,000. That may be even weaker in terms of commitment than the usual "I quote you $1,000." Further, she told him to send in a purchase order; she is probably in effect saying, "Make me an offer by sending in a Purchase Order" ("P.O."). In light of the lack of explicit terms and questionable commitment in Maxine's quote, it seems likely that her statements are no more than an invitation to Joe to make an offer, and not an offer themselves.

As a result, Joe made an offer when he sent in the P.O. We are told little of what the P.O. said, but the reason a person sends a P.O. is to purchase the items listed on the P.O. Thus the recipient of a P.O. is likely to see it as a manifestation of commitment to buy the item [Text § 3–1]. Indeed, UCC 2–206(1)(b) implies that an "order" for goods is an offer. Although the P.O. apparently contains only price, quantity, and subject matter, the UCC will fill in the other terms if the parties intend to contract with gap fillers, so there is no serious indefiniteness problem here.

The next issue turns on the objective theory of contracts. That is, Joe obviously was not seriously considering buying a photocopier when he ordered it from Maxine. Indeed, he told Maxine in his phone message that he was not interested in buying a copier; he just wanted to shoot his piece for *60 Minutes*. Thus, it is fair to say there was no *subjective* meeting of the minds to the contract even if Maxine accepted what appeared to be an offer. However, for at least the last century it has been established that the **objective** theory of governs contract formation in American courts. When one party has no reason to doubt that the other party intends to contract, the law does not permit the other party to avoid contractual liability simply because he or she did not actually intend to contract. Thus, because Joe's outward manifestations showed an intent to contract (i.e., a reasonable person in Maxine's shoes would believe that upon a valid acceptance a contract would be formed), his undisclosed subjective intent does not prevent his P.O. from being an offer that Maxine can accept [Text § 3–8].

Acceptance

(Note: The analysis immediately below is with reference to the original UCC's § 2–207. A section at the end provides an analysis of §§ R2–206(3) and R2–207.)

The next two issues are: (1) Whether Maxine's "acknowledgement" is an effective acceptance under UCC § 2–207(1); and (2) Whether Joe effectively revoked his offer before Maxine effectively accepted it.

Was Maxine's acknowledgement an effective acceptance under § 2–207(1)?

Maxine's acknowledgement added terms that as far as we know were not on Joe's P.O. That means the acknowledgement was an attempt to accept the offer and also add terms to the deal. § 2–207(1) deals with whether an attempted acceptance that tries to add or change terms is effective as an acceptance. § 2–207(1) states that so long as the offeree's writing is a reasonable and definite expression of acceptance, it **will** act as an effective acceptance despite the presence of additional or different terms, so long as there is no "acceptance is expressly made conditional on offeror's assent" to other terms clause in the offeree's document [Text § 5–7].

Accordingly, we must first ask whether the acknowledgement was **seasonable.** The offer had not lapsed; an offer received by mail which does not state how long it will be open ordinarily does not lapse until at least midnight of the day the offer was received [Text § 4–48]. Maxine mailed back the acknowledgement the same day she received the offer. Under the mailbox rule, the acceptance (if it was an acceptance) was effective when she posted it, because the mail was an invited means of acceptance and because it was correctly addressed [Text § 4–119]. It was an invited means of acceptance because the offer was sent by mail and nothing in the offer or the circumstances indicated that the mail was not a reasonable means of acceptance [Text § 4–94]. Thus, Maxine's power to accept the offer had not lapsed before acceptance. However, to be seasonable, an acceptance must become effective while the offer is still open to be accepted, and

SUGGESTED ANALYSIS OF SAMPLE ESSAY QUESTIONS

there is an issue to be discussed below about whether Joe revoked the offer before Maxine could accept it. Assuming he failed to revoke it effectively, the acknowledgement was a seasonable expression of acceptance.

Next we must ask if it was a **definite** expression of acceptance. A definite expression of acceptance is one that indicates commitment to the bargain going forward and which does not try to change one of the basic, typically negotiated terms of the offer, such as price, quantity, subject matter, or perhaps delivery terms. Here the acknowledgement indicated that Maxine would sell Joe a Z1000 for the same price as on the P.O., so it appears to be a definite expression of acceptance. The fact that it attempts to make material changes to the warranty portion of the deal by imposing a short express warranty and eliminating the implied warranty of merchantability does not prevent it from being an effective "acceptance" under § 2–207(1) for an acceptance is valid under § 2–207(1) even if the offeree's response contains additional or different terms [Text § 5–7].

However, the acknowledgement also attempts to add to the subject matter of the contract by requiring Joe to buy his supplies from Maxine. Unless the court sees supplies as being relatively minor compared to the copier itself, the court should decide that this addition makes the acknowledgement **not** a definite expression of acceptance, because one of the typically negotiated terms (quantity and subject matter) is affected, and Maxine's response would be deemed to propose a different deal. In that case, Maxine's letter would really be a counter-offer. That is, ultimately the issue in this case as to whether Maxine and Joe had a contract under § 2–207(1) comes down to whether the buyer and seller were buying and selling the same thing. If so, the presence of additional or different terms does not change the effectiveness of the acceptance. If not, then the purported acceptance becomes a counter-offer [Text § 5–8].

If the acknowledgement is a definite and seasonable expression of acceptance, the next issue is whether it is expressly made conditional on Joe's (the offeror's) assent to the added terms (thus involving the "unless" clause of Maxine's acknowledgement). If so, once again it is not an effective acceptance but a counter-offer [Text § 5–16]. The acknowledgement does say that its terms and only its terms will be the terms of the contract, but it does not say that Joe must **assent** to those terms for there to be a contract. It does not say, e.g., "No deal unless you assent to my terms," or "This acceptance is conditional on your agreeing to my terms," or anything along those lines. The acknowledgement did insist on

SUGGESTED ANALYSIS OF SAMPLE ESSAY QUESTIONS

its own terms, but such an insistence is insufficient to turn the offer into a counter-offer. § 2–207(1) makes clear that the key is whether the offeror's **assent** is needed before a contract is made. If it says that silence, or inaction, or any other thing short of affirmative agreement on the part of the offeror can lead to the offeror's acceptance of additional different terms, the document is an acceptance and not a counter-offer [Text § 5–16].

The analysis under revised UCC is similar. Under § R2–206(3), there must also be a "definite and seasonable expression of acceptance" in order for a contract to be formed. Hence the analysis above would apply here.

The revocation/acceptance issue

Joe attempted to revoke his offer by leaving the phone message for Maxine. Joe indicated he did not want the Z1000 so his statement is a sufficient manifestation of an intention not to enter into the deal he had offered to Maxine. As such, it would effectively revoke the offer and terminate Maxine's power of acceptance, so long as the revocation became effective before Maxine accepted the offer. However, once an offer has been accepted, the offeror can no longer revoke it [Text § 4–2].

As noted above, Maxine's acceptance would be effective under the mailbox rule when posted (dispatched) [Text § 4–119]. Maxine did not hear the message until after she mailed the letter, so if she is not deemed to have "received" it until then, so the revocation was too late. The facts do not say whether the message was left before she put the acknowledgement in the U.S. mail, and thus there is an issue as to whether the oral revocation was even "received" (albeit on an answering machine), before the acceptance's dispatch. While the legal answer to this issue is not that clear, for there are not a lot of cases on point, it is likely that a court would find that Maxine had not "received" the revocation until a reasonable time after she arrived back in the office so that she could check her messages.

Accordingly, as there was a valid offer by Joe in the P.O., a valid acceptance by Maxine, and consideration, an enforceable contract existed [Text § 1–13], and if Joe does not pay for the copier, he will be in breach.

Answer to Question No. 8

PART (1)

The first issue is whether Neighbor ("N") made an offer to Johnson ("J"). An offer is a manifestation of willingness to enter into a bargain so made as to justify another in understanding

SUGGESTED ANALYSIS OF SAMPLE ESSAY QUESTIONS

that his assent is invited and will conclude the bargain [Text § 3–1]. Central to the concept of offer is that in a valid offer the offeror is committed to the bargain and upon that offeree's acceptance, a contract will be formed. A statement is not an offer if the person to whom it is addressed (the offeree) knows or has reason to know that further communication by the person making the statement is needed to evidence sufficient willingness to enter into a bargain.

N's statement to J is an offer for several reasons. It shows commitment by N to a proposed deal—N says J "can have" the nails for $20 and invites him to take the nails. She would not do that unless she was willing to enter into the bargain of selling the nails to J for $20. She even specifies a means by which J can assent to the deal: by taking the nails in the garage. J will not reasonably believe any further assent by N is needed, since N did not indicate that further assent was needed; also since she is leaving, she will not be around to give any further assent before J takes the nails. The definiteness of the terms also shows N's commitment and that no further assent from N is needed: the price ($20), quantity (one bag), subject matter (nails), and time of delivery (whenever J takes the nails), and place of delivery (the garage) are all stated. Only time of payment is unstated, but since this is a contract for the sale of goods (and thus governed by the UCC), the UCC's time of payment gap filler, i.e., payment is due at the time and place of delivery, can be used to cure any indefiniteness problem [Text § 6–21]. Since no important terms are unstated, it makes sense to think N's statement is definite enough to be an offer.

Since N made an offer, the next issue is whether J accepted it. The offer specifies, or at least suggests, a method of acceptance—taking the nails from the garage [Text § 4–93]. Since J did that, it looks as though he accepted.

J's only defense is that he left the note specifying he would only pay $15. Under the objective theory of contracts, J would argue that no reasonable person in N's position could believe he was "accepting" N's offer as he specified a price change in the note. At most, J would argue he was making a counter-offer, indicating he was willing to go forward with the deal on different terms [Text § 4–29].

The problem with this argument, of course, is that J took the nails. He was not just making a counter-offer. Under Restatement 2d § 69(2), when an offeree exercises dominion over offered property ("does any act inconsistent with the offeror's ownership of offered property"), the offeree is bound to the offer's terms unless they are manifestly unreasonable. The rule is the same under the UCC § 2–606(1)(c) and § R2–608(4) [Text § 4–117]. $20 for a bag of nails that cost $15 at some unspecified time in the past is not manifestly unreasonable, given that J is saved the trouble of a trip to the store. Here the exercise of dominion was wrongful as against the offeror N because J manifested an intention not to accept, so there is an acceptance only if N ratifies J's taking of the nails. Thus, under the last sentences of § 69(2) or of UCC § 2–606(1)(c), N can choose to hold J to the contract and require him to pay $20. (Note N could also sue J for conversion, but that is a tort remedy, not a contractual one, and thus probably need not be mentioned in any answer to a contracts problem unless the tort has been discussed by your contracts Professor.)

(Note: The analysis immediately below is with reference to the original UCC's § 2–207. A section at the end provides an analysis of §§ R2–206(3) and R2–207.)

This agreement could also, of course, be discussed under UCC § 2–207(1). Under § 2–207(1), the question would be whether the effect of J's, i.e., the offeree's, note would be to turn his "acceptance" into a counter-offer (thus terminating J's power of acceptance). When an offeree changes a basic, typically negotiated term like price, the offeree has not made the definite expression of acceptance that § 2–207(1) requires [Text § 5–8]. That is, the buyer and seller simply are not part of the same deal. Accordingly, here J's note means that no contract was formed under § 2–207(1).

Once it is concluded that a contract was not formed under § 2–207(1), it might be tempting to argue that one was formed under § 2–207(3). However, § 2–207(3) is designed for the case in which the parties' communications do not show that a contract was formed, but where **both** parties thereafter go ahead and engage in conduct that recognizes the existence of a contract [Text § 5–23]. J engaged in such conduct (taking and presumably using the nails), but *N* did nothing after making her offer. Thus there is no contract formed under § 2–207(1) or (3). However, UCC § 1–103 allows general rules of contract law to supplement the Code. That includes the principle of Restatement 2d § 69(2). In addition, § 2–606(1)(c) also suggests acceptance. Thus, given the above analysis N can sue in contract for $20, or in tort for conversion for the value of the nails. There is a contract if N chooses there to be one.

The analysis under § 2–207(1) above would be the same under § R2–206(3) of the revised Code. Whether a contract was formed by conduct is determined by § R2–207 of the new Code. If a

SUGGESTED ANALYSIS OF SAMPLE ESSAY QUESTIONS

contract is formed under either provision, its terms are only those that both parties have agreed to [Text § 5–32].

PART (2)

The first issue is *whether Sales Co.'s 10/19 letter was an offer.*

The 10/19 letter uses the word "quote": the general rule is that "price quotes" are not offers [Text §§ 3–14; 3–15]. Also the letter does not have any **express** words of commitment that Sales Co. will sell the X14 to J (although the request for J to give an answer comes close to an express commitment). Many cases, especially older cases, look for such express words of commitment and ignore the context of the words. Further, it may be customary in the trade for sales of such complicated, expensive machines to be made pursuant to carefully drafted, written agreements.

However, the modern approach is to realize that: (1) use of the word "quote" does not prevent a communication from being an offer; and (2) commitment can be found in the communication based on its context, even if there are no express words of commitment. Here Sales Co.'s letter is in response to J's request for its "best **offer;**" the letter even states "Pursuant to your inquiry." A reasonable person will thus be inclined to consider a response to be an offer if the facts permit that conclusion. Sales Co. also implies that it is willing to sell the X14 for $30,000 when it says it does not **usually** sell them for the $30,000 price it quoted to J. Commitment to a bargain is also shown by Sales Co.'s invitation to J to give an answer. If Sales Co. is not proposing a bargain, what is Sales Co. asking him to answer? The invitation to give an answer also shows that Sales Co. is inviting J to assent. Nothing in the 10/19 letter indicates that any further assent by Sales Co. is needed before the bargain will be concluded. Indeed, the request for an answer indicates to the contrary. Enough terms are included with enough definiteness—price, quantity ("an" X14), and subject matter—that a reasonable person would have no problem believing that Sales Co. would be willing to be bound without any further clarification of terms [Text § 3–1].

The omitted terms—time and place of delivery, payment, quality—etc., are not essential under the UCC, which will fill the gaps with terms from §§ 2–308, 2–309, 2–310, and 2–314. Thus, likely the letter is definite enough to be an offer.

The next issue is *whether J accepted the offer.*

The first sub-issue is whether a mailed acceptance was an invited manner of acceptance [Text § 4–48]. The offer invited J to answer in person, but it did not clearly provide that J could

SUGGESTED ANALYSIS OF SAMPLE ESSAY QUESTIONS

only answer in person. Thus answering in person was probably only a suggested means of acceptance. That means that any means of acceptance reasonable under the circumstances is invited [Text § 4–93]. Since the offer was mailed, a mailed acceptance seems reasonable.

The only thing in this fact pattern that could be considered an acceptance is J's letter of 10/24. Since, once again, we are dealing with the sale of goods in which the offeree's response attempted to add a term to the deal, § 2–207 should be looked to so as to determine if a contract was made. J's 10/24 letter did not merely **suggest** that the attorney's fee provision should be added; it **insisted** that it be added to their deal. At common law, under the mirror image rule, it would *not* be acceptance but rather a counter-offer [Text § 5–1]. Under § 2–207(1), however, it is effective as an acceptance if:

(1) It is a **definite** expression of acceptance [Text § 5–6]. That means the response must **assent** to the **same** basic deal proposed in the offer, without changing any of the typically negotiated terms like price, quantity, or subject matter. "It's a deal" is an assent, and it doesn't change any of those typically negotiated terms. This requirement is satisfied, and thus the 10/24 letter acts as a definite expression of acceptance even though it adds an additional term.

(2) It is **seasonable.** That means that the acceptance had to become effective while the offer was still open to be accepted. The offer said J had until 10/29 to give an answer in person. Probably that means a mailed acceptance would have to be mailed early enough so that is would normally arrive by 10/29. J's mailing of his acceptance on 10/24 was thus seasonable, **unless** Sales Co. effectively revoked its offer, which is discussed below.

(3) It is not expressly conditional on the offeror's assent to the additional or different terms. Here J insisted that his additional attorney's fees term **must** apply, but he did not say that his acceptance would not be effective unless Sales Co. **"assented to"** the attorney's fee term. He did not say "no deal unless you agree to the attorney's fee clause." Just insisting that your terms apply is not enough to prevent your response from being an acceptance under § 2–207(1). It is essential that the terms of the offeree's document require the express assent of the offeror to the additional terms

SUGGESTED ANALYSIS OF SAMPLE ESSAY QUESTIONS

before the offeree's response becomes a counter-offer under this provision of § 2–207(1) [Text § 5–10].

Accordingly, assuming Sales Co. did not effectively revoke its offer, it appears J has a contract to buy an X14.

Hence, *whether the offer was effectively revoked* must be discussed.

The first sub-issue is whether the offer was irrevocable under UCC § 2–205, the merchant's firm offer provision [Text § 4–28]. Sales Co. is a merchant with respect to X14 machines, so **if** Sales Co. gave assurances that the offer would be held open until 10/29, the offer is irrevocable until then (assuming an authorized Sales Co representative signed the letter). However, the letter does **not** give that assurance, i.e., it does not *promise* that the offer will be held open, but, instead just indicates the time when the offeree's power to accept will lapse. Accordingly, it would be incorrect to conclude that Sales Co.'s offer was irrevocable.

The second sub-issue is the time at which J's acceptance became effective. A mailed acceptance where mailing is an authorized means is effective on dispatch [Text § 4–119]. Thus, J's letter was an effective acceptance as of 10/24.

Offers can only be revoked before they are accepted [Text § 4–2], so Sales Co.'s revocation was effective only if it occurred before J mailed his letter. Sales Co.'s letter of 10/22 was an attempted revocation of its offer since it manifested Sales Co.'s intent not to enter into the bargain proposed by its 10/19 offer. However, **a revocation is effective only when it is communicated to the offeree,** which in the case of mailed revocations means when the letter is *received,* **not** when it is mailed, or dispatched [Text § 4–120]. The revocation was not received by J until 10/26, two days **after** his acceptance became effective, and so it was too late. Thus, the offer was not effectively revoked, and J has a contract to buy an X14.

PART (3)

Part (3)(a)

(Note: The analysis immediately below is with reference to the original UCC's § 2–207. A section at the end provides an analysis of §§ R2–206(3) and R2–207.)

The terms of the contract for an X14 are determined under § 2–207(2) [Text § 5–14]. The first question is whether the attorney's fee provision will be included. § 2–207(2) states that between merchants, an additional term to a contract becomes part of the contract only if NONE of the following are true [Text § 5–16]:

SUGGESTED ANALYSIS OF SAMPLE ESSAY QUESTIONS

(1) The offeror's offer expressly limits acceptance to the terms of the offer, § 2–207(2)(a). Here, there was no express limitation in the 10/19 offer.

(2) The additional term materially alters the contract, § 2–207(2)(b). If the addition of an attorney's fee clause would materially alter the contract, then it cannot become part of the contract (unless Sales Co. expressly assents to it, which did not happen here). The tests that may be applied for whether a term materially alters a contract are:

(a) Whether it would cause unreasonable surprise or hardship if it became a part of the contract without Sales Co. actually being aware of it at the time of contracting (UCC § 2–207, Cmt. 4); and

(b) Whether the inclusion of the term would be likely to influence the decision of a reasonable person as to whether or not to enter into the contract.

An attorney's fee clause protects the innocent party in a dispute—it does not change the performance done by either party unless there is a dispute, and it probably is a fairly standard provision in contracts for sale of complicated machines. It therefore does not seem to create unreasonable hardship, nor should it be too surprising to Sales Co. that J might want such a term. On the other hand, attorney's fee clauses can make a party reluctant to litigate even when it believes it has a meritorious position if attorney's fees are likely to be quite large in comparison to the $30,000 cost of the X14.

It probably does not result in unreasonable surprise or hardship, but it *might* be a term that would influence a seller's decision to enter into or not enter into a contract to sell an X14. Hence, whatever the attorney's fee provision materially alters the terms of the contract it is a close question and one on which courts have disagreed. If the term is common in the trade, as it probably is, it probably does not materially alter the contract.

(3) The offeror has already objected to the term, or objects to it within a reasonable time, § 2–207(2)(c). The facts show no objection so far, but Sales Co. may still have a few days in which to object. If it does not, then this hurdle is passed.

SUGGESTED ANALYSIS OF SAMPLE ESSAY QUESTIONS

Under § R2–207 of the Code, only those terms agreed to (or terms implied by the Code) become part of the contract. Because there was no agreement to the attorneys' fees clause, it does not become part of the agreement.

Part (3)(b)

The offer J accepted was for sale of an X14 for $30,000. (Acceptance under 2–207(1) is an acceptance on the terms of the offer, as supplemented or changed by terms that pass the hurdles of 2–207(2).) Because Sales Co.'s attempted revocation by way of a price increase was not effective until after J's acceptance was effective (see Part (2)), the price increase is contractually ineffective. The analysis is similar under § R2–206(3).

Part (3)(c)

The offer J accepted did not require him to promise or commit himself to buy more items. It merely stated Sales Co.'s intent to sell him more ("We intend . . ."). It did not expressly ask J to make such a commitment, nor are there any circumstances that indicate a reasonable person would think he was giving such a commitment by accepting the offer. The indefiniteness of the stated intent ("lots of business") would lead a reasonable offeree to think it could not be asking for a commitment, since a reasonable person would not make such an indefinite commitment.

Answer to Question No. 9

The first issue is **whether Pete's has valid cause of action for breach of express warranty against Sam's as a result of there being no spare tire in the ambulance.**

If Pete, the owner of Pete's Ambulance Service, can surmount the parol evidence rule (see below), he can establish reasonably clearly the elements of a breach of express warranty claim [Text § 35–2]. Obviously, Sam made a representation that the tires would be included with the ambulance; the representation was part of the "basis of the bargain" (regardless of whether basis of bargain is defined as reliance or as something taking place before conclusion of the sale [Text § 35–4]), and the lack of the tires caused Pete's damages as measured by the difference in fair market value between the ambulance with the tires and the ambulance without.

The issue is whether or not the representation about the tires is admissible at all under the parol evidence rule.

SUGGESTED ANALYSIS OF SAMPLE ESSAY QUESTIONS

There seems to be no dispute that the contract they both signed contained a final expression of the parties as to at least most of the terms of the sales contract, price, delivery, etc. The question then becomes whether the writing was intended as a complete and exclusive statement of the terms of the agreement under § 2–202 [Text § 20–3]. While there is no evidence in the facts that the contract contained a merger clause, that fact alone is not determinative in deciding whether the contract was intended as a complete and exclusive statement [Text § 18–16]. In this case, both Pete's and Sam's are merchants executing a contract for the sale of a rather expensive good which is important to the running of their businesses. Thus, it would seem likely that the parties' would take care to scrutinize the contract carefully to ensure that written document would contain the final and exclusive statement of all the terms of their agreement. If so, then evidence of the oral promise to install the tire would be inadmissible under § 2–202(b) [Text § 20–3].

If a court were to construe a contract as not being a complete and exclusive statement of the terms of the agreement, i.e., not completely integrated, then the oral promise to equip the ambulance with new tires could be introduced under § 2–202(b) if it passed the "would certainly" test as set forth in Comment 3 to § 2–202 [Text § 20–6]. Under that test the court would ask, if the parties had really reached the agreement about the spare tires, can it be said that they would "would certainly" have included such a provision in their contract? It is likely that a judge would find that the evidence would be inadmissible given that test. That is, the installation of two spare tires was obviously quite important to Peter, and thus it is likely a judge would find that had the agreement in fact been made, Peter would have seen to it that the term "would certainly" have been included the final written contract. On the other hand, it is hardly a standard clause for a vehicle sale and a court might decide that it would *possibly,* but not certainly, be in the agreement if the parties in fact reached an accord about the tires and if Peter signed a standard printed automobile sales form contract. Nevertheless, although it is a close question, it seems likely that the evidence would be excluded.

This means that Pete would never be able to establish the first element of an express warranty claim, i.e., that a representation was made, because the parol evidence rule would bar the admissibility of such evidence in the trial.

The next issue is **whether Paragraph 6 of the sales agreement is valid and should be given full effect.**

SUGGESTED ANALYSIS OF SAMPLE ESSAY QUESTIONS

The resolution of this question is crucial as it is determinative of all remaining issues in the problem. To resolve the issue properly there must be a two-step analysis: first, whether the provision is facially valid under the Code must be discussed. If it is determined that the Paragraph is facially valid, then the issue of whether or not Sam's has lived up to its end of the bargain, thus entitling it to the benefits set forth in Paragraph 6, must be analyzed.

Paragraph 6 has two sentences, each of which is properly classified as a limitation of remedy, as opposed to a warranty disclaimer, and thus is governed by the rules of § 2–719 and not § 2–316 [Text § 32–54]. To be facially valid each of the sentences must be conscionable under § 2–719 and § 2–302. The analysis relating to each of the sentences is somewhat different, and thus they will have to be analyzed independently.

The first sentence ("repair/replacement provision") would likely be judged conscionable under § 2–302 [Text §§ 16–5; 32–52]. It is important to realize that in the repair/replacement provision Pete's has given up **all** remedies provided by the code, i.e., Pete's cannot reject the ambulance, cannot revoke its acceptance of the ambulance, cannot sue for breach of warranty, cannot sue for cover or market differential damages, etc. Its **sole** remedy under the contract is to have any defective part in the ambulance repaired or replaced. While such a provision would perhaps be held unconscionable in a consumer transaction, it is a different question when dealing between merchants. Here, Peter was buying a piece of machinery with which he was familiar in a type of transaction which he had entered into at least a few times previously. Additionally, it's not as if the provision takes all of Pete's remedies away and leaves it nothing in return. Instead of a lawsuit to recover market differential, warranty, or cover damages (as would be Pete's code-based remedies), Pete's has the right under the contract to have the ambulance fixed whenever a problem comes up. It may be that a court would nevertheless, find sufficient amounts of procedural unconscionability within the ambulance industry to void the provision (especially if the repair/replacement provision was adhesive as to Sam's and standard throughout all ambulance sellers), but if a retailer of ambulances cannot limit the remedies available in a transaction with an established ambulance company, sellers will likely never be able to do so in any transaction. Accordingly, the first sentence is facially valid and survives a conscionability attack [Text § 32–52].

The conscionability of the second sentence ("consequential damage provision") is governed by § 2–719(3). That provision states that a limitation on consequential damages between merchants is *prima facie* conscionable when the losses excluded by the provision are economic. Accordingly, to the extent the provision is interpreted to limit Pete's ability to recoup lost profits while the ambulance is being fixed, or economic loss suffered by Pete's as a result of the patient not getting to the hospital on time, the clause probably survives a conscionability attack. Of course, § 2–719(3) does not state that all economic consequential damage limitations are valid. It merely establishes a presumption of conscionability. However, this is a clause agreed to between two merchants in a transaction of some importance in their businesses. There is no evidence of oppression, unequal bargaining power, confidential relationship, etc., which might suggest unconscionability. Hence, it is unlikely that the presumption of conscionability will be rebutted [Text § 32–52].

To the extent Sam's tries to use the consequential damage provision to exclude recovery for non-economic damages, the clause is likely to be found *prima facie* unconscionable under § 2–719(3). That provision states that there is a presumption of unconscionability when a party attempts to limit consequential personal injury losses in consumer transactions. It is true that this is a merchant, not a consumer transaction, and there are reasons to treat the two differently. In a consumer transaction, the purchaser has only the seller to look to for personal injury recovery. In a case like this, the availability of corporate health benefits, worker's compensation rights, etc. means that Pete's driver has sources other than the seller from whom he can recover for his injuries. Nonetheless, courts have been understandably reluctant to permit exclusion of damages for personal injuries, and so I believe that to the extent the clause excludes personal injury damage, it is unconscionable.

Under § 2–302, a court is empowered to limit application of an unconscionable clause to avoid an unconscionable result [Text § 16–3]. As such, the consequential damages provision would likely be interpreted so as to include limitations on economic losses and to exclude limitations for personal injuries suffered by Pete's employees.

Just because the repair/replacement provision and a portion of the consequential damage provision in Paragraph 6 are valid against an attack of unconscionability does not necessarily mean that they are enforceable given this fact situation. The determination as to whether the clauses are enforceable turns on whether § 2–719(2) is satisfied. That provision provided that if the conduct of a party asserting the validity of an otherwise

SUGGESTED ANALYSIS OF SAMPLE ESSAY QUESTIONS

valid limitation of remedy provision is so delinquent that the limited remedy fails its essential purpose, the clause will be stricken. The purpose of repair/replacement clause is to ensure that the buyer has a working good, as opposed to having a nonconforming good and the right to reject, sue for breach of warranty, cover, etc. as provided in the Code. In the first five weeks that Pete's owned the ambulance, it was in the shop ten full days, plus it was going to need additional servicing after July 13th. While a day or two for repairs might be within the contemplation of § 2–719(2), it is likely that the intrusive interruptions in service that Pete's suffered has deprived it of the benefits of its bargain, i.e., a working ambulance, and thus the repair/replacement provision is unenforceable. In other words, Pete's has been able to realize neither the benefits of its code-based remedies or its contract-based remedies [Text § 32–52].

If the repair/replacement provision of Paragraph 6 is unenforceable, Pete's would have available to it any of the remedies set forth in § 2–711, with the possible exception of the ability to recover consequential damages, which will be discussed below. One of those remedies is to sue for breach of warranty under § 2–714. In such a case Pete's would have to give notice of its intention to sue to General Motors (now that Sam's in no longer in business), would have to keep the ambulance, but would be able to recover the difference between the value of the ambulance as promised and the value of the ambulance actually received, plus any incidental damages and possibly consequential damages as well. As a practical matter, if Pete's decided to keep the ambulance it would probably have the engine repaired by another mechanic so that it did not stall in traffic, and the repair bill would be the bulk of its damages. There should be no problem in recovering these damages against GM as the privity barriers for breach of warranty have long been abolished [Text § 35–18].

Pete's also would have the chance to exercise either its rejection or (possibly) revocation rights should it choose not to keep the ambulance [Text §§ 22–39; 22–45]. The first question that must be answered is whether Pete's has accepted the ambulance under § 2–606 [Text § 22–37]. The Comments to that section make it clear that neither possession nor payment, by themselves, signify acceptance. The idea behind acceptance is that the purchaser is given a reasonable period of time to test the product to ensure that it is a conforming good under the contract before it will be deemed to have been accepted. Here, Pete's has had the ambulance for approximately 6 weeks, but it has been in the shop often during that time. As automobiles are somewhat sophisticated pieces of machinery, and as courts have given automobile purchasers a fair amount of leeway to test a vehicle before acceptance, it is likely that Pete's will not be deemed to have accepted the car and thus be able to reject. There has been little controversy over a buyer's right to reject against a remote seller, and although that doctrine could be questioned (see below), based on existing precedent there should be no problem in Pete's exercising its rejection rights against GM [Text § 22–39].

Should Pete's be deemed to have accepted it under § 2–606(b), Pete's may be entitled to revoke its acceptance under § 2–608(1)(a) i.e., claiming that its acceptance was based on the reasonable assumption that the nonconformity would be cured [Text § 22–39]. Of course, to revoke Pete's would also have to establish that the value of the contract to it has been substantially impaired by the failure of the vehicle to run properly, but this should be no problem since it has obviously lost a good deal of money because of the defect.

While there has been no serious issue raised regarding rejection against remote sellers, there has been discussion as to whether or not it is proper in revocation situations [Text § 22–45]. Those who have argued in favor of revocation against remote sellers have stated that it is likely that the remote seller will have a better means of selling the revoked good in the used markets than will the buyer. This is probably true here as General Motors would seem to have better lines of distribution for used ambulances than Pete's. However, those who argue against a revocation remedy being available a remote seller point out that the remote seller only received wholesale purchase price from its dealer, yet would be forced to refund the full retail purchase price to the revoking buyer (this is also true for rejection against sellers but no one seems to have raised this issue in that context). While each of these arguments needs to be taken into account, the real issue appears to be who should bear the risk of the insolvency of the dealer—the manufacturer who chose to distribute its good though that retailer, or the consumer who chose to purchase from it? The manufacturer would seem to be in a better position to do the background checking so as to ensure the solvency of its dealers, and to get them to post bonds in case they go out of business, etc., rather than imposing on the consumer buyers the obligation to ensure that the dealer has sufficient resources to be in its location for the expected life of the car. Accordingly, it's probably the better rule that the buyer can revoke against a remote seller, at least when the retailer is bankrupt. Again, however, this is a close call.

SUGGESTED ANALYSIS OF SAMPLE ESSAY QUESTIONS

Upon rejection or revocation there is an issue as to whether or not Pete's has to pay any restitutionary recovery based on the value of any benefit Pete's received from using it during the six weeks. Most courts have held that such recovery is not available, but to the extent Pete's will receive back its full purchase price, plus any cover or market differential damages, it will have been put in a better position than it would have been had the contract been performed. That is, it will have all of its money, plus thirty days or so of using the ambulance for its business without having to pay for that use [Text § 22–52]. It would seem that its damages should be offset by its benefits, but it is difficult to find support for such a claim in the case law.

The fact that the repair/replacement position of Paragraph 6 is unenforceable does not necessarily answer the question as to whether or not the limitation on consequential damages for economic loss is unenforceable. The resolution of this question is determined by whether the repair/replacement and consequential damage provisions are considered dependent or independent. If they are deemed dependent, i.e., the only reason Pete's agreed to give up its rights to consequential damages was because it had been promised that a defective part would be promptly repaired or replaced, the consequential damage limitation must also be stricken and such damages would be recoverable. While this approach has been adopted by some courts, others have held that the provisions are independent, and thus the failure of the repair/replacement clause provision has no effect on the consequential damages provision. If so, then the economic loss suffered by Pete's both while the ambulance was being repaired, and by the patient who suffered additional damages while waiting for the substitute ambulance, would still not be recoverable [Text § 32–52].

CASE SQUIBS

(Listed Alphabetically by Subject Matter)

ANTICIPATORY REPUDIATION

Hochster v. De La Tour, 188 Eng. Rep. 922 (Q.B. 1853) [Text § 23–2]

McCloskey & Co. v. Minweld Steel Co., 220 F.2d 101 (3d Cir. 1955)

> This case demonstrates that a promisor's expression of anticipated difficulty in performing is not by enough itself to constitute an anticipatory repudiation. A subcontractor agreed to furnish and erect all of the structural steel on a certain project. The subcontractor experienced some difficulties with his supplier but promised delivery within approximately forty days. The general contractor would have experienced delays under the subcontractor's promised delivery schedule, so it requested delivery within thirty days. The subcontractor responded by explaining the difficulties he was having with his supplier. He also requested the general contractor's help in securing the steel from the supplier and indicated its desire to perform in a timely manner. The general contractor claimed that the subcontractor had anticipatorily breached. The court disagreed, stating that a party has not anticipatorily repudiated a contract absent "an absolute and unequivocal refusal to perform or a distinct and positive statement of an inability to do so." [Text § 23–12]

Oloffson v. Coomer, 296 N.E.2d 871 (Ill. App. Ct. 1973)

> This case illustrates the majority view of the proper measure of a buyer's recovery upon a seller's anticipatory repudiation. A farmer unequivocally repudiated a contract to sell corn when he stated he would not plant corn that season. The court held that the buyer could recover the difference between the price he contracted for and the price of the corn on the day of the repudiation, whether he replaced the corn immediately or waited until the date when the farmer's performance was due.
>
> UCC § 2–713 provides that the "market price" that should be used for purposes of a buyer's market differential damages is the market price pending on the date the buyer learned of the breach. The rationale for that rule, especially in a case like this one, is that it is not "commercially reasonable" to wait to replace a commodity sold in a volatile market when the price might substantially rise in the buyer's favor. [Text § 32–19]

CASE SQUIBS

Phelps v. Herro, 137 A.2d 159 (Md. 1957)

This case demonstrates that the doctrine of anticipatory repudiation does not apply to situations where one party has fully performed and the only obligation remaining for the other party is the duty to make payment for the performance. Thus, the aggrieved party must wait till the time for performance and then sue for damages. The plaintiffs agreed to sell certain interests they owned in real property and stock to the defendants for $37,500. The defendants paid a $5,000 down payment and signed a promissory note for the balance. The plaintiffs then fully performed by transferring their property interests to the defendants. However, the defendants notified the plaintiffs that they would not make the required payments on the promissory note, and the plaintiffs instituted an action for breach before even the first payment on the note was due. Plaintiffs claimed the right to sue immediately under the doctrine of anticipatory repudiation. The defendants asserted that plaintiffs' suit was premature since plaintiffs had performed all of their obligations under the contract, and all that remained was for defendants to tender their payment on the due date. The court ruled that with unilateral contracts, or with bilateral contracts that become unilateral by virtue of full performance by one of the parties, where the party still obligated has only a duty to pay money to fulfill his promise of performance, the doctrine of anticipatory repudiation has no application. Thus, plaintiffs' suit was premature, and their only remedy was to wait till the time for performance and sue for breach at that time. [Text § 23–5]

Reliance Cooperage Corp. v. Treat, 195 F.2d 977 (8th Cir. 1952)

The parties entered into an executory contract for the sale of bourbon staves. Treat breached before the time for performance arrived. The court opined that the proper time to measure the non-breaching party's damages in a case involving anticipatory repudiation is at the time set for performance, whether or not the non-breaching party accepts the anticipatory repudiation. That is, a party to an executory contract may refuse to accept an anticipatory repudiation of the contract and may instead insist upon performance. The contract then remains binding on both parties, and no actionable claim arises until the date set for performance. However, if the non-breaching party accepts the anticipatory repudiation, the damages will still be measured as of the time set for performance.

This is very much a minority position. Even the original UCC under which the case was decided stated that the proper "market price" to be used in the calculation of a buyer's market differential damages under § 2–713 is the market price pending on the day the seller learned of the breach, and not the day performance was due. The revised Code specifically deals with this issue and provides that the temporal market is one within a "reasonable time" after the buyer learns of the repudiation. [Text § 32–18]

United States v. Seacoast Gas Co., 204 F.2d 709 (5th Cir. 1953)

This case holds that a party may no longer retract his repudiation once the non-breaching party has materially changed his position in reliance on the repudiation or stated that it regards the repudiation as final. Seacoast contracted to supply gas to the United States for a certain period. During the period, Seacoast notified the United States that it would no longer perform under the contract. The United States sought out new suppliers, and when it secured a willing supplier, it notified Seacoast that unless its repudiation was retracted within three days, the United States would accept the new supplier's bid. Seacoast's retraction came after the three days had expired. The court held that Seacoast's retraction was ineffective because the United States materially changed its position when it accepted the new supplier's bid. Also, the United States had notified Seacoast that it intended to treat the repudiation as final after the three-day period expired. Thus, the repudiation could no longer be retracted after that point. [Text § 23–32]

ASSENT

Balfour v. Balfour, 2 K.B. 571 (1919)

In *Balfour*, a husband promised to make certain monthly payments to his wife, with whom he was living amicably at the time of the promise. After the parties separated, the wife sued for payments due under the agreement. The court held that the alleged contract was not enforceable because family members do not normally contemplate legal consequences when they make promises to each other. Such promises are unenforceable after domestic partners separate. Note, however, that there has been some relaxation of the presumption against legal consequences arising from these types of agreements in modern decisions. Thus, where the agreement is made between family members not living together amicably (e.g., where the agreement is entered into by separated marital partners or in a dissolution situation) or where the parties expressly agree to the agreement's enforceability, the contract is likely to be enforced. [Text § 2–7]

Varney v. Ditmars, 111 N.E. 822 (N.Y. 1916)

This early case is cited as one of the seminal cases setting forth the indefiniteness doctrine. An architectural draftsman sued his employer over a provision in his employment contract that he would be paid a "fair share of [the employer's] profits" in addition to his regular salary. The court refused to enforce the profit sharing provision, stating that its amount was a matter of "pure conjecture" and "may be any amount from a nominal sum to a material part according to the particular views of the person whose guess is considered. Such an executory contract must rest for performance on the honor and good faith of the parties making it." Accordingly, because the meaning of the term was too indefinite, the promise could not be enforced. [Text § 6–6]

ASSIGNMENT AND DELEGATION

Allhusen v. Caristo Construction Corp., 103 N.E.2d 891 (N.Y. 1952)

This case discusses the validity of a contract provision prohibiting the assignment of rights created by the contract. A general contractor contracted with a subcontractor for certain painting work on a project. The contract provided that "the assignment by [the subcontractor] of this contract or any interest therein, or of any money due or to become due . . . shall be void." The subcontractor assigned his right to payment under the contract to a bank, which thereafter assigned its interest to a third party. The assignment by the subcontractor was declared invalid. A freely bargained for "no assignment" clause is valid and will be enforced, so long as the clause is drafted in clear and plain language. However, note that most modern courts view no assignment clauses with hostility and thus construe them narrowly or find that the particular provision at issue was not drafted with the requisite clear and plain language for enforceability. Additionally, Article 9 of the UCC deems no assignment clauses within its purview as ineffective. This would include the assignment of accounts receivable. Thus, the result in *Allhusen* would be different if decided today. [Text § 27–21]

Chemical Bank v. Rinden Professional Association, 498 A.2d 706 (N.H. 1985)

The court in this case found that pursuant to UCC § 9–206(1) an obligor had waived its defenses against the assignee of a contract upon assignment of that contract. Chemical Bank was the assignee of a lease-purchase contract for an office phone system. The obligor on the contract was a law firm that refused to make payments once the phone system began to malfunction. The notice of assignment from the obligee contained a "hell or high water clause" which prohibited any defenses the obligor had against the obligee from being asserted against the assignee. However, any claims on the underlying contract could still be asserted against the obligee. This clause was included in the notice as a precondition to Chemical Bank's acceptance of the assignment. An agent of the law firm signed the waiver upon receipt. Chemical Bank brought suit three years later when the law firm refused to make any more payments because of the malfunction of the phone system. The court found that the notice of assignment and waiver were valid under § 9–206(1) because Chemical Bank took the assignment for value, in good faith and without notice of any claim or defense of the obligor against the obligee, i.e., it had holder in due course status. No consideration was required for the waiver to be effective upon assignment under § 2–209(1). Thus, the law firm could not assert the defense of malfunction of the phone system against Chemical Bank. [Text § 27–44]

Crane Ice Cream Co. v. Terminal Freezing & Heating Co., 128 A. 280 (Md. 1925)

The court in this case exemplified the pre-UCC view that output and requirements contracts cannot be assigned. The owner of an ice cream plant (the buyer) contracted with the seller to purchase his weekly requirements for ice, up to a maximum of 250 tons per week. The buyer agreed under the contract not to purchase ice from other suppliers. The buyer then sold his ice cream plant to a third party who owned several other ice cream plants, and the buyer assigned his rights to the contract with the seller to the third party. The third party sued the seller for breach of contract when the seller refused to make further deliveries. The court held that the contract between the buyer and the seller was not assignable to the third party. The reasoning was that the seller relied on the buyer's credit and the seller's past experience with the buyer in promising to meet the buyer's requirements. The third party might not have the same ability to pay or the same requirements since more ice cream plants were involved. Note, however, that the UCC may permit the assignment of an output or requirements contract if the assignee's output or requirements are not "unreasonably disproportionate" to the assignor's estimated output or requirements [UCC § 2–210, Comment 4].

Evening News Ass'n v. Peterson, 477 F. Supp. 77 (D.C. 1979)

This case demonstrates the assignability of certain personal service contracts. Peterson was a news anchor of a television station, which was sold. As part of the sale, the contracts of all the employees were assigned to the new owners. Peterson claimed his contract was not assignable because it was a personal service contract. The court held such contracts were freely assignable, so long as the assignment did not violate public policy, was not prohibited under the terms of the contract, and would not result in a materially greater burden to the employee (i.e., the "obligor"). While a personal service contract cannot usually be **delegated**, such contracts are freely assignable subject to the limitations stated above. Thus, so long as Peterson would not be required to appear on a greater number of newscasts, for example, his contract would be assignable. All that happened as a result of the assignment was that Peterson received his paycheck from the new owner of the station. Because his obligations under the contract remained the same, and because there was no prohibition against assignments in his contract with the old employer, the assignment was valid. [Text §§ 27–17; 28–10; 29–27]

CASE SQUIBS

Langell v. Betz, 164 N.E. 890 (N.Y. 1928)

This case exhibits an exception to the traditional rule that the assignment of a bilateral executory contract impliedly assigns the assignor's rights and duties under the contract. Seller contracted with purchaser for the sale of land. Purchaser assigned the contract to a third party. On the date set for performance, seller was ready to convey the property, but the third party refused to make payment for the land. The court held that the third party was not obligated to make payment on the assigned contract unless the third party promised he would perform the purchaser's obligations. This exception appears to apply only to contracts for the sale of land. [Text §§ 27–36; 28–6]

Taylor v. Barton-Child Co., 117 N.E. 43 (Mass. 1917)

This case demonstrates the traditional pre-UCC rule that a right based on a future expectation cannot be assigned. Thus, in *Taylor*, the court refused to recognize the assignment of after-acquired accounts receivable as valid. Today, use of such clauses is a routine business practice, and they are specifically provided for in the UCC. [Text § 27–14]

BREACH/CONSTRUCTIVE CONDITIONS

Holiday Inns of America, Inc. v. Knight, 450 P.2d 42 (Cal. 1969)

The court in this case discussed the potential forfeiture of payments made in the earlier years on a multi-year option contract. The parties' option agreement provided that the yearly option payments were to be made into a designated escrow account by July 1 in each of the five years covered by the agreement. In the fourth year, the plaintiffs mistakenly made payment directly to the seller after the due date for the option payment. Therefore, since the terms of the option agreement were not complied with, the seller returned the payment to the plaintiffs with a notice stating that the option had been cancelled. Thereafter, the plaintiff attempted to exercise the option, but this attempt was rejected. Normally, a breaching party is subject to forfeiture of all preceding payments made on a multi-year option contract if the option is cancelled. However, anti-forfeiture statutes may allow a party to avoid forfeiture and cancellation if the breach is not willful, grossly negligent, or fraudulent and the breaching party makes full compensation to the non-breaching party. This case was decided in California which has an anti-forfeiture statute in its Civil Code. Thus, the court declared that the plaintiffs had successfully exercised their option after the seller had attempted to cancel the option contract. [Text § 21–107]

Jacob & Youngs, Inc. v. Kent, 129 N.E. 889 (N.Y. 1921) [Text §§ 21–70; 30–35]

CASE SQUIBS

K & G Construction Co. v. Harris, 164 A.2d 451 (Md. 1960)

This case demonstrates the presumption made by courts that promises exchanged in a bilateral contract are mutually dependent. A subcontractor contracted to do some construction work for a general contractor. The general contractor agreed to make progress payments each month, and the subcontractor promised to perform all work in a "workmanlike manner." When the subcontractor's bulldozer damaged the house on the subject property, the general contractor refused to make any more progress payments. Then the subcontractor walked off the job because of the general contractor's failure to make payments. Thus, the general contractor was forced to pay a different contractor more money to complete the job. The court held that the general contractor was not in breach for failing to make the progress payments. The court presumed that the general contractor's promise to make progress payments was conditioned on the subcontractor's workmanlike performance. (Obviously the court assumed that the damage to the house was due to non-workmanlike performance.) Therefore, since the general contractor was not in breach, it was the subcontractor who breached by walking off the job. [Text § 21–66]

Kingston v. Preston, 99 Eng. Rep. 437 (K.B. 1773)

This was the first case to hold that, in a bilateral contract, one party's duty to perform is constructively conditioned on the other party's performance. Plaintiff and defendant entered an agreement for the sale of defendant's business. Plaintiff agreed to post a security bond (guaranteeing his payments), and defendant agreed to convey the property. Plaintiff failed to post the bond, so defendant refused to convey the property. Hence, plaintiff sued defendant for breach of contract. The court held that the defendant was excused from his promise to sell his business since the plaintiff breached his promise to post the security bond. The court reasoned that the defendant's performance was conditioned on the plaintiff performing his promise. [Text § 21–44]

Kirkland v. Archbold, 113 N.E.2d 496 (Ohio Ct. App. 1953)

If a contract is found to be divisible, i.e., the parties' agreement can be divided into a series of equal units of performance, then for purposes of determining whether a constructive condition has been performed, the contract will be hypothetically divided into a series of separate contracts. However, construction contracts are generally not considered divisible even if the owner is required to make periodic progress payments. This latter view was apparent in *Kirkland*, where the plaintiff agreed to do some construction work on the defendant's house. The contract provided for $1000 progress payments. However, the defendant claimed the plaintiff's work was shoddy and refused to make the first payment in full. Instead, he paid the plaintiff only $800 and ordered the plaintiff off the job. The court held that the plaintiff could only recover the reasonable value of his work for the period and not the entire progress payment due. This is because a construction project is deemed indivisible even if payments are scheduled periodically throughout the project. That is, the individual payments are not intended to equal the value of the work done in the corresponding period. [Text § 21–74]

Nolan v. Whitney, 88 N.Y. 648 (1882)

This case demonstrates the minority view in situations where a third party's satisfaction or approval is a condition precedent to another party's duty to perform. This minority view states that where the third party unreasonably withholds approval or unreasonably refuses to express satisfaction, the nonperformance of the condition is excused. In *Nolan*, an architect's certificate was required before a mason could request payment from the building's owner for his work. The architect honestly, but unreasonably, expressed his dissatisfaction and refused to issue the certificate. The court held that "[a]n unreasonable refusal on the part of the architect . . . to give the certificate dispenses with its necessity." This minority view is applied only where there is a possibility of forfeiture or unjust enrichment. [See gen. Text § 21–41]

Plante v. Jacobs, 103 N.W.2d 296 (Wis. 1960)

This court applied the doctrine of substantial performance. That is, once a contracting party has substantially performed, he or she may sue for his expectation damages if the other party refuses to perform. In other words, the constructive condition stating that one party's performance is constructively conditioned on there being no uncured material breach by the other is satisfied upon substantial performance. Here, when one party asserted that a minor breach on the part of the contractor justified his refusal to pay the contractor, it was **he** who materially breached the contract under the "first" material breach doctrine.

According to the court, a party has substantially performed once his or her performance "meets the essential purpose of the contract." Thus, where a contractor substantially performed a building project on a house, the contractor was entitled to recover the contract price, but was liable for damages resulting from his immaterial breach. Strict compliance with the building plans was not required. In this case, the deviation was the placement of a wall one foot off of the plan specifications, so the essential purpose of the contract had been fulfilled. [Text §§ 21–68]

CASE SQUIBS

Second National Bank v. Pan-American Bridge Co., 183 F. 391 (6th Cir. 1910)

This case illustrates the majority view that where a third party's approval of work completed is required as a condition of satisfaction under a construction contract, the unreasonable withholding of that approval will not excuse the performance of the condition unless the refusal is also made in bad faith. Plaintiff agreed to construct a building for the defendant, subject to approval of the plans and construction by the defendant's architect. The architect approved the plaintiff's plans which called for 8-hole rivet connections. However, after the plaintiff had constructed a substantial portion of the building, the architect insisted on 10-hole rivet connections. The defendant refused to pay the plaintiff until these changes were made so that its architect could issue the certificate of approval. The court held that it was not enough for the plaintiff to show that the architect's refusal to approve the project was unreasonable. The plaintiff had to also show that the architect was withholding approval in bad faith. Thus, if the architect was withholding his approval for safety reasons, for example, the plaintiff would not be successful in recovering against the defendant because the architect's approval was an express condition precedent to the defendant's liability for payment and express conditions are strictly enforced. [Text § 21–41]

Stewart v. Newbury, 115 N.E. 984 (N.Y. 1917)

This case illustrates the principle that, unless the parties agree otherwise, the duty to pay in a contract for services did not arise until the party to perform the services substantially completes the work. Thus, where plaintiff contracted to do construction work for the defendant, and the parties' agreement did not specify when payment was due from the defendant, plaintiff was not entitled to payment for his first month's work where the work performed was not yet close to completion. [Text § 21–50; 21–52]

CONSIDERATION/PROMISSORY ESTOPPEL

Allegheny College v. National Chatauqua County Bank of Jamestown, 159 N.E. 173 (N.Y. 1927)

In this case, Justice Cardozo set forth the requirements for valid consideration. A charitable donor promised to donate money to Allegheny College. In return, the College promised to name a scholarship fund after the donor. The court held that an enforceable bilateral contract, supported by valid consideration, had been formed.

Justice Cardozo opined that in order for a promise to be "supported by consideration," three requirements must be met: (1) the promisee must suffer a "legal detriment"; (2) the detriment must induce the promise; and (3) the promise must induce the detriment. Thus, a charitable organization's promise to name a scholarship after a donor is sufficient consideration to make the donor's promise enforceable if it is induced by the promised contribution and the promise to contribute is induced by the promised naming of the scholarship. Although the court held that an enforceable contract had been formed, the case is often noted for Justice Cardozo's statement that "we have adopted the doctrine of promissory estoppel as the equivalent of consideration in connection with our law of charitable subscriptions." Thus, as indicated now under § 90(2) of the Restatement 2d, promissory estoppel may be an alternative basis for enforcing the promise in similar cases. [Text §§ 7–4; 8–2; 8–5]

Bard v. Kent, 122 P.2d 8 (Cal. 1942)

This case illustrates the revocability of option contracts at common law where there is only a recital, but no actual payment, of consideration i.e., where there is "purported" consideration. The defendant offered the plaintiff a written option to extend his lease of the defendant's property. The option stated that it was granted "for consideration of ten dollars and other valuable consideration." The plaintiff never paid the stated consideration but hired an architect to draw up sketches for improvements to be made to the leased property. Before the plaintiff could exercise the option to renew the lease, the defendant died, and the defendant's estate refused to allow the plaintiff to renew. The court held that an option to renew a lease becomes an irrevocable offer only when consideration is actually paid by the offeree. In the absence of consideration, the option is revoked upon the death of the offeror, even if the offeree incurs expenses in reliance on the option. Thus, the fact that the plaintiff failed to pay the stated consideration prevented him from enforcing the option since it was revoked by the defendant's death.

Note, however, that under § 87 of the Restatement 2d of Contracts purported consideration in option contracts is sufficient to bind the party selling the option so long as the option is in writing, the deal is fair, and it is signed by the offeror. [Text § 4–78]

DeCicco v. Schweizer, 117 N.E. 807 (N.Y. 1917)

In *DeCicco*, Justice Cardozo wrote a controversial decision which held that a party's forbearance from exercising his right to rescind an agreement could be sufficient consideration to enforce the other party's promise. The opinion illustrates the general judicial hostility to the consideration requirement inherent in the pre-existing duty rule. In that case, a father promised his daughter's fiancé a $2,500/year payment if the fiancé and his daughter went through with their planned marriage. After making the payments for ten years, the father refused to make any more payments, claiming there was no consideration for his promise because his daughter and her fiancé were already engaged to be married when the agreement was entered into. Therefore, the parties were already bound to go through with the wedding (a pre-existing duty), and the fiancé's promise to get married could not then be adequate consideration for the promised payment from the father. However, the court found that the father's promise was supported by adequate consideration; it was not merely an unenforceable promise to make a gift. The court reasoned that the couple could have rescinded their engagement, and their forbearance from exercising this right was sufficient consideration for the father's promise. [Text § 7–12]

East Providence Credit Union v. Geremia, 239 A.2d 725 (R.I. 1968)

This case illustrates when a promise to procure insurance will be enforceable. The Geremias purchased a car with the help of a loan from the Credit Union. At the outset, the Geremias agreed to obtain insurance on the car. However, Mr. Geremia later became ill and could no longer pay the premiums on the insurance. The Credit Union promised to make the premium payments for the Geremias, and the Geremias agreed to allow the Credit Union to add the amount of these payments to their loan balance. However, the Credit Union failed to make the premium payments. When the car was subsequently destroyed, the Credit Union sued for the balance due on the loan, and the Geremias counterclaimed for the insurance proceeds. The court held for the Geremias on two grounds: (1) the agreement to pay interest on the money borrowed to pay the insurance premium was sufficient consideration to make the Credit Union's promise enforceable; and (2) the promise was enforceable by promissory estoppel, since the Geremias had relied on the Credit Union's promise to make the premium payments which caused the Geremias to forebear maintaining the insurance policy. This last basis for the court's decision is controversial since the facts indicate that the Geremias could not have continued to maintain the insurance policy anyway. Thus, there is a question of whether the Credit Union's promise caused a real forbearance by the Geremias. [Text § 7–18; 8–3]

Feinberg v. Pfeiffer Co., 322 S.W.2d 163 (Mo. Ct. App. 1959)

This case upholds by the principle that past consideration is insufficient consideration to make a contract enforceable. However, it also shows that where a contract cannot be enforced due to insufficient consideration, promissory estoppel can be used to enforce some or all of the promises of that agreement. After the plaintiff had worked for Pfeiffer Co. for 37 years, the company's board of directors passed a resolution entitling the plaintiff to a $200/month pension upon her retirement. Plaintiff continued working for another year and a half and then retired. She was paid her pension for seven years, but the company eventually cut the amount back to $100/month, and the plaintiff brought suit. The court held that the company's promise to pay her pension could not be enforced as a contract, for the company's promise was merely a gift promise based on past consideration. However, the company's promise could be enforced on promissory estoppel grounds, for the plaintiff reasonably, foreseeably, and detrimentally relied on the company's promise in deciding to retire when she did. [Text §§ 7–23; 8–3]

Fischer v. Union Trust Co., 101 N.W. 852 (Mich. 1904)

This case demonstrates that sham consideration will not suffice to make a gift promise enforceable. In *Fischer*, a daughter paid her father $1.00 at the time he deeded certain property to her in exchange for the father's promise that he would pay off the mortgages on the property when they became due. Following the father's death, the daughter sought to enforce her father's promise against his estate. The court held that the father's promise was an unenforceable gift due to lack of adequate consideration. The facts showed that the father's promise was intended as a gift, and thus the payment of $1.00 was merely sham consideration given the surrounding circumstances. As a result, the father's promise was unenforceable. [Text § 7–45]

Foakes v. Beer, 9 App. Cas. 605 (Eng. 1884)

Foakes is the preeminent pre-existing duty rule case. Foakes owed Beer money under a loan and did not have the money to repay the principal when it became due. The loan agreement contemplated this fact and called for him to pay interest on any sum not paid in full when due. Foakes entered into a modification with Beer, whereby they agreed he could repay the principal on fixed schedule, and as long as he stuck to the schedule, he would not have to pay any interest. Foakes stuck to the schedule, but after making the last payment, Beer sued for the interest called for in the original contract. The court held that Foakes had to pay the interest for there was no consideration for Beer's agreement to forego the interest. That is, under the preexisting duty rule, to be enforceable, a modification must be supported by new consideration. Because Foakes did not promise to do anything he had not already promised, Beer's promise to forego the interest was unenforceable. [Text §§ 7–80; 24–13]

Goodman v. Dicker, 169 F.2d 684 (D.C. Cir. 1948)

This case holds that reliance damages are recoverable in an action based on promissory estoppel where the defendant promised the plaintiff a franchise. A higher award of the plaintiff's expectation interest would be inappropriate given that there was no enforceable contract. In *Goodman*, the plaintiff applied to the defendant for a franchise to sell Emerson radios. The defendant led the plaintiff to believe that the franchise had been approved, and the plaintiff spent $1,150 to hire salesmen and advertise before he found out that the franchise had not in fact been approved. The court's holding, which allowed plaintiff his reliance damages, is significant for two reasons: (1) it allowed damages under a reliance measure, whereas the traditional rule would have allowed only a restitutionary recovery; and (2) recovery was permitted even though the franchise was terminable at will. [Text § 8–16]

Hamer v. Sidway, 27 N.E. 256 (N.Y. 1891)

This case demonstrates that the forbearance of a legal right is sufficient consideration to support a promise as a contract. An uncle promised to pay his nephew $5,000 if he refrained from smoking, drinking, and gambling until he turned age 21. After turning 21, the nephew sought to enforce this promise. The court held that the nephew's abstention from the specified activities was a sufficient consideration to support the uncle's promise. The fact that the nephew may have actually benefited from this forbearance does not mean that the nephew's performance did not amount to a "detriment." Rather, the nephew's agreement to limit his actions was a sufficient detriment for purposes of consideration. [Text § 4–95]

Harrington v. Taylor, 36 S.E.2d 227 (N.C. 1945)

This case holds that a humanitarian act, voluntarily performed, does not suffice as legal consideration for a subsequent promise. The defendant's wife was assaulting the defendant with an axe when the plaintiff intervened and saved the defendant's life. In the process, the plaintiff's hand was severely injured. The court held that the defendant's oral promise to compensate the plaintiff was unenforceable. That is, where the voluntary act occurs before the defendant's promise is made, the act does not constitute consideration for the promise. [Text § 7–30]

Hoffman v. Red Owl Stores, 133 N.W.2d 267 (Wis. 1965) [Text §§ 8–15; 8–18]

Kirksey v. Kirksey, 8 Ala. 131 (1845)

A gift promise is insufficient consideration to make a promise enforceable. Similarly, the fact that a promisee may have undertaken acts incidental to the receipt of the gift is not a sufficient detriment to make a gift promise enforceable. In *Kirksey*, a man promised his sister-in-law that he would provide a place for her to live at his home after the death of her husband. The sister-in-law thereafter incurred expenses in reliance on the promised place to live by moving her family several hundred miles to the defendant's home. Once she arrived, however, the brother-in-law changed his mind and refused to let her stay with him, and the sister-in-law brought suit.

The court held that the brother-in-law's promise was only a gift promise, and thus could not be enforced due to a lack of consideration.

Further, the sister-in-law's act of moving to Alabama could not be thought of as "substantial reliance" on the offer, which would have made it irrevocable. Rather, moving to Alabama was merely an act incidental to the gift, i.e., it is something the recipient had to do to take advantage of a gift. Since the brother-in-law's promise of a place to stay and the sister-in-law's moving to Alabama were in no way bargained for, the promise of a place to stay could not be enforced as an offer. Note, however, that at least the costs of the move would probably be recoverable on a promissory estoppel theory. [Text §§ 7–29; 8–3]

Kucera v. Kavan, 84 N.W.2d 207 (Neb. 1957)

This case illustrates the principle that reliance in the form of preparation for performance may render a unilateral offer irrevocable under the doctrine of promissory estoppel. The plaintiffs in *Kucera* were looking to purchase a farm. They began to negotiate with the defendant who suggested a joint ownership arrangement whereby the plaintiff and the defendant would become partners in the parcel of land, and the plaintiffs would obtain possession while paying the defendant rent. The defendant agreed that the plaintiffs would have an option to purchase the entire interest in the parcel once the defendant found another parcel to invest her money in. However, plaintiffs never paid consideration for the option. Plaintiffs took possession and began to make several thousand dollars' worth of improvements to the property. When the plaintiffs later attempted to exercise the option, however, the defendant refused to honor their right to accept his offer, stating that any such option was unenforceable due to the lack of consideration paid for it. Nevertheless, the court enforced the option agreement on the basis of the plaintiffs' reliance on the unenforceable option. The court quoted the Restatement which provided that "[a] promise which the promisor should reasonably expect to induce action or forbearance of a definite and substantial character on the part of the promisee and which does induce such action or forbearance is binding if injustice can be avoided only be enforcement of the promise." [Text § 4–85]

Mattei v. Hopper, 330 P.2d 625 (Cal. 1958)

The court in *Mattei* discussed the situation where one party's duty to perform is dependent on that party's subjective satisfaction with the other party's performance. In this case, one party agreed to purchase a shopping center subject to his satisfaction with leases that were to be secured for the shopping center. The court held that such a contract is supported by adequate consideration. "[T]he promisor's duty to exercise his judgment in good faith is an adequate consideration to support the contract." That is, the personal satisfaction clause did not render the promise illusory, for the determination of any such satisfaction had to be exercised in good faith. The party thus had bound himself to do something he did not have to do before the contract was entered into, i.e., decide in good faith whether he was satisfied with the lease terms, and thus consideration was present and the contract enforceable. [Text § 7–49]

Mills v. Wyman, 3 Pick. 207 (Mass. 1825) [Text §§ 7–32; 7–38]

Ricketts v. Scothorn, 77 N.W. 365 (Neb. 1898)

This case illustrates the application of the doctrine of promissory estoppel to enforce gifts that induce detrimental reliance by the donee. A grandfather did not want his granddaughter to have to work outside the home, so he gave her a promissory note as a kind of "nest egg." The daughter quit her job in reliance on the note. Subsequently, the grandfather died, and the daughter sought to enforce the note against his estate. The estate defended on the grounds that there was no consideration for the note, and thus its promise to pay was unenforceable. The court held that while the note could not be enforced as a contract because of the lack of consideration, the grandfather's promise to pay could be enforced on promissory estoppel grounds. That is, it was reasonable to foreseeably expect the daughter to rely on the note, she did in fact rely on the note, and injustice could only be avoided by enforcing the promise. [Text § 8–4]

Webb v. McGowin, 168 So. 196 (Ala. Ct. App. 1935) [Text § 7–35]

Wheeler v. White, 398 S.W.2d 93 (Tex. 1965)

A party to an otherwise unenforceable agreement may recover reliance damages under the Restatement 2d's view of promissory estoppel where the promise induced his "foreseeable, definite, and substantial reliance." Reliance will put him in the position he would have been in had he not relied on the promise. Plaintiff owned some land which he planned to develop as commercial property. Defendant promised the plaintiff a construction loan, and the parties signed a document which later turned out to be unenforceable as a contract because basic, material terms were omitted from the agreement. Before the loan was to come through, the defendant encouraged the plaintiff to demolish some buildings on the property which had a value around $58,000 so that construction could begin as soon as possible. The promised loan never materialized, and the plaintiff sued the defendant because he was unable to obtain alternative financing. The defendant asserted that plaintiff could have no recovery since the purported loan agreement was unenforceable as a contract. However, the court permitted plaintiff's recovery of his reliance damages in promissory estoppel under the above-stated principle. [Text §§ 8–3; 8–16]

Wood v. Lucy, Lady Duff Gordon, 222 N.Y. 88 (Ct. App. 1917) [Text § 7–54]

CASE SQUIBS

DAMAGES

Equitable Lumber Corp. v. IPA Land Development Corp., 344 N.E. 2d 391 (NY. 1976)

> This decision illustrates the more liberal view of the UCC toward liquidated damage provisions. A construction company contracted with a lumber company for the supply of lumber. The parties' contract specified that if the lumber company had to sue for the purchase price, the construction company would be liable for reasonable attorney's fees, liquidated at thirty percent of the amount recovered. The court held that liquidated damage provisions will be upheld if one of two tests are satisfied: (1) the liquidated damages are reasonable in light of anticipated harm from a breach viewed as of the time was contract was made; or (2) the liquidated damages are reasonable in light of the actual harm caused by the breach. The court remanded the case to determine whether one of these two tests was satisfied. Note that under the revised Code, § 2–718(1) because this was not a "consumer contract," the lumber company would not even have to establish that the amount of loss would be difficult to establish in order to expose the liquidated damages clause. [Text, §§ 30–80; 32–49]

Freeman & Mills v. Belcher Oils, 11 Cal. 4th 85 (1995)

> This case overruled that portion of *Seamen's Direct Buying Service v. Standard Oil* (see Case Squibs) holding a tort claim existed for the bad faith denial of the existence of a contract. Freeman & Mills ("Freeman") were accountants hired to work on a lawsuit filed against Belcher Oils ("Belcher"). The management at Belcher thereafter changed, the new CEO decided not to pay Freeman. Freeman brought suit claiming, among other things, the tort of bad faith denial of the existence of a contract established in *Seamen's*. The California Supreme Court agreed only to review the portion of the case involving the "bad faith denial" tort. It held that it had erred in *Seamen's* thus overruling a portion of its earlier decision and deciding that the tort of the bad faith denial of the existence of a contract no longer existed in California.

Hadley v. Baxendale, 156 Eng. Rep. 145 (1854) [Text § 30–55]

Hawkins v. McGee, 146 A. 641 (N.H. 1929)

> *Hawkins* demonstrates that a patient will be entitled to expectation damages where his or her doctor promises a certain result that does not occur. A young boy's hand was scarred from a severe burn, and the surgeon who was to perform a skin graft operation promised that the boy's hand would be "100% perfect" following the operation. The court held that the doctor made an enforceable promise, under the objective theory of contracts, which was breached when the surgery failed. The plaintiff was entitled to expectation damages equal to the

difference between the value of a "100% perfect" hand and the value of his hand in its post-surgery condition. [Text §§ 2–4; 3–25; 30–28]

Jacob & Youngs, Inc. v. Kent, 129 N.E. 889 (N.Y. 1921) [Text §§ 21–70; 30–35]

Neri v. Retail Marine Corp., 285 N.E.2d 311 (N.Y. 1972)

This case illustrates the proper measure of recovery against a breaching buyer by a lost volume seller. A boat retailer entered into an agreement with the plaintiff for the sale of a particular boat. Plaintiff provided a $4,250 deposit, and the retailer ordered the boat from the manufacturer. The plaintiff later rescinded the contract, and the retailer retained the entire deposit paid by the plaintiff. The retailer resold the boat to a third party at the same price the plaintiff originally agreed to pay, so the plaintiff sued to recover his deposit, claiming that the retailer had sustained no damages since it was able to secure the subsequent sale. However, the court noted that the retailer was a lost volume seller in that it could have obtained **two** sales had the plaintiff not breached the agreement. Therefore, under UCC § 2–708(2) the retailer was entitled to retain the amount of the profit it would have earned on the contract with the plaintiff, plus incidental damages, out of the plaintiff's deposit. Note, however, that this rule is only applicable if the seller has an excess supply of the goods. [Text §§ 30–46; 32–45]

Oloffson v. Coomer, 296 N.E.2d 871 (Ill. App. Ct. 1973) (See Case Squibs Section, Anticipatory Repudiation)

Parker v. Twentieth Century-Fox Film Corp., 474 P.2d 689 (Cal. 1970) [Text § 30–64]

Peevyhouse v. Garland Coal & Mining Co., 382 P.2d 109 (Okla. 1962)

This case illustrates the principle of economic waste by holding that the proper measure of expectation damages under a breached agreement to restore the value of property is the resulting diminution in the property value and not the disproportionately greater cost of restoration. The court held that landowners were entitled to expectation damages when a strip mining company breached a promise to restore their land. The proper measure of damages was the $300 difference between the value of the land if restored and the value in its unrestored state. The plaintiffs were not entitled to the $29,000 cost of restoration, which was clearly disproportionate to the benefit the owners would have received if the contract had been fully performed. [Text § 29–38]

Rockingham County v. Luten Bridge Co., 35 F.2d 301 (4th Cir. 1929)

This case applies the concept of avoidability of damages to limit a non-breaching party's recovery. A contractor who completed construction of a bridge could not recover the damages he incurred after the county issued a stop work order. The court reasoned that the county could not be held responsible for damages "which need not have been incurred," and could have been avoided without undue risk, burden, or humiliation to the non-breaching party. [Text § 30–60]

Seamen's Direct Buying Serv., Inc. v. Standard Oil Co., 686 P.2d 1158 (Cal. 1984)

The California Supreme Court has long recognized an implied covenant of good faith and fair dealing in every contract. A "bad faith" breach of this covenant by an insurance carrier gives rise to tort damages for breach of contract. The issue in this case was whether a plaintiff can recover tort damages for breach of the implied covenant of good faith and fair dealing in a commercial contract.

Seamen's entered into a lease of city marina property for the purpose of operating a marine fuel dealership, and then negotiated with Standard Oil to supply its fuel requirements for a ten-year period. Seamen's wished to lease a larger portion of the waterfront area in the city, but the city required evidence of a binding agreement with an oil company before this larger lease could be secured. In response to Seamen's request for a written, binding agreement, Standard Oil sent Seamen's an offer in which Standard promised to sign a fuel dealership agreement with Seamen's in the future. Seamen's accepted this offer and copies of the signed letter of intent were presented to the city which immediately approved Seamen's request to lease the larger space.

Shortly thereafter, fuel prices rose sharply, and the contemplated fuel dealership agreement was never executed. Then, federal regulations went into effect, mandating oil companies to allocate their fuel supplies between **existing** customers. Since Standard Oil had not yet begun to supply Seamen's requirements, Standard Oil claimed it need not go forward with the agreement. However, Standard indicated that the federal regulations were the only reason for its refusal to supply Seamen's, and requested Seamen's help in securing federal approval of their proposed agreement. Seamen's was able to secure this approval, but Standard thereafter changed its position by claiming no binding agreement had ever been reached and refused to go forward with the contract. Standard's refusal to go forward with the contract caused Seamen's to go out of business and lose the city marina project, and Seamen's brought suit seeking punitive damages for a "bad faith" breach.

In remanding the case, the California Supreme Court created a new tort in California, which was the bad faith denial of the existence of a contract. If Standard was found liable for this tort, Seamen's could recover tort damages, including punitive damages, if the requisite standards were met.

In addition, the court held that a breach of contract suit could also give rise to tort damages if the breach is of the covenant of good faith and fair dealing and if the contract is one in which the parties are in a "special relationship" with each other. However, it held that there were no indicia of such a "special relationship" in a commercial contract such as the one at issue in the case, and thus denied Seamen's tort damages for breach of contract in this action. [Text § 30–88]

Note, however, that *Seaman's* holding that a tort of "bad faith denial of the existence of a contract" existed in California was overruled by the California Supreme Court in *Freeman & Mills v. Belcher Oils* (see Case Squibs).

Southwest Engineering Co. v. United States, 341 F.2d 998 (8th Cir. 1965)

This case illustrates the enforcement of a liquidated damages provision where such a provision was a reasonable estimate of the potential loss resulting from a potential breach viewed at the time of contracting. The non-breaching party may collect under the liquidated damages provision even if the later breach results in no actual damages, provided the reasonable estimate requirement is met. In *Southwest Engineering*, the plaintiff contracted to build several projects for the defendant. Each contract between the parties provided for a $50–100 late charge for each day the project's completion was delayed by the plaintiff. Plaintiff was unable to complete some of the projects on time, so the defendant subtracted the late charges from payments made to the plaintiff. The plaintiff sued to recover the late charges because the defendant conceded that no actual loss was suffered by the delays. Nevertheless, the court upheld the defendant's withholding of liquidated damages, noting that liquidated damages provisions are enforceable if at the time of contracting they were a reasonable forecast of estimated losses from a breach of the contract and if actual damages will be difficult to prove with precision. It makes no difference that the defendant sustained no actual damages once the breach actually occurred. [Text § 30–80]

Sullivan v. O'Connor, 296 N.E.2d 183 (Mass. 1973)

The court in this case awarded reliance, rather than expectation, damages for a surgeon's breach of a promise to achieve a particular result for his patient, but also allowed the recovery of emotional distress damages as well. A plastic surgeon promised to improve his patient's appearance. The surgeon failed to achieve this result after two operations (in fact, the patient looked worse after the two operations than she did in her pre-surgery state), and a third operation was undertaken to attempt to restore the patient to her pre-surgery condition. The court allowed the patient's recovery of her reliance damages—the difference in value between her appearance before the operation and her appearance after the operation, in addition to the fees she paid and damages for pain and suffering. The court would not allow a recovery of the patient's expectation damages—the difference between the value of the patient's promised appearance and her appearance before the operation—because recovery of such damages would inhibit doctors from performing beneficial surgeries. [Text § 30–78]

Vitex Mfg. Corp. v. Caribtex Corp., 377 F.2d 795 (3d Cir. 1967)

Generally, a plaintiff's expectation damages are calculated by measuring the benefits the plaintiff would have received under the contract and subtracting any benefits the plaintiff received from not having to perform. An exception arises, however, in the calculation of the plaintiff's overhead costs. Overhead costs are generally considered fixed and not part of the costs saved by a non-breaching party who has not completed performance at the time of the breach. Thus, the non-breaching party's expectation damages will not be reduced by the proportion of overhead expenses allegedly saved because the work was left uncompleted. In *Vitex*, where the parties had a contract for the manufacture of cloth, the court refused to subtract the plaintiff's saved overhead costs as a result of the defendant's breach prior to the time plaintiff completed performance. [Text § 30–28]

White v. Benkowski, 155 N.W.2d 74 (Wis. 1967)

This case holds that punitive damages, i.e., damages beyond that required to compensate a party for his injured expectation interest, are generally not recoverable in contract. Thus, where a homeowner had a contract with his neighbor for the supply of water from the neighbor's well, and the neighbor had shut off the supply for several short periods causing odors to accumulate in the plaintiff's bathroom, the court refused to award punitive damages for the breach of the contract. The court noted that "without exception, punitive damages are not available in breach of contract actions." This is true even if the breach is willful. The court noted that the plaintiff would have to sue in tort if he wanted to recover punitive damages. [Text § 30–87]

DURESS

Austin Instrument, Inc. v. Loral Corp., 272 N.E.2d 533 (N.Y. 1971)

This case illustrates the principle that a contract modification will be unenforceable where the modification is secured through duress. A general contractor agreed to supply the U.S. Navy with $6,000,000 worth of radar sets. A subcontractor was to supply certain components necessary for the general contractor's performance. After the subcontractor began delivery of the components, the Navy granted the general contractor another contract to supply more radar sets. The subcontractor then threatened to stop further deliveries of the components unless it was guaranteed a portion of the work under the second contract and an increased price for the components under the original subcontract. There was no other supplier that could meet the general contractor's supply requirements in a timely manner, so the general contractor relented and agreed to the subcontractor's proposed modification. After full performance under both of the Navy contracts, the general contractor sought restitution of the excess payments made to the subcontractor as a result of the modification. The court held that the contract modification was voidable since the modification was the result of duress caused by the subcontractor. That is, the threat of non-delivery of the goods (which were not readily available from another source) and the requirement that the subcontractor be awarded a second subcontract constituted duress which sufficiently deprived the general contractor of its "free will" to reject the modification. [Text § 13–10]

EQUITABLE REMEDIES

Hilmor Sales Co. v. Helen Neushaefer Div. of Supronics Corp., 6 UCC Rep. Serv. 325 (N.Y. 1969)

This case discusses UCC § 2–716(1) which allows a buyer the right to specific performance "where the goods are unique or in other proper circumstances." Plaintiff contracted for the purchase of nail polish and lipsticks from the defendant at close-out prices. Defendant refused to perform, and plaintiff requested specific performance alleging that the goods were unique since they could not be replaced at the close out contract price. The court held, however, that the goods were not unique and that plaintiff's legal remedy of money damages would provide an adequate remedy so that the equitable remedy of specific performance was unnecessary. [Text §§ 29–8; 32–3]

Karpinski v. Ingrasci, 268 N.E.2d 751 (N.Y. 1971)

A covenant not to compete in an employment contract is enforceable if it is reasonable and not unduly broad. In *Karpinski*, plaintiff (an oral surgeon) hired defendant (another oral surgeon) to work for him, and the parties signed an agreement that the defendant would **never** practice oral surgery or general dentistry in competition with the plaintiff, within the same geographic region. The court held that the geographic region specified was not overly broad since it covered the area where plaintiff practiced. The lack of any time limit was also deemed reasonable. However, the court held that the covenant was unduly broad in that it prevented the defendant from practicing general dentistry in addition to oral surgery. Therefore, while the defendant was properly enjoined from practicing oral surgery in the same geographical region as his former employer, the provision that attempted to prevent the defendant from practicing general dentistry in the same geographical region was held to be unenforceable as unduly broad. [Text § 29–31]

Laclede Gas Co. v. Amoco Oil, 522 F.2d 33 (8th Cir. 1975) [Text § 29–10]

Lumley v. Wagner, 42 Eng. Rep. 687 (Ch. 1852) [Text § 29–5]

Peevyhouse v. Garland Coal & Mining Co., 382 P.2d 109 (Okla. 1962) (See Case Squibs, Damages)

EXPRESS CONDITIONS

J.N.A. Realty Corp. v. Cross Bay Chelsea, 366 N.E.2d 1313 (N.Y. 1977)

This case illustrates the "disproportionate forfeiture" exception to the general rule that an express condition must be literally complied with before the other party's obligation under a contract arises. The lessee of a building, through negligence or inadvertence, failed to exercise his option to renew a lease within the time specified in the lease agreement. The lessor brought an action to recover possession of the premises. The lessee, who operated a restaurant on the leased premises, had spent $55,000 on improvements and had built up a substantial amount of customer goodwill during the lease term. Generally, a notice exercising an option is ineffective if not given within the time specified in the lease agreement. However, the court granted equitable relief to prevent forfeiture of the improvements and goodwill. The court stated that if the lessee makes substantial improvements in good faith with an intent to renew the lease, and the lessor would not be prejudiced by the delay in giving notice, then equitable relief may be appropriate. No relief will be granted if the tenant's delay was intentional or undertaken in bad faith. [Text § 21–107]

ILLEGALITY

Bateman Eichler, Hill Richards, Inc. v. Berner, 472 U.S. 299 (1985)

This case illustrates the *in pari delicto* defense in a securities fraud action. A tippee filed a securities fraud action against a tipper for losses incurred on a securities purchase recommended by the tipper. The tipper defended that the tippee should be barred from recovery in the suit because the tippee was *in pari delicto* with the tipper, i.e., the tippee was guilty of wrongdoing since he traded on inside information along with the tipper.

The Court refused to apply the *in pari delicto* defense. The *in pari delicto* defense will only be allowed in a securities fraud case if: (1) as a direct result of his own actions, the plaintiff bears at least substantially equal responsibility for the violations he seeks to redress; and (2) preclusion of the suit would not significantly interfere with effective enforcement of the securities laws and protection on the investing public. The Court held that a tippee is not equally at fault with the tipper, so the *in pari delicto* defense is normally not allowed in these situations. Private enforcement of the securities should be encouraged to protect the public interest; therefore, tippees must be permitted to file suit against tippers. [Text § 17–24]

IMPOSSIBILITY, COMMERCIAL IMPRACTICABILITY, AND FRUSTRATION OF PURPOSE

Albre Marble & Tile Co. v. John Bowen Co., 155 N.E.2d 437 (Mass. 1959)

Albre established a non-breaching party's right to recover reliance damages for expenditures made in preparation for performance of a contract which is discharged because of impossibility, impracticality, or frustration. A general contractor entered into a contract with the state to build a state hospital. The general contractor hired a subcontractor to complete the marble and tile work on the project. Prior to the actual installation of the marble and tile, the subcontract called for the preparation of samples, shop drawings, tests, and affidavits. After preparation of these items, the hospital contract was cancelled because the general contractor failed to comply with statutory bidding requirements. The subcontractor sought recovery of the expenditures involved in preparing the samples and drawings. The general contractor counter-argued that recovery could only be had for labor and materials actually incorporated into the hospital construction. The court held that the non-breaching party to a contract which is discharged because of impossibility, impracticality, or frustration may recover his or her reliance damages if the party discharging the contract is "at greater fault" than the non-breaching party. The fair market value of any expenditures which "would have enured to the benefit" of the breaching party if the contract had been performed are recoverable in such a case. Since the drawings and samples would have enured to the general contractor's benefit had the contract been performed, the subcontractor may recover the fair market value of the expenditures related to that work. However, the court noted that if there is "equal fault" between a plaintiff and defendant, it may not award reliance damages. [See gen, Text § 30–65]

Alcoa v. Essex, 499 F. Supp. 53 (W.D. Pa. 1980) [Text § 25–43]

American Trading & Production Corp. v. Shell Int'l Marine, Ltd., 453 F.2d 939 (2d Cir. 1972)

The plaintiff in this case unsuccessfully sought to recover additional expenses incurred in shipping oil owned by the defendant by claiming that the agreed route for performance had become commercially impractical. The contract called for the oil to be transported from Texas to India and indicated a per ton charge "for passage through the Suez Canal." However, the Suez Canal was closed due to a state of war, and the shipper was forced to use the longer and more expensive route around the Cape of Good Hope. The court held that the plaintiff could not recover its additional expenses from the defendant because the contract had not become either impossible or impractical. Nothing in the contract provided that delivery **had** to go through the Suez Canal; hence, proceeding around the Cape of Good Hope was an alternative means of performance. The court acknowledged that an extreme increase in cost will excuse the performance of a commercial contract on impracticability grounds where the increase was not foreseeable and the contract did not specifically allocate the risk to the performing party. However, in this case, the increased cost was only a third over the agreed price, and that is an insufficient amount to trigger impracticability. [Text § 25–33]

Canadian Indus. Alcohol Co. v. Dunbar Molasses Co., 179 N.E. 383 (N.Y. 1932)

The performance of a contract is not excused on the grounds of impossibility when the seller is unable to obtain an adequate supply from his contemplated source. Here, the buyer and seller (a middleman) entered into a contract calling for the delivery of molasses. The seller contemplated, but did not contract for, receiving a supply of molasses from a particular refinery that it would re-sell to the buyer. The refinery output was not sufficient to meet the needs of the seller, so the seller claimed its delivery obligations under the contract with the buyer should be excused due to impossibility. Justice Cardozo disagreed, stating that where the seller makes an absolute promise to deliver and does not attempt to contract with others to insure an adequate supply of materials necessary to fulfill the obligation, the seller bears the risk that it will not be able to fulfill its promise. The seller may not shift this risk to the buyer after it has promised to deliver. Note, however, that if the seller **had** contracted directly with the refinery to assure an adequate supply, and the refinery had breached the supply contract, the seller would have a much stronger basis to claim impossibility of performance under the contract with the buyer. [Text § 25–21]

Iron Trade Products Co. v. Wilkoff Co., 116 A. 150 (Pa. 1922)

This court held that a contracting party who contracts to sell items which are in limited supply bears the risk that the market price on the items will rise and cannot claim impossibility as a result of such a price rise which occurs before the time for delivery arrives. In *Iron Trade*, it was the **buyer's** own purchase on the open market of the items in short supply which caused the seller's cost of performance to drastically rise. Claiming impossibility of performance, the seller refused to deliver the more expensive items at the lower contract price. However, the court concluded that the seller was in breach because there was no evidence that the buyer intended to interfere with the seller's performance. Additionally, the seller's performance, although more difficult to accomplish as a result of the price rise, was not impossible. [Text §§ 25–33; 25–40]

Krell v. Henry Coronation Cases, 2 K.B. 740 (1903) [Text § 25–56]

Lloyd v. Murphy, 153 P.2d 47 (Cal. 1944) [Text § 25–57]

Mineral Park Land Co. v. Howard, 172 Cal. 289 (1916)

This case illustrates the modern view that extreme impracticability may be an excuse for performance, whereas the traditional view allowed excuse only where a performance had been rendered impossible. The defendant was building a bridge and contracted for his supply of gravel under a requirements contract with the plaintiff. Under the agreement, the defendant was to excavate the gravel from plaintiff's land and pay a fixed price per yard. Once the defendant began to excavate below the water level on plaintiff's land, however, he refused to continue excavating as required by the contract because the cost to the defendant rose by ten times over the prior costs incurred with excavation above the water level. The court held that the defendant could be excused from excavating below the water level. Where changed or unexpected circumstances lead to a substantial increase in the cost of performance of a commercial contract rendering such performance extremely impracticable, performance may be excused just as though it were impossible. [Text § 25–32]

Paradine v. Jane, 82 Eng. Rep. 897 (K.B. 1647)

This case illustrates the traditional early common law doctrine of frustration of purpose. The court refused to excuse a lessee from paying rent on a contract where the lessee had been ousted from the leased property by a foreigner. The court noted that the ouster did not make the payment obligation impossible to perform. [Text § 25–45]

Stees v. Leonard, 20 Minn. 494 (1874)

This case illustrates that the impossibility defense will not be allowed where a contractor assumes the risk of poor soil conditions on a construction project. Defendant agreed to construct a building for the plaintiff. He began construction twice, and each time the building collapsed because the soil underneath was quicksand. Although it would have been possible to drain the land and construct a stable building at an increased expense, the defendant refused to make a third attempt at construction. The court held that the defendant could not be discharged from the contract on the basis of impossibility. A building contractor assumes the risk that he will have to drain the soil or reinforce the planned structure because the soil is unforeseeably less stable than expected. The contractor's performance will be excused only if it is absolutely impossible to remedy the condition. [Text § 25–14]

Taylor v. Caldwell, 122 Eng. Rep. 309 (K.B. 1863)

This case illustrates that, under the doctrine of impossibility, a contract will be discharged where essential subject matter of the contract is destroyed through no fault of either party. Thus, a singer was excused from his promise to perform in a music hall that was destroyed by fire prior to his scheduled performance. The court noted that the existence of the music hall was the "foundation of the contract," i.e., that it was a mutually shared basic assumption on which the contract was made, and that there was an implied condition that both parties would be excused if the hall no longer existed. [Text § 25–9]

United States v. Spearin, 248 U.S. 132 (1918)

This United States Supreme Court case allows discharge for impossibility of performance where one party requires the other party's performance to comply with its specifications that turn out to be defective. In *Spearin*, a contractor agreed to construct a sewer system for the United States government according to plans provided by the government. The Court held that the contractor could be discharged from the contract on impossibility grounds, and that the United States had breached an implied warranty that the specifications would be adequate. Therefore, the contractor could recover damages against the United States for breach of the implied warranty. [See gen. Text § 25–3]

United States v. Wegematic Corp., 360 F.2d 674 (2d Cir. 1966)

This case demonstrates that a vendor who promises a technological breakthrough will not be excused from performance when accomplishing the breakthrough becomes commercially impractical. The United States government advertised for bids on a digital computer system. Wegematic submitted a bid which promised an improved version of a present model on the market for the proposed price of $231,000. However, due to engineering difficulties, Wegematic was unable to deliver the computer by the delivery date in the contract, or even within a reasonable time thereafter. Wegematic requested that it be excused from performance because development of the necessary technology would take its engineers one to two years and would cost between $1,000,000 and $1,500,000 to accomplish. The government sued Wegematic for breach. The court held in favor of the government, stating that a vendor who promises new technology assumes the risk that it will prove impracticable to develop or produce. The court noted that to allow the defense of impracticability would require the bidding purchaser to be bound by contract, while the manufacturer would be "free to express what are only aspirations and gamble on mere probabilities of fulfillment without any risk of liability." In any event, the court noted that while the necessary expenses might seem large in relation to this one sale, economies of a scale would allow the manufacturer to recoup its costs once it sold more of the new systems to additional parties. [Text §§ 25–5; 25–14]

Watkins & Son v. Carrig, 21 A.2d 591 (N.H. 1941)

This case illustrates the general principle that the risk of adverse soil conditions on a building project generally rests with the building contractor. The building contractor usually cannot avoid the contract on the basis of mutual mistake because the builder is generally perceived to have expertise in sub-soil conditions. Hence, the risk is properly allocated to the builder. Thus, in *Watkins*, where a builder made a contract to construct a building and then discovered a large rock in the sub-soil that made his performance much more expensive, the court would not allow the builder to avoid the contract even though both parties adhered to the basic assumption that sub-soil conditions were normal. [Text § 25–14]

INTERPRETATION

Pacific Gas & Electric Co. v. G.W. Thomas Drayage & Rigging Co., 442 P.2d 641 (Cal. 1968)

This case follows the Corbin view and rejects Williston's "plain meaning rule" of contract interpretation. Defendant contracted to repair plaintiff's steam turbine. The parties' agreement stated that defendant promised to indemnify plaintiff "against all damage . . . resulting from injury to property. . . ." The defendant damaged the plaintiff's turbine while attempting to perform the repairs, and plaintiff sued for indemnity under the contract provision. The defendant argued that the parties meant that defendant was to be responsible only for damage to the property of third parties. Under the Williston view, the court would look to the plain meaning of the document and conclude that defendant was responsible for the damage to the turbine. However, the court in *Thomas Drayage* concluded that such a rule ignores the true (and possibly contrary) intention of the parties. Thus, the court held that oral testimony is admissible to ascertain the intent of the parties even if the language of their written document seems clear and unambiguous. However, before looking outside the four corners of the document, the court must preliminarily determine that the document is "fairly susceptible" of the asserted interpretation. [Text § 19–19]

CASE SQUIBS

MISREPRESENTATION

Kannavos v. Annino, 247 N.E.2d 708 (Mass. 1969)

Where the misrepresentation by the breaching party to a contract is fraudulent, the innocent party is entitled to avoid the contract even in the absence of proof of justifiable reliance. In *Kannavos*, the plaintiff contracted to purchase a house from the defendant who represented that the house was suitable for multi-family rental use. The plaintiff failed to confirm this representation with the public records, but there was evidence in the case that the defendant knew of the zoning regulation which prohibited multi-family use of the house. Therefore, the plaintiff was able to successfully rescind the contract. [Text § 15–22]

Laidlaw v. Organ, 15 U.S. (2 Wheat.) 178 (1817)

This United States Supreme Court case states the general rule (which is subject to several exceptions, none of which are present here) that a party has no duty to disclose beneficial facts during contract negotiations, especially when those facts are equally available to the other contracting party. In *Laidlaw*, a peace treaty was signed which effectively ended the War of 1812 and the British blockade of New Orleans. Organ lawfully learned of the treaty several hours before it became common knowledge. Knowing that with the blockade lifted the price of tobacco for export would rise, Organ purchased a large quantity of tobacco from Laidlaw without disclosing the fact of the peace treaty to Laidlaw. Laidlaw asked him whether he knew of any fact which would increase the value of the tobacco, and Organ simply did not answer. When the price of tobacco subsequently rose, Laidlaw sold the tobacco to another, and Organ sued for breach. However, Chief Justice Marshall stated that Laidlaw "was not bound to communicate" the facts that may be beneficial "where the means of intelligence are equally accessible to both parties" and where it is an arm's length transaction. That is, silence in such cases does not amount to an affirmative misrepresentation. Note the results could well have been different if Organ had affirmatively misled Laidlaw in answer to his question. [Text § 15–21]

MISTAKE

Elsinore Union Elementary School Dist. v. Kastorff, 353 P.2d 713 (Cal. 1960)

The court in *Elsinore* allowed relief for a unilateral mistake where a general contractor made a clerical error in his bid for construction work for a school district. The general contractor submitted a bid which mistakenly omitted a subcontractor's bid for the plumbing on the project. This omission amounted to almost ten percent of the general contractor's total bid, and made his bid of $89,994 more than

$11,000 less than the next lowest bid. The school district accepted the general contractor's bid, but before a written contract was sent to him, the general contractor requested to withdraw his bid. The school district was then forced to accept the next lowest bid, and it sued the general contractor for the difference. The court ruled that the general contractor should be released from the contract since the mistake was an honest clerical error. The court noted that the school district intended for the general contractor to furnish plumbing, and therefore the school district must have understood that the general contractor intended for his bid to include the plumbing work. Additionally, the sum omitted, almost ten percent of the general contractor's total bid, was a material amount. Note, however, that the court would be much less willing to grant relief where the mistake was due to an error in business judgment rather than a clerical error. [Text § 12–22]

Sherwood v. Walker, 33 N.W. 919 (Mich. 1887) [Text § 12–13]

Wood v. Boynton, 25 N.W. 42 (Wis. 1885) [Text § 12–14]

MISUNDERSTANDING

Frigaliment Importing Co. v. B.N.S. Int'l Sales Corp., 190 F. Supp. 116 (S.D.N.Y. 1960)

This case demonstrates that where the parties' contract contains an ambiguous term, the party claiming a breach of the contract has the burden of proving the meaning of the ambiguous term in his or her favor or there is no proven breach. The parties in *Frigaliment* entered into a contract calling for the sale and delivery of "chicken." The seller shipped "stewing chickens," and the buyer rejected them, claiming that the contract was for "broiling chickens," a much higher grade of chicken. The buyer later brought suit for breach. The court assumed that both parties acted in good faith and that they both believed the contract was on their own terms. The court held that the buyer could not sustain its burden of proof that there was a breach. The dictionary and the Department of Agriculture both supported the view that "chickens" meant "stewing chickens." Perhaps more significantly, given the prevailing prices at the time the contract was executed, it should have been clear to the buyer that the seller did not intend to provide broiling chickens. If it had, it would have entered into a losing contract. Thus, if the risk of mistaken views as to the meaning of the term "chicken" was to be allocated to one of the parties, it was properly allocated to the buyer under these facts. Accordingly, the buyer could not sustain its burden of establishing a breach in this case. [Text §§ 12–28; 12–30; 20–17]

Raffles v. Wichelhaus, 159 Eng. Rep. 375 (1864) [Text § 12–31]

CASE SQUIBS

MODIFICATION

Angel v. Murray, 322 A.2d 630 (R.I. 1974)

This case adopted section 89 of the Restatement 2d of Contracts as the proper rule to govern modifications and rejected the common law pre-existing duty rule requirement that consideration be present to make modifications enforceable. The defendant contracted with the City of Newport, Rhode Island to collect garbage. The contract provided that the defendant was to be compensated at the rate of $137,000 per year over a five-year term. During that term, the defendant's costs increased substantially, and the defendant requested an additional $10,000 per year to cover these increased costs. The City of Newport made the additional payments, but a citizen later sued to have the additional payments refunded to the city. The court held that the modification was enforceable despite the lack of additional consideration from the city. A promise modifying a pre-existing legal duty is valid without consideration where the contract has not been fully performed, and the modification is fair and equitable in view of circumstances unanticipated when the contract was formed. [Text § 9–20]

Universal Builders, Inc. v. Moon Motor Lodge, Inc., 244 A.2d 10 (Pa. 1968)

This case shows how a party may waive "no oral modifications" clause may be waived by a party. A provision in a construction contract required that all changes be in writing. The owner's agent requested a number of changes and promised to pay for them, although written change orders were never issued. This oral modification operated as an effective waiver of the condition that all modifications be in writing because the contractor materially changed his position by carrying out the requested changes in reliance on the agent's oral promise. [Text § 9–10]

Wisconsin Knife Works v. National Metal Crafters, 781 F.2d 1280 (7th Cir. 1986) [Text § 9–15]

OFFER AND ACCEPTANCE

Adams v. Lindsell, 106 Eng. Rep. 250 (K.B. 1818)

This case is cited as the original decision setting forth the mail box rule. The offeror mailed an offer to sell wool to the offeree. The offeree responded with a letter of acceptance. Subsequent to the offeree's dispatch of the acceptance, but before the offeror received it, the offeror sold the wool to another party and attempted to revoke the offer. The mail box rule says that: (1) properly addressed acceptances are effective upon dispatch, if acceptance by mail is a permissible mode of acceptance under the terms of the offer; and (2) rejections and revocations of offers are effective upon receipt. Thus, in this case, an enforceable contract was formed at the moment of the offeree's dispatch and the attempted revocation was without effect. [Text §§ 4–118; 4–123]

Allied Steel & Conveyors v. Ford Motor Co., 277 F.2d 907 (6th Cir. 1960)

This case details effective methods of acceptance where the offer is ambiguous as to whether it is to be accepted by a promise or performance. Ford contracted to buy machinery from Allied. It then sent an amended purchase order to Allied for the purchase of additional machines beyond the quantity agreed to in the original contract. The purchase order stated, "This purchase order agreement is not binding until accepted. Acceptance should be executed on [the] acknowledgment copy which should be returned to buyer." Allied began performance without returning an executed acknowledgment copy. A dispute later arose as to whether a contract had been formed. The key was how a reasonable offeree would construe the terms of the offer. Here, the court held that the offeree reasonably understood the offer not to state that return of the acknowledgment copy was the **exclusive** method of acceptance, but only one of the many permissible ways to accept. Hence, beginning performance was also a permissible method of acceptance, and a contract was formed for the additional machinery when performance was begun. Note that this case is not an exception to the general rule that the offeror is the "master of his offer;" it merely requires the offeror to be unmistakably clear in his or her terms, or risk alternative means of acceptance. [Text § 4–94]

Ammons v. Wilson & Co., 170 So. 227 (Miss. 1936)

This case illustrates a scenario where the prior course of dealing between the parties makes it reasonable that the offeree's silence be construed as an acceptance. The seller's salesman took an order from the buyer for prompt shipment "subject to acceptance by seller's authorized agent at point of shipment." The seller did not respond to the order for almost two weeks. During that time period, the market price of the ordered goods rose, and the seller subsequently refused to ship. The court held that a jury question was presented as to whether the seller's silence indicated an implied acceptance. An offer can be accepted by silence when such a pattern has been established by the course of dealing between the buyer and seller. In this case, the seller's salesman had previously taken orders from the buyer, and those orders "had been accepted and shipped not later than one week from the time they were given" without any notice of formal acceptance from the buyer. Therefore, it would have been reasonable for the buyer to assume that if the seller intended to reject the offer that notice would have been forthcoming during the usual time period required for shipping. Since no notice of rejection came, the buyer reasonably assumed that the seller had accepted the offer. [Text § 4–106]

Ayer v. Western Union Telegraph Co., 10 A. 495 (Me. 1887)

This case determined which party bears the risk of an incorrect price quote transmitted through the seller's agent. Ayer contracted with Western Union to transmit a price quote to the buyer as "two ten net cash," but Western Union mistakenly transmitted "two net cash." The buyer accepted Ayer's offer as transmitted, and Ayer supplied the goods at the lower price. The court held that the seller, not the buyer, bears the risk of an error committed by the telegraph company because an offeree must be able to rely on an offer communicated through an agent chosen by the offeror. Because the buyer had no reason to know of the error, and because the seller chose the agent, acceptance by the buyer at the lower price was valid under the objective theory of contracts. However, Western Union was held liable for the difference between the price Ayer quoted and the lower price, which Western Union mistakenly telegraphed. [Text § 4–3]

Brackenberry v. Hodgkin, 102 A. 106 (Me. 1917)

This case illustrates the irrevocability of offers looking to a unilateral contract once the offeree begins performance. A mother promised to leave her farm to her daughter if the daughter gave up her home to come and care for the mother. The court held that once the daughter began performance by complying with the request, an irrevocable option contract was formed which bound the mother to perform as promised in the offer, provided the daughter completed performance as specified in the offer. Note, however, that the offeree is not bound to complete his or her performance in such a situation, for the offeree may decline to exercise an option offered to him or her. [Text § 4–73]

C. Itoh & Co. (America), Inc. v. Jordan Int'l Co., 552 F.2d 1228 (7th Cir. 1977)

This case illustrates UCC § 2–207(3)'s role in determining the enforceability contract by conduct under the UCC, and in regulating what the terms of such a contract will be. The buyer in *Itoh* offered to purchase steel coils from the seller. The seller sent back an acknowledgment which included an additional arbitration clause and provided that "[s]eller's acceptance is . . . expressly conditional on [b]uyer's assent to the additional or different terms and conditions set forth below and printed on the reverse side." The buyer never notified the seller of his assent to the additional terms. Nonetheless, the seller shipped the steel coils, and the buyer paid for them. The court held that no contract was formed under UCC § 2–207(1), since the seller's acceptance fell within that provision's "expressly conditional" exception to the formation of a contract. However, a contract came into existence under UCC § 2–207(3), since the conduct of the parties recognized the existence of a contract. The terms of the contract were the terms on which the parties' forms agreed plus additional terms automatically provided by the UCC under the "knock out" rule. These terms would not include the arbitration clause. [Text § 5–13]

Under the revised Code, the result would be the same. A contract would be recognized by the conduct of the parties under § 2–206(3) and/or § 2–207, and only the terms on which the parties agreed, which would not include the arbitration clause.

Caldwell v. Cline, 156 S.E. 55 (W. Va. 1930)

This case determines the allowable time period for acceptance of an offer which provides that the offeree may accept for a specified time period. The offeror in *Caldwell* mailed an offer to the offeree on January 29 which stated that the offeree had eight days to accept or reject the offer. The offeree received the offer on February 2 and telegrammed his acceptance on February 8. This acceptance was received by the offeror on February 9. The court held that the offeree's acceptance was effective because an offer is deemed to be made when received by the offeree, and the period allowed for acceptance is calculated from the date of receipt, **unless otherwise specified in the offer**. [Text § 4–45]

Carlill v. Carbolic Smoke Ball Co., 1 Q.B. 256 (1893) [Text §§ 4–17; 4–26; 4–111]

Davis v. Jacoby, 34 P.2d 1026 (Cal. 1934)

If it is unclear whether an offer looks to a unilateral or a bilateral contract, the offer can be accepted either by performance or by a promise to perform. Thus, a letter which promised an inheritance to a niece and her husband if the couple would manage her uncle's affairs and care for his dying wife was an offer which could be accepted either by the couple's arrival, or by their promise to arrive, so long as they undertook preparations to fulfill that promise. The couple had thus accepted by sending a letter promising to perform, and hence the death of the uncle before they actually began did not affect their rights. That is, there is a general presumption in favor of bilateral contracts where the offeror's offer is unclear as to which type of contract was intended. The couple's acceptance of the bilateral contract meant that there was not an offer pending which would have resulted in the termination of the couple's power of acceptance upon the death of the offeror. Instead, they had entered into a contract, the terms of which were enforceable after the death of one party to the agreement (so long as they performed their promise to care for the uncle's wife). Thus, the niece had an enforceable right to an inheritance from her uncle's estate. [Text § 4–94]

CASE SQUIBS

Dickinson v. Dodds, 2 Ch. D. 463 (Eng. 1876)

This case sets forth the indirect revocation doctrine. The offeree was given "two days" to decide whether to accept an offer to sell some land. During that two-day period, the offeree learned from a reliable source that the land had been sold to another. The court held that as soon as the offeree learned of the sale from the reliable source, there was an effective, but indirect, revocation of the offeror's offer. [Text § 4–60]

Dorton v. Collins & Aikman Corp., 453 F.2d 1161 (6th Cir. 1972)

This case illustrates the tendency of the courts to strictly construe the "expressly conditional" exception of UCC § 2–207(1). The offeree's form in *Dorton* made its acceptance "**subject to** all of the terms and conditions" contained in the form. One of the terms in the form stated that any dispute arising under the parties' contract would be resolved by arbitration. The issue was whether the "subject to" language in the offeree's form made the offeree's acceptance "expressly conditional" on the offeror's assent to the additional terms. If so, the offeree's acknowledgement could not operate as an acceptance; rather, it would operate as a counter-offer. The court held that the "is subject to" language did not have such an effect. The court stated that for the "expressly conditional" exception of UCC § 2–207 (1) to become operative, "It is not enough than an acceptance is expressly conditional on additional or different terms; rather, an acceptance must be expressly conditional on the **offeror's assent** to those terms . . . [to make it a counter-offer]." Since the "is subject to" language in the offeree's form did not expressly require the offeror's separate and affirmative assent, the offeree's form operated as a valid acceptance of the offeror's offer. The case was then remanded to determine whether the arbitration clause "materially altered" the agreement under UCC § 2–207(2). [Text § 5–13]

Under the revised Code, the test is whether the parties signaled an intention to be bound, either by their contracts, § 2–206(3) or their conduct, § 2–207. It is likely the court would find a dividing agreement here under the revised Code using the same type of analysis. The arbitration clause would not become part of the agreement, however, as both parties did not agree to it.

Drennan v. Star Paving Co., 333 P.2d 757 (Cal. 1958) [Text §§ 4–86; 8–13]

Embry v. Hargardine, McKittrick Dry Goods Co., 105 S.W. 777 (Mo. Ct. App. 1907)

Embry was one of the first cases to usher in the objective theory of contracts. In that case, an employee threatened to quit if his employment contract was not renewed for another year. The employer replied, "Go ahead, you're all right. Get your men out, and don't let that worry you." Unbeknownst to the employee, however, the employer harbored an undisclosed intent not to renew the contract. Two months later, the employee was terminated, and he sued his employer, alleging that his employment contract had been renewed. The court held that a reasonable employee would have understood the employer's statement to mean that his employment contract was being renewed. Therefore, the employer's subjective intent when the statement was made was irrelevant and the alleged renewal was enforceable. [Text § 3–8]

Fairmount Glass Works v. Crunden-Martin Woodenware Co., 51 S.W. 196 (Ky. Ct. App. 1899)

This case demonstrates that in certain cases a "price quote" may amount to an "offer" which empowers the offeree to validly accept the bargain. The buyer in *Fairmount* requested the seller's price for ten carloads of mason jars. The seller wrote back, saying "we quote you" certain jars at specified prices "for immediate acceptance." The buyer accepted and requested delivery of the ten carloads. The seller refused to deliver the jars, claiming its letter did not constitute an offer, but was rather only a quotation of prices, which normally is deemed to be only a solicitation to make an offer. The court held, however, that an offer was created by the seller's correspondence, despite the fact that it never used the term "offer" and used the word "quote." Use of the language "for immediate acceptance" made it clear that the seller was willing to be bound to the terms in the correspondence, and thus the buyer was empowered to accept the seller's offer. [Text § 3–14]

Hamer v. Sidway, 27 N.E. 256 (N.Y. 1891) [Text § 4–95]

Hawkins v. McGee, 146 A. 641 (N.H. 1929)

Hawkins demonstrates that a patient will be entitled to expectation damages where his or her doctor promises a certain result that does not occur. A young boy's hand was scarred from a severe burn, and the surgeon who was to perform a skin graft operation promised that the boy's hand would be "100% perfect" following the operation. The court held that the doctor made an enforceable promise, under the objective theory of contracts, which was breached when the surgery failed. The plaintiff was entitled to expectation damages equal to the difference between the value of a "100% perfect" hand and the value of his hand in its post-surgery condition. [Text § 3–25]

Hays Merchandise, Inc. v. Dewey, 474 P.2d 270 (Wash. 1970)

This case illustrates UCC § 2–606(1)(c) which holds that a buyer has accepted goods once he or she does an act inconsistent with the seller's ownership of the goods. The retail buyer in *Hays* gave notice of revocation to the seller, but then proceeded to price, display, and sell the goods. These acts are clearly inconsistent with an intention to revoke the goods, and the court held that the buyer had thus accepted the goods. [Text § 22–41]

Humble Oil & Refining Co. v. Westside Investment Corp., 428 S.W.2d 92 (Tex. 1968)

This case demonstrates the principle that irrevocable offers are not terminated by the offeree's counter-offer. This is the case with option contracts which are formed when an offeree gives the offeror consideration to keep an offer open. In *Humble*, the seller and buyer agreed to a two-month option on certain real property. The buyer paid seller $50, which made the option irrevocable. During the two-month period, buyer sent a counter-offer stating that it would be willing to exercise its option on different terms. Later, buyer attempted to exercise the option according to its original terms, and seller claimed the option had been terminated by the buyer's counter-offer. The court held that an option contract is an irrevocable offer, and therefore the buyer's power of acceptance was not terminated by his interim counter offer. [Text § 4–74]

International Filter Co. v. Conroe Gin, Ice & Light Co., 277 S.W. 631 (Tex. Comm'n App. 1925)

The court in *Conroe* held that bilateral contracts may be effectively accepted without notice to the offeror where the offer expressly allows such an acceptance. The plaintiff sent the defendant a written proposal which stated that the proposal "becomes a contract when accepted by the purchaser and approved by an executive officer" at the plaintiff's office. An officer at the plaintiff's office accepted the proposal by writing "OK ... P.N. Engel" on the proposal. Subsequently, the defendant attempt to revoke its offer. The court held that the officer's endorsement on the proposal was sufficient to constitute an acceptance of the bilateral contract offer since the proposal expressly authorized acceptance in such a manner. Thus, the express language of the proposal made the officer's acceptance immediately effective without notification to the offeree. [Text § 4–115]

Jordan v. Dobbins, 122 Mass. 168 (1877)

This case illustrates the general principle that where either the offeror or offeree of a pending contract dies, the power to accept the contract is terminated. A third party wished to buy goods on credit from a department store. Dobbins executed a standing offer that he would guarantee any of the third party's debts to the department store. Dobbins died, a fact of which the department store was unaware, and the department store sued Dobbins's estate for debts owed by the third party. The court held, however, that the death of Dobbins (the guarantor) operated as a revocation of his guarantee whether or not the department store (the creditor) had notice of the death. Therefore, the debt owed by the third party could not be recovered from Dobbins's estate. [Text § 4–64]

Lefkowitz v. Great Minneapolis Surplus Stores, 86 N.W.2d 689 (Minn. 1957) [Text § 3–21]

Livingstone v. Evans, 4. D.L.R. 769 (Alta. 1925)

This case provides an example of a situation where an acceptance, which is mailed after the expiration of the offer, may be held to be a valid acceptance. In *Livingstone*, the offer stated no specific time period during which the offer would remain open, so the offer remained open for a reasonable time. The offeree failed to accept within a reasonable time, however, and mailed an acceptance at a later date. The late acceptance crossed in the mails with a letter from the offeror indicating that the offer was still open. Thus, the court held that the acceptance, though late according to the original offer's terms, was valid. [Text § 4–44]

Lonergan v. Skolnick, 276 P.2d 8 (Cal. Ct. App. 1954)

This case illustrates the general principle that a "quote" does not usually constitute an "offer" to sell. Thus, where there was a response to the plaintiff's inquiry about a certain piece of land with a disclaimer that the letter was a "form letter," the court held that the plaintiff was not reasonable in concluding that the price quote constituted an offer to sell. [Text § 3–9]

Lucy v. Zehmer, 84 S.E.2d 516 (Va. 1954)

This case illustrates the enforceability of a purported agreement under the objective theory of contracts even though one of the parties subjectively had no intention to enter the agreement. The plaintiff offered the defendants $50,000 for their farm. The defendants then drafted a written promise to sell the farm to the plaintiff at that price. The plaintiff took the defendants seriously and later sued them when they refused to convey the farm. The defendants asserted that they were only joking were intoxicated at the time they made the promise, and had no intention of actually selling the farm. The court held that the defendants were bound by the agreement, stating that "[a] person cannot set up that he was merely jesting when his conduct and words would warrant a reasonable person in believing that he intended a real agreement." [Text §§ 2–5; 3–23]

Marchiondo v. Scheck, 432 P.2d 405 (N.M. 1967)

This case holds that when an offer for a unilateral contract requests performance as the appropriate method for acceptance, the offeree's beginning of performance makes the offeror's offer irrevocable. The defendant offered to sell a piece of property to a third party (with a six-day time limit on the offer) and also offered the plaintiff (a real estate agent) a commission if the sale was consummated. The offer was made within the six-day limit, but the defendant subsequently revoked his offer to sell. The court held that the real estate agent was entitled to his commission because a seller's promise to pay a commission upon the sale of his property becomes irrevocable when the agent begins performance of the unilateral contract by securing a potential buyer. The commission is payable even if the seller later backs out of the sale. [Text § 4–61]

Morrison v. Thoelke, 155 So. 2d 889 (Fla. Dist. Ct. App. 1963)

This case illustrates the application of the mailbox rule to offerees. Buyer signed a contract for the purchase of real estate and mailed it to the seller. Seller signed (accepted) the contract and mailed it back to the Buyer. Before the buyer received the accepted contract through the mail, the seller contacted buyer's lawyer and attempted to repudiate his acceptance. The court held that the contract was enforceable at the moment of acceptance by the seller. Thus, an acceptance is effective upon dispatch by the offeree. A rejection dispatched after the acceptance is ineffective, even if received by the offeror before the acceptance. [Text § 4–118]

Petterson v. Pattberg, 161 N.E. 428 (N.Y. 1928)

This case holds that an acceptance of a contract offer unambiguously calling for a unilateral contract is not effective until performance actually starts. Prior to the time performance begins, the offeror can freely revoke his offer. The defendant held a mortgage on the plaintiff's property. The defendant offered plaintiff a partial reduction of principal if plaintiff paid off the mortgage before the end of the month. Before the end of month, plaintiff told defendant he had money to pay off the discounted mortgage, but defendant revoked before the plaintiff could physically tender the payment, stating that he had sold the mortgage to a third party. Plaintiff ended up paying the full principal amount to the third party, so he sued the defendant for the discount. The court held that the plaintiff never effectively accepted the defendant's offer because payment was never actually tendered. The court treated the attempted tender as a mere preparation to perform which was ineffective to accept the defendant's unilateral offer. The defendant was free to revoke his offer until an actual tender of payment was made. [Text § 4–98]

Roto-Lith v. F.P. Bartlett & Co., 297 F.2d 497 (1st Cir. 1962) [Text § 5–12]

Southwest Engineering Co. v. Martin Tractor Co., 473 P.2d 18 (Kan. 1970)

This court held, in accordance with UCC § 2–204(3), that the absence of an important term from an agreement is not necessarily fatal to the formation of the contract. Thus, where plaintiff and defendant failed to agree on a time for payment, the court inserted a "gap filler" payment term provided by UCC § 2–310(a) which requires that the goods be paid for upon delivery where the parties' contract fails to specify the payment term. Other indefiniteness problems concerning price and time for shipment or delivery may also be corrected by various gap filler provisions found in the UCC. In addition, it held that printed letterhead, or any other symbol adopted by a party with the present intention to authenticate a writing, is sufficient to meet the "signature" requirement of the statute of frauds. [Text §§ 6–17; 10–43]

PAROL EVIDENCE RULE

Danann Realty Corp. v. Harris, 157 N.E.2d 597 (N.Y. 1959)

The parol evidence rule ordinarily does not bar evidence of prior oral agreements which establish fraud in the transaction. However, *Danann* stands for an often criticized minority view that evidence of a misrepresentation is barred if the aggrieved party made a specific disclaimer regarding a particular misrepresentation. In that case, an aggrieved lessee signed a written agreement which contained a specific disclaimer that the lessee had made a "full investigation" and was not "relying upon any statement or representation" not contained in the written agreement. The lessor had made some oral misrepresentations regarding expenses which resulted in the lessee's tort action. Even though an ordinary merger clause does not bar evidence of a fraudulent misrepresentation, when the contract expressly states that the parties are relying only on specific representations mentioned in the contract, they may not later assert their reliance on oral representations not included in the contract. This is true even if the oral representations are fraudulent. [Text § 18–25]

Hicks v. Bush, 180 N.E.2d 425 (N.Y. 1962)

The holding in this case determines whether parol evidence is admissible to prove the existence of a condition precedent to the parties' written agreement. The plaintiff and the defendants held significant interests in various corporations. They drew up a written agreement which provided that both parties would tender their stock in the various enterprises in exchange for stock in what was to be a new, consolidated entity. The plaintiff tendered his stock according to the written agreement, but the defendants refused to tender theirs, claiming that there was an oral condition precedent to their duty to do so. This condition provided that the written document would have no effect unless additional capital from other sources could be obtained. The court held that parol testimony was admissible to prove the condition precedent because the condition asserted did not contradict the terms of the written agreement. The court noted that "[i]t is certainly not improbable that parties contracting in these circumstances would make the asserted oral agreement; the condition precedent at hand is the sort of condition which parties would not be inclined to incorporate into a written agreement intended for public consumption." [Text § 18–22]

Lee v. Joseph E. Seagram & Sons, Inc., 552 F.2d 447 (2d Cir. 1977)

This court followed the Corbin approach to the admissibility of parol evidence. The parties entered into a written agreement for the sale of plaintiff's liquor distributorship. The parties also had a collateral oral agreement that the defendant would find the plaintiff a liquor distributorship in another city. When the plaintiff sought to prove this oral agreement to the court, the defendant claimed that the parol evidence rule barred evidence of the agreement. The court rejected this contention and adopted the Corbin approach which allows extrinsic facts to be admitted to determine whether the parties intend a written document to be a full integration of their agreement or whether there is an enforceable collateral promise. The court held that the oral agreement in this case was not one which would ordinarily be included in the written agreement because it was based on the parties' personal relationship and would not be expected to appear in the parties' written agreement for the sale of corporate assets. Additionally, there was no merger clause in the written agreement, and the collateral promise did not contradict the terms of the written agreement. [Text § 18–11]

Masterson v. Sine, 436 P.2d 561 (Cal. 1968)

This case illustrates the Restatement position on whether parol evidence will be admitted to prove an oral agreement made contemporaneously with the parties' written contract. The plaintiffs conveyed their ranch to relatives. In the written deed, the plaintiffs reserved a ten-year repurchase option over the subject property. Subsequently, the plaintiff filed for bankruptcy, and the trustee in bankruptcy sued the relatives to exercise the repurchase option. The relatives wished to prove a contemporaneous oral agreement to the court that the option was understand to be of a "personal" nature only and was not assignable to persons outside the family. The court held that evidence of the oral agreement was admissible. The court determined that the oral agreement was one which would naturally be made as a separate agreement from the written contract. The deed in this case was a standard deed, and it would not be common for the parties to insert additional provisions regarding the non-assignability of the option. Thus, the court concluded that the deed was not a complete integration of the parties' agreement, and the oral agreement regarding the repurchase option was admissible in the relatives' defense. [Text § 18–13]

Mitchell v. Lath, 160 N.E. 646 (N.Y. 1928) [Text §§ 18–14, 20–7]

CASE SQUIBS

RESTITUTION

Britton v. Turner, 6 N.H. 481 (1834)

This case allows restitution to be awarded to a party in breach. An employer and employee entered into a one-year employment contract which called for $120 in compensation to be paid to the employee. The employee worked for 9 1/2 months and then breached the employment contract without justification. Nonetheless, the court held that the employee could recover $95 for the reasonable value of his services. The employee in this kind of situation is entitled to a restitutionary recovery of the reasonable value of his or her services because he or she has conferred a benefit upon the employer. Note that the jury in this case found the reasonable value of the employee's services to be equal to a *pro rata* amount of the contract price. [Text § 31–28]

STATUTE OF FRAUDS

Azevedo v. Minister, 471 P.2d 661 (Nev. 1970)

The UCC § 2–201 statute of frauds is satisfied by an accounting sent 10 weeks after the formation of an oral agreement, where performance began without objection after the oral agreement was formed. However, the burden of proving the oral agreement remains on the party alleging the contract, despite the other party's receipt of the written memoranda purportedly memorializing the contract. [Text § 10–54]

Crabtree v. Elizabeth Arden Sales Corp., 110 N.E.2d 551 (N.Y. 1953)

This case illustrates the modern view that the statute of frauds may be satisfied by combining the terms in an unsigned document with terms in a separate signed document to form a single memorandum if both documents clearly refer to the same transaction and there is external evidence that both parties assented to the unsigned document (the "merger" doctrine). In *Crabtree*, an employee sought to enforce an employment agreement against her employer which was evidenced by two payroll cards (signed by the employer) and the employer's memorandum of her oral offer (unsigned by the employer). The court rejected the view held by some jurisdictions that the signed writing must refer to the unsigned writing. It is enough "that a sufficient connection between the papers is established simply by a reference in them to the same subject matter or transaction and oral testimony is admitted to show the connection between the documents and to establish the acquiescence of the party to be charged, to the contents of the one unsigned." The court was satisfied that the alleged employment contract existed and was set forth in a series of documents some of which were signed by the party to be charged. Thus, the employee was allowed to introduce evidence explaining terms on the documents that were not signed by the employer. [Text § 10–11]

J.J. Brooksbank Co. v. American Motors Corp., 184 N.W.2d 796 (Minn. 1971)

Although the statute of frauds in this case barred the plaintiff's action to enforce the promise of the promisor to answer for the debt of a third party, it did not bar an action against the promisor for breach of an oral agreement to repurchase goods from the plaintiff. The plaintiff operated a Budget Rent-a-Car company. He entered into an oral agreement with American Motors under which plaintiff was to purchase new automobiles for use in his car-rental business, and American guaranteed that the cars would be repurchased by its franchised dealers at a depreciated price approximately one year after plaintiff purchased each car. A dispute arose over three of the cars purchased under the agreement after American's dealer in Minneapolis refused to repurchase its share of the cars. Plaintiff was forced to sell the three cars at an auction and thereafter brought suit for the difference in price between what he would have received if the cars had been sold under the oral repurchase agreement and what he realized at auction.

The trial court barred plaintiff's action, reasoning that American stood in the position of a surety of its dealers' obligations under the oral repurchase agreement. Since the statute of frauds limits the enforceability of oral suretyship promises, the trial court dismissed the plaintiff's suit.

The Minnesota Supreme Court, however, reversed, holding that this case presented an example of the "leading object" or definite interest" exception to the suretyship provisions of the Statute. That is, when the surety makes an oral promise to secure an economic advantage for the surety and not the principal, the transaction is outside the Statute, and thus enforceable even though oral. Here, American made its guarantee to further its own economic interest, and thus, under the "leading object" rule, the Statute did not apply. [Text § 10–31]

THIRD PARTY BENEFICIARY CONTRACTS

Dutton v. Poole, 83 Eng. Rep. 528 (K.B. 1677)

This early English case established the right of a third person to sue as a beneficiary of a contract to which that person was not a party. A father expressed his intention to sell wood to raise a dowry for his daughter. However, his son, who wanted to inherit the wood, promised to pay the father £ 1,000 if the father would promise not to sell the wood. The son never paid the promised sum, so the daughter sued him. The son defended, claiming the daughter had no standing to sue since she was not in privity with the contracting parties.

However, the court rejected this argument and allowed the daughter to sue as a third party beneficiary of the contract between the son and the father.

Note that Dutton was overruled in 1861 and the English rule now is that no beneficiary may enforce a contract. However, while a beneficiary is not entitled to enforce a promisor's promise directly in a breach action, the English courts allow an artificial use of trusts in this situation. That is, what the American courts would call a third party beneficiary, is called a beneficiary of an implied trust in the English courts. Thus, while the beneficiary may not sue the promisor on a third party beneficiary theory in the English courts, the beneficiary may sue the trustee of the implied trust (i.e., the promisor) for breach of trust. [Text §§ 26–1; 26–5]

Isbrandtsen Co. v. Local 1291, 204 F.2d 495 (3d Cir. 1953)

This case demonstrates than an "incidental" beneficiary, as opposed to "donee" or "creditor" beneficiaries, of a third party beneficiary contract is not entitled to sue to enforce the promisor's promise. Plaintiff chartered a ship to the Scott Paper Company ("Scott") for the purpose of transporting pulp. Scott agreed to load and unload the ship. Scott subsequently hired Lavino Shipping Company ("Lavino") to do the unloading. However, the employees of Lavino stopped work before the ship was fully unloaded. The work stoppage violated provisions of an agreement the employees' union had with Lavino. The delay in unloading the ship became expensive for the plaintiff, so the plaintiff sued the union for violation of the collective bargaining agreement with Lavino.

The court recognized the ability of donee and creditor beneficiaries to sue as third parties to enforce the obligations of a party under a contract. "If in buying the promise the promisee expresses an intent that some third party shall receive either the security of the executory promise or the benefit of performance as a gift, that party is a donee of . . . the contract right . . . If, on the other hand, the promisee's expressed intent is that some third party shall receive the performance in satisfaction and discharge of some actual or supposed duty or liability of the promisee, the third party is a creditor beneficiary." All others who may be benefited by a contract's performance are "incidental beneficiaries." The plaintiff could not qualify as either a donee beneficiary or a creditor beneficiary since the plaintiff was completely unknown to the labor union. Therefore, as an incidental beneficiary, plaintiff could not enforce the contract and recover his damages resulting from the work stoppage. [Text §§ 26–11; 26–17]

Lawrence v. Fox, 20 N.Y. 268 (1859) [Text §§ 26–10; 26–16]

CASE SQUIBS

Lucas v. Hamm, 364 P.2d 685 (Cal. 1961)

The intended third party beneficiary of a contract between two parties may sue for a breach of the contract. In *Lucas*, the intended beneficiaries of an invalidated trust sued the attorney who improperly drafted the document for the testator. Because the trust was intended for the beneficiaries' benefit, the court held that the beneficiaries had standing to sue for the attorney's breach. The court reasoned that the beneficiaries were the individuals under the contract to whom the attorney's "performance runs." Nevertheless, the beneficiaries were unable to recover against the attorney because the court determined that the attorney was not negligent and thus did not breach his contract to supply reasonably competent professional services. [Text § 26–14]

Martinez v. Socoma Co., 521 P.2d 841 (Cal. 1974)

Members of the public cannot sue as third party beneficiaries to recover for injuries resulting from a private party's failure to perform under a contract with a municipal, state, or federal governmental body, even though such contracts are entered into for the public benefit. Thus, in *Martinez*, where the defendants contracted with the federal government to supply job training and employment opportunities for disadvantaged persons, a class action suit brought by persons who would have qualified for the program which was filed as a result of the defendant's breach was dismissed. An exception arises, however, where the contract expresses the government's intent that individual citizens have the right to sue. [Text § 26–29]

Moch Co. v. Rensselaer Water Co., 159 N.E. 896 (1928)

This case illustrates the general presumption that parties intend to contract for their own benefit and not for the benefit of third parties. The defendant promised to supply water for the city's fire hydrants. Plaintiff's building was destroyed in a fire because the defendant failed to supply an adequate amount of water, resulting in a breach of defendant's contract with the city. For policy reasons, i.e., to prevent unlimited liability to all residents of the city, the court held that the plaintiff was not an intended beneficiary of the contract with the city. In general, however, members of the public cannot sue as third party beneficiaries to recover for injuries resulting from a private party's failure to perform under a contract with a municipal, state or federal government, even though such contracts may be viewed as entered into for the public benefit. [Text § 26–29]

Rouse v. United States, 215 F.2d 872 (D.C. Cir. 1954)

This case illustrates the application of the defense of fraudulent misrepresentation to a third party beneficiary (or its assignee) of a contract where that defense would be applicable to the original promisee. That is, the assignee merely "steps into the shoes" of the assignor. However, the promisor may not assert defenses the promisee could have asserted against the third party beneficiary (or its assignee) where the promisor expressly assumed liability for the promisee's debt.

As part of the purchase price of a home, Rouse agreed to make payments on a heating system installed by the seller (a contract which benefited the contractor that installed the heating system). Rouse then refused to pay on the contract, alleging that the seller (the promisee) fraudulently misrepresented the quality of the system. The United States sued Rouse as the assignee/guarantor of the contract between the seller and Rouse. Rouse could not assert the seller's defense of defective installation against the third party (the contractor) or its assignee because Rouse expressly assumed payment of the debt owed by the seller to the third party. However, the court held that Rouse could properly assert the defense of fraudulent misrepresentation against the United States (the third party's assignee) because a promisor may assert any defenses against the third party or its assignee that it could have asserted against the seller (the promisee). [Text § 26–34]

Seaver v. Ransom, 120 N.E. 639 (N.Y. 1918) [Text §§ 26–8, 26–15]

UNCONSCIONABILITY

A & M Produce Co. v. FMC Corp., 186 Cal. Rptr. 114 (Cal. App. Ct. 1982)

This court held that a disclaimer of express and implied warranties and a limitation on consequential damage recovery, which are in technical compliance with the requirements of the Uniform Commercial Code, may still be denied enforceability on unconscionability grounds. A small farming company entered into a contract with a large corporation for the sale of a weight-sizing machine for use by the farming company in harvesting a tomato crop. The farming company had never grown tomatoes before, so it relied on the corporate salesman's judgment regarding the specifications for the particular machine it would need. The salesman recommended a specific machine and assured the farming company that the one selected would work for their needs and that additional equipment would not be necessary.

The parties' written agreement was contained on a preprinted form produced by the corporation. The agreement contained two disclaimers: one disclaimed all warranties, and the other disclaimed consequential damages. Problems arose shortly after delivery of the machine because the machine was unable to properly harvest tomatoes without damaging them. Part of the problem was the need for additional equipment (a cooling unit), which the salesman had said the company would not need. The farming company ended up losing most of its tomato crop, so it wanted to return the weight-sizing machine to the corporation, but the corporation refused and demanded full payment of the balance due on the machine. The farming company subsequently sued for breach of express and implied warranties and for consequential damages, and the corporation defended that the warranties and consequential damage liability had been successfully disclaimed in the parties' written agreement.

The court refused, however, to enforce either the warranty disclaimers or the consequential damage limitation, stating that to do so would lead to an unconscionable result. The court held that the unconscionability doctrine applies to disclaimers of warranty and consequential damage provisions, just as it applies to any other contract provision, and that unconscionability is available to corporations just as it is to consumers. The court also held that that unconscionability has both procedural and substantive elements. The procedural element is met where the parties' agreement involves oppression and surprise for the party of lesser bargaining power. "Oppression . . . arises from an inequality of bargaining power which results . . . in 'an absence of meaningful choice.'" Surprise occurs when the contested terms "are hidden in a prolix printed form drafted by the party seeking to enforce the disputed terms." The substantive element is met where the agreement is "commercially unreasonable," i.e., where a contractual term causes an unjustifiable one-sided result, such as where the term "reallocates the risks of the bargain in an objectively unreasonable or unexpected manner." The procedural and substantive elements work together on a sliding scale, such that the more one of the elements can be shown, the less of the other that must be shown in order for the contested provision to be held unconscionable.

The contested provisions in the *A & M* case were unconscionable because the bargain took place between a large corporation and a small farming company (indicating oppression); both disclaimer provisions appeared on the middle of the back page of the preprinted form contract (indicating surprise); the provisions were never brought to the farming company's attention (indicating surprise); there was no opportunity for individual negotiation during the bargaining process (indicating oppression); the corporation knew the farming company had no expertise with weight-sizing machines and knew the farming company was relying on its expertise in selecting an appropriate machine (indicating oppression and commercial unreasonableness); and the disclaimer provisions resulted in the sale of an expensive piece of machinery with a corporation that guaranteed nothing about its performance (indicating commercial unreasonableness, i.e., a very one-sided bargain). Therefore, having found that the elements for the unconscionability doctrine were met, the court refused to give effect to the disclaimer provisions and upheld the lower court's damage award. [Text §§ 16–5; 16–13]

Campbell Soup Co. v. Wentz, 172 F.2d 80 (3d Cir. 1948)

This case illustrates the common law application of the unconscionability doctrine. Campbell Soup Company contracted with Wentz, a farmer, for his entire crop of a specific type of carrot at a fair price on the day the contract was signed. Subsequently, a market shortage occurred of the particular strain of carrots used for soup making, so the market price for Wentz's carrots rose sharply. As a consequence, Wentz breached the contract so that he could sell his carrots on the open market. Campbell's sued for specific performance. Normally, courts are amenable to granting specific performance in a shortage situation because the remedy of damages is inadequate where the plaintiff cannot buy a substitute performance in the open market. However, Campbell's had imposed a very one-sided bargain upon the plaintiff in that Campbell's could unilaterally cancel the contract with Wentz, while Wentz had to obtain Campbell's approval before he could sell any carrots it had even if Campbell's did not want them. Hence, the court stated that because one part of the contract was unconscionable, Campbell's was not entitled to equitable relief, even though the part of the contract that was unfair had nothing to do with the issue in the present case. Common law was very strict about requiring that plaintiffs who sought equity had "to do equity," and thus this case shows that unconscionability was more of a defense to equitable relief at common law than it was a doctrine by which parties sought affirmative relief. [Text § 16–3]

Weaver v. American Oil Co., 276 N.E.2d 144 (Ind. 1971)

Although many courts are reluctant to enforce adhesion contracts because of their inherent unfairness, a complaining party usually must show something more than a standardized form agreement to obtain relief from the contract. Courts, such as the court in *Weaver*, often require that the plaintiff additionally show the existence of a gross disparity in bargaining power. In that case, the defendant leased a gas station from the plaintiff, a large oil company. The lease signed by the parties was a standard form agreement which was drafted by the plaintiff's lawyers. The contested provision in the agreement provided that plaintiff could not be held liable for injuries to the defendant occurring on the premises, even if these injuries were caused by the plaintiff's negligence. In addition, the contract also provided that the defendant would be liable for any injuries occurring to the plaintiff, even if caused by the **plaintiff's** own negligence. An employee of the plaintiff spilled gasoline on the defendant and the defendant's employee, and the plaintiff brought a declaratory judgment action seeking a ruling that the plaintiff could not be held liable for the loss. The court held that the clause, which was located in the fine print of the contract, could not be enforced. The gross disparity in the parties' bargaining positions was apparent in that the plaintiff had no opportunity to negotiate any of the lease provisions. Moreover, plaintiff was not well educated, and the defendant never called the plaintiff's attention to the clause. Thus, the court concluded that there was no "real and voluntary meeting of the minds" and refused to enforce the contested provision. [Text § 16–5]

Williams v. Walker-Thomas Furniture Co., 350 F.2d 445 (D.C. Cir. 1965) [Text § 16–9]

UNDUE INFLUENCE

Methodist Mission Home v. N—A—B—, 451 S.W.2d 539 (Tex. Civ. App. 1970)

This case demonstrates the defense of undue influence to contract actions. A mother had a child out of wedlock, and shortly after the birth, while the mother was experiencing a period of emotional distress, representatives of the maternity home and the mother's counselor encouraged the mother to give up her child for adoption. The court allowed the mother's defense of undue influence to an adoption agreement, taking note of the fact that "an unwed mother who has just given birth is usually emotionally distraught and peculiarly vulnerable to efforts . . . to persuade her to give up her child." Thus, the elements of undue influence, i.e., that there be a "special relationship" between the contracting parties (the Woman and the Home); and that there be "improper persuasion" by the stronger party (the Home) were established. [Text § 14–4]

TABLE OF CASES

References are to page numbers. Case Squibs are in bold type.

A & M Produce v. FMC Corp., 271, 668, **859**
Adams v. Lindsell, 844
Albre Marble & Tile Co. v. John Bowen Co., 837
Alcoa v. Essex, 457, **837**
Allegheny College v. National Chatauqua County Bank of Jamestown, 823
Allhusen v. Caristo Construction Corp., 818
Allied Grape Growers v. Bronco Wine Co., 214
Allied Steel & Conveyors v. Ford Motor Co., 845
American Trading & Production Corp. v. Shell Int'l Marine, Ltd., 837
Ammons v. Wilson & Co., 845
Anderson v. May, 444
Angel v. Murray, 844
Austin Instrument, Inc. v. Loral Corp., 834
Autry v. Republic, Prod'ns, 466
Ayer v. Western Union Telegraph Co., 846
Azevedo v. Minister, 855
Balfour v. Balfour, 21, **817**
Bard v. Kent, 824
Baron v. Cain, 373
Bateman Eichler v. Berner, 278, **836**
Beall v. Beall, 24
Brackenberry v. Hodgkin, 846
Britton v. Turner, 855
Broadnax v. Ledbetter, 45
C. Itoh & Co. (America), Inc. v. Jordan Int'l Co., 99, **846**
Caldwell v. Cline, 847
Campbell Soup Co. v. Wentz, 861
Canadian Indus. Alcohol Co. v. Dunbar Molasses Co., 838
Carlill v. Carbolic Smoke Ball Co., 44, 47, 83, **847**
Chemical Bank v. Rinden Professional Association, 818
Crabtree v. Elizabeth Arden Sales Corp., 855

Crane Ice Cream Co. v. Terminal Freezing & Heating Co., 819
Danann Realty Corp. v. Harris, 853
Daubert v. Merrell Dow Pharmaceuticals, Inc., 595
Davis v. Jacoby, 847
DeCicco v. Schweizer, 824
Dickinson v. Dodds, 59, **848**
Dorton v. Collins & Aikman Corp., 99, **848**
Drennan v. Star Paving Co., 73, **848**
Dutton v. Poole, 856
East Providence Credit Union v. Geremia, 825
East River Steamship Corp. v. Transamerica Delaval, Inc., 645
Elsinore Union Elementary School Dist. v. Kastorff, 842
Embry v. Hargardine, McKittrick Dry Goods Co., 848
Equitable Lumber Corp. v. IPA Land Development Corp., 830
Evening News Ass'n v. Peterson, 819
Fairmount Glass Works v. Crunden-Martin Woodenware Co., 849
Feinberg v. Pfeiffer, 170, **825**
Fiege v. Boehm, 165
Fischer v. Union Trust Co., 826
Foakes v. Beer, 161, **826**
Freeman & Mills v. Belcher Oils, 830
Frigaliment Importing Co. v. B.N.S. International Sales Corp., 238, 315, **843**
Giant Food v. Washington Coca-Cola, 30
Goodman v. Dicker, 826
Hadley v. Baxendale, 598, 599, **830**
Hamer v. Sidway, 76, **827, 849**
Harrington v. Taylor, 827
Hauter v. Zogarts, 692
Hawkins v. McGee, 33, **830, 849**
Hays Merchandise, Inc. v. Dewey, 849
Hicks v. Bush, 853

863

TABLE OF CASES

Hilmor Sales Co. v. Helen Neushaefer Div. of Supronics Corp., 835
Hochster v. De La Tour, 408, 815
Hoffman v. Red Owl Stores, 174, 827
Holiday Inns of America, Inc. v. Knight, 820
Humble Oil & Refining Co. v. Westside Investment Corp., 850
International Filter Co. v. Conroe Gin, Ice & Light Co., 850
Iron Trade Products Co. v. Wilkoff Co., 838
Isbrandtsen Co. v. Local, 857
J.J. Brooksbank Co. v. American Motors Corp., 856
J.N.A. Realty Corp. v. Cross Bay Chelsea, 836
Jacob & Youngs v. Kent, 354, 585, 820, 831
Jordan v. Dobbins, 850
K & G Construction Co. v. Harris, 821
Kannavos v. Annino, 842
Karpinski v. Ingrasci, 835
Kingston v. Preston, 821
Kirkland v. Archbold, 821
Kirksey v. Kirksey, 827
Krell v. Henry, 463, 839
Kubik v. J & R Foods of Oregon, 149
Kucera v. Kavan, 828
Laclede Gas Co. v. Amoco Oil Co., 548, 836
LaCumbre Golf & Country Club v. Santa Barbara Hotel, 464
Laidlaw v. Organ, 260, 842
Langell v. Betz, 820
Lawrence v. Fox, 476, 857
Lee v. Joseph E. Seagram & Sons, Inc., 854
Lefkowitz v. Great Minneapolis Surplus Stores, 30, 851
Livingstone v. Evans, 851
Lloyd v. Murphy, 464, 839
Lonergan v. Scolnick, 26, 851
Lucas v. Hamm, 858
Lucy v. Zehmer, 20, 851
Lumley v. Wagner, 544, 836
Macke Co. v. Pizza of Gaithersburg, Inc., 532
Marchiondo v. Scheck, 851
Martinez v. Socoma Co., 858
Masterson v. Sine, 854
Mattei v. Hopper, 828

McCloskey & Co. v. Minweld Steel Co., 815
McDonald's Corp. v. Moore, 237
Methodist Mission Home v. N—A—B—, 862
Miami Coca-Cola Bottling Co. v. Orange Crush Co., 155
Mills v. Wyman, 140, 829
Mineral Park Land Co. v. Howard, 839
Mitchell v. Lath, 289, 854
Moch Co. v. Rensselaer Water Co., 858
Morrison v. Thoelke, 852
Nanakuli Paving & Rock Co. v. Shell Oil Co., Inc., 303
Neri v. Retail Marine Corp., 831
Nolan v. Whitney, 336, 822
Oloffson v. Coomer, 651, 815, 831
Ortelere v. Teacher's Ret. Bd., 226
Pacific Gas & Electric Co. v. G.W. Thomas Drayage & Rigging Co., 304, 841
Paradine v. Jane, 839
Parker v. Twentieth Century-Fox Film Corp., 608, 831
Peevyhouse v. Garland Coal & Mining Co., 562, 831, 836
Petterson v. Pattberg, 852
Phelps v. Herro, 816
Plante v. Jacobs, 822
Raffles v. Wichelhaus, 239, 843
Reliance Cooperage Corp. v. Treat, 816
Ricketts v. Scothorn, 171, 829
Rockingham County v. Luten Bridge Co., 606, 831
Roto-Lith, Ltd. v. F.P. Bartlett & Co., 98, 852
Rouse v. United States, 490, 858
Sally Beauty Co. v. Nexxus Prods. Co., Inc., 532
Seacoast Gas Co., United States v., 817
Seamen's Direct Buying Serv., Inc. v. Standard Oil Co., 622, 832
Seaver v. Ransom, 475, 859
Second National Bank v. Pan-American Bridge Co., 823
Sedmak v. Charlie's Chevrolet, Inc., 643
Sherwood v. Walker, 233, 843
Southwest Engineering Co. v. Martin Tractor Co., 852
Southwest Engineering Co. v. United States, 833
Spearin, United States v., 840
Stees v. Leonard, 839

TABLE OF CASES

Stewart v. Newbury, 823
Sullivan v. O'Connor, 833
Swartz v. War Memorial Comm'n, 374
Taylor v. Barton-Child Co., 820
Taylor v. Caldwell, 443, **840**
Trident Center v. Connecticut General Life Ins. Co., 305
U.S. for Use of Trane Co. v. Bond, 241
Universal Builders, Inc. v. Moon Motor Lodge, Inc., 844
Varney v. Ditmars, 117, **817**
Vitex Mfg. Corp. v. Caribtex Corp., 834
Walgreen Co. v. Sara Creek Prop. Co., 555
Wassenaar v. Panos, 617
Watkins & Son v. Carrig, 841
Weaver v. American Oil Co., 861
Webb v. McGowin, 141, **829**
Wegematic Corp., United States v., 442, **840**
Wheeler v. White, 829
White v. Benkowski, 834
Williams v. Walker-Thomas Furniture Co., 269, **862**
Wisconsin Knife Works v. National Metal Crafters, 186, **844**
Wood v. Boynton, 233, **843**
Wood v. Lucy, Lady Duff Gordon, 149, **829**
Wrench, LLC v. Taco Bell Corp., 12
Zabriskie Chevrolet, Inc. v. Smith, 391

TABLE OF RESTATEMENT OF CONTRACTS

Restatement 1st § 90 171
Restatement 1st § 133 473
Restatement 1st § 133(1) 474
Restatement 1st § 133(1)(a) 474
Restatement 1st § 133(1)(b) 476, 481
Restatement 1st § 133(1)(c) 477
Restatement 2nd § 1 8
Restatement 2nd § 12(1) 219
Restatement 2nd § 12(2)(a) 224
Restatement 2nd § 12(2)(b) 219
Restatement 2nd § 12(2)(c) 224
Restatement 2nd § 12(2)(d) 224
Restatement 2nd § 13 224
Restatement 2nd § 14 219
Restatement 2nd § 14, cmt. c 220, 221, 222
Restatement 2nd § 15(1)(a) 224, 225
Restatement 2nd § 15(1)(b) 224, 225
Restatement 2nd § 15(2) 225, 226
Restatement 2nd § 16 .... 32, 224, 227
Restatement 2nd § 16, cmt. b 32
Restatement 2nd § 17 .... 17, 19
Restatement 2nd § 18 .... 17, 19
Restatement 2nd § 19(1) 18
Restatement 2nd § 19(2) 18, 19
Restatement 2nd § 19, cmt. b 18
Restatement 2nd § 20 238
Restatement 2nd § 20(1)(a) 238, 239
Restatement 2nd § 20(1)(b) 238, 239
Restatement 2nd § 20(2) 238, 239
Restatement 2nd § 21 20
Restatement 2nd § 21, cmt. b, ill. 3 20
Restatement 2nd § 21, cmt. c 20
Restatement 2nd § 22(2) 21
Restatement 2nd § 23, cmt. c, ill. 2 44
Restatement 2nd § 23, cmt. d 41
Restatement 2nd § 24 .... 10, 23, 26
Restatement 2nd § 25 ...... 18, 24, 42, 64, 73
Restatement 2nd § 26 .... 27, 28, 53

Restatement 2nd § 26, cmt. b 29
Restatement 2nd § 26, cmt. c 28
Restatement 2nd § 26, cmt. d 27
Restatement 2nd § 28 36
Restatement 2nd § 28(1)(a) 36
Restatement 2nd § 28(1)(b) 36
Restatement 2nd § 28(1)(c) 37
Restatement 2nd § 29 .... 36, 41
Restatement 2nd § 29, cmt. b 35
Restatement 2nd § 29, cmt. b, ill. 1 43
Restatement 2nd § 30 .... 36, 75
Restatement 2nd § 30(2) 76, 78
Restatement 2nd § 32 .... 34, 76
Restatement 2nd § 33 .... 22, 122
Restatement 2nd § 33(1) 27, 115
Restatement 2nd § 33(2) 115, 118
Restatement 2nd § 33, cmt. a 122
Restatement 2nd § 33, cmts. d & e 122
Restatement 2nd § 35 65
Restatement 2nd § 35(1) 48
Restatement 2nd § 36 .... 54, 58
Restatement 2nd § 36(1) 48
Restatement 2nd § 36(1)(a) 49
Restatement 2nd § 36(1)(b) 48
Restatement 2nd § 36(1)(c) 48
Restatement 2nd § 36(1)(d) 49, 61
Restatement 2nd § 36(2) 62
Restatement 2nd § 36(2), cmt. b 49
Restatement 2nd § 36(2), cmt. c 49, 62
Restatement 2nd § 37 .... 73, 74
Restatement 2nd § 37, cmt. b, ill. 2 73
Restatement 2nd § 38 ...... 23, 48, 49, 50
Restatement 2nd § 38(2), cmt. b 54
Restatement 2nd § 38, cmt. a, ill. 1 50
Restatement 2nd § 39 ...... 23, 48, 49
Restatement 2nd § 39(2), cmt. c 50
Restatement 2nd § 39(2), cmt. c, ill. 3 54
Restatement 2nd § 39, cmt. a 51

TABLE OF RESTATEMENT OF CONTRACTS

Restatement 2nd § 39, cmt. b, ill. 2 53
Restatement 2nd § 41 48
Restatement 2nd § 41(1) 54
Restatement 2nd § 41(2) 55
Restatement 2nd § 41(3), cmt. e 56
Restatement 2nd § 41, cmt. b 55
Restatement 2nd § 42 ......23, 48, 58, 60
Restatement 2nd § 43 ....48, 59
Restatement 2nd § 43, cmt. d 59
Restatement 2nd § 45 ......25, 35, 64, 67, 68, 70, 72, 73, 77, 79, 736
Restatement 2nd § 45, cmt. d, ill. 8 47
Restatement 2nd § 45, cmt. e 68
Restatement 2nd § 45, cmt. f 69
Restatement 2nd § 46 ....46, 48, 60
Restatement 2nd § 48 ....49, 61
Restatement 2nd § 48, cmt. a 61
Restatement 2nd § 49 57
Restatement 2nd § 49, ill. 1 57
Restatement 2nd § 50 ....10, 39
Restatement 2nd § 50(1) 39
Restatement 2nd § 51 44
Restatement 2nd § 52 41
Restatement 2nd § 54 .....80, 82, 796
Restatement 2nd § 54(2) 79, 80
Restatement 2nd § 58 ....41, 75
Restatement 2nd § 59 .....95, 97, 112
Restatement 2nd § 60 ....36, 41, 75
Restatement 2nd § 61 112
Restatement 2nd § 62(1) 78
Restatement 2nd § 62(2) 78
Restatement 2nd § 63 ....85, 86
Restatement 2nd § 63(a) 85
Restatement 2nd § 63(b) 87
Restatement 2nd § 63, cmt. c 88
Restatement 2nd § 64 55
Restatement 2nd § 65 ....56, 86
Restatement 2nd § 66 86
Restatement 2nd § 67 ....86, 87
Restatement 2nd § 69(1)(a) 83
Restatement 2nd § 69(1)(b) 84
Restatement 2nd § 69(1)(c) 84
Restatement 2nd § 69(2) 84, 801, 802
Restatement 2nd § 69, cmt. a 83
Restatement 2nd § 69, cmt. e 85
Restatement 2nd § 69, cmt. e, ill. 7 85
Restatement 2nd § 69, cmt. e, ill. 8 85
Restatement 2nd § 71 ....10, 136
Restatement 2nd § 71–81 129
Restatement 2nd § 71(1) 131
Restatement 2nd § 71(2) 132, 133

Restatement 2nd § 71(3)(c) 164, 189
Restatement 2nd § 71(4) 136
Restatement 2nd § 73 ....156, 158, 159, 160, 163, 164, 188, 189, 192, 432
Restatement 2nd § 73, cmt. b 164
Restatement 2nd § 74 165
Restatement 2nd § 74(a) 165
Restatement 2nd § 74(b) 165
Restatement 2nd § 74, cmt. c 164
Restatement 2nd § 75 135
Restatement 2nd § 76, cmt. c 153
Restatement 2nd § 78 166
Restatement 2nd § 79(a) 131
Restatement 2nd § 79(b) 144
Restatement 2nd § 79, cmt. d 145
Restatement 2nd § 79, cmt. e 145
Restatement 2nd § 82 ....140, 142
Restatement 2nd §§ 82–96 130
Restatement 2nd § 83 ....140, 143
Restatement 2nd § 85 220
Restatement 2nd § 86 ....140, 167, 731
Restatement 2nd § 86, cmt. a, ill. 1 141
Restatement 2nd § 86, cmt. i 141
Restatement 2nd § 87 ....166, 292, 824
Restatement 2nd § 87(1) 66
Restatement 2nd § 87(1), cmt. c 66
Restatement 2nd § 87(2) 25, 64, 71, 72, 73, 172, 173, 613
Restatement 2nd § 87(2), cmt. e, ill. 4 25
Restatement 2nd § 87, cmt. c 166
Restatement 2nd § 89 ....188, 190, 368, 737, 743, 844
Restatement 2nd § 89(a) 161, 162, 188, 767
Restatement 2nd § 89(b) 161, 163, 189
Restatement 2nd § 89(c) 162, 189
Restatement 2nd § 89, cmt. d, ill. 7 163
Restatement 2nd § 90 ....11, 170, 171, 172, 199, 613
Restatement 2nd § 90(1) 175
Restatement 2nd § 90(2) 171, 172, 824
Restatement 2nd § 95 176
Restatement 2nd § 112 204
Restatement 2nd § 112, cmt. c ...204
Restatement 2nd § 116 205
Restatement 2nd § 116, cmt. b, ill. 1 205
Restatement 2nd § 116, cmt. b, ill. 2 205

TABLE OF RESTATEMENT OF CONTRACTS

Restatement 2nd § 124 203
Restatement 2nd § 125 197
Restatement 2nd § 125, cmt. e 198
Restatement 2nd § 127 198
Restatement 2nd § 129 199
Restatement 2nd § 131 ...... 199, 202, 206
Restatement 2nd § 132 ...... 199, 203, 206
Restatement 2nd § 134 ...... 199, 202, 206
Restatement 2nd § 139 ...... 172, 214, 613
Restatement 2nd § 148 436
Restatement 2nd § 149 .... 189, 215
Restatement 2nd § 151 229
Restatement 2nd § 151, cmt. b 230
Restatement 2nd § 152 ...... 230, 231, 234
Restatement 2nd § 152(1) 230, 233
Restatement 2nd § 152(2) 231
Restatement 2nd § 153 235
Restatement 2nd § 154 ...... 231, 232, 233, 235, 236, 237
Restatement 2nd § 154, cmt. b 233
Restatement 2nd § 159 253
Restatement 2nd § 160 257
Restatement 2nd § 161(a) 257
Restatement 2nd § 161(b) 258
Restatement 2nd § 161(c) 258
Restatement 2nd § 161(d) 258
Restatement 2nd § 161, cmt. e, ill. 12 259
Restatement 2nd § 162(1) 260
Restatement 2nd § 162(2) 262
Restatement 2nd § 163 252
Restatement 2nd § 164 253
Restatement 2nd § 168(1) 253
Restatement 2nd § 168(2) 254
Restatement 2nd § 169 254
Restatement 2nd § 169(b) 255
Restatement 2nd § 172 263
Restatement 2nd § 174 241
Restatement 2nd § 175 242
Restatement 2nd § 176(1) 242, 246
Restatement 2nd § 176(1)(a) 242
Restatement 2nd § 176(1)(b) 242
Restatement 2nd § 176(1)(c) 242
Restatement 2nd § 176(1)(d) 158, 243
Restatement 2nd § 176(2) 244, 245, 246
Restatement 2nd § 176, cmt. f, ill. 16 245

Restatement 2nd § 177 247
Restatement 2nd § 177, cmt. a 248
Restatement 2nd § 177, cmt. b 248
Restatement 2nd § 178 273
Restatement 2nd § 200 .... 297, 299
Restatement 2nd § 201(1) 299
Restatement 2nd § 202(1) 304
Restatement 2nd § 202(3)(a) 299
Restatement 2nd § 202(4) 300
Restatement 2nd § 202(5) 302
Restatement 2nd § 203(a) 297
Restatement 2nd § 203(b) 300
Restatement 2nd § 203(c) 298
Restatement 2nd § 203(d) 298
Restatement 2nd § 204 .... 122, 125
Restatement 2nd § 205 ...... 146, 159, 174, 188, 335, 351, 371, 409, 620
Restatement 2nd § 208 .... 265, 266
Restatement 2nd § 209(1) 285
Restatement 2nd § 210 .... 286, 287
Restatement 2nd § 210(1) 285
Restatement 2nd § 210(2) 285
Restatement 2nd § 210(3) 286
Restatement 2nd § 213 286
Restatement 2nd § 213(1) 291
Restatement 2nd § 213(2) 291
Restatement 2nd § 214 287
Restatement 2nd § 215 286
Restatement 2nd § 216 .... 286, 288
Restatement 2nd § 216(2)(b) 289
Restatement 2nd § 216, cmt. d, ill. 5 290
Restatement 2nd § 217 292
Restatement 2nd § 218(2) 292
Restatement 2nd §§ 219–222 124
Restatement 2nd §§ 219–223 300
Restatement 2nd § 222 124
Restatement 2nd § 224 .... 324, 328
Restatement 2nd § 225 325
Restatement 2nd § 226 337
Restatement 2nd § 226, cmt. c ... 323
Restatement 2nd § 227(1) 332
Restatement 2nd § 227(2) 332
Restatement 2nd § 227, cmt. d, ill. 9 332
Restatement 2nd § 228, cmt. a 335
Restatement 2nd § 228, cmt. b 335
Restatement 2nd § 228, cmt. b, ill. 4 335
Restatement 2nd § 229 .... 329, 374
Restatement 2nd § 229, cmt. a, ill. 1 375
Restatement 2nd § 229, cmt. c, ill. 3 375
Restatement 2nd § 230 .... 326, 328

TABLE OF RESTATEMENT OF CONTRACTS

Restatement 2nd § 230(1)............326
Restatement 2nd § 233................124
Restatement 2nd § 234(1)..........340, 341, 381
Restatement 2nd § 234(2)..........340, 341, 381
Restatement 2nd § 235(1)...........342
Restatement 2nd § 235(2)...........342
Restatement 2nd § 237.......344, 347
Restatement 2nd § 237, cmt. d 353
Restatement 2nd § 238......338, 339, 342
Restatement 2nd § 240...............358
Restatement 2nd § 241.......350, 773
Restatement 2nd § 242......344, 360, 361, 363, 773
Restatement 2nd § 243......360, 361, 410
Restatement 2nd § 243(2)..........360, 363
Restatement 2nd § 243(3)..........364, 411
Restatement 2nd § 243(3), cmt. d, ill. 4.............................411
Restatement 2nd § 243(4)..........361
Restatement 2nd § 243, cmt. b, ill. 3 364
Restatement 2nd § 243, cmt. d 365
Restatement 2nd § 243, cmt. d, ill. 4 365
Restatement 2nd § 245.......372, 374
Restatement 2nd § 245, cmt. a 372
Restatement 2nd § 245, cmt. b 374
Restatement 2nd § 246...............369
Restatement 2nd § 250...............410
Restatement 2nd § 250(a)..........413
Restatement 2nd § 250(b)..........415
Restatement 2nd § 250, cmt. b, ill. 3 414
Restatement 2nd § 251(1)..........422
Restatement 2nd § 251(2)..........422
Restatement 2nd § 253...............422
Restatement 2nd § 253(1)..........409
Restatement 2nd § 256.......423, 424
Restatement 2nd § 256(1)..........422
Restatement 2nd § 257...............422
Restatement 2nd § 261......441, 442, 451, 452, 465
Restatement 2nd § 261, cmt. d, ill. 6 449
Restatement 2nd § 261, cmt. e 442
Restatement 2nd § 262...............446
Restatement 2nd § 263...............447

Restatement 2nd § 263, cmt. a, ill. 3 449
Restatement 2nd § 263, cmt. a, ill. 4 456
Restatement 2nd § 264...............448
Restatement 2nd § 265.......459, 465
Restatement 2nd § 266...............465
Restatement 2nd § 269...............466
Restatement 2nd § 277...............428
Restatement 2nd § 277(1)...........435
Restatement 2nd § 278.......427, 428
Restatement 2nd § 279.......427, 429
Restatement 2nd § 279(2)..........430
Restatement 2nd § 280...............429
Restatement 2nd § 281...............427
Restatement 2nd § 281(1)..........430
Restatement 2nd § 281(2)..........430
Restatement 2nd § 281(3)..........431
Restatement 2nd § 283...............434
Restatement 2nd § 283, cmt. a 435
Restatement 2nd § 283, cmt. b 435, 436
Restatement 2nd § 284.......428, 436
Restatement 2nd § 284, cmt. a 436
Restatement 2nd § 284, cmt. b 436
Restatement 2nd § 302.......478, 739
Restatement 2nd § 302(1)..........478, 482, 483, 487
Restatement 2nd § 302(1)(a) 479, 481
Restatement 2nd § 302(1)(b) 479
Restatement 2nd § 302(2)..........480
Restatement 2nd § 302, cmt. a 472
Restatement 2nd § 304...............478
Restatement 2nd § 306...............485
Restatement 2nd § 306, cmt. a 485
Restatement 2nd § 308...............484
Restatement 2nd § 311(3)..........495
Restatement 2nd § 313...............487
Restatement 2nd § 313, cmt. a 487
Restatement 2nd § 315...............478
Restatement 2nd § 317...............499
Restatement 2nd § 317(2)..........505
Restatement 2nd § 317(2)(a) 505, 506
Restatement 2nd § 317(2)(b) 505
Restatement 2nd § 317(2)(c)......505, 508
Restatement 2nd § 318...............527
Restatement 2nd § 318(1)..........529, 530
Restatement 2nd § 318(2)..........529, 530

TABLE OF RESTATEMENT OF CONTRACTS

Restatement 2nd § 318(3) 529, 535
Restatement 2nd § 318, cmt. a, ill. 1 531
Restatement 2nd § 318, cmt. c, ill. 5 531
Restatement 2nd § 322(1) 509
Restatement 2nd § 322(2)(a) 509
Restatement 2nd § 322(2)(b) 509
Restatement 2nd § 322(2)(c) 509
Restatement 2nd § 324 503
Restatement 2nd § 324, cmt. b 515
Restatement 2nd § 326 512
Restatement 2nd § 327(1) 510
Restatement 2nd § 327(2) 510
Restatement 2nd § 327, cmt. a, ill. 1 511
Restatement 2nd § 328 .... 515, 529
Restatement 2nd § 330 503
Restatement 2nd § 331 513
Restatement 2nd § 332(1) 523
Restatement 2nd § 333(1) 521
Restatement 2nd § 333(2) 521
Restatement 2nd § 336(1) 517
Restatement 2nd § 338 516
Restatement 2nd § 342 524
Restatement 2nd § 344 .... 568, 609
Restatement 2nd § 344(a) 568
Restatement 2nd § 344(b) 569
Restatement 2nd § 344(c) 570, 625
Restatement 2nd § 346(2) 575
Restatement 2nd § 347 .... 576, 579, 583
Restatement 2nd § 347(b) 573
Restatement 2nd § 347, cmt. a 546, 576
Restatement 2nd § 348 .... 583, 584
Restatement 2nd § 348(2)(b) 583
Restatement 2nd § 348, cmt. c 583
Restatement 2nd § 348, cmt. c, ill. 4 585
Restatement 2nd § 349 611
Restatement 2nd § 349, cmt. b 612
Restatement 2nd § 350 .... 583, 593, 605, 610, 612
Restatement 2nd § 350(2) 605, 609
Restatement 2nd § 351 593
Restatement 2nd § 351(1) 598
Restatement 2nd § 351(2)(a) 602
Restatement 2nd § 351(2)(b) 603
Restatement 2nd § 351(3) 613
Restatement 2nd § 352 .... 593, 595, 610, 611

Restatement 2nd § 352, cmt. a 594, 595
Restatement 2nd § 352, cmt. a, ill. 1 598
Restatement 2nd § 352, cmt. b, ill. 6 598
Restatement 2nd § 353 .... 613, 614, 615
Restatement 2nd § 354 622
Restatement 2nd § 354(1) 622
Restatement 2nd § 354(2) 623
Restatement 2nd § 355 .... 620, 621
Restatement 2nd § 356 .... 574, 615, 617
Restatement 2nd § 356(1) 617, 618
Restatement 2nd § 356, cmt. a 616
Restatement 2nd § 359 546
Restatement 2nd § 360 547
Restatement 2nd § 360(1) 547
Restatement 2nd § 360(2) 549
Restatement 2nd § 360(3) 551
Restatement 2nd § 360(3), cmt. d, ill. 9 551
Restatement 2nd § 360, cmt. b, ill. 1 544
Restatement 2nd § 360, cmt. b, ill. 4 548
Restatement 2nd § 360, cmt. b, ill. 5 548
Restatement 2nd § 362 .... 546, 552
Restatement 2nd § 362, cmt. b, ill. 1 553
Restatement 2nd § 363 .... 560, 563
Restatement 2nd § 364 546
Restatement 2nd § 364(1)(a) 560, 561
Restatement 2nd § 364(1)(b) 560, 561
Restatement 2nd § 364, cmt. a, ill. 1 561
Restatement 2nd § 365 .... 546, 559, 560
Restatement 2nd § 366 .... 546, 552, 553
Restatement 2nd § 366, cmt. a, ill. 1 554
Restatement 2nd § 366, cmt. a, ill. 3 554
Restatement 2nd § 367 546
Restatement 2nd § 367(1) 552, 555
Restatement 2nd § 367(2) 556
Restatement 2nd § 367, cmt. b, ill. 1 557
Restatement 2nd § 371 630
Restatement 2nd § 371(a) 628
Restatement 2nd § 371(b) 629

TABLE OF RESTATEMENT OF CONTRACTS

Restatement 2nd § 371,
  cmt. b 630, 639
Restatement 2nd § 373(2) 632, 633, 636
Restatement 2nd § 373, cmt. a ... 632
Restatement 2nd § 373, cmt. a, ill. 2 632
Restatement 2nd § 374 636
Restatement 2nd § 374, cmt. b 630
Restatement 2nd §§ 375–377 640
Restatement 2nd § 384 630
Restatement 2nd § 384(1) 631
Restatement 2nd § 384(2) 631

TABLE OF UCC SECTIONS

§ 1–103	802
§ 1–103(b)	215
§ 1–201(b)(3)	10
§ 1–201(b)(12)	9
§ 1–201(b)(37)	66, 207, 209
§ 1–201(b)(43)	66, 207
§ 1–201(35)	525
§ 1–201(37)	732, 780
§ 1–202	60, 88
§ 1–210(b)(3)	9
§ 1–303(a)	124, 313
§ 1–303(b)	124
§ 1–303(c)	124, 314
§ 1–303(e)	302, 315
§ 1–304	146, 159, 175, 187, 335, 371, 409, 620, 695
§ 1–305	546, 576
§ 1–305(a)	644, 653
§ 1–306	368, 369, 432
§ 1–309	365, 411
§ 2–101	674
§ 2–102	6, 674, 675, 677
§ 2–104(1)	66, 100, 209, 696
§ 2–105	676, 677, 679, 786
§ 2–107	679
§ 2–107(1)	679
§ 2–107(2)	679
§ 2–201	180, 181, 206, 208, 215, 772, 780, 785, 855
§ 2–201(1)	206, 207, 208, 209, 210, 211, 212, 732, 780, 785
§ 2–201(1)–(3)	206, 207
§ 2–201(2)	180, 206, 209, 210, 211, 731, 732, 780, 781, 785
§ 2–201(3)	180, 206, 209, 212, 213, 214, 215, 785
§ 2–201(3)(a)	212, 214, 785
§ 2–201(3)(b)	212, 732
§ 2–201(3)(c)	213
§ 2–201, cmt. 3	211, 214
§ 2–201, cmt. 4	216
§ 2–201, cmt. 7	212
§ 2–202	281, 309, 310, 312, 316, 694, 808
§ 2–202(2)	211
§ 2–202(a)	309
§ 2–202(b)	808
§ 2–202, cmt. 3	310, 808
§ 2–203	176
§ 2–204	122
§ 2–204(2)	21
§ 2–204(3)	118, 852
§ 2–205	25, 64, 66, 73, 735, 805
§ 2–206	35, 77, 81
§ 2–206(1)	82
§ 2–206(1)(a)	76, 78
§ 2–206(1)(b)	81, 82, 797
§ 2–206(2)	79, 80, 784
§ 2–206(3)	847, 848
§ 2R–206(3)	112, 788, 789, 798, 800, 802, 805, 807
§ 2–207	6, 91, 92, 93, 94, 95, 97, 98, 102, 105, 106, 108, 109, 770, 788, 798, 802, 804, 805, 847, 848
§ 2–207(1)	94, 95, 96, 97, 98, 99, 101, 102, 103, 105, 106, 107, 108, 110, 111, 788, 789, 798, 799, 800, 802, 804, 805, 807, 846, 848
§ 2–207(2)	94, 98, 99, 100, 102, 103, 104, 105, 107, 108, 109, 110, 781, 790, 805, 807, 848
§ 2–207(2)(a)	100, 101, 108, 781, 806
§ 2–207(2)(a)–(c)	110
§ 2–207(2)(b)	100, 101, 107, 108, 110, 781, 806
§ 2–207(2)(c)	100, 102, 104, 107, 108, 781, 806
§ 2–207(3)	94, 96, 99, 103, 105, 106, 109, 111, 112, 789, 790, 802, 846
§ 2–207(a)	104
§ 2–207(a)–(c)	104
§ 2–207, cmt. 4	101, 806
§ 2–207, cmts. 4 & 5	101, 781
§ 2–207, cmt. 5	101
§ 2–207, cmt. 6	103
§ 2R–207	6, 91, 782, 788, 789, 790, 798, 802, 805, 807
§ 2–209	177, 178, 182, 186, 187, 190
§ 2–209(1)	161, 162, 178, 179, 180, 185, 368, 737, 782, 790, 819
§ 2–209(2)	178, 180, 181, 190
§ 2–209(3)	178, 179, 180, 181, 189, 734
§ 2–209(4)	178, 181, 182, 183, 184, 190, 215, 735
§ 2–209(5)	179, 185, 186, 735
§ 2–210	532

TABLE OF UCC SECTIONS

§	Pages
§ 2–210(1)	530, 535
§ 2–210(3)	509, 515
§ 2–210(4)	529
§ 2–210, cmt. 4	819
§ 2R–213	88
§ 2–302	265, 266, 695, 809, 810
§ 2–302(1)	266
§ 2–305	119, 120, 312, 731, 732
§ 2–305(4)	120
§ 2–305, cmt. 1	120
§ 2–306(1)	150, 151, 152
§ 2–306(2)	147, 149
§ 2–307	119, 121
§ 2–307, cmt. 3	121
§ 2–308	119, 121, 803
§ 2–308(a)	790
§ 2–309	105, 119, 121, 803
§ 2–309(3)	156
§ 2–310	119, 803
§ 2–310(a)	121, 790, 853
§ 2–312	689
§ 2–313	675, 689, 690, 692
§ 2–313(1)	689, 691
§ 2–313(1)(a)	690
§ 2–313(1)(b)	690
§ 2–313(1)(c)	690
§ 2–313, cmt. 3	693
§ 2–313, cmt. 5	693
§ 2–314	9, 689, 790, 803
§ 2–314(1)	786
§ 2–314(2)(a)	697
§ 2–314(2)(b)	697
§ 2–314(2)(c)	697
§ 2–315	110, 112, 675, 689, 698
§ 2–316	645, 669, 695, 809
§ 2–316(1)	694, 695
§ 2–316(2)	697, 699
§ 2–316(3)(a)	697
§ 2–316(3)(b)	698, 700
§ 2–318	702, 703
§ 2–319	685
§§ 2–319–320	685
§ 2–319(1)(a)	685
§ 2–319(1)(b)	686
§ 2–319(2)	686
§ 2–320	686
§ 2–320(1)	687
§ 2–320(3)	687
§ 2–320, cmt. 1	686
§ 2–326(1)(a)	147
§ 2–326(1)(b)	147
§ 2–326(3)	147
§ 2–328	36
§ 2–328(3)	36, 37
§ 2–501	676
§ 2–501(1)(a)	676
§ 2–501(1)(b)	676, 677
§ 2–504	682
§ 2–507	380
§ 2–507(1)	380
§ 2–508	391, 393
§ 2–508(1)	390, 745, 787
§ 2–508(2)	390, 745, 787
§ 2–509(1)(a)	682, 683
§ 2–509(1)(b)	682, 683
§ 2–510	683
§ 2–510(1)	683
§ 2–510(2)	684
§ 2–510(3)	684
§ 2–511(1)	380, 381
§ 2–511(2)	381
§ 2–513	398
§ 2–601	380, 382, 383, 384, 401, 404, 683
§ 2–602(1)	399
§ 2–602(1)(a)	401
§ 2–602(1)(c)	401
§ 2–602(2)(a)	400
§ 2–602(2)(b)	399
§ 2–603(1)	400
§ 2–603(2)	400
§ 2–604	401
§ 2–606	397, 811
§ 2–606(1)(a)	398
§ 2–606(1)(b)	398, 399
§ 2–606(1)(c)	84, 398, 787, 802, 849
§ 2–606(b)	812
§ 2–606, cmt. 3	398
§ 2–607	786
§ 2–607(1)	398, 653, 654, 655, 657, 658
§ 2–607(2)	399
§ 2–607(3)	399, 700, 786
§ 2–607(4)	399
§ 2–608	397, 402, 404
§ 2–608(1)	402
§ 2–608(1)(a)	402, 403, 787, 812
§ 2–608(1)(b)	402, 403
§ 2–608(2)	402, 403
§ 2–608(3)	404
§ 2R–608(4)	787, 802
§ 2–609	394, 395, 416, 417, 418, 419, 420, 421, 745, 746, 783
§ 2–609(1)	421
§ 2–609, cmt. 1	418, 422
§ 2–609, cmt. 3	418
§ 2–609, cmt. 4	420, 421
§ 2–610	409, 416, 421, 422, 783
§ 2–610(1)(a)	422
§ 2–610(1)(c)	423
§ 2–610, cmt. 1	415
§ 2–610, cmt. 4	422
§ 2–611	423
§ 2–611(1)	422, 424
§ 2–612	392, 402, 683
§ 2–612(1)	392
§ 2–612(2)	392

TABLE OF UCC SECTIONS

§ 2–612(3) 394, 395
§ 2–612, cmt. 6 395
§ 2–613 .... 62, 442, 444, 445, 447, 448
§ 2–614(2) 448
§ 2–615 .... 441, 442, 450, 451, 452, 459, 466
§ 2–615, cmt. 4 782
§ 2–616 .... 450, 451
§ 2–703 657
§ 2–704 665
§ 2–704(2) 423
§ 2–706 .... 591, 659, 660, 662, 663
§ 2–706(1) 659, 660
§ 2–706(2)–(4) 659, 660
§ 2–708 662
§ 2–708(1) 591, 661, 662, 663, 665
§ 2–708(2) 592, 662, 663, 664, 665, 786, 831
§ 2–709(1) 657, 786
§ 2–709(1)(a) 656, 657, 658
§ 2–709(1)(b) 656, 658, 785
§ 2–710 .... 646, 657
§ 2–711 .... 589, 811
§ 2–711(1) 653, 656
§ 2–712 .... 589, 590, 647, 648, 649, 650, 653, 659, 783
§ 2–712(1) 647
§ 2–712(3) 653
§ 2–712, cmt. 2 648
§ 2–713 .... 589, 590, 647, 650, 651, 652, 653, 661, 783, 815, 816
§ 2–713(1) 650
§ 2–713(1)(a) 652
§ 2–713(2) 651, 652
§ 2–714 .... 405, 655, 704, 811
§ 2–714(1) 655
§ 2–714(2) 409, 590, 654, 655, 702, 705, 786
§ 2–714(3) 590, 654
§ 2–715 .... 644, 646
§ 2–715(1) 646, 649
§ 2–715(2) 644, 645
§ 2–715(2)(a) 603, 605, 644, 645, 702
§ 2–715(2)(b) 613, 644, 645, 702
§ 2–716 .... 550, 551, 641, 642, 659
§ 2–716(1) 641, 643, 835
§ 2–716, cmt. 1 641
§ 2R–716(1) 544
§ 2–717 .... 393, 655, 786
§ 2–718 615
§ 2–718(1) 574, 617, 665, 666
§ 2–719 .... 645, 666, 667, 669, 809
§ 2–719(1) 666
§ 2–719(1)(b) 666
§ 2–719(2) 667, 668, 810, 811
§ 2–719(3) 666, 809, 810
§ 2–723 409

§ 2–723(1) 650, 651, 661
§ 2–725(1) 675
§ 2A–101 675
§ 3–302 519
§ 3–302(a) 519
§ 3–305 519
§ 3–311 433
§ 3–311(a) 434
§ 3–311(b) 434
§ 3–311(c) 434
§ 9–204 505
§ 9–206(1) 818
§§ 9–302 et seq. 526
§ 9–322 526

TABLE OF CISG SECTIONS

Article 8(3) 295
Article 11 195
Article 14(1) 37, 124
Article 14(2) 37
Article 19 113
Article 19(1) 113
Article 19(2) 113
Article 19(3) 113
Article 29(2) 190
Article 35 704
Article 35(1) 704
Article 35(2) 704
Article 35(2)(a) 704
Article 35(2)(b) 704
Article 35(2)(d) 704
Article 66 684
Article 67(1) 684
Article 69 684
Article 70 685

INDEX

References are to section numbers

ACCEPTANCE OF OFFERS
See OFFER AND ACCEPTANCE

ACCEPTANCE OF GOODS UNDER THE UCC
Generally, 22–37
Distinguished from "Acceptance" of offers, 22–37
Effect, 22–38
Revocation of acceptance, generally, 22–45
Ways to accept, 22–37

ACCORD AND SATISFACTION
See ACCORDS

ACCORDS
See also MUTUAL RESCISSION, RELEASES, SUBSTITUTED CONTRACTS, and SUBSTITUTED PERFORMANCE
Generally, 24–9
Breach of accord, effect of, 24–9
By check to compromise debt, 24–12 et seq.
Consideration, 24–13
Determination whether an agreement is an accord, 24–17
Distinguished from:
    mutual rescission, 24–24
    releases, 24–26
    substituted contract, 24–17
    third party beneficiary contracts, 26–49
Effect on original obligation, 24–9
Satisfaction, 24–9

ACCELERATION CLAUSE, 21–90

ADHESION CONTRACT, 16–12

ADVERTISEMENT
Characterized as a solicitation to make an offer, 3–18
Distinguished from offer, 3–18

ALEATORY PROMISES, 7–63

ALTERNATE PERFORMANCE CLAUSES
Distinguished from liquidated damage clauses, 30–86

"AMERICAN" RULE OF DAMGES IN BREACH OF REAL ESTATE CONTRACTS, 30–38

ANTICIPATORY BREACH
See ANTICIPATORY REPUDIATION

ANTICIPATORY REPUDIATION
Generally, Chapter 23
Bilateral Contract, Requirements of, 23–5
Conduct, repudiation by, 23–16
Effect, 23–2, 23–20, 23–31
Elements necessary to establish in non-UCC transactions, 23–4 et seq.
UCC transactions, 23–20 et seq.
Historical background, 23–2
Hochster case, 23–2
Reasonable assurances:
    acceptable responses to, 23–27 et seq.
    effect of failure to provide, 23–22
    elements, 23–22
    grounds to demand, 23–23 et seq.
Repudiation:
    distinguished from good faith difference of opinion, 23–15
    request for modification, 23–14
Retraction, 23–32
Suspend performance, right to, 23–28, 23–31
Words, repudiation by, 23–13

ANTI-ASSIGNMENT CLAUSE, 27–21

ANTI-DELEGATION CLAUSE, 28–16

APPLICABILITY OF ARTICLE 2 OF THE UCC TO A CONTRACT
See also UNIFORM COMMERCIAL CODE
Generally, Chapter 33

ASSIGNMENT OF RIGHTS
See also DELEGATION OF DUTIES
Generally, Chapter 27
After-acquired property clauses, 27–14

INDEX

Anti-assignment clause, effect of, 27–21
Assignee, defined, 27–2
Assignee "stands in the shoes" of the assignor, 27–42 et seq.
Assignee's rights against assignor, 27–49
Assignee's rights against obligor, 27–2, 27–40, 27–52
Assignment for value, defined, 27–8
"Assignment of contract" clause, effect of, 27–36, 28–6
Assignor, defined, 27–2
Claims of obligor in a suit against assignee, 27–42
Competing claims of assignees for same right:
    generally, 27–55 et seq.
    "English Rule," 27–58
    first to file and perfect rule, 27–62
    "Massachusetts Rule," 27–60
    "New York Rule," 27–56
    Restatement Rule, 27–60
    UCC approach, 27–62
Conditional, 27–31
Defenses of obligor in suit by assignee, 27–42
Defined, 27–2
Discharge of duties by obligor, 27–2, 27–40
Distinguished from:
    contracts to assign, 27–11
    third party beneficiary contracts, 26–52
Duties of obligor after valid assignment, 27–40
Elements for effective assignment, 27–10
"English Rule," regarding priority among competing assignments, 27–58
First to file approach, regarding priority among competing assignments, 27–62
Gratuitous assignment, defined, 27–5
Holder in due course, 27–44 et seq.
Limitations on right to assign, 27–15 et seq.
    material effect on obligor, 27–17
    "no assignment," clause, 27–21
    public policy, 27–16
"Massachusetts Rule," regarding priority among competing assignments, 27–60
Modification by assignee and obligor, 27–52 et seq.
    assignments for value, 27–53
    gratuitous assignments, 27–54
"New York" rule, regarding priority among competing assignments, 27–56
"No assignment" clause, effect of, 27–21
Notification to assignee, requirement of, 27–22
Notification to obligor, 27–28

Obligor:
    defined, 27–2
    discharge of duties where performance rendered to assignee, 27–40
    discharge of duties where performance rendered to assignor, 27–40
    duties of, 27–40
Option contracts, assignment of rights under, 4–10 et seq.
Oral, effectiveness of and interaction with Statute of Frauds, 27–38
Partial, 27–29
Revocability, 27–52 et seq.
Rights to Accept Offers, Assignment of, 4–8
Terminology, 27–2
Third party beneficiary contracts, relationship to, 26–52, 27–33
Warranties made in assignments for value, 27–49 et seq.
Writing, when required, 27–38

AUCTIONS
See OFFER AND ACCEPTANCE

BATTLE OF THE FORMS
Generally, Chapter 5
Under the CISG
    See CISG

BENEFICIARIES
See THIRD PARTY BENEFICIARY CONTRACTS

BEST EFFORTS
Illusory promises, effect on, 7–56, 7–52
Implied in:
    exclusive dealing contracts, 7–52
    output contracts, 7–56
    requirements contracts, 7–56

BILATERAL CONTRACTS
Anticipatory Repudiation, Necessity of, 23–5
Consideration for, 7–18, 7–6, 7–9
Constructive conditions of exchange under, 21–44
Defined, 1–16
Formed upon beginning performance under unilateral offer, 4–83
Material Breach, Necessity for, 21–62
Offers to enter into, 3–28

BREACH OF CONTRACT
    See also PERFORMANCE
    Generally Chapters, 21, 22, 23
Anticipatory repudiation as, 23–2, 23–20, 20–31
Consequences of, 21–60
Constructive conditions of exchange, relation to, 21–44 et seq., 21–58, 21–61, 22–2, 22–7 et seq.

INDEX

Definition, 21–55
Determining whether breach is material or partial, 21–56, 22–7 et seq.
Determining which party is in breach, 21–44, 21–60, 21–62, 21–66
Determining which party must perform first, 21–50, 22–2
Distinction between material and immaterial breach, when applicable, 21–62
Effect of breach, 21–60
Excuse of condition by, 21–92
First material breach doctrine, 21–66
Immaterial breach:
    constructive conditions of exchange, relationship with, 21–56
    defined, 21–57
    effect of declaring a breach "immaterial," 21–60
    substantial performance doctrine, 21–68
    turning material breach into immaterial breach by:
        cure, 21–77
        divisibility, 21–73
        part performance, 21–73
        waiver, 21–79
Material breach:
    anticipatory repudiation, relationship with, 23–2, 23–20, 23–31
    constructive conditions of exchange, relationship with, 21–55
    defined, 21–58
    determining whether breach is material or immaterial, 21–61, 21–56, 21–65 et seq.
    effect of declaring a breach "material," 21–60
    immaterial breach followed by repudiation constituting, 21–87
    material breach becoming partial breach, 21–72 et seq.
    material breach becoming total breach, 21–59, 21–87
    suspension of performance as a result of, 21–60
    "time is of the essence" clause, effect of, 21–86
    under the perfect tender rule, 22–7 et seq.
    when important to determine if breach is "material," 21–62
Partial breach
    See immaterial breach, above
Perfect tender rule:
    generally, 22–7 et seq.
    defined, 22–7
    effect, 22–7
    limitations, 22–11 et seq.
        course of dealing, 22–33
        course of performance, 22–33
        cure by seller, 22–12
        de minimus non curat lex, 22–30
        installment contracts, 22–23
        revocation of acceptance, 22–35
        usage of trade, 22–33
    relationship with material breach, 22–7
    statement of rule, 22–7
    when it applies, 22–7
Restitution available upon material breach, 21–91, 31–1, 31–4
    to the breaching party, 31–28
    to the non-breaching party, 31–21
Substantial performance doctrine, 21–68
Tender:
    generally, 21–47
    defined, 21–48
    of delivery, 22–3
    of payment, 22–5
    of performance, 22–2
    requirement of to trigger enforceable obligations, 21–47, 22–2
"Time is of the essence" clause, effect of, 21–86
Total breach:
    defined, 21–59
    when material breach becomes total breach, 21–56, 21–82
Under the UCC, generally, 22–1

"BROOKLYN BRIDGE" HYPOTHETICAL, 4–81 et seq.

BUILDING CONTRACTS
See CONSTRUCTION CONTRACTS

CAPACITY
See INCAPACITY

CATALOGUES
Distinguished from offers, 3–18

C & F, AS MERCANTILE TERM, 34–16

C.I.F., AS MERCANTILE TERM, 34–15

CISG
Applicability, 33–14
"Battle of the forms," 5–34
Indefiniteness, 6–27
Modification, 9–27
Offers, 3–38
Overview, 1–8
Parol Evidence Rule, 18–32
Risk of loss, 34–10
Warranties, 35–25

INDEX

COGNITION THEORY, 11–15

COMMERCIAL IMPRACTICABILITY
See IMPRACTICABILITY

COMMON LAW DECISION MAKING, 1–2

CONDITIONS
Generally, Chapter 21, 21–44, Chapter 23
Breach:
    As excuse for enforcing condition, 21–102
    Relationship with constructive conditions, 21–55
Constructive concurrent conditions:
    generally, 21–21, 21–50
    under UCC, 22–2
Constructive conditions, generally:
    defined, 21–8
    effect, 21–8, 21–44 et seq., 22–2 et seq.
    no strict construction rule, 21–24
Constructive conditions of ex-change:
    concurrent conditions, 21–21, 21–50, 22–2
    defined, 21–21
    immaterial breach, relationship to, 21–55, 21–57
    material breach, relationship to, 21–55, 21–58
    one party's performance constructively conditioned on there being no outstanding uncured material breach of the other, 21–58
    use to determine:
        material breach 21–55 et seq.
        order of performance, 21–50 et seq., 22–2, 22–6
Disproportionate forfeiture, as excuse for enforcing condition, 21–107
Effect of classifying a condition as precedent or subsequent, 21–17 et seq.
Excuses for enforcing conditions:
    generally, 21–92
    to avoid disproportionate forfeiture, 21–107
    waiver, 21–93
    wrongful non-cooperation, prevention, and hindrance, 21–102
Express conditions:
    defined, 21–4
    effect, 21–22
    strict construction rule, 21–23
        applies even in the absence of materiality, 21–24
        effect of reasonableness, 21–24
Forfeiture, disproportionate as excuse for enforcing condition, 21–107
Implied-in-fact conditions:
    defined, 21–6
    effect, 21–7
Implied-in-law conditions
    See Constructive Conditions, above
Interpretation, rules of applied to whether promise is subject to condition precedent or is unconditional, 21–27 et seq.
Order of performance, 21–50 et seq.
    under UCC, 22–6
Parol evidence rule, effect of condition precedent on, 18–22
Precedent:
    defined, 21–11
    distinguished from condition subsequent, 21–10 et seq.
    effect of construing condition as precedent rather than subsequent, 21–17, 21–13
    effect of construing promise as being subject to condition precedent versus being unconditional, 21–27
Promise/Duty:
    conditional, 21–27
    determining if conditional or unconditional, 21–27 et seq.
        rules of interpretation, 21–27
    effect of construction as being subject to a condition precedent, 21–12
    unconditional, 21–27 et seq.
Simultaneous performance, 21–47
    under UCC, 22–2
Strict construction rule applied to express conditions, 21–23
Strict construction rule not applied to constructive conditions, 21–24
Subsequent:
    defined, 21–15
    distinguished from condition precedent, 21–10 et seq.
    effect of construing condition as "subsequent" rather than precedent, 21–19
Types:
    concurrent, 21–21
    condition precedent, 21–11
    condition subsequent, 21–15
    constructive, 21–44
    express, 21–4
    implied-in-fact, 21–6
    implied-in-law, 21–8
Waiver:
    and modification, 9–10
    as excuse for enforcing condition, 21–93
    establishing, 21–93

INDEX

retraction, 9–16, 21–94
election, 21–97

CONDUCT
Anticipatory Repudiation by, 23–16
Contract by, 1–18, 5–23 et seq.
Ratification of contract entered into as minor by, 11–4
Ratification of contract entered into by mentally infirm by, 11–21 et seq.

CONSIDERATION
Generally, Chapter 7
Accords 24–9
    modern view, 24–12
Acts incidental to gift promises insufficient, 7–27
Adequacy of, 7–43
Aleatory promises, 7–63
Bilateral contracts, 7–7, 7–18, 7–6, 7–9
Defined, 7–2 et seq.
    bargain theory, 7–7
    benefit/detriment theory, 7–4
    criticism of definitions, 7–11
    will theory, 7–3
Exclusive dealing contracts, 7–52
Good faith, use with illusory promises, 7–47 et seq.
Gratuitous/gift promises, 7–23 et seq.
    acts incidental to gift promises, 7–27
Illusory promises:
    implied promises used to make enforceable:
        best efforts, 7–52
        good faith, 7–49
    in contracts with termination-at-will clauses, 7–66 et seq.
    modern view, 7–69
    UCC approach, 7–70
    in contracts with expressly conditional promises, 7–60
    in exclusive dealing contracts, 7–52
    in output contracts, 7–56
    in requirements contracts, 7–56
Implied best efforts promise, 7–52
Implied promise of good faith, 7–47 et seq.
Inadequate consideration, 7–43
    as evidence of fraud, duress, undue influence, 7–44
    as evidence of sham consideration, 7–45
    "peppercorn" theory, 7–43
Illusory promises, 7–47 et seq.
    modern approach, 7–49
    traditional approach, 7–48
Merchant's Firm Offer, 4–78
Modification of contracts, necessity of, 7–82, 9–3, 9–20
Moral obligation:
    generally, 7–30 et seq.
    Restatement 2d approach, 7–33
    traditional approach, 7–31
Option contracts, 4–8, 7–94
Output contracts:
    defined, 7–56
    implied ceiling, 7–58
    implied duty of good faith to make enforceable, 7–56
    implied floor, 7–58
Parol evidence rule, and unperformed consideration, 18–23
Past consideration:
    Restatement 2d approach, 7–33
    traditional approach, 7–30 et seq.
Past debts, 7–38, 24–12
Peppercorn theory, 7–43
Personal Satisfaction Clauses, 7–48 et seq.
Pre-existing duty rule, 7–71, 24–13
Promise as, 7–18 et seq.
Promise given to third party as, 7–20
Promises made unenforceable by bankruptcy or statute of limitations, enforceability of, 7–38
Promissory estoppel as "substitute" for, 8–2
Purported consideration, 4–77, 7–91
Requirements contracts:
    defined, 7–56
    implied ceiling, 7–58
    implied duty of good faith, 7–56
    implied floor, 7–58
Seal as substitute for, 8–20
Sham consideration, 7–45
"Substitutes" for, 8–2, 8–20
Third parties, promises made to, 7–20
Treatment under modern contract law, 7–10
Unilateral contracts, 7–5, 7–8, 7–12
Voidable promises as, 7–92

CONTRACTS
Defined:
    Restatement 2d, 1–10
    UCC, 1–11
    where different definitions would produce different results, 1–12
Elements, 1–13
Sources of contract law, 1–1 et seq.
Types:
    accords, 24–9
    assignments, 27–1 et seq.
    bilateral, 1–16
    delegations, 28–1 et seq.
    destination, 34–5
    exclusive dealing, 7–52
    express, 1–17
    implied-in-fact, 1–18
    implied-in-law, 1–20
    installment, 22–23
    novation, 24–5
    option, 4–74
    output, 7–56

quasi, 1–20
requirements, 7–56
shipment, 34–4
substituted contracts, 24–5
substituted performance, 24–2
third party beneficiary, 26–1 et. seq.
unilateral, 1–15

CONSTRUCTION CONTRACTS
Damages for Breach:
    breach by builder, 30–32
    breach by owner, 30–36
    special "lost value" calculation rules, 30–32
Frustration, applied to, 25–50
Impossibility, applied to, 25–25
Impracticability, applied to, 25–34, 25–37, 25–42
Losing contract, 30–47, 30–70, 31–23
Mistake in bid, 12–23
Offer by subcontractor to general contractor temporarily irrevocable, 4–86
Progress payments, 30–36
Substantial performance, 21–70, 30–35
Third party beneficiary contracts, contractor/subcontractor relationship, 26–30

CONSTRUCTIVE CONDITIONS OF EXCHANGE
See CONDITIONS

COUNTER-OFFER
See OFFER AND ACCEPTANCE

COURSE OF DEALING
Defined, 20–13
Indefiniteness, as cure for, 6–26
Interpretation, as aid to, 19–13
Parol evidence rule, relationship to, 20–9
Perfect tender rule, effect on, 22–33

COURSE OF PERFORMANCE
Defined, 20–10
Indefiniteness, as cure for, 6–26
Interpretation, as aid to, 19–13
Parol evidence rule, relationship to, 20–9
Perfect tender rule, effect on, 22–33

COVER
As remedy for buyer:
    defined, 32–12
    formula for recovery, 32–13, 30–41
As remedy for seller:
    defined, 32–35
    formula for recovery, 32–36, 30–41

CROSS-OFFERS, 4–5

CURE
Cash discount, cure by, 22–18
Defined, 21–77, 22–12
Effect, 21–77, 22–12 et seq.
Material breach, relationship to, 21–77
Money discount, cure by, 22–18
Perfect tender rule, relationship to, 22–12
Repair, cure by, 22–18
Replacement, cure by, 22–18
Seller's right to, 22–13
Total breach, relationship to, 21–78
Under UCC, 22–12
    buyer's duty to permit cure, 22–22
    in cases where buyer rejects, 22–12 et seq.
    in cases where buyer revokes acceptance, 22–51
    seller's right to cure after the "time for performance" has passed, 22–15
    seller's right to cure before the "time for performance" has passed, 22–13

DAMAGES
See also EQUITABLE REMEDIES, RESTITUTION
Generally, Chapters 30 and 32
Avoidability doctrine as limitation on recovery, 30–59
Benefit of the bargain damages, defined, 30–11, 30–17, 30–28
Buyer's damages:
    breach of warranty, 30–43, 32–24
    cover damages, 30–41, 32–13
    market differential damages, 30–44, 32–15
Certainty requirement as limitation on recovery, 30–49
    lost profits from collateral transactions, 30–51
    modern rules regarding certainty, 30–50
Consequential damages:
    defined, 30–12
    foreseeability test, 30–54 et seq.
    Hadley v. Baxendale, rule of, 30–53
    incidental loss as, 30–29
    lost profits as, 30–51, 30–57
    under UCC, 32–9
Construction contracts:
    breach by builder, 30–32
    breach by owner, 30–36
    special rules for calculating "lost value," 30–32
Cost avoided, defined, 30–28
Cover damages, buyer:
    defined, 32–12
    formula, 30–41, 32–12
Cover damages, seller:
    defined, 32–35
    formula, 30–44, 32–36
Direct damages:
    defined, 30–14
    foreseeability requirement, 30–54

INDEX

measure for breach of warranty, 30–43, 32–24
"ordinary course of events," 30–57
"Duty" to mitigate, 30–59
Emotional distress damages:
    general rule, 30–75, 30–76
    under UCC, 32–50
    where breach "particularly likely" to result in emotional distress, 30–79
    where breach results in personal injury, 30–76
Employment contracts:
    breach by employee, 30–31
    breach by employer, 30–30
Exemplary damages, defined, 30–16
    recoverability, 30–87
Expectation damages:
    avoidability, as limitation, 30–59
    calculation, 30–29
    certainty, as limitation, 30–49
    consequential damages, as component, 30–28, 30–29, 32–9
    construction contracts, 30–32, 30–36
    costs avoided, as component, 30–28, 30–29
    employment contracts, 30–30, 30–31
    foreseeability, as limitation, 30–54
    formula, general, 30–28, 30–29
    Hadley v. Baxendale, rule of, 30–55
    incidental damage, as component, 30–28, 30–29, 32–10
    land sale contracts, 30–37, 30–38
    limitations on recovery, 30–48 et seq.
    losing contract situations, 30–47
    loss avoided, as component, 30–28, 30–29
    lost value, as component, 30–28
Expectation interest defined, 30–4
General damages, defined, 30–18
Incidental damages:
    as consequential damage, 30–28, 30–29, 32–10
    defined, 30–19
    under UCC, 32–10
"Interest" analysis, 30–1
    expectation interest, defined, 30–4
    reliance interest, defined, 30–6
    restitution interest, defined, 30–8
Land sale contracts:
    "American Rule," 30–38
    breach by buyer, 30–37
    breach by seller, 30–38
    "English Rule," 30–38
Limitation of remedy clauses
    See LIMITATION OF REMEDIES
Limitations on recovery:
    avoidability, 30–59
    certainty, 30–49
    foreseeability, 30–54
Liquidated damages:
    defined, 30–21, 30–80
    distinguished from alternative performance clauses, 30–86
    standards for enforceable provision, 30–81, 32–49
    under UCC 32–49
Loss avoided, defined, 30–28
Lost value, defined, 30–28
Lost volume seller, 30–46, 32–46
Mitigation
    See Avoidability, above
Nominal damages:
    availability upon breach, 30–22
    defined, 30–22
Out-of-Pocket damages, defined, 30–10–30–23
Punitive damages:
    bad faith breach, 30–88
    commercial contracts, 30–88
    defined, 30–16, 30–24
    general rule, 30–87
    insurance contracts, 30–88
    under UCC, 32–50
    when breach is also a tort, 30–87
Reliance damages:
    generally, 30–65
    availability, 30–25
    certainty, as limitation, 30–69
    defined, 30–6, 30–25
    formula for recovering, 30–65
    limitations on recovery, 30–68 et seq.
    losing contract, effect on recovery, 30–70
    loss avoided, as limitation, 30–72
Reliance Interest, defined, 30–6
Restitution
    See RESTITUTION
Restitution interest, defined, 30–8
Seller's damages:
    cover, 30–44, 32–35, 32–36
    full contract price, 32–29
    lost profit, 32–45
    lost volume, 32–46
    market differential, 32–35 et seq.
Special damages, 30–26
Stipulated damages, defined, 30–27
Under UCC:
    buyer's breach of warranty recovery, 30–43, 32–24
    buyer's cover damages, 30–41, 32–12
    buyer's market differential damages, 30–41, 32–12, 32–15 et seq.
    consequential economic loss, 32–9
    consequential personal injury and personal property loss, 32–9
    emotional distress, 30–50

INDEX

incidental damages, 32–10
liquidated damages, 32–49
lost volume seller, 30–46, 32–46
punitive damages, 32–50
seller's cover damages, 30–45, 32–35
seller's lost profit recovery, 30–46, 32–45
seller's market differential damages, 30–44, 32–38
warranty damages, 32–23

DEATH
Of offeree:
  effect on irrevocable offer, 4–87
  effect on revocable offer, 4–64
Of offeror:
  effect on irrevocable offer, 4–87
  effect on revocable offer, 4–64
Of the party performing a specialized task in a personal services contract, 25–17
Of thing essential to performance of contract other than offeree or offeror, 4–71, 4–87

DELEGATION OF DUTIES
  See also ASSIGNMENT OF RIGHTS
Generally, Chapter 28
Anti-assignment clauses, effect of, 28–16
"Assignment of contract" clause, 28–6
Assumption of duty by delegate, 28–25, 28–31
Delegate, defined, 28–2
Delegating party, defined, 28–2
Delegator, defined, 28–2
Discharge of delegating party's duties upon performance of delegate, 28–23
Distinguished from novation, 28–31
Duties of delegate upon valid delegation, 28–19
Duties of delegating party after valid delegation, 28–19, 28–22
Elements of effective delegation, 28–4
Limitations on right to delegate:
  "no delegation" clause, 28–16
  public policy, 28–9
  substantial interest in performance by the obligor, 28–10
"No delegation" clauses, 28–16
Non-delegable duties, 28–10
Notification to obligee, 28–17
Novation, relationship with, 28–31
Obligee, defined, 28–2
Obligor, defined, 28–2
Rights of delegate after valid delegation, 28–19 et seq.
Terminology, 28–2
Third party beneficiary contracts, relationship with, 28–28

DEPENDENT PROMISES
Determination of, in contracts with two limitation of remedy clauses, 32–54

DESTINATION CONTRACT, 34–5

DETRIMENTAL RELIANCE
See PROMISSORY ESTOPPEL

DISCHARGE OF DUTIES
See ACCORDS, BREACH, FRUSTRATION OF PERFORMANCE, IMPOSSIBILITY, IMPRACTICABILITY, MODIFICATION, MUTUAL RESCISSION, NOVATION, PERFORMANCE, SUBSTITUTED CONTRACT, SUBSTITUTED PERFORMANCE, WAIVER

DOMESTIC SITUATION
Presumption against intent to contract, 2–6

DURESS
Generally, Chapter 13
Improper threat, compulsion by, 13–3 et seq.
  when terms appear fair, 13–5
  when terms are unfair, 13–10
Parol evidence rule, relationship with, 18–25
Physical compulsion, duress by, 13–2
Restitution allowed, 13–15

"DUTY" TO MITIGATE, 30–59

"EFFICIENT BREACH" DOCTRINE, 30–2

ELECTION
Waiver, relationship to, 21–97

ELEMENTS OF A CONTRACT, 1–13

"ENGLISH" RULE
Regarding damage recovery in seller breaches of land sale contracts, 30–38
Regarding multiple assignee claims for the same assigned right, 27–58

EQUAL PUBLICITY RULE, 4–23

EQUITABLE REMEDIES
  See also DAMAGES, RESTITUTION
Generally, Chapter 29, 32–2
Adequacy of damages, element of, 29–8
Difficulty of proving damages with reasonable certainty, 29–9
Inadequacy of damages as remedy, element of, 29–8
Injunction, 29–2

INDEX

Limitations on equitable relief:
    public policy, 29–32 et seq.
    risk of non-performance by non-breaching party, 29–39
    unfair business practices by non-breaching party, 29–35
    unreasonable hardship to breaching party, 29–37
Personal service contracts, 29–27
Practical limitations on equitable relief:
    disproportionate supervisory burden on court, 29–20, 29–23
    personal service contracts, 29–27
    terms of contract sufficiently uncertain, 29–21
Public policy limitations, 29–33
Real estate contracts, 29–13, 30–38
Replevin, 32–7
Requirements to obtain, 29–7 et seq.
    adequacy of money damages, 29–8
    difficulty of procuring adequate substitute performance, 29–13
    likelihood of collectible damages, 29–18
Specific performance, 29–3, 32–3
Types, 29–2
Under UCC:
    generally, 32–1
    replevin, 32–7
    specific performance, 32–3
Uniqueness of goods, 29–13, 32–3

EMPLOYMENT CONTRACTS
Damages for breach:
    breach by employee, 30–31
    breach by employer, 30–30
    emotional distress damages, 30–75 et seq.
Delegability of, 28–10
Incidental loss recoverable, 30–30
One year provision of statute of frauds, 10–14
Restitutionary recovery for breach of, 31–30
Specific performance, availability upon breach, 29–27 et seq.
Wrongful termination, 30–79

EXCLUSIVE DEALING CONTRACTS
Defined, 7–52
Implied "best efforts" promise to avoid illusory promise issue, 7–52

EXPECTATION DAMAGES
See DAMAGES

EXPRESS CONTRACTS
Defined, 1–17

EXPRESS WARRANTIES
See WARRANTIES

FACT
Distinguished from:
    opinion, 15–8
    prediction, 15–11
    puffing, 15–14
    statement of future intention, 15–12
    trade talk, 15–14
Express warranty claim, necessity of factual representation, 35–2, 35–3
Misrepresentation claim, necessity of factual representation, 15–7 et seq.
Mistake, necessity of mistaken belief as to existing fact, 12–2, 12–3
Mistake of law being mistake of fact, 12–4

FAMILY SETTING
Presumption against assent to contract in, 2–6

F.A.S., AS MERCANTILE TERM, 34–13

F.O.B., AS MERCANTILE TERM, 34–12

"FOUR CORNERS" TEST FOR INTERPRETATION, 18–9

FRAUD
See MISREPRESENTATION

FRUSTRATION OF PURPOSE
    See also IMPOSSIBILITY, IMPRACTICABILITY
    Generally, 25–45
Acceptance of the doctrine by American courts, 25–45
Buyer's defense, 25–45
Coronation cases, 25–56
Defined, 25–45
Destruction:
    of leased property, 25–50
    of partially completed building, 25–25
Elements necessary to establish the defense, 25–46 et seq.
In existence at time of making of contract, 25–59
Landlord/tenant cases, 25–50, 25–56, 25–57
Mistake, relation to, 25–59
Restitution permitted upon establishing, 25–65
Supervening, 25–59
Temporary, 25–60
Test for "frustration," 25–47

GAP FILLERS
See INDEFINITENESS

GENERAL OFFERS
Acceptance Problems under, 4–2
Defined, 3–32, 4–2

INDEX

GOOD FAITH
Implied in every contract, 7–49, 7–52, 7–56, 30–87
In exclusive dealing contracts, 7–52
In illusory promise cases, 7–49
In output contracts, 7–56
In requirement contracts, 7–56

"GRAVAMEN" TEST FOR UCC APPLICABILITY, 33–12

HOLDER IN DUE COURSE
Assignments, relationship with, 27–44 et seq.
Defined, 27–45
Elements to become, 27–45
Effect of becoming, 27–46
Limitations on applicability, 27–48

ILLEGALITY
Generally, Chapter 17
Definition, 17–2
Divisibility, as escape from effects of, 17–26
Enforceability:
    general rule, 17–17
    innocent party unaware of illegality, 17–18
    statute designed to protect a particular class, 17–20
In pari delicto doctrine, 17–23
Locus poenitentiae doctrine, 17–25
Part performance, 17–26
Restitutionary recovery in illegal contracts general rule, 17–23
    in pari delicto doctrine, 17–23
    locus poenitentiae doctrine, 17–25
    retraction by party, 17–25
Severability, 17–26
Types of illegal contracts, 17–3 et seq.
    bribery, 17–6
    criminal acts, contracts for, 17–4
    gambling contracts, 17–5
    release of tort liability, contract for, 17–8
    seller knows of buyer's illegal purpose, 17–13
    services provided by licensed parties, 17–10
"Void" contract, 17–1
Voidable contracts, 17–18, 17–20

IMMATERIAL BREACH
See BREACH

IMPLIED-IN-FACT CONTRACTS
Based on exchange of forms, 5–23
Defined, 1–18

IMPLIED-IN-LAW CONTRACTS
Defined, 1–20
Restitution available for breach of, 31–31

IMPLIED WARRANTY OF FITNESS FOR A PARTICULAR PURPOSE
See WARRANTIES

IMPLIED WARRANTY OF MERCHANTABILITY
See WARRANTIES

IMPOSSIBILITY
    See also IMPRACTICABILITY, FRUSTRATION OF PURPOSE
Generally, 25–3
Acceptance by American courts, 25–3
Caused by:
    crop destruction, 25–11
    death or destruction of thing necessary for performance, 25–20
    death or incapacity of a party, 25–17
    failure of subject matter to come into existence, 25–20
    government regulation, 25–23
    labor strikes, 25–27
Construction/repair contracts, 25–25
Defined, 25–3
Distinguished from: impracticability, 25–3, 25–31, 25–44
Elements necessary to establish the defense, 25–4 et seq.
In existence at the time the contract was made, 25–49
Mistake, relation to, 25–59
"Objective" impossibility, 25–5
Partial, 25–29
Personal services contracts, 25–17
Restitution permitted upon establishing, 25–64
Seller's doctrine, 25–3
"Subjective" impossibility, 25–5
Supervening, 25–49
Temporary, 25–60
Test for "impossibility," 25–5

IMPRACTICABILITY
    See also IMPOSSIBILITY, FRUSTRATION OF PURPOSE
Generally, 25–31
Acceptance by the American courts, 25–31
Alcoa case, 25–43
Construction cases, 25–34 et seq.
Defined, 25–31
Distinguished from impossibility, 25–3, 25–31, 25–44
Elements necessary to establish the defense, 25–32 et seq.
In existence at time contract was made, 25–49

INDEX

Restitution permitted upon establishing, 25–64
Seller's remedy, 25–3
Supervening, 25–49
Temporary, 25–60
Test for "impracticability," 25–32

INCAPACITY
Generally, Chapter 11
Due to:
    drug use, 11–24
    intoxication, 11–24
    mental incapacity, 11–15
        disaffirmance of contract by mentally incompetent, 11–24 et seq.
        ratification, 11–21
        restitution on disaffirmance general rule, 11–16
    minority, See Minors, below
Minors, 11–2 et seq.
    disaffirmance of contract by minor, 11–8 et seq.
    misrepresentation of age, 11–13
    ratification, 11–4 et seq.
        express, 11–5
        implied-in-fact, 11–6
        implied-in-law, 11–7
        silence upon reaching majority, effect of, 11–7
    restitution upon disaffirmance by minor:
        cash sales, 11–11
        credit sales, 11–9, 11–10
        for necessities, 11–12
        "New Hampshire" rule, 11–10
Of offeree under irrevocable offer, 4–87
Of offeree under revocable offer, 4–67
Of offeror under irrevocable offer, 4–87
Of offeror under revocable offer, 4–64
Of thing essential to performance of contract other than offeree or offeror, 4–87
Temporary, 11–24

INDEFINITENESS
Generally, Chapter 6
Agreed upon term too ambiguous, 6–6
Agreement to agree cases, 6–7
CISG
    See CISG
Common law rule, 6–10
Course of dealing as cure, 6–26
Course of performance as cure, 6–26
Defined, 6–1
Distinguished from failure to make a contract, 6–8
Essential terms, requirement of agreement upon, 6–9
Failure to agree as to a term, 6–5

Gap fillers:
    generally, 6–12, et seq.
    mode of delivery, 6–18
    place of delivery, 6–19
    place of payment, 6–21
    price, 6–17
    quantity, 6–22
    requirements before resorting to gap fillers, 6–12
    subject matter, 6–22
    time of delivery, 6–20
    time of payment 6–21
Modern rule, 6–11
    Restatement 2d approach, 6–23
    UCC approach, 6–12 et seq.
Past performance as cure, 6–25
Rationale for doctrine, 6–2
Types of cases subject to indefiniteness problems, 6–4
Usage of Trade as cure, 6–26

INDEPENDENT PROMISES
In contract with two limitation of remedy clauses, 32–54

INFANCY
See INCAPACITY

***IN PARI DEUCTO* DOCTRINE REGARDING ILLEGAL CONTRACTS, 17–23**

INTEGRATION CLAUSES
Defined, 18–7, 18–16
Parol evidence rule, effect on, 18–7, 18–16

INTEREST ANALYSIS OF CONTRACT DAMAGES, 30–1
Expectation interest, 30–4
Reliance interest, 30–6
Restitution interest, 30–8

INTERPRETATION
Generally, Chapter 19
Ambiguity as to time provisions in offer, 4–52
Construction, rules of, 19–2 et seq.
Course of dealing, 19–13, 19–14, 20–9
Course of performance, 19–13, 19–14, 20–9
    distinguished from waiver, 20–12
Duty unconditional or subject to condition precedent, 21–29 et seq.
Express terms, 19–14
Extrinsic evidence, admissibility of, 19–17
    Corbin/Restatement—reasonably susceptible test, 19–19
    Williston/Holmes—plain meaning test, 19–18
Hierarchy of interpretation rules, 19–14
Interpretation, rules of, 19–2 et seq.

INDEX

Interpretation under the UCC, 20–1 et seq.
Misunderstanding, distinguished from interpretation, 19–9
Plain meaning rule, 19–18
Reasonably susceptible test, 19–15
Usage of trade, 19–13, 19–14, 20–9

INTOXICATION
See INCAPACITY

IRREVOCABLE OFFER
See OFFER AND ACCEPTANCE

JEST, OFFER MADE IN
See OFFER AND ACCEPTANCE

KNOCKOUT RULE, 5–24, 5–31

LAND SALES CONTRACTS
Damages upon breach:
    "American Rule," 30–38
    breach by buyer, 30–37
    breach by seller, 30–38
    "English Rule," 30–38
Mistake applied to, 12–16
Not governed by UCC, 33–7
    Sales of goods attached to real estate, 33–13
Specific performance upon breach, 29–13
Statute of frauds, and, 10–6 et seq.
"Time is of the essence" clause in, 21–86

LAPSE OF OFFER
See OFFER AND ACCEPTANCE

"LAST SHOT" DOCTRINE, 5–4

"LEADING OBJECT" RULE AS EXCEPTION TO THE SURETYSHIP PROVISION OF STATUTE OF FRAUDS, 10–31

LIMITATION OF REMEDIES
Dependent promises in contract with two remedy limitation clauses, 32–54
Distinguished from disclaimer of warranties, 32–51
"Failure of essential purpose," 32–52
General rules regarding enforceability, 32–51 et seq.
Limitations on parties' ability to agree on enforceable limitation clause, 32–49, 32–51

LIQUIDATED DAMAGES
See DAMAGES

LOCUS POENITENTIAE **DOCTRINE**, 17–25

LOST VOLUME SELLER
Defined, 30–46, 32–46
Formula for recovery by, 32–47

MAILBOX RULE
See also OFFER AND ACCEPTANCE
Generally, 4–118 et seq.

"MAIN PURPOSE" RULE AS EXCEPTION TO SURETYSHIP PROVISION OF STATUTE OF FRAUDS, 10–31

"MASSACHUSETTS" RULE REGARDING PRIORITY AMONG ASSIGNMENTS, 27–60

MASTER OF THE OFFER, OFFEROR IS, 3–33

MATERIAL BREACH
See BREACH

MEETING OF THE MINDS, MUTUAL ASSENT, 2–3 et seq.

MERCANTILE TERMS
Generally, 34–6 et seq.
C & F, 34–16
C.I.F., 34–15
F.A.S., 34–13
F.O.B., 34–12

MERGER CLAUSES
Defined, 18–7, 18–16
Parol evidence rule, effect on, 18–16

"MERGER" DOCTRINE EFFECTING MEMORANDUM FOR STATUTE OF FRAUDS, 10–11

"MIGHT NATURALLY" TEST OF THE PAROL EVIDENCE RULE, 18–13

MIRROR IMAGE RULE
See OFFER AND ACCEPTANCE

MISREPRESENTATION
Generally, Chapter 15
Age, by minor, 11–13
Distinguished from misrepresentation in tort, 15–2, 15–3
Duty to disclose, silence actionable, 15–15, et seq.
Effect, 15–3
    fraud in the *factum*, 15–4
    fraud in the inducement, 15–6
Elements of actionable misrepresentation claim, 15–6 et seq.
Factual representation, 15–7
    distinguished from:
        opinion, 15–8
        prediction of future events, 15–11
        puffing, 15–14

statement of future
    intention, 15–12
  trade talk, 15–14
Fraud in the factum, 15–4
Fraud in the inducement, 15–6
  elements, 15–6 et seq.
Fraudulent, defined, 15–2
Limitation on right to sue: reasonable time after discovery, 15–33
Material, defined, 15–27
Of age by minor, 11–13
Opinion distinguished from fact, 15–8
Reliance:
  necessity of, 15–29
  reasonable, requirement of, 15–30
Restitution permitted upon establishing, 15–34
Silence as actionable factual misrepresentation, 15–15 et seq.
Types:
  fraudulent, 15–2
  innocent, 15–2
  negligent, 15–2

MISTAKE
Generally, Chapter 12
Conscious ignorance, distinguished from, 12–14, 12–15
Defined, 12–2
Distinguished from misunderstanding, 12–5, 12–29
Fact, requirement of, 12–2
  distinguished from erroneous belief as to future events, 12–3
  mistake of law can be mistake of fact, 12–4
Land sale cases, 12–16
Mistake of law, 12–4
Mutual mistake:
  defined, 12–7
  distinguished from "conscious ignorance," 12–14, 12–15
  distinguished from unilateral mistake, 12–6
  effect, 12–7
  elements to establish, 12–8 et seq.
  limitation on availability, reasonable time after discovery, 12–17
  restitution allowed, 12–19
Unavailability when party assumes risk, 12–11, 12–14, 12–15
Unilateral mistake:
  defined, 12–21
  distinguished from mutual mistake, 12–6
  effect, 12–26
  elements, 12–22
  limitations on availability: reasonable time after discovery, 12–25
  mistaken bid cases, 12–23, 12–24

restitution available upon establishing, 12–27

MISUNDERSTANDING
Generally, 12–28, et seq.
Distinguished from mistake, 12–5, 12–29
Effect, 12–30
Raffles v. Wichelhaus, 12–31 et seq.
Rules governing, 12–30

MITIGATION OF DAMAGES
See DAMAGES, Avoidability

MODIFICATION
Generally, Chapter 9
Assignments:
  for value, 27–8, 27–53
  gratuitous, 27–5, 27–54
CISG
  See CISG
Common Law Rules, 9–20 et seq.
Consideration, necessity of, 7–72 et seq., 9–4, 9–20
Defined, 9–25
Distinguished from:
  exception to parol evidence rule, 18–20, 9–28
  rescission, 9–25
Good Faith, requirements of, 9–15, 9–18
"No modification except in writing" clauses, effect of, 9–6
  waiver, 9–10
"No oral modification" clauses, effect of, 9–6
  waiver, 9–10
Pre-existing duty rule, relationship with, 7–71 et seq., 9–20, 9–23
Reliance damages available when modification unenforceable, 30–74
Third party beneficiary contracts, right of parties to modify, 26–44 et seq.
Waiver, compared 9–10 et seq.
  retraction, 9–16
Under Restatement, 9–20
Under UCC, 9–3 et seq.

MUTUAL ASSENT
Generally, Chapter 2
Assent required as to essential terms only, 2–9
Defined, 2–1
Family situations, presumption against, 2–6
Judged under objective theory of contract, 2–3
Meeting of the minds, 2–4
Social situations, presumption against, 2–6
Time of Contracting Unimportant, 2–8

MUTUAL MISTAKE
See MISTAKE

INDEX

MUTUAL RESCISSION
See also ACCORDS, NOVATIONS, RELEASES, SUBSTITUTED CONTRACTS, and SUBSTITUTED PERFORMANCE
Generally, 24–18 et seq.
Defined, 24–18
Distinguished from accords, 24–24
Distinguished from substituted contracts, 24–26
Distinguished from substituted performance, 24–24
Oral, 24–22

MUTUALITY OF OBLIGATION
See also MUTUAL ASSENT
Generally, Chapter 2
Discussed, 2–1

MUTUALITY OF REMEDY, 29–39

"NEW HAMPSHIRE" RULE REGARDING INCAPACITY, 11–10

"NEW YORK" RULE REGARDING PRIORITY AMONG ASSIGNMENTS, 27–56

NOMINAL DAMAGES, DEFINED, 30–22

"NO ORAL MODIFICATION" CLAUSE
See also MODIFICATION
Enforceability, 9–25

NOVATION
As type of substituted contract, 24–6
Defined, 24–5
Distinguished from Accords, 24–24
Distinguished from delegation, 28–31
Effect, 24–6

OBJECTIVE THEORY OF CONTRACT
Acceptance judged by, 4–3
Assent judged by, 2–3
Counter-offers judged by, 4–35
Defined, 2–3
Offer judged by, 3–8
Rejection of offers judged by, 4–35
Revocation of offers judged by, 4–57
Who may accept offers judged by, 4–6, 4–7

OFFER AND ACCEPTANCE
Generally, Chapters 3 and 4
Acceptance:
  by beginning performance, 4–98 et seq.
  by mail, 4–118 et seq.
  by performance, 4–92 et seq.
  by promising performance, 4–92 et seq.
  by silence, 4–112 et seq.
  defined, 4–1
  determined under objective theory of contract, 4–3
  distinction between power to accept and right to accept, 3–2, 4–6, 4–27, 4–87
  distinguished from cross-offers, 4–5
  duration of power of acceptance, 4–27 et seq.
  effect, 4–2
  grumbling, 4–41
  permissible method of acceptance, 4–92 et seq.
  power to accept created by offer, 3–2
  right to accept, 24, 4–87
  who is entitled to accept, 4–6 et seq.
Accommodation shipments, 4–107, 4–108
Advertisements, as offers, 3–18 et seq.
Anger, offers made in, 3–23
Auctions, 3–34 et seq.
  with reserve, 3–35
  withdrawal of bid, 3–37
  without reserve, 3–36
Beginning performance as method of acceptance:
  in response to ambiguous offer, effect of, 4–101
  in response to offer for bilateral contract, effect of, 4–100
  in response to offer for unilateral contract, effect of, 4–81, 4–99
  notice required upon beginning performance, 4–104, 4–106
  unilateral contract trick, 4–107
"Brooklyn Bridge" hypothetical, 4–81 et seq.
Carbolic Smoke Ball, rules of, 4–17, 4–26, 4–111
Catalogues, as offers, 3–18 et seq.
Conduct, offer and acceptance by:
  generally, 1–18, 4–113
  under UCC, 5–23, 5–24
Counter-offers:
  accommodation shipments as, 4–108
  defined, 4–29
  distinguished from:
    grumbling acceptances, 4–41
    mere inquiries, 4–39
    neutral comments, 4–38
    preliminary negotiation, 4–39
    requests for modification, 4–40

INDEX

statements that offer will be taken under further advisement, 4–42
effect on revocable offers, 4–29
effect on irrevocable offers, 4–27
judged by objective theory of contracts, 4–35
under UCC, 2–207, 5–7 et seq.
Cross-offers, 4–5
Death of offeree:
  irrevocable offers, effect on, 4–87
  revocable offers, effect on, 4–67
Death of offeror:
  irrevocable offers, effect on, 4–87
  revocable offers, effect on, 4–64
Delay in communication of offer, 4–53
Destruction of thing essential for performance, 4–68
Distinction between "power" to accept and "right" to accept, 3–2, 4–6, 4–27, 4–87
Equal publicity rule, 4–23, 4–62
General offers:
  acceptance by only the first party to do act, 4–13
  defined, 3–32, 4–12
  knowledge of offer by offeree, requirement of for acceptance, 4–18
  notice by offeree before acceptance, 4–17
  restrictive conditions in offer, effect of, 4–13
  revocation of general offers, 4–23, 4–62
Grumbling acceptances, 4–41
Grumbling manner, offers made in a, 3–23
Illegality of acts called for by offer, 4–69
Incapacity of offeree, 4–67
Incapacity of offeror:
  irrevocable offers, effect on, 4–87
  revocable offers, effect on, 4–64
Indirect revocation, 4–59 et seq.
Intoxicated, offers made while, 3–23
Irrevocable offers, termination of, 4–72 et seq.
  merchant's firm offers, 4–78, 4–27
  option contracts, 4–77 et seq.
Jest, offers made in, 3–23
Lapse of time:
  delay in transmission of offer, 4–53
  presumptions as to when power of acceptance has lapsed when offer made in:
    deals with price volatile goods, 4–50
    direct negotiations, 4–47
    expedited forms of communication, 4–49
    letter, 4–48

termination of power of acceptance through, in irrevocable offers, 4–27, 4–87
termination of power of acceptance through, in revocable offers, 4–44
Mailbox rule, 4–118 et seq.
  acceptances under option contracts, 4–124 statement of the rule, 4–118
  when acceptance of offer is effective, 4–118, 4–119, 4–120
    acceptance by mail as authorized method of acceptance, requirement of, 4–122
    proper address, requirement of, 4–121
  when rejection is effective, 4–126
    acceptance followed by rejection, 4–129
    rejection followed by acceptance, 4–128
  when revocation of offer is effective, 4–127
    revocation following acceptance, effect of, 4–118, 4–128
Merchant's firm offer, 4–78
Methods of acceptance, 4–92
  beginning performance, 4–98
    in response to ambiguous offer, effect of, 4–101
    in response to offer for bilateral contract, effect of, 4–100
    in response to offer for unilateral contract, effect of, 4–81, 4–99
  promissory acceptance, 4–92
  silence, 4–112 et seq.
  to offers seeking prompt shipment of goods under UCC, 4–97
  types, 4–92
  where method of acceptance not specified in offer, 4–94
  where method of acceptance specified in offer, 4–93
Mirror image rule, 5–1 et seq.
  "last shot" doctrine, 5–4
Mutual assent:
  as to material terms, 2–9
  defined, 2–1
  family situations, presumption against, 2–6
  meeting of the minds, elimination of, 2–4
  judged under objective theory of contracts, 2–3
  social situations, presumption against, 2–6

INDEX

time of contracting irrelevant, 2–8
Notice of acceptance:
    accomplished by beginning performance, 4–104
    effect of failure to give notice, 4–106
    general offer situations, 4–26, 4–111
    necessity when acceptance is unilateral contract situations, 4–109
Offer:
    advertisements as, 3–18 et seq.
    auction, made at, 3–34
    catalogues as, 3–18
    CISG
        See CISG
    creation of power of acceptance, 3–2, 4–6, 4–28, 4–87
    cross-offers, 4–5
    defined, 3–1
    determined under objective theory of contract, 3–8
    distinguished from:
        advertisements/catalogue descriptions, 3–18
        effect, 3–12
        invitations to make an offer, 3–16
        preliminary negotiations, 3–16
        request for price quotation, 3–14
        statements in jest, anger, a grumbling manner, or while intoxicated, 3–23
        statement of future intention, 3–12
    general offers, defined, 3–32, 4–12
Offeror "master of the offer," 3–33
Power of acceptance:
    created by offer, 3–2, 4–6, 4–27, 4–87
    determined by objective theory of contracts, 4–7
    distinction between "power" to accept and "right" to accept, 4–27, 4–87
    duration of, 4–27 et seq.
    transferability, 4–8
        option contracts, 4–10, 4–72 et seq.
    under general offers, 4–12, 4–13
    who may accept offer, 4–6 et seq.
Rejection of offers:
    defined, 4–29
    effect on irrevocable offers, 4–74, 4–87
    effect on revocable offers, 4–28, 4–29
    judged by objective theory of contracts, 4–35

mailbox rule, 4–112 et seq.
mere inquiries, 4–39
neutral comments, 4–38
preliminary negotiation, 4–39
requests for modification, 4–40
statements that offer will be taken under further advisement, 4–42
when effective, 4–37, 4–120
Revocation of offer:
    effect on irrevocable offers, 4–74, 4–87
    effect on revocable offers, 4–55
    general offers, 4–23
    indirect revocation, 4–59
    judged by objective theory of contracts, 4–57
    unilateral contract offers
        after offeree begins performance, 4–80 et seq.
        Brooklyn Bridge hypothetical, 4–81 et seq.
        unilateral option contract, 4–80 et seq.
    when effective, 4–57, 4–127
Silence as acceptance:
    generally, 4–112 et seq.
    acts inconsistent with offeror's ownership, 4–117
    general rule, 4–112
    previous conduct, effect of, 4–116
    requested by offeror, effect of, 4–115
    where offeree's acts evidence a contract, 1–18, 4–113
Smoke ball case, 4–17, 4–26
Termination of power of acceptance regarding irrevocable offers, 4–74
Termination of power of acceptance regarding revocable offers:
    by counter-offer, 4–29
    by death of offeree, 4–67
    by death of offeror, 4–64
    by death or destruction of thing essential for performance, 4–68
    by incapacity of offeree, 4–67
    by incapacity of offeror, 4–64
    by lapse of time, 4–44
    by non-occurrence of condition of acceptance, 4–69, 4–71
    by rejection by offeree, 4–29
    by revocation, 4–55
    by supervening illegality, 4–69
Unilateral contract trick under UCC, 4–107
    accommodation shipments, 4–108
Unilateral contracts:
    acceptance by beginning performance, 4–80, 4–98

INDEX

Under UCC, 2–207
    approach, 5–6 et seq.
    by conduct, 5–23
    by exchange of written forms, 5–6 et seq.
    confirmatory memorandum, effect of, 5–25
    determining terms of a contract formed under 2–207(2), 5–14
    determining terms of a contract formed under 2–207(3), 5–23
    "different" and "additional" terms, treatment of in 2–207(2), 5–21
    knock-out rule of 2–202(3), 5–23, 5–24

OFFEROR IS "MASTER OF THE OFFER," 3–33

OPTION CONTRACTS
Assignability of right to accept under, 4–10, 4–76
Consideration in, 4–77, 7–96
Defined, 4–74
Implied, 4–80
    on offeree's beginning of performance in response to unilateral contract offer, 4–99, 4–81
    on offeree's substantial reliance, 4–85, 7–91
Offer irrevocable under terms of contract, 4–74 et seq.
Purported consideration sufficient, 4–77, 7–96
Right to accept granted by, 4–74
Termination of offer under, 4–74
Transferability of right to accept under, 4–10, 4–72 et seq.
When mailed acceptance effective, 4–124

ORDER OF PERFORMANCE, 21–50 et seq.
Under UCC, 22–6

OUTPUT CONTRACTS
Defined, 7–56
Implied floor and ceiling on quantity, 7–58
Obligation of good faith, 7–56

PAROL EVIDENCE RULE
    Generally under common law, Chapter 18
    Generally under UCC, Chapter 20
Approach, 20–2
CISG
    See CISG
Common law rules, 18–4 et seq.
Contemporaneous "side" agreements, treatment of, 18–3
Contradictory terms, introduction of:
    "might naturally" test of common law, 18–13
    "would certainly" test under UCC, 20–6
Corbin view of integration, 18–11
Definition of parol evidence, 18–3
Determination as to whether writing is totally or partially integrated:
    analysis of different views, 18–8 et seq.
    Corbin/Restatement 2d view, 18–11
    Williston/four corners view, 18–9
Four corners view of integration, 18–9
"Ice house" case, 18–14, 20–7
Integration clause, effect of, 18–16
Merger clause, effect of, 18–16
"Might Naturally" Test for consistent additional terms at common law, 18–13
Modifications of existing contracts, distinguished from, 9–28, 18–20
Oral statements as parol evidence, 18–3
Parol evidence rule under the UCC, 20–1 et seq.
Partially integrated documents:
    defined, 18–6
    determination of, 18–8 et seq.
    effect of, 18–7, 20–5
Restatement 2d view on integration, 18–11
Side agreements, effect on, 18–3
Statement of rule, 18–4, 20–2
Statute of frauds, relation to, 18–29
Totally integrated documents:
    defined, 18–6
    determination of, 18–8 et seq.
    effect of determination, 18–7, 20–4
Typical problems under, 18–2
UCC rules, 22–2 et seq.
When rule does not apply:
    failure to provide consideration, 18–23
    modifications, 18–20
    no agreement was ever reached, 18–21
    occurrence of condition precedent, 18–22
    voidable agreements, 18–25
Williston/four corners view on integration, 18–9
"Would Certainly" Test for Consistent Additional Terms under UCC, 20–6
Written statements as parol evidence, 18–3

"PEPPERCORN THEORY" OF CONSIDERATION, 7–43

INDEX

PERFECT TENDER RULE
See also BREACH
Generally, 22–7 et seq.

PLAIN MEANING RULE OF CONTRACT INTERPRETATION, 19–18

PRIVITY
Defined, 35–16
Horizontal, 35–19
Vertical, 35–18

PRECEDENT CONDITIONS
See CONDITIONS

PREDICTION OF FUTURE EVENTS
As distinguished from factual representation, 15–11

"PREDOMINANT PURPOSE" TEST OF UCC APPLICABILITY, 33–11

PRE-EXISTING DUTY RULE
See also CONSIDERATION
Generally, 7–71 et seq., 9–3 et seq., 24–13

PRE-PERFORMANCE PREPARATION
As forming implied option contract, 4–80
Reliance damages for, 31–74

PRICE QUOTATIONS
Distinguished from offer, 3–14

PROMISSORY ESTOPPEL
Generally, Chapter 8
Approach, 8–19
As "substitute" for consideration, 8–2
Charitable subscriptions, enforceability of, 8–9
Damage measures, 8–16, 30–74
Defined, 8–1
Distinction between 1st and 2d restatement provisions, 8–5
Contractor/subcontractor cases, 4–85, 8–13
Effect:
    generally, 8–1
    on statute of frauds, 10–3, 10–58 et seq.
Elements under Restatement 2d, 8–3
    action or forbearance, 8–3
    avoiding injustice, 8–3
    foreseeable reliance, 8–3
Irrevocable offers, created by, 4–86, 8–11
Reliance damage recovery, 8–16, 30–74
Types of promises made enforceable as a result of:
    gift promises, 8–7
    offers by sub-contractors which induce substantial reliance, 4–86, 8–11
    oral promises to convey land, 8–8
    promises made in preliminary negotiations, 8–14

PUFFING
Distinguished from factual representations, 15–14, 35–3

QUASI-CONTRACTS
Defined, 1–20
Restitutionary recovery, 1–20, 31–31

"REASONABLY SUSCEPTIBLE" TEST UNDER INTERPRETATION RULES, 19–19

REJECTION OF GOODS UNDER THE UCC
See also REVOCATION OF ACCEPTANCE
Generally, 22–39 et seq.
Acts a buyer cannot take in order to have effective rejection, 22–41
Acts a buyer is permitted to take and still have effective rejection, 22–43
Acts a buyer must take in order to have effective rejection, 22–43
Cure, relationship with, 22–12
Effect, 22–39
Grounds for rejection, 22–44
Remedies available upon rightful and effective rejection, 32–11 et seq.
Right to reject, 22–39

REJECTION OF OFFERS
See OFFER AND ACCEPTANCE

RELEASES
See also ACCORDS, MUTUAL RESCISSION, SUBSTITUTED CONTRACTS, and SUBSTITUTED PERFORMANCE
Generally 24–25 et seq.
Defined, 24–25
Distinguished from:
    accords, 24–26
    substituted performance, 24–26
    substituted contracts, 24–26
Effect, 24–25

RELIANCE DAMAGES
See DAMAGES

REMEDIES
See EQUITABLE RELIEF, DAMAGES, RESTITUTION

REPUDIATION
See ANTICIPATORY REPUDIATION

REQUIREMENTS CONTRACTS
Defined, 7–56

INDEX

Implied floor and ceiling on quantity, 7-58

Obligation of good faith, 7-56

RESCISSION
See MUTUAL RESCISSION

RESTATEMENT OF CONTRACTS
Described, 1-4

RESTITUTION
    See also DAMAGES, EQUITABLE REMEDIES

Generally, Chapter 31

Award based on value of benefits actually received by benefited party, 31-1, 32-2

Breach, availability as remedy for:
    generally, 31-14
    limitations on recovery by non-breaching party:
        breach must be total breach, 31-15
        must be mutual, 31-11
        presumption of recovery using value calculation method yielding the greatest amount when non-breaching party sues, 31-10, 31-21
        presumption of recovery using value calculation method yielding the least amount when breaching party sues, 31-10, 31-28, 31-29
        where aggrieved party has performed and benefited party only has to pay money, 31-17

Cost Avoided method of value calculation, 31-5

Distinguished from reliance damages recovery, 31-1

Doctrine explained, 30-8, 31-1 et seq.

Duress, recovery upon, 13-15, 30-65

Frustration of purpose, recovery upon, 25-64, 31-33

Illegality, when recovery permitted, 17-7, 17-22, 31-33

Impossibility, recovery upon, 25-54, 31-33

Impracticability, recovery upon, 25-64, 31-33

Incapacity, when recovery permitted, 11-4, 11-8, 31-33

Losing contract situations, use in, 30-28, 30-70, 31-23

Measure of recovery:
    cost avoided method, 31-5
    net benefit method, 31-5

Mutual restitution, requirement of, 31-11

Net benefit method of value calculation, 31-5

Presumption of proper valuation method:
    recovery by breaching party, 31-10, 31-28, 31-29
    recovery by non-breaching party, 31-10, 31-21
    recovery in quasi-contract situations, 31-31

Quasi-contract, recovery in, 31-31

Recovery by breaching party:
    damages of non-breaching party must be subtracted from, 31-29
    presumption of recovery using value calculation method yielding the least amount, 31-6, 31-29

Unjust enrichment, goal to avoid, 31-1

Use where value of services exceeds contract price, 31-25

When Available, 31-3

REVOCATION OF ACCEPTANCE UNDER UCC
    See also REJECTION OF GOODS

Generally, 22-45 et seq.

Cure, relationship with, 22-51

Damages available upon rightful and effective revocation, 30-40 et seq., 32-11 et seq.

Effect, 22-45 et seq.

Elements necessary to establish, 22-46

Restitution, availability upon revocation, 22-52

REVOCATION OF OFFERS
See OFFER AND ACCEPTANCE

RISK OF LOSS
Generally, 34-1

CISG
    See CISG

In absence of breach:
    destination contracts, 34-3
    shipment contracts, 34-4

When breach has occurred:
    buyer's breach, 34-9
    seller's breach followed by revocation of acceptance, 34-8
    seller's breach that gives buyer right to reject, 34-7

SEAL, CONTRACTS UNDER, 8-20

SHIPMENT CONTRACT, 34-4

SILENCE
Acceptance by, 4-112 et seq.
Ratification by, 11-7

INDEX

When silence can trigger a duty to disclose in misrepresentation, 15–5 et seq.

SPECIFIC PERFORMANCE
See EQUITABLE REMEDIES

STATEMENT OF FUTURE INTENTION
As distinguished from factual statement at time of contracting in misrepresentation, 15–12

STATUTE OF FRAUDS
Generally, Chapter 10
Failure to satisfy, effect of, 10–3, 10–61
Marriage contracts, 10–24
    pre-nuptial agreements, 10–25
Memorandum, satisfying, 10–10 et seq.
"Merger" Doctrine to satisfy memorandum, 10–11
Modifications of contracts, 10–60, 9–3, 9–20
One year provision, 10–14
    contracts with early termination clauses, 10–19
    full performance by one party, effect of, 10–20
    part performance, 10–21
    satisfaction of one year provision, 10–22
Origins of, 10–1
Parol evidence rule, relation to, 18–29
Purpose, 10–2
Rationale, 10–2
Reliance, effect of, 10–58
Restitution, when required, 10–64
Sale of goods, 10–35 et seq.
    divisible contracts, 10–40
    limit enforcement to less than $500, 10–41
    quantity term, 10–42
    satisfaction by:
        admission, 10–53
        complete performance, 10–54
        merchant's confirmatory memorandum, 10–44
            objecting, effect of, 10–48
            party not a merchant, 10–49
        part performance, 10–55
        performance, 10–54
        specially manufactured goods, 10–52
"signed by" requirement, 10–43
Surety contracts, 10–26
    definition of "surety," 10–27
    leading object rule, 10–31
    main purpose rule, 10–31
Terminology, 10–5
Transfer of an interest in land, 10–6
    satisfying land portion of statute, 10–10
Waiver, relationship with, 9–29

STATUTE OF LIMITATIONS
Enforceability of promises to pay debt otherwise unenforceable by its running, 7–38
Under UCC, 33–6

SUB-CONTRACTORS
Bids to general contractors temporarily irrevocable, 4–86, 8–11 et seq.
Low bid to general contractor as unilateral mistake, 12–23

SUBSEQUENT AGREEMENTS
See ACCORDS, NOVATION, MUTUAL RESCISSION, RELEASES SUBSTITUTED CONTRACTS, SUBSTITUTED PERFORMANCE

SUBSEQUENT CONDITIONS
See CONDITIONS

SUBSTANTIAL PERFORMANCE DOCTRINE
See BREACH

SUBSTITUTED CONTRACTS
    See also ACCORDS, NOVATION, MUTUAL RESCISSION, RELEASES, and SUBSTITUTED PERFORMANCE
Generally, 24–5 et seq.
Defined, 24–5
Distinguished from:
    accords, 24–17
    mutual rescission, 24–24
    releases, 24–26
Effect on original duty, 24–6
Novation as type of, 24–5, 24–6

SUBSTITUTED PERFORMANCE
    See also ACCORDS, NOVATION, MUTUAL RESCISSION, RELEASES, and SUBSTITUTED CONTRACTS
Generally 24–2 et seq.
Defined, 24–2
Distinguished from:
    mutual rescission, 24–24
    releases, 24–26
Effect on original duty, 24–2

SURETY
Defined, 10–27

INDEX

Statute of frauds provision relating to, 10–26 et seq.

TENDER OF PERFORMANCE
Breach, relationship to, 21–47 et seq., 22–2 et seq.
Definition, 21–48, 22–3
Order of performance, relationship to, 21–50, 22–2
Under the UCC, 22–1 et seq.
    buyer's tender obligations, 22–5
    perfect tender rule, 22–7
    seller's tender obligations, 22–3

THIRD PARTY BENEFICIARY CONTRACTS
Generally, Chapter 26
Beneficiary's rights against promisor, 26–5 et seq.
    limited by promisor/promisee contract, 26–35
    limited by promisor's defenses assertable against promisee, 26–32
    recovery limited by immaterial breach of the promisee, 26–37
    subject to modification, 26–44
Beneficiary's right to disclaim beneficiary status, 26–26
Beneficiary "stands in the shoes" of the promisee, 26–32
Common law rule regarding enforceability, 26–6
Comparison between Restatement 1st and Restatement 2d approaches, 26–19
Construction contracts, 26–30
Contracts with municipalities, 26–29
Creditor beneficiary:
    defined, 26–9
    rights to enforce promisor's promise, 26–5 et seq., 26–13
"Creditor-like" intended beneficiary:
    defined, 26–14
    rights to enforce promisor's promise, 26–5 et seq., 26–28
Defenses against beneficiary, effect of, 26–31 et seq.
Defenses of promisee against promisor, 26–42 et seq.
Difference between Restatement 2d and Restatement 1st treatment of, 26–19
Disclaiming beneficiary status, 26–26
Distinguished from:
    accords, 26–49
    assignments, 26–52, 27–33
    novation, 26–49
Donee beneficiary:
    defined, 26–7
    rights to enforce beneficiary's promise, 26–5 et seq., 26–13
"Donee-like" intended beneficiary:
    defined, 26–14
    rights to enforce promisor's promise, 26–5 et seq., 26–28
Government contracts, 26–29
Identity of beneficiary unknown at time of making of the contract, 26–24
Incidental beneficiary:
    defined under Restatement 1st, 26–11
    defined under Restatement 2d, 26–17
    rights of beneficiary to enforce promisor's promise, 26–5 et seq.
Intended beneficiary:
    defined, 26–14
    rights of, 26–14
Modification of contract by promisee and promisor, 26–44
Municipal contract, 26–29
Promisee, defined, 26–2
Promisee's rights against promisor, 26–42
Promisor, defined, 26–2
Promisor's rights against beneficiary, 26–31
Restatement 2d approach compared to Restatement 1st approach, 26–19
Revocability by promisor and promisee, 26–44
Terminology, 26–2
When performance not rendered directly to beneficiary, 26–23

"TIME IS OF THE ESSENCE" CLAUSE, 21–86

TRADE TALK
As distinguished from factual representation, 15–14, 35–3

TRADE USAGE
See USAGE OF TRADE

"TRANSACTION IN GOODS" TEST FOR UCC APPLICABILITY, 33–3

TYPES OF CONTRACTS
Accord, 24–9
Bilateral, 1–16
Destination, 34–5
Exclusive dealing, 7–52
Express, 1–17
Implied-in-fact, 1–18
Implied-in-law, 1–20
Installment, 22–23
Novation, 24–5
Option, 4–73
Output, 7–56
Quasi, 1–20
Requirements, 7–56
Shipment, 34–4

INDEX

Substituted contract, 24–5
Substituted performance, 24–2
Third party beneficiary, 26–1
Unilateral, 1–15

UNCONSCIONABILITY
Generally, Chapter 16
Adhesion contracts, application to, 16–12
Circumstances must be present when contract is made, 16–11
Clauses that limit a party's remedies, applied to, 16–14
Cross-collateralization clauses, applied to, 16–9, 16–10
Defined, 16–1
Effect:
    At common law, 16–4
    Under modern law, 16–3
Elements, 16–5
In commercial transactions, 16–13
In consumer transactions, 16–9
Procedural unconscionability:
    as part of aggrieved's burden of proof, 16–6, 16–8
    defined, 16–6
Remedies once established, 16–3
"Sliding Scale" Test, 16–5, 16–8
Substantive unconscionability:
    as part of aggrieved's burden of proof, 16–7, 16–8
    defined, 16–7
Unilateral mistake, relationship with, 12–22 et seq.
Warranty disclaimers, applied to, 16–14, 32–51 et seq.

UNDUE INFLUENCE
Generally, Chapter 14
Elements, 14–2
    improper persuasion, 14–4
    special relationship, 14–3
Restitution allowed, 14–5

UNIFORM COMMERCIAL CODE
Acceptance of goods, 22–37
Anticipatory repudiation, 23–20 et seq.
Applicability of Article 2 to a contract:
    generally 33–3 et seq.
    goods attached to realty, 33–13
    lease transactions, 33–6
    merchants, 33–2
    sales/service "hybrid" transactions, 33–10
        gravamen test, 33–12
        predominant purpose test, 33–11
    sales transactions, 33–5
    "transactions in goods" test, 33–3
Approach upon multiple assignments of same right, 27–62
Buyer's money damage remedies:
    cover damages, 30–41, 32–12
    market differential damages, 30–41, 32–15
    warranty, 30–43, 32–23
Concurrent conditions of exchange, 22–2
Consequential damages, 32–9
Contract, defined, 1–11
Cure, 22–12
Damages under, generally, Chapter 32
Definition of contract, 1–11
Described, 1–5
Equitable remedies under, 29–2, 32–2
"First to file" rule regarding multiple assignments, 27–62
Incidental damages, 32–10
Indefiniteness, 6–11 et seq.
    gap fillers, 6–12 et seq.
Limitation of remedy clauses:
    generally, 32–51
    distinguished from warranty disclaimers, 32–54
    unconscionability applied to, 16–14, 32–51
Liquidated damages, 32–49
Mercantile Terms
    See also MERCANTILE TERMS
    Generally, 34–11, et seq.
Modification, 9–1 et seq.
Multiple assignments of the same right, approach of, 27–62
Offer and acceptance under 2–207, Chapter 5
Order of performance, 22–2 et seq.
Parol evidence rule, Chapter 20
Performance, Chapter 22
Rejection of goods, 22–39
Revocation of acceptance, 22–45
Risk of Loss
    See also RISK OF LOSS
    Generally, 34–1, et seq.
Seller's money damage remedies:
    cover damages, 30–44, 32–35
    full contract price, right to recover, 32–29 et seq.
    lost volume seller, 30–46, 32–46
    market differential damages, 30–44, 32–38
Statute of frauds in Article 2 transactions, 10–36 et seq.
Statute of Limitations, 33–6
Tender, 22–2 et seq.
Warranty:
    generally, Chapter 35
    damages recoverable upon breach of, 32–23
    defenses, 35–20 et seq.
    express warranty
        generally, 35–2 et seq.
        disclaiming, 35–11
        elements, 35–2
        horizontal privity and, 35–19

INDEX

implied warranty of fitness for a particular purpose
    disclaimer, 35–15
        generally, 35–12 et seq.
    disclaiming, 35–15
    elements, 35–12
implied warranty of merchantability:
    generally 35–8 et seq.
    disclaiming, 35–11
    elements, 35–8
notice by buyer, requirement of, 35–17
vertical privity, 35–18

UNIFORM SALES ACT, 1–6, 1–7

UNILATERAL CONTRACTS
Beginning performance as acceptance of, 4–100
Consideration in, 7–7, 7–8, 7–12
Defined, 1–15
Revocation of offers looking to, once performance has begun, 4–80
"Brooklyn Bridge" hypothetical, 4–81
"Unilateral contract" trick, 4–107
when notice of acceptance required, 4–26, 4–104, 4–109

UNILATERAL MISTAKE
See MISTAKE

USAGE OF TRADE
Defined, 20–15
Parol evidence rule, relationship to, 20–9
Indefiniteness, as a cure for, 6–26
Interpretation, effect on, 19–13
Perfect tender rule, effect on, 22–7, 22–23

VOID AND VOIDABLE AGREEMENTS
See DURESS, INCAPACITY, ILLEGALITY, MISTAKE, MISUNDERSTANDING, MISREPRESENTATION, STATUTE OF FRAUDS, UNDUE INFLUENCE

"VOID" CONTRACT
Defined, 13–2, 15–4, 17–1, Part IV, Introduction
Resulting from duress by physical compulsion, 13–2
Resulting from fraud in the *factum,* 15–4
Resulting from illegality, 17–1, 17–7

WAIVER
As excuse for enforcement of a condition, 21–92
Defined, 21–92
Distinguished from:
    course of performance, 20–5
    modification, 9–10
    parol evidence rule situations, 9–29
Election, when waiver becomes, 21–100
Modification, relationship to, 9–29 et seq.
Retraction of, 21–100

WARRANTIES
Generally, Chapter 35
Assignor's, made in assignments for value, 27–42
Buyer's damages upon breach, 32–23
By-standers, right to recover by, 35–19
CISG
    See CISG
Damages for breach, 32–23
Disclaimer:
    distinguished from limitation of remedy clauses, 32–51
    of express warranties, 35–7
    of the implied warranty of fitness for a particular purpose, 35–15
    of the implied warranty of merchantability, 35–11
Express warranty:
    generally, 35–2 et seq.
    disclaimer, 35–7
    elements, 35–2
Horizontal privity, 35–19
Implied warranty of fitness for a particular purpose:
    generally, 35–12 et seq.
    disclaimer, 35–15
    elements, 35–12
Implied warranty of merchantability:
    generally, 35–8 et seq.
    disclaimer, 35–11
    elements, 35–8
Limitation of remedy clause, 32–52, 32–54
Notice by buyer of breach, requirement of, 35–17
Puffing, 15–14, 35–3
Remote manufacturer, right to recover against, 35–18
Sample of model, basis for express warranty, 35–3
Vertical privity, 35–18

"WOULD CERTAINLY" TEST FOR UCC PAROL EVIDENCE RULE, 20–6